The new edition of DSM is bigger and more expensive than all previous editions. It cost the APA $25 million to produce, an amount that was immediately recouped by presales of 150,000 copies (Gorenstein, 2013).

Inside DSM-5

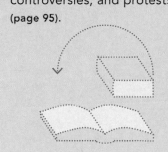

In 2013, the American Psychiatric Association (APA) published **DSM-5**, its new edition of the **Diagnostic and Statistical Manual of Mental Disorders** — the most widely used classification system in North America. DSM-5 is a **947-page** manual that lists **541 diagnoses** (Blashfield et al., 2014). The production of DSM-5 was a monumental 12-year undertaking, marked by long delays, controversies, and protests (page 95).

Outside advisors
300 persons

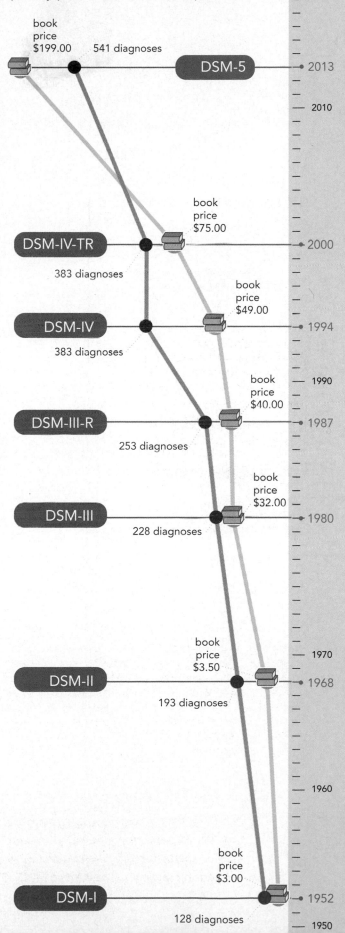

book price $199.00 · 541 diagnoses · **DSM-5** — 2013

— 2010

book price $75.00
DSM-IV-TR — 2000
383 diagnoses

book price $49.00
DSM-IV — 1994
383 diagnoses

— 1990
book price $40.00
DSM-III-R — 1987
253 diagnoses

book price $32.00
DSM-III — 1980
228 diagnoses

— 1970
book price $3.50
DSM-II — 1968
193 diagnoses

— 1960

book price $3.00
DSM-I — 1952
128 diagnoses

— 1950

(Blashfield et al., Gorenstein)

Gambling disorder is considered an *addiction* (page 342).

PRO Excessive gambling and substance addictions often share similar brain dysfunctioning.

CON Many other behaviors pursued excessively, such as sex, Internet use, and shopping, could eventually be considered behavioral addictions.

Mild neurocognitive disorder is added as a category (page 515).

PRO This diagnosis may help clinicians identify early symptoms of Alzheimer's disease.

CON People with normal age-related forgetfulness may receive a psychiatric diagnosis.

Application	Area of Use
Practice/research	North America
Practice/research	Worldwide
Research	United States

Fundamentals of
Abnormal Psychology

Fundamentals of
Abnormal Psychology

EIGHTH EDITION

Ronald J. Comer
Princeton University

worth publishers
Macmillan Learning

New York

Publisher: Rachel Losh
Executive Acquisitions Editor: Daniel McDonough
Editorial Assistant: Kimberly Morgan
Senior Marketing Manager: Lindsay Johnson
Marketing Assistant: Allison Greco
Executive Media Editor: Rachel Comerford
Associate Media Editor: Jessica Lauffer
Director, Content Management Enhancement: Tracey Kuehn
Managing Editor: Lisa Kinne
Senior Project Editor: Jane O'Neill
Media Producer: Eve Conte
Photo Editor: Jennifer Atkins
Permissions Editors: Felicia Ruocco, Melissa Pellerano
Permissions Associate: Chelsea Roden
Director of Design, Content Management: Diana Blume
Cover and Interior Designer: Babs Reingold
Layout Designer: Paul Lacy
Infographics Artist: Charles Yuen
Senior Production Supervisor: Sarah Segal
Composition: codeMantra
Printing and Binding: RR Donnelley
Cover Image: Ed Fairburn

Credits to use previously published material can be found in the Credits section, starting on page C-1.

Library of Congress Control Number: 2015957306

ISBN-13: 978-1-4641-7697-5
ISBN-10: 1-4641-7697-3

Worth Publishers
One New York Plaza
Suite 4500
New York, NY 10004-1562

http://www.macmillanhighered.com

To Delia and Emmett Comer,
The World Awaits

ABOUT THE AUTHOR

RON COMER has taught in Princeton University's Department of Psychology for the past 41 years, serving also as Director of Clinical Psychology Studies and as chair of the university's Institutional Review Board. His courses—Abnormal Psychology, Theories of Psychotherapy, Childhood Psychopathology, Experimental Psychopathology, and Controversies in Clinical Psychology—have been among the university's most popular offerings.

Professor Comer has received the President's Award for Distinguished Teaching at the university. He is also a practicing clinical psychologist and a consultant to Eden Autism Services and to hospitals and family practice residency programs throughout New Jersey.

In addition to writing *Fundamentals of Abnormal Psychology*, Eighth Edition, Professor Comer is the author of the textbook *Abnormal Psychology*, now in its ninth edition; coauthor of the introductory psychology textbook *Psychology Around Us*, Second Edition; and coauthor of *Case Studies in Abnormal Psychology*, Second Edition. He is the producer of numerous videos for courses in psychology and other fields of education, including The Higher Education Video Library Series, Video Anthology for Abnormal Psychology, Video Segments in Neuroscience, Introduction to Psychology Video Clipboard, and Developmental Psychology Video Clipboard. He also has published journal articles in clinical psychology, social psychology, and family medicine.

Professor Comer completed his undergraduate studies at the University of Pennsylvania and his graduate work at Clark University. He lives in Lawrenceville, New Jersey, with his wife, Marlene. From there he can keep a close eye on the Philadelphia sports teams with which he grew up.

Paul L. Bree

CONTENTS IN BRIEF

CONTENTS

CHAPTER : 3

Clinical Assessment, Diagnosis, and Treatment **77**

CHAPTER : 4

Anxiety, Obsessive-Compulsive, and Related Disorders **105**

CHAPTER : 8

Disorders Featuring Somatic Symptoms 249

CHAPTER : 9

Eating Disorders 279

CHAPTER : 10

Substance Use and Addictive Disorders — 309

CHAPTER : 11

Disorders of Sex and Gender — 347

PREFACE

I t was the spring of 1981. Over the previous eight months, the Philadelphia Phillies had won the World Series, and the Eagles, Sixers, and Flyers had made it to the Super Bowl, NBA Finals, and Stanley Cup Finals, respectively. I had two adorable children ages 5 and 3. I had been granted tenure at Princeton. My life was full—or so I thought.

Then, Linda Chaput, at that time an editor at W. H. Freeman and Company and Worth Publishers, walked into my office. During a lively discussion, she and I discovered that we had similar ideas about how abnormal psychology should be presented in a textbook. By the time Linda departed two hours later, we had outlined the principles that should underlie the "ideal" abnormal psychology textbook. We had, in effect, a deal. All that was left was for me to write the book. A decade later, the first edition of *Abnormal Psychology* ("the BOOK," as my family and I had come to call it) was published, followed a few years later by the first edition of *Fundamentals of Abnormal Psychology*.

As I look back to that fateful day in 1981, I cannot help but note that several things have changed. With a few exceptions, my Philadelphia sports teams have returned to form and have struggled year in, year out. My sons have become accomplished middle-aged men, and their previous "adorable" tag is now worn by my 2-year-old and 4-year-old grandchildren, Emmett and Delia. I am older, humbler, and a bit more fatigued than the person who met with Linda Chaput 35 years ago.

At the same time, several wonderful things remain the same. I am still at Princeton University. I am still married to the same near-perfect person—Marlene Comer. And I still have the privilege of writing abnormal psychology textbooks— *Fundamentals of Abnormal Psychology* and *Abnormal Psychology*. The current version, *Fundamentals of Abnormal Psychology,* Eighth Edition, represents my eighteenth edition of one or the other of the textbooks.

My textbook journey has been a labor of love, but I also must admit that each edition requires enormous effort, ridiculous pressure, and too many sleepless nights to count. I mention these labors not only because I am a world-class whiner but also to emphasize that I approach each edition as a totally new undertaking rather than as a cut-and-paste update of past editions. I work feverishly to make each edition fresh and to include innovative and enlightening pedagogical techniques.

With this in mind, I have added an enormous amount of new material and many exciting new features for this edition of *Fundamentals of Abnormal Psychology*—while at the same time retaining the successful themes, material, and techniques that have been embraced enthusiastically by past readers. The result is, I believe, a book that will excite readers and speak to them and their times. I have again tried to convey my passion for the field of abnormal psychology, and I have built on the generous feedback of my colleagues in this undertaking—the students and professors who have used this textbook over the years.

New and Expanded Features

In line with the many changes that have occurred over the past several years in the fields of abnormal psychology, education, and publishing, and in the world, I have brought the following new features and changes to the current edition.

•**NEW**• **DSM-5** With the publication of DSM-5, abnormal psychology is clearly a field in transition. To help students appreciate the field's current status and new directions, I present, integrate, and analyze DSM-5 material throughout the textbook. Controversy aside, this is now the field's classification and diagnostic system, and it is important that readers understand and master its categories and criteria, appreciate its strengths and weaknesses, and recognize its assumptions and implications, just as past readers learned about previous DSM editions.

DSM-5, as well as discussions of its implications and controversial nature, is presented in various ways throughout my textbook. First, its new categories, criteria, and information are woven smoothly into the narrative of each and every chapter. Second, reader-friendly pedagogical tools throughout the textbook, including a two-page infographic on the inside front cover and regular short features called *Dx Checklist* and *DSM-5 Controversy,* help students fully grasp the DSM-5 material. Third, special topic boxes highlight DSM-5 issues and controversies, such as *Premenstrual Dysphoric Disorder: Déjà Vu All Over Again* (page 209) and *Mass Murders: Where Does Such Violence Come From?* (page 434).

•NEW• TECHNOLOGY AND THE "MINDTECH" FEATURE The breathtaking rate of technological change that characterizes today's world has had significant effects on the mental health field. In this edition I cover this impact extensively, including many discussions in the book's narrative, boxes, photographs, and figures. The book examines, for example, how the Internet, texting, and social networks have become convenient tools for those who wish to bully others or pursue pedophilic desires (pages 373, 465, 466); how social networking may provide a new source for social anxiety (page 129); and how today's technology has helped create new psychological disorders such as Internet addiction (page 343). It also looks at dangerous new trends such as the posting of self-cutting videos on the Internet (page 225), and it informs the reader about *cybertherapy* in its ever-expanding forms—from Skype therapy and avatar therapy to virtual reality treatments (pages 57, 67, 163, 410).

In addition, I have added a new feature throughout the book called **MindTech**—sections in each chapter that give special attention to particularly provocative technological trends in engaging and enlightening ways. The **MindTech** features examine the following cutting-edge topics:

- Mental Health Apps Explode in the Marketplace (page 21)
- Social Networking Sites: A Researcher's Paradise? (page 24)
- Have Your Avatar Call My Avatar (page 67)
- Rorschach on Wikipedia: Psychology's Wiki Leaks? (page 83)
- Social Media Jitters (page 129)
- Virtual Reality Therapy: Better Than the Real Thing? (page 163)
- Texting: A Relationship Buster? (page 207)
- Crisis Texting (page 243)
- Can Social Media Spread "Mass Hysteria"? (page 255)
- Dark Sites of the Internet (page 294)
- Neknomination Goes Viral (page 315)
- "Sexting": Healthy or Pathological? (page 368)
- Can Computers Develop Schizophrenia? (page 396)
- Putting a Face on Auditory Hallucinations (page 410)
- Selfies: Narcissistic or Not? (page 446)
- Children Online: Parent Worries on the Rise (page 470)

- Remember to Tweet: Tweet to Remember (page 510)

- New Ethics for a Digital Age (page 549)

•**NEW**• "INFOCENTRALS" It is impossible to surf the Internet, watch TV, or flip through a magazine without coming across *infographics*, those graphic representations that present complex data in quick, stimulating, and visually appealing ways. Infographics present information in a way that allows us to easily recognize trends and patterns and make connections between related concepts. With the development of new digital tools over the past decade, the popularity of infographics has exploded. Readers and viewers like them and learn from them.

Thus *Fundamentals of Abnormal Psychology,* Eighth Edition, introduces a new feature called **InfoCentral**—numerous, lively infographics on important topics in the field. The infographics provide visual representations of data related to key topics and concepts in each chapter, repeatedly offering fascinating snippets of information to spur readers' interest. I am certain that readers will greatly enjoy these special offerings, while also learning from them.

Every chapter features a full-page *InfoCentral*, including the following ones:

- Happiness (page 19)

- Dietary Supplements: An Alternative Treatment (page 43)

- Common Factors in Therapy (page 101)

- Mindfulness (page 115)

- Sexual Assault (page 156)

- Sadness (page 185)

- The Right to Commit Suicide (page 240)

- Sleep and Sleep Disorders (page 264)

- Body Dissatisfaction (page 287)

- Smoking and Tobacco Use (page 320)

- Sex Throughout the Life Cycle (page 350)

- Hallucinations (page 390)

- Lying (page 457)

- Bullying (page 466)

- The Aging Population (page 506)

- Personal and Professional Issues (page 551)

•**NEW**• ADDITIONAL CUTTING-EDGE BOXES I have grouped the book's other boxes into two categories: *PsychWatch* boxes examine text topics in more depth, emphasize the effect of culture on mental disorders and treatment, and explore examples of abnormal psychology in movies, the news, and the real world. *MediaSpeak* boxes offer provocative pieces by news, magazine, and Web writers and bloggers on current issues in abnormal psychology. In addition to updating the *PsychWatch* and *MediaSpeak* boxes that have been retained from the previous edition, I have added many new ones. For example, new *MediaSpeak* boxes include the following:

- Flawed Study, Gigantic Impact (Chapter 1)

- Saving Minds Along with Souls (Chapter 2)

- The Fear Business (Chapter 4)

- Immigration and Depression in the 21st Century (Chapter 6)

- When Doctors Discriminate (Chapter 8)

•NEW• "CLINICAL CHOICES" INTERACTIVE CASE STUDIES This eighth edition of *Fundamentals of Abnormal Psychology* includes 11 new interactive case studies (one for each of the disorders chapters), available online through LaunchPad, our online course management system. Through an immersive mix of video, audio, and assessment, each interactive case allows the student to simulate the thought process of a clinician by identifying and evaluating a virtual "client's" symptoms, gathering information about the client's life situation and family history, determining a diagnosis, and formulating a treatment plan. The student will also answer various questions about each case to help reinforce the chapter material. Each answer will trigger feedback, guidance, and critical thinking in an active learning environment.

•NEW• ADDITIONAL AND EXPANDED TEXT SECTIONS Over the past few years, a number of topics in abnormal psychology have received special attention. In this edition, I have provided new sections on such topics, including *the psychology of mass killings* (pages 434), *the impact of the Affordable Care Act* (pages 17, 547), *the growing role of IRBs* (pages 32–33), *dimensional diagnoses* (pages 94, 456–459), *new treatments in the field* (pages 30, 57, 410), *spirituality and mental health* (pages 61, 62), *overuse of certain diagnoses* (pages 471, 492), *the psychological price of celebrity* (pages 200, 231), *transgender issues* (pages 376, 381), *alternative views of personality disorders* (pages 455–459), *self-injury* (pages 224, 437), *the pro-Ana movement* (page 294), *poor medical treatment for people with psychological disorders* (page 270), *ethics and psychology* (pages 544–546), *culture and abnormality* (pages 71, 454), *race and the clinical field* (pages 107–108), and *sexism in the clinical field* (pages 209, 365).

•NEW• ADDITIONAL CASE MATERIAL One of the hallmarks of my textbooks is the inclusion of numerous and culturally diverse clinical examples that bring theoretical and clinical issues to life. In my continuing quest for relevance to the reader and to today's world, I have replaced or revised more than one-third of the clinical material in this edition. The new clinical material includes the cases of Franco, major depressive disorder (pages 77, 79); Tonya, Munchausen syndrome by proxy (page 252); Meri, major depressive disorder (page 183); Eduardo, paranoid personality disorder (page 425); Luisa, dissociative personality disorder (page 170); Kay, bipolar disorder (page 216); Shani, anorexia nervosa (page 279); Ricky, ADHD (page 463); Lucinda, histrionic personality disorder (pages 441–442); Jonah, separation anxiety disorder (pages 467–468); and many others.

•NEW• CRITICAL THOUGHT QUESTIONS A very stimulating and popular feature of my previous edition of *Fundamentals of Abnormal Psychology* was the "critical thought questions"—questions that pop up within the text narrative, asking students to pause at precisely the right moment and think critically about the material they have just read. Given the enthusiastic response to this feature by professors and readers alike, I have added many new critical thought questions throughout the textbook, including ones in the *MindTech* and *MediaSpeak* features.

•NEW• "BETWEEN THE LINES" The textbook not only retains but also expands a fun and thought-provoking feature from past editions that has been very popular among students and professors—reader-friendly elements called "Between the Lines," consisting of text-relevant tidbits, surprising facts, current events, historical notes, interesting trends, enjoyable lists, and stimulating quotes.

•NEW• THOROUGH UPDATE In this edition I present the most current theories, research, and events, including more than 2,000 new references from the years 2013–2015, as well as hundreds of new photos, tables, and figures.

•**EXPANDED COVERAGE**• PREVENTION AND MENTAL HEALTH PROMOTION In accord with the clinical field's growing emphasis on prevention, positive psychology, and psychological wellness, I have increased the textbook's attention to these important approaches (for example, pages 16–17, 19, 524).

•**EXPANDED COVERAGE**• MULTICULTURAL ISSUES Over the past 30 years, clinical theorists and researchers increasingly have become interested in ethnic, racial, gender, and other cultural factors, and my previous editions of *Fundamentals of Abnormal Psychology* certainly have included these important factors. The study of such factors has, appropriately, been elevated to a broad perspective in recent years—the *multicultural perspective*. Consistent with this clinical movement, the current edition includes yet additional multicultural material and research throughout the text. Even a quick look through the pages of this textbook will reveal that it truly reflects the diversity of our society and of the field of abnormal psychology.

•**EXPANDED COVERAGE**• "NEW-WAVE" COGNITIVE AND COGNITIVE-BEHAVIORAL THEORIES AND TREATMENTS The current edition of *Abnormal Psychology* has expanded its coverage of the "new-wave" cognitive and cognitive-behavioral theories and therapies, including *mindfulness-based cognitive therapy* and *Acceptance and Commitment Therapy* (ACT), presenting their propositions, techniques, and research in chapters throughout the text (for example, pages 56, 114, 115, 410).

•**EXPANDED COVERAGE**• NEUROSCIENCE The clinical field continues to witness the growth and impact of remarkable brain-imaging techniques, genetic mapping strategies, and other neuroscience approaches, all of which are expanding our understanding of the brain. Correspondingly, the new edition of *Fundamentals of Abnormal Psychology* has further expanded its coverage of how biochemical factors, brain structure, brain function, and genetic factors contribute to abnormal behavior (for example, pages 39, 116, 118, 393).

Continuing Strengths

As I noted earlier, in this edition I have also retained the themes, material, and techniques that have worked successfully and have been embraced enthusiastically by past readers.

BREADTH AND BALANCE The field's many theories, studies, disorders, and treatments are presented completely and accurately. All major models—psychological, biological, and sociocultural—receive objective, balanced, up-to-date coverage, without bias toward any single approach.

INTEGRATION OF MODELS Discussions throughout the text, particularly those headed "Putting It Together," help students better understand where and how the various models work together and how they differ.

EMPATHY The subject of abnormal psychology is people—very often people in great pain. I have tried therefore to write always with empathy and to impart this awareness to students.

INTEGRATED COVERAGE OF TREATMENT Discussions of treatment are presented throughout the book. In addition to a complete overview of treatment in the opening chapters, each of the pathology chapters includes a full discussion of relevant treatment approaches.

RICH CASE MATERIAL As I mentioned earlier, the textbook features hundreds of culturally diverse clinical examples to bring theoretical and clinical issues to life.

More than 25 percent of the clinical material in this edition is new or revised significantly.

MARGIN GLOSSARY Hundreds of key words are defined in the margins of pages on which the words appear. In addition, a traditional glossary is available at the back of the book.

ROLLING SUMMARIES Instead of waiting until the end of a chapter for a summary, *SUMMING UP* sections appear throughout each chapter, at the completion of each major section, helping students to better retain the material under discussion.

"PUTTING IT TOGETHER" A section toward the end of each chapter, "Putting It Together," asks whether competing models can work together in a more integrated approach and also summarizes where the field now stands and where it may be going.

FOCUS ON CRITICAL THINKING The textbook provides tools for thinking critically about abnormal psychology. As I mentioned earlier, in this edition, "critical thought" questions appear at carefully selected locations within the text discussions. The questions ask readers to stop and think critically about the material they have just read.

CHAPTER-ENDING KEY TERMS AND QUICK QUIZ SECTIONS These sections, keyed to appropriate pages in the chapter for easy reference, allow students to review and test their knowledge of chapter materials.

STRIKING PHOTOS AND STIMULATING ILLUSTRATIONS Concepts, disorders, treatments, and applications are brought to life for the reader with stunning photographs, diagrams, graphs, and anatomical figures—all reflecting the most up-to-date data available. The photos range from historical to today's world to pop culture. They do more than just illustrate topics: they touch and move readers.

ADAPTABILITY Chapters are self-contained, so they can be assigned in any order that makes sense to the professor.

MEDIA and Other Supplements

I have been delighted by the enthusiastic responses of both professors and students to the supplements that accompany my textbooks. This edition offers those supplements once again, revised and enhanced, and adds a number of exciting new ones.

FOR PROFESSORS

WORTH VIDEO COLLECTION FOR ABNORMAL PSYCHOLOGY *Produced and edited by Ronald J. Comer, Princeton University, and Gregory Comer, Princeton Academic Resources. Faculty Guide included.* This incomparable video series offers 128 clips that depict disorders, show historical footage, and illustrate clinical topics, pathologies, treatments, experiments, and dilemmas. Videos are available in LaunchPad and on the *Video Collection for Abnormal Psychology* Flash Drive. I also have written an accompanying guide that fully describes and discusses each video clip, so that professors can make informed decisions about the use of the segments in lectures.

INSTRUCTOR'S RESOURCE MANUAL *by Charlie Harris, Clayton State University and Danielle Gunraj, SUNY Binghamton.* This comprehensive guide ties together the ancillary package for professors and teaching assistants. The manual includes detailed chapter summaries, lists of principal learning objectives, topic overviews, ideas for lectures, lecture outlines, discussion launchers, classroom activities, extra credit projects, and DSM criteria for each of the disorders discussed in the text. It also offers strategies for using the accompanying media, including the video collection. Finally, it includes a comprehensive set of valuable materials that can be obtained from outside sources—items such as relevant feature films, documentaries, teaching references, and Internet sites related to abnormal psychology.

- **Lecture Slides** *available at http://www.macmillanhighered.com/Catalog/product/ fundamentalsofabnormalpsychology-eighthedition-comer.* These slides focus on key concepts and themes from the text and can be used as-is or customized to fit a professor's needs.

- **Illustration Slides** *available at http://www.macmillanhighered.com/Catalog/product/ fundamentalsofabnormalpsychology-eighthedition-comer.* These slides featuring all chapter photos and illustrations can be used as is or customized to fit a professor's needs.

- **Chapter Figures, Photos, and Tables** *available at http://www.macmillanhighered. com/Catalog/product/fundamentalsofabnormalpsychology-eighthedition-comer.* This collection gives professors access to all of the photographs, illustrations, and tables from *Fundamentals of Abnormal Psychology,* Eighth Edition.

ASSESSMENT TOOLS

TEST BANK *by Chrysalis Wright, University of Central Florida.* A comprehensive test bank offers more than 2,200 multiple-choice, fill-in-the-blank, and essay questions. Each question is graded according to difficulty, the Bloom's level is identified, and keyed to the topic and page in the text where the source information appears.

DIPLOMA ONLINE COMPUTERIZED TEST BANK Available for both *Windows and Macintosh at http://www.macmillanhighered.com/Catalog/product/fundamentalsofabnormalpsychology-eighthedition-comer.* This downloadable Test Bank guides professors step-by-step through the process of creating a test and allows them to add an unlimited number of questions, edit or scramble questions, format a test, and include pictures and multimedia links. The accompanying grade book enables them to record students' grades throughout the course and includes the capacity to sort student records and view detailed analyses of test items, curve tests, generate reports, add weights to grades, and more. These Test Bank files also provide tools for converting the Test Bank into a variety of useful formats as well as Blackboard- and WebCT-formatted versions of the Test Bank for *Fundamentals of Abnormal Psychology,* Eighth Edition.

FOR STUDENTS

CASE STUDIES IN ABNORMAL PSYCHOLOGY, SECOND EDITION, by Ethan E. Gorenstein, Behavioral Medicine Program, New York–Presbyterian Hospital, and Ronald J. Comer, Princeton University. This new edition of our popular case study book provides 20 case histories—all of them updated and several of them brand new—each going beyond DSM diagnoses to describe the individual's history and symptoms, a theoretical discussion of treatment, a specific treatment plan, and the actual treatment conducted. The casebook also provides three cases without diagnoses or treatment, so that students can identify disorders and suggest appropriate therapies. Wonderful case material, particularly for somatic symptom disorder, hoarding disorder, and gender dysphoria, has been added for this edition by Danae Hudson and Brooke Whisenhunt, professors at Missouri State University.

LAUNCHPAD **with LearningCurve Quizzing—Multimedia to Support Teaching and Learning** *Available at www.launchpadworks.com.*
   A comprehensive Web resource for teaching and learning psychology, *Launch-Pad* combines Worth Publishers' award-winning media with an innovative platform

for easy navigation. For students, it is the ultimate online study guide with rich interactive tutorials, videos, e-Book, and the LearningCurve adaptive quizzing system. For instructors, LaunchPad is a full-course space where class documents can be posted, quizzes are easily assigned and graded, and students' progress can be assessed and recorded. Whether you are looking for the most effective study tools or a robust platform for an online course, LaunchPad is a powerful way to enhance your class.

LaunchPad to Accompany *Fundamentals of Abnormal Psychology,* Eighth Edition, can be previewed at www.launchpadworks.com.

Fundamentals of Abnormal Psychology, Eighth Edition, and LaunchPad can be ordered together with:

ISBN-10: 1-319-06179-6
ISBN-13: 978-1-319-06179-1

LaunchPad for *Fundamentals of Abnormal Psychology,* Eighth Edition, includes the following resources:

- The **LearningCurve** quizzing system was designed based on the latest findings from learning and memory research. It combines adaptive question selection, immediate and valuable feedback, and a gamelike interface to engage students in a learning experience that is unique to them. Each LearningCurve quiz is fully integrated with other resources in LaunchPad through the Personalized Study Plan, so students will be able to review with Worth's extensive library of videos and activities. And state-of-the-art question analysis reports allow instructors to track the progress of individual students as well as their class as a whole.

- **An interactive e-Book** allows students to highlight, bookmark, and make their own notes, just as they would with a printed textbook.

- **Clinical Choices**, *authored by Taryn Myers, of Virginia Wesleyan College.* In these 11 interactive case studies in LaunchPad, students simulate the role of clinical psychologist, engaging with virtual clients to identify psychological disorders (based on DSM-5 criteria) and think critically about diagnosis and treatment options.

- *Abnormal Psychology Video Activities*, *produced and edited by Ronald J. Comer, Princeton University, and Gregory Comer, Princeton Academic Resources.* These intriguing video cases run three to seven minutes each and focus on persons affected by disorders discussed in the text. Students first view a video case and then answer a series of thought-provoking questions about it.

- **Deep integration** is available between LaunchPad products and Blackboard, Brightspace by D2Learn, Canvas, and Moodle. These deep integrations offer educators single sign-on and gradebook sync, now with auto-refresh. Also, these best-in-class integrations offer deep linking to all Macmillan digital content at the chapter and asset level, giving professors ultimate flexibility and customization capability within their learning management system.

Acknowledgments

I am very grateful to the many people who have contributed to writing and producing this book. I particularly thank Marlene Comer for her usual outstanding work on the manuscript. In addition, I am indebted to Marlene Glissmann for her fast, furious, and fantastic work on the references. And I sincerely appreciate the superb work of the book's assistants—actually collaborators—Greg Comer and Jon Comer.

I am indebted greatly to those outstanding academicians and clinicians who have provided feedback on this new edition of *Fundamentals of Abnormal Psychology,* along with that of its partner, *Abnormal Psychology,* and have commented with great insight and wisdom on its clarity, accuracy, and completeness. Their collective knowledge has in large part shaped the current edition: David Alfano, Community College of Rhode Island; Jeffrey Armstrong, Northampton Community College; Wendy Bartkus, Albright College; Jennifer Bennett, University of New Mexico; Christine Browning, Victory University; Megan Davies, NOVA-Woodbridge Campus; Pernella Deams, Grambling State University; Frederick Ernst, University of Texas Pam America; Jessica Goodwin Jolly, Gloucester County College; Abby Hill, Trinity International University; Tony Hoffman, University of California, Santa Cruz; Craig Knapp, College of St. Joseph; Sally Kuhlenschmidt, Western Kentucky University; Paul Lewis, Bethel College; Gregory Mallis, University of Indianapolis; Taryn Myers, Virginia Wesleyan College; Edward O'Brien, Marywood University; Mary Pelton-Cooper, Northern Michigan University; Ginger Pope, South Piedmont Community College; Lisa Riley, Southwest Wisconsin Technical College; Ty Schepis, Texas State University; and Elizabeth Seebach, Saint Mary's University of Minnesota.

Earlier I also received valuable feedback from academicians and clinicians who reviewed portions of the previous editions of *Fundamentals of Abnormal Psychology* and *Abnormal Psychology.* Certainly their collective knowledge has also helped shape this new edition, and I gratefully acknowledge their important contributions: Christopher Adams, Fitchburg State University; Dave W. Alfano, Community College of Rhode Island; Alisa Aston, University of North Florida; Kent G. Bailey, Virginia Commonwealth University; Stephanie Baralecki, Chestnut Hill College; Sonja Barcus, Rochester College; Marna S. Barnett, Indiana University of Pennsylvania; Jillian Bennett, University of Massachusetts Boston; Otto A. Berliner, Alfred State College; Allan Berman, University of Rhode Island; Douglas Bernstein, University of Toronto, Mississauga; Sarah Bing, University of Maryland Eastern Shore; Greg Bolich, Cleveland Community College; Stephen Brasel, Moody Bible Institute; Conrad Brombach, Christian Brothers University; Barbara Brown, Georgia Perimeter College; Jeffrey A. Buchanan, Minnesota State University, Mankato; Gregory M. Buchanan, Beloit College; Laura Burlingame-Lee, Colorado State University; Loretta Butehorn, Boston College; Glenn M. Callaghan, San Jose State University; E. Allen Campbell, University of St. Francis; Julie Carboni, San Jose College and National University; David N. Carpenter, Southwest Texas University; Marc Celentana, The College of New Jersey; Edward Chang, University of Michigan; Daniel Chazin, Rutgers University; Sarah Cirese, College of Marin; June Madsen Clausen, University of San Francisco; Victor B. Cline, University of Utah; E. M. Coles, Simon Fraser University; Michael Connor, California State University, Long Beach; Frederick L. Coolidge, University of Colorado, Colorado Springs; Patrick J. Courtney, Central Ohio Technical College; Charles Cummings, Asheville Buncombe Technical Community College; Dennis Curtis, Metropolitan Community College; Timothy K. Daugherty, Missouri State University; Lauren Doninger, Gateway Community College; Mary Dosier, University of Delaware; S. Wayne Duncan, University of Washington, Seattle; Anne Duran, California State University Bakersfield; Morris N. Eagle, York University; Miriam Ehrenberg, John Jay College of Criminal Justice; Jon Elhai, University of Toledo; Daniella K. C. Errett, Pennsylvania Highlands Community College; Carlos A. Escoto, Eastern Connecticut State University; William Everist, Pima Community College; Jennifer Fiebig, Loyola University Chicago; David M. Fresco, Kent State University; Anne Fisher, University of Southern Florida; William E. Flack Jr., Bucknell University; John Forsyth, State University of New York, Albany; Alan Fridlund, University of California, Santa Barbara; Stan Friedman, Southwest Texas State University; Dale Fryxell, Chaminade University; Lawrence L. Galant,

Gaston College; Kathryn E. Gallagher, Georgia State University; Rosemarie B. Gilbert, Brevard Community College; Karla Gingerich, Colorado State University; Nicholas Greco, College of Lake County; Jane Halonen, University of West Florida; James Hansell, University of Michigan; Neth Hansjoerg, Rensselaer Polytechnic Institute; David Harder, Tufts University; Morton G. Harmatz, University of Massachusetts; Jinni A. Harrigan: California State University, Fullerton; Jumi Hayaki, College of the Holy Cross; RaNae Healy, Gateway Community College; Anthony Hermann, Kalamazoo College; Paul Hewitt, University of British Columbia; David A. Hoffinan, University of California, Santa Cruz; Art Hohmuth, The College of New Jersey; Art Houser, Fort Scott Community College; Danae Hudson, Missouri State University; William G. Iacono, University of Minnesota; Ashleigh E. Jones, University of Illinois at Urbana-Champaign; Ricki E. Kantrowitz, Westfield State University; Barbara Kennedy, Brevard Community College; Lynn M. Kernen, Hunter College; Audrey Kim, University of California, Santa Cruz; Guadalupe Vasquez King, Milwaukee Area Technical College; Tricia Z. King, Georgia State University; Bernard Kleinman, University of Missouri, Kansas City; Futoshi Kobayashi, Northern State University; Alan G. Krasnoff, University of Missouri, St. Louis; Robert D. Langston, University of Texas, Austin; Kimberlyn Leary, University of Michigan; Harvey R. Lerner, Kaiser-Permanente Medical Group; Arnold D. LeUnes, Texas A&M University; Michael P. Levin, Kenyon College; Barbara Lewis, University of West Florida; Mary Margaret Livingston, Louisiana Technical University; Karsten Look, Columbus State Community College; Joseph LoPiccolo, University of Missouri, Columbia; L. E. Lowenstein, Southern England Psychological Services; Jerald J. Marshall, University of Central Florida; Toby Marx, Union County College; Janet R. Matthews, Loyola University; Robert J. McCaffrey, State University of New York, Albany; Rosemary McCullough, Ave Maria University; E. Dudley McGlynn, Auburn University; Tara McKee, Hamilton College; Lily D. McNair, University of Georgia; Mary W. Meagher, Texas A&M University; Dorothy Mercer, Eastern Kentucky University; Michele Metcalf, Coconino Community College; Joni L. Mihura, University of Toledo; Andrea Miller, Georgia Southwestern State University; Antoinette Miller, Clayton State University; Regina Miranda, Hunter College; John Mitchell, Lycoming College; Robin Mogul, Queens University; Linda M. Montgomery, University of Texas, Permian Basin; Jeri Morris, Roosevelt University; Karen Mottarella, University of Central Florida; Maria Moya, College of Southern Nevada; Karla Klein Murdock, University of Massachusetts, Boston; Sandy Naumann, Delaware Technical & Community College; David Nelson, Sam Houston State University; Paul Neunuebel, Sam Houston State University; Ryan Newell, Oklahoma Christian University; Katherine M. Nicolai, Rockhurst University; Susan A. Nolan, Seton Hall University; Fabian Novello, Purdue University; Ryan O'Loughlin, Nazareth College; Mary Ann M. Pagaduan, American Osteopathic Association; Crystal Park, University of Connecticut; Dominic J. Parrott, Georgia State University; Daniel Paulson, Carthage College; Paul A. Payne, University of Cincinnati; David V. Perkins, Ball State University; Julie C. Piercy, Central Virginia Community College; Lloyd R. Pilkington, Midlands Technical College; Harold A. Pincus, chair, DSM-IV, University of Pittsburgh, Western Psychiatric Institute and Clinic; Chris Piotrowski, University of West Florida; Debbie Podwika, Kankakee Community College; Norman Poppel, Middlesex County College; David E. Powley, University of Mobile; Laura A. Rabin, Brooklyn College; Max W. Rardin, University of Wyoming, Laramie; Lynn P. Rehm, University of Houston; Leslie A. Rescorla, Bryn Mawr College; R. W. Rieber, John Jay College, CUNY; George Esther Rothblum, University of Vermont; Vic Ryan, University of Colorado, Boulder; Randall Salekin, Florida International University; Edie Sample, Metropolitan Community College; Jackie Sample, Central Ohio Technical College; A. A. Sappington, University of Alabama, Birmingham; Martha Sauter, McLennan Community College; Laura Scaletta, Niagara County Community College; George W. Shardlow, City College of San

Francisco; Shalini Sharma, Manchester Community College; Roberta S. Sherman, Bloomington Center for Counseling and Human Development; Wendy E. Shields, University of Montana; Sandra T. Sigmon, University of Maine, Orono; Susan J Simonian, College of Charleston; Janet A. Simons, Central Iowa Psychological Services; Jay R. Skidmore, Utah State University; Rachel Sligar, James Madison University; Katrina Smith, Polk Community College; Robert Sommer, University of California, Davis; Jason S. Spiegelman, Community College of Baltimore County; John M. Spores, Purdue University, South Central; Caroline Stanley, Wilmington College; Wayne Stein, Brevard Community College; Arnit Steinberg, Tel Aviv University; David Steitz, Nazareth College; B. D. Stillion, Clayton College and State University; Deborah Stipp, Ivy Tech College; Joanne H. Stohs, California State University, Fullerton; Jaine Strauss, Macalester College; Mitchell Sudolsky, University of Texas at Austin; John Suler, Rider University; Sandra Todaro, Bossier Parish Community College; Terry Trepper, Purdue University Calumet; Thomas A. Tutko, San Jose State University; Arthur D. VanDeventer, Thomas Nelson Community College; Maggie VandeVelde, Grand Rapids Community College; Jennifer Vaughn, Metropolitan Community College; Norris D. Vestre, Arizona State University; Jamie Walter, Roosevelt University; Steve Wampler, Southwestern Community College; Eleanor M. Webber, Johnson State College; Lance L. Weinmann, Canyon College; Doug Wessel, Black Hills State University; Laura Westen, Emory University; Brook Whisenhunt, Missouri State University; Joseph L. White, University of California, Irvine; Justin Williams, Georgia State University; Amy C. Willis, Veterans Administration Medical Center, Washington, DC; James M. Wood, University of Texas, El Paso; Lisa Wood, University of Puget Sound; Lucinda E. Woodward, Indiana University Southeast; Kim Wright, Trine University; David Yells, Utah Valley State College; Jessica Yokely, University of Pittsburgh; Carlos Zalaquett, University of South Florida; and Anthony M. Zoccolillo, Rutgers University.

I would also like to thank a small group of talented professors who provided valuable feedback that shaped the development of our new, exciting interactive case studies, Clinical Choices, in this new edition: David Berg, Community College of Philadelphia; Christopher J. Dyszelski, Madison Area Technical College; Paul Deal, Missouri State University; Urminda Firlan, Kalamazoo Valley Community College; Julie Hanauer, Suffolk County Community College; Sally Kuhlenschmidt, Western Kentucky University; Erica Musser, Florida International University; Garth Neufeld, Highline Community College; and Jeremy Pettit, Florida International University.

A special thank you to the authors of the book's supplements package for doing splendid jobs with their respective supplements: Chrysalis Wright, University of Central Florida (*Test Bank*); Charlie Harris, Clayton State University, and Danielle Gunraj, SUNY Binghamton (*Instructor's Resource Manual*); Taryn Myers, Virginia Wesleyan College (*Clinical Choices*); Mallory Malkin, Mississippi University for Women (*Research Exercises*); Jennifer Bennett, University of New Mexico (*Chapter Quizzes*); Ann Brandt-Williams, Glendale Community College; Elaine Cassel, Marymount University and Lord Fairfax Community College; Danae L. Hudson, Missouri State University; John Schulte, Cape Fear Community College and University of North Carolina; and Brooke L. Whisenhunt, Missouri State University (additional Web site materials).

I also extend my deep appreciation to the core team of professionals at Worth Publishers and W. H. Freeman and Company who have worked so closely with me to produce this edition and many previous editions. The team consists of truly extraordinary people—each extremely talented, each committed to excellence, each dedicated to the education of readers, each bound by a remarkable work ethic, and each a wonderful person. It is accurate to say that these members of the core team were once again my co-authors and co-teachers in this enterprise, and I am in their debt.

They are Rachel Losh, publisher; Daniel McDonough, executive acquisitions editor; Mimi Melek, senior development editor; Tracey Kuehn, director, content management enhancement; Jane O'Neill, senior project editor; Sarah Segal, senior production supervisor; Paul Lacy, layout designer; Jennifer Atkins, photo editor; Rachel Comerford, executive media editor; Jessica Lauffer, associate media editor; Eve Conte, media producer; Babs Reingold, cover and interior designer; Blake Logan, design manager; Diana Blume, director of design, content management; and Chuck Yuen, infographics designer.

I also am indebted to Kevin Feyen, vice president, digital product development, and Catherine Woods, vice president, content management, who have been so closely involved with my books for many years. In addition, still other professionals at Worth and at W. H. Freeman to whom I am indebted are Lisa Kinne, managing editor; Chuck Linsmeier, vice president editorial, sciences and social sciences; Todd Elder, director of advertising; Kimberly Morgan, editorial assistant; Hilary Newman, director of rights and permissions; Melissa Pellerano and Felicia Ruocco, permissions editors; Chelsea Roden, permissions associate; Michele Kornegay, copy editor; Tina Hastings, proofreader; Ellen Brennan and Marlene Glissmann, indexers; and John Philp, for his outstanding work on the video supplements for professors and students. Not to be overlooked are the superb professionals at Worth and at Freeman who continuously work with great passion, skill, and judgment to bring my books to the attention of professors across the world: Kate Nurre, executive marketing manager; Lindsay Johnson, senior marketing manager; Allison Greco, marketing assistant; Craig Bleyer, national sales manager; and the company's wonderful sales representatives. Thank you so much.

One final note. As I mentioned in the prefaces of the past few editions, with each passing year I have become increasingly aware of just how fortunate I am. So, once again, at the risk of sounding like a walking cliché, let me say with a clarity that at my current age is sharper and better informed than at earlier points in my life, how appreciative I am that I have the opportunity each day to work with so many interesting and stimulating students during this important and exciting stage of their lives. Similarly, I am grateful beyond words for my extraordinary family, particularly my wonderful sons, Greg and Jon; my fantastic daughters-in-law, Emily and Jami; my perfect grandchildren, Delia and Emmett; and my truly magnificent wife, Marlene.

Ron Comer
Princeton University
January 2016

Fundamentals of
Abnormal Psychology

Ed Fairburn

Abnormal Psychology: Past and Present

Johanne cries herself to sleep every night. She is certain that the future holds nothing but misery. Indeed, this is the only thing she does feel certain about. "I'm going to suffer and suffer and suffer, and my daughters will suffer as well. We're doomed. The world is ugly. I hate every moment of my life." She has great trouble sleeping. She is afraid to close her eyes. When she does, the hopelessness of her life—and the ugly future that awaits her daughters—becomes all the clearer to her. When she drifts off to sleep, her dreams are nightmares filled with terrible images—bodies, decay, death, destruction.

Some mornings Johanne even has trouble getting out of bed. The thought of facing another day overwhelms her. She wishes that she and her daughters were dead. "Get it over with. We'd all be better off." She feels paralyzed by her depression and anxiety, overwhelmed by her sense of hopelessness, and filled with fears of becoming ill, too tired to move, too negative to try anymore. On such mornings, she huddles her daughters close to her and sits away the day in the cramped tent she shares with them. She feels she has been deserted by the world and left to rot. She is both furious at life and afraid of it at the same time.

During the past year Alberto has been hearing mysterious voices that tell him to quit his job, leave his family, and prepare for the coming invasion. These voices have brought tremendous confusion and emotional turmoil to Alberto's life. He believes that they come from beings in distant parts of the universe who are somehow wired to him. Although it gives him a sense of purpose and specialness to be the chosen target of their communications, the voices also make him tense and anxious. He does all he can to warn others of the coming apocalypse. In accordance with instructions from the voices, he identifies online articles that seem to be filled with foreboding signs, and he posts comments that plead with other readers to recognize the articles' underlying messages. Similarly, he posts long, rambling YouTube videos that describe the invasion to come. The online comments and feedback that he receives typically ridicule and mock him. If he rejects the voices' instructions and stops his online commentary and videos, then the voices insult and threaten him and turn his days into a waking nightmare.

Alberto has put himself on a sparse diet as protection against the possibility that his enemies may be contaminating his food. He has found a quiet apartment far from his old haunts, where he has laid in a good stock of arms and ammunition. After witnessing the abrupt and troubling changes in his behavior and watching his ranting and rambling videos, his family and friends have tried to reach out to Alberto, to understand his problems, and to dissuade him from the disturbing course he is taking. Every day, however, he retreats further into his world of mysterious voices and imagined dangers.

Most of us would probably consider Johanne's and Alberto's emotions, thoughts, and behaviors psychologically abnormal. They are the result of a state sometimes called *psychopathology, maladjustment, emotional disturbance,* or *mental illness* (see *PsychWatch* on the next page). These terms have been applied to the many problems that seem closely tied to the human brain or mind. Psychological abnormality affects the famous and the unknown, the rich and the poor. Celebrities, writers, politicians, and other public figures of the present and the past have struggled with it. Psychological problems can bring great suffering, but they can also be the source of inspiration and energy.

PsychWatch

Verbal Debuts

We use words like "abnormal" and "mental disorder" so often that it is easy to forget that there was a time not that long ago when these terms did not exist. When did these and similar words (including slang terms) make their debut in print as expressions of psychological dysfunctioning? The *Oxford English Dictionary* offers the following dates.

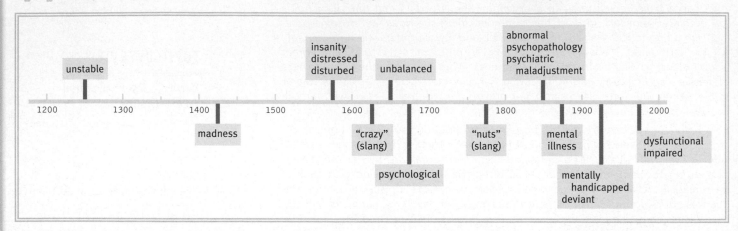

Because they are so common and so personal, these problems capture the interest of us all. Hundreds of novels, plays, films, and television programs have explored what many people see as the dark side of human nature, and self-help books flood the market. Mental health experts are popular guests on both television and radio, and some even have their own shows, Web sites, and blogs.

The field devoted to the scientific study of the problems we find so fascinating is usually called **abnormal psychology.** As in any science, workers in this field, called *clinical scientists,* gather information systematically so they can describe, predict, and explain the phenomena they study. The knowledge that they acquire is then used by *clinical practitioners,* whose role is to detect, assess, and treat abnormal patterns of functioning.

> **Why do actors who portray characters with psychological disorders tend to receive more awards for their performances?**

What Is Psychological Abnormality?

Although their general goals are similar to those of other scientific professionals, clinical scientists and practitioners face problems that make their work especially difficult. One of the most troubling is that psychological abnormality is very hard to define. Consider once again Johanne and Alberto. Why are we so ready to call their responses abnormal?

While many definitions of abnormality have been proposed over the years, none has won total acceptance (Bergner & Bunford, 2014). Still, most of the definitions have certain features in common, often called "the four Ds": deviance, distress, dysfunction, and danger. That is, patterns of psychological abnormality are typically *deviant* (different, extreme, unusual, perhaps even bizarre), *distressing* (unpleasant and upsetting to the person), *dysfunctional* (interfering with the person's ability to conduct daily activities in a constructive way), and possibly *dangerous.* This definition offers a useful starting point from which to explore the phenomena of psychological abnormality. As you will see, however, it has limitations.

Deviance

Abnormal psychological functioning is *deviant*, but deviant from what? Johanne's and Alberto's behaviors, thoughts, and emotions are different from those that are considered normal in our place and time. We do not expect people to cry themselves to sleep each night, hate the world, wish themselves dead, or obey voices that no one else hears.

In short, abnormal behavior, thoughts, and emotions are those that differ markedly from a society's ideas about proper functioning. Each society establishes **norms**—stated and unstated rules for proper conduct. Behavior that breaks legal norms is considered to be criminal. Behavior, thoughts, and emotions that break norms of psychological functioning are called abnormal.

Judgments of abnormality vary from society to society. A society's norms grow from its particular **culture**—its history, values, institutions, habits, skills, technology, and arts. A society that values competition and assertiveness may accept aggressive behavior, whereas one that emphasizes cooperation and gentleness may consider aggressive behavior unacceptable and even abnormal. A society's values may also change over time, causing its views of what is psychologically abnormal to change as well. In Western society, for example, a woman seeking the power of running a major corporation or indeed of leading the country would have been considered inappropriate and even delusional a hundred years ago. Today the same behavior is valued.

Judgments of abnormality depend on *specific circumstances* as well as on cultural norms. What if, for example, we were to learn that Johanne is a citizen of Haiti and that her desperate unhappiness began in the days, weeks, and months following the massive earthquake that struck her country, already the poorest country in the Western hemisphere, on January 12, 2010? The quake, one of the worst natural disasters in history, killed 250,000 Haitians and left 1.5 million homeless. Half of Haiti's homes and buildings were immediately turned into rubble, and its electricity and other forms of power disappeared. Tent cities replaced homes for most people (Granitz, 2014; Wilkinson, 2011).

In the weeks and months that followed the earthquake, Johanne came to accept that she wouldn't get all of the help she needed and that she might never again see the friends and neighbors who had once given her life so much meaning. As she and her daughters moved from one temporary tent or hut to another throughout the country, always at risk of developing serious diseases, she gradually gave up all hope that her life would ever return to normal. In this light, Johanne's reactions do not seem quite so inappropriate. If anything is abnormal here, it is her situation. Many human experiences produce intense reactions—financial ruin, large-scale catastrophes and disasters, rape, child abuse, war, terminal illness, chronic pain (Janssen et al., 2015). Is there an "appropriate" way to react to such things? Should we ever call reactions to such experiences abnormal?

Distress

Even functioning that is considered unusual does not necessarily qualify as abnormal. According to many clinical theorists, behavior, ideas, or emotions usually have to cause *distress* before they can be labeled abnormal. Consider the Ice Breakers, a group of people in Michigan who go swimming in lakes throughout the state every weekend from November through February. The colder the weather, the better they like it. One man, a member of the group for 17 years, says he loves the challenge of human against nature. A 37-year-old lawyer believes that the weekly shock is good for her health. "It cleanses me," she says. "It perks me up and gives me strength."

Chaideer Mahyuddin/AFP/Getty Images

Dealing with deviance
Each culture identifies and deals with deviant behavior in its own way. For example, uncomfortable with the deviant appearance of young punk rockers—mohawks, tattoos, nose piercings, tight jeans, and chains—shari'a police in Aceh province on Sumatra Island in Indonesia arrested 60 such youth in 2011 and made them undergo a 10-day "moral rehabilitation" camp. There the rockers were forced to have their heads shaved, bathe in a lake, wear traditional clothes, remove their piercings, and pray.

▶ **abnormal psychology** The scientific study of abnormal behavior undertaken to describe, predict, explain, and change abnormal patterns of functioning.

▶ **norms** A society's stated and unstated rules for proper conduct.

▶ **culture** A people's common history, values, institutions, habits, skills, technology, and arts.

AP Photo/David Guttenfelder

Context is key On the morning after Japan's devastating earthquake and tsunami in 2011, Reiko Kikuta (right) and her husband Takeshi watch workers try to attach ropes to their home and pull it ashore. Anxiety and depression were common and seemingly normal reactions in the wake of this extraordinary disaster, rather than being clear symptoms of psychopathology.

Certainly these people are different from most of us, but is their behavior abnormal? Far from experiencing distress, they feel energized and challenged. Their positive feelings must cause us to hesitate before we decide that they are functioning abnormally.

Should we conclude, then, that feelings of distress must always be present before a person's functioning can be considered abnormal? Not necessarily. Some people who function abnormally maintain a positive frame of mind. Consider once again Alberto, the young man who hears mysterious voices. What if he enjoyed listening to the voices, felt honored to be chosen, loved sending out warnings on the Internet, and looked forward to saving the world? Shouldn't we still regard his functioning as abnormal?

Dysfunction

Abnormal behavior tends to be *dysfunctional;* that is, it interferes with daily functioning (Bergner & Bunford, 2014). It so upsets, distracts, or confuses people that they cannot care for themselves properly, participate in ordinary social interactions, or work productively. Alberto, for example, has quit his job, left his family, and prepared to withdraw from the productive life he once led. Because our society holds that it is important to carry out daily activities in an effective manner, Alberto's behavior is likely to be regarded as abnormal and undesirable. In contrast, the Ice Breakers, who continue to perform well in their jobs and enjoy fulfilling relationships, would probably be considered simply unusual.

Danger

Perhaps the ultimate in psychological dysfunctioning is behavior that becomes *dangerous* to oneself or others. Individuals whose behavior is consistently careless, hostile, or confused may be placing themselves or those around them at risk. Alberto, for example, seems to be endangering both himself, with his diet, and others, with his buildup of arms and ammunition.

Although danger is often cited as a feature of abnormal psychological functioning, research suggests that it is actually the exception rather than the rule (Stuber et al., 2014). Most people struggling with anxiety, depression, and even bizarre thinking pose no immediate danger to themselves or to anyone else.

The Elusive Nature of Abnormality

Efforts to define psychological abnormality typically raise as many questions as they answer. Ultimately, a society selects general criteria for defining abnormality and then uses those criteria to judge particular cases. One clinical theorist, Thomas Szasz (1920–2012), placed such emphasis on society's role that he found the whole concept of mental illness to be invalid, a *myth* of sorts (Szasz, 2011, 1963, 1960). According to Szasz, the deviations that society calls abnormal are simply "problems in living," not signs of something wrong within the person.

Even if we assume that psychological abnormality is a valid concept and that it can indeed be defined, we may be unable to apply our definition consistently. If a behavior—excessive use of alcohol among college students, say—is familiar enough,

> **What behaviors fit the criteria of deviant, distressful, dysfunctional, or dangerous but would not be considered abnormal by most people?**

▶ **treatment** A systematic procedure designed to change abnormal behavior into more normal behavior. Also called *therapy.*

the society may fail to recognize that it is deviant, distressful, dysfunctional, and dangerous. Thousands of college students throughout the United States are so dependent on alcohol that it interferes with their personal and academic lives, causes them great discomfort, jeopardizes their health, and often endangers them and the people around them (Merrill et al., 2014). Yet their problem often goes unnoticed and undiagnosed. Alcohol is so much a part of the college subculture that it is easy to overlook drinking behavior that has become abnormal.

Conversely, a society may have trouble separating an abnormality that requires intervention from an *eccentricity,* an unusual pattern with which others have no right to interfere. From time to time we see or hear about people who behave in ways we consider strange, such as a man who lives alone with two dozen cats and rarely talks to other people. The behavior of such people is deviant, and it may well be distressful and dysfunctional, yet many professionals think of it as eccentric rather than abnormal (see *PsychWatch* on the next page).

In short, while we may agree to define psychological abnormalities as patterns of functioning that are deviant, distressful, dysfunctional, and sometimes dangerous, we should be clear that these criteria are often vague and subjective. In turn, few of the current categories of abnormality that you will meet in this book are as clear-cut as they may seem, and most continue to be debated by clinicians.

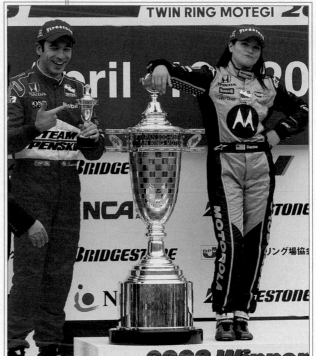

AP Photo/Katsumi Kasahara

Changing times Just decades ago, a woman's love for race car driving would have been considered strange, perhaps even abnormal. Today, Danica Patrick (right) is one of America's finest race car drivers. The size difference between her first-place trophy at the Indy Japan 300 auto race and that of second-place male driver Hélio Castroneves symbolizes just how far women have come in this sport.

➤ *Summing Up*

WHAT IS PSYCHOLOGICAL ABNORMALITY? The field devoted to the scientific study of abnormal behavior is called abnormal psychology. Abnormal functioning is generally considered to be deviant, distressful, dysfunctional, and dangerous. Behavior must also be considered in the context in which it occurs, however, and the concept of abnormality depends on the norms and values of the society in question.

What Is Treatment?

Once clinicians decide that a person is indeed suffering from some form of psychological abnormality, they seek to treat it. **Treatment,** or **therapy,** is a procedure designed to change abnormal behavior into more normal behavior; it, too, requires careful definition. For clinical scientists, the problem is closely related to defining abnormality. Consider the case of Bill:

February: *He cannot leave the house; Bill knows that for a fact. Home is the only place where he feels safe—safe from humiliation, danger, even ruin. If he were to go to work, his coworkers would somehow reveal their contempt for him. A pointed remark, a quizzical look—that's all it would take for him to get the message. If he were to go shopping at the store, before long everyone would be staring at him. Surely others would see his dark mood and thoughts; he wouldn't be able to hide them. He dare not even go for a walk alone in the woods—his heart would probably start racing again, bringing him to his knees and leaving him breathless, incoherent, and unable to get home. No, he's much better off staying in his room, trying to get*

(continues on the next page)

through another evening of this curse called life. Thank goodness for the Internet. Were it not for his reading of news sites and blog posts and online forums, he would, he knows, be cut off from the world altogether.

July: Bill's life revolves around his circle of friends: Bob and Jack, whom he knows from the office, where he was recently promoted to director of customer relations, and Frank and Tim, his weekend tennis partners. The gang meets for dinner every week at someone's house, and they chat about life, politics, and their jobs. Particularly special in Bill's life is Janice. They go to movies, restaurants, and shows together. She thinks Bill's just terrific, and Bill finds himself beaming whenever she's around. Bill looks forward to work each day and to his one-on-one dealings with customers. He is taking part in many activities and relationships and more fully enjoying life.

Bill's thoughts, feelings, and behavior interfered with all aspects of his life in February. Yet most of his symptoms had disappeared by July. All sorts of factors may have contributed to Bill's improvement—advice from friends and family members, a new job or vacation, perhaps a big change in his diet or exercise regimen. Any or all of these things may have been useful to Bill, but they could not be considered treatment or therapy. Those terms are usually reserved for special, systematic procedures

PsychWatch

Marching to a Different Drummer: Eccentrics

➤ Writer **James Joyce** always carried a tiny pair of lady's bloomers, which he waved in the air to show approval.

➤ **Benjamin Franklin** took "air baths" for his health, sitting naked in front of an open window.

➤ **Alexander Graham Bell** covered the windows of his house to keep out the rays of the full moon. He also tried to teach his dog how to talk.

➤ Writer **D. H. Lawrence** enjoyed removing his clothes and climbing mulberry trees.

These famous persons have been called eccentrics. The dictionary defines an *eccentric* as a person who deviates from common behavior patterns or displays odd or whimsical behavior. But how can we separate a psychologically healthy person who has unusual habits from a person whose oddness is a symptom of psychopathology? Little research has been done on eccentrics, but a few studies offer some insights (Stares, 2005; Pickover, 1999; Weeks & James, 1995).

Researcher David Weeks studied 1,000 eccentrics and estimated that as many as 1 in 5,000 persons may be "classic, full-time eccentrics." Weeks

pinpointed 15 characteristics common to the eccentrics in his study: *nonconformity, creativity, strong curiosity, idealism, extreme interests and hobbies, lifelong awareness of being different, high intelligence, outspokenness, noncompetitive-*

Lance Manion/Retna Ltd./Corbis

ness, unusual eating and living habits, disinterest in others' opinions or company, mischievous sense of humor, nonmarriage, eldest or only child, and *poor spelling skills.*

Weeks suggests that eccentrics do not typically suffer from mental disorders. Whereas the unusual behavior of persons with mental disorders is thrust upon them and usually causes them suffering, eccentricity is chosen freely and provides pleasure. In short, "Eccentrics know they're different and glory in it" (Weeks & James, 1995, p. 14). Similarly, the thought processes of eccentrics are not severely disrupted and do not leave these persons dysfunctional. In fact, Weeks found that eccentrics in his study actually had fewer emotional problems than individuals in the general population. Perhaps being an "original" is good for mental health.

Musical eccentric Pop superstar Lady Gaga is known far and wide for her eccentric behavior, outrageous sense of fashion, and unusual performing style. Her millions of fans enjoy her unusual persona every bit as much as the lyrics and music that she writes and sings.

for helping people overcome their psychological difficulties. According to clinical theorist Jerome Frank, all forms of therapy have three key features:

1. A *sufferer* who seeks relief from the healer.
2. A trained, socially accepted *healer,* whose expertise is accepted by the sufferer and his or her social group.
3. A *series of contacts* between the healer and the sufferer, through which the healer . . . tries to produce certain changes in the sufferer's emotional state, attitudes, and behavior.

(Frank, 1973, pp. 2–3)

Despite this straightforward definition, clinical treatment is surrounded by conflict and confusion. Carl Rogers, a pioneer in the modern clinical field (you will meet him in Chapter 2), noted that "therapists are not in agreement as to their goals or aims. . . . They are not in agreement as to what constitutes a successful outcome of their work. They cannot agree as to what constitutes a failure. It seems as though the field is completely chaotic and divided."

Some clinicians view abnormality as an illness and so consider therapy a procedure that helps *cure* the illness. Others see abnormality as a problem in living and therapists as *teachers* of more functional behavior and thought. Clinicians even differ on what to call the person who receives therapy: those who see abnormality as an illness speak of the "patient," while those who view it as a problem in living refer to the "client." Because both terms are so common, this book will use them interchangeably.

Despite their differences, most clinicians do agree that large numbers of people need therapy of one kind or another. Later you will encounter evidence that therapy is indeed often helpful.

AP Photo/Paul White

Therapy . . . not Recently, a hotel in Spain that was about to undergo major renovations invited members of the public to relieve their stress by destroying the rooms on one floor of the hotel. This activity may indeed have been therapeutic for some, but it was not *therapy.* It lacked, among other things, a "trained healer" and a series of systematic contacts between healer and sufferer.

> ## ➤ *Summing Up*
>
> **WHAT IS TREATMENT?** Therapy is a systematic process for helping people overcome their psychological difficulties. It typically requires a patient, a therapist, and a series of therapeutic contacts.

How Was Abnormality Viewed and Treated in the Past?

In any given year, as many as 30 percent of the adults and 19 percent of the children and adolescents in the United States display serious psychological disturbances and are in need of clinical treatment (Merikangas et al., 2013; Kessler et al., 2012, 2009). The rates in other countries are similarly high. It is tempting to conclude that something about the modern world is responsible for these many emotional problems—perhaps rapid technological change, the growing threat of terrorism, or a decline in religious, family, or other support systems (Paslakis et al., 2015; Gelkopf et al., 2013). But every society, past and present, has witnessed psychological abnormality. Perhaps, then, the proper place to begin our examination of abnormal behavior and treatment is in the past.

Ancient Views and Treatments

Historians who have examined the unearthed bones, artwork, and other remnants of ancient societies have concluded that these societies probably regarded abnormal behavior as the work of evil spirits. People in prehistoric societies apparently

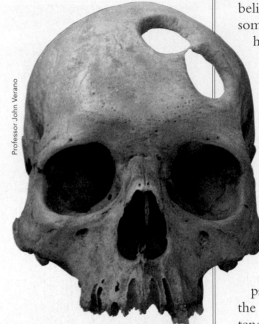

Professor John Verano

Expelling evil spirits The two holes in this skull recovered from ancient times indicate that the person underwent trephination, possibly for the purpose of releasing evil spirits and curing mental dysfunctioning.

believed that all events around and within them resulted from the actions of magical, sometimes sinister, beings who controlled the world. In particular, they viewed the human body and mind as a battleground between external forces of good and evil. Abnormal behavior was typically interpreted as a victory by evil spirits, and the cure for such behavior was to force the demons from a victim's body.

This supernatural view of abnormality may have begun as far back as the Stone Age, a half-million years ago. Some skulls from that period recovered in Europe and South America show evidence of an operation called **trephination,** in which a stone instrument, or *trephine,* was used to cut away a circular section of the skull (Heeramun-Aubeeluck & Lu, 2013). Some historians have concluded that this early operation was performed as a treatment for severe abnormal behavior—either hallucinations, in which people saw or heard things not actually present, or melancholia, characterized by extreme sadness and immobility. The purpose of opening the skull was to release the evil spirits that were supposedly causing the problem (Selling, 1940).

Later societies also explained abnormal behavior by pointing to possession by demons. Egyptian, Chinese, and Hebrew writings all account for psychological deviance this way, and the Bible describes how an evil spirit from the Lord affected King Saul and how David pretended to be mad to convince his enemies that he was visited by divine forces.

The treatment for abnormality in these early societies was often *exorcism*. The idea was to coax the evil spirits to leave or to make the person's body an uncomfortable place in which to live. A *shaman,* or priest, might recite prayers, plead with the evil spirits, insult the spirits, perform magic, make loud noises, or have the person drink bitter potions. If these techniques failed, the shaman performed a more extreme form of exorcism, such as whipping or starving the person.

> **What demonological explanations or treatments, besides exorcism, are still around today, and why do they persist?**

Greek and Roman Views and Treatments

In the years from roughly 500 B.C. to 500 A.D., when the Greek and Roman civilizations thrived, philosophers and physicians often offered different explanations and treatments for abnormal behaviors. Hippocrates (460–377 B.C.), often called the father of modern medicine, taught that illnesses had *natural* causes. He saw abnormal behavior as a disease arising from internal physical problems. Specifically, he believed that some form of brain pathology was the culprit and that it resulted—like all other forms of disease, in his view—from an imbalance of four fluids, or **humors,** that flowed through the body: *yellow bile, black bile, blood,* and *phlegm* (Wolters, 2013). An excess of yellow bile, for example, caused frenzied activity; an excess of black bile was the source of unshakable sadness.

To treat psychological dysfunctioning, Hippocrates sought to correct the underlying physical pathology. He believed, for instance, that the excess of black bile underlying sadness could be reduced by a quiet life, a diet of vegetables, exercise, celibacy, and even bleeding. Hippocrates' focus on internal causes for abnormal behavior was shared by the great Greek philosophers Plato (427–347 B.C.) and Aristotle (384–322 B.C.) and by influential Greek and Roman physicians.

Europe in the Middle Ages: Demonology Returns

The enlightened views of Greek and Roman physicians and scholars were not enough to shake ordinary people's belief in demons. And with the decline of Rome, demonological views and practices became popular once again. A growing distrust of science spread throughout Europe.

▶ **trephination** An ancient operation in which a stone instrument was used to cut away a circular section of the skull, perhaps to treat abnormal behavior.

▶ **humors** According to the Greeks and Romans, bodily chemicals that influence mental and physical functioning.

From 500 to 1350 A.D., the period known as the Middle Ages, the power of the clergy increased greatly throughout Europe. In those days the church rejected scientific forms of investigation, and it controlled all education. Religious beliefs, which were highly superstitious and demonological, came to dominate all aspects of life. Deviant behavior, particularly psychological dysfunctioning, was seen as evidence of Satan's influence.

The Middle Ages were a time of great stress and anxiety—of war, urban uprisings, and plagues. People blamed the devil for these troubles and feared being possessed by him (Sluhovsky, 2011). Abnormal behavior apparently increased greatly during this period. In addition, there were outbreaks of *mass madness,* in which large numbers of people apparently shared absurd false beliefs and imagined sights or sounds. In one such disorder, *tarantism* (also known as *Saint Vitus' dance*), groups of people would suddenly start to jump, dance, and go into convulsions (Prochwicz & Sobczyk, 2011; Sigerist, 1943). All were convinced that they had been bitten and possessed by a wolf spider, now called a tarantula, and they sought to cure their disorder by performing a dance called a tarantella. In another form of mass madness, *lycanthropy,* people thought they were possessed by wolves or other animals. They acted wolflike and imagined that fur was growing all over their bodies.

Not surprisingly, some of the earlier demonological treatments for psychological abnormality reemerged during the Middle Ages. Once again the key to the cure was to rid the person's body of the devil that possessed it. Exorcisms were revived, and clergymen, who generally were in charge of treatment during this period, would plead, chant, or pray to the devil or evil spirit (Sluhovsky, 2011, 2007). If these techniques did not work, they had others to try, some amounting to torture.

It was not until the Middle Ages drew to a close that demonology and its methods began to lose favor. Towns throughout Europe grew into cities, and government officials gained more power and took over nonreligious activities. Among their other responsibilities, they began to run hospitals and direct the care of people suffering from mental disorders. Medical views of abnormality gained favor once again, and many people with psychological disturbances received treatment in medical hospitals, such as the Trinity Hospital in England (Allderidge, 1979).

> **How might Twitter, text messaging, Instagram, Facebook, the Internet, or other technologies facilitate current forms of mass madness?**

Bewitched or bewildered? A great fear of witchcraft swept Europe beginning in the 1300s and extending through the "enlightened" Renaissance. Tens of thousands of people, mostly women, were thought to have made a pact with the devil. Some appear to have had mental disorders, which caused them to act strangely (Zilboorg & Henry, 1941). This woman is being "dunked" repeatedly until she confesses to witchery.

© Bettmann/Cortis

The Renaissance and the Rise of Asylums

During the early part of the Renaissance, a period of flourishing cultural and scientific activity from about 1400 to 1700, demonological views of abnormality continued to decline. German physician Johann Weyer (1515–1588), the first physician to specialize in mental illness, believed that the mind was as susceptible to sickness as the body was. He is now considered the founder of the modern study of psychopathology.

The care of people with mental disorders improved in this atmosphere. In England, such individuals might be kept at home while their families were aided financially by the local parish. Across Europe, religious shrines were devoted to the humane and loving treatment of people with mental disorders. Perhaps the best known of these shrines was at Gheel in Belgium. Beginning in the fifteenth century, people came to Gheel from all over the world for psychic healing. Local residents welcomed these pilgrims into their homes, and many stayed on to form the world's first "colony" of mental patients. Gheel was the forerunner of today's *community mental health programs* (Guarnieri, 2009; Aring, 1975, 1974). Many patients still live in foster homes there, interacting with other residents, until they recover.

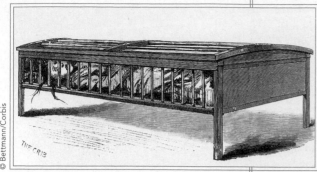

The "crib" Outrageous devices and techniques, such as the "crib," were used in asylums, and some continued to be used even during the reforms of the nineteenth century.

Unfortunately, these improvements in care began to fade by the mid-sixteenth century. Government officials discovered that private homes and community residences could house only a small percentage of those with severe mental disorders and that medical hospitals were too few and too small. More and more, they converted hospitals and monasteries into **asylums,** institutions whose primary purpose was to care for people with mental illness. These institutions were begun with the intention that they would provide good care (Kazano, 2012). Once the asylums started to overflow, however, they became virtual prisons where patients were held in filthy conditions and treated with unspeakable cruelty.

In 1547, for example, Bethlehem Hospital was given to the city of London by Henry VIII for the sole purpose of confining the mentally ill. In this asylum, patients bound in chains cried out for all to hear. The hospital even became a popular tourist attraction; people were eager to pay to look at the howling and gibbering inmates. The hospital's name, pronounced "Bedlam" by the local people, has come to mean a chaotic uproar (Selling, 1940).

The Nineteenth Century: Reform and Moral Treatment

Historians usually point to La Bicêtre, an asylum in Paris for male patients, as the first site of asylum reform. In 1793, during the French Revolution, Philippe Pinel (1745–1826) was named the chief physician there. He argued that the patients were sick people whose illnesses should be treated with sympathy and kindness rather than chains and beatings (Yakushev & Sidorov, 2013). He allowed them to move freely about the hospital grounds; replaced the dark dungeons with sunny, airy rooms; and offered support and advice. Pinel's approach proved remarkably successful. Many patients who had been shut away for decades improved greatly over a short period of time and were released. Pinel later brought similar reforms to a mental hospital in Paris for female patients, La Salpetrière.

Meanwhile, an English Quaker named William Tuke (1732–1819) was bringing similar reforms to northern England. In 1796 he founded the York Retreat, a rural estate where about 30 mental patients lived as guests in quiet country houses and were treated with a combination of rest, talk, prayer, and manual work (Kibria & Metcalfe, 2014).

The Spread of Moral Treatment

The methods of Pinel and Tuke, called **moral treatment** because they emphasized moral guidance and humane and respectful techniques, caught on throughout Europe and the United States. Patients with psychological problems were increasingly perceived as potentially productive human beings who deserved individual care, including discussions of their problems, useful activities, work, companionship, and quiet.

The person most responsible for the early spread of moral treatment in the United States was Benjamin Rush (1745–1813), an eminent physician at Pennsylvania Hospital who is now considered the father of American psychiatry. Limiting his practice to mental illness, Rush developed humane approaches to treatment (Grossman, 2013; Rush, 2010). For example, he required that the hospital hire intelligent and sensitive attendants to work closely with patients, reading and talking to them and taking them on regular walks. He also suggested that it would be therapeutic for doctors to give small gifts to their patients now and then.

Rush's work was influential, but it was a Boston schoolteacher named Dorothea Dix (1802–1887) who made humane

Dance in a madhouse A popular feature of moral treatment was the "lunatic ball." Hospital officials would bring patients together to dance and enjoy themselves. One such ball is shown in this painting, *Dance in a Madhouse,* by George Bellows.

care a public and political concern in the United States. From 1841 to 1881, Dix went from state legislature to state legislature and to Congress speaking of the horrors she had observed at asylums and calling for reform. Dix's campaign led to new laws and greater government funding to improve the treatment of people with mental disorders (Davidson et al., 2010). Each state was made responsible for developing effective public mental hospitals, or **state hospitals,** all of which were intended to offer moral treatment. Similar hospitals were established throughout Europe.

The Decline of Moral Treatment By the 1850s, a number of mental hospitals throughout Europe and America reported success using moral approaches. By the end of that century, however, several factors led to a reversal of the moral treatment movement (Kazano, 2012). One factor was the speed with which the movement had spread. As mental hospitals multiplied, severe money and staffing shortages developed, recovery rates declined, and overcrowding in the hospitals became a major problem. Another factor was the assumption behind moral treatment that all patients could be cured if treated with humanity and dignity. For some, this was indeed sufficient. Others, however, needed more effective treatments than any that had yet been developed. An additional factor contributing to the decline of moral treatment was the emergence of a new wave of prejudice against people with mental disorders. The public came to view them as strange and dangerous, undeserving of donations or government funds. Moreover, many of the patients entering public mental hospitals in the United States in the late nineteenth century were poor foreign immigrants, whom the public had little interest in helping.

By the early years of the twentieth century, the moral treatment movement had ground to a halt in both the United States and Europe. Public mental hospitals were providing only custodial care and ineffective medical treatments and were becoming more overcrowded every year. Long-term hospitalization became the rule once again.

The Early Twentieth Century: The Somatogenic and Psychogenic Perspectives

As the moral movement was declining in the late 1800s, two opposing perspectives emerged and began to compete for the attention of clinicians: the **somatogenic perspective,** the view that abnormal psychological functioning has physical causes, and the **psychogenic perspective,** the view that the chief causes of abnormal functioning are psychological. These perspectives came into full bloom during the twentieth century.

The Somatogenic Perspective The somatogenic perspective has at least a 2,400-year history—remember Hippocrates' view that abnormal behavior resulted from brain disease and an imbalance of humors? Not until the late 1800s, however, did this perspective make a triumphant return and begin to gain wide acceptance.

Two factors were responsible for this rebirth. One was the work of a distinguished German researcher, Emil Kraepelin (1856–1926). In 1883, Kraepelin published an influential textbook arguing that physical factors, such as fatigue, are responsible for mental dysfunction. In addition, as you will see in Chapter 3, he developed the first modern system for classifying abnormal behaviors, listing their physical causes and discussing their course (Hoff, 2015; Jäger et al., 2013).

New biological discoveries also triggered the rise of the somatogenic perspective. One of the most important discoveries was that an organic disease, *syphilis,* led to *general paresis,* an irreversible disorder that featured both mental symptoms such as delusions of grandeur and physical ones like paralysis (Hogebrug et al., 2013). In 1897, German neurologist Richard von Krafft-Ebing (1840–1902) injected matter from syphilis sores into patients suffering from general paresis and found that none

///// BETWEEN THE LINES /////

Early Asylums

Most of the patients in Middle Age asylums, from all classes and circumstances, were women.

The first asylum in colonial America was established in Williamsburg, Virginia, in 1773.

(faqs.org, 2014; Barton, 2004)

▶ **asylum** A type of institution that first became popular in the sixteenth century to provide care for persons with mental disorders. Most became virtual prisons.

▶ **moral treatment** A nineteenth-century approach to treating people with mental dysfunction that emphasized moral guidance and humane and respectful treatment.

▶ **state hospitals** State-run public mental institutions in the United States.

▶ **somatogenic perspective** The view that abnormal psychological functioning has physical causes.

▶ **psychogenic perspective** The view that the chief causes of abnormal functioning are psychological.

of the patients developed symptoms of syphilis. Their immunity could have been caused only by an earlier case of syphilis. Since all of his patients with general paresis were now immune to syphilis, Krafft-Ebing theorized that syphilis had been the cause of their general paresis. The work of Kraepelin and the new understanding of general paresis led many researchers and practitioners to suspect that physical factors were responsible for many mental disorders, perhaps all of them.

Despite the general optimism, biological approaches yielded mostly disappointing results throughout the first half of the twentieth century. Although many medical treatments were developed for patients in mental hospitals during that time, most of the techniques failed to work. Physicians tried tooth extraction, tonsillectomy, hydrotherapy (alternating hot and cold baths), and lobotomy, a surgical cutting of certain nerve fibers in the brain. Even worse, biological views and claims led, in some circles, to proposals for immoral solutions such as *eugenic sterilization,* the elimination (through medical or other means) of individuals' ability to reproduce (see Table 1-1). Not until the 1950s, when a number of effective medications were finally discovered, did the somatogenic perspective truly begin to pay off for patients.

The Psychogenic Perspective The late 1800s also saw the emergence of the psychogenic perspective, the view that the chief causes of abnormal functioning are often psychological. This view, too, had a long history, but it did not gain much of a following until studies of *hypnotism* demonstrated its potential.

Hypnotism is a procedure in which a person is placed in a trancelike mental state during which he or she becomes extremely suggestible. It was used to help treat psychological disorders as far back as 1778, when an Austrian physician named Friedrich Anton Mesmer (1734–1815) set up a clinic in Paris. His patients suffered from *hysterical disorders,* mysterious bodily ailments that had no apparent physical basis. Mesmer had his patients sit in a darkened room filled with music; then he

table: 1-1

Eugenics and Mental Disorders

Year	Event
1896	Connecticut became the first state in the United States to prohibit persons with mental disorders from marrying.
1896–1933	Every state in the United States passed a law prohibiting marriage by persons with mental disorders.
1907	Indiana became the first state to pass a bill calling for people with mental disorders, as well as criminals and other "defectives," to undergo sterilization.
1927	The U.S. Supreme Court ruled that eugenic sterilization was constitutional.
1907–1945	Approximately 45,000 Americans were sterilized under eugenic sterilization laws; 21,000 of them were patients in state mental hospitals.
1929–1932	Denmark, Norway, Sweden, Finland, and Iceland passed eugenic sterilization laws.
1933	Germany passed a eugenic sterilization law, under which 375,000 people were sterilized by 1940.
1940	Nazi Germany began to use "proper gases" to kill people with mental disorders; 70,000 or more people were killed in less than 2 years.

Information from: Fischer, 2012; Whitaker, 2002.

▶ **psychoanalysis** Either the theory or the treatment of abnormal mental functioning that emphasizes unconscious psychological forces as the cause of psychopathology.

appeared, dressed in a colorful costume, and touched the troubled area of each patient's body with a special rod. A surprising number of patients seemed to be helped by this treatment, called *mesmerism* (Musikantow, 2011; Dingfelder, 2010). Their pain, numbness, or paralysis disappeared. Several scientists believed that Mesmer was inducing a trancelike state in his patients and that this state was causing their symptoms to disappear. The treatment was so controversial, however, that eventually Mesmer was banished from Paris.

It was not until years after Mesmer died that many researchers had the courage to investigate his procedure, later called *hypnotism* (from *hypnos*, the Greek word for "sleep"), and its effects on hysterical disorders. The experiments of two physicians practicing in the city of Nancy in France, Hippolyte-Marie Bernheim (1840–1919) and Ambroise-Auguste Liébault (1823–1904), showed that hysterical disorders could actually be induced in otherwise normal people while they were under the influence of hypnotism. That is, the physicians could make normal people experience deafness, paralysis, blindness, or numbness by means of hypnotic suggestion—and they could remove these artificial symptoms by the same means. Thus they established that a *mental* process—hypnotic suggestion—could both cause and cure even a physical dysfunction. Leading scientists concluded that hysterical disorders were largely psychological in origin, and the psychogenic perspective rose in popularity.

Among those who studied the effects of hypnotism on hysterical disorders was Josef Breuer (1842–1925) of Vienna. Breuer, a physician, discovered that his patients sometimes awoke free of hysterical symptoms after speaking openly under hypnosis about past upsetting events. During the 1890s, Breuer was joined in his work by another Viennese physician, Sigmund Freud (1856–1939). As you will see in Chapter 2, Freud's work eventually led him to develop the theory of **psychoanalysis,** which holds that many forms of abnormal and normal psychological functioning are psychogenic. In particular, Freud believed that *unconscious* psychological processes are at the root of such functioning.

Freud also developed the *technique* of psychoanalysis, a form of discussion in which clinicians help troubled people gain insight into their unconscious psychological processes. He believed that such insight, even without hypnotic procedures, would help the patients overcome their psychological problems. Freud and his

Hypnotism update Hypnotism, the procedure that opened the door for the psychogenic perspective, continues to influence many areas of modern life, including the fields of psychotherapy, entertainment, and law enforcement. Here a forensic clinician uses hypnosis to help a witness recall the details of a crime. Recent research has clarified, however, that hypnotic procedures are as capable of creating false memories as they are of uncovering real memories.

The more things change . . . Patients at a modern-day mental hospital in Bangladesh eat their lunch off of the floor of their ward. Such conditions are similar to those that existed in some state hospitals throughout the United States well into the twentieth century.

All About Freud

Freud's parents often favored Sigmund over his siblings.

Freud's fee for one session of therapy was $20.

For almost 40 years, Freud treated patients 10 hours per day, 5 or 6 days per week.

Freud's four sisters died in Nazi concentration camps.

Freud was nominated for the Nobel Prize in 12 different years, but never won.

(Nobel Media, 2014; Cherry, 2010; Hess, 2009; Gay, 2006, 1999; Jacobs, 2003)

followers offered treatment to patients in their offices for sessions of approximately an hour—a format now known as *outpatient therapy*. By the early twentieth century, psychoanalytic theory and treatment were widely accepted throughout the Western world (Messias, 2014).

➤ *Summing Up*

HOW WAS ABNORMALITY VIEWED AND TREATED IN THE PAST? The history of psychological disorders stretches back to ancient times. Prehistoric societies apparently viewed abnormal behavior as the work of evil spirits. There is evidence that Stone Age cultures used trephination, a primitive form of brain surgery, to treat abnormal behavior. People of early societies also sought to drive out evil spirits by exorcism.

Physicians of the Greek and Roman empires offered more enlightened explanations of mental disorders. Hippocrates believed that abnormal behavior was caused by an imbalance of the four bodily fluids, or humors.

Unfortunately, throughout history each period of enlightened thinking about psychological functioning has been followed by a period of backward thinking. In the Middle Ages, for example, Europeans returned to demonological explanations of abnormal behavior. The clergy was very influential and held that mental disorders were the work of the devil. As the Middle Ages drew to a close, such explanations and treatments began to decline, and care of people with mental disorders improved during the early part of the Renaissance. Certain religious shrines became dedicated to the humane treatment of such individuals. Unfortunately, this enlightened approach was short-lived, and by the middle of the sixteenth century persons with mental disorders were being warehoused in asylums.

Care of people with mental disorders started to improve again in the nineteenth century. In Paris, Philippe Pinel started the movement toward moral treatment. In the United States, Dorothea Dix spearheaded a movement to ensure legal rights and protection for people with mental disorders and to establish state hospitals for their care. Unfortunately, the moral treatment movement disintegrated by the late nineteenth century, and mental hospitals again became warehouses where inmates received minimal care.

The turn of the twentieth century saw the return of the somatogenic perspective, the view that abnormal psychological functioning is caused primarily by physical factors. The same period saw the rise of the psychogenic perspective, the view that the chief causes of abnormal functioning are psychological. Sigmund Freud's psychogenic approach, psychoanalysis, eventually gained wide acceptance and influenced future generations of clinicians.

Lunar Myths

Although it is popularly believed that a full moon is regularly accompanied by significant increases in crime, strange and abnormal behaviors, and admissions to mental hospitals, decades of research have failed to support this notion.

(Bakalar, 2013, 2011; Schafer et al., 2010; McLay et al., 2006)

Current Trends

It would hardly be accurate to say that we now live in a period of great enlightenment about or dependable treatment of mental disorders. In fact, surveys have found that 43 percent of respondents believe that people bring mental disorders on themselves, and 35 percent consider such disorders to be caused by sinful behavior (Stuber et al., 2014; NMHA, 1999). Nevertheless, there have been major changes over the past 50 years in the ways clinicians understand and treat abnormal functioning. There are more theories and types of treatment, more research studies, more information, and—perhaps because of those increases—more disagreements about abnormal functioning today than at any time in the past.

How Are People with Severe Disturbances Cared for?

In the 1950s, researchers discovered a number of new **psychotropic medications**—drugs that primarily affect the brain and reduce many symptoms of mental dysfunctioning. They included the first *antipsychotic drugs,* which correct extremely confused and distorted thinking; *antidepressant drugs,* which lift the mood of depressed people; and *antianxiety drugs,* which reduce tension and worry.

When given these drugs, many patients who had spent years in mental hospitals began to show signs of improvement. Hospital administrators, encouraged by these results and pressured by a growing public outcry over the terrible conditions in public mental hospitals, began to discharge patients almost immediately.

Since the discovery of these medications, mental health professionals in most of the developed nations of the world have followed a policy of **deinstitutionalization,** releasing hundreds of thousands of patients from public mental hospitals. On any given day in 1955, close to 600,000 people were confined in public mental institutions across the United States (see Figure 1-1). Today the daily patient population in the same kinds of hospitals is less than 40,000 (Althouse, 2010).

In short, outpatient care has now become the primary mode of treatment for people with severe psychological disturbances as well as for those with more moderate problems. When severely disturbed people do need institutionalization these days, they are usually hospitalized for a short period of time. Ideally, they are then provided with outpatient psychotherapy and medication in community programs and residences (Stein et al., 2015).

Chapters 2 and 12 will look more closely at this recent emphasis on community care for people with severe psychological disturbances—a philosophy called the *community mental health approach.* The approach has been helpful for many patients, but too few community programs are available to address current needs in the United States (Dixon & Schwarz, 2014). As a result, hundreds of thousands of persons with severe disturbances fail to make lasting recoveries, and they shuttle back and forth between the mental hospital and the community. After release from the hospital, they at best receive minimal care and often wind up living in decrepit rooming houses or on the streets. At least 100,000 people with such disturbances are homeless on any given day; another 135,000 or more are inmates of jails and prisons (Kooyman & Walsh, 2011; Althouse, 2010). Their abandonment is truly a national disgrace.

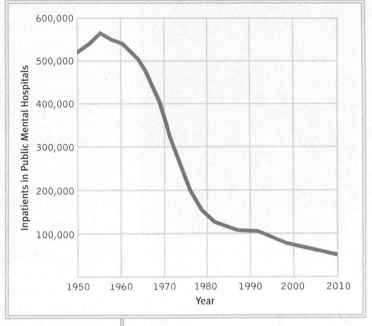

figure 1-1

The impact of deinstitutionalization
The number of patients (fewer than 40,000) now hospitalized in public mental hospitals in the United States is a small fraction of the number hospitalized in 1955. (Information from: Althouse, 2010; Torrey, 2001; Lang, 1999.)

How Are People with Less Severe Disturbances Treated?

The treatment picture for people with moderate psychological disturbances has been more positive than that for people with severe disorders. Since the 1950s, outpatient care has continued to be the preferred mode of treatment for them, and the number and types of facilities that offer such care have expanded to meet the need.

Before the 1950s, outpatient care exclusively took the form of **private psychotherapy,** in which individuals seek out a self-employed therapist for counseling services. Since the 1950s, most health insurance plans have expanded coverage to include private psychotherapy, so that it is now widely available to people of all incomes. Today, outpatient therapy is also offered in a number of less expensive settings, such as community mental health centers, crisis intervention centers, family service centers, and other social service agencies. Surveys suggest that nearly one of every six adults in the United States receives outpatient treatment for psychological disorders in the course of a year (NIMH, 2010).

▶ **psychotropic medications**
Drugs that mainly affect the brain and reduce many symptoms of mental dysfunctioning.

▶ **deinstitutionalization** The practice, begun in the 1960s, of releasing hundreds of thousands of patients from public mental hospitals.

▶ **private psychotherapy** An arrangement in which a person directly pays a therapist for counseling services.

From Juilliard to the streets Nathaniel Ayers, subject of the book and movie *The Soloist*, plays his violin on the streets of Los Angeles while living as a homeless person in 2005. Once a promising musical student at the Juilliard School in New York, Ayers developed schizophrenia and eventually found himself without treatment and without a home.

Outpatient treatments are also becoming available for more and more kinds of problems. When Freud and his colleagues first began to practice, most of their patients suffered from anxiety or depression. Almost half of today's clients suffer from those same problems, but people with other kinds of disorders are also receiving therapy. In addition, at least 20 percent of clients enter therapy because of milder problems in living—problems with marital, family, job, peer, school, or community relationships (Ten Have et al., 2013; Druss & Bornemann, 2010).

Yet another change in outpatient care since the 1950s has been the development of programs devoted exclusively to one kind of psychological problem. We now have, for example, suicide prevention centers, substance abuse programs, eating disorder programs, phobia clinics, and sexual dysfunction programs. Clinicians in these programs have the kind of expertise that can be acquired only by concentration in a single area.

A Growing Emphasis on Preventing Disorders and Promoting Mental Health

Although the community mental health approach has often failed to address the needs of people with severe disorders, it has given rise to an important principle of mental health care—**prevention** (Grill & Monsell, 2014). Rather than wait for psychological disorders to occur, many of today's community programs try to correct the social conditions that underlie psychological problems (poverty or violence in the community, for example) and to help individuals who are at risk for developing emotional problems (for example, teenage mothers or the children of people with severe psychological disorders). As you will see later, community prevention programs are not always successful, but they have grown in number, offering great promise as the ultimate form of intervention.

> Why do you think it has taken psychologists so long to start studying positive behaviors?

Prevention programs have been further energized in the past few years by the field of psychology's ever-growing interest in **positive psychology** (Ramirez et al., 2014; Seligman & Fowler, 2011). Positive psychology is the study and promotion of positive feelings such as optimism and happiness, positive traits like hard work and

Green spaces and mental health A young woman soaks in the green environment at Battersea Park in London. Recent positive psychology research has found that people who live in urban areas feel less distress and more life satisfaction if they reside in greener areas of their cities (White et al., 2013). Small wonder that Londoners with easy access to parks and green spaces report having a better quality of life than those living without it.

wisdom, positive abilities, and group-directed virtues, including altruism and tolerance (see *InfoCentral* on page 19).

While researchers study and learn more about positive psychology in the laboratory, clinical practitioners with this orientation are teaching people coping skills that may help protect them from stress and encouraging them to pursue psychological wellness, meaningful activities, and enriching relationships—thus preventing mental disorders (Sergeant & Mongrain, 2014).

Multicultural Psychology

We are, without question, a society of multiple cultures, races, and languages. Members of racial and ethnic minority groups in the United States collectively make up 35 percent of the population, a percentage that is expected to grow to more than 50 percent in the coming decades (Santa-Cruz, 2010; U.S. Census Bureau, 2010). This change is partly because of shifts in immigration trends and partly because of higher birth rates among minority groups in the United States (NVSR, 2010).

In response to this growing diversity, a new area of study called **multicultural psychology** has emerged. Multicultural psychologists seek to understand how culture, race, ethnicity, gender, and similar factors affect behavior and thought and how people of different cultures, races, and genders may differ psychologically (Alegría et al., 2013, 2010). As you will see throughout this book, the field of multicultural psychology has begun to have a powerful effect on our understanding and treatment of abnormal behavior.

The Increasing Influence of Insurance Coverage

So many people now seek therapy that insurance companies have changed their coverage for mental health patients. Today the dominant form of coverage is the **managed care program**—a program in which the insurance company determines such key issues as which therapists its clients may choose, the cost of sessions, and the number of sessions for which a client may be reimbursed (Domino, 2012; Glasser, 2010).

At least 75 percent of all privately insured persons in the United States are currently enrolled in managed care programs (Deb et al., 2006). The coverage for mental health treatment under such programs follows the same basic principles as coverage for medical treatment, including a limited pool of practitioners from which patients can choose, preapproval of treatment by the insurance company, strict standards for judging whether problems and treatments qualify for reimbursement, and ongoing reviews. In the mental health realm, both therapists and clients typically dislike managed care programs (Lustig et al., 2013). They fear that the programs inevitably shorten therapy (often for the worse), unfairly favor treatments whose results are not always lasting (for example, drug therapy), pose a special hardship for those with severe mental disorders, and result in treatments determined by insurance companies rather than by therapists (Turner, 2013).

A key problem with insurance coverage—both managed care and other kinds of insurance programs—is that reimbursements for mental disorders tend to be lower than those for medical disorders. This places persons with psychological difficulties at a distinct disadvantage (Sipe et al., 2015). Thus, in 2008 the U.S. Congress passed a federal *parity* law that directed insurance companies to provide equal coverage for mental and medical problems, and in 2014 the mental health provisions of the Affordable Care Act (the ACA)—referred to colloquially as "Obamacare"—went into effect and extended the reach of the earlier law. The ACA designates mental health care as 1 of 10 types of "essential health benefits" that *must* be provided by all insurers (SAMHSA, 2014; Pear, 2013). It also requires all health plans to provide *preventive* mental health services at no additional cost (for example, free screenings

AP Photo/Matthew S. Gunby

Positive psychology in action Often positive psychology and multicultural psychology work together. Here, for example, two young girls come together as one at the end of a "slave reconciliation" walk by 400 people in Maryland. The walk was intended to promote racial understanding and to help Americans overcome the lasting psychological effects of slavery.

▸ **prevention** Interventions aimed at deterring mental disorders before they can develop.

▸ **positive psychology** The study and enhancement of positive feelings, traits, and abilities.

▸ **multicultural psychology** The field that examines the impact of culture, race, ethnicity, and gender on behaviors and thoughts and focuses on how such factors may influence the origin, nature, and treatment of abnormal behavior.

▸ **managed care program** Health care coverage in which the insurance company largely controls the nature, scope, and cost of medical or psychological services.

for depressive disorders) and to allow membership to individuals who have preexisting mental conditions. It is not yet clear whether such provisions will in fact result in better treatment for people with psychological problems.

What Are Today's Leading Theories and Professions?

One of the most important developments in the clinical field has been the growth of numerous theoretical perspectives that now coexist in the field. Before the 1950s, the *psychoanalytic* perspective, with its emphasis on unconscious psychological problems as the cause of abnormal behavior, was dominant. Since then, additional influential perspectives have emerged, particularly the *biological, behavioral, cognitive, humanistic-existential,* and *sociocultural* schools of thought. At present, no single viewpoint dominates the clinical field as the psychoanalytic perspective once did. In fact, the perspectives often conflict and compete with one another.

In addition, a variety of professionals now offer help to people with psychological problems. Before the 1950s, psychotherapy was offered only by *psychiatrists,* physicians who complete three to four additional years of training after medical school (a *residency*) in the treatment of abnormal mental functioning. After World War II, however, with millions of soldiers returning home to countries throughout North America and Europe, the demand for mental health services expanded so rapidly that other professional groups had to step in to fill the need.

Among those other groups are *clinical psychologists*—professionals who earn a doctorate in clinical psychology by completing four to five years of graduate training in abnormal functioning and its treatment and also complete a one-year internship in a mental health setting. Psychotherapy is also provided by *counseling psychologists, educational* and *school psychologists, psychiatric nurses, marriage therapists, family therapists,* and—the largest group—*psychiatric social workers* (see Table 1-2). Each of these specialties has its own graduate training program. Theoretically, each conducts therapy in a distinctive way, but in reality clinicians from the various specialties often use similar techniques.

A related development in the study and treatment of mental disorders since World War II has been a growing appreciation of the need for effective research. *Clinical researchers* have tried to determine which concepts best explain and predict abnormal behavior, which treatments are most effective, and what kinds of changes may be required. Well-trained clinical researchers conduct studies in universities, medical schools, laboratories, mental hospitals, mental health centers, and other clinical settings throughout the world. Their work has produced important discoveries and has changed many of our ideas about abnormal psychological functioning.

table: 1-2

Profiles of Mental Health Professionals in the United States

	Degree	Began to Practice	Current Number	Average Annual Salary	Percent Female
Psychiatrists	MD, DO	1840s	50,000	$144,020	25
Psychologists	PhD, PsyD, EdD	Late 1940s	174,000	$63,000	52
Social workers	MSW, DSW	Early 1950s	607,000	$43,040	77
Counselors	Various	Early 1950s	475,000	$47,530	90

Information from: Cherry, 2014; U.S. Bureau of Labor Statistics, 2014, 2011, 2002; AMA, 2011; Carey, 2011; Weissman, 2000.

HAPPINESS

Positive psychology is the study of positive feelings, traits, and abilities. A better understanding of constructive functioning enables clinicians to better promote psychological wellness. **Happiness** is the positive psychology topic currently receiving the most attention. Many, but far from all, people are happy. In fact, only **one-third** of adults declare themselves "very happy." Let's take a look at some of today's leading facts, figures, and notions about happiness.

WHO Is "Very Happy?"

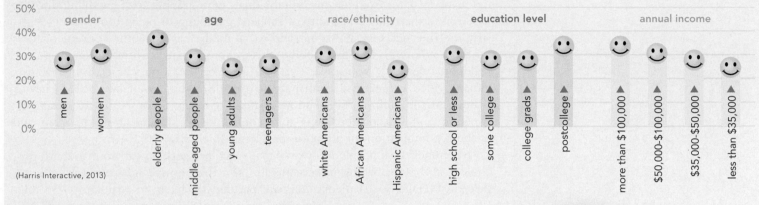

gender · age · race/ethnicity · education level · annual income

men · women · elderly people · middle-aged people · young adults · teenagers · white Americans · African Americans · Hispanic Americans · high school or less · some college · college grads · postcollege · more than $100,000 · $50,000-$100,000 · $35,000-$50,000 · less than $35,000

(Harris Interactive, 2013)

Happiness Building Blocks

Are people born with a happy disposition? Or do their surroundings and life circumstances make them more or less happy? Researchers of this **nature-versus-nurture** question have learned that both sets of factors **interact** to determine one's degree of happiness. But the factors have different degrees of impact.

Life events **40%**
Values (family, friends, community, work) **12%**
Genes **48%**
(Brooks, 2013)

Who Tends to Be *Happier*?

Politically conservative people	Politically liberal people
Unashamed people	Guilt-ridden people
Peaceful people	Angry people
Extroverts	Introverts
Regular church attenders	Church nonattenders

(Brooks, 2013; DePaulo, 2013; *The Economist*, 2010)

The Pursuit of Happiness

People tend to pursue a happy life. For some, that means pursuit of a **pleasant life** – filled with as many pleasures as possible. Others pursue an **engaging life**, characterized by satisfaction in work, parenting, love, and leisure. Still others pursue a **meaningful life** – recognizing and using their strengths in the service of others. (Seligman, 2002)

WHAT Do Happy People Do?

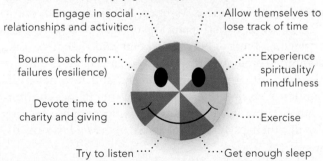

- Engage in social relationships and activities
- Allow themselves to lose track of time
- Bounce back from failures (resilience)
- Experience spirituality/mindfulness
- Devote time to charity and giving
- Exercise
- Try to listen
- Get enough sleep

(Bratskeir, 2013)

Social Contact and Happiness

The more social contact, the happier we are – up to a point!

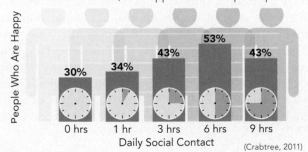

People Who Are Happy

30% (0 hrs) · 34% (1 hr) · 43% (3 hrs) · 53% (6 hrs) · 43% (9 hrs)

Daily Social Contact

(Crabtree, 2011)

Work and Happiness

Certain jobs have a higher percentage of happy people than others.

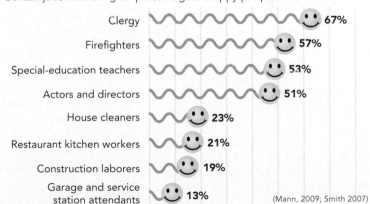

- Clergy **67%**
- Firefighters **57%**
- Special-education teachers **53%**
- Actors and directors **51%**
- House cleaners **23%**
- Restaurant kitchen workers **21%**
- Construction laborers **19%**
- Garage and service station attendants **13%**

(Mann, 2009; Smith 2007)

Marriage and Happiness

Married people are, on average, a bit happier than people with a different marital status.

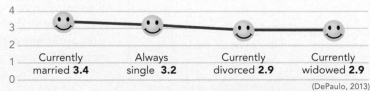

Currently married **3.4** · Always single **3.2** · Currently divorced **2.9** · Currently widowed **2.9**

(DePaulo, 2013)

Technology and Mental Health

The breathtaking rate of technological change that characterizes today's world has begun to have significant effects—both positive and negative—on the mental health field, and it will undoubtedly affect the field even more in the coming years. Let's consider just a small sample of these effects.

Our digital world provides new triggers for abnormal behavior. As you'll see in Chapter 10, for example, many individuals who grapple with gambling disorder have found the ready availability of Internet gambling to be all too inviting. Similarly, the Internet, text messaging, and social media have become convenient tools for those who wish to stalk or bully others, express sexual exhibitionism, or pursue pedophilic desires (Aboujaoude et al., 2015). Likewise, some clinicians believe that violent video games may contribute to the development of antisocial behavior (Zhuo, 2010). And, in the opinion of many clinicians, constant text messaging, tweeting, and Internet browsing may contribute to shorter attention spans and establish a foundation for attention problems (Richtel, 2010).

A number of clinicians also worry that social networking can contribute to psychological dysfunctioning in certain cases. On the positive side, research indicates that, on average, social media users are particularly likely to maintain close relationships, receive social support, be trusting, and lead active lives (Hampton et al., 2011; Rainie et al., 2011). On the negative side, however, is research suggesting that social networking sites may increase peer pressure and social anxiety in some adolescents (Charles, 2011; Hampton et al., 2011). The sites may, for example, cause some people to develop fears that others in their network will exclude them socially. Similarly, there is clinical concern that sites such as Facebook may facilitate shy people's withdrawal from valuable face-to-face relationships.

Bruce Eric Kaplan/The New Yorker Collection/www.cartoonbank.com

"We don't go to therapists—we just watch them on TV."

In addition, the face of clinical treatment is constantly changing in our fast-moving digital world. The use of **cybertherapy,** for example, is growing by leaps and bounds as a treatment option (Blanken et al., 2015; Pope & Vasquez, 2011). As you'll see in Chapter 2, cybertherapy takes such forms as long-distance therapy between clients and therapists using Skype, therapy offered by computer programs, treatment enhanced by the use of video game–like avatars and other virtual reality experiences, and Internet-based support groups. Similarly, countless Web sites offer a wealth of mental health information. And literally thousands of apps are devoted to relaxing people, cheering them up, or otherwise improving their psychological states (see *MindTech* on the next page).

Unfortunately, as you'll also see throughout the book, the cybertherapy movement is not without its problems. Along with the body of mental health information now available online comes an enormous amount of misinformation about psychological problems and their treatments, offered by persons and sites that are far from knowledgeable. Similarly, the issue of quality control is a major problem for Internet-based therapy, support groups, and the like. Moreover, there are now numerous anti-treatment Web sites that try to guide people away from seeking help for their psychological problems (Davey, 2010). In Chapters 3, 7, and 9, for example, you will read about the growing phenomenon of pro-anorexia and pro-suicide Web sites and their dangerous effects on vulnerable people. Clearly, the impact of technological change presents formidable challenges for clinicians and researchers alike.

▶ **cybertherapy** The use of computer technology, such as Skype or avatars, to provide therapy.

MindTech

Mental Health Apps Explode in the Marketplace

Oleksiy Mark/Shutterstock

About a decade ago, some clinicians and researchers began using text messages to help track the behaviors, thoughts, and emotions of clients with psychological problems (Bauer, 2003). That pioneering work has mushroomed into an industry of smartphone apps that often help provide mental health assistance to consumers (Sifferlin, 2013). There are, in fact, now thousands of such apps in the marketplace—many of them free, the rest low in cost (Saedi, 2012).

Many of these apps provide individuals with mental health education and resources; others help users to keep track of their shifting moods, thoughts, and bodily changes (called *biometrics*); still others are interactive and are designed to serve as co-therapists or even substitute therapists, offering reminders, advice, and exercises in response to the needs and input of users. Some of today's more popular apps include *My Mood Tracker, MindShift, PTSD Coach, Moody Me, Live Happy, Optimism, Moodscope,* and *Mood 24/7* (Kiume, 2013; Szalavitz, 2013; Landau, 2012; Saedi, 2012).

Many of today's apps are promising (Konrath, 2013) and have increasingly been recommended by therapists and mental health researchers, even by the National Institutes of Health. But be aware: most of them are *unregulated.* Only in the past year has the FDA announced its intention to systematically regulate smartphone apps that monitor health and mental health (Alter, 2013). In the meantime, in the absence of regulation and proper research, consumers and therapists alike would be wise to investigate the reputation, manufacturer, content, and therapeutic principles of apps that they are considering (Sifferlin, 2013).

> **What kinds of problems might result from the growing availability and use of mental health apps in today's world?**

➤ *Summing Up*

CURRENT TRENDS In the 1950s, researchers discovered a number of new psychotropic medications, drugs that mainly affect the brain and reduce many symptoms of mental dysfunctioning. Their success contributed to a policy of deinstitutionalization, under which hundreds of thousands of patients were released from public mental hospitals. In addition, outpatient treatment has become the primary approach for most people with mental disorders, both mild and severe; prevention programs are growing in number and influence; the field of multicultural psychology has begun to influence how clinicians view and treat abnormality; and insurance coverage is having a significant impact on the way treatment is conducted.

It is also the case that a variety of perspectives and professionals have come to operate in the field of abnormal psychology, and many well-trained clinical researchers now investigate the field's theories and treatments. And finally, the remarkable technological advances of recent times have affected the mental health field.

What Do Clinical Researchers Do?

Research is the key to accuracy in all fields of study; it is particularly important in abnormal psychology because a wrong belief in this field can lead to great suffering. At the same time, clinical researchers, also called clinical scientists, face certain challenges that make their work very difficult. They must, for example, figure out how to measure such elusive concepts as private thoughts, mood changes, and human potential. They must consider the different cultural backgrounds, races, and genders of the people they choose to study. And they must always ensure that the rights of their research participants, both human and animal, are not violated. Let us examine the leading methods used by today's researchers.

Clinical researchers try to discover broad laws, or principles, of abnormal psychological functioning. They search for a general, or *nomothetic,* understanding of the nature, causes, and treatments of abnormality. They do not typically assess, diagnose, or treat individual clients; that is the job of clinical practitioners. To gain a broad insight, clinical researchers, like scientists in other fields, use the **scientific method**—that is, they collect and evaluate information through careful observations. These observations in turn enable them to pinpoint and explain relationships between *variables.*

Simply stated, a variable is any characteristic or event that can vary, whether from time to time, from place to place, or from person to person. Age, sex, and race are human variables. So are eye color, occupation, and social status. Clinical researchers are interested in variables such as childhood upsets, present life experiences, moods, social functioning, and responses to treatment. They try to determine whether two or more such variables change together and whether a change in one variable causes a change in another. Will the death of a parent cause a child to become depressed? If so, will a given treatment reduce that depression?

Such questions cannot be answered by logic alone because scientists, like all human beings, frequently make errors in thinking. Thus, clinical researchers must depend mainly on three methods of investigation: the *case study,* which typically is focused on one individual, and the *correlational method* and *experimental method,* approaches that are usually used to gather information about many individuals. Each is best suited to certain kinds of circumstances and questions. As a group, these methods enable scientists to form and test **hypotheses,** or hunches, that certain variables are related in certain ways—and to draw broad conclusions as to why. More properly, a hypothesis is a tentative explanation offered to provide a basis for an investigation.

The Case Study

A **case study** is a detailed description of a person's life and psychological problems. It describes the person's history, present circumstances, and symptoms. It may also include speculation about why the problems developed, and it may describe the person's treatment (Yin, 2013). As you will see in Chapter 5, one of the field's best-known case studies, called *The Three Faces of Eve,* describes a woman with three alternating personalities, each having a distinct set of memories, preferences, and personal habits (Thigpen & Cleckley, 1957).

Most clinicians take notes and keep records in the course of treating their patients, and some further organize such notes into a formal case study to be shared with other professionals. The clues offered by a case study may help a clinician better understand or treat the person under discussion (Yin, 2013). In addition, case studies may play nomothetic roles that go far beyond the individual clinical case.

How Are Case Studies Helpful?
Case studies can be a source of *new ideas* about behavior and "open the way for discoveries" (Bolgar, 1965). Freud's theory of psychoanalysis was based mainly on the patients he saw in private practice. In

Case study, Hollywood style Case studies often find their way into the arts or media and capture the public's attention. Unfortunately, as this movie poster of *The Three Faces of Eve* illustrates, the studies may be trivialized or sensationalized in those ventures.

addition, a case study may offer *tentative support* for a theory. Freud used case studies in this way as well, regarding them as evidence for the accuracy of his ideas. Conversely, case studies may serve to *challenge a theory's assumptions* (Yin, 2013).

Case studies may also show the value of *new therapeutic techniques*. And finally, case studies may offer opportunities to study *unusual problems* that do not occur often enough to permit a large number of observations (Goodwin & Goodwin, 2012). Investigators of problems such as personality disorder once relied entirely on case studies for information.

What Are the Limitations of Case Studies? Case studies also have limitations (Yin, 2013). First, they are reported by *biased observers,* that is, by therapists who have a personal stake in seeing their treatments succeed. These therapists must choose what to include in a case study, and their choices may at times be self-serving. Second, case studies rely on *subjective evidence*. Is a client's problem really caused by the events that the therapist or client says are responsible? After all, those are only a fraction of the events that may be contributing to the situation. Finally, case studies provide *little basis for generalization*. Events or treatments that seem important in one case may be of no help at all in efforts to understand or treat others.

> **Why do case studies and other anecdotal offerings influence people so much, often more than systematic research does?**

The limitations of the case study are largely addressed by two other methods of investigation: the *correlational method* and the *experimental method*. These methods do not offer the rich details that make case studies so interesting, but they do help investigators draw broad conclusions about abnormality in the population at large. Thus they are now the preferred methods of clinical investigation.

Three features of the correlational and experimental methods enable clinical investigators to gain general insights: (1) The researchers typically observe many individuals (see *MindTech* on the next page). (2) The researchers apply procedures uniformly and can thus repeat, or *replicate,* their investigations. And (3) the researchers use *statistical tests* to analyze the results of a study.

The Correlational Method

Correlation is the degree to which events or characteristics vary with each other. The **correlational method** is a research procedure used to determine this "co-relationship" between variables. This method can be used, for example, to answer the question, "Is there a correlation between the amount of stress in people's lives and the degree of depression they experience?" That is, as people keep experiencing stressful events, are they increasingly likely to become depressed?

To test this question, researchers have collected life stress scores (for example, the number of threatening events experienced during a certain period of time) and depression scores (for example, scores on a depression survey) from individuals and have correlated these scores. The people who are chosen for a study are its subjects, or *participants,* the term preferred by today's investigators. Typically, investigators have found that life stress and depression variables do indeed increase or decrease together (Monroe et al., 2014). That is, the greater someone's life stress score, the higher his or her score on the depression scale. When variables change the same way, their correlation is said to have a positive *direction* and is referred to as a *positive correlation*. Alternatively, correlations can have a negative rather than a positive direction. In a *negative correlation,* the value of one variable increases as the value of the other variable decreases. Researchers have found, for example, a

▸ **scientific method** The process of systematically gathering and evaluating information through careful observations to understand a phenomenon.

▸ **hypothesis** A hunch or prediction that certain variables are related in certain ways.

▸ **case study** A detailed account of a person's life and psychological problems.

▸ **correlation** The degree to which events or characteristics vary along with each other.

▸ **correlational method** A research procedure used to determine how much events or characteristics vary along with each other.

Twins, correlation, and inheritance These healthy twin sisters are participating in a twin cultural festival at Honglingjin Park in Beijing, China. Correlational studies of many pairs of twins have suggested a link between genetic factors and certain psychological disorders. Identical twins (who have identical genes) display a higher correlation for some disorders than do fraternal twins (whose genetic makeup is not identical).

Imaginechina via AP Images

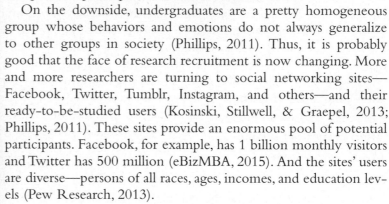

MindTech

A Researcher's Paradise?

Two of the biggest problems for researchers are finding enough participants for their studies and obtaining a sufficient range of participants. Until recent years, undergraduates were the most common participants in behavioral research—even clinical research (Gosling, 2011). This was largely a matter of convenience. Undergraduates are, after all, just down the hall, often in need of money, and typically interested in joining research studies. Moreover, at many universities, undergraduates are *required* to participate in research studies.

Jan Haas/picture-alliance/dpa/AP Images

On the downside, undergraduates are a pretty homogeneous group whose behaviors and emotions do not always generalize to other groups in society (Phillips, 2011). Thus, it is probably good that the face of research recruitment is now changing. More and more researchers are turning to social networking sites—Facebook, Twitter, Tumblr, Instagram, and others—and their ready-to-be-studied users (Kosinski, Stillwell, & Graepel, 2013; Phillips, 2011). These sites provide an enormous pool of potential participants. Facebook, for example, has 1 billion monthly visitors and Twitter has 500 million (eBizMBA, 2015). And the sites' users are diverse—persons of all races, ages, incomes, and education levels (Pew Research, 2013).

One recent study demonstrates the power and potential of social media participant pools (Kosinski et al., 2013). In this investigation, 58,000 Facebook subscribers allowed the researchers access to their list of "likes," and the subscribers further filled out online personality tests. The study found that information about a participant's likes could predict with considerable accuracy his or her personality traits, level of happiness, use of addictive substances, and level of intelligence, among other variables. Similarly, other social media site studies have tested various psychological theories "about relationships, identity, self-esteem, popularity, collective action, race, and political engagement" (Rosenbloom, 2007).

What a great resource, right? Not so fast. The studies above asked social media users whether they were willing to participate, but in a number of other studies, the users do *not* know that their posted information is being examined and tested. Inasmuch as posted information is publicly available, some researchers believe it is ethical to study that information without informing users that they are indeed being studied.

Facebook and most other social media sites do not have policies prohibiting scholars from studying user profiles without permission (Rosenbloom, 2007). In contrast, many research institutes have concluded that postings on social networking sites should be considered private, and they require their researchers at their institutions to obtain explicit permission from social media users when network information is being examined. While this technology-driven question of what's public and what's private is under debate, it is probably best that posters follow a new version of that most sacred rule of consumerism—"poster beware."

negative correlation between depression and activity level. The greater one's depression, the lower the number of one's activities.

There is yet a third possible outcome for a correlational study. The variables under study may be *unrelated*, meaning that there is no consistent relationship between them. As the measures of one variable increase, those of the other variable sometimes increase and sometimes decrease. Studies have found that depression and intelligence are unrelated, for example.

In addition to knowing the direction of a correlation, researchers need to know its *magnitude,* or strength. That is, how closely do the two variables correspond? Does one *always* vary along with the other, or is their relationship less exact? When two variables are found to vary together very closely in person after person, the correlation is said to be high, or strong.

The direction and magnitude of a correlation are often calculated numerically and expressed by a statistical term called the *correlation coefficient.* The correlation coefficient can vary from +1.00, which indicates a perfect positive correlation between two variables, down to −1.00, which represents a perfect negative correlation. The *sign* of the coefficient (+ or −) signifies the direction of the correlation; the *number* represents its magnitude. The closer the correlation is to .00, the weaker, or lower in magnitude, it is. Thus correlations of +.75 and −.75 are of equal magnitude and equally strong, whereas a correlation of +.25 is weaker than either.

Everyone's behavior is changeable, and many human responses can be measured only approximately. Most correlations found in psychological research, therefore, fall short of perfect positive or negative correlation. For example, one early study of life stress and depression, with a sample of 68 adults, found a correlation of +.53 (Miller, Ingham, & Davidson, 1976). Although hardly perfect, a correlation of this magnitude is considered large in psychological research.

When Can Correlations Be Trusted?

Scientists must decide whether the correlation they find in a given sample of participants accurately reflects a real correlation in the general population. Could the observed correlation have occurred by mere chance? They can test their conclusions with a *statistical analysis* of their data, using principles of probability. In essence, they ask how likely it is that the study's particular findings have occurred by chance. If the statistical analysis indicates that chance is unlikely to account for the correlation they found, researchers may conclude that their findings reflect a real correlation in the general population.

What Are the Merits of the Correlational Method?

The correlational method has certain advantages over the case study (see Table 1-3). Because researchers measure their variables, observe many participants, and apply statistical analyses, they are in a better position to generalize their correlations to people beyond the ones they have studied. Furthermore, researchers can easily repeat correlational studies using new samples of participants to check the results of earlier studies.

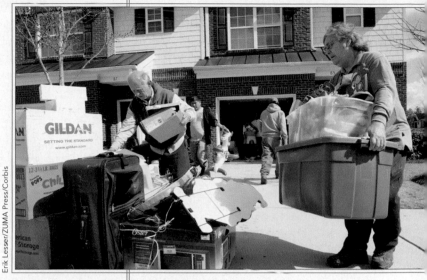

Erik Lesser/ZUMA Press/Corbis

Stress and depression In Norcross, Georgia, friends and workers bring all of this family's possessions to the curb after their bank has foreclosed on their mortgage, another casualty of the subprime loan crisis and economic downturn. Researchers have found that the stress produced by the loss of one's home is often accompanied by the onset of depression and other psychological symptoms.

table: 1-3

Relative Strengths and Weaknesses of Research Methods

	Provides Individual Information	Provides General Information	Provides Causal Information	Statistical Analysis Possible	Replicable
Case study	Yes	No	No	No	No
Correlational method	No	Yes	No	Yes	Yes
Experimental method	No	Yes	Yes	Yes	Yes

"Recalculating . . . recalculating . . ."

Although correlations allow researchers to describe the relationship between two variables, they do not *explain* the relationship (Jackson, 2012). When we look at the positive correlation found in many life stress studies, we may be tempted to conclude that increases in recent life stress cause people to feel more depressed. In fact, however, the two variables may be correlated for any one of three reasons: (1) Life stress may cause depression. (2) Depression may cause people to experience more life stress (for example, a depressive approach to life may cause people to perform poorly at work or may interfere with social relationships). (3) Depression and life stress may each be caused by a third variable, such as financial problems (Gutman & Nemeroff, 2011).

> **Can you think of other correlations in life that are interpreted mistakenly as causal?**

Although correlations say nothing about causation, they can still be of great use to clinicians. Clinicians know, for example, that suicide attempts increase as people become more depressed. Thus, when they work with severely depressed clients, they stay on the lookout for signs of suicidal thinking. Perhaps depression directly causes suicidal behavior, or perhaps a third variable, such as a sense of hopelessness, causes both depression and suicidal thoughts. Whatever the cause, just knowing that there is a correlation may enable clinicians to take measures (such as hospitalization) to help save lives.

Special Forms of Correlational Research Epidemiological studies and longitudinal studies are two kinds of correlational research used widely by clinical investigators. **Epidemiological studies** reveal the incidence and prevalence of a disorder in a particular population. *Incidence* is the number of new cases that emerge during a given period of time. *Prevalence* is the total number of cases in the population during a given period; prevalence includes both existing and new cases.

Over the past 40 years, clinical researchers throughout the United States have worked on one of the largest epidemiological studies of mental disorders ever conducted, called the Epidemiologic Catchment Area Study (Ramsey et al., 2013). They have interviewed more than 20,000 people in five cities to determine the prevalence of many psychological disorders and the treatment programs used. Two other large-scale epidemiological studies in the United States, the National Comorbidity Survey and the National Comorbidity Survey Replication, have questioned more than 9,000 individuals (Martin, Neighbors, & Griffith, 2013). All these studies have been further compared with epidemiological studies of specific groups, such as Hispanic and Asian American populations, or with epidemiological studies conducted in other countries, to see how rates of mental disorders and treatment programs vary from group to group and from country to country (Jimenez et al., 2010).

Such epidemiological studies have helped researchers identify groups at risk for particular disorders. Women, it turns out, have a higher rate of anxiety disorders and depression than men, while men have a higher rate of alcoholism than women. Elderly people have a higher rate of suicide than young people. Hispanic Americans experience posttraumatic stress disorder more than other racial and ethnic groups in the United States. And persons in some countries have higher rates of certain mental disorders than those in other countries. Eating disorders such as anorexia nervosa, for example, appear to be more common in Western countries than in non-Western ones.

In **longitudinal studies**, correlational studies of another kind, researchers observe the same individuals on many occasions over a long period of time. In several such studies, investigators have observed the progress over the years of normally functioning children whose mothers or fathers suffered from schizophrenia (Rasic et al., 2014; Mednick, 1971). The researchers have found, among other things, that

▶ **epidemiological study** A study that measures the incidence and prevalence of a disorder in a given population.

▶ **longitudinal study** A study that observes the same participants on many occasions over a long period of time.

▶ **experiment** A research procedure in which a variable is manipulated and the effect of the manipulation is observed.

▶ **independent variable** The variable in an experiment that is manipulated to determine whether it has an effect on another variable.

▶ **dependent variable** The variable in an experiment expected to change as the independent variable is manipulated.

▶ **confound** In an experiment, a variable other than the independent variable that is also acting on the dependent variable.

▶ **control group** In an experiment, a group of participants who are not exposed to the independent variable.

▶ **experimental group** In an experiment, the participants who are exposed to the independent variable under investigation.

the children of the parents with the most severe cases of schizophrenia were particularly likely to develop a psychological disorder and to commit crimes at later points in their development.

The Experimental Method

An **experiment** is a research procedure in which a variable is manipulated and the manipulation's effect on another variable is observed. The manipulated variable is called the **independent variable** and the variable being observed is called the **dependent variable.**

To examine the experimental method more fully, let's consider a question that is often asked by clinicians (Toth et al., 2014): "Does a particular therapy relieve the symptoms of a particular disorder?" Because this question is about a causal relationship, it can be answered only by an experiment (see Table 1-4). That is, experimenters must give the therapy in question to people who are suffering from a disorder and then observe whether they improve. Here the therapy is the independent variable, and psychological improvement is the dependent variable.

As with correlational studies, investigators who conduct experiments must do a statistical analysis on their data and find out how likely it is that the observed improvement is due to chance. Again, if that likelihood is very low, the improvement is considered to be statistically significant, and the experimenter may conclude with some confidence that it is due to the independent variable.

If the true cause of changes in the dependent variable cannot be separated from other possible causes, then an experiment gives very little information. Thus, experimenters must try to eliminate all **confounds** from their studies—variables other than the independent variable that may also be affecting the dependent variable. When there are confounds in an experiment, they, rather than the independent variable, may be causing the observed change.

For example, situational variables, such as the location of the therapy office (say, a quiet country setting) or soothing background music in the office, may have a therapeutic effect on participants in a therapy study. Or perhaps the participants are unusually motivated or have high expectations that the therapy will work, factors that thus account for their improvement. To guard against confounds, researchers should include three important features in their experiments—a *control group, random assignment,* and a *blind design* (see *MediaSpeak* on the next page).

The Control Group A **control group** is a group of research participants who are not exposed to the independent variable under investigation but whose experience is similar to that of the experimental group, the participants who are exposed to the independent variable. By comparing the two groups, an experimenter can better determine the effect of the independent variable.

To study the effectiveness of a particular therapy, for example, experimenters typically divide participants into two groups. The **experimental group** may come into an office and receive the therapy for an hour, while the control group may simply come into

table: 1-4

Most Investigated Questions in Clinical Research
Most Common *Correlational* Questions
Are stress and onset of mental disorders related?
Is culture (or gender or race) generally linked to mental disorders?
Are income and mental disorders related?
Are social skills tied to mental disorders?
Is social support tied to mental disorders?
Are family conflict and mental disorders related?
Is treatment responsiveness tied to culture?
Which symptoms of a disorder appear together?
How common is a disorder in a particular population?
Most Common *Causal* Questions
Does factor X cause a disorder?
Is cause A more influential than cause B?
How does family communication and structure affect family members?
How does a disorder affect the quality of a person's life?
Does treatment X alleviate a disorder?
Is treatment X more helpful than no treatment at all?
Is treatment A more helpful than treatment B?
Why does treatment X work?
Can an intervention prevent abnormal functioning?

MediaSpeak

Flawed Study, Gigantic Impact

By David DiSalvo, *Forbes*, May 19, 2012

In 2001, Dr. Robert L. Spitzer, psychiatrist and professor emeritus of Columbia University, presented a paper at a meeting of the American Psychiatric Association about something called "reparative therapy" [also known as "conversion therapy"] for gay men and women. By undergoing reparative therapy, the paper claimed, gay men and women could change their sexual orientation. Spitzer had interviewed 200 allegedly former-homosexual men and women that he claimed had shown varying degrees of such change; all of the participants provided Spitzer with self reports of their experience with the therapy.

Spitzer, now 79 years old, was no stranger to the controversy surrounding his chosen subject. Thirty years earlier, he had played a leading role in removing homosexuality from the list of mental disorders in the association's diagnostic manual [DSM-III]. Clearly, his interest in the topic was more than a passing academic curiosity. . . .

Fast forward to 2012, and Spitzer is of quite a different mind. Last month he told a reporter with *The American Prospect* that he regretted the 2001 study and the effect it had on the gay community, and that he owed the community an apology. And this month he sent a letter to the *Archives of Sexual Behavior*, which published his work in 2003, asking that the journal retract his paper.

Spitzer's mission to clean the slate is commendable, but the effects of his work have been coursing through the homosexual community like acid since it made headlines a decade ago. His study was seized upon by anti-homosexual activists and therapists who held up Spitzer's paper as proof that they could "cure" patients of their sexual orientation.

Spitzer didn't invent reparative therapy, and he isn't the only researcher to have conducted studies claiming that it works, but as an influential psychiatrist from a prestigious university, his words carried a lot of weight.

In his recantation of the study, he says that it contained at least two fatal flaws: the self reports from those he surveyed were not verifiable, and he didn't include a control group of men and women who didn't undergo the therapy for comparison. Self reports are notoriously unreliable. . . . Lacking a control group is a fundamental no-no in social science research across the board. The conclusion is inescapable—Spitzer's study was simply bad science. . . .

The object lesson worth drawing from this story is that just one instance of bad science given the blessing of recognized experts can lead to years of damaging lies that snowball out of control. Spitzer cannot be held solely responsible for what happened after his paper was published, but he'd probably agree now that the study should never have been presented in the first place. At the very least, his example may help prevent future episodes of the same.

Mike Clarke/AFP/Getty Images

Protesting reparative therapy Protestors from a gay rights group in Hong Kong hold up a banner outside a social welfare department in 2011 to protest the department's endorsement of reparative therapy.

the office for an hour. If the experimenters find later that the people in the experimental group improve more than the people in the control group, they may conclude that the therapy was effective, above and beyond the effects of time, the office setting, and any other confounds. To guard against confounds, experimenters try to provide all participants, both control and experimental, with experiences that are identical in every way—except for the independent variable.

Random Assignment

Researchers must also watch out for differences in the *makeup* of the experimental and control groups since those differences may also confound a study's results. In a therapy study, for example, the experimenter may unintentionally put wealthier participants in the experimental group and poorer ones in the control group. This difference, rather than their therapy, may be the cause of the greater improvement later found among the experimental participants. To reduce the effects of preexisting differences, experimenters typically use **random assignment.** This is the general term for any selection procedure that ensures that every participant in the experiment is as likely to be placed in one group as the other. Researchers might, for example, assign people to groups by flipping a coin or picking names out of a hat.

Blind Design

A final confound problem is *bias.* Participants may bias an experiment's results by trying to please or help the experimenter. In a therapy experiment, for example, if those participants who receive the treatment know the purpose of the study and which group they are in, they might actually work harder to feel better or fulfill the experimenter's expectations. If so, *subject,* or *participant, bias* rather than therapy could be causing their improvement.

To avoid this bias, experimenters can prevent participants from finding out which group they are in. This experimental strategy is called a **blind design** because the individuals are blind as to their assigned group. In a therapy study, for example, control participants could be given a *placebo* (Latin for "I shall please"), something that looks or tastes like real therapy but has none of its key ingredients. This "imitation" therapy is called *placebo therapy.* If the experimental (true therapy) participants improve more than the control (placebo therapy) participants, experimenters have more confidence that the true therapy has caused their improvement.

> **Why might sugar pills or other kinds of placebo treatments help some people feel better?**

An experiment may also be confounded by *experimenter bias*—that is, experimenters may have expectations that they unintentionally transmit to the participants in their studies. In a drug therapy study, for example, the experimenter might smile and act confident while providing real medications to the experimental participants but frown and appear hesitant while offering placebo drugs to the control participants. This kind of bias is sometimes referred to as the *Rosenthal effect,* after the psychologist who first identified it (Rosenthal, 1966). Experimenters can eliminate their own bias by arranging to be blind themselves. In a drug therapy study, for example, an aide could make sure that the real medication and the placebo drug look identical. The experimenter could then administer treatment without knowing which participants were receiving true medications and which were receiving false medications. While either the participants or the experimenter may be kept blind in

Holger Hollemann/picture-alliance/dpa/AP Images

Is animal companionship a form of therapy? A patient (right) and therapist (left) feed ring-tailed lemurs at Serengeti Park near Hodenhagen, Germany, as part of a monthly program called "Psychiatric Animal Days." The program is based on the assumption that animals have a calming and therapeutic effect on people. An experimental design is needed to determine whether this or any other form of treatment actually causes clients to improve.

▶**random assignment** A selection procedure that ensures that participants are randomly placed either in the control group or in the experimental group.

▶**blind design** An experiment in which participants do not know whether they are in the experimental or the control condition.

Natural experiments In this famous photograph, a woman carries her daughter to safety after a massive tornado carved its way through Moore, Oklahoma, in 2013, leveling the town, killing 25 people, and injuring 377 others. Natural experiments conducted in the aftermath of such catastrophes have found that many survivors experience lingering feelings of anxiety and depression.

Sue Ogrocki/AP Photo

an experiment, it is best that both be blind—a research strategy called a *double-blind design*. In fact, most medication experiments now use double-blind designs to test promising drugs (Pratley, Fleck, & Wilson, 2014).

Alternative Experimental Designs Clinical researchers must often settle for experimental designs that are less than ideal (Manton et al., 2014). The most common such variations are the *quasi-experimental design,* the *natural experiment,* the *analogue experiment,* and the *single-subject experiment.*

In **quasi-experiments,** or **mixed designs,** investigators do not randomly assign participants to control and experimental groups but instead make use of groups that already exist in the world at large (Girden & Kabacoff, 2011). Consider, for example, research into the effects of child abuse. Because it would be unethical for investigators of this issue to actually abuse a randomly chosen group of children, they must instead compare children who already have a history of abuse with children who do not. To make this comparison as valid as possible, they may further use *matched control participants.* That is, they match the experimental participants with control participants who are similar in age, sex, race, number of children in the family, socioeconomic status, type of neighborhood, or other characteristics. When the data from studies of this kind show that abused children are typically sadder and have lower self-esteem than matched control participants who have not been abused, the investigators can conclude with some confidence that abuse is causing the differences (Lindert et al., 2013).

In **natural experiments,** nature itself manipulates the independent variable, and the experimenter observes the effects. Natural experiments must be used for studying the psychological effects of unusual and unpredictable events, such as floods, earthquakes, plane crashes, and fires. Because the participants in these studies are selected by an accident of fate rather than by the investigators' design, natural experiments are actually a kind of quasi-experiment.

On December 26, 2004, an earthquake occurred beneath the Indian Ocean off the coast of Sumatra, Indonesia. The earthquake triggered a series of massive tsunamis that flooded the ocean's coastal communities, killed more than 225,000 people, and injured and left millions of survivors homeless, particularly in Indonesia, Sri Lanka, India, and Thailand. Within months of this disaster, researchers conducted natural experiments in which they collected data from hundreds of survivors and from control groups of people who lived in areas not directly affected by the tsunamis. The disaster survivors scored significantly higher on anxiety and depression measures (dependent variables) than the controls did. The survivors also experienced more sleep problems, feelings of detachment, arousal, difficulties concentrating, startle responses, and guilt feelings than the controls did (Musa et al., 2014; Heir et al., 2010). Over the past several years, other natural experiments have focused on survivors of the 2010 Haitian earthquake, the massive earthquake and tsunami in Japan in 2011, the Northeast's Superstorm Sandy in 2012, and the unprecedented Oklahoma tornados in 2013. These studies have also revealed lingering psychological symptoms among survivors of those disasters (Iwadare et al., 2013).

Experimenters often run **analogue experiments.** Here they induce laboratory participants to behave in ways that seem to resemble real-life abnormal behavior and then conduct experiments on the participants in the hope of shedding light on the real-life abnormality. For example, as you'll see in Chapter 6, investigator Martin Seligman, in a classic body of work, has produced

© Mikel Roberts/Sygma/Corbis

Similar enough? Celebrity chimpanzee Cheetah, age 59, does some painting along with her friend and trainer. Chimps and human beings share more than 90 percent of their genetic material, but their brains and bodies are very different, as are their perceptions and experiences. Thus, abnormal-like behavior produced in animal analogue experiments may differ from the human abnormality under investigation.

depression-like symptoms in laboratory participants—both animals and humans—by repeatedly exposing them to negative events (shocks, loud noises, task failures) over which they have no control. In these "learned helplessness" analogue studies, the participants seem to give up, lose their initiative, and become sad—suggesting to some clinicians that human depression itself may indeed be caused by loss of control over the events in one's life.

Finally, scientists sometimes do not have the luxury of experimenting on many participants. They may, for example, be investigating a disorder so rare that few participants are available. Experimentation is still possible, however, with a **single-subject experimental design.** Here a single participant is observed both before and after the manipulation of an independent variable (Richards, Taylor, & Ramasamy, 2014).

For example, using a particular kind of single-subject design, called an *ABAB,* or *reversal, design,* one researcher sought to determine whether the systematic use of rewards would reduce a teenage boy's habit of disrupting his special education class with loud talk (Deitz, 1977). He rewarded the boy, who suffered from intellectual disability (previously called mental retardation), with extra teacher time whenever he went 55 minutes without interrupting the class more than three times. In condition A, the student was observed prior to receiving any reward, and he was found to disrupt the class frequently with loud talk. In condition B, the boy was given a series of teacher reward sessions (introduction of the independent variable); as expected, his loud talk decreased dramatically. Next, the rewards from the teacher were stopped (condition A again), and the student's loud talk increased once again. Apparently the independent variable had indeed been the cause of the improvement. To be still more confident about this conclusion, the researcher had the teacher apply reward sessions yet again (condition B again). Once again the student's behavior improved.

What Are the Limits of Clinical Investigations?

We began this section by noting that clinical scientists look for general laws that will help them understand, treat, and prevent psychological disorders. As we have seen, however, circumstances can interfere with their progress.

Each method of investigation that we have observed addresses some of the problems involved in studying human behavior, but no one approach overcomes

▶ **quasi-experiment** An experiment in which investigators make use of control and experimental groups that already exist in the world at large. Also called a *mixed design.*

▶ **natural experiment** An experiment in which nature, rather than an experimenter, manipulates an independent variable.

▶ **analogue experiment** A research method in which the experimenter produces abnormal-like behavior in laboratory participants and then conducts experiments on the participants.

▶ **single-subject experimental design** A research method in which a single participant is observed and measured both before and after the manipulation of an independent variable.

A national disgrace In a 1997 White House ceremony, President Bill Clinton offers an official apology to 94-year-old Herman Shaw and other African American men whose syphilis went untreated by government doctors and researchers in the Tuskegee Syphilis Study, a research undertaking conducted from 1932 to 1972, prior to the emergence of Institutional Review Boards. In this infamous study, 399 participants were not informed that they had the disease, and they continued to go untreated even after it was discovered that penicillin is an effective intervention for syphilis.

them all. Thus it is best to view each research method as part of a team of approaches that together may shed light on abnormal human functioning. When more than one method has been used to investigate a disorder, it is important to ask whether all the results seem to point in the same direction. If they do, clinical scientists are probably making progress toward understanding and treating that disorder. Conversely, if the various methods seem to produce conflicting results, the scientists must admit that knowledge in that particular area is still limited.

Protecting Human Participants

Human research participants have needs and rights that must be respected. In fact, researchers' primary obligation is to avoid harming the human participants in their studies—physically or psychologically.

The vast majority of researchers are conscientious about fulfilling this obligation. They try to conduct studies that test their hypotheses and further scientific knowledge in a safe and respectful way. But there have been some notable exceptions to this over the years, particularly several infamous studies conducted in the mid-1900s. Partly because of such exceptions, the government and the institutions in which research is conducted now take careful measures to ensure that the safety and rights of human research participants are properly protected.

Who, beyond researchers themselves, might directly watch over the rights and safety of human participants? For the past few decades, that responsibility has been given to **Institutional Review Boards,** or **IRBs.** Each research facility has an IRB—a committee of five or more members who review and monitor every study conducted at that institution, starting when the studies are first proposed. The institution may be a university, medical school, psychiatric or medical hospital, private research facility, mental health center, or the like. If research is conducted there, the institution must have an IRB, and that IRB has the responsibility and power to require changes in a proposed study as a condition of approval. If acceptable changes are not made by the researcher, then the IRB can disapprove the study altogether. Similarly, if, over the course of the study, the safety or rights of the participants are placed in jeopardy, the IRB must intervene and can even stop the study if necessary. These powers are granted to IRBs (or similar ethics committees) by nations around the world. In the United States, for example, IRBs are empowered by two agencies of the federal government—the Office for Human Research Protections and the Food and Drug Administration.

> Do outside restrictions on research—either animal or human studies—interfere with necessary investigations and thus limit potential gains for human beings?

It turns out that protecting the rights and safety of human research participants is a complex undertaking. Thus, IRBs often are forced to conduct a kind of risk-benefit analysis in their reviews. They may, for example, approve a study that poses minimal or slight risks to participants if that "acceptable" level of risk is offset by the study's potential benefits to society. In general, IRBs try to ensure that each study grants the following rights to its participants (NIJ, 2010):

➤ The participants enlist voluntarily.

➤ Before enlisting, the participants are adequately informed about what the study entails ("*informed consent*").

➤ The participants can end their participation in the study at any time.

➤ The benefits of the study outweigh its costs/risks.

➤ The participants are protected from physical and psychological harm.

▶**Institutional Review Board (IRB)** An ethics committee in a research facility that is empowered to protect the rights and safety of human research participants.

➤ The participants have access to information about the study.

➤ The participants' privacy is protected by principles such as confidentiality or anonymity.

Unfortunately, even with IRBs on the job, these rights can be in jeopardy. Consider, for example, the right of informed consent. To help ensure that participants understand what they are getting into when they enlist for a study, IRBs typically require that the individuals read and sign an "informed consent form" that spells out everything they need to know. But how clear are such forms? Not very, according to some investigations (Albala, Doyle, & Appelbaum, 2010; Mathew & McGrath, 2002).

It turns out that most such forms—the very forms deemed acceptable by IRBs—are written at an advanced college level, making them incomprehensible to a large percentage of participants. In fact, fewer than half of all participants may fully understand the informed consent forms they are signing. Still other investigations indicate that only around 10 percent of human participants carefully read the informed consent forms before signing them, and only 30 percent ask questions of the researchers during the informed consent phase of their studies (CISCRP, 2013).

In short, the IRB system is flawed, much like the research undertakings it oversees. There are various reasons for this. One is that ethical principles are subtle and elusive notions that do not always translate into simple regulations and guidelines. Another reason is that ethical decisions—whether by IRB members or by researchers—are subject to differences in perspective, interpretation, decision-making style, and the like. Despite such problems and limitations, most observers agree that the creation and work of IRBs have helped improve the rights and safety of human research participants over the years. The boards may reflect an imperfect system, but they play a necessary and important role in monitoring the quality and appropriateness of research undertakings.

Paul Sakuma/AP Photo

Making a point The rights of animal subjects must also be considered. Here, members of an organization called In Defense of Animals wear monkey masks and sit in locked cages in front of the University of California, San Francisco, to protest the use of monkeys in research.

➤ Summing Up

WHAT DO CLINICAL RESEARCHERS DO? Researchers use the scientific method to uncover nomothetic principles of abnormal psychological functioning. They attempt to identify and examine relationships between variables and depend primarily on three methods of investigation: the case study, the correlational method, and the experimental method.

A case study is a detailed account of a person's life and psychological problems.

Correlational studies are used to systematically observe the degree to which events or characteristics vary together. This method allows researchers to draw broad conclusions about abnormality in the population at large. Two widely used forms of the correlational method are epidemiological studies and longitudinal studies.

In experiments, researchers manipulate suspected causes to see whether expected effects will result. This method allows researchers to determine the causes of various conditions or events. Clinical experimenters must often settle for experimental designs that are less than ideal, including the quasi-experiment, the natural experiment, the analogue experiment, and the single-subject experiment.

Each research facility has an Institutional Review Board (IRB) that has the power and responsibility to protect the rights and safety of human participants in all studies conducted at that facility. Members of the IRB review each study

(continues on the next page)

during the planning stages and can require changes in the proposed study before granting approval for the undertaking. If the required changes are not made, the IRB has the authority to disapprove the study. Among the important participant rights that the IRB protects is the right of informed consent, an acceptable risk/benefit balance, and privacy (confidentiality or anonymity).

PUTTING IT...*together*

A Work in Progress

Since ancient times, people have tried to explain, treat, and study abnormal behavior. By examining the responses of past societies to such behaviors, we can better understand the roots of our present views and treatments. In addition, a look backward helps us appreciate just how far we have come—how humane our present views are, how impressive our recent discoveries are, and how important our current emphasis on research is.

At the same time, we must recognize the many problems in abnormal psychology today. The field has yet to agree on one definition of abnormality. It is currently made up of conflicting schools of thought and treatment whose members are often unimpressed by the claims and accomplishments of the others. Clinical practice is carried out by a variety of professionals trained in different ways. And current research methods each have flaws that limit our knowledge and use of clinical information.

As you travel through the topics in this book, keep in mind the field's current strengths and weaknesses, the progress that has been made, and the journey that lies ahead. Perhaps the most important lesson to be learned from our look at the history of this field is that our current understanding of abnormal behavior represents a work in progress. The clinical field stands at a crossroads, with some of the most important insights, investigations, and changes yet to come.

KEY TERMS

abnormal psychology, p. 2
deviance, p. 3
norms, p. 3
culture, p. 3
distress, p. 3
dysfunction, p. 4
danger, p. 4
treatment, p. 5
trephination, p. 8
humors, p. 8
asylum, p. 10
moral treatment, p. 10
state hospitals, p. 11
somatogenic perspective, p. 11
psychogenic perspective, p. 11
general paresis, p. 11
hypnosis, p. 13

psychoanalysis, p. 13
psychotropic medications, p. 15
deinstitutionalization, p. 15
private psychotherapy, p. 15
prevention, p. 16
positive psychology, p. 16
multicultural psychology, p. 17
managed care program, p. 17
cybertherapy, p. 20
scientific method, p. 22
hypothesis, p. 22
case study, p. 22
correlation, p. 23
correlational method, p. 23
epidemiological study, p. 26
incidence, p. 26
prevalence, p. 26

longitudinal study, p. 26
experiment, p. 27
independent variable, p. 27
dependent variable, p. 27
confound, p. 27
control group, p. 27
experimental group, p. 27
random assignment, p. 29
blind design, p. 29
placebo therapy, p. 29
double-blind design, p. 30
quasi-experiment, p. 30
natural experiment, p. 30
analogue experiment, p. 30
single-subject experimental design, p. 31
Institutional Review Board (IRB), p. 32
informed consent, p. 32

QuickQuiz

1. What features are common to abnormal psychological functioning? *pp. 2–5*

2. Name two forms of past treatments that reflect a demonological view of abnormal behavior. *pp. 7–9*

3. Give examples of the somatogenic view of psychological abnormality from Hippocrates, the Renaissance, the nineteenth century, and the recent past. *pp. 8–12*

4. Describe the role of hypnotism and hysterical disorders in the development of the psychogenic view. *pp. 12–14*

5. How did Sigmund Freud come to develop the theory and technique of psychoanalysis? *pp. 13–14*

6. Describe the major changes that have occurred since the 1950s in the treatment of people with mental disorders. *pp. 14–21*

7. What are the advantages and disadvantages of the case study, correlational method, and experimental method? *pp. 22–31*

8. What techniques do researchers include in experiments to guard against the influence of confounds? *pp. 27–31*

9. Describe four alternative kinds of experiments that researchers often use. *pp. 30–31*

10. What are Institutional Review Boards, and what are their responsibilities and goals? *pp. 32–33*

Visit *LaunchPad*
www.macmillanhighered.com/launchpad/comerfund8e
to access the e-book, new interactive case studies, videos, activities, and LearningCurve quizzes, as well as study aids including flashcards, FAQs, and research exercises.

Macmillan Education LaunchPad

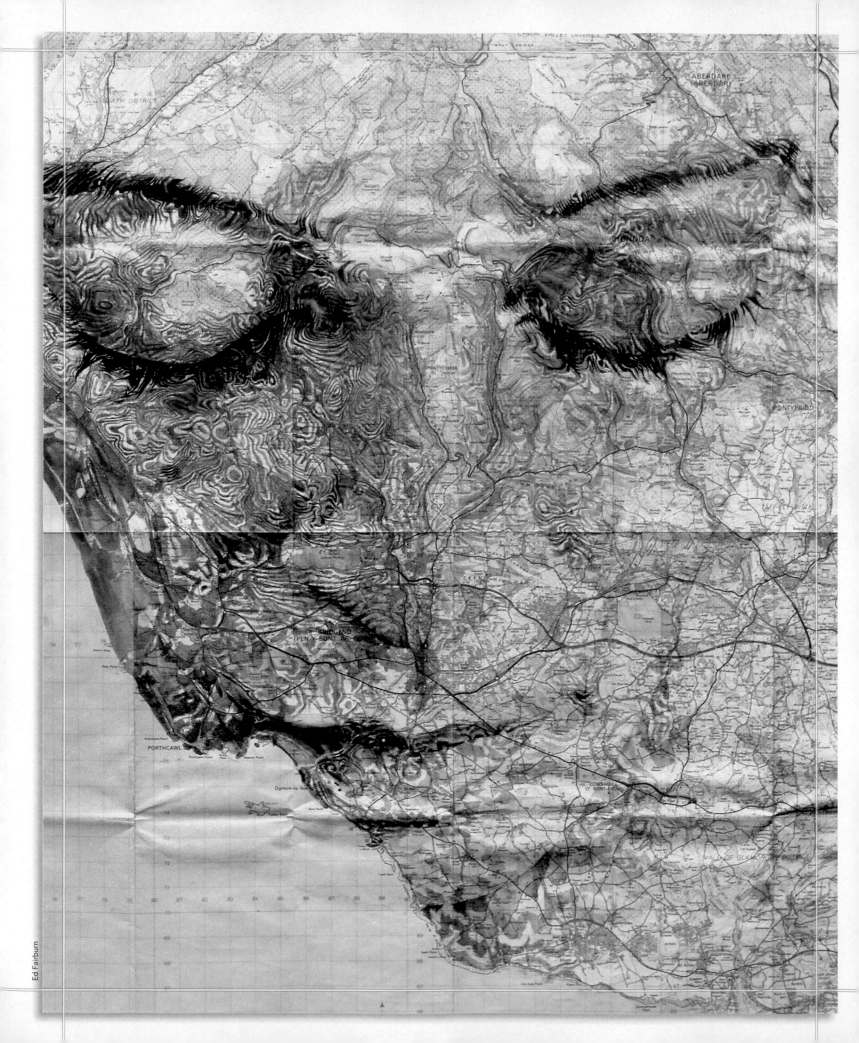

Models of Abnormality

Philip Berman, a 25-year-old single unemployed former copy editor for a large publishing house . . . had been hospitalized after a suicide attempt in which he deeply gashed his wrist with a razor blade. He described [to the therapist] how he had sat on the bathroom floor and watched the blood drip into the bathtub for some time before he [contacted] his father at work for help. He and his father went to the hospital emergency room to have the gash stitched, but he convinced himself and the hospital physician that he did not need hospitalization. The next day when his father suggested he needed help, he knocked his dinner to the floor and angrily stormed to his room. When he was calm again, he allowed his father to take him back to the hospital.

The immediate precipitant for his suicide attempt was that he had run into one of his former girlfriends with her new boyfriend. The patient stated that they had a drink together, but all the while he was with them he could not help thinking that "they were dying to run off and jump in bed." He experienced jealous rage, got up from the table, and walked out of the restaurant. He began to think about how he could "pay her back."

Mr. Berman had felt frequently depressed for brief periods during the previous several years. He was especially critical of himself for his limited social life and his inability to have managed to have sexual intercourse with a woman even once in his life. As he related this to the therapist, he lifted his eyes from the floor and with a sarcastic smirk said, "I'm a 25-year-old virgin. Go ahead, you can laugh now." He has had several girlfriends to date, whom he described as very attractive, but who he said had lost interest in him. On further questioning, however, it became apparent that Mr. Berman soon became very critical of them and demanded that they always meet his every need, often to their own detriment. The women then found the relationship very unrewarding and would soon find someone else.

During the past two years Mr. Berman had seen three psychiatrists briefly, one of whom had given him a drug, the name of which he could not remember, but that had precipitated some sort of unusual reaction for which he had to stay in a hospital overnight. . . . Concerning his hospitalization, the patient said that "It was a dump," that the staff refused to listen to what he had to say or to respond to his needs, and that they, in fact, treated all the patients "sadistically." The referring doctor corroborated that Mr. Berman was a difficult patient who demanded that he be treated as special, and yet was hostile to most staff members throughout his stay. After one angry exchange with an aide, he left the hospital without [permission], and subsequently signed out against medical advice.

Mr. Berman is one of two children of a middle-class family. His father is 55 years old and employed in a managerial position for an insurance company. He perceives his father as weak and ineffectual, completely dominated by the patient's overbearing and cruel mother. He states that he hates his mother with "a passion I can barely control." He claims that his mother used to call him names like "pervert" . . . when he was growing up, and that in an argument she once "kicked me in the balls." Together, he sees his parents as rich, powerful, and selfish, and, in turn, thinks that they see him as lazy, irresponsible, and a behavior problem. When his parents called the therapist to discuss their son's treatment, they stated that his problem began with the birth of his younger brother, Arnold, when Philip was 10 years old. After Arnold's birth Philip apparently became [a disagreeable] child who cursed a lot and was difficult to discipline. Philip recalls this period only vaguely. He reports that his mother once was hospitalized for depression, but that now "she doesn't believe in psychiatry."

Mr. Berman had graduated from college with average grades. Since graduating he had worked at three different publishing houses, but at none of them for more than one year. He always found some justification for quitting. He usually sat around his house doing very little for two or three months after quitting a job, until his parents

▸ **model** A set of assumptions and concepts that helps scientists explain and interpret observations. Also called a *paradigm*.

▸ **neuron** A nerve cell.

▸ **synapse** The tiny space between the nerve ending of one neuron and the dendrite of another.

▸ **neurotransmitter** A chemical that, released by one neuron, crosses the synaptic space to be received at receptors on the dendrites of neighboring neurons.

prodded him into getting a new one. He described innumerable interactions in his life with teachers, friends, and employers in which he felt offended or unfairly treated . . . and frequent arguments that left him feeling bitter . . . and [he] spent most of his time alone, "bored." He was unable to commit himself to any person, he held no strong convictions, and he felt no allegiance to any group.

The patient appeared as a very thin, bearded . . . young man with pale skin who maintained little eye contact with the therapist and who had an air of angry bitterness about him. Although he complained of depression, he denied other symptoms of the depressive syndrome. He seemed preoccupied with his rage at his parents, and seemed particularly invested in conveying a despicable image of himself. . . .

Spitzer et al., 1983, pp. 59–61

Philip Berman is clearly a troubled person, but how did he come to be that way? How do we explain and correct his many problems? To answer these questions, we must first look at the wide range of complaints we are trying to understand: Philip's depression and anger, his social failures, his lack of employment, his distrust of those around him, and the problems within his family. Then we must sort through all kinds of potential causes—internal and external, biological and interpersonal, past and present.

Although we may not realize it, we all use theoretical frameworks as we read about Philip. Over the course of our lives, each of us has developed a perspective that helps us make sense of the things other people say and do. In science, the perspectives used to explain events are known as **models**, or **paradigms**. Each model spells out the scientist's basic assumptions, gives order to the field under study, and sets guidelines for its investigation (Kuhn, 1962). It influences what the investigators observe as well as the questions they ask, the information they seek, and how they interpret this information. To understand how a clinician explains or treats a specific set of symptoms, such as Philip's, we must know his or her preferred model of abnormal functioning.

Until recently, clinical scientists of a given place and time tended to agree on a single model of abnormality—a model greatly influenced by the beliefs of their culture. The *demonological model* that was used to explain abnormal functioning during the Middle Ages, for example, borrowed heavily from medieval society's concerns with religion, superstition, and warfare. Medieval practitioners would have seen the devil's guiding hand in Philip Berman's efforts to commit suicide and his feelings of depression, rage, jealousy, and hatred. Similarly, their treatments for him—from prayers to whippings—would have sought to drive foreign spirits from his body.

Today several models are used to explain and treat abnormal functioning. This variety has resulted both from shifts in values and beliefs over the past half-century and from improvements in clinical research. At one end of the spectrum is the *biological model,* which sees physical processes as key to human behavior. In the middle are four models that focus on more psychological and personal aspects of human functioning: the *psychodynamic model* looks at people's unconscious internal processes and conflicts, the *behavioral model* emphasizes behavior and the ways in which it is learned, the *cognitive model* concentrates on the thinking that underlies behavior, and the *humanistic-existential model* stresses the role of values and choices. At the far end of the spectrum is the *sociocultural model,* which looks to social and cultural forces as the keys to human functioning. This model includes the *family-social perspective,* which focuses on an individual's family and social interactions, and the *multicultural perspective,* which emphasizes an individual's culture and the shared beliefs, values, and history of that culture.

Given their different assumptions and principles, the models are sometimes in conflict. Those who follow one perspective often scoff at the "naïve" interpretations,

//// **BETWEEN THE LINES** ////

In Their Words

"Mental illness is so much more complicated than any pill that any mortal could invent."

Elizabeth Wurtzel, *Prozac Nation*

investigations, and treatment efforts of the others. Yet none of the models is complete in itself. Each focuses mainly on one aspect of human functioning, and none can explain all aspects of abnormality.

The Biological Model

Philip Berman is a biological being. His thoughts and feelings are the results of biochemical and bioelectrical processes throughout his brain and body. Proponents of the *biological model* believe that a full understanding of Philip's thoughts, emotions, and behavior must therefore include an understanding of their biological basis. Not surprisingly, then, they believe that the most effective treatments for Philip's problems will be biological ones.

How Do Biological Theorists Explain Abnormal Behavior?

Adopting a medical perspective, biological theorists view abnormal behavior as an illness brought about by malfunctioning parts of the organism. Typically, they point to problems in brain anatomy or brain chemistry as the cause of such behavior.

Brain Anatomy and Abnormal Behavior The brain is made up of approximately 100 billion nerve cells, called **neurons**, and thousands of billions of support cells, called *glia* (from the Greek word for "glue"). Within the brain large groups of neurons form distinct areas, or *brain regions*. Toward the top of the brain, for example, is a cluster of regions, collectively referred to as the *cerebrum*, which includes the *cortex, corpus callosum, basal ganglia, hippocampus,* and *amygdala* (see Figure 2-1). The neurons in each of these brain regions control important functions. The cortex is the outer layer of the brain, the corpus callosum connects the brain's two cerebral hemispheres, the basal ganglia plays a crucial role in planning and producing movement, the hippocampus helps regulate emotions and memory, and the amygdala plays a key role in emotional memory. Clinical researchers have discovered connections between certain psychological disorders and problems in specific areas of the brain. One such disorder is *Huntington's disease,* a disorder marked by violent emotional outbursts, memory loss, suicidal thinking, involuntary body movements, and absurd beliefs. This disease has been traced to a loss of cells in the basal ganglia and cortex.

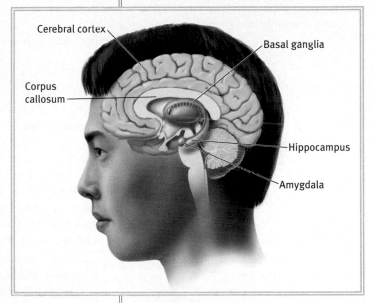

figure 2-1

The cerebrum Some psychological disorders can be traced to abnormal functioning of neurons in the cerebrum, which includes brain structures such as the cerebral cortex, corpus callosum, basal ganglia, hippocampus, and amygdala.

Brain Chemistry and Abnormal Behavior Biological researchers have also learned that psychological disorders can be related to problems in the transmission of messages from neuron to neuron. Information is communicated throughout the brain in the form of electrical impulses that travel from one neuron to one or more others. An impulse is first received by a neuron's *dendrites,* antenna-like extensions located at one end of the neuron. From there it travels down the neuron's *axon,* a long fiber extending from the neuron's body. Finally, it is transmitted through the *nerve ending* at the end of the axon to the dendrites of other neurons (see Figure 2-2).

But how do messages get from the nerve ending of one neuron to the dendrites of another? After all, the neurons do not actually touch each other. A tiny space, called the **synapse**, separates one neuron from the next, and the message must somehow move across that space. When an electrical impulse reaches a neuron's ending, the nerve ending is stimulated to release a chemical, called a **neurotransmitter**, that

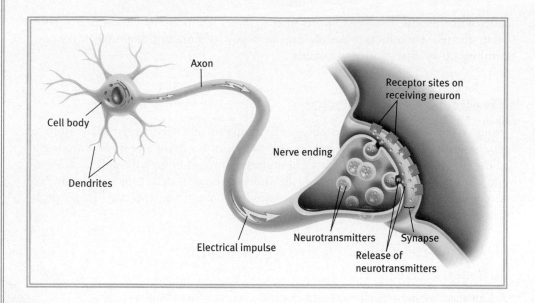

figure 2-2

A neuron communicating information
A message in the form of an electrical impulse travels down the sending neuron's axon to its nerve ending, where neurotransmitters are released and carry the message across the synaptic space to the dendrites of a receiving neuron.

travels across the synaptic space to **receptors** on the dendrites of the neighboring neurons. After binding to the receiving neuron's receptors, some neurotransmitters give a message to receiving neurons to "fire," that is, to trigger their own electrical impulse. Other neurotransmitters carry an inhibitory message; they tell receiving neurons to stop all firing. As you can see, neurotransmitters play a key role in moving information through the brain.

Researchers have identified dozens of neurotransmitters in the brain, and they have learned that each neuron uses only certain kinds. Studies indicate that abnormal activity by certain neurotransmitters can lead to specific mental disorders. Depression, for example, has been linked to low activity of the neurotransmitters *serotonin* and *norepinephrine.* Perhaps low serotonin activity is partly responsible for Philip Berman's pattern of depression and rage.

In addition to focusing on neurons and neurotransmitters, researchers have learned that mental disorders are sometimes related to abnormal chemical activity in the body's *endocrine system.* Endocrine glands, located throughout the body, work along with neurons to control such vital activities as growth, reproduction, sexual activity, heart rate, body temperature, energy, and responses to stress. The glands release chemicals called **hormones** into the bloodstream, and these chemicals then propel body organs into action. During times of stress, for example, the *adrenal glands,* located on top of the kidneys, secrete the hormone *cortisol* to help the body deal with the stress. Abnormal secretions of this chemical have been tied to anxiety and mood disorders.

Sources of Biological Abnormalities Why do some people have brain structures or biochemical activities that differ from the norm? Three factors have received particular attention in recent years—*genetics, evolution,* and *viral infections.*

GENETICS AND ABNORMAL BEHAVIOR Abnormalities in brain anatomy or chemistry are sometimes the result of genetic inheritance. Each cell in the human brain and body contains 23 pairs of *chromosomes,* with each chromosome in a pair inherited from one of the person's parents. Every chromosome contains numerous **genes**— segments that control the characteristics and traits a person inherits. Altogether, each cell contains around 30,000 genes (NIH, 2015; Emig et al., 2013). Scientists have known for years that genes help determine such physical characteristics as hair color, height, and eyesight. Genes can make people more prone to heart disease, cancer, or diabetes and perhaps to possessing artistic or musical skill. Studies suggest that

▶**receptor** A site on a neuron that receives a neurotransmitter.

▶**hormones** The chemicals released by endocrine glands into the bloodstream.

▶**gene** Chromosome segments that control the characteristics and traits we inherit.

inheritance also plays a part in mood disorders, schizophrenia, and other mental disorders. It appears that in most cases, several genes combine to help produce our actions and reactions, both functional and dysfunctional.

The precise contributions of various genes to mental disorders have become clearer in recent years, thanks in part to the completion of the *Human Genome Project* in 2000. In this major undertaking, scientists used the tools of molecular biology to *map*, or *sequence*, all of the genes in the human body in great detail. With this information in hand, researchers hope eventually to be able to prevent or change genes that help cause medical or psychological disorders.

EVOLUTION AND ABNORMAL BEHAVIOR Genes that contribute to mental disorders are typically viewed as unfortunate occurrences—almost mistakes of inheritance. The responsible gene may be a *mutation*, an abnormal form of the appropriate gene that emerges by accident. Or the problematic gene may be inherited by an individual after it has initially entered the family line as a mutation. According to some theorists, however, many of the genes that contribute to abnormal functioning are actually the result of normal *evolutionary* principles (Sipahi et al., 2014; Fábrega, 2010).

In general, evolutionary theorists argue that human reactions and the genes responsible for them have survived over the course of time because they have helped individuals to thrive and adapt. Ancestors who had the ability to run fast, for example, or the craftiness to hide were most able to escape their enemies and to reproduce. Thus, the genes responsible for effective walking, running, or problem solving were particularly likely to be passed on from generation to generation to the present day.

Similarly, say evolutionary theorists, the capacity to experience fear was, and in many instances still is, adaptive. Fear alerted our ancestors to dangers, threats, and losses so that persons could avoid or escape potential problems. People who were particularly sensitive to danger—those with greater fear responses—were more likely to survive catastrophes, battles, and the like and to reproduce and pass on their fear genes. Of course, in today's world, pressures are more numerous, subtle, and complex than they were in the past, condemning many individuals with such genes to a near-endless stream of fear and arousal. That is, the very genes that helped their ancestors to survive and reproduce might now leave these individuals particularly prone to fear reactions, anxiety disorders, or related psychological disorders.

The evolutionary perspective is controversial in the clinical field and has been rejected by many theorists. Imprecise and at times impossible to research, this explanation requires leaps of faith that many scientists find unacceptable.

VIRAL INFECTIONS AND ABNORMAL BEHAVIOR Another possible source of abnormal brain structure or biochemical dysfunctioning is *viral infections*. As you will see in Chapter 14, for example, research suggests that *schizophrenia*, a disorder marked by delusions, hallucinations, or other departures from reality, may be related to exposure to certain viruses during childhood or before birth (Liu et al., 2014; Arias et al., 2012). Studies have found that the mothers of many individuals with this disorder contracted influenza or related viruses during their pregnancy. This and related pieces of circumstantial evidence suggest that a damaging virus may enter the fetus' brain and remain dormant there until the individual reaches adolescence or young adulthood. At that time, the virus may produce the symptoms of schizophrenia. During the past decade, researchers have sometimes linked viruses to anxiety, depressive, and bipolar disorders, as well as to psychotic disorders (Liu et al., 2014).

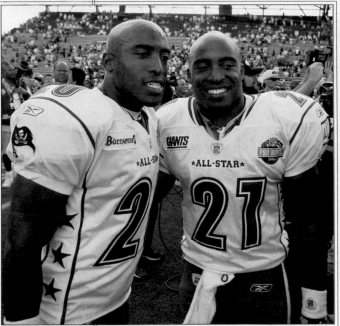

AP Photo/Ted S. Warren

More than coincidence? Identical twins Ronde and Tiki Barber, shown here at the 2006 NFL Pro Bowl, each had a successful football career—Ronde with the Tampa Bay Buccaneers and Tiki with the New York Giants. Studies of twins suggest that some aspects of behavior and personality are influenced by genetic factors. Many identical twins, like the Barbers, have similar tastes, behave in similar ways, and make similar life choices. Some even develop similar abnormal behaviors.

▸ **psychotropic medications** Drugs that primarily affect the brain and reduce many symptoms of mental dysfunctioning.

▸ **electroconvulsive therapy (ECT)** A biological treatment in which a brain seizure is triggered as an electric current passes through electrodes attached to the patient's forehead.

▸ **psychosurgery** Brain surgery for mental disorders. Also called *neurosurgery*.

Biological Treatments

Biological practitioners look for certain kinds of clues when they try to understand abnormal behavior. Does the person's family have a history of that behavior, and hence a possible genetic predisposition to it? (Philip Berman's case history mentions that his mother was once hospitalized for depression.) Is the behavior produced by events that could have had a physiological effect? (Philip was having a drink when he flew into a jealous rage at the restaurant.)

Once the clinicians have pinpointed physical sources of dysfunctioning, they are in a better position to choose a biological course of treatment. The three leading kinds of biological treatments used today are *drug therapy, electroconvulsive therapy,* and *psychosurgery.* Drug therapy is by far the most common of these approaches.

In the 1950s, researchers discovered several effective **psychotropic medications**, drugs that mainly affect emotions and thought processes. These drugs have greatly changed the outlook for a number of mental disorders and today are used widely, either alone or with other forms of therapy. However, the psychotropic drug revolution has also produced some major problems. Many people believe, for example, that the drugs are overused. Moreover, while drugs are effective in many cases, they do not help everyone. Thus many people seek out a biological alternative to drug therapy—the enormously popular *herbal supplements* (see *InfoCentral* on the next page).

> **What might the popularity of psychotropic drugs suggest about coping styles and problem-solving skills in our society?**

Four major psychotropic drug groups are used in therapy: antianxiety, antidepressant, antibipolar, and antipsychotic drugs. *Antianxiety drugs,* also called *minor tranquilizers* or *anxiolytics,* help reduce tension and anxiety. *Antidepressant drugs* help improve the mood of people who are depressed. *Antibipolar drugs,* also called *mood stabilizers,* help steady the moods of those with a bipolar disorder, a condition marked by mood swings from mania to depression. And *antipsychotic drugs* help reduce the confusion, hallucinations, and delusions of psychotic disorders, disorders (such as schizophrenia) marked by a loss of contact with reality.

Psychotropic drugs, like all medications, reach the marketplace only after systematic research and careful review. It takes an average of 12 years and hundreds of millions of dollars for a pharmaceutical company in the United States to bring a newly identified chemical compound to market. Along the way, the drug is vigorously tested in study after study—first on animals and then on humans—to determine its efficacy, safety, dosage, and side effects, until finally it receives approval by the U.S. Food and Drug Administration. Only 3 percent of newly discovered chemical compounds make it to animal testing, only 2 percent of animal-tested compounds reach human testing, and only 21 percent of human-tested drugs are eventually approved (FDA, 2014).

A second form of biological treatment, used primarily on depressed patients, is **electroconvulsive therapy (ECT)**. Two electrodes are attached to a patient's forehead, and an electrical current of 65 to 140 volts is passed briefly through the brain. The current causes a brain seizure that lasts up to a few minutes. After seven to nine ECT sessions, spaced two or three days apart, many patients feel considerably less depressed. The treatment is used on tens of thousands of depressed persons annually, particularly those whose depression fails to respond to other treatments (Dukart et al., 2014).

A third form of biological treatment is **psychosurgery**, or **neurosurgery**, brain surgery for mental disorders. It is thought to have roots as far back as trephining, the prehistoric practice of chipping a hole in the skull of a person who behaved strangely. Modern procedures are derived from a technique first developed in the late 1930s by a

The ultimate brain The human brain increasingly has captured the attention of both neuroscientists and the public at large. This image, taken from a screenshot of a popular iPad app, shows brain tissue from the renowned physicist Albert Einstein.

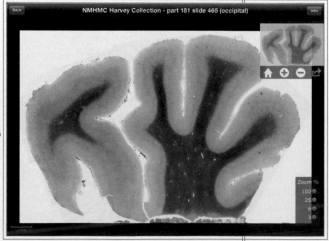

NMHMC Harvey Collection - part 181 slide 465 (occipital)

DIETARY SUPPLEMENTS: AN ALTERNATIVE TREATMENT

Dietary supplements, also known as **nutraceuticals**, are non–pharmaceutical and nonfood substances that people may take to supplement their diets, often to help prevent or treat psychological or physical ailments. Depression is the psychological problem for which nutraceuticals are used most often.

NUTRACEUTICALS ARE...

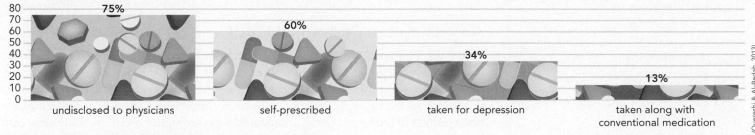

- **75%** undisclosed to physicians
- **60%** self-prescribed
- **34%** taken for depression
- **13%** taken along with conventional medication

(Qureshi & Al-Bedah, 2013)

POPULAR NUTRACEUTICALS FOR DEPRESSION

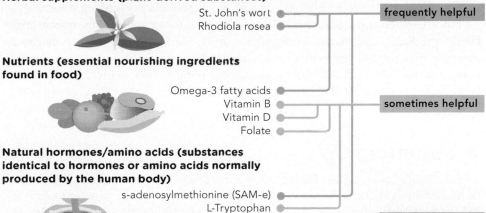

Herbal supplements (plant-derived substances)
- St. John's wort
- Rhodiola rosea

Nutrients (essential nourishing ingredients found in food)
- Omega-3 fatty acids
- Vitamin B
- Vitamin D
- Folate

Natural hormones/amino acids (substances identical to hormones or amino acids normally produced by the human body)
- s-adenosylmethionine (SAM-e)
- L-Tryptophan
- Melatonin

- **frequently helpful**
- **sometimes helpful**
- **rarely helpful**

How Effective Are Nutraceuticals for Unipolar Depression?

Nutraceuticals do not appear to be helpful for people with severe depression. However, according to research, several types of supplements are effective for mild or moderate depression.

(Qureshi & Al-Bedah, 2013; Howland, 2012; Lakhan & Vieira, 2008)

Many other countries (Canada, Germany, China) regulate supplements more strictly than the United States.

Depressed people take nutraceuticals because...
- they are not helped by conventional treatments
- they developed major side effects to antidepressant drugs
- they cannot afford conventional treatments
- they dislike modern medications
- they prefer more natural treatments

(Qureshi & Al-Bedah, 2013)

NUTRACEUTICALS AND CONVENTIONAL MEDICATIONS

To receive approval for a conventional drug, its manufacturer must prove it safe and effective through a testing process that costs hundreds of millions of dollars.

The 1994 Dietary Supplement Health and Education Act states that dietary supplements are not bound by the same legal requirements as conventional medications. Since then more than 4,000 manufacturers have rushed supplements to market, typically without research and often with extraordinary claims about their healing powers.

- Nutraceuticals are assumed to be safe unless the FDA can prove them harmful.
- Nutraceuticals can be potent, and even interact dangerously with conventional medications (NIH, 2011; Magee, 2007).
- Patients are often misinformed by friends or the Internet and may take nutraceuticals incorrectly.
- Many patients are reluctant to discuss their use of supplements with their therapists or physicians (Niv et al., 2010; Kessler, 2002).

WHO CONSUMES NUTRACEUTICALS?

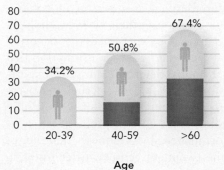
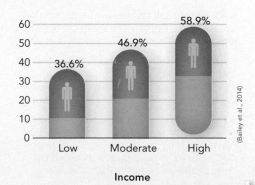

Age: 20-39: 34.2%, 40-59: 50.8%, >60: 67.4%

Race/ethnicity: White American: 53.8%, African American: 37.8%, Hispanic American: 33.3%

Income: Low: 36.6%, Moderate: 46.9%, High: 58.9%

(Bailey et al., 2014)

BETWEEN THE LINES

Big Dates in Drug Approval

1954	Thorazine (first antipsychotic)
1955	Ritalin (first ADHD drug)
1958	MAO inhibitors (first antidepressant)
1960	Librium (first benzodiazepine antianxiety drug)
1961	Elavil (first tricyclic antidepressant)
1963	Valium (second benzodiazepine antianxiety drug)
1970	Lithium (first mood stabilizer/ antibipolar drug)
1987	Prozac (first SSRI antidepressant)
1998	Viagra (first erectile disorder drug)

Portuguese neuropsychiatrist, António Egas Moniz. In that procedure, known as a *lobotomy,* a surgeon would cut the connections between the brain's frontal lobes and the lower regions of the brain. Today's psychosurgery procedures are much more precise than the lobotomies of the past. Even so, they are considered experimental and are used only after certain severe disorders have continued for years without responding to any other form of treatment.

Assessing the Biological Model

Today the biological model enjoys considerable respect. Biological research constantly produces valuable new information. And biological treatments often bring great relief when other approaches have failed. At the same time, this model has its shortcomings. Some of its proponents seem to expect that all human behavior can be explained in biological terms and treated with biological methods. This view can limit rather than enhance our understanding of abnormal functioning. Our mental life is an interplay of biological and nonbiological factors, and it is important to understand that interplay rather than to focus on biological variables alone.

Another shortcoming is that several of today's biological treatments are capable of producing significant undesirable effects. Certain antipsychotic drugs, for example, may produce movement problems such as severe shaking, bizarre-looking contractions of the face and body, and extreme restlessness. Clearly such costs must be addressed and weighed against the drug's benefits.

> ### ➤ *Summing Up*
>
> **THE BIOLOGICAL MODEL** Biological theorists look at the biological processes of human functioning to explain abnormal behavior, pointing to anatomical or biochemical problems in the brain and body. Such abnormalities are sometimes the result of genetic inheritance, evolution, or viral infections. Biological therapists use physical and chemical methods to help people overcome their psychological problems. The leading methods are drug therapy, electroconvulsive therapy, and, on rare occasions, psychosurgery.

The Psychodynamic Model

The *psychodynamic model* is the oldest and most famous of the modern psychological models. Psychodynamic theorists believe that a person's behavior, whether normal or abnormal, is determined largely by underlying psychological forces of which he or she is not consciously aware. These internal forces are described as *dynamic*—that is, they interact with one another—and their interaction gives rise to behavior, thoughts, and emotions. Abnormal symptoms are viewed as the result of conflicts between these forces.

Psychodynamic theorists would view Philip Berman as a person in conflict. They would want to explore his past experiences because, in their view, psychological conflicts are tied to early relationships and to traumatic experiences that occurred during childhood. Psychodynamic theories rest on the *deterministic* assumption that no symptom or behavior is "accidental": All behavior is determined by past experiences. Thus Philip's hatred for his mother, his memories of her as cruel and overbearing, the weakness of his father, and the birth of a younger brother when Philip was 10 may all be important to the understanding of his current problems.

The psychodynamic model was first formulated by Viennese neurologist Sigmund Freud (1856–1939) at the turn of the twentieth century. After studying

▶ **id** According to Freud, the psychological force that produces instinctual needs, drives, and impulses.

▶ **ego** According to Freud, the psychological force that employs reason and operates in accordance with the reality principle.

▶ **ego defense mechanisms** According to psychoanalytic theory, strategies developed by the ego to control unacceptable id impulses and to avoid or reduce the anxiety they arouse.

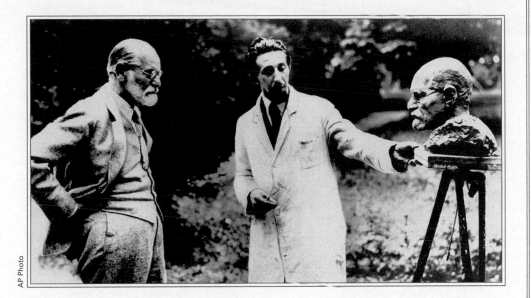

AP Photo

Freud takes a closer look at Freud Sigmund Freud, founder of psychoanalytic theory and therapy, contemplates a sculptured bust of himself in 1931 at his village home in Potzlein, near Vienna. As Freud and the bust go eyeball to eyeball, one can only imagine what conclusions each is drawing about the other.

hypnosis, Freud developed the theory of *psychoanalysis* to explain both normal and abnormal psychological functioning as well as a corresponding method of treatment, a conversational approach also called psychoanalysis. During the early 1900s, Freud and several of his colleagues in the Vienna Psychoanalytic Society—including Carl Gustav Jung (1875–1961)—became the most influential clinical theorists in the Western world.

How Did Freud Explain Normal and Abnormal Functioning?

Freud believed that three central forces shape the personality—instinctual needs, rational thinking, and moral standards. All of these forces, he believed, operate at the *unconscious level,* unavailable to immediate awareness; he further believed these forces to be dynamic, or interactive. Freud called the forces the *id,* the *ego,* and the *superego.*

The Id Freud used the term **id** to denote instinctual needs, drives, and impulses. The id operates in accordance with the *pleasure principle;* that is, it always seeks gratification. Freud also believed that all id instincts tend to be sexual, noting that from the very earliest stages of life a child's pleasure is obtained from nursing, defecating, masturbating, or engaging in other activities that he considered to have sexual ties. He further suggested that a person's *libido,* or sexual energy, fuels the id.

The Ego During our early years we come to recognize that our environment will not meet every instinctual need. Our mother, for example, is not always available to do our bidding. A part of the id separates off and becomes the **ego**. Like the id, the ego unconsciously seeks gratification, but it does so in accordance with the *reality principle,* the knowledge we acquire through experience that it can be unacceptable to express our id impulses outright. The ego, employing reason, guides us to know when we can and cannot express those impulses.

The ego develops basic strategies, called **ego defense mechanisms**, to control unacceptable id impulses and avoid or reduce the anxiety they arouse. The most basic defense mechanism, *repression,* prevents unacceptable impulses from ever reaching consciousness. There are many other ego defense mechanisms, and each of us tends to favor some over others (see Table 2-1 on the next page).

"I'm doing a lot better now that I'm back in denial."

Pat Byrnes/The New Yorker Collection/www.cartoonbank.com

table: **2-1**

The Defense Never Rests: Defense Mechanisms to the Rescue

Defense	Operation	Example
Repression	Person avoids anxiety by simply not allowing painful or dangerous thoughts to become conscious.	An executive's desire to run amok and attack his boss and colleagues at a board meeting is denied access to his awareness.
Denial	Person simply refuses to acknowledge the existence of an external source of anxiety.	You are not prepared for tomorrow's final exam, but you tell yourself that it's not actually an important exam and that there's no good reason not to go to a movie tonight.
Projection	Person attributes own unacceptable impulses, motives, or desires to other individuals.	The executive who repressed his destructive desires may project his anger onto his boss and claim that it is actually the boss who is hostile.
Rationalization	Person creates a socially acceptable reason for an action that actually reflects unacceptable motives.	A student explains away poor grades by citing the importance of the "total experience" of going to college and claiming that too much emphasis on grades would actually interfere with a well-rounded education.
Displacement	Person displaces hostility away from a dangerous object and onto a safer substitute.	After a perfect parking spot is taken by a person who cuts in front of your car, you release your pent-up anger by starting an argument with your roommate.
Intellectualization	Person represses emotional reactions in favor of overly logical response to a problem.	A woman who has been beaten and raped gives a detached, methodical description of the effects that such attacks may have on victims.
Regression	Person retreats from an upsetting conflict to an early developmental stage at which no one is expected to behave maturely or responsibly.	A boy who cannot cope with the anger he feels toward his rejecting mother regresses to infantile behavior, soiling his clothes and no longer taking care of his basic needs.

The Superego The **superego** grows from the ego, just as the ego grows out of the id. This personality force operates by the *morality principle,* a sense of what is right and what is wrong. As we learn from our parents that many of our id impulses are unacceptable, we unconsciously adopt our parents' values. Judging ourselves by their standards, we feel good when we uphold their values; conversely, when we go against them, we feel guilty. In short, we develop a *conscience.*

According to Freud, these three parts of the personality—the id, the ego, and the superego—are often in some degree of conflict. A healthy personality is one in which an effective working relationship, an acceptable compromise, has formed among the three forces. If the id, ego, and superego are in excessive conflict, the person's behavior may show signs of dysfunction.

Freudians would therefore view Philip Berman as someone whose personality forces have a poor working relationship. His ego and superego are unable to control his id impulses, which lead him repeatedly to act in impulsive and often dangerous ways—suicidal gestures, jealous rages, job resignations, outbursts of temper, frequent arguments.

Developmental Stages Freud proposed that at each stage of development, from infancy to maturity, new events challenge individuals and require adjustments in their id, ego, and superego. If the adjustments are successful, they lead to personal growth. If not, the person may become **fixated**, or stuck, at an early stage of development. Then all subsequent development suffers, and the individual may well be headed for abnormal functioning in the future. Because parents are the key figures during the early years of life, they are often seen as the cause of improper development.

▸**superego** According to Freud, the psychological force that represents a person's values and ideals.

▸**fixation** According to Freud, a condition in which the id, ego, and superego do not mature properly and are frozen at an early stage of development.

▸**free association** A psychodynamic technique in which the patient describes any thought, feeling, or image that comes to mind, even if it seems unimportant.

Freud named each stage of development after the body area that he considered most important to the child at that time. For example, he referred to the first 18 months of life as the *oral stage*. During this stage, children fear that the mother who feeds and comforts them will disappear. Children whose mothers consistently fail to gratify their oral needs may become fixated at the oral stage and display an "oral character" throughout their lives, one marked by extreme dependence or extreme mistrust. Such persons are particularly prone to develop depression. As you will see in later chapters, Freud linked fixations at the other stages of development—*anal* (18 months to 3 years of age), *phallic* (3 to 5 years), *latency* (5 to 12 years), and *genital* (12 years to adulthood)—to yet other kinds of psychological dysfunction.

How Do Other Psychodynamic Explanations Differ from Freud's?

Personal and professional differences between Freud and his colleagues led to a split in the Vienna Psychoanalytic Society early in the twentieth century. Carl Jung and others developed new theories. Although the new theories departed from Freud's ideas in important ways, each held on to Freud's belief that human functioning is shaped by dynamic (interacting) psychological forces. Thus all such theories, including Freud's, are referred to as *psychodynamic*.

Three of today's most influential psychodynamic theories are ego theory, self theory, and object relations theory. *Ego theorists* emphasize the role of the ego and consider it a more independent and powerful force than Freud did (Sharf, 2015). *Self theorists,* in contrast, give the greatest attention to the role of the *self*—the unified personality. They believe that the basic human motive is to strengthen the wholeness of the self (Dunn, 2013; Kohut, 2001, 1977). *Object relations theorists* propose that people are motivated mainly by a need to have relationships with others and that severe problems in the relationships between children and their caregivers may lead to abnormal development (Yun et al., 2013; Kernberg, 2005, 1997).

"Luke, I am your father." This light saber fight between Luke Skywalker and Darth Vader highlights the most famous, and contentious, father–son relationship in movie history. According to Sigmund Freud, however, all fathers and sons have significant tensions and conflicts that they must work through, even in the absence of the special pressures faced by Luke and his father in the *Star Wars* series.

Psychodynamic Therapies

Psychodynamic therapies range from Freudian psychoanalysis to modern therapies based on self theory or object relations theory. Psychodynamic therapists seek to uncover past traumas and the inner conflicts that have resulted from them. They try to help clients resolve, or settle, those conflicts and to resume personal development.

According to most psychodynamic therapists, therapists must subtly guide therapy discussions so that the patients discover their underlying problems for themselves. To aid in the process, the therapists rely on such techniques as *free association, therapist interpretation, catharsis,* and *working through*.

Free Association In psychodynamic therapies, the patient is responsible for starting and leading each discussion. The therapist tells the patient to describe any thought, feeling, or image that comes to mind, even if it seems unimportant. This practice is known as **free association**. The therapist expects that the patient's associations will eventually uncover unconscious events. In the following excerpts from a famous psychodynamic case, notice how free association helps a woman to discover threatening impulses and conflicts within herself:

▶ **resistance** An unconscious refusal to participate fully in therapy.

▶ **transference** According to psychodynamic theorists, the redirection toward the psychotherapist of feelings associated with important figures in a patient's life, now or in the past.

▶ **dream** A series of ideas and images that form during sleep.

▶ **catharsis** The reliving of past repressed feelings in order to settle internal conflicts and overcome problems.

▶ **working through** The psychoanalytic process of facing conflicts, reinterpreting feelings, and overcoming one's problems.

> **Patient:** *So I started walking, and walking, and decided to go behind the museum and walk through [New York's] Central Park. So I walked and went through a back field and felt very excited and wonderful. I saw a park bench next to a clump of bushes and sat down. There was a rustle behind me and I got frightened. I thought of men concealing themselves in the bushes. I thought of the sex perverts I read about in Central Park. I wondered if there was someone behind me exposing himself. The idea is repulsive, but exciting too. I think of father now and feel excited. I think of an erect penis. This is connected with my father. There is something about this pushing in my mind. I don't know what it is, like on the border of my memory. (Pause)*
>
> **Therapist:** *Mm-hmm. (Pause) On the border of your memory?*
>
> **Patient:** *(The patient breathes rapidly and seems to be under great tension.) As a little girl, I slept with my father. I get a funny feeling. I get a funny feeling over my skin, tingly-like. It's a strange feeling, like a blindness, like not seeing something. My mind blurs and spreads over anything I look at. I've had this feeling off and on since I walked in the park. My mind seems to blank off like I can't think or absorb anything.*
>
> *(Wolberg, 2005, 1967, p. 662)*

Therapist Interpretation Psychodynamic therapists listen carefully as patients talk, looking for clues, drawing tentative conclusions, and sharing interpretations when they think the patient is ready to hear them. Interpretations of three phenomena are particularly important—*resistance, transference,* and *dreams.*

Patients are showing **resistance**, an unconscious refusal to participate fully in therapy, when they suddenly cannot free associate or when they change a subject to avoid a painful discussion. They demonstrate **transference** when they act and feel toward the therapist as they did or do toward important persons in their lives, especially their parents, siblings, and spouses. Consider again the woman who walked in Central Park. As she continues talking, the therapist helps her to explore her transference:

> **Patient:** *I get so excited by what is happening here. I feel I'm being held back by needing to be nice. I'd like to blast loose sometimes, but I don't dare.*
>
> **Therapist:** *Because you fear my reaction?*
>
> **Patient:** *The worst thing would be that you wouldn't like me. You wouldn't speak to me friendly; you wouldn't smile; you'd feel you can't treat me and discharge me from treatment. But I know this isn't so, I know it.*
>
> **Therapist:** *Where do you think these attitudes come from?*
>
> **Patient:** *When I was nine years old, I read a lot about great men in history. I'd quote them and be dramatic. I'd want a sword at my side; I'd dress like an Indian. Mother would scold me. Don't frown, don't talk so much. Sit on your hands, over and over again. I did all kinds of things. I was a naughty child. She told me I'd be hurt. Then at fourteen I fell off a horse and broke my back. I had to be in bed. Mother told me on the day I went riding not to, that I'd get hurt because the ground was frozen. I was a stubborn, self-willed child. Then I went against her will and suffered an accident that changed my life, a fractured back. Her attitude was, "I told you so." I was put in a cast and kept in bed for months.*
>
> *(Wolberg, 2005, 1967, p. 662)*

Finally, many psychodynamic therapists try to help patients interpret their **dreams** (Russo, 2014) (see Table 2-2). Freud (1924) called dreams the "royal road to the unconscious." He believed that repression and other defense mechanisms operate less completely during sleep and that dreams, if correctly interpreted, can reveal unconscious instincts, needs, and wishes. Freud identified two kinds of dream content—manifest and latent. *Manifest content* is the consciously remembered dream; *latent content* is its symbolic meaning. To interpret a dream, therapists must translate its manifest content into its latent content.

> **Why do you think most people try to interpret and make sense of their own dreams?**

table: 2-2

Percent of Research Participants Who Have Had Common Dreams		
	Men	Women
Being chased or pursued, not injured	78%	83%
Sexual experiences	85	73
Falling	73	74
School, teachers, studying	57	71
Arriving too late, e.g., for a train	55	62
Trying to do something repeatedly	55	53
Flying or soaring through the air	58	44
Failing an examination	37	48
Being physically attacked	40	44
Being frozen with fright	32	44

Information from: Robert & Zadra, 2014; Copley, 2008; Kantrowitz & Springen, 2004.

Catharsis Insight must be an emotional as well as an intellectual process. Psychodynamic therapists believe that patients must experience **catharsis**, a reliving of past repressed feelings, if they are to settle internal conflicts and overcome their problems.

Working Through A single episode of interpretation and catharsis will not change the way a person functions. The patient and therapist must examine the same issues over and over in the course of many sessions, each time with greater clarity. This process, called **working through**, usually takes a long time, often years.

Current Trends in Psychodynamic Therapy The past 40 years have witnessed significant changes in the way many psychodynamic therapists conduct sessions. An increased demand for focused, time-limited psychotherapies has resulted in efforts to make psychodynamic therapy more efficient and affordable. Two current psychodynamic approaches that illustrate this trend are *short-term psychodynamic therapies* and *relational psychoanalytic therapy*.

SHORT-TERM PSYCHODYNAMIC THERAPIES In several short versions of psychodynamic therapy, patients choose a single problem—a *dynamic focus*—to work on, such as difficulty getting along with other people (Frederickson, 2013). The therapist and patient focus on this problem throughout the treatment and work only on the psychodynamic issues that relate to it (such as unresolved oral needs). Only a limited number of studies have tested the effectiveness of these short-term psychodynamic therapies, but their findings do suggest that the approaches are sometimes quite helpful to patients (Knekt et al., 2015; Wolitzky, 2011).

RELATIONAL PSYCHOANALYTIC THERAPY Whereas Freud believed that psychodynamic therapists should take on the role of a neutral, distant expert during a treatment session, a contemporary school of psychodynamic therapy referred to as *relational psychoanalytic therapy* argues that therapists are key figures in the lives of patients—figures whose reactions and beliefs should be included in the therapy process (Ringstrom, 2014; Luborsky et al., 2011). Thus, a key principle of relational therapy is that therapists should also disclose things about themselves, particularly their own reactions to patients, and try to establish more equal relationships with patients.

Assessing the Psychodynamic Model

Freud and his followers have helped change the way abnormal functioning is understood. Largely because of their work, a wide range of theorists today look for answers outside of biological processes. Psychodynamic theorists have also helped us to understand that abnormal functioning may be rooted in the same processes

> /////BETWEEN THE LINES/////
>
> **In Their Words**
>
> "Fortunately, analysis is not the only way to resolve inner conflicts. Life itself still remains a very effective therapist."
> Karen Horney, *Our Inner Conflicts*, 1945

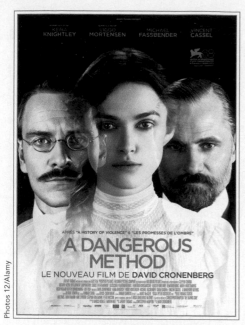

Photos 12/Alamy

A cultural phenomenon The history and practice of psychoanalysis have been very popular subjects in the arts over the years. For example, the critically acclaimed 2011 film *A Dangerous Method* portrays complex personal and professional reasons for the collapse of Sigmund Freud's relationship with his close colleague and friend, Carl Jung.

▸ **conditioning** A simple form of learning.

▸ **operant conditioning** A process of learning in which behavior that leads to satisfying consequences is likely to be repeated.

▸ **modeling** A process of learning in which an individual acquires responses by observing and imitating others.

▸ **classical conditioning** A process of learning in which two events that repeatedly occur close together in time become fused in a person's mind and produce the same response.

as normal functioning. Psychological conflict is a common experience; it leads to abnormal functioning only if the conflict becomes excessive.

> **What are some of the ways that Freud's theories have affected literature, film and television, child rearing, and education in Western society?**

Freud and his many followers have also had a monumental impact on treatment. They were the first to apply theory systematically to treatment. They were also the first to demonstrate the potential of psychological, as opposed to biological, treatment, and their ideas have served as starting points for many other psychological treatments.

At the same time, the psychodynamic model has its shortcomings. Its concepts are hard to research (Prochaska & Norcross, 2013; Levy et al., 2012). Because processes such as id drives, ego defenses, and fixation are abstract and supposedly operate at an unconscious level, there is no way of knowing for certain if they are occurring. Not surprisingly, then, psychodynamic explanations and treatments have received limited research support over the years, and psychodynamic theorists rely largely on evidence provided by individual case studies. Nevertheless, recent research evidence suggests that long-term psychodynamic therapy may be helpful for many persons with long-term complex disorders (Lorentzen et al., 2015; Kunst, 2014), and 18 percent of today's clinical psychologists identify themselves as psychodynamic therapists (Prochaska & Norcross, 2013, 2010).

➤ *Summing Up*

THE PSYCHODYNAMIC MODEL Psychodynamic theorists believe that an individual's behavior, whether normal or abnormal, is determined by underlying psychological forces. They consider psychological conflicts to be rooted in early parent–child relationships and traumatic experiences. The psychodynamic model was formulated by Sigmund Freud, who said that three dynamic forces—the id, ego, and superego—interact to produce thought, feeling, and behavior. Other psychodynamic theories are ego theory, self theory, and object relations theory.

Psychodynamic therapists help people uncover past traumas and the inner conflicts that have resulted from them. They use a number of techniques, including free association and interpretations of psychological phenomena such as resistance, transference, and dreams. The leading contemporary psychodynamic approaches include short-term psychodynamic therapies and relational psychoanalytic therapy.

The Behavioral Model

Like psychodynamic theorists, behavioral theorists believe that our actions are determined largely by our experiences in life. However, the *behavioral model* concentrates on *behaviors,* the responses an organism makes to its environment. Behaviors can be external (going to work, say) or internal (having a feeling or thought). In turn, behavioral theorists base their explanations and treatments on *principles of learning,* the processes by which these behaviors change in response to the environment.

Many learned behaviors help people to cope with daily challenges and to lead happy, productive lives. However, abnormal behaviors also can be learned. Behaviorists who try to explain Philip Berman's problems might view him as a man who has received improper training: he has learned behaviors that offend others and repeatedly work against him.

© Corey Perrine/ZUMA Press/Corbis

Whereas the psychodynamic model had its beginnings in the clinical work of physicians, the behavioral model began in laboratories where psychologists were running experiments on **conditioning**, simple forms of learning. The researchers manipulated *stimuli* and *rewards,* then observed how their manipulations affected the responses of their research participants.

During the 1950s, many clinicians became frustrated with what they viewed as the vagueness and slowness of the psychodynamic model. Some of them began to apply the principles of learning to the study and treatment of psychological problems. Their efforts gave rise to the behavioral model of abnormality.

How Do Behaviorists Explain Abnormal Functioning?

Learning theorists have identified several forms of conditioning, and each may produce abnormal behavior as well as normal behavior. In **operant conditioning**, for example, humans and animals learn to behave in certain ways as a result of receiving *rewards*—consequences of one kind or another—whenever they do so. In **modeling**, individuals learn responses simply by observing other individuals and repeating their behaviors.

In a third form of conditioning, **classical conditioning**, learning occurs when two events repeatedly occur close together in time. The events become fused in a person's mind, and before long the person responds in the same way to both events. If one event produces a response of joy, the other brings joy as well; if one event brings feelings of relief, so does the other. A closer look at this form of conditioning illustrates how the behavioral model can account for abnormal functioning.

Ivan Pavlov (1849–1936), a famous Russian physiologist, first demonstrated classical conditioning with animal studies. He placed a bowl of meat powder before a dog, producing the natural response that all dogs have to meat: They start to salivate (see Figure 2-3). Next Pavlov added a step: Just before presenting the dog with meat powder, he sounded a bell. After several such pairings of bell tone and presentation of meat powder, Pavlov noted that the dog began to salivate as soon as it heard the bell. The dog had learned to salivate in response to a sound.

In the vocabulary of classical conditioning, the meat in this demonstration is an *unconditioned stimulus (US)*. It elicits the *unconditioned response (UR)* of salivation, that is, a natural response with

figure 2-3
Working for Pavlov In Ivan Pavlov's experimental device, the dog's saliva was collected in a tube as it was secreted, and the amount was recorded on a revolving cylinder. The experimenter observed the dog through a one-way glass window.

A. Bandura, Stanford University

See and do Modeling may account for some forms of abnormal behavior. A well-known study by Albert Bandura and his colleagues (1963) demonstrated that children learned to abuse a doll by observing an adult hit it. Children who had not been exposed to the adult model did not mistreat the doll.

which the dog is born. The sound of the bell is a *conditioned stimulus (CS),* a previously neutral stimulus that comes to be linked with meat in the dog's mind. As such, it too produces a salivation response. When the salivation response is produced by the conditioned stimulus rather than by the unconditioned stimulus, it is called a *conditioned response (CR).*

Before Conditioning	After Conditioning
CS: Tone → No response	CS: Tone → CR: Salivation
US: Meat → UR: Salivation	US: Meat → UR: Salivation

Classical conditioning explains many familiar behaviors. The romantic feelings a young man experiences when he smells his girlfriend's perfume, say, may represent a conditioned response. Initially, this perfume may have had little emotional effect on him, but because the fragrance was present during several romantic encounters, it came to elicit a romantic response.

Abnormal behaviors, too, can be acquired by classical conditioning. Consider a young boy who is repeatedly frightened by a neighbor's large German shepherd dog. Whenever the child walks past the neighbor's front yard, the dog barks loudly and lunges at him, stopped only by a rope tied to the porch. In this unfortunate situation, the boy's parents are not surprised to discover that he develops a fear of dogs. They are stumped, however, by another intense fear the child displays, a fear of sand. They cannot understand why he cries whenever they take him to the beach and screams in fear if sand even touches his skin.

Where did this fear of sand come from? Classical conditioning. It turns out that a big sandbox is set up in the neighbor's front yard for the dog to play in. Every time the dog barks and lunges at the boy, the sandbox is there too. After repeated pairings of this kind, the child comes to fear sand as much as he fears the dog.

Behavioral Therapies

Behavioral therapists aim to identify the behaviors that are causing a person's problems and then try to replace them with more appropriate ones by applying the principles of classical conditioning, operant conditioning, or modeling (Antony, 2014). The therapist's attitude toward the client is that of teacher rather than healer.

Classical conditioning treatments, for example, may be used to change abnormal reactions to particular stimuli. **Systematic desensitization** is one such method, often applied in cases of *phobia*—a specific and unreasonable fear. In this step-by-step procedure, clients learn to react calmly instead of with intense fear to the objects or situations they dread (Tellez et al., 2015; Wolpe, 1997, 1995, 1990). First, they are taught the skill of relaxation over the course of several sessions. Next, they construct a *fear hierarchy,* a list of feared objects or situations, starting with those that are less

▶ **systematic desensitization** A behavioral treatment in which clients with phobias learn to react calmly instead of with intense fear to the objects or situations they dread.

feared and ending with the ones that are most dreaded. Here is the hierarchy developed by a man who was afraid of dogs:

1. Read the word "dog" in a book.
2. Hear a neighbor's barking dog.
3. See photos of small dogs.
4. See photos of large dogs.
5. See a movie in which a dog is prominently featured.
6. Be in the same room with a quiet, small dog.
7. Pet a small, cuddly dog.
8. Be in the same room with a large dog.
9. Pet a big, frisky dog.
10. Play roughhouse with a dog.

Desensitization therapists next have their clients either imagine or actually confront each item on the hierarchy while in a state of relaxation. In step-by-step pairings of feared items and relaxation, clients move up the hierarchy until at last they can face every one of the items without experiencing fear. As you will read in Chapter 4, research has shown systematic desensitization and other classical conditioning techniques to be effective in treating phobias (Antony, 2014).

Assessing the Behavioral Model

The behavioral model has become a powerful force in the clinical field. Various behavioral theories have been proposed over the years, and many treatment techniques have been developed. As you can see in Figure 2-4, approximately 15 percent of today's clinical psychologists report that their approach is mainly behavioral (Prochaska & Norcross, 2013).

Perhaps the greatest appeal of the behavioral model is that it can be tested in the laboratory, whereas psychodynamic theories generally cannot. The behaviorists' basic concepts—stimulus, response, and reward—can be observed and measured. Experimenters have, in fact, successfully used the principles of learning to create clinical symptoms in laboratory participants, suggesting that psychological disorders may indeed develop in the same way. In addition, research has found that behavioral treatments can be helpful to people with specific fears, compulsive behavior, social deficits, mental retardation, and other problems (Antony, 2014).

At the same time, research has also revealed weaknesses in the model. Certainly behavioral researchers have produced specific symptoms in participants. But are these symptoms *ordinarily* acquired in this way? There is still no indisputable evidence that most people with psychological disorders are victims of improper conditioning. Similarly, behavioral therapies have limitations. The improvements noted in the therapist's office do not always extend to real life. Nor do they necessarily last without continued therapy.

Finally, some critics hold that the behavioral view is too simplistic, that its concepts fail to account for the complexity of human functioning. In 1977 Albert Bandura, a leading behaviorist, argued that in order to feel happy and function effectively people must develop a positive sense of *self-efficacy*. That is, they must know that they can master and perform needed behaviors whenever necessary. Other behaviorists of the 1960s and 1970s similarly recognized that human beings engage in *cognitive processes,* such as anticipating or interpreting—ways of thinking that until then had been largely ignored in behavioral theory and therapy. These

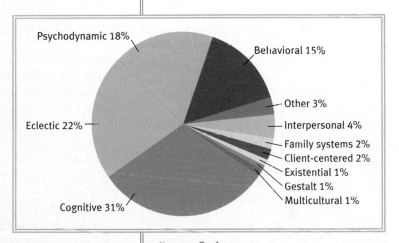

figure 2-4
Theoretical orientations of today's clinical psychologists In one survey, 22 percent of clinical psychologists labeled their approach as "eclectic," 31 percent considered their model "cognitive," and 18 percent called their orientation "psychodynamic." (Information from: Prochaska & Norcross, 2013.)

individuals developed *cognitive-behavioral explanations* that took both behaviors and unseen cognitions into account and *cognitive-behavioral therapies* that helped clients to change both counterproductive behaviors and dysfunctional ways of thinking (Redding, 2014; Meichenbaum, 1993; Goldiamond, 1965). Cognitive-behavioral theorists and therapists bridge the behavioral model and the cognitive model, the view to which we turn next.

> ## ➤ *Summing Up*
>
> **THE BEHAVIORAL MODEL** Behaviorists focus on behaviors and propose that they develop in accordance with the principles of learning. These theorists hold that three types of conditioning—classical conditioning, operant conditioning, and modeling—account for all behavior, whether normal or dysfunctional. The goal of the behavioral therapies is to identify the client's problematic behaviors and replace them with more appropriate ones, using techniques based on one or more of the principles of learning. The classical conditioning approach of systematic desensitization, for example, has been effective in treating phobias.

BETWEEN THE LINES

In Their Words

"The greatest discovery of my generation is that human beings can alter their lives by altering their attitudes of mind."
William James (1842–1910)

The Cognitive Model

Philip Berman, like the rest of us, has *cognitive* abilities—special intellectual capacities to think, remember, and anticipate. These abilities can help him accomplish a great deal in life. Yet they can also work against him. As he thinks about his experiences, Philip may misinterpret them in ways that lead to poor decisions, maladaptive responses, and painful emotions.

In the early 1960s two clinicians, Albert Ellis (1962) and Aaron Beck (1967), proposed that cognitive processes are at the center of behaviors, thoughts, and emotions and that we can best understand abnormal functioning by looking to cognition—a perspective known as the *cognitive model*. Ellis and Beck claimed that clinicians must ask questions about the assumptions and attitudes that color a client's perceptions, the thoughts running through that person's mind, and the conclusions to which they are leading. Other theorists and therapists soon embraced and expanded these ideas and techniques.

How Do Cognitive Theorists Explain Abnormal Functioning?

According to cognitive theorists, abnormal functioning can result from several kinds of cognitive problems. Some people may make *assumptions* and adopt *attitudes* that are disturbing and inaccurate (Beck & Weishaar, 2014; Ellis, 2014). Philip Berman, for example, often seems to assume that his past history has locked him in his present situation. He believes that he was victimized by his parents and that he is now forever doomed by his past. He seems to approach all new experiences and relationships with expectations of failure and disaster.

Illogical thinking processes are another source of abnormal functioning, according to cognitive theorists. Beck, for example, has found that some people consistently think in illogical ways and keep arriving at self-defeating conclusions (Beck & Weishaar, 2014). As you will see in Chapter 6, he has identified a number of illogical thought processes regularly found in depression, such as *overgeneralization,* the drawing of broad negative conclusions on the basis of a single insignificant event.

One depressed student couldn't remember the date of Columbus' third voyage to America during a history class. Overgeneralizing, she spent the rest of the day in despair over her wide-ranging ignorance.

Cognitive Therapies

According to cognitive therapists, people with psychological disorders can overcome their problems by developing new, more functional ways of thinking. Because different forms of abnormality may involve different kinds of cognitive dysfunctioning, cognitive therapists have developed a number of strategies. Beck, for example, has developed an approach that is widely used, particularly in cases of depression (Beck & Weishaar, 2014).

In Beck's approach, called simply **cognitive therapy**, therapists help clients recognize the negative thoughts, biased interpretations, and errors in logic that dominate their thinking and, according to Beck, cause them to feel depressed. Therapists also guide clients to challenge their dysfunctional thoughts, try out new interpretations, and ultimately apply the new ways of thinking in their daily lives. As you will see in Chapter 6, people with depression who are treated with Beck's approach improve much more than those who receive no treatment.

> **How might your efforts to reason with a depressed friend differ from Beck's cognitive therapy strategies for people with depression?**

In the excerpt that follows, a cognitive therapist guides a depressed 26-year-old graduate student to see the link between the way she interprets her experiences and the way she feels and to begin questioning the accuracy of her interpretations:

Therapist: *How do you understand it?*

Patient: *I get depressed when things go wrong. Like when I fail a test.*

Therapist: *How can failing a test make you depressed?*

Patient: *Well, if I fail I'll never get into law school.*

Therapist: *So failing the test means a lot to you. But if failing a test could drive people into clinical depression, wouldn't you expect everyone who failed the test to have a depression? . . . Did everyone who failed get depressed enough to require treatment?*

Patient: *No, but it depends on how important the test was to the person.*

Therapist: *Right, and who decides the importance?*

Patient: *I do.*

Therapist: *And so, what we have to examine is your way of viewing the test (or the way that you think about the test) and how it affects your chances of getting into law school. Do you agree?*

Patient: *Right. . . .*

Therapist: *Now what did failing mean?*

Patient: *(Tearful) That I couldn't get into law school.*

Therapist: *And what does that mean to you?*

Patient: *That I'm just not smart enough.*

Therapist: *Anything else?*

Patient: *That I can never be happy.*

Therapist: *And how do these thoughts make you feel?*

Patient: *Very unhappy.*

▶ **cognitive therapy** A therapy developed by Aaron Beck that helps people recognize and change their faulty thinking processes.

(continues on the next page)

> **Therapist:** *So it is the meaning of failing a test that makes you very unhappy. In fact, believing that you can never be happy is a powerful factor in producing unhappiness. So, you get yourself into a trap—by definition, failure to get into law school equals "I can never be happy."*
>
> *(Beck et al., 1979, pp. 145–146)*

Assessing the Cognitive Model

The cognitive model has had very broad appeal. In addition to a large number of cognitive-behavioral clinicians who apply both cognitive and learning principles in their work, many cognitive clinicians focus exclusively on client interpretations, attitudes, assumptions, and other cognitive processes. Altogether approximately 31 percent of today's clinical psychologists identify their approach as cognitive (Prochaska & Norcross, 2013).

The cognitive model is popular for several reasons. First, it focuses on a process unique to human beings—the process of human thought—and many theorists from varied backgrounds find themselves drawn to a model that considers thought to be the primary cause of normal and abnormal behavior.

Cognitive theories also lend themselves to research. Investigators have found that people with psychological disorders often make the kinds of assumptions and errors in thinking the theorists claim (Ingram et al., 2007). Yet another reason for the popularity of this model is the impressive performance of cognitive and cognitive-behavioral therapies in formats ranging from individual and group therapy to cybertherapy (see *PsychWatch* on the next page). They have proved very effective for treating depression, panic disorder, social phobia, and sexual dysfunctions, for example (Barlow, 2014; Zu et al., 2014).

Nevertheless, the cognitive model, too, has its drawbacks. First, although disturbed cognitive processes are found in many forms of abnormality, their precise role has yet to be determined. The cognitions seen in psychologically troubled people could well be a result rather than a cause of their difficulties. Second, although cognitive and cognitive-behavioral therapies are clearly of help to many people, they do not help everyone. Is it enough simply to change cognitions? Can such changes make a general and lasting difference in the way people feel and behave? A growing body of research suggests that it is not always possible to achieve the kinds of cognitive changes proposed by Beck and other cognitive therapists (Sharf, 2015).

In response to such limitations, a new group of cognitive and cognitive-behavioral therapies, sometimes called the *new wave of cognitive therapies,* has emerged in recent years (Prochaska & Norcross, 2013). These new approaches, such as the widely used *Acceptance and Commitment Therapy (ACT),* help clients to *accept* many of their problematic thoughts rather than judge them, act on them, or try fruitlessly to change them (Levin et al., 2015; Hayes & Lillis, 2012). The hope is that by recognizing such thoughts for what they are—just thoughts—clients will eventually be able to let them pass through their awareness without being particularly troubled by them.

As you will see in Chapter 4, ACT and other new-wave cognitive therapies often employ *mindfulness-based* techniques to help clients achieve such acceptance. These techniques borrow heavily from a form of meditation called *mindfulness meditation,* which teaches individuals to pay attention to the thoughts and feelings that are flowing through their minds during meditation and to accept such thoughts in a

"What did I tell you about destroying Mommy's inner balance?"

PsychWatch

Cybertherapy: Surfing for Help

As you read in Chapter 1, computer-based treatment, or *cybertherapy*, has come to complement, and in some instances replace, traditional face-to-face therapy over the past few decades (Ringwood, 2013). The clinical field's first journey into the digital world took the form of *computer software therapy programs* (Harklute, 2010; Tantam, 2006). These programs, which continue to be popular, are designed to reduce emotional distress through typed conversations between human "clients" and their computers. One software program, for example, helps people state their problems in "if–then" statements, a technique similar to that used by cognitive therapists. As

you will see later in this chapter, a number of software therapy programs also have users interact with *avatars*, on-screen virtual human figures (Reamer, 2013). Advocates of software therapy programs argue that many people find it easier to disclose sensitive personal information to a computer than to a therapist, and indeed research indicates that some of the programs are helpful to a degree (Emmelkamp, 2011; Harklute, 2010).

Another form of cybertherapy, *e-mail therapy*, has exploded in popularity over the past decade. Thousands of therapists have set up online services that invite people with problems to e-mail their questions and concerns (Murphy et al., 2011;

Mulhauser, 2010). However, services of this kind have raised concerns about the quality of care and about confidentiality (Fenichel, 2011). Many e-mail therapists do not even have advanced clinical training.

Also on the rise is *visual e-therapy* (Khatri, 2014; Hoffman, 2011), which more closely mimics the conventional therapy experience. A client sets up an appointment with a therapist, and, with the aid of Skype or a webcam, the two proceed to have a face-to-face session. The advantage? Clients can receive counseling conveniently while sitting at home or in their office, and they can have access to a counselor who is located even thousands of miles away. The key disadvantage? Once again, quality control (Fenichel, 2011).

Still more common than either e-mail therapy or visual e-therapies are Internet chat groups and "virtual" support groups. Tens of thousands of these groups are currently "in session" around the clock for everything from depression to substance abuse, anxiety, sexual dysfunctions, and eating disorders (Hucker & McCabe, 2014; Moskowitz, 2008, 2001). Like in-person self-help groups, the online chat groups provide opportunities for people with similar problems to communicate with one another and freely trade information, advice, and empathy.

Cybertherapy is still being developed, and its effectiveness has yet to be fully determined. At the same time, the rapid growth of this approach serves as a reminder of digital technology's increasing impact on the mental health field.

Helen H. Richardson/Denver Post via Getty Images

Meeting at your place . . . and mine Colorado psychiatrist Robert Chalfant and his office administrator demonstrate the simple digital setup that enables him to conduct treatment with many distant clients each week.

nonjudgmental way. Early research indicates that ACT and other new–wave cognitive therapies are often helpful in the treatment of anxiety and depression (A–Tjak et al., 2015; Swain et al., 2013).

A final drawback of the cognitive model is that, like the other models you have read about, it is narrow in certain ways. Although cognition is a very special human dimension, it is still only one part of human functioning. Aren't human beings more than the sum of their thoughts, emotions, and behaviors? Shouldn't explanations of human functioning also consider broader issues, such as how people approach life, what value they extract from it, and how they deal with the question of life's meaning? This is the position of the humanistic–existential model.

▸**self-actualization** The humanistic process by which people fulfill their potential for goodness and growth.

▸**client-centered therapy** The humanistic therapy developed by Carl Rogers in which clinicians try to help clients by conveying acceptance, accurate empathy, and genuineness.

Actualizing the self Humanists suggest that self-actualized people show concern for the welfare of humanity. This 89-year-old social services volunteer (right), one of 65 million Americans who perform volunteer work each year (CNCS, 2013), has participated for the past 20 years as a companion to elderly persons with intellectual disability and developmental disabilities.

AP Photo/Columbus Daily Dispatch, Eric Albrecht

➤ *Summing Up*

THE COGNITIVE MODEL According to the cognitive model, we must understand human thought to understand human behavior. When people display abnormal patterns of functioning, cognitive theorists point to cognitive problems, such as maladaptive assumptions and illogical thinking processes. Cognitive therapists try to help people recognize and change their faulty ideas and thinking processes. In addition to traditional cognitive therapies, such as Beck's cognitive therapy, a new wave of cognitive and cognitive-behavioral therapies has emerged in recent years. The new therapies teach clients to be mindful of and accept many of their problematic thoughts.

The Humanistic-Existential Model

Philip Berman is more than the sum of his psychological conflicts, learned behaviors, or cognitions. Being human, he also has the ability to pursue philosophical goals such as self-awareness, strong values, a sense of meaning in life, and freedom of choice. According to humanistic and existential theorists, Philip's problems can be understood only in the light of such complex goals. Humanistic and existential theorists are often grouped together—in an approach known as the *humanistic-existential model*—because of their common focus on these broader dimensions of human existence. At the same time, there are important differences between them.

Humanists, the more optimistic of the two groups, believe that human beings are born with a natural tendency to be friendly, cooperative, and constructive. People, these theorists propose, are driven to **self-actualize**—that is, to fulfill this potential for goodness and growth. They can do so, however, only if they honestly recognize and accept their weaknesses as well as their strengths and establish satisfying personal values to live by. Humanists further suggest that self-actualization leads naturally to a concern for the welfare of others and to behavior that is loving, courageous, spontaneous, and independent (Maslow, 1970).

Existentialists agree that human beings must have an accurate awareness of themselves and live meaningful—they say "authentic"—lives in order to be psychologically well adjusted. These theorists do not believe, however, that people are naturally inclined to live positively. They believe that from birth we have total freedom, either to face up to our existence and give meaning to our lives or to shrink from that responsibility. Those who choose to "hide" from responsibility and choice will view themselves as helpless and may live empty, inauthentic, and dysfunctional lives as a result.

The humanistic and existential views of abnormality both date back to the 1940s. At that time Carl Rogers (1902–1987), often considered the pioneer of the humanistic perspective, developed **client-centered therapy**, a warm and supportive approach that contrasted sharply with the psychodynamic techniques of the day. He also proposed a theory of personality that paid little attention to irrational instincts and conflicts.

The existential view of personality and abnormality appeared during this same period. Many of its principles came from the ideas of nineteenth-century European existential philosophers who held that human beings are constantly defining and so giving meaning to their existence through their actions (Yalom, 2014).

The humanistic and existential theories, and their uplifting implications, were extremely popular during the 1960s and 1970s, years of considerable soul-searching and social upheaval in Western society. They have since lost some of their popularity, but they continue to influence the ideas and work of many clinicians. In particular, humanistic principles are apparent throughout positive psychology (the study and enhancement of positive feelings, traits, abilities, and selfless virtues), an area of psychology that, as you read in Chapter 1, has gained much momentum in recent years (see pages 16–17).

Rogers' Humanistic Theory and Therapy

According to Carl Rogers, the road to dysfunction begins in infancy (Raskin, Rogers, & Witty, 2014; Rogers, 1987, 1951). We all have a basic need to receive *positive regard* from the important people in our lives (primarily our parents). Those who receive *unconditional* (nonjudgmental) *positive regard* early in life are likely to develop *unconditional self-regard.* That is, they come to recognize their worth as persons, even while recognizing that they are not perfect. Such people are in a good position to actualize their positive potential.

Unfortunately, some children repeatedly are made to feel that they are not worthy of positive regard. As a result, they acquire *conditions of worth,* standards that tell them they are lovable and acceptable only when they conform to certain guidelines. To maintain positive self-regard, these people have to look at themselves very selectively, denying or distorting thoughts and actions that do not measure up to their conditions of worth. They thus acquire a distorted view of themselves and their experiences. They do not know what they are truly feeling, what they genuinely need, or what values and goals would be meaningful for them. Problems in functioning are then inevitable.

Rogers might view Philip Berman as a man who has gone astray. Rather than striving to fulfill his positive human potential, he drifts from job to job and relationship to relationship. In every interaction he is defending himself, trying to interpret events in ways he can live with, usually blaming his problems on other people. Nevertheless, his basic negative self-image continually reveals itself. Rogers would probably link this problem to the critical ways Philip was treated by his mother throughout his childhood.

Clinicians who practice Rogers' client-centered therapy try to create a supportive climate in which clients feel able to look at themselves honestly and accepting (Raskin et al., 2014). The therapist must display three important qualities throughout the therapy—*unconditional positive regard* (full and warm acceptance for

AP Photo/Amel Emric

Unconditional positive regard Carl Rogers argued that clients must receive unconditional positive regard in order to feel better about themselves and to overcome their problems. In this spirit, a number of organizations now arrange for individuals to have close relationships with gentle and nonjudgmental animals. Here a Bosnian child hugs her horse during rehabilitation therapy at the Therapeutic and Leisure Center in Kakrinje, near Sarajevo.

"Just remember, son, it doesn't matter whether you win or lose—unless you want Daddy's love."

the client), *accurate empathy* (skillful listening and restating), and *genuineness* (sincere communication). In the following classic case, the therapist uses all these qualities to move the client toward greater self-awareness:

> **Client:** Yes, I know I shouldn't worry about it, but I do. Lots of things—money, people, clothes. In classes I feel that everyone's just waiting for a chance to jump on me. . . . When I meet somebody I wonder what he's actually thinking of me. Then later on I wonder how I match up to what he's come to think of me.
>
> **Therapist:** You feel that you're pretty responsive to the opinions of other people.
>
> **Client:** Yes, but it's things that shouldn't worry me.
>
> **Therapist:** You feel that it's the sort of thing that shouldn't be upsetting, but they do get you pretty much worried anyway.
>
> **Client:** Just some of them. Most of those things do worry me because they're true. The ones I told you, that is. But there are lots of little things that aren't true. . . . Things just seem to be piling up, piling up inside of me. . . . It's a feeling that things were crowding up and they were going to burst.
>
> **Therapist:** You feel that it's a sort of oppression with some frustration and that things are just unmanageable.
>
> **Client:** In a way, but some things just seem illogical. I'm afraid I'm not very clear here but that's the way it comes.
>
> **Therapist:** That's all right. You say just what you think.
>
> *(Snyder, 1947, pp. 2–24)*

In such an atmosphere, clients are expected to feel accepted by their therapists. They then may be able to look at themselves with honesty and acceptance. They begin to value their own emotions, thoughts, and behaviors, and so they are freed from the insecurities and doubts that prevent self-actualization.

Client-centered therapy has not fared very well in research (Prochaska & Norcross, 2013). Although some studies show that participants who receive this therapy improve more than control participants, many other studies have failed to find any such advantage. All the same, Rogers' therapy has had a positive influence on clinical practice (Raskin et al., 2014). It was one of the first major alternatives to psychodynamic therapy, and it helped open up the clinical field to new approaches. Rogers also helped pave the way for *psychologists* to practice psychotherapy, which had previously been considered the exclusive territory of psychiatrists. And his commitment to clinical research helped promote the systematic study of treatment. Approximately 2 percent of today's clinical psychologists, 1 percent of social workers, and 3 percent of counseling psychologists report that they employ the client-centered approach (Prochaska & Norcross, 2013).

Gestalt Theory and Therapy

Gestalt therapy, another humanistic approach, was developed in the 1950s by a charismatic clinician named Frederick (Fritz) Perls (1893–1970). Gestalt therapists, like client-centered therapists, guide their clients toward self-recognition and self-acceptance (Yontef & Jacobs, 2014). But unlike client-centered therapists, they often try to achieve this goal by challenging and even frustrating their clients. Some of Perls' favorite techniques were skillful frustration, role playing, and employing numerous rules and exercises.

In the technique of *skillful frustration*, gestalt therapists refuse to meet their clients' expectations or demands. This use of frustration is meant to help people see how

▶ **gestalt therapy** The humanistic therapy developed by Fritz Perls in which clinicians actively move clients toward self-recognition and self-acceptance by using techniques such as role playing and self-discovery exercises.

often they try to manipulate others into meeting their needs. In the technique of *role playing,* the therapists instruct clients to act out various roles. A person may be told to be another person, an object, an alternative self, or even a part of the body. Role playing can become intense, as individuals are encouraged to express emotions fully. Many cry out, scream, kick, or pound. Through this experience they may come to "own" (accept) feelings that previously made them uncomfortable.

Perls also developed a list of *rules* to ensure that clients will look at themselves more closely. In some versions of gestalt therapy, for example, clients may be required to use "I" language rather than "it" language. They must say, "I am frightened" rather than "The situation is frightening." Yet another common rule requires clients to stay in the *here and now.* They have needs now, are hiding their needs now, and must observe them now.

Approximately 1 percent of clinical psychologists and other kinds of clinicians describe themselves as gestalt therapists (Prochaska & Norcross, 2013). Because they believe that subjective experiences and self-awareness cannot be measured objectively, proponents of gestalt therapy have not often performed controlled research on this approach (Yontef & Jacobs, 2014; Leung, Leung, & Ng, 2013).

Spiritual Views and Interventions

For most of the twentieth century, clinical scientists viewed religion as a negative—or at best neutral—factor in mental health (Bonelli & Koenig, 2013; Van Praag, 2011). In the early 1900s, for example, Freud argued that religious beliefs were defense mechanisms, "born from man's need to make his helplessness tolerable" (1961, p. 23). This negative view of religion now seems to be ending, however. During the past decade, many articles and books linking spiritual issues to clinical treatment have been published, and the ethical codes of psychologists, psychiatrists, and counselors have each concluded that religion is a type of diversity that mental health professionals must respect (Peteet, Lu, & Narrow, 2011).

> **What various explanations might account for the correlation between spirituality and mental health?**

Researchers have learned that spirituality does, in fact, often correlate with psychological health. In particular, studies have examined the mental health of people who are devout and who view God as warm, caring, helpful, and dependable. Repeatedly, these individuals are found to be less lonely, pessimistic, depressed, or anxious than people without any religious beliefs or those who view God as cold and unresponsive (Koenig, 2015; Day, 2010; Loewenthal, 2007). Such people also seem to cope better with major life stressors—from illness to war—and to attempt suicide less often. In addition, they are less likely to abuse drugs.

Do such correlations indicate that spirituality helps *produce* greater mental health? Not necessarily. As you'll recall from Chapter 1, correlations do not indicate causation. It may be, for example, that a sense of optimism leads to more spirituality and that, independently, optimism contributes to greater mental health. Whatever the proper interpretation, many therapists now make a point of including spiritual issues when they treat religious clients, and some further encourage clients to use their spiritual resources to help them cope with current stressors (Gonçalves et al., 2015; Koenig, 2015). Similarly, a number of religious institutions offer counseling services to their members (see *MediaSpeak* on the next page).

Existential Theories and Therapy

Like humanists, existentialists believe that psychological dysfunctioning is caused by self-deception; existentialists, however, are talking about a kind of self-deception in which people hide from life's responsibilities and fail to recognize that it is up

Lad Strayer/The Daily Telegram/AP Photo

Beating the blues Gestalt therapists often guide clients to express their needs and feelings in their full intensity by banging on pillows, crying out, kicking, or pounding things. Building on these techniques, a new approach, *drum therapy,* teaches clients, such as this woman, how to beat drums in order to help release traumatic memories, change beliefs, and feel more liberated.

MediaSpeak
Saving Minds Along with Souls

By T. M. Luhrmann, *The New York Times*, April 18, 2014

A few weeks ago, one year after his son took his life while struggling with depression, [Rick] Warren, the founding pastor of Saddleback Church, one of the nation's largest evangelical churches, teamed up with his local Roman Catholic Diocese and the National Alliance on Mental Illness for an event that announced a new initiative to involve the church in the care of serious mental illness.

Their goal is not only to reduce stigma for people with schizophrenia, bipolar disorder, depression and the like, though that is an important part of it. "We are all broken," Mr. Warren said in his remarks. . . . "We're all a little bit mentally ill."

The larger goal is to get the church directly involved with the care of people with serious psychiatric illness by training administrators and pastors to handle psychiatric crises, to set up groups within the church for people with serious mental illness and to establish services within the church for people who need them. . . .

. . . The public mental health system is a woefully underfunded crazy-quilt of uncoordinated agencies. . . . It can be hideously difficult to navigate even for someone who is not hearing hallucinated voices. . . . [And] many psychiatric clients hate the idea of being forcibly medicated.

But they do often go to church. . . . In an urban Chicago neighborhood where I did many months of research with homeless psychotic women, I found that these women often refused psychiatric care. . . . But fully half of them said that they had a church and that they went to that church at least twice each month, and over 80 percent of them said that God was their best friend—some, that he was their only friend.

Mr. Warren's . . . interest in training the ordinary people who work in church offices and hold prayer circles to be actively involved in mental health care . . . can sound a little alarming. But in fact . . . a study just published in *The Lancet* demonstrated that this [kind of] community care [sometimes] produced modestly better outcomes for patients with schizophrenia than care in the psychiatric facility.

AP Photo/John Amis

Actualizing the self A few years ago, Tibetan spiritual leader the Dalai Lama (right) met with professor of psychiatry Zindel Segal (left) and other mental health researchers at a conference examining possible ties between science, mental health, and spirituality.

. . . Psychiatrists are the least religious of all physicians, and the new initiative may leave them cold. But Mr. Warren has made an impact before: His initiative on H.I.V.-AIDS was partially responsible for generating George W. Bush's President's Emergency Plan for AIDS Relief. If this works, it could have a real impact on the mental health system.

We're desperately in need of something that does.

(T. M. Lurhman is a professor of anthropology at Stanford University.)

to them to give meaning to their lives. According to existentialists, many people become overwhelmed by the pressures of present-day society and so look to others for explanations, guidance, and authority. They overlook their personal freedom of choice and avoid responsibility for their lives and decisions (Yalom, 2014). Such people are left with empty, inauthentic lives. Their dominant emotions are anxiety, frustration, boredom, alienation, and depression.

Existentialists might view Philip Berman as a man who feels overwhelmed by the forces of society. He sees his parents as "rich, powerful, and selfish," and he perceives teachers, acquaintances, and employers as oppressing. He fails to appreciate his choices in life and his capacity for finding meaning and direction. Quitting becomes a habit with him—he leaves job after job, ends every romantic relationship, and flees difficult situations.

In **existential therapy**, people are encouraged to accept responsibility for their lives and for their problems. Therapists try to help clients recognize their freedom so that they may choose a different course and live with greater meaning (Yalom, 2014; van Deurzen, 2012; Schneider & Krug, 2010). The precise techniques used in existential therapy vary from clinician to clinician. At the same time, most existential therapists place great emphasis on the *relationship* between therapist and client and try to create an atmosphere of honesty, hard work, and shared learning and growth.

> **Patient:** *I don't know why I keep coming here. All I do is tell you the same thing over and over. I'm not getting anywhere.*
> **Doctor:** *I'm getting tired of hearing the same thing over and over, too.*
> **Patient:** *Maybe I'll stop coming.*
> **Doctor:** *It's certainly your choice.*
> **Patient:** *What do you think I should do?*
> **Doctor:** *What do you want to do?*
> **Patient:** *I want to get better.*
> **Doctor:** *I don't blame you.*
> **Patient:** *If you think I should stay, ok, I will.*
> **Doctor:** *You want me to tell you to stay?*
> **Patient:** *You know what's best; you're the doctor.*
> **Doctor:** *Do I act like a doctor?*
>
> *(Keen, 1970, p. 200)*

Existential therapists do not believe that experimental methods can adequately test the effectiveness of their treatments. To them, research dehumanizes individuals by reducing them to test measures. Not surprisingly, then, very little controlled research has been devoted to the effectiveness of this approach (Vos et al., 2015; Schneider & Krug, 2010). Nevertheless, around 1 percent of today's clinical psychologists use an approach that is primarily existential (Prochaska & Norcross, 2013).

Assessing the Humanistic-Existential Model

The humanistic-existential model appeals to many people in and out of the clinical field. In recognizing the special challenges of human existence, humanistic and existential theorists tap into an aspect of psychological life that typically is missing from the other models (Watson et al., 2011). Moreover, the factors that they say are essential to effective functioning—self-acceptance, personal values, personal meaning, and personal choice—are certainly lacking in many people with psychological disturbances.

▸ **existential therapy** A therapy that encourages clients to accept responsibility for their lives and to live with greater meaning and value.

BETWEEN THE LINES

Is Niceness in the Genes?

Research suggests that people with particular versions of the receptor genes for two hormones, *oxytocin* and *vasopressin*, are consistently nicer than people without such gene versions.

(Poulin, Homan, & Buffone, 2012)

The optimistic tone of the humanistic-existential model is also an attraction. Such optimism meshes quite well with the goals and principles of positive psychology (Rashid & Seligman, 2014). Theorists who follow the principles of the humanistic-existential model offer great hope when they assert that, despite past and present events, we can make our own choices, determine our own destiny, and accomplish much. Still another attractive feature of the model is its emphasis on health. Unlike clinicians from some of the other models who see individuals as patients with psychological illnesses, humanists and existentialists view them simply as people who have yet to fulfill their potential.

At the same time, the humanistic-existential focus on abstract issues of human fulfillment gives rise to a major problem from a scientific point of view: these issues are difficult to research. In fact, with the notable exception of Rogers, who tried to investigate his clinical methods carefully, humanists and existentialists have traditionally rejected the use of empirical research. This antiresearch position is just now beginning to change among some humanistic and existential researchers—a change that may lead to important insights about the merits of this model in the coming years (Vos et al., 2015; Schneider & Krug, 2010; Strumpfel, 2006).

➤ Summing Up

THE HUMANISTIC-EXISTENTIAL MODEL The humanistic-existential model focuses on the human need to successfully deal with philosophical issues such as self-awareness, values, meaning, and choice.

Humanists believe that people are driven to self-actualize. When this drive is interfered with, abnormal behavior may result. One group of humanistic therapists, client-centered therapists, tries to create a very supportive therapy climate in which people can look at themselves honestly and acceptingly, thus opening the door to self-actualization. Another group, gestalt therapists, uses more active techniques to help people recognize and accept their needs. Recently the role of religion as an important factor in mental health and in psychotherapy has caught the attention of researchers and clinicians.

According to existentialists, abnormal behavior results from hiding from life's responsibilities. Existential therapists encourage people to accept responsibility for their lives, to recognize their freedom to choose a different course, and to choose to live with greater meaning.

The Sociocultural Model: Family-Social and Multicultural Perspectives

Philip Berman is also a social and cultural being. He is surrounded by people and by institutions, he is a member of a family and a cultural group, he participates in social relationships, and he holds cultural values. Such forces are always operating upon Philip, setting rules and expectations that guide or pressure him, helping to shape his behaviors, thoughts, and emotions.

According to the *sociocultural model*, abnormal behavior is best understood in light of the broad forces that influence an individual. What are the norms of the individual's society and culture? What roles does the person play in the social environment? What kind of family structure or cultural background is the person a part of? And how do other people view and react to him or her? In fact, the sociocultural model is composed of two major perspectives—the *family-social perspective* and the *multicultural perspective*.

How Do Family-Social Theorists Explain Abnormal Functioning?

Proponents of the family-social perspective argue that clinical theorists should concentrate on those broad forces that operate *directly* on an individual as he or she moves through life—that is, family relationships, social interactions, and community events. They believe that such forces help account for both normal and abnormal behavior, and they pay particular attention to three kinds of factors: *social labels and roles, social networks,* and *family structure and communication.*

Social Labels and Roles Abnormal functioning can be influenced greatly by the labels and roles assigned to troubled people (Rüsch et al., 2014; Yap et al., 2013). When people stray from the norms of their society, the society calls them deviant and, in many cases, "mentally ill." Such labels tend to stick. Moreover, when people are viewed in particular ways, reacted to as "crazy," and perhaps even encouraged to act sick, they gradually learn to accept and play the assigned social role. Ultimately the label seems appropriate.

A famous study called "On Being Sane in Insane Places" by clinical investigator David Rosenhan (1973) supports this position. Eight normal people, actually colleagues of Rosenhan, presented themselves at various mental hospitals, complaining that they had been hearing voices say the words "empty," "hollow," and "thud." On the basis of this complaint alone, each was diagnosed as having schizophrenia and admitted.

Moreover, the pseudopatients had a hard time convincing others that they were well once they had been given the diagnostic label. Their hospitalizations ranged from 7 to 52 days, even though they behaved normally and stopped reporting symptoms as soon as they were admitted. In addition, the label "schizophrenia" kept influencing the way the staff viewed and dealt with them. For example, one pseudopatient who paced the corridor out of boredom was, in clinical notes, described as "nervous." For their part, the pseudopatients came to feel powerless, invisible, and bored.

Social Connections and Supports Family-social theorists are also concerned with the social environments in which people operate, including their social and professional relationships. How well do they communicate with others? What kind of signals do they send to or receive from others? Researchers have often found ties between deficiencies in social networks and a person's functioning (Schwarzbach et al., 2013; Paykel, 2008, 2006, 2003). They have observed, for example, that people who are isolated and lack social support or intimacy in their lives are more likely to become depressed when under stress and to remain depressed longer than are people with supportive spouses or warm friendships.

Some clinical theorists believe that people who are unwilling or unable to communicate and develop relationships in their everyday lives will often find adequate social contacts online, using social networking sites like Facebook. Although this may be true for some such individuals, research suggests that people's online relationships tend to parallel their offline relationships (Dolan, 2011). One survey of 172 college students, for example, found that those students with the most friends on Facebook also were particularly social offline, while those who were less willing to communicate with other people offline also tended to initiate far fewer relationships on Facebook (Sheldon, 2008).

Niall Carson/Press Association via AP Images

Are friends more influential than relatives? Yes, according to the work of researchers Jerome Micheletta and Bridget Waller. Their studies indicate that macaque monkeys, such as those shown here, are more responsive to and more likely to imitate the behaviors of friends than relatives.

▶ **family systems theory** A theory that views the family as a system of interacting parts whose interactions exhibit consistent patterns and unstated rules.

▶ **group therapy** A therapy format in which a group of people with similar problems meet together with a therapist to work on those problems.

Family Structure and Communication Of course, one of the important social networks for an individual is his or her family. According to **family systems theory**, the family is a system of interacting parts—the family members—who interact with one another in consistent ways and follow rules unique to each family (Goldenberg, Goldenberg, & Pelavin, 2014). Family systems theorists believe that the *structure* and *communication* patterns of some families actually force individual members to behave in a way that otherwise seems abnormal. If the members were to behave normally, they would severely strain the family's usual manner of operation and would actually increase their own and their family's turmoil.

Family systems theory holds that certain family systems are particularly likely to produce abnormal functioning in individual members. Some families, for example, have an *enmeshed* structure in which the members are grossly overinvolved in one another's activities, thoughts, and feelings. Children from this kind of family may have great difficulty becoming independent in life (Santiseban et al., 2001). Some families display *disengagement,* which is marked by very rigid boundaries between the members. Children from these families may find it hard to function in a group or to give or request support (Corey, 2012, 2004).

> **How might family theorists react to writer Leo Tolstoy's famous claim that "every unhappy family is unhappy in its own fashion"?**

Philip Berman's angry and impulsive personal style might be seen as the product of a disturbed family structure. According to family systems theorists, the whole family—Philip's mother, father, and brother, and Philip himself—relate in such a way as to maintain Philip's behavior. Family theorists might be particularly interested in the conflict between Philip's mother and father and the imbalance between their parental roles. They might see Philip's behavior as both a reaction to and stimulus for his parents' behaviors. With Philip acting out the role of the misbehaving child, or scapegoat, his parents may have little need or time to question their own relationship.

Family systems theorists would also seek to clarify the precise nature of Philip's relationship with each parent. Is he enmeshed with his mother and/or disengaged from his father? They would look too at the rules governing the sibling relationship in the family, the relationship between Philip's parents and brother, and the nature of parent–child relationships in previous generations of the family.

Today's TV families Unlike television viewers of the 1950s, when problem-free families like the Nelsons (of *Ozzie & Harriet*) and the Andersons (of *Father Knows Best*) ruled the airwaves, today's viewers prefer more complex, sometimes dysfunctional, families, like the Pritchetts, whose trials and tribulations are on display in ABC's popular series *Modern Family*.

Danny Feld/ABC via Getty Images

Family-Social Treatments

The family-social perspective has helped spur the growth of several treatment approaches, including *group, family,* and *couple therapy* and *community treatment.* Therapists of any orientation may work with clients in these various formats, applying the techniques and principles of their preferred models (see *MindTech* below). However, more and more of the clinicians who use these formats believe that psychological problems emerge in family and social settings and are best treated in such settings, and they include special sociocultural strategies in their work.

Group Therapy Thousands of therapists specialize in **group therapy,** a format in which a therapist meets with a group of clients who have similar problems. One survey of clinical psychologists showed that almost one-third of them devoted some portion of their practice to group therapy (Norcross & Goldfried, 2005). Typically, members of a therapy group meet together with a therapist and discuss the problems of one or more of the people in the group. Together they develop important insights,

MindTech

Have Your Avatar Call My Avatar

The sociocultural model holds that abnormal behavior is best understood and treated in a social context. Thus, some proponents of this perspective are particularly interested in a relatively new feature in cybertherapy—the use of *avatars,* three-dimensional graphical representations of the users and/or other key persons in their lives (Reamer, 2013; Pagliari et al., 2012; Carey, 2010). A growing number of computer software therapy programs have users interact with on-screen virtual human figures who ask questions such as "What kinds of things do you dislike about yourself?", who nod sympathetically when users offer self-criticisms, and who reinforce certain user statements with smiles or encouraging words.

In another use of avatars, some real-life therapists guide their clients to enter virtual environments on their computers, acquire virtual bodies, and interact with animated figures who resemble their parents, bosses, or friends—in situations that can feel very real. Theoretically, experiences in virtual worlds of this kind can help clients change their reactions in the real world (Reamer, 2013).

Guia Besana/Anzenberger/Redux

Clients know they are entering a make-believe world when they receive avatar therapy, so why do so many apparently make real-life progress?

In one highly publicized case, for example, a woman with agoraphobia—a fear of leaving the house—was guided by her therapist to adopt an avatar and enter into a virtual world of other avatars, a journey that eventually enabled her to venture outside into the real world (Smith, 2008). Similarly, therapists have used avatar therapy to help individuals who suffer from social anxiety, trauma aftereffects, substance abuse, and even hallucinations—often with considerable success (Leff et al., 2014, 2013; Kedmey, 2013).

Sharing and supporting Clients often benefit from group therapy and self-help groups. Many such groups focus on particular client populations, such as bereaved persons, abused spouses, or people with social skills deficits.

Zigy Kaluzny/Stone/Getty Images

build social skills, strengthen feelings of self-worth, and share useful information or advice (Corey, 2016). Many groups are created with particular client populations in mind; for example, there are groups for people with alcoholism, for those who are physically handicapped, and for people who are divorced, abused, or bereaved.

Research suggests that group therapy is of help to many clients, often as helpful as individual therapy (Green et al., 2015). The group format also has been used for purposes that are educational rather than therapeutic, such as "consciousness raising" and spiritual inspiration.

> **Why might group therapy actually be more helpful to some people with psychological problems than individual therapy would be?**

A format similar to group therapy is the **self-help group** (or **mutual help group**). Here people who have similar problems (for example, bereavement, substance abuse, illness, unemployment, or divorce) come together to help and support one another without the direct leadership of a professional clinician (Lake, 2014; Mueller et al., 2007). According to estimates, there are now between 500,000 and 3 million such groups in the United States alone, attended each year by as many as 3 to 4 percent of the population. In addition, numerous self-help chat groups have emerged on the Internet.

Family Therapy **Family therapy** was first introduced in the 1950s. A therapist meets with all members of a family, points out problem behaviors and interactions, and helps the whole family to change its ways (Goldenberg et al., 2014). Here, the entire family is viewed as the unit under treatment, even if only one of the members receives a clinical diagnosis. The following is a typical interaction between family members and a therapist:

> Tommy sat motionless in a chair gazing out the window. He was fourteen and a bit small for his age. . . . Sissy was eleven. She was sitting on the couch between her Mom and Dad with a smile on her face. Across from them sat Ms. Fargo, the family therapist.
>
> Ms. Fargo spoke. "Could you be a little more specific about the changes you have seen in Tommy and when they came about?"
>
> Mrs. Davis answered first. "Well, I guess it was about two years ago. Tommy started getting in fights at school. When we talked to him at home he said it was

none of our business. He became moody and disobedient. He wouldn't do anything that we wanted him to. He began to act mean to his sister and even hit her."

"What about the fights at school?" Ms. Fargo asked.

This time it was Mr. Davis who spoke first. "Ginny was more worried about them than I was. I used to fight a lot when I was in school and I think it is normal. . . . But I was very respectful to my parents, especially my Dad. If I ever got out of line he would smack me one."

"Have you ever had to hit Tommy?" Ms. Fargo inquired softly.

"Sure, a couple of times, but it didn't seem to do any good."

All at once Tommy seemed to be paying attention, his eyes riveted on his father. "Yeah, he hit me a lot, for no reason at all!"

"Now, that's not true, Thomas." Mrs. Davis has a scolding expression on her face. "If you behaved yourself a little better you wouldn't get hit. Ms. Fargo, I can't say that I am in favor of the hitting, but I understand sometimes how frustrating it may be for Bob."

"You don't know how frustrating it is for me, honey." Bob seemed upset. "You don't have to work all day at the office and then come home to contend with all of this. Sometimes I feel like I don't even want to come home."

Ginny gave him a hard stare. "You think things at home are easy all day? I could use some support from you. You think all you have to do is earn the money and I will do everything else. Well, I am not about to do that anymore." . . . [She] began to cry. "I just don't know what to do anymore. Things just seem so hopeless. Why can't people be nice in this family anymore? I don't think I am asking too much, am I?"

Ms. Fargo . . . looked at each person briefly and was sure to make eye contact. "There seems to be a lot going on . . . . I think we are going to need to understand a lot of things to see why this is happening."

(Sheras & Worchel, 1979, pp. 108–110)

Family therapists may follow any of the major theoretical models, but many of them adopt the principles of family systems theory (Riina & McHale, 2014). Today 2 percent of all clinical psychologists, 5 percent of counseling psychologists, and 14 percent of social workers identify themselves mainly as *family systems therapists* (Prochaska & Norcross, 2013).

As you read earlier, family systems theory holds that each family has its own rules, structure, and communication patterns that shape the individual members' behavior. In one family systems approach, *structural family therapy*, therapists try to change the family power structure, the roles each person plays, and the relationships between members (Goldenberg et al., 2014; Minuchin, 2007, 1987, 1974). In another, *conjoint family therapy*, therapists try to help members recognize and change harmful patterns of communication (Sharf, 2015; Satir, 1987, 1967, 1964).

Family therapies of various kinds are often helpful to individuals, although research has not yet clarified how helpful (Goldenberg et al., 2014; Nichols, 2013). Some studies have found that as many as 65 percent of individuals treated with family approaches improve, while other studies suggest much lower success rates. Nor has any one type of family therapy emerged as consistently more helpful than the others (Bitter, 2013; Alexander et al., 2002).

Couple Therapy

In **couple therapy**, or **marital therapy**, the therapist works with two individuals who are in a long-term relationship. Often they are husband and wife, but the couple need not be married or even living together. Like family therapy, couple therapy often focuses on the structure and communication patterns in the relationship (Baucom et al., 2015, 2010, 2009). A couple approach may also be used when a child's psychological problems are traced to problems in the parents' relationship.

▶ **self-help group** A group made up of people with similar problems who help and support one another without the direct leadership of a clinician. Also called a *mutual help group*.

▶ **family therapy** A therapy format in which the therapist meets with all members of a family and helps them to change in therapeutic ways.

▶ **couple therapy** A therapy format in which the therapist works with two people who share a long-term relationship. Also called *marital therapy*.

BETWEEN THE LINES

Shifting Family Values

59% Percentage of adults who say their families have fewer family dinners than when they were growing up

10 Average number of weekly hours today's fathers spend doing housework, compared with 4 hours a half-century ago

18 Average number of weekly hours today's mothers spend doing housework, compared with 32 hours a half-century ago

(Harris Interactive, 2013; Pew Research Center, 2013)

▶ **community mental health treatment** A treatment approach that emphasizes community care.

▶ **multicultural perspective** The view that each culture within a larger society has a particular set of values and beliefs, as well as special external pressures, that help account for the behavior and functioning of its members. Also called *culturally diverse perspective.*

Although some degree of conflict exists in any long-term relationship, many couples in our society have serious marital discord. The divorce rate in Canada, the United States, and Europe is now close to 50 percent of the marriage rate. Many couples who live together without marrying apparently have similar levels of difficulty (Martins et al., 2014).

Couple therapy, like family and group therapy, may follow the principles of any of the major therapy orientations. *Cognitive-behavioral couple therapy,* for example, uses many techniques from the cognitive and behavioral perspectives (Baucom & Boeding, 2013; Becvar & Becvar, 2012). Therapists help spouses recognize and change problem behaviors largely by teaching specific problem-solving and communication skills. A broader, more sociocultural version, called *integrative couple therapy,* further helps partners accept behaviors that they cannot change and embrace the whole relationship nevertheless (Christensen et al., 2014, 2010). Partners are asked to see such behaviors as an understandable result of basic differences between them.

Couples treated by couple therapy seem to show greater improvement in their relationships than couples with similar problems who do not receive treatment, but no one form of couple therapy stands out as superior to others (Christensen et al., 2014, 2010). Although marital functioning improved in two-thirds of treated couples by the end of therapy, fewer than half of those who are treated achieve "distress free" or "happy" relationships. One-fourth of all treated couples eventually separate or divorce.

Community Treatment **Community mental health treatment** programs allow clients to receive treatment in nearby social surroundings as they try to recover. Such community-based treatments, including *community day programs* and *residential services,* seem to be of special value to people with severe mental disorders (Stein et al., 2015; Cuddeback et al., 2013). A number of other countries have launched similar community movements over the past several decades.

As you read in Chapter 1, a key principle of community treatment is *prevention.* This involves clinicians actively reaching out to clients rather than waiting for them to seek treatment. Research suggests that such efforts are often very successful (Urben et al., 2015; Beardslee et al., 2013) Community workers recognize three types of prevention, which they call *primary, secondary,* and *tertiary.*

Primary prevention consists of efforts to improve community attitudes and policies. Its goal is to prevent psychological disorders altogether. Community workers may, for example, consult with a local school board, offer public workshops on stress reduction, or construct Web sites on how to cope effectively.

Secondary prevention consists of identifying and treating psychological disorders in the early stages, before they become serious. Community workers may work with teachers, ministers, or police to help them recognize the early signs of psychological dysfunction and teach them how to help people find treatment. Similarly, hundreds of mental health Web sites provide this same kind of information to family members, teachers, and the like.

© Najlah Feanny/Corbis

The community way At the Queens Community Center, a program in New York City funded by Catholic Charities, counselors such as the man on the right teach computer and broader life skills to people with mental health challenges or developmental disabilities.

The goal of *tertiary prevention* is to provide effective treatment as soon as it is needed so that moderate or severe disorders do not become long-term problems. Community agencies across the United States successfully offer tertiary care for millions of people with moderate psychological problems, but, as you read in Chapter 1, they often fail to provide the services needed by hundreds of thousands with severe disturbances (Althouse, 2010). One of the reasons for this failure is lack of funding, an issue that you will read about in later chapters.

How Do Multicultural Theorists Explain Abnormal Functioning?

Culture refers to the set of values, attitudes, beliefs, history, and behaviors shared by a group of people and communicated from one generation to the next (Matsumoto & Hwang, 2012, 2011; Matsumoto, 2007, 2001). We are, without question, a society of multiple cultures. Indeed, by the year 2050, the number of racial and ethnic minority group members in the United States will collectively equal or surpass the number of white Americans (U.S. Census Bureau, 2014; Kaiser Family Foundation, 2010).

Partly in response to this growing diversity, the **multicultural**, or **culturally diverse, perspective** has emerged (Leong, 2014, 2013). Multicultural psychologists seek to understand how culture, race, ethnicity, gender, and similar factors affect behavior and thought and how people of different cultures, races, and genders differ psychologically (Alegría et al., 2014, 2012, 2007). Today's multicultural view is different from past—less enlightened—cultural perspectives: it does not imply that members of racial, ethnic, and other minority groups are in some way inferior or culturally deprived in comparison with a majority population. Rather, the model holds that an individual's behavior, whether normal or abnormal, is best understood when examined in the light of that individual's unique cultural context, from the values of that culture to the special external pressures faced by members of the culture.

The groups in the United States that have received the most attention from multicultural researchers are ethnic and racial minority groups (African American, Hispanic American, American Indian, and Asian American groups) and groups such as economically disadvantaged persons, gays and lesbians, and women (although women are not technically a minority group). Each of these groups is subjected to special pressures in American society that may contribute to feelings of stress and, in some cases, to abnormal functioning. Researchers have learned, for example, that psychological abnormality, especially severe psychological abnormality, is indeed more common among poorer people than among wealthier people (Wittayanukorn, 2013; Sareen et al., 2011) (see Figure 2-5). Perhaps the pressures of poverty explain this relationship.

Of course, membership in these various groups overlaps. Many members of minority groups, for example, also live in poverty. The higher rates of crime, unemployment, overcrowding, and homelessness; the inferior medical care; and the limited educational opportunities typically available to poor people may place great stress on many members of such minority groups (Alegria et al., 2014; Miller et al., 2011).

Multicultural researchers have also noted that the prejudice and discrimination faced by many minority groups may contribute to various forms of abnormal functioning (McDonald et al., 2014; Guimón, 2010). Women in Western society receive diagnoses of anxiety disorders and of depression at least twice as often as men (NIMH, 2015). Similarly, African Americans, Hispanic Americans, and American Indians are more likely than white Americans to experience serious psychological distress or extreme sadness. American Indians also have exceptionally high alcoholism and suicide rates (Maza, 2015; Horwitz, 2014). Although many factors may combine to produce these differences, prejudice based on race and sexual orientation, and the problems such prejudice poses, may contribute to abnormal patterns of tension, unhappiness, low self-esteem, and escape (Guimón, 2010).

figure 2-5

Poverty and mental health Recent surveys in the United States find that people with low annual incomes have a greater risk of experiencing mental disorders than do those with higher incomes. For example, 10 percent of low-income people have persistent symptoms of anxiety, compared with 6 percent of higher-income people. (Information from: Sareen et al., 2011.)

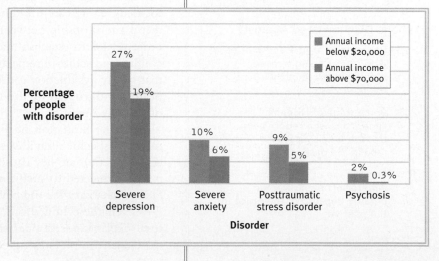

An unacceptable difference Dressed in traditional American Indian clothing, a high school student from the Mescalero Apache Reservation in New Mexico testifies before Congress on "The Preventable Epidemic: Youth Suicides and the Urgent Need for Mental Health Care Resources in Indian Country."

Multicultural Treatments

Studies conducted throughout the world have found that members of ethnic and racial minority groups tend to show less improvement in clinical treatment, make less use of mental health services, and stop therapy sooner than members of majority groups (Cook et al., 2014; Comas-Diaz, 2012, 2011).

A number of studies suggest that two features of treatment can increase a therapist's effectiveness with minority clients: (1) greater sensitivity to cultural issues and (2) inclusion of cultural morals and models in treatment, especially in therapies for children and adolescents (Comas-Diaz, 2014; Inman & DeBoer, 2013). Given such findings, some clinicians have developed **culture-sensitive therapies**, approaches that are designed to help address the unique issues faced by members of cultural minority groups. Therapies geared to the pressures of being female, called **gender-sensitive**, or **feminist**, **therapies**, follow similar principles (Sharf, 2015).

Culture-sensitive approaches typically include the following elements (Prochaska & Norcross, 2013; Wyatt & Parham, 2007):

1. Special cultural instruction for therapists in their graduate training program
2. The therapist's awareness of a client's cultural values
3. The therapist's awareness of the stress, prejudices, and stereotypes to which minority clients are exposed
4. The therapist's awareness of the hardships faced by the children of immigrants
5. Helping clients recognize the impact of both their own culture and the dominant culture on their self-views and behaviors
6. Helping clients identify and express suppressed anger and pain
7. Helping clients achieve a bicultural balance that feels right for them
8. Helping clients raise their self-esteem—a sense of self-worth that has often been damaged by generations of negative messages

Assessing the Sociocultural Model

The family-social and multicultural perspectives have added greatly to the understanding and treatment of abnormal functioning. Today most clinicians take family, cultural, social, and societal issues into account, factors that were overlooked just 35 years ago. In addition, clinicians have become more aware of the impact of clinical and social roles. Finally, the treatment formats offered by the sociocultural model sometimes succeed where traditional approaches have failed.

At the same time, the sociocultural model has certain problems. To begin with, sociocultural research findings are often difficult to interpret. Indeed, research may reveal a relationship between certain family or cultural factors and a particular disorder yet fail to establish that they are its *cause*. Studies show a link between family conflict and schizophrenia, for example, but that finding does not necessarily mean that family dysfunction causes schizophrenia. It is equally possible that family functioning is disrupted by the tension and conflict created by the psychotic behavior of a family member.

Another limitation of the sociocultural model is its inability to predict abnormality in specific individuals. If, for example, social conditions such as prejudice and discrimination are key causes of anxiety and depression, why do only some of the people subjected to such forces experience psychological disorders? Are still other factors necessary for the development of the disorders?

Given these limitations, most clinicians view the family-social and multicultural explanations as operating in conjunction with the biological or psychological explanations. They agree that family, social, and cultural factors may create a

BETWEEN THE LINES

Who Is Discriminated Against?

35% Percentage of African Americans who report being treated unfairly because of their race in the past year

20% Percentage of Hispanic Americans who report being treated unfairly because of their race in the past year

10% Percentage of white Americans who report being treated unfairly because of their race in the past year

(Pew Research Center, 2013)

climate favorable to the development of certain disorders. They believe, however, that biological or psychological conditions—or both—must also be present for the disorders to evolve.

> ## Summing Up

THE SOCIOCULTURAL MODEL One sociocultural perspective, the family-social perspective, looks outward to three kinds of factors: social labels and roles, social connections and supports, and the family system. Practitioners from the family-social perspective may practice group, family, or couple therapy or community treatment.

The multicultural perspective, another perspective from the sociocultural model, holds that an individual's behavior, whether normal or abnormal, is best understood when examined in the light of his or her unique cultural context, including the values of that culture and the special external pressures faced by members of that culture. Practitioners of this perspective may practice culture-sensitive therapies, approaches that seek to address the unique issues faced by members of cultural minority groups.

PUTTING IT...*together*

Integration of the Models

Today's leading models vary widely (see Table 2-3 on the next page), and none of the models has proved consistently superior. Each helps us appreciate a key aspect of human functioning, and each has important strengths as well as serious limitations.

With all their differences, the conclusions and techniques of the various models are often compatible. Certainly our understanding and treatment of abnormal behavior are more complete if we appreciate the biological, psychological, *and* sociocultural aspects of a person's problem rather than only one of them. Not surprisingly, a growing number of clinicians favor explanations of abnormal behavior that consider more

▶ **culture-sensitive therapies** Approaches that are designed to help address the unique issues faced by members of cultural minority groups.

▶ **gender-sensitive therapies** Approaches geared to the pressures of being a woman in Western society. Also called *feminist therapies*.

Community mental health: Argentine style Staff members and patients from Borda Neuropsychiatric Hospital in Buenos Aires set up a laptop and begin broadcasting on the popular radio station Radio La Colifata (*colifa* is slang for "crazy one"). The station was started more than 20 years ago to help patients pursue therapeutic activities and reach out to the community.

AP Photo/Ali Burafi

than one kind of cause at a time. These explanations, sometimes called *biopsychosocial theories*, state that abnormality results from the interaction of genetic, biological, developmental, emotional, behavioral, cognitive, social, cultural, and societal influences (Calkins & Dollar, 2014). A case of depression, for example, might best be explained by pointing collectively to an individual's inheritance of unfavorable genes, traumatic losses during childhood, negative ways of thinking, and social isolation.

Some biopsychosocial theorists favor a *diathesis-stress* explanation of how the various factors work together to cause abnormal functioning ("diathesis" means a predisposed tendency). According to this theory, people must *first* have a biological, psychological, or sociocultural predisposition to develop a disorder and must *then* be subjected to episodes of severe stress. In a case of depression, for example, we might find that unfavorable genes and related biochemical abnormalities predispose the individual to develop the disorder, while the loss of a loved one actually triggers its onset.

In a similar quest for integration, many therapists are now combining treatment techniques from several models (Norcross & Beutler, 2014). In fact, 22 percent of today's clinical psychologists, 34 percent of counseling psychologists, and 26 percent of social workers describe their approach as "eclectic" or "integrative" (Prochaska & Norcross, 2013). Studies confirm that clinical problems often respond better to combined approaches than to any one therapy alone. For example, as you will see, drug therapy combined with cognitive therapy is sometimes the most effective treatment for depression.

Given the recent rise in biopsychosocial theories and combination treatments, our examinations of abnormal behavior throughout this book will take two directions. As different disorders are presented, we will look at how today's models explain each disorder, how clinicians who endorse each model treat people with the disorder, and how well these explanations and treatments are supported by research. Just as important, however, we will also be observing how the explanations and treatments may build upon and strengthen one another, and we will examine current efforts toward integration of the models.

table: **2-3**

Comparing the Models

	Biological	Psychodynamic	Behavioral	Cognitive	Humanistic	Existential	Family-Social	Multicultural
Cause of dysfunction	Biological malfunction	Underlying conflicts	Maladaptive learning	Maladaptive thinking	Self-deceit	Avoidance of responsibility	Family or social stress	External pressures or cultural conflicts
Research support	Strong	Modest	Strong	Strong	Weak	Weak	Moderate	Moderate
Consumer designation	Patient	Patient	Client	Client	Patient or client	Patient or client	Client	Client
Therapist role	Doctor	Interpreter	Teacher	Persuader	Observer	Collaborator	Family/social facilitator	Cultural advocate/teacher
Key therapy technique	Biological intervention	Free association and interpretation	Conditioning	Reasoning	Reflection	Varied	Family/social intervention	Culture-sensitive intervention
Therapy goal	Biological repair	Broad psychological change	Functional behaviors	Adaptive thinking	Self-actualization	Authentic life	Effective family or social system	Cultural awareness and comfort

KEY TERMS

model, p. 38
neuron, p. 39
synapse, p. 39
neurotransmitter, p. 39
receptors, p. 40
endocrine system, p. 40
hormone, p. 40
gene, p. 40
psychotropic medication, p. 42
electroconvulsive therapy (ECT), p. 42
psychosurgery, p. 42
unconscious, p. 45
id, p. 45
ego, p. 45
ego defense mechanism, p. 45
superego, p. 46

fixation, p. 46
object relations theory, p. 47
free association, p. 47
resistance, p. 48
transference, p. 48
dream, p. 49
catharsis, p. 49
working through, p. 49
short-term psychodynamic therapies, p. 49
relational psychoanalytic therapy, p. 49
conditioning, p. 51
operant conditioning, p. 51
modeling, p. 51
classical conditioning, p. 51
systematic desensitization, p. 52
self-efficacy, p. 53

cognitive therapy, p. 55
self-actualization, p. 58
client-centered therapy, p. 58
gestalt therapy, p. 60
existential therapy, p. 63
family systems theory, p. 66
group therapy, p. 67
self-help group, p. 68
family therapy, p. 68
couple therapy, p. 69
community mental health treatment, p. 70
multicultural perspective, p. 71
culture-sensitive therapy, p. 72
gender-sensitive therapy, p. 72
biopsychosocial theories, p. 74
diathesis-stress explanation, p. 74

QuickQuiz

1. What are the key regions of the brain, and how do messages travel throughout the brain? Describe the biological treatments for psychological disorders. *pp. 39–44*

2. Identify the models associated with learned responses (*p. 50*), values (*p. 58*), responsibility (*p. 63*), spirituality (*p. 61*), underlying conflicts (*p. 44*), and maladaptive assumptions (*p. 54*).

3. Identify the treatments that use unconditional positive regard (*p. 59*), free association (*p. 47*), classical conditioning (*p. 52*), skillful frustration (*p. 60*), and dream interpretation (*p. 49*).

4. What are the key principles of the psychodynamic (*pp. 44–50*), behavioral

(*pp. 50–54*), cognitive (*pp. 54–58*), and humanistic-existential (*pp. 58–64*) models?

5. According to psychodynamic theorists, what roles do the id, ego, and superego play in the development of both normal and abnormal behavior? What are the key techniques used by psychodynamic therapists? *pp. 45–49*

6. What forms of conditioning do behaviorists rely on in their explanations and treatments of abnormal behaviors? *pp. 51–53*

7. What kinds of cognitive dysfunctioning can lead to abnormal behavior, and which treatment approaches are used

to address such cognitive dysfunctions? *pp. 54–58*

8. How do humanistic theories and therapies differ from existential ones? *pp. 58–63*

9. How might societal labels and roles, social connections, family factors, and culture relate to psychological functioning? *pp. 64–66, 71*

10. What are the key features of culture-sensitive therapy, group therapy, family therapy, couple therapy, and community treatment? How effective are these various approaches? *pp. 67–73*

Visit *LaunchPad*

www.macmillanhighered.com/launchpad/comerfund8e
to access the e-book, new interactive case studies, videos, activities, and LearningCurve quizzes, as well as study aids including flashcards, FAQs, and research exercises.

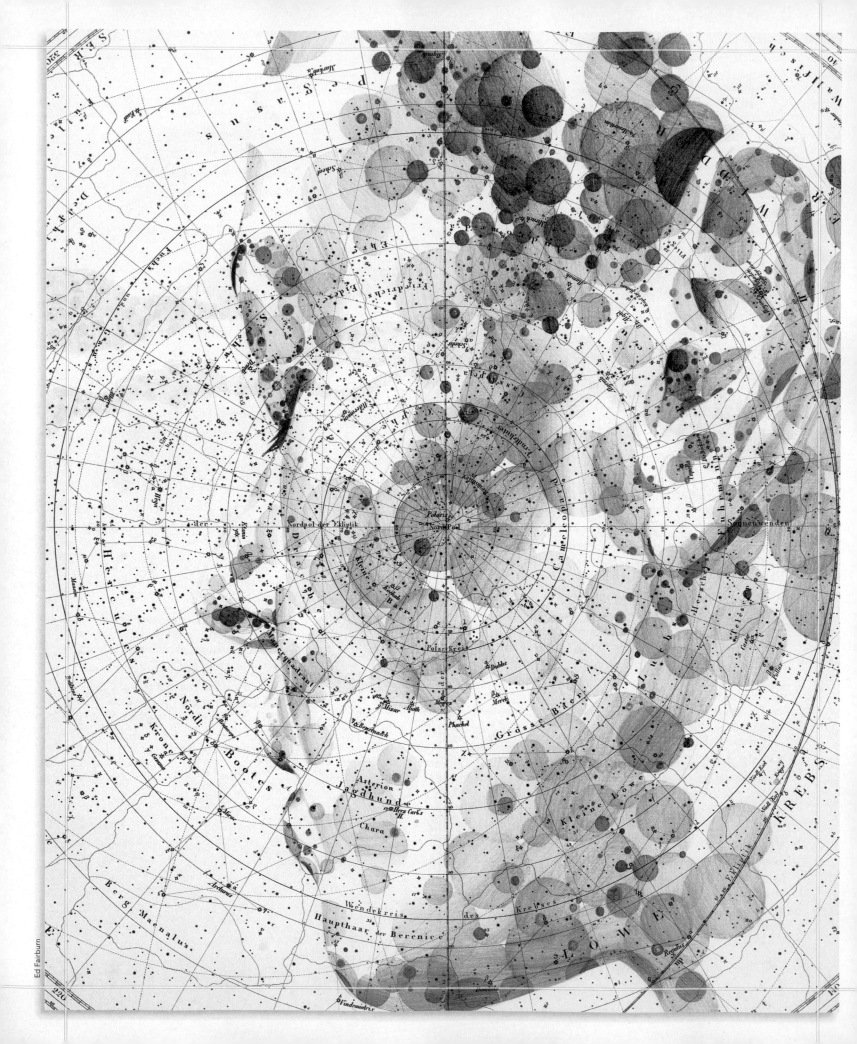

Clinical Assessment, Diagnosis, and Treatment

F ranco started seeing a therapist at the urging of his friend Jesse. It had been almost four months since Franco broke up with his girlfriend, and he still seemed unable to pull himself together. He had totally stopped playing sports and attending concerts, things he normally did on a regular basis. When he finally returned Jesse's calls, he mentioned several serious and avoidable mistakes that he had made at work recently, but he barely seemed to care. He also confided to his friend that he felt very tired and was unable to touch his food. Jesse suspected that Franco was clinically depressed, but, then again, he was not a therapist.

Feelings of despondency led Franco to make an appointment with a therapist at a local counseling center. His clinician's first step was to learn as much as possible about Franco and his disturbance. Who is he, what is his life like, and what are his symptoms? The answers might help to reveal the causes and probable course of his present dysfunction and suggest what kinds of strategies would be most likely to help him. Treatment could then be tailored to Franco's needs and particular pattern of abnormal functioning.

In Chapters 1 and 2 you read about how researchers in abnormal psychology build a general understanding of abnormal functioning. Clinical practitioners apply this broad information in their work, but their main focus when faced with new clients is to gather **idiographic,** or individual, information about them (Zheng et al., 2015). To help a client overcome problems, clinicians must fully understand the client and his or her particular difficulties. To gather such individual information, clinicians use the procedures of *assessment* and *diagnosis*. Then they are in a position to offer *treatment*.

Clinical Assessment: How and Why Does the Client Behave Abnormally?

Assessment is simply the collecting of relevant information in an effort to reach a conclusion. It goes on in every realm of life. We make assessments when we decide what cereal to buy or which presidential candidate to vote for. College admissions officers, who have to select the "best" of the students applying to their college, depend on academic records, recommendations, achievement test scores, interviews, and application forms to help them decide. Employers, who have to predict which applicants are most likely to be effective workers, collect information from résumés, interviews, references, and perhaps on-the-job observations.

Clinical assessment is used to determine whether, how, and why a person is behaving abnormally and how that person may be helped. It also enables clinicians to evaluate people's progress after they have been in treatment for a while and decide whether the treatment should be changed. The hundreds of clinical assessment techniques and tools that have been developed fall into three categories: *clinical interviews, tests,* and *observations.* To be useful, these tools must be *standardized* and must have clear *reliability* and *validity.*

Characteristics of Assessment Tools

All clinicians must follow the same procedures when they use a particular type of assessment tool. To **standardize** such a tool is to set up common steps to be followed whenever it is administered. Similarly, clinicians must standardize the way they interpret the results of an assessment tool in order to be able to understand what a particular score means. They may standardize the scores of a test, for example, by first administering it to a group of research participants whose performance will then serve as a common standard, or norm, against which later individual scores can be measured. The group that initially takes the test must be typical of the larger population for whom the test is intended. If an aggressiveness test meant for the public at large were standardized on a group of Marines, for example, the resulting "norm" might turn out to be misleadingly high (Hogan, 2014).

Reliability refers to the *consistency* of assessment measures. A good assessment tool will always yield similar results in the same situation (Dehn, 2013). An assessment tool has high *test–retest reliability,* one kind of reliability, if it yields similar results every time it is given to the same people. If a woman's responses on a particular test indicate that she is generally a heavy drinker, the test should produce a similar result when she takes it again a week later. To measure test–retest reliability, participants are tested on two occasions and the two scores are correlated (Holden & Bernstein, 2013). The higher the correlation (see Chapter 1), the greater the test's reliability.

An assessment tool shows high *interrater* (or *interjudge*) *reliability,* another kind of reliability, if different judges independently agree on how to score and interpret it. True–false and multiple-choice tests yield consistent scores no matter who evaluates them, but other tests require that the evaluator make a judgment. Consider a test that requires the person to draw a copy of a picture, which a judge then rates for accuracy. Different judges may give different ratings to the same drawing.

Finally, an assessment tool must have **validity:** it must *accurately* measure what it is supposed to measure (Dehn, 2013). Suppose a weight scale reads 12 pounds every time a 10-pound bag of sugar is placed on it. Although the scale is reliable because its readings are consistent, those readings are not valid, or accurate.

A given assessment tool may appear to be valid simply because it makes sense and seems reasonable. However, this sort of validity, called *face validity,* does not by itself mean that the instrument is trustworthy. A test for depression, for example, might include questions about how often a person cries. Because it makes sense that depressed people would cry, these test questions have face validity. It turns out, however, that many people cry a great deal for reasons other than depression, and some extremely depressed people do not cry at all. Thus an assessment tool should not be used unless it has high *predictive validity* or *concurrent validity* (Dehn, 2013).

Predictive validity is a tool's ability to predict future characteristics or behavior. Let's say that a test has been developed to identify elementary schoolchildren who are likely to take up cigarette smoking in high school. The test gathers information about the children's parents—their personal characteristics, smoking habits, and attitudes toward smoking—and on that basis identifies high-risk children. To establish the test's predictive validity, investigators could administer it to a group of elementary school students, wait until they were in high school, and then check to see which children actually did become smokers.

Concurrent validity is the degree to which the measures gathered from one tool agree with the measures gathered from other assessment techniques. Participants' scores on a new test designed to measure anxiety, for example, should correlate

Reliable assessments Former National Basketball Association stars Clyde Drexler, James Worthy, Brent Barry, Dominique Wilkins, and Julius Erving served as judges at the 2011 All-Star slam dunk contest. Holding up their scores after each dunk, they displayed high interrater reliability and showed they still know a great dunk when they see one.

© Icon SMI/Corbis

How reliable and valid are the tests you take in school? What about the tests you see online and in print magazines?

highly with their scores on other anxiety tests or with their behavior during clinical interviews.

Before any assessment technique can be fully useful, it must meet the requirements of standardization, reliability, and validity. No matter how insightful or clever a technique may be, clinicians cannot profitably use its results if they are uninterpretable, inconsistent, or inaccurate. Unfortunately, more than a few clinical assessment tools fall short, suggesting that at least some clinical assessments, too, miss their mark.

Clinical Interviews

Most of us feel instinctively that the best way to get to know people is to meet with them face to face. Under these circumstances, we can see them react to what we do and say, observe as well as listen as they answer, and generally get a sense of who they are. A *clinical interview* is just such a face-to-face encounter (Miller, 2015; Goldfinger & Pomerantz, 2014). If during a clinical interview a man looks as happy as can be while describing his sadness over the recent death of his mother, the clinician may suspect that the man actually has conflicting emotions about this loss.

Conducting the Interview The interview is often the first contact between client and clinician. Clinicians use it to collect detailed information about the person's problems and feelings, lifestyle and relationships, and other personal history. They may also ask about the person's expectations of therapy and motives for seeking it. The clinician who worked with Franco began with a face-to-face interview:

> *Franco arrived for his appointment in gray sweatpants and a T-shirt. His stubble suggested that he had not shaved, and the many food stains on his shirt indicated he had not washed it for quite some time. Franco spoke without emotion. He slouched into the chair, sending signals that he did not want to be there.*
>
> *When pressed, he talked about his two-year relationship with Maria, who, at 25, was 13 years younger than he was. Franco had believed that he had met his future wife, but Maria's domineering mother was unhappy about the age difference and kept telling her daughter that she could find someone better. Franco wanted Maria to stand up to her mother and to move in with him, but this was not easy for her to do. Believing that Maria's mother had too much influence over her and frustrated that she would not commit to him, he had broken up with Maria during a fight. He soon realized that he had acted impulsively, but Maria refused to take him back.*
>
> *When asked about his childhood, Franco described his father's death in a gruesome car crash on his way to pick up 12-year-old Franco from soccer practice. Initially, his father had told Franco that he could not come get him from practice, but Franco "threw a tantrum" and his father agreed to rearrange his schedule. Franco believed himself responsible for his father's death.*
>
> *Franco stated that, over the years, his mother had encouraged this feeling of self-blame by complaining that she had been forced to "give up her life" to raise Franco alone. She was always nasty to Franco and nasty to every woman he later dated. She even predicted that Franco would "die alone."*
>
> *Franco described being very unhappy throughout his school years. He hated school and felt less smart than the other kids. On occasion, a teacher's critique—meant as encouragement—left him unable to do his homework for days, and his grades suffered. He truly believed he was stupid. Similarly, later in life, he interpreted his rise to a position as bank manager as due entirely to hard work. "I know I'm not as smart as the others there."*

▶ **idiographic understanding** An understanding of a particular individual.

▶ **assessment** The process of collecting and interpreting relevant information about a client or research participant.

▶ **standardization** The process in which a test is administered to a large group of people whose performance then serves as a standard or norm against which any individual's score can be measured.

▶ **reliability** A measure of the consistency of test or research results.

▶ **validity** A measure of the accuracy of a test's or study's results.

BETWEEN THE LINES

The Stigma Continues

33% Americans who would not seek counseling for fear of being labeled "mentally ill"

67% Americans who would not tell their employer that they were seeking mental health treatment

37% Americans who would be reluctant to seek treatment because of confidentiality concerns

(Opinion Research Corporation, 2011, 2004)

(continues on the next page)

Franco explained that since the breakup with Maria, he had experienced more unhappiness than ever before. He often spent all night watching television. At the same time, he could barely pay attention to what was happening on the screen. He said that some days he actually forgot to eat. He had no wish to see his friends. At work, the days blurred into one another, distinguished only by a growing number of reprimands from his bank supervisors. He attributed these work problems to his basic lack of ability. His supervisors had simply figured out that he had not been good enough for the job all along.

Beyond gathering basic background data of this kind, clinical interviewers give special attention to those topics they consider most important (Miller, 2015; Segal, June, & Marty, 2010). Psychodynamic interviewers try to learn about the person's needs and memories of past events and relationships. Behavioral interviewers try to pinpoint information about the stimuli that trigger responses and their consequences. Cognitive interviewers try to discover assumptions and interpretations that influence the person. Humanistic clinicians ask about the person's self-evaluation, self-concept, and values. Biological clinicians look for signs of biochemical or brain dysfunction. And sociocultural interviewers ask about the family, social, and cultural environments.

Interviews can be either unstructured or structured. In an *unstructured interview,* the clinician asks mostly open-ended questions, perhaps as simple as "Would you tell me about yourself?" The lack of structure allows the interviewer to follow leads and explore relevant topics that could not be anticipated before the interview.

In a *structured interview,* clinicians ask prepared—mostly specific—questions. Sometimes they use a published *interview schedule*—a standard set of questions designed for all interviews. Many structured interviews include a **mental status exam,** a set of questions and observations that systematically evaluate the client's awareness, orientation with regard to time and place, attention span, memory, judgment and insight, thought content and processes, mood, and appearance (Sommers-Flanagan & Sommers-Flanagan, 2013). A structured format ensures that clinicians will cover the same kinds of important issues in all of their interviews and enables them to compare the responses of different individuals.

Military concerns U.S. Army troops await their turn for psychological assessment at the Soldier Readiness Processing Center at Fort Hood, Texas. Many soldiers have developed significant psychological problems in recent years as a result of their repeated deployments to Iraq and Afghanistan, leading the Army to conduct assessments that might predict which individuals are particularly vulnerable to such reactions.

© Erich Schlegel/Corbis

Although most clinical interviews have both unstructured and structured portions, many clinicians favor one kind over the other. Unstructured interviews typically appeal to psychodynamic and humanistic clinicians, while structured formats are widely used by behavioral and cognitive clinicians, who need to pinpoint behaviors, attitudes, or thinking processes that may underlie abnormal behavior (Segal & Hersen, 2010).

What Are the Limitations of Clinical Interviews?
Although interviews often produce valuable information about people, there are limits to what they can accomplish. One problem is that they sometimes lack validity, or accuracy (Sommers-Flanagan & Sommers-Flanagan, 2013). Individuals may intentionally mislead in order to present themselves in a positive light or to avoid discussing embarrassing topics (Gold & Castillo, 2010). Or people may be unable to give an accurate report in their interviews. Individuals who suffer from depression, for example, take a pessimistic view of themselves and may describe themselves as poor workers or inadequate parents when that isn't the case at all.

Interviewers too may make mistakes in judgments that slant the information they gather (Clinton, Fernandez, & Alicea, 2010). They usually rely too heavily on first impressions, for example, and give too much weight to unfavorable information about a client (Wu & Shi, 2005). Interviewer biases, including gender, race, and age biases, may also influence the interviewers' interpretations of what a client says (Ungar et al., 2006).

Interviews, particularly unstructured ones, may also lack reliability (Sommers-Flanagan & Sommers-Flanagan, 2013). People respond differently to different interviewers, providing, for example, less information to a cold interviewer than to a warm and supportive one (Quas et al., 2007). Similarly, a clinician's race, gender, age, and appearance may influence a client's responses (Davis et al., 2010; Springman, Wherry, & Notaro, 2006).

Because different clinicians can obtain different answers and draw different conclusions even when they ask the same questions of the same person, some researchers believe that interviewing should be discarded as a tool of clinical assessment. As you'll see, however, the two other kinds of clinical assessment methods also have serious limitations.

"I'll say a normal word, then you say the first sick thing that pops into your head."

Clinical Tests

Clinical tests are devices for gathering information about a few aspects of a person's psychological functioning, from which broader information about the person can be inferred. On the surface, it may look easy to design an effective test. Every month, magazines and Web sites present new tests that supposedly tell us about our personalities, relationships, sex lives, reactions to stress, or ability to succeed. Such tests might sound convincing, but most of them lack reliability, validity, and standardization. That is, they do not yield consistent, accurate information or say where we stand in comparison with others.

More than 500 clinical tests are currently in use throughout the United States. Clinicians use six kinds most often: *projective tests, personality inventories, response inventories, psychophysiological tests, neurological and neuropsychological tests,* and *intelligence tests.*

Projective Tests
Projective tests require that clients interpret vague stimuli, such as inkblots or ambiguous pictures, or follow open-ended instructions such as "Draw a person." Theoretically, when clues and instructions are so general, people will "project" aspects of their personality into the task (Cherry, 2015; Hogan, 2014).

▶ **mental status exam** A set of interview questions and observations designed to reveal the degree and nature of a client's abnormal functioning.

▶ **clinical test** A device for gathering information about a few aspects of a person's psychological functioning from which broader information about the person can be inferred.

▶ **projective test** A test consisting of ambiguous material that people interpret or respond to.

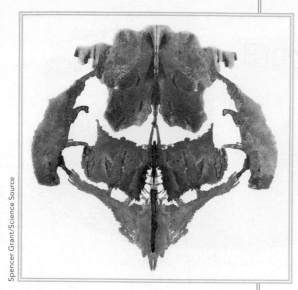

figure 3-1

An inkblot similar to those used in the Rorschach test. In this test, individuals view and react to a total of 10 inkblot images.

Projective tests are used primarily by psychodynamic clinicians to help assess the unconscious drives and conflicts they believe to be at the root of abnormal functioning (Baer & Blais, 2010). The most widely used projective tests are the *Rorschach test,* the *Thematic Apperception Test, sentence-completion tests,* and *drawings.*

RORSCHACH TEST In 1911 Hermann Rorschach, a Swiss psychiatrist, experimented with the use of inkblots in his clinical work. He made thousands of blots by dropping ink on paper and then folding the paper in half to create a symmetrical but wholly accidental design, such as the one shown in Figure 3-1. Rorschach found that everyone saw images in these blots. In addition, the images a viewer saw seemed to correspond in important ways with his or her psychological condition. People diagnosed with schizophrenia, for example, tended to see images that differed from those described by people experiencing depression.

> Despite its limitations, just about everyone has heard of the Rorschach. Why do you think it is so famous and popular?

Rorschach selected 10 inkblots and published them in 1921 with instructions for their use in assessment. This set was called the *Rorschach Psychodynamic Inkblot Test.* Rorschach died just 8 months later, at the age of 37, but his work was continued by others, and his inkblots took their place among the most widely used projective tests of the twentieth century (see *MindTech* on the next page).

Clinicians administer the "Rorschach," as it is commonly called, by presenting one inkblot card at a time and asking respondents what they see, what the inkblot seems to be, or what it reminds them of. In the early years, Rorschach testers paid special attention to the themes and images that the inkblots brought to mind (Butcher, 2010). Testers now also pay attention to the style of the responses: Do the clients view the design as a whole or see specific details? Do they focus on the blots or on the white spaces between them?

THEMATIC APPERCEPTION TEST The Thematic Apperception Test (TAT) is a pictorial projective test (Aronow, Weiss, & Reznikoff, 2011; Morgan & Murray, 1935). People who take the TAT are commonly shown 30 cards with black-and-white pictures of individuals in vague situations and are asked to make up a dramatic story about each card. They must tell what is happening in the picture, what led up to it, what the characters are feeling and thinking, and what the outcome of the situation will be.

Clinicians who use the TAT believe that people always identify with one of the characters on each card. The stories are thought to reflect the individuals' own circumstances, needs, and emotions. For example, a female client seems to be revealing her own feelings when telling this story about a TAT picture similar to the image shown in Figure 3-2:

figure 3-2

A picture similar to one used in the Thematic Apperception Test.

> This is a woman who has been quite troubled by memories of a mother she was resentful toward. She has feelings of sorrow for the way she treated her mother, her memories of her mother plague her. These feelings seem to be increasing as she grows older and sees her children treating her the same way that she treated her mother.
>
> *(Aiken, 1985, p. 372)*

SENTENCE-COMPLETION TEST In the sentence-completion test, first developed in the 1920s (Payne, 1928), the test-taker completes a series of unfinished sentences, such as "I wish . . ." or "My father. . . ." The test is considered a good springboard for discussion and a quick and easy way to pinpoint topics to explore.

Psychology's Wiki Leaks?

In 2009, an emergency room physician posted the images of all 10 Rorschach cards, along with common responses to each card, on *Wikipedia,* the online encyclopedia. The publisher of the test, Hogrefe Publishing, immediately threatened to take *Wikipedia* to court, saying that the encyclopedia's willingness to post the images was "unbelievably reckless" (Cohen, 2009). However, no legal actions took place, and to this day, the 10 cards remain on *Wikipedia* for the entire world to see.

Many psychologists have criticized the Wikipedia posting, arguing that the Rorschach test responses of patients who have previously seen the test on *Wikipedia* cannot be trusted. In support of their concerns, a recent study found that reading the *Wikipedia* Rorschach test article did indeed help many individuals perform more positively on the test itself (Schultz & Brabender, 2012). These clinical concerns are consistent with the long-standing positions of the British, Canadian, and American Psychological Associations, who hold that nonprofessional publications of psychological test answers are wrong and potentially harmful to patients (CPA, 2009; BPS, 2007; APA, 1996).

Still other critics point out that the online publication of the Rorschach cards jeopardizes the usefulness of thousands of published studies—studies that have tried to link patients' Rorschach responses to particular psychological disorders (Cohen, 2009). These studies were conducted on first-time inkblot observers, not on people who had already viewed the cards online.

Why do you think this Rorschach debate has led to an increase in the distribution of psychological tests?

On the other hand, more than a few test skeptics seem very pleased by the online posting, hoping that it will lower the public's regard for the test and lessen its clinical use (Radford, 2009). In fact, one recent study suggests that the Rorschach–Wikipedia debate has already led to unfavorable opinions of the test among many individuals (Schultz & Loving, 2012).

It appears that this debate is actually leading to an increase—rather than a decrease—in the distribution of psychological tests. Several newspapers reporting on the controversy have themselves published photos of the Rorschach cards (Simple, 2009; White, 2009). And as you will read later in this chapter, intelligence tests, among the most widely used of all psychological tests, are now available—on eBay of all places—to anyone who is willing to pay the price. 💬

Drawing test Drawing tests are commonly used to assess the functioning of children. One is the Kinetic Family Drawing test, in which children draw their household members performing some activity ("kinetic" means "active").

DRAWINGS On the assumption that a drawing tells us something about its creator, clinicians often ask clients to draw human figures and talk about them (McGrath & Carroll, 2012). Evaluations of these drawings are based on the details and shape of the drawing, the solidity of the pencil line, the location of the drawing on the paper, the size of the figures, the features of the figures, the use of background, and comments made by the respondent during the drawing task. In the *Draw-a-Person* (*DAP*) *test,* the most popular of the drawing tests, individuals are first told to draw "a person" and then are instructed to draw a person of the other sex.

The art of assessment In the spirit of projective tests, the sometimes bizarre cat portraits of early-twentieth-century artist Louis Wain have been interpreted as reflections of the psychosis with which he struggled for many years.

WHAT ARE THE MERITS OF PROJECTIVE TESTS? Until the 1950s, projective tests were the most commonly used method for assessing personality. In recent years, however, clinicians and researchers have relied on them largely to gain "supplementary" insights (McGrath & Carroll, 2012). One reason for this shift is that practitioners who follow the newer models have less use for the tests than psychodynamic clinicians do. Even more important, the tests have not consistently shown much reliability or validity (Hogan, 2014).

In reliability studies, different clinicians have tended to score the same person's projective test quite differently. Similarly, in validity studies, when clinicians try to describe a client's personality and feelings on the basis of responses to projective tests, their conclusions often fail to match the self-report of the client, the view of the psychotherapist, or the picture gathered from an extensive case history (Cherry, 2015; Bornstein, 2007).

Another validity problem is that projective tests are sometimes biased against minority ethnic groups (Costantino et al., 2007) (see Table 3-1). For example, people are supposed to identify with the characters in the TAT when they make up stories about them, yet no members of minority groups are in the TAT pictures. In response to this problem, some clinicians have developed other TAT-like tests with African American or Hispanic figures (Costantino et al., 2007, 1992).

Personality Inventories An alternative way to collect information about individuals is to ask them to assess themselves. Respondents to a **personality inventory** answer a wide range of questions about their behavior, beliefs, and feelings. In the typical personality inventory, individuals indicate whether each of a long list of statements applies to them. Clinicians then use the responses to draw conclusions about the person's personality and psychological functioning (Hogan, 2014; Watson, 2012).

By far the most widely used personality inventory is the *Minnesota Multiphasic Personality Inventory (MMPI)* (Butcher, 2011). Two adult versions are available—the original test, published in 1945, and the *MMPI-2,* a 1989 revision that was itself revised in 2001. There is also a streamlined version of the inventory called the *MMPI-2-Restructured Form* and a special version of the test for adolescents called the *MMPI-A* (Williams & Butcher, 2011).

The MMPI consists of more than 500 self-statements, to be labeled "true," "false," or "cannot say." The statements cover issues ranging from physical concerns to mood, sexual behaviors, and social activities. Altogether the statements make up 10 clinical scales, on each of which an individual can score from 0 to 120. When people score above 70 on a scale, their functioning on that scale is considered deviant. When the 10 scale scores are considered side by side, a pattern called a *profile* takes shape, indicating the person's general personality. The 10 scales on the MMPI measure the following:

Hypochondriasis Items showing abnormal concern with bodily functions ("I have chest pains several times a week.")

Depression Items showing extreme pessimism and hopelessness ("I often feel hopeless about the future.")

Hysteria Items suggesting that the person may use physical or mental symptoms as a way of unconsciously avoiding conflicts and responsibilities ("My heart frequently pounds so hard I can feel it.")

Psychopathic deviate Items showing a repeated and gross disregard for social customs and an emotional shallowness ("My activities and interests are often criticized by others.")

Masculinity-femininity Items that are thought to separate male and female respondents ("I like to arrange flowers.")

Paranoia Items that show abnormal suspiciousness and delusions of grandeur or persecution ("There are evil people trying to influence my mind.")

Psychasthenia Items that show obsessions, compulsions, abnormal fears, and guilt and indecisiveness ("I save nearly everything I buy, even after I have no use for it.")

Schizophrenia Items that show bizarre or unusual thoughts or behavior ("Things around me do not seem real.")

Hypomania Items that show emotional excitement, overactivity, and flight of ideas ("At times I feel very 'high' or very 'low' for no apparent reason.")

Social introversion Items that show shyness, little interest in people, and insecurity ("I am easily embarrassed.")

The MMPI and other personality inventories have several advantages over projective tests (Cherry, 2015; Hogan, 2014). Because they are computerized or paper–and–pencil tests, they do not take much time to administer, and they are objectively scored. Most of them are standardized, so one person's scores can be compared with those of many others. Moreover, they often display greater test–retest reliability than projective tests. For example, people who take the MMPI a second time after a period of less than 2 weeks receive approximately the same scores (Graham, 2014, 2006).

▶ **personality inventory** A test, designed to measure broad personality characteristics, consisting of statements about behaviors, beliefs, and feelings that people evaluate as either characteristic or uncharacteristic of them.

table: 3-1

Multicultural Hot Spots in Assessment and Diagnosis

Cultural Hot Spot	Effect on Assessment or Diagnosis
• Immigrant Client	**• Dominant-Culture Assessor**
Homeland culture may differ from current country's dominant culture	May misread culture-bound reactions as pathology
May have left homeland to escape war or oppression	May overlook client's vulnerability to posttraumatic stress
May have weak support systems in this country	May overlook client's heightened vulnerability to stressors
Lifestyle (wealth and occupation) in this country may fall below lifestyle in homeland	May overlook client's sense of loss and frustration
May refuse or be unable to learn dominant language	May misunderstand client's assessment responses, or may overlook or misdiagnose client's symptoms
• Ethnic-Minority Client	**• Dominant-Culture Assessor**
May reject or distrust members of dominant culture, including assessor	May experience little rapport with client, or may misinterpret client's distrust as pathology
May be uncomfortable with dominant culture's values (e.g., assertiveness, confrontation) and so find it difficult to apply clinician's recommendations	May view client as unmotivated
May manifest stress in culture-bound ways (e.g., somatic symptoms such as stomachaches)	May misinterpret symptom patterns
May hold cultural beliefs that seem strange to dominant culture (e.g., belief in communication with dead)	May misinterpret cultural responses as pathology (e.g., a delusion)
May be uncomfortable during assessment	May overlook and feed into client's discomfort
• Dominant-Culture Assessor	**• Ethnic-Minority Client**
May be unknowledgeable or biased about ethnic-minority culture	Cultural differences may be pathologized, or symptoms may be overlooked
May nonverbally convey own discomfort to ethnic-minority client	May become tense and anxious

Information from: Rose et al., 2011; Bhattacharya et al., 2010; Dana, 2005, 2000; Westermeyer, 2004, 2001, 1993; López & Guarnaccia, 2005, 2000; Kirmayer, 2003, 2002, 2001; Sue & Sue, 2003; Tsai et al., 2001; Thakker & Ward, 1998.

"We're going to run some tests: blood work, a cat-scan, and the S.A.T.'s."

Personality inventories also appear to have more validity, or accuracy, than projective tests (Cherry, 2015; Butcher, 2011, 2010). However, they can hardly be considered *highly* valid. When clinicians have used these tests alone, they have not regularly been able to judge a respondent's personality accurately (Braxton et al., 2007). One problem is that the personality traits that the tests seek to measure cannot be examined directly. How can we fully know a person's character, emotions, and needs from self-reports alone?

Another problem is that despite the use of more diverse standardization groups by the MMPI-2 designers, this and other personality tests continue to have certain cultural limitations. Responses that indicate a psychological disorder in one culture may be normal responses in another (Butcher, 2010; Dana, 2005, 2000). In Puerto Rico, for example, where it is common to practice spiritualism, it would be normal to answer "true" to the MMPI item "Evil spirits possess me at times." In other populations, that response could indicate psychopathology (Rogler et al., 1989).

Despite such limits in validity, personality inventories continue to be popular. Research indicates that they can help clinicians learn about people's personal styles and disorders as long as they are used in combination with interviews or other assessment tools.

Response Inventories Like personality inventories, **response inventories** ask people to provide detailed information about themselves, but these tests focus on one specific area of functioning (Wang & Gorenstein, 2013; Vaz et al., 2013; Watson, 2012). For example, one such test may measure affect (emotion), another social skills, and still another cognitive processes. Clinicians can use the inventories to determine the role such factors play in a person's disorder.

Affective inventories measure the severity of such emotions as anxiety, depression, and anger. In one of the most widely used affective inventories, the Beck Depression Inventory, people rate their level of sadness and its effect on their functioning. For *social skills inventories,* used particularly by behavioral and family-social clinicians, respondents indicate how they would react in a variety of social situations. *Cognitive inventories* reveal a person's typical thoughts and assumptions and can help uncover counterproductive patterns of thinking. They are, not surprisingly, often used by cognitive therapists and researchers.

Both the number of response inventories and the number of clinicians who use them have increased steadily in the past 30 years. At the same time, however, these inventories have major limitations. With the notable exceptions of the Beck Depression Inventory and a few others, many of the tests have not been subjected to careful standardization, reliability, and validity procedures (Blais & Baer, 2010). Often they are created as a need arises, without being tested for accuracy and consistency.

Psychophysiological Tests Clinicians may also use **psychophysiological tests,** which measure physiological responses as possible indicators of psychological problems (Daly et al., 2014). This practice began three decades ago, after several studies suggested that states of anxiety are regularly accompanied by physiological changes, particularly increases in heart rate, body temperature, blood pressure, skin reactions (*galvanic skin response*), and muscle contractions. The measuring of physiological changes has since played a key role in the assessment of certain psychological disorders.

One psychophysiological test is the *polygraph,* popularly known as a *lie detector* (Bhutta et al., 2015; Rosky, 2013). Electrodes attached to various parts of a

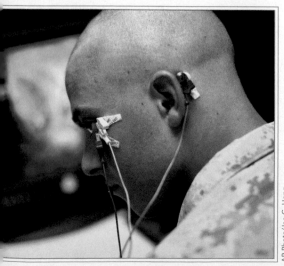

Blink of the eye Before entering combat duty, this Marine takes an eyeblink test—a psychophysiological test in which sensors are attached to the eyelid and other parts of the face. The test tries to detect physical indicators of tension and anxiety and to predict which Marines might be particularly susceptible to posttraumatic stress disorder.

person's body detect changes in breathing, perspiration, and heart rate while the person answers questions. The clinician observes these functions while the person answers "yes" to *control questions*—questions whose answers are known to be yes, such as "Are both your parents alive?" Then the clinician observes the same physiological functions while the person answers *test questions,* such as "Did you commit this robbery?" If breathing, perspiration, and heart rate suddenly increase, the person is suspected of lying.

> **Why might an innocent person "fail" a lie detector test? How might a guilty person manage to "pass" the test?**

Like other kinds of clinical tests, psychophysiological tests have their drawbacks (Rusconi & Mitchener-Nissen, 2013). Many require expensive equipment that must be carefully tuned and maintained. In addition, psychophysiological measurements can be inaccurate and unreliable (see *PsychWatch* below). The laboratory equipment itself—elaborate and sometimes frightening—may arouse a participant's nervous system and thus change his or her physical responses. Physiological responses may also change when they are measured repeatedly in a single session. Galvanic skin responses, for example, often decrease during repeated testing.

▸ **response inventories** Tests that measure a person's responses in one specific area of functioning, such as affect, social skills, or cognitive processes.

▸ **psychophysiological test** A test that measures physical responses (such as heart rate and muscle tension) as possible indicators of psychological problems.

PsychWatch

The Truth, the Whole Truth, and Nothing but the Truth

In movies, criminals being grilled by the police reveal their guilt by sweating, shaking, cursing, or twitching. When they are hooked up to a *polygraph* (a lie detector), the needles bounce all over the paper. This image has been with us since World War I, when some clinicians developed the theory that people who are telling lies display systemic changes in their breathing, perspiration, and heart rate (Marston, 1917).

The danger of relying on polygraph tests is that, according to researchers, they do not work as well as we would like (Rosky, 2015, 2013; Rusconi & Mitchener-Nissen, 2013; Meijer & Verschuere, 2010).

The public did not pay much attention to this inconvenient fact until the mid-1980s, when the American Psychological Association officially reported that polygraphs were often inaccurate and the U.S. Congress voted to restrict their use in criminal prosecution and employment screening (Krapohl, 2002). Research indicates that 8 out of 100 truths, on average, are called lies in polygraph testing (Grubin, 2010; Raskin & Honts, 2002; MacLaren, 2001). Imagine, then, how many innocent people might be convicted of crimes if polygraph findings were taken as valid evidence in criminal trials.

Given such findings, polygraphs are less trusted and less popular today than they once were. For example, few courts now admit results from such tests as evidence of criminal guilt (Grubin, 2010; Daniels, 2002). Polygraph testing has by no means disappeared, however. The FBI uses it extensively, parole boards and probation offices routinely use it to help decide whether to release convicted offenders, and in public-sector hiring (such as for police officers), the use of polygraph screening may actually be on the increase (Meijer & Verschuere, 2010; Kokish et al., 2005).

AP Photo/Fernando Vergara

All the rage A student learns to administer polygraph exams at the Latin American Polygraph Institute in Bogota, Colombia. Despite evidence that these tests are often invalid, they are widely used by businesses in Colombia, where deception by employees has become a major problem.

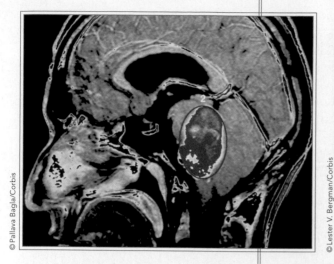

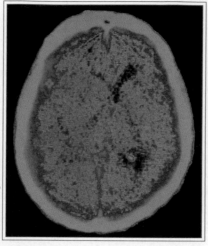

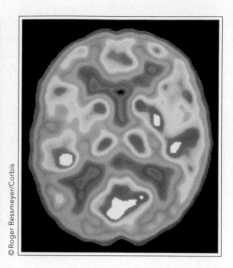

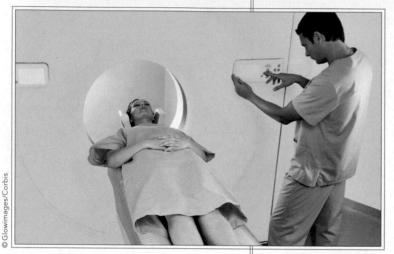

Traditional scanning The most widely used neuroimaging techniques in clinical practice—the MRI (bottom), CAT, and PET—take pictures of the living brain. Here, an MRI scan (above left) reveals a large tumor, colored in orange; a CAT scan (above center) reveals a mass of blood within the brain; and a PET scan (above right) shows which areas of the brain are active (those colored in red, orange, and yellow) when an individual is being stimulated.

Neurological and Neuropsychological Tests

Some problems in personality or behavior are caused primarily by damage to the brain or by changes in brain activity. Head injuries, brain tumors, brain malfunctions, alcoholism, infections, and other disorders can all cause such impairment. If a psychological dysfunction is to be treated effectively, it is important to know whether its primary cause is a physical abnormality in the brain.

A number of techniques may help pinpoint brain abnormalities. Some procedures, such as brain surgery, biopsy, and X ray, have been used for many years. More recently, scientists have developed a number of **neurological tests,** which are designed to measure brain structure and activity directly. One neurological test is the *electroencephalogram* (*EEG*), which records *brain waves*, the electrical activity that takes place within the brain as a result of neurons firing. In an EEG, electrodes placed on the scalp send brain-wave impulses to a machine that records them.

Other neurological tests actually take "pictures" of brain structure or brain activity. These tests, called **neuroimaging,** or **brain scanning, techniques,** include *computerized axial tomography* (*CAT scan* or *CT scan*), in which X rays of the brain's structure are taken at different angles and combined; *positron emission tomography* (*PET scan*), a computer-produced motion picture of chemical activity throughout the brain; and *magnetic resonance imaging* (*MRI*), a procedure that uses the magnetic property of certain hydrogen atoms in the brain to create a detailed picture of the brain's structure.

One version of the MRI, *functional magnetic resonance imaging* (*fMRI*), converts MRI pictures of brain structures into detailed pictures of neuron activity, thus offering a picture of the *functioning* brain. Partly because fMRI-produced images of brain functioning are so much clearer than PET scan images, the fMRI has produced enormous enthusiasm among brain researchers since it was first developed in 1990.

Though widely used, these techniques are sometimes unable to detect subtle brain abnormalities. Clinicians have therefore developed less direct but sometimes more revealing **neuropsychological tests** that measure cognitive, perceptual, and motor performances on certain tasks; clinicians interpret abnormal performances as an indicator of underlying brain problems (Hogan, 2014). Brain damage is especially likely to affect visual perception, memory, and visual-motor coordination, so neuropsychological tests focus particularly on these areas. The famous *Bender Visual-Motor Gestalt Test,* for example, consists of nine cards, each displaying a simple geometrical design. Patients look at the designs one at a time and copy each one on a piece of paper. Later they try to redraw the designs from memory. Notable errors in accuracy by individuals older than 12 are thought to reflect organic brain impairment. Clinicians often use a *battery,* or series, of neuropsychological tests, each targeting a specific skill area (Flanagan et al., 2013; Reitan & Wolfson, 2005, 1996).

The EEG Electrodes pasted to the scalp help measure the brain waves of this baby boy.

Intelligence Tests

Intelligence Tests An early definition of intelligence described it as "the capacity to judge well, to reason well, and to comprehend well" (Binet & Simon, 1916, p. 192). Because intelligence is an *inferred* quality rather than a specific physical process, it can be measured only indirectly. In 1905, French psychologist Alfred Binet and his associate Théodore Simon produced an **intelligence test** consisting of a series of tasks requiring people to use various verbal and nonverbal skills. The general score derived from this and later intelligence tests is termed an **intelligence quotient (IQ).** There are now more than 100 intelligence tests available. As you will see in Chapter 14, intelligence tests play a key role in the diagnosis of intellectual disability (mental retardation), and they can also help clinicians identify other problems (Hogan, 2014; Mishak, 2014).

Intelligence tests are among the most carefully produced of all clinical tests (Bowden et al., 2011). Because they have been standardized on large groups of people, clinicians have a good idea how each individual's score compares with the performance of the population at large. These tests have also shown very high reliability: people who repeat the same IQ test years later receive approximately the same score. Finally, the major IQ tests appear to have fairly high validity: children's IQ scores often correlate with their performance in school, for example.

How might IQ scores be misused by school officials, parents, or other individuals? Why is society preoccupied with these scores?

Nevertheless, intelligence tests have some key shortcomings. Factors that have nothing to do with intelligence, such as low motivation or high anxiety, can greatly influence test performance (Chaudhry & Ready, 2012) (see *MediaSpeak* on the next page). In addition, IQ tests may contain cultural biases in their language or tasks that place people of one background at an advantage over those of another (Goldfinger & Pomerantz, 2014). Similarly, members of some minority groups may have little experience with this kind of test, or they may be uncomfortable with test examiners of a majority ethnic background. Either way, their performances may suffer.

Clinical Observations

In addition to interviewing and testing people, clinicians may systematically observe their behavior. In one technique, called *naturalistic observation,* clinicians observe clients in their everyday environments. In another, *analog observation,* they observe them in an artificial setting, such as a clinical office or laboratory. Finally, in *self-monitoring,* clients are instructed to observe themselves.

▶ **neurological test** A test that directly measures brain structure or activity.

▶ **neuroimaging techniques** Neurological tests that provide images of brain structure or activity, such as CT scans, PET scans, and MRIs. Also called *brain scans.*

▶ **neuropsychological test** A test that detects brain impairment by measuring a person's cognitive, perceptual, and motor performances.

▶ **intelligence test** A test designed to measure a person's intellectual ability.

▶ **intelligence quotient (IQ)** An overall score derived from intelligence tests.

MediaSpeak

Intelligence Tests Too? eBay and the Public Good

Michelle Roberts, Associated Press

Intelligence tests . . . are for sale on eBay Inc.'s online auction site, and the test maker is worried they will be misused.

The series of Wechsler intelligence tests, made by San Antonio-based Harcourt Assessment, Inc., are supposed to be sold to and administered by only clinical psychologists and trained professionals.

Given more than a million times a year nationwide, according to Harcourt, the intelligence tests often are among numerous tests ordered by prosecutors and defense attorneys to determine the mental competence of criminal defendants. A low IQ, for example, can be used to argue leniency in sentencing.

Schools use the tests to determine whether to place a student in a special program, whether for gifted or struggling students. Harcourt officials say they fear the tests for sale on eBay will be misused for coaching by lawyers or parents.

But eBay has denied their request to restrict the sale of the tests. eBay officials say there is nothing illegal about selling the tests, and it cannot monitor every possible misuse of items sold through its network of 248 million buyers and sellers. [The tests continue to be available on eBay as of 2015.] Five of the tests were listed for sale . . . for

When free enterprise principles conflict with psychological well-being, how should the matter be resolved?

The Wechsler Adult Intelligence Scale-Revised (WAIS-R) This widely used intelligence test has 11 subtests, which cover such areas as factual information, memory, vocabulary, arithmetic, design, and eye–hand coordination.

about $175 to $900. The latest edition of the adult test, which retails for $939, was offered on eBay for $249.99.

"In order for it to maintain its integrity, there needs to be limited availability," said [a] Harcourt spokesman. . . . "Misinterpreting the results [of questions and tasks on the tests], even without malicious intent, could lead to mistakes in assessing a child's intelligence. . . ."

IQ Tests for Sale on eBay by Michelle Roberts, The Associated Press, 12/18/2007. Used with permission of The Associated Press Copyright © 2014. All rights reserved.

Naturalistic and Analog Observations Naturalistic clinical observations usually take place in homes, schools, institutions such as hospitals and prisons, or community settings. Most of them focus on parent–child, sibling–sibling, or teacher–child interactions and on fearful, aggressive, or disruptive behavior (Hughes et al., 2014; Lindhiem et al., 2011). Often such observations are made by *participant observers*—key people in the client's environment—and reported to the clinician.

When naturalistic observations are not practical, clinicians may resort to analog observations, often aided by special equipment such as a video camera or one-way mirror. Analog observations often have focused on children interacting with their parents, married couples attempting to settle a disagreement, speech-anxious people giving a speech, and fearful people approaching an object they find frightening.

Although much can be learned from actually witnessing behavior, clinical observations have certain disadvantages. For one thing, they are not always reliable. It is possible for various clinicians who observe the same person to focus on different aspects of behavior, assess the person differently, and arrive at different conclusions (Meersand, 2011). Careful training of observers and the use of observer checklists can help reduce this problem.

Similarly, observers may make errors that affect the validity, or accuracy, of their observations (Wilson et al., 2010). The observer may suffer from *overload* and be unable to see or record all of the important behaviors and events. Or the observer may experience *observer drift*, a steady decline in accuracy as a result of fatigue or of a gradual unintentional change in the standards used when an observation continues for a long period of time. Another possible problem is *observer bias*—the observer's judgments may be influenced by information and expectations he or she already has about the person (Hróbjartsson et al., 2014).

A client's *reactivity* may also limit the validity of clinical observations; that is, his or her behavior may be affected by the very presence of the observer (Antal et al., 2015). If schoolchildren are aware that someone special is watching them, for example, they may change their usual classroom behavior, perhaps in the hope of creating a good impression (Lane et al., 2011).

Finally, clinical observations may lack *cross-situational validity*. A child who behaves aggressively in school is not necessarily aggressive at home or with friends after school. Because behavior is often specific to particular situations, observations in one setting cannot always be applied to other settings (Kagan, 2007).

Self-Monitoring As you saw earlier, personality and response inventories are tests in which individuals report their own behaviors, feelings, or cognitions. In a related assessment procedure, *self-monitoring*, people observe themselves and carefully record the frequency of certain behaviors, feelings, or thoughts as they occur over time (Newcomb & Mustanski, 2014; Huh et al., 2013). How frequently, for instance, does a drug user have an urge for drugs or a headache sufferer have a headache? Self-monitoring is especially useful in assessing behavior that occurs so infrequently that it is unlikely to be seen during other kinds of observations. It is also useful for behaviors that occur so frequently that any other method of observing them in detail would be impossible—for example, smoking, drinking, or other drug use. Finally, self-monitoring may be the only way to observe and measure private thoughts or perceptions.

Like all other clinical assessment procedures, however, self-monitoring has drawbacks (Huh et al., 2013). Here too validity is often a problem. People do not always manage or try to record their observations accurately. Furthermore, when people monitor themselves, they may change their behaviors unintentionally. Smokers, for example, often smoke fewer cigarettes than usual when they are monitoring themselves, and teachers give more positive and fewer negative comments to their students.

An ideal observation Using a one-way mirror, a clinical observer is able to view a mother interacting with her child without distracting the duo or influencing their behaviors.

Spencer Grant/PhotoEdit

➤ *Summing Up*

CLINICAL ASSESSMENT Clinical practitioners are interested primarily in gathering individual information about each client. They seek an understanding of the specific nature and origins of a client's problems through clinical assessment.

To be useful, assessment tools must be standardized, reliable, and valid. Most clinical assessment methods fall into three general categories: clinical interviews, tests, and observations. A clinical interview may be either unstructured or structured. Types of clinical tests include projective, personality, response, psychophysiological, neurological, neuropsychological, and intelligence tests. Types of observation include naturalistic observation, analog observation, and self-monitoring.

/////// BETWEEN THE LINES ///////

In Their Words

"You can observe a lot just by watching."

Yogi Berra

▸**diagnosis** A determination that a person's problems reflect a particular disorder.

▸**syndrome** A cluster of symptoms that usually occur together.

▸**classification system** A list of disorders, along with descriptions of symptoms and guidelines for making appropriate diagnoses.

Diagnosis: Does the Client's Syndrome Match a Known Disorder?

Clinicians use the information from interviews, tests, and observations to construct an integrated picture of the factors that are causing and maintaining a client's disturbance, a construction sometimes known as a *clinical picture* (Goldfinger & Pomerantz, 2014). Clinical pictures also may be influenced to a degree by the clinician's theoretical orientation (Garb, 2010, 2006). The psychologist who worked with Franco held a cognitive-behavioral view of abnormality and so produced a picture that emphasized modeling and reinforcement principles and Franco's expectations, assumptions, and interpretations:

Franco's mother had reinforced his feelings of insecurity and his belief that he was unintelligent and inferior. When teachers tried to encourage and push Franco, his mother actually called him "an idiot." Although he was the only one in his family to attend college and did well there, she told him he was too inadequate to succeed in the world. When he received a B in a college algebra course, his mother told him, "You'll never have money." She once told him, "You're just like your father, dumb as a post," and railed against "the dumb men I got stuck with."

As a child Franco had watched his parents argue. Between his mother's self-serving complaints and his father's rants about his backbreaking work to provide for his family, Franco had decided that life would be unpleasant. He believed it was natural for couples to argue and blame each other. Using his parents as models, Franco believed that when he was displeased with a girlfriend—Maria or a prior girlfriend—he should yell at her. At the same time, he was confused that several of his girlfriends had complained about his temper.

He took the termination of his relationship with Maria as proof that he was "stupid." He felt foolish to have broken up with her. He interpreted his behavior and the break-up as proof that he would never be loved and that he would never find happiness. In his mind, all he had to look forward to from here on out was a lifetime of problematic relationships, fights, and getting fired from lesser and lesser jobs. This hopelessness fed his feelings of depression and also made it hard for him to try to make himself feel better.

With the assessment data and clinical picture in hand, clinicians are ready to make a **diagnosis**—that is, a determination that a person's psychological problems constitute a particular disorder. When clinicians decide, through diagnosis, that a client's pattern of dysfunction reflects a particular disorder, they are saying that the pattern is basically the same as one that has been displayed by many other people, has been investigated in a variety of studies, and perhaps has responded to particular forms of treatment. They can then apply what is generally known about the disorder to the particular individual they are trying to help. They can, for example, better predict the future course of the person's problem and the treatments that are likely to be helpful.

Classification Systems

The principle behind diagnosis is straightforward. When certain symptoms occur together regularly— a cluster of symptoms is called a **syndrome**—and follow a particular course, clinicians agree that those symptoms make up a particular mental disorder (see Table 3-2). If people display this particular pattern of symptoms,

> **Why do you think many clinicians prefer the label "person with schizophrenia" over "schizophrenic person"?**

///// BETWEEN THE LINES /////

What Is a Nervous Breakdown?

The term "nervous breakdown" is used by laypersons, not clinicians. Most people use it to refer to a *sudden* psychological disturbance that incapacitates a person, perhaps requiring hospitalization (Hall-Flavin, 2011; Padwa, 1996).

diagnosticians assign them to that diagnostic category. A list of such categories, or disorders, with descriptions of the symptoms and guidelines for assigning individuals to the categories, is known as a **classification system.**

In 1883, Emil Kraepelin developed the first modern classification system for abnormal behavior (see Chapter 1). His categories formed the foundation for the *Diagnostic and Statistical Manual of Mental Disorders (DSM),* the classification system currently written by the American Psychiatric Association (APA, 2013). The DSM is the most widely used classification system in North America. Most other countries rely primarily on a system called the *International Classification of Diseases (ICD),* developed by the World Health Organization, which lists both medical and psychological disorders.

The content of the DSM has been changed significantly over time. The current edition, called *DSM-5,* was published in 2013. It features a number of changes from the previous edition, DSM-IV-TR, and the editions prior to that.

DSM-5

DSM-5 lists more than 500 mental disorders (see Figure 3-3). Each entry describes the criteria for diagnosing the disorder and the key clinical features of the disorder. The system also describes features that are often but not always related to the disorder. The classification system is further accompanied by background information such as research findings; age, culture, or gender trends; and each disorder's prevalence, risk, course, complications, predisposing factors, and family patterns.

DSM-5 requires clinicians to provide both categorical and dimensional information as part of a proper diagnosis. *Categorical information* refers to the name of the particular category (disorder) indicated by the client's symptoms. *Dimensional information* is a rating of how severe a client's symptoms are and how dysfunctional the client is across various dimensions of personality.

Categorical Information First, the clinician must decide whether the person is displaying one of the hundreds of psychological disorders listed in the manual. Some of the most frequently diagnosed disorders are the anxiety disorders and depressive disorders.

ANXIETY DISORDERS People with anxiety disorders may experience general feelings of anxiety and worry (*generalized anxiety disorder*); fears of specific situations, objects, or activities (*phobias*); anxiety about social situations (*social anxiety disorder*); repeated outbreaks of panic (*panic disorder*); or anxiety about being separated from one's parents or other key individuals (*separation anxiety disorder*).

DEPRESSIVE DISORDERS People with depressive disorders may experience an episode of extreme sadness and related symptoms (*major depressive disorder*), persistent and chronic sadness (*persistent depressive disorder*), or severe premenstrual sadness and related symptoms (*premenstrual dysphoric disorder*).

Although people may receive just one diagnosis from the DSM-5 list, they often receive more than one. Franco would likely receive

table: **3-2**

Mental Health Awareness Dates	
January	Mental Wellness Month
March	Developmental Disabilities Awareness Month
	National Self-Injury Awareness Month
April	Alcohol Awareness Month
	National Autism Awareness Month
	National Stress Awareness Month
May	Children's Mental Health Awareness Week
	National Anxiety and Depression Awareness Week
	Schizophrenia Awareness Week
June	Panic Awareness Day (June 17)
	Posttraumatic Stress Disorder Awareness Day (June 27)
September	World Suicide Prevention Day (September 10)
October	National Depression Awareness Month
	World Mental Health Day (October 10)
	National Bipolar Awareness Day (October 10)
	OCD Awareness Week
	ADHD Awareness Month
November	National Alzheimer's Disease Awareness Month

Information from: *Disabled World,* 2014.

figure 3-3

How many people in the United States qualify for a DSM diagnosis during their lives? Almost half, according to some surveys. Some people even experience two or more different disorders, which is known as comorbidity. (Information from: Greenberg, 2011; Kessler et al., 2005.)

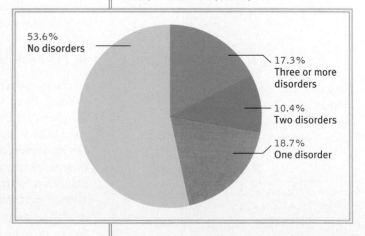

53.6% No disorders

17.3% Three or more disorders

10.4% Two disorders

18.7% One disorder

"Am I a happy man or just an asymptomatic one?"

a diagnosis of *major depressive disorder.* In addition, let's suppose the clinician judged that Franco's worries about his teachers' opinions of him and his later concerns that supervisors at work would discover his inadequate skills were really but two examples of a much broader, persistent pattern of excessive worry, concern, and avoidance. He might then receive an additional diagnosis of *generalized anxiety disorder.* Alternatively, if Franco's anxiety symptoms did not rise to the level of generalized anxiety disorder, his diagnosis of major depressive disorder might simply specify that he is experiencing some features of anxiety (*major depressive disorder with anxious distress*).

Dimensional Information In addition to deciding what disorder a client is displaying, diagnosticians assess the current severity of the client's disorder—that is, how much the symptoms impair the client. For each disorder, the framers of DSM-5 have suggested various rating scales that may prove useful for evaluating the severity of the particular disorder (APA, 2013). In cases of major depressive disorder, for example, two scales are suggested by DSM-5: the *Cross-Cutting Symptom Measure* and the *Emotional Distress–Depression Scale.* The former scale indicates the current frequency of general negative feelings and behaviors (for example, "I do not know what I want out of life"), and the latter indicates the frequency of depression-specific feelings and behaviors (for example, "I feel worthless"). Using scores from these scales, the diagnostician then rates the client's depression as "mild," moderate," or "severe." Based on his clinical interview, tests, and observations, Franco might warrant a rating of *moderate* depression from his therapist. DSM-5 is the first edition of the DSM to consistently seek both categorical and dimensional information as equally important parts of the diagnosis, rather than categorical information alone.

Additional Information Clinicians also may include other useful information when making a diagnosis. They may, for example, indicate special psychosocial problems the client has. Franco's recent breakup with his girlfriend might be noted as *relationship distress.* Altogether, Franco might receive the following diagnosis:

> **Diagnosis: Major depressive disorder with anxious distress**
> *Severity:* Moderate
> *Additional information:* Relationship distress

Each diagnostic category also has a numerical code that clinicians must state—a code listed in ICD-10, the current edition of the international classification system mentioned earlier. Thus if Franco were assigned the DSM-5 diagnosis indicated above, his clinician would also state a numerical code of *F32.1*—the code corresponding to *major depressive disorder, moderate severity.*

Is DSM-5 an Effective Classification System?

A classification system, like an assessment method, is judged by its reliability and validity. Here *reliability* means that different clinicians are likely to agree on the diagnosis when they use the system to diagnose the same client. Early versions of the DSM were at best moderately reliable (Regier et al., 2011). In the early 1960s, for example, four clinicians, each relying on DSM-I, the first edition of the DSM, independently interviewed 153 patients (Beck et al., 1962). Only 54 percent of their diagnoses were in agreement. Because all four clinicians were experienced diagnosticians, their failure to agree suggested deficiencies in the classification system.

The framers of DSM-5 followed certain procedures in their development of the new manual to help ensure that DSM-5 would have greater reliability than

BETWEEN THE LINES

By the Numbers

1 Number of categories of psychological dysfunctioning listed in the 1840 U.S. census ("idiocy/insanity")

60 Number of categories listed in DSM-I in 1952

541 Number of categories listed in DSM-5

the previous DSMs (APA, 2013). For example, they conducted extensive reviews of research to pinpoint which categories in past DSMs had been too vague and unreliable. In addition, they gathered input from a wide range of experienced clinicians and researchers. They then developed a number of new diagnostic criteria and categories, expecting that the new criteria and categories were in fact reliable. Despite such efforts, some critics continue to have concerns about the procedures used in the development of DSM-5 (Wakefield, 2015; Brown et al., 2014; Frances, 2013). They worry, for example, that the framers failed to run a sufficient number of their own studies—in particular, *field studies* that test the merits of the new criteria and categories. In turn, the critics fear that DSM-5 may have retained several of the reliability problems that were on display in the past DSMs.

The *validity* of a classification system is the accuracy of the information that its diagnostic categories provide. Categories are of most use to clinicians when they demonstrate *predictive validity*—that is, when they help predict future symptoms or events. A common symptom of major depressive disorder is either insomnia or excessive sleep. When clinicians give Franco a diagnosis of major depressive disorder, they expect that he may eventually develop sleep problems even if none are present now. In addition, they expect him to respond to treatments that are effective for other depressed persons. The more often such predictions are accurate, the greater a category's predictive validity.

DSM-5's framers tried to also ensure the validity of this new edition by conducting extensive reviews of research and consulting with numerous clinical advisors. As a result, its criteria and categories may have stronger validity than those of the earlier versions of the DSM. But, again, many clinical theorists worry that at least some of the criteria and categories in DSM-5 are based on weak research and that others may reflect gender or racial bias (Koukopoulos & Sani, 2014; Rhebergen & Graham, 2014). In fact, one important organization, the National Institute of Mental Health (NIMH), has already concluded that the validity of DSM-5 is sorely lacking and is acting accordingly (Insel & Lieberman, 2013; Lane, 2013). The world's largest funding agency for mental health research, NIMH has announced that it will no longer give financial support to clinical studies that rely exclusively on DSM-5 criteria.

Wave of criticism Although researchers are still conducting studies to sort out the merits and problems of DSM-5, many clinical theorists have already voiced criticism regarding its new categories, diagnostic criteria, and possible validity problems. Two outspoken and respected critics, clinicians Gary Greenberg and Allen Frances, have written the books *The Book of Woe* and *Saving Normal*.

Call for Change

The effort to produce DSM-5 took more than a decade. After years of preliminary work, a DSM-5 task force and numerous work groups were formed in 2006, seeking to develop a DSM that addressed the limitations of previous DSM editions. Finally, in 2013, DSM-5, the new diagnostic and classification system, was published. The categories and criteria of DSM-5 are featured throughout this textbook (APA, 2013).

Some of the key changes in DSM-5 are the following:

➤ Adding a new category, "autism spectrum disorder," that combines certain past categories such as "autistic disorder" and "Asperger's syndrome" (see Chapter 14).

➤ Viewing "obsessive-compulsive disorder" as a problem that is different from the anxiety disorders and grouping it instead along with other obsessive-compulsive-like disorders such as "hoarding disorder," "body dysmorphic disorder," "trichotillomania" (hair-pulling disorder), and "excoriation (skin-picking) disorder" (see Chapter 4).

➤ Viewing "posttraumatic stress disorder" as a problem that is distinct from the anxiety disorders (see Chapter 5).

New Pop Psychology Labels

- **"Online disinhibition effect"** The tendency of people to show less restraint when on the Internet (Sitt, 2013; Suler, 2004).

- **"Drunkorexia"** A diet fad, particularly among young women, in which the individual restricts food intake during the day so that she can party and get drunk at night without gaining weight from the alcohol (Archer, 2013).

➤ Adding new categories, "disruptive mood dysregulation disorder," "persistent depressive disorder," and "premenstrual dysphoric disorder," and grouping them with other kinds of depressive disorders (see Chapter 6).

➤ Adding a new category, "somatic symptom disorder" (see Chapter 8).

➤ Replacing the term "hypochondriasis" with the new term "illness anxiety disorder" (see Chapter 8).

➤ Adding a new category, "binge eating disorder" (see Chapter 9).

➤ Adding a new category, "substance use disorder," that combines past categories "substance abuse" and "substance dependence" (see Chapter 10).

➤ Viewing "gambling disorder" as a problem that should be grouped as an addictive disorder alongside the substance use disorders (see Chapter 10).

➤ Replacing the term "gender identity disorder" with the new term "gender dysphoria" (see Chapter 11).

➤ Replacing the term "mental retardation" with the new term "intellectual disability" (see Chapter 14).

➤ Adding a new category, "specific learning disorder," that combines past categories "reading disorder," "mathematics disorder," and "disorder of written expression" (see Chapter 14).

➤ Replacing the term "dementia" with the new term "neurocognitive disorder" (see Chapter 15).

➤ Adding a new category, "mild neurocognitive disorder" (see Chapter 15).

Can Diagnosis and Labeling Cause Harm?

Even with trustworthy assessment data and reliable and valid classification categories, clinicians will sometimes arrive at a wrong conclusion (Faust & Ahern, 2012; Trull & Prinstein, 2012). Like all human beings, they are flawed information processors. Studies show that they may be overly influenced by information gathered early in the assessment process. In addition, they may pay too much attention to certain sources of information, such as a parent's report about a child, and too little to others, such as the child's point of view. Finally, their judgments can be distorted by any number of personal biases—gender, age, race, and socioeconomic status, to

The power of labeling When looking at this late-nineteenth-century photograph of a baseball team at the State Homeopathic Asylum for the Insane in Middletown, New York, most observers assume that the players are patients. As a result, they tend to "see" depression or confusion in the players' faces and posture. In fact, the players are members of the asylum staff, some of whom even sought their jobs for the express purpose of playing for the hospital team.

Elizabeth Eckert, Middletown, NY. Courtesy Tracy DeMichiel

name just a few. Given the limitations of assessment tools, assessors, and classification systems, it is small wonder that studies sometimes uncover shocking errors in diagnosis, especially in hospitals (Mitchell, 2010; Vickrey et al., 2010).

> **Why are medical diagnoses usually valued, while the use of psychological diagnoses is often criticized?**

Beyond the potential for misdiagnosis, the very act of classifying people can lead to unintended results. As you read in Chapter 2, for example, many family-social theorists believe that diagnostic labels can become self-fulfilling prophecies. When people are diagnosed as mentally disturbed, they may be perceived and reacted to correspondingly. If others expect them to take on a sick role, they may begin to consider themselves sick as well and act that way. Furthermore, our society attaches a stigma to abnormality (Hansson et al., 2014). People labeled mentally ill may find it difficult to get a job, especially a position of responsibility, or to be welcomed into social relationships. Once a label has been applied, it may stick for a long time.

Because of these problems, some clinicians would like to do away with diagnoses. Others disagree. They believe we must simply work to increase what is known about psychological disorders and improve diagnostic techniques. They hold that classification and diagnosis are critical to understanding and treating people in distress.

➤ *Summing Up*

DIAGNOSIS After collecting assessment information, clinicians form a clinical picture and decide upon a diagnosis. The diagnosis is chosen from a classification system. The system used most widely in North America is the *Diagnostic and Statistical Manual of Mental Disorders* (DSM). The most recent version of the DSM, known as DSM-5, lists more than 500 disorders. DSM-5 contains numerous additions and changes to the diagnostic categories, criteria, and organization found in past editions of the DSM. The reliability and validity of this revised diagnostic and classification system are currently receiving clinical review and, in some circles, criticism.

Even with trustworthy assessment data and reliable and valid classification categories, clinicians will not always arrive at the correct conclusion. They are human and so fall prey to various biases, misconceptions, and expectations. Another problem related to diagnosis is the prejudice that labels arouse, which may be damaging to the person who is diagnosed.

Treatment: How Might the Client Be Helped?

Over the course of 10 months, Franco was treated for depression and related symptoms. He improved considerably during that time, as the following report describes:

> *During therapy, Franco's debilitating depression relented. Increasingly, he came to appreciate that his mother's accusations against him—and his self-accusations—were not accurate. He also started to consider the possibility that Maria's reluctance to commit to him had been more about where she was in her life than a sign that he was a terrible or inadequate person. Eventually, Maria and Franco talked again, although they did not renew their relationship. Franco felt better realizing that she did not hate him. She even told him that her mother had said some kind things about him after their breakup.*

(continues on the next page)

▶ **empirically supported treatment**
Therapy that has received clear research support for a particular disorder and has corresponding treatment guidelines. Also known as *evidence-based treatment*.

Franco also managed to straighten out his problems at work. He explained his recent difficulties to his immediate supervisor at the bank and committed himself to improving his recent performance. His supervisor, with whom he had been friendly before his recent struggles, said she was glad that he was communicating openly and emphasized that he would be given the opportunity to improve his performance. He was surprised to hear how highly he had been regarded over the years, although as she put it, "Why would you have been promoted otherwise?"

Over the course of therapy, Franco also forced himself to spend more time having fun with his friends. He found his mood on the upswing as a result of these reestablished relationships. In addition, he began dating a woman he met through Jesse. He often considered the lessons he learned in treatment, trying to handle this new relationship in ways different from the destructive patterns of his past.

Clearly, treatment helped Franco, and by its conclusion he was a happier, more functional person than the man who had first sought help 10 months earlier. But how did his therapist decide on the treatment program that proved to be so helpful?

Treatment Decisions

Franco's therapist began, like all therapists, with assessment information and diagnostic decisions. Knowing the specific details and background of Franco's problem (*idiographic data*) and combining this individual information with broad information about the nature and treatment of depression, the clinician arrived at a treatment plan for him.

Yet therapists may be influenced by additional factors when they make treatment decisions. Their treatment plans typically reflect their theoretical orientations and how they have learned to conduct therapy (Sharf, 2015). As therapists apply a favored model in case after case, they become more and more familiar with its principles and treatment techniques and tend to use them in work with still other clients.

Current research may also play a role. Most clinicians say that they value research as a guide to practice (Beutler et al., 1995). However, not all of them actually read research articles, so they cannot be directly influenced by them (Rivett, 2011; Stewart & Chambless, 2007). In fact, according to surveys, therapists gather much of their information about the latest developments in the field from colleagues, professional newsletters, workshops, conferences, Web sites, books, and the like (Simon, 2011; Corrie & Callanan, 2001). Unfortunately, the accuracy and usefulness of these sources vary widely.

To help clinicians become more familiar with and apply research findings, there is an ever-growing movement in North America, the United Kingdom, and elsewhere toward **empirically supported,** or **evidence-based, treatment** (Holt et al., 2015; Pope & Wedding, 2014). Proponents of this movement have formed task forces that seek to identify which therapies have received clear research support for each disorder, to propose corresponding treatment guidelines, and to spread such information to clinicians. Critics of the movement worry that such efforts have thus far been simplistic, biased, and at times misleading (Jager & Leek, 2013; Nairn, 2012). However, the empirically supported treatment movement has been gaining considerable momentum over the past decade.

The Effectiveness of Treatment

Altogether, more than 400 forms of therapy are currently practiced in the clinical field (Wedding & Corsini, 2014). Naturally, the most important question to ask about each of them is whether it does what it is supposed to do. Does a particular treatment really help people overcome their psychological problems? On the surface, the question may seem simple. In fact, it is one of the most difficult questions for clinical researchers to answer.

////// BETWEEN THE LINES //////

Famous Movie Clinicians

Dr. Benjamin (*Still Alice, 2014*)

Dr. Banks (*Side Effects, 2013*)

Dr. Patel (*Silver Linings Playbook, 2012*)

Dr. Cawley (*Shutter Island, 2010*)

Dr. Steele (*Changeling, 2008*)

Dr. Rosen (*A Beautiful Mind, 2001*)

Dr. Crowe (*The Sixth Sense, 1999*)

Dr. Maguire (*Good Will Hunting, 1997*)

Dr. Lecter (*The Silence of the Lambs, 1991*)

Dr. Marvin (*What About Bob?, 1991*)

Dr. Sayer (*Awakenings, 1990*)

Dr. Sobel (*Analyze This, 1999*)

Dr. Berger (*Ordinary People, 1980*)

Dr. Dysart (*Equus, 1977*)

Nurse Ratched (*One Flew Over the Cuckoo's Nest, 1975*)

The first problem is how to *define* "success." If, as Franco's therapist implies, he still has much progress to make at the conclusion of therapy, should his recovery be considered successful? The second problem is how to *measure* improvement (Hunsley & Lee, 2014; Lambert, 2010). Should researchers give equal weight to the reports of clients, friends, relatives, therapists, and teachers? Should they use rating scales, inventories, therapy insights, observations, or some other measure?

Perhaps the biggest problem in determining the effectiveness of treatment is the *variety* and *complexity* of the treatments currently in use. People differ in their problems, personal styles, and motivations for therapy. Therapists differ in skill, experience, orientation, and personality. And therapies differ in theory, format, and setting. Because an individual's progress is influenced by all these factors and more, the findings of a particular study will not always apply to other clients and therapists.

Proper research procedures address some of these problems. By using control groups, random assignment, matched research participants, and the like, clinicians can draw certain conclusions about various therapies. Even in studies that are well designed, however, the variety and complexity of treatment limit the conclusions that can be reached (Kazdin, 2015, 2013, 2006).

Despite these difficulties, the job of evaluating therapies must be done, and clinical researchers have plowed ahead with it. Investigators have, in fact, conducted thousands of *therapy outcome studies,* studies that measure the effects of various treatments. The studies typically ask one of three questions: (1) Is therapy *in general* effective? (2) Are *particular* therapies generally effective? (3) Are *particular* therapies effective for *particular* problems?

"Batman is getting more press than me."

Is Therapy Generally Effective? Studies suggest that therapy often is more helpful than no treatment or than placebos. A pioneering review examined 375 controlled studies, covering a total of almost 25,000 people seen in a wide assortment of therapies (Smith, Glass, & Miller, 1980; Smith & Glass, 1977). The reviewers combined the findings of these studies by using a special statistical technique called *meta-analysis.* According to this analysis, the average person who received treatment was better off than 75 percent of the untreated persons (see Figure 3-4). Other meta-analyses have found similar relationships between treatment and improvement (Sharf, 2015).

Some clinicians have concerned themselves with an important related question: Can therapy be harmful? A number of studies suggest that 5 to 10 percent of patients actually seem to get worse because of therapy (Lambert, 2010). Their symptoms may become more intense, or they may develop new ones, such as a sense of failure, guilt, reduced self-concept, or hopelessness, because of their inability to profit from therapy (Lambert, 2010; Lambert et al., 1986).

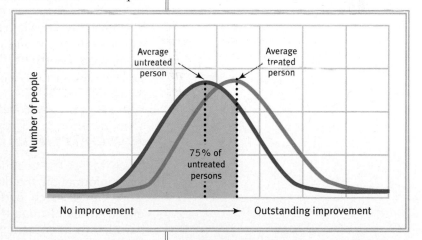

figure 3-4
Does therapy help? Combining participants and results from hundreds of studies, investigators have determined that the average person who receives psychotherapy improves more than do 75 percent of all untreated people with similar problems. (Information from: Prochaska & Norcross, 2013; Lambert et al., 1993; Smith et al., 1980.)

Are Particular Therapies Generally Effective? The studies you have read about so far have lumped all therapies together to consider their general effectiveness. Many researchers, however, consider it wrong to treat all therapies alike. Some critics suggest that these studies are operating under a *uniformity myth*—a false belief that all therapies are equivalent despite differences in the therapists' training, experience, theoretical orientations, and personalities (Good & Brooks, 2005; Kiesler, 1995, 1966).

▶ **rapprochement movement**
A movement to identify a set of common factors, or common strategies, that run through all successful therapies.

▶ **psychopharmacologist** A psychiatrist who primarily prescribes medications.

Thus, an alternative approach examines the effectiveness of *particular* therapies. Most research of this kind shows each of the major forms of therapy to be superior to no treatment or to placebo treatment (Prochaska & Norcross, 2013). A number of other studies have compared particular therapies with one another and found that no one form of therapy generally stands out over all others (Luborsky et al., 2006, 2002, 1975).

If different kinds of therapy have similar successes, might they have something in common? People in the **rapprochement movement** have tried to identify a set of *common factors,* or *common strategies,* that may run through all effective therapies, regardless of the clinicians' particular orientations (Sharf, 2015) (see *InfoCentral* on the next page). Surveys of highly successful therapists suggest, for example, that most give feedback to clients, help clients focus on their own thoughts and behavior, pay attention to the way they and their clients are interacting, and try to promote self-mastery in their clients. In short, effective therapists of any type may practice more similarly than they preach.

Are Particular Therapies Effective for Particular Problems?

People with different disorders may respond differently to the various forms of therapy (Norcross & Beutler, 2014; Beutler, 2011). In an oft-quoted statement, influential clinical theorist Gordon Paul said decades ago that the most appropriate question regarding the effectiveness of therapy may be "*What* specific treatment, by *whom,* is most effective for *this* individual with *that* specific problem, and under *which* set of circumstances?" (Paul, 1967, p. 111). Researchers have investigated how effective particular therapies are at treating particular disorders, and they often have found sizable differences among the various therapies. Behavioral therapies, for example, appear to be the most effective of all in treating phobias (Antony, 2014), whereas drug therapy is the single most effective treatment for schizophrenia (Minzenberg et al., 2011).

As you read previously, studies also show that some clinical problems may respond better to *combined* approaches (Norcross & Beutler, 2014; Valencia et al., 2013). Drug therapy is sometimes combined with certain forms of psychotherapy, for example, to treat depression. In fact, it is now common for clients to be seen by two therapists—one of them a **psychopharmacologist,** a psychiatrist who primarily prescribes medications, and the other a psychologist, social worker, or other therapist who conducts psychotherapy.

Obviously, knowledge of how particular therapies fare with particular disorders can help therapists and clients alike make better decisions about treatment (Holt et al., 2015; Beutler, 2011, 2002, 2000). We will keep returning to this issue as we examine the various disorders throughout the book.

➤ SUMMING UP

TREATMENT The treatment decisions of therapists may be influenced by assessment information, the diagnosis, the clinician's theoretical orientation and familiarity with research, and the state of knowledge in the field. Determining the effectiveness of treatment is difficult. Nevertheless, therapy outcome studies have led to three general conclusions: (1) people in therapy are usually better off than people with similar problems who receive no treatment; (2) the various therapies do not appear to differ dramatically in their general effectiveness; and (3) certain therapies or combinations of therapies do appear to be more effective than others for certain disorders. Some therapists currently advocate empirically supported treatment—the active identification, promotion, and teaching of those interventions that have received clear research support.

COMMON FACTORS IN THERAPY

The **evidence-based treatment** approach identifies the "specific therapies and techniques" that are most helpful for a particular disorder. In contrast, the **common factors treatment** approach contends that successful therapies share common components that greatly influence the outcome of therapy. Both likely contribute to the success of treatment (Hofman & Barlow, 2014; Weinberger, 2014; Laska et al., 2013).

What Factors Contribute to Therapy Outcomes?

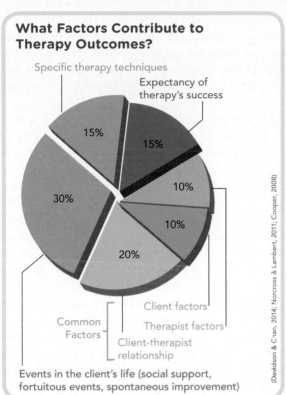

Specific therapy techniques — 15%
Expectancy of therapy's success — 15%
10%
30%
10%
20%

Common Factors
Client factors
Therapist factors
Client-therapist relationship

Events in the client's life (social support, fortuitous events, spontaneous improvement)

(Davidson & Chan, 2014; Norcross & Lambert, 2011; Cooper, 2008)

Evidence-Based Treatments: High Batting Averages

According to numerous studies, just about all of today's leading treatments are highly effective for at least one psychological disorder.

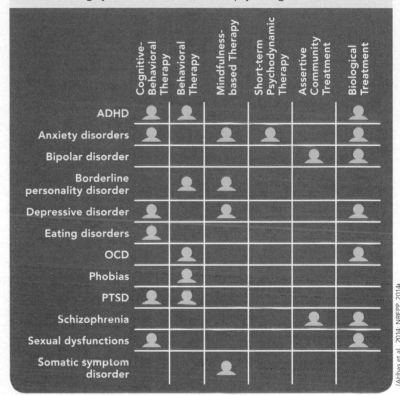

	Cognitive-Behavioral Therapy	Behavioral Therapy	Mindfulness-based Therapy	Short-term Psychodynamic Therapy	Assertive Community Treatment	Biological Treatment
ADHD	👤	👤				👤
Anxiety disorders	👤		👤	👤		👤
Bipolar disorder					👤	👤
Borderline personality disorder		👤	👤			
Depressive disorder	👤		👤			👤
Eating disorders	👤					
OCD		👤				👤
Phobias		👤				
PTSD	👤	👤				
Schizophrenia					👤	👤
Sexual dysfunctions	👤					👤
Somatic symptom disorder			👤			

(Abbas et al., 2014; NREPP, 2014)

Common Factors

There are three kinds of common factors that help contribute to a positive treatment outcome: client factors, therapist factors, and client-therapist relationship.

Client Factors:

Strongly related to positive outcome
High motivation
High involvement

Moderately related to positive outcome
Positive attitude
Accurate expectation of what therapy will be like
Comfortable in close relationships
Good interpersonal skills
Nonperfectionism
Openness

Client-Therapist Relationship:

Strongly related to positive outcome
Agreement on goals
Collaboration
Therapist empathizes with client
Therapist offers accurate interpretations

Moderately related to positive outcome
Therapist is positive, warm, and accepting toward client
Therapist listens to, guides, and advises client
Therapist gives mostly positive feedback to client
Therapist manages own feelings toward client

Modestly related to positive outcome
Therapist is genuine
Therapist discloses information about self
Therapist interprets relationship (a little bit)

Therapist Factors:

Moderately related to positive outcome
Sense of well-being
Training and experience
Supervision during treatment
Confidence about course of therapy

Despite conventional wisdom, research does not indicate that the following factors affect the outcome of therapy: the client's gender, age, sexual orientation, or income; and the therapist's gender, age, specific personality traits, or personal background.

(Davidson & Chan, 2014; Norcross, 2011; Cooper, 2008)

What kind of empathy do clients want from their therapist?

Appreciates how I feel — 30%
Shares personal information with me — 18%
8%
44%
Is nurturing
Appreciates how I think

(Duncan et al., 2010; Bachelor, 1988)

What do clients say is most important when choosing a therapist?

52% — Common factors
16% — Specific evidence-based techniques
32% — No preference

(Swan & Heesacker, 2013)

Raising public awareness Believing that more public awareness about psychological disorders will lead to better assessment and treatment, the Gadsden Museum of Art in Gadsden, Alabama, sponsored an exhibit called "Heads Up Alabama! Psychology Promotes Healthy Living." Artists designed 20 heads, including these two, to bring attention to psychological issues faced by children and adults.

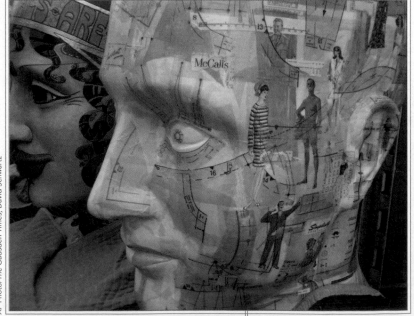

AP Photo/*The Gadsden Times*, David Schwartz

PUTTING IT...*together*

Assessment and Diagnosis at a Crossroads

In Chapter 2 you read that today's leading models of abnormal behavior often differ widely in their assumptions, conclusions, and treatments. It should not surprise you, then, that clinicians also differ considerably in their approaches to assessment and diagnosis. Yet when all is said and done, no single assessment technique stands out as superior to the rest. Each of the hundreds of available tools has major limitations, and each produces at best an incomplete picture of how a person is functioning and why.

In short, the present state of assessment and diagnosis argues against relying exclusively on any one approach. That is why the majority of today's clinicians use *batteries* of assessment tools in their work. Some of these batteries provide invaluable information and guidance, as in the assessment of Alzheimer's disease and certain other disorders that are particularly difficult to diagnose, as you shall see later in the book.

Attitudes toward clinical assessment have shifted back and forth over the past several decades. Before the 1950s, assessment was a highly regarded part of clinical practice. As the number of clinical models grew during the 1960s and 1970s, however, followers of each model favored certain tools over others, and the practice of assessment became fragmented. Meanwhile, research began to reveal that a number of tools were inaccurate or inconsistent. In this atmosphere, many clinicians lost confidence in and abandoned systematic assessment and diagnosis.

Today, however, respect for assessment and diagnosis is on the rise once again. One reason for this renewal of interest is the development of more precise diagnostic criteria. Another is the drive by researchers for more rigorous tests to help them select appropriate participants for clinical studies. Still another factor is the awareness in the clinical field that certain disorders can be properly identified only after careful assessment procedures. A final factor is the growing confidence in the field that brain-scanning techniques may soon offer assessment information about a wide range of psychological disorders.

Along with heightened respect for assessment and diagnosis has come increased research. Indeed, today's researchers are carefully examining every major kind of assessment tool—from projective tests to personality inventories to scanning procedures. This work is helping many clinicians perform their work with more accuracy and consistency—welcome news for people with psychological problems.

Ironically, just as today's clinicians and researchers are rediscovering systematic assessment, rising costs and economic factors may be conspiring to discourage the use of assessment tools. As you read in Chapter 1, insurance parity and treatment coverage for people with psychological problems are expected to improve as a result of recent federal parity laws and the Affordable Care Act (see pages 17–18). However, many experts fear that clinical testing procedures will continue to receive only limited insurance support. Which forces will ultimately have a stronger influence on clinical assessment and diagnosis—promising research or economic pressure? Only time will tell.

Finally, the practice of assessment and diagnosis of psychological disorders is expected to be affected tremendously by the use of DSM-5. Will this new edition of the classification system prove to be an improvement over past systems? Will it be embraced by more clinicians? Will it unite or divide the clinical field? What impact will DSM-5 have on the use of assessment procedures? The answers to these important questions should emerge soon, as current studies reach fruition and lead to journal publications. Clearly, the practice of clinical assessment and diagnosis is currently at a crossroads.

KEY TERMS

idiographic understanding, p. 77
assessment, p. 77
standardization, p. 78
reliability, p. 78
validity, p. 78
clinical interview, p. 79
mental status exam, p. 80
clinical test, p. 81
projective test, p. 81
Rorschach test, p. 82
Thematic Apperception Test (TAT), p. 82
personality inventory, p. 84
Minnesota Multiphasic Personality
    Inventory (MMPI), p. 84

response inventories, p. 86
psychophysiological test, p. 86
neurological test, p. 88
EEG, p. 88
neuroimaging techniques, p. 88
CAT scan, p. 88
PET scan, p. 88
MRI, p. 88
fMRI, p. 88
neuropsychological test, p. 88
battery, p. 89
intelligence test, p. 89
intelligence quotient (IQ), p. 89
naturalistic observation, p. 89

analog observation, p. 89
self-monitoring, p. 89
diagnosis, p. 92
syndrome, p. 92
classification system, p. 93
DSM-5, p. 93
categorical information, p. 93
dimensional information, p. 94
empirically supported
    treatment, p. 98
therapy outcome study, p. 99
rapprochement movement, p. 100
common factors, p. 100
psychopharmacologist, p. 100

QuickQuiz

1. What forms of reliability and validity should clinical assessment tools display? *pp. 78–79*

2. What are the strengths and weaknesses of structured and unstructured interviews? *pp. 80–81*

3. List and describe today's leading projective tests. *pp. 82–83*

4. What are the key features of the MMPI? *pp. 84–85*

5. What are the strengths and weaknesses of projective tests (*p. 84*), personality inventories (*pp. 85–86*), and other kinds of clinical tests (*pp. 86–89*)?

6. How do clinicians determine whether psychological problems are linked to brain damage? *pp. 88–89*

7. Describe the ways in which clinicians may make observations of clients' behaviors. *pp. 89–91*

8. What is the purpose of clinical diagnoses? *p. 92*

9. Describe DSM-5. What problems may accompany the use of classification systems and the process of clinical diagnosis? *pp. 93–95, 96–97*

10. According to therapy outcome studies, how effective is therapy? *pp. 99–100*

Visit *LaunchPad*

www.macmillanhighered.com/launchpad/comerfund8e
to access the e-book, new interactive case studies, videos, activities, and LearningCurve quizzes, as well as study aids including flashcards, FAQs, and research exercises.

Anxiety, Obsessive-Compulsive, and Related Disorders

Tomas, a 25-year-old Web designer, was afraid that he was "losing his mind." He had always been a worrier. He worried about his health, his girlfriend, his work, his social life, his future, his finances, and so on. Would his best friend get angry at him? Was his girlfriend tiring of him? Was he investing his money wisely? Were his clients pleased with his work? But, lately, those worries had increased to an unbearable level. He was becoming consumed with the notion that something terrible was about to happen to him. Within an hour's time, he might have intense concerns about going broke, developing cancer, losing one of his parents, offending his friends, and more. He was certain that disaster awaited him at every turn. No amount of reassurance, from himself or from others, brought relief for very long.

He started therapy with Dr. Adena Morven, a clinical psychologist. Dr. Morven immediately noticed how disturbed Tomas appeared. He looked tense and frightened and could not sit comfortably in his chair; he kept tapping his feet and jumped when he heard traffic noise from outside the office building. He kept sighing throughout the visit, fidgeting and shifting his position, and he appeared breathless while telling Dr. Morven about his difficulties.

Tomas described his frequent inability to concentrate to the therapist. When designing client Web sites, he would lose his train of thought. Less than 5 minutes into a project, he'd forget much of his overall strategy. During conversations, he would begin a sentence and then forget the point he was about to make. TV watching had become impossible. He found it almost impossible to concentrate on anything for more than 5 minutes; his mind kept drifting away from the task at hand.

To say the least, he was worried about all of this. "I'm worried about being so worried," he told Dr. Morven, almost laughing at his own remark. At this point, Tomas expected the worst whenever he began a conversation, task, plan, or outing. If an event or interaction did in fact start to go awry, he would find himself overwhelmed with uncomfortable feelings—his heart would beat faster, his breathing would increase, and he'd sweat profusely. On some occasions, he thought he was actually having a heart attack—at the ripe old age of 25.

Typically, such physical reactions lasted but a matter of seconds. However, those few seconds felt like an eternity to Tomas. He acknowledged coming back down to earth after those feelings subsided—but, for him, "back down to earth" meant back to worrying and then worrying some more.

Dr. Morven empathized with Tomas about how upsetting this all must be. She asked him why he had decided to come into therapy now—as opposed to last year, last month, or last week. Tomas was able to pinpoint several things. First, all the worrying and anxiety seemed to be on the increase. Second, he was finding it hard to sleep. His nights were filled by tossing and turning—and, of course, more worrying. Third, he suspected that all of his worrying, physical symptoms, and lack of sleep were bad for his health. Wouldn't they eventually lead to a major medical problem of some kind? And finally, his constant anxiety had begun to interfere with his life. Although his girlfriend and other acquaintances did not seem to realize how much he was suffering, he was growing weary of covering it all up. He found himself turning down social invitations and work opportunities more and more. He had even quit his once-beloved weekly poker game. Not that staying home helped in any real way. He wondered how much longer he could go on this way.

▶**fear** The central nervous system's physiological and emotional response to a serious threat to one's well-being.

▶**anxiety** The central nervous system's physiological and emotional response to a vague sense of threat or danger.

▶**generalized anxiety disorder** A disorder marked by persistent and excessive feelings of anxiety and worry about numerous events and activities.

You don't need to be as troubled as Tomas to experience fear and anxiety. Think about a time when your breathing quickened, your muscles tensed, and your heart pounded with a sudden sense of dread. Was it when your car almost skidded off the road in the rain? When your professor announced a pop quiz? What about when the person you were in love with went out with someone else or your boss suggested that your job performance ought to improve? Any time you face what seems to be a serious threat to your well-being, you may react with the state of immediate alarm known as **fear.** Sometimes you cannot pinpoint a specific cause for your alarm, but still you feel tense and edgy, as if you expect something unpleasant to happen. The vague sense of being in danger is usually called **anxiety,** and it has the same features—the same increases in breathing, muscular tension, perspiration, and so forth—as fear.

Although everyday experiences of fear and anxiety are not pleasant, they often are useful. They prepare us for action—for "fight or flight"—when danger threatens. They may lead us to drive more cautiously in a storm, keep up with our reading assignments, treat our friends more sensitively, and work harder at our jobs. Unfortunately, some people suffer such disabling fear and anxiety that they cannot lead normal lives. Their discomfort is too severe or too frequent, lasts too long, or is triggered too easily. These people are said to have an *anxiety disorder* or a related kind of disorder.

> **If fear is so unpleasant, why do many people seek out the feelings of fear brought about by amusement park rides, scary movies, bungee jumping, and the like?**

Anxiety disorders are the most common mental disorders in the United States. In any given year around 18 percent of the adult population suffer from one or another of the anxiety disorders identified by DSM-5, while close to 29 percent of all people develop one of the disorders at some point in their lives (Kessler et al., 2012, 2010, 2009; Daitch, 2011). Only around one-fifth of these individuals seek treatment (Wang et al., 2005).

People with *generalized anxiety disorder* experience general and persistent feelings of worry and anxiety. People with *specific phobias* have a persistent and irrational fear of a particular object, activity, or situation. People with *agoraphobia* fear traveling to public places such as stores or movie theaters. Those with *social anxiety disorder* are intensely afraid of social or performance situations in which they may become embarrassed. And people with *panic disorder* have recurrent attacks of terror. Most individuals with one anxiety disorder suffer from a second one as well (Leyfer et al., 2013; Merikangas & Swanson, 2010) (see Figure 4-1). Tomas, for example, has the excessive worry found in generalized anxiety disorder and the repeated attacks of terror that mark panic disorder. In addition, many of those with an anxiety disorder also experience depression (Starr et al., 2014).

Anxiety also plays a major role in a different group of problems, called *obsessive-compulsive and related disorders.* People with these disorders feel overrun by recurrent thoughts that cause anxiety or by the need to perform certain repetitive actions to reduce anxiety. Because anxiety is so prominent in these disorders, they will be examined in this chapter along with the anxiety disorders.

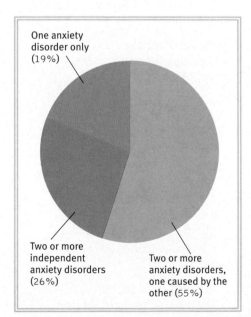

One anxiety disorder only (19%)

Two or more independent anxiety disorders (26%)

Two or more anxiety disorders, one caused by the other (55%)

figure 4-1

Does anxiety beget anxiety? People with one anxiety disorder usually experience another as well, either simultaneously or at another point in their lives. (Information from: Merikangas & Swanson, 2010; Ruscio et al., 2007; Rodriguez et al., 2004; Hunt & Andrews, 1995.)

Generalized Anxiety Disorder

People with **generalized anxiety disorder** experience excessive anxiety under most circumstances and worry about practically anything. In fact, their problem is sometimes described as *free-floating anxiety.* Like the young Web designer Tomas, they typically feel restless, keyed up, or on edge; tire easily; have difficulty concentrating; suffer from muscle tension; and have sleep problems (see Table 4-1). The symptoms last at least 6 months (APA, 2013). Nevertheless, most people with the disorder are able, although with some difficulty, to carry on social relationships and job activities.

Generalized anxiety disorder is common in Western society. Surveys suggest that as much as 4 percent of the U.S. population has the symptoms of this disorder in any given year, a rate that holds across Canada, Britain, and other Western countries (Kessler et al., 2012, 2010; Ritter et al., 2010). Altogether, more than 6 percent of all people develop generalized anxiety disorder sometime during their lives. It may emerge at any age, but usually it first appears in childhood or adolescence. Women diagnosed with the disorder outnumber men 2 to 1. Around one-quarter of the people who have generalized anxiety disorder are currently in treatment (NIMH, 2011; Wang et al., 2005).

A variety of factors have been cited to explain the development of this disorder. Here you will read about the views and treatments offered by the sociocultural, psychodynamic, humanistic, cognitive, and biological models. We will examine the behavioral perspective when we turn to phobias later in the chapter because that model approaches generalized anxiety disorder and phobias in basically the same way.

The Sociocultural Perspective: Societal and Multicultural Factors

According to sociocultural theorists, generalized anxiety disorder is most likely to develop in people who are faced with ongoing societal conditions that are dangerous. Studies have found that people in highly threatening environments are indeed more likely to develop the general feelings of tension, anxiety, and fatigue and the sleep disturbances found in this disorder (Slopen et al., 2012).

Take, for example, a classic study that was done on the psychological impact of living near the Three Mile Island nuclear power plant after the nuclear reactor accident of March 1979 (Baum et al., 2004; Wroble & Baum, 2002). In the months following the accident, local mothers of preschool children were found to display five times as many anxiety or depression disorders as mothers living elsewhere. Although the number of disorders decreased during the next year, the Three Mile Island mothers still displayed high levels of anxiety or depression a year later. Similarly, studies conducted more recently have found that in the months and years following Hurricane Katrina in 2005 and the Haitian earthquake in 2010, the rate of generalized and other anxiety disorders was twice as high among area residents who lived through the disasters as among unaffected persons living elsewhere (Cénat & Derivois, 2015; Shultz et al., 2012; Galea et al., 2007).

One of the most powerful forms of societal stress is poverty. People without financial means are likely to live in rundown communities with high crime rates, have fewer educational and job opportunities, and run a greater risk for health problems (Moore, Radcliffe, & Liu, 2014). As sociocultural theorists would predict, such people also have a higher rate of generalized anxiety disorder (McLaughlin et al., 2012). In the United States, the rate is almost twice as high among people with low incomes as among those with higher incomes (Sareen et al., 2011). As wages decrease, the rate of generalized anxiety disorder steadily increases (see Table 4–2 on the next page).

Since race is closely tied to stress in the United States (related to discrimination, low income, and reduced job opportunities), it is not surprising that it too is sometimes tied to the prevalence of generalized anxiety disorder (Sibrava et al., 2013; Soto et al., 2011). In any given year, African Americans are 30 percent more likely than white Americans to suffer from this disorder. Moreover, although researchers have not consistently found a heightened rate of generalized anxiety disorder among Hispanic Americans, they have noted

table: 4-1

Dx Checklist

Generalized Anxiety Disorder

1. For six months or more, person experiences disproportionate, uncontrollable, and ongoing anxiety and worry about multiple matters.

2. The symptoms include at least three of the following: edginess, fatigue, poor concentration, irritability, muscle tension, sleep problems.

3. Significant distress or impairment.

Information from: APA, 2013.

The role of society Bishop Richard Garcia hugs the father of a 6-year-old child who was killed by a stray bullet fired by gang members outside his house. People who live in dangerous environments experience greater anxiety and have a higher rate of generalized anxiety disorder than those who live in other settings.

AP Photo/The Monterey County Herald/Orville Myers

table: **4-2**

Eye on Culture:

Prevalence of Anxiety Disorders and Obsessive-Compulsive Disorder (Compared to Rate in Total Population)

	Female	Low Income	African American	Hispanic American	Elderly
Generalized anxiety disorder	Higher	Higher	Higher	Same	Higher
Specific phobias	Higher	Higher	Higher	Higher	Lower
Agoraphobia	Higher	Higher	Same	Same	Higher
Social anxiety disorder	Higher	Higher	Higher	Lower	Lower
Panic disorder	Higher	Higher	Same	Same	Lower
Obsessive-compulsive disorder	Same	Higher	Same	Same	Lower

Information from: Polo et al., 2011; Sareen et al., 2011; Bharani & Lantz, 2008; Hopko et al., 2008; Nazarian & Craske, 2008; Schultz et al., 2008.

////// BETWEEN THE LINES //////

Google's Most Searched Symptoms

1. Pregnancy symptoms

2. Influenza symptoms

3. Diabetes symptoms

4. **Anxiety symptoms**

5. Thyroid symptoms

(Sifferlin, 2013)

that many Hispanics in both the United States and Latin America suffer from *nervios* ("nerves"), a pattern that bears great similarity to generalized anxiety disorder (López & Guarnaccia, 2005, 2000). People with *nervios* experience enormous emotional distress, somatic symptoms such as headaches and stomachaches, so-called brain aches marked by poor concentration and nervousness, and symptoms of irritability, tearfulness, and trembling.

Although poverty and various societal and cultural pressures may help create a climate in which generalized anxiety disorder is more likely to develop, sociocultural variables are not the only factors at work. After all, most people in poor or dangerous environments do not develop this disorder. Even if sociocultural factors play a broad role, theorists still must explain why some people develop the disorder and others do not. The psychodynamic, humanistic-existential, cognitive, and biological schools of thought have all tried to explain why and have offered corresponding treatments.

The Psychodynamic Perspective

Sigmund Freud (1933, 1917) believed that all children experience some degree of anxiety as part of growing up and that all use ego defense mechanisms to help control such anxiety (see pages 45–47). Children feel *realistic anxiety* when they face actual danger; *neurotic anxiety* when they are repeatedly prevented, by parents or by circumstances, from expressing their id impulses; and *moral anxiety* when they are punished or threatened for expressing their id impulses. According to Freud, some children have particularly high levels of such anxiety, or their defense mechanisms are particularly inadequate, and these individuals may develop generalized anxiety disorder.

Psychodynamic Explanations: When Childhood Anxiety Goes Unresolved According to Freud, when a child is overrun by neurotic or moral anxiety, the stage is set for generalized anxiety disorder. Early developmental experiences may produce an unusually high level of anxiety in such a child. Say that a boy is spanked every time he cries for milk as an infant, messes his pants as a 2-year-old, and explores his genitals as a toddler. He may eventually come to believe that his various id impulses are very dangerous, and he may feel overwhelming anxiety whenever he has such impulses.

Alternatively, a child's ego defense mechanisms may be too weak to cope with even normal levels of anxiety. Overprotected children, shielded by their parents from all frustrations and threats, have little opportunity to develop effective defense mechanisms. When they face the pressures of adult life, their defense mechanisms may be too weak to cope with the resulting anxieties.

Today's psychodynamic theorists often disagree with specific aspects of Freud's explanation for generalized anxiety disorder. Most continue to believe, however, that the disorder can be traced to inadequacies in the early relationships between children and their parents (Sharf, 2015). Researchers have tested the psychodynamic explanations in various ways. In one strategy, they have tried to show that people with generalized anxiety disorder are particularly likely to use defense mechanisms. For example, one team of investigators examined the early therapy transcripts of patients with this diagnosis and found that the patients often reacted defensively. When asked by therapists to discuss upsetting experiences, they would quickly forget (*repress*) what they had just been talking about, change the direction of the discussion, or deny having negative feelings (Luborsky, 1973).

In another line of research, investigators have studied people who as children suffered extreme punishment for id impulses. As psychodynamic theorists would predict, these people have higher levels of anxiety later in life (Busch et al., 2010; Chiu, 1971). In addition, several studies have supported the psychodynamic position that extreme protectiveness by parents may often lead to high levels of anxiety in their children (Manfredi et al., 2011; Hudson & Rapee, 2004).

Although these studies are consistent with psychodynamic explanations, some scientists question whether they show what they claim to show. When people have difficulty talking about upsetting events early in therapy, for example, they are not necessarily repressing those events. They may be focusing purposely on the positive aspects of their lives, or they may be too embarrassed to share personal negative events until they develop trust in the therapist.

Psychodynamic Therapies Psychodynamic therapists use the same general techniques to treat all psychological problems: *free association* and the therapist's interpretations of *transference, resistance,* and *dreams. Freudian psychodynamic therapists*

Alex Gregory/The New Yorker Collection/www.cartoonbank.com

GREGORY

"Since my mother was rarely home, I guess I blame my nanny."

use these methods to help clients with generalized anxiety disorder become less afraid of their id impulses and more successful in controlling them. Other psychodynamic therapists, particularly *object relations therapists,* use them to help anxious patients identify and settle the childhood relationship problems that continue to produce anxiety in adulthood (Blass, 2014; Lucas, 2006).

Controlled studies have typically found psychodynamic treatments to be of only modest help to persons with generalized anxiety disorder (Craske, 2010). An exception to this trend is *short-term psychodynamic therapy* (see Chapter 2), which has in some cases significantly reduced the levels of anxiety, worry, and social difficulty of patients with this disorder (Bressi et al., 2014; Salzer et al., 2011).

The Humanistic Perspective

Humanistic theorists propose that generalized anxiety disorder, like other psychological disorders, arises when people stop looking at themselves honestly and acceptingly. Repeated denials of their true thoughts, emotions, and behavior make these people extremely anxious and unable to fulfill their potential as human beings.

The humanistic view of why people develop this disorder is best illustrated by Carl Rogers' explanation. As you saw in Chapter 2, Rogers believed that children who fail to receive *unconditional positive regard* from others may become overly critical of themselves and develop harsh self-standards, what Rogers called *conditions of worth.* They try to meet these standards by repeatedly distorting and denying their true thoughts and experiences. Despite such efforts, however, threatening self-judgments keep breaking through and causing them intense anxiety. This onslaught of anxiety sets the stage for generalized anxiety disorder or some other form of psychological dysfunctioning.

Practitioners of Rogers' treatment approach, **client–centered therapy** (also called *person-centered therapy*), try to show unconditional positive regard for their clients and to empathize with them. The therapists hope that an atmosphere of genuine acceptance and caring will help clients feel secure enough to recognize their true needs, thoughts, and emotions. When clients eventually are honest and comfortable with themselves, their anxiety or other symptoms will subside. In the following excerpt, Rogers describes the progress made by a client with anxiety and related symptoms:

> Therapy was an experiencing of her self, in all its aspects, in a safe relationship . . . the experiencing of self as having a capacity for wholeness . . . a self that cared about others. This last followed . . . the realization that the therapist cared, that it really mattered to him how therapy turned out for her, that he really valued her. . . . She gradually became aware of the fact that . . . there was nothing fundamentally bad, but rather, at heart she was positive and sound.
>
> *(Rogers, 1954, pp. 261–264)*

▶ **client-centered therapy** The humanistic therapy developed by Carl Rogers in which clinicians try to help clients by being accepting, empathizing accurately, and conveying genuineness. Also known as *person-centered therapy.*

▶ **basic irrational assumptions** The inaccurate and inappropriate beliefs held by people with various psychological problems, according to Albert Ellis.

Despite such optimistic case reports, controlled studies have failed to offer strong support for this approach. Although research does suggest that client–centered therapy is usually more helpful to anxious clients than no treatment, the approach is only sometimes superior to placebo therapy (Prochaska & Norcross, 2013, 2006, 2003). In addition, researchers have found, at best, only limited support for Rogers' explanation of generalized anxiety disorder and other forms of abnormal behavior. Nor have other humanistic theories and treatment received much research support.

The Cognitive Perspective

Followers of the cognitive model suggest that psychological problems are often caused by dysfunctional ways of thinking (see *PsychWatch* on page 113). Given that excessive worry—a cognitive symptom—is a key characteristic of generalized anxiety disorder (see Figure 4-2), it is not surprising that cognitive theorists have had much to say about the causes of and treatments for this particular disorder.

Maladaptive Assumptions Initially, cognitive theorists suggested that generalized anxiety disorder is primarily caused by *maladaptive assumptions,* a notion that continues to be influential. Albert Ellis, for example, proposed that many people are guided by irrational beliefs that lead them to act and react in inappropriate ways (Ellis, 2014, 2002, 1962). Ellis called these **basic irrational assumptions,** and he claimed that people with generalized anxiety disorder often hold the following ones:

> "It is a dire necessity for an adult human being to be loved or approved of by virtually every significant other person in his community."

> "It is awful and catastrophic when things are not the way one would very much like them to be."

> "If something is or may be dangerous or fearsome, one should be terribly concerned about it and should keep dwelling on the possibility of its occurring."

> "One should be thoroughly competent, adequate, and achieving in all possible respects if one is to consider oneself worthwhile."

> *(Ellis, 1962)*

When people who make these assumptions are faced with a stressful event, such as an exam or a first date, they are likely to interpret it as dangerous, to overreact, and to feel fear. As they apply the assumptions to more and more events, they may begin to develop generalized anxiety disorder.

Similarly, cognitive theorist Aaron Beck argued that people with generalized anxiety disorder constantly hold silent assumptions (for example, "A situation or a person is unsafe until proven to be safe" or "It is always best to assume the worst") that imply they are in imminent danger (Clark & Beck, 2012, 2010; Beck & Emery, 1985). Since the time of Ellis' and Beck's initial proposals, researchers have repeatedly found that people with generalized anxiety disorder do indeed hold maladaptive assumptions, particularly about dangerousness (Clark & Beck, 2012, 2010).

New-Wave Cognitive Explanations In recent years, several new explanations for generalized anxiety disorder, sometimes called the *new-wave cognitive explanations,* have emerged. Each of them builds on the work of Ellis and Beck and their emphasis on danger.

> **Why might many people believe, at least implicitly, that worrying is useful— even necessary—for problems to work out?**

The *metacognitive theory,* developed by researcher Adrian Wells (2014, 2011, 2005), suggests that people with generalized anxiety disorder implicitly hold both positive and negative beliefs about worrying. On the positive side, they believe that worrying is a useful way of appraising and coping with threats in life. And so they look for and examine all possible signs of danger—that is, they worry constantly.

At the same time, Wells argues, people with generalized anxiety disorder also hold negative beliefs about worrying, and these negative attitudes are the ones that open the door to the disorder. Because society teaches them that worrying is a bad thing, they come to believe that their repeated worrying is in fact harmful (mentally and physically) and uncontrollable. Now they further worry about the fact that they always seem to be worrying (so-called *meta-worries*). Their meta-worries may

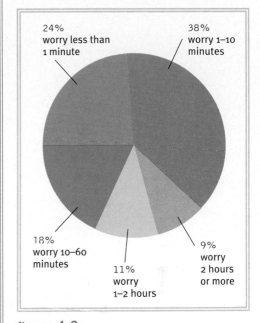

figure 4-2

How long do your worries last? In one survey, 62 percent of college students said they spend less than 10 minutes at a time worrying about something. In contrast, 20 percent worry for more than an hour. (Information from: Tallis et al., 1994.)

▶ **rational-emotive therapy** A cognitive therapy developed by Albert Ellis that helps clients identify and change the irrational assumptions and thinking that help cause their psychological disorder.

include concerns that they are going crazy with worry, making themselves ill with worry, and losing out in life because of worrying. The net effect of all this worrying: generalized anxiety disorder.

This explanation has received considerable research support. Studies indicate, for example, that people who generally hold both positive and negative beliefs about worrying are particularly prone to developing generalized anxiety disorder and that repeated meta-worrying is a powerful predictor of developing the disorder (Wells, 2014, 2011, 2005).

According to another new explanation for generalized anxiety disorder, the *intolerance of uncertainty theory,* certain individuals cannot tolerate the knowledge that negative events *may* occur, even if the possibility of occurrence is very small. Inasmuch as life is filled with uncertain events, these individuals worry constantly that such events are about to occur. Such intolerance and worrying leave them highly vulnerable to the development of generalized anxiety disorder (Dugas et al., 2012, 2010, 2004; Fisher & Wells, 2011). Think of when you meet someone you're attracted to and how you then feel prior to texting or calling call him or her for the first time—or how you feel while you're waiting for that person to contact you for the first time. The worry that you experience in such instances—the sense of sometimes unbearable uncertainty over the possibility of an unacceptable negative outcome—is, according to this theory, how people with generalized anxiety disorder feel all the time.

Proponents of this theory believe people with generalized anxiety disorder keep worrying and worrying in their efforts to find "correct" solutions for various situations in their lives and to restore certainty to the situations. However, because they can never really be sure that a given solution is a correct one, they are always left to grapple with intolerable levels of uncertainty, triggering new rounds of worrying and new efforts to find correct solutions. Like the metacognitive theory of worry, considerable research supports this theory. Studies have found, for example, that people with generalized anxiety disorder display higher levels of intolerance of uncertainty than people with normal degrees of anxiety (Dugas et al., 2012, 2004).

Worry-free workers This famous Bill Jones motivational poster, displayed in workplaces throughout the United States in the 1920s, reflects the view of today's new-wave cognitive theorists—that worrying is a dysfunctional process that can be brought under control.

Finally, a third new explanation for generalized anxiety disorder, the *avoidance theory,* developed by researcher Thomas Borkovec, suggests that people with this disorder have greater bodily arousal (higher heart rate, perspiration, respiration) than other people and that worrying actually serves to *reduce* this arousal, perhaps by distracting the individuals from their unpleasant physical feelings (Liera & Newman, 2014; Borkovec et al., 2004). In short, the avoidance theory holds that people with generalized anxiety disorder worry repeatedly in order to reduce or avoid uncomfortable states of bodily arousal. When, for example, they find themselves in an uncomfortable job situation or social relationship, they implicitly choose to intellectualize (that is, worry about) losing their job or losing their friend rather than having to stew in a state of intense negative arousal. The worrying serves as a quick, though ultimately maladaptive, way of coping with unpleasant bodily states.

Borkovec's explanation has also been supported by numerous studies. Research reveals that people with generalized anxiety disorder experience particularly fast and intense bodily reactions, find such reactions overwhelming and unpleasant, worry more than other people upon becoming aroused, and successfully reduce their arousal whenever they worry (Liera & Newman, 2014; Hirsch et al., 2012).

Cognitive Therapies Two kinds of cognitive approaches are used in cases of generalized anxiety disorder. In one, based on the pioneering work of Ellis and Beck, therapists help clients change the maladaptive assumptions that characterize their disorder. In the other, new-wave cognitive therapists

PsychWatch

Fears, Shmears: The Odds Are Usually on Our Side

People with anxiety disorders have many unreasonable fears, but millions of other people, too, worry about disaster every day. Most of the catastrophes they fear are not probable. Perhaps the ability to live by laws of *probability* rather than *possibility* is what separates the fearless from the fearful. What are the odds, then, that commonly feared events will happen? The range of probability is wide, but the odds are usually heavily in our favor.

A city resident will be a victim of a violent crime: 1 in 237

A suburbanite will be a victim of a violent crime: 1 in 408

A child will suffer a high-chair injury this year: 1 in 6,000

The IRS will audit you this year: 1 in 100

You will be murdered this year: 1 in 20,000

You will be a victim of burglary this year: 1 in 35

You will be a victim of robbery this year: 1 in 885

You will be killed on your next bus ride: 1 in 500 million

You will be hit by a baseball at a major-league game: 1 in 42,000

You will drown in the tub this year: 1 in 685,000

Your house will have a fire this year: 1 in 200

Watch out! The statistical chance of being hit by a foul ball at a major league baseball game is 1 in 42,000. But try telling that to these fans.

Otto Greule Jr./Getty Images

Your carton will contain a broken egg: 1 in 10

You will develop a tooth cavity: 1 in 6

You will contract AIDS from a blood transfusion: 1 in 286,000

You will die in a tsunami: 1 in 500,000

You will be attacked by a shark: 1 in 4 million

You will receive a diagnosis of cancer this year: 1 in 8,000

A woman will develop breast cancer during her lifetime: 1 in 8

A piano player will eventually develop lower back pain: 1 in 3

You will be killed on your next automobile outing: 1 in 4 million

Condom use will eventually fail to prevent pregnancy: 1 in 8

An IUD will eventually fail to prevent pregnancy: 1 in 167

Coitus interruptus will eventually fail to prevent pregnancy: 1 in 5

You will die as a result of a lightning strike: 1 in 10 million

(Information from: FBI, 2014; Glovin, 2014; CDC, 2013; Quillian & Pager, 2012; Britt, 2005)

help clients to understand the special role that worrying may play in their disorder and to change their views about and reactions to worrying.

CHANGING MALADAPTIVE ASSUMPTIONS In Ellis' technique of **rational–emotive therapy,** therapists point out the irrational assumptions held by clients, suggest more appropriate assumptions, and assign homework that gives the clients practice at challenging old assumptions and applying new ones (Ellis, 2014, 2008, 2005). Studies suggest that this approach and similar cognitive approaches bring at least modest relief to those suffering from generalized anxiety (Clark & Beck, 2012, 2010). Ellis' approach is illustrated in the following discussion between him and an anxious client who fears failure and disapproval at work, especially over a testing procedure that she has developed for her company:

> **Client:** I'm so distraught these days that I can hardly concentrate on anything for more than a minute or two at a time. My mind just keeps wandering to that damn testing procedure I devised, and that they've put so much money into; and whether it's going to work well or be just a waste of all that time and money. . . .
>
> **Ellis:** Point one is that you must admit that you are telling yourself something to start your worrying going, and you must begin to look, and I mean really look, for the specific nonsense with which you keep reindoctrinating yourself. . . . The false statement is: "If, because my testing procedure doesn't work and I am functioning inefficiently on my job, my co-workers do not want me or approve of me, then I shall be a worthless person." . . .
>
> **Client:** But if I want to do what my firm also wants me to do, and I am useless to them, aren't I also useless to me?
>
> **Ellis:** No—not unless you think you are. You are frustrated, of course, if you want to set up a good testing procedure and you can't. But need you be desperately unhappy because you are frustrated? And need you deem yourself completely unworthwhile because you can't do one of the main things you want to do in life?
>
> *(Ellis, 1962, pp. 160–165)*

BREAKING DOWN WORRYING Alternatively, some of today's new-wave cognitive therapists specifically guide clients with generalized anxiety disorder to recognize and change their dysfunctional use of worrying (Wells, 2014, 2010; Newman et al., 2011). They begin by educating the clients about the role of worrying in their disorder and have them observe their bodily arousal and cognitive responses across various life situations. In turn, the clients come to appreciate the triggers of their worrying, their misconceptions about worrying, and their misguided efforts to control their lives by worrying. As their insights grow, clients are expected to see the world as less threatening (and so less arousing), try out more constructive ways of dealing with arousal, and worry less about the fact that they worry so much. Research has begun to indicate that a concentrated focus on worrying is indeed a helpful addition to the traditional cognitive treatment for generalized anxiety disorder (Wells, 2014, 2011, 2010).

Treating individuals with generalized anxiety disorder by helping them to recognize their inclination to worry is similar to another cognitive approach that has gained popularity in recent years. The approach, *mindfulness-based cognitive therapy,* was developed by psychologist Steven Hayes and his colleagues as part of their broader treatment approach called *acceptance and commitment therapy* (Hayes et al., 2013). Here therapists help clients to become aware of their streams of thoughts, including their worries, as they are occurring and to *accept* such thoughts as mere events of the mind. By accepting their thoughts rather than trying to eliminate them, the clients are expected to be less upset and affected by them.

Mindfulness-based cognitive therapy has also been applied to a range of other psychological problems, such as depression, posttraumatic stress disorder, personality disorders, and substance use disorders, often with promising results (Roemer & Orsillo, 2014). This cognitive approach borrows heavily from a form of meditation called *mindfulness meditation,* which teaches people to pay attention to the thoughts and feelings that flow through their mind during meditation and to accept such thoughts in a nonjudgmental way (see *InfoCentral* on the next page).

The Kobal Collection/Blumhouse Productions

Fearful delights Many people enjoy the feeling of fear as long as it occurs under controlled circumstances, as when they are safely watching the tension grow in the hugely popular series of movies *Paranormal Activity 1, 2, 3,* and *4* (plus the Latino-oriented spinoff *Paranormal Activity: The Marked Ones*), among the most profitable films ever made. In this shot from a scene in the first film, the lead character Katie tries to escape a supernatural presence in her house.

MINDFULNESS

Over the past decade, **mindfulness** has become one of the most common terms in psychology. Mindfulness involves being in the present moment, intentionally and nonjudgmentally. **Mindfulness training programs** use mindfulness **meditation** techniques to help treat people suffering from pain, anxiety disorders, and depressive disorders, as well as a variety of other psychological disorders.

MINDFULNESS TRAINING PROGRAMS

- Have the goal of achieving a state of intentional, non-judgmental attention on the present.

attention to body sensations

attention to **breathing** sensations

attention to wandering and busy thoughts

8 weeks of instruction

simple **yoga**

homework **assignments**
(practice and **journal** keeping)

(Noonan, 2014; Russell, 2014; Chan, 2013; Kerr et al., 2013; Plaza et al., 2013)

- Help treat other disorders, including:

pain conditions

PTSD and other stress disorders

depressive disorders

obsessive-compulsive disorder

substance use disorders

borderline personality disorder

(Kerr et al., 2013; King et al., 2013; Hanstede et al., 2008)

Amount that U.S. adults spend on mindfulness programs each year $8 billion

- Help reduce the anxiety found in . . .

generalized **anxiety** disorder

social **anxiety** disorder

panic disorder

test **anxiety**

illness anxiety

depressive disorder with **anxious** distress

(Kraemer et al., 2014; Hoge et al., 2013; Kerr et al., 2013; Khoury et al., 2013; Carlson, 2012; Cunha & Paiva, 2012)

Percentage of the U.S. population that practice mindfulness meditation techniques 10%

Number of medical schools in North America that teach mindfulness >100

Why Do People Seek Out Mindfulness?

"Cell phones, texting, social networking, emailing, etc., easily distract me from what I'm doing."

Millennials 61%
Gen Xers 46%
Boomers 32%
Total Adults 47%

(Palley, 2014)

Number of scientific papers and books on mindfulness 9,300

Number of certified instructors around the world in mindfulness-based stress reduction 1,000

(Brewer, 2014; Marchand 2014; Noonan, 2014; Pickert, 2014)

RESEARCH-SUPPORTED EFFECTS OF MINDFULNESS

Mindfulness appears to

- improve control over anxiety and related emotions (*amygdala*)

- promote more peaceful sleep

- improve functioning of the autonomic nervous system

- produce *alpha rhythm brain waves* tied to an alert, but non-anxious, mental state

- improve functioning of the *thalamus*, which heightens sensory signaling and consciousness

MINDFUL LIFE STRATEGIES

(Noonan, 2014; Russell, 2014)

Employ conscious awareness each morning—notice how you feel before starting the day.

Practice mindful breathing for 5 to 30 minutes throughout the day.

Take regular breaks from sitting at your desk.

Choose an object in your environment and observe it carefully.

Take a slow 10-minute walk, synchronizing your breathing with your steps.

Unplug from technology periodically before starting the day.

At the end of the day, reflect about the day, without judgment.

Eat lunch slowly, savoring every bite and body sensation.

Do nothing for at least 5 minutes each day.

Inhale and exhale deeply and focus on your breath.

Slow yourself down throughout the day.

- lower stress

- improve decision-making under stress (*frontal cortex*)

- heighten attention (*basal ganglia*)

- improve working memory and verbal reasoning (*frontal cortex* and *hippocampus*)

- improve functioning of the immune system

- increase enjoyment and experience of music

- decrease feelings of loneliness among elderly people

(Noonan, 2014; Chan, 2013; Plaza et al., 2013)

▶ **family pedigree study** A research design in which investigators determine how many and which relatives of a person with a disorder have the same disorder.

▶ **benzodiazepines** The most common group of antianxiety drugs, which includes Valium and Xanax.

▶ **gamma-aminobutyric acid (GABA)** A neurotransmitter whose low activity has been linked to generalized anxiety disorder.

▶ **sedative-hypnotic drugs** Drugs that calm people at lower doses and help them to fall asleep at higher doses.

The Biological Perspective

Biological theorists believe that generalized anxiety disorder is caused chiefly by biological factors. For years this claim was supported primarily by **family pedigree studies,** in which researchers determine how many and which relatives of a person with a disorder have the same disorder. If biological tendencies toward generalized anxiety disorder are inherited, people who are biologically related should have similar probabilities of developing this disorder. Studies have in fact found that biological relatives of persons with generalized anxiety disorder are more likely than nonrelatives to have the disorder also (Schienle et al., 2011). Approximately 15 percent of the relatives of people with the disorder display it themselves—a much higher prevalence rate than that found in the general population. And the closer the relative (an identical twin, for example), the greater the likelihood that he or she will also have the disorder.

Biological Explanations: GABA Inactivity In recent decades, important discoveries by brain researchers have offered clearer evidence that generalized anxiety disorder is related to biological factors (Bergado-Acosta et al., 2014; Craig & Chamberlain, 2010). One of the first such discoveries was made in the 1950s, when researchers determined that **benzodiazepines,** the family of drugs that includes *alprazolam* (Xanax), *lorazepam* (Ativan), and *diazepam* (Valium), provide relief from anxiety. At first, no one understood why benzodiazepines reduce anxiety. Eventually, however, the development of radioactive techniques enabled researchers to pinpoint the exact sites in the brain that are affected by benzodiazepines (Mohler & Okada, 1977). Apparently certain neurons have receptors that receive the benzodiazepines, just as a lock receives a key.

Investigators soon discovered that these benzodiazepine receptors ordinarily receive **gamma-aminobutyric acid (GABA),** a common neurotransmitter in the brain. As you read in Chapter 2, neurotransmitters are chemicals that carry messages from one neuron to another. GABA carries *inhibitory* messages: when GABA is received at a receptor, it causes the neuron to stop firing.

On the basis of such findings, biological researchers eventually pieced together several scenarios of how fear reactions may occur. A leading one began with the notion that in normal fear reactions, key neurons throughout the brain fire more rapidly, triggering the firing of still more neurons and creating a general state of excitability throughout the brain and body. Perspiration, breathing, and muscle tension increase. This state is experienced as fear or anxiety. Continuous firing of neurons eventually triggers a feedback system—that is, brain and body activities that reduce the level of excitability. Some neurons throughout the brain release the neurotransmitter GABA, which then binds to GABA receptors on certain neurons and instructs those neurons to stop firing. The state of excitability ceases, and the experience of fear or anxiety subsides (Atack, 2010; Costa, 1985, 1983).

Some researchers have concluded that a malfunction in this feedback system can cause fear or anxiety to go unchecked (Salari et al., 2015; Bremner & Charney, 2010). In fact, when investigators reduced GABA's ability to bind to GABA receptors, they found that animal subjects reacted with a rise in anxiety (Costa, 1985; Mohler et al., 1981). This finding suggested that people with generalized anxiety disorder might have ongoing problems in their anxiety feedback system. Perhaps they have too few GABA receptors, or perhaps their GABA receptors do not readily capture the neurotransmitter.

This explanation continues to have many supporters, but it is also problematic. First, according to recent biological discoveries, other neurotransmitters may also play important roles in anxiety and generalized anxiety disorder, either acting alone or in conjunction with GABA (Mandrioli & Mercolini, 2015; Baldwin et al., 2013). Second, biological theorists are faced with the problem of establishing a causal relationship. The abnormal GABA responses of anxious persons may be the result, rather than the cause, of their anxiety disorders. Perhaps long-term anxiety eventually leads to poorer GABA reception, for example.

In fact, research conducted in recent years indicates that the root of generalized anxiety disorder is probably more complicated than the activity of a single neurotransmitter or group of neurotransmitters. Researchers have determined, for example, that emotional reactions of various kinds are tied to *brain circuits*—networks of brain structures that work together, triggering each other into action with the help of neurotransmitters and producing a particular kind of emotional reaction. It turns out that the circuit that produces anxiety reactions includes the *prefrontal cortex;* the *anterior cingulate cortex;* and the *amygdala,* a small almond-shaped brain structure that usually starts the emotional ball rolling. Recent studies suggest that this circuit often functions improperly in people with generalized anxiety disorder (Lang, McTeague, & Bradley, 2014; Schienle et al., 2011) (see Figure 4-3).

Biological Treatments The leading biological treatment for generalized anxiety disorder is *drug therapy* (see Table 4-3). Other biological interventions are *relaxation training* and *biofeedback*.

ANTIANXIETY DRUG THERAPY In the late 1950s, benzodiazepines were originally marketed as **sedative-hypnotic drugs**—drugs that calm people in low doses and help them fall asleep in higher doses. These new antianxiety drugs seemed less addictive than previous sedative-hypnotic medications, such as *barbiturates,* and they appeared to produce less tiredness. Thus, they were quickly embraced by both doctors and patients.

Only years later did investigators come to understand the reasons for the effectiveness of benzodiazepines. As you have read, researchers eventually learned that there are specific neuron sites in the brain that receive benzodiazepines and that these same receptor sites ordinarily receive the neurotransmitter GABA. Apparently,

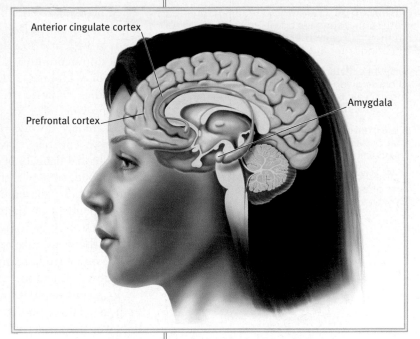

Anterior cingulate cortex

Prefrontal cortex

Amygdala

figure 4-3

The biology of anxiety The circuit in the brain that helps produce anxiety reactions includes areas such as the amygdala, the prefrontal cortex, and the anterior cingulate cortex.

table: **4-3**

Some Benzodiazepine Drugs

Generic Name	Trade Name(s)	Generic Name	Trade Name(s)
Alprazolam	Xanax, Xanax XR	Halazepam	Paxipam
Bromazepam	Lectopam, Lexotan, Bromaze	Lorazepam	Ativan
Chlordiazepoxide	Librium	Midazolam	Versed
Clonazepam	Klonopin	Nitrazepam	Mogadon, Alodorm, Pacisyn, Dumolid
Clorazepate	Tranxene	Oxazepam	Serax
Diazepam	Valium	Prazepam	Lysanxia, Centrax
Estazolam	ProSom	Quazepam	Doral
Flunitrazepam	Rohypnol	Temazepam	Restoril
Flurazepam	Dalmadorm, Dalmane	Triazolam	Halcion

▶ **relaxation training** A treatment procedure that teaches clients to relax at will so they can calm themselves in stressful situations.

▶ **biofeedback** A technique in which a client is given information about physiological reactions as they occur and learns to control the reactions voluntarily.

▶ **electromyograph (EMG)** A device that provides feedback about the level of muscular tension in the body.

▶ **phobia** A persistent and unreasonable fear of a particular object, activity, or situation.

when benzodiazepines bind to these neuron receptor sites, particularly those receptors known as *GABA-A receptors,* they increase the ability of GABA to bind to them as well, and so improve GABA's ability to stop neuron firing and reduce anxiety (Griebel & Holmes, 2013).

Studies indicate that benzodiazepines often provide relief for people with generalized anxiety disorder (Islam et al., 2014). However, clinicians have come to realize the potential dangers of these drugs. First, for many people, when the medications are stopped, anxiety returns as strong as ever. Second, we now know that people who take benzodiazepines in large doses for an extended time can become physically dependent on them. Third, the drugs can produce undesirable effects such as drowsiness, lack of coordination, memory loss, depression, and aggressive behavior. Finally, the drugs mix badly with certain other drugs or substances. If, for example, people on benzodiazepines drink even small amounts of alcohol, their breathing can slow down dangerously (Chollet et al., 2013).

> Why are antianxiety drugs so popular in today's world? Does their popularity say something about our society?

In recent decades, still other kinds of drugs have become available for people with generalized anxiety disorder. In particular, it has been discovered that a number of *antidepressant* medications, drugs that are usually used to lift the moods of depressed persons, and *antipsychotic* medications, drugs commonly given to people who lose touch with reality, are also helpful to many people with generalized anxiety disorder (Chollet et al., 2013; Comer et al., 2011).

RELAXATION TRAINING A nonchemical biological technique commonly used to treat generalized anxiety disorder is **relaxation training.** The notion behind this approach is that physical relaxation will lead to a state of psychological relaxation. In one version, therapists teach clients to identify individual muscle groups, tense them, release the tension, and ultimately relax the whole body. With continued practice, they can bring on a state of deep muscle relaxation at will, reducing their state of anxiety.

Research indicates that relaxation training is more effective than no treatment or placebo treatment in cases of generalized anxiety disorder (Hayes-Skelton et al., 2013). The improvement it produces, however, tends to be modest (Leahy, 2004), and other techniques that are known to relax people, such as basic meditation, often seem to be equally effective (Bourne et al., 2004). Relaxation training is of greatest help to people with generalized anxiety disorder when it is combined with cognitive therapy or with biofeedback (Cuijpers et al., 2014).

BIOFEEDBACK In **biofeedback,** therapists use electrical signals from the body to train people to control physiological processes such as heart rate or muscle tension. Clients are connected to a monitor that gives them continuous information about their bodily activities. By attending to the signals from the monitor, they may gradually learn to control even seemingly involuntary physiological processes.

The most widely applied method of biofeedback for the treatment of anxiety uses a device called an **electromyograph (EMG),** which provides feedback about the level of muscular tension in the body. Electrodes are attached to the client's muscles—usually the forehead muscles—where they detect the minute electrical activity that accompanies muscle tension (see Figure 4-4). The device then converts the electric energy, or *potentials,* coming from the muscles into an image, such as lines on a screen, or into a tone whose pitch changes along

figure 4-4
Biofeedback at work This biofeedback system records tension in the forehead muscles of an anxious person. The system receives, amplifies, converts, and displays information about the tension, allowing the client to "observe" it and to try to reduce his tension responses.

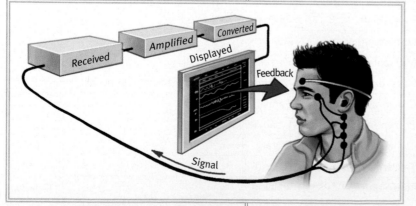

with changes in muscle tension. Thus clients "see" or "hear" when their muscles are becoming more or less tense. Through repeated trial and error, the individuals become skilled at voluntarily reducing muscle tension and, theoretically, at reducing tension and anxiety in everyday stressful situations.

Research finds that, in most cases, EMG biofeedback, like relaxation training, has only a modest effect on a person's anxiety level (Brambrink, 2004). As you will see in Chapter 8, biofeedback has had its greatest impact when it plays an *adjunct* role in the treatment of certain medical problems, including headaches and back pain (Flor, 2014; Young & Kemper, 2013).

➤ *Summing Up*

GENERALIZED ANXIETY DISORDER People with generalized anxiety disorder experience excessive anxiety and worry about a wide range of events and activities. Various explanations and treatments for this anxiety disorder have been offered.

According to the sociocultural view, societal dangers, economic stress, or related racial and cultural pressures may create a climate in which cases of generalized anxiety disorder are more likely to develop.

In the original psychodynamic explanation, Freud said that generalized anxiety disorder may develop when anxiety is excessive and defense mechanisms break down and function poorly. Psychodynamic therapists use free association, interpretation, and related psychodynamic techniques to help people overcome this problem.

Carl Rogers, the leading humanistic theorist, believed that people with generalized anxiety disorder fail to receive unconditional positive regard from significant others during their childhood and so become overly critical of themselves. He treated such individuals with client-centered therapy.

Cognitive theorists believe that generalized anxiety disorder is caused by maladaptive assumptions and beliefs. Many cognitive theorists further believe that implicit beliefs about the power and value of worrying are particularly important in the development and maintenance of this disorder. Cognitive therapists help their clients to change such thinking and to find more effective ways of coping during stressful situations.

Biological theorists hold that generalized anxiety disorder results from low activity of the neurotransmitter GABA. A common biological treatment is anti-anxiety drugs. Certain antidepressant drugs and antipsychotic drugs may also be of help. Relaxation training and biofeedback are also applied in many cases.

Phobias ///////////////////////////////// / / / /

A **phobia** (from the Greek word for "fear") is a persistent and unreasonable fear of a particular object, activity, or situation. People with a phobia become fearful if they even think about the object or situation they dread, but they usually remain comfortable as long as they avoid it or thoughts about it.

We all have our areas of special fear, and it is normal for some things to upset us more than other things (see *MediaSpeak* on page 121). How do such common fears differ from phobias? DSM-5 indicates that a phobia is more intense and persistent and the desire to avoid the object or situation is stronger (APA, 2013). People with phobias often feel so much distress that their fears may interfere dramatically with their lives.

table: **4-4**

Dx Checklist

Specific Phobia

1. Marked, persistent, and disproportionate fear of a particular object or situation, usually lasting at least six months.

2. Immediate fear is produced by exposure to the object.

3. Avoidance of the feared situation.

4. Significant distress or impairment.

Information from: APA, 2013.

Most phobias technically fall under the category of *specific phobias*, DSM-5's label for an intense and persistent fear of a specific object or situation. In addition, there is a broader kind of phobia called *agoraphobia*, a fear of venturing into public places or situations where escape might be difficult if one were to become panicky or incapacitated.

Specific Phobias

A **specific phobia** is a persistent fear of a specific object or situation (see Table 4–4). When sufferers are exposed to the object or situation, they typically experience immediate fear. Common specific phobias are intense fears of specific animals or insects, heights, enclosed spaces, thunderstorms, and blood. Here Andrew talks about his phobic fear of flying:

> *We got on board, and then there was the take-off. There it was again, that horrible feeling as we gathered speed. It was creeping over me again, that old feeling of panic. I kept seeing everyone as puppets, all strapped to their seats with no control over their destinies, me included. Every time the plane did a variation of speed or route, my heart would leap and I would hurriedly ask what was happening. When the plane started to lose height, I was terrified that we were about to crash.*
>
> *(Melville, 1978, p. 59)*

Each year around 12 percent of all people in the United States have the symptoms of a specific phobia (Kessler et al., 2012). Almost 14 percent of individuals develop such phobias at some point during their lives, and many people have more than one at a time. Women with the disorder outnumber men by at least 2 to 1. For reasons that are not clear, the prevalence of specific phobias also differs among racial and ethnic minority groups. In some studies, African Americans and Hispanic Americans report having at least 50 percent more specific phobias than do white Americans, even when economic factors, education, and age are held steady across the groups (Stein & Williams, 2010; Breslau et al., 2006). It is worth noting, however, that these heightened rates are at work only among African and Hispanic Americans who were born in the United States, not those who emigrated to the United States at some point during their lives (Hopko et al., 2008).

The impact of a specific phobia on a person's life depends on what arouses the fear (Costa et al., 2014). People whose phobias center on dogs, insects, or water will keep encountering the objects they dread. Their efforts to avoid them must be elaborate and may greatly restrict their activities. Urban residents with snake phobias have a much easier time. The vast majority of people with a specific phobia do not seek treatment (NIMH, 2011). They try instead to avoid the objects they fear.

Agoraphobia

People with **agoraphobia** are afraid of being in public places or situations where escape might be difficult or help unavailable, should they experience panic or become incapacitated (APA, 2013) (see Table 4–5 on page 122). This is a pervasive and complex phobia, which usually begins in one's twenties or thirties. In any given year, 1.7 percent of the population experience agoraphobia, women twice as frequently as men (Kessler et al., 2012). The disorder also is twice as common among poor people as wealthy people (Sareen et al., 2011). At least one–fifth of those with agoraphobia are currently in treatment (NIMH, 2011).

▶ **specific phobia** A severe and persistent fear of a specific object or situation.

▶ **agoraphobia** An anxiety disorder in which a person is afraid to be in public situations from which escape might be difficult or help unavailable if paniclike or embarrassing symptoms were to occur.

MediaSpeak

The Fear Business

By Beth Accomando, NPR, October 6, 2013

Every job requires a special skill set.

In this business, screaming is one of those skills. Also, being certified on a chainsaw.

"We're always looking for folks who have a passion for wielding a chainsaw while wearing makeup and costume and just scaring the heck out of people," says Jennifer Struever.

Streuver is the event manager for Scream Zone at the Del Mar Fairgrounds in San Diego County, Calif. Haunted houses are part of the multibillion-dollar business of Halloween—and they need employees.

Streuver is conducting interviews inside the Scream Zone's tented maze, in a room that could be Leatherface's kitchen. It has a slab of meat hanging from the ceiling and impressive cutlery on the wall.

"We do ask people if they have any problem with chainsaw fumes, moving floors, strobe lights, loud noises," Streuver says. "We need to know if they're allergic to stage blood or latex, because they will be experiencing that in their costumes and makeup."

Over at the haunted castle end of the Scream Zone tent, a huge green demon salivates over potential victims—ahem, applicants—as they wait to be called for their interview. It's so hot that the multiple fans do little to help, and the heat feels like it could melt the flesh off the living dead.

Geraldo Figueroa could get into that. "I'd like to be a zombie," he says. "It seems like it'd be really fun, especially with the new attraction"—zombie paintball safari. . . .

. . . Lung power [is important]—as Samantha Topacio demonstrates. "I mean, I haven't screamed in awhile because no one really recreationally screams just for fun," she says. Topacio performed better at her audition. "I did one that was a victim-type thing," she says, "and then the other one was more like a creepy

Geoff Caddick/Press Association via AP Images

Yikes! Phobophobia, a Halloween show at the London Bridge Experience in London, brings the worst and most typical phobic objects to patrons and has them handle the creatures. Here, a patron confronts a clown, a big spider, and a snake simultaneously.

antagonist-type character." The screams landed her the job and got her a high-five from Ashley Amaral, who's been working at the Scream Zone for years. The petite, perky blond takes wicked delight in her job.

"It is so awesome to see big burly men crumble to the ground," she says. "You think they're so tough. They come in like, 'Oh, you're just a girl, please.' And they just crumble. They will run out of this and say, 'Oh, blank, no, I'm out of here.'"

Each time someone flees for an emergency exit, it's a bloody feather in her co-workers' cap. There's a scoreboard where they keep a tally of victims who don't make it through the House of Horror. Last year it was 523. It gives a whole new meaning to customer satisfaction.

"The Fear Business." Source: "In This Business, Scaredy Cats Need Not Apply," by Beth Accomando, NPR, October 6, 2013 (from KPBS).

It is typical of people with agoraphobia to avoid entering crowded streets or stores, driving in parking lots or on bridges, and traveling on public transportation or in airplanes. If they venture out of the house at all, it is usually only in the company of close relatives or friends. Some insist that family members or friends stay with them at home, but even at home and in the company of others they may continue to feel anxious.

In many cases the intensity of the agoraphobia fluctuates. In severe cases, people become virtual prisoners in their own homes. Their social life dwindles and they

table: 4-5

Dx Checklist

Agoraphobia

1. Pronounced, disproportionate, and repeated fear about being in at least two of the following situations: Public transportation (e.g., auto or plane travel) • Parking lots, bridges, or other open spaces • Shops, theaters, or other confined places • Lines or crowds • Away from home unaccompanied.

2. Fear of such agoraphobic situations derives from a concern that it would be hard to escape or get help if panic, embarrassment, or disabling symptoms were to occur.

3. Avoidance of the agoraphobic situations.

4. Symptoms usually continue for at least six months.

5. Significant distress or impairment.

Information from: APA, 2013.

---

cannot hold a job. People with agoraphobia may also become depressed, sometimes as a result of the severe limitations that their disorder places on their lives.

Many people with agoraphobia do, in fact, have extreme and sudden explosions of fear, called *panic attacks,* when they enter public places, a problem that may have first set the stage for their development of agoraphobia. Such individuals may receive two diagnoses—agoraphobia and *panic disorder,* an anxiety disorder that you will read about later in this chapter—because their difficulties extend considerably beyond an excessive fear of venturing away from home into public places (APA, 2013).

What Causes Phobias?

Each of the models offers explanations for phobias. Evidence tends to support the behavioral explanations. Behaviorists believe that people with phobias first learn to fear certain objects, situations, or events through conditioning (Cherry, 2014; Field & Purkis, 2012). Once the fears are acquired, the individuals avoid the dreaded object or situation, permitting the fears to become all the more entrenched.

Behavioral Explanations: How Are Fears Learned? Behaviorists propose **classical conditioning** as a common way of acquiring phobic reactions. Here, two events that occur close together in time become strongly associated in a person's mind, and, as you saw in Chapter 2, the person then reacts similarly to both of them. If one event triggers a fear response, the other may also.

In the 1920s, a clinician described the case of a young woman who apparently acquired a specific phobia of running water through classical conditioning (Bagby, 1922). When she was 7 years old she went on a picnic with her mother and aunt and ran off by herself into the woods after lunch. While she was climbing over some large rocks, her feet were caught between two of them. The harder she tried to free herself, the more trapped she became. No one heard her screams, and she grew more and more terrified. In the language of behaviorists, the entrapment was eliciting a fear response.

Entrapment → Fear response

As she struggled to free her feet, the girl heard a waterfall nearby. The sound of the running water became linked in her mind to her terrifying battle with the rocks, and she developed a fear of running water as well.

Running water → Fear response

Eventually the aunt found the screaming child, freed her from the rocks, and comforted her, but the psychological damage had been done. From that day forward, the girl was terrified of running water. For years family members had to hold her down to bathe her. When she traveled on a train, friends had to cover the windows so that she would not have to look at any streams. The young woman had apparently acquired a specific phobia through classical conditioning.

In conditioning terms, the entrapment was an *unconditioned stimulus* (US) that understandably elicited an *unconditioned response* (UR) of fear. The running water represented a *conditioned stimulus* (CS), a formerly neutral stimulus that became associated with entrapment in the child's mind and came also to elicit a fear reaction. The newly acquired fear was a *conditioned response* (CR).

US: Entrapment → UR: Fear

CS: Running water → CR: Fear

Another way of acquiring a fear reaction is through **modeling** that is, through observation and imitation (Bandura & Rosenthal, 1966). A person may observe that others are afraid of certain objects or events and develop fears of the same things.

Consider a young boy whose mother is afraid of illnesses, doctors, and hospitals. If she frequently expresses those fears, before long the boy himself may fear illnesses, doctors, and hospitals.

Why should one or a few upsetting experiences or observations develop into a long-term phobia? Shouldn't the trapped girl see later that running water will bring her no harm? Shouldn't the boy see later that illnesses are temporary and doctors and hospitals helpful? Behaviorists believe that after acquiring a fear response, people try to *avoid* what they fear. They do not get close to the dreaded objects often enough to learn that the objects are really quite harmless.

Behaviorists also propose that learned fears of this kind will blossom into a generalized anxiety disorder if a person acquires a large number of them. This development is presumed to come about through **stimulus generalization:** responses to one stimulus are also elicited by similar stimuli. The fear of running water acquired by the girl in the rocks could have generalized to such similar stimuli as milk being poured into a glass or even the sound of bubbly music. Perhaps a person experiences a series of upsetting events, each event produces one or more feared stimuli, and the person's reactions to each of these stimuli generalize to yet other stimuli. That person may then build up a large number of fears and eventually develop generalized anxiety disorder.

How Have Behavioral Explanations Fared In Research?
Some laboratory studies have found that animals and humans can indeed be taught to fear objects through classical conditioning (Miller, 1948; Mowrer, 1947, 1939). In one famous report, psychologists John B. Watson and Rosalie Rayner (1920) described how they taught a baby boy called Little Albert to fear white rats. For weeks Albert was allowed to play with a white rat and appeared to enjoy doing so. One time when Albert reached for the rat, however, the experimenter struck a steel bar with a hammer, making a very loud noise that frightened Albert. The next several times that Albert reached for the rat, the experimenter again made the loud noise. Albert acquired a fear and avoidance response to the rat.

> **What concerns might today's human-participant research review boards raise about the study on Little Albert?**

Research has also supported the behavioral position that fears can be acquired through modeling. Psychologists Albert Bandura and Theodore Rosenthal (1966), for example, had human research participants observe a person apparently being shocked by electricity whenever a buzzer sounded. The victim was actually the experimenter's accomplice—in research terminology, a *confederate*—who pretended to feel pain by twitching and yelling whenever the buzzer went on. After the unsuspecting participants had observed several such episodes, they themselves had a fear reaction whenever they heard the buzzer.

Although these studies support behaviorists' explanations of phobias, other research has called those explanations into question (Gamble et al., 2010). Several laboratory studies with children and adults have failed to condition fear reactions. In addition, although most case studies trace phobias to incidents of classical conditioning or modeling, quite a few fail to do so. So, although it appears that a phobia *can* be acquired by classical conditioning or modeling, researchers have not established that the disorder is *ordinarily* acquired in this way.

A Behavioral-Evolutionary Explanation
Some phobias are much more common than others. Phobic reactions to animals, heights, and darkness are more common than phobic reactions to meat, grass, and houses. Theorists often account for these differences by proposing that human beings, as a species, have a predisposition to develop certain fears (Cherry,

▶ **classical conditioning** A process of learning in which two events that repeatedly occur close together in time become tied together in a person's mind and so produce the same response.

▶ **modeling** A process of learning in which a person observes and then imitates others. Also, a therapy approach based on the same principle.

▶ **stimulus generalization** A phenomenon in which responses to one stimulus are also produced by similar stimuli.

New best friends? Is a mouse's fear of cats a conditioned reaction or genetically hardwired? Scientists at Tokyo University used genetic engineering to switch off this rodent's instinct to cower at the smell or presence of cats. But mouse beware! The cat has not been genetically engineered correspondingly.

AP Photo/Ko and Reiko Kobayakawa, Tokyo University Department of Biophysics and Biochemistry Graduate School of Science

▶ **preparedness** A predisposition to develop certain fears.

▶ **exposure treatments** Behavioral treatments in which persons are exposed to the objects or situations they dread.

▶ **systematic desensitization** A behavioral treatment that uses relaxation training and a fear hierarchy to help clients with phobias react calmly to the objects or situations they dread.

▶ **flooding** A treatment for phobias in which clients are exposed repeatedly and intensively to a feared object and made to see that it is actually harmless.

2014; Lundqvist & Ohman, 2005). This idea is referred to as **preparedness** because human beings, theoretically, are "prepared" to acquire some phobias and not others. The following case makes the point:

> *A four-year-old girl was playing in the park. Thinking that she saw a snake, she ran to her parents' car and jumped inside, slamming the door behind her. Unfortunately, the girl's hand was caught by the closing car door, the results of which were severe pain and several visits to the doctor. Before this, she may have been afraid of snakes, but not phobic. After this experience, a phobia developed, not of cars or car doors, but of snakes. The snake phobia persisted into adulthood, at which time she sought treatment from me.*
>
> *(Marks, 1977, p. 192)*

Where might such predispositions to fear come from? According to some theorists, the predispositions have been transmitted genetically through an evolutionary process. Among our ancestors, the ones who more readily acquired fears of animals, darkness, heights, and the like were more likely to survive long enough to reproduce and to pass on their fear inclinations to their offspring (Cherry, 2014; Ohman & Mineka, 2003).

How Are Phobias Treated?

Every theoretical model has its own approach to treating phobias, but behavioral techniques are more widely used than the rest, particularly for specific phobias. In addition, research has shown such techniques to fare better than other approaches in most head-to-head comparisons. Thus we shall focus here primarily on the behavioral interventions.

Treatments for Specific Phobias Specific phobias were among the first anxiety disorders to be treated successfully. The major behavioral approaches to treating them are *systematic desensitization, flooding,* and *modeling.* Together, these approaches are called **exposure treatments** because in all of them people are exposed to the objects or situations they dread (Gordon et al., 2013; Abramowitz et al., 2011).

People treated by **systematic desensitization,** a technique developed by Joseph Wolpe (1987, 1969), learn to relax while gradually facing the objects or situations they fear. Since relaxation and fear are incompatible, the new relaxation response is thought to substitute for the fear response. Desensitization therapists first offer *relaxation training* to clients, teaching them how to bring on a state of deep muscle relaxation at will. In addition, the therapists help clients create a *fear hierarchy,* a list of feared objects or situations, ordered from mildly to extremely upsetting.

Then clients learn how to pair relaxation with the objects or situations they fear. While the client is in a state of relaxation, the therapist has the client face the event at the bottom of his or her hierarchy. This may be an actual confrontation, a process called *in vivo desensitization.* A person who fears heights, for example, may stand on a chair or climb a stepladder. Or the confrontation may be imagined, a process called *covert desensitization.* In this case, the person imagines the frightening event while the therapist describes it. The client moves through the entire list, pairing his or

Recovering lost revenues These riders scream out as they experience a sudden steep drop from the top of an amusement park ride. Several parks offer behavioral programs to help prospective customers overcome their fears of roller coasters and other horror rides. After "treatment," some clients are able to ride the rails with the best of them. For others, it's back to the relative calm of the Ferris wheel.

Ocean/Corbis

REUTERS/Rick Wilking/Corbis

Flight without fear No, these people are not sleeping, or worse. They are going through relaxation and meditation exercises prior to going on an airplane flight from Kansas City to Denver. They are students in an eight-week course called "Flight Without Fear" that applies the principles of behavioral desensitization to help people overcome their phobic fear of flying.

her relaxation responses with each feared item. Because the first item is only mildly frightening, it is usually only a short while before the person is able to relax totally in its presence. Over the course of several sessions, clients move up the ladder of their fears until they reach and overcome the one that frightens them most of all.

Another behavioral treatment for specific phobias is **flooding.** Therapists who use flooding believe that people will stop fearing things when they are exposed to them repeatedly and made to see that they are actually quite harmless. Clients are forced to face their feared objects or situations without relaxation training and without a gradual buildup. The flooding procedure, like desensitization, can be either in vivo or covert.

When flooding therapists guide clients in imagining feared objects or situations, they often exaggerate the description so that the clients experience intense emotional arousal. In the case of a woman with a snake phobia, the therapist had her imagine the following scene, among others:

> *Close your eyes again. Picture the snake out in front of you, now make yourself pick it up. Reach down, pick it up, put it in your lap, feel it wiggling around in your lap, leave your hand on it, put your hand out and feel it wiggling around. Kind of explore its body with your fingers and hand. You don't like to do it, make yourself do it. Make yourself do it. Really grab onto the snake. Squeeze it a little bit, feel it. Feel it kind of start to wind around your hand. Let it. Leave your hand there, feel it touching your hand and winding around it, curling around your wrist.*
>
> *(Hogan, 1968, p. 423)*

In *modeling* it is the therapist who confronts the feared object or situation while the fearful person observes (Bandura, 2011, 1977, 1971; Bandura et al., 1977). The behavioral therapist acts as a model to demonstrate that the person's fear is groundless. After several sessions many clients are able to approach the objects or situations calmly. In one version of modeling, *participant modeling,* the client is actively encouraged to join in with the therapist.

Clinical researchers have repeatedly found that each of the exposure treatments helps people with specific phobias (Tellez et al., 2015; Antony & Roemer, 2011). The key to greater success in all of these therapies appears to be *actual* contact with the feared object or situation. In vivo desensitization is more effective than covert desensitization, in vivo flooding more effective than covert flooding, and participant modeling more helpful than strictly observational modeling. In addition, a growing number of therapists are using *virtual reality*—3D computer graphics that simulate real-world objects and situations—as a useful exposure tool (Dunsmoor et al., 2014).

Treatments for Agoraphobia

For years clinicians made little impact on agoraphobia, the fear of leaving one's home and entering public places. However, approaches have now been developed that enable many people with agoraphobia to venture out with less anxiety. These new approaches do not always bring as much relief to sufferers as the highly successful treatments for specific phobias, but they do offer considerable relief to many people.

Behaviorists have again led the way, this time by developing a variety of exposure approaches for agoraphobia (Gloster et al., 2014, 2011). Therapists typically help clients to venture farther and farther from their homes and to gradually enter outside places, one step at a time. Sometimes the therapists use support, reasoning, and coaxing to get clients to confront the outside world. They also use more systematic exposure methods, such as those described in the following case study:

> [Lenita] was a young woman who, shortly after she married, found herself unable to leave home. Even walking a few yards from her front door terrified her. . . .
>
> It is not surprising . . . that this young woman found herself unable to function independently after leaving home to marry. Her inability to leave her new home was reinforced by an increasing dependence on her husband and by the solicitous overconcern of her mother, who was more and more frequently called in to stay with her. . . . Since she was cut off from her friends and from so much enjoyment in the outside world, depression added to her misery. . . .
>
> [After several years of worsening symptoms, Lenita was admitted to our psychiatric hospital.] To measure [her] improvement, we laid out a mile-long course from the hospital to downtown, marked at about 25-yard intervals. Before beginning [treatment], we asked the patient to walk as far as she could along the course. Each time she balked at the front door of the hospital. Then the first phase of [treatment] began: we held two sessions each day in which the patient was praised for staying out of the hospital for a longer and longer time. The reinforcement schedule was simple. If the patient stayed outside for 20 seconds on one trial and then on the next attempt stayed out for 30 seconds, she was praised enthusiastically. Now, however, the criterion for praise was raised—without the patient's knowledge—to 25 seconds. If she met the criterion she was again praised, and the time was increased again. If she did not stay out long enough, the therapist simply ignored her performance. To gain the therapist's attention, which she valued, she had to stay out longer each time.
>
> This she did, until she was able to stay out for almost half an hour. But was she walking farther each time? Not at all. She was simply circling around in the front drive of the hospital, keeping the "safe place" in sight at all times. We therefore changed the reinforcement to reflect the distance walked. Now she began to walk farther and farther each time. Supported by this simple therapeutic procedure, the patient was progressively able to increase her self-confidence. . . .
>
> Praise was then thinned out, but slowly, and the patient was encouraged to walk anywhere she pleased. Five years later, she [is] still perfectly well. We might assume that the benefits of being more independent maintained the gains and compensated for the loss of praise from the therapist.
>
> *(Agras, 1985, pp. 77–80)*

Exposure therapy for people with agoraphobia often includes additional features—particularly the use of support groups and home-based self-help programs—to motivate clients to work hard at their treatment. In the *support group* approach, a small number of people with agoraphobia go out together for exposure sessions that last for several hours. The group members support and encourage one another and eventually coax one another to move away from the safety of the group and perform exposure tasks on their own. In the *home-based self-help programs,* clinicians give clients and their families detailed instructions for carrying out exposure treatments themselves.

Between 60 and 80 percent of agoraphobic clients who receive exposure treatment find it easier to enter public places, and the improvement persists for years after the beginning of treatment (Craske & Barlow, 2014; Gloster et al., 2014, 2011). Unfortunately, these improvements are often partial rather than complete, and as many as half of successfully treated clients have relapses, although these people readily recapture previous gains if they are treated again. Those whose agoraphobia is accompanied by a panic disorder seem to benefit less than others from exposure therapy alone. We shall take a closer look at this group when we investigate treatments for panic disorder.

➤ *Summing Up*

PHOBIAS A phobia is a severe, persistent, and unreasonable fear of a particular object, activity, or situation. There are two main categories of phobias: specific phobias and agoraphobia. Behaviorists believe that phobias are often learned from the environment through classical conditioning or through modeling, and then are maintained by avoidance behaviors.

Specific phobias have been treated most successfully with behavioral exposure techniques by which people are led to confront the objects they fear. The exposure may be gradual and relaxed (desensitization), intense (flooding), or vicarious (modeling). Agoraphobia is also treated effectively by exposure therapy. However, for people with both agoraphobia and panic disorder, exposure therapy alone is not as effective.

Social Anxiety Disorder

Many people are uncomfortable when interacting with others or talking or performing in front of others. A number of entertainers and sports figures, from singer Barbra Streisand to baseball pitcher Zack Greinke, have described episodes of significant anxiety before performing. Social fears of this kind certainly are unpleasant, but usually the people who have them manage to function adequately.

People with **social anxiety disorder,** by contrast, have severe, persistent, and irrational anxiety about social or performance situations in which they may face scrutiny by others and possibly feel embarrassment (APA, 2013) (see Table 4-6). The social anxiety may be narrow, such as a fear of talking in public or eating in front of others, or it may be broad, such as a general fear of functioning poorly in front of others. In both forms, people repeatedly judge themselves as performing less competently than they actually do (see *MindTech* on page 129). It is because of its wide-ranging scope that this disorder is now called social anxiety disorder rather than *social phobia,* the label it had in past editions of the DSM (Heimberg et al., 2014).

Why do so many professional performers seem prone to performance anxiety?

Social anxiety disorder can interfere greatly with one's life (Cooper, Hildebrandt, & Gerlach, 2014). A person who cannot interact with others or speak in public may fail to carry out important responsibilities. One who cannot eat in public may reject

▶ **social anxiety disorder** A severe and persistent fear of social or performance situations in which embarrassment may occur.

table: **4-6**

Dx Checklist

Social Anxiety Disorder

1. Pronounced, disproportionate, and repeated anxiety about social situation(s) in which individual could be exposed to possible scrutiny by others, typically lasting six months or more.

2. Fear of being negatively evaluated by or offensive to others.

3. Anxiety is almost always produced by exposure to the social situation.

4. Avoidance of feared situations.

5. Significant distress or impairment.

Information from: APA, 2013.

meal invitations and other social offerings. Since many people with this disorder keep their fears secret, their social reluctance is often misinterpreted as snobbery, lack of interest, or hostility.

Surveys reveal that 7.4 percent of people in the United States and other Western countries (around 60 percent of them female) experience social anxiety disorder in any given year (see Table 4-7). Around 13 percent develop this disorder at some point in their lives (Kessler et al., 2012; Alfano & Beidel, 2011). It tends to begin in late childhood or adolescence and may continue into adulthood. At least one-quarter of individuals with social anxiety disorder are currently in treatment (NIMH, 2011).

table: **4-7**

Profile of Anxiety Disorders and Obsessive-Compulsive Disorder

	One-Year Prevalence	Female-to-Male Ratio	Typical Age at Onset	Prevalence Among Close Relatives	Percentage Currently Receiving Clinical Treatment
Generalized anxiety disorder	4.0%	2:1	0–20 years	Elevated	25.5%
Specific phobia	12.0%	2:1	Variable	Elevated	19.0%
Agoraphobia	1.7%	2:1	15–35 years	Elevated	20.9%
Social anxiety disorder	7.4%	3:2	10–20 years	Elevated	24.7%
Panic disorder	2.4%	5:2	15–35 years	Elevated	34.7%
Obsessive-compulsive disorder	1.0–2.0%	1:1	4–25 years	Elevated	41.3%

Information from: NIMH, 2011; Kessler et al., 2010, 2005, 1999, 1994; Ritter et al., 2010; Ruscio et al., 2007; Wang et al., 2005; Regier et al., 1993.

Research finds that poor people are 50 percent more likely than wealthier people to have social anxiety disorder (Sareen et al., 2011). Moreover, in several studies, African Americans and Asian Americans, but not Hispanic Americans, have scored higher than white Americans on surveys of social anxiety (Polo et al., 2011; Stein & Williams, 2010). In addition, a culture-bound disorder called *taijin kyofusho* seems to be particularly common in Asian countries such as Japan and Korea. Although this disorder is traditionally defined as a fear of making other people feel uncomfortable, a number of clinicians now suspect that its sufferers primarily fear being evaluated negatively by other people, a key feature of social anxiety disorder.

What Causes Social Anxiety Disorder?

The leading explanation for social anxiety disorder has been proposed by cognitive theorists and researchers (Iza et al., 2014; Heimberg et al., 2010). They contend that people with this disorder hold a group of social beliefs and expectations that consistently work against them. These include:

➤ They hold unrealistically high social standards and so believe that they must perform perfectly in social situations.

➤ They view themselves as unattractive social beings.

➤ They view themselves as socially unskilled and inadequate.

➤ They believe they are always in danger of behaving incompetently in social situations.

➤ They believe that inept behaviors in social situations will inevitably lead to terrible consequences.

➤ They believe that they have no control over feelings of anxiety that emerge in social situations.

MindTech

Social Media Jitters

In recent years, researchers have learned that computer and mobile device use can unintentionally produce various forms of anxiety, including social and generalized anxiety (Lepp et al., 2014; Smith, 2014; Krasnova et al., 2013).

The biggest culprit here seems to be spending too much time on social networks such as Facebook. Although frequenting social network sites helps many people feel supported and included, for others, the visits seem to produce significant insecurities and fears. Surveys suggest, for example, that more than one-third of Facebook users develop a fear that others will post or use information or photos of them without their permission (Smith, 2014; Szalavitz, 2013). In addition, a fourth of all users feel a constant pressure to disclose too much personal information on their social networks, and a number feel intense pressure to post material that will be popular and get numerous comments and "likes." More than a few users also worry that they will discover posts about social activities from which they were excluded.

> **Can you think of other negative feelings that might be triggered by social networking?**

One study found that a third of users feel distinctly worse after visiting Facebook—more anxious, more envious, and more dissatisfied with their lives (Krasnova et al., 2013). These feelings are particularly triggered when users observe vacation photos of other users, read birthday greetings received by other users, and see how many "likes" or comments others receive for their postings or photos. Such experiences seem to lead some users to worry that they are less desirable, less interesting, or less capable than most other social media users.

Of course, many of today's users do feel more positive about their social network visits. But even these people may have some social network–induced anxiety and tension. Around two-thirds, for example, are truly afraid that they will miss something if they don't check their social networks constantly—a phenomenon known as FOMO ("fear of missing out") (Cool Infographics, 2013; Szalavitz, 2013).

© Gu/Corbis

Social networking is not the only digital source of anxiety. Recent studies show that excessive cell phone use often results in high levels of anxiety and tension (Lepp et al., 2014). Why? Some theorists speculate that frequent phone users feel *obligated* to stay in touch with friends, another version of FOMO. Others believe that the rise in anxiety among heavy cell phone users is really the result of other cell phone effects, such as poorer performance in school or a reduction in positive time spent alone and self-reflecting (Archer, 2013). Whatever the explanation, two-thirds of cell phone users report feeling "panicked" when they misplace or lose their phones, even for a few minutes. Many experience "nomophobia" (*no-mobile-phone-phobia*), a pop term for the rush of fear that people have when they realize that they are disconnected from the world, friends, and family (Archer, 2013). 💬

Cognitive theorists hold that, because of these beliefs, people with social anxiety disorder keep anticipating that social disasters will occur, and they repeatedly perform "avoidance" and "safety" behaviors to help prevent or reduce such disasters (Moscovitch et al., 2013). Avoidance behaviors include, for example, talking only to people they already know well at gatherings or parties. Safety behaviors include wearing makeup to cover up blushing.

Jim Urguhart/Reuters/Landov

Man's best therapist? Dan McManus and his service dog Shadow hang glide together outside Salt Lake City, Utah, in 2013. McManus experiences anxiety, and Shadow's presence and companionship help him to confront feared objects and situations. The two have been flying together for about nine years with a specially made harness for Shadow.

In Their Words

"When all by myself, I can think of all kinds of clever remarks, quick comebacks to what no one said, and flashes of witty sociability with nobody. But all of this vanishes when I face someone in the flesh. . . ."

Fernando Pessoa

Beset by such beliefs and expectations, people with social anxiety disorder find that their anxiety levels increase as soon as they enter into a social situation. Moreover, because they are convinced that their social flaws are the cause of the anxiety, certain that they do not have the social skills to deal with the situation, and concerned that they cannot contain their negative arousal, they become filled with anxiety.

Later, after the social event has taken place, the individuals repeatedly review the details of the event. They overestimate how poorly things went and what negative results may take place. These persistent thoughts actually keep the event alive and further increase the individuals' fears about future social situations.

Researchers have indeed found that people with social anxiety disorder manifest the beliefs, expectations, interpretations, and feelings listed here (Moscovitch et al., 2013; Rosenberg et al., 2010). At the same time, cognitive theorists often differ on why some individuals have such cognitions and others do not. Various factors have been uncovered by researchers, including genetic predispositions, trait tendencies, biological abnormalities, traumatic childhood experiences, and overprotective parent–child interactions during childhood (Heimberg & Magee, 2014; Rapee, 2014).

Treatments for Social Anxiety Disorder

Only in the past 15 years have clinicians been able to treat social anxiety disorder successfully. Their newfound success is due in part to the growing recognition that the disorder has two distinct features that may feed upon each other: (1) sufferers have overwhelming social fears, and (2) they often lack skill at starting conversations, communicating their needs, or meeting the needs of others. Armed with this insight, clinicians now treat social anxiety disorder by trying to reduce social fears, by providing training in social skills, or both.

How Can Social Fears Be Reduced? Social fears are often reduced through medication (Pelissolo & Moukheiber, 2013). Somewhat surprisingly, it is *antidepressant medications* that seem to be the drugs of most help for this disorder, often more helpful than benzodiazepines or other kinds of antianxiety medications. At the same time, several types of psychotherapy have proved to be at least as effective as medication at reducing social fears, and people helped by such psychological treatments appear less likely to relapse than those treated with medications alone (Abramowitz et al., 2011). This finding suggests to some clinicians that the psychological approaches should always be included in the treatment of social fears.

One psychological approach is *exposure therapy,* the behavioral intervention so effective with phobias (Heimberg & Magee, 2014; Anderson et al., 2013). Exposure therapists encourage clients with social fears to expose themselves to the dreaded social situations and to remain until their fears subside. Usually the exposure is gradual, and it often includes homework assignments that are carried out in the social situations. In addition, group therapy offers an ideal setting for exposure treatments by allowing people to face social situations in an atmosphere of support and caring (McEvoy, 2007). In one group, for example, a man who was afraid that his hands would tremble in the presence of other people had to write on a blackboard in front of the group and serve tea to the other members (Emmelkamp, 1982).

Cognitive therapies have also been widely used to treat social fears, often in combination with behavioral techniques (Heimberg & Magee, 2014; Goldin et al., 2013, 2012). In the following discussion, cognitive therapist Albert Ellis uses rational-emotive therapy to help a man who fears he will be rejected if he speaks up at gatherings. The discussion took place after the man had done a homework assignment in which he was asked to identify his negative social expectations and force himself to say anything he had on his mind in social situations, no matter how stupid it might seem to him:

After two weeks of this assignment, the patient came into his next session of therapy and reported: "I did what you told me to do. . . . [Every] time, just as you said, I found myself retreating from people, I said to myself: 'Now, even though you can't see it, there must be some sentences. What are they?' And I finally found them. And there were many of them! And they all seemed to say the same thing."

"What thing?"

"That I, uh, was going to be rejected. . . . [If] I related to them I was going to be rejected. And wouldn't that be perfectly awful if I was to be rejected. And there was no reason for me, uh, to take that, uh, sort of thing, and be rejected in that awful manner." . . .

"And did you do the second part of the homework assignment?"

"The forcing myself to speak up and express myself?"

"Yes, that part."

"That was worse. That was really hard. Much harder than I thought it would be. But I did it."

"And?"

"Oh, not bad at all. I spoke up several times; more than I've ever done before. Some people were very surprised. Phyllis was very surprised, too. But I spoke up." . . .

"And how did you feel after expressing yourself like that?"

"Remarkable! I don't remember when I last felt this way. I felt, uh, just remarkable—good, that is. It was really something to feel! But it was so hard. I almost didn't make it. And a couple of other times during the week I had to force myself again. But I did. And I was glad!"

(Ellis, 1962, pp. 202–203)

Studies show that rational-emotive therapy and other cognitive approaches do indeed help reduce social fears (Heimberg & Magee, 2014; Ollendick, 2014). And these reductions typically persist for years. On the other hand, research also suggests that while cognitive therapy often reduces social fears, it does not consistently help people perform effectively in social settings. This is where social skills training has come to the forefront.

How Can Social Skills Be Improved? In **social skills training,** therapists combine several behavioral techniques in order to help people improve their social skills. They usually *model* appropriate social behaviors for clients and encourage the individuals to try them out. The clients then *role-play* with the therapists, *rehearsing* their new behaviors until they become more effective. Throughout the process, therapists provide frank *feedback* and *reinforce* (praise) the clients for effective performances.

Reinforcement from other people with similar social difficulties is often more powerful than reinforcement from a therapist alone. In *social skills training groups* and *assertiveness training groups,* members try out and rehearse new social behaviors with other group members. The group can also provide guidance on what is socially appropriate. According to research, social skills training, both individual and group formats, has helped many people perform better in social situations (Sarver, Beidel, & Spitalnick, 2014).

▶ **social skills training** A therapy approach that helps people learn or improve social skills and assertiveness through role playing and rehearsing of desirable behaviors.

➤ *Summing Up*

SOCIAL ANXIETY DISORDER People with social anxiety disorder experience severe and persistent anxiety about social or performance situations in which they may be scrutinized by others or be embarrassed. Cognitive theorists believe that the disorder is particularly likely to develop among people who hold and act on certain dysfunctional social beliefs and expectations.

Therapists who treat social anxiety disorder typically distinguish two components of this disorder: social fears and poor social skills. They try to reduce social fears by drug therapy, exposure techniques, group therapy, various cognitive approaches, or a combination of these interventions. They may try to improve social skills by social skills training.

Panic Disorder

Sometimes an anxiety reaction takes the form of a smothering, nightmarish panic in which people lose control of their behavior and, in fact, are practically unaware of what they are doing. Anyone can react with panic when a real threat looms up suddenly. Some people, however, experience **panic attacks**—periodic, short bouts of panic that occur suddenly, reach a peak within minutes, and gradually pass (APA, 2013).

The attacks feature at least four of the following symptoms of panic: palpitations of the heart, tingling in the hands or feet, shortness of breath, sweating, hot and cold flashes, trembling, chest pains, choking sensations, faintness, dizziness, and a feeling of unreality (APA, 2013). Small wonder that during a panic attack many people fear they will die, go crazy, or lose control.

> *My first panic attack happened when I was traveling for spring break with my mom. . . . [W]hile I was driving . . . , a random thought entered my head, . . . and BOOM—it was like my body . . . had been waiting for an invitation and jumped me right in to a full-blown panic attack. I felt huge waves of warm adrenaline surging across my chest and back, my hands were shaking, and I felt scared that I was losing control—whatever that meant. "I've got to pull over," I said. . . . Catching my breath, a part of me knew I had experienced a panic attack, but was still utterly bewildered at why it happened and how quickly it came on, taking over body and mind. . . . If you've never had a panic attack before, it feels as scary as if someone jumped out from a dark alley and put a gun to your head, leaving you pleading for your life. You would do whatever it took to get away and fast. . . . It's so intense that in the height of panic, the survival instinct kicks in and it seems like a toss-up whether you'll make it out alive or with your mental faculties in place. . . .*
>
> *(LeCroy & Holschuh, 2012)*

More than one-quarter of all people have one or more panic attacks at some point in their lives (Kessler et al., 2010, 2006). Some people, however, have panic attacks repeatedly and unexpectedly and without apparent reason. They may be suffering from **panic disorder.** In addition to the panic attacks, people who are diagnosed with panic disorder experience dysfunctional changes in their thinking or behavior as a result of the attacks (see Table 4-8). They may, for example, worry persistently about having additional attacks, have concerns about what such attacks mean ("Am I losing my mind?"), or plan their lives around the possibility of future attacks (APA, 2013).

table: **4-8**

Dx Checklist

Panic Disorder

1. Unforeseen panic attacks occur repeatedly.

2. One or more of the attacks precedes either of the following symptoms:

   (a) At least a month of continual concern about having additional attacks.

   (b) At least a month of dysfunctional behavior changes associated with the attacks (for example, avoiding new experiences).

Information from: APA, 2013.

Around 2.4 percent of all people in the United States suffer from panic disorder in a given year; more than 5 percent develop it at some point in their lives (Kessler et al., 2012). The disorder tends to develop in late adolescence or early adulthood and is at least twice as common among women as among men. Poor people are 50 percent more likely than wealthier people to experience panic disorder (Sareen et al., 2011).

For reasons that are not understood, the prevalence of this disorder is somewhat higher among white Americans than among minority groups in the United States (Levine et al., 2013). In addition, the features of panic attacks seem to differ somewhat from group to group (Barrera et al., 2010). For example, Asian Americans appear more likely than white Americans to experience dizziness, unsteadiness, and choking, while African Americans seem less likely than white Americans to have those particular symptoms. Surveys indicate that at least one-third of those with panic disorder in the United States are currently in treatment (NIMH, 2011; Wang et al., 2005).

As you read earlier, panic disorder is often accompanied by agoraphobia, the broad phobia in which people are afraid to travel to public places where escape might be difficult should they have panic symptoms or become incapacitated. In such cases, the panic disorder typically sets the stage for the development of agoraphobia. That is, after experiencing multiple unpredictable panic attacks, a person becomes increasingly fearful of having new attacks in public places.

At any time The golfing world was shocked when professional golfer Charlie Beljan—usually a cool customer during competitions—had to sit down and wait for a panic attack to pass on the 18th fairway during a tournament in Lake Buena Vista, Florida, in 2012. Beljan successfully completed the competition, and has since received enormous praise for his comfortable and public candor about his problem.

The Biological Perspective

In the 1960s, clinicians made the surprising discovery that panic disorder was helped more by certain *antidepressant drugs,* drugs that are usually used to reduce the symptoms of depression, than by most of the benzodiazepine drugs, the drugs useful in treating generalized anxiety disorder (Klein, 1964; Klein & Fink, 1962). This observation led to the first biological explanations and treatments for panic disorder.

What Biological Factors Contribute to Panic Disorder? To understand the biology of panic disorder, researchers worked backward from their understanding of the antidepressant drugs that seemed to control it. They knew that these particular antidepressant drugs operate in the brain primarily by changing the activity of **norepinephrine,** yet another one of the neurotransmitters that carries messages between neurons. Given that the drugs were so helpful in eliminating panic attacks, researchers began to suspect that panic disorder might be caused in the first place by abnormal norepinephrine activity.

Several studies produced evidence that norepinephrine activity is indeed irregular in people who suffer from panic attacks. For example, the **locus coeruleus** is a brain area rich in neurons that use norepinephrine, and it serves as a kind of "on–off" switch for most norepinephrine-using neurons throughout the brain (Hedaya, 2011). When this area is electrically stimulated in monkeys, the monkeys have a paniclike reaction, suggesting that panic reactions may be related to increases in norepinephrine activity in the locus coeruleus (Redmond, 1981, 1979, 1977). Similarly, in another line of research, scientists were able to produce panic attacks in human beings by injecting them with chemicals known to increase the activity of norepinephrine (Bourin et al., 1995; Charney et al., 1990, 1987).

These findings strongly tied norepinephrine and the locus coeruleus to panic attacks. However, research conducted in recent years suggests that the root of panic attacks is probably more complicated than a single neurotransmitter or a single brain area. It turns out that panic reactions are produced in part by a brain circuit consisting of areas such as the *amygdala, hippocampus, ventromedial nucleus of the*

▶ **panic attacks** Periodic, short bouts of panic that occur suddenly, reach a peak within minutes, and gradually pass.

▶ **panic disorder** An anxiety disorder marked by recurrent and unpredictable panic attacks.

▶ **norepinephrine** A neurotransmitter whose abnormal activity is linked to panic disorder and depression.

▶ **locus coeruleus** A small area of the brain that seems to be active in the regulation of emotions. Many of its neurons use norepinephrine.

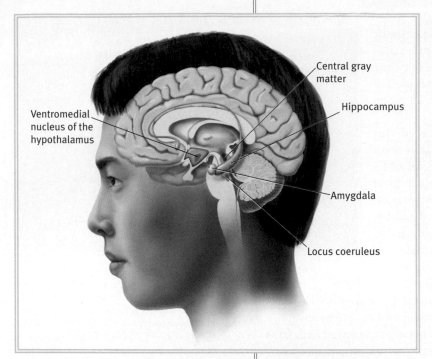

figure 4-5

The biology of panic The circuit in the brain that produces panic reactions includes areas such as the amygdala, hippocampus, ventromedial nucleus of the hypothalamus, central gray matter, and locus coeruleus. This circuit appears to be different from the one limited to anxiety reactions, although the panic and anxiety circuits do share the amygdala.

hypothalamus, central gray matter, and *locus coeruleus* (Henn, 2013; Etkin, 2010) (see Figure 4-5). When a person confronts a frightening object or situation, the amygdala is stimulated. In turn, the amygdala stimulates the other brain areas in the circuit, temporarily setting into motion an "alarm and escape" response (increased heart rate, respiration, blood pressure, and the like) that is very similar to a panic reaction (Gray & McNaughton, 1996). Most of today's researchers believe that this brain circuit—including the neurotransmitters at work throughout the circuit—probably functions improperly in people who experience panic disorder (Henn, 2013; Bremner & Charney, 2010).

Note that the brain circuit responsible for panic reactions appears to be different from the one responsible for broad and worry-dominated *anxiety* reactions—the circuit that was discussed on page 117. Although some of the brain areas and neurotransmitters in the two circuits obviously overlap—particularly the amygdala, which seems to be at the center of each circuit—the finding that the panic brain circuit and the anxiety brain circuit are different has further convinced many researchers that panic disorder is biologically different from generalized anxiety disorder and, for that matter, from other kinds of anxiety disorders.

Why might some people have abnormalities in norepinephrine activity, locus coeruleus functioning, and other parts of the panic brain circuit? One possibility is that a predisposition to develop such abnormalities is inherited (Gloster et al., 2015; Torgersen, 1990, 1983). Once again, if a genetic factor is at work, close relatives should have higher rates of panic disorder than more distant relatives. Studies do find that among identical twins (twins who share all of their genes), if one twin has panic disorder, the other twin has the same disorder in as many as 31 percent of cases (Tsuang et al., 2004). Among fraternal twins (who share only some of their genes), if one twin has panic disorder, the other twin has the same disorder in only 11 percent of cases (Kendler et al., 1995, 1993).

Panic's aftermath Flowers and photos are placed in front of the Kiss nightclub in Santa Maria, Brazil, on January 29, 2013, to pay tribute to the victims of a horrific fire at the club a few days earlier. A total of 242 clubbers were killed and 112 injured in the fire, many as a result of crowd panic, stampeding, and crushing. Catastrophes such as this remind us that people with panic disorder are not the only ones to experience panic.

© Marcelo Sayao/epa/Corbis

Drug Therapies As you have just read, researchers discovered in 1962 that certain antidepressant drugs could prevent panic attacks or reduce their frequency. Since the time of this surprising finding, studies across the world have repeatedly confirmed the initial observation (Cuijpers et al., 2014; Stein et al., 2010).

It appears that all antidepressant drugs that restore proper activity of norepinephrine in the locus coeruleus and other parts of the panic brain circuit are able to help prevent or reduce panic symptoms (Pollack, 2005; Redmond, 1985). Such drugs bring at least some improvement to 80 percent of patients who have panic disorder, and the improvement can last indefinitely, as long as the drugs are continued. In addition, *alprazolam* (Xanax) and other powerful benzodiazepine drugs have also proved effective in the treatment of panic disorder (NIMH, 2013; Bandelow & Baldwin, 2010). Apparently, the benzodiazepines help individuals with this disorder by *indirectly* affecting the activity of norepinephrine throughout the brain. Clinicians also have found the same antidepressant drugs and powerful benzodiazepines to be helpful in cases of panic disorder accompanied by agoraphobia.

The Cognitive Perspective

Cognitive theorists have come to recognize that biological factors are only part of the cause of panic attacks. In their view, full panic reactions are experienced only by people who further *misinterpret* the physiological events that are taking place within their bodies. Cognitive treatments are aimed at correcting such misinterpretations.

The Cognitive Explanation: Misinterpreting Bodily Sensations

Cognitive theorists believe that panic-prone people may be very sensitive to certain bodily sensations; when they unexpectedly experience such sensations, they misinterpret them as signs of a medical catastrophe (Gloster et al., 2014; Clark & Beck, 2012, 2010). Rather than understanding the probable cause of their sensations as "something I ate" or "a fight with the boss," those prone to panic grow increasingly upset about losing control, fear the worst, lose all perspective, and rapidly plunge into panic. For example, many people with panic disorder seem to "overbreathe," or hyperventilate, in stressful situations. The abnormal breathing makes them think that they are in danger of suffocation, so they panic. They further develop the belief that these and other "dangerous" sensations may return at any time and so set themselves up for future panic attacks.

In **biological challenge tests,** researchers produce hyperventilation or other biological sensations by administering drugs or by instructing clinical research participants to breathe, exercise, or simply think in certain ways. As you might expect, participants with panic disorder experience greater upset during these tests than participants without the disorder, particularly when they believe that their bodily sensations are dangerous or out of control (Bunaciu et al., 2012).

Why might some people be prone to such misinterpretations? One possibility is that panic-prone individuals generally experience, through no fault of their own, more frequent or more intense bodily sensations than other people do (Nillni et al., 2012; Nardi et al., 2001). In fact, the kinds of sensations that are most often misinterpreted in panic disorders seem to be carbon dioxide increases in the blood, shifts in blood pressure, and rises in heart rate—bodily events that are controlled in part by the locus coeruleus and other regions of the panic brain circuit. Another possibility, supported by some research, is that people prone to bodily misinterpretations have had more trauma-filled events over the course of their lives than other persons (Hawks et al., 2011).

Whatever the precise causes of such misinterpretations may be, research suggests that panic-prone individuals generally have a high degree of what is called **anxiety sensitivity;** that is, they focus on their bodily sensations much of the time, are unable to assess them logically, and interpret them as potentially harmful. Studies

//// **BETWEEN THE LINES** ////

In Their Words

"Neither a man nor a crowd nor a nation can be trusted to act humanely or to think sanely under the influence of a great fear."

Bertrand Russell

▶ **biological challenge test** A procedure used to produce panic in participants or clients by having them exercise vigorously or perform some other potentially panic-inducing task in the presence of a researcher or therapist.

▶ **anxiety sensitivity** A tendency to focus on one's bodily sensations, assess them illogically, and interpret them as harmful.

have found that people who scored high on anxiety-sensitivity surveys are up to five times more likely than other people to develop panic disorder (Hawks et al., 2011; Maller & Reiss, 1992). Other studies have found that individuals with panic disorder typically earn higher anxiety-sensitivity scores than other persons do (Allan et al., 2014; Reinecke et al., 2011).

Cognitive Therapy Cognitive therapists try to correct people's misinterpretations of their bodily sensations (Craske & Barlow, 2014; Clark & Beck, 2012, 2010). The first step is to educate clients about the general nature of panic attacks, the actual causes of bodily sensations, and the tendency of clients to misinterpret their sensations. The next step is to teach clients to apply more accurate interpretations during stressful situations, thus short-circuiting the panic sequence at an early point.

"Weekends I like to be able to panic without having all the distractions."

Therapists may also teach clients to cope better with anxiety—for example, by using relaxation and breathing techniques—and to distract themselves from their sensations, perhaps by striking up a conversation with someone.

In addition, cognitive therapists may use biological challenge procedures to induce panic sensations, so that clients can apply their new skills under watchful supervision (Gloster et al., 2014). Individuals whose attacks typically are triggered by a rapid heart rate, for example, may be told to jump up and down for several minutes or to run up a flight of stairs. They can then practice interpreting the resulting sensations appropriately, without dwelling on them.

According to research, cognitive treatments often help people with panic disorder (Wesner et al., 2015; Craske & Barlow, 2014). In studies across the world, around 80 percent of participants given these treatments have become free of panic, compared with only 13 percent of control participants. Cognitive therapy has proved to be at least as helpful as antidepressant drugs or alprazolam in the treatment of panic disorder, sometimes even more so (Bandelow et al., 2015; Baker, 2011). In view of the effectiveness of both cognitive and drug treatments, many clinicians have tried, with some success, to combine them (Cuijpers et al., 2014). For individuals who display both panic disorder and agoraphobia, research suggests that it is most helpful to combine behavioral exposure techniques with cognitive treatments and/or drug therapy (Gloster et al., 2014, 2011).

➤ Summing Up

PANIC DISORDER Panic attacks are periodic, discrete bouts of panic that occur suddenly. Sufferers of panic disorder experience panic attacks repeatedly and unexpectedly and without apparent reason. Panic disorder may be accompanied by agoraphobia in some cases, leading to two diagnoses.

Some biological theorists believe that abnormal norepinephrine activity in the brain's locus coeruleus may be central to panic disorder. Others believe that related neurotransmitters or a panic brain circuit may also play key roles. Biological therapists use certain antidepressant drugs or powerful benzodiazepines to treat people with this disorder.

Cognitive theorists suggest that panic-prone people become preoccupied with some of their bodily sensations and misinterpret them as signs of medical catastrophe. In turn, they panic and in some cases develop panic disorder. Cognitive therapists teach patients to interpret their physical sensations more accurately and to cope better with anxiety.

Obsessive-Compulsive Disorder

Obsessions are persistent thoughts, ideas, impulses, or images that seem to invade a person's consciousness. **Compulsions** are repetitive and rigid behaviors or mental acts that people feel they must perform in order to prevent or reduce anxiety. As Figure 4-6 indicates, minor obsessions and compulsions are familiar to almost everyone. You may find yourself filled with thoughts about an upcoming performance or exam or keep wondering whether you forgot to turn off the stove or lock the door. You may feel better when you avoid stepping on cracks, turn away from black cats, or arrange your closet in a particular manner. Repetitive thoughts or behaviors of this kind, however, are hardly a reflection of abnormality.

According to DSM-5, a diagnosis of **obsessive-compulsive disorder** is called for when obsessions or compulsions feel excessive or unreasonable, cause great distress, take up much time, and interfere with daily functions (see Table 4-9 on the next page). Although obsessive-compulsive disorder is not classified as an anxiety disorder in DSM-5, anxiety does play a major role in this pattern. The obsessions cause intense anxiety, while the compulsions are aimed at preventing or reducing anxiety. In addition, anxiety rises if a person tries to resist his or her obsessions or compulsions.

An individual with this disorder observed: "I can't get to sleep unless I am sure everything in the house is in its proper place so that when I get up in the morning, the house is organized. I work like mad to set everything straight before I go to bed, but, when I get up in the morning, I can think of a thousand things that I ought to do. . . . I can't stand to know something needs doing and I haven't done it" (McNeil, 1967, pp. 26–28). Research indicates that several additional disorders are closely related to obsessive-compulsive disorder in their features, causes, and treatment responsiveness, and so, as you will soon see, DSM-5 has grouped them together with obsessive-compulsive disorder.

Between 1 and 2 percent of the people in the United States and other countries throughout the world suffer from obsessive-compulsive disorder in any given year (Kessler et al., 2012; Björgvinsson & Hart, 2008). As many as 3 percent develop the disorder at some point during their lives. It is equally common in men and women and among people of different races and ethnic groups (Matsunaga & Seedat, 2011). The disorder usually begins by young adulthood and typically persists for many years, although its symptoms and their severity may fluctuate over time. It is estimated that more than 40 percent of people with obsessive-compulsive disorder may seek treatment, many for an extended period (Patel et al., 2014; Kessler et al., 1999, 1994).

What Are the Features of Obsessions and Compulsions?

Obsessive thoughts feel both intrusive and foreign to the people who experience them. Attempts to ignore or resist these thoughts may arouse even more anxiety, and before long they come back more strongly than ever. People with obsessions typically are quite aware that their thoughts are excessive.

Certain basic themes run through the thoughts of most people troubled by obsessive thinking (Bokor & Anderson, 2014). The most common theme appears to be dirt or contamination (Torres et al., 2013). Other common ones are violence and aggression, orderliness, religion, and sexuality.

Compulsions are similar to obsessions in many ways. For example, although compulsive behaviors are technically under voluntary control, the people who feel

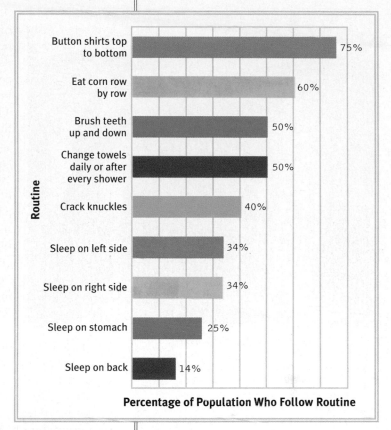

figure 4-6
Normal routines Most people find it comforting to follow set routines when they carry out everyday activities, and, in fact, 40 percent become irritated if they must depart from their routines. (Information from: Kanner, 2005, 1998, 1995.)

▶ **obsession** A persistent thought, idea, impulse, or image that is experienced repeatedly, feels intrusive, and causes anxiety.

▶ **compulsion** A repetitive and rigid behavior or mental act that a person feels driven to perform in order to prevent or reduce anxiety.

▶ **obsessive-compulsive disorder** A disorder in which a person has recurrent and unwanted thoughts, a need to perform repetitive and rigid actions, or both.

Cultural rituals Rituals do not necessarily reflect compulsions. Indeed, cultural and religious rituals often give meaning and comfort to their practitioners. Here Buddhist monks splash water over themselves during their annual winter prayers at a temple in Tokyo. This cleansing ritual is performed to pray for good luck.

they must do them have little sense of choice in the matter. Most of these individuals recognize that their behavior is unreasonable, but they believe at the same time something terrible will happen if they don't perform the compulsions. After performing a compulsive act, they usually feel less anxious for a short while. For some people the compulsive acts develop into detailed *rituals*. They must go through the ritual in exactly the same way every time, according to certain rules.

Like obsessions, compulsions take various forms. *Cleaning compulsions* are very common. People with these compulsions feel compelled to keep cleaning themselves, their clothing, or their homes. The cleaning may follow ritualistic rules and be repeated dozens or hundreds of times a day. People with *checking compulsions* check the same items over and over—door locks, gas taps, important papers—to make sure that all is as it should be. Another common compulsion is the constant effort to seek *order* or *balance*. People with this compulsion keep placing certain items (clothing, books, foods) in perfect order in accordance with strict rules. *Touching, verbal,* and *counting* compulsions are also common.

Although some people with obsessive-compulsive disorder experience obsessions only or compulsions only, most experience both. In fact, compulsive acts are often a response to obsessive thoughts. One study found that in most cases, compulsions seemed to represent a *yielding* to obsessive doubts, ideas, or urges (Akhtar et al., 1975). A woman who keeps doubting that her house is secure may yield to that obsessive doubt by repeatedly checking locks and gas jets, or a man who obsessively fears contamination may yield to that fear by performing cleaning rituals. The study also found that compulsions sometimes serve to help *control* obsessions. A teenager describes how she tried to control her obsessive fears of contamination by performing counting and verbal rituals:

> **Patient:** If I heard the word, like, something that had to do with germs or disease, it would be considered something bad, and so I had things that would go through my mind that were sort of like "cross that out and it'll make it okay" to hear that word.
>
> **Interviewer:** What sort of things?
>
> **Patient:** Like numbers or words that seemed to be sort of like a protector.
>
> **Interviewer:** What numbers and what words were they?
>
> **Patient:** It started out to be the number 3 and multiples of 3 and then words like "soap and water," something like that; and then the multiples of 3 got really high, and they'd end up to be 124 or something like that. It got real bad then.
>
> *(Spitzer et al., 1981, p. 137)*

table: 4-9

Dx Checklist
Obsessive-Compulsive Disorder
1. Occurrence of repeated obsessions, compulsions, or both.
2. The obsessions or compulsions take up considerable time.
3. Significant distress or impairment.
Information from: APA, 2013.

Obsessive-compulsive disorder was once among the least understood of the psychological disorders. In recent decades, however, researchers have begun to learn more about it. The most influential explanations and treatments come from the psychodynamic, behavioral, cognitive, and biological models.

The Psychodynamic Perspective

As you have seen, psychodynamic theorists believe that an anxiety disorder develops when children come to fear their own id impulses and use ego defense mechanisms to lessen the resulting anxiety. What distinguishes obsessive-compulsive disorder from other anxiety disorders, in their view, is that here the battle between anxiety-provoking id impulses and anxiety-reducing defense mechanisms is not buried in the unconscious but is played out in overt thoughts and actions. The id impulses usually take the form of obsessive thoughts, and the ego defenses appear as counter-thoughts or compulsive actions. A woman who keeps imagining her mother lying broken and bleeding, for example, may counter those thoughts with repeated safety checks throughout the house.

Sigmund Freud traced obsessive-compulsive disorder to the *anal stage* of development (occurring at about 2 years of age). He proposed that during this stage some children experience intense rage and shame as a result of negative toilet-training experiences. Other psychodynamic theorists have argued instead that such early rage reactions are rooted in feelings of insecurity (Erikson, 1963; Sullivan, 1953; Horney, 1937). Either way, these children repeatedly feel the need to express their strong aggressive id impulses while at the same time knowing they should try to restrain and control the impulses. If this conflict between the id and ego continues, it may eventually blossom into obsessive-compulsive disorder. Overall, research has not clearly supported the psychodynamic explanation (Busch et al., 2010; Fitz, 1990).

When treating patients with obsessive-compulsive disorder, psychodynamic therapists try to help the individuals uncover and overcome their underlying conflicts and defenses, using the customary techniques of free association and therapist interpretation. Research has offered little evidence, however, that a traditional psychodynamic approach is of much help (Ponniah, Magiati, & Hollon, 2013). Thus some psychodynamic therapists now prefer to treat these patients with short-term psychodynamic therapies, which, as you saw in Chapter 2, are more direct and action-oriented than the classical techniques.

The Behavioral Perspective

Behaviorists have concentrated on explaining and treating compulsions rather than obsessions. They propose that people happen upon their compulsions quite randomly. In a fearful situation, they happen just coincidentally to wash their hands, say, or dress a certain way. When the threat lifts, they link the improvement to that particular action. After repeated accidental associations, they believe that the action is bringing them good luck or actually changing the situation, and so they perform the same actions again and again in similar situations. The act becomes a key method of avoiding or reducing anxiety (Grayson, 2014; Frost & Steketee, 2001).

> **Have you ever tried an informal version of exposure and response prevention in order to stop behaving in certain ways?**

Famous clinical scientist Stanley Rachman and his associates have shown that compulsions do appear to be rewarded by a reduction in anxiety. In one of their experiments, for example, 12 research participants with compulsive hand-washing rituals were placed in contact with objects that they considered contaminated (Hodgson & Rachman, 1972). As behaviorists would predict, the hand-washing rituals of these participants seemed to lower their anxiety.

If people keep performing compulsive behaviors in order to prevent bad outcomes and ensure positive outcomes, can't they be taught that such behaviors are not really serving this purpose? In a behavioral treatment called **exposure and response prevention** (or **exposure and ritual prevention**), first developed by psychiatrist Victor Meyer (1966), clients are repeatedly exposed to objects or situations that produce anxiety, obsessive fears, and compulsive behaviors, but they are told to *resist*

▶ **exposure and response prevention** A behavioral treatment for obsessive-compulsive disorder that exposes a client to anxiety-arousing thoughts or situations and then prevents the client from performing his or her compulsive acts. Also called *exposure and ritual prevention*.

Getting down and dirty In one *exposure and response prevention* assignment, clients with cleaning compulsions might be instructed to do heavy-duty gardening and then resist washing their hands or taking a shower. They may never go so far as to participate in and enjoy mud wrestling, like these delightfully filthy individuals at the annual Mud Day event in Westland, Michigan, but you get the point.

Bill Pugliano/ Getty Images

performing the behaviors they feel so bound to perform. Because people find it very difficult to resist such behaviors, therapists may set an example first.

Many behavioral therapists now use exposure and response prevention in both individual and group therapy formats. Some of them also have people carry out *self-help* procedures at home (Franklin & Foa, 2014). That is, they assign homework in exposure and response prevention, such as these assignments given to a woman with a cleaning compulsion:

➤ Do not mop the floor of your bathroom for a week. After this, clean it within three minutes, using an ordinary mop. Use this mop for other chores as well without cleaning it.

➤ Buy a fluffy mohair sweater and wear it for a week. When taking it off at night do not remove the bits of fluff. Do not clean your house for a week.

➤ You, your husband, and children all have to keep shoes on. Do not clean the house for a week.

➤ Drop a cookie on the contaminated floor, pick the cookie up and eat it.

➤ Leave the sheets and blankets on the floor and then put them on the beds. Do not change these for a week.

(Emmelkamp, 1982, pp. 299–300)

Eventually this woman was able to set up a reasonable routine for cleaning herself and her home.

Between 55 and 85 percent of clients with obsessive-compulsive disorder have been found to improve considerably with exposure and response prevention, improvements that often continue indefinitely (Abramowitz et al., 2011, 2008; McKay, Taylor, & Abramowitz, 2010). The effectiveness of this approach suggests that people with this disorder are like the superstitious man in the old joke who keeps snapping his fingers to keep elephants away. When someone points out, "But there aren't any elephants around here," the man replies, "See? It works!" One review concludes, "With hindsight, it is possible to see that the [obsessive-compulsive] individual has been snapping his fingers, and unless he stops (response prevention) and takes a look around at the same time (exposure), he isn't going to learn much of value about elephants" (Berk & Efran, 1983, p. 546).

The Cognitive Perspective

Cognitive theorists begin their explanation of obsessive-compulsive disorder by pointing out that everyone has repetitive, unwanted, and intrusive thoughts. Anyone might have thoughts of harming others or being contaminated by germs, for example, but most people dismiss or ignore them with ease. Those who develop this disorder, however, typically blame themselves for such thoughts and expect that somehow terrible things will happen (Grayson, 2014; Salkovskis, 1999, 1985). To avoid such negative outcomes, they try to **neutralize** the thoughts—thinking or behaving in ways meant to put matters right or to make amends (Jacob et al., 2014; Salkovskis et al., 2003).

Neutralizing acts might include requesting special reassurance from others, deliberately thinking "good" thoughts, washing one's hands, or checking for possible sources of danger. When a neutralizing effort brings about a temporary reduction in discomfort, it is reinforced and will likely be repeated. Eventually the neutralizing thought or act is used so often that it becomes, by definition, an obsession or compulsion. At the same time, the individual becomes more and more convinced that his or her unpleasant intrusive thoughts are dangerous. As the person's fear of such thoughts increases, the thoughts begin to occur more frequently and they, too, become obsessions.

The Kobal Collection at Art Resource, NY

Personal knowledge The HBO hit series *Girls* follows the struggles of Hannah Horvath and her friends as they navigate their 20s, "one mistake at a time." The show's creator and star, Lena Dunham, says that Hannah's difficulties often are inspired by her own real-life experiences, including her childhood battle with OCD and anxiety.

In support of this explanation, studies have found that people with obsessive-compulsive disorder have intrusive thoughts more often than other people, resort to more elaborate neutralizing strategies, and experience reductions in anxiety after using neutralizing techniques (Jacob et al., 2014; Salkovskis et al., 2003).

Although everyone sometimes has undesired thoughts, only some people develop obsessive-compulsive disorder. Why do these individuals find such normal thoughts so disturbing to begin with? Researchers have found that this population tends (1) to have exceptionally high standards of conduct and morality (Whitton, Henry, & Grisham, 2014; Rachman, 1993), (2) to believe intrusive negative thoughts are equivalent to actions and capable of causing harm (Lawrence & Williams, 2011), and (3) to believe that they should have perfect control over all of their thoughts and behaviors in life (Gelfand & Radomsky, 2013).

THE ETERNAL QUESTION

Should I obsessively check my e-mail or my appearance?

Cognitive therapists help clients focus on the cognitive processes involved in their obsessive-compulsive disorder. Initially, they educate the clients, pointing out how misinterpretations of unwanted thoughts, an excessive sense of responsibility, and neutralizing acts help produce and maintain their symptoms. The therapists then guide the clients to identify, challenge, and change their distorted cognitions. It appears that cognitive techniques of this kind often help reduce the number and impact of obsessions and compulsions (Franklin & Foa, 2014). While the behavioral approach (exposure and response prevention) and the cognitive approach have each been of help to clients with obsessive-compulsive disorder, some research suggests that a combination of the two approaches is often more effective than either intervention alone (Grayson, 2014; McKay et al., 2010).

The Biological Perspective

In recent years, two lines of research have uncovered more direct evidence that biological factors play a key role in obsessive-compulsive disorder, and promising biological treatments for the disorder have been developed as well. This research points to (1) abnormally low activity of the neurotransmitter *serotonin* and (2) abnormal functioning in key regions of the brain.

Serotonin, like GABA and norepinephrine, is a brain chemical that carries messages from neuron to neuron. The first clue to its role in obsessive-compulsive disorder was, once again, a surprising finding by clinical researchers—this time that two antidepressant drugs, *clomipramine* and *fluoxetine* (Anafranil and Prozac), reduce obsessive and compulsive symptoms (Bokor & Anderson, 2014). Since these particular drugs increase serotonin activity, some researchers concluded that the disorder might be caused by low serotonin activity. In fact, only those antidepressant drugs that increase serotonin activity help in cases of obsessive-compulsive disorder; antidepressants that mainly affect other neurotransmitters typically have little or no effect on it (Jenike, 1992). Although serotonin is the neurotransmitter most often cited in explanations of obsessive-compulsive disorder, recent studies have suggested that other neurotransmitters, particularly *glutamate, GABA,* and *dopamine,* may also play important roles in the development of the disorder (Bokor & Anderson, 2014).

Another line of research has linked obsessive-compulsive disorder to the abnormal functioning of specific regions of the brain, particularly the **orbitofrontal cortex** (just above each eye) and the **caudate nuclei** (structures located within the brain region known as the *basal ganglia*). These regions are part of a brain circuit that usually converts sensory information into thoughts and actions. The

▶ **neutralizing** A person's attempt to eliminate unwanted thoughts by thinking or behaving in ways that put matters right internally, making up for the unacceptable thoughts.

▶ **serotonin** A neurotransmitter whose abnormal activity is linked to depression, obsessive-compulsive disorder, and eating disorders.

▶ **orbitofrontal cortex** A region of the brain in which impulses involving excretion, sexuality, violence, and other primitive activities normally arise.

▶ **caudate nuclei** Structures in the brain, within the region known as the basal ganglia, that help convert sensory information into thoughts and actions.

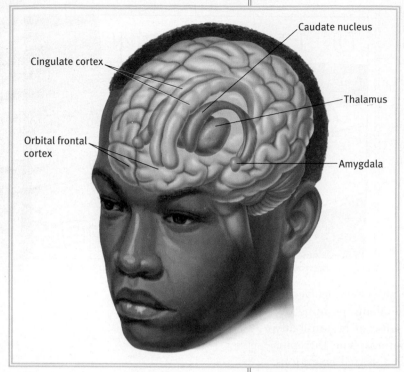

figure 4-7
The biology of obsessive-compulsive disorder Brain structures that have been linked to obsessive-compulsive disorder include the orbitofrontal cortex, caudate nucleus, thalamus, amygdala, and cingulate cortex. The structures may be too active in people with the disorder.

Image labels: Cingulate cortex, Caudate nucleus, Thalamus, Orbital frontal cortex, Amygdala

circuit begins in the orbitofrontal cortex, where sexual, violent, and other primitive impulses normally arise. These impulses next move on to the caudate nuclei, which act as filters that send only the most powerful impulses on to the *thalamus,* the next stop on the circuit (see Figure 4-7). If impulses reach the thalamus, the person is driven to think further about them and perhaps to act. Many theorists now believe that either the orbitofrontal cortex or the caudate nuclei of some people are too active, leading to a constant eruption of troublesome thoughts and actions (Endrass et al., 2011). Additional parts of this brain circuit have also been identified in recent years, including the *cingulate cortex* and, yet again, the *amygdala* (Via et al., 2014; Stein & Fineberg, 2007).

In support of this brain circuit explanation, medical scientists have observed for years that obsessive-compulsive symptoms do sometimes arise or subside after the orbitofrontal cortex, caudate nuclei, or other regions in the circuit are damaged by accident or illness (Hofer et al., 2013). Similarly, brain scan studies have shown that the caudate nuclei and the orbitofrontal cortex of research participants with obsessive-compulsive disorder are more active than those of control participants (Marsh et al., 2014; Baxter et al., 2001, 1990).

The serotonin and brain circuit explanations may themselves be linked. It turns out that serotonin—along with the neurotransmitters glutamate, GABA, and dopamine—plays a key role in the operation of the orbitofrontal cortex, caudate nuclei, and other parts of the brain circuit; certainly abnormal activity by one or more of these neurotransmitters could be contributing to the improper functioning of the circuit.

Ever since researchers first discovered that particular antidepressant drugs help to reduce obsessions and compulsions, these drugs have been used to treat obsessive-compulsive disorder (Bokor & Anderson, 2014). We now know that the drugs not only increase brain serotonin activity but also help produce more normal activity in the orbitofrontal cortex and caudate nuclei (McCabe & Mishor, 2011). Studies have found that these antidepressant drugs bring improvement to between 50 and 80 percent of those with obsessive-compulsive disorder (Bareggi et al., 2004). The obsessions and compulsions do not usually disappear totally, but on average they are cut almost in half within 8 weeks of treatment (DeVeaugh-Geiss et al., 1992).

People who are treated with such drugs alone, however, tend to relapse if their medication is stopped. Thus, more and more individuals with obsessive-compulsive disorder are now being treated by a combination of behavioral, cognitive, and drug therapies. According to research, such combinations often yield higher levels of symptom reduction and bring relief to more clients than do each of the approaches alone—improvements that may continue for years (Romanelli et al., 2014; Simpson et al., 2013).

Obviously, the treatment picture for obsessive-compulsive disorder has improved greatly over the past 15 years, and indeed, this disorder is now helped by several forms of treatment, often used in combination. In fact, some studies suggest that the behavioral, cognitive, and biological approaches may ultimately have the same effect on the brain. In these investigations, both participants who responded to cognitive-behavioral treatments and those who responded to antidepressant drugs showed marked reductions in activity in the caudate nuclei and other parts of the obsessive-compulsive brain circuit (Jabr, 2013; Baxter et al., 2000, 1992).

Obsessive-Compulsive-Related Disorders

Some people perform particular patterns of repetitive and excessive behavior that greatly disrupt their lives. Among the most common such patterns are excessive appearance-checking, hoarding, hair-pulling, and skin-picking. DSM-5 has created the group name *obsessive-compulsive-related disorders* and assigned four of these patterns to that group: *hoarding disorder, trichotillomania (hair-pulling disorder), excoriation (skin-picking) disorder,* and *body dysmorphic disorder.* Collectively, these four disorders are displayed by at least 5 percent of all people (Frost et al., 2012; Keuthen et al., 2012, 2010; Wolrich, 2011).

People who display **hoarding disorder** feel that they must save items, and they become very distressed if they try to discard them (APA, 2013). These feelings make it difficult for them to part with possessions, resulting in an extraordinary accumulation of items that clutters their lives and living areas. This pattern causes the individuals significant distress and may greatly impair their personal, social, or occupational functioning (Ong et al., 2015; Frost et al., 2012). It is common for them to wind up with numerous useless and valueless items, from junk mail to broken objects to unused clothes. Parts of their homes may become inaccessible because of the clutter. For example, sofas, kitchen appliances, or beds may be unusable. In addition, the pattern often results in fire hazards, unhealthful sanitation conditions, or other dangers.

People with **trichotillomania,** also known as **hair-pulling disorder**, repeatedly pull out hair from their scalp, eyebrows, eyelashes, or other parts of the body (APA, 2013). The disorder usually centers on just one or two of these body sites, most often the scalp. Typically, those with the disorder pull one hair at a time. It is common for anxiety or stress to trigger or accompany the hair-pulling behavior. Some sufferers follow specific rituals as they pull their hair, including pulling until the hair feels "just right" and selecting certain types of hairs for pulling (Starcevic, 2015; Keuthen et al., 2012). Because of the distress, impairment, or embarrassment caused by this behavior, the individuals often try to reduce or stop the hair-pulling. The term "trichotillomania" is derived from the Greek for "frenzied hair-pulling."

People with **excoriation (skin-picking) disorder** keep picking at their skin, resulting in significant sores or wounds (APA, 2013). Like those with hair-pulling

> ▸ **hoarding disorder** A disorder in which individuals feel compelled to save items and become very distressed if they try to discard them, resulting in an excessive accumulation of items.

> ▸ **trichotillomania** A disorder in which people repeatedly pull out hair from their scalp, eyebrows, eyelashes, or other parts of the body. Also called *hair-pulling disorder.*

> ▸ **excoriation disorder** A disorder in which people repeatedly pick at their skin, resulting in significant sores or wounds. Also called *skin-picking disorder.*

© Sandy Huffaker/Corbis

A messy aftermath This man prepares to clean out his mother's home after her death. This is not an easy task—emotionally or physically—under the best of circumstances, but it is particularly difficult in this instance: his mother had suffered from hoarding disorder.

▶ **body dysmorphic disorder** A disorder in which individuals become preoccupied with the belief that they have certain defects or flaws in their physical appearance. Such defects or flaws are imagined or greatly exaggerated.

disorder, they often try to reduce or stop the behavior. Most sufferers pick with their fingers and center their picking on one area, most often the face (Grant et al., 2015, 2012; Odlaug & Grant, 2012). Other common areas of focus include the arms, legs, lips, scalp, chest, and extremities such as fingernails and cuticles. The behavior is typically triggered or accompanied by anxiety or stress.

People with **body dysmorphic disorder** become preoccupied with the belief that they have a particular defect or flaw in their physical appearance. Actually, the perceived defect or flaw is imagined or greatly exaggerated in the person's mind (APA, 2013). Such beliefs drive the individuals to repeatedly check themselves in the mirror, groom themselves, pick at the perceived flaw, compare themselves with others, seek reassurance, or perform other, similar behaviors. Here, too, those with the problem experience significant distress or impairment.

Body dysmorphic disorder is the obsessive-compulsive-related disorder that has received the most study to date. Researchers have found that, most often, individuals with this problem focus on wrinkles; spots on the skin; excessive facial hair; swelling of the face; or a misshapen nose, mouth, jaw, or eyebrow (Fang & Wilhelm, 2015; Veale & Bewley, 2015). Some worry about the appearance of their feet, hands, breasts, penis, or other body parts. Still others, like the woman described here, are concerned about bad odors coming from sweat, breath, genitals, or the rectum.

> A woman of 35 had for 16 years been worried that her sweat smelled terrible. . . . For fear that she smelled, for 5 years she had not gone out anywhere except when accompanied by her husband or mother. She had not spoken to her neighbors for 3 years. . . . She avoided cinemas, dances, shops, cafes, and private homes. . . . Her husband was not allowed to invite any friends home; she constantly sought reassurance from him about her smell. . . . Her husband bought all her new clothes as she was afraid to try on clothes in front of shop assistants. She used vast quantities of deodorant and always bathed and changed her clothes before going out, up to 4 times daily.
>
> *(Marks, 1987, p. 371)*

Worldwide influence A lingerie ad in a subway station in Shanghai, China, displays a woman in a push-up bra. As West meets East, Asian women have been bombarded by ads encouraging them to make Western-like changes to their various body parts. Perhaps not so coincidentally, cases of body dysmorphic disorder among Asians are becoming more and more similar to those among Westerners.

Mark Henley/ Panos

Of course, it is common in our society to worry about appearance (see Figure 4-8). Many teenagers and young adults worry about acne, for instance. The concerns of people with body dysmorphic disorder, however, are extreme. Sufferers may severely limit contact with other people, be unable to look others in the eye, or go to great lengths to conceal their "defects"—say, always wearing sunglasses to cover their supposedly misshapen eyes. As many as half of people with the disorder seek plastic surgery or dermatology treatment, and often they feel worse rather than better afterward (Dey et al., 2015; McKay et al., 2008). A large number are housebound, and more than 10 percent may attempt suicide (Buhlmann et al., 2010; Phillips et al., 1993).

As with the other obsessive-compulsive-related disorders, theorists typically account for body dysmorphic disorder by using the same kinds of explanations, both psychological and biological, that have been applied to obsessive-compulsive disorder (Hartmann et al., 2015; Witthöft & Hiller, 2010). Similarly, clinicians typically treat clients with this disorder by applying the kinds of treatment used with obsessive-compulsive disorder, particularly

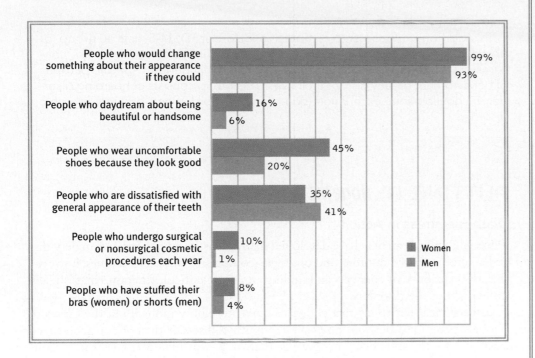

figure 4-8
"Mirror, mirror, on the wall ..." People with body dysmorphic disorder are not the only ones who have concerns about their appearance. Surveys find that in our appearance-conscious society, large percentages of people regularly think about and try to change the way they look. (Information from: ASAPS, 2015; Samorodnitzky-Naveh et al., 2007; Noonan, 2003; Kimball, 1993; Poretz & Sinrod, 1991; Weiss, 1991; Simmon, 1990.)

antidepressant drugs, exposure and response prevention, and cognitive therapy (Fang & Wilhelm, 2015; Krebs et al., 2012).

In one study, for example, 17 clients with this disorder were treated with exposure and response prevention. Over the course of 4 weeks, the clients were repeatedly reminded of their perceived physical defects and, at the same time, prevented from doing anything to help reduce their discomfort (such as checking their appearance) (Neziroglu et al., 2004, 1996). By the end of treatment, these individuals were less concerned with their "defects" and spent less time checking their body parts and avoiding social interactions.

➤ Summing Up

OBSESSIVE-COMPULSIVE DISORDER People with obsessive-compulsive disorder are beset by obsessions, perform compulsions, or both. Compulsions are often a response to a person's obsessive thoughts.

According to the psychodynamic view, obsessive-compulsive disorder arises out of a battle between id impulses and ego defense mechanisms. Behaviorists believe that compulsive behaviors develop through chance associations. The leading behavioral treatment combines prolonged exposure with response prevention. Cognitive theorists believe that obsessive-compulsive disorder grows from a normal human tendency to have unwanted and unpleasant thoughts. The efforts of some people to understand, eliminate, or avoid such thoughts actually lead to obsessions and compulsions. Cognitive therapists educate clients and help them correct their misinterpretations of the unwanted thoughts. Research suggests that a combined cognitive-behavioral approach may be more effective than either therapy alone.

Biological researchers have tied obsessive-compulsive disorder to low serotonin activity and abnormal functioning in the orbitofrontal cortex and caudate nuclei. Antidepressant drugs that raise serotonin activity are a useful form of treatment.

BETWEEN THE LINES

Losing Battle

People who try to avoid all contamination and rid themselves and their world of all germs are fighting a losing battle. While talking, the average person sprays 300 microscopic saliva droplets per minute, or 2.5 per word.

(continues on the next page)

In addition to obsessive-compulsive disorder, DSM-5 lists a group of obsessive-compulsive-related disorders, disorders in which obsessive-like concerns drive individuals to repeatedly and excessively perform specific patterns of behavior that greatly disrupt their lives. This group consists of hoarding disorder, trichotillomania, excoriation (skin-picking) disorder, and body dysmorphic disorder.

PUTTING IT...*together*

Diathesis-Stress in Action

Clinicians and researchers have developed many ideas about generalized anxiety disorder, phobias, panic disorder, and obsessive-compulsive disorder. At times, however, the sheer quantity of concepts and findings makes it difficult to grasp what is really known about the disorders.

Overall, it is fair to say that clinicians currently know more about the causes of phobias, panic disorder, and obsessive-compulsive disorder than about generalized anxiety disorder and social anxiety disorder. It is worth noting that the insights about panic disorder and obsessive-compulsive disorder—once among the field's most puzzling patterns—did not emerge until clinical theorists took a look at the disorders from more than one perspective and integrated those views. Today's cognitive explanation of panic disorder, for example, builds squarely on the biological theorists' idea that the disorder begins with abnormal brain activity and unusual physical sensations. Similarly, the cognitive explanation of obsessive-compulsive disorder takes its lead from the biological position that some people are predisposed to having more unwanted and intrusive thoughts than others do.

It may be that a fuller understanding of generalized anxiety disorder and social anxiety disorder awaits a similar integration of the various models. In fact, such integrations have already begun. Recall, for example, that one of the new-wave cognitive explanations for generalized anxiety disorder links the cognitive process of worrying to heightened bodily arousal in people with the disorder.

Similarly, a growing number of theorists are adopting a *diathesis-stress* view of generalized anxiety disorder. They believe that certain individuals have a biological vulnerability toward developing the disorder—a vulnerability that is eventually brought to the surface by psychological and sociocultural factors. Indeed, genetic investigators have discovered that certain genes may determine whether a person reacts to life's stressors calmly or in a tense manner, and developmental researchers have found that even during the earliest stages of life some infants become particularly aroused when stimulated (Burijon, 2007; Kalin, 1993). Perhaps these easily aroused infants have inherited defects in GABA functioning or other biological limitations that predispose them to generalized anxiety disorder. If, over the course of their lives, they also face intense societal pressures, learn to interpret the world as a dangerous place, or come to regard worrying as a useful tool, they may be candidates for developing generalized anxiety disorder.

In the treatment realm, integration of the models is already on display for each of the anxiety disorders and for obsessive-compulsive disorder. Therapists have discovered, for example, that treatment is at least sometimes more effective when medications are combined with cognitive techniques to treat panic disorder and when medications are combined with cognitive-behavioral techniques to treat obsessive-compulsive disorder. Similarly, cognitive techniques are often combined

CLINICAL CHOICES

Now that you've read about anxiety, obsessive-compulsive and related disorders, try the interactive case study for this chapter. See if you are able to identify Priya's symptoms and suggest a diagnosis based on her symptoms. What kind of treatment would be most effective for Priya? Go to LaunchPad to access *Clinical Choices*.

▶ **stress-management program** An approach to treating generalized and other anxiety disorders that teaches clients techniques for reducing and controlling stress.

Stress and Arousal: The Fight-or-Flight Response

The features of arousal and fear are set in motion by the brain area called the *hypothalamus*. When our brain interprets a situation as dangerous, neurotransmitters in the hypothalamus are released, triggering the firing of neurons throughout the brain and the release of chemicals throughout the body. Actually, the hypothalamus activates two important systems—the *autonomic nervous system* and the *endocrine system* (Biran et al., 2015). The **autonomic nervous system (ANS)** is the extensive network of nerve fibers that connect the *central nervous system* (the brain and spinal cord) to all the other organs of the body. These fibers help control the *involuntary* activities of the organs—breathing, heartbeat, blood pressure, perspiration, and the like (see Figure 5-1). The **endocrine system** is the network of *glands* located throughout the body. (As you read in Chapter 2, glands release *hormones* into the bloodstream and on to the various body organs.) The ANS and the endocrine system often overlap in their responsibilities. There are two pathways, or routes, by which these systems produce arousal and fear reactions—the *sympathetic nervous system* pathway and the *hypothalamic-pituitary-adrenal* pathway.

When we face a dangerous situation, the hypothalamus first excites the **sympathetic nervous system,** a group of ANS fibers that work to quicken our heartbeat and produce the other changes that we experience as fear or anxiety. These nerves may stimulate the organs of the body directly—for example, they may

▸ **autonomic nervous system (ANS)** The network of nerve fibers that connect the central nervous system to all the other organs of the body.

▸ **endocrine system** The system of glands located throughout the body that help control important activities such as growth and sexual activity.

▸ **sympathetic nervous system** The nerve fibers of the autonomic nervous system that quicken the heartbeat and produce other changes experienced as arousal and fear.

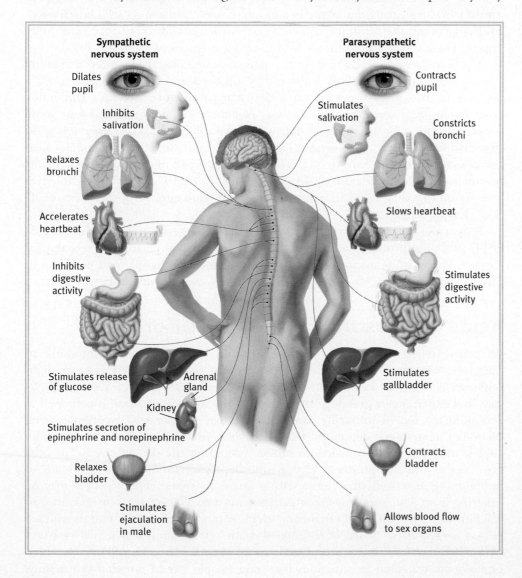

figure 5-1

The autonomic nervous system (ANS) When the sympathetic division of the ANS is activated, it stimulates some organs and inhibits others. The result is a state of general arousal. In contrast, activation of the parasympathetic division leads to an overall calming effect.

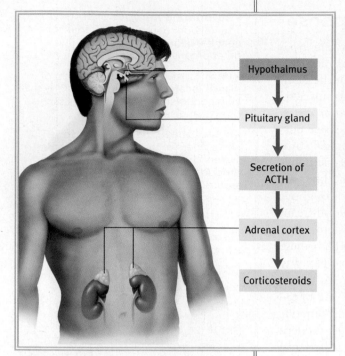

figure 5-2

The endocrine system: The HPA pathway When a person perceives a stressor, the hypothalamus activates the pituitary gland to secrete the adrenocorticotropic hormone, or ACTH, which stimulates the adrenal cortex. The adrenal cortex releases stress hormones called corticosteroids that act on other body organs to trigger arousal and fear reactions.

▸**parasympathetic nervous system** The nerve fibers of the autonomic nervous system that help return bodily processes to normal.

▸**hypothalamic-pituitary-adrenal (HPA) pathway** One route by which the brain and body produce arousal and fear.

▸**corticosteroids** A group of hormones, including cortisol, released by the adrenal glands at times of stress.

▸**acute stress disorder** A disorder in which a person experiences fear and related symptoms soon after a traumatic event but for less than a month.

▸**posttraumatic stress disorder (PTSD)** A disorder in which a person continues to experience fear and related symptoms long after a traumatic event.

directly stimulate the heart and increase heart rate. The nerves may also influence the organs indirectly, by stimulating the *adrenal glands* (glands located on top of the kidneys), particularly an area of these glands called the *adrenal medulla*. When the adrenal medulla is stimulated, the chemicals *epinephrine* (*adrenaline*) and *norepinephrine* (*noradrenaline*) are released. You have already seen that these chemicals are important neurotransmitters when they operate in the brain (see pages 133–134). When released from the adrenal medulla, however, they act as hormones and travel through the bloodstream to various organs and muscles, further producing arousal and fear.

When the perceived danger passes, a second group of autonomic nervous system fibers, called the **parasympathetic nervous system,** helps return our heartbeat and other body processes to normal. Together the sympathetic and parasympathetic nervous systems help control our arousal and fear reactions.

The second pathway by which arousal and fear reactions are produced is the **hypothalamic-pituitary-adrenal (HPA) pathway** (see Figure 5-2). When we are faced by stressors, the hypothalamus also signals the *pituitary gland,* which lies nearby, to secrete the *adrenocorticotropic hormone* (*ACTH*), sometimes called the body's "major stress hormone." ACTH, in turn, stimulates the outer layer of the adrenal glands, an area called the *adrenal cortex,* triggering the release of a group of stress hormones called **corticosteroids,** including the hormone *cortisol.* These corticosteroids travel to various body organs, where they further produce arousal and fear reactions (Seaward, 2013).

The reactions on display in these two pathways are collectively referred to as the *fight-or-flight* response, precisely because they arouse our body and prepare us for a response to danger. Each person has a particular pattern of autonomic and endocrine functioning and so a particular way of experiencing arousal and fear. Some people are almost always relaxed, while others typically feel tension, even when no threat is apparent. A person's general level of arousal and anxiety is sometimes called *trait anxiety* because it seems to be a general trait that each of us brings to the events in our lives (Tolmunen et al., 2014; Spielberger, 1985, 1972, 1966). Psychologists have found that differences in trait anxiety appear soon after birth (Schwartz et al., 2015; Kagan, 2003).

People also differ in their sense of which situations are threatening (Moore et al., 2014). Walking through a forest may be fearsome for one person but relaxing for another. Flying in an airplane may arouse terror in some people and boredom in others. Such variations are called differences in *situation,* or *state, anxiety.*

Acute and Posttraumatic Stress Disorders

Of course when we actually confront stressful situations, we do not think to ourselves, "Oh, there goes my autonomic nervous system" or "My fight-or-flight response seems to be kicking in." We just feel aroused psychologically and physically and experience a growing sense of fear. If the stressful situation is perceived as extraordinary and/or unusually dangerous, we may temporarily experience levels of arousal, anxiety, and depression that are beyond anything we have ever known.

For most people, such reactions subside soon after the danger passes. For others, however, the symptoms of anxiety and depression, as well as other kinds of symptoms, persist well after the upsetting situation is over. These people may be suffering from *acute stress disorder* or *posttraumatic stress disorder,* patterns that arise in reaction to a psychologically traumatic event. A traumatic event is one in which a person is exposed to actual or threatened death, serious injury, or sexual violation (APA, 2013). Unlike the anxiety disorders that you read about in Chapter 4, which typically are triggered by situations that most people would not find threatening, the situations that cause acute stress disorder or posttraumatic stress disorder—combat, rape, an earthquake, an airplane crash—would be traumatic for anyone.

If the symptoms begin within four weeks of the traumatic event and last for less than a month, DSM-5 assigns a diagnosis of **acute stress disorder** (APA, 2013). If the symptoms continue longer than a month, a diagnosis of **posttraumatic stress disorder (PTSD)** is given. The symptoms of PTSD may begin either shortly after the traumatic event or months or years afterward (see Table 5-1).

Studies indicate that at least half of all cases of acute stress disorder develop into posttraumatic stress disorder (Bryant et al., 2015, 2005). Think back to Latrell, the soldier in Iraq whose case opened this chapter. As you'll recall, Latrell became overrun by anxiety, insomnia, worry, anger, depression, irritability, intrusive thoughts, flashback memories, and social detachment within days of the attack on his convoy mission—thus qualifying him for a diagnosis of acute stress disorder. As his symptoms worsened and continued beyond one month—even long after his return to the United States—this diagnosis became PTSD. Aside from the differences in onset and duration, the symptoms of acute stress disorder and PTSD are almost identical:

REEXPERIENCING THE TRAUMATIC EVENT People may be battered by recurring thoughts, memories, dreams, or nightmares connected to the event (APA, 2013). A few relive the event so vividly in their minds (flashbacks) that they think it is actually happening again.

AVOIDANCE People usually avoid activities that remind them of the traumatic event and try to avoid related thoughts, feelings, or conversations (APA, 2013).

REDUCED RESPONSIVENESS People feel detached from other people or lose interest in activities that once brought enjoyment. Some experience symptoms of *dissociation*, or psychological separation: they feel dazed, have trouble remembering things, or have a sense of derealization (feeling that the environment is unreal or strange) (APA, 2013).

INCREASED AROUSAL, NEGATIVE EMOTIONS, AND GUILT People with these disorders may feel overly alert (hyperalertness), be easily startled, have trouble concentrating, and develop sleep problems (APA, 2013). They may display anxiety, anger, or depression and feel extreme guilt because they survived the traumatic event while others did not (Worthen et al., 2014). Some also feel guilty about what they may have had to do to survive.

You can see these symptoms in the recollections of a Vietnam combat veteran years after he returned home:

I can't get the memories out of my mind! The images come flooding back in vivid detail, triggered by the most inconsequential things, like a door slamming or the smell of stir-fried pork. Last night I went to bed, was having a good sleep for a change. Then in the early morning a storm-front passed through and there was a bolt of crackling thunder. I awoke instantly, frozen in fear. I am right back in Vietnam, in the middle of the monsoon season at my guard post. I am sure I'll get hit in the next volley and convinced I will die. My hands are freezing, yet sweat pours from my entire body. I feel each hair on the back of my neck standing on end. I can't catch my breath and my heart is pounding. I smell a damp sulfur smell.

(Davis, 1992)

table: **5-1**

Dx Checklist

Posttraumatic Stress Disorder

1. Person is exposed to a traumatic event—death or threatened death, severe injury, or sexual violation.

2. Person experiences at least one of the following intrusive symptoms: • Repeated, uncontrolled, and distressing memories • Repeated and upsetting trauma-linked dreams • Dissociative experiences such as flashbacks • Significant upset when exposed to trauma-linked cues • Pronounced physical reactions when reminded of the event(s).

3. Person continually avoids trauma-linked stimuli.

4. Person experiences negative changes in trauma-linked cognitions and moods, such as being unable to remember key features of the event(s) or experiencing repeated negative emotions.

5. Person displays conspicuous changes in arousal and reactivity, such as excessive alertness, extreme startle responses, or sleep disturbances.

6. Person experiences significant distress or impairment, with symptoms lasting more than a month.

Information from: APA, 2013.

▶**rape** Forced sexual intercourse or another sexual act committed against a nonconsenting person or intercourse between an adult and an underage person.

What Triggers Acute and Posttraumatic Stress Disorders?

An acute or posttraumatic stress disorder can occur at any age, even in childhood, and can affect one's personal, family, social, or occupational life (Alisic et al., 2014; Monson et al., 2014). People with these stress disorders may also experience depression, another anxiety disorder, or substance abuse or become suicidal. Surveys indicate that at least 3.5 percent of people in the United States have one of the stress disorders in any given year; 7 to 9 percent suffer from one of them during their lifetimes (Kessler et al., 2012; Peterlin et al., 2011). Around two-thirds of these individuals seek treatment at some point in their lives, but relatively few do so when they first develop the disorder (Hoge et al., 2014; Wang et al., 2005).

> **What types of events in modern society might trigger acute stress disorder and posttraumatic stress disorder?**

Women are at least twice as likely as men to develop stress disorders: around 20 percent of women who are exposed to a serious trauma may develop one, compared with 8 percent of men (Perrin et al., 2014; Russo & Tartaro, 2008). Moreover, people with low incomes are twice as likely as people with higher incomes to experience one of the stress disorders (Sareen et al., 2011).

Any traumatic event can trigger a stress disorder; however, some are particularly likely to do so. Among the most common are combat, disasters, and abuse and victimization.

Combat For years clinicians have recognized that many soldiers develop symptoms of severe anxiety and depression *during* combat. It was called "shell shock" during World War I and "combat fatigue" during World War II and the Korean War (Figley, 1978). Not until after the Vietnam War, however, did clinicians learn that a great many soldiers also experience serious psychological symptoms *after* combat (Ruzek et al., 2011).

By the late 1970s, it became apparent that many Vietnam combat veterans were still experiencing war-related psychological difficulties (Roy-Byrne et al., 2004). We now know that as many as 29 percent of all Vietnam veterans, male and female, suffered an acute or posttraumatic stress disorder, while another 22 percent have had at least some stress symptoms (Hermes et al., 2014; Krippner & Paulson, 2006). In fact, 10 percent of the veterans of that war still deal with posttraumatic stress symptoms, including flashbacks, night terrors, nightmares, and persistent images and thoughts.

A similar pattern unfolded among the nearly 2 million veterans of the wars in Afghanistan and Iraq (Ruzek et al., 2011). For example, a few years ago, the RAND Corporation, a nonprofit research organization, conducted a large-scale study of military service members who served in those wars (Zoroya, 2013; RAND Corporation, 2010, 2008). It found that around 20 percent of the Americans deployed to the wars had so far reported symptoms of posttraumatic stress disorder. Given that not all of those studied were in fact exposed to prolonged periods of combat-related stress, this is indeed a very large percentage. Half of the veterans interviewed in this study described traumas in which they had seen friends seriously wounded or killed, 45 percent reported seeing dead or gravely wounded civilians, and 10 percent said they themselves had been injured and hospitalized.

It is also worth noting that the wars in Afghanistan and Iraq involved repeated deployments of many of the combat veterans and that the soldiers who served such multiple deployments were 50 percent more likely than those with one tour of service to have experienced severe combat stress, significantly raising their risk of developing posttraumatic stress disorder (Tyson, 2006).

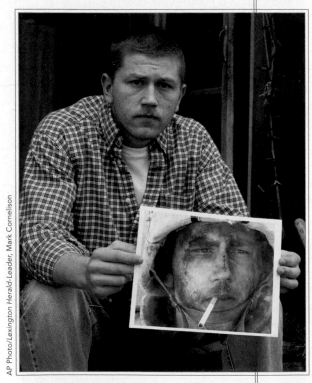

AP Photo/Lexington Herald-Leader, Mark Cornelison

"Marlboro Man" One of the most famous photos to emerge from the war in Iraq was that of a U.S. Marine, dubbed "the Marlboro Man" by the news media, taken during the battle for Fallujah in 2004. In the photo—praised by the president, military commanders, and national media, among millions of others—the soldier's face was smeared with dirt and blood, and a cigarette dangled from his lips. Two years after the photo was taken, 21-year-old James Blake Miller was sitting outside his home in Kentucky, holding the famous picture of himself and revealing that he had since received a diagnosis of posttraumatic stress disorder.

Disasters Acute and posttraumatic stress disorders may also follow natural and accidental disasters such as earthquakes, floods, tornadoes, fires, airplane crashes, and serious car accidents (see Table 5-2). Researchers have found, for example, unusually high rates of posttraumatic stress disorder among the survivors of 2005's Hurricane Katrina, 2010's BP Gulf Coast oil spill, and the devastating tornado that struck Moore, Oklahoma, in 2013 (Cherry et al., 2015; Pearson, 2013; Voelker, 2010). In fact, because they occur more often, civilian traumas have been the trigger of stress disorders at least 10 times as often as combat traumas (Bremner, 2002). Studies have even found that between 15 and 40 percent of people involved in traffic accidents—adult or child—may develop PTSD within a year of the accident (Noll-Hussong et al., 2013; Hickling & Blanchard, 2007).

Victimization People who have been abused or victimized often have stress symptoms that linger. Research suggests that more than one-third of all victims of physical or sexual assault develop posttraumatic stress disorder (Walsh et al., 2014; Koss et al., 2011) and that as many as half of all people who are directly exposed to terrorism or torture may develop the disorder (Basoglu et al., 2001).

SEXUAL ASSAULT A common form of victimization in our society today is sexual assault (see *InfoCentral* on the next page). **Rape** is forced sexual intercourse or another sexual act committed against a nonconsenting person or intercourse between an adult and an underage person. In the United States, approximately 100,000 cases of rape or attempted rape are reported to the police each year (Berzofsky et al., 2013; Koss et al., 2011). Most experts believe that these are but a fraction of the actual number of rapes and rape attempts, given the reluctance of many victims to report their sexual assaults. Most rapists are men and most victims are women. Around one in six women is raped at some time during her life. Approximately 73 percent of the victims are raped by acquaintances, intimates, or relatives (BJS, 2013).

The rates of rape differ from race to race. Around 27 percent of American Indian women and 22 percent of African American women have been raped at some point in their lives, compared with 19 percent of white American women, 15 percent of Hispanic American women, and 12 percent of Asian American women (Black et al., 2011).

The psychological impact of rape on a victim is immediate and may last a long time (Koss et al., 2011, 2008; Koss, 2005, 1993). Rape victims typically experience enormous distress during the week after the assault. Stress continues to rise for the next three weeks, maintains a peak level for another month or so, and then starts to improve. In one study, 94 percent of rape victims fully qualified for a clinical diagnosis of acute stress disorder when they were observed around 12 days after the assault (Rothbaum et al., 1992). Although some rape victims improve psychologically within three or four months, for many others, the profound effects of their assault persist for up to 18 months or longer. Victims typically continue to have higher-than-average levels of

> How might physicians, police, and the courts better meet the psychological needs of rape victims?

table: 5-2

Worst Natural Disasters of the Past 100 Years

Disaster	Year	Location	Number Killed
Flood	1931	Huang He River, China	3,700,000
Tsunami	2004	South Asia	280,000
Earthquake	1976	Tangshan, China	255,000
Heat wave	2003	Europe	35,000
Volcano	1985	Nevado del Ruiz, Colombia	23,000
Hurricane	1998	(Mitch) Central America	18,277
Landslide	1970	Yungay, Peru	17,500
Avalanche	1916	Italian Alps	10,000
Blizzard	1972	Iran	4,000
Tornado	1989	Shaturia, Bangladesh	1,300

Information from: USGS, 2011; CBC, 2008; Ash, 2001.

Raising awareness and sensitivity This woman joins a rally in front of Ireland's national parliament to protest "jokes" made by three policemen about raping women they had recently arrested. A recording of the police conversation was leaked to the public in 2011, causing a public uproar.

Julien Behal/PA Wire via AP Images

SEXUAL ASSAULT

People who are **sexually assaulted** have been forced to engage in a sexual act against their will. According to most definitions, people who are **raped** have been forced into sexual intercourse or other forms of sexual penetration. Rape victims often experience **rape trauma syndrome (RTS),** a pattern of problematic physical and psychological symptoms. RTS is actually a form of PTSD. Approximately **one-third** of rape victims develop PTSD.

THE PSYCHOLOGICAL EFFECTS OF RAPE

suicidal thoughts
attempted **suicide**
vulnerability to develop **psychological disorders**
feelings of self-blame and **betrayal**
flashbacks
panic attacks
sleep problems
memory problems

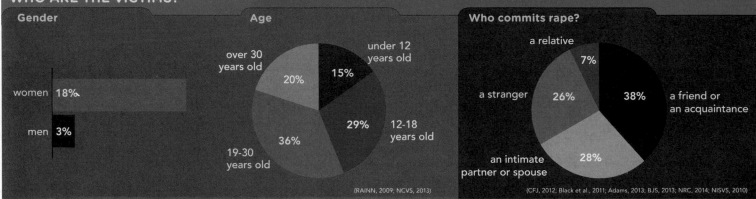

Rape victims are more likely to:

3 X 🙜🙜🙜 suffer from depression

4 X 🙜🙜🙜🙜 contemplate suicide

6 X 🙜🙜🙜🙜🙜🙜 suffer from PTSD

12 X abuse alcohol

26 X abuse drugs

(Adams, 2013; RAINN, 2009)

WHO ARE THE VICTIMS?

Gender

women **18%**

men **3%**

Age

over 30 years old **20%**

under 12 years old **15%**

12-18 years old **29%**

19-30 years old **36%**

(RAINN, 2009; NCVS, 2013)

Who commits rape?

a relative **7%**

a stranger **26%**

a friend or an acquaintance **38%**

an intimate partner or spouse **28%**

(CFJ, 2012; Black et al., 2011; Adams, 2013; BJS, 2013; NRC, 2014; NISVS, 2010)

SEXUAL ASSAULT ON COLLEGE CAMPUSES

The White House has criticized the poor job that colleges are doing preventing sexual assault on campus, punishing perpetrators, and providing proper support for victims. It has pushed colleges to develop guidelines to help prevent sexual assaults (Anderson, 2014). Among other measures, the White House initiative encourages all students and university staff to sign the **"It's On Us"** pledge, which makes everyone on campus responsible for preventing and intervening in sexual assaults.

(White House Task Force, 2014; RAINN, 2009)

IT'S ON
US

I pledge:

To RECOGNIZE that nonconsensual sex is sexual assault.

To IDENTIFY situations in which sexual assault may occur.

To INTERVENE in situations where consent has not or cannot be given.

To CREATE an environment in which sexual assault is unacceptable and survivors are supported.

Crisis on College Campuses

20% women sexually assaulted in college

95% college rapes estimated to be unreported

47% college rape victims who sustain bodily injuries

(Anderson, 2014; CRCC, 2014; Weiner, 2014; Adams, 2013; BJS, 2013; Statistic Brain, 2013; CDC, 2012; RAINN, 2009)

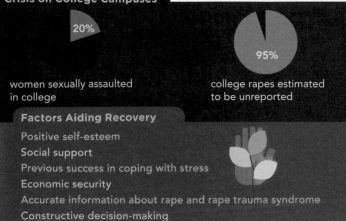

Factors Aiding Recovery

Positive self-esteem
Social support
Previous success in coping with stress
Economic security
Accurate information about rape and rape trauma syndrome
Constructive decision-making

Factors Delaying Recovery

Prior victimization
Chronic life stressors
Lack of social support
Low self-esteem
Degree of violence during attack

(NCVS, 2014)

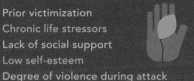

89,000 rapes are reported to police per year, but the number of rapes per year is estimated to be *at least* 225,000

(CFJ, 2012; Black et al., 2011; Adams, 2013; BJS, 2013; NRC, 2014; NISVS, 2010)

(NCVS, 2014)

anxiety, suspiciousness, depression, self-esteem problems, self-blame, flashbacks, sleep problems, and sexual dysfunction (Pietrzak et al., 2014; Street et al., 2011).

Female victims of rape and other crimes also are much more likely than other women to suffer serious long-term health problems (Morgan et al., 2015; Koss & Heslet, 1992). Interviews with 390 women revealed that such victims had poorer physical well-being for at least five years after the crime and made twice as many visits to physicians.

Ongoing victimization and abuse in the family—specifically child and spouse abuse—may also lead to psychological stress disorders. Because these forms of abuse may occur over the long term and violate family trust, many victims develop other symptoms and disorders as well (Koss et al., 2011).

TERRORISM People who are victims of terrorism or who live under the threat of terrorism often experience posttraumatic stress symptoms (Stene et al., 2015). Unfortunately, this source of traumatic stress is on the rise in our society. Few will ever forget the events of September 11, 2001, when hijacked airplanes crashed into and brought down the World Trade Center in New York City and partially destroyed the Pentagon in Washington, DC, killing thousands of victims and rescue workers and forcing thousands more to desperately run, crawl, and even dig their way to safety. A number of studies have indicated that in the aftermath of that fateful day, many individuals developed immediate and long-term psychological effects, ranging from brief stress reactions, such as shock, fear, and anger, to enduring psychological disorders, such as posttraumatic stress disorder (Ruggero et al., 2013; Mitka, 2011; Galea et al., 2007).

Follow-up studies suggest that many of these individuals continue to struggle with terrorism-related stress reactions (Cone et al., 2015; Adams & Boscarino, 2005). Indeed, even years after the attacks, 42 percent of all adults in the United States and 70 percent of all New York adults report high terrorism fears; 23 percent of all adults in the United States report feeling less safe in their homes; 15 percent of all U.S. adults report drinking more alcohol than they did prior to the attacks; and 9 percent of New York adults display PTSD, compared with the national annual prevalence of 3.5 percent. Studies of subsequent acts of terrorism, such as the 2004 commuter train bombings in Madrid, the 2005 London subway and bus bombings, and the 2013 Boston Marathon bombing, tell a similar story (Comer et al., 2014; Chacón & Vecina, 2007).

Gender and Posttraumatic Stress Disorder

Many researchers believe that women's higher rates of posttraumatic stress disorder are tied to the types of violent traumas they experience—namely, interpersonal assaults such as rape or sexual abuse (Street et al., 2011; Russo & Tartaro, 2008).

©Goran Tomasevic/Reuters/Corbis

The horror of terrorism Fearful shoppers at the Westgate shopping center in Kenya scramble for safety as armed police hunt the terrorist gunmen who went on a 4-day shooting spree in 2013, leaving 67 people dead and 175 wounded.

▶ **torture** The use of brutal, degrading, and disorienting strategies to reduce victims to a state of utter helplessness.

TORTURE **Torture** refers to the use of "brutal, degrading, and disorienting strategies in order to reduce victims to a state of utter helplessness" (Okawa & Hauss, 2007). Often, it is done on the orders of a government or another authority to force persons to yield information or make a confession (Gerrity et al., 2001). As you will see in Chapter 16, the question of the morality of torturing prisoners who are considered suspects in the "war on terror" has been the subject of much discussion over the past several years.

It is hard to know how many people are in fact tortured around the world because such numbers are typically hidden by governments (Basoglu et al., 2001). It has been estimated, however, that between 5 and 35 percent of the world's 15 million refugees have suffered at least one episode of torture and that more than 400,000 torture survivors from around the world now live in the United States (ORR, 2011, 2006; AI, 2000; Baker, 1992). Of course, these numbers do not take into account the many thousands of victims who have remained in their countries even after being tortured.

People from all walks of life are subjected to torture worldwide—from suspected terrorists to student activists and members of religious, ethnic, and cultural minority groups. The techniques used on them may include *physical torture* (beatings, waterboarding, electrocution), *psychological torture* (threats of death, mock executions, verbal abuse, degradation), *sexual torture* (rape, violence to the genitals, sexual humiliation), or *torture through deprivation* (sleep, sensory, social, nutritional, medical, or hygiene deprivation).

Torture victims often experience physical ailments as a result of their ordeal, from scarring and fractures to neurological problems and chronic pain. But many theorists believe that the lingering psychological effects of torture are even more problematic (Gjini et al., 2013; Punamäki et al., 2010). It appears that between 30 and 50 percent of torture victims develop posttraumatic stress disorder. Even for those who do not develop a full-blown disorder, symptoms such as nightmares, flashbacks, repressed memories, depersonalization, poor concentration, anger outbursts, sadness, and suicidal thoughts are common (Taylor et al., 2013).

Why Do People Develop Acute and Posttraumatic Stress Disorders?

Clearly, extraordinary trauma can cause a stress disorder. The stressful event alone, however, may not be the entire explanation. Certainly, anyone who experiences an unusual trauma will be affected by it, but only some people develop a stress disorder (see *PsychWatch* on the next page). To understand the development of these disorders more fully, researchers have looked to the survivors' biological processes, personalities, childhood experiences, social support systems, and cultural backgrounds and to the severity of the traumas.

Biological and Genetic Factors Investigators have learned that traumatic events trigger physical changes in the brain and body that may lead to severe stress reactions and, in some cases, to stress disorders (Yehuda et al., 2015; Pace & Heim, 2011). They have, for example, found abnormal activity of the hormone *cortisol* and the neurotransmitter/hormone *norepinephrine* in the urine, blood, and saliva of combat soldiers, rape victims, concentration camp survivors, and survivors of other severe stresses (Groer et al., 2015; Gola et al., 2012).

Evidence from brain studies also shows that once a stress disorder sets in, it may lead to further biochemical arousal, and this continuing arousal may eventually damage key brain areas (Lee et al., 2014; Pace & Heim, 2011). As we have seen in earlier chapters, researchers have determined that emotional reactions of various kinds are tied to brain circuits—networks

Children, too A 10-year-old boy sits in a devastated area of Japan after the 2011 earthquake and tsunami. Children also may develop posttraumatic stress disorder after natural disasters, leading clinicians to worry about the mental health of the many Japanese children who experienced the magnitude 9.0 earthquake.

Kimimasa Mayama/epa/Corbis

PsychWatch

Adjustment Disorders: A Category of Compromise?

Some people react to a major stressor in their lives with extended and excessive feelings of anxiety, depressed mood, or antisocial behaviors. The symptoms do not quite add up to acute stress disorder or posttraumatic stress disorder, nor do they reflect an anxiety or mood disorder, but they do cause considerable distress or interfere with the person's job, schoolwork, or social life. Should we consider such reactions normal? No, says DSM-5. Somewhere between effective coping strategies and stress disorders lie the *adjustment disorders*, patterns that are included in DSM-5's group of trauma- and stressor-related disorders (APA, 2013).

DSM-5 lists several types of adjustment disorders, including *adjustment disorder with anxiety* and *adjustment disorder with depressed mood*. People receive such diagnoses if they develop their symptoms within three months of the onset of a stressor. If the stressor is long-term, such as a medical condition, the adjustment disorder may last indefinitely.

Almost any kind of stressor may trigger an adjustment disorder. Common ones are the breakup of a relationship, marital problems, business difficulties, and living in a crime-ridden neighborhood. The disorder may also be triggered by developmental events such as going away to school, getting married, or retiring from a job.

Up to 30 percent of all people in outpatient therapy receive this diagnosis; it accounts for far more treatment claims submitted to insurance companies than any other. However, some experts doubt that adjustment disorders are as common as this figure suggests. Rather, the diagnosis seems to be a favorite among clinicians—it can easily be applied to a range of problems yet is less stigmatizing than many other categories.

Candidates for dysfunction? A stock trader reacts with exhaustion, worry, and disbelief at the stock exchange in Chicago after a particularly bad—stock-plummeting—day in 2011. Business difficulties are among the most common stressors known to trigger adjustment disorders.

AP Photo/M. Spencer Green

of brain structures that, with the help of neurotransmitters, trigger each other into action to produce various emotions. It appears that abnormal activity in one such circuit may contribute to posttraumatic stress reactions. This circuit includes the *hippocampus* and *amygdala,* which send and receive messages to and from each other (Li et al., 2014; Bremner & Charney, 2010).

Normally, the hippocampus plays a major role both in memory and in the regulation of the body's stress hormones. Clearly, a dysfunctional hippocampus may help produce the intrusive memories and constant arousal found in posttraumatic stress disorder (Bremner et al., 2004). Similarly, as you read in Chapter 4, the amygdala helps control anxiety and many other emotional responses. It also works with the hippocampus to produce the emotional components of memory. Thus, a dysfunctional amygdala may help produce the repeated emotional symptoms and strong emotional memories common to people with posttraumatic stress disorder (Protopopescu et al., 2005). In short, the arousal produced by extraordinarily traumatic events may lead to stress disorders in some people, and the stress disorders may produce yet further brain abnormalities, locking in the disorders all the more firmly.

//// BETWEEN THE LINES ////

The Smell of Stress?

Stress is odorless. The bacteria that feed off of our sweat are what give our bodies odor during very stressful events.

It may also be that posttraumatic stress disorder leads to the transmission of biochemical abnormalities to the children of people with the disorder (Yehuda et al., 2015). One team of researchers examined the cortisol levels of women who had been pregnant during the September 11, 2001, terrorist attacks and had developed PTSD (Yehuda & Bierer, 2007). Not only did these women have higher-than-average cortisol levels, but the babies to whom they gave birth after the attacks also displayed higher cortisol levels, suggesting that the babies inherited a predisposition to develop the same disorder.

Many theorists believe that people whose biochemical reactions to stress are unusually strong are more likely than others to develop acute and posttraumatic stress disorders. But why would certain people be prone to such strong biological reactions? One possibility is that the propensity is inherited (Clark et al., 2013). Clearly, this is suggested by the mother–offspring studies just discussed. Similarly, studies conducted on thousands of pairs of twins who have served in the military find that if one twin develops stress symptoms after combat, an identical twin is more likely than a fraternal twin to develop the same problem (Koenen et al., 2003; True & Lyons, 1999).

Building resiliency Noting that a resilient, or "hardy," personality style may help protect people from developing stress disorders, many programs now claim to build resiliency. Here young South Korean schoolchildren fall on a mud flat at a five-day winter military camp designed to strengthen them mentally and physically.

AP Photo/Ahn Young-joon

Personality Some studies suggest that people with certain personalities, attitudes, and coping styles are particularly likely to develop acute and posttraumatic stress disorders (DiGangi et al., 2013). In the aftermath of Hurricane Hugo in 1989, for example, children who had been highly anxious before the storm were more likely than other children to develop severe stress reactions (Hardin et al., 2002). Research has also found that people who generally view life's negative events as beyond their control tend to develop more severe stress symptoms after sexual or other kinds of traumatic events than people who feel that they have more control over their lives (Catanesi et al., 2013; Bremner, 2002). Similarly, people who generally find it difficult to derive anything positive from unpleasant situations adjust more poorly after traumatic events than people who are generally resilient and who typically find value in negative events (Kunst, 2011).

> Do the vivid images seen daily on the Web, on TV, and in video games make people more vulnerable to developing psychological stress disorders or less vulnerable?

Childhood Experiences Researchers have found that certain childhood experiences seem to leave some people at risk for later acute and posttraumatic stress disorders (Pervanidou & Chrousos, 2014). People whose childhoods have been marked by poverty appear more likely to develop these disorders in the face of later trauma. So do people who went through an assault, abuse, or a catastrophe at an early age; who were younger than 10 when their parents separated or divorced; or whose family members suffered from psychological disorders (Ogle et al., 2014; Yehuda et al., 2010).

Social Support People whose social and family support systems are weak are also more likely to develop acute or posttraumatic stress disorder after a traumatic event (DiGangi et al., 2013). Rape victims who feel loved, cared for, valued, and accepted by their friends and relatives recover more successfully (Street et al., 2011). So do those treated with dignity and respect by the criminal justice system (Patterson, 2011). In contrast, clinical reports have suggested that poor social support contributes to the development of posttraumatic stress disorder in some combat veterans (Schumm et al., 2014).

Multicultural Factors There is a growing suspicion among clinical researchers that the rates of posttraumatic stress disorder may differ among ethnic groups in the United States. In particular, Hispanic Americans may be more vulnerable to the disorder than other cultural groups (Hinton & Lewis-Fernandez, 2011; Koch & Haring, 2008). Some cases in point: (1) Studies of combat veterans from the wars in Afghanistan, Iraq, and Vietnam have found higher rates of posttraumatic stress disorder among Hispanic American veterans than among white American and African American veterans (RAND Corporation, 2010, 2008; Kulka et al., 1990). (2) In surveys of police officers, Hispanic American officers typically report more severe duty-related stress symptoms than their non-Hispanic counterparts (Pole et al., 2001). (3) Data on hurricane victims reveal that after some hurricanes Hispanic American victims have had a significantly higher rate of PTSD than victims from other ethnic groups (Perilla et al., 2002). (4) Surveys of New York City residents conducted in the months following the terrorist attacks of September 11, 2001, revealed that 14 percent of Hispanic American residents developed PTSD, compared with 9 percent of African American residents and 7 percent of white American residents (Hinton & Lewis-Fernandez, 2011; Galea et al., 2002).

Why might Hispanic Americans be more vulnerable to posttraumatic stress disorder than other racial or ethnic groups? Several explanations have been suggested. One holds that as part of their cultural belief system, many Hispanic Americans tend to view traumatic events as inevitable and unalterable, a coping response that may heighten their risk for posttraumatic stress disorder (Perilla et al., 2002). Another explanation suggests that their culture's emphasis on social relationships and social support may place Hispanic American victims at special risk when traumatic events deprive them—temporarily or permanently—of important relationships and support systems. Indeed, a study conducted almost three decades ago found that among Hispanic American Vietnam combat veterans with stress disorders, those with poor family and social relationships suffered the most severe symptoms (Escobar et al., 1983).

Severity of Trauma As you might expect, the severity and nature of the traumatic event that a person goes through help determine whether the person will develop a stress disorder. Some events can override even a nurturing childhood, positive attitudes, and social support (Ogle, Rubin, & Siegler, 2014). One study examined 253 Vietnam War prisoners five years after their release. Some 23 percent qualified for a clinical diagnosis of posttraumatic stress disorder, though all had been evaluated as well adjusted before their imprisonment (Ursano et al., 1981).

Generally, the more severe the trauma and the more direct one's exposure to it, the higher the likelihood of developing a stress disorder (Ogle et al., 2014). Mutilation, severe physical injury, or sexual abuse in particular seem to increase the risk of stress reactions, as does witnessing the injury or death of other people (Perrin et al., 2014; Ursano et al., 2003).

How Do Clinicians Treat Acute and Posttraumatic Stress Disorders?

Treatment can be very important for people who have been overwhelmed by traumatic events (Church, 2014). Overall, about half of all cases of posttraumatic stress disorder improve within six months (Asnis et al., 2004). The remainder of cases may

Spencer Platt/Getty Images

Cultural disparity The horror of witnessing the World Trade Center's twin towers burn and collapse on September 11, 2001, was shared by millions of onlookers that fateful day. However, for reasons not fully understood, Hispanic Americans developed more cases of PTSD in the aftermath of this event than did other cultural groups — a difference also on display after other mass traumas (Hinton & Lewis-Fernandez, 2011).

BETWEEN THE LINES

Top Stressors in the United States

1. Job pressure

2. Money

3. Health

4. Relationships

5. Poor nutrition

6. Media overload

7. Sleep deprivation

(APA, 2013)

persist for years, and, indeed, more than one-third of people with PTSD do not respond to treatment even after many years (Byers et al., 2014).

Today's treatment procedures for troubled survivors typically vary from trauma to trauma. Was it combat, an act of terrorism, sexual molestation, or a major accident? Yet all the programs share basic goals: they try to help survivors put an end to their stress reactions, gain perspective on their painful experiences, and return to constructive living (Taylor, 2010). Programs for combat veterans who suffer from PTSD illustrate how these issues may be addressed.

Treatment for Combat Veterans Therapists have used a variety of techniques to reduce veterans' posttraumatic symptoms. Among the most common are *drug therapy, behavioral exposure techniques, insight therapy, family therapy,* and *group therapy.* Typically the approaches are combined, as no one of them successfully reduces all the symptoms (Mott et al., 2014; Rothbaum et al., 2014).

Antianxiety drugs help control the tension that many veterans experience (Writer et al., 2014). In addition, antidepressant medications may reduce the occurrence of nightmares, panic attacks, flashbacks, and feelings of depression (Morgan et al., 2012).

Behavioral exposure techniques, too, have helped reduce specific symptoms, and they have often led to improvements in overall adjustment (Steenkamp et al., 2015). In fact, some studies indicate that exposure treatment is the single most helpful intervention for people with posttraumatic stress disorder (Haagen et al., 2015). This finding suggests to many clinical theorists that exposure of one kind or another should always be part of the treatment picture (see *MindTech* on the next page). In a classic case, the exposure technique of *flooding,* along with relaxation training, helped rid a 31-year-old veteran of frightening flashbacks and nightmares (Fairbank & Keane, 1982). The therapist and the veteran first singled out combat scenes that the man had been reexperiencing frequently. The therapist then helped the veteran to imagine one of these scenes in great detail and urged him to hold on to the image until his anxiety stopped. After each of these flooding exercises, the therapist had the veteran switch to a positive image and led him through relaxation exercises.

A widely applied form of exposure therapy is **eye movement desensitization and reprocessing (EMDR),** in which clients move their eyes in a rhythmic

Standing down To help prevent, reduce, or treat combat-related PTSD, the U.S. military and other organizations now offer stress- and trauma-release exercises for soldiers and ex-soldiers to perform. Here relaxation training and yoga are taught to veterans during the 2013 Veteran Stand Down hosted by Goodwill Southern California.

Brian Cahn/ZUMA Press/Corbis

MindTech

Virtual Reality Therapy: Better Than the Real Thing?

As you have read, exposure-based treatment may be the single most helpful intervention for people with PTSD (Le et al., 2014). However, *in vivo* (actual) exposure to upsetting stimuli is more effective in treating PTSD than covert (imaginary) exposure. For years, this meant that treatment for PTSD for combat veterans was less than optimal. Unable to revisit real-life battle settings, veterans had to imagine rifle fire, bomb explosions, dead bodies, and/or other traumatic stimuli for their treatment.

All that changed a decade ago, when "virtual" exposure to combat conditions became available for veterans with PTSD. The Office of Naval Research funded the development of "Virtual Iraq," a war simulation treatment game (McIlvaine, 2011). This game was able to produce sights and sounds that seemed every bit as real and produced as much—or more—alarm as real battle conditions. The use of virtual reality as an exposure technique has since become a standard in PTSD treatment.

In *virtual reality therapy,* PTSD clients use wraparound goggles and joysticks to navigate their way through a computer-generated military convoy, battle, or bomb attack in a landscape that looks like Iraq or Afghanistan.

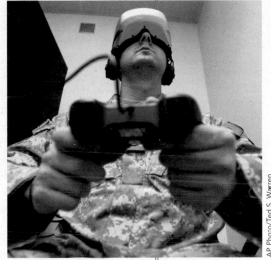

AP Photo/Ted S. Warren

"Virtual" exposure An ex-soldier's headset and video game–type controller take him back to a battle scene in Iraq.

Can you design a virtual reality exposure treatment program for people with social anxiety disorder?

The therapist controls the intensity of the horrifying sights, terrifying sounds, and awful smells of combat, triggering very real feelings of fear or panic in the client. Exposure therapy proceeds with the therapist applying the exposures to these stimuli in either *gradual steps* or a *flooding* approach (see pages 124–126).

Study after study has suggested that virtual reality therapy is extremely helpful for combat veterans with PTSD, much more so than covert exposure therapy (Nauert, 2014; McLay, 2013; Rauch, Eftekhari, & Ruzek, 2012). In addition, the improvements produced by this intervention appear to last for extended periods, perhaps indefinitely. Small wonder that virtual reality therapy is now also becoming common in the treatment of other anxiety disorders and phobias, including social anxiety disorder and fears of heights, flying, and closed spaces (Anderson et al., 2013).

manner from side to side while flooding their minds with images of the objects and situations they ordinarily try to avoid. Case studies and controlled studies suggest that this treatment can often be helpful to people with posttraumatic stress disorder (Chen et al., 2015; Rothbaum et al., 2011). Many theorists argue that it is the exposure feature of EMDR, rather than the eye movement, that accounts for its success as a treatment for PTSD (Lamprecht et al., 2004).

Although drug therapy and exposure techniques bring some relief, most clinicians believe that veterans with posttraumatic stress disorder cannot fully recover with these approaches alone: they must also come to grips in some way with their

▶ **eye movement desensitization and reprocessing (EMDR)** An exposure treatment in which clients move their eyes in a rhythmic manner from side to side while flooding their minds with images of objects and situations they ordinarily avoid.

Personal Impact of Stress

33	Percentage of people who feel they are living with extreme stress
48	Percentage of people who lie awake at night due to stress
48	Percentage of people who say stress negatively affects their personal and professional lives
54	Percentage of people who say stress has caused them to fight with close friends or relatives

(APA, 2013)

combat experiences and the impact those experiences continue to have. Thus clinicians often try to help veterans bring out deep-seated feelings, accept what they have done and experienced, become less judgmental of themselves, and learn to trust other people once again (Rothbaum et al., 2011; Turner et al., 2005). In a similar vein, cognitive therapists typically guide such veterans to examine and change the dysfunctional attitudes and styles of interpretation that they have developed as a result of their traumatic experiences (Spence et al., 2014).

Veterans who have posttraumatic stress disorder may be further helped in a couple, family, or group therapy format (Shnaider et al., 2014; Vogt et al., 2011). The symptoms of PTSD are particularly apparent to family members, who may be directly affected by the client's anxieties, depressed mood, or angry outbursts (Owens et al., 2014). With the help and support of their family members, they may come to examine their impact on others, learn to communicate better, and improve their problem-solving skills.

In group therapy sessions, called *rap groups* when initiated during the 1980s, the veterans meet with others like themselves to share experiences and feelings (particularly guilt and rage), develop insights, and give mutual support (Ellis et al., 2014). Today hundreds of small *Veterans Outreach Centers* across the country, as well as treatment programs in Veterans Administration hospitals and mental health clinics, provide group treatment (Schumm et al., 2015; Ruzek & Batten, 2011). These agencies also offer individual therapy, counseling for spouses and children, family therapy, and aid in seeking jobs, education, and benefits (Mott et al., 2014). Clinical reports suggest that these programs offer a necessary, sometimes life-saving, treatment opportunity.

Psychological Debriefing People who are traumatized by disasters, victimization, or accidents profit from many of the same treatments that are used to help survivors of combat (Monson et al., 2014). In addition, because their traumas occur in their own community, where mental health resources are close at hand, they may, according to many clinicians, further benefit from immediate community interventions.

One of the leading such approaches is called **psychological debriefing,** or **critical incident stress debriefing**, an intervention applied widely over the past 30 years. The use of this intervention has, however, come under careful scrutiny in recent years, reminding the clinical field of the ongoing need for systematic research into its assumptions and applications.

Psychological debriefing is a form of crisis intervention that has victims of trauma talk extensively about their feelings and reactions within days of the critical incident (Tuckey & Scott, 2014; Mitchell, 2003, 1983). Based on the assumption that such sessions prevent or reduce stress reactions, they are often provided to trauma victims who have not yet displayed any symptoms at all, as well as to those who have. During the sessions, often conducted in a group format, counselors guide the individuals to describe the details of the recent trauma, to vent and relive the emotions provoked at the time of the event, and to express their current feelings. The clinicians then clarify to the victims that their reactions are perfectly normal responses to a terrible event, offer stress management tips, and, in some cases, refer the victims to professionals for long-term counseling.

Many thousands of counselors, both professionals and nonprofessionals, have been trained in psychological debriefing since its beginnings in the early 1980s, and the intense approach has been applied in the aftermath of countless traumatic events (Pfefferbaum, Newman, & Nelson, 2014; Wei et al., 2010). Indeed, when a traumatic incident affects numerous individuals, debriefing-trained counselors may come from far and wide to conduct debriefing sessions with the victims. Large mobilizations of this kind have offered free emergency mental health services at disaster sites such

▶ **psychological debriefing** A form of crisis intervention in which victims are helped to talk about their feelings and reactions to traumatic incidents. Also called *critical incident stress debriefing*.

as the 1999 shooting of 23 people at Columbine High School in Colorado, the 2001 World Trade Center attack, the 2004 tsunami in South Asia, the floods caused by Hurricane Katrina in 2005, and the Haitian and Japanese earthquakes in 2010 and 2011.

In such community-wide mobilizations, the counselors may knock on doors or approach victims at shelters. Although victims from all socioeconomic groups may be engaged, those who live in poverty have been viewed traditionally as most in need and so have been targeted for psychological debriefing most often.

Does Psychological Debriefing Work? Over the years, personal testimonials for rapid mobilization programs have often been favorable (Watson & Shalev, 2005; Mitchell, 2003). However, as you read earlier, a growing number of studies conducted in the twenty-first century have called into question the effectiveness of this kind of intervention (Tuckey & Scott, 2014; Gist & Devilly, 2010).

Actually, an investigation conducted in the early 1990s was the first to raise concerns about disaster debriefing programs (Bisson & Deahl, 1994). Crisis counselors offered immediate debriefing sessions to 62 British soldiers whose job during the Gulf War was to handle and identify the bodies of people who had been killed. Despite such sessions, half of the soldiers displayed posttraumatic stress symptoms when interviewed nine months later.

In a properly controlled study conducted a few years later on hospitalized burn victims, researchers separated the victims into two groups (Bisson et al., 1997). One group received a single one-on-one debriefing session within days of their burn accidents, while the other (control) group of burn victims received no such intervention. Three months later, it was found that the debriefed and the control patients had similar rates of posttraumatic stress disorder. Moreover, researchers found that 13 months later, the rate of posttraumatic stress disorder was actually *higher* among the debriefed burn victims (26 percent) than among the control victims (9 percent).

More recent studies, focusing on yet other kinds of disasters, have yielded similar patterns of findings, raising important questions about the effectiveness of psychological debriefing (Tuckey & Scott, 2014; Szumilas et al., 2010). Some clinicians have come to believe that the early intervention programs may encourage victims to dwell too long on the traumatic events that they have experienced. And a number worry that early disaster counseling may unintentionally "suggest" problems to certain victims, thus helping to produce stress disorders (McNally, 2004; McClelland, 1998).

Many mental health professionals continue to believe in psychological debriefing programs. However, given the unsupportive and even contradictory research findings of recent years, the current clinical climate is moving away from outright acceptance. A number of clinical theorists now believe that certain *high-risk* individuals may profit from debriefing programs, and that those people should receive debriefing techniques immediately after a traumatic event, but that other trauma victims should not receive such interventions (Delahanty, 2011). Of course, a key to this notion is the ability to effectively identify the risk factors that predict PTSD and the personality factors that predict responsiveness to psychological debriefing. Research into these issues is now under way (North & Pfefferbaum, 2013; Delahanty, 2011).

AP Photo/Chilean government, Hugo Infante

A change of direction A Chilean miner is helped by rescue workers after being pulled out of the gold and copper mine in which he and 32 other miners had been trapped for more than two months in 2010. On the advice of international psychologists, Chilean officials decided to make counseling *available*, but not required, for the rescued miners. This advice was a departure from the widely used procedure of psychological debriefing, which has failed to receive consistent research support in recent years.

▸ **dissociative disorders** Disorders marked by major changes in memory that do not have clear physical causes.

▸ **memory** The faculty for recalling past events and past learning.

▸ **dissociative amnesia** A disorder marked by an inability to recall important personal events and information.

At risk A U.S. Marine takes a short break before going on patrol in southern Afghanistan in 2011. Combat soldiers are particularly vulnerable to amnesia and other dissociative reactions. They may forget specific horrors, personal information, or even their identities.

Shamil Zhumatov/Reuters/Corbis

➤ *Summing Up*

ACUTE AND POSTTRAUMATIC STRESS DISORDERS When we view a stressor as threatening, we often experience a stress response consisting of arousal and a sense of fear. The features of arousal and fear are set in motion by the hypothalamus, a brain area that activates the autonomic nervous system and the endocrine system. There are two pathways by which these systems produce arousal and fear—the sympathetic nervous system pathway and the hypothalamic-pituitary-adrenal pathway.

People with acute stress disorder or posttraumatic stress disorder react with arousal, anxiety, and other stress symptoms after a traumatic event, including reexperiencing the traumatic event, avoiding related events, being markedly less responsive than normal, and feeling guilt. The symptoms of acute stress disorder begin soon after the trauma and last less than a month. Those of post-traumatic stress disorder may begin at any time (even years) after the trauma and may last for months or years.

In attempting to explain why some people develop a psychological stress disorder and others do not, researchers have focused on biological factors, personality, childhood experiences, social support, multicultural factors, and the severity of the traumatic event. Techniques used to treat the stress disorders include drug therapy, behavioral exposure, cognitive and other insight thera-pies, family therapy, and group therapy. Rapidly mobilized community inter-ventions often follow the principles of critical incident stress debriefing. Such approaches initially appeared helpful after large-scale disasters; however, some recent studies have raised questions about their usefulness.

Dissociative Disorders

As you have just read, people with acute and posttraumatic stress disorders may have symptoms of dissociation along with their other symptoms. They may, for example, feel dazed, have trouble remembering things, or have a sense of derealization. Symp-toms of this kind are also on display in **dissociative disorders,** another group of disorders triggered by traumatic events (Armour et al., 2014). In fact, the memory difficulties and other dissociative symptoms found in these disor-ders are particularly intense, extensive, and disruptive. Moreover, in such disorders, dissociative reactions are the main or only symptoms. People with dissociative disorders do not typically have the significant arousal, negative emotions, sleep difficulties, and other problems that characterize acute and posttraumatic stress disorders. Nor are there clear physical factors at work in dissociative disorders.

Most of us experience a sense of wholeness and continuity as we interact with the world. We perceive ourselves as being more than a collection of isolated sensory experiences, feelings, and behaviors. In other words, we have an *identity,* a sense of who we are and where we fit in our environment. **Memory** is a key to this sense of identity, the link between our past, present, and future. Without a memory, we would always be starting over; with it, our life and our identity move forward. In dissociative disorders, one part of a person's memory or identity becomes *dissociated,* or separated, from other parts of his or her memory or identity.

There are several kinds of dissociative disorders. People with *dis-sociative amnesia* are unable to recall important personal events and information. People with *dissociative identity disorder,* once known as *multiple personality disorder,* have two or more separate identities that may not always be aware of each other's memories, thoughts, feelings, and behavior. And people with *depersonalization-derealization disorder* feel as though they have become detached from their own mental processes or bodies or are observing themselves from the outside.

Several famous books and movies have portrayed dissociative disorders. Two classics are *The Three Faces of Eve* and *Sybil,* each about a woman who developed multiple personalities after having been subject to traumatic events in childhood. The topic is so fascinating that most television drama series seem to include at least one case of dissociation every season, creating the impression that the disorders are very common. Many clinicians, however, believe that they are rare.

Dissociative Amnesia

People with **dissociative amnesia** are unable to recall important information, usually of a stressful nature, about their lives (APA, 2013). The loss of memory is much more extensive than normal forgetting and is not caused by physical factors such as a blow to the head (see Table 5-3). Typically, an episode of amnesia is directly triggered by a traumatic or upsetting event (Kikuchi et al., 2010).

Dissociative amnesia may be *localized, selective, generalized,* or *continuous.* In *localized amnesia,* the most common type of dissociative amnesia, a person loses all memory of events that took place within a limited period of time, almost always beginning with some very disturbing occurrence. A soldier, for example, may awaken a week after a horrific combat battle and be unable to recall the battle or any of the events surrounding it. She may remember everything that happened up to the battle and may recall everything that has occurred over the past several days, but the events in between remain a total blank. The forgotten period is called the *amnestic episode.* During an amnestic episode, people may appear confused; in some cases they wander about aimlessly. They are already experiencing memory difficulties but seem unaware of them.

People with *selective amnesia,* the second most common form of dissociative amnesia, remember some, but not all, events that took place during a period of time. If the combat soldier mentioned in the previous paragraph had selective amnesia, she might remember certain interactions or conversations that occurred during the battle, but not more disturbing events such as the death of a friend or the screams of enemy soldiers.

In some cases the loss of memory extends back to times long before the upsetting period. In addition to forgetting battle-linked events, the soldier may not remember events that occurred earlier in her life. In this case, she would have what is called *generalized amnesia.* In extreme cases, she might not even recognize relatives and friends.

In the forms of dissociative amnesia just discussed, the period affected by the amnesia has an end. In *continuous amnesia,* however, forgetting continues into the present. The soldier might forget new and ongoing experiences as well as what happened before and during the battle.

These various forms of dissociative amnesia are similar in that the amnesia interferes mostly with a person's memory of personal material. Memory for abstract or encyclopedic information usually remains. People with dissociative amnesia are as likely as anyone else to know the name of the president of the United States and how to read or drive a car.

Clinicians do not know how common dissociative amnesia is (Pope et al., 2007), but they do know that many cases seem to begin during serious threats to health and safety, as in wartime and natural disasters. Like the soldier in the earlier examples, combat veterans often report memory gaps of hours or days, and some forget personal information, such as their name and address (Bremner, 2002).

Why do many people question the authenticity of individuals who seem to lose their memories at times of severe stress?

table: 5-3

Dx Checklist

Dissociative Amnesia

1. Person cannot recall important life-related information, typically traumatic or stressful information. The memory problem is more than simple forgetting.

2. Significant distress or impairment.

3. The symptoms are not caused by a substance or medical condition.

Dissociative Identity Disorder

1. Person experiences a disruption to his or her identity, as reflected by at least two separate personality states or experiences of possession.

2. Person repeatedly experiences memory gaps regarding daily events, key personal information, or traumatic events, beyond ordinary forgetting.

3. Significant distress or impairment.

4. The symptoms are not caused by a substance or medical condition.

Information from: APA, 2013.

Lost and found Cheryl Ann Barnes is helped off a plane by her grandmother and stepmother upon arrival in Florida in 1996. The 17-year-old high school honor student had disappeared from her Florida home and was found one month later in a New York City hospital listed as Jane Doe, apparently suffering from a dissociative fugue.

Childhood abuse, particularly child sexual abuse, can also trigger dissociative amnesia; indeed, in the 1990s there were many reports in which adults claimed to recall long-forgotten experiences of childhood abuse (Wolf & Nochajski, 2013) (see *PsychWatch* on the next page). In addition, dissociative amnesia may occur under more ordinary circumstances, such as the sudden loss of a loved one through rejection or death or extreme guilt over certain actions (for example, an extramarital affair) (Koh et al., 2000).

The personal impact of dissociative amnesia depends on how much is forgotten. Obviously, an amnestic episode of two years is more of a problem than one of two hours. Similarly, an amnestic episode during which a person's life changes in major ways causes more difficulties than one that is quiet.

An extreme version of dissociative amnesia is called *dissociative fugue*. Here persons not only forget their personal identities and details of their past lives but also flee to an entirely different location. Some people travel a short distance and make few social contacts in the new setting (APA, 2013). Their fugue may be brief—a matter of hours or days—and end suddenly. In other cases, however, the person may travel far from home, take a new name, and establish a new identity, new relationships, and even a new line of work. Such people may also display new personality characteristics; often they are more outgoing. This pattern is seen in the century-old case of the Reverend Ansel Bourne, whose last name was the inspiration for Jason Bourne, the memory-deprived secret agent in the modern-day Bourne books and movies.

On January 17, 1887, [the Reverend Ansel Bourne, of Greene, R.I.] drew 551 dollars from a bank in Providence with which to pay for a certain lot of land in Greene, paid certain bills, and got into a Pawtucket horsecar. This is the last incident which he remembers. He did not return home that day, and nothing was heard of him for two months. He was published in the papers as missing, and foul play being suspected, the police sought in vain his whereabouts. On the morning of March 14th, however, at Norristown, Pennsylvania, a man calling himself A. I. Brown who had rented a small shop six weeks previously, stocked it with stationery, confectionery, fruit and small articles, and carried on his quiet trade without seeming to any one unnatural or eccentric, woke up in a fright and called in the people of the house to tell him where he was. He said that his name was Ansel Bourne, that he was entirely ignorant of Norristown, that he knew nothing of shop keeping, and that the last thing he remembered—it seemed only yesterday—was drawing the money from the bank, etc. in Providence. . . . He was very weak, having lost apparently over twenty pounds of flesh during his escapade, and had such a horror of the idea of the candy-store that he refused to set foot in it again.

(James, 1890, pp. 391–393)

Fugues tend to end abruptly. In some cases, as with Reverend Bourne, the person "awakens" in a strange place, surrounded by unfamiliar faces, and wonders how he or she got there. In other cases, the lack of personal history may arouse suspicion. Perhaps a traffic accident or legal problem leads police to discover the false identity; at other times friends search for and find the missing person. When people are found before their state of fugue has ended, therapists may find it necessary to ask them many questions about the details of their lives, repeatedly remind them who they are, and even begin psychotherapy before they recover their memories (Igwe, 2013; Mamarde et al., 2013). As these people recover their past, some forget the events of the fugue period.

BETWEEN THE LINES

In Their Words

"There are lots of people who mistake their imagination for their memory."

Josh Billings

PsychWatch

Repressed Childhood Memories or False Memory Syndrome?

Throughout the 1990s, reports of *repressed childhood memory of abuse* attracted much public attention. Adults with this type of *dissociative amnesia* seemed to recover buried memories of sexual and physical abuse from their childhood. A woman might claim, for example, that her father had sexually molested her repeatedly between the ages of 5 and 7. Or a young man might remember that a family friend had made sexual advances on several occasions when he was very young. Often the repressed memories surfaced during therapy for another problem.

Although the number of such claims has declined in recent years, experts remain split on this issue (Wolf & Nochajski, 2013; Birrell, 2011). Some believe that recovered memories are just what they appear to be—horrible memories of abuse that have been buried for years in the person's mind. Other experts believe that the memories are actually illusions—false images created by a mind that is confused. Opponents of the repressed memory concept hold that the details of childhood sexual abuse are often remembered all too well, not completely wiped from memory (Loftus & Cahill, 2007). They also point out that memory in general is often flawed (Haaken & Reavey, 2010; Lindsay et al., 2004). Moreover, false memories of various kinds can be created in the laboratory by tapping into research participants' imaginations (Weinstein & Shanks, 2010; Brainerd et al., 2008).

Early recall These three siblings, all born on the same day in different years, have very different reactions to their cakes at a 1958 birthday party. But how do they each remember that party today? Research suggests that our memories of early childhood may be influenced by the reminiscences of family members, our dreams, television and movie plots, and our present self-image.

Bettmann/Corbis

If the alleged recovery of childhood memories is not what it appears to be, what is it? According to opponents of the concept, it may be a powerful case of suggestibility (Loftus & Cahill, 2007; Loftus, 2003, 2001). These theorists hold that the attention paid to the phenomenon by both clinicians and the public has led some therapists to make the diagnosis without sufficient evidence (Haaken & Reavey, 2010). The therapists may actively search for signs of early abuse in clients and even encourage clients to produce repressed memories (McNally & Garaerts, 2009). Certain therapists in fact use special memory recovery techniques, including hypnosis, regression therapy, journal writing, dream interpretation, and interpretation of bodily symptoms. Perhaps some clients respond to the techniques by unknowingly forming false memories of abuse. The apparent memories may then become increasingly familiar to them as a result of repeated therapy discussions of the alleged incidents.

Of course, repressed memories of childhood sexual abuse do not emerge only in clinical settings. Many individuals come forward on their own. Opponents of the repressed memory concept explain these cases by pointing to various books, articles, Web sites, and television shows that seem to validate repressed memories of childhood abuse (Haaken & Reavey, 2010; Loftus, 1993). Still other opponents of the repressed memory concept believe that, for biological or other reasons, some individuals are more prone than others to experience false memories—either of childhood abuse or of other kinds of events (McNally et al., 2005).

It is important to recognize that the experts who question the recovery of repressed childhood memories do not in any way deny the problem of child sexual abuse. In fact, proponents and opponents alike are greatly concerned that the public may take this debate to mean that clinicians have doubts about the scope of the problem of child sexual abuse. Whatever may be the final outcome of the repressed memory debate, the problem of childhood sexual abuse is all too real and all too common.

The majority of people who go through a dissociative fugue regain most or all of their memories and never have a recurrence. Since fugues are usually brief and totally reversible, those who have experienced them tend to have few aftereffects. People who have been away for months or years, however, often do have trouble adjusting to the changes that took place during their flight. In addition, some people commit illegal or violent acts in their fugue state and later must face the consequences.

Dissociative Identity Disorder

Dissociative identity disorder is both dramatic and disabling, as we see in the case of Luisa:

Luisa was first brought in for treatment after she was found walking in circles by the side of the road in a suburban neighborhood near Denver. Agitated, malnourished, and dirty, this 30-year-old woman told police that her name was Franny and that she was a 15-year-old who was running away from her home in Telluride. At first, the police officers suspected she was giving a false identity to avoid prosecution for prostitution or drug possession, but there really was no evidence for either crime when she was found.

Once it became apparent that she fully believed what she was saying, the woman, who carried no identification of any kind, was transferred to a psychiatric hospital for observation. By the time she met with a therapist, she was no longer a young child speaking rapidly about a terrible family situation. She was now calling herself Luisa, and she spoke in slow, measured, and sad tones—eloquent but often confused.

Luisa described how she had been sexually abused for years by her stepfather, starting when she was six. She said she had run away from home at the age of 15 and had not spoken since to either her mother or stepfather. She claimed that, although she had spent considerable time living on the streets over the years, she was currently living with her boyfriend, Tim, in a small apartment. However, when pressed, she was unable to say what Tim did for a living, nor could she provide his address or last name. Thus she remained in treatment.

Over the course of treatment, as her therapist continued to probe for details of her unhappy childhood and sexual abuse, Luisa became more and more agitated, until finally, she actually transformed back into 15-year-old Franny during one session. Her therapist wrote in his notes, "Her entire physical presence transformed itself suddenly and almost violently. Her face, previously relaxed and even flat, became tense and scrunched up, and her entire body hunched over. She moved her chair back almost two feet and repeatedly flinched from me if I even gestured in her direction. Her voice became high-pitched, clipped, and fast, spitting out words, and her vocabulary became limited, to that which a child would display. She seemed to be a different person in every way possible."

Over the following several sessions, Luisa's therapist wound up meeting still other personalities. One was Miss Johnson, a strict school principal who claimed to have taught Luisa when she was younger. Another was Roger—homeless, tough, and threatening—who made it clear that he was in charge of Luisa and the other personalities. In addition there was Sarah, aged 55 and divorced, and Lilly, aged 24, a math genius and accountant who seemed to appear whenever Luisa needed to deal with money or complex mathematical issues.

A person with **dissociative identity disorder,** known in the past as *multiple personality disorder,* develops two or more distinct personalities, often called **subpersonalities,** or **alternate personalities**, each with a unique set of memories, behaviors, thoughts, and emotions (see again Table 5-3). At any given time, one of the subpersonalities takes center stage and dominates the person's functioning. Usually one subpersonality, called the *primary,* or *host,* personality, appears more often than the others.

The transition from one subpersonality to another, called *switching,* is usually sudden and may be dramatic (Barlow & Chu, 2014). Luisa, for example, twisted her face and hunched her shoulders and body forward violently. Switching is usually triggered by a stressful event, although clinicians can also bring about the change with hypnotic suggestion.

▶ **dissociative identity disorder** A dissociative disorder in which a person develops two or more distinct personalities. Also known as *multiple personality disorder.*

▶ **subpersonalities** The two or more distinct personalities found in individuals suffering with dissociative identity disorder. Also known as *alternate personalities.*

Cases of dissociative identity disorder were first reported almost three centuries ago (Rieber, 2006, 2002). Many clinicians consider the disorder to be rare, but some reports suggest that it may be more common than was once thought (Dorahy et al., 2014). Most cases are first diagnosed in late adolescence or early adulthood, but more often than not, the symptoms actually began in early childhood after episodes of trauma or abuse (often sexual abuse) (Sar et al., 2014; Steele, 2011; Ross & Ness, 2010). Women receive this diagnosis at least three times as often as men.

> **Why might women be much more likely than men to receive a diagnosis of dissociative identity disorder?**

How Do Subpersonalities Interact? How subpersonalities relate to or recall one another varies from case to case (Barlow & Chu, 2014). Generally, however, there are three kinds of relationships. In *mutually amnesic relationships,* the subpersonalities have no awareness of one another (Ellenberger, 1970). Conversely, in *mutually cognizant patterns,* each subpersonality is well aware of the rest. They may hear one another's voices and even talk among themselves. Some are on good terms, while others do not get along at all.

In *one-way amnesic relationships,* the most common relationship pattern, some subpersonalities are aware of others, but the awareness is not mutual. Those who are aware, called *coconscious subpersonalities,* are "quiet observers" who watch the actions and thoughts of the other subpersonalities but do not interact with them. Sometimes while another subpersonality is present, the coconscious personality makes itself known through indirect means, such as auditory hallucinations (perhaps a voice giving commands) or "automatic writing" (the current personality may find itself writing down words over which it has no control).

Investigators used to believe that most cases of dissociative identity disorder involved two or three subpersonalities. Studies now suggest, however, that the average number of subpersonalities per patient is much higher—15 for women and 8 for men (APA, 2000). In fact, there have been cases in which 100 or more subpersonalities were observed. Often the subpersonalities emerge in groups of two or three at a time.

In the case of "Eve White," made famous in the book and movie *The Three Faces of Eve,* a woman had three subpersonalities—Eve White, Eve Black, and Jane (Thigpen & Cleckley, 1957). Eve White, the primary personality, was quiet and serious; Eve Black was carefree and mischievous; and Jane was mature and intelligent. According to the book, these three subpersonalities eventually merged into Evelyn, a stable personality who was really an integration of the other three.

The book was mistaken, however; this was not to be the end of Eve's dissociation. In an autobiography 20 years later, she revealed that altogether 22 subpersonalities had come forth during her life, including 9 subpersonalities after Evelyn. Usually they appeared in groups of three, and so the authors of *The Three Faces of Eve* apparently never knew about her previous or subsequent subpersonalities. She has now overcome her disorder, achieving a single, stable identity, and has been known as Chris Sizemore for more than 35 years (Ramsland & Kuter, 2011; Sizemore, 1991).

How Do Subpersonalities Differ? As in Chris Sizemore's case, subpersonalities often exhibit dramatically different characteristics. They may also have their own names and different *identifying features, abilities and preferences,* and even *physiological responses.*

IDENTIFYING FEATURES The subpersonalities may differ in features as basic as age, gender, race, and family history, as in the case of Sybil Dorsett, whose disorder is described in the famous novel *Sybil* (Schreiber, 1973). According to the novel, Sybil displayed 17 subpersonalities, all with different identifying features. They included adults, a teenager, and even a baby. One subpersonality, Vicky, saw herself as attractive and blonde, while another, Peggy Lou, believed herself to be "a pixie with a pug nose." Yet another, Mary, was plump with dark hair, and Vanessa was a tall, thin

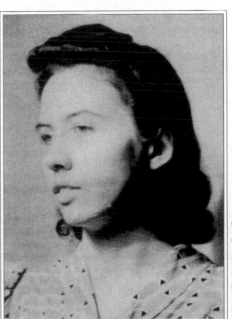

The real Sybil Clinical historians have identified painter Shirley A. Mason (shown here) as the real-life person on whom the famous work of fiction *Sybil* was based.

AP Photo/The Mankato Free Press

redhead. (It is worth noting that the accuracy of the real-life case on which this novel was based has been challenged in recent years.)

ABILITIES AND PREFERENCES Although memories of abstract or encyclopedic information are not usually affected in dissociative amnesia, they are often disturbed in dissociative identity disorder. It is not uncommon for the different subpersonalities to have different abilities: one may be able to drive, speak a foreign language, or play a musical instrument, while the others cannot (Coons & Bowman, 2001). Their handwriting can also differ. In addition, the subpersonalities usually have different tastes in food, friends, music, and literature. Chris Sizemore ("Eve") later pointed out, "If I had learned to sew as one personality and then tried to sew as another, I couldn't do it. Driving a car was the same. Some of my personalities couldn't drive" (Sizemore & Pitillo, 1977, p. 4).

PHYSIOLOGICAL RESPONSES Researchers have discovered that subpersonalities may have physiological differences, such as differences in blood pressure levels and allergies (Spiegel, 2009; Putnam et al., 1990). A pioneering study looked at the brain activities of different subpersonalities by measuring their *evoked potentials*—that is, brain-response patterns recorded on an electroencephalograph (Putnam, 1984). The brain pattern a person produces in response to a specific stimulus (such as a flashing light) is usually unique and consistent. However, when an evoked potential test was administered to four subpersonalities of each of 10 people with dissociative identity disorder, the results were dramatic. The brain-activity pattern of each subpersonality was unique, showing the kinds of variations usually found in totally different people. A number of other studies conducted over the past two decades have yielded similar findings (Boysen & VanBergen, 2014).

How Common Is Dissociative Identity Disorder?

As you have seen, dissociative identity disorder has traditionally been thought of as rare. Some researchers even argue that many or all cases are *iatrogenic*—that is, unintentionally produced by practitioners (Lynn & Deming, 2010; Piper & Merskey, 2005, 2004). They believe that therapists create this disorder by subtly suggesting the existence of other personalities during therapy or by explicitly asking a patient to produce different personalities while under hypnosis. In addition, they believe, a therapist who is looking for multiple personalities may reinforce these patterns by displaying greater interest when a patient displays symptoms of dissociation.

> **What verdict is appropriate for accused criminals with dissociative identity disorder whose crimes are committed by one of their subpersonalities?**

These arguments seem to be supported by the fact that many cases of dissociative identity disorder first come to attention while the person is already in treatment for a less serious problem. But such is not true of all cases; many people seek treatment because they have noticed time lapses throughout their lives or because relatives and friends have observed their subpersonalities (Putnam, 2006, 2000).

The number of people diagnosed with dissociative identity disorder increased dramatically in the 1980s and 1990s, only to decrease again over the past 15 years (Paris, 2012). Not withstanding this decline, thousands of cases have now been diagnosed in the United States and Canada alone, and some clinical theorists estimate that as much as 1 percent of the population in the United States and other Western countries displays the disorder (Dorahy et al., 2014). On the other side of the coin, many clinicians continue to question the legitimacy of this category.

How Do Theorists Explain Dissociative Amnesia and Dissociative Identity Disorder?

A variety of theories have been proposed to explain dissociative amnesia and dissociative identity disorder. Older explanations, such as those offered by psychodynamic and behavioral theorists, have not received much investigation (Merenda, 2008).

However, newer viewpoints, which combine cognitive-behavioral and biological principles and highlight such factors as *state-dependent learning* and *self-hypnosis,* have captured the interest of clinical scientists.

The Psychodynamic View

Psychodynamic theorists believe that these dissociative disorders are caused by *repression,* the most basic ego defense mechanism: people fight off anxiety by unconsciously preventing painful memories, thoughts, or impulses from reaching awareness. Everyone uses repression to a degree, but people with dissociative amnesia and dissociative identity disorder are thought to repress their memories excessively (Henderson, 2010).

In the psychodynamic view, dissociative amnesia is a *single episode* of massive repression. A person unconsciously blocks the memory of an extremely upsetting event to avoid the pain of facing it (Kikuchi et al., 2010). Repressing may be his or her only protection from overwhelming anxiety.

In contrast, dissociative identity disorder is thought to result from a *lifetime* of excessive repression (Howell, 2011; Wang & Jiang, 2007). Psychodynamic theorists believe that this continuous use of repression is motivated by traumatic childhood events, particularly abusive parenting (Baker, 2010; Ross & Ness, 2010). Children who experience such traumas may come to fear the dangerous world they live in and take flight from it by pretending to be another person who is looking on safely from afar. Abused children may also come to fear the impulses that they believe are the reasons for their excessive punishments. Whenever they experience "bad" thoughts or impulses, they unconsciously try to disown and deny them by assigning them to other personalities.

Most of the support for the psychodynamic explanation of dissociative identity disorder is drawn from case histories, which report such brutal childhood experiences as beatings, cuttings, burnings with cigarettes, imprisonment in closets, rape, and extensive verbal abuse (Ross & Ness, 2010). Yet some individuals with this disorder do not seem to have experiences of abuse in their background (Ross & Ness, 2010; Bliss, 1980). For example, Chris Sizemore, the subject of *The Three Faces of Eve,* has reported that her disorder first emerged during her preschool years after she witnessed two deaths and a horrifying accident within a three-month period.

The Behavioral View

Behaviorists believe that dissociation grows from normal memory processes such as drifting of the mind or forgetting (see *PsychWatch* on page 175). Specifically, they hold that dissociation is a response learned through *operant conditioning* (Casey, 2001). People who experience a horrifying event may later find temporary relief when their mind drifts to other subjects. For some, this momentary forgetting, leading to a drop in anxiety, increases the likelihood of future forgetting. In short, they are reinforced for the act of forgetting and learn—without being aware that they are learning—that such acts help them escape anxiety. Thus,

"I think I accidentally repressed my good memories."

▶ **state-dependent learning** Learning that becomes associated with the conditions under which it occurred, so that it is best remembered under the same conditions.

▶ **self-hypnosis** The process of hypnotizing oneself, sometimes for the purpose of forgetting unpleasant events.

like psychodynamic theorists, behaviorists see dissociation as escape behavior. But behaviorists believe that a reinforcement process rather than a hardworking unconscious is keeping the individuals unaware that they are using dissociation as a means of escape. Like psychodynamic theorists, behaviorists have relied largely on case histories to support their view. Moreover, the behavioral explanation fails to explain precisely how temporary and normal escapes from painful memories grow into a complex disorder or why more people do not develop dissociative disorders.

State-Dependent Learning If people learn something when they are in a particular situation or state of mind, they are likely to remember it best when they are again in that same condition. If they are given a learning task while under the influence of alcohol, for example, their later recall of the information may be strongest under the influence of alcohol. Similarly, if they smoke cigarettes while learning, they may later have better recall when they are again smoking.

This link between state and recall is called **state-dependent learning.** It was initially observed in animals who learned things during experiments while under the influence of certain drugs (Ardjmand et al., 2011; Overton, 1966, 1964). Research with human participants later showed that state-dependent learning can

> **Might it be possible to use the principles of state-dependent learning to produce better results in school or at work?**

be associated with mood states as well: material learned during a happy mood is recalled best when the participant is again happy, and sad-state learning is recalled best during sad states (de l'Etoile, 2002; Bower, 1981) (see Figure 5-3).

What causes state-dependent learning? One possibility is that *arousal* levels are an important part of learning and memory. That is, a particular level of arousal will have a set of remembered events, thoughts, and skills attached to it. When a situation produces that particular level of arousal, the person is more likely to recall the memories linked to it.

Although people may remember certain events better in some arousal states than in others, most can recall events under a variety of states. However, perhaps people who are prone to develop dissociative disorders have state-to-memory links that are unusually rigid and narrow (Barlow, 2011). Maybe each of their thoughts, memories, and skills is tied *exclusively* to a particular state of arousal, so that they recall a given event only when they experience an arousal state almost identical to the state in which the memory was first acquired. When such people are calm, for example, they may forget what happened during stressful times, thus laying the groundwork for dissociative amnesia. Similarly, in dissociative identity disorder, different arousal levels may produce entirely different groups of memories, thoughts, and abilities—that is, different subpersonalities (Dorahy & Huntjens, 2007). This could explain why personality transitions in dissociative identity disorder tend to be sudden and stress-related.

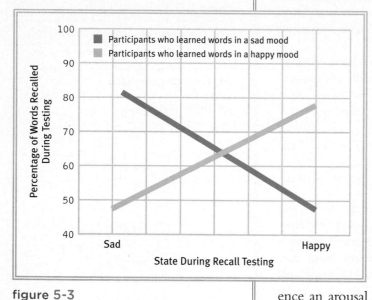

figure 5-3

State-dependent learning In one study, participants who learned a list of words while in a hypnotically induced happy state remembered the words better if they were in a happy mood when tested later than if they were in a sad mood. Conversely, participants who learned the words when in a sad mood recalled them better if they were sad during testing than if they were happy. (Information from: Bower, 1981.)

Self-Hypnosis As you first saw in Chapter 1, people who are *hypnotized* enter a sleeplike state in which they become very suggestible. While in this state, they can behave, perceive, and think in ways that would ordinarily seem impossible. They may, for example, become temporarily blind, deaf, or insensitive to pain. Hypnosis can also help people remember events that occurred and were forgotten years ago, a capability used by many psychotherapists. Conversely, it can make people forget facts, events, and even their personal identities—an effect called *hypnotic amnesia.*

The parallels between hypnotic amnesia and the dissociative disorders we have been examining are striking (van der Kruijs et al., 2014). Both are conditions in which people forget certain material for a period of time yet later remember it. And

PsychWatch

Peculiarities of Memory

Usually memory problems must interfere greatly with a person's functioning before they are considered a sign of a disorder. Peculiarities of memory, on the other hand, fill our daily lives. Memory investigators have identified a number of these peculiarities—some familiar, some useful, some problematic, but none abnormal.

➤ **Absentmindedness** Often we fail to register information because our thoughts are focusing on other things. If we haven't absorbed the information in the first place, it is no surprise that later we can't recall it.

➤ **Déjà vu** Almost all of us have at some time had the strange sensation of recognizing a scene that we happen upon for the first time. We feel sure we have been there before.

➤ **Jamais vu** Sometimes we have the opposite experience: a situation or scene that is part of our daily life seems suddenly unfamiliar. "I knew it was my car, but I felt as if I'd never seen it before."

➤ **The tip-of-the-tongue phenomenon** To have something on the tip of the tongue is an acute "feeling of knowing": we are unable to recall some piece of information, but we know that we know it.

➤ **Eidetic images** Some people have such vivid visual afterimages that they can describe a picture in detail after looking at it just once. The images may be memories of pictures, events, fantasies, or dreams.

"Did you ever start to do something and then forget what the heck it was?"

➤ **Memory while under anesthesia** As many as 2 of every 1,000 anesthetized patients process enough of what is said in their presence during surgery to affect their recovery. In many such cases, the ability to understand language has continued under anesthesia, even though the patient cannot explicitly recall it.

➤ **Memory for music** Even as a small child, Mozart could memorize and reproduce a piece of music after having heard it only once. While no one yet has matched the genius of Mozart, many musicians can mentally hear whole pieces of music and can rehearse anywhere, far from their instruments.

➤ **Visual memory** Most people recall visual information better than other kinds of information: they easily can bring to their mind the appearance of places, objects, faces, or the pages of a book. They almost never forget a face, yet they may well forget the name attached to it. Other people have stronger verbal memories: they remember sounds or words particularly well, and the memories that come to their minds are often puns or rhymes.

---

in both, the people forget without any insight into why they are forgetting or any awareness that something is being forgotten. These parallels have led some theorists to conclude that dissociative disorders may be a form of **self-hypnosis** in which people hypnotize themselves to forget unpleasant events (Dell, 2010). Dissociative amnesia may develop, for example, in people who, consciously or unconsciously, hypnotize themselves into forgetting horrifying experiences that have recently taken place in their lives. If the self-induced amnesia covers all memories of a person's past and identity, that person may undergo a dissociative fugue.

The self-hypnosis theory might also be used to explain dissociative identity disorder. On the basis of several investigations, some theorists believe that this disorder often begins between the ages of 4 and 6, a time when children are generally very suggestible and excellent hypnotic subjects (Kohen & Olness, 2011; Kluft, 2001, 1987). These theorists argue that some children who experience abuse or other horrifying events manage to escape their threatening world by self-hypnosis, mentally separating themselves from their bodies and fulfilling their wish to become some other person or persons (Giesbrecht & Merckelbach, 2009). One patient with multiple personalities observed, "I was in a trance often [during my childhood]. There was a little place where I could sit, close my eyes and imagine, until I felt very relaxed just like hypnosis" (Bliss, 1980, p. 1392).

How Are Dissociative Amnesia and Dissociative Identity Disorder Treated?

As you have seen, people with dissociative amnesia often recover on their own. Only sometimes do their memory problems linger and require treatment. In contrast, people with dissociative identity disorder usually require treatment to regain their lost memories and develop an integrated personality. Treatments for dissociative amnesia tend to be more successful than those for dissociative identity disorder, probably because the former pattern is less complex.

How Do Therapists Help People with Dissociative Amnesia?

The leading treatments for dissociative amnesia are *psychodynamic therapy*, *hypnotic therapy*, and *drug therapy*, although support for these interventions comes largely from case studies rather than controlled investigations (Gentile et al., 2014, 2013). Psychodynamic therapists guide patients to search their unconscious in the hope of bringing forgotten experiences back to consciousness (Howell, 2011). The focus of psychodynamic therapy seems particularly well suited to the needs of people with dissociative amnesia. After all, the patients need to recover lost memories, and the general approach of psychodynamic therapists is to try to uncover memories—as well as other psychological processes—that have been repressed. Thus many theorists, including some who do not ordinarily favor psychodynamic approaches, believe that psychodynamic therapy may be the most appropriate treatment for dissociative amnesia.

Erin Painter/Midland Daily News/AP Photo

Hypnotic recall Northwood University students react while under hypnosis to the suggestion of being on a beach in Hawaii and needing suntan lotion. Many clinicians use hypnotic procedures to help clients recall past events, but research reveals that such procedures often create false memories.

Another common treatment for dissociative amnesia is **hypnotic therapy,** or **hypnotherapy**. Therapists hypnotize patients and then guide them to recall their forgotten events (Rathbone et al., 2014). Given the possibility that dissociative amnesia may be a form of self-hypnosis, hypnotherapy may be a particularly useful intervention. It has been applied both alone and in combination with other approaches (Colletti et al., 2010).

Sometimes injections of barbiturates such as *sodium amobarbital* (Amytal) or *sodium pentobarbital* (Pentothal) have been used to help patients with dissociative amnesia regain their lost memories. These drugs are often called "truth serums," but actually their effect is to calm people and free their inhibitions, thus helping them to recall anxiety-producing events (Ahern et al., 2000). These drugs do not always work, however, and if used at all, they are likely to be combined with other treatment approaches.

How Do Therapists Help People with Dissociative Identity Disorder?

Unlike victims of dissociative amnesia, people with dissociative identity disorder do not typically recover without treatment. Treatment for this pattern is complex and difficult, much like the disorder itself. Therapists usually try to help the clients (1) recognize fully the nature of their disorder, (2) recover the gaps in their memory, and (3) integrate their subpersonalities into one functional personality (Gentile et al., 2014, 2013; Howell, 2011).

RECOGNIZING THE DISORDER Once a diagnosis of dissociative identity disorder is made, therapists typically try to bond with the primary personality and with each of the subpersonalities (Howell, 2011). As bonds are formed, therapists try to educate patients and help them to recognize fully the nature of their disorder.

▶**hypnotic therapy** A treatment in which the patient undergoes hypnosis and is then guided to recall forgotten events or perform other therapeutic activities. Also known as *hypnotherapy*.

▶**fusion** The final merging of two or more subpersonalities in dissociative identity disorder.

▶**depersonalization-derealization disorder** A dissociative disorder marked by the presence of persistent and recurrent episodes of depersonalization, derealization, or both.

Some therapists actually introduce the subpersonalities to one another, by hypnosis, for example, or by having patients look at videos of their other personalities (Howell, 2011; Ross & Gahan, 1988). A number of therapists have also found that group therapy helps to educate patients (Fine & Madden, 2000). In addition, family therapy may be used to help educate spouses and children about the disorder and to gather helpful information about the patient (Kluft, 2001, 2000).

RECOVERING MEMORIES To help patients recover the missing pieces of their past, therapists typically use the same approaches applied in dissociative amnesia, including psychodynamic therapy, hypnotherapy, and drug treatment (Brand et al., 2014; Kluft, 2001, 1991). These techniques work slowly for patients with dissociative identity disorder, however, as some subpersonalities may keep denying experiences that the others recall. One of the subpersonalities may even assume a "protector" role to prevent the primary personality from suffering the pain of recollecting traumatic experiences.

INTEGRATING THE SUBPERSONALITIES The final goal of therapy is to merge the different subpersonalities into a single, integrated identity. Integration is a continuous process that occurs throughout treatment until patients "own" all of their behaviors, emotions, sensations, and knowledge. **Fusion** is the final merging of two or more subpersonalities. Many patients distrust this final treatment goal, and their subpersonalities may see integration as a form of death (Howell, 2011; Kluft, 2001, 1991). Therapists have used a range of approaches to help merge subpersonalities, including psychodynamic, supportive, cognitive, and drug therapies (Cronin et al., 2014; Baker, 2010).

Once the subpersonalities are integrated, further therapy is typically needed to maintain the complete personality and to teach social and coping skills that may help prevent later dissociations. In case reports, some therapists note high success rates (Brand et al., 2014; Dorahy et al., 2014), but others find that patients continue to resist full integration. A few therapists have in fact questioned the need for full integration.

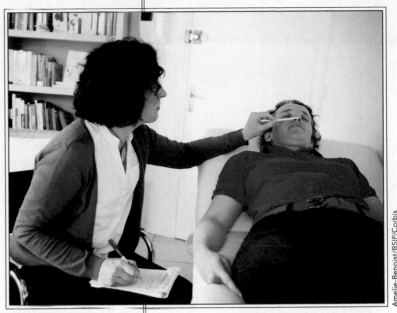

Sensory memories Sensory stimuli often trigger important memories. Thus some clinicians practice *olfactotherapy*, a method that uses the smells and vibrations of essential oils to help elicit memories from clients.

Amelie-Benoist/BSIP/Corbis

Depersonalization-Derealization Disorder

As you read earlier, DSM-5 categorizes **depersonalization–derealization disorder** as a dissociative disorder, even though it is not characterized by the memory difficulties found in the other dissociative disorders. Its central symptoms are persistent and recurrent episodes of *depersonalization* (the sense that one's own mental functioning or body is unreal or detached) and/or *derealization* (the sense that one's surroundings are unreal or detached).

> A 24-year-old graduate student . . . had begun to doubt his own reality. He felt he was living in a dream in which he saw himself from without, and did not feel connected to his body or his thoughts. When he saw himself through his own eyes, he perceived his body parts as distorted—his hands and feet seemed quite large. As he walked across campus, he often felt the people he saw might be robots. . . .
>
> [By] his second session, he . . . had begun to perceive [his girlfriend] in a distorted manner. He . . . hesitated before returning, because he wondered whether his therapist was really alive.
>
> *(Kluft, 1988, p. 580)*

Like this graduate student, people experiencing depersonalization feel as though they have become separated from their body and are observing themselves from outside. Occasionally their mind seems to be floating a few feet above them—a sensation known as *doubling*. Their body parts feel foreign to them, their hands and feet smaller or bigger than usual. Many sufferers describe their emotional state as "mechanical," "dreamlike," or "dizzy." Throughout the whole experience, however, they are aware that their perceptions are distorted, and in that sense they remain in contact with reality. In some cases this sense of unreality also extends to other sensory experiences and behavior. People may, for example, have distortions in their sense of touch or smell or their judgments of time or space, or they may feel that they have lost control over their speech or actions.

In contrast to depersonalization, derealization is characterized by feeling that the external world is unreal and strange. Objects may seem to change shape or size; other people may seem removed, mechanical, or even dead. The graduate student, for example, saw other people as robots, perceived his girlfriend in a distorted manner, and hesitated to return for a second session of therapy because he wondered whether his therapist was really alive.

Depersonalization and derealization experiences by themselves do not indicate a depersonalization–derealization disorder. Transient depersonalization or derealization reactions are fairly common (Michal, 2011). One-third of all people say that on occasion they have felt as though they were watching themselves in a movie. Similarly, one-third of individuals who confront a life-threatening danger experience feelings of depersonalization or derealization (van Duijl et al., 2010). People sometimes have feelings of depersonalization after practicing meditation or after traveling to new places. Young children may also experience depersonalization from time to time as they are developing their capacity for self-awareness. In most such cases, the affected people are able to compensate for the distortion and continue to function with reasonable effectiveness until the temporary episode eventually ends.

The symptoms of depersonalization-derealization disorder, in contrast, are persistent or recurrent, cause considerable distress, and may impair social relationships

> **If you have ever experienced feelings of depersonalization or derealization, how did you explain them at the time?**

Religious dissociations As part of religious or cultural practices, many people voluntarily enter into trances that are similar to the symptoms found in dissociative identity disorder and depersonalization-derealization disorder. Here, voodoo followers sing and flail about in trances inside a sacred pool at a temple in Souvenance, Haiti.

Daniel Morel/Reuters

and job performance (Gentile et al., 2014; Michal, 2011). The disorder occurs most frequently in adolescents and young adults, hardly ever in people over 40 (Moyano, 2010). It usually comes on suddenly and may be triggered by extreme fatigue, physical pain, intense stress, or recovery from substance abuse. Survivors of traumatic experiences or people caught in life-threatening situations, such as hostages or kidnap victims, seem to be particularly vulnerable to this disorder. The disorder tends to be long-lasting; the symptoms may improve and even disappear for a time, only to return or intensify during times of severe stress. Like the graduate student in our case discussion, many sufferers fear that they are losing their minds and become preoccupied with worry about their symptoms. Few theories have been offered to explain this disorder.

➤ *Summing Up*

DISSOCIATIVE DISORDERS People with dissociative disorders experience major changes in memory and identity that are not caused by clear physical factors—changes that often emerge after a traumatic event. Typically, one part of the memory or identity is dissociated, or separated, from the other parts. People with dissociative amnesia are unable to recall important personal information or past events in their lives. Those with dissociative fugue, an extreme form of dissociative amnesia, not only fail to remember personal information but also flee to a different location and may establish a new identity. In another dissociative disorder, dissociative identity disorder (previously called multiple personality disorder), a person develops two or more distinct subpersonalities.

Dissociative amnesia and dissociative identity disorder are not well understood. Among the processes that have been cited to explain them are extreme repression, operant conditioning, state-dependent learning, and self-hypnosis.

Dissociative amnesia may end on its own or may require treatment. Dissociative identity disorder typically requires treatment. Approaches commonly used to help people with dissociative amnesia recover their lost memories are psychodynamic therapy, hypnotic therapy, and sodium amobarbital or sodium pentobarbital. Therapists who treat people with dissociative identity disorder use the same approaches and also try to help the clients recognize the nature and scope of their disorder, recover the gaps in their memory, and integrate their subpersonalities into one functional personality.

People with yet another kind of dissociative disorder, depersonalization-derealization disorder, feel as though they are detached from their own mental processes or body and are observing themselves from the outside or feel as though the people or objects around them are unreal or detached. Transient depersonalization and derealization experiences seem to be relatively common, while depersonalization-derealization disorder is not.

PUTTING IT...*together*

Getting a Handle on Trauma and Stress

The concepts of trauma and stress have been prominent in the field of abnormal psychology since its earliest days. Dating back to Sigmund Freud, for example, psychodynamic theorists have proposed that most forms of psychopathology—from depression to schizophrenia—begin with traumatic losses or events. Even theorists from the other clinical models agree that people under stress are particularly vulnerable to psychological disorders of various kinds, including anxiety

CLINICAL CHOICES

Now that you've read about disorders of trauma and stress, try the interactive case study for this chapter. See if you are able to identify Michelle's symptoms and suggest a diagnosis based on her symptoms. What kind of treatment would be most effective for Michelle? Go to LaunchPad to access *Clinical Choices*.

disorders, depressive disorders, eating disorders, substance use disorders, and sexual dysfunctions.

But why and how do trauma and stress translate into psychopathology? That question has, in fact, eluded clinical theorists and researchers—until recent times. In part because of the identification and study of acute and posttraumatic stress disorders, researchers now better understand the relationship between trauma, stress, and psychological dysfunction—viewing it as a complex interaction of many variables, including biological and genetic factors, personality traits, childhood experiences, social support, multicultural factors, and environmental events. Similarly, clinicians are now developing more effective treatment programs for people with acute and posttraumatic stress disorders—programs that *combine* biological, behavioral, cognitive, family, and social interventions.

Insights and treatments for the dissociative disorders, the other group of trauma-triggered disorders discussed in this chapter, have not moved as quickly. Although these disorders were among the field's earliest identified problems, the clinical field stopped paying much attention to them during the latter part of the twentieth century, with some clinicians even questioning the legitimacy of the diagnoses. However, the field's focus on dissociative disorders has surged during the past two decades—partly because of intense clinical interest in stress reactions and partly because of the growing effort to understand physically rooted memory disorders such as Alzheimer's disease. Researchers have begun to appreciate that dissociative disorders may be more common than clinical theorists had previously recognized. In fact, there is growing evidence that the disorders may be rooted in processes that are already well known from other areas of study, such as state-dependent learning and self-hypnosis.

Amidst the rapid developments in the realms of trauma and stress lies a cautionary tale. When problems are studied heavily, it is common for the public, as well as some researchers and clinicians, to draw conclusions that may be too bold. For example, many people—perhaps too many—are now receiving diagnoses of posttraumatic stress disorder, partly because the symptoms of PTSD are many and because PTSD has received so much attention (Holowka et al., 2014; Wakefield & Horwitz, 2010). Similarly, some of today's clinicians worry that the resurging interest in dissociative disorders may be creating a false impression of their prevalence. We shall see such potential problems again when we look at other forms of pathology that are currently receiving great focus, such as bipolar disorder among children and attention deficit/hyperactivity disorder. The line between enlightenment and overenthusiasm is often thin.

"I'm more interested in hearing about the eggs you're hiding from yourself."

Paul Noth/The New Yorker Collection/www.cartoonbank.com

KEY TERMS

stressor, p. 149

hypothalamus, p. 151

autonomic nervous system (ANS), p. 151

endocrine system, p. 151

sympathetic nervous system, p. 151

epinephrine, p. 152

norepinephrine, p. 152

parasympathetic nervous system, p. 152

hypothalamic-pituitary-adrenal (HPA) pathway, p. 152

corticosteroids, p. 152

acute stress disorder, p. 153

posttraumatic stress disorder (PTSD), p. 153

rape, p. 155

torture, p. 158

eye movement desensitization and reprocessing (EMDR), p. 162

rap groups, p. 164

psychological debriefing, p. 164

dissociative disorders, p. 166

memory, p. 166

dissociative amnesia, p. 167

amnestic episode, p. 167

dissociative fugue, p. 168

dissociative identity disorder, p. 170

subpersonalities, p. 170

iatrogenic disorder, p. 172

state-dependent learning, p. 173

self-hypnosis, p. 173

repression, p. 173

hypnotic therapy, p. 176

fusion, p. 177

depersonalization-derealization disorder, p. 177

QuickQuiz

1. What factors determine how people react to stressors in life? *pp. 149–152*

2. What factors seem to help influence whether persons will develop acute and posttraumatic stress disorders after experiencing a traumatic event? *pp. 158–161*

3. What treatment approaches have been used with people suffering from acute or posttraumatic stress disorder? *pp. 161–165*

4. List and describe the different dissociative disorders. What is dissociative fugue? *pp. 166–179*

5. What are the various patterns of dissociative amnesia? *pp. 167–169*

6. What are the different kinds of relationships that the subpersonalities may have in dissociative identity disorder? *p. 171*

7. Describe the psychodynamic, behavioral, state-dependent learning, and self-hypnosis explanations of dissocia-tive amnesia and dissociative identity disorder. How well is each explanation supported by research? *pp. 172–175*

8. What approaches have been used to treat dissociative amnesia? *p. 176*

9. What are the key features of treatment for dissociative identity disorder? Is treatment successful? *pp. 176–177*

10. Define and describe depersonalization-derealization disorder. How well is this problem understood? *pp. 177–179*

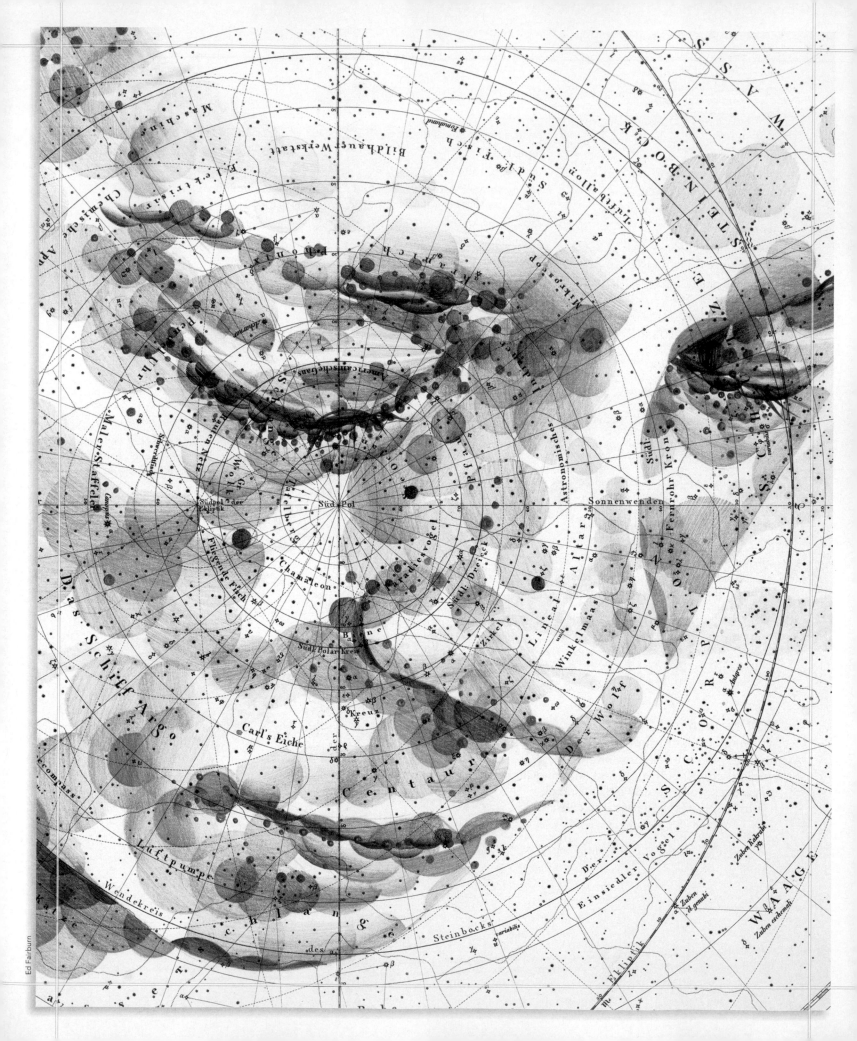

Ed Fairburn

Depressive and Bipolar Disorders

> The first conscious thought that all was not well with me came . . . when I was twenty-two. I had been living in Los Angeles for two years, working various temp jobs while trying to establish myself as a writer and performance artist. Out of nowhere and for no apparent reason—or so it seemed—I started feeling strong sensations of grief. I don't remember the step-by-step progression of the illness. What I can recall is that my life disintegrated; first, into a strange and terrifying space of sadness and then, into a cobweb of fatigue. I gradually lost my ability to function. It would take me hours to get up out of bed, get bathed, put clothes on. By the time I was fully dressed, it was well into the afternoon. . . .
>
> After a while I stopped showing up at my temp job, stopped going out altogether, and locked myself in my home. It was over three weeks before I felt well enough to leave. During that time, I cut myself off from everything and everyone. Days would go by before I bathed. I did not have enough energy to clean up myself or my home. There was a trail of undergarments and other articles of clothing that ran from the living room to the bedroom to the bathroom of my tiny apartment. Dishes with decaying food covered every counter and tabletop in the place. Even watching TV or talking on the phone required too much concentration. . . . All I could do was. . . wait for whatever I was going through to pass. And it did. Slowly. . . .
>
> . . . Deep down, I knew that something had gone wrong with me, in me. But what could I do? Stunned and defenseless, the only thing I felt I could do was move on. I assured myself that my mind and the behaviors it provoked were well within my control. In the future I would just have to be extremely aware. I would make sure that what happened did not happen again. But it did. Again and again, no matter how aware, responsible, or in control I tried to be. . . .
>
> Each wave of the depression cost me something dear. I lost my job because the temp agencies where I was registered could no longer tolerate my lengthy absences. Unable to pay rent, I lost my apartment and ended up having to rent a small room in a boarding house. I lost my friends. Most of them found it too troublesome to deal with my sudden moodiness and passivity so they stopped calling and coming around.
>
> (Danquah, 1998)

Most people's moods come and go. Their feelings of elation or sadness are understandable reactions to daily events and do not affect their lives greatly. However, the moods of certain people last a long time. As in the case of Meri Nana-Ama Danquah, a performance artist and poet who described her disorder in the opening of this chapter, their moods color all of their interactions with the world and even interfere with normal functioning. Such people struggle in particular with depression, mania, or both. **Depression** is a low, sad state in which life seems dark and its challenges overwhelming. **Mania,** the opposite of depression, is a state of breathless euphoria, or at least frenzied energy, in which people may have an exaggerated belief that the world is theirs for the taking.

Mood problems of these kinds are at the center of two groups of disorders—depressive disorders and bipolar disorders (APA, 2013). These groups are examined in this chapter. People with **depressive disorders** suffer only from depression, a pattern called **unipolar depression**. They have no history of mania and return to a normal or nearly normal mood when their depression

► **depression** A low, sad state marked by significant levels of sadness, lack of energy, low self-worth, guilt, or related symptoms.

► **mania** A state or episode of euphoria or frenzied activity in which people may have an exaggerated belief that the world is theirs for the taking.

► **depressive disorders** The group of disorders marked by unipolar depression.

► **unipolar depression** Depression without a history of mania.

► **bipolar disorder** A disorder marked by alternating or intermixed periods of mania and depression.

lifts. In contrast, those with **bipolar disorders** have periods of mania that alternate with periods of depression.

Mood problems have always captured people's interest, in part because so many famous people have suffered from them. The Bible speaks of the severe depressions of Nebuchadnezzar, Saul, and Moses. Queen Victoria of England and Abraham Lincoln seem to have experienced recurring depressions. Mood difficulties also have plagued writers Ernest Hemingway and Sylvia Plath, comedian Jim Carrey, and musical performers Eminem and Beyoncé. Their problems have been shared by millions (NAMI, 2014).

Unipolar Depression: The Depressive Disorders

Whenever we feel particularly unhappy, we are likely to describe ourselves as "depressed." In all likelihood, we are merely responding to sad events, fatigue, or unhappy thoughts. This loose use of the term confuses a perfectly normal mood swing with a clinical syndrome (see *InfoCentral*). All of us experience dejection from time to time, but only some experience a depressive disorder. Such disorders bring severe and long-lasting psychological pain that may intensify as time goes by. Those who suffer from them may lose their will to carry out the simplest of life's activities; some even lose their will to live.

> Almost every day we have ups and downs in mood. How can we distinguish the everyday blues from clinical depression?

How Common Is Unipolar Depression?

Around 9 percent of adults in the United States suffer from a severe unipolar pattern of depression in any given year, while as many as 5 percent suffer from mild forms (Kessler et al., 2012, 2010). Around 18 percent of all adults experience an episode of severe unipolar depression at some point in their lives. These prevalence rates are similar in Canada, England, and many other countries. Moreover, the rate of depression—mild or severe—is higher among poor people than wealthier people (Sareen et al., 2011).

Women are at least twice as likely as men to have episodes of severe unipolar depression (WHO, 2014; Astbury, 2010). As many as 26 percent of women have an episode at some time in their lives, compared with 12 percent of men. As you will see in Chapter 14, among children the prevalence of unipolar depression is similar for girls and boys.

Approximately 85 percent of people with unipolar depression recover, some without treatment. At least 40 percent of them have at least one other episode of depression later in their lives (Halverson et al., 2015; Monroe, 2010).

What Are the Symptoms of Depression?

The picture of depression may vary from person to person. Earlier you saw how Meri's profound sadness, fatigue, and cognitive deterioration brought her job and social life to a standstill. Some depressed people have symptoms that are less severe. They manage to function, although their depression typically robs them of much effectiveness or pleasure.

As the case of Meri indicates, depression has many symptoms other than sadness. The symptoms, which often exacerbate one another, span five areas of functioning: emotional, motivational, behavioral, cognitive, and physical.

Emotional Symptoms Most people who are depressed feel sad and dejected. They describe themselves as feeling "miserable," "empty," and "humiliated." They tend to lose their sense of humor, report getting little pleasure from anything, and in

Laura Fortune/Rex Features via AP Images

Taking a bite out of depression To raise public awareness about depression, a charity cake shop in London sells cakes and cookies with decorations that reflect the symptoms of depressive disorders. Some of the decorations are even unfinished in order to echo how depression decreases the ability to pursue or complete work tasks and other activities.

SADNESS

Depression, a clinical disorder that causes considerable distress and impairment, features a range of symptoms, including emotional, motivational, behavioral, cognitive, and physical symptoms. **Sadness** is often one of the symptoms found in depression, but most often it is a perfectly normal negative emotion triggered by a loss or other painful circumstance.

(Horwitz & Wakefield, 2012, 2007)

SADNESS DIFFERS FROM CLINICAL DEPRESSION

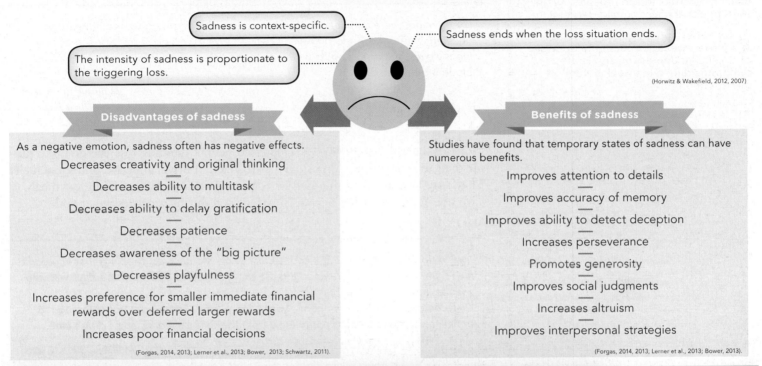

Sadness is context-specific.

The intensity of sadness is proportionate to the triggering loss.

Sadness ends when the loss situation ends.

(Horwitz & Wakefield, 2012, 2007)

Disadvantages of sadness

As a negative emotion, sadness often has negative effects.

Decreases creativity and original thinking

Decreases ability to multitask

Decreases ability to delay gratification

Decreases patience

Decreases awareness of the "big picture"

Decreases playfulness

Increases preference for smaller immediate financial rewards over deferred larger rewards

Increases poor financial decisions

(Forgas, 2014, 2013; Lerner et al., 2013; Bower, 2013; Schwartz, 2011).

Benefits of sadness

Studies have found that temporary states of sadness can have numerous benefits.

Improves attention to details

Improves accuracy of memory

Improves ability to detect deception

Increases perseverance

Promotes generosity

Improves social judgments

Increases altruism

Improves interpersonal strategies

(Forgas, 2014, 2013; Lerner et al., 2013; Bower, 2013).

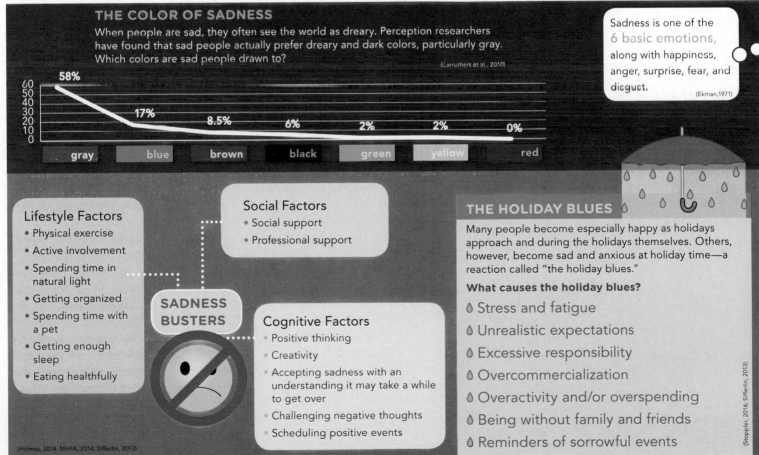

THE COLOR OF SADNESS

When people are sad, they often see the world as dreary. Perception researchers have found that sad people actually prefer dreary and dark colors, particularly gray. Which colors are sad people drawn to?

(Carruthers et al., 2010)

Sadness is one of the **6 basic emotions,** along with happiness, anger, surprise, fear, and disgust.

(Ekman, 1971)

gray	blue	brown	black	green	yellow	red
58%	17%	8.5%	6%	2%	2%	0%

Lifestyle Factors
- Physical exercise
- Active involvement
- Spending time in natural light
- Getting organized
- Spending time with a pet
- Getting enough sleep
- Eating healthfully

Social Factors
- Social support
- Professional support

SADNESS BUSTERS

Cognitive Factors
- Positive thinking
- Creativity
- Accepting sadness with an understanding it may take a while to get over
- Challenging negative thoughts
- Scheduling positive events

(Holmes, 2014; MHFA, 2014; Sifferlin, 2013)

THE HOLIDAY BLUES

Many people become especially happy as holidays approach and during the holidays themselves. Others, however, become sad and anxious at holiday time—a reaction called "the holiday blues."

What causes the holiday blues?

◊ Stress and fatigue

◊ Unrealistic expectations

◊ Excessive responsibility

◊ Overcommercialization

◊ Overactivity and/or overspending

◊ Being without family and friends

◊ Reminders of sorrowful events

(Stoppler, 2014; Sifferlin, 2013)

major depressive disorder A severe pattern of depression that is disabling and is not caused by such factors as drugs or a general medical condition.

persistent depressive disorder A chronic form of unipolar depression marked by ongoing and repeated symptoms of either major or mild depression.

premenstrual dysphoric disorder A disorder marked by repeated episodes of significant depression and related symptoms during the week before menstruation.

some cases display *anhedonia,* an inability to experience any pleasure at all. A number also experience anxiety, anger, or agitation. Terrie Williams, author of *Black Pain,* a book about depression in African Americans, describes the agony she went through each morning as her depression was unfolding:

> My mornings were unmanageable. To wake up each morning was to remember once again that the world by which I defined myself was no more. Soon after opening my eyes, the crying bouts would start and I'd sit alone for hours, weeping and mourning my losses.
>
> *(Williams, 2008, p. 9)*

Motivational Symptoms Depressed people typically lose the desire to pursue their usual activities. Almost all report a lack of drive, initiative, and spontaneity. They may have to force themselves to go to work, talk with friends, eat meals, or have sex. Terrie describes her social withdrawal during a depressive episode:

> I woke up one morning with a knot of fear in my stomach so crippling that I couldn't face light, much less day, and so intense that I stayed in bed for three days with the shades drawn and the lights out.
>
> Three days. Three days not answering the phone. Three days not checking my e-mail. I was disconnected completely from the outside world, and I didn't care.
>
> *(Williams, 2008, p. xxiv)*

Suicide represents the ultimate escape from life's challenges. As you will see in Chapter 7, many depressed people become uninterested in life or wish to die; others wish they could kill themselves, and some actually do. It has been estimated that between 6 and 15 percent of people who suffer from severe depression commit suicide (MHF, 2014; Alridge, 2012).

Behavioral Symptoms Depressed people are usually less active and less productive. They spend more time alone and may stay in bed for long periods. One man recalls, "I'd awaken early, but I'd just lie there—what was the use of getting up to a miserable day?" (Kraines & Thetford, 1972, p. 21). Depressed people may also move and even speak more slowly (Behrman, 2014).

Cognitive Symptoms Depressed people hold extremely negative views of themselves. They consider themselves inadequate, undesirable, inferior, perhaps evil (Lopez Molina et al., 2014). They also blame themselves for nearly every unfortunate event, even things that have nothing to do with them, and they rarely credit themselves for positive achievements.

Another cognitive symptom of depression is pessimism. Sufferers are usually convinced that nothing will ever improve, and they feel helpless to change any aspect of their lives. Because they expect the worst, they are likely to procrastinate. Their sense of hopelessness and helplessness makes them especially vulnerable to suicidal thinking (Shiratori et al., 2014).

People with depression frequently complain that their intellectual ability is poor. They feel confused, unable to remember things, easily

Dear diary, Sorry to bother you again.

LOW SELF-ESTEEM

distracted, and unable to solve even the smallest problems. In laboratory studies, depressed people do perform more poorly than nondepressed people on some tasks of memory, attention, and reasoning (Chen et al., 2013). It may be, however, that these difficulties sometimes reflect motivational problems rather than cognitive ones.

Physical Symptoms People who are depressed frequently have such physical ailments as headaches, indigestion, constipation, dizzy spells, and general pain (Bai et al., 2014; Goldstein et al., 2011). In fact, many depressions are misdiagnosed as medical problems at first (Parker & Hyett, 2010). Disturbances in appetite and sleep are particularly common (Jackson et al., 2014). Most depressed people eat less, sleep less, and feel more fatigued than they did prior to the disorder. Some, however, eat and sleep excessively.

Diagnosing Unipolar Depression

According to DSM-5, a *major depressive episode* is a period of two or more weeks marked by at least five symptoms of depression, including sad mood and/or loss of pleasure (see Table 6-1 on the next page). In extreme cases, the episode may include psychotic symptoms, ones marked by a loss of contact with reality, such as *delusions*—bizarre ideas without foundation—or *hallucinations*—perceptions of things that are not actually present. A depressed man with psychotic symptoms may imagine that he cannot eat "because my intestines are deteriorating and will soon stop working," or he may believe that he sees his dead wife.

DSM-5 lists several types of depressive disorders. People who go through a major depressive episode without having any history of mania receive a diagnosis of **major depressive disorder** (APA, 2013) (see Table 6-1 again). The disorder may be further described as *seasonal* if it changes with the seasons (for example, if the depression recurs each winter), *catatonic* if it is marked by either immobility or excessive activity, *peripartum* if it occurs during pregnancy or within four weeks of giving birth, or *melancholic* if the person is almost totally unaffected by pleasurable events.

People whose unipolar depression is particularly long-lasting receive a diagnosis of **persistent depressive disorder** (APA, 2013) (see Table 6-1 again). Some people with this chronic disorder have repeated major depressive episodes, a pattern technically called *persistent depressive disorder with major depressive episodes*. Others have less severe and less disabling symptoms, a pattern called *persistent depressive disorder with dysthymic syndrome*.

A third type of depressive disorder is **premenstrual dysphoric disorder,** a diagnosis given to certain women who repeatedly have clinically significant depressive and related symptoms during the week before menstruation. The inclusion of this pattern in DSM-5 is controversial, as you will see later (see page 209).

Yet another kind of depressive disorder, *disruptive mood dysregulation disorder,* is characterized by a combination of persistent depressive symptoms and recurrent outbursts of severe temper. This disorder emerges during mid-childhood or adolescence and so is discussed in Chapter 14, "Disorders Common Among Children and Adolescents."

Stress and Unipolar Depression

Episodes of unipolar depression often seem to be triggered by stressful events (Fried et al., 2015). In fact, researchers have found that depressed people have a larger number of stressful life events during the month just before the onset of their disorder than do other people during the same period of time. Of course, stressful life events also precede other psychological disorders, but depressed people often report more such events than anybody else.

Lincoln's private war In 1841 Abraham Lincoln wrote to a friend, "I am now the most miserable man living. If what I feel were equally distributed to the whole human family, there would be not one cheerful face on earth."

George P. A. Healy 1887, The National Portrait Gallery, Smithsonian Institution/Art Resource, NY

table: **6-1**

Dx Checklist

Major Depressive Episode

1. For a 2-week period, person displays an increase in depressed mood for the majority of each day and/or a decrease in enjoyment or interest across most activities for the majority of each day.

2. For the same 2 weeks, person also experiences at least 3 or 4 of the following symptoms: • Considerable weight change or appetite change • Daily insomnia or hypersomnia • Daily agitation or decrease in motor activity • Daily fatigue or lethargy • Daily feelings of worthlessness or excessive guilt • Daily reduction in concentration or decisiveness • Repeated focus on death or suicide, a suicide plan, or a suicide attempt.

3. Significant distress or impairment.

Major Depressive Disorder

1. Presence of a major depressive episode

2. No pattern of mania or hypomania.

Persistent Depressive Disorder

1. Person experiences the symptoms of Major Depressive Disorder or Dysthymic Disorder for at least 2 years.

2. During the two-year period, symptoms not absent for more than two months at a time.

3. No history of mania or hypomania.

4. Significant distress or impairment.

Information from: APA, 2013.

Some clinicians consider it important to distinguish a *reactive (exogenous) depression,* which follows clear-cut stressful events, from an *endogenous depression,* which seems to be a response to internal factors. But can one ever know for certain whether a depression is reactive or not? Even if stressful events occurred before the onset of depression, that depression may not be reactive. The events could actually be a coincidence. Thus, today's clinicians usually concentrate on recognizing both the situational and the internal aspects of any given case of unipolar depression.

> Why do you think stressful events or periods in life might trigger depressed feelings and other negative emotions?

The Biological Model of Unipolar Depression

Medical researchers have been aware for years that certain diseases and drugs produce mood changes. Could unipolar depression itself have biological causes? Evidence from genetic, biochemical, anatomical, and immune system studies suggests that often it does.

Genetic Factors Four kinds of research—family pedigree, twin, adoption, and molecular biology gene studies—suggest that some people inherit a predisposition to unipolar depression (McGuffin, 2014). *Family pedigree studies* select people with unipolar depression, examine their relatives, and see whether depression also afflicts other members of the family. If a predisposition to unipolar depression is inherited, the relatives should have a higher rate of depression than the population at large. Researchers have in fact found that as many as 30 percent of those relatives are depressed (see Table 6-2), compared with fewer than 10 percent of the general population (Levinson & Nichols, 2014; Berrettini, 2006).

If a predisposition to unipolar depression is inherited, you might also expect to find a particularly large number of cases among the close relatives of a proband. *Twin studies* have supported this expectation (Levinson & Nichols, 2014). One study looked at nearly 200 pairs of twins. When an identical twin had unipolar depression, there was a 46 percent chance that the other twin would have the same disorder. In contrast, when a fraternal twin had unipolar depression, the other twin had only a 20 percent chance of developing the disorder (McGuffin et al., 1996).

Finally, today's scientists have at their disposal techniques from the field of molecular biology to help them directly identify genes and determine whether certain gene abnormalities are related to depression. Using such techniques, researchers have found evidence that unipolar depression may be tied to genes on chromosomes 1, 4, 9, 10, 11, 12, 13, 14, 17, 18, 20, 21, 22, and X (Jansen et al., 2015; Preuss et al., 2013). For example, a number of researchers have found that people who are depressed often have an abnormality of their *5-HTT* gene, a gene located on chromosome 17 that is responsible for the activity of the neurotransmitter serotonin. As you will read in the next section, low activity of serotonin is closely tied to depression.

Biochemical Factors Low activity of two neurotransmitter chemicals, **norepinephrine** and **serotonin,** has been strongly linked to unipolar depression. In the 1950s, several pieces of evidence began to point to this relationship. First, medical researchers discovered that certain medications for high blood pressure often caused depression (Ayd, 1956). As it turned out, some of these medications lowered norepinephrine activity and others lowered serotonin. A second piece of evidence was the discovery of the first truly effective antidepressant drugs. Although these drugs were discovered by accident, researchers soon learned that they relieve depression by increasing either norepinephrine or serotonin activity.

For years it was thought that low activity of *either* norepinephrine or serotonin was capable of producing depression, but investigators now believe that their relation to depression is more complicated (Ding et al., 2014; Goldstein et al., 2011). Research suggests that interactions between serotonin and norepinephrine activity, or between these and other kinds of neurotransmitters in the brain, rather than the operation of any one neurotransmitter alone, may account for unipolar depression.

▸ **norepinephrine** A neurotransmitter whose abnormal activity is linked to depression and panic disorder.

▸ **serotonin** A neurotransmitter whose abnormal activity is linked to depression, obsessive-compulsive disorder, and eating disorders.

table: **6-2**

Comparing Depressive and Bipolar Disorders

	One-Year Prevalence (Percent)	Female-to-Male Ratio	Typical Age at Onset (Years)	Prevalence among First-Degree Relatives	Percentage Currently Receiving Treatment
Major depressive disorder	8.0%	2:1	24–29	Elevated	50.0%
Persistent depressive disorder (with dysthymic syndrome)	1.5–5.0%	Between 3:2 and 2:1	10–25	Elevated	36.8%
Bipolar I disorder	1.6%	1:1	15–44	Elevated	33.8%
Bipolar II disorder	1.0%	1:1	15–44	Elevated	33.8%
Cyclothymic disorder	0.4%	1:1	15–25	Elevated	Unknown

Information from: APA, 2013, 2000; Kessler et al., 2012, 2010, 2005; Gonzalez et al., 2010; Taube-Schiff & Lau, 2008; Regier et al., 1993; Weissman et al., 1991.

Biological researchers have also learned that the body's *endocrine system* may play a role in unipolar depression (see *PsychWatch*). As you have seen, endocrine glands throughout the body release *hormones,* chemicals that in turn spur body organs into action (see Chapter 5). People with unipolar depression have been found to have abnormally high levels of *cortisol,* one of the hormones released by the adrenal glands during times of stress (Owens et al., 2014; Treadway & Pizzagalli, 2014). This relationship is not all that surprising, given that stressful events often seem to trigger depression. Another hormone that has been tied to depression is *melatonin,*

PsychWatch

Sadness at the Happiest of Times

Women usually expect the birth of a child to be a happy experience. But for 10 to 30 percent of new mothers, the weeks and months after childbirth bring clinical depression (Guintivano et al., 2014). *Peripartum depression,* popularly called *postpartum depression,* typically begins within four weeks after the birth of a child; many cases actually begin during pregnancy (APA, 2013). This disorder is far more severe than simple "baby blues." It is also different from other postpartum syndromes such as *postpartum psychosis,* a problem that is examined in Chapter 12.

The "baby blues" are so common—as many as 80 percent of women experience them—that most researchers consider them normal. As new mothers try to cope with the wakeful nights and other stresses that accompany the arrival of a new baby, they may have crying spells, fatigue, anxiety, insomnia, and sadness (Enatescu et al., 2014). These symptoms usually disappear within days or weeks (Kendall-Tackett, 2010).

In postpartum depression, however, depressive symptoms continue and may last up to a year or more. The symptoms include extreme sadness, despair, tearfulness, insomnia, anxiety, intrusive thoughts, compulsions, panic attacks, feelings of inability to cope, and suicidal thoughts. Women who have an episode of postpartum depression have a 25 to 50 percent chance of developing it again with a subsequent birth (Stevens et al., 2002).

Many clinicians believe that the hormonal changes accompanying childbirth trigger postpartum depression. All women go through a kind of hormone "withdrawal" after delivery, as estrogen and progesterone levels, which rise as

much as 50 times above normal during pregnancy, now drop sharply to levels far below normal (Horowitz et al., 2005, 1995). Perhaps some women are particularly influenced by these dramatic hormone changes (Mehta et al., 2014). Other theorists suggest that some women may have a genetic predisposition to postpartum depression (Guintivano et al., 2014).

At the same time, psychological and sociocultural factors may play important roles in the disorder (Mauthner, 2010). The birth of a baby brings enormous changes for women—changes in her marital relationship, daily routines, and social roles. Sleep and relaxation are likely to decrease, and financial pressures may increase. Perhaps she feels the added stress of giving up a career—or of trying to maintain one. This pileup of stress may heighten the risk of depression (Phillips, 2011; Kendall-Tackett, 2010). Mothers whose infants are sick or temperamentally "difficult" may be under yet additional pressure.

Fortunately, treatment can make a big difference for most women with postpartum depression. Self-help support groups have proved extremely helpful for many women who have or who are at risk for postpartum depression (Dennis, 2014; Evans et al., 2012). In addition, many respond well to the same approaches that are applied to other forms of depression—antidepressant medications, cognitive therapy, interpersonal psychotherapy, or a combination of these approaches (Hou et al., 2014; Kim et al., 2014).

However, many women who would benefit from treatment do not seek help because they feel ashamed about being sad at a time that is supposed to be joyous and are concerned about being

Bryan Bedder/WireImage/Getty Images

"I felt like a failure." Accomplished actress and musician Gwyneth Paltrow, seen here performing at the Annual Country Music Awards in Nashville, Tennessee, recently revealed that she suffered from postpartum depression for a number of months after giving birth to her second child in 2006. Said Paltrow, "I felt like a zombie. . . . I couldn't connect. . . . I thought it meant I was a terrible mother and person. . . . I felt like a failure."

judged harshly (Bina, 2014; Mauthner, 2010). For them, a large dose of education is in order. Even positive events, such as the birth of a child, can be stressful if they also bring major change to one's life. Recognizing and addressing such feelings are in everyone's best interest.

Lighting up depression In London's Trafalgar Square, people sit and stand around an art installation called the Trafalgar Sun during the gloomy days of January, basking in the rays of the artificial sun. Winter depression has been linked to a decrease in the amount of light people are exposed to at that time of the year and to an accompanying shift in secretions of the hormone *melatonin*.

sometimes called the "Dracula hormone" because it is released only in the dark. People who experience a recurrence of depression each winter (a pattern called *seasonal affective disorder*) may secrete more melatonin during the winter's long nights than other individuals do.

Still other biological researchers are starting to believe that unipolar depression is tied more closely to what happens *within* neurons than to the chemicals that carry messages between neurons. They believe that activity by key neurotransmitters or hormones ultimately leads to deficiencies of certain proteins and other chemicals within neurons—deficiencies that may impair the health of the neurons and lead in turn to depression (Duman, 2014).

The biochemical explanations of unipolar depression have produced much enthusiasm, but research in this area has certain limitations. Some of it has relied on *analogue studies,* which create depression-like symptoms in laboratory animals. Researchers cannot be certain that these symptoms do in fact reflect the human disorder. Similarly, until recent years, technology was limited, and studies of human depression had to measure brain biochemical activity indirectly. As a result, investigators could never be certain of the biochemical events that were taking place in the brain. Current studies using newer technology, such as PET and MRI scans, are helping to eliminate such uncertainties about such brain activity.

Brain Anatomy and Brain Circuits In earlier chapters, you read that many biological researchers now believe that emotional reactions of various kinds are tied to brain *circuits*—networks of brain structures that work together, triggering each other into action and producing a particular kind of emotional reaction. Although research is far from complete, a brain circuit responsible for unipolar depression has begun to emerge (Treadway & Pizzagalli, 2014; Brockmann et al., 2011). An array of brain-imaging studies point to several brain areas that are likely members of this circuit, including the *prefrontal cortex,* the *hippocampus,* the *amygdala,* and *Brodmann Area 25,* an area located just under the brain part called the *cingulate cortex* (see Figure 6-1). Research suggests that, among depressed people, activity and blood flow are low in certain parts of the prefrontal cortex (Vialou et al., 2014), yet high in other parts (Lemogne et al., 2010); the hippocampus is undersized and its production of new neurons is low

figure 6-1

The biology of depression Researchers believe that the brain circuit involved in unipolar depression includes the prefrontal cortex, the hippocampus, the amygdala, and Brodmann Area 25.

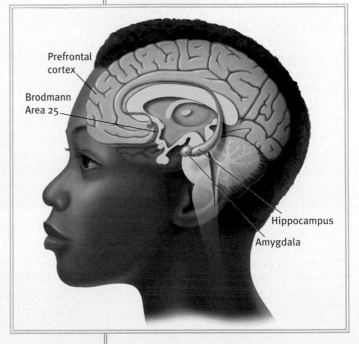

▸ **electroconvulsive therapy (ECT)** A treatment for depression in which electrodes attached to a patient's head send an electrical current through the brain, causing a convulsion.

▸ **MAO inhibitor** An antidepressant drug that prevents the action of the enzyme monoamine oxidase.

▸ **tricyclic** An antidepressant drug such as imipramine that has three rings in its molecular structure.

(Kubera et al., 2011; Campbell et al., 2004); activity and blood flow are elevated in the amygdala (Treadway & Pizzagalli, 2014; Goldstein et al., 2011); and Brodmann Area 25 is relatively small and overactive (Eggers, 2014; Mayberg et al., 2005).

The Immune System As you will see in Chapter 8, the *immune system* is the body's network of activities and body cells that fight off bacteria, viruses, and other foreign invaders. When people are under intense stress for a while, their immune systems may become dysregulated, leading to lower functioning of important white blood cells called *lymphocytes* and to increased production of *C-reactive protein* (*CRP*), a protein that spreads throughout the body and causes inflammation and various illnesses. There is a growing belief among some researchers that immune system dysregulation of this kind helps produce depression (Anderson et al., 2014; Yoon et al., 2012).

What Are the Biological Treatments for Unipolar Depression?

Usually biological treatment means *antidepressant drugs* or popular herbal supplements, but for severely depressed people who do not respond to other forms of treatment, it sometimes means *electroconvulsive therapy,* or a relatively new group of approaches called *brain stimulation.*

ELECTROCONVULSIVE THERAPY One of the most controversial forms of treatment for depression is **electroconvulsive therapy (ECT).** In this procedure, two electrodes are attached to the patient's head, and 65 to 140 volts of electricity are passed through the brain for half a second or less. This results in a *brain seizure* that lasts from 25 seconds to a few minutes. After 6 to 12 such treatments, spaced over two to four weeks, most patients feel less depressed (Fink, 2014, 2007).

The discovery that electric shock can be therapeutic was made by accident. In the 1930s, clinical researchers mistakenly came to believe that brain seizures, or the *convulsions* (severe body spasms) that accompany them, could cure schizophrenia and other psychotic disorders, and so they searched for ways to induce seizures as a treatment for patients with psychosis. One early technique was to give patients the drug *metrazol.* Another was to give them large doses of insulin (*insulin coma therapy*). These procedures produced the desired brain seizures, but each was quite dangerous and sometimes even caused death. Finally, an Italian psychiatrist named Ugo Cerletti discovered that he could produce seizures more safely by applying electric currents to a patient's head. ECT soon became popular and was tried out on a wide range of psychological problems, as new techniques so often are. Its effectiveness with severe depression in particular became apparent.

In the early years of ECT, broken bones and dislocations of the jaw or shoulders sometimes resulted from patients' severe convulsions. Today's practitioners avoid these problems by giving patients strong *muscle relaxants* to minimize convulsions. They also use *anesthetics* to put patients to sleep during the procedure, reducing their terror.

Patients who receive ECT often have difficulty remembering certain events, most often events that took place immediately before and after their treatments (Martin et al., 2015; Merkl et al., 2011). In most cases, this memory loss clears up within a few months, but some patients are left with gaps in more distant memory, and this form of amnesia can be permanent (Hanna et al., 2009; Wang, 2007).

ECT is clearly effective in treating unipolar depression, although it has been difficult to determine why it works so well (Baldinger et al., 2014; Fink et al., 2014). The procedure seems to be particularly effective in cases of depression that include delusions (Rothschild, 2010).

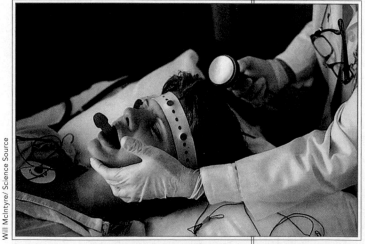

Will McIntyre/ Science Source

ECT today The techniques for administering ECT have changed significantly since the treatment's early days. Today, patients are given drugs to help them sleep, muscle relaxants to prevent severe jerks of the body and broken bones, and oxygen to guard against brain damage.

ANTIDEPRESSANT DRUGS Two kinds of drugs discovered in the 1950s reduce the symptoms of depression: *monoamine oxidase (MAO) inhibitors* and *tricyclics*. These drugs have now been joined by a third group, the so-called *second-generation antidepressants* (see Table 6-3).

The effectiveness of **MAO inhibitors** as a treatment for unipolar depression was discovered accidentally. Physicians noted that *iproniazid,* a drug being tested on patients with tuberculosis, had an interesting effect: it seemed to make the patients happier (Sandler, 1990). It was found to have the same effect on depressed patients (Kline, 1958; Loomer et al., 1957). What this and several related drugs had in common biochemically was that they slowed the body's production of the enzyme *monoamine oxidase (MAO)*. Thus they were called MAO inhibitors.

Normally, brain supplies of the enzyme MAO break down, or degrade, the neurotransmitter norepinephrine. MAO inhibitors block MAO from carrying out this activity and thereby stop the destruction of norepinephrine. The result is a rise in norepinephrine activity and, in turn, a reduction of depressive symptoms. Approximately half of depressed patients who take MAO inhibitors are helped by them (Ciraulo et al., 2011; Thase et al., 1995). There is, however, a potential danger with regard to these drugs. When people who take MAO inhibitors eat foods containing the chemical *tyramine*—including such common foods as cheeses, bananas, and certain wines—their blood pressure rises dangerously. Thus people on these drugs must stick to a rigid diet.

The discovery of **tricyclics** in the 1950s was also accidental. Researchers who were looking for a new drug to combat schizophrenia ran some tests on a drug called *imipramine* (Kuhn, 1958). They discovered that imipramine was of no help in cases of schizophrenia, but it did relieve unipolar depression in many people. The new drug (trade name Tofranil) and related ones became known as tricyclic antidepressants because they all share a three-ring molecular structure.

In hundreds of studies, depressed patients taking tricyclics have improved much more than similar patients taking placebos, although the drugs must be taken for at least 10 days before such improvements take hold (Advokat et al., 2014). About 65 percent of patients who take tricyclics are helped by them (FDA, 2014). If the patients stop taking tricyclics immediately after obtaining relief, they run a high risk of relapsing within a year. If, however, they continue taking the drugs for five

"Katia, I know that with the right combination of therapy and medication I could have a committed relationship with you."

table: 6-3

Drugs That Reduce Unipolar Depression

Generic Name	Trade Name
Monoamine oxidase inhibitors	
Isocarboxazid	Marplan
Phenelzine	Nardil
Tranylcypromine	Parnate
Selegiline	Eldepryl
Tricyclics	
Imipramine	Tofranil
Amitriptyline	Elavil
Doxepin	Sinequan; Silenor
Trimipramine	Surmontil
Desipramine	Norpramin
Nortriptyline	Aventil; Pamelor
Protriptyline	Vivactil
Clomipramine	Anafranil
Amoxapine	Asendin
Mirtazapine	Remeron
Second-Generation Antidepressants	
Maprotiline	Ludiomil
Trazodone	Desyrel
Fluoxetine	Prozac
Sertraline	Zoloft
Paroxetine	Paxil
Venlafaxine	Effexor
Fluvoxamine	Luvox
Bupropion	Wellbutrin, Aplenzin
Citalopram	Celexa
Escitalopram	Lexapro
Duloxetine	Cymbalta
Desvenlafaxine	Pristiq
Atomoxetine	Strattera

▶ **selective serotonin reuptake inhibitors (SSRIs)** A group of second-generation antidepressant drugs that increase serotonin activity specifically, without affecting other neurotransmitters.

▶ **vagus nerve stimulation** A treatment procedure for depression in which an implanted pulse generator sends regular electrical signals to a person's vagus nerve; the nerve then stimulates the brain.

▶ **transcranial magnetic stimulation (TMS)** A treatment procedure for depression in which an electromagnetic coil, which is placed on or above a patient's head, sends a current into the individual's brain.

months or more after being free of depressive symptoms—"continuation therapy" or "maintenance therapy"—their chances of relapse decrease considerably (Borges et al., 2014; FDA, 2014).

Most researchers have concluded that tricyclics reduce depression by acting on neurotransmitter "reuptake" mechanisms (Ciraulo et al., 2011). Remember from Chapter 2 that messages are carried from the "sending" neuron across the synaptic space to a receiving neuron by a neurotransmitter, a chemical released from the axon ending of the sending neuron. However, there is a complication in this process. While the sending neuron releases the neurotransmitter, a pumplike mechanism in the neuron's ending immediately starts to reabsorb it in a process called *reuptake*. The purpose of this reuptake process is to control how long the neurotransmitter remains in the synaptic space and to prevent it from overstimulating the receiving neuron. Unfortunately, the reuptake mechanism may be too successful in some people—cutting off norepinephrine or serotonin activity too soon, preventing messages from reaching the receiving neurons, and producing clinical depression. Tricyclics *block* this reuptake process, thus increasing their neurotransmitter activity (see Figure 6-2).

> If antidepressant drugs are effective, why do many people seek out herbal supplements for depression?

A third group of effective antidepressant drugs, structurally different from the MAO inhibitors and tricyclics, has been developed during the past few decades. Most of these second-generation antidepressants are called **selective serotonin reuptake inhibitors (SSRIs)** because they increase serotonin activity specifically, without affecting norepinephrine or other neurotransmitters. The SSRIs include *fluoxetine* (trade name Prozac), *sertraline* (Zoloft), and *escitalopram* (Lexapro). More recently developed *selective norepinephrine reuptake inhibitors,* such as *atomoxetine* (Strattera), which increase norepinephrine activity only, and *serotonin-norepinephrine reuptake inhibitors,* such as *venlafaxine* (Effexor), which increase both serotonin and norepinephrine activity, are also now available (Advokat et al., 2014).

In effectiveness and speed of action, the second-generation antidepressant drugs are about on a par with the tricyclics, yet they are prescribed more often and their sales have skyrocketed. They do not pose the dietary problems of the MAO inhibitors or produce some of the unpleasant effects of the tricyclics, such as dry mouth and constipation. At the same time, the new antidepressants can produce undesirable

figure 6-2

Reuptake and antidepressants (Left) Soon after a neuron releases neurotransmitters such as norepinephrine or serotonin into its synaptic space, it activates a pumplike reuptake mechanism to reabsorb excess neurotransmitters. In depression, however, this reuptake process is too active, removing too many neurotransmitters before they can bind to a receiving neuron. (Right) Tricyclic and most second-generation antidepressant drugs block the reuptake process, enabling norepinephrine or serotonin to remain in the synapse longer and bind to the receiving neuron.

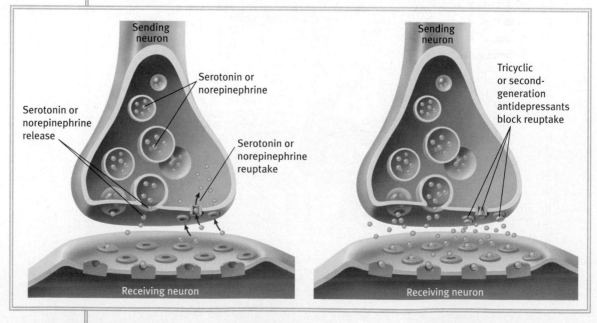

side effects of their own. Some people gain weight or have a reduced sex drive, for example (Stahl, 2014).

As popular as the antidepressants are, it is important to recognize that they do not work for everyone. In fact, as you have read, even the most successful of them *fails* to help at least 35 percent of clients with depression. In fact, some recent reviews have raised the possibility that the failure rate is higher still (Hegerl et al., 2012; Isacsson & Alder, 2012). How are clients who do not respond to antidepressant drugs treated currently? Researchers have noted that, all too often, their psychiatrists or family physicians simply prescribe alternative antidepressants or antidepressant mixtures—one after another—without directing the clients to psychotherapy or counseling of some kind. Melissa, a depressed woman for whom psychotropic drug treatment has failed to work over many years, reflects on this issue:

> [S]he spoke, in a wistful manner, of how she wished her treatment could have been different. "I do wonder what might have happened if [at age 16] I could have just talked to someone, and they could have helped me learn about what I could do on my own to be a healthy person. . . . Instead, it was you have this problem with your neurotransmitters, and so here, take this pill Zoloft, and when that didn't work, it was take this pill Prozac, and when that didn't work, it was take this pill Effexor, and then when I started having trouble sleeping, it was take this sleeping pill," she says, her voice sounding more wistful than ever. "I am so tired of the pills."
>
> (Whitaker, 2010)

BRAIN STIMULATION In recent years, three additional biological approaches have been developed for the treatment of depressive disorders—*vagus nerve stimulation, transcranial magnetic stimulation,* and *deep brain stimulation.*

The vagus nerve, the longest nerve in the human body, runs from the brain stem through the neck down the chest and on to the abdomen. A number of years ago, a group of depression researchers surmised that they might be able to stimulate the brain by electrically stimulating the vagus nerve with ECT. Their efforts gave birth to a new treatment for depression—**vagus nerve stimulation.**

In this procedure, a surgeon implants a small device called a *pulse generator* under the skin of the chest. The surgeon then guides a wire, which extends from the pulse generator, up to the neck and attaches it to the vagus nerve (see Figure 6-3). Electrical signals travel from the pulse generator through the wire to the vagus nerve. The stimulated vagus nerve then delivers electrical signals to the brain. In 2005, the U.S. Food and Drug Administration (FDA) approved this procedure.

Ever since vagus nerve stimulation was first tried on depressed human beings, research has found that it brings significant relief to many depressed people. In fact, in studies of severely depressed people who have not responded to any other form of treatment, as many as 40 percent improve significantly when treated with this procedure (Howland, 2014; Berry et al., 2013).

Transcranial magnetic stimulation (TMS) is another technique that is used to try to stimulate the brain without subjecting depressed patients to the undesired effects or trauma of ECT. In this procedure, the clinician places an electromagnetic coil on or above the patient's head. The coil sends a current into the prefrontal cortex. As you'll remember, some parts of the prefrontal cortex of depressed people

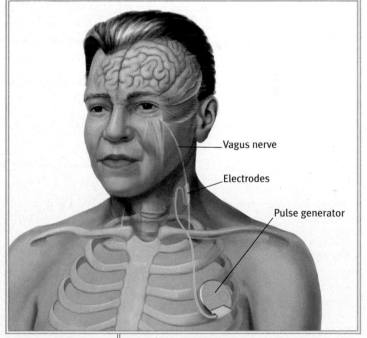

figure 6-3

Vagus nerve stimulation In the procedure called vagus nerve stimulation, an implanted pulse generator sends electrical signals to the vagus nerve, which then delivers electrical signals to the brain. This stimulation of the brain helps reduce depression in many patients.

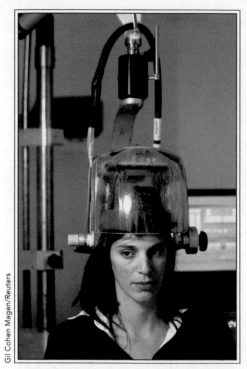

Gil Cohen Magen/Reuters

Stimulating the brain In this version of transcranial magnetic stimulation, a woman sits under a helmet. The helmet contains an electromagnetic coil that sends currents into and stimulates her brain.

are underactive; TMS appears to increase neuron activity in those regions. A number of studies have found that TMS reduces depression for many patients when it is administered daily for two to four weeks (Dunner et al., 2014; Fox et al., 2012).

As you read earlier, researchers have recently linked depression to high activity in *Brodmann Area 25*. This finding led neurologist Helen Mayberg and her colleagues (2005) to administer an experimental treatment called **deep brain stimulation (DBS)** to six severely depressed patients who had previously been unresponsive to all other forms of treatment. The Mayberg team drilled two tiny holes into the patient's skull and implanted electrodes in Area 25. The electrodes were connected to a battery, or "pacemaker," that was implanted in the patient's chest (for men) or stomach (for women). The pacemaker powered the electrodes, sending a steady stream of low-voltage electricity to Area 25. Mayberg's expectation was that this repeated stimulation would reduce Area 25 activity to a normal level and "recalibrate" and regulate the depression brain circuit.

In the initial study of DBS, four of the six severely depressed patients became almost depression-free within a matter of months (Mayberg et al., 2005). Subsequent research with other severely depressed individuals has also yielded promising findings (Berlim et al., 2014; Taghva, Malone, & Rezai, 2013). Understandably, this work has produced considerable enthusiasm in the clinical field, but it is important to recognize that research on DBS is in its early stages.

Psychological Models of Unipolar Depression

The psychological models that have been most widely applied to unipolar depression are the psychodynamic, behavioral, and cognitive models. The psychodynamic model has not been strongly supported by research, and the behavioral model has received moderate support. In contrast, the cognitive model has received considerable research support and gained a large following.

The Psychodynamic Model
Sigmund Freud (1917) and his student Karl Abraham (1916, 1911) developed the first psychodynamic explanation and treatment for depression. Their emphasis on dependence and loss continues to influence today's psychodynamic clinicians.

PSYCHODYNAMIC EXPLANATIONS Freud and Abraham began by noting the similarity between clinical depression and grief in people who lose loved ones: constant weeping, loss of appetite, difficulty sleeping, loss of pleasure in life, and social withdrawal. According to the theorists, a series of unconscious processes is set in motion when a loved one dies. Unable to accept the loss, mourners at first regress to the *oral stage* of development, the period of total dependency when infants cannot distinguish themselves from their parents. By regressing to this stage, the mourners merge their own identity with that of the person they have lost, and so symbolically regain the lost person. They direct all their feelings for the loved one, including sadness and anger, toward themselves. For most mourners, this reaction is temporary. For some, however, grief worsens over time, and they, in fact, become depressed.

> Why do you think so many comedians and other entertainers report having been depressed earlier in their lives?

Of course, many people become depressed without losing a loved one. To explain why, Freud proposed the concept of **symbolic,** or **imagined, loss,** in which a person equates other kinds of events with the loss of a loved one. A college student may, for example, experience failure in a calculus course as the loss of her parents, believing that they love her only when she excels academically.

Although many psychodynamic theorists have parted company with Freud and Abraham's theory of depression, it continues to influence current psychodynamic thinking (Desmet, 2013; Zuckerman, 2011). For example, *object relations theorists* (the psychodynamic theorists who emphasize relationships) propose that depression results when people's relationships leave them feeling unsafe and insecure (Schattner & Sharar, 2011; Blatt, 2004). People whose parents pushed them toward either excessive dependence or excessive self-reliance are more likely to become depressed when they later lose important relationships.

The following description by the therapist of a depressed middle-aged woman illustrates the psychodynamic concepts of dependence, loss of a loved one, and symbolic loss:

> Marie Carls . . . had always felt very attached to her mother. . . . She always tried to placate her volcanic [emotions], to please her in every possible way. . . .
>
> After marriage [to Julius], she continued her pattern of submission and compliance. Before her marriage she had difficulty in complying with a volcanic mother, and after her marriage she almost automatically assumed a submissive role. . . .
>
> [W]hen she was thirty years old . . . [Marie] and her husband invited Ignatius, who was single, to come and live with them. Ignatius and [Marie] soon discovered that they had an attraction for each other. They both tried to fight that feeling; but when Julius had to go to another city for a few days, the so-called infatuation became much more than that. There were a few physical contacts. . . . There was an intense spiritual affinity. . . . A few months later everybody had to leave the city. . . . Nothing was done to maintain contact. Two years later . . . Marie heard that Ignatius had married. She felt terribly alone and despondent. . . .
>
> Her suffering had become more acute as she [came to believe] that old age was approaching and she had lost all her chances. Ignatius remained as the memory of lost opportunities. . . . Her life of compliance and obedience had not permitted her to reach her goal. . . . When she became aware of these ideas, she felt even more depressed. . . . She felt that everything she had built in her life was false or based on a false premise.
>
> *(Arieti & Bemporad, 1978, pp. 275–284)*

Studies have offered general support for the psychodynamic idea that major losses, especially ones suffered early in life, may set the stage for later depression (Gilman, 2013; Gutman & Nemeroff, 2011). When, for example, a depression scale was administered to 1,250 medical patients during visits to their family physicians, the patients whose fathers had died during their childhood scored higher on depression (Barnes & Prosen, 1985). At the same time, research does not indicate that loss is always at the core of depression. In fact, it is estimated that less than 10 percent of all people who have major losses in life actually become depressed (Bonanno, 2004; Paykel & Cooper, 1992). Moreover, research into the loss–depression link has yielded inconsistent findings. Though some studies find evidence of a relationship between childhood loss and later depression, others do not.

WHAT ARE THE PSYCHODYNAMIC TREATMENTS FOR UNIPOLAR DEPRESSION? Believing that unipolar depression results from unconscious grief over real or imagined losses, compounded by excessive dependence on other people, psychodynamic therapists seek to help clients bring these underlying issues to consciousness and work through them. They encourage the depressed client to associate freely during therapy; suggest interpretations of the client's associations, dreams, and displays of resistance and transference; and help the person review past events and

▶ **deep brain stimulation (DBS)** A treatment procedure for depression in which a pacemaker powers electrodes that have been implanted in Brodmann Area 25, thus stimulating that brain area.

▶ **symbolic loss** According to Freudian theory, the loss of a valued object (for example, a loss of employment) that is unconsciously interpreted as the loss of a loved one. Also called *imagined loss*.

Early loss The young daughter of a police officer killed during the September 11, 2001, terrorist attacks stands onstage holding her father's hand while the names of attack victims are read during ceremonies at Ground Zero marking the fifth anniversary of the event. Research has found that people who lose their parents as children have an increased likelihood of experiencing depression as adults.

Spencer Platt/Getty Images

Across the species Researcher Harry Harlow and his colleagues found that infant monkeys reacted with apparent despair to separation from their mothers. Even monkeys raised with surrogate mothers—wire cylinders wrapped with foam rubber and covered with terry cloth—formed an attachment to them and mourned their absence.

University of Wisconsin Primate Laboratory, Madison

///// BETWEEN THE LINES /////

Loss of Confidants

Intimate social contact has been declining over the past 30 years. When research participants were asked in 1985 how many confidants they turned to for discussion of important matters, most answered 3. Today, the most common response to the same question is 2 (Bryner, 2011; McPherson, Smith-Lovin, & Brashears, 2006).

feelings (Busch et al., 2004). Free association, for example, helped one man recall the early experiences of loss that, according to his therapist, had set the stage for his depression:

> Among his earliest memories, possibly the earliest of all, was the recollection of being wheeled in his baby cart under the elevated train structure and left there alone. Another memory that recurred vividly during the analysis was of an operation around the age of five. He was anesthetized and his mother left him with the doctor. He recalled how he had kicked and screamed, raging at her for leaving him.
>
> *(Lorand, 1968, pp. 325–326)*

Despite successful case reports such as this, researchers have found that long-term psychodynamic therapy is only occasionally helpful in cases of unipolar depression (Prochaska & Norcross, 2013). Two features of the approach may help limit its effectiveness. First, depressed clients may be too passive and feel too weary to join fully into the subtle therapy discussions. And second, they may become discouraged and end treatment too early when this long-term approach is unable to provide the quick relief that they desperately seek. Short-term psychodynamic therapies have performed better than traditional, longer-term approaches (Midgley et al., 2013; Lemma et al., 2011).

The Behavioral Model Behaviorists believe that unipolar depression results from significant changes in the number of rewards and punishments people receive in their lives, and they treat depressed people by helping them build more desirable patterns of reinforcement (Dygdon & Dienes, 2013). Clinical researcher Peter Lewinsohn was one of the first clinical theorists to develop a behavioral explanation (Lewinsohn et al., 1990, 1984).

THE BEHAVIORAL EXPLANATION Lewinsohn suggested that the positive rewards in life dwindle for some people, leading them to perform fewer and fewer constructive behaviors. The rewards of campus life, for example, disappear when a young woman graduates from college and takes a job; and an aging baseball player loses the rewards of high salary and adulation when his skills deteriorate. Although many people manage to fill their lives with other forms of gratification, some become particularly disheartened. The positive features of their lives decrease even more, and the decline in rewards leads them to perform still fewer constructive behaviors. In this manner, they spiral toward depression.

In a number of studies, behaviorists have found that the number of rewards people receive in life is indeed related to the presence or absence of depression. Not only do depressed participants typically report fewer positive rewards than nondepressed participants, but when their rewards begin to increase, their mood improved as well (Bylsma et al., 2011; Lewinsohn et al., 1979). Similarly, other investigations have found a strong relationship between positive life events and feelings of life satisfaction and happiness (Carvalho & Hopko, 2011).

Lewinsohn and other behaviorists have further proposed that *social* rewards are particularly important in the downward spiral of depression (Martell et al., 2010). This claim has been supported by research showing that depressed persons receive fewer social rewards than nondepressed persons and that as their mood improves, their social rewards increase. Although depressed people are sometimes the victims of social circumstances (see *MediaSpeak* on the next page), it may also be that their dark mood and flat behaviors help produce a decline in social rewards (Constantino et al., 2012; Coyne, 2001).

MediaSpeak

Immigration and Depression in the 21st Century

By Andrew Solomon, *New York Times*, December 8, 2013

A Canadian woman was denied entry to the United States last month because she had been hospitalized for depression in 2012. Ellen Richardson could not visit, she was told, unless she obtained "medical clearance" from one of three Toronto doctors approved by the Department of Homeland Security. Endorsement by her own psychiatrist, which she could presumably have obtained more efficiently, "would not suffice." She had been en route to New York, where she had intended to board a cruise to the Caribbean. . . .

The border agent told her he was acting in accordance with the United States Immigration and Nationality Act, Section 212, which allows patrols to block people from visiting the United States if they have a physical or mental disorder that threatens anyone's "property, safety or welfare." The [*Toronto*] *Star* reported that the agent produced a signed document stating that Ms. Richardson would need a medical evaluation because of her "mental illness episode." . . .

This is not the first time such measures have been reported. In 2011, Lois Kamenitz, a Canadian and a former teacher, was barred from entering the United States because she had once attempted suicide. [A police official] told the *Star* that he had heard of eight similar cases that year. After the incident, he wrote to me: "My sense is that there are a great many people being turned away. . . ."

People in treatment for mental illnesses do not have a higher rate of violence than people without mental illnesses. Furthermore, depression affects one in 10 American adults. . . . Pillorying depression is regressive, a swoop back into a period when any sign of mental illness was the basis for social exclusion. . . . [T]his border policy is not only unfair to visitors, but also constitutes an affront to the millions of Americans who are grappling with mental-health challenges.

Stigmatizing the condition is bad; stigmatizing the treatment is even worse. . . . Yet this incident will serve only to warn people against seeking treatment for

"Give me your tired, your poor, your huddled masses . . ." An Italian immigrant and her family arrive at Ellis Island in New York City in 1905. Today's U.S. immigration policies for persons with mental disorders are sometimes less generous than they were more than 100 years ago.

What kind of roles should mental health experts play in the development of immigration, gun, or other laws that target people with mental disorders?

mental illness. . . . Ms. Richardson, who attempted suicide in 2001 and as a result is paraplegic, has asserted that she has had appropriate treatment, and that she now has a fulfilling, purposeful life. We should applaud people who get treatment and manage to live deeply despite their challenges [and] put to rest the idea that people with mental health conditions who pose no danger are unwelcome in our country.

When the applause stops According to behaviorists, the reduction in rewards brought about by retirement places high achievers at particular risk for depression. Former New York Giants running back Tiki Barber, seen here eluding a defender, recently described the severe depression he went through after he retired from pro football in 2006, lost his job as a TV network correspondent, and ended his marriage, in quick succession. "I remember there were days where I would literally . . . sit on the couch and do nothing for 10 hours. . . . I started to shrivel. . . . I didn't have . . . that aura any more."

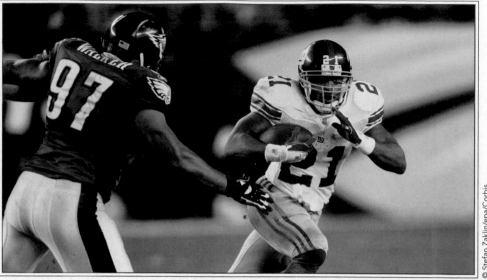

© Stefan Zaklin/epa/Corbis

WHAT ARE THE BEHAVIORAL TREATMENTS FOR UNIPOLAR DEPRESSION? Behavioral therapists use a variety of strategies to help increase the number of rewards experienced by their depressed clients (Dimidjian et al., 2014; Martell et al., 2010): (1) First the therapist selects activities that the client considers pleasurable, such as going shopping or taking photos, and encourages the person to set up a weekly schedule for engaging in them. Studies have shown that adding positive activities to a person's life—sometimes called *behavioral activation*—can indeed lead to a better mood. (2) Second, while reintroducing pleasurable events into a client's life, the therapist makes sure that the person's various behaviors are reinforced correctly. Behaviorists argue that when people become depressed, their negative behaviors—crying, ruminating, complaining, or self-criticism—keep others at a distance, reducing chances for rewarding interactions. To change this pattern, therapists guide clients to monitor their negative behaviors and to try new, more positive ones. In addition, the therapist may try to systematically ignore a client's depressive behaviors while praising or otherwise rewarding constructive statements and behavior, such as going to work. (3) Finally, behavioral therapists may train clients in effective social skills. In group therapy programs, for example, members may work together to improve eye contact, facial expression, posture, and other behaviors that send social messages.

These behavioral techniques seem to be of only limited help when just one of them is applied. However, when two or more such techniques are combined, behavioral treatment does appear to reduce depressive symptoms, particularly if the depression is mild. It is worth noting that Lewinsohn himself has combined behavioral techniques with cognitive strategies in recent years in an approach similar to the cognitive-behavioral treatments discussed in the next section.

The Cognitive Model

Cognitive theorists believe that people with unipolar depression persistently view events in negative ways and that such perceptions lead to their disorder. The two most influential cognitive explanations are the *theory of learned helplessness* and the *theory of negative thinking*.

LEARNED HELPLESSNESS Feelings of helplessness fill this account of a young woman's depression:

Mary was 25 years old and had just begun her senior year in college. . . . Asked to recount how her life had been going recently, Mary began to weep. Sobbing, she said that for the last year or so she felt she was losing control of her life and that *recent stresses (starting school again, friction with her boyfriend) had left her feeling worthless and frightened. Because of a gradual deterioration in her vision, she was now forced to wear glasses all day. "The glasses make me look terrible," she said, and "I don't look people in the eye much any more." Also, to her dismay, Mary had gained 20 pounds in the past year. She viewed herself as overweight and unattractive. At times she was convinced that with enough money to buy contact lenses and enough time to exercise she could cast off her depression; at other times she believed nothing would help. . . . Mary saw her life deteriorating in other spheres, as well. She felt overwhelmed by schoolwork and, for the first time in her life, was on academic probation. . . . In addition to her dissatisfaction with her appearance and her fears about her academic future, Mary complained of a lack of friends. Her social network consisted solely of her boyfriend, with whom she was living. Although there were times she experienced this relationship as almost unbearably frustrating, she felt helpless to change it and was pessimistic about its permanence.*

(Spitzer et al., 1983, pp. 122–123)

▶ **learned helplessness** The perception, based on past experiences, that one has no control over one's reinforcements.

Mary feels that she is "losing control of her life." According to psychologist Martin Seligman (1975), such feelings of helplessness are at the center of her depression. Since the mid-1960s Seligman has been developing the **learned helplessness** theory of depression. It holds that people become depressed when they think (1) that they no longer have control over the reinforcements (the rewards and punishments) in their lives and (2) that they themselves are responsible for this helpless state.

Seligman's theory first began to take shape when he was working with laboratory dogs. In one procedure, he strapped dogs into an apparatus called a hammock, in which they received shocks periodically no matter what they did. The next day each dog was placed in a *shuttle box,* a box divided in half by a barrier over which the animal could jump to reach the other side (see Figure 6-4). Seligman applied shocks to the dogs in the box, expecting that they, like other dogs in this situation, would soon learn to escape by jumping over the barrier. However, most of these dogs failed to learn anything in the shuttle box. After a flurry of activity, they simply "lay down and quietly whined" and accepted the shock.

Seligman decided that while receiving inescapable shocks in the hammock the day before, the dogs had learned that they had no control over unpleasant events (shocks) in their lives. That is, they had learned that they were helpless to do anything to change negative situations. Thus, when later they were placed in a new situation (the shuttle box) where they could in fact control their fate, they continued to believe that they were generally helpless. Seligman noted that the effects of learned helplessness greatly resemble the symptoms of human depression, and he proposed that people in fact become depressed after developing a general belief that they have no control over reinforcements in their lives.

In numerous human and animal studies, participants who undergo helplessness training have displayed reactions similar to depressive symptoms (Dygdon & Dienes, 2013). When, for example, human participants are exposed to uncontrollable negative events, they later score higher than other individuals on a depressive mood survey (Miller & Seligman, 1975). Similarly, helplessness-trained animal subjects lose interest in sexual and social activities—a common symptom of human depression (Lindner, 1968).

The learned helplessness explanation of depression has been revised somewhat over the past several decades. According to a newer version of the theory, the *attribution-helplessness theory,* when people view events as beyond their control, they

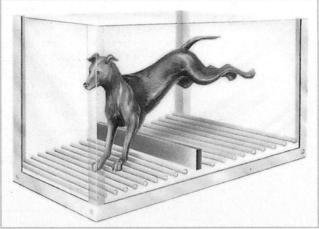

figure 6-4
Jumping to safety Experimental animals learn to escape or avoid shocks that are administered on one side of a shuttle box by jumping to the other (safe) side.

ask themselves why this is so (Abramson et al., 2002, 1989, 1978). If they attribute their present lack of control to some *internal* cause that is both *global* and *stable* ("I am inadequate at everything and I always will be"), they may well feel helpless to prevent future negative outcomes and they may experience depression. If they make other kinds of attributions, they are unlikely to have this reaction.

Consider a college student whose girlfriend breaks up with him. If he attributes this loss of control to an internal cause that is both global and stable—"It's my fault [internal], I ruin everything I touch [global], and I always will [stable]"—he then has reason to expect similar losses of control in the future and may generally experience a sense of helplessness. According to the learned helplessness view, he is a prime candidate for depression. If the student had instead attributed the breakup to causes that were more *specific* ("The way I've behaved the past couple of weeks blew this relationship"), *unstable* ("I don't usually act like that"), or *external* ("She never did know what she wanted"), he might not expect to lose control again and would probably not experience helplessness and depression. Hundreds of studies have supported the relationship between styles of attribution, helplessness, and depression (Rotenberg et al., 2012).

Some theorists have refined the helplessness model yet again in recent years. They suggest that attributions are likely to cause depression only when they further produce a sense of *hopelessness* in a person (Wain et al., 2011). By taking this factor into consideration, clinicians are often able to predict depression with still greater precision (Wang et al., 2013).

Although the learned helplessness theory of unipolar depression has been very influential, it too has imperfections. First, much of the learned helplessness research relies on animal subjects. It is impossible to know whether the animals' symptoms do in fact reflect the clinical depression found in humans. Second, the attributional feature of the theory raises difficult questions. What about the dogs and rats who learn helplessness? Can animals make attributions, even implicitly?

NEGATIVE THINKING Like Seligman, Aaron Beck believes that negative thinking lies at the heart of depression (Beck & Weishaar, 2014; Beck, 2002, 1991, 1967). According to Beck, maladaptive attitudes, a cognitive triad, errors in thinking, and automatic thoughts combine to produce the clinical syndrome.

Beck believes that some people develop *maladaptive attitudes* as children, such as "My general worth is tied to every task I perform" or "If I fail, others will feel repelled by me." The attitudes result from their early interactions and experiences (see Figure 6-5). Many failures are inevitable in a full, active life, so such attitudes are inaccurate and set the stage for all kinds of negative thoughts and reactions. Beck suggests that later in these people's lives, upsetting situations may trigger an extended round of negative thinking. That thinking typically takes three forms, which he calls the **cognitive triad:** the individuals repeatedly interpret (1) their *experiences,* (2) *themselves,* and (3) their *futures* in negative ways that lead them to feel depressed. The cognitive triad is at work in the thinking of this depressed person:

> One-third of people who felt unhappy as children continue to feel unhappy as adults. Why might this be so?

> *I can't bear it. I can't stand the humiliating fact that I'm the only woman in the world who can't take care of her family, take her place as a real wife and mother, and be respected in her community. When I speak to my young son Billy, I know I can't let him down, but I feel so ill-equipped to take care of him; that's what frightens me. I don't know what to do or where to turn; the whole thing is too overwhelming. . . . I must be a laughing stock. It's more than I can do to go out and meet people and have the fact pointed up to me so clearly.*
>
> *(Fieve, 1975)*

▶ **cognitive triad** The three forms of negative thinking that Aaron Beck theorizes lead people to feel depressed. The triad consists of a negative view of one's experiences, oneself, and the future.

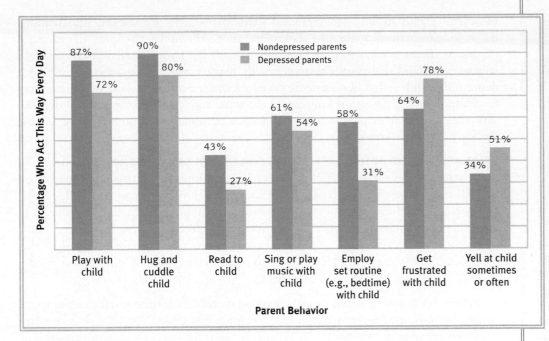

figure 6-5
How depressed parents and their children interact Depressed parents are less likely than nondepressed parents to play with, hug, read to, or sing to their young children each day or to employ the same routine each day. They are also more likely to get frustrated with their children on a daily basis. (Information from: Turney, 2011; Princeton Survey Research Associates, 1996.)

According to Beck, depressed people also make *errors in their thinking.* In one common error of logic, they draw arbitrary inferences—negative conclusions based on little evidence. A man walking through the park, for example, passes a woman who is looking at nearby flowers and concludes, "She's avoiding looking at me." Similarly, depressed people often minimize the significance of positive experiences or magnify that of negative ones. A college student receives an A on a difficult English exam, for example, but concludes that the grade reflects the professor's generosity rather than her own ability (minimization). Later in the week the same student must miss an English class and is convinced that she will be unable to keep up the rest of the semester (magnification).

Finally, depressed people have *automatic thoughts,* a steady train of unpleasant thoughts that keep suggesting to them that they are inadequate and that their situation is hopeless. Beck labels these thoughts "automatic" because they seem to just happen, as if by reflex. In the course of only a few hours, depressed people may be visited by hundreds of such thoughts: "I'm worthless. . . . I'll never amount to anything . . . I let everyone down. . . . Everyone hates me. . . . My responsibilities are overwhelming. . . . I've failed as a parent. . . . I'm stupid. . . . Everything is difficult for me. . . . Things will never change."

Many studies have produced evidence in support of Beck's explanation (Pössel & Black, 2014). Several of them confirm that depressed people hold maladaptive attitudes and that the more of these maladaptive attitudes they hold, the more depressed they tend to be (Thomas & Altareb, 2012). Still other research has found the cognitive triad at work in depressed people (Lai et al., 2014). And still other studies have supported Beck's claims about errors in logic (Alcalar et al., 2012). In one study, female participants—some depressed, some not—were asked to read and interpret paragraphs about women in difficult situations. Depressed participants made more errors in logic (such as arbitrary inference) in their interpretations than nondepressed women did (Hammen & Krantz, 1976).

Finally, research has supported Beck's claim that automatic thoughts are tied to depression (Alcalar et al., 2012).

"You're sad about the wrong things, Albert."

Topham/The Image Works

Flower power Despite the effectiveness of antidepressant drugs and certain kinds of psychotherapy, many depressed people turn to herbal remedies such as *Saint-John's-wort*, a low, wild-growing shrub. Studies indicate that this herb can be quite helpful in cases of mild or moderate depression.

In several classic studies, nondepressed participants who are tricked into reading negative automatic-thought-like statements about themselves become increasingly depressed (Bates et al., 1999; Strickland et al., 1975). In a related line of research, it has been found that people who generally make *ruminative responses* during their depressed moods—that is, repeatedly dwell mentally on their mood without acting to change it—feel dejection longer and are more likely to develop clinical depression later in life than people who avoid such ruminations (Johnson et al., 2014; Watkins & Nolen-Hoeksema, 2014).

WHAT ARE THE COGNITIVE TREATMENTS FOR UNIPOLAR DEPRESSION? To help clients overcome this negative thinking, Beck has developed a treatment approach that he calls **cognitive therapy** (Beck & Weishaar, 2014). However, as you will see, the approach also includes a number of behavioral techniques, particularly as therapists try to get clients moving again and encourage them to try out new behaviors. Thus, many theorists consider this approach a *cognitive-behavioral therapy* rather than the purely cognitive intervention implied by its name. The approach follows four phases and usually requires fewer than 20 sessions.

PHASE 1: Increasing activities and elevating mood Using behavioral techniques to set the stage for cognitive treatment, therapists first encourage clients to become more active and confident. Clients spend time during each session preparing a detailed schedule of hourly activities for the coming week. As they become more active from week to week, their mood is expected to improve.

PHASE 2: Challenging automatic thoughts Once people are more active and feeling some emotional relief, cognitive therapists begin to educate them about their negative automatic thoughts. The individuals are instructed to recognize and record automatic thoughts as they occur and to bring their lists to each session. Therapist and client then test the reality behind the thoughts, often concluding that they are groundless.

PHASE 3: Identifying negative thinking and biases As people begin to recognize the flaws in their automatic thoughts, cognitive therapists show them how illogical thinking processes are contributing to these thoughts. The therapists also guide clients to recognize that almost all their interpretations of events have a negative bias and to change that style of interpretation.

PHASE 4: Changing primary attitudes Therapists help clients change the maladaptive attitudes that set the stage for their depression in the first place. As part of the process, therapists often encourage clients to test their attitudes, as in the following therapy discussion:

> **Therapist:** *On what do you base this belief that you can't be happy without a man?*
> **Patient:** *I was really depressed for a year and a half when I didn't have a man.*
> **Therapist:** *Is there another reason why you were depressed?*
> **Patient:** *As we discussed, I was looking at everything in a distorted way. But I still don't know if I could be happy if no one was interested in me.*
> **Therapist:** *I don't know either. Is there a way we could find out?*
> **Patient:** *Well, as an experiment, I could not go out on dates for a while and see how I feel.*
> **Therapist:** *I think that's a good idea. Although it has its flaws, the experimental method is still the best way currently available to discover the facts. You're fortunate in being able to run this type of experiment. Now, for the first time in your adult life you aren't attached to a man. If you find you can be happy without a man, this will greatly strengthen you and also make your future relationships all the better.*
>
> *(Beck et al., 1979, pp. 253–254)*

▶ **cognitive therapy** A therapy developed by Aaron Beck that helps people identify and change the maladaptive assumptions and ways of thinking that help cause their psychological disorders.

Over the past several decades, hundreds of studies have shown that Beck's therapy and similar cognitive and cognitive-behavioral approaches help with unipolar depression. Depressed adults who receive these therapies improve much more than those who receive placebos or no treatment at all (Young et al., 2014; Hollon & Cuijpers, 2013). Around 50 to 60 percent show a near-total elimination of their symptoms.

It is worth noting that a growing number of today's cognitive-behavioral therapists do not agree with Beck's proposition that individuals must fully discard their negative cognitions in order to overcome depression. These therapists, the new-wave cognitive-behavioral therapists about whom you read in Chapters 2 and 4, including those who practice *acceptance and commitment therapy (ACT)*, guide depressed clients to recognize and accept their negative cognitions simply as streams of thinking that flow through their minds, rather than as valuable guides for behavior and decisions. As clients increasingly accept their negative thoughts for what they are, they can better work around the thoughts as they navigate their way through life (Levin et al., 2014; Hayes et al., 2006).

The Sociocultural Model of Unipolar Depression

Sociocultural theorists propose that unipolar depression is strongly influenced by the social context that surrounds people. Their belief is supported by the finding, discussed earlier, that depression is often triggered by outside stressors. Once again, there are two kinds of sociocultural views—the *family-social perspective* and the *multicultural perspective*.

The Family-Social Perspective
Earlier you read that some behaviorists believe that a decline in social rewards is particularly important in the development of depression. Although presented as part of their behavioral explanation, this view is consistent with the family-social perspective. Depression has been tied repeatedly to the unavailability of social support such as that found in a happy marriage (Ito & Sagara, 2014). People who are separated or divorced display at least three times the depression rate of married or widowed people and double the rate of those who have never been married (Schultz, 2007; Weissman et al., 1991). In some cases, the spouse's depression may contribute to marital discord, a separation, or divorce, but often the interpersonal conflicts and low social support found in troubled relationships seem to lead to depression (Najman et al., 2014).

> **Why might problems in the social arena—e.g., social loss, social ties, and social rewards—be tied to depression?**

Researchers have also found that people whose lives are isolated and without intimacy are particularly likely to become depressed at times of stress (Hölzel et al., 2011; Nezlek et al., 2000). Some highly publicized studies conducted in England several decades ago showed that women who had three or more young children, lacked a close confidante, and had no outside employment were more likely than other women to become depressed after going through stressful events (Brown, 2002; Brown & Harris, 1978). Studies have also found that depressed people who lack social support remain depressed longer than those who have a supportive spouse or warm friendships.

Family-Social Treatments
Therapists who use family and social approaches to treat depression help clients change how they deal with the close relationships in their lives. The most effective family-social approaches are *interpersonal psychotherapy* and *couple therapy*.

BETWEEN THE LINES

In Their Words

"No one can make you feel inferior without your consent."

Eleanor Roosevelt

The "dogtor" will see you now A client talks through his problems and concerns to "Dogtor" Schnauzer at the first ever "Dogtor's Surgery" program. According to research, many pet owners satisfy their basic need for social contact, and help thwart off depressed feelings, by talking to and confiding in their pets. Indeed, millions of pet owners say that they confide in their pets before their spouses, and one-quarter talk to their pets more than their spouses. The Dogtor's Surgery program is designed to offer similar pet-related emotional benefits to people who are not pet owners.

More Than/Rex Features via AP Images

▶**interpersonal psychotherapy (IPT)**
A treatment for unipolar depression that is based on the belief that clarifying and changing one's interpersonal problems helps lead to recovery.

INTERPERSONAL PSYCHOTHERAPY Developed by clinical researchers Gerald Klerman and Myrna Weissman, **interpersonal psychotherapy (IPT)** holds that various interpersonal situations may lead to depression and must be addressed. Particularly problematic are interpersonal loss, interpersonal role dispute, interpersonal role transition, and interpersonal deficits (Bleiberg & Markowitz, 2014; Verdeli, 2014). Over the course of around 16 sessions, IPT therapists address these areas.

First, depressed people may, as psychodynamic theorists suggest, be having a grief reaction over an important *interpersonal loss,* the loss of a loved one. In such cases, IPT therapists encourage clients to look closely at their relationship with the lost person and express any feelings of anger they may discover. Eventually clients develop new ways of remembering the lost person and also look for new relationships.

Second, depressed people may find themselves in the midst of an *interpersonal role dispute.* Role disputes occur when two people have different expectations of their relationship and of the role each should play. IPT therapists help clients examine whatever role disputes they may be involved in and then develop ways of resolving them.

Depressed people may also be going through an *interpersonal role transition,* brought about by major life changes such as divorce or the birth of a child. They may feel overwhelmed by the role changes that accompany the life change. In such cases, IPT therapists help them develop the social supports and skills the new roles require.

Finally, some depressed people display *interpersonal deficits,* such as extreme shyness or social awkwardness, that prevent them from having intimate relationships (see *MindTech* on the next page). IPT therapists may help such clients identify their deficits and teach them social skills and assertiveness in order to improve their social effectiveness. In the following discussion, the therapist encourages a depressed man to recognize the effect his behavior has on others:

Role transition Major life changes such as marriage, the birth of a child, or divorce can create difficulties in role transition, one of the interpersonal problem areas addressed by IPT therapists in their work with depressed clients.

Tom Moran

> **Client:** *(After a long pause with eyes downcast, a sad facial expression, and slumped posture) People always make fun of me. I guess I'm just the type of guy who really was meant to be a loner, damn it. (Deep sigh)*
>
> **Therapist:** *Could you do that again for me?*
>
> **Client:** *What?*
>
> **Therapist:** *The sigh, only a bit deeper.*
>
> **Client:** *Why? (Pause) Okay, but I don't see what . . . okay. (Client sighs again and smiles)*
>
> **Therapist:** *Well, that time you smiled, but mostly when you sigh and look so sad I get the feeling that I better leave you alone in your misery, that I should walk on eggshells and not get too chummy or I might hurt you even more.*
>
> **Client:** *(A bit of anger in his voice) Well, excuse me! I was only trying to tell you how I felt.*
>
> **Therapist:** *I know you felt miserable, but I also got the message that you wanted to keep me at a distance, that I had no way to reach you.*
>
> **Client:** *(Slowly) I feel like a loner, I feel that even you don't care about me—making fun of me.*
>
> **Therapist:** *I wonder if other folks need to pass this test, too?*
>
> *(Beier & Young, 1984, p. 270)*

Studies suggest that IPT and related interpersonal treatments for depression have a success rate similar to that of cognitive and cognitive-behavioral therapies (Bleiberg & Markowitz, 2014). That is, symptoms almost totally disappear in 50 to 60 percent of clients who receive treatment. Not surprisingly, IPT is considered especially useful for depressed people who are struggling with social conflicts or undergoing changes in their careers or social roles (Ravitz et al., 2013).

MindTech

Texting: A Relationship Buster?

Texting has now become the leading way that most people communicate with others (Pew Research Center, 2015; Cocotas, 2013). The average 18- to 24-year-old sends and receives a total of 4,000 texts each month. Many people text almost constantly throughout the day. In fact, surveys suggest that people often fail to fully attend to their current activities in order to juggle their text con-

> **Can you think of ways in which texting might sometimes be helpful to relationships and communications?**

versations. Some clinicians worry that excessive texting may damage our relationships—relationships with the people we are texting and relationships with those we are ignoring while texting.

Based on her studies, MIT professor Sherry Turkle (2013, 2012) has concluded that communicating primarily via text does indeed affect relationships negatively. Many of her participants reported, "I'd rather text than talk." Turkle concludes from her research that people often use texting as a crutch to avoid direct communication and possible confrontations. Moreover, her participants said that texting saves valuable time over face-to-face conversations. However, concludes Turkle, "People who feel they are too busy to have conversations in person are not making the important emotional connections they otherwise would."

In related work, researcher Karla Klein Murdock (2013) interviewed 83 college freshmen about their daily texting habits, along with their levels of social and personal stress, sleep patterns, and happiness. She found that hastily written texts (which is to say, most texts) often lend themselves to misunderstandings between senders and receivers—misunderstandings that can quickly spin out of control. Murdock also noted that many participants in her study felt the need to constantly keep up with ongoing text conversations, interrupting their in-person conversations—thus inviting damage to those relationships as well. Small wonder that the participants who averaged the most daily texts were more likely than other participants to report more stress, unhappiness, anxiety, and sleeping problems. Murdock believes that in many such cases, the negative effects of texting on the participants' personal relationships are leading to broader feelings of stress and unhappiness.

"Huh? Oh, yeah—I do."

None of this suggests that texting per se is a detriment to social or personal happiness. Rather, it seems to be the exclusive and excessive use of it that is the problem. It just may be that many important discussions are better served by in-person, or at least phone, conversations. 💬

Tom Cheney The New Yorker Collection/www.cartoonbank.com

► **couple therapy** A therapy format in which the therapist works with two people who share a long-term relationship.

COUPLE THERAPY As you have read, depression can result from marital discord, and recovery from depression is often slower for people who do not receive support from their spouse (Park & Unützer, 2014). In fact, as many as half of all depressed clients may be in a dysfunctional relationship. Thus many cases of depression have been treated by **couple therapy,** the approach in which a therapist works with two people who share a long-term relationship (Cohen et al., 2014).

Therapists who offer *integrative behavioral couples therapy* teach specific communication and problem-solving skills to couples and further guide them to be more accepting of each other (see Chapter 2). When a depressed person's relationship is filled with conflict, couple treatments such as this may be as effective as individual cognitive therapy, interpersonal psychotherapy, or drug therapy in helping to reduce depression (Lebow et al., 2012, 2010).

The Multicultural Perspective

Two issues have captured the interest of multicultural theorists: (1) links between *gender and depression* and (2) ties between *cultural and ethnic background and depression.*

GENDER AND DEPRESSION As you have read, there is a strong link between gender and depression. Women in places as far apart as France, Sweden, Lebanon, New Zealand, and the United States are at least twice as likely as men to receive a diagnosis of unipolar depression (Schuch et al., 2014). Why the huge difference between the sexes? A variety of theories have been offered.

The *artifact theory* holds that women and men are equally prone to depression but that clinicians often fail to detect depression in men (Emmons, 2010). Perhaps depressed women display more emotional symptoms, such as sadness and crying, which are easily diagnosed, while depressed men mask their depression behind traditionally "masculine" symptoms such as anger. Although a popular explanation, this view has failed to receive consistent research support. It turns out that women are actually no more willing or able than men to identify their depressive symptoms and to seek treatment (McSweeney, 2004; Nolen-Hoeksema, 1990).

The *hormone explanation* holds that hormone changes trigger depression in many women (Kurita et al., 2013). A woman's biological life from her early teens to middle age is marked by frequent changes in hormone levels. Gender differences in rates of depression also span these same years. Research suggests, however, that hormone changes alone are not responsible for the high levels of depression in women (Whiffen & Demidenko, 2006). Important social and life events that occur at puberty, pregnancy, and menopause could likewise have an effect. Hormone explanations have also been criticized as sexist, since they imply that a woman's normal biology is flawed (see *PsychWatch* on the next page).

The *life stress theory* suggests that women in our society are subject to more stress than men (Astbury, 2010). On average they face more poverty, more menial jobs, less adequate housing, and more discrimination than men—all factors that have been linked to depression. And in many homes, women bear a disproportionate share of responsibility for child care and housework.

The *body dissatisfaction explanation* states that females in Western society are taught, almost from birth, to seek a low body weight and slender body shape—goals that are unreasonable, unhealthy, and often unattainable. As you will observe in Chapter 9, the cultural standard for males is much more lenient. As girls approach adolescence, peer pressure may result in them becoming more and more dissatisfied with their weight and body, increasing the likelihood of depression. Consistent with this theory, gender differences in depression do indeed first appear during adolescence (Naninck et al., 2011), and people with eating disorders often have high levels of depression (Calugi et al., 2014). However, it is not clear that eating and weight concerns actually cause depression; they may instead be the result of depression.

BETWEEN THE LINES

Paternal Postpartum Depression

Considerable research has already indicated that a mother's postpartum depression can lead to disturbances in a child's social, behavioral, and cognitive development. Research suggests that a father's postpartum depression can have similar effects (Koh et al., 2014; Edoka et al., 2011).

PsychWatch

Premenstrual Dysphoric Disorder: Déjà Vu All Over Again

Back in the early 1990s, one of the biggest controversies in the development of DSM-IV centered on the category *premenstrual dysphoric disorder* (*PMDD*). The DSM-IV work group recommended that PMDD be formally listed as a new kind of depressive disorder. The category was to be applied when a woman was regularly impaired by at least 5 of 11 symptoms during the week before menstruation: depressed or hopeless feelings; tense or anxious feelings; marked mood changes; frequent irritability or anger and increased interpersonal conflicts; decreased interest in her usual activities; poor concentration; lack of energy; changes in appetite; insomnia or sleepiness; a sense of being overwhelmed or out of control; and physical symptoms such as swollen breasts, headaches, muscle pain, a "bloated" sensation, or weight gain.

This recommendation set off an uproar. Many clinicians (including some dissent-

David Chaskin/PA Wire via AP Images

ing members of the work group), several national organizations, interest groups, and the media warned that this diagnostic category would "pathologize" severe cases of *premenstrual syndrome*, or *PMS*, the premenstrual discomforts that are common and normal, and might cause women's behavior in general to be at-

tributed largely to "raging hormones" (a stereotype that society was finally rejecting). They argued that data were lacking to include the new category (Chase, 1993; DeAngelis, 1993).

The solution? A compromise. PMDD was not listed as a formal category in DSM-IV, but the pattern was listed in the DSM-IV appendix, with the suggestion that it be studied more thoroughly. Critics hoped that PMDD would die a quiet death there. However, two decades later the category gained new life. When, in 2011, the DSM-5 task force published a list of changes being considered for the new edition of the DSM, premenstrual dysphoric disorder was included as one of the depressive disorders. The reaction? Another uproar among many clinicians and interest groups. This time, however, the proponents prevailed, citing several studies conducted over the past 20 years. PMDD is now an official category in DSM-5.

The *lack-of-control theory* draws on the learned helplessness research and proposes that women may be more prone to depression because they feel less control than men over their lives. It has been found that victimization of any kind, from burglary to rape, often produces a general sense of helplessness and increases the symptoms of depression. Women in our society are more likely than men to be victims, particularly of sexual assault and child abuse (Astbury, 2010).

A final explanation for the gender differences found in depression is the *rumination theory*. As you read earlier, rumination is the tendency to keep focusing on one's feelings when depressed and to consider repeatedly the causes and consequences of that depression ("Why am I so down? . . . I won't be able to finish my work if I keep going like this. . . ."). It turns out that women are more likely than men to ruminate when their mood darkens, perhaps making them more vulnerable to the onset of clinical depression (Johnson & Whisman, 2013; Nolen-Hoeksema, 2002, 2000).

Each of these explanations for the gender difference in unipolar depression offers food for thought. Each has gathered just enough supporting evidence to make it interesting and just enough evidence to the contrary to raise questions about its usefulness. Thus, at present, the gender difference in depression remains one of the most talked-about but least understood phenomena in the clinical field.

CULTURAL BACKGROUND AND DEPRESSION Depression is a worldwide phenomenon, and certain symptoms of this disorder seem to be constant across all countries. A landmark study of four countries—Canada, Switzerland, Iran, and Japan—found that the great majority of depressed people in these very different countries reported symptoms of sadness, joylessness, tension, lack of energy, loss of interest, loss of

////// BETWEEN THE LINES //////

Parental Impact

It has been estimated that 400,000 infants are born each year to depressed mothers (Murray & Nyp, 2011).

ability to concentrate, ideas of insufficiency, and thoughts of suicide (Matsumoto & Juang, 2008). Beyond such core symptoms, however, research suggests that the precise picture of depression varies from country to country (Kok et al., 2012; Kleinman, 2004). Depressed people in non-Western countries—China and Nigeria, for example—are more likely to be troubled by physical symptoms such as fatigue, weakness, sleep disturbances, and weight loss. Depression in those countries is less often marked by cognitive symptoms such as self-blame, low self-esteem, and guilt.

Within the United States, researchers have found few differences in the symptoms of depression among members of different ethnic or racial groups. Nor have they found significant differences in the *overall* rates of depression between such minority groups. On the other hand, recent research has revealed that there are often striking differences between ethnic/racial groups in the *recurrence* of depression. Hispanic Americans and African Americans are 50 percent more likely than white Americans to have recurrent episodes of depression (González et al., 2010). Why this difference? Around 54 percent of depressed white Americans receive treatment for their disorders (medication and/or psychotherapy), compared with 34 percent of depressed Hispanic Americans and 40 percent of depressed African Americans (González et al., 2010). It may be that minority groups in the United States are more vulnerable to repeated experiences of depression partly because many of their members have more limited treatment opportunities when they are depressed.

Research has also revealed that depression is distributed unevenly within some minority groups. This is not totally surprising, given that each minority group itself consists of people of varied backgrounds and cultural values. For example, depression is more common among Hispanic and African Americans born in the United States than among Hispanic and African American immigrants (González et al., 2010; Miranda et al., 2005). Moreover, within the Hispanic American population, Puerto Ricans have a higher rate of depression than do Mexican Americans or Cuban Americans.

Multicultural Treatments In Chapter 2, you read that *culture-sensitive therapies* seek to address the unique issues faced by members of cultural minority groups (Comas-Díaz, 2014). For such approaches, therapists typically have special cultural training and a heightened awareness of their clients' cultural values and the culture-related stressors, prejudices, and stereotypes that their clients face. They make an effort to help clients develop a comfortable (for them) bicultural balance and to recognize the impact of their own culture and the dominant culture on their views of themselves and on their behaviors (Prochaska & Norcross, 2013).

> Do you think culture-sensitive therapies might be more useful for some kinds of disorders than for other kinds?

In the treatment of unipolar depression, culture-sensitive approaches increasingly are being combined with traditional forms of psychotherapy to help minority clients overcome their disorders (Aguilera et al., 2010; Stacciarini et al., 2007). A number of today's therapists, for example, offer cognitive-behavioral therapy for depressed minority clients while also focusing on the clients' economic pressures, minority identity, and related cultural issues. A range of studies indicate that Hispanic American, African American, American Indian, and Asian American clients are more likely to overcome their depressive disorders when a culture-sensitive focus is added to the form of psychotherapy that they are otherwise receiving (Comas-Díaz, 2014).

Is laughter the best medicine? A man laughs during a 2013 session of laughter therapy in a public plaza in Caracas, Venezuela. He is one of many who attended this open session of laughter therapy, a relatively new group treatment being offered around the world, based on the belief that laughing at least 15 minutes each day drives away depression and other ills.

AP Photo/Ariana Cubillos

➤ *Summing Up*

UNIPOLAR DEPRESSION: THE DEPRESSIVE DISORDERS People with unipolar depression, the most common pattern of mood disorder, suffer from depression only. The various disorders characterized by unipolar depression are called depressive disorders in DSM-5. The symptoms of depression span five areas of functioning: emotional, motivational, behavioral, cognitive, and physical. Women are at least twice as likely as men to experience severe unipolar depression.

According to the biological view, low activity of two neurotransmitters, norepinephrine and serotonin, helps cause depression. Hormonal factors may also be at work. So, too, may deficiencies of key proteins and other chemicals within certain neurons. Brain-imaging research has also tied depression to abnormalities in a circuit of brain areas, including the prefrontal cortex, hippocampus, amygdala, and Brodmann Area 25. All such biological problems may be linked to genetic factors. Most biological treatments consist of antidepressant drugs, but electroconvulsive therapy is still used to treat some severe cases of depression, and several brain stimulation techniques have been developed to treat depressed patients who are unresponsive to other forms of treatment.

According to the psychodynamic view, certain people who experience real or imagined losses may regress to an earlier stage of development, fuse with the person they have lost, and eventually become depressed. Psychodynamic therapists try to help persons with unipolar depression recognize and work through their losses and excessive dependence on others.

The behavioral view says that when people experience a large reduction in their positive rewards in life, they become more and more likely to become depressed. Behavioral therapists try to reintroduce clients to activities that they once found pleasurable, reward nondepressive behaviors, and teach effective social skills.

The leading cognitive views focus on learned helplessness and negative thinking. According to Seligman's learned helplessness theory, people become depressed when they believe that they have lost control over the reinforcements in their lives and when they attribute this loss to causes that are internal, global, and stable. According to Beck's theory of negative thinking, maladaptive attitudes, the cognitive triad, errors in thinking, and automatic thoughts help produce unipolar depression. Cognitive therapists help depressed persons identify and change their dysfunctional cognitions, and cognitive-behavioral therapists try to reduce depression by combining cognitive and behavioral techniques.

Sociocultural theories propose that unipolar depression is influenced by social and cultural factors. Family-social theorists point out that a low level of social support is often linked to unipolar depression. Correspondingly, interpersonal psychotherapy and couple therapy are often helpful in cases of depression. Multicultural theories have noted that the character and prevalence of depression often vary by gender and sometimes by culture, an issue that culture-sensitive therapies for depression seek to address.

Non-Western depression Depressed people in non-Western countries tend to have fewer cognitive symptoms, such as self-blame, and more physical symptoms, such as fatigue, weakness, and sleep disturbances.

Bipolar Disorders

People with a *bipolar disorder* experience both the lows of depression and the highs of mania. Many describe their life as an emotional roller coaster, as they shift back and forth between extreme moods. A number of sufferers eventually become suicidal. Their roller coaster ride also has a dramatic impact on relatives and friends (Barron et al., 2014).

BETWEEN THE LINES

Clinical Oversight

Around 70 percent of people with a bipolar disorder are misdiagnosed at least once (Statistic Brain, 2012).

▶ **bipolar I disorder** A type of bipolar disorder marked by full manic and major depressive episodes.

▶ **bipolar II disorder** A type of bipolar disorder marked by mildly manic (hypomanic) episodes and major depressive episodes.

▶ **cyclothymic disorder** A disorder marked by numerous periods of hypomanic symptoms and mild depressive symptoms.

table: **6-4**

Dx Checklist

Manic Episode

1. For one week or more, person displays a continually abnormal, inflated, unrestrained, or irritable mood as well as continually heightened energy or activity, for most of every day.

2. Person also experiences at least three of the following symptoms: • grandiosity or overblown self-esteem • reduced sleep need • increased talkativeness, or drive to continue talking • rapidly shifting ideas or the sense that one's thoughts are moving very fast • attention pulled in many directions • heightened activity or agitated movements • excessive pursuit of risky and potentially problematic activities.

3. Significant distress or impairment.

Bipolar I Disorder

1. Occurrence of a manic episode.

2. Hypomanic or major depressive episodes may precede or follow the manic episode.

Bipolar II Disorder

1. Presence or history of major depressive episode(s).

2. Presence or history of hypomanic episode(s).

3. No history of a manic episode.

Information from: APA, 2013.

What Are the Symptoms of Mania?

Unlike people sunk in the gloom of depression, those in a state of mania typically experience dramatic and inappropriate rises in mood. The symptoms of mania span the same areas of functioning—*emotional, motivational, behavioral, cognitive,* and *physical*—as those of depression, but mania affects those areas in an opposite way.

A person in the throes of mania has powerful emotions in search of an outlet. The mood of euphoric joy and well-being is out of all proportion to the actual happenings in the person's life. Not every person with mania is a picture of happiness, however. Some instead become very irritable and angry, especially when others get in the way of their exaggerated ambitions.

In the motivational realm, people with mania seem to want constant excitement, involvement, and companionship. They enthusiastically seek out new friends and old, new interests and old, and have little awareness that their social style is overwhelming, domineering, and excessive.

The behavior of people with mania is usually very active. They move quickly, as though there were not enough time to do everything they want to do. They may talk rapidly and loudly, their conversations filled with jokes and efforts to be clever or, conversely, with complaints and verbal outbursts. Flamboyance is not uncommon: dressing in flashy clothes, giving large sums of money to strangers, or even getting involved in dangerous activities.

In the cognitive realm, people with mania usually show poor judgment and planning, as if they feel too good or move too fast to consider possible pitfalls. Filled with optimism, they rarely listen when others try to slow them down. They may also hold an inflated opinion of themselves, and sometimes their self-esteem approaches grandiosity. During severe episodes of mania, some have trouble remaining coherent or in touch with reality.

Finally, in the physical realm, people with mania feel remarkably energetic. They typically get little sleep yet feel and act wide awake (Armitage & Arnedt, 2011). Even if they miss a night or two of sleep, their energy level may remain high.

Diagnosing Bipolar Disorders

People are considered to be in a full *manic episode* when for at least one week they display an abnormally high or irritable mood, increased activity or energy, and at least three other symptoms of mania (see Table 6-4). The episode may even include psychotic features such as delusions or hallucinations. When the symptoms of mania are less severe (causing little impairment), the person is said to be having a *hypomanic episode* (APA, 2013).

DSM-5 distinguishes two kinds of bipolar disorders—bipolar I and bipolar II. People with **bipolar I disorder** have full manic and major depressive episodes. Most of them experience an *alternation* of the episodes; for example, weeks of mania followed by a period of wellness, followed in turn by an episode of depression. Some, however, have *mixed* features, in which they display both manic and depressive symptoms within the same episode—for example, having racing thoughts amidst feelings of extreme sadness. In **bipolar II disorder**, hypomanic—that is, mildly manic—episodes alternate with major depressive episodes over the course of time. Some people with this pattern accomplish huge amounts of work during their mild manic periods (see *PsychWatch* on page 214).

Without treatment, the mood episodes tend to recur for people with either type of bipolar disorder. If a person has four or more episodes within a one-year period, his or her disorder is considered to be *rapid cycling*. A woman describes her rapid cycling in the following excerpt, taken from a journal article she wrote anonymously several years ago.

> My mood may swing from one part of the day to another. I may wake up low at 10 am, but be high and excitable by 3 pm. I may not sleep for more than 2 hours one night, being full of creative energy, but by midday be so fatigued it is an effort to breathe.
>
> If my elevated states last more than a few days, my spending can become uncontrollable. . . . I will sometimes drive faster than usual, need less sleep and can concentrate well, making quick and accurate decisions. At these times I can also be sociable, talkative and fun, focused at times, distracted at others. If this state of elevation continues I often find that feelings of violence and irritability towards those I love will start to creep in. . . .
>
> My thoughts speed up. . . . I frequently want to be able to achieve several tasks at the same moment. . . . Physically my energy levels can seem limitless. The body moves smoothly, there is little or no fatigue. I can go mountain biking all day when I feel like this and if my mood stays elevated not a muscle is sore or stiff the next day. But it doesn't last, my elevated phases are short. . . . [T]he shift into severe depression or a mixed mood state occurs sometimes within minutes or hours, often within days and will last weeks often without a period of normality. . . .
>
> Initially my thoughts become disjointed and start slithering all over the place. . . . I start to believe that others are commenting adversely on my appearance or behaviour. . . . My sleep will be poor and interrupted by bad dreams. . . . The world appears bleak. . . . I become repelled by the proximity of people. . . . I will be overwhelmed by the slightest tasks, even imagined tasks. . . . Physically there is immense fatigue: my muscles scream with pain. . . . . Food becomes totally uninteresting. . . .
>
> I start to feel trapped, that the only escape is death. . . . I become passionate about one subject only at these times of deep and intense fear, despair and rage: suicide. . . . I have made close attempts on my life . . . over the last few years. . . .
>
> Then inexplicably, my mood will shift again. The fatigue drops from my limbs like shedding a dead weight, my thinking returns to normal, the light takes on an intense clarity, flowers smell sweet and my mouth curves to smile at my children, my husband and I am laughing again. Sometimes it's for only a day but I am myself again, the person that I was a frightening memory. I have survived another bout of this dreaded disorder. . . .
>
> *(Anonymous, 2006)*

Surveys from around the world indicate that between 1 and 2.6 percent of all adults are suffering from a bipolar disorder at any given time (Kessler et al., 2012; Merikangas et al., 2011). As many as 4 percent experience one of the bipolar disorders at some time in their life. The bipolar disorders are equally common in women and men, but they are more common among people with low incomes than those with higher incomes (Sareen et al., 2011). Onset usually occurs between the ages of 15 and 44 years. In most untreated cases, the manic and depressive episodes eventually subside, only to recur at a later time.

Some people have numerous periods of hypomanic symptoms and *mild* depressive symptoms, a pattern that is called **cyclothymic disorder** in DSM-5. The symptoms of this milder form of bipolar disorder continue for two or more years, interrupted occasionally by normal moods that may last for only days or weeks. This disorder, like bipolar I and bipolar II disorders, usually begins in adolescence or early adulthood and is equally common among women and men. At least 0.4 percent of the population develops cyclothymic disorder. In some cases, the milder symptoms eventually blossom into a bipolar I or II disorder (Zeschel et al., 2015; Goto et al., 2011).

Andrew H. Walker/Getty Images

Going public In June 2010, an exuberant Catherine Zeta-Jones received a Tony Award for her performance in the Broadway musical *A Little Night Music*. Less than a year later, she announced that she was receiving treatment for bipolar disorder, a public acknowledgment that received enormous praise from mental health advocacy groups. Entering a treatment program after the extended stress of helping her husband Michael Douglas battle apparent throat cancer, Jones said there was no need to suffer in silence and she hoped the publicity surrounding her treatment would help others.

What Causes Bipolar Disorders?

Throughout the first half of the twentieth century, the search for the causes of bipolar disorders made little progress. More recently, biological research has produced some promising clues. The biological insights have come from research into neurotransmitter activity, ion activity, brain structure, and genetic factors.

Neurotransmitters Could *overactivity* of norepinephrine be related to mania? This was the expectation of clinicians back in the 1960s after investigators first found a relationship between low norepinephrine activity and unipolar depression. Indeed, some research did find the norepinephrine activity of people with mania to be higher than that of control participants (Post et al., 1980, 1978; Schildkraut, 1965).

Because serotonin activity often parallels norepinephrine activity in unipolar depression, theorists at first expected that mania would also be related to high serotonin activity, but no such relationship has been found. Instead, research suggests

PsychWatch

Abnormality and Creativity: A Delicate Balance

The ancient Greeks believed that various forms of "divine madness" inspired creative acts, from poetry to performance (Ludwig, 1995). Even today many people expect "creative geniuses" to be psychologically disturbed. A popular image of the artist includes a glass of liquor, a cigarette, and a tormented expression. Classic examples include writer William Faulkner, who suffered from alcoholism and received electroconvulsive therapy for depression; poet Sylvia Plath, who was depressed for most of her life and eventually committed suicide at age 31; and dancer Vaslav Nijinsky, who suffered from schizophrenia and spent many years in institutions. In fact, a number of studies indicate that artists and writers are somewhat more likely than others to suffer from certain mental disorders, particularly bipolar disorders (Kyaga et al., 2013, 2011; Galvez et al., 2011; Sample, 2005).

Why might creative people be prone to such psychological disorders? Some may be predisposed to such disorders long before they begin their artistic careers (Simonton, 2010; Ludwig, 1995). Indeed, creative people often have a family history of psychological problems (Kyaga et al., 2013, 2011). A number also have experienced intense psychological trauma

AP Photo/Akira Suemori

The price of creativity? Like many other writers and artists, J. K. Rowling has had periods of depression and even suicidal feelings at certain times in her life. Here, the *Harry Potter* author looks at the laptop of a child while launching her new Web project, Pottermore, at a London museum in 2011.

during childhood. English writer Virginia Woolf, for example, endured sexual abuse as a child.

A second explanation for the link between creativity and psychological disorders is that the creative professions offer a welcome climate for those with psychological disturbances. In the worlds of poetry, painting, and acting, for example, emotional expression, unusual thinking,

and/or personal turmoil are valued as sources of inspiration and success (Galvez et al., 2011; Sample, 2005).

Much remains to be learned about the relationship between emotional turmoil and creativity, but work in this area has already clarified two important points. First, psychological disturbance is hardly a requirement for creativity. Most "creative geniuses" are, in fact, psychologically stable and happy throughout their entire lives (Kaufman, 2013). Second, *mild* psychological disturbances relate to creative achievement much more strongly than severe disturbances do (Galvez et al., 2011). For example, nineteenth-century composer Robert Schumann produced 27 works during one hypomanic year but next to nothing during years when he was severely depressed and suicidal (Jamison, 1995).

Some artists worry that their creativity would disappear if their psychological suffering were to stop. In fact, however, research suggests that successful treatment for severe psychological disorders more often than not improves the creative process (Jamison, 1995; Ludwig, 1995). Romantic notions aside, severe mental dysfunctioning has little redeeming value, in the arts or anywhere else.

that mania, like depression, may be linked to *low* serotonin activity (Hsu et al., 2014; Nugent et al., 2013). Perhaps low activity of serotonin opens the door to a mood disorder and *permits* the activity of norepinephrine (or perhaps other neurotransmitters) to define the particular form the disorder will take. That is, low serotonin activity accompanied by low norepinephrine activity may lead to depression; low serotonin activity accompanied by high norepinephrine activity may lead to mania.

Ion Activity While neurotransmitters play a significant role in the communication *between* neurons, electrically charged *ions* seem to play a critical role in relaying messages *within* a neuron. When a neuron receives an incoming message, its *sodium ions* (Na^+) and *potassium ions* (K+) flow back and forth between the outside and inside of the neuron's membrane, producing a wave of electrical activity that travels down the length of the neuron (the axon) and results in its "firing."

If messages are to travel effectively down the axon, the ions must be able to move easily between the outside and the inside of the neural membrane. Some studies suggest that, among bipolar individuals, irregularities in the transport of these ions may cause neurons to fire too easily (resulting in mania) or to stubbornly resist firing (resulting in depression) (Manji & Zarate, 2011; Li & El-Mallakh, 2004).

Brain Structure Brain imaging and postmortem studies have identified a number of abnormal brain structures in people with bipolar disorders (Eker et al., 2014; Chen et al., 2011; Savitz & Drevets, 2011). For example, the basal ganglia and cerebellum of these people tend to be smaller than those of other people, and their dorsal raphe nucleus, striatum, amygdala, hippocampus, and prefrontal cortex each have structural abnormalities. It is not clear what role such structural abnormalities play in bipolar disorders.

Genetic Factors Many theorists believe that people inherit a biological predisposition to develop bipolar disorders (Wiste et al., 2014; Gershon & Nurnberger, 1995). Family pedigree studies support this idea. Identical twins of those with a bipolar disorder have a 40 percent likelihood of developing the same disorder, and fraternal twins, siblings, and other close relatives of such persons have a 5 to 10 percent likelihood, compared with the 1 to 2.6 percent prevalence rate in the general population.

Researchers have also used techniques from *molecular biology* to more directly examine possible genetic factors. These various undertakings have linked bipolar disorders to genes on chromosomes 1, 4, 6, 10, 11, 12, 13, 15, 18, 20, 21, and 22 (Sinkus et al., 2015; Green et al., 2013; Bigdeli et al., 2013). Such wide-ranging findings suggest that a number of genetic abnormalities probably combine to help bring about bipolar disorders.

What Are the Treatments for Bipolar Disorders?

Until the latter part of the twentieth century, people with bipolar disorders were destined to spend their lives on an emotional roller coaster. Psychotherapists reported almost no success, and antidepressant drugs were of limited help. In fact, the drugs sometimes triggered a manic episode (Courtet et al., 2011; Post, 2011, 2005).

Lithium and Other Mood Stabilizers This gloomy picture changed dramatically in 1970 when the FDA approved the use of **lithium,** a silvery-white element found in various simple mineral salts throughout the natural world, as a treatment for bipolar disorders. Additional **mood stabilizing,** or **antibipolar, drugs**

© Sunset Boulevard/Corbis

War of a different kind While starring as Princess Leia, the invincible heroine in the *Star Wars* movies from 1977 to 1983, actress Carrie Fisher was diagnosed with bipolar disorder. The disorder is now under control with the help of medication, and Fisher says, "I don't want peace [in my life], I just don't want war" (Epstein, 2001, p. 36).

▶ **lithium** A metallic element that occurs in nature as a mineral salt and is an effective treatment for bipolar disorders.

▶ **mood stabilizing drugs** Psychotropic drugs that help stabilize the moods of people suffering from bipolar disorder. Also known as *antibipolar drugs*.

▶ **second messengers** Chemical changes within a neuron just after the neuron receives a neurotransmitter message and just before it responds.

have since been developed, including the antiseizure drugs *carbamazepine* (Tegretol) and *valproate* (Depoakote), and several of them are now used as widely as lithium, either because they produce fewer undesired effects or because they are even more effective than lithium.

Nevertheless, it was lithium that first brought hope to those suffering from bipolar disorders. In her widely read memoir, *An Unquiet Mind*, psychiatric researcher Kay Redfield Jamison describes how lithium, combined with psychotherapy, enabled her to overcome her bipolar disorder:

> I took [lithium] faithfully and found that life was a much stabler and more predictable place than I had ever reckoned. My moods were still intense and my temperament rather quick to the boil, but I could make plans with far more certainty and the periods of absolute blackness were fewer and less extreme. . . .
>
> At this point in my existence, I cannot imagine leading a normal life without both taking lithium and having had the benefits of psychotherapy. Lithium prevents my seductive but disastrous highs, diminishes my depressions, clears out the wool and webbing from my disordered thinking, slows me down, gentles me out, keeps me from ruining my career and relationships, keeps me out of a hospital, alive, and makes psychotherapy possible. [At the same time], ineffably, psychotherapy heals. It makes some sense of the confusion, reins in the terrifying thoughts and feelings, returns some control and hope and possibility of learning from it all. . . . No pill can help me deal with the problem of not wanting to take pills; likewise, no amount of psychotherapy alone can prevent my manias and depressions. I need both. . . .
>
> (Jamison, 1995)

All manner of research has attested to the effectiveness of lithium and other mood stabilizers in treating *manic* episodes (Galling et al., 2015; Geddes & Miklowitz, 2013). More than 60 percent of patients with mania improve on these medications. In addition, most such patients have fewer new episodes as long as they continue taking the medications (Malhi et al., 2013). One study found that the risk of relapse is 28 times higher if patients stop taking a mood stabilizer (Suppes et al., 1991). Thus, today's clinicians usually continue patients on some level of a mood stabilizing drug even after their manic episodes subside (Gao et al., 2010).

Powerful plot device In *Homeland*, one of television's most popular series, actress Claire Danes plays Carrie Mathison, a CIA operative who is obsessed with Marine-turned-terrorist Nicholas Brody (played by actor Damian Lewis). One of the show's key features is Mathison's bipolar disorder, which both heightens and hinders her effectiveness in the pursuit of terrorists.

In the limited body of research that has been done on this subject, the mood stabilizers also seem to help those with bipolar disorder overcome their *depressive* episodes, though to a lesser degree than they help with their manic episodes (Malhi et al., 2013; Post, 2011). Given the drugs' less powerful impact on depressive episodes, many clinicians use a combination of mood stabilizers and antidepressant drugs to treat bipolar depression (Nivoli et al., 2011).

Researchers do not fully understand how mood stabilizing drugs operate (Malhi et al., 2013; Aiken, 2010). They suspect that the drugs change synaptic activity in neurons, but in a way different from that of antidepressant drugs. The firing of a neuron actually consists of several phases that ensue at lightning speed. When the neurotransmitter binds to a receptor on the receiving neuron, a series of changes occur *within* the receiving neuron to set the stage for firing. The substances in the neuron that carry out those changes are often called **second messengers** because they relay the original message from the receptor site to the firing mechanism of the neuron. (The neurotransmitter itself is considered the *first messenger*.) Whereas antidepressant drugs affect a neuron's initial reception of neurotransmitters, mood stabilizers appear to affect a neuron's second messengers.

"He's bipolar."

Lee Lorenz/The New Yorker Collection/www.cartoonbank.com

In a similar vein, it has been found that lithium and other mood stabilizing drugs also increase the production of *neuroprotective proteins*—key proteins within certain neurons whose job is to prevent cell death. The drugs may increase the health and functioning of those cells and thus reduce bipolar symptoms (Malhi et al., 2013; Gray et al., 2003).

Adjunctive Psychotherapy As Jamison stated in her memoir, psychotherapy alone is rarely helpful for persons with bipolar disorders. At the same time, clinicians have learned that mood stabilizing drugs alone are not always sufficient either. Thirty percent or more of patients with these disorders may not respond to lithium or a related drug, may not receive the proper dose, or may relapse while taking it. In addition, a number of patients stop taking mood stabilizers on their own (Advokat et al., 2014).

In view of these problems, many clinicians now use individual, group, or family therapy as an *adjunct* to mood stabilizing drugs (Reinares et al., 2014; Geddes & Miklowitz, 2013). Most often, therapists use these formats to emphasize the importance of continuing to take medications; to improve social skills and relationships that may be affected by bipolar episodes; to educate patients and families about bipolar disorders; to help patients solve the family, school, and occupational problems caused by their disorder; and to help prevent patients from attempting suicide (Hollon & Ponniah, 2010). Few controlled studies have tested the effectiveness of such adjunctive therapy, but those that have been done, along with numerous clinical reports, suggest that it helps reduce hospitalization, improves social functioning, and increases patients' ability to obtain and hold a job (Culver & Pratchett, 2010).

///// **BETWEEN THE LINES** /////

Frenzied Masterpiece

George Frideric Handel wrote his *Messiah* in less than a month during a manic episode (Roesch, 1991).

➤ *Summing Up*

BIPOLAR DISORDERS In bipolar disorders, episodes of mania alternate or intermix with episodes of depression. These disorders are much less common than unipolar depression. They may take the form of bipolar I, bipolar II, or cyclothymic disorder.

(continues on the next page)

Mania may be related to high norepinephrine activity along with a low level of serotonin activity. Some researchers have also linked bipolar disorders to improper transport of ions back and forth between the outside and the inside of a neuron's membrane, others have focused on deficiencies of key proteins and other chemicals within certain neurons, and still others have uncovered abnormalities in key brain structures. Genetic studies suggest that people may inherit a predisposition to these biological abnormalities.

Lithium and other mood stabilizing drugs have proved to be very effective in reducing and preventing the manic and the depressive episodes of bipolar disorders. These drugs may reduce bipolar symptoms by affecting the activity of second messengers or key proteins or other chemicals within certain neurons throughout the brain. Patients tend to fare better when mood stabilizing and/or other psychotropic drugs are combined with adjunctive psychotherapy.

PUTTING IT...*together*

Making Sense of All That Is Known

During the past 40 years, researchers and clinicians have made tremendous gains in the understanding and treatment of depressive and bipolar disorders. These are now among the most treatable of all psychological disorders. The choice of treatment for bipolar disorders is narrow and simple: drug therapy, ideally accompanied by psychotherapy, is the single most successful approach. The picture for unipolar depression is more varied and complex, although no less promising. Cognitive, cognitive-behavioral, interpersonal, and antidepressant drug therapy are all helpful in cases of any severity; couple therapy is helpful in select cases; pure behavioral therapy helps in mild to moderate cases; and ECT is useful and effective in severe cases.

Several factors have been tied closely to unipolar depression, including biological abnormalities, a reduction in positive reinforcements, negative ways of thinking, a perception of helplessness, and life stress and other sociocultural influences. Precisely how all of these factors relate to unipolar depression, however, is unclear. Several relationships are possible:

1. *One of the factors* may be the key cause of unipolar depression.

2. *Different factors* may be capable of initiating unipolar depression in different people. Some people may, for example, begin with low serotonin activity, which predisposes them to react helplessly in stressful situations, interpret events negatively, and enjoy fewer pleasures in life. Others may first suffer a severe loss, which triggers helplessness reactions, low serotonin activity, and reductions in positive rewards.

3. An *interaction between two or more specific factors* may be necessary to produce unipolar depression. Perhaps people will become depressed only if they have low levels of serotonin activity, feel helpless, *and* repeatedly blame themselves for negative events.

4. The *various factors may play different roles* in unipolar depression. Some may cause the disorder, some may result from it, and some may keep it going.

As with unipolar depression, clinicians and researchers have learned much about bipolar disorders during the past 40 years. But bipolar disorders appear to be best explained by a focus on *one* kind of variable—biological factors. The evidence suggests that biological abnormalities, perhaps inherited and perhaps triggered by life stress, cause bipolar disorders. Whatever roles other factors may play, the primary one appears to lie in this realm.

CLINICAL CHOICES

Now that you've read about disorders of mood, try the interactive case study for this chapter. See if you are able to identify John's symptoms and suggest a diagnosis based on his symptoms. What kind of treatment would be most effective for John? Go to LaunchPad to access *Clinical Choices.*

There is no question that investigations into depressive and bipolar disorders have been fruitful and enlightening. And it is more than reasonable to expect that important research findings and insights will continue to unfold in the years ahead. Now that clinical researchers have gathered so many important pieces of the puzzle, they must put the pieces together into a still more meaningful picture that will suggest even better ways to predict, prevent, and treat these disorders.

KEY TERMS

depression, p. 183

mania, p. 183

depressive disorders, p. 183

unipolar depression, p. 183

bipolar disorders, p. 184

anhedonia, p. 186

major depressive disorder, p. 187

persistent depressive disorder, p. 187

premenstrual dysphoric disorder, p. 187

disruptive mood dysregulation disorder, p. 187

norepinephrine, p. 189

serotonin, p. 189

cortisol, p. 190

melatonin, p. 190

seasonal affective disorder, p. 191

Brodmann Area 25, p. 191

electroconvulsive therapy (ECT), p. 192

MAO inhibitors, p. 193

tyramine, p. 193

tricyclics, p. 193

selective serotonin reuptake inhibitors (SSRIs), p. 194

vagus nerve stimulation, p. 195

transcranial magnetic stimulation (TMS), p. 195

deep brain stimulation (DBS), p. 196

symbolic loss, p. 196

behavioral activation, p. 200

learned helplessness, p. 201

attribution, p. 201

cognitive triad, p. 202

automatic thoughts, p. 202

rumination, p. 204

cognitive therapy, p. 204

interpersonal psychotherapy (IPT), p. 206

couple therapy, p. 208

hypomanic episode, p. 212

bipolar I disorder, p. 212

bipolar II disorder, p. 212

cyclothymic disorder, p. 213

ions, p. 215

lithium, p. 215

mood stabilizing drugs, p. 215

second messengers, p. 217

neuroprotective proteins, p. 217

adjunctive psychotherapy, p. 217

QuickQuiz

1. What is the difference between depressive disorders and bipolar disorders? *pp. 183–184*

2. What are the key symptoms of depression and mania? *pp. 184–188, 212*

3. Describe the role of norepinephrine and serotonin in unipolar depression. *pp. 189–191*

4. Describe Freud and Abraham's psychodynamic theory of depression and the evidence that supports it. *pp. 196–197*

5. How do behaviorists describe the role of rewards in depression? *p. 198*

6. How might learned helplessness be related to human depression? *pp. 200–202*

7. What kinds of negative thinking may lead to mood problems? *pp. 202–204*

8. How do sociocultural theorists account for unipolar depression? *pp. 205, 208–210*

9. What roles do biological and genetic factors seem to play in bipolar disorders? *pp. 214–215*

10. Discuss the leading treatments for unipolar depression and bipolar disorders. How effective are these various approaches? *pp. 192–198, 200, 204–208, 210, 215–217*

Visit *LaunchPad*

www.macmillanhighered.com/launchpad/comerfund8e

to access the e-book, new interactive case studies, videos, activities, and LearningCurve quizzes, as well as study aids including flashcards, FAQs, and research exercises.

Ed Fairburn

Suicide

> T he war in Iraq never ended for Jonathan Michael Boucher. Not when he flew home from Baghdad, not when he moved to Saratoga Springs for a fresh start and, especially, not when nighttime arrived.
>
> Tortured by what he saw as an 18-year-old Army private during the 2003 invasion and occupation, Boucher was diagnosed with post-traumatic stress disorder (PTSD) and honorably discharged from the military less than two years later.
>
> On May 15, three days before his 24th birthday, the young veteran committed suicide in his apartment's bathroom, stunning friends and family. . . . There was no note. . . .
>
> Johnny Boucher joined the Army right after graduating from East Lyme High School in Connecticut in 2002 because he was emotionally moved by the Sept. 11, 2001, terrorist attacks. "He felt it was his duty to do what he could for America," his father, Steven Boucher, 50, said.
>
> Shortly after enlisting, the 6-foot-2-inch soldier deployed with the "Wolf Pack"— 1st Battalion, 41st Field Artillery—and fought his way north in Iraq. He landed with his unit at Baghdad International Airport and was responsible for helping guard it. The battalion earned a Presidential Unit Citation for "exceptional bravery and heroism in the liberation of Baghdad."
>
> But it was during those early months of the war that Johnny Boucher had the evils of combat etched into his mind. The soldier was devastated by seeing a young Iraqi boy holding his dead father, who had been shot in the head. Later, near the airport, the soldier saw four good friends in his artillery battery killed in a vehicle accident minutes after one of them relieved him from duty, his father said.
>
> Boucher tried to rescue the soldiers. Their deaths and other things his son saw deeply impacted his soul after he returned because he was sensitive about family and very patriotic, Steven Boucher said. . . .
>
> But when the sun set, memories of combat and lost friends rose to the top, causing the former artilleryman severe nightmares. Sometimes he would curl up in a ball and weep, causing his parents to try to comfort him. . . . "At nighttime, he was just haunted," Steven Boucher said. . . . "Haunted, I think, by war." Bitterness about the war had crept in, and the troubled former soldier started drinking to calm himself. . . .
>
> Supported by a huge family he adored . . . Johnny Boucher recently got his own apartment on Franklin Street and appeared to be getting back on track. He seemed to be calm and enjoying life. But it was difficult to tell, and he was still fearful of sleep, his father said. They had plans for a hike, a birthday party and attending his brother Jeffrey's graduation. . . . Then, without warning, Johnny Boucher was gone. He hanged himself next to a Bible, his Army uniform and a garden statue of an angel, said his mother, who discovered him after he failed to show up to work for two days. . . .
>
> *Yusko, 2008*

Salmon spawn and then die, after an exhausting upstream swim to their breeding ground. Lemmings rush to the sea and drown. But only humans knowingly take their own lives. The actions of salmon and lemmings are instinctual responses that may even help their species survive in the long run. Only in the human act of suicide do beings act for the specific purpose of putting an end to their lives.

Suicide has been recorded throughout history. The Old Testament described King Saul's suicide: "There Saul took a sword and fell on it." The ancient Chinese, Greeks, and Romans also provided examples. In more recent times, suicides by such celebrated individuals as writer Ernest Hemingway, actress

table: **7-1**

Most Common Causes of Death in the United States

Rank	Cause	Deaths Per Year
1	Heart disease	597,689
2	Cancer	574,743
3	Chronic respiratory diseases	138,080
4	Stroke	129,476
5	Accidents	120,859
6	Alzheimer's	83,494
7	Diabetes	69,071
8	Kidney disease	50,476
9	Pneumonia and influenza	50,097
10	**Suicide**	**38,364**

Information from: CDC, 2013

Marilyn Monroe, rock star Kurt Cobain, and comedian Robin Williams have both shocked and fascinated the public.

Today suicide is one of the leading causes of death in the world. By the time you finish reading this page and the next, someone in the United States will have killed himself or herself (AFSP, 2014). In fact, at least 100 Americans will have taken their own lives by this time tomorrow.

It has been estimated that 1 million people die by suicide each year, more than 38,000 in the United States alone (AFSP, 2014; CDC, 2013) (see Table 7-1). Around 25 million other people throughout the world—as many as 1 million in the United States—make unsuccessful attempts to kill themselves; such attempts are called **parasuicides.** Actually, it is difficult to obtain accurate figures on suicide, and many investigators believe that estimates are often low. For one thing, suicide can be difficult to distinguish from unintentional drug overdoses, automobile crashes, drownings, and other accidents (Björkenstam et al., 2014). Many apparent "accidents" are probably intentional. For another, since suicide is frowned on in our society, relatives and friends often refuse to acknowledge that loved ones have taken their own lives.

Suicide is not officially classified as a mental disorder, although DSM-5's framers have proposed that a category called *suicidal behavior disorder* be studied for possible inclusion in future revisions of DSM-5 (APA, 2013). Regardless of whether suicidal acts themselves represent a distinct disorder, psychological dysfunctioning—a breakdown of coping skills, emotional turmoil, a distorted view of life—usually plays a role in such acts. For example, the young combat veteran about whom you read at the beginning of this chapter had intense feelings of depression, developed a severe drinking problem, and displayed posttraumatic stress disorder.

What Is Suicide?

Not every self-inflicted death is a suicide. A man who crashes his car into a tree after falling asleep at the steering wheel is not trying to kill himself. Thus Edwin Shneidman (2005, 1993, 1963), a pioneer in this field, defined **suicide** as an intentioned death—a self-inflicted death in which one makes an intentional, direct, and conscious effort to end one's life.

Intentioned deaths may take various forms. Consider the following examples. All three of these people intended to die, but their motives, concerns, and actions differed greatly:

> **Dave** was a successful man. By the age of 50 he had risen to the vice presidency of a small but profitable investment firm. He had a caring wife and two teenage sons who respected him. They lived in an upper-middle-class neighborhood, had a spacious house, and enjoyed a life of comfort.
>
> In August of his fiftieth year, everything changed. Dave was fired. Just like that. The economy had gone bad once again, the firm's profits were down, and the president wanted to try new, fresher investment strategies and marketing approaches. Dave had been "old school." He didn't fully understand today's investors—didn't know how to reach out to them with Web-based advertising, engage them online in the investment process, or give his firm a high-tech look. Dave's boss wanted to try a younger person.
>
> The experience of failure, loss, and emptiness was overwhelming for Dave. He looked for another position, but found only low-paying jobs for which he was overqualified. Each day as he looked for work Dave became more depressed, anxious, and desperate. He thought of trying to start his own investment company or to be a

▶ **parasuicide** A suicide attempt that does not result in death.

▶ **suicide** A self-inflicted death in which the person acts intentionally, directly, and consciously.

consultant of some kind, but in the cold of night, he knew he was just fooling himself with such notions. He kept sinking, withdrew from others, and felt increasingly hopeless.

Six months after losing his job, Dave began to consider ending his life. The pain was too great, the humiliation unending. He hated the present and dreaded the future. Throughout February he went back and forth. On some days he was sure he wanted to die. On other days, an enjoyable evening or uplifting conversation might change his mind temporarily. On a Monday late in February he heard about a job possibility, and the anticipation of the next day's interview seemed to lift his spirits. But Tuesday's interview did not go well. He knew there'd be no job offer. He went home, took a recently purchased gun from his locked desk drawer, and shot himself.

Demaine never truly recovered from his mother's death. He was only seven years old and unprepared for such a loss. His father sent him to live with his grandparents for a time, to a new school with new kids and a new way of life. In Demaine's mind, all these changes were for the worse. He missed the joy and laughter of the past. He missed his home, his father, and his friends. Most of all he missed his mother.

He did not really understand her death. His father said that she was in heaven now, at peace, happy. Demaine's unhappiness and loneliness continued day after day and he began to put things together in his own way. He believed he would be happy again if he could join his mother. He felt she was waiting for him, waiting for him to come to her. The thoughts seemed so right to him; they brought him comfort and hope. One evening, shortly after saying good night to his grandparents, Demaine climbed out of bed, went up the stairs to the roof of their apartment house, and jumped to his death. In his mind he was joining his mother in heaven.

Tya and Noah had met on a speed date. On a lark, Tya and a friend had registered at the speed date event, figuring, "What's the worst thing that can happen?" On the night of the big event, Tya talked to dozens of guys, none of whom appealed to her—except for Noah! He was quirky. He was witty. And he seemed as turned off by the whole speed date thing as she was. His was the only name that she put on her list. As it turned out, he also put her name down on his list, and a week later each of them received an email with contact information about the other. A flurry of email exchanges followed, and before long, they were going together. She marveled at her luck. She had beaten the odds. She had had a successful speed date experience.

It was Tya's first serious relationship; it became her whole life. Thus she was truly shocked and devastated when, on the one-year anniversary of their speed date, Noah told her that he no longer loved her and was leaving her for someone else.

As the weeks went by, Tya was filled with two competing feelings—depression and anger. Several times she texted or called Noah, begged him to reconsider, and pleaded for a chance to win him back. At the same time, she hated him for putting her through such misery.

Tya's friends became more and more worried about her. At first they sympathized with her pain, assuming it would soon lift. But as time went on, her depression and anger worsened, and Tya began to act strangely. Always a bit of a drinker, she started to drink heavily and to mix her drinks with various kinds of drugs.

One night Tya went into her bathroom, reached for a bottle of sleeping pills, and swallowed a handful of them. She wanted to make her pain go away, and she wanted Noah to know just how much pain he had caused her. She continued swallowing pill after pill, crying and swearing as she gulped them down. When she began to feel drowsy, she decided to call her close friend Dedra. She was not sure why she was calling, perhaps to say good-bye, to explain her actions, or to make sure that Noah was told; or perhaps to be talked out of it. Dedra pleaded and reasoned with her and tried to motivate her to live. Tya was trying to listen, but she became less and less coherent. Dedra hung up the phone and quickly called Tya's neighbor and the police. When reached by her neighbor, Tya was already in a coma. Seven hours later, while her friends and family waited for news in the hospital lounge, Tya died.

Hindustan Times/Newscom

Legitimate protest or attempted suicide? Civil rights activist Irom Sharmila, seen here at a press conference in New Delhi, has been on a hunger strike for almost 15 years to protest an Indian law that suspends many human rights protections. A form of attempted suicide? Not in Sharmila's mind, but the Indian government has charged her with attempted suicide and mandated that she be force-fed through a tube.

BETWEEN THE LINES

Shocking Comparison

Each year, more deaths in the United States result from suicide (38,364) than from motor vehicle crashes (33,687) (CDC, 2013).

▸ **subintentional death** A death in which the victim plays an indirect, hidden, partial, or unconscious role.

While Tya seemed to have mixed feelings about her death, Dave was clear in his wish to die. Whereas Demaine viewed death as a trip to heaven, Dave saw it as an end to his existence. Such differences can be important in efforts to understand and treat suicidal persons. Accordingly, Shneidman distinguished four kinds of people who intentionally end their lives: the death seeker, death initiator, death ignorer, and death darer.

> **How should clinicians decide whether to hospitalize a person who is considering suicide?**

Death seekers clearly intend to end their lives at the time they attempt suicide. This singleness of purpose may last only a short time. It can change to confusion the very next hour or day, and then return again in short order. Dave, the middle-aged investment counselor, was a death seeker. He had many misgivings about suicide and was ambivalent about it for weeks, but on Tuesday night he was a death seeker—clear in his desire to die and acting in a manner that virtually guaranteed a fatal outcome.

Death initiators also clearly intend to end their lives, but they act out of a belief that the process of death is already under way and that they are simply hastening the process. Some expect that they will die in a matter of days or weeks. Many suicides among the elderly and very sick fall into this category. Robust novelist Ernest Hemingway was profoundly concerned about his failing body as he approached his sixty-second birthday—a concern that some observers believe was at the center of his suicide.

Death ignorers do not believe that their self-inflicted death will mean the end of their existence. They believe they are trading their present lives for a better or happier existence. Many child suicides, like Demaine's, fall into this category, as do those of adult believers in a hereafter who commit suicide to reach another form of life. In 1997, for example, the world was shocked to learn that 39 members of an unusual cult named Heaven's Gate had committed suicide at an expensive house outside San Diego. It turned out that these members had acted out of the belief that their deaths would free their spirits and enable them to ascend to a "higher kingdom."

Death darers experience mixed feelings, or ambivalence, about their intent to die, even at the moment of their attempt, and they show this ambivalence in the act itself. Although to some degree they wish to die, and they often do die, their risk-taking behavior does not guarantee death. The person who plays Russian roulette—that is, pulls the trigger of a revolver randomly loaded with one bullet—is a death darer. Tya might be considered a death darer. Although her unhappiness and anger were great, she was not sure that she wanted to die. Even while taking pills, she called her friend, reported her actions, and listened to her friend's pleas.

When people play *indirect, covert, partial,* or *unconscious* roles in their own deaths, Shneidman (2001, 1993, 1981) classified them in a suicide-like category called **subintentional deaths.** Traditionally, clinicians have cited drug, alcohol, or tobacco use; promiscuous sexual behavior; recurrent physical fighting; and medication mismanagement as behaviors that may contribute to subintentional deaths (Juan et al., 2011).

In recent years, another behavioral pattern, *self-injury* or *self-mutilation,* has been added to this list—for example, cutting or burning oneself or banging one's head. Although this pattern is not officially classified as a mental disorder, the framers of DSM-5 proposed that a category called *nonsuicidal self-injury* be studied for possible inclusion in future revisions of the DSM (APA, 2013).

Self-injurious behavior is more common than previously recognized, particularly among teenagers and young adults, and it may be on the increase (Rodav, Levy, & Hamdan, 2014). It appears that this behavior becomes addictive in nature. The pain brought on by self-injury seems to offer some relief from emotional suffering, the behavior serves as a temporary distraction from problems, and the scars

Death darers? A sky surfer tries to ride the perfect cloud, high above the hustle and bustle of the city below. Are thrill seekers daredevils searching for new highs, as many of them claim, or are some actually death darers?

Digital Vision/Getty Images

that result may document the person's distress (Wilkinson & Goodyer, 2011). More generally, self-injury may help a person deal with chronic feelings of emptiness and boredom. Although self-injury and the other risky behaviors mentioned earlier may indeed represent an indirect attempt at suicide (Victor & Klonsky, 2014), the true intent behind them is unclear, so, other than the commentary in *MediaSpeak*, these behaviors are not included in the discussions of this chapter.

MediaSpeak

Videos of Self-Injury Find an Audience

By Roni Caryn Rabin, *New York Times*

YouTube videos are spreading word of a self-destructive behavior already disturbingly common among many teenagers and young adults—"cutting" and other forms of self-injury that stop short of suicide, a new study reports.

As many as one in five young men and women are believed to have engaged at least once in what psychologists call nonsuicidal self-injury. Now the behavior is being depicted in hundreds of YouTube clips—most of which don't carry any warnings about the content—that show explicit videos and photographs of people injuring themselves, usually by cutting. They also depict burning, hitting and biting oneself, picking at one's skin, disturbing wounds and embedding objects under the skin. Most of the injuries are inflicted on the wrists and arms and, less commonly, on the legs, torso or other parts of the body.

Some of the videos weave text, music and photography together, which may glamorize self-harming behaviors even more, the paper's authors warn.

And the videos are popular. Many viewers rated the videos positively, selecting them as favorites more than 12,000 times, according to the new study, . . . whose authors reviewed the 100 most-viewed videos on self-harm.

Stephen P. Lewis, assistant professor of psychology at the University of Guelph in Ontario and the paper's lead author, calls the YouTube depictions of self-harm "an alarming new trend," especially considering how popular Internet use is among the population

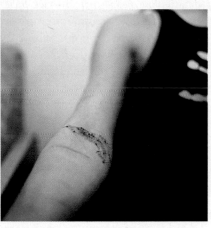

Self-mutilation online The self-inflicted knife wounds of this patient are evident. The phenomenon of self-injury is growing and now extends even to the Internet and social networks.

Elena Dorfman/Redux Pictures

that engages most in self-injury already: teenagers and young adults.

"The risk is that these videos normalize self-injury, and foster a virtual community for some people in which self-injury is accepted, and the message of getting help is not necessarily conveyed," Dr. Lewis said. "There's another risk, which is the phenomenon of 'triggering,' when someone who has a history of self-injury then watches a video or sees a picture, his or her urge to self-injure might actually increase in the moment."

Only about one in four of the 100 most-viewed videos sent a clear message against self-injury, the paper's analysis showed, and about the same proportion had an encouraging message that suggested the behavior could be overcome. About half the videos had a sad, melancholic tone, while about half described the behavior in a straightforward and factual manner.

About a quarter of the videos conveyed a mixed message about self-injury, while 42 percent were deemed neutral and 7 percent were clearly favorable toward self-injury. Only 42 percent of the videos warned viewers about the content.

> **Why do you think certain individuals decide to display their acts of self-injury online?**

Retrospective analysis The very public retrospective analysis of the 1994 suicide of rock star Kurt Cobain, leader of the grunge band Nirvana, was given new impetus in 2002 with the publication of *Journals*—a collection of notebook pages in which Cobain had written about his thoughts and concerns, bouts with depression, and drug addiction during the final years of his life.

▶ retrospective analysis A psychological autopsy in which clinicians piece together information about a person's suicide from the person's past.

How Is Suicide Studied?

Suicide researchers face a major obstacle: the people they study are no longer alive. How can investigators draw accurate conclusions about the intentions, feelings, and circumstances of those who can no longer explain their actions? Two research methods attempt to deal with this problem, each with only partial success.

One strategy is **retrospective analysis,** a kind of psychological autopsy in which clinicians and researchers piece together data from the suicide victim's past (Schwartz, 2011). Relatives, friends, therapists, or physicians may remember past statements, conversations, and behaviors that shed light on a suicide. Retrospective information may also be provided by the suicide notes that some victims leave behind (Cerel et al., 2015). However, such sources of information are not always available or reliable (Kelleher & Campbell, 2011; Wurst et al., 2011).

Because of these limitations, many researchers also use a second strategy—*studying people who survive their suicide attempts.* It is estimated that there are 12 nonfatal suicide attempts for every fatal suicide (AFSP, 2014). However, it may be that people who survive suicide attempts differ in important ways from those who do not. Many of them may not really have wanted to die, for example. Nevertheless, suicide researchers have found it useful to study survivors of suicide attempts, and this chapter shall consider those who attempt suicide and those who commit suicide as more or less alike.

Patterns and Statistics

Suicide happens within a larger social setting, and researchers have gathered many statistics regarding the social contexts in which such deaths take place. They have found, for example, that suicide rates vary from country to country (Kirkcaldy et al., 2010). South Korea, Russia, Hungary, Germany, Austria, Finland, Denmark, China, and Japan have very high rates—more than 20 suicides annually per 100,000 persons; conversely, Egypt, Mexico, Greece, and Spain have relatively low rates, fewer than 5 per 100,000. The United States and Canada fall in between, each with a suicide rate of 12.1 per 100,000 persons; England has a rate of 9 per 100,000 (AFSP, 2014; CDC, 2013).

Religious affiliation and beliefs may help account for these national differences (Foo et al., 2014). For example, countries that are largely Catholic, Jewish, or Muslim tend to have low suicide rates. Perhaps in these countries, strict prohibitions against suicide or a strong religious tradition deter many people from committing suicide. Yet there are exceptions to this tentative rule. Austria, a largely Roman Catholic country, has one of the highest suicide rates in the world.

> **What factors besides religious affiliation and beliefs might help account for national variations in suicide rates?**

Research is beginning to suggest that religious doctrine may not help prevent suicide as much as the degree of an individual's *devoutness.* Regardless of their particular persuasion, very religious people seem less likely to commit suicide (Cook, 2014; Güngörmüs et al., 2014). Similarly, it seems that people who have a greater reverence for life are less prone to consider or attempt self-destruction (Lee, 1985).

The suicide rates of men and women also differ. Three times as many women attempt suicide as men, yet men succeed at more than four times the rate of women (AFSP, 2014; CDC, 2013). Around the world 19 of every 100,000 men kill themselves each year; the suicide rate for women is 4 per 100,000 (Levi et al., 2003).

Although various explanations have been proposed for this gender difference, a popular one points to the different methods used by men and women (Stack &

Wasserman, 2009). Men tend to use more violent methods, such as shooting, stabbing, or hanging themselves, whereas women use less violent methods, such as drug overdose. Guns are used in 56 percent of the male suicides in the United States, compared with 31 percent of the female suicides (CDC, 2014).

Suicide is also related to social environment and marital status (You et al., 2011). In one study, around half of the individuals who had committed suicide were found to have no close personal friends (Maris, 2001), although they may be active on Internet and social networks. Fewer still had close relationships with parents and other family members. In a related vein, research has revealed that divorced persons have a higher suicide rate than married or cohabiting individuals (Roskar et al., 2011).

Finally, in the United States at least, suicide rates seem to vary according to race (see Figure 7-1). The overall suicide rate of white Americans is more than twice as high as that of African Americans, Hispanic Americans, and Asian Americans (AFSP, 2014; CDC, 2013). A major exception to this pattern is the very high suicide rate of American Indians, which is at least 20 percent higher than that of white Americans (Herne et al., 2014; SPRC, 2013). Although the extreme poverty of many American Indians may partly explain their high suicide rate, studies show that factors such as alcohol use, modeling, and the availability of guns may also play a role (Lanier, 2010). In addition to differences across racial groups, researchers have found that suicide rates sometimes differ within groups. Among Hispanic Americans, for example, Puerto Ricans are significantly more likely to attempt suicide than any other Hispanic American group (Baca-Garcia et al., 2011).

Some of these statistics on suicide have been questioned. Analyses suggest, for example, that the actual rate of suicide may be 15 percent higher for African Americans and 6 percent higher for women than usually reported (Barnes, 2010; Phillips & Ruth, 1993). People in these groups are more likely than others to use methods of suicide that can be mistaken for causes of accidental death, such as poisoning, drug overdose, single-car crashes, and pedestrian accidents.

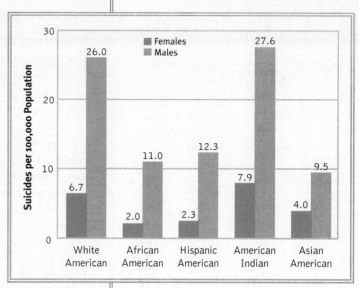

figure 7-1

Suicide, race, and gender In the United States, American Indians have the highest suicide rates among both males and females. (Information from: CDC, 2014, 2010; SPRC, 2013.)

➤ *Summing Up*

WHAT IS SUICIDE? Suicide is a self-inflicted death in which a person makes an intentional, direct, and conscious effort to end his or her life. Four kinds of people who intentionally end their lives have been distinguished: the death seeker, the death initiator, the death ignorer, and the death darer.

Two major strategies are used in the study of suicide: retrospective analysis and the study of people who survive suicide attempts. Suicide ranks among the top 10 causes of death in Western societies. Rates vary from country to country. One reason seems to be cultural differences in religious affiliation, beliefs, and degree of devoutness. Suicide rates also vary according to race, gender, and marital status.

What Triggers a Suicide?

Suicidal acts may be connected to recent events or current conditions in a person's life. Although such factors may not be the basic motivation for the suicide, they can precipitate it. Common triggering factors include *stressful events, mood and thought changes, alcohol and other drug use, mental disorders,* and *modeling.*

///// BETWEEN THE LINES /////

Deal Breaker

If clients state an intention to commit suicide, therapists may break the doctor–patient confidentiality agreement that usually governs treatment discussions.

Stressful Events and Situations

Researchers have counted more stressful events in the recent lives of suicide attempters than in the lives of nonattempters (McFeeters et al., 2014; Pompili et al., 2011). At the beginning of this chapter, for example, you read about a young man who committed suicide upon returning to civilian life, after experiencing the enormous stressors of combat in Iraq. However, the stressors that help lead to suicide do not need to be as horrific as those tied to combat. Common forms of *immediate stress* seen in cases of suicide are the loss of a loved one through death, divorce, or rejection (Roskar et al., 2011); loss of a job (Milner el al., 2014); significant financial loss (Houle & Light, 2014); and stress caused by hurricanes or other natural disasters, even among very young children. People may also attempt suicide in response to *long-term* rather than recent stress. Four such stressors are particularly common—social isolation, serious illness, an abusive environment, and occupational stress.

Social Isolation As you saw in the cases of Dave, Demaine, and Tya, people from loving families or supportive social systems may commit suicide. However, those without such social supports are particularly vulnerable to suicidal thinking and actions. Researchers have found a heightened risk for suicidal behavior among those who feel little sense of "belongingness," believe that they have limited or no social support, live alone, and have ongoing conflicts with other people (You et al., 2011).

Serious Illness People whose illnesses cause them great pain or severe disability may try to commit suicide, believing that death is unavoidable and imminent (Schneider & Shenassa, 2008). They may also believe that the suffering and problems caused by their illnesses are more than they can endure. Studies suggest that as many as one-third of those who die by suicide have been in poor physical health during the months prior to their suicidal acts (MacLean et al., 2011; Conwell et al., 1990).

Abusive or Repressive Environment Victims of an abusive or repressive environment from which they have little or no hope of escape sometimes commit suicide. For example, some prisoners of war, inmates of concentration camps, abused spouses, abused children, and prison inmates try to end their lives (Fazel et al., 2011). Like those who have serious illnesses, these people may feel that they can endure no more suffering and believe that there is no hope for improvement in their condition.

Occupational Stress Some jobs create feelings of tension or dissatisfaction that may trigger suicide attempts. Research has found particularly high suicide rates among psychiatrists and psychologists, physicians, nurses, dentists, lawyers, police officers, farmers, and unskilled laborers (Milner et al., 2013; Kleespies et al., 2011). Such correlations do not necessarily mean that occupational pressures directly cause suicidal actions. Perhaps unskilled workers are responding to financial insecurity rather than job stress when they attempt suicide. Similarly, rather than reacting to the emotional strain of their work, suicidal psychiatrists and psychologists may have long-standing emotional problems that stimulated their career interest in the first place.

Mood and Thought Changes

Many suicide attempts are preceded by a change in mood. The change may not be severe enough to warrant a diagnosis of a mental disorder, but it does represent a significant shift from the person's past mood. The most common change is an increase in sadness (Kim et al., 2015). Also common are increases in feelings of anxiety, tension, frustration, anger, or shame (Reisch et al., 2010). In fact, Shneidman (2005, 2001) believed that the key to suicide is "psychache," a feeling of psychological pain

Famous prison suicide People around the country expressed outrage when they learned that Ariel Castro, shown here at his 2013 trial, had kidnapped three young women in Cleveland, Ohio, and imprisoned them in his house for more than a decade, repeatedly raping them. Sentenced to 1,000 years without parole for his crimes, Castro killed himself by hanging just a month into his sentence. Around 5.5 percent of all prison deaths are due to suicide (Smith, 2013).

that seems intolerable to the person. A study of 88 patients found that those who scored higher on a measure called the Psychological Pain Assessment Scale were indeed more likely than others to commit suicide (Pompili et al., 2008).

Suicide attempts may also be preceded by shifts in patterns of thinking. People may become preoccupied with their problems, lose perspective, and see suicide as the only effective solution to their difficulties (Shneidman, 2005, 2001). They often develop a sense of **hopelessness**—a pessimistic belief that their present circumstances, problems, or mood will not change. Some clinicians believe that a feeling of hopelessness is the single most likely indicator of suicidal intent, and they take special care to look for signs of hopelessness when they assess the risk of suicide (Rosellini & Bagge, 2014).

Many people who attempt suicide fall victim to **dichotomous thinking,** viewing problems and solutions in rigid either/or terms (Shneidman, 2005, 2001, 1993). Indeed, Shneidman said that the "four-letter word" in suicide is "only," as in "suicide was the *only* thing I could do" (Maris, 2001). In the following statement a woman who survived her leap from a building describes her dichotomous thinking at the time. She saw death as the only alternative to her pain:

> *I was so desperate. I felt, my God, I couldn't face this thing. Everything was like a terrible whirlpool of confusion. And I thought to myself: There's only one thing to do. I just have to lose consciousness. That's the only way to get away from it. The only way to lose consciousness, I thought, was to jump off something good and high. . . .*
>
> *(Shneidman, 1987, p. 56)*

Alcohol and Other Drug Use

Studies indicate that as many as 70 percent of the people who attempt suicide drink alcohol just before they do so (Crosby et al., 2009; McCloud et al., 2004). Autopsies reveal that about one-quarter of these people are legally intoxicated (Flavin et al., 1990). It may be that the use of alcohol lowers a person's fears of committing suicide, releases underlying aggressive feelings, or impairs his or her judgment and problem-solving ability. Research shows that the use of other kinds of drugs may have a similar tie to suicide, particularly in teenagers and young adults (Darke et al., 2005). A high level of heroin, for example, was found in the blood of Kurt Cobain at the time of his suicide in 1994 (Colburn, 1996).

Mental Disorders

Although people who attempt suicide may be troubled or anxious, they do not necessarily have a psychological disorder. Nevertheless, the majority of all suicide attempters do have such a disorder (Singhal et al., 2014; Nock et al., 2013). Research suggests that as many as 70 percent of all suicide attempters had been experiencing severe *depression,* 20 percent *chronic alcoholism,* and 10 percent *schizophrenia.* Correspondingly, as many as 25 percent of people with each of these disorders try to kill themselves. People who are both depressed and dependent on alcohol seem particularly prone to suicidal impulses (Nenadic´-Šviglin et al., 2011). It is also the case that many people with borderline personality disorder, a pattern that you will read about in Chapter 13, try to harm themselves or make suicidal gestures as part of their disorder (Amore et al., 2014).

As you saw in Chapter 6, people with major depressive disorder often have suicidal thoughts. Indeed, one review has found that treatments for depression consistently reduce the rate of suicidal thinking, attempts, and completions among

Kevin Winter/Getty Images

Acting happy Fans of megastar, comedian, and actor Robin Williams were shocked when he committed suicide by hanging in 2014. Close friends reported that Williams had been battling depression and the early stages of Parkinson's disease for some time—a painful emotional state that he managed to conceal from the public with his joyful performances. Williams' autopsy also revealed a type of neurocognitive disorder called Lewy body disease.

▶ **hopelessness** A pessimistic belief that one's present circumstances, problems, or mood will not change.

▶ **dichotomous thinking** Viewing problems and solutions in rigid either/or terms.

patients (Sakinofsky, 2011). Even when depressed people are showing improvements in mood, however, they may remain at high risk for suicide. In fact, among those who are severely depressed, the risk of suicide may actually increase as their mood improves and they have more energy to act on their suicidal wishes. Recall, for example, the combat veteran whose case opened this chapter. Just before he committed suicide, he had seemed to be calm and enjoying life again, according to family members and friends.

Severe depression also may play a key role in suicide attempts made by those with serious physical illnesses (Werth, 2004). A study of 44 patients with terminal illnesses revealed that fewer than one-quarter of them had thoughts of suicide or wished for an early death and that those who did were all suffering from major depressive disorder (Brown et al., 1986).

A number of the people who drink alcohol or use drugs just before a suicide attempt actually have a long history of abusing such substances (Kim et al., 2015; Ries, 2010). The basis for the link between substance-related disorders and suicide is not clear. Perhaps the tragic lifestyle of many persons with these disorders or their sense of being hopelessly trapped by a substance leads to suicidal thinking. Alternatively, a third factor—psychological pain, for instance, or desperation—may cause both substance abuse and suicidal thinking (Sher et al., 2005). Such people may be caught in a downward spiral: they are driven toward substance use by psychological pain or loss, only to find themselves caught in a pattern of substance abuse that aggravates rather than solves their problems (Maris, 2001).

People with schizophrenia, as you will see in Chapter 12, may hear voices that are not actually present (hallucinations) or hold beliefs that are clearly false and perhaps bizarre (delusions). The popular notion is that when such people kill themselves, they must be responding to an imagined voice commanding them to do so or to a delusion that suicide is a grand and noble gesture. Research indicates, however, that suicides by people with schizophrenia more often reflect feelings of demoralization or fears of further mental deterioration (Meltzer, 2011). Many young and unemployed people with schizophrenia who have had relapses over several years come to believe that the disorder will forever disrupt their lives. Still others seem to be disheartened by their substandard living conditions. Suicide is the leading cause of premature death among people with schizophrenia.

Modeling: The Contagion of Suicide

It is not unusual for people, particularly teenagers, to try to commit suicide after observing or reading about someone else who has done so (Hagihara et al., 2014). Perhaps they have been struggling with major problems and the other person's suicide seems to reveal a possible solution, or perhaps they have been thinking about suicide and the other person's suicide seems to give them permission or finally persuades them to act. Either way, one suicidal act apparently serves as a *model* for another. Suicides by family members and friends, those by celebrities, other highly publicized suicides, and those by coworkers or colleagues are particularly common triggers.

Family Members and Friends A recent suicide by a family member or friend increases the likelihood that a person will attempt suicide (Ali et al., 2011). Of course, the death of a family member or friend, especially when self-inflicted, is a life-changing event, and suicidal thoughts or attempts may be tied largely to that trauma or sense of loss. Indeed, such losses typically have a lifelong impact on surviving relatives and friends, including a heightened risk of suicide that can continue for years (Roy, 2011). However, even when researchers factor out these issues, they find increases in the risk of suicide among the relatives and friends of people who recently committed suicide (Ali et al., 2011). This additional risk factor is often called the *social contagion effect*.

Celebrities Research suggests that suicides by entertainers, political figures, and other well-known people are regularly followed by unusual increases in the number of suicides across the nation (Queinec et al., 2011). During the week after the suicide of Marilyn Monroe in 1963, for example, the national suicide rate rose 12 percent (Phillips, 1974).

Other Highly Publicized Cases Suicides with bizarre or unusual aspects often receive intense coverage by the news media. Such highly publicized accounts may lead to similar suicides (Hagihara et al., 2014). During the year after a widely publicized, politically motivated suicide by self-burning in England, for example, 82 other people set themselves on fire, with equally fatal results (Ashton & Donnan, 1981). Inquest reports revealed that most of those people had histories of emotional problems and that none of the suicides had the political motivation of the publicized suicide. The imitators seemed to be responding to their own problems in a manner triggered by the suicide they had observed or read about.

Some clinicians argue that more responsible reporting could reduce this frightening impact of highly publicized suicides (Sullivan et al., 2015). A careful approach to reporting was seen in the media's coverage of the suicide of Kurt Cobain. MTV's repeated theme on the evening of the suicide was "Don't do it!" In fact, thousands of upset, frightened, and in some cases suicidal young people called MTV and other radio and television stations in the hours after Cobain's death. Some of the stations responded by posting the phone numbers of suicide prevention centers, presenting interviews with suicide experts, and offering counseling services and advice directly to callers. Perhaps because of such efforts, the usual rate of suicide both in Seattle, where Cobain lived, and elsewhere held steady during the weeks that followed (Colburn, 1996).

Coworkers and Colleagues The word-of-mouth publicity that attends suicides in a school, workplace, or small community may trigger suicide attempts. The suicide of a recruit at a U.S. Navy training school, for example, was followed within two weeks by another and also by an attempted suicide at the school. To head off what threatened to become a suicide epidemic, the school began a program of staff education on suicide and group therapy sessions for recruits who had been close to the suicide victims (Grigg, 1988). Today, a number of schools, for individuals of all ages, put into action programs of this kind after a student commits suicide (Joshi et al., 2015). Such postsuicide programs are often referred to by clinicians as *postvention*.

Eye of the storm In a celebrated case, the British press blamed the music of the emo group My Chemical Romance for the suicide of a 13-year-old girl in 2008. For years, the lyrics and melodies of various songs have been pointed to as negative influences, particularly on teenagers, that can contribute to suicide attempts. However, little research has been conducted on this issue and lawsuits making such claims have typically been dismissed.

© Tim Mosenfelder/Corbis

➤ *Summing Up*

WHAT TRIGGERS A SUICIDE? Many suicidal acts are triggered by the current events or conditions in a person's life. The acts may be triggered by recent stressors, such as loss of a loved one and job loss, or long-term stressors, such as social isolation, serious illness, an abusive environment, and job stress. They may also be preceded by changes in mood or thought, particularly increases in one's sense of hopelessness. In addition, the use of alcohol or other kinds of substances, mental disorders, or news of another's suicide may precede suicide attempts.

What Are the Underlying Causes of Suicide?

Most people faced with difficult situations never try to kill themselves. In an effort to understand why some people are more prone to suicide than others, theorists have proposed more fundamental explanations for self-destructive actions than the immediate triggers considered in the previous section. The leading theories come from the psychodynamic, sociocultural, and biological perspectives. As a group, however, these hypotheses have received limited research support and fail to address the full range of suicidal acts. Thus the clinical field currently lacks a satisfactory understanding of suicide.

The Psychodynamic View

Many psychodynamic theorists believe that suicide results from depression and from anger at others that is redirected toward oneself. This theory was first stated by Wilhelm Stekel at a meeting in Vienna in 1910, when he proclaimed that "no one kills himself who has not wanted to kill another or at least wished the death of another" (Shneidman, 1979). Agreeing with this notion, influential psychiatrist Karl Menninger called suicide "murder in the 180th degree."

As you read in Chapter 6, Freud (1917) and Abraham (1916, 1911) proposed that when people experience the real or symbolic loss of a loved one, they unconsciously incorporate the person into their own identity and feel toward themselves as they had felt toward the other. For a short while, negative feelings toward the lost loved one are experienced as self-hatred. Anger toward the loved one may turn into intense anger against oneself and finally into depression. Suicide is thought to be an extreme expression of this self-hatred (Campbell, 2010). The following description of a suicidal patient demonstrates how such forces may operate:

> *A 27-year-old conscientious and responsible woman took a knife to her wrists to punish herself for being tyrannical, unreliable, self-centered, and abusive. She was perplexed and frightened by this uncharacteristic self-destructive episode and was enormously relieved when her therapist pointed out that her invective described her recently deceased father much better than it did herself.*
>
> *(Gill, 1982, p. 15)*

In support of Freud's view, researchers have often found a relationship between childhood losses—real or symbolic—and later suicidal behaviors (Alonzo et al., 2014). A classic study of 200 family histories, for example, found that early parental loss was much more common among suicide attempters (48 percent) than among nonsuicidal individuals (24 percent) (Adam et al., 1982). Common forms of loss were death of the father and divorce or separation of the parents. Similarly, a study of 343 depressed individuals found that those who had felt rejected or neglected as children by their parents were more likely than other people to attempt suicide as adults (Ehnvall et al., 2008).

Late in his career, Freud proposed that human beings have a basic "death instinct." He called this instinct *Thanatos* and said that it opposes the "life instinct." According to Freud, while most people learn to redirect their death instinct by aiming it toward others, suicidal people, caught in a web of self-anger, direct it squarely toward themselves.

Sociological findings are consistent with this explanation of suicide. National suicide rates have been found to drop in times of war (Maris, 2001), when, one could argue, people are encouraged to direct their self-destructive energy against

Murder-suicide in the air Nowhere is the link between homicidal and suicidal behavior more evident than in cases of murder–suicide. On March 24, 2015, Andreas Lubitz, a depressed 27-year-old copilot, deliberately crashed a Germanwings Airbus A320 (above) into the French Alps, killing himself and 149 passengers and crew members. Around 2 percent of all suicides occur in the context of murder–suicide, usually involving spouses or lovers.

© Xinhua/Xinhua Press/Corbis

"the enemy." In addition, in many parts of the world, societies with high rates of homicide tend to have low rates of suicide, and vice versa (Bills & Li, 2005). However, research has failed to establish that suicidal people are in fact dominated by intense feelings of anger. Although hostility is an important element in some suicides, several studies find that other emotional states are even more prevalent (Conner & Weisman, 2011).

> **Why might towns and countries in past times have been inclined to punish those who attempted suicide and their relatives?**

By the end of his career, Freud himself expressed dissatisfaction with his theory of suicide. Other psychodynamic theorists have also challenged his ideas over the years, yet themes of loss and self-directed aggression generally remain at the center of most psychodynamic explanations (King, 2003).

Durkheim's Sociocultural View

Toward the end of the nineteenth century, Emile Durkheim (1897), a sociologist, developed a broad theory of suicidal behavior. Today this theory continues to be influential and is often supported by research (Fernquist, 2007). According to Durkheim, the probability of suicide is determined by how attached a person is to such social groups as the family, religious institutions, and community. The more thoroughly a person belongs, the lower the risk of suicide. Conversely, people who have poor relationships with their society are at higher risk of killing themselves. He defined several categories of suicide, including *egoistic, altruistic,* and *anomic* suicide.

Egoistic suicides are committed by people over whom society has little or no control. These people are not concerned with the norms or rules of society, nor are they integrated into the social fabric. According to Durkheim, this kind of suicide is more likely in people who are isolated, alienated, and nonreligious. The larger the number of such people living in a society, the higher that society's suicide rate.

Altruistic suicides, in contrast, are committed by people who are so well integrated into the social structure that they intentionally sacrifice their lives for its well-being. Soldiers who threw themselves on top of a live grenade to save others, Japanese kamikaze pilots who crashed their planes into enemy ships during World War II, and Buddhist monks and nuns who protested the Vietnam War by setting themselves on fire may have been committing altruistic suicide (Leenaars, 2004; Stack, 2004). According to Durkheim, societies that encourage people to sacrifice themselves for others and to preserve their own honor (as East Asian societies do) are likely to have higher suicide rates.

Anomic suicides, another category proposed by Durkheim, are those committed by people whose social environment fails to provide stable structures, such as family and religion, to support and give meaning to life. Such a societal condition, called *anomie* (literally, "without law"), leaves people without a sense of belonging. Unlike egoistic suicide, which is the act of a person who rejects the structures of a society, anomic suicide is the act of a person who has been let down by a disorganized, inadequate, often decaying society.

Durkheim argued that when societies go through periods of anomie, their suicide rates increase. Historical trends support this claim. Periods of economic depression may bring about some degree of anomie in a country, and national suicide rates tend to rise during such times (Noh, 2009; Maris, 2001). Periods of population change and increased immigration, too, tend to bring about a state of anomie, and again suicide rates rise (Kposowa et al., 2008).

A major change in a person's immediate surroundings, rather than general societal problems, can also lead to anomic suicide. People who suddenly inherit a great deal of money, for example, may go through a period of anomie as their relationships with social, economic, and occupational structures are changed. Thus Durkheim

Thaier Al-Sudani/Reuters

Altruistic suicide? A clay sculpture of a suicide bomber is displayed at a Baghdad art gallery. Some sociologists believe that the acts of such bombers fit Durkheim's definition of altruistic suicide, arguing that the bombers believe they are sacrificing their lives for the well-being of their society. Other theorists, however, point out that many such bombers seem indifferent to the innocent lives they are destroying and categorize the bombers instead as mass murderers motivated by hatred rather than by feelings of altruism (Humphrey, 2006).

John Storey/San Francisco Chronicle/Corbis

Not just another bridge This man, one of only 26 people to survive jumping off the Golden Gate Bridge, returns to the site of his suicide attempt—made at the age of 19. The bridge is believed to be the site of more jumping suicides than any other location in the world—with an estimated 1,400 suicides since the bridge opened in 1937.

predicted that societies with more opportunities for change in individual wealth or status would have higher suicide rates; this prediction is also supported by research (Cutright & Fernquist, 2001; Lester, 2000, 1985). Conversely, people who are removed from society and sent to a prison environment may experience anomie. As you read earlier, research confirms that such people have a heightened suicide rate (Fazel et al., 2011).

Although today's sociocultural theorists do not always embrace Durkheim's particular ideas, most agree that social structure and cultural stress often play major roles in suicide. In fact, the sociocultural view pervades the study of suicide. Recall the earlier discussion of the many studies linking suicide to broad factors such as religious affiliation, marital status, gender, race, and societal stress. You will also see the impact of such factors when you read about the ties between suicide and age.

Despite the influence of sociocultural theories such as Durkheim's, these theories cannot by themselves explain why some people who face particular societal pressures commit suicide while the majority do not. Durkheim himself concluded that the final explanation probably lies in the interaction between societal and individual factors.

The Biological View

For years, biological researchers have relied largely on family pedigree studies to support their position that biological factors contribute to suicidal behavior. They repeatedly have found higher rates of suicide among the parents and close relatives of suicidal people than among those of nonsuicidal people (Petersen et al., 2014; Roy, 2011). Such findings may suggest that genetic, and so biological, factors are at work.

> Suicide sometimes runs in families. How might clinicians and researchers explain such family patterns?

In the past three decades, laboratory studies have offered more direct support for a biological view of suicide. One promising line of research focuses on *serotonin*. The activity level of this neurotransmitter has often been found to be low in people who commit suicide (Fabio Di Narzo et al., 2014; Mann & Currier, 2007). An early hint of this relationship came from a study by psychiatric researcher Marie Asberg and her colleagues (1976). They studied 68 depressed patients and found that 20 of the patients had particularly low levels of serotonin activity. It turned out that 40 percent of the research participants with such serotonin levels attempted suicide, compared with 15 percent of those with higher serotonin levels. The researchers interpreted this to mean that low serotonin activity may be "a predictor of suicidal acts." Later studies found that suicide attempters with low serotonin activity are 10 times more likely to make a repeat attempt and succeed than are suicide attempters with higher serotonin activity (Roy, 1992).

At first glance, these and related studies may appear to tell us only that depressed people often attempt suicide. After all, depression is itself related to low serotonin activity. On the other hand, there is evidence of low serotonin activity even among suicidal people who have no history of depression (Mann & Currier, 2007). That is, low serotonin activity also seems to play a role in suicide separate from depression.

How, then, might low serotonin activity increase the likelihood of suicidal behavior? One possibility is that it contributes to aggressive and impulsive behaviors

(Preti, 2011). It has been found, for example, that serotonin activity is lower in aggressive men than in nonaggressive men and that serotonin activity is often low in those who commit such aggressive acts as arson and murder (Oquendo et al., 2006, 2004; Stanley et al., 2000). Such findings suggest that low serotonin activity helps produce aggressive feelings and impulsive behavior. In people who are clinically depressed, low serotonin activity may produce aggressive tendencies that cause them to be particularly vulnerable to suicidal thoughts and acts. Even in the absence of a depressive disorder, however, people with low serotonin activity may develop such aggressive feelings that they, too, are dangerous to themselves or to others. Still other research indicates that low serotonin activity *combined* with key psychosocial factors (such as childhood traumas) may be the strongest suicide predictor of all (Moberg et al., 2011).

Is aggression the key? Biological theorists believe that heightened feelings of aggression and impulsivity, produced by low serotonin activity, are key factors in suicide. In 2007, professional wrestling champion Chris Benoit (right) killed his wife and son and then hanged himself, a tragedy that seemed consistent with this theory. In addition, toxicology reports found steroids, drugs known to help cause aggression and impulsivity, in Benoit's body.

➤ *Summing Up*

WHAT ARE THE UNDERLYING CAUSES OF SUICIDE? The leading explanations for suicide come from the psychodynamic, sociocultural, and biological models. Each has received only limited support. Psychodynamic theorists believe that suicide usually results from depression and self-directed anger. Emile Durkheim's sociocultural theory defines three categories of suicide, based on the person's relationship with society: egoistic, altruistic, and anomic suicides. And biological theorists suggest that the activity of the neurotransmitter serotonin is particularly low in people who commit suicide.

Is Suicide Linked to Age?

Although people of all ages may try to kill themselves, the likelihood of committing suicide steadily increases with age up through middle age, then decreases during the early stages of old age, and then increases again beginning at age 85 (see Figure 7-2 on page 237). Currently, 1 of every 100,000 people under 15 years of age in the United States kills himself or herself each year, compared with 11 of every 100,000 people between 15 and 24 years old, 19 of every 100,000 between 45 and 64 years old, 15 of every 100,000 between 65 and 84, and 18 of every 100,000 people over age 85 (AFSP, 2014; CDC, 2013). The exceptional rate of suicide among those who are middle-aged is a recent phenomenon and is not fully understood. Up until 2006, that rate had been considerably lower than the current rate and always lower than that of elderly people.

Clinicians have paid particular attention to self-destructive behavior in three age groups: *children, adolescents,* and the *elderly.* Although the features and theories of suicide discussed throughout this chapter apply to all age groups, each group faces unique problems that may play key roles in the suicidal acts of its members.

Children

Although suicide is infrequent among children, it has been increasing over the past several decades (Dervic et al., 2008). Indeed, more than 6 percent of all deaths among children between the ages of 10 and 14 years are caused by suicide (Arias et al., 2003). Boys outnumber girls by as much as 5 to 1. In addition, it has been estimated that 1 of every 100 children tries to harm himself or herself, and many thousands of children are hospitalized each year for deliberately self-destructive

///// **BETWEEN THE LINES** /////

Additional Punishment

Up through the nineteenth century, the bodies of suicide victims in France and England were sometimes dragged through the streets on a frame, head downward, the way criminals were dragged to their executions.

In the United States, the last prosecution for attempted suicide occurred in 1961; the prosecution was not successful.

(Wertheimer, 2001; Fay, 1995)

Student stress The intense training and testing that characterize Japan's educational system produce high levels of stress in many students. This child, wearing a headband that translates to "Struggle to Pass," participates in summer *juku*, a camp where children receive special academic training, extra lessons, and exam practice 11 hours a day.

acts, such as stabbing, cutting, burning, or shooting themselves; overdosing; or jumping from high places (Fortune & Hawton, 2007).

Researchers have found that suicide attempts by the very young are commonly preceded by such behavioral patterns as running away from home; accident-proneness; aggressive acting out; temper tantrums; self-criticism; social withdrawal and loneliness; extreme sensitivity to criticism by others; low tolerance of frustration; sleep problems; dark fantasies, daydreams, or hallucinations; marked personality change; and overwhelming interest in death and suicide (Soole et al., 2015; Wong et al., 2011; Dervic et al., 2008). Studies further have linked child suicides to the recent or anticipated loss of a loved one, family stress and a parent's unemployment, abuse by parents, victimization by peers (for example, bullying), and a clinical level of depression (van Geel et al., 2014; Renaud et al., 2008).

Most people find it hard to believe that children fully comprehend the meaning of a suicidal act. They argue that because a child's thinking is so limited, children who attempt suicide fall into Shneidman's category of "death ignorers," like Demaine, who sought to join his mother in heaven. Many child suicides, however, appear to be based on a clear understanding of death and on a clear wish to die (Pfeffer, 2003). In addition, suicidal thinking among even normal children is apparently more common than most people once believed. Clinical interviews with schoolchildren have revealed that between 6 and 33 percent have thought about suicide (Riesch et al., 2008; Culp et al., 1995). Small wonder that many of today's elementary schools have tried to develop tools and procedures for better identifying and assessing suicide risk among their students (Miller, 2011; Whitney et al., 2011).

Adolescents

> *Dear Mom, Dad, and everyone else,*
>   *I'm sorry for what I've done, but I loved you all and I always will, for eternity. Please, please, please don't blame it on yourselves. It was all my fault and not yours or anyone else's. If I didn't do this now, I would have done it later anyway. We all die some day, I just died sooner.*
>   *Love,*
>   *John*
>
>   (Berman, 1986)

The suicide of John, age 17, was not an unusual occurrence. Suicidal actions become much more common after the age of 13 than at any earlier age. According to official records, approximately 1,400 teenagers (age 13 to 18), or 7 of every 100,000, commit suicide in the United States each year (Nock et al., 2013). In addition, at least 12 percent of teenagers have persistent suicidal thoughts and 4 percent make suicide attempts (Nock et al., 2013). Because fatal illnesses are uncommon among the young, suicide has become the third leading cause of death in this age group, after accidents and homicides (CDC, 2015). Around 10 percent of all adolescent deaths are the result of suicide.

More than half of teenage suicides have been tied to clinical depression (see *PsychWatch* on page 238), low self-esteem, and feelings of hopelessness, but many teenagers who try to kill themselves also appear to struggle with anger and impulsiveness or to have serious alcohol or drug problems (Orri et al., 2014; Renaud et al., 2008). Some also have deficiencies in their ability to sort out and solve problems.

Teenagers who consider or attempt suicide are often under great stress. They may be dealing with long-term pressures such as poor (or missing) relationships

BETWEEN THE LINES

Therapeutic Failure

More than 55% of suicidal teens actually started therapy before the onset of their suicidal behaviors, but it failed to prevent their actions (Nock et al., 2013).

with parents, family conflict, inadequate peer relationships, and social isolation (Orri et al., 2014; Capuzzi & Gross, 2008). Alternatively, their actions also may be triggered by more immediate stress, such as a parent's unemployment or medical illness, financial setbacks for the family, or a social loss such as a breakup with a boyfriend or girlfriend (Orbach & Iohan, 2007). Stress at school seems to be a particularly common problem for teenagers who attempt suicide. Some have trouble keeping up at school, while others may be high achievers who feel pressured to be perfect and to stay at the top of the class (Frazier & Cross, 2011; Miller, 2011).

Some theorists believe that the period of adolescence itself produces a stressful climate in which suicidal actions are more likely. Adolescence is often marked by conflicts, depressed feelings, tensions, and difficulties at home and school. Adolescents tend to react to events more sensitively, angrily, dramatically, and impulsively than individuals in other age groups; thus the likelihood of their engaging in suicidal acts during times of stress is higher (Greening et al., 2008). Finally, the eagerness of adolescents to imitate others, including others who attempt suicide, may set the stage for suicidal action (Apter & Wasserman, 2007). One pioneering study found that 93 percent of adolescent suicide attempters had known someone who had attempted suicide (Conrad, 1992).

Teen Suicides: Attempts Versus Completions Far more teenagers attempt suicide than actually kill themselves—most experts believe that the ratio is 25 to 1 (AFSP, 2014), although estimates range as high as 200 to 1. The unusually large number of unsuccessful teenage suicides may mean that adolescents are less certain than middle-age and elderly people who make such attempts. While some do indeed wish to die, many may simply want to make others understand how desperate they are, or they may want to get help or teach others a lesson (Apter & Wasserman, 2007). Up to half of teenagers who make a suicide attempt try again in the future, and as many as 14 percent eventually die by suicide (Horwitz et al., 2014; Wong et al., 2008).

Why is the rate of suicide attempts so high among teenagers (as well as among young adults)? Several explanations, most pointing to societal factors, have been proposed. First, as the number and proportion of teenagers and young adults in the general population have risen, the competition for jobs, college positions, and academic and athletic honors has intensified for them, leading increasingly to shattered dreams and ambitions (Holinger & Offer, 1993, 1991, 1982). Other explanations point to weakening ties in the family (which may produce feelings of alienation and rejection in many of today's young people) and to the easy availability of alcohol and other drugs and the pressure to use them among teenagers and young adults (Brent, 2001; Cutler et al., 2001).

The mass media coverage of suicides by teenagers and young adults may also contribute to the high rate of suicide attempts among the young (Gerard et al., 2012). The detailed descriptions of teenage suicide that the media and the arts often offer may serve as models for young people who are contemplating suicide (Cheng et al., 2007). In one of the most famous examples of this phenomenon, just days after the highly publicized suicides of four adolescents in a New Jersey town in 1987, dozens of teenagers across the United States took similar actions (at least 12 of them fatal)—two in the same garage just one week later.

It is worth noting here that a number of *pro-suicide* forums and chat rooms have popped up on the Internet in recent

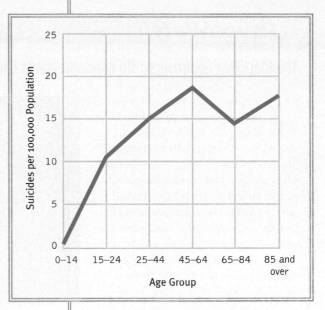

figure 7-2
Suicide and age In the United States, suicide rates keep rising up to the age of 64, then fall during the first two decades of old age, then rise again among people over the age of 84. (Information from: AFSP, 2014.)

Telling his story College student Bryce Mackie watches as his film, *Eternal High*, is played for a group of mental health professionals in Ohio. He made the film in high school, chronicling his struggle with bipolar disorder and suicidal thoughts.

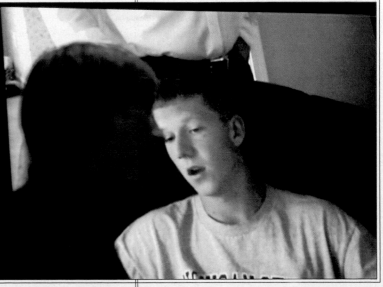

AP Photo/Ron Schwane

PsychWatch

The Black Box Controversy: Do Antidepressants Cause Suicide?

A major controversy in the clinical field is whether antidepressant drugs are highly dangerous for depressed children and teenagers. Throughout the 1990s, most psychiatrists believed that antidepressants—particularly the second-generation antidepressants—were safe and effective for children and adolescents, just as they seemed to be for adults, and they prescribed those medications readily (Cooper et al., 2014). However, after reviewing a large number of clinical reports and studying 3,300 patients on antidepressants, the U.S. Food and Drug Administration (FDA) concluded in 2004 that the drugs produce a real, though small, increase in the risk of suicidal behavior for certain children and adolescents, especially during the first few months of treatment, and it ordered that all antidepressant containers carry "black box" warnings stating that the drugs "increase the risk of suicidal thinking and behavior in children." In 2007 the FDA expanded this warning to include young adults.

Although many clinicians have been pleased by the FDA order, others worry that it may be ill-advised (Isacsson & Rich, 2014; Haliburn, 2010). They argue that while the drugs may indeed increase the risk of suicidal thoughts and attempts

Ocean/Corbis

in as many as 2 to 3 percent of young patients, the risk of suicide is actually reduced in the vast majority of children and teenagers who take the drugs (Christiansen et al., 2015; Mulder, 2010). To support this argument, they point out that the overall rate of teenage suicides decreased by 30 percent in the decade leading up to 2004, as the number of antidepressant prescriptions provided to children and teenagers was soaring (Isacsson & Rich, 2014; Isacsson et al., 2010).

The critics of the black box warnings also point to the initial effect that the warnings had on prescription patterns and teenage suicide rates in the United States and other countries. Some studies suggest that during the first two years

following the institution of the black box warnings, the number of antidepressant prescriptions fell 22 percent in the United States and the Netherlands, while the rate of teenage suicides rose 14 percent in the United States, the largest suicide rate increase since 1979 (Fawcett, 2007). Although other studies challenge these numbers (Wheeler et al., 2008), it is certainly possible that black box warnings were indirectly depriving many young patients of a medication that they truly needed to help fight depression and head off suicide. Antidepressant prescriptions for depressed teenagers now seem to be rising again, and the effect of this trend reversal on teenage suicide rates certainly awaits careful scrutiny.

A major outgrowth and benefit of the black box controversy is that the FDA recently has expanded its interest in suicidal side effects to drugs other than antidepressants. It now requires pharmaceutical companies to test for suicidal side effects in certain newly developed drugs, such as those for obesity and epilepsy, before such drugs receive FDA approval (Carey, 2008; Harris, 2008). In the past, lethal effects of this kind never came to light until well after drugs had been approved and used by millions of patients.

years. Some pro-suicide Web sites celebrate former users who have committed suicide, others help set up appointments for joint or partner suicides, and several offer specific instructions about suicide methods and locations and writing suicide notes (Daine et al., 2013; Davey, 2010). Although such sites are growing in number and influence, they do not appear to be a major factor in the rise of teenage suicide attempts—at least not yet. One study found that pro-suicide sites were visited by suicidal people relatively infrequently, whereas sites dedicated to suicide-related information, prevention, or treatment were visited very often (Kemp & Collings, 2011).

Teen Suicides: Multicultural Issues Teenage suicide rates vary by ethnicity in the United States. Around 7.5 of every 100,000 white American teenagers commit suicide each year, compared with 5 of every 100,000 African American teens and 5 of every 100,000 Hispanic American teens (Goldston et al., 2008; NAHIC, 2006). Although these numbers certainly indicate that white American teens are more prone to suicide, the rates of the three groups are in fact becoming closer (Baca-Garcia et al., 2011). This closing trend may reflect increasingly similar pressures on young African, Hispanic, and white Americans—competition for grades and college opportunities, for example, is now intense for all three groups (Barnes, 2010). The growing suicide rates for young African and Hispanic Americans may also be linked to their rising unemployment, the many anxieties and economic pressures of inner-city life, and the rage many feel over racial inequities in our society (Baca-Garcia et al., 2011; Barnes, 2010). Recent studies further indicate that 4.5 of every 100,000 Asian American teens now commit suicide each year.

The highest teenage suicide rate of all is displayed by American Indians. Currently, more than 15 of every 100,000 American Indian teenagers commit suicide each year, double the rate of white American teenagers and triple that of other minority teenagers. Clinical theorists attribute this extraordinarily high rate to factors such as the extreme poverty faced by most American Indian teens, their limited educational and employment opportunities, their particularly high rate of alcohol abuse, and the geographical isolation of those who live on reservations (Alcántara & Gone, 2008; Goldston et al., 2008). In addition, it appears that certain American Indian reservations have extreme suicide rates—called *cluster suicides*—and that teenagers who live in such communities are unusually likely to be exposed to suicide, to have their lives disrupted, to observe suicidal models, and to be at risk for suicide contagion (Bender, 2006; Chekki, 2004).

The Elderly

More than 15 of every 100,000 people over the age of 65 in the United States commit suicide, a rate that rises to 18 per 100,000 among the very elderly, as you read earlier (AFSD, 2014). Elderly people commit over 19 percent of all suicides in the United States, yet they account for only 14 percent of the total population (U.S. Census Bureau, 2014).

AP Photo/Michael Albans

Continuing trend The rate of suicide among American Indians is much higher than the national average. Here a memorial is held for a young suicide victim at a middle school on the Fort Peck Indian Reservation in Poplar, Montana.

Why do people often view the suicides of elderly or chronically sick people as less tragic than that of young or healthy people?

Many factors contribute to this high suicide rate. As people grow older, all too often they become ill, lose close friends and relatives, lose control over their lives, and lose status in our society (Draper, 2014; O'Riley et al., 2014). Such experiences may result in feelings of hopelessness, loneliness, depression, "burdensomeness," or inevitability among aged persons and so increase the likelihood that they will attempt suicide (Kim et al., 2014; Cukrowicz et al., 2011). One study found that two-thirds of particularly elderly individuals (those over 80 years old) who committed suicide had been hospitalized for medical reasons within two years preceding the suicide (Erlangsen et al., 2005), and another found a heightened rate of vascular or respiratory illnesses among elderly people who attempted suicide (Levy et al., 2011). Still other research has shown that the suicide rate of elderly people who have recently lost a spouse is particularly high (Ajdacic-Gross et al., 2008).

Elderly people are typically more determined than younger people in their decision to die and give fewer warnings, so their success rate is much higher (Dennis & Brown, 2011). An estimated one of every four elderly persons who attempts suicide succeeds (AFSD, 2014). Given the determination of aged persons and their physical decline, some people argue that older persons who want to die are clear in their thinking and should be allowed to carry out their wishes (see *InfoCentral* on the next page). However, clinical depression appears to play an important role in as many as 60 percent of suicides by the elderly, suggesting that more elderly people who are suicidal should be receiving treatment for their depressive disorders (Levy

THE RIGHT TO COMMIT SUICIDE

In ancient Greece, citizens with a grave illness or mental anguish could obtain official permission from the Senate to take their own lives (Humphry & Wickett, 1986). In contrast, most Western countries have traditionally discouraged suicide, based on their belief in the "sanctity of life" (Dickens et al., 2008). Today, however, a person's **"right to commit suicide"** is receiving more and more support from the public, particularly in connection with ending great pain and terminal illness (Breitbart et al., 2011; Werth, 2004, 2000).

WHO SUPPORTS THE RIGHT OF TERMINALLY ILL PATIENTS TO COMMIT SUICIDE?

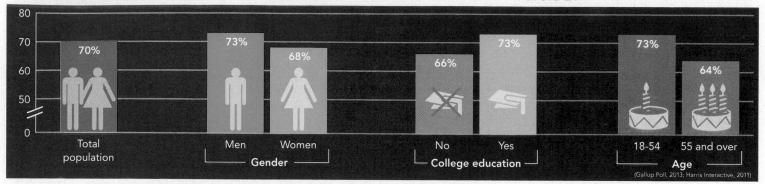

(Gallup Poll, 2013; Harris Interactive, 2011)

EUTHANASIA AND PHYSICIAN-ASSISTED SUICIDE

Euthanasia, also called "mercy killing," is the practice of killing someone who is terminally sick or badly injured to stop the suffering. Euthanasia is not necessarily initiated by the patient. **Physician-assisted suicide** is a particular form of euthanasia, in which a physician helps a patient to end his or her life, in response to the patient's request.

Should physicians provide indirect or direct assistance?

Physicians may *advise* patients about how to end their life (indirect assistance) or may *actually end* a patient's life (direct assistance). Many people who support physician-assisted suicide remain uncomfortable with the prospect of a doctor directly inducing a patient's death.

Jack Kevorkian, the Michigan physician who claimed to have assisted in the deaths of 130 progressively ill patients, was convicted of second-degree murder and sentenced to prison after he administered a lethal injection to a terminally ill patient on a *60 Minutes* broadcast in 2008.

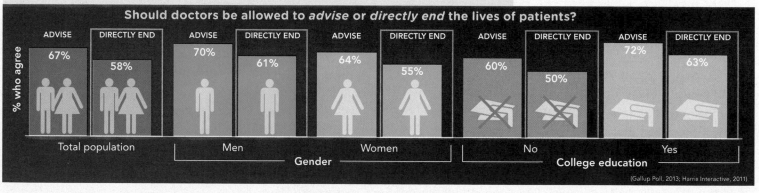

(Gallup Poll, 2013; Harris Interactive, 2011)

WHERE IS EUTHANASIA AND PHYSICIAN-ASSISTED SUICIDE LEGAL?

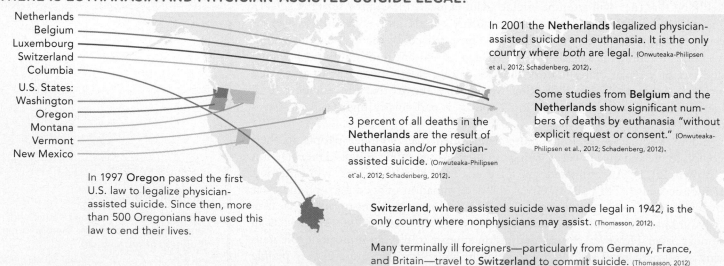

Netherlands
Belgium
Luxembourg
Switzerland
Columbia

U.S. States:
Washington
Oregon
Montana
Vermont
New Mexico

In 1997 **Oregon** passed the first U.S. law to legalize physician-assisted suicide. Since then, more than 500 Oregonians have used this law to end their lives.

3 percent of all deaths in the **Netherlands** are the result of euthanasia and/or physician-assisted suicide. (Onwuteaka-Philipsen et al., 2012; Schadenberg, 2012).

In 2001 the **Netherlands** legalized physician-assisted suicide and euthanasia. It is the only country where *both* are legal. (Onwuteaka-Philipsen et al., 2012; Schadenberg, 2012).

Some studies from **Belgium** and the **Netherlands** show significant numbers of deaths by euthanasia "without explicit request or consent." (Onwuteaka-Philipsen et al., 2012; Schadenberg, 2012).

Switzerland, where assisted suicide was made legal in 1942, is the only country where nonphysicians may assist. (Thomasson, 2012).

Many terminally ill foreigners—particularly from Germany, France, and Britain—travel to **Switzerland** to commit suicide. (Thomasson, 2012)

Lawrence Migdale/Pix

et al., 2011). In fact, research suggests that treating depression in older persons helps reduce their risk of suicide markedly (Draper, 2014).

The suicide rate among the elderly in the United States is lower in some minority groups (Joe et al., 2014; Alcántara & Gone, 2008). Although American Indians have the highest overall suicide rate, for example, the rate among elderly American Indians is relatively low. The aged are held in high esteem by American Indians and are looked to for the wisdom and experience they have acquired over the years, and this may help account for their low suicide rate. Such high regard is in sharp contrast to the loss of status often experienced by elderly white Americans.

Similarly, the suicide rate is only one-third as high among elderly African Americans as among elderly white Americans (Joe et al., 2014; Barnes, 2010). One reason for this low suicide rate may be the pressures faced by African Americans, of whom it is sometimes said: "only the strongest survive" (Seiden, 1981). Those who reach an advanced age often have overcome significant adversity, and many feel proud of what they have accomplished. Because reaching old age is not in itself a form of success for white Americans, their attitude toward aging may be more negative. Another possible explanation is that aged African Americans have successfully overcome the rage that prompts many suicides in younger African Americans.

Attitudes Toward Suicide

Hispanic and African Americans have certain beliefs that may make them less likely to attempt suicide. Both groups hold stronger moral objections to suicide than other groups do. In addition, Hispanic Americans have firmer beliefs about the need to cope and survive and feel more responsibility to their families (Oquendo et al., 2005). And African Americans have higher degrees of orthodox religious belief and personal devotion and express more concern about giving others the power to end one's life (MacDonald, 1998; Neeleman et al., 1998).

➤ *Summing Up*

IS SUICIDE LINKED TO AGE? The likelihood of suicide varies with age. It is uncommon among children, although it has been increasing in that group during the past several decades. Suicide by adolescents is more common than suicide by children, but the numbers have been decreasing over the past decade. Adolescent suicide has been linked to clinical depression, anger, impulsiveness, major stress, and adolescent life itself. Suicide attempts by this age group are numerous. The high attempt rate among adolescents and young adults may be related to the growing number and proportion of young people in the general population, the weakening of family ties, the increased availability and use of drugs among young people, and the broad media coverage of suicide attempts

(continues on the next page)

by the young. The rate of suicide among American Indian teens is twice as high as that among white American teens and three times as high as those of African, Hispanic, and Asian American teens.

In Western societies, the elderly are more likely to commit suicide than people in most other age groups. The loss of health, friends, control, and status may produce feelings of hopelessness, loneliness, depression, or inevitability in this age group.

Treatment and Suicide

Treatment of suicidal people falls into two major categories: *treatment after suicide has been attempted* and *suicide prevention*. Treatment may also be beneficial to relatives and friends of those who commit or attempt to commit suicide. Their feelings of loss, guilt, or anger after a suicide fatality or attempt can be intense (Kramer et al., 2015), but the discussion here is limited to the treatment afforded suicidal people themselves.

What Treatments Are Used After Suicide Attempts?

After a suicide attempt, most victims need medical care. Close to one-half million people in the United States are admitted to a hospital each year for injuries resulting from efforts to harm themselves (AFSP, 2014). Some are left with severe injuries, brain damage, or other medical problems. Once the physical damage is treated, psychotherapy or drug therapy may begin, on either an inpatient or outpatient basis.

Unfortunately, even after trying to kill themselves, many suicidal people fail to receive systematic follow-up care (Stanley et al., 2015). In some cases, health care professionals are at fault for this lack of follow-up. In others, the person who has attempted suicide refuses therapy. According to one review, the average number of therapy sessions attended by teenagers who receive follow-up care is 8; around 18 percent of such teens stop treatment against their therapists' advice (Spirito et al., 2011).

The goals of therapy for those who have attempted suicide are to keep the individuals alive, reduce their psychological pain, help them achieve a nonsuicidal state of mind, provide them with hope, and guide them to develop better ways of handling stress (Rudd & Brown, 2011). Various therapies have been employed, including drug, psychodynamic, cognitive-behavioral, group, and family therapies (Baldessarini & Tondo, 2011, 2007; Spirito et al., 2011). Research indicates that cognitive-behavioral therapy may be particularly helpful (Rudd et al., 2015; Brown et al., 2011, 2010). This approach focuses largely on the painful thoughts, sense of hopelessness, dichotomous thinking, poor coping skills, weak problem-solving abilities, and other cognitive and behavioral features that characterize suicidal people.

What Is Suicide Prevention?

During the past 60 years, emphasis around the world has shifted from suicide treatment to suicide prevention. In some respects this change is most appropriate: the last opportunity to keep many potential suicide victims alive comes before their first attempt.

The first **suicide prevention program** in the United States was founded in Los Angeles in 1955; the first in England, called the *Samaritans*, was started in 1953. There are now hundreds of suicide prevention centers in the United States and England. In addition, many of today's mental health centers, hospital emergency rooms, pastoral counseling centers, and poison control centers include suicide prevention programs among their services.

Working with suicide Pedestrians and police work to rescue a young woman who had attempted to drown herself in a river in 2010. Police departments across the world typically provide special crisis intervention training so that officers can develop the skills to help suicidal individuals.

Zhang Xiaoli/Color China Photo/AP Images

There are also hundreds of *suicide hotlines,* 24-hour-a-day telephone services, in the United States. Callers reach a counselor, typically a *paraprofessional*—a person trained in counseling but without a formal degree—who provides services under the supervision of a mental health professional.

Suicide prevention programs and hotlines respond to suicidal people as individuals *in crisis*—that is, under great stress, unable to cope, feeling threatened or hurt, and interpreting their situations as unchangeable. Thus the programs offer **crisis intervention:** they try to help suicidal people see their situations more accurately, make better decisions, act more constructively, and overcome their crises (Lester, 2011). Because crises can occur at any time, the centers advertise their hotlines and also welcome people who walk in without appointments (see *MindTech*).

▸ **suicide prevention program** A program that tries to identify people who are at risk of killing themselves and to offer them crisis intervention.

▸ **crisis intervention** A treatment approach that tries to help people in a psychological crisis to view their situation more accurately, make better decisions, act more constructively, and overcome the crisis.

MindTech

Crisis Texting

Suicide hotlines and drop-in centers have dominated the field of suicide prevention for decades. Over the past year or so, however, texting has emerged as an additional tool in the fight against self destruction. More and more therapists are conducting crisis intervention sessions via text, especially with young people. There are some limitations to this form of counseling, but there are also advantages, including the following (Kaufman, 2014):

What limitations or problems might result from attempts to prevent suicides by the use of texting?

(1) While it is difficult to create the personal connection that even a phone conversation with a counselor can provide, most people under 20 are very familiar—and comfortable—with texting as a form of communication (Momtaz, 2014).

(2) If a person's crisis involves an abusive situation with a family member, the person does not need to wait until he or she is alone to communicate with a counselor. The texter can be in the same room with their abuser, who might not be any the wiser (Lublin, 2014).

(3) Similarly, a person in crisis who might be out in public does not need to wait until alone to seek help. He or she can still look "cool" to peers or friends while receiving desperately needed assistance (Weichman, 2014).

(4) A session conducted by text can be interrupted and picked back up more naturally than a phone conversation. Likewise, a counselor can hand over a session to another expert with less interruption of flow than there would be in a phone conversation.

LuminaStock/Getty Images

(5) Because texts are retained, the person in crisis can go back and reread the texts during difficult moments in the future and revisit the advice and coping mechanisms discussed (Weichman, 2014). Also, saved texts may provide valuable data for researchers studying suicide trends and may lead to unanticipated treatment insights.

One nonprofit service, the Crisis Text Line in New York, has been offering text counseling since the fall of 2013, in partnership with a number of hotlines across the United States (Kaufman, 2014; Lubin, 2014). In the first half year of operation, it exchanged nearly a million texts with 19,000 teenagers, with only minimal advertising. Google now links users to the Crisis Text Line's contact information whenever they do searches for suicide-related topics. 💬

Raising public awareness In order to better educate the public about suicide's far reach, many organizations now hold special remembrances. Here the organization Active Minds sponsors an exhibit of 1,100 backpacks at Montclair State University in New Jersey. The backpacks represent the number of college students who die by suicide each year.

Some prevention centers and hotlines reach out to particular suicidal populations. The *Trevor Lifeline,* for example, is a nationwide, around-the-clock hotline available for LGBTQ (lesbian, gay, bisexual, transgender, and questioning) teenagers who are thinking about suicide. This hotline is one of several services offered by the *Trevor Foundation,* a wide-reaching organization dedicated to providing support, guidance, and information and promoting acceptance of LGBTQ teens.

The public sometimes confuses suicide prevention centers and hotlines with online chat rooms and forums (message boards) to which some suicidal people turn. However, chat rooms and forums operate quite differently, and in fact, most of them do not seek out suicidal people or try to prevent suicide. Typically, these sites are not prepared to deal with suicidal people, do not offer face-to-face support, do not involve professionals or paraprofessionals, and do not have ways of keeping out inappropriate users.

Today, suicide prevention takes place not only at prevention centers and hotlines but also in therapists' offices. Suicide experts encourage all therapists to look for and address signs of suicidal thinking in their clients, regardless of the broad reasons that the clients are seeking treatment (McGlothlin, 2008). With this in mind, a number of guidelines have been developed to help therapists effectively uncover, assess, prevent, and treat suicidal thinking and behavior in their daily work (de Beurs et al., 2015; Van Orden et al., 2008; Shneidman & Farberow, 1968).

Although specific techniques vary from therapist to therapist and from prevention center to prevention center, the approach developed originally by the Los Angeles Suicide Prevention Center continues to reflect the goals and techniques of many clinicians and organizations. During the initial contact at the center, the counselor has several tasks:

Establish a Positive Relationship As callers must trust counselors in order to confide in them and follow their suggestions, counselors try to set a positive and comfortable tone for the discussion. They convey that they are listening, understanding, interested, nonjudgmental, and available.

Understand and Clarify the Problem Counselors first try to understand the full scope of the caller's crisis and then help the person see the crisis in clear and constructive terms. In particular, they try to help callers see the central issues and the transient nature of their crises and recognize the alternatives to suicide.

Assess Suicide Potential Crisis workers at the Los Angeles Suicide Prevention Center fill out a questionnaire, often called a *lethality scale,* to estimate the caller's potential for suicide. It helps them determine the degree of stress the caller is under, the caller's relevant personality characteristics, how detailed the suicide plan is, the severity of symptoms, and the coping resources available to the caller.

Assess and Mobilize the Caller's Resources Although they may view themselves as ineffectual, helpless, and alone, people who are suicidal usually have many strengths and resources, including relatives and friends. It is the counselor's job to recognize, point out, and activate those resources.

Formulate a Plan Together the crisis worker and caller develop a plan of action. In essence, they are agreeing on a way out of the crisis, an alternative to suicidal action. Most plans include a series of follow-up counseling sessions over the next few days or weeks, either in person at the center or by phone. Each plan also requires the caller to take certain actions and make certain changes in his or her personal life. Counselors usually negotiate a *no-suicide contract* with the caller—a promise not to attempt suicide, or at least a promise to reestablish contact if the caller again considers suicide. Although such contracts are popular, their effectiveness has been called into question

BETWEEN THE LINES

Still at Risk

Approximately 4 percent of all suicides are committed by people who are inpatients at mental hospitals or other psychiatric facilities.

(Rudd et al., 2006). In addition, if callers are in the midst of a suicide attempt, counselors try to find out their whereabouts and get medical help to them immediately.

Although crisis intervention may be sufficient treatment for some suicidal people, longer-term therapy is needed for most (Lester et al., 2007). If a crisis intervention center does not offer this kind of therapy, its counselors will refer the clients elsewhere.

Yet another way to help prevent suicide may be to reduce the public's access to common means of suicide (Anestis & Anestis, 2015; Lester, 2011). In 1960, for example, around 12 of every 100,000 people in Britain killed themselves by inhaling coal gas (which contains carbon monoxide). In the 1960s, Britain replaced coal gas with natural gas (which contains no carbon monoxide) as an energy source, and by the mid-1970s the rate of coal gas suicide fell to 0 (Maris, 2001). In fact, England's overall rate of suicide dropped as well. On the other hand, the Netherlands' drop in gas-induced suicides was compensated for by an increase in other methods, particularly drug overdoses.

Similarly, ever since Canada passed a law in the 1990s restricting the availability of and access to certain firearms, there has been a decrease in firearm suicides across the country (Leenaars, 2007). Some studies suggest that this decrease has not been displaced by increases in other kinds of suicides; other studies, however, have found an increase in the use of other suicide methods (Caron et al., 2008). Thus, although many clinicians hope that measures such as gun control, safer medications, better bridge barriers, and car emission controls will lower suicide rates, there is no guarantee that they will.

Do Suicide Prevention Programs Work?

It is difficult for researchers to measure the effectiveness of suicide prevention programs (Sanburn, 2013; Lester, 2011). There are many kinds of programs, each with its own procedures and each serving populations that vary in number, age, and the like. Communities with high suicide risk factors, such as a high elderly population or economic problems, may continue to have higher suicide rates than other communities regardless of the effectiveness of their local prevention centers.

Do suicide prevention centers reduce the number of suicides in a community? Clinical researchers do not know (Sanburn, 2013). Studies comparing local suicide rates before and after the establishment of community prevention centers have yielded different findings. Some find a decline in a community's suicide rates, others no change, and still others an increase (De Leo & Evans, 2004; Leenaars & Lester, 2004). Of course, even an increase may represent a positive impact, if it is lower than the larger society's overall increase in suicidal behavior.

Do suicidal people contact prevention centers? Apparently only a small percentage do (Sanburn, 2013). Moreover, the typical caller to an urban prevention center appears to be young, African American, and female, whereas the greatest number of suicides are committed by older white men (Maris, 2001). A key problem is that people who are suicidal do not necessarily admit to or talk about their feelings in discussions with others, even professionals (Stolberg et al., 2002).

Prevention programs do seem to reduce the number of suicides among those high-risk people who do call. One study identified 8,000 high-risk individuals who contacted the Los Angeles Suicide Prevention Center (Farberow & Litman, 1970). Approximately 2 percent of these callers later committed suicide, compared with the 6 percent suicide rate usually found in similar high-risk groups. Clearly, centers need to be more visible and available to people who are thinking of suicide. The growing number of advertisements and

A different kind of military threat Concerned about the growing number of suicides by military personnel, the U.S. Army has distributed this antisuicide poster to soldiers in military bases around the country. The fear and pain of repeated military deployments has apparently been a major factor in the serious rise of depression and suicidal actions among members of the military (Nock et al., 2014).

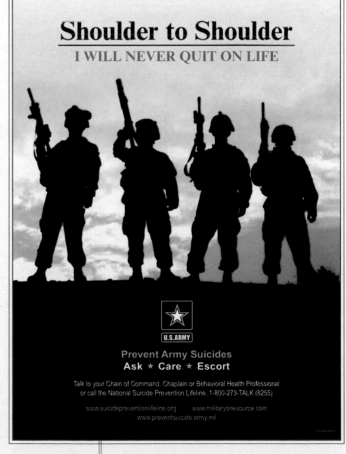

U.S. Army Public Health Command

BETWEEN THE LINES

Clinical Encounters

Suicide is the most common clinical emergency encountered in mental health practice (Stolberg et al., 2002; Beutler et al., 2000).

Suicidal behavior or thinking is the most common reason for admission to a mental hospital. Around two-thirds of patients who are admitted have aroused concern that they will harm themselves (Miret et al., 2011; Jacobson, 1999).

BETWEEN THE LINES

Highest National Suicide Rates

Lithuania (31.5 per 100,000 people)

South Korea (31)

Kazakhstan (26.9)

Belarus (25.3)

Japan (24.4)

Russia (23.5)

Guyana (22.9)

Ukraine (22.6)

(WHO, 2011)

announcements on the Web, television, radio, and billboards indicate movement in this direction.

Many theorists have called for more effective public education about suicide as the ultimate form of prevention, and a number of *suicide education programs* have emerged. Most of these programs take place in schools and concentrate on students and their teachers (Joshi et al., 2015; Schilling et al., 2014). There are also a growing number of online sites that provide education about suicide—targeting troubled persons, their family members, and friends (Lai et al., 2014). These offerings agree with the following statement by Shneidman:

> **Why might some schools be reluctant to offer suicide education programs?**

> *The primary prevention of suicide lies in education. The route is through teaching one another and . . . the public that suicide can happen to anyone, that there are verbal and behavioral clues that can be looked for . . . and that help is available. . . . In the last analysis, the prevention of suicide is everybody's business.*
>
> *(Shneidman, 1985, p. 238)*

➤ *Summing Up*

TREATMENT AND SUICIDE Treatment may follow a suicide attempt. When it does, therapists try to help the person achieve a nonsuicidal state of mind and develop better ways of handling stress and solving problems.

Over the past 60 years, emphasis has shifted to suicide prevention. Suicide prevention programs include 24-hour-a-day hotlines and walk-in centers staffed largely by paraprofessionals. During their initial contact with a suicidal person, counselors try to establish a positive relationship, understand and clarify the problem, assess the potential for suicide, assess and mobilize the caller's resources, and formulate a plan for overcoming the crisis. Beyond such crisis intervention, most suicidal people also need longer-term therapy. In a still broader attempt at prevention, suicide education programs for the public are on the increase.

PUTTING IT...*together*

Psychological and Biological Insights Lag Behind

Once a mysterious and hidden problem that was hardly acknowledged by the public and barely investigated by professionals, suicide today is the focus of much attention. During the past 40 years in particular, investigators have learned a great deal about this life–or–death problem.

In contrast to most other problems covered in this textbook, suicide has received much more examination from the sociocultural model than from any other. Sociocultural theorists have, for example, highlighted the importance of societal change and stress, national and religious affiliation, marital status, gender, race, and the mass media. The insights and information gathered by psychological and biological researchers have been more limited.

Although sociocultural factors certainly shed light on the general background and triggers of suicide, they typically leave us unable to predict that a given person will attempt suicide. Clinicians do not yet fully understand why some people kill themselves while others in similar circumstances manage to find better ways of addressing their problems. Psychological and biological insights must catch up to the sociocultural insights if clinicians are truly to understand suicide.

Treatments for suicide also pose some difficult problems. Clinicians have yet to develop clearly successful therapies for suicidal people. Although suicide prevention programs certainly show the clinical field's commitment to helping those who are suicidal, it is not yet clear how much such programs actually reduce the overall risk or rate of suicide.

At the same time, the growth in the amount of research on suicide offers great promise. And perhaps most promising of all, clinicians are now enlisting the public in the fight against this problem. They are calling for broader public education about suicide—for programs aimed at both young and old. It is reasonable to expect that the current commitment will lead to a better understanding of suicide and to more successful interventions. Such goals are of importance to everyone. Although suicide itself is typically a lonely and desperate act, the impact of such acts is very broad indeed.

KEY TERMS

parasuicide, p. 222

suicidal behavior disorder, p. 222

suicide, p. 222

death seeker, p. 224

death initiator, p. 224

death ignorer, p. 224

death darer, p. 224

subintentional death, p. 224

nonsuicidal self injury, p. 224

retrospective analysis, p. 226

hopelessness, p. 229

dichotomous thinking, p. 229

postvention, p. 231

Thanatos, p. 232

egoistic suicide, p. 233

altruistic suicide, p. 233

anomic suicide, p. 233

serotonin, p. 234

suicide prevention program, p. 242

suicide hotline, p. 243

paraprofessional, p. 243

crisis intervention, p. 243

suicide education program, p. 246

QuickQuiz

1. Define suicide and subintentional death. Describe four different kinds of people who attempt suicide. What is nonsuicidal self-injury? *pp. 222–225*

2. What techniques do researchers use to study suicide? *p. 226*

3. How do statistics on suicide vary according to country, religion, gender, marital status, and race? *pp. 226–227*

4. What kinds of immediate and long-term stressors have been linked to suicide? *pp. 227–228*

5. What other conditions or events may help trigger suicidal acts? *pp. 228–231*

6. How do psychodynamic, sociocultural, and biological theorists explain suicide, and how well supported are their theories? *pp. 232–235*

7. Compare the risk, rate, and causes of suicide among children, adolescents, and elderly persons. *pp. 235–241*

8. How do theorists explain the high rate of suicide attempts by adolescents and young adults? *pp. 236–239*

9. Describe the nature and goals of treatment given to people after they have attempted suicide. Do such people often receive this treatment? *p. 242*

10. Describe the principles of suicide prevention programs. What procedures are used by counselors in these programs? How effective are the programs? *pp. 242–246*

Visit *LaunchPad*

www.macmillanhighered.com/launchpad/comerfund8e
to access the e-book, new interactive case studies, videos, activities, and LearningCurve quizzes, as well as study aids including flashcards, FAQs, and research exercises.

 Macmillan Education LaunchPad

Ed Fairburn

Disorders Featuring Somatic Symptoms

I t was Wednesday. The big day. Midterms in history and physics back to back, beginning at 11:30, and an oral presentation in psych at 3:30. Jarell had been preparing for, and dreading, this day for weeks, calling it "D-Day" to his friends. He had been up until 3:30 A.M. the night before, studying, trying to nail everything down. It seemed like he had fallen asleep only minutes ago, yet here it was 9:30 A.M. and the killer day was under way.

As soon as he woke, Jarell felt a tight pain grip his stomach. He also noticed buzzing in his ears, a lightheadedness, and even aches throughout his body. He wasn't surprised, given the day he was about to face. One test might bring a few butterflies of anxiety; two and a presentation were probably good for a platoon of dragonflies.

As he tried to get going, however, Jarell began to suspect that this was more than butterflies. His stomach pain soon turned to spasms, and his lightheadedness became outright dizziness. He could barely make it to the bathroom without falling. Thoughts of breakfast made him nauseous. He knew he couldn't keep anything down.

Jarell began to worry, even panic. This was hardly the best way to face what was in store for him today. He tried to shake it off, but the symptoms stayed. Finally, his roommate convinced him that he had better go to a doctor. At 10:30, just an hour before the first exam, he entered the big brick building called "Student Health." He felt embarrassed, like a wimp, but what could he do? Persevering and taking two tests under these conditions wouldn't prove anything—except maybe that he was foolish.

Psychological factors may contribute to somatic, or bodily, illnesses in a variety of ways. The physician who sees Jarell has some possibilities to sort out. Jarell could be *faking* his pain and dizziness to avoid taking some tough tests. Alternatively, he may be *imagining* his illness, that is, faking to himself. Or he could be *overreacting* to his pain and dizziness. Then again, his physical symptoms could be both real and significant, yet triggered by *stress*: whenever he feels extreme pressure, such as a person can feel before an important test, Jarell's gastric juices may become more active and irritate his intestines, and his blood pressure may rise and cause him to become dizzy. Finally, he may be coming down with the flu. Even this "purely medical" problem, however, could be linked to psychological factors. Perhaps weeks of constant worry about the exams and presentation have weakened Jarell's body so that he was not able to fight off the flu virus. Whatever the diagnosis, Jarell's state of mind is affecting his body. The physician's view of the role played by psychological factors will in turn affect the treatment Jarell receives.

You have observed throughout the book that psychological disorders frequently have physical causes. Abnormal neurotransmitter activity, for example, contributes to generalized anxiety disorder, panic disorder, and posttraumatic stress disorder. Is it surprising, then, that bodily illnesses may have psychological causes? Today's clinicians recognize the wisdom of Socrates' fourth century B.C.E. assertion: "You should not treat body without soul."

The idea that psychological factors may contribute to somatic illnesses has ancient roots, yet it had few proponents before the twentieth century. It

▶**factitious disorder** A disorder in which a person feigns or induces physical symptoms, typically for the purpose of assuming the role of a sick person.

was particularly unpopular during the Renaissance, when medicine began to be a physical science and scientists became committed to the pursuit of objective "fact" (Conti, 2014). At that time, the mind was considered the territory of priests and philosophers, not of physicians and scientists. By the seventeenth century, French philosopher René Descartes went so far as to claim that the mind, or soul, is totally separate from the body—a position called *mind-body dualism*. Over the course of the twentieth century, however, numerous studies convinced medical and clinical researchers that psychological factors such as stress, worry, and perhaps even unconscious needs can contribute in major ways to bodily illness.

DSM-5 lists a number of psychological disorders in which bodily symptoms or concerns are the primary features of the disorders. These include *factitious disorder*, in which patients intentionally produce or feign physical symptoms; *conversion disorder*, which is characterized by medically unexplained physical symptoms that affect voluntary motor or sensory functioning; *somatic symptom disorder*, in which people become disproportionately concerned, distressed, and disrupted by bodily symptoms; *illness anxiety disorder*, in which people who are anxious about their health become preoccupied with the notion that they are seriously ill despite the absence of bodily symptoms; and *psychological factors affecting other medical conditions*, disorders in which psychological factors adversely affect a person's general medical condition.

Factitious Disorder

Like Jarell, people who become physically sick usually go to a physician. Sometimes, however, the physician cannot find a medical cause for the problem and may suspect that other factors are involved. Perhaps the patient is *malingering*—intentionally feigning illness to achieve some external gain, such as financial compensation or deferment from military service (Crighton et al., 2014).

Alternatively, a patient may intentionally produce or feign physical symptoms from a wish to be a patient; that is, the motivation for assuming the sick role may be the role itself (Baig et al., 2015). Physicians would then decide that the patient is manifesting **factitious disorder** (see Table 8-1). Consider, for example, the symptoms of this lab technician:

> A 29-year-old female laboratory technician was admitted to the medical service via the emergency room because of bloody urine. The patient said that she was being treated for lupus erythematosus by a physician in a different city. She also mentioned that she had had Von Willebrand's disease (a rare hereditary blood disorder) as a child. On the third day of her hospitalization, a medical student mentioned to the resident that she had seen this patient several weeks before at a different hospital in the area, where the patient had been admitted for the same problem. A search of the patient's belongings revealed a cache of anticoagulant medication. When confronted with this information she refused to discuss the matter and hurriedly signed out of the hospital against medical advice.
>
> (Spitzer et al., 1981, p. 33)

Factitious disorder is known popularly as *Munchausen syndrome*, a label derived from the exploits of Baron von Münchhausen, an eighteenth-century cavalry officer who journeyed from tavern to tavern in Europe telling fantastical tales about his supposed military adventures (Ayoub, 2010). People with factitious disorder often go to extremes to create the appearance of illness (APA, 2013). Many give themselves medications secretly. Some, like the woman just described, inject drugs to cause bleeding (Mucha et al., 2014). Still others use laxatives to produce chronic diarrhea.

table: 8-1

Dx Checklist

Factitious Disorder Imposed on Self

1. False creation of physical or psychological symptoms, or deceptive production of injury or disease, even without external rewards for such ailments.

2. Presentation of oneself as ill, damaged, or hurt.

Factitious Disorder Imposed on Another

1. False creation of physical or psychological symptoms, or deceptive production of injury or disease, in another person, even without external rewards for such ailments.

2. Presentation of another person (victim) as ill, damaged, or hurt.

(Information from: APA, 2013)

"You're not ill yet, Mr. Blandell, but you've got potential."

High fevers are especially easy to create. In a classic study of patients with prolonged mysterious fever, more than 9 percent were eventually diagnosed with factitious disorder (Feldman et al., 1994).

People with factitious disorder often research their supposed ailments and are impressively knowledgeable about medicine (Miner & Feldman, 1998). Many eagerly undergo painful testing or treatment, even surgery (McDermott et al., 2012). When confronted with evidence that their symptoms are factitious, they typically deny the charges and leave the hospital; they may enter another hospital the same day.

Clinical researchers have had a hard time determining the prevalence of factitious disorder, since patients with the disorder hide the true nature of their problem (Kenedi, Sames, & Paice, 2013). Overall, the pattern appears to be more common in women than men. Men, however, may more often have severe cases. The disorder usually begins during early adulthood.

Factitious disorder seems to be particularly common among people who (1) received extensive treatment for a medical problem as children, (2) carry a grudge against the medical profession, or (3) have worked as a nurse, laboratory technician, or medical aide. A number have poor social support, few enduring social relationships, and little family life (McDermott et al., 2012; Feldman et al., 1994).

The precise causes of factitious disorder are not understood (Lawlor & Kirakowski, 2014), although clinical reports have pointed to factors such as depression, unsupportive parental relationships during childhood, and an extreme need for social support that is not otherwise available (McDermott et al., 2012; Ozden & Canat, 1999; Feldman et al., 1995, 1994). Nor have clinicians been able to develop dependably effective treatments for this disorder.

Psychotherapists and medical practitioners often report feelings of annoyance or anger toward people with factitious disorder, feeling that these people are, at the very least, wasting their time. Yet people with the disorder feel they have no control over the problem, and they often experience great distress.

In a related pattern, *factitious disorder imposed on another*, known popularly as *Munchausen syndrome by proxy*, parents or caretakers make up or produce physical illnesses in their children, leading in some cases to repeated painful

//// BETWEEN THE LINES ////

In Their Words

"I would rather have anything wrong with my body than something wrong with my head."

Sylvia Plath, *The Bell Jar*

Should society treat or punish those parents who produce Munchausen syndrome by proxy in their children?

diagnostic tests, medication, and surgery (Koetting, 2015; Ayoub, 2010). If the children are removed from their parents and placed in the care of others, their symptoms disappear (see *PsychWatch*).

➤ Summing Up

FACTITIOUS DISORDER People with factitious disorder feign or induce physical disorders, typically for the purpose of assuming the role of a sick person. The disorder is neither well understood nor well treated. In a related pattern, factitious disorder imposed on another, a parent fabricates or induces a physical illness in his or her child.

PsychWatch

Munchausen Syndrome by Proxy

Tanya, a mere 8 years old, had been hospitalized 127 times over the past five years and undergone 28 different medical procedures—from removal of her spleen to exploratory surgery of her intestines. Two months ago, her mother was arrested, charged with child endangerment. When Tanya's grandmother gently tried to talk to the girl about her mother's arrest (or, as she put, "Mommy's going away"), Tanya was upset and confused. "I miss Mommy so much. She's the best person in the world. She spent all her time with me in the hospital. She made the doctors pay attention to me. They say Mommy was making me feel bad, putting bad stuff in my tube. But there's no way Mommy made me feel bad."

Convalescent, 1867, by Frank Holl

Frank Holl, Convalescent. Private Collection © Christopher Wood Gallery, London, UK/Bridgeman Images

Cases like Tanya's have horrified the public and called attention to *Munchausen syndrome by proxy*. This form of factitious disorder is caused by a caregiver who uses various techniques to induce symptoms in a child—giving the child drugs, tampering with medications, contaminating a feeding tube, or even smothering the child, for example. The illness can take almost any form, but the most common symptoms are bleeding, seizures, asthma, comas, diarrhea, vomiting, "accidental" poisonings, infections, fevers, and sudden infant death syndrome.

Between 6 and 30 percent of the victims of Munchausen syndrome by proxy die as a result of their symptoms, and 8 percent of those who survive are permanently disfigured or physically impaired (Flaherty & Macmillan, 2013; Ayoub, 2006). Psychological, educational, and physical development are also affected (Bass & Glaser, 2014; Schreier et al., 2010).

The syndrome is very hard to diagnose and may be more common than clinicians once thought (Ashraf & Thevasagayam, 2014; Feldman, 2004). The parent (usually the mother) seems to be so devoted and caring that others sympathize with and admire her. Yet the physical problems disappear when the child and parent are separated (Koetting, 2015; Scheuerman et al., 2013). In many cases, siblings of the sick child are also victimized (Ayoub, 2010, 2006).

What kind of parent carefully inflicts pain and illness on her own child? The typical Munchausen mother is emotionally needy: she craves the attention and praise she receives for her devoted care of her sick child (Asraf & Thevasagayam, 2014; Noeker, 2004). She may have little social support outside the medical system. Often the mothers have a medical background of some kind—perhaps having worked formerly in a doctor's office. A number have medically unexplained physical problems of their own (Bass & Glaser, 2014). Typically they deny their actions, even in the face of clear evidence, and refuse to undergo therapy (Bluglass, 2001).

Law enforcement authorities approach Munchausen syndrome by proxy as a crime—a carefully planned form of child abuse (Flaherty & Macmillan, 2013; Schreier et al., 2010). They almost always require that the child be separated from the mother (Koetting, 2015; Ayoub, 2010, 2006). At the same time, a parent who resorts to such actions is seriously disturbed and greatly in need of clinical help. Thus clinical researchers and practitioners must now work to develop clearer insights and more effective treatments for such parents and their young victims.

Conversion Disorder and Somatic Symptom Disorder

When a bodily ailment has an excessive and disproportionate impact on the person, has no apparent medical cause, or is inconsistent with known medical diseases, physicians may suspect a *conversion disorder* or a *somatic symptom disorder*. Consider the plight of Brian:

> Brian was spending Saturday sailing with his wife, Helen. The water was rough but well within what they considered safe limits. They were having a wonderful time and really didn't notice that the sky was getting darker, the wind blowing harder, and the sailboat becoming more difficult to control. After a few hours of sailing, they found themselves far from shore in the middle of a powerful and dangerous storm.
>
> The storm intensified very quickly. Brian had trouble controlling the sailboat amidst the high winds and wild waves. He and Helen tried to put on the safety jackets they had neglected to wear earlier, but the boat turned over before they were finished. Brian, the better swimmer of the two, was able to swim back to the overturned sailboat, grab the side, and hold on for dear life, but Helen simply could not overcome the rough waves and reach the boat. As Brian watched in horror and disbelief, his wife disappeared from view.
>
> After a time, the storm began to lose its strength. Brian managed to right the sailboat and sail back to shore. Finally he reached safety, but the personal consequences of this storm were just beginning. The next days were filled with pain and further horror: the Coast Guard finding Helen's body . . . texts, emails, and conversations with family members and friends . . . self-blame . . . grief . . . and more. Compounding this horror, the accident had left Brian with a severe physical impairment—he could not walk properly. He first noticed this terrible impairment when he sailed the boat back to shore, right after the accident. As he tried to run from the sailboat to get help, he could hardly make his legs work. By the time he reached the nearby beach restaurant, all he could do was crawl. Two patrons had to lift him to a chair, and after he told his story and the authorities were alerted, he had to be taken to a hospital.
>
> At first Brian and the hospital physician assumed that he must have been hurt during the accident. One by one, however, the hospital tests revealed nothing—no broken bones, no spinal damage, nothing. Nothing that could explain such severe impairment.
>
> By the following morning, the weakness in his legs had become near paralysis. Because the physicians could not pin down the nature of his injuries, they decided to keep his activities to a minimum. He was not allowed to talk long with the police. To his deep regret, he was not even permitted to attend Helen's funeral.
>
> The mystery deepened over the following days and weeks. As Brian's paralysis continued, he became more and more withdrawn, unable to see more than a few friends and family members and unable to take care of the many unpleasant tasks attached to Helen's death. He could not bring himself to return to work or get on with his life. Texting, emailing, and phone conversations slowly came to a halt. At most, he was able to go online and surf the Internet. Almost from the beginning, Brian's paralysis had left him self-absorbed and drained of emotion, unable to look back and unable to move forward.

Conversion Disorder

Eventually, Brian received a diagnosis of **conversion disorder** (see Table 8-2). People with this disorder display physical symptoms that affect voluntary motor or sensory functioning, but the symptoms are inconsistent with known medical diseases (APA, 2013). In short, they have neurological-like symptoms—for example, paralysis, blindness, or loss of feeling—that have no neurological basis.

▸ **conversion disorder** A disorder in which a person's bodily symptoms affect his or her voluntary motor and sensory functions, but the symptoms are inconsistent with known medical diseases.

table: **8-2**

Dx Checklist

Conversion Disorder

1. Presence of at least one symptom or deficit that affects voluntary or sensory function.

2. Symptoms are found to be inconsistent with known neurological or medical disease.

3. Significant distress or impairment.

(Information from: APA, 2013)

Conversion disorder often is hard, even for physicians, to distinguish from a genuine medical problem (Ali et al., 2015; Parish & Yutzy, 2011). In fact, it is always possible that a diagnosis of conversion disorder is a mistake and that the patient's problem has an undetected neurological or other medical cause (de Schipper et al., 2014). Because conversion disorders are so similar to "genuine" medical ailments, physicians sometimes rely on oddities in the patient's medical picture to help distinguish the two (Boone, 2011). The symptoms of a conversion disorder may, for example, be at odds with the way the nervous system is known to work. In a conversion symptom called *glove anesthesia,* numbness begins sharply at the wrist and extends evenly right to the fingertips. As Figure 8-1 shows, real neurological damage is rarely as abrupt or evenly spread out.

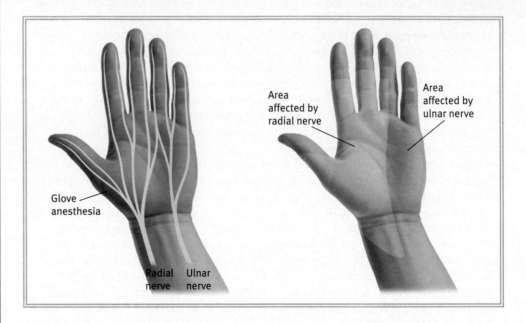

figure 8-1

Glove anesthesia In this conversion symptom (left), the entire hand, extending from the fingertips to the wrist, becomes numb. Actual physical damage (right) to the ulnar nerve, in contrast, causes anesthesia in the ring finger and little finger and beyond the wrist partway up the arm; damage to the radial nerve causes loss of feeling only in parts of the ring, middle, and index fingers and the thumb and partway up the arm. (Information from: Gray, 1959.)

The physical effects of a conversion disorder may also differ from those of the corresponding medical problem (Ali et al., 2015; Scheidt et al., 2014). For example, when paralysis from the waist down, or paraplegia, is caused by damage to the spinal cord, a person's leg muscles may *atrophy,* or waste away, unless physical therapy is applied. The muscles of people whose paralysis is the result of a conversion disorder, in contrast, do not usually atrophy. Perhaps those with a conversion disorder exercise their muscles without being aware that they are doing so. Similarly, people with conversion blindness have fewer accidents than people who are organically blind, an indication that they have at least some vision even if they are unaware of it.

Unlike people with factitious disorder, those with conversion disorder do not consciously want or purposely produce their symptoms. Like Brian, they almost always believe that their problems are genuinely medical (Lahman et al., 2010). This pattern is called "conversion" disorder because clinical theorists used to believe that individuals with the disorder are converting psychological needs or conflicts into their neurological-like symptoms. Although some theorists still believe that conversion is at work in the disorder, others prefer alternative kinds of explanations, as you'll see later.

Conversion disorder usually begins between late childhood and young adulthood; it is diagnosed at least twice as often in women as in men (Raj et al., 2014). It typically appears suddenly, at times of extreme stress, and lasts a matter of weeks (Kukla et al., 2010). Some research suggests that people who develop the disorder tend to be generally suggestible (see *MindTech* on the next page); many are highly susceptible to hypnotic procedures, for example (Parish & Yutzy, 2011; Roelofs et al., 2002). It is thought to be a rare problem, occurring in at most 5 of every 1,000 persons.

▶ **somatic symptom disorder** A disorder in which people become excessively distressed, concerned, and anxious about bodily symptoms that they are experiencing, and their lives are greatly and disproportionately disrupted by the symptoms.

MindTech

Can Social Media Spread "Mass Hysteria"?

In Chapter 1, you read about outbreaks during the Middle Ages of *mass madness,* also called *mass hysteria* or *mass psychogenic illness,* in which large numbers of people would share psychological or physical maladies that had no apparent cause (see page 9). Periodic outbreaks of mysterious illnesses are not a thing of the past. In fact, the number of such cases currently seems to be on the increase (Vitelli, 2013). Most of today's clinicians consider these outbreaks to be a form of conversion disorder.

New Zealand sociologist Robert Bartholomew (2014) has been studying mass psychogenic illnesses that date back over 400 years, and he argues that social media is a major factor in the current increase. One notable 2011 outbreak in Le Roy, New York, demonstrates the suggestive role played by social media (Vitelli, 2013; Dominus, 2012). A local high school student began having facial spasms. After several weeks, others started having similar symptoms, and eventually 18 girls from the high school were affected. Apparently, a number of these teenagers began to show symptoms after they saw a YouTube video featuring a girl from a nearby town who had significant tics. Doctors eventually concluded that this was an example of mass psychogenic illness.

An unusual aspect of the Le Roy case that further points to the likely role of social media is that in addition to the 18 high school girls, a 36-year-old woman with no connection to the teenage girls also began having the same symptoms during the same period of time (NBC, 2012). She stated that she first saw the facts of the case on a Facebook post.

This case mirrors others in recent years, such as an outbreak of hiccups and vocal tics in early 2013 among teenagers in Danvers, Massachusetts, and the case of 400 garment workers in a Bangladesh factory who had severe gastrointestinal symptoms for which there was ultimately no physical explanation (Vitelli, 2013). In these and other cases, the symptoms seemed to be spread, at least in part, by social media exposure.

Bartholomew (2014) believes that due to the power of social media, future outbreaks of mass psychogenic illness may be more numerous, wide ranging, and severe than any yet recorded. He observes that in the distant past "the local priests, who were . . . summoned to [treat mass psychogenic illnesses], faced a daunting task . . . but they were fortunate in one regard: they did not have to contend with mobile phones, Twitter, and Facebook." 💬

Science Source

Coming around again? This lithograph depicts Saint Vitus' Dance, a widespread form of mass psychogenic illness during the Middle Ages, characterized by rapid, uncoordinated, jerking movements of the face, feet, and hands. Similar symptoms were on display in Le Roy, New York, in 2011, during an outbreak of mass psychogenic illness attributed to the impact of social media.

> **In what ways could social media itself help to prevent or reduce cases of mass psychogenic illness?**

Somatic Symptom Disorder

People with **somatic symptom disorder** become excessively distressed, concerned, and anxious about bodily symptoms that they are experiencing, and their lives are greatly disrupted by the symptoms (APA, 2013) (see Table 8-3 on the next page). The symptoms last longer but are less dramatic than those found in conversion disorder. In some cases, the somatic symptoms have no known cause; in others,

table: 8-3

Dx Checklist

Somatic Symptom Disorder

1. Person experiences at least one upsetting or repeatedly disruptive physical (somatic) symptom.

2. Person experiences an unreasonable number of thoughts, feelings, and behaviors regarding the nature or implications of the physical symptoms, including one of the following:

   (a) Repeated, excessive thoughts about their seriousness.

   (b) Continual high anxiety about their nature or health implications.

   (c) Disproportionate amounts of time and energy spent on the symptoms or their health implications.

3. Physical symptoms usually continue to some degree for more than 6 months.

(Information from: APA, 2013)

the cause can be identified. Either way, the person's concerns are disproportionate to the seriousness of the bodily problems.

Two patterns of somatic symptom disorder have received particular attention. In one, sometimes called a *somatization pattern*, the individual experiences a large and varied number of bodily symptoms. In the other, called a *predominant pain pattern*, the person's primary bodily problem is the experience of pain.

Somatization Pattern Sheila baffled medical specialists with the wide range of her symptoms:

> Sheila reported having abdominal pain since age 17, necessitating exploratory surgery that yielded no specific diagnosis. She had several pregnancies, each with severe nausea, vomiting, and abdominal pain; she ultimately had a hysterectomy for a "tipped uterus." Since age 40 she had experienced dizziness and "blackouts," which she eventually was told might be multiple sclerosis or a brain tumor. She continued to be bedridden for extended periods of time, with weakness, blurred vision, and difficulty urinating. At age 43 she was worked up for a hiatal hernia because of complaints of bloating and intolerance of a variety of foods. She also had additional hospitalizations for neurological, hypertensive, and renal workups, all of which failed to reveal a definitive diagnosis.
>
> *(Spitzer et al., 1994, 1981, pp. 185, 260)*

Like Sheila, people with a somatization pattern of somatic symptom disorder experience many long-lasting physical ailments—ailments that typically have little or no physical basis. This pattern, first described by Pierre Briquet in 1859, is also known as *Briquet's syndrome*. A sufferer's ailments often include pain symptoms (such as headaches or chest pain), gastrointestinal symptoms (such as nausea or diarrhea), sexual symptoms (such as erectile or menstrual difficulties), and neurological-type symptoms (such as double vision or paralysis).

People with a somatization pattern usually go from doctor to doctor in search of relief. They often describe their many symptoms in dramatic and exaggerated terms. Most also feel anxious and depressed (Taycan et al., 2014; Dimsdale & Creed, 2010). The pattern typically lasts for many years, fluctuating over time but rarely disappearing completely without therapy (Parish & Yutzy, 2011; Abbey, 2005).

"I can't watch. It makes me sick." These fans are "watching" the 2010 World Cup match between Spain and Germany. The stress of big games in soccer and other sports causes many fans to develop a range of physical symptoms, such as fainting, throwing up, stomach pain, headaches, and chest pains. No wonder these people closed their eyes as the tension mounted.

© Tobias Schwarz /Reuters/Corbis

Between 0.2 and 2.0 percent of all women in the United States may experience a somatization pattern in any given year, compared with less than 0.2 percent of men (North, 2005; APA, 2000). The pattern often runs in families; as many as 20 percent of the close female relatives of women with the pattern also develop it. It usually begins between adolescence and young adulthood.

Predominant Pain Pattern If the primary feature of somatic symptom disorder is pain, the person is said to have a predominant pain pattern. Patients with conversion disorder or another pattern of somatic symptom disorder may also experience pain, but it is the key symptom in this pattern. The source of the pain may be known or unknown. Either way, the concerns and disruption produced by the pain are disproportionate to its severity and seriousness.

Although the precise prevalence has not been determined, this pattern appears to be fairly common (Nickel et al., 2010). It may begin at any age, and women seem more likely than men to experience it (APA, 2000). Often it develops after an accident or during an illness that has caused genuine pain, which then takes on a life of its own. For example, Laura, a 36-year-old woman, reported pains that went far beyond the usual symptoms of her tubercular disease, called sarcoidosis:

> *Before the operation I would have little joint pains, nothing that really bothered me that much. After the operation I was having severe pains in my chest and in my ribs, and those were the type of problems I'd been having after the operation, that I didn't have before. . . . I'd go to an emergency room at night, 11:00, 12:00, 1:00 or so. I'd take the medicine, and the next day it stopped hurting, and I'd go back again. In the meantime this is when I went to the other doctors, to complain about the same thing, to find out what was wrong; and they could never find out what was wrong with me either. . . .*
>
> *. . . At certain points when I go out or my husband and I go out, we have to leave early because I start hurting. . . . A lot of times I just won't do things because my chest is hurting for one reason or another. . . . Two months ago when the doctor checked me and another doctor looked at the x-rays, he said he didn't see any signs of the sarcoid then and that they were doing a study now, on blood and various things, to see if it was connected to sarcoid. . . .*
>
> *(Green, 1985, pp. 60–63)*

What Causes Conversion and Somatic Symptom Disorders?

For many years, conversion and somatic symptom disorders were referred to as *hysterical* disorders. This label was meant to convey the prevailing belief that excessive and uncontrolled emotions underlie the bodily symptoms found in these disorders.

Why do the terms "hysteria" and "hysterical" currently have such negative connotations in our society?

Work by Ambroise-Auguste Liébault and Hippolyte Bernheim in the late nineteenth century helped foster the notion that such psychological factors were at the root of hysterical disorders. These researchers founded the Nancy School in Paris for the study and treatment of mental disorders. There they were able to produce hysterical symptoms in normal people—deafness, paralysis, blindness, and numbness—by hypnotic suggestion, and they could remove the symptoms by the same means (see Chapter 1). If hypnotic suggestion could both produce and reverse physical dysfunctioning, they concluded, hysterical disorders might themselves be caused by psychological processes.

Today's leading explanations for conversion and somatic symptom disorders come from the psychodynamic, behavioral, cognitive, and multicultural models. None has received much research support, however, and the disorders are still poorly understood.

The Psychodynamic View As you read in Chapter 1, Freud's theory of psychoanalysis began with his efforts to explain hysterical symptoms. Indeed, he was one of the few clinicians of his day to treat patients with these symptoms seriously, as people with genuine problems. After studying hypnosis in Paris, Freud became interested in the work of an older physician, Josef Breuer (1842–1925). Breuer had successfully used hypnosis to treat a woman he called Anna O., who suffered from hysterical deafness, disorganized speech, and paralysis (Ellenberger, 1972). On the basis of this and similar cases, Freud (1894) came to believe that hysterical disorders represented a *conversion* of underlying emotional conflicts into physical symptoms and concerns.

Observing that most of his patients with hysterical disorders were women, Freud centered his explanation of such disorders on the needs of girls during their *phallic stage* (ages 3 through 5). At that time in life, he believed, all girls develop a pattern of desires called the *Electra complex:* each girl experiences sexual feelings for her father and at the same time recognizes that she must compete with her mother for his affection. However, aware of her mother's more powerful position and of cultural taboos, the child typically represses her sexual feelings and rejects these early desires for her father.

Freud believed that if a child's parents overreact to her sexual feelings—with strong punishments, for example—the Electra conflict will be unresolved and the child may reexperience sexual anxiety throughout her life. Whenever events trigger sexual feelings, she may feel an unconscious need to hide them from both herself and others. Freud concluded that some women hide their sexual feelings by unconsciously converting them into physical symptoms and concerns.

Hero Images/Getty Images

Electra complex goes awry Freud argued that a hysterical disorder may result when parents overreact to their daughter's early displays of affection for her father, by repeatedly punishing her, for example. The child may go on to exhibit sexual repression in adulthood and convert sexual feelings into physical ailments.

Most of today's psychodynamic theorists take issue with parts of Freud's explanation of conversion and somatic symptom disorders (Nickel et al., 2010), but they continue to believe that sufferers of the disorders have unconscious conflicts carried forth from childhood, which arouse anxiety, and that they convert this anxiety into "more tolerable" physical symptoms (Brown et al., 2005).

Psychodynamic theorists propose that two mechanisms are at work in these disorders—primary gain and secondary gain. People derive **primary gain** when their bodily symptoms keep their internal conflicts out of awareness. During an argument, for example, a man who has underlying fears about expressing anger may develop a conversion paralysis of the arm, thus preventing his feelings of rage from reaching consciousness. People derive **secondary gain** when their bodily symptoms further enable them to avoid unpleasant activities or to receive sympathy from others. When, for example, a conversion paralysis allows a soldier to avoid combat duty or conversion blindness prevents the breakup of a relationship, secondary gain may be at work. Similarly, the conversion paralysis of Brian, the man who lost his wife in the boating accident, seemed to help him avoid many painful duties after the accident, such as attending her funeral and returning to work.

The Behavioral View Behavioral theorists propose that the physical symptoms of conversion and somatic symptom disorders bring *rewards* to sufferers (see Table 8-4). Perhaps the symptoms remove those with the disorders from an unpleasant relationship, or perhaps the symptoms bring attention from other people (Witthöft & Hiller, 2010). In response to such rewards, the sufferers learn to display the bodily

▶ **primary gain** In psychodynamic theory, the gain people derive when their somatic symptoms keep their internal conflicts out of awareness.

▶ **secondary gain** In psychodynamic theory, the gain people derive when their somatic symptoms elicit kindness from others or provide an excuse to avoid unpleasant activities.

table: **8-4**

Disorders That Have Somatic Symptoms

Disorder	Voluntary Control of Symptoms?	Symptoms Linked to Psychosocial Factor?	An Apparent Goal?
Malingering	Yes	Maybe	Yes
Factitious disorder	Yes	Yes	No*
Conversion disorder	No	Yes	Maybe
Somatic symptom disorder	No	Yes	Maybe
Illness anxiety disorder	No	Yes	No
Psychophysiological disorder	No	Yes	No
Physical illness	No	Maybe	No

*Except for medical attention.

symptoms more and more prominently. Behaviorists also hold that people who are familiar with an illness will more readily adopt its physical symptoms. In fact, studies find that many sufferers develop their bodily symptoms after they or their close relatives or friends have had similar medical problems (Marshall et al., 2007).

Clearly, the behavioral focus on the role of rewards is similar to the psychodynamic notion of secondary gain. The key difference is that psychodynamic theorists view the gains as indeed secondary—that is, as gains that come only after underlying conflicts produce the disorders. Behaviorists view them as the primary cause of the development of the disorders.

Like the psychodynamic explanation, the behavioral view of conversion and somatic symptom disorders has received little research support. Even clinical case reports only occasionally support this position. In many cases the pain and upset that surround the disorders seem to outweigh any rewards the symptoms might bring.

The Cognitive View

Some cognitive theorists propose that conversion and somatic symptom disorders are forms of *communication*, providing a means for people to express emotions that would otherwise be difficult to convey (Koo et al., 2014; Hallquist et al., 2010). Like their psychodynamic colleagues, these theorists hold that the emotions of people with the disorders are being converted into physical symptoms. They suggest, however, that the purpose of the conversion is not to defend against anxiety but to communicate extreme feelings—anger, fear, depression, guilt, jealousy—in a "physical language" that is familiar and comfortable for the person with the disorder.

According to this view, people who find it particularly hard to recognize or express their emotions are candidates for conversion and somatic symptom disorders. So are those who "know" the language of physical symptoms through firsthand experience with a genuine physical ailment. Because children are less able to express their emotions verbally, they are particularly likely to develop physical symptoms as a form of communication (Shaw et al., 2010). Like the other explanations, this cognitive view has not been widely tested or supported by research.

The Multicultural View

Most Western clinicians believe that it is inappropriate to produce or focus excessively on somatic symptoms in response to personal

The positive side of swearing Famous English soccer player Wayne Rooney yells out in pain after being struck by a ball in the groin. Research indicates that swearing can help reduce pain, and not just pain on display in conversion and somatic symptom disorders, but even pain like Rooney's (Stephens et al., 2009).

Martin Rickett/Press Association via AP Images

Mind over matter The opposite of somatic symptom disorder are instances in which people "ignore" pain or other physical symptoms. Here a London performance artist smiles comfortably while her skin is pierced with sharp hooks that help suspend her from the ceiling above. Her action was part of a protest to end shark finning—the practice of cutting off a shark's fin and throwing its still-living body back into the sea so that the fin can be used in the production of shark fin soup (a food delicacy) and other goods.

AP Photo/Lefteris Pitarakis

distress (Shaw et al., 2010; So, 2008; Escobar, 2004). That is, in part, why conversion and somatic symptom disorders are included in DSM-5. Some theorists believe, however, that this position reflects a Western bias—a bias that sees somatic reactions as an *inferior* way of dealing with emotions (Moldavsky, 2004; Fábrega, 1990).

In fact, the transformation of personal distress into somatic complaints is the norm in many non-Western cultures (Draguns, 2006; Kleinman, 1987). In such cultures, the formation of such complaints is viewed as a socially and medically correct—and less stigmatizing—reaction to life's stressors. Studies have found very high rates of stress-caused bodily symptoms in non-Western medical settings throughout the world, including those in China, Korea, Japan, and Arab countries (Zhou et al., 2015; Matsumoto & Juang, 2008). People throughout Latin America seem to display the most somatic reactions (Escobar, 2004, 1995; Escobar et al., 1998, 1992). Even within the United States, Hispanic Americans display more somatic reactions in the face of stress than do other populations.

The lesson to be learned from such multicultural findings is not that somatic reactions to stress are superior to psychological ones or vice versa, but rather, once again, that both bodily and psychological reactions to life events are often influenced by one's culture. Overlooking this point can lead to knee-jerk mislabels or misdiagnoses.

How Are Conversion and Somatic Symptom Disorders Treated?

People with conversion and somatic symptom disorders usually seek psychotherapy only as a last resort. They believe that their problems are completely medical and at first reject all suggestions to the contrary (Lahmann et al., 2010). When a physician tells them that their symptoms or concerns have a psychological dimension, they often go to another physician. Eventually, however, many patients with these disorders do consent to psychotherapy, psychotropic drug therapy, or both (Raj et al., 2014).

Many therapists focus on the *causes* of these disorders (the trauma or anxiety tied to the physical symptoms) and apply insight, exposure, and drug therapies (Ali et al., 2015; Boone, 2011). Psychodynamic therapists, for example, try to help those with somatic symptoms become conscious of and resolve their underlying fears, thus eliminating the need to convert anxiety into physical symptoms (Nickel et al., 2010; Hawkins, 2004). Alternatively, behavioral therapists use exposure treatments. They expose clients to features of the horrific events that first triggered their physical symptoms, expecting that the clients will become less anxious over the course of repeated exposures and more able to face those upsetting events directly rather than through physical channels (Stuart et al., 2008). And biological therapists use antianxiety drugs or certain antidepressant drugs to help reduce the anxiety of clients with conversion and somatic symptom disorders (Raj et al., 2014).

Other therapists try to address the *physical symptoms* of these disorders rather than the causes, using techniques such as suggestion, reinforcement, or confrontation (Ali et al., 2015; Parish & Yutzy, 2011). Those who employ *suggestion* offer emotional support to patients and tell them persuasively (or hypnotically) that their physical symptoms will soon disappear (Hallquist et al., 2010; Lahmann et al., 2010). Therapists who take a *reinforcement* approach arrange for the removal of rewards for

///// BETWEEN THE LINES /////

Diagnostic Confusion

Many medical problems with vague or confusing symptoms—multiple sclerosis, hyperparathyroidism, lupus, and chronic fatigue syndrome are examples—frequently have been misdiagnosed as conversion or somatic symptom disorder. In the past, whiplash was regularly misdiagnosed in this way (Shaw et al., 2010; Ferrari, 2006; Nemecek, 1996).

a client's "sickness" symptoms and an increase of rewards for healthy behaviors (Raj et al., 2014; North, 2005). And therapists who take a *confrontational* approach try to force patients out of the sick role by straightforwardly telling them that their bodily symptoms are without medical basis (Sjolie, 2002). Researchers have not fully evaluated the effects of these particular approaches on conversion and somatic symptom disorders (Martlew, Pulman, & Marson, 2014; Boone, 2011).

▶ **illness anxiety disorder** A disorder in which people are chronically anxious about and preoccupied with the notion that they have or are developing a serious medical illness, despite the absence of somatic symptoms. Previously known as *hypochondriasis*.

➤ *Summing Up*

CONVERSION DISORDER AND SOMATIC SYMPTOM DISORDER Conversion disorder involves bodily symptoms that affect voluntary motor and sensory functions, but the symptoms are inconsistent with known medical diseases. Diagnosticians are sometimes able to distinguish conversion disorder from a "true" medical problem by observing oddities in the patient's medical picture. In somatic symptom disorder, people become excessively distressed, concerned, and anxious about bodily symptoms that they are experiencing, and their lives are greatly and disproportionately disrupted by the symptoms.

Freud developed the initial psychodynamic view of conversion and somatic symptom disorders, proposing that the disorders represent a conversion of underlying emotional conflicts into physical symptoms. According to behaviorists, the physical symptoms of these disorders bring rewards to the sufferer, and such reinforcement helps maintain the symptoms. Some cognitive theorists propose that the disorders are forms of communication and that people express their emotions through their physical symptoms. Treatments for these disorders include insight, exposure, and drug therapies and may include techniques such as suggestion, reinforcement, or confrontation.

Illness Anxiety Disorder

People with **illness anxiety disorder,** previously known as *hypochondriasis,* are chronically anxious about their health and are convinced that they have or are developing a serious medical illness, despite the absence of somatic symptoms (see Table 8-5). They repeatedly check their body for signs of illness and misinterpret various bodily events as signs of serious medical problems. Typically the events are merely normal bodily changes, such as occasional coughing, sores, or sweating. Those with illness anxiety disorder persist in such misinterpretations no matter what friends, relatives, and physicians say. Many of these individuals recognize that their concerns are excessive, but many do not.

Although illness anxiety disorder can begin at any age, it starts most often in early adulthood, among men and women in equal numbers. Between 1 and 5 percent of all people experience the disorder (Weck et al., 2015; Abramowitz & Braddock, 2011). Their symptoms tend to rise and fall over the years. Physicians report seeing many cases (Dimsdale et al., 2011). As many as 7 percent of all patients seen by primary care physicians may display the disorder.

Theorists typically explain illness anxiety disorder much as they explain various anxiety disorders (see Chapter 4). Behaviorists, for example, believe that the illness fears are acquired through classical conditioning or modeling (Marshall et al., 2007). Cognitive theorists suggest that people with the disorder are so sensitive to and threatened by bodily cues that they come to misinterpret them (Witthöft & Hiller, 2010).

People with illness anxiety disorder usually receive the kinds of treatments that are used to treat obsessive-compulsive disorder (see pages 139–142). Studies reveal, for example, that clients with the disorder often improve considerably when given

table: 8-5

Dx Checklist
Illness Anxiety Disorder
1. Person is preoccupied with thoughts about having or getting a significant illness. In reality, person has no or, at most, mild somatic symptoms.
2. Person has easily triggered, high anxiety about health.
3. Person displays unduly high number of health-related behaviors (e.g., keeps focusing on body) or dysfunctional health-avoidance behaviors (e.g., avoids doctors).
4. Person's concerns continue to some degree for at least 6 months.
(Information from: APA, 2013)

▶ **psychophysiological disorders** Disorders in which biological, psychological, and sociocultural factors interact to cause or worsen a physical illness. Also known as *psychological factors affecting other medical conditions*.

▶ **ulcer** A lesion that forms in the wall of the stomach or of the duodenum.

▶ **asthma** A medical problem marked by narrowing of the trachea and bronchi, which results in shortness of breath, wheezing, coughing, and a choking sensation.

▶ **insomnia** Difficulty falling or staying asleep.

▶ **muscle contraction headache** A headache caused by a narrowing of muscles surrounding the skull. Also known as *tension headache*.

▶ **migraine headache** A severe, near-paralyzing headache that occurs on one side of the head.

table: 8-6

Dx Checklist

Psychological Factors Affecting Other Medical Conditions

1. The presence of a medical condition.

2. Psychological factors negatively affect the medical condition by:
   - Affecting the course of the medical condition.
   - Providing obstacles for the treatment of the medical condition.
   - Posing new health risks.
   - Triggering or worsening the medical condition.

(Information from: APA, 2013)

the same *antidepressant drugs* that are helpful in cases of obsessive-compulsive disorder (Bouman, 2008). Many clients also improve when treated with the behavioral approach of *exposure and response prevention* (Weck et al., 2015). In this approach, the therapists repeatedly point out bodily variations to the clients while, at the same time, preventing them from seeking their usual medical attention. In addition, cognitive therapists guide the clients to identify, challenge, and change their beliefs about illness that are helping to maintain their disorder.

➤ *Summing Up*

ILLNESS ANXIETY DISORDER People with illness anxiety disorder are chronically anxious about and preoccupied with the notion that they have or are developing a serious medical illness, despite the absence of substantial somatic symptoms. Theorists explain this disorder much as they do anxiety disorders. Treatment includes drug, behavioral, and cognitive approaches originally developed for obsessive-compulsive disorder.

Psychophysiological Disorders: Psychological Factors Affecting Other Medical Conditions

About 85 years ago, clinicians identified a group of physical illnesses that seemed to be caused or worsened by an *interaction* of biological, psychological, and sociocultural factors (Dunbar, 1948; Bott, 1928). Early editions of the DSM labeled these illnesses **psychophysiological,** or **psychosomatic, disorders,** but DSM-5 labels them as **psychological factors affecting other medical conditions** (see Table 8-6). The more familiar term "psychophysiological" will be used in this chapter.

It is important to recognize that significant medical symptoms and conditions are involved in psychophysiological disorders and that the disorders often result in serious physical damage (APA, 2013). They are different from the factitious, conversion, and illness anxiety disorders that are accounted for primarily by psychological factors.

Traditional Psychophysiological Disorders

Before the 1970s, clinicians believed that only a limited number of illnesses were psychophysiological. The best known and most common of these disorders were ulcers, asthma, insomnia, chronic headaches, high blood pressure, and coronary heart disease. Recent research, however, has shown that many other physical illnesses—including bacterial and viral infections—may also be caused by an interaction of psychosocial and physical factors. Let's look first at the traditional psychophysiological disorders and then at the illnesses that are newer to this category.

Ulcers are lesions (holes) that form in the wall of the stomach or of the duodenum, resulting in burning sensations or pain in the stomach, occasional vomiting, and stomach bleeding. More than 25 million people in the United States have ulcers at some point during their lives, and ulcers cause an estimated 6,500 deaths each year (Stratemeier & Vignogna, 2014). Ulcers often are caused by an interaction of stress factors, such as environmental pressure or intense feelings of anger or anxiety (see Figure 8-2), and physiological factors, such as the bacteria *H. pylori* (Marks, 2014; Fink, 2011).

Asthma causes the body's airways (the trachea and bronchi) to narrow periodically, making it hard for air to pass to and from the lungs. The resulting symptoms are shortness of breath, wheezing, coughing, and a terrifying choking sensation. Some 235 million people in the world—25 million in the United States alone—currently suffer from asthma (WHO, 2013; Akinbami et al., 2011), and most were children or young teenagers at the time of the first attack. Seventy percent of all cases appear to be caused by an interaction of stress factors, such as environmental pressures or anxiety, and physiological factors, such as allergies to specific substances, a slow-acting sympathetic nervous system, or a weakened respiratory system (CDC, 2013; Dhabhar, 2011).

Insomnia, difficulty falling asleep or maintaining sleep, plagues more than one-third of the population each year (Heffron, 2014). Although many of us have temporary bouts of insomnia that last a few nights or so, a large number of people—10 percent of the population—have insomnia that lasts months or years (see *InfoCentral* on the next page). Chronic insomniacs feel as though they are almost constantly awake. They often are very sleepy during the day and may have difficulty functioning. Their problem may be caused by a combination of psychosocial factors, such as high levels of anxiety or depression, and physiological problems, such as an overactive arousal system or certain medical ailments (Trauer et al., 2015; Belleville et al., 2011).

Chronic headaches are frequent intense aches of the head or neck that are not caused by another physical disorder. There are two major types. **Muscle contraction,** or **tension, headaches** are marked by pain at the back or front of the head or the back of the neck. These occur when the muscles surrounding the skull tighten, narrowing the blood vessels. Approximately 45 million Americans suffer from such headaches (CDC, 2010).

Migraine headaches are extremely severe, often nearly paralyzing headaches that are located on one side of the head and are sometimes accompanied by dizziness, nausea, or vomiting. Migraine headaches are thought by some medical theorists to develop in two phases: (1) blood vessels in the brain narrow, so that the flow of blood to parts of the brain is reduced, and (2) the same blood vessels later expand, so that blood flows through them rapidly, stimulating many neuron endings and causing pain. Twenty-three million people in the United States suffer from migraines.

Research suggests that chronic headaches are caused by an interaction of stress factors, such as environmental pressures or general feelings of helplessness, anger, anxiety, or depression, and physiological factors, such as abnormal activity of the

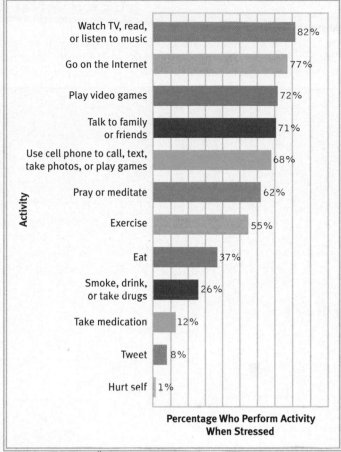

Percentage Who Perform Activity When Stressed

figure 8-2

What do people do to relieve stress? According to surveys, most of us go on the Internet, watch television, read, or listen to music. Tweeting is on the rise. (Information from: IWS, 2011; Pew Research Center, 2011, 2010; MHA, 2008; NPD Group, 2008.)

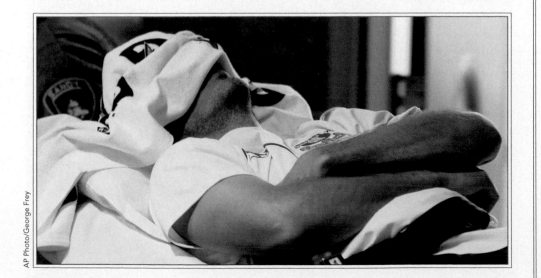

More than head pain Beyond intense head pain, the symptoms of migraine headaches may range from dizziness, nausea, and vomiting to physical ailments that virtually paralyze the individual. Here soccer star Freddie Ljungberg is taken from the Major League Soccer All-Star game to a nearby hospital in 2009. A long-time migraine sufferer, he lost his vision temporarily as a consequence of a migraine that he developed during the game.

SLEEP AND SLEEP DISORDERS

Sleep is a naturally recurring state that features altered conscious- ness, suspension of voluntary bodily functions, muscle relaxation, and reduced perception of environmental stimuli. Researchers have acquired much data about the stages, cycles, brain waves, and mechanics of sleep, but they do not fully understand its precise purpose. We do know, however, that humans and other animals need sleep to survive and function properly.

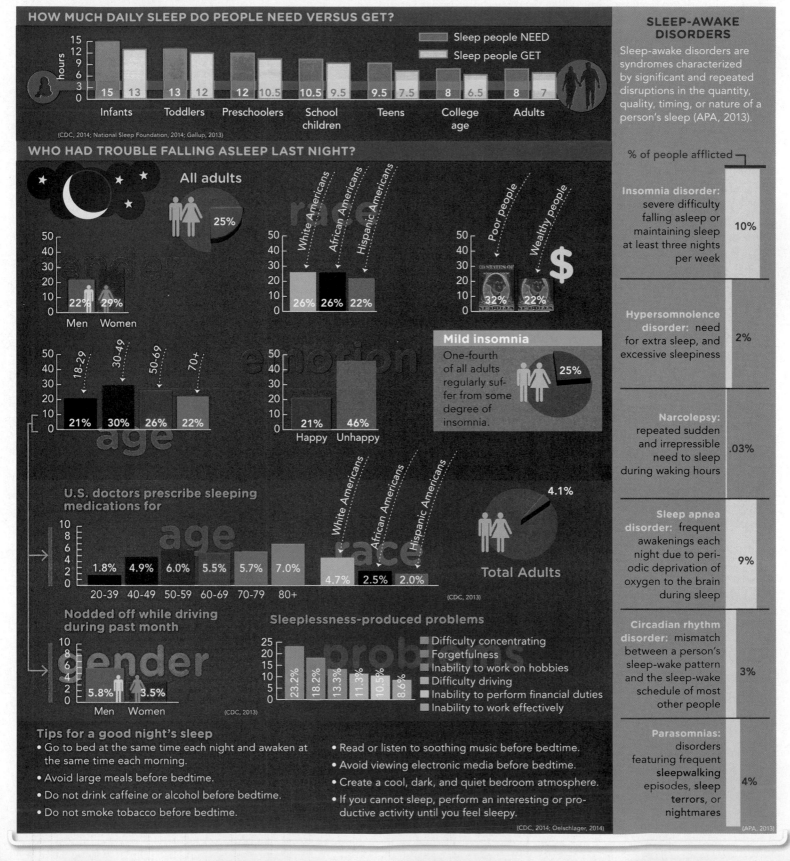

HOW MUCH DAILY SLEEP DO PEOPLE NEED VERSUS GET?

Sleep people NEED
Sleep people GET

	Infants	Toddlers	Preschoolers	School children	Teens	College age	Adults
NEED	15	13	12	10.5	9.5	8	8
GET	13	12	10.5	9.5	7.5	6.5	7

(CDC, 2014; National Sleep Foundation, 2014; Gallup, 2013)

WHO HAD TROUBLE FALLING ASLEEP LAST NIGHT?

All adults 25%

Men 22% Women 29%

White Americans 26% African Americans 26% Hispanic Americans 22%

Poor people 32% Wealthy people 22%

18-29 21% 30-49 30% 50-69 26% 70+ 22%

Happy 21% Unhappy 46%

Mild insomnia
One-fourth of all adults regularly suf- fer from some degree of insomnia. 25%

U.S. doctors prescribe sleeping medications for

20-39 1.8% 40-49 4.9% 50-59 6.0% 60-69 5.5% 70-79 5.7% 80+ 7.0%

White Americans 4.7% African Americans 2.5% Hispanic Americans 2.0%

Total Adults 4.1%

(CDC, 2013)

Nodded off while driving during past month

Men 5.8% Women 3.5%

(CDC, 2013)

Sleeplessness-produced problems

- Difficulty concentrating 23.2%
- Forgetfulness 18.2%
- Inability to work on hobbies 13.3%
- Difficulty driving 11.3%
- Inability to perform financial duties 10.5%
- Inability to work effectively 8.6%

Tips for a good night's sleep

- Go to bed at the same time each night and awaken at the same time each morning.
- Avoid large meals before bedtime.
- Do not drink caffeine or alcohol before bedtime.
- Do not smoke tobacco before bedtime.
- Read or listen to soothing music before bedtime.
- Avoid viewing electronic media before bedtime.
- Create a cool, dark, and quiet bedroom atmosphere.
- If you cannot sleep, perform an interesting or pro- ductive activity until you feel sleepy.

(CDC, 2014; Oelschlager, 2014)

SLEEP-AWAKE DISORDERS

Sleep-awake disorders are syndromes characterized by significant and repeated disruptions in the quantity, quality, timing, or nature of a person's sleep (APA, 2013).

% of people afflicted

Insomnia disorder: severe difficulty falling asleep or maintaining sleep at least three nights per week — 10%

Hypersomnolence disorder: need for extra sleep, and excessive sleepiness — 2%

Narcolepsy: repeated sudden and irrepressible need to sleep during waking hours — .03%

Sleep apnea disorder: frequent awakenings each night due to peri- odic deprivation of oxygen to the brain during sleep — 9%

Circadian rhythm disorder: mismatch between a person's sleep-wake pattern and the sleep-wake schedule of most other people — 3%

Parasomnias: disorders featuring frequent sleepwalking episodes, sleep terrors, or nightmares — 4%

(APA, 2013)

neurotransmitter serotonin, vascular problems, or muscle weakness (Bruffaerts et al., 2015; Young & Skorga, 2011; Engel, 2009).

Hypertension is a state of chronic high blood pressure. That is, the blood pumped through the body's arteries by the heart produces too much pressure against the artery walls. Hypertension has few outward signs, but it interferes with the proper functioning of the entire cardiovascular system, greatly increasing the likelihood of stroke, heart disease, and kidney problems. It is estimated that 75 million people in the United States have hypertension, thousands die directly from it annually, and millions more perish because of illnesses caused by it (CDC, 2014, 2011). Around 10 percent of all cases are caused by physiological abnormalities alone; the rest result from a combination of psychological and physiological factors and are called *essential hypertension*. Some of the leading psychosocial causes of essential hypertension are constant stress, environmental danger, and general feelings of anger or depression. Physiological factors include obesity, smoking, poor kidney function, and an unusually high proportion of the gluey protein *collagen* in a person's blood vessels (Hu et al., 2015; Brooks et al., 2011).

Coronary heart disease is caused by a blocking of the *coronary arteries,* the blood vessels that surround the heart and are responsible for carrying oxygen to the heart muscle. The term actually refers to several problems, including blockage of the coronary arteries and *myocardial infarction* (a "heart attack"). In the United States, nearly 18 million people have some form of coronary heart disease. It is the leading cause of death for both men and women in the nation, accounting for 600,000 deaths each year, around 40 percent of all deaths (CDC, 2014; AHA, 2011). The majority of all cases of coronary heart disease are related to an interaction of psychosocial factors, such as job stress or high levels of anger or depression, and physiological factors, such as high cholesterol, obesity, hypertension, smoking, or lack of exercise (Rhéaume et al., 2015; Bekkouche et al., 2011).

> **What jobs and/or lifestyles in our society might be particularly stressful and traumatizing?**

▶ **hypertension** Chronic high blood pressure.

▶ **coronary heart disease** Illness of the heart caused by a blockage in the coronary arteries.

What Factors Contribute to Psychophysiological Disorders?

Over the years, clinicians have identified a number of variables that may generally contribute to the development of psychophysiological disorders. The variables can be grouped as biological, psychological, and sociocultural factors.

BIOLOGICAL FACTORS You saw in Chapter 5 that one way the brain activates body organs is through the operation of the *autonomic nervous system* (*ANS*), the network of nerve fibers that connect the central nervous system to the body's organs. Defects in this system are believed to contribute to the development of psychophysiological disorders (Lundberg, 2011; Hugdahl, 1995). If one's ANS is stimulated too easily, for example, it may overreact to situations that most people find only mildly stressful, eventually damaging certain organs and causing a psychophysiological disorder. Other more specific biological problems may also contribute to psychophysiological disorders. A person with a weak gastrointestinal system, for example, may be a prime candidate for an ulcer, whereas someone with a weak respiratory system may develop asthma readily.

In a related vein, people may display "favored" biological reactions that raise their chances of developing psychophysiological disorders. Some individuals perspire in response to stress, others develop stomachaches, and still others have a rise in blood pressure (Lundberg, 2011). Research has indicated, for example, that some people are particularly likely to have temporary rises in blood pressure when stressed (Su et al., 2014). It may be that they are prone to develop hypertension.

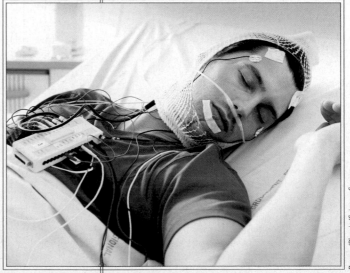

Studying sleep Clinicians and researchers use special techniques to assess and learn about sleep and sleep disorders. This man is undergoing a *polysomnographic* examination, a procedure that measures a person's physiological activity during sleep, including measurements of lung, heart, and brain activity.

Burger/Phanie/Science Source

"I'm sure it's nothing."

Bruce Eric Kaplan/The New Yorker Collection/www.cartoonbank.com

PSYCHOLOGICAL FACTORS According to many theorists, certain needs, attitudes, emotions, or coping styles may cause people to overreact repeatedly to stressors and thus increase their chances of developing psychophysiological disorders (Williams et al., 2011). Researchers have found, for example, that men with a *repressive coping style* (a reluctance to express discomfort, anger, or hostility) tend to have a particularly sharp rise in blood pressure and heart rate when they are stressed (Trapp et al., 2014).

Another personality style that may contribute to psychophysiological disorders is the **Type A personality style,** an idea introduced a half-century ago by two cardiologists, Meyer Friedman and Ray Rosenman (1959). People with this style are said to be consistently angry, cynical, driven, impatient, competitive, and ambitious. They interact with the world in a way that, according to Friedman and Rosenman, produces continual stress and often leads to coronary heart disease. People with a **Type B personality style,** by contrast, are thought to be more relaxed, less aggressive, and less concerned about time and thus are less likely to develop cardiovascular deterioration.

The link between the Type A personality style and coronary heart disease has been supported by many studies. In one well-known investigation of more than 3,000 people, Friedman and Rosenman (1974) separated healthy men in their forties and fifties into Type A and Type B categories and then followed their health over the next eight years. More than twice as many Type A men developed coronary heart disease. Later studies found that Type A functioning correlates similarly with heart disease in women (Haynes et al., 1980).

Recent studies indicate that the link between the Type A personality style and heart disease may not be as strong as the earlier studies suggested. These studies do suggest, however, that several of the characteristics that supposedly make up the Type A style, particularly *hostility* and *time urgency,* may indeed be strongly related to heart disease (Allan, 2014; Williams et al., 2013).

SOCIOCULTURAL FACTORS: THE MULTICULTURAL PERSPECTIVE Adverse social conditions may set the stage for psychophysiological disorders (Su et al., 2014). Such conditions produce ongoing stressors that trigger and interact with the biological and personality factors just discussed. One of society's most negative social conditions, for example, is poverty. In study after study, it has been found that relatively wealthy people have fewer psychophysiological disorders, better health in general, and better health outcomes than poor people (Singh & Siahpush, 2014; Chandola & Marmot, 2011). One obvious reason for this relationship is that poorer people typically experience higher rates of crime, unemployment, overcrowding, and other negative stressors than wealthier people. In addition, they typically receive inferior medical care.

The relationship between race and psychophysiological and other health problems is complicated. On the one hand, as one might expect from the economic trends just discussed, African Americans have more such problems than do white Americans. African Americans have, for example, higher rates of high blood pressure, diabetes, and asthma (Wang et al., 2014; CDC, 2011). They are also more likely than white Americans to die of heart disease and stroke. Certainly, economic factors may help explain this racial difference. Many African Americans live in poverty; those who do often must contend with the high rates of crime and unemployment that often result in poor health conditions (Greer et al., 2014).

Research further suggests that the high rate of psychophysiological and other medical disorders among African Americans probably extends beyond economic factors. Consider, for example, the finding that 42 percent of African Americans have high blood pressure, compared with 29 percent of white Americans (CDCP, 2011). Although this difference may be explained in part by the dangerous environments

▶ **Type A personality style** A personality pattern characterized by hostility, cynicism, drivenness, impatience, competitiveness, and ambition.

▶ **Type B personality style** A personality pattern in which a person is more relaxed, less aggressive, and less concerned about time.

in which so many African Americans live and the unsatisfying jobs at which so many must work (Gilbert et al., 2011), other factors may also be operating. A physiological predisposition among African Americans may, for example, increase their risk of developing high blood pressure. Or it may be that repeated experiences of racial discrimination constitute special stressors that help raise the blood pressure of African Americans (Dolezsar et al., 2014) (see Figure 8-3). In fact, some recent investigations have found that the more discrimination people experience over a one-year period, the greater their daily rise in blood pressure (Smart-Richman et al., 2010).

Looking at the health picture of African Americans, one might expect to find a similar trend among Hispanic Americans. After all, a high percentage of Hispanic Americans also live in poverty, are exposed to discrimination, are affected by high rates of crime and unemployment, and receive inferior medical care (BLS, 2015; Travis & Meltzer, 2008). However, despite such disadvantages, the health of Hispanic Americans is, on average, at least as good and often better than that of both white Americans and African Americans (CDC, 2015). As you can see in Table 8-7, for example, Hispanic Americans have lower rates of high blood pressure, high cholesterol, asthma, and cancer than white Americans or African Americans do.

The relatively positive health picture for Hispanic Americans in the face of clear economic disadvantage has been referred to in the clinical field as the "Hispanic Health Paradox." Generally, researchers are puzzled by this pattern, but a few explanations have been offered. It may be, for example, that the strong emphasis on social relationships, family support, and religiousness that often characterize Hispanic American cultures increase health resilience among their members (Dubowitz et al., 2010; Gallo et al., 2009), or Hispanic Americans may have a physiological predisposition that improves their likelihood of having better health outcomes.

New Psychophysiological Disorders

Clearly, biological, psychological, and sociocultural factors combine to produce psychophysiological disorders. In fact, the interaction of such factors is now considered the *rule* of bodily functioning, not the exception. As the years have passed, more and more illnesses have been added to the list of traditional psychophysiological disorders, and researchers have found many links between psychosocial stress and a wide range of physical illnesses. Let's look at how these links were established and then at *psychoneuroimmunology*, the area of study that ties stress and illness to the body's immune system.

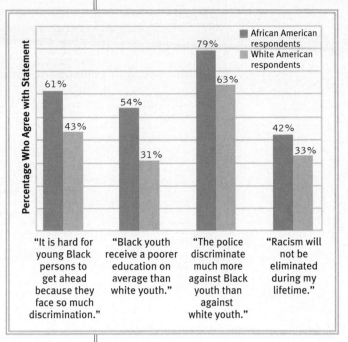

figure 8-3

How much discrimination do racial minority teenagers face? It depends on who's being asked the question. In a recent survey of 1,590 teenagers and young adults, African American respondents were more likely than white American respondents to recognize that African American teens experience various forms of discrimination. (Information from: Black Youth Project, 2011.)

table: **8-7**

Dx Checklist

Prevalence of Medical Disorders Among U.S. Racial Groups

	High Blood Pressure	High Cholesterol	Diabetes	Asthma	Cancer
African Americans	42%	24%	16%	13%	5%
White Americans	29%	30%	11%	11%	8%
Hispanic Americans	21%	20%	11%	9%	3%

(Information from: CDCP, 2011; Mendes, 2010)

table: **8-8**

Most Stressful Life Events

Adults: Social Readjustment Rating Scale*

1. Death of spouse
2. Divorce
3. Marital separation
4. Jail term
5. Death of close family member
6. Personal injury or illness
7. Marriage
8. Fired at work
9. Marital reconciliation
10. Retirement
11. Change in health of family member
12. Pregnancy

*Full scale has 43 items.
(Reprinted from *Journal of Psychosomatic Research*, Vol. 11, Holmes, T. H., & Rahe, R. H., The Social Readjustment Rating Scale, 213–218, Copyright 1967, with permission from Elsevier.)

Students: Undergraduate Stress Questionnaire†

1. Death (family member or friend)
2. Had a lot of tests
3. It's finals week
4. Applying to graduate school
5. Victim of a crime
6. Assignments in all classes due the same day
7. Breaking up with boy/girlfriend
8. Found out boy/girlfriend cheated on you
9. Lots of deadlines to meet
10. Property stolen
11. You have a hard upcoming week
12. Went into a test unprepared

†Full scale has 83 items.
(Information from: Crandall, C. S., Preisler, J. J., & Aussprung, J. (1992). Measuring life event stress in the lives of college students: The Undergraduate Stress Questionnaire (USQ). *Journal of Behavioral Medicine*, 15(6), 627–662.)

Are Physical Illnesses Related to Stress? Back in 1967 two researchers, Thomas Holmes and Richard Rahe, developed the *Social Readjustment Rating Scale,* which assigns numerical values to the stresses that most people experience at some time in their lives (see Table 8-8). Answers given by a large sample of participants indicated that the most stressful event on the scale is the death of a spouse, which receives a score of 100 *life change units* (*LCUs*). Lower on the scale is retirement (45 LCUs), and still lower is a minor violation of the law (11 LCUs). This scale gave researchers a yardstick for measuring the total amount of stress a person faces over a period of time. If, for example, in the course of a year a woman started a new business (39 LCUs), sent her son off to college (29 LCUs), moved to a new house (20 LCUs), and had a close friend die (37 LCUs), her stress score for the year would be 125 LCUs, a considerable amount of stress for such a period of time.

With this scale in hand, Holmes and Rahe (1989, 1967) examined the relationship between life stress and the onset of illness. They found that the LCU scores of sick people during the year before they fell ill were much higher than those of healthy people. If a person's life changes totaled more than 300 LCUs over the course of a year, he or she was particularly likely to develop serious health problems.

Using the Social Readjustment Rating Scale or similar scales, studies have since linked stresses of various kinds to a wide range of physical conditions, from trench mouth and upper respiratory infections to cancer (Baum et al., 2011; Rook et al., 2011) (see *MediaSpeak* on page 270). Overall, the greater the amount of life stress, the greater the likelihood of illness. Researchers even have found a relationship between traumatic stress and death. Widows and widowers, for example, display an increased risk of death during their period of bereavement (Moon et al., 2014; Möller et al., 2011).

▶ **psychoneuroimmunology** The study of the connections between stress, the body's immune system, and illness.

▶ **immune system** The body's network of activities and cells that identify and destroy antigens and cancer cells.

▶ **antigen** A foreign invader of the body, such as a bacterium or virus.

▶ **lymphocytes** White blood cells that circulate through the lymph system and bloodstream, helping the body identify and destroy antigens and cancer cells.

Student stress-busters: East and West According to research, frequent testing is the second most stressful life event for high school and college students. To reduce such stress, college applicants from Beijing give one another head massages in preparation for China's college entrance exams (left). In the meantime, students at a dorm at Northwestern University in the United States try to blow off steam by performing "primal screams" during their final exam period (right).

One shortcoming of Holmes and Rahe's Social Readjustment Rating is that it does not take into consideration the particular life stress reactions of specific populations. For example, in their development of the scale, the researchers sampled white Americans predominantly. Few of the respondents were African Americans or Hispanic Americans. But since their ongoing life experiences often differ in key ways, might not members of minority groups and white Americans differ in their stress reactions to various kinds of life events? Research indicates that indeed they do (Bennett & Olugbala, 2010; Johnson, 2010). One study found, for example, that African Americans experience greater stress than white Americans in response to a major personal injury or illness, a major change in work responsibilities, or a major change in living conditions (Komaroff et al., 1989, 1986). Similarly, studies have shown that women and men differ in their reactions to a number of life changes (APA, 2010; Wang et al., 2007).

Finally, college students may face stressors that are different from those listed in the Social Readjustment Rating Scale. Instead of having marital difficulties, being fired, or applying for a job, a college student may have trouble with a roommate, fail a course, or apply to graduate school. When researchers use special scales to measure life events in this population, they find the expected relationships between stressful events and illness (Anders et al., 2012; Hurst et al., 2012) (see Table 8-8 again).

Psychoneuroimmunology How do stressful events result in a viral or bacterial infection? Researchers in an area of study called **psychoneuroimmunology** seek to answer this question by uncovering the links between psychosocial stress, the immune system, and health. The **immune system** is the body's network of activities and cells that identify and destroy **antigens**—foreign invaders, such as bacteria, viruses, fungi, and parasites—and cancer cells. Among the most important cells in this system are billions of **lymphocytes,** white blood cells that circulate through the lymph system and the bloodstream. When antigens strike, lymphocytes spring into action to help the body overcome the invaders.

One group of lymphocytes, called *helper T-cells,* identifies antigens and then multiplies and triggers the production of other kinds of immune cells. Another group, *natural killer T-cells,* seeks out and destroys body cells that have already been infected by viruses, thus helping to stop the spread of a viral infection. A third group of lymphocytes, *B-cells,* produces *antibodies,* protein molecules that recognize and bind to antigens, mark them for destruction, and prevent them from causing infection.

Researchers now believe that stress can interfere with the activity of lymphocytes, slowing them down and thus increasing a person's susceptibility to viral and

---

BETWEEN THE LINES

The Immune System at Work

Marital Stress During and after marital spats, women typically release more stress hormones than men, and so have poorer immune functioning (Gouin et al., 2009; Kiecolt-Glaser et al., 1996).

Virtues of Laughter After watching a humorous video, research participants who laughed at the film showed decreases in stress and improvements in natural killer cell activity (Bennett, 1998).

MediaSpeak
When Doctors Discriminate

By Juliann Garey, *New York Times*, August 10, 2013

The first time it was an ear, nose and throat doctor. I had an emergency visit for an ear infection, which was causing a level of pain I hadn't experienced since giving birth. He looked at the list of drugs I was taking for my bipolar disorder and closed my chart.

"I don't feel comfortable prescribing anything," he said. "Not with everything else you're on." He said it was probably safe to take Tylenol and politely but firmly indicated it was time for me to go. The next day my eardrum ruptured and I was left with minor but permanent hearing loss.

Another time I was lying on the examining table when a gastroenterologist I was seeing for the first time looked at my list of drugs and shook her finger in my face. "You better get yourself together psychologically," she said, "or your stomach is never going to get any better." . . .

I was surprised when, after one of these run-ins, my psychopharmacologist said this sort of behavior was all too common. At least 14 studies have shown that patients with a serious mental illness receive worse medical care than "normal" people. . . . I never knew it until I started poking around, but this particular kind of discriminatory doctoring has a name. It's called "diagnostic overshadowing." . . . [P]eople with a serious mental illness—including bipolar disorder, major depression, schizophrenia and schizoaffective disorder—end up with wrong diagnoses and are under-treated.

That is a problem, because if you are given one of these diagnoses you probably also suffer from one or more chronic physical conditions: though no one quite knows why, migraines, irritable bowel syndrome and mitral valve prolapse often go hand in hand with bipolar disorder. . . .

It's little wonder that many people with a serious mental illness don't seek medical attention when they need it. As a result, many of us end up in emergency rooms—where doctors, confronted with an endless stream of drug addicts who come to their door looking for an easy fix—are often all too willing to equate mental illness with drug-seeking behavior and refuse to prescribe pain medication. . . .

Indeed, given my experience over the last two decades, I shouldn't have been surprised by the statistics I found in . . . a review of studies . . . . The take-away: people who suffer from a serious mental illness and use the public health care system die 25 years earlier than those without one.

True, suicide is a big factor, accounting for 30 to 40 percent of early deaths. But 60 percent die of preventable or treatable conditions. First on the list is, unsurprisingly, cardiovascular disease. Two studies showed that patients with both a mental illness and a cardiovascular condition received about half the number of follow-up interventions, like bypass surgery or cardiac catheterization, after having a heart attack than did the "normal" cardiac patients.

The report also contains a list of policy recommendations, including designating patients with serious mental illnesses as a high-priority population; coordinating and integrating mental and physical health care for such people; education for health care workers and patients; and a quality-improvement process that . . . ensures appropriate prevention, screening and treatment services. . . .

We can only hope that humanizing programs like this . . . become a requirement for all health care workers. Maybe then "first, do no harm" will apply to everyone, even the mentally ill.

PhotoAlto/Odilon Dimier/Getty Images

bacterial infections (Dhabhar, 2014, 2011). In a landmark study, investigator Roger Bartrop and his colleagues (1977) in New South Wales, Australia, compared the immune systems of 26 people whose spouses had died eight weeks earlier with those of 26 matched control group participants whose spouses had not died. Blood samples revealed that lymphocyte functioning was much lower in the bereaved people than in the controls. Still other studies have shown slow immune functioning in people who are exposed to long-term stress. For example, researchers have found poorer immune functioning among those who provide ongoing care for a relative with Alzheimer's disease (Fonareva & Oken, 2014; Kiecolt-Glaser et al., 2002, 1996).

These studies seem to be telling a remarkable story. During periods when healthy people happened to have unusual levels of stress, they remained healthy on the surface, but their stressors apparently slowed their immune systems so that they became susceptible to illness. If stress affects our capacity to fight off illness, it is no wonder that researchers have repeatedly found a relationship between life stress and illnesses of various kinds. But why and when does stress interfere with the immune system? Several factors influence whether stress will result in a slowdown of the system, including *biochemical activity, behavioral changes, personality style,* and *degree of social support.*

BIOCHEMICAL ACTIVITY Excessive activity of the neurotransmitter *norepinephrine* apparently contributes to slowdowns of the immune system. Remember from Chapter 5 that stress leads to increased activity by the sympathetic nervous system, including an increase in the release of norepinephrine throughout the brain and body. Research indicates that if stress continues for an extended time, norepinephrine eventually travels to receptors on certain lymphocytes and gives them an *inhibitory message* to stop their activity, thus slowing down immune functioning (Dhabhar, 2014; Lekander, 2002).

In a similar manner, *corticosteroids*—that is, cortisol and other so-called stress hormones—apparently contribute to poorer immune system functioning. Recall that when a person is under stress, the adrenal glands release corticosteroids (see page 152). As in the case of norepinephrine, if stress continues for an extended time, the stress hormones eventually travel to receptor sites located on certain lymphocytes and give an inhibitory message, again causing a slowdown of the activity of the lymphocytes (Dhabhar, 2014; Groër et al., 2010).

Recent research has further indicated that another action of the corticosteroids is to trigger an increase in the production of *cytokines,* proteins that bind to receptors throughout the body. At moderate levels of stress, the cytokines, another key player in the immune system, help combat infection. But as stress continues and more corticosteroids are released, the growing production and spread of cytokines lead to *chronic inflammation* throughout the body, contributing at times to heart disease, stroke, and other illnesses (Dhabhar, 2014; Brooks et al., 2011).

BEHAVIORAL CHANGES Stress may set in motion a series of behavioral changes that indirectly affect the immune system. Some people under stress may, for example, become anxious or depressed, perhaps even develop an anxiety or mood disorder. As a result, they may sleep badly, eat poorly, exercise less, or smoke or drink more—behaviors known to slow down the immune system (Brooks et al., 2011; Kibler et al., 2010).

PERSONALITY STYLE According to research, people who generally respond to life stress with optimism, constructive coping, and resilience—that is, people who welcome challenges and are willing to take control in their daily encounters—experience better immune system functioning and are

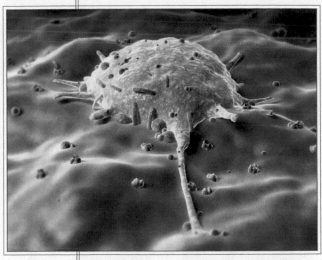

First line of defense How do lymphocytes meet up with invading antigens? The lymphocytes are first alerted by *macrophages,* big white blood cells in the immune system that recognize an antigen, engulf it, break it down, and hand off its dissected parts to the lymphocytes. Here a macrophage stretches its long "arms" (pseudopods) to detect and capture the suspected antigens.

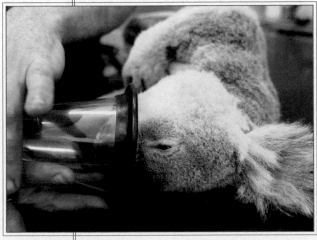

Everyone Is vulnerable to stress A male koala receives a swab test at the Sydney Wildlife World in Australia to detect an often-fatal disease called chlamydiosis. Chlamydiosis is caused by a virus that often breaks out in koalas when their immune systems are weakened during times of stress, such as when they are forced to find a new habitat. Fewer than 100,000 koalas are now left in Australia, down from millions of them two centuries ago.

©J. Dennis Thomas/Corbis

Attitude is key During a four-month period in 2012, stand-up comedian Tig Notaro developed breast cancer and underwent a double mastectomy, lost her mother, developed pneumonia, and also went through other significant life changes. Shortly after, she changed her comedy act to include descriptions of her ordeal and disease process. Her presentations have entertained and enthralled audiences and catapulted her career to new heights. They also appear to have played a role in helping her to fight her medical problems and regain her health.

///// BETWEEN THE LINES /////

New Pop-Culture Diagnosis

Phantom cell phone vibration syndrome: a false sense that one's cell phone is vibrating (Archer, 2013)

better prepared to fight off illness (Kim, Chopik, & Smith, 2014; Williams et al., 2011). Some studies have found, for example, that people with "hardy" or resilient personalities remain healthy after stressful events, while those whose personalities are less hardy seem more susceptible to illness (Bonanno & Mancini, 2012; Ouellette & DiPlacido, 2001). Researchers have even discovered that men with a general sense of hopelessness die at above-average rates from heart disease and other causes (Kangelaris et al., 2010; Everson et al., 1996). Similarly, a growing body of research suggests that people who are spiritual tend to be healthier than people without spiritual beliefs, and a few studies have linked spirituality to better immune system functioning (Jackson & Bergeman, 2011; Cadge & Fair, 2010).

In related work, researchers have found a relationship between certain personality characteristics and a person's ability to cope effectively with cancer (Baum et al., 2011; Floyd et al., 2011). They have found, for example, that patients with certain forms of cancer who display a helpless coping style and who cannot easily express their feelings, particularly anger, tend to have a poorer quality of life in the face of their disease than patients who do express their emotions. A few investigators have even suggested a relationship between personality and cancer *outcome,* but this claim has not been supported clearly by research (Pillay et al., 2014; Kern & Friedman, 2011; Urcuyo et al., 2005).

SOCIAL SUPPORT Finally, people who have few social supports and feel lonely tend to have poorer immune functioning in the face of stress than people who do not feel lonely (Hicks, 2014; Cohen, 2002). In a pioneering study, medical students were given the *UCLA Loneliness Scale* and then divided into "high" and "low" loneliness groups (Kiecolt-Glaser et al., 1984). The high-loneliness group showed lower lymphocyte responses during a final exam period.

Other studies have found that social support and affiliation may actually help protect people from stress, poor immune system functioning, and subsequent illness or help speed up recovery from illness or surgery (Hicks, 2014; Rook et al., 2011). Similarly, some studies have suggested that patients with certain forms of cancer who receive social support in their personal lives or supportive therapy often have better immune system functioning and more successful recoveries than patients without such supports (Dagan et al., 2011; Kim et al., 2010).

➤ *Summing Up*

PSYCHOPHYSIOLOGICAL DISORDERS Psychophysiological disorders are those in which biological, psychosocial, and sociocultural factors interact to cause or worsen a physical problem. Factors linked to these disorders are biological factors, such as defects in the autonomic nervous system or particular organs; psychological factors, such as particular needs, attitudes, or personality styles; and sociocultural factors, such as aversive social conditions and cultural pressures.

For years, clinical researchers singled out a limited number of physical illnesses as psychophysiological. These traditional psychophysiological disorders include ulcers, asthma, insomnia, chronic headaches, hypertension, and coronary heart disease. Recently many other psychophysiological disorders have been identified. Indeed, scientists have linked many physical illnesses to stress and have developed a new area of study called psychoneuroimmunology. Stress can slow lymphocyte activity, thereby interfering with the immune system's ability to protect against illness during times of stress. Factors that seem to affect immune functioning include norepinephrine and corticosteroid activity, behavioral changes, personality style, and social support.

Psychological Treatments for Physical Disorders

As clinicians have discovered that stress and related psychological and sociocultural factors may contribute to physical disorders, they have applied psychological treatments to more and more medical problems. The most common of these interventions are relaxation training, biofeedback, meditation, hypnosis, cognitive interventions, support groups, and therapies to increase awareness and expression of emotions. The field of treatment that combines psychological and physical approaches to treat or prevent medical problems is known as **behavioral medicine**.

Relaxation Training

As you saw in Chapter 4, people can be taught to relax their muscles at will, a process that sometimes reduces feelings of anxiety. Given the positive effects of relaxation on anxiety and the nervous system, clinicians believe that *relaxation training* can help prevent or treat medical illnesses that are related to stress.

Relaxation training, often in combination with medication, has been widely used in the treatment of high blood pressure (Moffatt et al., 2010). It has also been of some help in treating headaches, insomnia, asthma, diabetes, pain, certain vascular diseases, and the undesirable effects of certain cancer treatments (McKenna et al., 2015; Nezu et al., 2011).

Biofeedback

As you also saw in Chapter 4, patients given *biofeedback training* are connected to machinery that gives them continuous readings about their involuntary body activities. This information enables them gradually to gain control over those activities. Somewhat helpful in the treatment of anxiety disorders, the procedure has also been applied to a growing number of physical disorders.

In a classic study, *electromyograph (EMG)* feedback was used to treat 16 patients who had facial pain caused in part by tension in their jaw muscles (Dohrmann & Laskin, 1978). In an EMG procedure, electrodes are attached to a person's muscles so that the muscle contractions are detected and converted into a tone (see pages 118–119). Changes in the pitch and volume of the tone indicate changes in muscle tension. After "listening" to EMG feedback repeatedly, the 16 patients in this study learned how to relax their jaw muscles at will and later reported that they had less facial pain.

EMG feedback has also been used successfully in the treatment of headaches and muscular disabilities caused by strokes or accidents. Still other forms of biofeedback training have been of some help in the treatment of heartbeat irregularities, asthma, high blood pressure, stuttering, and pain (McKenna et al., 2015; Freitag, 2013; Young & Kemper, 2013).

Meditation

Although meditation has been practiced since ancient times, Western health care professionals have only recently become aware of its effectiveness in relieving physical distress. *Meditation* is a technique of turning one's concentration inward, achieving a slightly changed state of consciousness, and temporarily ignoring all stressors. In the most common approach, meditators go to a quiet place, assume a comfortable posture, utter or think a particular sound (called a *mantra*) to help focus their attention, and allow their mind to turn away from all outside thoughts and concerns. Many people who meditate regularly report feeling more peaceful, engaged, and creative. Meditation has been used to help manage pain and to treat high blood pressure, heart problems, asthma, skin disorders, diabetes, insomnia, and even viral infections (Manchanda & Madan, 2014; Stein, 2003; Andresen, 2000).

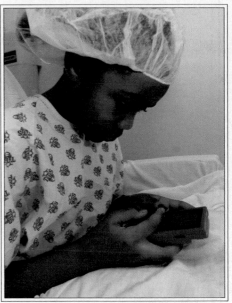

AP Photo/Mike Derer

The power of distraction Researchers at a medical center in New Jersey had this 10-year-old girl and other young patients play with handheld Game Boys while waiting for their anesthesia to take effect before their surgery. Such game-playing was found to be more effective at relaxing the young patients than antianxiety drugs or holding hands with parents. Additional research suggests that patients who are more relaxed often have better surgical outcomes.

▶ **behavioral medicine** A field that combines psychological and physical interventions to treat or prevent medical problems.

Fighting HIV on all fronts As part of his treatment at the Wellness Center in San Francisco, this man meditates and writes letters to his HIV virus.

Joe McNally/Time & Life Pictures/Getty Images

One form of meditation that has been used in particular by patients suffering from severe pain is *mindfulness meditation* (Barker, 2014; Kabat-Zinn, 2005). Here, as you read in Chapters 2 and 4, meditators pay attention to the feelings, thoughts, and sensations that are flowing through their mind during meditation, but they do so with detachment and objectivity and, most importantly, without judgment. By just being mindful but not judgmental of their feelings and thoughts, including feelings of pain, they are less inclined to label them, fixate on them, or react negatively to them.

Hypnosis

As you saw in Chapter 1, people who undergo *hypnosis* are guided by a hypnotist into a sleeplike, suggestible state during which they can be directed to act in unusual ways, feel unusual sensations, remember seemingly forgotten events, or forget remembered events. With training, some people are even able to induce their own hypnotic state (*self-hypnosis*). Hypnosis is now used as an aid to psychotherapy and to help treat many physical conditions.

The hypnotic way Hypnosis is now widely used in medical procedures, particularly to help reduce and control pain. At the Cliniques Universitaires Saint-Luc Hospital in Brussels, a surgeon prepares a patient for her thyroid procedure while anesthesiologist Dr. Fabienne Roelants hypnotizes the patient. One-third of all thyroid-removal surgeries and one-quarter of all breast cancer surgeries at the hospital are conducted using a combination of hypnosis and a local anesthetic rather than general anesthesia.

Hypnosis seems to be particularly helpful in the control of pain (Jensen et al., 2014, 2011). One case study describes a patient who underwent dental surgery under hypnotic suggestion. After a hypnotic state was induced, the dentist suggested to the patient that he was in a pleasant and relaxed setting listening to a friend describe his own success at undergoing similar dental surgery under hypnosis. The dentist then proceeded to perform a successful 25-minute operation (Gheorghiu & Orleanu, 1982). Although only some people are able to go through surgery while anesthetized by hypnosis alone, hypnosis combined with chemical forms of anesthesia is apparently helpful to many patients (Lang, 2010). Beyond its use in the control of pain, hypnosis has been used successfully to help treat such problems as skin diseases, asthma, insomnia, high blood pressure, warts, and other forms of infection (Becker, 2015; McBride, Vlieger, & Anbar, 2014; Modlin, 2002).

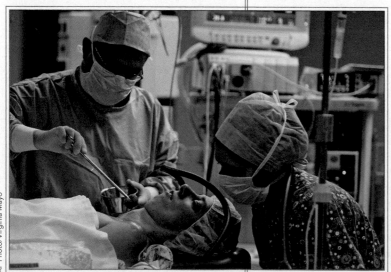

AP Photo/Virginia Mayo

Cognitive Interventions

People with physical ailments have sometimes been taught new attitudes or cognitive responses toward their ailments as part of treatment (Hampel et al., 2014; Syrjala et al., 2014). For example, an approach called *self-instruction training,* or *stress inoculation training,* has helped patients cope with severe pain (D'Arienzo, 2010; Meichenbaum, 1993, 1977, 1975). In this training, therapists teach people to identify and eventually rid themselves of unpleasant thoughts that keep emerging during pain episodes (so-called *negative self-statements,* such as "Oh no, I can't take this pain") and to replace them with *coping self-statements* instead (for example, "When pain comes, just pause; keep focusing on what you have to do").

Support Groups and Emotion Expression

If anxiety, depression, anger, and the like contribute to a person's physical ills, interventions to reduce these negative emotions should help reduce the ills. Thus it is not surprising that some medically ill people have profited from support groups and from therapies that guide them to become more aware of and express their emotions and needs (Bell et al., 2010; Hsu et al., 2010). Research suggests that the discussion, or even the writing down, of past and present emotions or upsets may help improve a person's health, just as it may help one's psychological functioning (Kelly & Barry, 2010; Smyth & Pennebaker, 2001). In one study, asthma and arthritis patients who wrote down their thoughts and feelings about stressful events for a handful of days showed lasting improvements in their conditions. Similarly, stress-related writing was found to be beneficial for patients with either HIV or cancer (Corter & Petrie, 2011; Petrie et al., 2004).

Combination Approaches

Studies have found that the various psychological interventions for physical problems tend to be equally effective (Devineni & Blanchard, 2005). Relaxation and biofeedback training, for example, are equally helpful (and more helpful than placebos) in the treatment of high blood pressure, headaches, and asthma. Psychological interventions are, in fact, often most helpful when they are combined with other psychological interventions and with medical treatments (Jensen et al., 2014, 2011; Hembree & Foa, 2010). In a classic study, ulcer patients who were given relaxation, self-instruction, and assertiveness training along with medication were found to be less anxious and more comfortable, to have fewer symptoms, and to have a better long-term outcome than patients who received medication only (Brooks & Richardson, 1980). Combination interventions have also been helpful in changing Type A patterns and in reducing the risk of coronary heart disease among people who display Type A kinds of behavior (Ladwig et al., 2014; Harlapur et al., 2010).

Clearly, the treatment picture for physical illnesses has been changing dramatically. While medical treatments continue to dominate, today's medical practitioners are traveling a course far removed from that of their counterparts in centuries past.

BETWEEN THE LINES

Room with a View

According to one hospital's records of individuals who underwent gallbladder surgery, those in rooms with a good view from their window had shorter hospitalizations and needed fewer pain medications than those in rooms without a good view (Ulrich, 1984).

BETWEEN THE LINES

Strictly a Coincidence?

On February 17, 1673, French actor-playwright Molière collapsed onstage and died while performing in *Le Malade Imaginaire* (*The Hypochondriac*).

➤ *Summing Up*

PSYCHOLOGICAL TREATMENTS FOR PHYSICAL DISORDERS Behavioral medicine combines psychological and physical interventions to treat or prevent medical problems. Psychological approaches such as relaxation training, biofeedback training, meditation, hypnosis, cognitive techniques, support groups, and therapies that heighten the awareness and expression of emotions and needs are increasingly being included in the treatment of various medical problems.

PUTTING IT...*together*

Expanding the Boundaries of Abnormal Psychology

Once considered outside the field of abnormal psychology, bodily ailments and physical illnesses are now seen as problems that fall squarely within its boundaries. Just as physical factors have long been recognized as playing a role in abnormal mental functioning, psychological conditions are now considered important contributors to abnormal physical functioning. In fact, many of today's clinicians believe that psychological and sociocultural factors contribute to some degree to the onset and course of virtually all physical ailments.

The number of studies devoted to this relationship has risen steadily during the past 40 years. What researchers once saw as a vague connection between stress and physical illness is now understood as a complex interaction of many variables. Such factors as life changes, a person's particular psychological state, social support, biochemical activity, and slowing of the immune system are all recognized as contributors to disorders once considered purely physical.

Insights into the treatment of physical illnesses have been accumulating just as rapidly. Psychological approaches such as relaxation training and cognitive therapy are being applied to more and more physical ills, usually in combination with traditional medical treatments. Small wonder that many practitioners are convinced that such treatment combinations will eventually be the norm in treating the majority of physical ailments.

One of the most exciting aspects of these recent developments is the field's growing emphasis on the *interrelationship* of the social environment, the brain, and the rest of the body. Researchers have observed repeatedly that mental disorders are often best understood and treated when sociocultural, psychological, and biological factors are all taken into consideration. They now know that this interaction also helps explain medical problems. We are reminded that the brain is part of the body and that both are part of a social context. For better and for worse, the three are intertwined.

CLINICAL CHOICES

Now that you've read about disorders featuring somatic symptoms, try the interactive case study for this chapter. See if you are able to identify Joanne's symptoms and suggest a diagnosis based on her symptoms. What kind of treatment would be most effective for Joanne? Go to LaunchPad to access *Clinical Choices.*

KEY TERMS

mind-body dualism, p. 250
malingering, p. 250
factitious disorder, p. 250
Munchausen syndrome, p. 250
Munchausen syndrome by proxy, p. 251
conversion disorder, p. 253
somatic symptom disorder, p. 253
Electra complex, p. 258
primary gain, p. 258
secondary gain, p. 258
illness anxiety disorder, p. 261
psychophysiological disorder, p. 262

psychological factors affecting other medical conditions, p. 262
ulcer, p. 262
asthma, p. 262
insomnia, p. 263
muscle contraction headaches, p. 263
migraine headaches, p. 263
hypertension, p. 265
coronary heart disease, p. 265
Type A personality style, p. 266
Type B personality style, p. 266
Social Readjustment Rating Scale, p. 268

psychoneuroimmunology, p. 269
immune system, p. 269
antigen, p. 269
lymphocyte, p. 269
cytokines, p. 271
behavioral medicine, p. 273
relaxation training, p. 273
biofeedback training, p. 273
meditation, p. 273
hypnosis, p. 274
self-instruction training, p. 275

QuickQuiz

1. What are the symptoms of factitious disorder, conversion disorder, and somatic symptom disorder? *pp. 250–257*

2. How do practitioners distinguish conversion disorder from a "genuine" medical problem? What are two different patterns of somatic symptom disorder? *pp. 254, 256–257*

3. What are the leading explanations and treatments for conversion and somatic symptom disorder? How well does research support them? *pp. 257–261*

4. What are the symptoms, causes, and treatments of illness anxiety disorder? *pp. 261–262*

5. What are the specific causes of ulcers, asthma, insomnia, headaches, hypertension, and coronary heart disease? *pp. 262–265*

6. What kinds of biological, psychological, and sociocultural factors appear to contribute to psychophysiological disorders? *pp. 265–267*

7. What kind of relationship has been found between life stress and physical illnesses? What scale has helped researchers investigate this relationship? *pp. 268–269*

8. Describe the connection between stress, the immune system, and physical illness. Explain the specific roles played by various types of lymphocytes. *pp. 269–271*

9. Discuss how immune system functioning at times of stress may be affected by a person's biochemical activity, behavioral changes, personality style, and social support. *pp. 271–272*

10. What psychological treatments have been used to help treat physical illnesses? To which specific illnesses has each been applied? *pp. 273–275*

Visit *LaunchPad*
www.macmillanhighered.com/launchpad/comerfund8e
to access the e-book, new interactive case studies, videos, activities, and LearningCurve quizzes, as well as study aids including flashcards, FAQs, and research exercises.

Macmillan Education LaunchPad

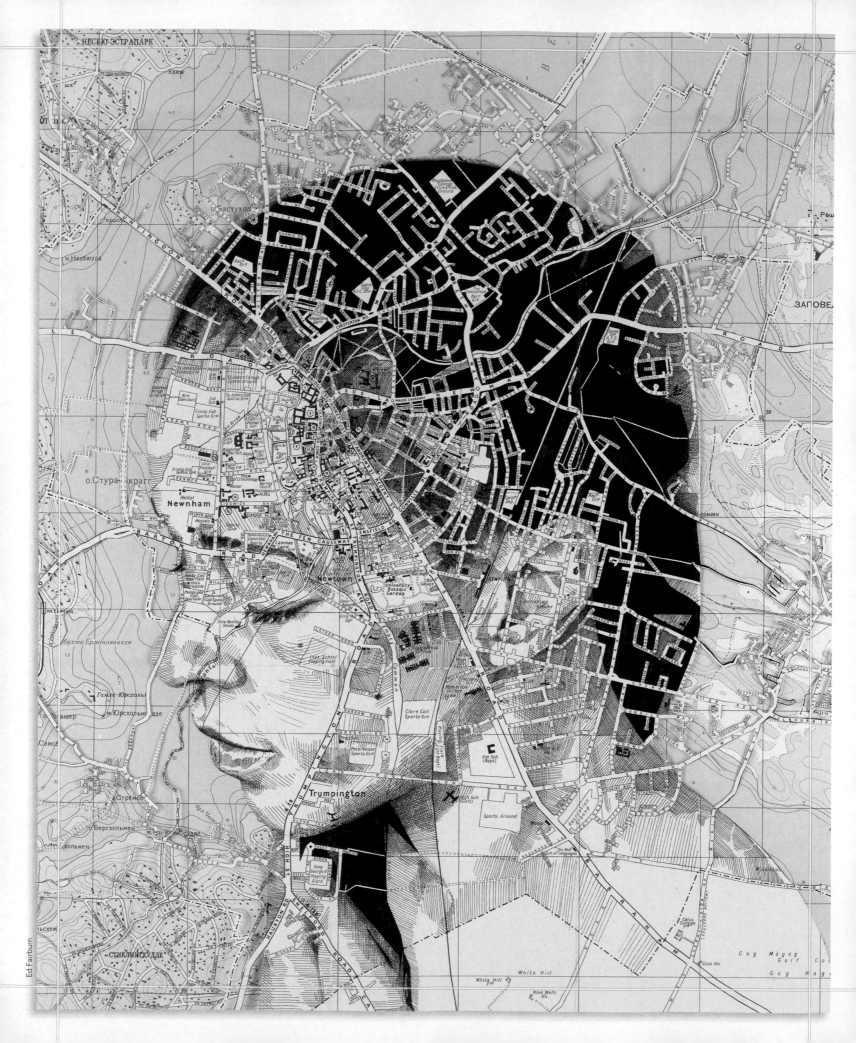

Ed Fairburn

Eating Disorders

Shani, age 15: *I walked into the kitchen when no one was around, took a slice of bread out of the packet, toasted it, spread butter on it, took a deep breath and bit. Guilty. I spat it in the trash and tossed the rest of it in and walked away. Seconds later I longed for the toast, walked back to the trash, popped open the lid and sifted around in the debris. I found it and contemplated, for minutes, whether to eat it. I brought it close to my nose and inhaled the smell of melted butter. Guilty. Guilty for trashing it. Guilty for craving it. Guilty for tasting it. I threw it back in the trash and walked away. No is no, I told myself. No is no.*

. . . And no matter how hard I would try to always have The Perfect Day in terms of my food, I would feel the guilt every second of every day. . . . It was my desire to escape the guilt that perpetuated my compulsion to starve.

In time I formulated a more precise list of "can" and "can't" in my head that dictated what I was allowed or forbidden to consume. . . . It became my way of life. My manual. My blueprint. But more than that, it gave me false reassurance that my life was under control. I was managing everything because I had this list in front of me telling me what—and what not—to do. . . .

In the beginning, starving was hard work. It was not innate. Day by day I was slowly lured into another world, a world that was . . . as rewarding as it was challenging. . . .

That summer, despite the fact that I had lost a lot of weight, my mother agreed to let me go to summer camp with my fifteen-year-old peers, after I swore to her that I would eat. I broke that promise as soon as I got there. . . . At breakfast time when all the teens raced into the dining hall to grab cereal boxes and bread loaves and jelly tins and peanut butter jars, I sat alone cocooned in my fear. I fingered the plastic packet of a loaf of white sliced bread, took out a piece and tore off a corner, like I was marking a page in a book, onto which I dabbed a blob of peanut butter and jelly the size of a Q-tip. That was my breakfast. Every day. For three weeks.

I tried to get to the showers when everyone else was at the beach so nobody would see me. I heard girls behind me whispering, "That's the girl I told you about that looks so disgusting." Someone invariably walked in on me showering and covered her mouth with her hand like I was a dead body. I wished I could disappear into the drain like my hair that was falling out in chunks. . . .

[Upon returning to school] I was labeled the "concentration camp victim." On my return, over the months everyone watched my body shrink as though it were being vacuum packed in slow motion. . . . At my lowest weight my hipbones protruded like knuckle bones under my dress and I had to minimize the increments of the belt holes until there was so much extra belt material dangling down that I did away with the belt completely. My shoes were too big for my feet; my ankles were so thin that I wore three pairs of socks at a time and still my shoes would slide off my heels. And my panties were so baggy I secured them with safety pins on the sides so they wouldn't fall down. . . .

On the home front things were worse than ever. . . . I locked my door and forbade anyone from entering. Even so, my mother and I had screaming matches every day, with her trying to convince me that "your body needs food as fuel" and me retaliating with "I'm not hungry." . . .

For nine months my mother stood by, forbidden to interfere, while I starved myself. She had no idea what was going on, nor did I. . . . She watched me transform from an innocent, soft, kind, loving girl into a reclusive, vicious, aggressive, defiant teenager. . . . And there was nothing she could say or do to stop me. She knew that if my weight continued to drop radically that she might lose me. But despite all her desperate attempts to reach out to me . . . she had no way of getting through to me. . . .

(Raviv, 2010)

▶ **anorexia nervosa** A disorder marked by the pursuit of extreme thinness and by extreme weight loss.

It has not always done so, but Western society today equates thinness with health and beauty. In fact, in the United States thinness has become a national obsession. Most of us are as preoccupied with how much we eat as with the taste and nutritional value of our food. Thus it is not surprising that during the past three decades we have also witnessed an increase in two eating disorders that have at their core a morbid fear of gaining weight. Sufferers of *anorexia nervosa,* like Shani, are convinced that they need to be extremely thin, and they lose so much weight that they may starve themselves to death. People with *bulimia nervosa* go on frequent eating binges, during which they uncontrollably consume large quantities of food, and then force themselves to vomit or take other extreme steps to keep from gaining weight. A third eating disorder, *binge-eating disorder,* in which people frequently go on eating binges but do not force themselves to vomit or engage in other such behaviors, also appears to be on the rise. People with binge-eating disorder do not fear weight gain to the same degree as those with anorexia nervosa and bulimia nervosa, but they do have many of the other features found in those disorders (Alvarenga et al., 2014).

> Are girls and women in Western society destined to struggle with at least some issues of eating and appearance?

The news media have published many reports about eating disorders. One reason for the surge in public interest is the frightening medical consequences that can result from the disorders. The public first became aware of such consequences in 1983 when Karen Carpenter died from medical problems related to anorexia. Carpenter, the 32-year-old lead singer of the soft-rock brother-and-sister duo called the Carpenters, had been enormously successful and was admired by many as a wholesome and healthy model to young women everywhere. Another reason for the current concern is the disproportionate prevalence of anorexia nervosa and bulimia nervosa among adolescent girls and young women.

Anorexia Nervosa

Shani, 15 years old and in the ninth grade, displays many symptoms of **anorexia nervosa** (APA, 2013). She purposely maintains a significantly low body weight, intensely fears becoming overweight, has a distorted view of her weight and shape, and is excessively influenced by her weight and shape in her self-evaluations (see Table 9-1).

Like Shani, at least half of the people with anorexia nervosa reduce their weight by restricting their intake of food, a pattern called *restricting-type anorexia nervosa.* First they tend to cut out sweets and fattening snacks; then, increasingly, they eliminate other foods. Eventually people with this kind of anorexia nervosa show almost no variability in diet. Others, however, lose weight by forcing themselves to vomit after meals or by abusing laxatives or diuretics, and they may even engage in eating binges, a pattern called *binge-eating/purging-type anorexia nervosa,* which you will read about in more detail in the section on bulimia nervosa.

Ninety to 95 percent of all cases of anorexia nervosa occur in females. Although the disorder can appear at any age, the peak age of onset is between 14 and 20 years. Between 0.5 and 4.0 percent of all females in Western countries develop the disorder in their lifetime, and many more display at least some of its symptoms (Ekern, 2014; Stice et al., 2013). It seems to be on the increase in North America, Europe, and Japan.

Typically the disorder begins after a person who is slightly overweight or of normal weight has been on a diet (APA, 2015; Stice & Presnell, 2010). The escalation toward anorexia nervosa may follow a stressful event such as separation of parents, a move away from home, or an experience of personal failure (APA, 2015;

table: 9-1

Dx Checklist

Anorexia Nervosa

1. Individual purposely takes in too little nourishment, resulting in body weight that is very low and below that of other people of similar age and gender.

2. Individual is very fearful of gaining weight, or repeatedly seeks to prevent weight gain despite low body weight.

3. Individual has a distorted body perception, places inappropriate emphasis on weight or shape in judgments of herself or himself, or fails to appreciate the serious implications of her or his low weight.

(Information from: APA, 2013.)

Wilson et al., 2003). Although most people with the disorder recover, between 2 and 6 percent of them become so seriously ill that they die, usually from medical problems brought about by starvation or from suicide (Suokas et al., 2013; Forcano et al., 2010).

The Clinical Picture

Becoming thin is the key goal for people with anorexia nervosa, but *fear* provides their motivation. People with this disorder are afraid of becoming obese, of giving in to their growing desire to eat, and more generally of losing control over the size and shape of their bodies. In addition, despite their focus on thinness and the severe restrictions they may place on their food intake, people with anorexia are *preoccupied with food*. They may spend considerable time thinking and even reading about food and planning their limited meals (Herzig, 2004). Many report that their dreams are filled with images of food and eating (Knudson, 2006).

This preoccupation with food may in fact be a result of food deprivation rather than its cause. In a famous "starvation study" conducted in the late 1940s, 36 normal-weight conscientious objectors were put on a semi-starvation diet for six months (Keys et al., 1950). Like people with anorexia nervosa, the volunteers became preoccupied with food and eating. They spent hours each day planning their small meals, talked more about food than about any other topic, studied cookbooks and recipes, mixed food in odd combinations, and dawdled over their meals. Many also had vivid dreams about food.

Persons with anorexia nervosa also *think in distorted ways*. They usually have a low opinion of their body shape, for example, and consider themselves unattractive (Boone et al., 2014; Siep et al., 2011). In addition, they are likely to overestimate their actual proportions. While most women in Western society over-estimate their body size, the estimates of those with anorexia nervosa are particularly high. In one of her classic books on eating disorders, Hilde Bruch, a pioneer in this field, recalled the self-perceptions of a 23-year-old patient:

> I look in a full-length mirror at least four or five times daily and I really cannot see myself as too thin. Sometimes after several days of strict dieting, I feel that my shape is tolerable, but most of the time, odd as it may seem, I look in the mirror and believe that I am too fat.
>
> *(Bruch, 1973)*

This tendency to overestimate body size has been tested in the laboratory (Delinsky, 2011). In a popular assessment technique, research participants look at a photograph of themselves through an adjustable lens. They are asked to adjust the lens until the image that they see matches their actual body size. The image can be made to vary from 20 percent thinner to 20 percent larger than actual appearance. In one study, more than half of the individuals with anorexia nervosa overestimated their body size, stopping the lens when the image was larger than they actually were.

The distorted thinking of anorexia nervosa also takes the form of certain mal-adaptive attitudes and misperceptions (Alvarenga et al., 2014). Sufferers tend to hold such beliefs as "I must be perfect in every way," "I will become a better person if I deprive myself," and "I can avoid guilt by not eating."

Laboratory starvation Thirty-six conscientious objectors who were put on a semistarvation diet for six months developed many of the symptoms seen in anorexia nervosa and bulimia nervosa (Keys et al., 1950).

Wallace Kirkland/Time Life Pictures/Getty Images

Turning point When soft-rock star Karen Carpenter (right) received an award from fellow musician Emmylou Harris at the 1977 Billboard Music Awards, few people paid much attention to her symptoms. Carpenter's 1983 death helped change the public's view of anorexia nervosa.

► **amenorrhea** The absence of menstrual cycles.

► **bulimia nervosa** A disorder marked by frequent eating binges that are followed by forced vomiting or other extreme compensatory behaviors to avoid gaining weight. Also known as *binge-purge syndrome.*

► **binge** An episode of uncontrollable eating during which a person ingests a very large quantity of food.

People with anorexia nervosa also have certain *psychological problems,* such as depression, anxiety, low self-esteem, and insomnia or other sleep disturbances (Forsén Mantilla et al., 2014; Holm-Denoma et al., 2014). A number grapple with substance abuse (Mann et al., 2014). And many display obsessive-compulsive patterns (Degortes et al., 2014). They may set rigid rules for food preparation or even cut food into specific shapes. Broader obsessive-compulsive patterns are common as well. Many, for example, exercise compulsively, prioritizing exercise over most other activities in their lives (Fairburn et al., 2008). In some research, people with anorexia nervosa and others with obsessive-compulsive disorder score equally high for obsessiveness and compulsiveness. Finally, persons with anorexia nervosa tend to be perfectionistic, a characteristic that typically precedes the onset of the disorder (Boone et al., 2014).

Medical Problems

The starvation habits of anorexia nervosa cause medical problems (Faje et al., 2014; Suokas et al., 2014). Women develop **amenorrhea**, the absence of menstrual cycles. Other problems include lowered body temperature, low blood pressure, body swelling, reduced bone mineral density, and slow heart rate. Metabolic and electrolyte imbalances also may occur and can lead to death by heart failure or circulatory collapse. The poor nutrition of people with anorexia nervosa may also cause skin to become rough, dry, and cracked; nails to become brittle; and hands and feet to be cold and blue. Some people lose hair from the scalp, and some grow *lanugo* (the fine, silky hair that covers some newborns) on their trunk, extremities, and face. Shani, the young woman whose self-description opened this chapter, recalls how her body deteriorated as her disorder was progressing: "Nobody knew that I was always cold no matter how many layers I wore, that my hair came out in thick wads whenever I wet it or washed it, that I stopped menstruating, [and] that my hipbones hurt to lie on my stomach and my coccyx hurt to sit on the floor" (Raviv, 2010).

➤ *Summing Up*

ANOREXIA NERVOSA Rates of eating disorders have increased dramatically as thinness has become a national obsession. People with anorexia nervosa pursue extreme thinness and lose dangerous amounts of weight. They may follow a pattern of restricting-type anorexia nervosa or binge-eating/purging-type anorexia nervosa. The central features of anorexia nervosa are a drive for thinness, intense fear of weight gain, and disturbed body perception and other cognitive disturbances. Ninety to 95 percent of all cases occur among females. Most sufferers develop significant medical problems, including amenorrhea.

Bulimia Nervosa

People with **bulimia nervosa**—a disorder also known as **binge-purge syndrome**—engage in repeated episodes of uncontrollable overeating, or **binges.** A binge episode takes place over a limited period of time, often two hours, during which the person eats much more food than most people would eat during a similar time span (APA, 2013). In addition, people with this disorder repeatedly perform inappropriate *compensatory behaviors,* such as forcing themselves to vomit; misusing laxatives, diuretics, or enemas; fasting; or exercising excessively (see Table 9-2). Lindsey, a woman who has since recovered from bulimia nervosa, describes a morning during her disorder:

> *Today I am going to be really good and that means eating certain predetermined portions of food and not taking one more bite than I think I am allowed. I am very careful to see that I don't take more than Doug does. I judge by his body. I can feel the tension building. I wish Doug would hurry up and leave so I can get going!*
>
> *As soon as he shuts the door, I try to get involved with one of the myriad of responsibilities on the list. I hate them all! I just want to crawl into a hole. I don't want to do anything. I'd rather eat. I am alone, I am nervous, I am no good, I always do everything wrong anyway, I am not in control, I can't make it through the day, I just know it. It has been the same for so long.*
>
> *I remember the starchy cereal I ate for breakfast. I am into the bathroom and onto the scale. It measures the same, but I don't want to stay the same! I want to be thinner! I look in the mirror, I think my thighs are ugly and deformed looking. I see a lumpy, clumsy, pear-shaped wimp. There is always something wrong with what I see. I feel frustrated trapped in this body and I don't know what to do about it.*
>
> *I float to the refrigerator knowing exactly what is there. I begin with last night's brownies. I always begin with the sweets. At first I try to make it look like nothing is missing, but my appetite is huge and I resolve to make another batch of brownies. I know there is half of a bag of cookies in the bathroom, thrown out the night before, and I polish them off immediately. I take some milk so my vomiting will be smoother. I like the full feeling I get after downing a big glass. I get out six pieces of bread and toast one side in the broiler, turn them over and load them with patties of butter and put them under the broiler again till they are bubbling. I take all six pieces on a plate to the television and go back for a bowl of cereal and a banana to have along with them. Before the last toast is finished, I am already preparing the next batch of six more pieces. Maybe another brownie or five, and a couple of large bowlfuls of ice cream, yogurt or cottage cheese. My stomach is stretched into a huge ball below my ribcage. I know I'll have to go into the bathroom soon, but I want to postpone it. I am in never-never land. I am waiting, feeling the pressure, pacing the floor in and out of the rooms. Time is passing. Time is passing. It is getting to be time.*
>
> *I wander aimlessly through each of the rooms again tidying, making the whole house neat and put back together. I finally make the turn into the bathroom. I brace my feet, pull my hair back and stick my finger down my throat, stroking twice, and get up a huge pile of food. Three times, four and another pile of food. I can see everything come back. I am glad to see those brownies because they are SO fattening. The rhythm of the emptying is broken and my head is beginning to hurt. I stand up feeling dizzy, empty and weak. The whole episode has taken about an hour.*
>
> *(Hall & Cohn, 2010, p. 1; Hall, 1980, pp. 5–6)*

table: **9-2**

Dx Checklist

Bulimia Nervosa

1. Repeated binge-eating episodes.

2. Repeated performance of ill-advised compensatory behaviors (e.g., forced vomiting) to prevent weight gain.

3. Symptoms take place at least weekly for a period of 3 months.

4. Inappropriate influence of weight and shape on appraisal of oneself.

(Information from: APA, 2013.)

Like anorexia nervosa, bulimia nervosa usually occurs in females, again in 90 to 95 percent of the cases (ANAD, 2015; Sanftner & Tantillo, 2011). It begins in adolescence or young adulthood (most often between 15 and 20 years of age) and often lasts for years, with periodic letup (Stice et al., 2013). The weight of people with bulimia nervosa usually stays within a normal range, although it may fluctuate markedly within that range. Some people with this disorder, however, become seriously underweight and may eventually qualify for a diagnosis of anorexia nervosa instead (see Figure 9-1 on the next page).

Many teenagers and young adults go on occasional eating binges or experiment with vomiting or laxatives after they hear about these behaviors from their friends or the media. Indeed, according to global studies, 25 to 50 percent of all students report periodic binge eating or self-induced vomiting (Ekern, 2014; McDermott & Jaffa, 2005). Only some of these individuals, however, qualify for a diagnosis of bulimia nervosa. Surveys in several Western countries suggest that as many as 5 percent

BETWEEN THE LINES

In Their Words

"To be born woman is to know—Although they do not talk of it at school—Women must labour to be beautiful."

W. B. Yeats, 1904

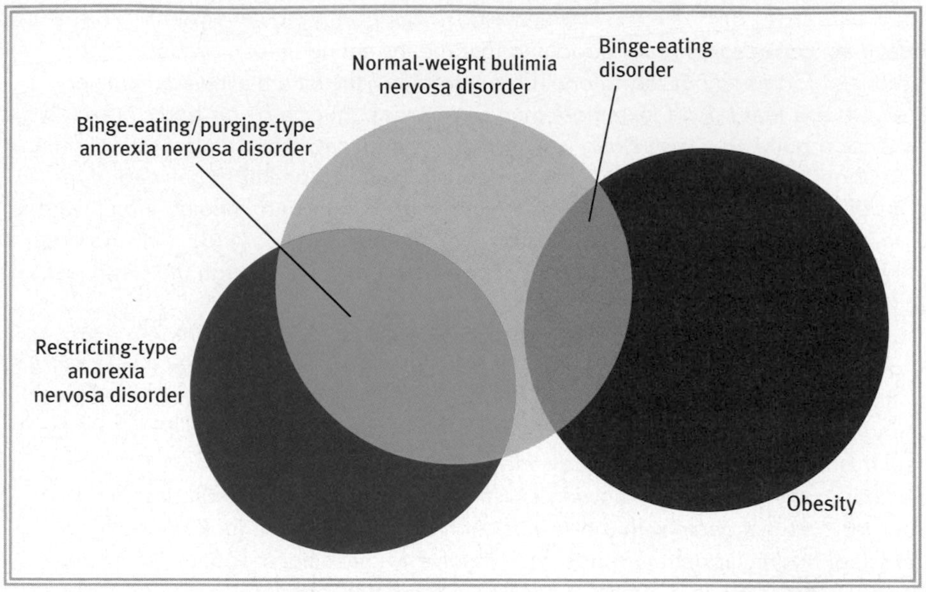

figure 9-1
Overlapping patterns of anorexia nervosa, bulimia nervosa, and obesity Some people with anorexia nervosa binge and purge their way to weight loss, and some obese people binge eat. However, most people with bulimia nervosa are not obese, and most overweight people do not binge eat.

of women develop the full syndrome (Ekern, 2014; Touchette et al., 2011). Among college students the rate may be much higher (Zerbe, 2008).

Binges

People with bulimia nervosa may have between 1 and 30 binge episodes per week (Fairburn et al., 2008). In most cases, they carry out the binges in secret. The person eats massive amounts of food very rapidly, with minimal chewing—usually sweet, high-calorie foods with a soft texture, such as ice cream, cookies, doughnuts, and sandwiches. The food is hardly tasted or thought about. Binge eaters consume an average of 3,400 calories during an episode. Some individuals consume as many as 10,000 calories.

Binges are usually preceded by feelings of great tension. The person feels irritable, "unreal," and powerless to control an overwhelming need to eat "forbidden" foods. During the binge, the person feels unable to stop eating (APA, 2013). Although the binge itself may be experienced as pleasurable in the sense that it relieves the unbearable tension, it is followed by feelings of extreme self-blame, shame, guilt, and depression, as well as fears of gaining weight and being discovered (Sanftner & Tantillo, 2011; Goss & Allan, 2009).

Compensatory Behaviors

After a binge, people with bulimia nervosa try to compensate for and undo its effects. Many resort to vomiting, for example. But vomiting actually fails to prevent the absorption of half of the calories consumed during a binge. Furthermore, repeated vomiting affects one's general ability to feel satiated; thus it leads to greater hunger and more frequent and intense binges. Similarly, the use of laxatives or diuretics largely fails to undo the caloric effects of bingeing (Fairburn et al., 2008).

Vomiting and other compensatory behaviors may temporarily relieve the uncomfortable physical feelings of fullness or reduce the feelings of anxiety and self-disgust attached to binge eating (Stewart & Williamson, 2008). Over time, however, a cycle develops in which purging allows more bingeing, and bingeing necessitates more purging. The cycle eventually causes people with the disorder to feel powerless and disgusted with themselves (Sanftner & Tantillo, 2011; Hayaki et al., 2002). Most recognize fully that they have an eating disorder. Lindsey, the woman we met

BETWEEN THE LINES

Royal Bulimia?

During her three years as queen of England, Anne Boleyn, King Henry VIII's second wife, displayed a habit, first observed during her coronation banquet, of vomiting during meals. In fact, she assigned a lady-in-waiting the task of holding up a sheet when the queen looked likely to vomit (Shaw, 2004).

earlier, recalls how the pattern of binge eating, purging, and self-disgust took hold while she was a teenager in boarding school.

> *Every bite that went into my mouth was a naughty and selfish indulgence, and I became more and more disgusted with myself. . . .*
>
> *The first time I stuck my fingers down my throat was during the last week of school. I saw a girl come out of the bathroom with her face all red and her eyes puffy. She had always talked about her weight and how she should be dieting even though her body was really shapely. I knew instantly what she had just done and I had to try it. . . .*
>
> *I began with breakfasts which were served buffet-style on the main floor of the dorm. I learned which foods I could eat that would come back up easily. When I woke in the morning, I had to make the decision whether to stuff myself for half an hour and throw up before class, or whether to try and make it through the whole day without overeating. . . . I always thought people noticed when I took huge portions at mealtimes, but I figured they assumed that because I was an athlete, I burned it off. . . . Once a binge was under way, I did not stop until my stomach looked pregnant and I felt like I could not swallow one more time.*
>
> *That year was the first of my nine years of obsessive eating and throwing up. . . . I didn't want to tell anyone what I was doing, and I didn't want to stop. . . . [Though] being in love or other distractions occasionally lessened the cravings, I always returned to the food.*
>
> *(Hall & Cohn, 2010, p. 55; Hall, 1980, pp. 9–12)*

As with anorexia nervosa, a bulimic pattern typically begins during or after a period of intense dieting, often one that has been successful and earned praise from family members and friends (APA, 2015; Stice & Presnell, 2010; Couturier & Lock, 2006). Studies of both animals and humans have found that normal research participants placed on very strict diets also develop a tendency to binge (Pankevich et al., 2010; Eifert et al., 2007). Some of the participants in the conscientious objector

Curtis Means/NBC NewsWire/Getty Images

Eating for sport Many people go on occasional eating binges. In fact, sometimes binges are officially endorsed, as you see in this photo from the annual Nathan's Famous International Hot Dog Eating Contest in Brooklyn's Coney Island, New York. However, people are considered to have an eating disorder only when the binges recur, the pattern endures, and the issues of weight or shape dominate self-evaluation.

AP Photo/Disney-ABC Domestic Television, Ida Mae Astute

Across the generations When famous television journalist Katie Couric interviewed popular singer Demi Lovato in 2012, it turned out that the two had an important thing in common—eating disorders. Lovato has spoken openly for years about her body image issues and eating struggles, but not until this interview did Couric reveal that she had experienced similar problems in the past. She noted, "I wrestled with bulimia all through college and for two years after that."

"starvation study," for example, later binged when they were allowed to return to regular eating, and a number of them continued to be hungry even after large meals (Keys et al., 1950).

Bulimia Nervosa Versus Anorexia Nervosa

Bulimia nervosa is similar to anorexia nervosa in many ways. Both disorders typically begin after a period of dieting by people who are fearful of becoming obese; driven to become thin; preoccupied with food, weight, and appearance; and struggling with depression, anxiety, obsessiveness, and the need to be perfect (Boone et al., 2014; Holm-Denoma et al., 2014). People with either of the disorders have a heightened risk of suicide attempts (Suokas et al., 2014). Substance abuse may accompany either disorder, perhaps beginning with the excessive use of diet pills (Mann et al., 2014). People with either disorder believe that they weigh too much and look too heavy regardless of their actual weight or appearance (Boone et al., 2014) (see *InfoCentral* on the next page). And both disorders are marked by disturbed attitudes toward eating (Alvarenga et al., 2014).

Yet the two disorders also differ in important ways. Although people with either disorder worry about the opinions of others, those with bulimia nervosa tend to be more concerned about pleasing others, being attractive to others, and having intimate relationships (Zerbe, 2010, 2008). They also tend to be more sexually experienced and active than people with anorexia nervosa (Gonidakis et al., 2014). Particularly troublesome, they are more likely to have long histories of mood swings, become easily frustrated or bored, and have trouble coping effectively or controlling their impulses and strong emotions (Boone et al., 2014; Lilenfeld, 2011). As many as one-third of those with bulimia nervosa display the characteristics of a personality disorder, particularly borderline personality disorder, which you will be looking at more closely in Chapter 13 (Reas et al., 2013).

Another difference is the nature of the medical complications that accompany the two disorders (Corega et al., 2014; Mitchell & Crow, 2010). Only half of women with bulimia nervosa are amenorrheic or have very irregular menstrual periods, compared with almost all of those with anorexia nervosa. On the other hand, repeated vomiting bathes teeth and gums in hydrochloric acid, leading some women with bulimia nervosa to have serious dental problems, such as breakdown of enamel and even loss of teeth. Moreover, frequent vomiting or chronic diarrhea (from the use of laxatives) can cause dangerous potassium deficiencies, which may lead to weakness, intestinal disorders, kidney disease, or heart damage.

BETWEEN THE LINES

Sending a (Bad) Message

- Prior to 1995, eating problems were rare in the Fiji Islands in the South Pacific.

- Soon after satellite television began beaming Western shows and fashions to the islands in 1995, Fijian teenage girls who regularly watched TV became increasingly likely to feel "too big or fat," to diet regularly, and to vomit to control weight.

- As more and more young Fijians have participated on Facebook and other forms of online social networking in recent years, the prevalence of eating disorders among teenagers there has further risen dramatically.

(Becker et al., 2011, 2010, 2007, 2003, 2002, 1999)

BODY DISSATISFACTION

People who evaluate their weight and shape negatively are experiencing **body dissatisfaction**. Around 73% of all girls and women are dissatisfied with their bodies, compared with 56% of all boys and men (Mintem et al., 2014). The vast majority of dissatisfied females believe they are overweight; in contrast, half of dissatisfied males consider themselves overweight and half consider themselves underweight. The factors most closely tied to body dissatisfaction are perfectionism and unrealistic expectations (Wade & Tiggemann, 2013). Body dissatisfaction is the single most powerful contributor to dieting and to the development of eating disorders.

BODY DISSATISFACTION CORRELATES WITH...

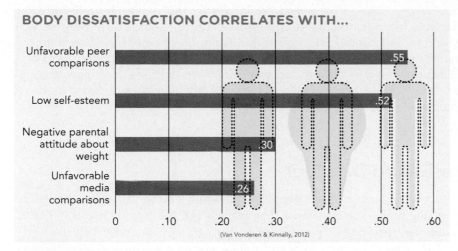

Unfavorable peer comparisons	.55
Low self-esteem	.52
Negative parental attitude about weight	.30
Unfavorable media comparisons	.26

0   .10   .20   .30   .40   .50   .60

(Van Vonderen & Kinnally, 2012)

PEOPLE WITH HIGH BODY DISSATISFACTION ARE MORE PRONE TO...

- Eating disorders
- Depressive disorders
- Anxiety disorders
- Body dysmorphic disorder
- Problems in interpersonal relationships
- Difficulties at work

(Marques et al., 2012; Dyl et al., 2006; Ohring et al., 2002)

ADULTS AND BODY DISSATISFACTION

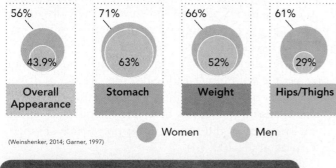

56% / 43.9%	71% / 63%	66% / 52%	61% / 29%
Overall Appearance	Stomach	Weight	Hips/Thighs

● Women ● Men

(Weinshenker, 2014; Garner, 1997)

NEGATIVE BODY THOUGHTS

97% of women have at least one negative thought about their bodies each day.

On average, a woman has **13** negative body thoughts each day.

Examples of negative body thoughts:

• • • "I hate my thighs, my stomach, and my arms."

"I look disgusting." • • •

• • • "I'm obese. All the pretty girls are size 2."

(Dreisbach, 2011)

ADOLESCENTS AND BODY DISSATISFACTION

Females of all ages tend to be dissatisfied with their bodies, but the biggest leap in dissatisfaction occurs when girls transition from early to mid-adolescence (Mäkinen et al., 2012).

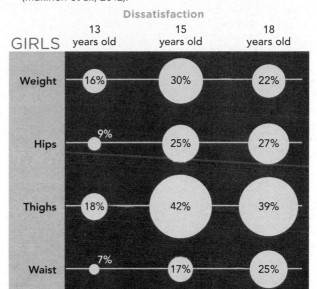

Dissatisfaction

GIRLS	13 years old	15 years old	18 years old
Weight	16%	30%	22%
Hips	9%	25%	27%
Thighs	18%	42%	39%
Waist	7%	17%	25%

BOYS	13 years old	15 years old	18 years old
Weight	17%	25%	20%
Hips	12%	2%	4%
Thighs	10%	9%	6%
Waist	21%	11%	10%

(Weinshenker, 2014; Rosenblum & Lewis, 1999)

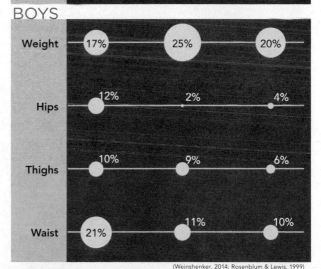

SOCIAL MEDIA AND BODY DISSATISFACTION

- The more time teenage girls spend on social media, the higher their body dissatisfaction.
- 86% of teens say that social network sites hurt their body confidence.

(PROUD2BME, 2013; Tiggemann & Slater, 2013)

▶ **binge-eating disorder** A disorder marked by frequent binges but not extreme compensatory behaviors.

▶ **multidimensional risk perspective** A theory that identifies several kinds of risk factors that are thought to combine to help cause a disorder. The more factors present, the greater the risk of developing the disorder.

➤ *Summing Up*

BULIMIA NERVOSA People with bulimia nervosa go on frequent eating binges and then force themselves to vomit or perform other inappropriate compensatory behaviors. The binges are often in response to increasing tension and are followed by feelings of guilt and self-blame.

Compensatory behavior is at first reinforced by the temporary relief from uncomfortable feelings of fullness or the reduction of feelings of anxiety, self-disgust, and loss of control attached to bingeing. Over time, however, sufferers generally feel disgusted with themselves, depressed, and guilty. People with bulimia nervosa may have mood swings or have difficulty controlling their impulses. Some display a personality disorder. Many develop significant medical problems.

Binge-Eating Disorder

Like those with bulimia nervosa, people with **binge-eating disorder** engage in repeated eating binges during which they feel no control over their eating (APA, 2013). However, they do *not* perform inappropriate compensatory behavior (see Table 9-3). As a result of their frequent binges, around two-thirds of people with binge-eating disorder become overweight or even obese (Brauhardt et al., 2014).

Binge-eating disorder was first identified more than 50 years ago as a pattern common among many overweight people (Stunkard, 1959). It is important to recognize, however, that most overweight people do not engage in repeated binges; their weight results from frequent overeating and/or a combination of biological, psychological, and sociocultural factors (ANAD, 2014).

Between 2 and 7 percent of the population have binge-eating disorder (Brownley et al., 2015; Smink et al., 2013). The binges that characterize this pattern are similar to those seen in bulimia nervosa, particularly the amount of food eaten and the sense of loss of control experienced during the binge. Moreover, like people with bulimia nervosa or anorexia nervosa, those with binge-eating disorder typically are preoccupied with food, weight, and appearance; base their evaluation of themselves largely on their weight and shape; misperceive their body size and are extremely dissatisfied with their body; struggle with feelings of depression, anxiety, and perfectionism; may abuse substances; and typically first develop the disorder in adolescence or young adulthood (Brauhardt et al., 2014; Pearl et al., 2014). On the other hand, although they aspire to limit their eating, people with binge-eating disorder are not as driven to thinness as those with anorexia nervosa and bulimia nervosa. Also, unlike the other eating disorders, binge-eating disorder does not necessarily begin with efforts at extreme dieting, nor are there large gender differences in the prevalence of binge-eating disorder (Davis, 2015; Grucza et al., 2007).

table: **9-3**

Dx Checklist
Binge-Eating Disorder
1. Recurrent binge-eating episodes.
2. Binge-eating episodes include at least three of these features: • Unusually fast eating • Absence of hunger • Uncomfortable fullness • Secret eating due to sense of shame • Subsequent feelings of self-disgust, depression, or severe guilt.
3. Significant distress.
4. Binge-eating episodes take place at least weekly over the course of 3 months.
5. Absence of excessive compensatory behaviors.
(Information from: APA, 2013.)

➤ *Summing Up*

BINGE-EATING DISORDER People with binge-eating disorder have frequent binge-eating episodes but do not display inappropriate compensatory behaviors. Although most overweight people do not have binge-eating disorder, two-thirds of those with binge-eating disorder become overweight. Between 2 and 7 percent of the population display binge-eating disorder. Unlike anorexia nervosa and bulimia nervosa, this disorder is more evenly distributed among males and females and people of different races.

What Causes Eating Disorders?

Most of today's theorists and researchers use a **multidimensional risk perspective** to explain eating disorders. That is, they identify several key factors that place a person at risk for these disorders (Jacobi & Fittig, 2010). The more of these factors that are present, the more likely it is that a person will develop an eating disorder. As you will see, most of the factors that have been cited and investigated center on anorexia nervosa and bulimia nervosa. Binge-eating disorder, identified as a clinical syndrome more recently, is only now being broadly investigated. Which of these factors are also at work in this "newer" disorder will probably become clearer in the coming years.

Psychodynamic Factors: Ego Deficiencies

Hilde Bruch, a pioneer in the study and treatment of eating disorders, was mentioned earlier in this chapter. Bruch developed a largely psychodynamic theory of the disorders. She argued that disturbed mother–child interactions lead to serious *ego deficiencies* in the child (including a poor sense of independence and control) and to severe *perceptual disturbances* that jointly help produce disordered eating (Bruch, 2001, 1991, 1962).

According to Bruch, parents may respond to their children either effectively or ineffectively. *Effective parents* accurately attend to their children's biological and emotional needs, giving them food when they are crying from hunger and comfort when they are crying out of fear. *Ineffective parents,* by contrast, fail to attend to their children's needs, deciding that their children are hungry, cold, or tired without correctly interpreting the children's actual condition. They may feed their children when their children are anxious rather than hungry or comfort them when they are tired rather than anxious. Children who receive such parenting may grow up confused and unaware of their own internal needs, not knowing for themselves when they are hungry or full and unable to identify their own emotions.

Because they cannot rely on internal signals, these children turn instead to external guides, such as their parents. They seem to be "model children," but they fail to develop genuine self-reliance and "experience themselves as not being in control of their behavior, needs, and impulses, as not owning their own bodies" (Bruch, 1973, p. 55). Adolescence increases their basic desire to establish independence, yet they feel unable to do so. To overcome their sense of helplessness, they seek excessive control over their body size and shape and over their eating habits. Helen, an 18-year-old patient of Bruch's, described such needs and efforts:

> There is a peculiar contradiction—everybody thinks you're doing so well and everybody thinks you're great, but your real problem is that you think that you are not good enough. You are afraid of not living up to what you think you are expected to do. You have one great fear, namely that of being ordinary, or average, or common—just not good enough. This peculiar dieting begins with such anxiety. You want to prove that you have control, that you can do it. The peculiar part of it is that it makes you feel good about yourself, makes you feel "I can accomplish something." It makes you feel "I can do something nobody else can do."
>
> (Bruch, 1978, p. 128)

Clinical reports and research have provided some support for Bruch's theory (Holtom-Viesel & Allan, 2014; Schultz & Laessle, 2012). Clinicians have observed that the parents of teenagers with eating disorders do tend to define their children's

Wrong message Supermodel Kate Moss arrives at a New York City fashion gala. Asked during a 2009 online interview whether she had any life mottos, Moss set off a firestorm by replying, "Nothing tastes as good as skinny feels." Noting that this phrase often appears on pro-anorexia Web sites, many critics accused the model of giving legitimacy to the pro-Ana movement. Moss countered that her answer had been misrepresented and clarified that she does not support self-starvation as a lifestyle choice.

AP Photo/Evan Agostini

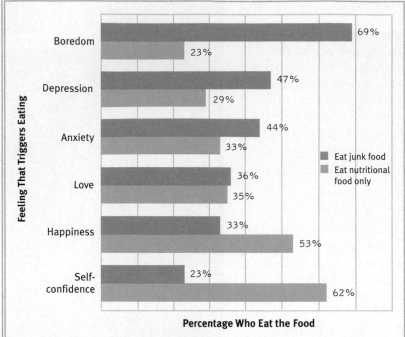

figure 9-2

When do people seek junk food?
Apparently, when they feel bad. People who eat junk food when they are feeling bad outnumber those who eat nutritional food under similar circumstances. In contrast, more people seek nutritional food when they are feeling good. (Information from: Isasi et al., 2013; Haberman, 2007; Rowan, 2005; Hudd et al., 2000; Lyman, 1982.)

▶ **hypothalamus** A part of the brain that helps regulate various bodily functions, including eating and hunger.

▶ **lateral hypothalamus (LH)** A brain region that produces hunger when activated.

▶ **ventromedial hypothalamus (VMH)** A brain region that depresses hunger when activated.

needs rather than allow the children to define their own needs (Ihle et al., 2005; Steiner et al., 1991). When Bruch interviewed the mothers of 51 children with anorexia nervosa, many proudly recalled that they had always "anticipated" their young child's needs, never permitting the child to "feel hungry" (Bruch, 1973).

Research has also supported Bruch's belief that people with eating disorders perceive internal cues, including emotional cues, inaccurately (Lavender et al., 2014; Fairburn et al., 2008). When research participants with an eating disorder are anxious or upset, for example, many of them mistakenly think they are also hungry (see Figure 9-2), and they respond as they might respond to hunger—by eating. In fact, people with eating disorders are often described by clinicians as *alexithymic*, meaning they have great difficulty putting descriptive labels on their feelings (D'Agata et al., 2015; Zerbe, 2010, 2008). And finally, studies support Bruch's argument that people with eating disorders rely excessively on the opinions, wishes, and views of others. They are more likely than other people to worry about how others view them, to seek approval, to be conforming, and to feel a lack of control over their lives (Amianto et al., 2011; Travis & Meltzer, 2008).

Cognitive Factors

If you look closely at Bruch's explanation of eating disorders, you'll see that it contains several *cognitive* ideas. She held, for example, that as a result of ineffective parenting, people with eating disorders improperly label their internal sensations and needs, generally feel little control over their lives, and, in turn, want to have excessive levels of control over their body size, shape, and eating habits. According to cognitive theorists, these deficiencies contribute to a broad cognitive distortion that lies at the center of disordered eating, namely, people with anorexia nervosa and bulimia nervosa judge themselves—often exclusively—based on their shape and weight and their ability to control them (Fairburn et al., 2015, 2008; Murphy et al., 2010). This "core pathology," say cognitive theorists, gives rise to all other aspects of the disorders, including the repeated efforts to lose weight and the preoccupation with thoughts about shape, weight, and eating.

As you saw earlier in the chapter, research indicates that people with eating disorders do indeed display such cognitive deficiencies (Siep et al., 2011). Although studies have not clarified that such deficiencies are the *cause* of eating disorders, many cognitive-behavioral therapists proceed from this assumption and center their treatment for the disorders on correcting the clients' cognitive distortions and accompanying behaviors. As you'll soon see, cognitive-behavioral therapies of this kind are among the most widely used of all treatments for eating disorders (Fairburn et al., 2015, 2008).

> **How might you explain the finding that eating disorders tend to be less common in cultures that restrict a woman's freedom to make decisions about her life?**

Depression

Many people with eating disorders, particularly those with bulimia nervosa, have symptoms of depression (Harrington et al., 2015). This finding has led some theorists to suggest that depressive disorders set the stage for eating disorders.

Their claim is supported by four kinds of evidence. First, many more people with an eating disorder qualify for a clinical diagnosis of major depressive disorder than do people in the general population. Second, the close relatives of people with eating disorders seem to have a higher rate of depressive disorders than do close relatives of people without such disorders. Third, as you will soon see, many people with eating disorders, particularly bulimia nervosa, have low activity of the neurotransmitter serotonin, similar to the serotonin abnormalities found in people with depression. And finally, people with eating disorders are often helped by some of the same antidepressant drugs that reduce depression. Of course, although such findings suggest that depression may help cause eating disorders, other explanations are possible. For example, the pressure and pain of having an eating disorder may *cause* depression.

Biological Factors

Biological theorists suspect that certain genes may leave some people particularly susceptible to eating disorders (Starr & Kreipe, 2014). Consistent with this idea, relatives of people with eating disorders are up to six times more likely than other people to develop the disorders themselves (Thornton et al., 2011; Strober et al., 2001, 2000). Moreover, if one identical twin has anorexia nervosa, the other twin also develops the disorder in as many as 70 percent of cases; in contrast, the rate for fraternal twins, who are genetically less similar, is 20 percent. Similarly, in the case of bulimia nervosa, identical twins display a concordance rate of 23 percent, compared with a rate of 9 percent among fraternal twins (Thornton et al., 2011; Kendler et al., 1995, 1991).

One factor that has interested investigators is the possible role of *serotonin*. Several research teams have found a link between eating disorders and the genes responsible for the production of this neurotransmitter, and still others have measured low serotonin activity in many people with eating disorders (Phillips et al., 2014; Starr & Kreipe, 2014). Thus some theorists suspect that abnormal serotonin activity causes the bodies of some people to crave and binge on high-carbohydrate foods (Kaye et al., 2013, 2011, 2005).

Other biological researchers explain eating disorders by pointing to the **hypothalamus,** a part of the brain that regulates many bodily functions (Berthoud, 2012). Researchers have located two separate areas in the hypothalamus that help control eating. One, the **lateral hypothalamus (LH),** produces hunger when it is activated. When the LH of a laboratory animal is stimulated electrically, the animal eats, even if it has been fed recently. In contrast, another area, the **ventromedial hypothalamus (VMH),** reduces hunger when it is activated. When the VMH is electrically stimulated, laboratory animals stop eating.

These areas of the hypothalamus and related brain structures are apparently activated by chemicals from the brain and body, depending on whether the person is eating or fasting (Schwartz, 2014; Petrovich, 2011). Two such brain chemicals are the natural appetite suppressants *cholecystokinin* (*CCK*) and *glucagon-like peptide-1* (*GLP-1*) (Dossat et al., 2015; Turton et al., 1996). When one team of researchers collected and injected GLP-1 into the brains of rats, the chemical traveled to receptors in the hypothalamus and caused the rats to reduce their food intake almost entirely even though they had not eaten for 24 hours. Conversely, when "full" rats were injected with a substance that blocked the reception of GLP-1 in the hypothalamus, they more than doubled their food intake.

Some researchers believe that the hypothalamus, related brain areas, and chemicals such as CCK and GLP-1, working together, comprise a "weight thermostat"

"*What do you eat for anxiety?*"

/////// **BETWEEN THE LINES** ///////

Smoking, Eating, and Weight

75 percent of people who quit smoking gain weight.

Nicotine, a stimulant substance, suppresses appetites and increases metabolic rate, perhaps because of its impact on the lateral hypothalamus.

(Kroemer et al., 2013; Higgins & George, 2007)

Laboratory obesity Biological theorists believe that certain genes leave some individuals particularly susceptible to eating disorders. To help support this view, researchers have created mutant ("knockout") mice—mice without certain genes. The mouse on the left is missing a gene that helps produce obesity, and it is thin. In contrast, the mouse on the right, which retains that gene, is obese.

of sorts in the body, which is responsible for keeping an individual at a particular weight level called the **weight set point.** Genetic inheritance and early eating practices seem to determine each person's weight set point (Yu et al., 2015; Sullivan et al., 2011). When a person's weight falls below his or her particular set point, the LH and certain other brain areas are activated and seek to restore the lost weight by producing hunger and lowering the body's *metabolic rate,* the rate at which the body expends energy. When a person's weight rises above his or her set point, the VMH and certain other brain areas are activated, and they try to remove the excess weight by reducing hunger and increasing the body's metabolic rate.

According to the weight set point theory, when people diet and fall to a weight below their weight set point, their brain starts trying to restore the lost weight. Hypothalamic and related brain activity produce a preoccupation with food and a desire to binge. They also trigger bodily changes that make it harder to lose weight and easier to gain weight, however little is eaten (Yu et al., 2015; Higgins & George, 2007). Once the brain and body begin conspiring to raise weight in this way, dieters actually enter into a battle against themselves. Some people apparently manage to shut down the inner "thermostat" and control their eating almost completely. These people move toward restricting-type anorexia nervosa. For others, the battle spirals toward a binge-purge or binge-only pattern. Although the weight set point explanation has received considerable debate in the clinical field, it remains widely accepted by theorists and practitioners.

Societal Pressures

Eating disorders are more common in Western countries than in other parts of the world. Thus, many theorists believe that Western standards of female attractiveness are partly responsible for the emergence of the disorders (MacNeill & Best, 2015). Western standards of female beauty have changed throughout history, with a noticeable shift in preference toward a thin female frame in recent decades (Gilbert et al., 2005). One study that tracked the height, weight, and age of contestants in the Miss America Pageant from 1959 through 1978 found an average decline of 0.28 pound per year among the contestants and 0.37 pound per year among winners (Garner et al., 1980). The researchers also examined data on all *Playboy* magazine centerfold models over the same time period and found that the average weight, bust, and hip measurements of these women had decreased steadily. More recent studies of Miss America contestants and *Playboy* centerfolds indicate that these trends have continued (Rubinstein & Caballero, 2000).

Because thinness is especially valued in the subcultures of performers, fashion models, and certain athletes, members of these groups are likely to be particularly concerned and/or criticized about their weight. For example, after undergoing an inpatient treatment program for eating disorders, the popular singer and rapper Kesha recently wrote, "The music industry has set unrealistic expectations for what a body is supposed to look like, and I started becoming overly critical of my own body because of that" (Sebert, 2014).

> **Why do you think that fashion models, often called supermodels, have risen to celebrity status in recent decades?**

Studies have found that performers, models, and athletes are indeed more prone than others to anorexia nervosa and bulimia nervosa (Arcelus, Witcomb, & Mitchell, 2014; Martinsen & Sundgot-Borgen, 2013). In fact, many famous young women from these fields have publicly acknowledged grossly disordered eating patterns over the years. Surveys of athletes at colleges around the United States reveal that more than 9 percent of female college athletes suffer from an eating disorder and at least another 33 percent display eating behaviors that put them at risk for such disorders (Ekern, 2014; Kerr et al., 2007). A full 20 percent of surveyed gymnasts appear to have an eating disorder (Van Durme et al., 2012).

▶ **weight set point** The weight level that a person is predisposed to maintain, controlled in part by the hypothalamus.

▶ **enmeshed family pattern** A family system in which members are overinvolved with each other's affairs and overconcerned about each other's welfare.

Attitudes toward thinness may also help explain economic differences in the rates of eating disorders. In the past, women in the upper socioeconomic classes expressed more concern about thinness and dieting than women of the lower socioeconomic classes (Margo, 1985). Correspondingly, anorexia nervosa and bulimia nervosa were more common among women higher on the socioeconomic scale (Foreyt et al., 1996; Rosen et al., 1991). In recent years, however, dieting and preoccupation with thinness have increased to some degree in all socioeconomic classes, as has the prevalence of these eating disorders (Starr & Kreipe, 2014; Ernsberger, 2009).

Western society not only glorifies thinness but also creates a climate of prejudice against overweight people (Puhl et al., 2015). Whereas slurs based on ethnicity, race, and gender are considered unacceptable, cruel jokes about obesity are standard fare on the Web and television and in movies, books, and magazines. Research indicates that the prejudice against obese people is deep-rooted (Grilo et al., 2005). Prospective parents who were shown pictures of a chubby child and a medium-weight or thin child rated the former as less friendly, energetic, intelligent, and desirable than the latter. In another study, preschool children who were given a choice between a chubby and a thin rag doll chose the thin one, although they could not say why.

Given these trends, it is not totally surprising that a recent survey of 248 adolescent girls directly tied eating disorders and body dissatisfaction to social networking, Internet activity, and television browsing (Latzer, Katz, & Spivak, 2011) (see *MindTech* on the next page). The survey found that the respondents who spent more time on Facebook were more likely to display eating disorders, have negative body image, eat in dysfunctional ways, and want to diet. Those who spent more time on fashion and music Web sites and those who viewed more gossip- and leisure-related television programs showed similar tendencies.

A.B./Getty Images

Models and mannequins Mannequins were once made extra-thin to show the lines of the clothing for sale to best advantage. Today the shape of the ideal woman is indistinguishable from that of a mannequin (right), and a growing number of young women try to achieve this ideal.

Family Environment

Families may play an important role in the development and maintenance of eating disorders (Hoste, Lebow, & Le Grange, 2014). Research suggests that as many as half of the families of people with anorexia nervosa or bulimia nervosa have a long history of emphasizing thinness, physical appearance, and dieting. In fact, the mothers in these families are more likely to diet themselves and to be generally perfectionistic than are the mothers in other families (Zerbe, 2008; Woodside et al., 2002).

Abnormal interactions and forms of communication within a family may also set the stage for an eating disorder (Holtom-Viesel, & Allan, 2014). Family systems theorists argue that the families of people who develop eating disorders are often dysfunctional to begin with and that the eating disorder of one member is a reflection of the larger problem. Influential family theorist Salvador Minuchin, for example, believes that what he calls an **enmeshed family pattern** often leads to eating disorders (Olson, 2011; Minuchin et al., 2006).

In an enmeshed system, family members are overinvolved in each other's affairs and overconcerned with the details of each other's lives. On the positive side, enmeshed families can be affectionate and loyal. On the negative side, they can be clingy and foster dependency. Parents are too involved in the lives of their children, allowing little room for individuality and independence. Minuchin argues that adolescence poses a special problem for these families. The teenager's normal push for independence threatens the family's apparent harmony and closeness. In response, the family may subtly force the child to take on a "sick" role—to develop an eating disorder or some other illness. The child's disorder enables the family to maintain its appearance of harmony. A sick child needs her family, and family members can rally to protect her. Some case studies have supported such family systems explanations, but systematic research fails to show that particular family patterns consistently set the stage for the development of eating disorders (Holtom-Viesel & Allan, 2014). In fact, the families of people with either anorexia nervosa or bulimia nervosa vary widely.

MindTech

Dark Sites of the Internet

Clinicians, researchers, and other mental health practitioners try to combat psychological disorders—in person, in journals and books, and online. Unfortunately, today there are also other—more negative—forces operating that run counter to the work of mental health professionals. Among the most common are so-called *dark sites* of the Internet—sites with the goal of promoting behaviors that the clinical community, and most of society, consider abnormal and destructive. *Pro-anorexia sites* are a prime example of this phenomenon (Wooldridge et al., 2014).

The Eating Disorders Association reports that there are more than 500 pro-anorexia Internet sites, with names such as "Dying to Be Thin" and "Starving for Perfection" (Borzekowski et al., 2010). These sites are commonly called *pro-Ana* sites, using a girl named Ana as the personification of this eating disorder. Some of the sites view anorexia nervosa (and bulimia nervosa) as lifestyles rather than psychological disorders; others present themselves as nonjudgmental sites for people with anorexic features. Either way, the sites are enormously popular and appear to greatly outnumber "pro-recovery" Web sites. This worries professionals and parents alike, although it is not yet clear how influential the sites actually are (Delforterie et al., 2014).

Besides promoting eating disorders, might there be other ways in which pro-Ana sites are potentially harmful to regular visitors?

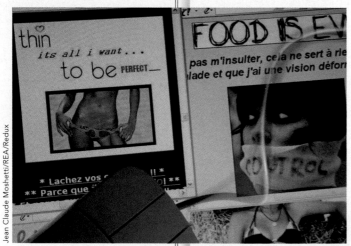

Jean Claude Moshetti/REA/Redux

Many users of the sites exchange tips on how they can starve themselves and disguise their weight loss from family, friends, and doctors (Christodoulou, 2012). The sites may also offer support and feedback about starvation diets. Many of the sites offer mottos, emotional messages, and photos and videos of extremely thin actresses and models as "thinspiration" (Mathis, 2014).

The pro-Ana movement and its messages actually appear throughout the Internet—for example, on Web forums; social networks such as Facebook, Tumblr, and Live Journal; and video platforms such as YouTube, Vimeo, and Veoh (Syed-Abdul et al, 2013). Most online enterprises try to seek out and delete pro-Ana material and groups, taking the position that such messages promote self-harm (Peng, 2008). However, despite such efforts, the sites—and their pro-Ana messages—continue to flourish.

Many people worry that pro-Ana sites place vulnerable people at great risk, and they have called for more active efforts to ban these sites. Others argue, however, that despite their potential dangers, the sites represent basic freedoms that should not be violated—freedom of speech, for example, and perhaps even the freedom to do oneself harm. 💬

Multicultural Factors: Racial and Ethnic Differences

In the popular 1995 movie *Clueless,* Cher and Dionne, wealthy teenage friends of different races, have similar tastes, beliefs, and values about everything from boys to schoolwork. In particular, they have the same kinds of eating habits and beauty ideals, and they are even similar in weight and physical form. But does the story of these young women reflect the realities of white American and African American females in our society?

In the early 1990s, the answer to this question appeared to be a resounding no. Most studies conducted up to the time of the movie's release indicated that the eating behaviors, values, and goals of young African American women were considerably healthier than those of young white American women (Lovejoy, 2001; Cash & Henry, 1995; Parker et al., 1995). A widely publicized 1995 study at the University of Arizona, for example, found that the eating behaviors and attitudes of young African American women were more positive than those of young white American women. It found, specifically, that nearly 90 percent of the white American respondents were dissatisfied with their weight and body shape, compared with around 70 percent of the African American teens.

The study also suggested that white American and African American adolescent girls had different ideals of beauty. The white American teens, asked to define the "perfect girl," described a girl of 5' 7" weighing between 100 and 110 pounds—proportions that mirror those of so-called supermodels. Attaining a perfect weight, many said, was the key to being happy and popular. In contrast, the African American respondents emphasized personality traits over physical characteristics. They defined the "perfect" African American girl as smart, fun, easy to talk to, not conceited, and funny; she did not necessarily need to be "pretty," as long as she was well groomed. The body dimensions the African American teens described were more attainable for the typical girl; they favored fuller hips, for example. Moreover, the African American respondents were less likely than the white American respondents to diet for extended periods.

Unfortunately, research conducted over the past decade suggests that body image concerns, dysfunctional eating patterns, and anorexia nervosa and bulimia nervosa are on the rise among young African American women as well as among women of other minority groups (Starr & Kreipe, 2014; Gilbert, 2011). For example, a survey conducted by *Essence*—the largest-circulation magazine geared toward African Americans—and studies by several teams of researchers have found that the risk of today's African American women developing these eating disorders is approaching

Dangerous profession The fashion world was shocked when 21-year-old Brazilian model Ana Carolina Reston died in 2006 of complications from anorexia nervosa. Told during a 2004 casting call that she was "too fat," Reston began restricting her diet to only apples and tomatoes, culminating in a generalized infection and eventually death. The 5'8" model weighed 88 pounds at the time of her death.

SPARK Movement Members of SPARK Movement, a group of high school girls dedicated to changing how female shapes and weight are portrayed in the media, recently conducted a mock fashion show on the streets of New York City. The group called on the editors of *Teen Vogue* magazine to stop altering the bodies and faces of girls displayed in the magazine's photos.

/////BETWEEN THE LINES/////

Climate Control

Women who live in warmer climates (where more revealing clothing is worn) have lower weight, engage in more binge eating and purging, and have more body image concerns than women who live in cooler climates (Sloan, 2002).

that of white American women. Similarly, African American women's attitudes about body image, weight, and eating are closing in on those of white American women (Annunziato et al., 2007). In the *Essence* survey, 65 percent of African American respondents reported dieting, 39 percent said that food controlled their lives, 19 percent avoided eating when hungry, 17 percent used laxatives, and 4 percent vomited to lose weight.

The shift in the eating behaviors and eating problems of African American women appears to be partly related to their *acculturation* (Kroon Van Diest et al., 2014). One study compared African American women at a predominately white American university with those at a predominately African American university. Those at the former school had significantly higher depression scores, and those scores were positively correlated with eating problems (Ford, 2000).

Still other studies indicate that Hispanic American female adolescents and young adults engage in disordered eating behaviors and express body dissatisfaction at rates about equal to those of white American women (Blow & Cooper, 2014; Levine & Smolak, 2010). Moreover, those who consider themselves more oriented to white American culture have particularly high rates of anorexia nervosa and bulimia nervosa (Cachelin et al., 2006). These eating disorders also appear to be on the increase among young Asian American women and young women in several Asian countries (Pike et al., 2013; Stewart & Williamson, 2008). In one Taiwanese study, for example, 65 percent of the underweight girls aged 10 to 14 years said they wished they were thinner (Wong & Huang, 2000).

Multicultural Factors: Gender Differences

Males account for only 5 to 10 percent of all people with anorexia nervosa and bulimia nervosa. The reasons for this striking gender difference are not entirely clear, but Western society's double standard for attractiveness is, at the very least, one reason. Our society's emphasis on a thin appearance is clearly aimed at women much more than men, and some theorists believe that this difference has made women much more inclined to diet and more prone to eating disorders. Surveys of college men have, for example, found that the majority select "muscular, strong and broad shoulders" to describe the ideal male body and "thin, slim, slightly underweight" to describe the ideal female body (Mayo & George, 2014; Toro et al., 2005).

Salt-N-Pepa: Behind the scenes When the pioneering female rap group Salt-N-Pepa suddenly disbanded in 2002, it was viewed by most as a "typical" band breakup. In fact, however, one of the performers, Cheryl "Salt" James (shown here), had been suffering from bulimia nervosa. She quit performing in order to recover from the disorder and to escape the pressures of her fame, including, in her words, "the pressure to be beautiful and management telling me 'You're gaining weight.'" With James now recovered, the group has reunited and is touring again.

Scott Gries/Getty Images

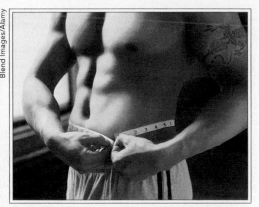

Not for women only A growing number of today's men are developing eating disorders. Some of them aspire to a very lean body shape, such as that displayed by a new breed of ultra-thin male models (left), and develop anorexia nervosa or bulimia nervosa. Others want the ultramuscular look displayed by bodybuilders (above) and develop a new kind of eating disorder called *muscle dysmorphobia*. The men in this latter category inaccurately consider themselves to be scrawny and small and keep striving for a "perfect" body through excessive weight lifting and abuse of steroids.

A second reason for the different rates of anorexia nervosa and bulimia nervosa between men and women may be the different methods of weight loss favored by the two genders. According to some clinical observations, men are more likely to use exercise to lose weight, whereas women more often diet (Gadalla, 2009; Toro et al., 2005). And, as you have read, dieting often precedes the onset of these eating disorders.

Why do some men develop anorexia nervosa or bulimia nervosa? In a number of cases, the disorder is linked to the *requirements and pressures of a job or sport* (Morgan, 2012; Thompson & Sherman, 2011). According to one study, 37 percent of men with these eating disorders had jobs or played sports for which weight control was important, compared with 13 percent of women with such disorders (Braun, 1996). The highest rates of male eating disorders have been found among jockeys, wrestlers, distance runners, body builders, and swimmers. Jockeys commonly spend hours before a race in a sauna, shedding up to seven pounds of weight, and may restrict their food intake, abuse laxatives and diuretics, and force vomiting (Kerr et al., 2007).

> **Why do you think that the prevalence of eating disorders among men has been on the increase in recent years?**

For other men who develop anorexia nervosa or bulimia nervosa, *body image* appears to be a key factor, just as it is in women (Mayo & George, 2014; Mond et al., 2014). Many report that they want a "lean, toned, thin" shape similar to the ideal female body, rather than the muscular, broad-shouldered shape of the typical male ideal (Morgan, 2012; Hildebrandt & Alfano, 2009).

Still other men seem to be caught up in a different kind of eating disorder, called *reverse anorexia nervosa* or *muscle dysmorphobia*. Men with this disorder are very muscular but still see themselves as scrawny and small and therefore continue to strive for a "perfect" body through extreme measures such as excessive weight lifting or the abuse of steroids (Lin & DeCusati, 2015; Morgan, 2012). People with muscle

BETWEEN THE LINES

Saintly Restraint

During the Middle Ages, restrained eating, prolonged fasting, or purging by a number of female saints was greatly admired and was even counted among their miracles. Catherine of Siena sometimes pushed twigs down her throat to bring up food, Mary of Oignies and Beatrice of Nazareth vomited from the mere smell of meat, and Columba of Rieti died of self-starvation (Brumberg, 1988).

dysmorphobia typically feel shame about their bodies, and many have a history of depression, anxiety, and self-destructive compulsive behavior. About one-third of them also engage in related dysfunctional behaviors such as binge eating.

➤ *Summing Up*

WHAT CAUSES EATING DISORDERS? Most theorists now use a multidimensional risk perspective to explain anorexia nervosa and bulimia nervosa and to identify several key contributing factors. These factors include ego deficiencies; cognitive factors; depression; biological factors such as activity of the hypothalamus, biochemical activity, and the body's weight set point; society's emphasis on thinness and bias against obesity; family environment; racial and ethnic differences; and gender differences. Which of these factors are also involved in binge-eating disorder is not yet clear.

How Are Eating Disorders Treated?

Today's treatments for eating disorders have two goals. The first is to correct the dangerous eating pattern as quickly as possible. The second is to address the broader psychological and situational factors that have led to and maintain the eating problem. Family and friends can also play an important role in helping to overcome the disorder.

Treatments for Anorexia Nervosa

The immediate aims of treatment for anorexia nervosa are to help people regain their lost weight, recover from malnourishment, and eat normally again. Therapists must then help them to make psychological and perhaps family changes to lock in those gains.

How Are Proper Weight and Normal Eating Restored? A variety of treatment methods are used to help patients with anorexia nervosa gain weight quickly and return to health within weeks. In the past, treatment almost always took place in a hospital, but now it is often offered in day hospitals or outpatient settings (Raveneau et al., 2014; Keel & McCormick, 2010).

In life-threatening cases, clinicians may need to force *tube and intravenous feedings* on a patient who refuses to eat (Rocks et al., 2014; Touyz & Carney, 2010). Unfortunately, this use of force may cause the client to distrust the clinician. In contrast, clinicians using behavioral weight-restoration approaches offer *rewards* whenever patients eat properly or gain weight and offer no rewards when they eat improperly or fail to gain weight (Tacón & Caldera, 2001).

Perhaps the most popular weight-restoration technique in recent years has been a combination of *supportive nursing care,* nutritional counseling, and a relatively high-calorie diet—often called a nutritional rehabilitation program (Leclerc et al., 2013). Here nurses *gradually* increase a patient's diet over the course of several weeks to more than 3,000 calories a day (Zerbe, 2010, 2008; Herzog et al., 2004). The nurses educate patients about the program, track their progress, provide encouragement, and help them recognize that their weight gain is under control and will not lead to obesity. In some programs, the nurses also use *motivational interviewing,* an intervention in which they motivate clients to actively make and follow through on constructive choices regarding their eating behaviors and their lives (Dray et al., 2014). Studies

"Normal Barbie" For years, the ultra-slim measurements and proportions of the widely popular Barbie doll have introduced women to an unattainable ideal at a very young age. Hoping to demonstrate instead that "average is beautiful," artist Nickolay Lamm recently designed a Normal Barbie (right), using the CDC measurements of the average 19-year-old American woman. Normal Barbie turns out to be shorter, curvier, and bustier than the doll sitting on store shelves around the world.

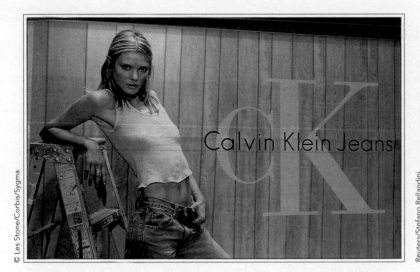

find that patients in nursing-care programs usually gain the necessary weight over 8 to 12 weeks.

How Are Lasting Changes Achieved? Clinical researchers have found that people with anorexia nervosa must overcome their underlying psychological problems in order to create lasting improvement. Therapists typically use a combination of education, psychotherapy, and family therapy to help reach this broader goal (Knatz et al., 2015; Wade & Watson, 2012). Psychotropic drugs have also been helpful in some cases, but research has found that such medications are typically of limited benefit over the long-term course of anorexia nervosa (Starr & Kreipe, 2014).

COGNITIVE-BEHAVIORAL THERAPY A combination of behavioral and cognitive interventions is included in most treatment programs for anorexia nervosa. Such techniques are designed to help clients appreciate and change the behaviors and thought processes that help keep their restrictive eating going (Fairburn & Cooper, 2014; Evans & Waller, 2011). On the behavioral side, clients are typically required to monitor (perhaps by keeping a diary) their feelings, hunger levels, and food intake and the ties between these variables. On the cognitive side, they are taught to identify their "core pathology"—the deep-seated belief that they should in fact be judged by their shape and weight and by their ability to control these physical characteristics. The clients may also be taught alternative ways of coping with stress and of solving problems.

The therapists who use these approaches are particularly careful to help patients with anorexia nervosa recognize their need for independence and teach them more appropriate ways to exercise control (Pike et al., 2010). The therapists may also teach them to identify better and trust their internal sensations and feelings (Wilson, 2010). In the following session, a therapist tries to help a 15-year-old client recognize and share her feelings:

Patient: *I don't talk about my feelings; I never did.*
Therapist: *Do you think I'll respond like others?*
Patient: *What do you mean?*
Therapist: *I think you may be afraid that I won't pay close attention to what you feel inside, or that I'll tell you not to feel the way you do—that it's foolish to*

(continues on the next page)

A story of two billboards In 1995, the Calvin Klein clothing brand posed young teenagers in sexually suggestive clothing ads (left). A public uproar forced the company to remove the ads from magazines and billboards across the United States, but by then, a point had been made—that extreme thinness was in vogue for female fashion and, indeed, for females of all ages. In contrast, the Nolita clothing brand launched a major ad campaign *against* excessive thinness in 2007, displaying anti-anorexia billboards throughout Italy (right). Here two young women stare at one such billboard—that of an emaciated naked woman appearing beneath the words "No Anorexia." The billboard model, Isabelle Caro, died in 2010 of complications from anorexia nervosa.

BETWEEN THE LINES

Fashion Downsizing

In 1968, the average fashion model was 8 percent thinner than the typical woman. Today, models are 23 percent thinner (Tashakova, 2011; Derenne & Beresin, 2006).

© Berliner Verlag/Steinach/dpa/Corbis

Calling for more assertive action
According to many people, efforts to change the negative impact of the fashion industry and media on women have been woefully ineffective to date. Thus a feminist movement has emerged to more aggressively fight society's "obsession with female thinness." The movement's slogan, "Riots Not Diets," has already caught fire and now adorns bags, T-shirts, patches, cookies, glassware, and many other objects around the world.

> *feel frightened, to feel fat, to doubt yourself, considering how well you do in school, how you're appreciated by teachers, how pretty you are.*
>
> **Patient:** (Looking somewhat tense and agitated) *Well, I was always told to be polite and respect other people, just like a stupid, faceless doll.* (Affecting a vacant, doll-like pose)
>
> **Therapist:** *Do I give you the impression that it would be disrespectful for you to share your feelings, whatever they may be?*
>
> **Patient:** *Not really; I don't know.*
>
> **Therapist:** *I can't, and won't, tell you that this is easy for you to do. . . . But I can promise you that you are free to speak your mind, and that I won't turn away.*
>
> *(Strober & Yager, 1985, pp. 368–369)*

Finally, cognitive-behavioral therapists help clients with anorexia nervosa change their attitudes about eating and weight (Fairburn & Cooper, 2014; Evans & Waller, 2012) (see Table 9-4). The therapists may guide clients to identify, challenge, and change maladaptive assumptions, such as "I must always be perfect" or "My weight and shape determine my value" (Fairburn et al., 2015, 2008). They may also educate clients about the body distortions typical of anorexia nervosa and help them see that their own assessments of their size are incorrect.

Although cognitive-behavioral techniques are often of great help to clients with anorexia nervosa, research suggests that the techniques typically must be supplemented by other approaches to bring about better results (Zerbe, 2010, 2008). Family therapy, for example, is often included in treatment.

CHANGING FAMILY INTERACTIONS Family therapy can be an invaluable part of treatment for anorexia nervosa, particularly for children and adolescents with the disorder. As in other family therapy situations, the therapist meets with the family as a whole, points out troublesome family patterns, and helps the members make appropriate changes. In particular, family therapists may try to help the person with anorexia nervosa separate her feelings and needs from those of other members of her

table: 9-4

Sample Items from the Eating Disorder Inventory

For each item, decide if the item is true about you ALWAYS (A), USUALLY (U), OFTEN (O), SOMETIMES (S), RARELY (R), or NEVER (N). Circle the letter that corresponds to your rating.

A	U	O	S	R	N	I eat when I am upset.
A	U	O	S	R	N	I stuff myself with food.
A	U	O	S	R	N	I think about dieting.
A	U	O	S	R	N	I think that my thighs are too large.
A	U	O	S	R	N	I feel extremely guilty after overeating.
A	U	O	S	R	N	I am terrified of gaining weight.
A	U	O	S	R	N	I get confused as to whether or not I am hungry.
A	U	O	S	R	N	I have the thought of trying to vomit in order to lose weight.
A	U	O	S	R	N	I think my buttocks are too large.
A	U	O	S	R	N	I eat or drink in secrecy.

(Information from: Clausen et al., 2011; Garner, 2005, 1991; Garner, Olmsted, & Polivy, 1984.)

family. Although the role of family in the development of anorexia nervosa is not yet clear, research strongly suggests that family therapy (or at least parent counseling) can be helpful in the treatment of this disorder (Knatz et al., 2015; Ambresin et al., 2014).

> **Mother:** *I think I know what [Susan] is going through: all the doubt and insecurity of growing up and establishing her own identity. (Turning to the patient, with tears) If you just place trust in yourself, with the support of those around you who care, everything will turn out for the better.*
>
> **Therapist:** *Are you making yourself available to her? Should she turn to you, rely on you for guidance and emotional support?*
>
> **Mother:** *Well, that's what parents are for.*
>
> **Therapist:** *(Turning to patient) What do you think?*
>
> **Susan:** *(To mother) I can't keep depending on you, Mom, or everyone else. That's what I've been doing, and it gave me anorexia. . . .*
>
> **Therapist:** *Do you think your mom would prefer that there be no secrets between her and the kids—an open door, so to speak?*
>
> **Older sister:** *Sometimes I do.*
>
> **Therapist:** *(To patient and younger sister) How about you two?*
>
> **Susan:** *Yeah. Sometimes it's like whatever I feel, she has to feel.*
>
> **Younger sister:** *Yeah.*
>
> *(Strober & Yager, 1985, pp. 381–382)*

What Is the Aftermath of Anorexia Nervosa?

The use of combined treatment approaches has greatly improved the outlook for people with anorexia nervosa, although the road to recovery can be difficult. The course and outcome of this disorder vary from person to person, but researchers have noted certain trends.

On the positive side, weight is often quickly restored once treatment for the disorder begins, and treatment gains may continue for years (Isomaa & Isomaa, 2014; Haliburn, 2005). As many as 85 percent of patients continue to show improvement—either full or partial—when they are interviewed several years or more after their initial recovery (Isomaa & Isomaa, 2014; Brewerton & Costin, 2011).

Another positive note is that most females with anorexia nervosa menstruate again when they regain their weight, and other medical improvements follow (Mitchell & Crow, 2010). Also encouraging is that the death rate from anorexia nervosa seems to be falling (van Son et al., 2010). Earlier diagnosis and safer and faster weight-restoration techniques may account for this trend. Deaths that do occur are usually caused by suicide, starvation, infection, gastrointestinal problems, or electrolyte imbalance.

Donald Kravitz/Getty Images

Miss America speaks out Kirsten Haglund is crowned Miss America at the January 2008 pageant. During her one-year reign, Haglund openly acknowledged her past struggles with anorexia nervosa. In recent years, she has continued to travel and speak about body image issues and eating disorders. She also has started a foundation to provide treatment services for women who have eating disorders.

On the negative side, as many as 25 percent of persons with anorexia nervosa remain seriously troubled for years (Isomaa & Isomaa, 2014; Steinhausen, 2009). Furthermore, recovery, when it does occur, is not always permanent. At least one-third of recovered patients have recurrences of anorexic behavior, usually triggered by new stresses, such as marriage, pregnancy, or a major relocation (Stice et al., 2013; Fennig et al., 2002). Even years later, many who have recovered continue to express concerns about their weight and appearance. Some still restrict their diets to a degree, feel anxiety when they eat with other people, or hold some distorted ideas about food, eating, and weight (Isomaa & Isomaa, 2014; Fairburn et al., 2008).

About half of those who have suffered from anorexia nervosa continue to have certain emotional problems—particularly depression, obsessiveness, and social anxiety—years after treatment. Such problems are particularly common in those who had not reached a fully normal weight by the end of treatment (Bodell & Mayer, 2011; Steinhausen, 2002).

The more weight persons have lost and the more time that passes before they enter treatment, the poorer the recovery rate (Fairburn et al., 2008). People who had psychological or sexual problems before the onset of the disorder tend to have a poorer recovery rate than those without such a history (Zerwas et al., 2013; Amianto et al., 2011). People whose families are dysfunctional have less positive treatment outcomes (Holtom-Viesel & Allan, 2014). Teenagers seem to have a better recovery rate than older patients (Richard, 2005).

Treatments for Bulimia Nervosa

Treatment programs for bulimia nervosa are often offered in eating disorder clinics (Henderson et al., 2014). Such programs share the immediate goals of helping clients to eliminate their binge-purge patterns and establish good eating habits and the more general goal of eliminating the underlying causes of bulimic patterns. The programs emphasize education as much as therapy (Fairburn & Cooper, 2014). Cognitive-behavioral therapy is particularly helpful in cases of bulimia nervosa—perhaps even more helpful than in cases of anorexia nervosa (Fairburn & Cooper, 2014; Wonderlich et al., 2014). And antidepressant drug therapy, which is of limited help to people with anorexia nervosa, appears to be quite effective in many cases of bulimia nervosa (Starr & Kreipe, 2014).

Cognitive-Behavioral Therapy

When treating clients with bulimia nervosa, cognitive-behavioral therapists employ many of the same techniques that they use to help treat people with anorexia nervosa. However, they tailor the techniques to the unique features of bulimia (for example, bingeing and purging behavior) and to the specific beliefs at work in bulimia nervosa.

BEHAVIORAL TECHNIQUES Therapists often instruct clients with bulimia nervosa to keep diaries of their eating behavior, changes in sensations of hunger and fullness, and the ebb and flow of other feelings (Stewart & Williamson, 2008). This helps the clients to observe their eating patterns more objectively and recognize the emotions and situations that trigger their desire to binge.

One team of researchers studied the effectiveness of an online version of the diary technique (Shapiro et al., 2010). They had 31 clients with bulimia nervosa, each an outpatient in a 12-week cognitive-behavioral therapy program, send nightly texts to their therapists, reporting on their bingeing and purging urges and episodes. The clients received feedback messages, including reinforcement and encouragement for the treatment goals they had been able to reach that day. The clinical researchers reported that by the end of therapy, the clients showed significant decreases in binges, purges, other bulimic symptoms, and feelings of depression.

Cognitive-behavioral therapists may also use the behavioral technique of *exposure and response prevention* to help break the binge-purge cycle. As you read in Chapter 4, this approach consists of exposing people to situations that would ordinarily raise anxiety and then preventing them from performing their usual compulsive responses until they learn that the situations are actually harmless and their compulsive acts unnecessary. For bulimia nervosa, the therapists require clients to eat particular kinds and amounts of food and then prevent them from vomiting to show that eating can be a harmless and even constructive activity that needs no undoing (Wilson, 2010). Typically the therapist sits with the client while the client eats the forbidden foods and stays until the urge to purge has passed. Studies find that this treatment often helps reduce eating-related anxieties, bingeing, and vomiting.

Eric Young/Winona Daily News/AP Photo

COGNITIVE TECHNIQUES Beyond such behavioral techniques, a primary focus of cognitive-behavioral therapists is to help clients with bulimia nervosa recognize and change their maladaptive attitudes toward food, eating, weight, and shape (Waller et al., 2014; Wonderlich et al., 2014). The therapists typically teach the clients to identify and challenge the negative thoughts that regularly precede their urge to binge—"I have no self-control"; "I might as well give up"; "I look fat" (Fairburn & Cooper, 2014; Fairburn, 1985). They may also guide clients to recognize, question, and eventually change their perfectionistic standards, sense of helplessness, and low self-concept (see *PsychWatch* on the next page). Cognitive-behavioral approaches seem to help as many as 65 percent of patients stop bingeing and purging (Poulsen et al., 2014; Eifert et al., 2007).

Other Forms of Psychotherapy Because of its effectiveness in the treatment of bulimia nervosa, cognitive-behavioral therapy is often tried first, before other therapies are considered. If clients do not respond to it, other approaches with promising but less impressive track records may then be tried. A common alternative is *interpersonal psychotherapy,* the treatment described in Chapter 6 that is used to help improve interpersonal functioning (Fairburn et al., 2015; Kass et al., 2013). *Psychodynamic therapy* has also been used in cases of bulimia nervosa, but only a few research studies have tested and supported its effectiveness (Poulsen et al., 2014; Tasca et al., 2014). The various forms of psychotherapy—cognitive-behavioral, interpersonal, and psychodynamic—are often supplemented by family therapy (Ambresin et al., 2014; Starr & Kreipe, 2014).

Cognitive-behavioral, interpersonal, and psychodynamic therapy may each be offered in either an individual or a group therapy format, including self-help groups. Research suggests that group formats are at least somewhat helpful for as many as 75 percent of people with bulimia nervosa (Valbak, 2001).

Antidepressant Medications During the past 15 years, antidepressant drugs—all forms of antidepressant drugs—have been used to help treat bulimia nervosa (Starr & Kreipe, 2014). In contrast to people with anorexia nervosa, those with bulimia nervosa are often helped considerably by these drugs. According to research, the drugs help as many as 40 percent of patients, reducing their binges by an average of 67 percent and vomiting by 56 percent. Once again, drug therapy seems to work best in combination with other forms of therapy, particularly cognitive-behavioral

New efforts at prevention A number of innovative educational programs have been developed to help promote healthy body images and prevent eating disorders. Here, a first-year Winona State University student swings a maul over her shoulder and into bathroom scales as part of Eating Disorders Awareness Week. The scale smashing is an annual event.

The Sugar Plum Fairy

In a November 2010 review of the New York City Ballet production of *The Nutcracker, New York Times* critic Alastair Macauley wrote that Jenifer Ringer, the 37-year-old dancer who played the part of the Sugar Plum Fairy, "looked as if she'd eaten one sugar plum too many" (Macauley, 2010). That harsh critique of the dancer's weight and body set off a storm of protest throughout the country. Many regarded the reviewer's comments as cruel, an example of the absurd aesthetic standards by which women are judged in our society—even a lithe and graceful ballet artist. The reviewer defended his position, arguing, "If you want to make your appearance irrelevant to criticism, do not choose ballet as a career" (Macauley, 2010). But, in the eyes of most observers, he had gone too far.

About the only person who reacted calmly in the face of this uproar was the dancer herself, Jenifer Ringer. She even noted that "as a dancer, I do put myself out there to be criticized, and my body is part of my art form" (Ringer, 2010). It turns out that the 2010 flak was hardly the first time that Ringer's weight and appearance had been described in unflattering terms. In a 2014 autobiography, she has revealed that her body had been an object of criticism throughout much of her professional life.

Ringer began with the City Ballet as a teenager in 1989, and by 1995 she was soloing. According to her memoir, she was also developing bulimia nervosa

Unfair critique Ballet dancer Jenifer Ringer performs with partner Jared Angle in *The Nutcracker.*

while her career was on the rise. She fell into a pattern of overeating and overexercising to compensate. As she puts it, "I had lost any sense of a center for self-esteem and self-worth" (Ringer, 2014).

Decades before Macauley's 2010 critique, many of Ringer's dance mentors were urging her to lose weight. She recalls how legendary choreographer Jerome Robbins exhorted her, "Come on. You just need to get the weight off. Just do it. We need you" (Ringer, 2014). In fact, after a warning from a ballet master that she must "stop eating cheesecake," Ringer's contract with the ballet company was not renewed in 1997 (Ringer, 2014). She left dance at that time for a brief stint as an office worker.

After overcoming her eating disorder and regaining her self-esteem, Ringer rejoined the City Ballet in 1998. The next 16 years of dance represented a personal and professional triumph for her—a triumph that those harsh and unfair words in 2010 could not penetrate. By then, she was no longer an insecure person who judged herself and her body by the standards of others. Rather, as she states in her memoir, "I didn't feel I was heavy, and someone else's opinion of me had no power over me unless I allowed it" (Ringer, 2014).

therapy (Stewart & Williamson, 2008). Alternatively, some therapists wait to see whether cognitive-behavioral therapy or another form of psychotherapy is effective before trying antidepressants (Wilson, 2010, 2005).

What Is the Aftermath of Bulimia Nervosa? Left untreated, bulimia nervosa can last for years, sometimes improving temporarily but then returning. Treatment, however, produces immediate, significant improvement in approximately 40 percent of clients: they stop or greatly reduce their bingeing and purging, eat properly, and maintain a normal weight (Isomaa & Isomaa, 2014; Richard, 2005). Another 40 percent show a moderate response—at least some decrease in binge eating and purging. As many as 20 percent show little immediate improvement. Follow-up studies, conducted years after treatment, suggest that as many as 85 percent of people with bulimia nervosa have recovered, either fully or partially (Isomaa & Isomaa, 2014; Brewerton & Costin, 2011).

Relapse can be a problem even among people who respond successfully to treatment (Stice et al., 2013; Olmsted et al., 2005). As with anorexia nervosa, relapses are usually triggered by a new life stress (Liu, 2007; Abraham & Llewellyn-Jones, 1984). One study found that close to one-third of those who had recovered from bulimia nervosa relapsed within two years of treatment, usually within six months (Olmsted et al., 1994). Relapse is more likely among people who had longer histories of bulimia nervosa before treatment, had vomited more frequently during their disorder, continued to vomit at the end of treatment, had histories of substance abuse, and continue to be lonely or to distrust others after treatment (Vall & Wade, 2015; Brewerton & Costin, 2011; Fairburn et al., 2004).

> **Why do some people who recover from anorexia nervosa and bulimia nervosa remain vulnerable to relapse after recovery?**

Treatments for Binge-Eating Disorder

Given the key role of binges in both bulimia nervosa and binge-eating disorder (bingeing without purging), today's treatments for binge-eating disorder are often similar to those for bulimia nervosa. In particular, cognitive-behavioral therapy, other forms of psychotherapy, and antidepressant medications have been provided—with some success—to help reduce or eliminate the binge-eating patterns and to change disturbed thinking such as being overly concerned with weight and shape (Fischer et al., 2014; Fairburn, 2013). Of course, many people with binge-eating disorder also are overweight, a problem that requires additional kinds of intervention and is often resistant to long-term improvement (Grilo et al., 2014; Claudino & Morgan, 2012).

Now that binge-eating disorder has been identified and is receiving considerable study, it is likely that specialized treatment programs that target the disorder's unique issues will emerge in the coming years (Grilo et al., 2014). In the meantime, relatively little is known about the aftermath of this disorder (Claudino & Morgan, 2012). In one follow-up study of hospitalized patients with severe symptoms, one-third of those who had been treated still displayed the disorder 12 years after hospitalization, and 36 percent were still significantly overweight (Fichter et al., 2008). As with the other eating disorders, many of those who initially recover from binge-eating disorder continue to have a relatively high risk of relapse (ANAD, 2014).

The Biggest Loser phenomenon Contestant Hannah Curlee proudly observes the results of her weigh-in on the 2011 season finale of the popular reality show *The Biggest Loser*. In this TV series, overweight contestants compete to lose the most weight for cash prizes. Most overweight people do not display binge-eating disorder, but most people with the disorder are overweight.

➤ *Summing Up*

HOW ARE EATING DISORDERS TREATED? The first step in treating anorexia nervosa is to increase calorie intake and quickly restore the person's weight, using a strategy such as supportive nursing care. The second step is to deal with the underlying psychological and family problems, often using a combination of education, cognitive-behavioral approaches, and family therapy. As many as 90 percent of people who are successfully treated for anorexia nervosa continue to show full or partial improvements years later. However, some of them relapse along the way.

Treatments for bulimia nervosa focus first on stopping the binge-purge pattern and then on addressing the underlying causes of the disorder. Often several treatment strategies are combined, including education, psychotherapy

(continues on the next page)

(particularly cognitive-behavioral therapy), and antidepressant medications. As many as 75 percent of those who receive treatment eventually improve either fully or partially. Relapse can be a problem and may be precipitated by a new stress. Similar treatments are used to help people with binge-eating disorder. These individuals, however, may also require interventions to address their excessive weight.

PUTTING IT...*together*

A Standard for Integrating Perspectives

You have observed throughout this book that it is often useful to consider socio-cultural, psychological, and biological factors jointly when trying to explain or treat various forms of abnormal functioning. Nowhere is the argument for combining these perspectives more powerful than in the case of eating disorders. According to the multidimensional risk perspective embraced by many theorists, varied factors act together to spark the development of eating disorders, particularly anorexia nervosa and bulimia nervosa. One case may result from societal pressures, autonomy issues, the physical and emotional changes of adolescence, and hypothalamic overactivity, while another case may result from family pressures, depression, and the effects of dieting. No wonder that the most helpful treatment programs for eating disorders combine sociocultural, psychological, and biological approaches. When the multidimensional risk perspective is applied to eating disorders, it demonstrates that scientists and practitioners who follow very different models can work together productively in an atmosphere of mutual respect.

Research on eating disorders keeps revealing new surprises that force clinicians to adjust their theories and treatment programs. For example, researchers have learned that people with eating disorders sometimes feel strangely positive about their symptoms (Williams & Reid, 2010). One recovered patient said, "I still miss my bulimia as I would an old friend who has died" (Cauwels, 1983, p. 173). Given such feelings, many therapists now help clients work through grief reactions over their lost symptoms, reactions that may emerge as the clients begin to overcome their eating disorders (Zerbe, 2008).

While clinicians and researchers seek more answers about eating disorders, clients themselves have begun to take an active role in the identification and treatment of the disorders. A number of patient-run organizations now provide information, education, and support through Web sites, national telephone hot lines, schools, professional referrals, newsletters, workshops, and conferences (Musiat & Schmidt, 2010; Sinton & Taylor, 2010).

CLINICAL CHOICES

Now that you've read about eating disorders, try the interactive case study for this chapter. See if you are able to identify Jenny's symptoms and suggest a diagnosis based on her symptoms. What kind of treatment would be most effective for Jenny? Go to LaunchPad to access *Clinical Choices.*

KEY TERMS

anorexia nervosa, p. 280

restricting-type anorexia nervosa, p. 280

amenorrhea, p. 282

bulimia nervosa, p. 282

binge, p. 282

compensatory behavior, p. 284

binge-eating disorder, p. 288

multidimensional risk perspective, p. 289

effective parents, p. 289

hypothalamus, p. 291

lateral hypothalamus (LH), p. 291

ventromedial hypothalamus (VMH), p. 291

cholecystokinin (CCK), p. 291

glucagon-like peptide-1 (GLP-1), p. 291

weight set point, p. 292

enmeshed family pattern, p. 293

supportive nursing care, p. 298

QuickQuiz

1. What are the symptoms and main features of anorexia nervosa and bulimia nervosa? *pp. 280–286*

2. How are people with anorexia nervosa similar to those with bulimia nervosa? How are they different? *p. 286*

3. What are the symptoms and main features of binge-eating disorder? How is this disorder different from bulimia nervosa? *p. 288*

4. According to Hilde Bruch, how might parents' failure to attend appropriately to their baby's internal needs and emotions contribute to the later development of an eating disorder? *pp. 289–290*

5. How might a person's hypothalamus and weight set point contribute to the development of an eating disorder? *pp. 291–292*

6. What evidence suggests that sociocultural pressures and factors may set the stage for eating disorders? *pp. 292–298*

7. When clinicians treat people with anorexia nervosa, what are their short-term and long-term goals? What approaches do they use to accomplish them? *pp. 298–301*

8. How well do people with anorexia nervosa recover from their disorder? What factors affect a person's recovery? What risks and problems may linger after recovery? *pp. 301–302*

9. What are the key goals and approaches used in the treatment of bulimia nervosa, and how successful are they? What factors affect a person's recovery? What risks and problems may linger after recovery? *pp. 302–305*

10. How are treatments for binge-eating disorder similar to and different from treatments for bulimia nervosa? *p. 305*

Visit *LaunchPad*
www.macmillanhighered.com/launchpad/comerfund8e
to access the e-book, new interactive case studies, videos, activities, and LearningCurve quizzes, as well as study aids including flashcards, FAQs, and research exercises.

Macmillan Education
LaunchPad

Substance Use and Addictive Disorders

"I am Duncan. I am an alcoholic." The audience settled deeper into their chairs at these familiar words. Another chronicle of death and rebirth would shortly begin [at] Alcoholics Anonymous. . . .

"I must have been just past my 15th birthday when I had that first drink that everybody talks about. And like so many of them . . . it was like a miracle. With a little beer in my gut, the world was transformed. I wasn't a weakling anymore, I could lick almost anybody on the block. And girls? Well, you can imagine how a couple of beers made me feel like I could have any girl I wanted. . . .

"Though it's obvious to me now that my drinking even then, in high school, and after I got to college, was a problem, I didn't think so at the time. After all, everybody was drinking and getting drunk and acting stupid, and I didn't really think I was different. . . . I guess the fact that I hadn't really had any blackouts and that I could go for days without having to drink reassured me that things hadn't gotten out of control. And that's the way it went, until I found myself drinking even more—and more often—and suffering more from my drinking, along about my third year of college. . . .

"My roommate, a friend from high school, started bugging me about my drinking. It wasn't even that I'd have to sleep it off the whole next day and miss class, it was that he had begun to hear other friends talking about me, about the fool I'd made of myself at parties. He saw how shaky I was the morning after, and he saw how different I was when I'd been drinking a lot—almost out of my head was the way he put it. And he could count the bottles that I'd leave around the room, and he knew what the drinking and carousing was doing to my grades. . . . [P]artly because I really cared about my roommate and didn't want to lose him as a friend, I did cut down on my drinking by half or more. I only drank on weekends—and then only at night. . . . And that got me through the rest of college and, actually, through law school as well. . . .

"Shortly after getting my law degree, I married my first wife, and . . . for the first time since I started, my drinking was no problem at all. I would go for weeks at a time without touching a drop. . . .

"My marriage started to go bad after our second son, our third child, was born. I was very much career- and success-oriented, and I had little time to spend at home with my family . . . My traveling had increased a lot, there were stimulating people on those trips, and, let's face it, there were some pretty exciting women available, too. So home got to be little else but a nagging, boring wife and children I wasn't very interested in. My drinking had gotten bad again, too, with being on the road so much, having to do a lot of entertaining at lunch when I wasn't away, and trying to soften the hassles at home. I guess I was putting down close to a gallon of very good scotch a week, with one thing or another.

"And as that went on, the drinking began to affect both my marriage and my career. With enough booze in me and under the pressures of guilt over my failure to carry out my responsibilities to my wife and children, I sometimes got kind of rough physically with them. I would break furniture, throw things around, then rush out and drive off in the car. I had a couple of wrecks, lost my license for two years because of one of them. Worst of all was when I tried to stop. By then I was totally hooked, so every time I tried to stop drinking, I'd experience withdrawal in all its horrors . . . with the vomiting and the 'shakes' and being unable to sit still or to lie down. And that would go on for days at a time. . . .

"Then, about four years ago, with my life in ruins, my wife given up on me and the kids with her, out of a job, and way down on my luck, [Alcoholics Anonymous] and I found each other. . . . I've been dry now for a little over two years, and with luck and support, I may stay sober. . . ."

(Spitzer et al., 1983, pp. 87–89)

Human beings enjoy a remarkable variety of foods and drinks. Every substance on earth probably has been tried by someone, somewhere, at some time. We also have discovered substances that have interesting effects—both medical and pleasurable—on our brains and the rest of our bodies. We may swallow an aspirin to quiet a headache, an antibiotic to fight an infection, or a tranquilizer to calm us down. We may drink coffee to get going in the morning or wine to relax with friends. We may smoke cigarettes to soothe our nerves. However, many of the substances we consume can harm us or disrupt our behavior or mood. The misuse of such substances has become one of society's biggest problems; it has been estimated that the cost of substance misuse is more than $600 billion each year in the United States alone (Johnston et al., 2014).

Not only are numerous substances available in our society, but new ones are also introduced almost every day. Some are harvested from nature, others derived from natural substances, and still others produced in the laboratory. Some, such as anti-anxiety drugs, require a physician's prescription for legal use. Others, such as alcohol and nicotine, are legally available to adults. Still others, such as heroin, are illegal under all circumstances. In 1962, only 4 million people in the United States had ever used marijuana, cocaine, heroin, or another illegal substance; today the number has climbed to more than 100 million (SAMHSA, 2014). In fact, 24 million people have used illegal substances within the past month. Almost 24 percent of all high school seniors have used an illegal drug within the past month (Johnston et al., 2014).

A *drug* is defined as any substance other than food that affects our bodies or minds. It need not be a medicine or be illegal. The term "substance" is now frequently used in place of "drug," in part because many people fail to see that such substances as alcohol, tobacco, and caffeine are drugs, too. When a person ingests a substance—whether it be alcohol, cocaine, marijuana, or some form of medication—trillions of powerful molecules surge through the bloodstream and into the brain. Once there, the molecules set off a series of biochemical events that disturb the normal operation of the brain and body. Not surprisingly, then, substance misuse may lead to various kinds of abnormal functioning.

Substances may cause *temporary* changes in behavior, emotion, or thought; this cluster of changes is called **substance intoxication** in DSM-5. As Duncan found out, for example, an excessive amount of alcohol may lead to *alcohol intoxication,* a temporary state of poor judgment, mood changes, irritability, slurred speech, and poor coordination. Similarly, drugs such as LSD may produce *hallucinogen intoxication,* sometimes called *hallucinosis,* which consists largely of perceptual distortions and hallucinations.

Some substances can also lead to *long-term* problems. People who regularly ingest them may develop **substance use disorders,** patterns of maladaptive behaviors and reactions brought about by the repeated use of substances (Higgins et al., 2014; APA, 2013). People with a substance use disorder may come to crave a particular substance and rely on it excessively, resulting in damage to their family and social relationships, poor functioning at work, and/or danger to themselves or others (see Table 10-1). In many cases, people with such a disorder also become physically dependent on the substance, developing a *tolerance* for it and experiencing *withdrawal* reactions. When people develop **tolerance,** they need increasing doses of the substance to produce the desired effect. **Withdrawal** reactions consist of unpleasant and sometimes

table: **10-1**

Dx Checklist
Substance Use Disorder
1. Individual displays a maladaptive pattern of substance use leading to significant impairment or distress.
2. Presence of at least 2 of the following symptoms within a 1-year period:
(a) Substance is often taken in larger amounts or over a longer period than intended.
(b) Unsuccessful efforts or persistent desire to reduce or control substance use.
(c) Much time spent trying to obtain, use, or recover from the effects of substance.
(d) Failure to fulfill major role obligations at work, school, or home as a result of repeated substance use.
(e) Continued use of substance despite persistent social or interpersonal problems caused by it.
(f) Cessation or reduction of important social, occupational, or recreational activities because of substance use.
(g) Continuing to use substance in situations where use poses physical risks.
(h) Continuing to use substance despite awareness that it is causing or worsening a physical or psychological problem.
(i) Craving for substance.
(j) Tolerance effects.
(k) Withdrawal reactions.
(Information from: APA, 2013)

dangerous symptoms—cramps, anxiety attacks, sweating, nausea—that occur when the person suddenly stops taking or cuts back on the substance. Duncan, who described his problems to fellow members at an Alcoholics Anonymous meeting, was caught in a form of substance use disorder called *alcohol use disorder.* When he was a college student and later a lawyer, alcohol damaged his family, social, academic, and work life. He also built up a tolerance for alcohol over time and had withdrawal symptoms such as vomiting and shaking when he tried to stop using it.

In any given year, 8.9 percent of all teens and adults in the United States, over 23 million people, have a substance use disorder (SAMHSA, 2014; NSDUH, 2013). American Indians have the highest rate of substance use disorders in the United States (21.8 percent), while Asian Americans have the lowest (3.2 percent). White Americans, Hispanic Americans, and African Americans have rates close to 9 percent (see Figure 10-1). Only 11 percent (around 2.5 million people) of all those with substance use disorders receive treatment from a mental health professional (Belendiuk & Riggs, 2014; NSDUH, 2013).

The substances people misuse fall into several categories: *depressants, stimulants, hallucinogens,* and *cannabis.* In this chapter you will read about some of the most problematic substances and the abnormal patterns they may produce. In addition, at the end of the chapter, you'll read about *gambling disorder,* a problem that DSM-5 lists as an additional addictive disorder. By listing this behavioral pattern alongside the substance use disorders, DSM-5 is suggesting that this problem has addictive-like symptoms and causes that share more than a passing similarity to those at work in substance use disorders.

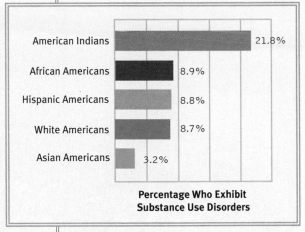

Percentage Who Exhibit Substance Use Disorders

figure 10-1
How do races differ in substance use disorders? In the United States, American Indians are much more likely than members of other ethnic or cultural groups to have substance use disorders. (Information from: NSDUH, 2013.)

Depressants

Depressants slow the activity of the central nervous system. They reduce tension and inhibitions and may interfere with a person's judgment, motor activity, and concentration. The three most widely used groups of depressants are *alcohol, sedative-hypnotic drugs,* and *opioids.*

Alcohol

The World Health Organization estimates that 2 billion people worldwide consume **alcohol.** In the United States more than half of all residents at least from time to time drink beverages that contain alcohol (SAMHSA, 2014). Purchases of beer, wine, and liquor amount to tens of billions of dollars each year in the United States alone.

When people consume five or more drinks on a single occasion, it is called a *binge-drinking* episode. Twenty-three percent of people in the United States over the age of 11, most of them male, binge-drink each month (SAMHSA, 2014). Around 6.5 percent of people over 11 years of age binge-drink at least five times each month. They are considered heavy drinkers. Among heavy drinkers, males outnumber females by at least 3 to 2.

All alcoholic beverages contain *ethyl alcohol,* a chemical that is quickly absorbed into the blood through the lining of the stomach and the intestine. The ethyl alcohol immediately begins to take effect as it is carried in the bloodstream to the central nervous system (the brain and spinal cord), where it acts to depress, or slow, functioning by binding to various neurons. One important group of neurons to which ethyl alcohol binds are those that normally receive the neurotransmitter GABA. As you saw in Chapter 4, GABA carries an *inhibitory* message—a message to stop firing—when it is received at certain neurons. When alcohol binds to receptors on those neurons, it apparently helps GABA to shut down the neurons, thus helping to relax the drinker (Filip et al., 2014; Nace, 2011, 2005).

▸**substance intoxication** A cluster of temporary undesirable behavioral or psychological changes that develop during or shortly after the ingestion of a substance.

▸**substance use disorder** A pattern of long-term maladaptive behaviors and reactions brought about by repeated use of a substance.

▸**tolerance** The brain and body's need for ever larger doses of a drug to produce earlier effects.

▸**withdrawal** Unpleasant, sometimes dangerous reactions that may occur when people who use a drug regularly stop taking or reduce their dosage of the drug.

▸**alcohol** Any beverage containing ethyl alcohol, including beer, wine, and liquor.

Aris Messinis/AP Photo

Substance misuse and sports fans A problem that has received growing attention in recent years is excessive drinking by fans at sports events. While two soccer players were jumping for a high ball at this 2002 playoff game in Athens, Greece, fans—many of them intoxicated—ripped out plastic seats, threw flares on the field, and hurled coins and rocks at the players.

At first ethyl alcohol depresses the areas of the brain that control judgment and inhibition; people become looser, more talkative, and often more friendly. As their inner control breaks down, they may feel relaxed, confident, and happy. When more alcohol is absorbed, it slows down additional areas in the central nervous system, leaving drinkers less able to make sound judgments, their speech less careful and less coherent, and their memory weaker. Many people become highly emotional and perhaps loud and aggressive.

Motor difficulties increase as a person continues drinking, and reaction times slow. People may be unsteady when they stand or walk and clumsy in performing even simple activities. They may drop things, bump into doors and furniture, and misjudge distances. Their vision becomes blurred, particularly their peripheral, or side, vision, and they have trouble hearing. As a result, people who have drunk too much alcohol may have great difficulty driving or solving simple problems.

The extent of the effect of ethyl alcohol is determined by its *concentration*, or proportion, in the blood. Thus a given amount of alcohol has less effect on a large person than on a small one. Gender also affects the concentration of alcohol in the blood. Women have less of the stomach enzyme *alcohol dehydrogenase*, which breaks down alcohol in the stomach before it enters the blood. So women become more intoxicated than men on equal doses of alcohol (Hart & Ksir, 2014).

Levels of impairment are closely related to the concentration of ethyl alcohol in the blood. When the alcohol concentration reaches 0.06 percent of the blood volume, a person usually feels relaxed and comfortable. By the time it reaches 0.09 percent, however, the drinker crosses the line into intoxication. If the level goes as high as 0.55 percent, the drinker will likely die. Most people lose consciousness before they can drink enough to reach this level; nevertheless, more than 1,000 people in the United States die each year from too high a blood alcohol level (Hart & Ksir, 2014).

The effects of alcohol subside only when the alcohol concentration in the blood declines. Most of the alcohol is broken down, or *metabolized*, by the liver into carbon dioxide and water, which can be exhaled and excreted. The average rate of this metabolism is 25 percent of an ounce per hour, but different people's livers work at different speeds; thus rates of "sobering up" vary. Despite popular belief, only time and metabolism can make a person sober. Drinking black coffee, splashing cold water on one's face, or "pulling oneself together" cannot hurry the process.

Alcohol Use Disorder Though legal, alcohol is actually one of the most dangerous of recreational drugs, and its reach extends across the life span. In fact, around 28 percent of middle school students admit to some alcohol use, while 39 percent of high school seniors drink alcohol each month (most to the point of intoxication) and 2.2 percent report drinking every day (Johnston et al., 2014). Alcohol misuse is also a major problem on college campuses (see *PsychWatch* on the next page).

> If alcohol is highly addictive and capable of causing so many problems, why does it remain legal in most countries?

Surveys indicate that over a one-year period, 6.8 percent of all adults in the United States display *alcohol use disorder,* known in popular terms as *alcoholism* (NSDUH, 2013). Men with this disorder outnumber women by at least 2 to 1. Many teenagers also experience the disorder (Johnston et al., 2014).

PsychWatch

College Binge Drinking: An Extracurricular Crisis

Drinking large amounts of alcohol in a short time, or *binge drinking*, is a serious problem on college campuses, as well as in many other settings (SAMHSA, 2014; NSDUH, 2013). Studies show that 40 percent of college students binge-drink at least once each year, one-third of them six times or more per month. In many circles, alcohol use is an accepted part of college life, but consider some of the following statistics (Abbey et al., 2014; Statistic Brain, 2012; Howland et al., 2010; NCASA, 2007; Abbey, 2002):

➤ Alcohol-related arrests account for 83 percent of all campus arrests.

➤ More than half of all sexual assaults on college campuses involve the heavy consumption of alcohol.

➤ Alcohol may be a factor in nearly 40 percent of academic problems and 28 percent of all instances of dropping out of college.

➤ Approximately 700,000 students each year are physically or emotionally traumatized or assaulted by a student drinker.

➤ Half of college students say "drinking to get drunk" is an important reason for drinking.

➤ Binge drinking often has a lingering effect on mood, memory, brain functioning, and heart functioning.

➤ Binge drinking is tied to 1,700 deaths and 500,000 injuries, every year.

➤ The number of female binge drinkers among college students has increased 31 percent over the past decade.

Testing the limits College binge drinking, which involves behaviors similar to that shown here, has led to a number of deaths in recent years.

These findings have led some educators to describe binge drinking as "the number one public health hazard" for full-time college students, and many researchers and clinicians have turned their attention to it. Researchers at the Harvard School of Public Health, for example, have surveyed more than 50,000 students at 120 college campuses around the United States (Wechsler & Nelson, 2008; Wechsler et al., 2004, 1995, 1994). One of their surveys found that the students most likely to binge-drink were those who lived in a fraternity or sorority house, pursued a party-centered lifestyle, and engaged in high-risk behaviors such as substance misuse or having multiple sex partners. Other surveys have also suggested that students who were binge drinkers in high school were more likely to binge-drink in college.

Efforts to change such patterns have begun. For example, some universities now provide substance-free dorms: 36 percent of the residents in such dorms continue to be occasional binge drinkers, according to one study, compared with 75 percent of those who live in a fraternity or sorority house (Wechsler et al., 2002). This and other current research efforts are promising. However, most people in the clinical field agree that much more work is needed to help us fully understand, prevent, and treat what has become a major societal problem.

The current prevalence of alcoholism is around 7.6 percent for white Americans, 5.1 percent for Hispanic Americans, and 4.5 percent for African Americans (NSDUH, 2013). American Indians, particularly men, tend to display a higher rate of alcohol use disorder than any of these groups. Overall, 8.5 percent of them experience the disorder, although specific prevalence rates differ widely across the various American Indian reservation communities. Generally, Asians in the United States and elsewhere have a lower rate of alcoholism (1.7 percent) than do people from other cultures. As many as half of these individuals have a deficiency of alcohol dehydrogenase, the chemical responsible for breaking down alcohol, so they react quite negatively to even a modest intake of alcohol. Such reactions in turn help prevent extended use (Tsuang & Pi, 2011).

**DSM-5 Controversy:
Is All Drug Misuse the Same?**

DSM-5 has combined two past disorders, *substance abuse* (excessive and chronic reliance on drugs) and *substance dependence* (excessive reliance accompanied by tolerance and withdrawal symptoms) into a single category—*substance use disorder*. Critics worry that clinicians may now fail to recognize and address the different prognoses and treatment needs of people who abuse substances and those who depend on substances.

CLINICAL PICTURE Generally speaking, people with alcohol use disorder drink large amounts regularly and rely on it to enable them to do things that would otherwise make them anxious (McCrady, 2014). Eventually the drinking interferes with their social behavior and ability to think and work. They may have frequent arguments with family members or friends, miss work repeatedly, and even lose their jobs. MRI scans of chronic heavy drinkers have revealed damage in various regions of their brains and, correspondingly, impairments in their memory, speed of thinking, attention skills, and balance (Sifferlin, 2014).

Individually, people's patterns of alcoholism vary. Some drink large amounts of alcohol every day and keep drinking until intoxicated. Others go on periodic binges of heavy drinking that can last weeks or months. They may remain intoxicated for days and later be unable to remember anything about the period. Still others may limit their excessive drinking to weekends, evenings, or both.

TOLERANCE AND WITHDRAWAL For many people, alcohol use disorder includes the symptoms of tolerance and withdrawal reactions (McCrady, 2014). As their bodies build up a tolerance for alcohol, they need to drink ever larger amounts to feel its effects. In addition, they have withdrawal symptoms when they stop drinking. Within hours their hands, tongue, and eyelids begin to shake; they feel weak and nauseated; they sweat and vomit; their heart beats rapidly; and their blood pressure rises. They may also become anxious, depressed, unable to sleep, or irritable (APA, 2013).

A small percentage of people with alcohol use disorder go through a particularly dramatic withdrawal reaction called **delirium tremens ("the DTs").** It consists of terrifying visual hallucinations that begin within a few days after they stop or reduce their drinking. Some people see small, frightening animals chasing or crawling on them or objects dancing about in front of their eyes. Like most other alcohol withdrawal symptoms, the DTs usually run their course in two to three days. However, people who have severe withdrawal reactions such as this may also have seizures, lose consciousness, suffer a stroke, or even die. Today certain medical procedures can help prevent or reduce such extreme reactions.

What Is the Personal and Social Impact of Alcoholism?
Alcoholism destroys millions of families, social relationships, and careers (see *MindTech* on the next page). Medical treatment, lost productivity, and losses due to deaths from alcoholism cost society many billions of dollars annually. The disorder also plays a role in more than one-third of all suicides, homicides, assaults, rapes, and accidental deaths, including 30 percent of all fatal automobile accidents in the United States (NIAAA, 2015; Gifford et al., 2010). Altogether, intoxicated drivers are responsible for 10,000 deaths each year. More than 11 percent of all adults have driven while intoxicated at least once in the past year (SAMHSA, 2014).

Alcoholism has serious effects on the 30 million children of people with this disorder. Home life for these children is likely to include much conflict and perhaps sexual or other forms of abuse. In turn, the children themselves have higher rates of psychological problems (Kelley et al., 2014; Watt, 2002). Many have low self-esteem, poor communication skills, poor sociability, and marital problems.

Long-term excessive drinking can also seriously damage a person's physical health (Nace, 2011, 2005). It so overworks the liver that people may develop an irreversible condition called *cirrhosis,* in which the liver becomes scarred and dysfunctional. Cirrhosis accounts for more than 36,000 deaths

Simulating alcohol's effects A 16-year-old student weaves her way through an obstacle course while wearing a pair of goggles that produce alcohol-like impairment. The exercise is part of a DUI-prevention program at her New Mexico high school, designed to give students hands-on experience with alcohol's effects on vision and balance.

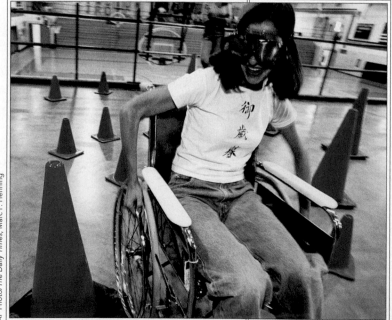

Neknomination Goes Viral

Binge drinking and other risky alcohol-related behaviors have long been associated with peer pressure. But in the past few years, a popular new "game"—made possible by the Internet and social media—has taken the impact of peer pressure to new heights.

In early 2013, an online drinking game called *Neknominate* (or *Neknomination*), believed to have originated in Australia, emerged on Internet sites like YouTube and Facebook (Wilkinson and Soares, 2014). In this game, a person records a video of himself or herself drinking an entire bottle of hard liquor (known in Australia as "necking") and then challenges ("nominates") a friend by name to post his or her own drinking video, one that will top the level and danger of the initial drinking act, and to then pass the challenge on to another person (James, 2014).

In most cases, the drink being consumed in the videos has an unusually high alcohol content, to make the "achievement" all the more "impressive." Some of the videos also involve people exhibiting other dangerous or reckless behavior along with the drinking, such as driving while drinking, stripping in public, shoplifting, or consuming motor oil or even small animals both alive and dead (Wilkinson and Soares, 2014).

runzelkorn/Shutterstock

Given the nature of the game, you may not be surprised that Neknominate was tied with a number of deaths within a very short period after its emergence, as it spread to Great Britain, Canada, the United States, and other parts of the world (James, 2014). In February 2014, for example, five unrelated men, three in England and two in Ireland, died while making videos of themselves completing Neknominate challenges.

> **What psychological factors, besides peer pressure, might induce a person to participate in an activity as risky as Neknominate?**

A public outcry regarding the practice of Neknominate has emerged, with politicians, doctors, and others calling on Facebook and YouTube to ban discussions or presentations of the game. Facebook, however, has declined to ban discussions or postings associated with it, stating that its policy is only to ban content that is directly harmful, not to censor content that discusses potentially dangerous or offensive behavior (Wilkinson and Soares, 2014). The practice and uproar surrounding Neknominate has begun to die down a bit in recent months—while many Neknominate players have moved on to other high-risk Internet crazes such as *Punch4Punch*, in which people video themselves punching each other until one gives up.

each year (CDC, 2015). Alcohol use disorder may also damage the heart and lower the immune system's ability to fight off cancer, bacterial infections, and AIDS.

Long-term excessive drinking also causes major nutritional problems. Alcohol makes people feel full and lowers their desire for food, yet it has no nutritional value. As a result, chronic drinkers become malnourished, weak, and prone to disease. Their vitamin and mineral deficiencies may also cause problems. An alcohol-related

▶ **delirium tremens (DTs)** A dramatic withdrawal reaction that some people who are dependent on alcohol have. It consists of confusion, clouded consciousness, and terrifying visual hallucinations.

▶ **Korsakoff's syndrome** An alcohol-related disorder marked by extreme confusion, memory impairment, and other neurological symptoms.

▶ **fetal alcohol syndrome** A cluster of problems in a child, including low birth weight, irregularities in the head and face, and intellectual deficits, caused by excessive alcohol intake by the mother during pregnancy.

▶ **sedative-hypnotic drug** A drug used in low doses to reduce anxiety and in higher doses to help people sleep. Also called an *anxiolytic drug.*

▶ **barbiturates** Addictive sedative-hypnotic drugs that reduce anxiety and help people sleep.

▶ **benzodiazepines** The most common group of sedative-hypnotic drugs, which includes Valium and Xanax.

▶ **opioid** Opium or any of the drugs derived from opium, including morphine, heroin, and codeine.

▶ **opium** A highly addictive substance made from the sap of the opium poppy.

▶ **morphine** A highly addictive substance derived from opium that is particularly effective in relieving pain.

▶ **heroin** One of the most addictive substances derived from opium.

▶ **endorphins** Neurotransmitters that help relieve pain and reduce emotional tension. They are sometimes referred to as the body's own opioids.

deficiency of vitamin B (thiamine), for example, may lead to **Korsakoff's syndrome,** a disease marked by extreme confusion, memory loss, and other neurological symptoms. People with Korsakoff's syndrome cannot remember the past or learn new information and may make up for their memory losses by *confabulating*—reciting made-up events to fill in the gaps.

Women who drink during pregnancy place their fetuses at risk (Bakoyiannis et al., 2014; Hart & Ksir, 2014; Gifford et al., 2010). Excessive alcohol use during pregnancy may cause a baby to be born with **fetal alcohol syndrome,** a pattern of abnormalities that can include intellectual disability disorder, hyperactivity, head and face deformities, heart defects, and slow growth. It has been estimated that in the overall population, around 1 of every 1,000 babies is born with this syndrome. The rate may increase to as many as 29 of every 1,000 babies of women who are problem drinkers. If all alcohol-related birth defects (known as *fetal alcohol spectrum disorder*) are counted, the rate becomes 80 to 200 such births per 1,000 heavy-drinking women. In addition, heavy drinking early in pregnancy often leads to a miscarriage. According to surveys, 8.5 percent of pregnant American women have drunk alcohol during the past month and 2.7 percent of pregnant women have had binge-drinking episodes (SAMHSA, 2014; NSDUH, 2013).

Sedative-Hypnotic Drugs

Sedative-hypnotic drugs, also called **anxiolytic** (meaning "anxiety-reducing") **drugs,** produce feelings of relaxation and drowsiness. At low dosages, the drugs have a calming or sedative effect. At higher dosages, they are sleep inducers, or hypnotics. For the first half of the twentieth century, a group of drugs called **barbiturates** were the most widely prescribed sedative-hypnotic drugs. Although still prescribed by some physicians, these drugs have been largely replaced by **benzodiazepines**, which are generally safer and less likely to lead to intoxication, tolerance effects, and withdrawal reactions (Filip et al., 2014).

As Chapter 4 noted, benzodiazepines, developed in the 1950s, are the most popular sedative-hypnotic drugs available. Xanax, Ativan, and Valium are just three of the dozens of these compounds in clinical use. Altogether, 130 million prescriptions are written annually for benzodiazepines (Grohol, 2012). Like alcohol, they calm people by binding to receptors on the neurons that receive GABA and by increasing GABA's activity at those neurons (Filip et al., 2014). Benzodiazepines relieve anxiety without making people as drowsy as other kinds of sedative-hypnotics. They are also less likely to slow a person's breathing, so they are less likely to cause death during sleep in the event of an overdose.

When benzodiazepines were first discovered, they seemed so safe and effective that physicians prescribed them generously, and their use spread. Eventually, however, it became clear that in high enough doses the drugs can, like barbiturates, cause intoxication and lead to *sedative-hypnotic use disorder,* a pattern marked by craving for the drugs, tolerance effects, and withdrawal reactions. Over a one-year period, 0.03 percent of all adults in the United States display this disorder, and as many as 1 percent develop the pattern over the course of their lives (SAMHSA, 2014).

Opioids

Opioids include opium—taken from the sap of the opium poppy—and the drugs derived from it, such as heroin, morphine, and codeine. **Opium** itself has been in use for thousands of years. In the past it was used widely in the treatment of medical disorders because of its ability to reduce both physical and emotional pain. Eventually, however, physicians discovered that the drug was addictive.

In 1804 a new substance, **morphine,** was derived from opium. Named after Morpheus, the Greek god of sleep, this drug relieved pain even better than opium did and initially was considered safe. However, wide use of the drug eventually revealed that it, too, could lead to addiction. So many wounded soldiers in the United States received morphine injections during the Civil War that morphine addiction became known as "soldiers' disease."

In 1898, morphine was converted into yet another new pain reliever, **heroin.** For several years heroin was viewed as a wonder drug and was used as a cough medicine and for other medical purposes. Eventually, however, physicians learned that heroin is even more addictive than the other opioids. By 1917, the U.S. Congress had concluded that all drugs derived from opium were addictive, and it passed a law making opioids illegal except for medical purposes.

Still other drugs have been derived from opium, and *synthetic* (laboratory-blended) opioids such as *methadone* have also been developed (Dilts & Dilts, 2011, 2005). All these opioid drugs—natural and synthetic—are known collectively as *narcotics.* Each drug has a different strength, speed of action, and tolerance level. Morphine, *codeine,* and *oxycodone* (the key ingredient in OxyContin and Percocet) are medical narcotics usually prescribed to relieve pain. In contrast to these narcotics, heroin is illegal in the United States in all circumstances.

Most narcotics are smoked, inhaled, snorted, injected by needle just beneath the skin ("skin popped"), or injected directly into the bloodstream ("mainlined"), the most powerful form of intake. An injection quickly brings on a *rush*—a spasm of warmth and ecstasy that is sometimes compared with orgasm. The brief spasm is followed by several hours of a pleasant feeling called a *high* or *nod.* During a high, the drug user feels relaxed, happy, and unconcerned about food, sex, or other bodily needs.

> **Can you think of other substances or activities that, like opioids, can be helpful in controlled portions but dangerous when used excessively?**

Opioids create these effects by depressing the central nervous system, particularly the centers that help control emotion. The drugs attach to brain receptor sites that ordinarily receive **endorphins**—neurotransmitters that help relieve pain and reduce emotional tension. When neurons at these receptor sites receive opioids, they produce pleasurable and calming feelings just as they would do if they were receiving endorphins. In addition to reducing pain and tension, opioids cause nausea, narrowing of the pupils ("pinpoint pupils"), and constipation.

Opioid Use Disorder

Heroin use exemplifies the kinds of problems posed by opioids. After taking heroin repeatedly for just a few weeks, users may develop *opioid use disorder.* Their use of heroin interferes significantly with their social and occupational functioning, and their lives center around the drug. They may also build a tolerance for heroin and experience a withdrawal reaction when they stop taking it (Hart & Ksir, 2014). At first the withdrawal symptoms are anxiety, restlessness, sweating, and rapid breathing; later they include severe twitching, aches, fever, vomiting, diarrhea, loss of appetite, high blood pressure, and weight loss of up to 15 pounds (due to loss of bodily fluids). These symptoms usually peak by the third day, gradually subside, and disappear by the eighth day. A person in heroin withdrawal can either wait out the symptoms or end withdrawal by taking the drug again.

Such people soon need heroin just to avoid going into withdrawal, and they must continually increase their doses in order to achieve even that relief. The temporary high becomes less intense and less important. Heroin users may spend much of their time planning their next dose, in

Purer blend Heroin, derived from poppies such as this one in a poppy field in southern Afghanistan, is purer and stronger today than it was three decades ago (65 percent pure versus 5 percent pure).

© Stringer/epa/Corbis

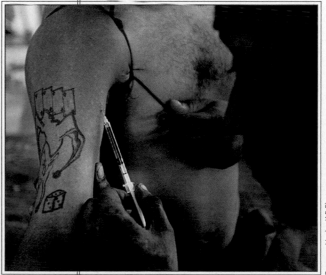

Injecting heroin Opioids may be taken by mouth, inhaled, snorted, injected just beneath the surface of the skin, or injected intravenously. Here, one addict injects another with heroin inside one of the many so-called shooting galleries where addicts gather in downtown San Juan, Puerto Rico.

Brennan Linsley/AP Photo

many cases turning to criminal activities, such as theft and prostitution, to support the expensive "habit" (Cadet et al., 2014; Koetzle, 2014).

Surveys suggest that more than 1 percent of adults in the United States display an opioid use disorder within a given year (SAMHSA, 2014; NSDUH, 2013). Most of these persons (80 percent) are addicted to the pain-reliever opioids such as oxycodone and morphine (see Figure 10-2). Around 20 percent of those with opioid use disorder (a half-million people) are addicted to heroin. The rate of opioid dependence dropped considerably during the 1980s, rose in the early 1990s, fell in the late 1990s, and now seems to be relatively high once again. The actual number of opioid-dependent people may be even higher, however, as many people are reluctant to admit an illegal activity.

What Are the Dangers of Opioid Use? Once again, heroin provides a good example of the dangers of opioid use. The most immediate danger of heroin use is an overdose, which closes down the respiratory center in the brain, almost paralyzing breathing and in many cases causing death (Christensen, 2014). Death is particularly likely during sleep, when a person is unable to fight this effect by consciously working to breathe. People who resume heroin use after having avoided it for some time often make the fatal mistake of taking the same dose they had built up to before. Because their bodies have been without heroin for some time, however, they can no longer tolerate this high level (Gray, 2014). Each year approximately 2 percent of those addicted to heroin and other opioids die under the drug's influence, usually from an overdose.

Heroin users run other risks as well. Drug dealers often mix heroin with a cheaper drug or even a deadly substance such as cyanide or battery acid. In addition, dirty needles and other unsterilized equipment spread infections such as AIDS, hepatitis C, and skin abscesses (NIDA, 2014; Dilts & Dilts, 2011). In some areas of the United States, the HIV infection rate among active heroin users is reported to be as high as 60 percent.

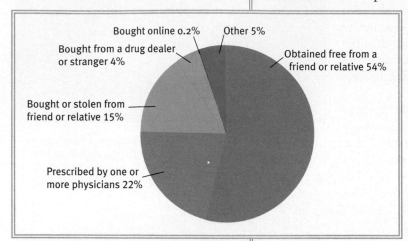

figure 10-2

Where do people obtain pain killers for nonmedical use? More than half get the drugs from friends or relatives, and more than 20 percent obtain them from a doctor. Fewer than 5 percent buy them from a drug dealer. (Information from: SAMHSA, 2014; NSDUH, 2013.)

BETWEEN THE LINES

Nonmedical Use of Pain Relievers

In the United States, the largest increase in illicit drug use during the past few years has been the nonmedical use of medications, mostly pain relievers (SAMHSA, 2014).

➤ Summing Up

SUBSTANCE MISUSE AND DEPRESSANTS Repeated and excessive use of certain substances (or drugs) can lead to substance use disorders. Many people with such disorders also develop a tolerance for the substance in question and/or have unpleasant withdrawal symptoms when they abstain from it.

Depressants are substances that slow the activity of the central nervous system. Repeated and excessive use of these substances can lead to problems such as alcohol use disorder, sedative-hypnotic use disorder, or opioid use disorder. Alcoholic beverages contain ethyl alcohol, which is carried by the blood to the central nervous system, depressing its function. Intoxication occurs when the concentration of alcohol in the bloodstream reaches 0.09 percent. Among other actions, alcohol increases the activity of the neurotransmitter GABA at key sites in the brain. Sedative-hypnotic drugs, which produce feelings of relaxation and drowsiness, include barbiturates and benzodiazepines. These drugs also increase the activity of GABA. Opioids include opium and drugs derived from it, such as morphine and heroin, as well as laboratory-made opioids. They all reduce tension and pain and cause other reactions. Opioids operate by binding to neurons that ordinarily receive endorphins.

Stimulants

Stimulants are substances that increase the activity of the central nervous system, resulting in increased blood pressure and heart rate, more alertness, and sped-up behavior and thinking. Among the most troublesome stimulants are *cocaine* and *amphetamines,* whose effects on people are very similar. When users report different effects, it is often because they have ingested different amounts of the drugs. Two other widely used and legal stimulants are *caffeine* and *nicotine* (see *InfoCentral* on the next page).

Cocaine

Cocaine—the central active ingredient of the coca plant, found in South America—is the most powerful natural stimulant now known (Acosta et al., 2011, 2005). The drug was first separated from the plant in 1865. Native people of South America, however, have chewed the leaves of the plant since prehistoric times for the energy and alertness the drug offers. Processed cocaine is an odorless, white, fluffy powder. For recreational use, it is most often snorted so that it is absorbed through the mucous membrane of the nose. Some users prefer the more powerful effects of injecting cocaine intravenously or smoking it in a pipe or cigarette.

For years people believed that cocaine posed few problems aside from intoxication and, on occasion, temporary psychosis (see Table 10-2). Only later did researchers come to appreciate its many dangers (Haile, 2012). Their insights came after society witnessed a dramatic surge in the drug's popularity and in problems related to its use. In the early 1960s, an estimated 10,000 people in the United States had tried cocaine. Today 28 million people have tried it, and 1.6 million—most of them teenagers or young adults—are using it currently (SAMHSA, 2014; NSDUH, 2013). In fact, 1.1 percent of all high school seniors have used cocaine within the past month and almost 2.6 percent have used it within the past year (Johnston et al., 2014).

Cocaine brings on a euphoric rush of well-being and confidence. Given a high enough dose, this rush can be almost orgasmic, like the one produced by heroin. At first cocaine stimulates the higher centers of the central nervous system, making

▸ **cocaine** An addictive stimulant obtained from the coca plant. It is the most powerful natural stimulant known.

table: **10-2**

Risks and Consequences of Drug Misuse

	Potential Intoxication	Addiction Potential	Risk of Organ Damage or Death	Risk of Severe Social or Economic Consequences	Risk of Severe or Long-Lasting Mental and Behavioral Change
Opioids	High	High	Moderate	High	Low to moderate
Sedative-hypnotics Barbiturates Benzodiazepines	Moderate Moderate	Moderate to high Moderate	Moderate to high Low	Moderate to high Low	Low Low
Stimulants (cocaine, amphetamines)	High	High	Moderate	Low to moderate	Moderate to high
Alcohol	High	Moderate	High	High	High
Cannabis	High	Low to moderate	Low	Low to moderate	Low
Mixed drugs	High	High	High	High	High

Information from: Hart & Ksir, 2014; APA, 2013; Hart et al., 2010.

SMOKING, TOBACCO, AND NICOTINE

Around **27%** percent of all Americans over the age of 11 regularly smoke tobacco—a total of **70 million** people (NSDUH, 2013).

Similarly, **22%** of the world population over 11 smoke regularly—a total of **1.1 billion** people (WHO, 2014).

WHO SMOKES REGULARLY IN THE UNITED STATES?

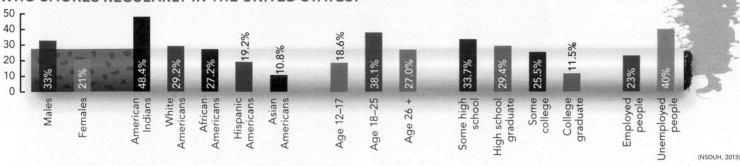

Males	33%
Females	21%
American Indians	48.4%
White Americans	29.2%
African Americans	27.2%
Hispanic Americans	19.2%
Asian Americans	10.8%
Age 12–17	18.6%
Age 18–25	38.1%
Age 26 +	27.0%
Some high school	33.7%
High school graduate	29.4%
Some college	25.5%
College graduate	11.5%
Employed people	23%
Unemployed people	40%

(NSDUH, 2013)

SMOKING AND HEALTH

438,000 Annual U.S. deaths caused by **smoking-related diseases**

5 million Annual worldwide deaths caused by **smoking-related diseases**

42,000 Annual U.S. deaths caused by **secondhand cigarette smoke**

479,000 Annual worldwide deaths caused by **secondhand cigarette smoke**

(CDC, 2014)

WHY DO PEOPLE CONTINUE TO SMOKE?

Between **50%** and **75%** of smokers keep smoking because they are addicted to **nicotine**, the active substance in tobacco (WHO, 2014). Nicotine is a stimulant of the central nervous system that acts on the same neurotransmitters and reward centers in the brain as amphetamines and cocaine. It is as addictive as those drugs and heroin (Hart & Ksir, 2014). Smokers addicted to nicotine are said to have **tobacco use disorder** (APA, 2013).

U.S. smokers with tobacco use disorder 32.5 million

Worldwide smokers with tobacco use disorder 770 million

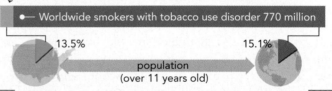

13.5% — population (over 11 years old) — 15.1%

(WHO, 2014; NSDUH, 2013)

QUITTING SMOKING

More and more smokers try to quit each year. One reason is that many studies have identified the severe health dangers smoking poses. Another is the outstanding job that health agencies have done spreading the word about these dangers. With the declining acceptability of smoking, a market for products and techniques to help people kick the habit has emerged.

Getting the Message

Teens who believe that smoking is harmful

% 12th graders

- 1997: 68.7%
- 2008: 74.0%
- 2013: 78.2%

(Johnson et al., 2014)

Common Aids for Quitting

RAPID SMOKING — Puffing frequently and rapidly until becoming ill.

NICOTINE GUM — Releases nicotine when chewed.

NICOTINE PATCH — Releases nicotine through the skin.

NICOTINE LOZENGES — Dissolves in the mouth and releases nicotine.

NASAL SPRAY — Delivers aerosol nicotine into the nostrils.

ANTIDEPRESSANTS (BUPROPION AND NORTRIPTYLINE) — Reduce craving for nicotine.

SELF-HELP GROUPS — Offer psychological support.

Trying to Stop

% of smokers

- Want to stop smoking: 69%
- Make an attempt to quit each year: 43%
- Eventually able to stop permanently: 46%

(CDC, 2014; NSDUH, 2013).

Most Popular New Aid: e-Cigarettes

Smoking an e-cigarette, a battery-operated cigarette, is called **vaping**.

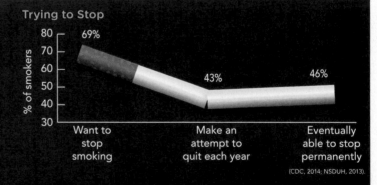

LED end glows when smoker inhales

Heater vaporizes nicotine

Smoker exhales a cloud of vapor

Tobacco Cigarette (vs.) e-Cigarette

Tobacco Cigarette	e-Cigarette
10 mg of nicotine	0.34 mg of nicotine
Smoke poses biggest danger	No actual burning or smoke
Very addictive	Mildly addictive
$35 billion annual earnings	$1 billion annual earnings

(CDC, 2014; Griffin, 2014; Schroeder & Hoffman, 2014; Bullen et al., 2013)

users feel excited, energetic, talkative, and even euphoric. As more is taken, it stimulates other centers of the central nervous system, producing a faster pulse, higher blood pressure, faster and deeper breathing, and further arousal and wakefulness.

Cocaine apparently produces these effects largely by increasing supplies of the neurotransmitter *dopamine* at key neurons throughout the brain (Haile, 2012). Excessive amounts of dopamine travel to receiving neurons throughout the central nervous system and overstimulate them. Cocaine appears to also increase the activity of the neurotransmitters *norepinephrine* and *serotonin* in some areas of the brain (Hart & Ksir, 2014).

High doses of the drug produce *cocaine intoxication,* whose symptoms are poor muscle coordination, grandiosity, bad judgment, anger, aggression, compulsive behavior, anxiety, and confusion. Some people have hallucinations, delusions, or both.

> *A young man described how, after free-basing, he went to his closet to get his clothes, but his suit asked him, "What do you want?" Afraid, he walked toward the door, which told him, "Get back!" Retreating, he then heard the sofa say, "If you sit on me, I'll kick your ass." With a sense of impending doom, intense anxiety, and momentary panic, the young man ran to the hospital where he received help.*
>
> *(Allen, 1985, pp. 19–20)*

As the stimulant effects of cocaine subside, the user goes through a depression-like letdown, popularly called *crashing,* a pattern that may also include headaches, dizziness, and fainting (NIH, 2015; Acosta et al., 2011, 2005). For occasional users, the aftereffects usually disappear within 24 hours, but they may last longer for people who have taken a particularly high dose. These people may sink into a stupor, deep sleep, or, in some cases, coma.

Ingesting Cocaine In the past, cocaine use and impact were limited by the drug's high cost. Moreover, cocaine was usually snorted, a form of ingestion that has less powerful effects than either smoking or injection (Haile, 2012). Since 1984, however, the availability of newer, more powerful, and sometimes cheaper forms of cocaine has produced an enormous increase in the use of the drug. For example, many people now ingest cocaine by **free-basing,** a technique in which the pure cocaine basic alkaloid is chemically separated, or "freed," from processed cocaine, vaporized by heat from a flame, and inhaled through a pipe.

Millions more people use **crack,** a powerful form of free-base cocaine that has been boiled down into crystalline balls. It is smoked with a special pipe and makes a crackling sound as it is inhaled (hence the name). Crack is sold in small quantities at a fairly low cost, which has resulted in crack epidemics among people who previously could not have afforded cocaine, primarily those in poor, urban areas (Acosta et al., 2011, 2005). Around 1.1 percent of high school seniors report having used crack within the past year, down from a peak of 2.7 percent in 1999 (Johnston et al., 2014).

What Are the Dangers of Cocaine? Aside from cocaine's harmful effects on behavior, cognition, and emotion, the drug poses serious physical dangers (NIH, 2015; Paczynski & Gold, 2011). The growth in the use of the powerful forms of cocaine has caused the annual number of cocaine-related emergency room incidents in the United States to multiply more than 125 times since 1982, from around 4,000 cases to 505,000 (SAMHSA, 2013). Cocaine use has also been linked to many suicides (San Nicolas & Lemos, 2015).

▶ **free-basing** A technique for ingesting cocaine in which the pure cocaine basic alkaloid is chemically separated from processed cocaine, vaporized by heat from a flame, and inhaled with a pipe.

▶ **crack** A powerful, ready-to-smoke free-base cocaine.

Smoking crack Crack, a powerful form of freebase cocaine, is produced by boiling cocaine down into crystalline balls and is smoked with a crack pipe.

© Boris Roessler/dpa/Corbis

▶ **amphetamine** A stimulant drug that is manufactured in the laboratory.

▶ **methamphetamine** A powerful amphetamine drug that has surged in popularity in recent years, posing major health and law enforcement problems.

▶ **hallucinogen** A substance that causes powerful changes primarily in sensory perception, including strengthening perceptions and producing illusions and hallucinations. Also called a *psychedelic drug.*

▶ **LSD (lysergic acid diethylamide)** A hallucinogenic drug derived from ergot alkaloids.

Methamphetamine dependence: spreading the word This powerful ad shows the degenerative effects of methamphetamine addiction on a woman over a four-year period—from age 36 in the top photo to age 40 in the bottom one.

DON'T LET DRUG DEALERS CHANGE THE FACE OF YOUR NEIGHBOURHOOD.
Call Crimestoppers anonymously on 0800 555 111.

The greatest danger of cocaine use is an overdose. Excessive doses have a strong effect on the respiratory center of the brain, at first stimulating it and then depressing it to the point where breathing may stop. Cocaine can also create major, even fatal, heart irregularities or brain seizures that bring breathing or heart functioning to a sudden stop (Acosta et al., 2011, 2005). In addition, pregnant women who use cocaine run the risk of having a miscarriage and of having children with predispositions to later drug use and with abnormalities in immune functioning, attention and learning, thyroid size, and dopamine and serotonin activity in the brain (Minnes et al., 2014; Kosten et al., 2008).

Amphetamines

Amphetamines are stimulant drugs that are manufactured in the laboratory. Some common examples are amphetamine (Benzedrine), dextroamphetamine (Dexedrine), and methamphetamine (Methedrine). First produced in the 1930s to help treat asthma, amphetamines soon became popular among people trying to lose weight; athletes seeking an extra burst of energy; soldiers, truck drivers, and pilots trying to stay awake; and students studying for exams through the night (Haile, 2012). Physicians now know the drugs are far too dangerous to be used so casually, and they prescribe them much less freely.

Amphetamines are most often taken in pill or capsule form, although some people inject the drugs intravenously or smoke them for a quicker, more powerful effect. Like cocaine, amphetamines increase energy and alertness and reduce appetite when taken in small doses; produce a rush, intoxication, and psychosis in high doses; and cause an emotional letdown as they leave the body. Also like cocaine, amphetamines stimulate the central nervous system by increasing the release of the neurotransmitters dopamine, norepinephrine, and serotonin throughout the brain, although the actions of amphetamines differ somewhat from those of cocaine (Hart & Ksir, 2014; Haile, 2012).

One kind of amphetamine, **methamphetamine** (nicknamed *crank*), has surged in popularity in recent years and so warrants special focus. Almost 6 percent of all people over the age of 11 in the United States have used methamphetamine at least once. Around 0.2 percent use it currently (NSDUH, 2013). It is available in the form of crystals (also known by the street names *ice* and *crystal meth*), which users smoke.

Most of the nonmedical methamphetamine in the United States is made in small "stovetop laboratories," which typically operate for a few days in a remote area and then move on to a new—safer—location (Hart & Ksir, 2014). Such laboratories have been around since the 1960s, but they have increased eightfold—in number, production, and in being confiscated by authorities—over the past decade. A major health concern is that the secret laboratories expel dangerous fumes and residue (Burgess, 2001).

Since 1989, when the media first began reporting about the dangers of smoking methamphetamine crystals, the rise in usage has been dramatic. Correspondingly, methamphetamine-linked emergency room visits are increasing in hospitals throughout all parts of the country (SAMHSA, 2013).

Methamphetamine is about as likely to be used by women as men. Around 40 percent of current users are women (NSDUH, 2013). The drug is particularly popular today among biker gangs, rural Americans, and urban gay communities and has gained wide use as a "club drug," the term for those drugs that regularly find their way to all-night dance parties, or "raves" (Hart & Ksir, 2014; Hopfer, 2011).

Like other kinds of amphetamines, methamphetamine increases activity of the neurotransmitters dopamine, serotonin, and norepinephrine, producing increased arousal, attention, and related effects (Yu et al., 2015; Acosta et al., 2011, 2005). It can have serious negative effects on a user's physical, mental, and social life. Of particular concern is that it damages nerve endings. But users focus more on methamphetamine's immediate positive impact, including perceptions by many that it makes them feel hypersexual and uninhibited (Washton & Zweben, 2008; Jefferson, 2005).

Stimulant Use Disorder

Regular use of either cocaine or amphetamines may lead to *stimulant use disorder.* The stimulant comes to dominate the person's life, and the person may remain under the drug's effects much of each day and function poorly in social relationships and at work. Regular stimulant use may also cause problems in short-term memory and attention (Lundqvist, 2010). People may develop tolerance and withdrawal reactions to the drug—in order to gain the desired effects, they must take higher doses, and when they stop taking it, they may go through deep depression, fatigue, sleep problems, irritability, and anxiety (Barr et al., 2011). These withdrawal symptoms can last for weeks or even months after drug use has ended. In a given year, 0.4 percent of all people over the age of 11 display stimulant use disorder that is centered on cocaine, and 0.2 percent display stimulant use disorder centered on amphetamines (SAMHSA, 2014; NSDUH, 2013).

Cocaine and the heart Pop icon Whitney Houston died in her bathtub on February 11, 2012. The coroner's report ruled that the cause of her death was accidental drowning caused in part by heart disease and her abuse of cocaine and perhaps other drugs. The suspicion is that her long-term use of cocaine helped produce her heart problems (Dolak & Murphy, 2012).

Ebet Roberts/Redferns/Getty Images

➤ *Summing Up*

STIMULANTS Stimulants, including cocaine, amphetamines, caffeine, and nicotine, are substances that increase the activity of the central nervous system. Abnormal use of cocaine or amphetamines can lead to stimulant use disorder. Stimulants produce their effects by increasing the activity of dopamine, norepinephrine, and serotonin in the brain.

Hallucinogens, Cannabis, and Combinations of Substances

Other kinds of substances may also cause problems for their users and for society. *Hallucinogens* produce delusions, hallucinations, and other sensory changes. *Cannabis* produces sensory changes, but it also has depressant and stimulant effects, and so it is considered apart from hallucinogens in DSM-5. And many people take *combinations of substances.*

Hallucinogens

Hallucinogens are substances that cause powerful changes in sensory perception, from strengthening a person's normal perceptions to inducing illusions and hallucinations. They produce sensations so out of the ordinary that they are sometimes called "trips." The trips may be exciting or frightening, depending on how a person's mind interacts with the drugs. Also called *psychedelic drugs,* the hallucinogens include LSD, mescaline, psilocybin, and MDMA (Ecstasy) (see *PsychWatch* on page 325). Many of these substances come from plants or animals; others are produced in laboratories.

LSD (lysergic acid diethylamide), one of the most famous and most powerful hallucinogens, was derived by Swiss chemist Albert Hoffman in 1938 from a group of naturally occurring drugs called *ergot alkaloids.* During the 1960s, a decade of social rebellion and experimentation, millions of people turned to the drug as a way of expanding their experience. Within two hours of being swallowed, LSD brings on a state of *hallucinogen intoxication,* sometimes called *hallucinosis,* marked by a general strengthening of perceptions, particularly visual perceptions, along with psychological changes and physical symptoms. People may focus on small details— the pores of the skin, for example, or individual blades of grass. Colors may seem enhanced or take on a shade of purple. People may have illusions in which objects seem distorted and appear to move, breathe, or change shape. A person under the influence of LSD may also hallucinate—seeing people, objects, or forms that are not actually present.

Hallucinosis may also cause one to hear sounds more clearly, feel tingling or numbness in the limbs, or confuse the sensations of hot and cold. Some people have been badly burned after touching flames that felt cool to them under the influence of LSD. The drug may also cause different senses to cross, an effect called *synesthesia.* Colors, for example, may be "heard" or "felt."

LSD can also induce strong emotions, from joy to anxiety or depression. The perception of time may slow dramatically. Long-forgotten thoughts and feelings may resurface. Physical symptoms can include sweating, palpitations, blurred vision, tremors, and poor coordination. All of these effects take place while the user is fully awake and alert, and they wear off in about six hours.

It seems that LSD produces these symptoms primarily by binding to some of the neurons that normally receive the neurotransmitter *serotonin,* changing the neurotransmitter's activity at those sites (Advokat et al., 2014). These neurons ordinarily help the brain send visual information and control emotions (as you saw in Chapter 6); thus LSD's activity there produces various visual and emotional symptoms.

> **Why do various club drugs (for example, Ecstasy and crystal meth), often used at "raves," fall in and out of favor rather quickly?**

More than 14 percent of all people in the United States have used LSD or another hallucinogen at some point in their lives. Around 0.4 percent, or 1.1 million people, are currently using them (NSDUH, 2013). Although people do not usually develop tolerance to LSD or have withdrawal symptoms when they stop taking it, the drug poses dangers for both one-time and long-term users. It is so powerful that any dose, no matter how small, is likely to produce enormous perceptual, emotional, and behavioral reactions. Sometimes the reactions are extremely unpleasant—a so-called bad trip (when LSD users injure themselves or others, for instance, usually they are in the midst of a bad trip). Witness, for example, this description of a young woman who took LSD during the 1960s, when so many people thought of the drug as a problem-free mind expander, only to learn about its dark side through personal use:

> *A 21-year-old woman was admitted to the hospital along with her lover. He had had a number of LSD experiences and had convinced her to take it to make her less constrained sexually. About half an hour after ingestion of approximately 200 microgm., she noticed that the bricks in the wall began to go in and out and that light affected her strangely. She became frightened when she realized that she was unable to distinguish her body from the chair she was sitting on or from her lover's body. Her fear became more marked after she thought that she would not get back into herself. At the time of admission she was hyperactive and laughed inappropriately. Her stream of talk was illogical and affect labile. Two days later, this reaction had ceased.*
>
> *(Frosch, Robbins, & Stern, 1965)*

Lingering popularity Although less popular than in the 1960s, LSD continues to be a drug of some favor, especially among younger people, at many raves, rock concerts, and similar events. This participant at the 2012 Boom Festival, a gathering of boomers who share "the universal spirit of psychedelic trance," wrote a message on his back that leaves no doubt about how important the drug is to him.

© Fernando Mendes/Demotix/Corbis

PsychWatch

Club Drugs: X Marks the (Wrong) Spot

You probably know of the drug *MDMA (3,4-methylenedioxymeth-amphetamine)* by its common street name, *Ecstasy.* This laboratory-produced drug is technically a *stimulant,* similar to amphetamines, but it also produces hallucinogenic effects and so is often considered a *hallucinogenic* drug (Litjens et al., 2014; McDowell, 2011, 2005). MDMA was developed as far back as 1910, but only in the past 25 years has it gained life as a club drug. Today, in the United States alone, consumers collectively take hundreds of thousands of doses of MDMA weekly (Johnston et al., 2014). Altogether, 12 million Americans over the age of 11 have now tried the drug at least once in their lifetime (NSDUH, 2013, 2010).

What is Ecstasy's allure? As a stimulant and hallucinogen, it helps to raise the mood of many partygoers and provides them with an energy boost that enables them to keep dancing and partying. It may also produce strong feelings of attachment and connectedness in users. However, it can be a dangerous drug, particularly when taken repeatedly.

What Are the Dangers of Using Ecstasy?

As MDMA has become more widely used, it has received more research scrutiny. As it turns out, the mood and energy lift produced by MDMA comes at a high price (Downey et al., 2015; Koczor et al., 2015; Hart & Ksir, 2014; Parrott et al., 2014). The problems that the drug may cause include the following:

➤ Psychological problems such as confusion, depression, sleep difficulties, severe anxiety, and paranoid thinking.

➤ Impairment of memory and other cognitive skills.

➤ Physical symptoms such as muscle tension, nausea, blurred vision, faintness, and chills or sweating.

➤ Increases in heart rate and blood pressure, which place people with heart disease at special risk.

➤ Reduced sweat production. At a hot, crowded dance party, taking Ecstasy can even cause heat stroke, or *hyperthermia.* Users generally try to remedy this problem by drinking lots of water, but since the body cannot sweat under the drug's influence, the excess fluid intake can result in an equally perilous condition known as *hyponatremia,* or "water intoxication."

➤ Potential liver damage.

How Does MDMA Operate in the Brain?

MDMA works by causing the neurotransmitters *serotonin* and (to a lesser extent) *dopamine* to be released all at once throughout the brain, at first increasing and then depleting a person's overall supply of the neurotransmitters. MDMA also interferes with the body's ability to produce new supplies of serotonin. With repeated use, the brain eventually produces less and less serotonin (Lizarraga et al., 2014; McDowell, 2011, 2005). Ecstasy's impact on these neurotransmitters accounts for its various psychological effects and associated problems (Lizarraga et al., 2014; Zakzanis et al., 2007).

End of the Honeymoon?

Although it is no longer used as much as it was in the early 2000s, MDMA seems to have regained considerable popularity in recent years, finding its way back to raves, dance clubs, and various college settings (Johnston et al., 2014; Palamar & Kamboukos, 2014). Clearly, despite the alarming research results, the honeymoon for MDMA is not yet over.

Feeling the effects
Shortly after taking MDMA, this couple manifests a shift in mood, energy, and behavior. Although MDMA can feel pleasurable and energizing, often it produces undesired immediate effects, including confusion, depression, anxiety, sleep difficulties, and paranoid thinking.

© Scott Houston/Corbis Sygma

Another danger is the long-term effect that LSD may have (Lerner et al., 2014; Weaver & Schnoll, 2008). Some users eventually develop psychosis or a mood or anxiety disorder. And a number have *flashbacks*—a recurrence of the sensory and emotional changes after the LSD has left the body. Flashbacks may occur days or even months after the last LSD experience.

The source of marijuana Marijuana is made from the leaves of the hemp plant, *Cannabis sativa*. The plant is an annual herb, reaches a height of between 3 and 15 feet, and is grown in a wide range of altitudes, climates, and soils.

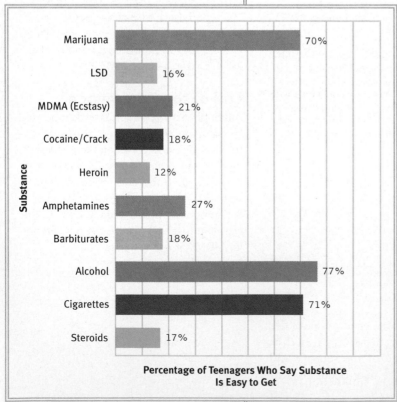

Vaughan Fleming/Science Photo Library/Science Source

Cannabis

Cannabis sativa, the hemp plant, grows in warm climates throughout the world. The drugs produced from varieties of hemp are, as a group, called **cannabis.** The most powerful of them is *hashish;* the weaker ones include the best-known form of cannabis, **marijuana,** a mixture derived from the buds, crushed leaves, and flowering tops of hemp plants. More than 19 million people over the age of 11 (7.3 percent of the population) currently smoke marijuana at least monthly; more than 5 million smoke it daily (SAMHSA, 2014; NSDUH, 2013).

Each of the cannabis drugs is found in various strengths because the potency of a cannabis drug is greatly affected by the climate in which the plant is grown, the way it was prepared, and the manner and duration of its storage. Of the several hundred active chemicals in cannabis, **tetrahydrocannabinol (THC)** appears to be the one most responsible for its effects. The higher the THC content, the more powerful the cannabis; hashish contains a large portion, while marijuana's is small.

When smoked, cannabis produces a mixture of hallucinogenic, depressant, and stimulant effects. At low doses, the smoker typically has feelings of joy and relaxation and may become either quiet or talkative. Some smokers, however, become anxious, suspicious, or irritated, especially if they have been in a bad mood or are smoking in an upsetting environment. Many smokers report sharpened perceptions and fascination with the intensified sounds and sights around them. Time seems to slow down, and distances and sizes seem greater than they actually are. This overall "high" is technically called *cannabis intoxication.* Physical changes include reddening of the eyes, fast heartbeat, increases in blood pressure and appetite, dryness in the mouth, and dizziness. Some people become drowsy and may fall asleep.

In high doses, cannabis produces odd visual experiences, changes in body image, and hallucinations. Smokers may become confused or impulsive. Some worry that other people are trying to hurt them. Most of the effects of cannabis last two to six hours. The changes in mood, however, may continue longer.

Cannabis Use Disorder Until the early 1970s, the use of marijuana, the weak form of cannabis, rarely led to a pattern of *cannabis use disorder.* Today, however, many people, including large numbers of high school students, are developing the disorder, getting high on marijuana regularly and finding their social and occupational or academic lives very much affected (see Figure 10-3). Many regular users also develop a tolerance for marijuana and may feel restless and irritable and have flulike symptoms when they stop smoking (Chen et al., 2005). Around 1.7 percent of all teenagers and adults in the United States have displayed cannabis use disorder within the past month (SAMHSA, 2014; NSDUH, 2013).

Why have more and more marijuana users developed cannabis use disorder over the past three decades? Mainly

figure 10-3

How easy is it for teenagers to acquire substances? Most surveyed tenth graders say it is easy to get cigarettes, alcohol, and marijuana, and more than one-fifth say it is easy to get Ecstasy and amphetamines. (Information from: Johnston et al., 2014.)

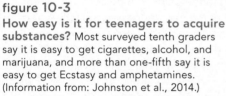

Marijuana 70%
LSD 16%
MDMA (Ecstasy) 21%
Cocaine/Crack 18%
Heroin 12%
Amphetamines 27%
Barbiturates 18%
Alcohol 77%
Cigarettes 71%
Steroids 17%

Substance

Percentage of Teenagers Who Say Substance Is Easy to Get

because marijuana has changed. The marijuana widely available in the United States today is at least four times more powerful than that used in the early 1970s. The average THC content of today's marijuana is 8 percent, compared with 2 percent in the late 1960s. Marijuana is now grown in places with a hot, dry climate, which increases the THC content.

Is Marijuana Dangerous?
As the strength and use of marijuana have increased, researchers have discovered that smoking it may pose certain dangers (NIDA, 2015; Price, 2011). It occasionally causes panic reactions similar to the ones caused by hallucinogens, and some smokers may fear they are losing their minds (APA, 2000). Typically such reactions end in two to six hours, along with marijuana's other effects.

Marijuana use can also adversely affect sensorimotor and cognitive functioning, especially among teenagers and children, whose brains are still developing (Barcott & Schererk, 2015). In turn, it has caused many automobile accidents (Brady & Li, 2014). Moreover, people on a marijuana high often fail to remember information, especially anything that has been recently learned, no matter how hard they try to concentrate; thus heavy marijuana smokers are at a serious disadvantage at school or work (Budney et al., 2011; Jaffe & Klein, 2010).

One study compared blood flow in the brain arteries of chronic marijuana users and nonusers (Herning et al., 2005). After one month of abstinence from smoking marijuana, chronic users continued to have higher blood flow than nonusers. Though still higher than normal, the blood flow of light marijuana users (fewer than 16 smokes per week) and of moderate users (fewer than 70 smokes per week) did improve somewhat over the course of the abstinence month. The blood flow of heavy users, however, showed no improvement. This lingering effect may help explain the memory and thinking problems of chronic heavy users of marijuana.

There are research indications that regular marijuana smoking may also lead to long-term health problems (NIDA, 2015; Budney et al., 2011; Whitten, 2010). It may, for example, contribute to lung disease, although there is considerable debate on this issue (Pletcher et al., 2012; Tashkin, 2001). Some studies suggest that marijuana smoking reduces the ability to expel air from the lungs, perhaps even more than tobacco smoking does. Another concern is the effect of regular marijuana smoking on human reproduction. Studies since the late 1970s have discovered lower sperm counts in men who are chronic smokers and abnormal ovulation in women who are chronic smokers (Hartney, 2014; Schuel et al., 2002).

Efforts to educate the public about the dangers of repeated marijuana use appeared to have paid off throughout the 1980s. The percentage of high school seniors who smoked marijuana on a daily basis decreased from 11 percent in 1978 to 2 percent in 1992. Today, however, 6.5 percent of high school seniors smoke it daily, and more than 50 percent of seniors do not believe that regular use poses a great risk (Johnston et al., 2014; NSDUH, 2013).

Cannabis and Society: A Rocky Relationship
For centuries, cannabis played a respected role in medicine. It was recommended as a surgical anesthetic by Chinese physicians 2,000 years ago and was used in other lands to treat cholera, malaria, coughs, insomnia, and rheumatism. When cannabis entered the United States in the early twentieth century, mainly in the form of marijuana, it was likewise used for various medical purposes. Soon, however, more effective medicines replaced it, and the favorable view of cannabis began to change. Marijuana began to be used as a recreational drug, and its illegal distribution became a law enforcement problem. Authorities assumed it was highly dangerous and outlawed the "killer weed."

▸ **cannabis drugs** Drugs produced from the varieties of the hemp plant *Cannabis sativa*. They cause a mixture of hallucinogenic, depressant, and stimulant effects.

▸ **marijuana** One of the cannabis drugs, derived from the buds, leaves, and flowering tops of the hemp plant *Cannabis sativa*.

▸ **tetrahydrocannabinol (THC)** The main active ingredient of cannabis substances.

"Medibles" ready for sale At his store "TH Candy" in Washington State, this confectioner displays a number of popular medical marijuana edibles ("medibles"), including candies, chocolates, teas, tinctures, and baked goods.

© Anthony Bolante/Reuters/Corbis

Sniffing for drugs An increasingly common scene in schools, airports, storage facilities, and similar settings is that of trained dogs sniffing for marijuana, cocaine, opioids, and other substances. Here one such animal sniffs lockers at a school in Texas to see whether students have hidden any illegal substances among their books or other belongings.

In the 1980s, researchers developed precise techniques for measuring THC and for extracting pure THC from cannabis; they also developed laboratory forms of THC. These inventions opened the door to new medical applications for cannabis (Mack & Joy, 2001), such as its use in treating glaucoma, a severe eye disease. Cannabis was also found to help patients with chronic pain or asthma, to reduce the nausea and vomiting of cancer patients in chemotherapy, and to improve the appetites of people with AIDS and so help them combat weight loss.

In light of these findings, several interest groups began campaigning during the late 1980s for the *medical legalization* of marijuana, which operates on the brain and body more quickly than the THC capsules developed in the laboratory. Government agencies initially resisted this movement, saying prescriptions for pure THC served all needed medical functions. However, medical marijuana advocates pressed on, and in 2009 the U.S. Attorney General directed federal prosecutors to not pursue cases against medical marijuana users or their caregivers who are complying with state laws. Currently, 23 states have laws allowing marijuana to be used for medical purposes, and several more have such laws pending (Tilak, 2014).

Canada's federal government has taken a more lenient position on the medical marijuana issue than the U.S. federal government. Based on a series of studies and trial programs, Health Canada, the country's health care regulator, now legally permits people who are suffering from severe and debilitating illnesses to use marijuana for medical purposes. It allows the sale of medical marijuana in select pharmacies, and it licenses numerous companies to produce medical marijuana (Tilak, 2014).

Heartened by such developments in the realm of medical marijuana, a movement to legalize the *recreational* use of marijuana has gained enormous momentum in recent years. In fact, since 2012 residents in the states of Colorado, Washington, Alaska, and Oregon have voted to legalize marijuana for use of any kind. Moreover, according to recent polls, more than half of Americans believe that marijuana should be made legal, up from 12 percent in 1969 and 41 percent in 2010 (Pew Research Center, 2013).

Combinations of Substances

Because people often take more than one drug at a time, a pattern called *polysubstance use,* researchers have studied the ways in which drugs interact with one another (Murray et al., 2015; De La Garza & Kalechstein, 2012). When different drugs are in the body at the same time, they may *multiply,* or potentiate, each other's effects. The combined impact, called a **synergistic effect,** is often greater than the sum of the effects of each drug taken alone: a small dose of one drug mixed with a small dose of another can produce an enormous change in body chemistry.

One kind of synergistic effect occurs when two or more drugs have *similar actions* (McCance-Katz, 2010). For instance, alcohol, benzodiazepines, barbiturates, and opioids—all depressants—may severely depress the central nervous system when mixed (Hart & Ksir, 2014). Combining them, even in small doses, can lead to extreme intoxication, coma, and even death. A young man may have just a few alcoholic drinks at a party, for example, and shortly afterward take a moderate dose of barbiturates to help him fall asleep. He believes he has acted with restraint and good judgment—yet he may never wake up.

A different kind of synergistic effect results when drugs have *opposite,* or *antagonistic, actions.* Stimulant drugs, for example, interfere with the liver's usual disposal of barbiturates and alcohol. Thus people who combine barbiturates or alcohol with

▶ **synergistic effect** In pharmacology, an increase of effects that occurs when more than one substance is acting on the body at the same time.

Paul Howell/Liaison/Getty Images

AP Photo/Ross D. Franklin

Real life versus acting Most fans of the television series *Glee* were shocked by the 2013 death of 31-year-old actor Cory Monteith (center), caused by a toxic combination of heroin and alcohol. One reason for their shock was that Finn Hudson, the *Glee* character played by Monteith, was so wholesome and happy. But Monteith himself had waged a long battle against substance use disorder, dating back to age 12. He had most recently pursued intense treatment for the disorder just four months before his death.

cocaine or amphetamines may build up toxic, even lethal, levels of the depressant substances in their systems. Students who take amphetamines to help them study late into the night and then take barbiturates to help them fall asleep are unknowingly placing themselves in serious danger.

Each year tens of thousands of people are admitted to hospitals with a multiple-drug emergency, and several thousand of them die (SAMHSA, 2013). Sometimes the cause is carelessness or ignorance. Often, however, people use multiple drugs precisely because they enjoy the synergistic effects. In fact, as many as 90 percent of those who use one illegal drug are also using another to some extent (Rosenthal & Levounis, 2011, 2005).

Fans mourn the deaths of many celebrities who have died from polysubstance use. For example, in 2014 the New York City medical examiner ruled that actor Philip Seymour Hoffman died of "acute mixed drug intoxication," citing the presence of heroin, cocaine, benzodiazepines, and amphetamines in his system (Coleman, 2014). In the more distant past, Elvis Presley's delicate balancing act of stimulants and depressants, Janis Joplin's mixtures of wine and heroin, and John Belushi's and Chris Farley's liking for the combined effect of cocaine and opioids ("speedballs") each ended in tragedy.

> **Who has more impact on the drug behaviors of teenagers and young adults: rock performers who speak out against drugs or rock performers who praise drugs?**

➤ *Summing Up*

HALLUCINOGENS, CANNABIS, AND COMBINATIONS OF SUBSTANCES Hallucinogens, such as LSD, are substances that cause powerful changes primarily in sensory perception. People's perceptions are intensified and they may have illusions and hallucinations. LSD apparently causes such effects by disturbing the release of the neurotransmitter serotonin.

The main ingredient of *Cannabis sativa*, a hemp plant, is tetrahydrocannabinol (THC). Marijuana, the most popular form of cannabis, is more powerful today than it was in years past. It can cause intoxication, and regular use can lead to cannabis use disorder.

Many people take more than one drug at a time, and the drugs interact. The use of two or more drugs at the same time—polysubstance use—has become increasingly common.

What Causes Substance Use Disorders?

Clinical theorists have developed sociocultural, psychological, and biological explanations for why people develop substance use disorders. No single explanation, however, has gained broad support. Like so many other disorders, excessive and chronic drug use is increasingly viewed as the result of a combination of these factors.

Sociocultural Views

A number of sociocultural theorists propose that people are most likely to develop substance use disorders when they live under stressful socioeconomic conditions (Fink et al., 2015; Marsiglia & Smith, 2010). Studies have found that poorer people tend to have higher rates of substance use disorder than wealthier people. In a related vein, 18 percent of unemployed adults currently use an illegal drug, compared with 9 percent of full-time employed workers and 12.5 percent of part-time employees (SAMHSA, 2014; NSDUH, 2013).

Sociocultural theorists hold that people confronted regularly by other kinds of stress also have a heightened risk of developing substance use disorders. A range of studies conducted with Hispanic and African American people, for example, find higher rates of substance use disorders among those participants who live or work in environments of particularly intense discrimination (Clark, 2014; Hurd et al., 2014; Unger et al., 2014).

Still other sociocultural theorists propose that people are more likely to develop substance use disorders if they are part of a family or social environment in which substance use is valued or at least accepted (Chung et al., 2014; Washburn et al., 2014). Researchers have learned that problem drinking is more common among teenagers whose parents and peers drink, as well as among teenagers whose family environments are stressful and unsupportive (Wilens et al., 2014; Andrews & Hops, 2011). Moreover, lower rates of alcoholism are found among Jews and Protestants, groups in which drinking is typically acceptable only as long as it remains within clear limits, whereas alcoholism rates are higher among the Irish and Eastern Europeans, who do not, in general, draw as clear a line (Hart & Ksir, 2014; Ledoux et al., 2002).

Why might different ethnic, religious, and national groups have different rates of alcohol use disorder?

Common substance, uncommon danger
A 13-year-old boy sniffs glue as he lies dazed near a garbage heap. In the United States, at least 6 percent of all people have tried to get high by inhaling the hydrocarbons found in common substances such as glue, gasoline, paint thinner, cleaners, and spray-can propellants (APA, 2013). Such behavior may lead to *inhalant use disorder* and poses a number of serious medical dangers.

Steven Rubin/The Image Works

Psychodynamic Views

Psychodynamic theorists believe that people with substance use disorders have powerful *dependency* needs that can be traced to their early years (Iglesias et al., 2014; Dodes & Khantzian, 2011, 2005). They suggest that when parents fail to satisfy a young child's need for nurturance, the child is likely to grow up depending excessively on others for help and comfort, trying to find the nurturance that was lacking during the early years. If this search for outside support includes experimentation with a drug, the person may well develop a dependent relationship with the substance.

Some psychodynamic theorists also believe that certain people respond to their early deprivations by developing a *substance abuse personality* that leaves them particularly prone to drug abuse. Personality inventories, patient interviews, and even animal studies have in fact indicated that people who abuse drugs tend to be more dependent, antisocial, impulsive, novelty-seeking, risk-taking, and depressive than other people (Hicks et al., 2014). However, these findings are correlational (at least, the findings from human studies are) and do not clarify whether such traits lead to chronic drug use or whether repeated drug use causes people to be dependent, impulsive, and the like.

In an effort to establish clearer causation, one pioneering longitudinal study measured the personality traits of a large group of nonalcoholic young men and then kept track of each man's development (Jones, 1971, 1968). Years later, the traits of the men who developed alcohol problems in middle age were compared with the traits of those who did not. The men who developed alcohol problems had been more impulsive as teenagers and continued to be so in middle age, a finding suggesting that impulsive men are indeed more prone to develop alcohol problems. Similarly, in some laboratory investigations, "impulsive" rats—those that generally have trouble delaying their rewards—have been found to drink more alcohol when offered it than other rats (Stein et al., 2013; Poulos et al., 1995).

A major weakness of this line of argument is the wide range of personality traits that have been tied to substance use disorders. Different studies point to different "key" traits (Wills & Ainette, 2010). Inasmuch as some people with these disorders appear to be dependent, others impulsive, and still others antisocial, researchers cannot presently conclude that any one personality trait or group of traits stands out in the development of the disorders (Chassin et al., 2001).

Cognitive-Behavioral Views

According to behaviorists, *operant conditioning* may play a key role in substance use disorders. They argue that the temporary reduction of tension or raising of spirits produced by a drug has a rewarding effect, thus increasing the likelihood that the user will seek this reaction again (Urošević et al., 2015; Clark, 2014). Similarly, the rewarding effects may eventually lead users to try higher dosages or more powerful methods of ingestion. Cognitive theorists further argue that such rewards eventually produce an *expectancy* that substances will be rewarding, and this expectation helps motivate people to increase drug use at times of tension (Sussman, 2010).

In support of these behavioral and cognitive views, studies have found that many people do drink more alcohol or seek heroin when they feel tense (Kassel et al., 2010; McCarthy et al., 2010). In one study, as participants worked on a difficult anagram task, a confederate planted by the researchers unfairly criticized and belittled them (Marlatt et al., 1975). The participants were then asked to participate in an "alcohol taste task," supposedly to compare and rate alcoholic beverages. Those who had been harassed drank more alcohol during the taste task than did the control participants who had not been criticized.

In a manner of speaking, the cognitive-behavioral theorists are arguing that many people take drugs to "medicate" themselves when they feel tense. If so, one would expect higher rates of substance use disorders among people who suffer from anxiety, depression, and other such problems. And, in fact, at least 19 percent of all adults who suffer from psychological disorders also display substance use disorders (Keyser-Marcus et al., 2015; NSDUH, 2013).

A number of behaviorists have proposed that *classical conditioning* may also play a role in these disorders (O'Brien, 2013; Cunningham et al., 2011). As you'll remember from Chapters 2 and 4, classical conditioning occurs when two stimuli that appear close together in time become connected in a person's mind, so that eventually, the person responds similarly to each stimulus. Cues or objects present in the environment at the time a person takes a drug may act as classically conditioned stimuli and come to produce some of the same pleasure brought on by the drugs themselves. Just the sight of a hypodermic needle, drug buddy, or regular supplier,

▶ **reward center** A dopamine-rich pathway in the brain that produces feelings of pleasure when activated.

for example, has been known to comfort people who are addicted to heroin or amphetamines and to relieve their withdrawal symptoms. In a similar manner, cues or objects that are present during withdrawal distress may *produce* withdrawal-like symptoms. One man who had formerly been dependent on heroin became nauseated and had other withdrawal symptoms when he returned to the neighborhood where he had gone through withdrawal in the past—a reaction that led him to start taking heroin again (O'Brien et al., 1975). Although classical conditioning certainly appears to be at work in particular cases of substance use disorder, it has not received widespread research support as the *key* factor in such disorders (Grimm, 2011).

Biological Views

In recent years, researchers have come to suspect that drug misuse may have biological causes. Studies on genetic predisposition and specific biochemical processes have provided some support for these suspicions.

Genetic Predisposition

For years, breeding experiments have been conducted to see whether certain animals are genetically predisposed to become addicted to drugs (Saba et al., 2015; Carroll & Meisch, 2011; Weiss, 2011). In several studies, for example, investigators have first identified animals that prefer alcohol to other beverages and then mated them to one another. Generally, the offspring of these animals have been found also to display an unusual preference for alcohol.

Similarly, some research with human twins has suggested that people may inherit a predisposition to misuse substances (Ystrom et al., 2014). One classic study found an alcoholism *concordance* rate of 54 percent in a group of identical twins; that is, if one identical twin displayed alcoholism, the other twin also did in 54 percent of the cases. In contrast, a group of fraternal twins had a concordance rate of only 28 percent (Kaij, 1960). Other studies have found similar twin patterns (Koskinen et al., 2011; Tsuang et al., 2001). As you have read, however, such findings do not rule out other interpretations. For one thing, the parenting received by two identical twins may be more similar than that received by two fraternal twins.

A clearer indication that genetics may play a role in substance use disorders comes from studies of alcoholism rates in people adopted shortly after birth (Samek et al., 2014; Walters, 2002). These studies have compared adoptees whose biological parents abuse alcohol with adoptees whose biological parents do not. By adulthood, the individuals whose biological parents abuse alcohol typically show higher rates of alcoholism than those with nonalcoholic biological parents.

Genetic linkage strategies and *molecular biology* techniques provide more direct evidence in support of a genetic explanation (Pieters et al., 2012; Gelernter & Kranzler, 2008). One line of investigation has found an abnormal form of the so-called *dopamine-2 (D2) receptor gene* in a majority of research participants with substance use disorders but in less than 20 percent of participants who do not have such disorders (Cosgrove, 2010; Blum et al., 1996, 1990). Other studies have tied still other genes to substance use disorders.

Crack cookies? Researchers at Connecticut College found that the lab-induced addiction of rats to Oreo cookies—particularly the creamy center—was as strong as their lab-induced addiction to cocaine and morphine in many ways. The study was conducted to test the growing theory that many high-fat, high-sugar foods stimulate the brain in the same ways and locations that addictive drugs do.

Biochemical Factors

Over the past few decades, researchers have pieced together several biological explanations of drug tolerance and withdrawal symptoms (Chung et al., 2012; Kosten et al., 2011, 2005). According to one of the leading explanations, when a particular drug is ingested, it increases the activity of certain neurotransmitters whose normal purpose is to calm, reduce pain, lift mood, or increase alertness. When a person keeps on taking the drug, the brain apparently makes an adjustment and reduces its own production of the neurotransmitters.

Because the drug is increasing neurotransmitter activity or efficiency, the brain's release of the neurotransmitter is less necessary. As drug intake increases, the body's production of the neurotransmitters continues to decrease, leaving the person in need of progressively more of the drug to achieve its effects. In this way, drug takers build tolerance for a drug, becoming more and more reliant on it rather than on their own biological processes to feel comfortable, happy, or alert. If they suddenly stop taking the drug, their natural supply of neurotransmitters will be low for a time, producing the symptoms of withdrawal. Withdrawal continues until the brain resumes its normal production of the neurotransmitters.

Which neurotransmitters are affected depends on the drug used. Repeated and excessive use of alcohol or benzodiazepines may lower the brain's production of the neurotransmitter GABA, regular use of opioids may reduce the brain's production of endorphins, and regular use of cocaine or amphetamines may lower the brain's production of dopamine (Kosten et al., 2011, 2005). In addition, researchers have identified a neurotransmitter called *anandamide* that operates much like THC; excessive use of marijuana may reduce the production of anandamide (Janis, 2015; Budney et al., 2011).

This theory helps explain why people who regularly take substances have tolerance and withdrawal reactions. But why are drugs so rewarding, and why do certain people turn to them in the first place? A number of brain-imaging studies suggest that many, perhaps all, drugs eventually activate a **reward center,** or "pleasure pathway," in the brain (Urošević et al., 2014) (see Figure 10-4). A key neurotransmitter in this pleasure pathway appears to be *dopamine* (Trifilieff & Martinez, 2014). When dopamine is activated along the pleasure pathway, a person feels pleasure. Music may activate dopamine in the reward center. So may a hug or a word of praise. And so do drugs. Some researchers believe that other neurotransmitters may also play important roles in the reward center (McClure et al., 2014).

Certain drugs apparently stimulate the reward center directly. Remember that cocaine and amphetamines directly increase dopamine activity. Other drugs seem to stimulate it in roundabout ways. The biochemical reactions triggered by alcohol, opioids, and marijuana probably set in motion a series of chemical events that eventually lead to increased dopamine activity in the reward center. A number of studies further suggest that when substances repeatedly stimulate this reward center, the center develops a hypersensitivity to the substances. That is, neurons in the center fire more readily when later stimulated by the substances, contributing to future desires for them. (Urošević et al., 2014).

Still other theorists suspect that people who chronically use drugs may suffer from a *reward-deficiency syndrome:* their reward center is not readily activated by the usual events in their lives, so they turn to drugs to stimulate this pleasure pathway, particularly in times of stress (Garfield et al., 2014; Blum et al., 2000). Abnormal genes, such as the abnormal D2 receptor gene, have been cited as a possible cause of this syndrome (Trifilieff & Martinez, 2014).

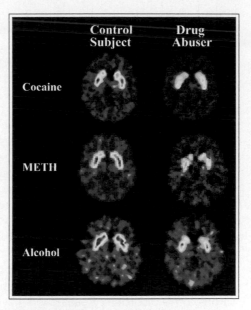

Victims of a reward deficiency syndrome? The brain reward centers of people who develop substance use disorders may be inadequately activated by events in life—a problem called the *reward deficiency syndrome.* With the colors red and orange indicating more brain activity, these PET scans show that before abusers of cocaine, methamphetamine, and alcohol use drugs, their reward centers (right) are generally less active than the reward centers of nonabusers (left) (Volkow et al., 2004, 2002).

Reprinted from *Neurobiology of Learning and Memory*, N. D. Volkow et al. Role of Dopamine, the Frontal Cortex and Memory Circuits in Drug Addiction: Insight from Imaging Studies, 610–624, © 2002, with permission from Elsevier. http://www.sciencedirect.com/science/article/pii/S1074742702940992

figure 10-4

Pleasure centers in the brain One of the reasons drugs produce feelings of pleasure is because they increase levels of the neurotransmitter dopamine along a "pleasure pathway" in the brain that extends from the ventral tegmental area to the nucleus accumbens and then to the frontal cortex. This activation of pleasure centers plays a role in addiction.

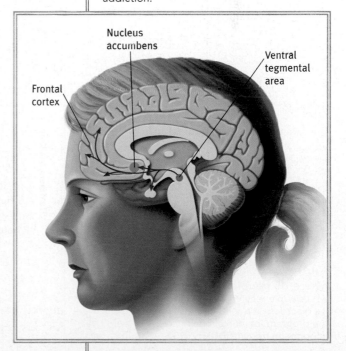

Songs of Substance

Substance use is a popular theme in music. Hit songs include Amy Winehouse's "Rehab," the Velvet Underground's "Heroin," the Rolling Stones' "Sister Morphine," Snoop Dogg's "Gin and Juice," Eric Clapton's "Cocaine," Eminem's "Drug Ballad," Lil' Kim's "Drugs," Jay Z's "I Know," Miley Cyrus' "We Can't Stop," and Rihanna's "Diamonds."

➤ *Summing Up*

WHAT CAUSES SUBSTANCE USE DISORDERS? Several explanations for substance use disorders have been put forward. Together they are beginning to shed light on the disorders.

According to sociocultural theorists, the people most likely to develop these disorders are those living in stressful socioeconomic conditions or people whose families value or accept drug use. In the psychodynamic view, people who develop substance use disorders have excessive dependency needs traceable to the early stages of life. Some psychodynamic theorists also believe that certain people have a substance abuse personality that makes them prone to drug use. In the leading behavioral view, drug use is seen as being reinforced initially because it reduces tensions and lifts spirits. According to cognitive theorists, such effects may also lead to an expectancy that drugs will be comforting and helpful.

The biological explanations are supported by twin, adoptee, genetic linkage, and molecular biology studies, suggesting that people may inherit a predisposition to the disorders. Researchers have also learned that drug tolerance and withdrawal symptoms may be caused by cutbacks in the brain's production of particular neurotransmitters during excessive and repeated drug use. Biological studies suggest that many, perhaps all, drugs may ultimately lead to increased dopamine activity in the brain's reward center.

How Are Substance Use Disorders Treated?

Many approaches have been used to treat substance use disorders (see *MediaSpeak* on page 336), including psychodynamic, behavioral, cognitive-behavioral, and biological approaches, along with several sociocultural therapies. Although these treatments sometimes meet with great success, more often they are only moderately helpful (Belendiuk & Riggs, 2014). Today the treatments are typically used on either an outpatient or inpatient basis or a combination of the two (see Figure 10-5).

figure 10-5

Where do people receive treatment?
Most people receive treatment for substance use disorders in a self-help group, rehabilitation program, or mental health center. (Information from: NSDUH, 2013.)

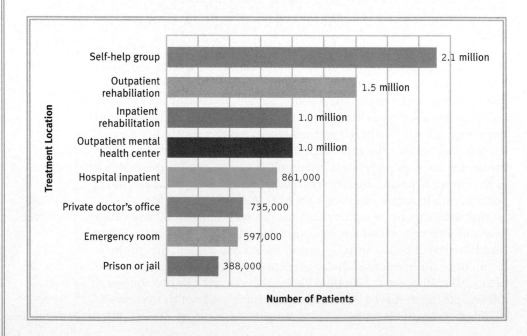

Treatment Location	Number of Patients
Self-help group	2.1 million
Outpatient rehabiliation	1.5 million
Inpatient rehabilitation	1.0 million
Outpatient mental health center	1.0 million
Hospital inpatient	861,000
Private doctor's office	735,000
Emergency room	597,000
Prison or jail	388,000

Psychodynamic Therapies

Psychodynamic therapists first guide clients to uncover and work through the underlying needs and conflicts that they believe have led to the substance use disorder. Although this approach is often used, it has not been found to be particularly effective (McCrady, 2014). It may be that substance use disorders, regardless of their causes, eventually become stubborn independent problems that must be the direct target of treatment if people are to become drug-free. Psychodynamic therapy tends to be of more help when it is combined with other approaches in a multidimensional treatment program (Lightdale et al., 2011, 2008).

Behavioral Therapies

A widely used behavioral treatment for substance use disorders is **aversion therapy,** an approach based on the principles of classical conditioning. Clients are repeatedly presented with an unpleasant stimulus (for example, an electric shock) at the very moment that they are taking a drug. After repeated pairings, they are expected to react negatively to the substance itself and to lose their craving for it.

Aversion therapy has been used to treat alcoholism more than it has to treat other substance use disorders. In one version of this therapy, drinking is paired with drug-induced nausea and vomiting (McCrady et al., 2014; Welsh & Liberto, 2001). The pairing of nausea with alcohol is expected to produce negative responses to alcohol itself. Another version of aversion therapy requires people with alcoholism to imagine extremely upsetting, repulsive, or frightening scenes while they are drinking. The pairing of the imagined scenes with alcohol is expected to produce negative responses to alcohol itself. Here is the kind of scene therapists may guide a client to imagine:

> I'd like you to vividly imagine that you are tasting the (beer, whiskey, etc.). See yourself tasting it, capture the exact taste, color and consistency. Use all of your senses. After you've tasted the drink you notice that there is something small and white floating in the glass—it stands out. You bend closer to examine it more carefully, your nose is right over the glass now and the smell fills your nostrils as you remember exactly what the drink tastes like. Now you can see what's in the glass. There are several maggots floating on the surface. As you watch, revolted, one manages to get a grip on the glass and, undulating, creeps up the glass. There are even more of the repulsive creatures in the glass than you first thought. You realise that you have swallowed some of them and you're very aware of the taste in your mouth. You feel very sick and wish you'd never reached for the glass and had the drink at all.
>
> (Clarke & Saunders, 1988, pp. 143–144)

A behavioral approach that has been effective in the short-term treatment of people who are addicted to cocaine and several other drugs is *contingency management,* which makes incentives (such as cash, vouchers, prizes, or privileges) contingent on the submission of drug-free urine specimens (Godley et al., 2014). In one pioneering study, 68 percent of cocaine abusers who completed a six-month contingency training program achieved at least eight weeks of continuous abstinence (Higgins et al., 2011, 1993).

Behavioral interventions for substance use disorders have usually had only limited success when they are the sole form of treatment (Belendiuk & Riggs, 2014; Carroll, 2008). A major problem is that the approaches can be effective only when people are motivated to continue using them despite their unpleasantness or demands.

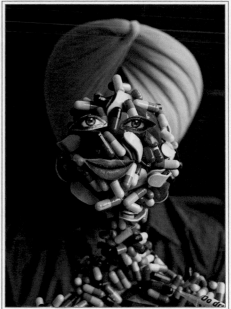

Spreading the word In a particularly innovative effort to increase public awareness about the dangers of drug abuse, Harwinder Singh Gill, an artist in India, created a model of the human body made up of capsule shells. Gill did this on the eve of the 2012 International Day Against Drug Abuse and Illicit Trafficking.

▶ **aversion therapy** A treatment in which clients are repeatedly presented with unpleasant stimuli while they are performing undesirable behaviors such as taking a drug.

MediaSpeak

Enrolling at Sober High

by Jeff Forester

Jeff has been sober 22 months, he tells me. Without blinking or ducking, his clear blue eyes looking straight at me, he says that if it were not for Sobriety High, he'd be dead. I believe him. . . . Sobriety High started in Minneapolis in 1989 with just two students. It has 100 more today, and 33 sober high schools have sprung up in eight other states. . . . According to a National Institute on Drug Abuse study, 78% of the students in sober high schools attend after receiving formal rehab. . . .

While [Sobriety High] undoubtedly feels like a school, the wall banners feature phrases like "Turning It Over Is A Turning Point" rather than, say, a sign for the prom. The students are diverse, with hair of all different lengths and colors; some have the seemingly requisite addict tattoos while others are decked out in Goth garb and still others project a distinctly Midwestern Wonder Bread aura. Their journeys are also diverse, with the lucky ones landing here after treatment but many coming from the courts, detox or the streets. . . .

. . . The classes are small so that teachers can check in with each student regularly and the curriculum flexible so as to help them with what they missed while they were using or in treatment. Some programs help students—many with hair-raising records—find work. Some also work with chemically dependent parents and older siblings as well. Students typically have "group" each day, and while it is not an AA meeting, the DNA of AA is evident. . . .

All teenagers have low impulse control but the stakes are higher for chemically dependent kids trying to stay sober. Says Joe Schrank, . . . a board member of the National Youth Recovery Foundation, . . . "When you put pot and booze on top of adolescent stupidity, kids are at risk." . . .

Just try adding acne, constant temptation and regularly being heckled that you're a "pussy" to a standard newcomer's recovery and you'll see just how high the deck is stacked against teenage sobriety; the notion of placing them in an environment that caters to clean living thus makes sense. . . .

Purestock/SuperStock

Ninety percent of students at Sobriety High have other mental health issues besides chemical dependency [and] need the extra support of counselors, psychologists, and ongoing mental health support, and this is costly. . . . "It takes more money per student, and the schools must be on a segregated site if they are to have a drug and alcohol free campus." . . .

For barely sober teens . . . closing recovery schools would be disastrous. "Many of them will go back to the streets, or prison, or they will be dead," says . . . the Sobriety High social worker. . . . Supporters . . . point out that closing recovery schools makes little fiscal sense. "Recovery school is a fraction of the cost of incarceration," says Joe Schrank. . . . "Look at Drug Courts," adds former Congressman Jim Ramstad. "The recidivism rate for those who complete the course is 24% while the rate for criminal court is 75%." . . .

[Social worker Debbie Bolton] says plainly, "What we do is important. We save lives."

"Most Sober High Schools Are Very Successful. So Why Are They Facing the Ax?" By Jeff Forester, TheFix.com (addiction website), 6/18/2011.

> **What advantages might sober schools have over other substance abuse interventions?**

Generally, behavioral treatments work best in combination with either biological or cognitive approaches (Belendiuk & Riggs, 2014; Carroll & Kiluk, 2012).

Cognitive-Behavioral Therapies

Cognitive-behavioral treatments for substance use disorders help clients identify and change the behaviors and cognitions that keep contributing to their patterns of substance misuse (Gregg et al., 2014; Yoon et al., 2012). Practitioners of these approaches also help the clients develop more effective coping skills—skills that can be applied during times of stress, temptation, and substance craving.

Perhaps the most prominent cognitive-behavioral approach to substance misuse is **relapse-prevention training** (Jhanjee, 2014; Daley et al., 2011). The overall goal of this approach is for clients to gain *control* over their substance-related behaviors. To help reach this goal, clients are taught to identify high-risk situations, appreciate the range of decisions that confront them in such situations, change their dysfunctional lifestyles, and learn from mistakes and lapses.

Several strategies typically are included in relapse-prevention training for alcohol use disorder: (1) *Therapists have clients keep track of their drinking* by writing down the times, locations, emotions, bodily changes, and other circumstances of their drinking. (2) *Therapists teach clients coping strategies to use when such situations arise,* strategies such as employing relaxation techniques, spacing their drinks, or sipping drinks rather than gulping. (3) *Therapists teach clients to plan ahead of time,* determining beforehand how many drinks are appropriate, what to drink, and under which circumstances to drink.

Relapse-prevention training has been found to lower some people's frequency of intoxication and of binge drinking (Jhanjee, 2014; Borden et al., 2011). People who are young and do not have the tolerance and withdrawal features of chronic alcohol use seem to do best with this approach (Hart & Ksir, 2014; Deas et al., 2008).

Another form of cognitive-behavioral treatment that has been used in cases of substance use disorder is *acceptance and commitment therapy (ACT),* the mindfulness-based approach that helps clients become *aware* of their streams of thoughts as they are occurring and to accept such thoughts as mere events of the mind (see Chapters 2 and 4). For people with substance use disorders, that means increasing their awareness and acceptance of their drug cravings, worries, and depressive thoughts. By accepting such thoughts rather than trying to eliminate them, the clients are expected to be less upset by them and less likely to act on them by seeking out drugs. Research indicates that ACT often is as effective as other cognitive-behavioral treatments for substance use disorders, and sometimes more effective (Lee et al., 2015; Bowen et al., 2014; Chiesa & Serretti, 2014).

Biological Treatments

Biological treatments may be used to help people withdraw from substances, abstain from them, or simply maintain their level of use without increasing it further. As with the other forms of treatment, biological approaches alone rarely bring long-term improvement, but they can be helpful when combined with other approaches.

Detoxification **Detoxification** is systematic and medically supervised withdrawal from a drug. Some detoxification programs are offered on an outpatient basis. Others are located in hospitals and clinics and may also include individual

Better ways to cope Several treatments for substance use disorders, including relapse-prevention training, teach clients alternative—more functional—ways of coping with stress and negative emotions. In that spirit, this patient at a drug rehabilitation center in China developed the practice of kicking a punching dummy to help release his pent-up anger.

▶ **relapse-prevention training** A cognitive-behavioral approach to treating alcohol use disorder in which clients are taught to keep track of their drinking behavior, apply coping strategies in situations that typically trigger excessive drinking, and plan ahead for risky situations and reactions.

▶ **detoxification** Systematic and medically supervised withdrawal from a drug.

Patrick Davison/The Dallas Morning News

Forced detoxification Abstinence is not always medically supervised, nor is it necessarily planned or voluntary. This person, who is suffering from alcoholism, begins to have symptoms of withdrawal soon after being imprisoned for public intoxication.

and group therapy, a "full-service" institutional approach that has become popular. One detoxification approach is to have clients withdraw gradually from the substance, taking smaller and smaller doses until they are off the drug completely. A second—often medically preferred—detoxification strategy is to give clients other drugs that reduce the symptoms of withdrawal (Bisaga et al., 2015; Day & Strang, 2011). Antianxiety drugs, for example, are sometimes used to reduce severe alcohol withdrawal reactions such as delirium tremens and seizures. Detoxification programs seem to help motivated people withdraw from drugs (Müller et al., 2010). However, relapse rates tend to be high for those who do not receive a follow-up form of treatment—psychological, biological, or sociocultural—after successfully detoxifying (Blodgett et al., 2014).

Antagonist Drugs After successfully stopping a drug, people must avoid falling back into a pattern of misuse. As an aid to resisting temptation, some people with substance use disorders are given **antagonist drugs,** which block or change the effects of the addictive drug. *Disulfiram* (Antabuse), for example, is often given to people who are trying to stay away from alcohol. By itself, a low dose of disulfiram seems to have few negative effects, but a person who drinks alcohol while taking it will have intense nausea, vomiting, blushing, a faster heart rate, dizziness, and perhaps fainting. People taking disulfiram are less likely to drink alcohol because they know the terrible reaction that awaits them should they have even one drink. Disulfiram has proved helpful, but again only with people who are motivated to take it as prescribed (Diclemente et al., 2008).

For substance use disorders centered on opioids, several *narcotic antagonists,* such as *naloxone,* are used (Alter, 2014). These antagonists attach to *endorphin* receptor sites throughout the brain and make it impossible for the opioids to have their usual effect. Without the rush or high, continued drug use becomes pointless. Although narcotic antagonists have been helpful—particularly in emergencies, to rescue people from an overdose of opioids—they can in fact be dangerous for people who are addicted to opioids. The antagonists must be given very carefully because of their ability to throw such persons into severe withdrawal. Research indicates that narcotic antagonists may also be useful in the treatment of substance use disorders involving alcohol or cocaine (Crits-Christoph et al., 2015; Harrison & Petrakis, 2011).

Drug Maintenance Therapy A drug-related lifestyle may be a bigger problem than the drug's direct effects. Much of the damage caused by heroin addiction,

▶ **antagonist drugs** Drugs that block or change the effects of an addictive drug.

▶ **methadone maintenance program** A treatment approach in which clients are given legally and medically supervised doses of methadone—a heroin substitute—to treat heroin-centered substance use disorder.

▶ **Alcoholics Anonymous (AA)** A self-help organization that provides support and guidance for people with alcohol use disorder.

for example, comes from overdoses, unsterilized needles, and an accompanying life of crime. Thus clinicians were very enthusiastic when **methadone maintenance programs** were developed in the 1960s to treat heroin addiction (Dole & Nyswander, 1967, 1965). In these programs, people with an addiction are given the laboratory opioid *methadone* as a substitute for heroin. Although they then become dependent on methadone, their new addiction is maintained under safe medical supervision. Unlike heroin, methadone produces a moderate high, can be taken by mouth (thus eliminating the dangers of needles), and needs to be taken only once a day.

> **Why has the legal, medically supervised use of heroin (in Great Britain) or heroin substitutes (in the United States) sometimes failed to combat drug problems?**

At first, methadone programs seemed very effective, and many of them were set up throughout the United States, Canada, and England. These programs became less popular during the 1980s, however, because of the dangers of methadone itself. Many clinicians came to believe that substituting one addiction for another is not an acceptable "solution" for a substance use disorder, and many people with an addiction complained that methadone addiction was creating an additional drug problem that simply complicated their original one (Winstock, Lintzeris, & Lea, 2011). Methadone is sometimes harder to withdraw from than heroin because the withdrawal symptoms can last longer (Hart & Ksir, 2014; Day & Strang, 2011). Moreover, pregnant women maintained on methadone have the added concern of the drug's effect on their fetus.

Despite such concerns, maintenance treatment with methadone—or with other opioid substitute drugs—has again sparked interest among clinicians in recent years, partly because of new research support (Balhara, 2014; Fareed et al., 2011) and partly because of the rapid spread of the HIV and hepatitis C viruses among intravenous drug abusers and their sex partners and children (Lambdin et al., 2014; Galanter & Kleber, 2008). Not only is methadone treatment safer than street opioid use, but many methadone programs now include AIDS education and other health instructions in their services. Research suggests that methadone maintenance programs are most effective when they are combined with education, psychotherapy, family therapy, and employment counseling (Jhanjee, 2014). Today thousands of clinics provide methadone treatment across the United States.

Sociocultural Therapies

As you have read, sociocultural theorists—both *family-social* and *multicultural* theorists—believe that psychological problems emerge in a social setting and are best treated in a social context. Three sociocultural approaches have been used to help people overcome substance use disorders: (1) *self-help programs,* (2) *culture- and gender-sensitive programs,* and (3) *community prevention programs.*

Self-Help and Residential Treatment Programs

Many people with substance use disorders have organized among themselves to help one another recover without professional assistance. The drug self-help movement dates back to 1935, when two Ohio men suffering from alcoholism met and wound up discussing alternative treatment possibilities. The first discussion led to others and to the eventual formation of a self-help group whose members discussed alcohol-related problems, traded ideas, and provided support. The organization became known as **Alcoholics Anonymous (AA).**

Today AA has more than 2 million members in 114,000 groups across the world (AA World Services, 2014). It offers peer support along with moral and spiritual guidelines to help people overcome alcoholism. Different members apparently find different aspects of AA helpful. For some it is the peer support; for others it is the

Pros and cons of methadone treatment Methadone is itself a narcotic that can be as dangerous as other opioids when not taken under safe medical supervision. Here a couple protests against a proposed methadone treatment facility in Maine. Their 19-year-old daughter, who was not an opioid addict, had died months earlier after taking methadone to get high.

Shawn Patrick Ouelette/Maine Sunday Telegram/AP Photo

////// BETWEEN THE LINES //////

Staying Sober

• 48% of current AA members have been sober for more than five years.

• 37% of current AA members have been sober for less than one year.

(AA World Services, 2014)

spiritual dimension (Tusa & Burgholzer, 2013). Meetings take place regularly, and members are available to help each other 24 hours a day.

By offering guidelines for living, the organization helps members abstain "one day at a time," urging them to accept as fact the ideas that they have a disease, are powerless over alcohol, and must stop drinking entirely and permanently if they are to live normal lives. Related self-help organizations, *Al-Anon* and *Alateen,* offer support for people who live with and care about people with alcoholism. Self-help programs such as *Narcotics Anonymous* and *Cocaine Anonymous* have been developed for other substance use disorders.

Fighting drug abuse while in prison
Inmates at a county jail in Texas exercise and meditate as part of a drug and alcohol rehabilitation program. The program also includes psychoeducation and other interventions to help inmates address their substance use disorders.

It is worth noting that the abstinence goal of AA directly opposes the controlled-drinking goal of relapse-prevention training and several other interventions for substance misuse (see page 337). In fact, this issue—abstinence versus controlled drinking—has been debated for years (Hart & Ksir, 2014; Rosenthal, 2011, 2005). Feelings about it have run so strongly that in the 1980s the people on one side challenged the motives and honesty of those on the other (Sobell & Sobell, 1984, 1973; Pendery et al., 1982).

Research indicates, however, that both controlled drinking and abstinence may be useful treatment goals, depending on the nature of the particular drinking problem. Studies suggest that abstinence may be a more appropriate goal for people who have a long-standing alcohol use disorder, whereas controlled drinking can be helpful to younger drinkers whose pattern does not include tolerance and withdrawal reactions. Many of those in the latter group may respond to treatments that teach a nonabusive form of drinking (Hart & Ksir, 2014; Witkiewitz & Marlatt, 2007, 2004).

Many self-help programs have expanded into **residential treatment centers,** or **therapeutic communities**—such as *Daytop Village* and *Phoenix House*—where people formerly addicted to drugs live, work, and socialize in a drug-free environment while undergoing individual, group, and family therapies and making a transition back to community life (Relf et al., 2014; Bonetta, 2010).

The evidence that keeps self-help and residential treatment programs going comes largely in the form of individual testimonials. Many tens of thousands of people have revealed that they are members of these programs and credit them with turning their lives around. Studies of the programs have also had favorable findings, but their numbers have been limited (Galanter, 2014).

Culture- and Gender-Sensitive Programs

Many people with substance use disorders live in a poor and perhaps violent setting. A growing number of today's treatment programs try to be sensitive to the special sociocultural pressures and problems faced by drug abusers who are poor, homeless, or members of minority groups (Hadland & Baer, 2014; Hurd et al., 2014). Therapists who are sensitive to their clients' life challenges can do more to address the stresses that often lead to relapse.

> **What different kinds of issues might be confronted by drug abusers from different minority groups or genders?**

Similarly, therapists have become more aware that women often require treatment methods different from those designed for men (Lund, Brendryen, & Ravndal, 2014; Greenfield et al., 2011). Women and men often have different physical and psychological reactions to drugs, for example. In addition, treatment of women with substance use disorders may be complicated by the impact of sexual abuse, the possibility that they may be or may

▶ **residential treatment center** A place where people formerly addicted to drugs live, work, and socialize in a drug-free environment. Also called a *therapeutic community.*

become pregnant while taking drugs, the stresses of raising children, and the fear of criminal prosecution for abusing drugs during pregnancy (Finnegan & Kandall, 2008). Thus many women with such disorders feel more comfortable seeking help at gender-sensitive clinics or residential programs; some such programs also allow children to live with their recovering mothers.

Community Prevention Programs Perhaps the most effective approach to substance use disorders is to prevent them (Sandler et al., 2014). The first drug-prevention programs were conducted in schools (Espada et al., 2015). Today such programs are also offered in workplaces, activity centers, and other community settings and even through the media (NSDUH, 2013). Around 75 percent of adolescents report that they have seen or heard a substance use–prevention message within the past year. And almost 60 percent have talked to their parents in the past year about the dangers of alcohol and other drugs.

Prevention programs may focus on the *individual* (for example, by providing education about unpleasant drug effects), the *family* (by teaching parenting skills), the *peer group* (by teaching resistance to peer pressure), the *school* (by setting up firm enforcement of drug policies), or the *community* at large. The most effective prevention efforts focus on several of these areas to provide a consistent message about drug misuse in all areas of people's lives (Wambeam et al., 2014). Some prevention programs have even been developed for preschool children.

> **What impact might admissions by celebrities about their past drug use have on people's willingness to seek treatment?**

Two of today's leading community-based prevention programs are TheTruth.com and Above the Influence. The Truth.com is an antismoking campaign, aimed at young people in particular, that has "edgy" ads on the Web (on YouTube, for instance), on television, and in magazines and newspapers. Above the Influence is a similar advertising campaign that focuses on a range of substances abused by teenagers. One recent nationwide survey of 3,000 students has suggested that watching Above the Influence ads may help reduce marijuana use by teenagers (Slater et al., 2011). The survey found that 8 percent of eighth-graders familiar with the campaign have taken up marijuana use, in contrast to 12 percent of students who have never seen the ads.

Listen to my story A prisoner stands shackled before students at an Ohio high school and discusses his drunk-driving conviction (his intoxicated driving resulted in a fatal automobile crash). These visits by inmates are part of the school's "Make the Right Choice" prevention program.

Fred Squillante/The Columbus Dispatch

➤ *Summing Up*

HOW ARE SUBSTANCE USE DISORDERS TREATED? Treatments for substance use disorders vary widely. Usually several approaches are combined. Psychodynamic therapies are used to try to help clients become aware of and correct the underlying needs and conflicts that may have led to their use of drugs. A common behavioral technique is aversion therapy, in which an unpleasant stimulus is paired with the drug that the person is abusing. Cognitive and behavioral techniques have been combined in such forms as relapse-prevention training. Biological treatments include detoxification, antagonist drugs, and drug maintenance therapy. Sociocultural treatments approach substance use disorders in a social context by means of self-help groups (e.g., Alcoholics Anonymous), culture- and gender-sensitive treatments, and community prevention programs.

///// BETWEEN THE LINES /////

Cocaine Alert

Cocaine accounts for more drug treatment admissions than any other drug (Hart & Ksir, 2014; SAMHSA, 2014).

Other Addictive Disorders

As you read at the beginning of this chapter, DSM-5 lists *gambling disorder* as an addictive disorder alongside the substance use disorders. This represents a significant broadening of the concept of addiction, which in previous editions of the DSM referred only to the misuse of substances. In essence, DSM-5 is suggesting that people may become addicted to behaviors and activities beyond substance use.

Gambling Disorder

It is estimated that as many as 4 percent of adults and 3 to 10 percent of teenagers and college students suffer from **gambling disorder** (Nowak & Aloe, 2013; Black et al., 2012). Clinicians are careful to distinguish between this disorder and social gambling (APA, 2013). Gambling disorder is defined less by the amount of time or money spent gambling than by the addictive nature of the behavior. People with gambling disorder are preoccupied with gambling and typically cannot walk away from a bet. When they lose money repeatedly, they often gamble more in an effort to win the money back and continue gambling even in the face of financial, social, occupational, educational, and health problems (see Table 10-3). They usually gamble more when feeling distressed and often lie to cover up the extent of their gambling. Many people with gambling disorder need to gamble with ever-larger amounts of money to reach the desired excitement, and they feel restless or irritable when they try to reduce or stop gambling—symptoms that are similar to the tolerance and withdrawal reactions displayed in cases of substance use disorder (APA, 2013).

The explanations proposed for gambling disorder often parallel those for substance use disorders. Some studies suggest, for example, that people with gambling disorder may (1) inherit a genetic predisposition to develop the disorder (Vitaro et al., 2014); (2) experience heightened dopamine activity and operation of the brain's reward center when they gamble (Jabr, 2013); (3) have impulsive, novelty-seeking, and other personality styles that leave them prone to gambling disorder (Leeman et al., 2014); and (4) make repeated cognitive mistakes such as inaccurate

table: **10-3**

Dx Checklist

Gambling Disorder

1. Individual displays a maladaptive pattern of gambling, featuring at least four of the following symptoms over the course of a full year:

   (a) Can achieve desired excitement only by gambling more and more money.

   (b) Feels restless or irritable when tries to reduce gambling.

   (c) Repeatedly tries and fails at efforts to control, reduce, or cease gambling.

   (d) Consumed with gambling thoughts or plans.

   (e) Gambling is often triggered by upset feelings.

   (f) Frequently returns to gambling to try to recoup previous losses.

   (g) Covers up amount of gambling by lying.

   (h) Gambling has put important relationships, job, or educational/career opportunities at risk.

   (i) Seeks money from others to address gambling-induced financial problems.

2. Individual experiences significant distress or impairment.

(Information from: APA, 2013)

expectations and misinterpretations of their emotions and bodily states (Spada et al., 2015; Williams et al., 2012). However, the research on these theories has been limited thus far, leaving such explanations tentative for now.

Several of the leading treatments for substance use disorders have been adapted for use with gambling disorder. These treatments include cognitive-behavioral approaches like relapse-prevention training and biological approaches such as narcotic antagonists (Jabr, 2013; Bosco et al., 2012). In addition, the self-help group program *Gamblers Anonymous,* a network modeled after *Alcoholics Anonymous,* is available to the many thousands of people with gambling disorder (Marceaux & Melville, 2011). People who attend such groups seem to have a better recovery rate.

Internet Gaming Disorder: Awaiting Official Status

As people increasingly turn to the Internet for activities that used to take place in the "real world"—communicating, networking, shopping, playing games, and participating in a community—a new psychological problem has emerged: an uncontrollable need to be online (Hsu et al., 2014; Young, 2011). This pattern has been called *Internet use disorder, Internet addiction,* and *problematic Internet use,* among other names.

For people who have this pattern—at least 1 percent of all people—the Internet has become a black hole. They spend all or most of their waking hours texting, tweeting, networking, gaming, Internet browsing, e-mailing, blogging, visiting virtual worlds, shopping online, or viewing online pornography (Yoo et al., 2014) Specific symptoms of this pattern parallel those found in substance use disorders and gambling disorder, extending from the loss of outside interests to possible withdrawal reactions when Internet use is not possible (APA, 2013).

Although clinicians, the media, and the public have shown enormous interest in this problem, it is not included as a disorder in DSM-5. Rather, the DSM workgroup has recommended that one version of the pattern, which it calls **Internet gaming disorder,** receive further study for possible inclusion in future editions (APA, 2013). Time—and research—will tell whether this pattern reaches the status of a formal clinical disorder.

David Sacks/The Image Bank/Getty Images

Increase in gambling venues This woman is playing a slot machine while vacationing on a cruise ship. Harmless fun for her, but not for everyone. Some theorists believe the recent increases in the prevalence of gambling disorder are related to the explosion of new gambling venues, in particular the many casinos that have been built in every part of the country, and the legalization and spread of online gambling.

➤ *Summing Up*

OTHER ADDICTIVE DISORDERS DSM-5 groups gambling disorder alongside the substance use disorders as an addictive disorder. The explanations for this disorder, which are parallel to those for substance use disorders, include genetic factors, dopamine activity, personality styles, and cognitive factors. Treatments for gambling disorder include cognitive-behavioral approaches, narcotic antagonists, and self-help groups. The DSM-5 task force recommended that another addictive pattern, Internet gaming disorder, receive further study for possible inclusion in future DSM revisions.

PUTTING IT...*together*

New Wrinkles to a Familiar Story

In some respects, the story of the misuse of drugs is the same today as in the past. Substance use is still rampant, often creating damaging psychological disorders. New drugs keep emerging, and the public goes through periods of believing, naïvely, that the new drugs are "safe." Only gradually do people learn that these, too, pose dangers. And treatments for substance-use disorders continue to have only limited effect.

▶ **gambling disorder** A disorder marked by persistent and recurrent gambling behavior, leading to a range of life problems.

▶ **Internet gaming disorder** A disorder marked by persistent, recurrent, and excessive Internet gaming. Recommended for further study by the DSM-5 task force.

Yet there are positive new wrinkles in this familiar story. Researchers have begun to develop a clearer understanding of how drugs act on the brain and body. In treatment, self-help groups and rehabilitation programs are flourishing. And preventive education to make people aware of the dangers of drug misuse is also expanding and seems to be having an effect. One reason for these improvements is that investigators and clinicians have stopped working in isolation and are instead looking for intersections between their own work and work from other models.

Perhaps the most important insight to be gained from these integrated efforts is that several of the models were already on the right track. Social pressures, personality characteristics, rewards, and genetic predispositions all seem to play roles in substance use disorders, and in fact to operate together. For example, some people may inherit a malfunction of the biological reward center and so may need special doses of external stimulation—which can be provided by, for example, gambling, intense relationships, an abundance of certain foods, or drugs—to stimulate their reward center. Their pursuit of external rewards may take on the character of an addictive personality. Such people may be especially prone to experimenting with drugs, particularly when their social group makes the drugs available or when they are faced with intense stress.

Just as each model has identified important factors in the development of substance use disorders, each has made important contributions to treatment. As you have seen, the various forms of treatment seem to work best when they are combined with approaches from the other models, making integrated treatment the most productive approach.

Yet another new wrinkle to the addiction story is that the clinical field has now formally proclaimed that substances are not the only things to which people may develop an addiction. By grouping gambling disorder with the substance use disorders and targeting Internet gaming disorder for possible inclusion in the future, DSM-5 has opened the door for a broader view and perhaps broader treatments of addictive patterns—whether they are induced by substances or by other kinds of experiences.

CLINICAL CHOICES

Now that you've read about substance use and addictive disorders, try the interactive case study for this chapter. See if you are able to identify Jorge's symptoms and suggest a diagnosis based on his symptoms. What kind of treatment would be most effective for Jorge? Go to LaunchPad to access *Clinical Choices*.

KEY TERMS

QuickQuiz

1. What are substance use disorders? *pp. 310–311*

2. How does alcohol act on the brain and body? What are the problems and dangers of alcohol misuse? *pp. 311–316*

3. Describe the features and problems of the misuse of barbiturates and benzodiazepines. *p. 316*

4. Compare the various opioids (opium, heroin, morphine). What problems may result from their use? *pp. 316–318*

5. List and compare two kinds of stimulant drugs. Describe their biological actions and the problems caused by each of them. *pp. 319–323*

6. What are the effects of hallucinogens, particularly LSD? *pp. 323–325*

7. What are the effects of marijuana and other cannabis substances? Why is marijuana a greater danger today than it was decades ago? *pp. 326–328*

8. What special problems does polysubstance use pose? *pp. 328–329*

9. Describe the leading explanations and treatments for substance use disorders. How well supported are these explanations and treatments? *pp. 330–341*

10. Name and describe two addictive patterns that are not triggered by substance misuse. *pp. 342–343*

Visit *LaunchPad*
www.macmillanhighered.com/launchpad/comerfund8e
to access the e-book, new interactive case studies, videos, activities, and LearningCurve quizzes, as well as study aids including flashcards, FAQs, and research exercises.

Macmillan Education
LaunchPad

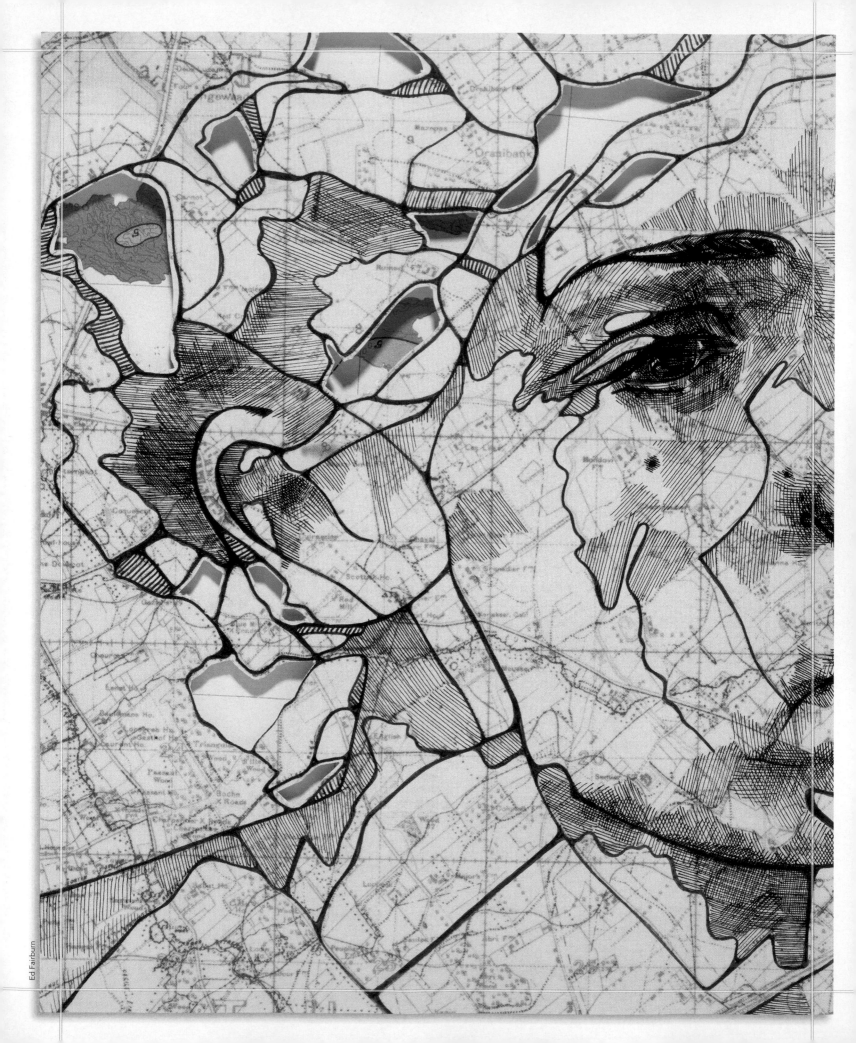

Ed Fairburn

Disorders of Sex and Gender

R obert, a 57-year-old man, came to sex therapy with his wife because of his inability to get erections. He had not had a problem with erections until six months earlier, when they attempted to have sex after an evening out, during which he had had several drinks. They attributed his failure to get an erection to his being "a little drunk," but he found himself worrying over the next few days that he was perhaps becoming impotent. When they next attempted intercourse, he found himself unable to get involved in what they were doing because he was so intent on watching himself to see if he would get an erection. Once again he did not, and they were both very upset. His failure to get an erection continued over the next few months. Robert's wife was very upset and frustrated, accusing him of having an affair or of no longer finding her attractive. Robert wondered if he was getting too old or if his medication for high blood pressure, which he had been taking for about a year, might be interfering with erections. When they came for sex therapy, they had not attempted any sexual activity for over two months.

Sexual behavior is a major focus of both our private thoughts and public discussions. Sexual feelings are a crucial part of our development and daily functioning, sexual activity is tied to the satisfaction of our basic needs, and sexual performance is linked to our self-esteem. Most people are fascinated by the abnormal sexual behavior of others and worry about the normality of their own sexuality.

Experts recognize two general categories of sexual disorders: sexual dysfunctions and paraphilic disorders. People with *sexual dysfunctions* have problems with their sexual responses. Robert, for example, had a dysfunction known as erectile disorder, a repeated failure to attain or maintain an erection during sexual activity. People with *paraphilic disorders* have repeated and intense sexual urges or fantasies in response to objects or situations that society deems inappropriate, and they may behave inappropriately as well. They may be aroused by the thought of sexual activity with a child, for example, or of exposing their genitals to strangers, and they may act on those urges. In addition to the sexual disorders, DSM-5 includes a diagnosis called *gender dysphoria,* a pattern in which people persistently feel that they have been born to the wrong sex, identify with the other gender, and experience significant distress or impairment as a consequence of these feelings.

As you will see throughout this chapter, relatively little is known about racial and other cultural differences in sexuality. This is true for normal sexual patterns, sexual dysfunctions, and paraphilic disorders alike. Although different cultural groups have for years been labeled hypersexual, "hot blooded," exotic, passionate, submissive, and the like, such incorrect stereotypes have grown strictly from ignorance or prejudice, not from objective observations or research (McGoldrick et al., 2007). In fact, sex therapists and sex researchers have only recently begun to attend systematically to the importance of culture and race.

▸**sexual dysfunction** A disorder marked by a persistent inability to function normally in some area of the sexual response cycle.

▸**desire phase** The phase of the sexual response cycle consisting of an urge to have sex, sexual fantasies, and sexual attraction.

▸**male hypoactive sexual desire disorder** A male dysfunction marked by a persistent reduction or lack of interest in sex and hence a low level of sexual activity.

▸**female sexual interest/arousal disorder** A female dysfunction marked by a persistent reduction or lack of interest in sex, as well as, in some cases, limited excitement and few sexual sensations during sexual activity.

Sexual Dysfunctions

Sexual dysfunctions, disorders in which people cannot respond normally in key areas of sexual functioning, make it difficult or impossible to enjoy sexual intercourse. Studies suggest that as many as 30 percent of men and 45 percent of women around the world suffer from such a dysfunction during their lives (Lewis et al., 2010). Sexual dysfunctions are typically very distressing, and they often lead to sexual frustration, guilt, loss of self-esteem, and interpersonal problems (Faubion & Rullo, 2015; McCarthy & McCarthy, 2012). Often these dysfunctions are interrelated; many patients with one dysfunction have another as well. Sexual dysfunctioning is described here for heterosexual couples, the majority of couples seen in therapy. Gay and lesbian couples have the same dysfunctions, however, and therapists use the same basic techniques to treat them.

> Rates for sexual behavior are typically based on population surveys. What factors might affect the accuracy of such surveys?

The human sexual response can be described as a *cycle* with four phases: *desire, excitement, orgasm,* and *resolution* (see Figure 11-1). Sexual dysfunctions affect one or more of the first three phases. Resolution consists simply of the relaxation and reduction in arousal that follow orgasm. Some people struggle with a sexual dysfunction their whole lives; in other cases, normal sexual functioning preceded the dysfunction. In some cases the dysfunction is present during all sexual situations; in others it is tied to particular situations (APA, 2013).

Disorders of Desire

The **desire phase** of the sexual response cycle consists of an interest in or urge to have sex, sexual attraction to others, and, for many people, sexual fantasies. Two dysfunctions affect the desire phase—*male hypoactive sexual desire disorder* and *female sexual interest/arousal disorder*. The latter disorder actually cuts across both the desire and excitement phases of the sexual response cycle. It is considered a single disorder in DSM-5 because, according to research, desire and arousal overlap particularly highly for women, and many women express difficulty distinguishing feelings of desire from those of arousal (APA, 2013).

A number of people have normal sexual interest but choose, as a matter of lifestyle rather than sexual desire, to avoid engaging in sexual relations (see *InfoCentral* on page 350). These people are not diagnosed as having one of the sexual desire disorders.

figure 11-1

The normal sexual response cycle Researchers have found a similar sequence of phases in both males and females. Sometimes, however, women do not experience orgasm; in that case, the resolution phase is less sudden. And sometimes women have two or more orgasms in succession before the resolution phase. (Information from: Kaplan, 1974; Masters & Johnson, 1970, 1966.)

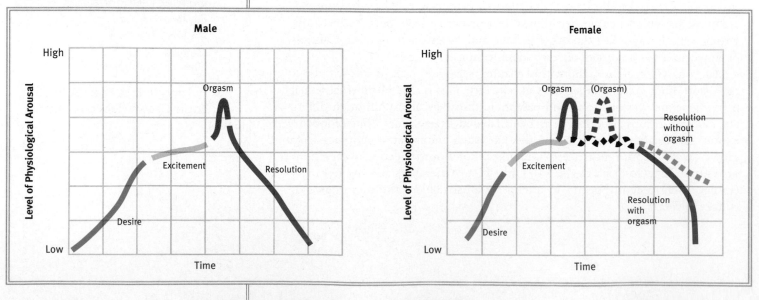

Men with **male hypoactive sexual desire disorder** persistently lack or have reduced interest in sex and engage in little sexual activity (see Table 11-1). Nevertheless, when they do have sex, their physical responses may be normal and they may enjoy the experience. While most cultures portray men as wanting all the sex they can get, as many as 18 percent of men worldwide have this disorder, and the number seeking therapy has increased during the past decade (Martin et al., 2014; Lewis et al., 2010).

Women with **female sexual interest/arousal disorder** also lack normal interest in sex and rarely initiate sexual activity (see Table 11-1 again). In addition, many such women feel little excitement during sexual activity, are unaroused by erotic cues, and have few genital or nongenital sensations during sexual activity (APA, 2013). As many as 38 percent of women worldwide have reduced sexual interest and arousal (Christensen et al., 2011; Laumann et al., 2005, 1999, 1994). It is important to note that many sex researchers and therapists believe it is inaccurate to combine desire and excitement symptoms into a single female disorder (Sungur & Gündüz, 2014).

A person's sex drive is determined by a combination of biological, psychological, and sociocultural factors, any of which may reduce sexual desire. Most cases of low sexual desire are caused primarily by sociocultural and psychological factors, but biological conditions can also lower sex drive significantly.

Biological Causes of Low Sexual Desire A number of hormones interact to help produce sexual desire and behavior (see Figure 11-2), and abnormalities in their activity can lower a person's sex drive (Randolph et al., 2015; Giraldi et al., 2013; Laan et al., 2013). In both men and women, a high level of the hormone *prolactin,* a low level of the male sex hormone *testosterone,* and either a high or low level of the female sex hormone *estrogen* can lead to low sex drive. Low sex drive has been linked to the high levels of estrogen contained in some birth control pills, for example. Conversely, it has also been tied to the low level of estrogen found in many postmenopausal women or women who have recently given birth. Long-term physical illness can also lower a person's sex drive (Berry & Berry, 2013). The

table: 11-1

> ### Dx Checklist
>
> #### Male Hypoactive Sexual Desire Disorder
>
> 1. For at least 6 months, individual repeatedly experiences few or no sexual thoughts, fantasies, or desires.
>
> 2. Individual experiences significant distress about this.
>
> #### Female Sexual Interest/Arousal Disorder
>
> 1. For at least 6 months, individual usually displays reduced or no sexual interest and arousal, characterized by the reduction or absence of at least three of the following: • Sexual interest • Sexual thoughts or fantasies • Sexual initiation or receptiveness • Excitement or pleasure during sex • Responsiveness to sexual cues • Genital or nongenital sensations during sex.
>
> 2. Individual experiences significant distress.
>
> (Information from: APA, 2013.)

figure 11-2
Normal female sexual anatomy Changes in the female anatomy take place during the different phases of the sexual response cycle. (Information from: Hyde, 1990, p. 200.)

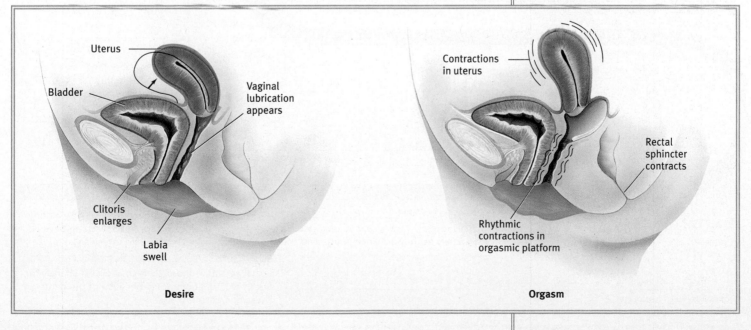

Uterus
Bladder
Vaginal lubrication appears
Clitoris enlarges
Labia swell

Desire

Contractions in uterus
Rectal sphincter contracts
Rhythmic contractions in orgasmic platform

Orgasm

SEX THROUGHOUT THE LIFE CYCLE

Sexual dysfunctions are different from the usual patterns of sexual functioning. But in the sexual realm, what is "the usual"? Studies conducted over the past two decades have provided a wealth of enlightening information about sexual behavior in the "normal" populations of North America. As you might expect, sexual behavior often differs by age and by gender.

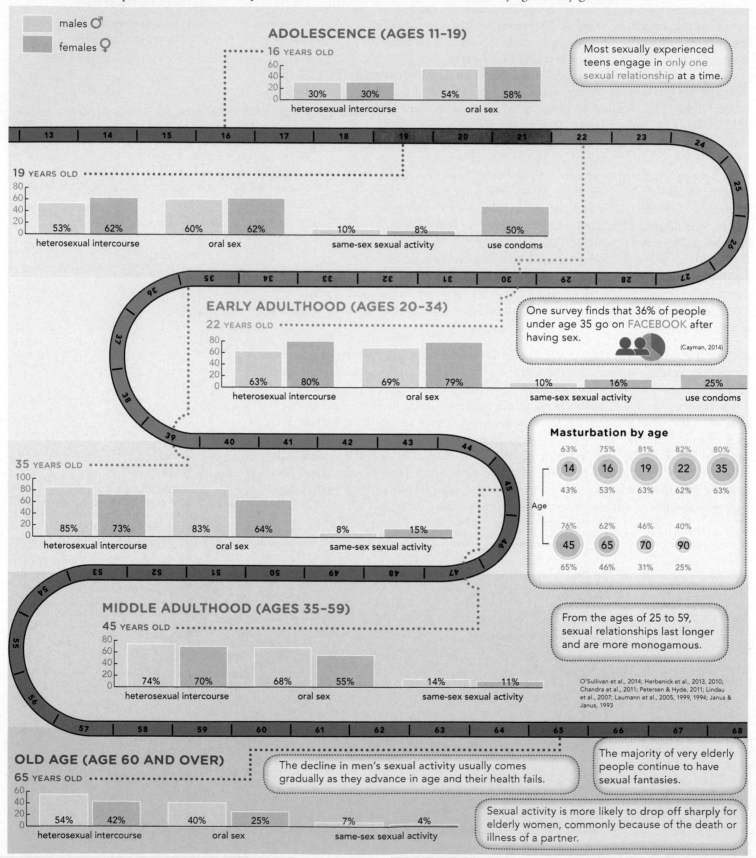

males ♂
females ♀

ADOLESCENCE (AGES 11–19)

16 YEARS OLD

heterosexual intercourse: 30% / 30%
oral sex: 54% / 58%

Most sexually experienced teens engage in only one sexual relationship at a time.

19 YEARS OLD

heterosexual intercourse: 53% / 62%
oral sex: 60% / 62%
same-sex sexual activity: 10% / 8%
use condoms: 50%

EARLY ADULTHOOD (AGES 20–34)

22 YEARS OLD

heterosexual intercourse: 63% / 80%
oral sex: 69% / 79%
same-sex sexual activity: 10% / 16%
use condoms: 25%

One survey finds that 36% of people under age 35 go on FACEBOOK after having sex.
(Cayman, 2014)

Masturbation by age

	63%	75%	81%	82%	80%
	14	16	19	22	35
	43%	53%	63%	62%	63%

Age

	76%	62%	46%	40%
	45	65	70	90
	65%	46%	31%	25%

35 YEARS OLD

heterosexual intercourse: 85% / 73%
oral sex: 83% / 64%
same-sex sexual activity: 8% / 15%

MIDDLE ADULTHOOD (AGES 35–59)

45 YEARS OLD

heterosexual intercourse: 74% / 70%
oral sex: 68% / 55%
same-sex sexual activity: 14% / 11%

From the ages of 25 to 59, sexual relationships last longer and are more monogamous.

O'Sullivan et al., 2014; Herbenick et al., 2013, 2010; Chandra et al., 2011; Petersen & Hyde, 2011; Lindau et al., 2007; Laumann et al., 2005, 1999, 1994; Janus & Janus, 1993

OLD AGE (AGE 60 AND OVER)

65 YEARS OLD

heterosexual intercourse: 54% / 42%
oral sex: 40% / 25%
same-sex sexual activity: 7% / 4%

The decline in men's sexual activity usually comes gradually as they advance in age and their health fails.

The majority of very elderly people continue to have sexual fantasies.

Sexual activity is more likely to drop off sharply for elderly women, commonly because of the death or illness of a partner.

reduced drive may be a direct result of the illness or an indirect result because of stress, pain, or depression brought on by the illness.

Clinical practice and research have further indicated that sex drive can be lowered by certain pain medications, psychotropic drugs, and illegal drugs such as cocaine, marijuana, amphetamines, and heroin (Glina et al., 2013). Low levels of alcohol may enhance the sex drive by lowering a person's inhibitions, but high levels may reduce it (George et al., 2011).

Psychological Causes of Low Sexual Desire A general increase in anxiety, depression, or anger may reduce sexual desire in both men and women (Rajkumar & Kumaran, 2015; Štulhofer et al., 2013). Frequently, as cognitive theorists have noted, people with low sexual desire have particular attitudes, fears, or memories that contribute to their dysfunction, such as a belief that sex is immoral or dangerous (Giraldi et al., 2013). Other people are so afraid of losing control over their sexual urges that they try to resist them completely. And still others fear pregnancy.

Certain psychological disorders may also contribute to low sexual desire. Even a mild level of depression can interfere with sexual desire, and some people with obsessive-compulsive symptoms find contact with another person's body fluids and odors to be highly unpleasant (Rubio-Aurioles & Bivalacqua, 2013).

Sociocultural Causes of Low Sexual Desire The attitudes, fears, and psychological disorders that contribute to low sexual desire occur within a social context, and thus certain sociocultural factors have also been linked to disorders of sexual desire. Many people who have low sexual desire are feeling situational pressures—for example, divorce, a death in the family, job stress, infertility difficulties, or having a baby (Hamilton & Meston, 2013). Other people may be having problems in their relationships (Witherow et al., 2015; Brenot, 2011). People who are in an unhappy relationship, have lost affection for their partner, or feel powerless and dominated by their partner can lose interest in sex. Even in basically happy relationships, if one partner is a very unskilled, unenthusiastic lover, the other can begin to lose interest in sex (Jiann, Su, & Tsai, 2013). And sometimes partners differ in their needs for closeness. The one who needs more personal space may develop low sexual desire as a way of keeping distance.

Cultural standards can also set the stage for low sexual desire. Some men adopt our culture's double standard and thus cannot feel sexual desire for a woman they love and respect (Maurice, 2007). More generally, because our society equates sexual attractiveness with youthfulness, many middle-aged and older men and women lose interest in sex as their self-image or their attraction to their partner diminishes with age (Leiblum, 2010).

The trauma of sexual molestation or assault is especially likely to produce the fears, attitudes, and memories found in disorders of sexual desire. Some survivors of sexual abuse may feel repelled by sex, sometimes for years, even decades (Turchik & Hassija, 2014; Giraldi et al., 2013). In some cases, survivors may have vivid flashbacks of the assault during adult consensual sexual activity.

Disorders of Excitement

The **excitement phase** of the sexual response cycle is marked by changes in the pelvic region, general physical arousal, and increases in heart rate, muscle tension, blood pressure, and rate of breathing. In men, blood pools in the pelvis and leads to erection of the penis; in women, this phase produces swelling of the clitoris and labia, as well as lubrication of the vagina. As you read earlier, female sexual interest/arousal disorder may include dysfunction during the excitement phase. In addition, a male disorder—*erectile disorder*—involves dysfunction during the excitement phase only.

▶ **excitement phase** The phase of the sexual response cycle marked by changes in the pelvic region, general physical arousal, and increases in heart rate, muscle tension, blood pressure, and rate of breathing.

Paul Sakuma/AP Photo

Grand Theft Auto: **The sexual controversy** With 15 different titles, *Grand Theft Auto* is one of today's most popular video game series. But it was almost derailed in 2004 with the release of one of the titles, *Grand Theft Auto: San Andreas.* Fearing that the sexual material in this game was too graphic for children and an unhealthy developmental influence, parents and politicians pressured the producer to develop enhanced security measures and, eventually, to remove the sexual material.

table: **11-2**

> ## Dx Checklist
>
> ### Erectile Disorder
>
> 1. For at least 6 months, individual usually finds it very difficult to obtain an erection, maintain an erection, and/or achieve past levels of erectile rigidity during sex.
>
> 2. Individual experiences significant distress.
>
> (Information from: APA, 2013.)

Erectile Disorder Men with **erectile disorder** persistently fail to attain or maintain an erection during sexual activity (see Table 11-2). This problem occurs in as much as 25 percent of the male population, including Robert, the man whose difficulties opened this chapter (Martin et al., 2014; Christensen et al., 2011). Carlos Domera also has erectile disorder:

> *Carlos Domera is a 30-year-old dress manufacturer who came to the United States from Argentina at age 22. He is married to . . . Phyllis, also age 30. They have no children. Mr. Domera's problem was that he had been unable to have sexual intercourse for over a year due to his inability to achieve or maintain an erection. He had avoided all sexual contact with his wife for the prior five months, except for two brief attempts at lovemaking which ended when he failed to maintain his erection.*
>
> *The couple separated a month ago by mutual agreement due to the tension that surrounded their sexual problem and their inability to feel comfortable with each other. Both professed love and concern for the other, but had serious doubts regarding their ability to resolve the sexual problem. . . .*
>
> *[Carlos] conformed to the stereotype of the "macho Latin lover," believing that he "should always have erections easily and be able to make love at any time." Since he couldn't "perform" sexually, he felt humiliated and inadequate, and he dealt with this by avoiding not only sex, but any expression of affection for his wife.*
>
> *[Phyllis] felt "he is not trying; perhaps he doesn't love me, and I can't live with no sex, no affection, and his bad moods." She had requested the separation temporarily, and he readily agreed. However, they had recently been seeing each other twice a week. . . .*
>
> *During the evaluation he reported that the onset of his erectile difficulties was concurrent with a tense period in his business. After several "failures" to complete intercourse, he concluded he was "useless as a husband" and therefore a "total failure." The anxiety of attempting lovemaking was too much for him to deal with.*
>
> *He reluctantly admitted that he was occasionally able to masturbate alone to a full, firm erection and reach a satisfying orgasm. However, he felt ashamed and guilty about this, from both childhood masturbatory guilt and a feeling that he was "cheating" his wife. It was also noted that he had occasional firm erections upon awakening in the morning. Other than the antidepressant, the patient was taking no drugs, and he was not using much alcohol. There was no evidence of physical illness.*
>
> *(Spitzer et al., 1983, pp. 105–106)*

Unlike Carlos, most men with an erectile disorder are over the age of 50, largely because so many cases are associated with ailments or diseases of older adults (Regal, 2015). Around 7 percent of men who are under 40 years old also have the disorder; that number increases to as many as 40 percent of men in their sixties and 75 percent of those in their seventies and eighties (Lewis et al., 2010; Rosen, 2007). Moreover, according to surveys, half of all adult men experience erectile difficulty during intercourse at least some of the time. Most cases of erectile disorder result from an interaction of biological, psychological, and sociocultural processes.

> **Why do you think the clinical field has been slow to investigate possible cultural and racial differences in sexual behaviors?**

BIOLOGICAL CAUSES The same hormonal imbalances that can cause male hypoactive sexual desire disorder can also produce erectile disorder (Glina et al., 2013; Hyde, 2005). More commonly, however, vascular problems—problems with the body's blood vessels—are involved (Lewis et al., 2010; Rosen, 2007). An erection occurs

▶ **erectile disorder** A dysfunction in which a man repeatedly fails to attain or maintain an erection during sexual activity.

▶ **nocturnal penile tumescence (NPT)** Erection during sleep.

▶ **performance anxiety** The fear of performing inadequately and a related tension experienced during sex.

▶ **spectator role** A state of mind that some people experience during sex, focusing on their sexual performance to such an extent that their performance and their enjoyment are reduced.

when the chambers in the penis fill with blood, so any condition that reduces blood flow into the penis, such as heart disease or clogging of the arteries, may lead to erectile disorder (Glina et al., 2013). It can also be caused by damage to the nervous system as a result of diabetes, spinal cord injuries, multiple sclerosis, kidney failure, or treatment by dialysis (da Silva et al., 2015; Berry & Berry, 2013). In addition, as is the case with male hypoactive sexual desire disorder, the use of certain medications and various forms of substance abuse, from alcohol abuse to cigarette smoking, may interfere with erections (Glina et al., 2013; Herrick et al., 2011).

Medical procedures, including ultrasound recordings and blood tests, have been developed for diagnosing biological causes of erectile disorder. Measuring **nocturnal penile tumescence (NPT),** or erections during sleep, is particularly useful in assessing whether physical factors are responsible. Men typically have erections during *rapid eye movement (REM) sleep,* the phase of sleep in which dreaming takes place. A healthy man is likely to have two to five REM periods each night, and several penile erections as well. Abnormal or absent nightly erections usually (but not always) indicate some physical basis for erectile failure. As a rough screening device, a patient may be instructed to fasten a simple "snap gauge" band around his penis before going to sleep and then check it the next morning. A broken band indicates that he has had an erection during the night. An unbroken band indicates that he did not have nighttime erections and suggests that his general erectile problem may have a physical basis. A newer version of this device further attaches the band to a computer, which provides precise measurements of erections throughout the night (Wincze et al., 2008). Such assessment devices are less likely to be used in clinical practice today than in past years. As you'll see later in the chapter, Viagra and other drugs for erectile disorder are typically given to patients without much formal evaluation of their problem (Rosen, 2007).

PSYCHOLOGICAL CAUSES Any of the psychological causes of male hypoactive sexual desire disorder can also interfere with arousal and lead to erectile disorder. As many as 90 percent of all men with severe depression, for example, experience some degree of erectile dysfunction (Montejo et al., 2011; Stevenson & Elliott, 2007).

One well-supported psychological explanation for erectile disorder is the cognitive-behavioral theory developed by William Masters and Virginia Johnson (1970). The explanation emphasizes **performance anxiety** and the **spectator role.** Once a man begins to have erectile problems, for whatever reason, he becomes fearful about failing to have an erection and worries during each sexual encounter. Instead of relaxing and enjoying the sensations of sexual pleasure, he remains distanced from the activity, watching himself and focusing on the goal of reaching erection. Instead of being an aroused participant, he becomes a judge and spectator. Whatever the initial reason for the erectile dysfunction, the resulting spectator role becomes the reason for the ongoing problem. In this vicious cycle, the original cause of the erectile failure becomes less important than fear of failure.

SOCIOCULTURAL CAUSES Each of the sociocultural factors that contribute to male hypoactive sexual desire disorder has also been tied to erectile disorder. Men who have lost their jobs and are under financial stress, for example, are more likely to develop erectile difficulties than other men (Štulhofer et al., 2013). Marital stress, too, has been tied to this dysfunction (Brenot, 2011; Rosen, 2007; LoPiccolo, 2004, 1991). Two relationship patterns in particular may contribute to it. In one, a wife provides too little physical

"Well, how convenient."

Joe Dator/The New Yorker Collection/The Cartoon Bank

▶ **orgasm phase** The phase of the sexual response cycle during which a person's sexual pleasure peaks and sexual tension is released as muscles in the pelvic region contract rhythmically.

▶ **premature ejaculation** A dysfunction in which a man persistently reaches orgasm and ejaculates within one minute of beginning sexual activity with a partner and before he wishes to. Also called *early* or *rapid* ejaculation.

▶ **delayed ejaculation** A male dysfunction characterized by persistent inability to ejaculate or very delayed ejaculations during sexual activity with a partner.

stimulation for her aging husband, who, because of normal aging changes, now requires more intense, direct, and lengthy physical stimulation of the penis in order to have an erection. In the second relationship pattern, a couple believes that only intercourse can give the wife an orgasm. This idea increases the pressure on the man to have an erection and makes him more vulnerable to erectile dysfunction. If the wife reaches orgasm manually or orally during their sexual encounter, his pressure to perform is reduced.

Disorders of Orgasm

During the **orgasm phase** of the sexual response cycle, a person's sexual pleasure peaks and sexual tension is released as the muscles in the pelvic region contract, or draw together, rhythmically (see Figure 11-3). The man's semen is ejaculated, and the outer third of the woman's vaginal wall contracts. Dysfunctions of this phase of the sexual response cycle are *premature ejaculation* and *delayed ejaculation* in men and *female orgasmic disorder* in women.

Premature Ejaculation Eduardo is typical of many men in his experience of premature ejaculation:

> Eduardo, a 20-year-old student, sought treatment after his girlfriend ended their relationship because his premature ejaculation left her sexually frustrated. Eduardo had had only one previous sexual relationship, during his senior year in high school. With two friends he would drive to a neighboring town and find a certain prostitute. After picking her up, they would drive to a deserted area and take turns having sex with her, while the others waited outside the car. Both the prostitute and his friends urged him to hurry up because they feared discovery by the police, and besides, in the winter it was cold. When Eduardo began his sexual relationship with his girlfriend, his entire sexual history consisted of this rapid intercourse, with virtually no foreplay. He found caressing his girlfriend's breasts and genitals and her touching of his penis to be so arousing that he sometimes ejaculated before complete entry of the penis, or after at most only a minute or so of intercourse.

figure 11-3
Normal male sexual anatomy Changes in the male anatomy occur during the different phases of the sexual response cycle. (Information from: Hyde, 1990, p. 199.)

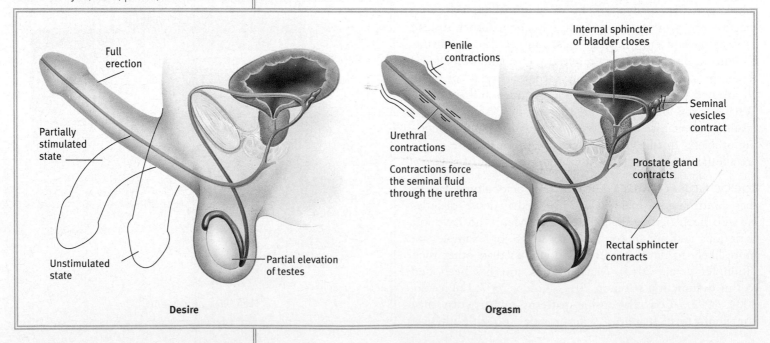

Desire

Orgasm

A man suffering from **premature ejaculation** (also called *early*, or *rapid*, ejaculation) persistently reaches orgasm and ejaculates within one minute of beginning sexual activity with a partner and before he wishes to (see Table 11-3). As many as 30 percent of men worldwide ejaculate early at some time (Lewis et al., 2010; Laumann et al., 2005, 1999, 1994). The typical duration of intercourse in our society has increased over the past several decades, which has caused more distress among men who ejaculate prematurely. Although many young men certainly contend with the dysfunction, research suggests that men of any age may suffer from it (Sansone et al., 2015; Rowland, 2012).

Psychological, particularly behavioral, explanations of premature ejaculation have received more research support than other kinds of explanations. The dysfunction is common, for example, among young, sexually inexperienced men such as Eduardo, who simply have not learned to slow down, control their arousal, and extend the pleasurable process of making love (Althof, 2007). In fact, young men often ejaculate prematurely during their first sexual encounter. With continued sexual experience, most men acquire more control over their sexual responses. Men of any age who have sex only occasionally are also prone to ejaculate early.

Clinicians have also suggested that premature ejaculation may be related to anxiety, hurried masturbation experiences during adolescence (in fear of being "caught" by parents), or poor recognition of one's own sexual arousal (Althof, 2007). However, these theories have only sometimes received clear research support.

There is a growing belief among many clinical theorists that biological factors may also play a key role in many cases of premature ejaculation. Three biological theories have emerged from the limited investigations done so far (Althof, 2007; Mirone et al., 2001). One theory states that some men are born with a genetic predisposition to develop this dysfunction. Indeed, one study found that 91 percent of a small sample of men suffering from early ejaculation had first-degree relatives who also had the dysfunction. A second theory, based on animal studies, argues that the brains of men who ejaculate prematurely contain certain serotonin receptors that are overactive and others that are underactive. A third explanation holds that men with this dysfunction have greater sensitivity or nerve conduction in the area of their penis, a notion that has received inconsistent research support thus far.

table: 11-3

Dx Checklist

Premature Ejaculation

1. For at least 6 months, individual usually ejaculates within 1 minute of beginning sex with a partner and earlier than he wants to.

2. Individual experiences significant distress.

Delayed Ejaculation

1. For at least 6 months, individual usually displays a significant delay, infrequency, or absence of ejaculation during sexual activity with a partner.

2. Individual experiences significant distress.

Female Orgasmic Disorder

1. For at least 6 months, individual usually displays a significant delay, infrequency, or absence of orgasm, and/or is unable to achieve past orgasmic intensity.

2. Individual experiences significant distress.

(Information from: APA, 2013.)

Delayed Ejaculation A man with **delayed ejaculation** (previously called *male orgasmic disorder* or *inhibited male orgasm*) persistently is unable to ejaculate or has very delayed ejaculations during sexual activity with a partner (see Table 11-3 again). Around 10 percent of men worldwide have this disorder (Lewis et al., 2010; Laumann et al., 2005, 1999). It is typically a source of great frustration and upset, as in the case of John:

> John, a 38-year-old sales representative, had been married for 9 years. At the insistence of his 32-year-old wife, the couple sought counseling for their sexual problem—his inability to ejaculate during intercourse. During the early years of the marriage, his wife had experienced difficulty reaching orgasm until he learned to delay his ejaculation for a long period of time. To do this, he used mental distraction techniques and regularly smoked marijuana before making love. Initially, John felt very satisfied that he could make love for longer and longer periods of time without ejaculation and regarded his ability as a sign of masculinity.

(continues on the next page)

▶**female orgasmic disorder** A dysfunction in which a woman persistently fails to reach orgasm, has very low intensity orgasms, or has very delayed orgasms.

> *About 3 years prior to seeking counseling, after the birth of their only child, John found that he was losing his erection before he was able to ejaculate. His wife suggested different intercourse positions, but the harder he tried, the more difficulty he had in reaching orgasm. Because of his frustration, the couple began to avoid sex altogether. John experienced increasing performance anxiety with each successive failure, and an increasing sense of helplessness in the face of his problem.*
>
> *Rosen & Rosen, 1981, pp. 317–318)*

A low testosterone level, certain neurological diseases, and some head or spinal cord injuries can interfere with ejaculation (Lewis et al., 2010; Stevenson & Elliott, 2007). Substances that slow down the sympathetic nervous system (such as alcohol, some medications for high blood pressure, and certain psychotropic medications) can also affect ejaculation (Herrick et al., 2011). For example, certain serotonin-enhancing antidepressant drugs appear to interfere with ejaculation in at least 30 percent of men who take them (Glina et al., 2013; Montejo et al., 2011).

> **Are there other problem areas in life that might also be explained by performance anxiety and the spectator role?**

A leading psychological cause of delayed ejaculation appears to be performance anxiety and the spectator role, the cognitive-behavioral factors also involved in erectile disorder (Kashdan et al., 2011). Once a man begins to focus on reaching orgasm, he may stop being an aroused participant in his sexual activity and instead become an unaroused, self-critical, and fearful observer (Rowland, 2012; Wiederman, 2001).

Another psychological cause of delayed ejaculation may be past masturbation habits. If, for example, a man has masturbated all his life by rubbing his penis against sheets, pillows, or other such objects, he may have difficulty reaching orgasm in the absence of the sensations tied to those objects (Wincze et al., 2008). Finally, delayed ejaculation may develop out of male hypoactive sexual desire disorder (Apfelbaum, 2000). A man who engages in sex largely because of pressure from his partner, without any real desire for it, simply may not get aroused enough to ejaculate.

Female Orgasmic Disorder Janel and Isaac, married for three years, went for sex therapy because of her lack of orgasm.

> *Janel had never had an orgasm in any way, but because of Isaac's concern, she had been faking orgasm during intercourse until recently. Finally she told him the truth, and they sought therapy together. Janel had been raised by a strictly religious family. She could not recall ever seeing her parents kiss or show physical affection for each other. She was severely punished on one occasion when her mother found her looking at her own genitals, at about age 7. Janel received no sex education from her parents, and when she began to menstruate, her mother told her only that this meant that she could become pregnant, so she mustn't ever kiss a boy or let a boy touch her. Her mother restricted her dating severely, with repeated warnings that "boys only want one thing." While her parents were rather critical and demanding of her (asking her why she got one B among otherwise straight As on her report card, for example), they were loving parents and their approval was very important to her.*

Nightly Visits

People can sometimes have an orgasm during sleep. Ancient Babylonians said that such nocturnal orgasms were caused by a "maid of the night" who visited men in their sleep and a "little night man" who visited women (Kahn & Fawcett, 1993).

Women with **female orgasmic disorder** persistently fail to reach orgasm, have very low intensity orgasms, or have a very delayed orgasm (see Table 11-3 again). As many as 25 percent of women apparently have this problem to some degree—including more than a third of postmenopausal women (Lewis et al., 2010; Heiman, 2007, 2002). Studies indicate that 10 percent or more of women have never had an orgasm, either alone or during intercourse, and at least another 9 percent rarely have orgasms (Bancroft et al., 2003). At the same time, half of all women experience orgasm in intercourse at least fairly regularly (de Sutter et al., 2014; SOGC, 2014). Women who are more sexually assertive and more comfortable with masturbation tend to have orgasms more regularly (Carrobles et al., 2011; Hurlbert, 1991). Female orgasmic disorder appears to be more common among single women than among women who are married or living with someone (Lewis et al., 2010; Laumann et al., 2005, 1999, 1994). In one study, when participants with female orgasmic disorder were asked to pick a word that best describes their feelings about it, two-thirds of them chose "frustration" (Kingsberg et al., 2013).

> **How might the women's movement have helped to enlighten clinical views of sexual disorders?**

Most clinicians agree that orgasm during intercourse is not mandatory for normal sexual functioning (Meana, 2012). Many women instead reach orgasm with their partners by direct stimulation of the clitoris. Although early psychoanalytic theory considered a lack of orgasm during intercourse to be pathological, evidence suggests that women who rely on stimulation of the clitoris for orgasm are entirely normal and healthy (Laan, Rellini, & Barnes, 2013; Heiman, 2007).

Biological, psychological, and sociocultural factors may combine to produce female orgasmic disorder (Berry & Berry, 2013; Jiann, Su, & Tsai, 2013). Because arousal plays a key role in orgasms, arousal difficulties often are featured prominently in explanations of female orgasmic disorder.

BIOLOGICAL CAUSES A variety of physiological conditions can affect a woman's orgasm. Diabetes can damage the nervous system in ways that interfere with arousal, lubrication of the vagina, and orgasm. Lack of orgasm has sometimes been linked to multiple sclerosis and other neurological diseases, to the same drugs and medications that may interfere with ejaculation in men, and to changes, often postmenopausal, in skin sensitivity and structure of the clitoris, vaginal walls, or the labia—the folds of skin on each side of the vagina (Cordeau & Courtois, 2014; Blackmore et al., 2011; Lombardi et al., 2011).

PSYCHOLOGICAL CAUSES The psychological causes of female sexual interest/arousal disorder, including depression, may also lead to female orgasmic disorder (Kalmbach et al., 2014; Laan et al., 2013). In addition, as both psychodynamic and cognitive theorists might predict, memories of childhood traumas or problematic childhood relationships have sometimes been associated with orgasm problems. In one large study, memories of an unhappy childhood or loss of a parent during childhood were tied to lack of orgasm in adulthood (Raboch & Raboch, 1992). In other studies, childhood memories of a dependable father, a positive relationship with one's mother, affection between the parents, the mother's positive personality, and the mother's expression of positive emotions were all predictors of positive orgasm outcomes (Heiman, 2007; Heiman et al., 1986).

SOCIOCULTURAL CAUSES For years many clinicians have believed that female orgasmic problems may result from society's recurrent message to women that they should repress and deny their sexuality, a message that has often led to "less permissive" sexual attitudes and behavior among women than among men. In fact, many women with both arousal and orgasmic difficulties report that they had an overly strict religious upbringing, were punished for childhood masturbation, received no preparation for the onset of menstruation, were restricted in their dating as teenagers, and were told that "nice girls don't" (Laan et al., 2013; LoPiccolo & Van Male, 2000).

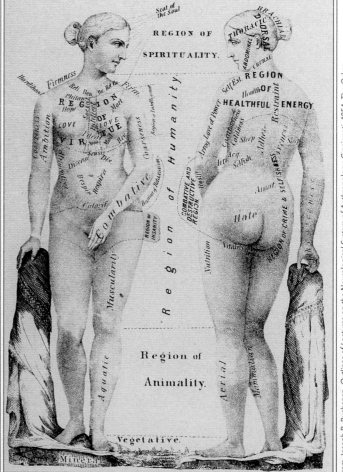

"The region of insanity" Medical authorities described "excessive passion" in Victorian women as dangerous and as a possible cause of insanity (Gamwell & Tomes, 1995). This illustration from a nineteenth-century medical textbook even labels a woman's reproductive organs as her "region of insanity."

From Joseph R. Buchanan, *Outlines of Lectures on the Neurological System of Anthropology*, Cincinnati, 1854. The Oskar Diethelm Library, Department of Psychiatry, Cornell University Medical College and The New York Hospital, New York

▶**genito-pelvic pain/penetration disorder** A sexual dysfunction characterized by significant physical discomfort during intercourse.

A sexually restrictive history, however, is just as common among women who function well during sexual activity (LoPiccolo, 2002, 1997). In addition, cultural messages about female sexuality have been more positive in recent years, while the rate of arousal and orgasmic problems remains the same for women. Why, then, do some women and not others develop such problems? Researchers suggest that unusually stressful events, traumas, or relationships may help produce the fears, memories, and attitudes that often characterize these sexual problems (Meana, 2012; Westheimer & Lopater, 2005). For example, many women molested as children or raped as adults have female orgasmic disorder (Hall, 2007; Heiman, 2007).

Research has also related orgasmic behavior to certain qualities in a woman's intimate relationships (Laan et al., 2013; Brenot, 2011). Studies have found, for example, that the likelihood of reaching orgasm may be tied to how much emotional involvement a woman had during her first experience of intercourse and how long that relationship lasted, the pleasure the woman felt during the experience, her current attraction to her partner's body, and her marital happiness. Interestingly, the same studies have found that orgasmic women more often have erotic fantasies during sex with their current partner than do nonorgasmic women.

Disorders of Sexual Pain

Certain sexual dysfunctions are characterized by enormous physical discomfort during intercourse, a difficulty that does not fit neatly into a specific part of the sexual response cycle. Women have such dysfunctions, collectively called **genito-pelvic pain/penetration disorder,** much more often than men do (APA, 2013).

For some women with genito-pelvic pain/penetration disorder, the muscles around the outer third of the vagina involuntarily contract, preventing entry of the penis (see Table 11-4). This problem, known in medical circles as *vaginismus,* can prevent a couple from ever having intercourse. The problem has received relatively little research, but estimates are that fewer than 1 percent of all women have vaginismus (Christensen et al., 2011). A number of women with vaginismus enjoy sex greatly, have a strong sex drive, and reach orgasm with stimulation of the clitoris (Cherner & Reissing, 2013). They just fear the discomfort of penetration of the vagina.

Most clinicians agree with the cognitive-behavioral position that this form of genito-pelvic pain/penetration disorder is usually a learned fear response, set off by a woman's expectation that intercourse will be painful and damaging (Simonelli et al., 2014; Cherner & Reissing, 2013). A variety of factors apparently can set the stage for this fear, including anxiety and ignorance about intercourse, exaggerated stories about how painful and bloody the first occasion of intercourse is for women, trauma caused by an unskilled lover who forces his penis into the vagina before the woman is aroused and lubricated, and the trauma of childhood sexual abuse or adult rape (Jiann et al., 2013; Fugl-Meyer et al., 2013).

Alternatively, women may have this form of genito-pelvic pain/penetration disorder because of an infection of the vagina or urinary tract, a gynecological disease such as herpes simplex, or the physical effects of menopause. In such cases, the dysfunction can be overcome only if the women receive medical treatment for these conditions.

Other women with genito-pelvic pain/penetration disorder do not have involuntary contractions of their vaginal muscles, but they do experience severe vaginal or pelvic pain during sexual intercourse, a pattern known medically as *dyspareunia* (from Greek words meaning "painful mating"). Surveys suggest that more than 14 percent of women suffer from this problem to some degree (Antony & Barlow, 2010, 2004; Laumann et al., 2005, 1999). Women with dyspareunia typically enjoy sex and get aroused but find their sex lives very limited by the pain that accompanies what used to be a positive event (Huijding et al., 2011).

table: 11-4

Dx Checklist

Genito-Pelvic Pain/ Penetration Disorder

1. For at least 6 months, individual repeatedly experiences at least one of the following problems:
   • Difficulty having vaginal penetration during intercourse
   • Significant vaginal or pelvic pain when trying to have intercourse or penetration • Significant fear that vaginal penetration will cause vaginal or pelvic pain • Significant tensing of the pelvic muscles during vaginal penetration.

2. Individual experiences significant distress from this.

(Information from: APA, 2013.)

This form of genito-pelvic pain/penetration disorder usually has a physical cause (Fugl-Meyer et al., 2013). Among the most common is an injury (for example, to the vagina or pelvic ligaments) during childbirth. The scar left by an episiotomy (a cut often made to enlarge the vaginal entrance and ease delivery) also can cause pain. Around 16 percent of women have severe vaginal or pelvic pain during intercourse for up to a year after giving birth (Bertozzi et al., 2010). More generally, such pain has also been tied to the penis colliding with remaining parts of the hymen, vaginal infections, wiry pubic hair rubbing against the labia during intercourse, pelvic diseases, tumors, cysts, allergic reactions to the chemicals in vaginal douches and contraceptive creams, the rubber in condoms and diaphragms, and the protein in semen (Tripoli et al., 2011).

Although psychological factors (for instance, heightened anxiety or overattentiveness to one's body) or relationship problems may contribute to dyspareunia (Granot et al., 2011), psychosocial factors alone are rarely responsible for it (Dewitte, Van Lankveld, & Crombez, 2011). In cases that are truly psychogenic, the woman may in fact be suffering from female sexual interest/arousal disorder. That is, penetration into an unaroused, unlubricated vagina is painful (Fugl-Meyer et al., 2013). It also is the case that at least 3 percent of men suffer from pain in the genitals during intercourse, and many of these men also qualify for a diagnosis of genito-pelvic pain/penetration disorder.

➤ *Summing Up*

SEXUAL DYSFUNCTIONS Sexual dysfunctions make it difficult or impossible for a person to have or enjoy sexual activity.

DSM-5 lists two disorders of the desire phase of the sexual response cycle: male hypoactive sexual desire disorder and female sexual interest/arousal disorder. Biological causes for these disorders include abnormal hormone levels, certain drugs, and some medical illnesses. Psychological and sociocultural causes include specific fears, situational pressures, relationship problems, and the trauma of having been sexually molested or assaulted.

Disorders of the excitement phase include erectile disorder. Biological causes of the disorder include abnormal hormone levels, vascular problems, medical conditions, and certain medications. Psychological and sociocultural causes include the combination of performance anxiety and the spectator role, situational pressures such as job loss, and relationship problems.

Premature ejaculation, a disorder of the orgasm phase, has been attributed most often to behavioral causes, such as inappropriate early learning and inexperience. In recent years, possible biological factors have been identified as well. Delayed ejaculation, another orgasm disorder, can have biological causes, such as low testosterone levels, neurological diseases, and certain drugs, and psychological causes, such as performance anxiety and the spectator role. The dysfunction may also develop from male hypoactive sexual desire disorder. Female orgasmic disorder, which is often accompanied by arousal difficulties, has been tied to biological causes such as medical diseases and changes that occur after menopause, psychological causes such as memories of childhood traumas, and sociocultural causes such as relationship problems.

Genito-pelvic pain/penetration disorder involves significant pain during intercourse. In one form of this disorder, vaginismus, involuntary contractions of the muscles around the outer third of the vagina prevent entry of the penis. In another form, dyspareunia, the person has severe vaginal or pelvic pain during intercourse. This form of the disorder usually occurs in women and typically has a physical cause, such as injury resulting from childbirth.

Treatments for Sexual Dysfunctions

The last 40 years have brought major changes in the treatment of sexual dysfunctions. For the first half of the twentieth century, the leading approach was long-term psychodynamic therapy. Clinicians assumed that sexual dysfunctioning was caused by failure to progress properly through the psychosexual stages of development, and they used techniques of free association and therapist interpretations to help clients gain insight about themselves and their problems. Although it was expected that broad personality changes would lead to improvement in sexual functioning, psychodynamic therapy was typically unsuccessful (Bergler, 1951).

In the 1950s and 1960s, behavioral therapists offered new treatments for sexual dysfunctions. Usually they tried to reduce the fears that they believed were causing the dysfunctions. They did so through such procedures as relaxation training and systematic desensitization (Lazarus, 1965; Wolpe, 1958). These approaches had some success, but they failed to work in cases where the key problems included misinformation, negative attitudes, and lack of effective sexual techniques (LoPiccolo, 2002, 1995).

A revolution in the treatment of sexual dysfunctions took place with the publication of William Masters and Virginia Johnson's landmark book *Human Sexual Inadequacy* in 1970. The *sex therapy* program they introduced has evolved into a complex approach, which now includes interventions from the various models, particularly cognitive-behavioral, couple, and family systems therapies (McCarthy & McCarthy, 2012; Leiblum, 2010, 2007). In recent years, biological interventions, particularly drug therapies, have been added to the treatment arsenal (Berry & Berry, 2013).

> **Sex is one of the topics most commonly searched on the Internet. Why might it be such a popular search topic?**

What Are the General Features of Sex Therapy?

Modern sex therapy is short-term and instructive, typically lasting 15 to 20 sessions. It centers on specific sexual problems rather than on broad personality issues (Recordon & Köhl, 2014). Carlos Domera, the Argentine man with erectile disorder whom you met earlier, responded successfully to the multiple techniques of modern sex therapy:

> At the end of the evaluation session the psychiatrist reassured the couple that Mr. Domera had a "reversible psychological" sexual problem that was due to several factors, including his depression, but also more currently his anxiety and embarrassment, his high standards, and some cultural and relationship difficulties that made communication awkward and relaxation nearly impossible. The couple was advised that a brief trial of therapy, focused directly on the sexual problem, would very likely produce significant improvement within ten to fourteen sessions. They were assured that the problem was almost certainly not physical in origin, but rather psychogenic, and that therefore the prognosis was excellent.
>
> Mr. Domera was shocked and skeptical, but the couple agreed to commence the therapy on a weekly basis, and they were given a typical first "assignment" to do at home: a caressing massage exercise to try together with specific instructions not to attempt genital stimulation or intercourse at all, even if an erection might occur.
>
> Not surprisingly, during the second session Mr. Domera reported with a cautious smile that they had "cheated" and had had intercourse "against the rules." This was their first successful intercourse in more than a year. Their success and happiness were acknowledged by the therapist, but they were cautioned strongly that rapid initial improvement often occurs, only to be followed by increased performance anxiety in subsequent weeks and a return of the initial problem. They were humorously chastised and encouraged to try again to have sexual contact involving caressing

and non-demand light genital stimulation, without an expectation of erection or orgasm, and to avoid intercourse.

During the second and fourth weeks [Carlos] did not achieve erections during the love play, and the therapy sessions dealt with helping him to accept himself with or without erections and to learn to enjoy sensual contact without intercourse. His wife helped him to believe genuinely that he could please her with manual or oral stimulation and that, although she enjoyed intercourse, she enjoyed these other stimulations as much, as long as he was relaxed.

[Carlos] struggled with his cultural image of what a "man" does, but he had to admit that his wife seemed pleased and that he, too, was enjoying the nonintercourse caressing techniques. He was encouraged to view his new lovemaking skills as a "success" and to recognize that in many ways he was becoming a better lover than many husbands, because he was listening to his wife and responding to her requests.

By the fifth week the patient was attempting intercourse successfully with relaxed confidence, and by the ninth session he was responding regularly with erections. If they both agreed, they would either have intercourse or choose another sexual technique to achieve orgasm. Treatment was terminated after ten sessions.

(Spitzer et al., 1983, pp. 106–107)

As Carlos Domera's treatment indicates, modern sex therapy includes a variety of principles and techniques. The following ones are used in almost all cases, regardless of the dysfunction:

1. **Assessing and conceptualizing the problem.** Patients are initially given a medical examination and are interviewed concerning their "sex history." The therapist's focus during the interview is on gathering information about past life events and, in particular, current factors that are contributing to the dysfunction (Althof et al., 2013; Berry & Berry, 2013). Sometimes proper assessment requires a team of specialists, perhaps including a psychologist, urologist, and neurologist.

2. **Mutual responsibility.** Therapists stress the principle of *mutual responsibility.* Both partners in the relationship share the sexual problem, regardless of who has the actual dysfunction, so treatment is likely to be more successful when both are in therapy (Laan et al., 2013; McCarthy & McCarthy, 2012).

3. **Education about sexuality.** Many patients who suffer from sexual dysfunctions know very little about the physiology and techniques of sexual activity (Hucker & McCabe, 2015; Rowland, 2012). Thus sex therapists may discuss these topics and offer educational materials, including instructional books, videos, and Internet sites.

4. **Emotion identification.** Sex therapists help patients identify and express upsetting emotions tied to past events that may keep interfering with sexual arousal and enjoyment (Kleinplatz, 2010).

5. **Attitude change.** Following a cardinal principle of cognitive therapy, sex therapists help patients examine and change any beliefs about sexuality that are preventing sexual arousal and pleasure (McCarthy & McCarthy, 2012; Hall, 2010). Some of these mistaken beliefs are widely shared in our society and can result from past traumatic events, family attitudes, or cultural ideas.

6. **Elimination of performance anxiety and the spectator role.** Therapists often teach couples *sensate focus,* or *nondemand pleasuring,* a series of sensual tasks, sometimes called "petting" exercises, in which the partners focus on the sexual pleasure

"It's not you, babe—I've been neutered."

that can be achieved by exploring and caressing each other's body at home, without demands to have intercourse or reach orgasm—demands that may be interfering with arousal (Hucker & McCabe, 2015). Couples are told at first to refrain from intercourse at home and to restrict their sexual activity to kissing, hugging, and sensual massage of various parts of the body, but not of the breasts or genitals. Over time, they learn how to give and receive greater sexual pleasure and they build back up to the activity of sexual intercourse.

7. **Increasing sexual and general communication skills.** Couples are taught to use their sensate-focus skills and apply new sexual techniques and positions at home. They may, for example, try sexual positions in which the person being caressed can guide the other's hands and control the speed, pressure, and location of sexual contact (Heiman, 2007). Couples are also taught to give instructions to each other in a nonthreatening, informative manner ("It feels better over here, with a little less pressure"), rather than a threatening uninformative manner ("The way you're touching me doesn't turn me on"). Moreover, couples are often given broader training in how best to communicate with each other (Brenot, 2011).

8. **Changing destructive lifestyles and marital interactions.** A therapist may encourage a couple to change their lifestyle or take other steps to improve a situation that is having a destructive effect on their relationship—to distance themselves from interfering in-laws, for example, or to change a job that is too demanding. Similarly, if the couple's general relationship is marked by conflict, the therapist will try to help them improve it, often before work on the sexual problems per se begins (Brenot, 2011).

9. **Addressing physical and medical factors.** Systematic increases in physical activity have proved helpful for persons with various kinds of sexual dysfunctions (Lewis et al., 2010). In addition, when sexual dysfunctions are caused by a medical problem, such as disease, injury, medication, or substance abuse, therapists try to address that problem (Korda et al., 2010). If antidepressant medications are causing erectile disorder, for example, the clinician may suggest lowering the dosage of the medication, changing the time of day when the drug is taken, or turning to a different antidepressant.

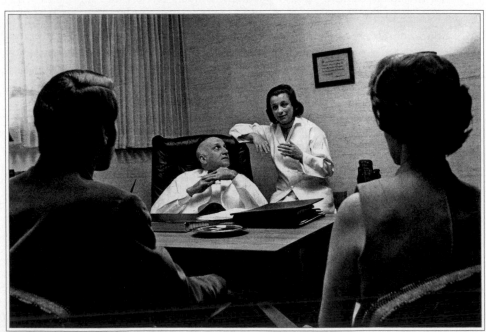

Sexual pioneers William Masters and Virginia Johnson work with a couple in their office. The two researchers, the field's most important figures in the study of the human sexual response and the treatment of sexual dysfunctions, conducted their work from 1967 until the 1990s, writing two classic books, *Human Sexual Response* and *Human Sexual Inadequacy*. Their work and personal lives are currently portrayed—in largely fictional form—in the Showtime series *Masters of Sex*.

George Tames/The New York Times/Redux

What Techniques Are Used to Treat Particular Dysfunctions?

In addition to the general components of sex therapy, specific techniques can help in each of the sexual dysfunctions.

Disorders of Desire

Male hypoactive sexual desire disorder and female sexual interest/arousal disorder are among the most difficult dysfunctions to treat because of the many issues that may feed into them (Leiblum, 2010). Thus therapists typically use a combination of techniques. In a technique called *affectual awareness,* patients visualize sexual scenes in order to discover any feelings of anxiety, vulnerability, and other negative emotions they may have concerning sex (McCarthy & McCarthy, 2012; Kleinplatz, 2010). In another technique, patients receive cognitive *self-instruction training* to help them change their negative reactions to sex. That is, they learn to replace negative statements during sex with "coping statements," such as "I can allow myself to enjoy sex; it doesn't mean I'll lose control."

"When I touch him he rolls into a ball."

© Callahan/Levin Represents

Therapists may also use behavioral approaches to help heighten a patient's sex drive. They may instruct clients to keep a "desire diary" in which they record sexual thoughts and feelings, to read books and view films with erotic content, and to fantasize about sex. They also may encourage pleasurable shared activities such as dancing and walking together (Rubio-Aurioles & Bivalacqua, 2013). If the reduced sexual desire has resulted from sexual assault or childhood molestation, additional techniques may be needed (Hall, 2010, 2007). A patient may, for example, be encouraged to remember, talk about, and think about the assault until the memories no longer arouse fear or tension. These and related psychological approaches apparently help many women and men with low sexual desire eventually to have intercourse more than once a week (Meana, 2012; Rowland, 2012). However, only a few controlled studies have been conducted.

Finally, biological interventions can have a role in the treatment for desire problems. *Hormone* treatments have been used and received some research support (Wright & O'Connor, 2015; Rubio-Aurioles & Bivalacqua, 2013). In addition, in 2015 the FDA approved the drug *flibanserin* (brand name Addyi), as a treatment for women distressed by low sexual desire.

Erectile Disorder

Treatments for erectile disorder focus on reducing a man's performance anxiety, increasing his stimulation, or both, using a range of behavioral, cognitive, and relationship interventions (Mola, 2015; Rowland, 2012; Carroll, 2011). In one treatment, the couple may be instructed to try the *tease technique* during sensate-focus exercises: the partner keeps caressing the man, but if the man gets an erection, the partner stops caressing him until he loses it. This exercise reduces pressure on the man to perform and at the same time teaches the couple that erections occur naturally in response to stimulation, as long as the partners do not keep focusing on performance. In another technique, the couple may be instructed to use manual or oral sex to try to achieve the woman's orgasm, again reducing pressure on the man to perform (LoPiccolo, 2004, 2002, 1995).

Biological approaches gained great momentum with the development in 1998 of *sildenafil* (trade name Viagra). This drug increases blood flow to the penis within one hour of ingestion; the increased blood flow enables the user to attain an erection during sexual activity (see *PsychWatch* on page 365). In general, sildenafil appears to be safe; however, it may not be so for men with certain coronary heart diseases and cardiovascular diseases, particularly those who are taking nitroglycerin and other heart medications (Stevenson & Elliott, 2007). Soon after Viagra emerged, two other erectile dysfunction drugs were also approved—*tadalafil* (Cialis) and *vardenafil*

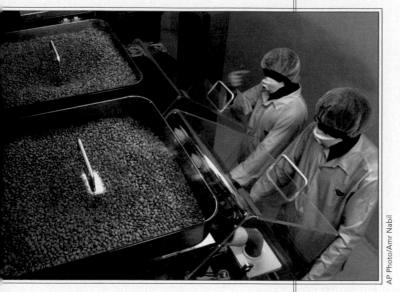

AP Photo/Amr Nabil

Viagra around the world Few drugs have had the worldwide impact of Viagra (and its cousins Cialis and Levitra). Here technicians at a pharmaceutical factory in Cairo sort thousands of Viagra pills for distribution and marketing in Egypt's pharmacies.

(Levitra)—that are now actively competing with Viagra for a share of the lucrative marketplace. Collectively, the three drugs are the most common form of treatment for erectile disorder. They effectively restore erections in 75 percent of men who use them. Some research, though, suggests that a combination of one of these erectile dysfunction drugs and a psychological intervention such as those mentioned above may be more helpful than either kind of treatment alone (Schmidt et al., 2014).

Prior to the development of Viagra, Cialis, and Levitra, a range of other medical procedures were developed for erectile disorder. These procedures are now viewed as "second line"—often costly— treatments that are used primarily when the medications are unsuccessful or too risky for individuals (Martin et al., 2013). Such treatments include gel suppositories, injections of drugs into the penis, and a *vacuum erection device (VED)*, a hollow cylinder that is placed over the penis. Here a man uses a hand pump to pump air out of the cylinder, drawing blood into his penis and producing an erection.

Premature Ejaculation

Early ejaculation has been treated successfully for years by behavioral procedures (McMahon et al., 2013; Masters & Johnson, 1970). In one such approach, the *stop-start,* or *pause, procedure,* the penis is manually stimulated until the man is highly aroused. The couple then pauses until his arousal subsides, after which the stimulation is resumed. This sequence is repeated several times before stimulation is carried through to ejaculation, so the man ultimately experiences much more total time of stimulation than he has ever experienced before (LoPiccolo, 2004, 1995). Eventually the couple progresses to putting the penis in the vagina, making sure to withdraw it and to pause whenever the man becomes too highly aroused. According to clinical reports, after two or three months, many couples can enjoy prolonged intercourse without any need for pauses (Althof, 2007).

Some clinicians treat premature ejaculation with SSRIs, the serotonin-enhancing antidepressant drugs. Because these drugs often reduce sexual arousal or orgasm, the reasoning goes, they may be helpful to men who ejaculate prematurely. Many studies report positive results with this approach (McMahon et al., 2013). The effect of this approach is consistent with the biological theory, mentioned earlier, that serotonin receptors in the brains of men with early ejaculation may function abnormally.

Delayed Ejaculation

Therapies for delayed ejaculation include techniques to reduce performance anxiety and increase stimulation (Rowland, 2012; LoPiccolo, 2004). In one of many such techniques, a man may be instructed to masturbate to orgasm in the presence of his partner or to masturbate just short of orgasm before inserting his penis for intercourse (Marshall, 1997). This increases the likelihood that he will ejaculate during intercourse. He then is instructed to insert his penis at ever earlier stages of masturbation.

When delayed ejaculation is caused by physical factors such as neurological damage or injury, treatment may include a drug to increase arousal of the sympathetic nervous system (Stevenson & Elliott, 2007). However, few studies have systematically tested the effectiveness of such treatments (Hartmann & Waldinger, 2007).

Female Orgasmic Disorder

Specific treatments for female orgasmic disorder include cognitive-behavioral techniques, self-exploration, enhancement of body awareness, and directed masturbation training (Laan et al., 2013; McCarthy & McCarthy, 2012). These procedures are especially useful for women who have never had an orgasm under any circumstances. Biological treatments, including hormone therapy or the use of sildenafil (Viagra), have also been tried, but research has not consistently found these to be helpful (Wright & O'Connor, 2015; Laan et al., 2013).

PsychWatch

Sexism, Viagra, and the Pill

Many of us believe that we live in an enlightened world, where sexism is declining and where health care and benefits are available to men and women in equal measure. However, the responses of government agencies and insurance companies to the discovery and marketing of Viagra in 1998 called this belief into question (Goldstein, 2014).

Consider, first, the nation of Japan. In early 1999, just six months after it was introduced in the United States, Viagra was approved for use among men in Japan (Goldstein, 2014; Martin, 2000). In contrast, low-dose contraceptives—"the pill"—were not approved for use among women in Japan until June 1999—a full 40 years after their introduction elsewhere! Many observers believe that birth control pills would still be unavailable to women in Japan had Viagra not received its quick approval.

Has the United States been able to avoid such an apparent double standard in its health care system? Not really. Before Viagra was introduced, insurance companies were not required to reimburse women for the cost of prescription contraceptives. As a result, women had to pay 68 percent more out-of-pocket expenses for health care than did men, largely because of uncovered reproductive health care costs (Hayden, 1998). In contrast, when Viagra was introduced in 1998, many insurance companies readily agreed to cover the new drug. As the public outcry grew over the contrast between coverage of Viagra for men and lack of coverage of oral contraceptives for women, laws across the country finally began to change. Today 28 states require female contraceptive coverage by private insurance companies (Guttmacher, 2011). The Affordable Care Act—the federal health care law passed in 2010 and enacted in 2013—includes provisions that require *all* insurance companies to cover contraceptives. However, in the so-called "Hobby Lobby" decision, the Supreme Court ruled in 2014 that corporation owners can refuse to provide such insurance coverage for their employees based on religious grounds.

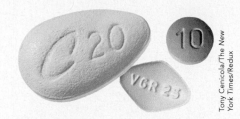

"The pills": Cialis, Viagra, and Levitra

Tony Cenicola/The New York Times/Redux

"The pill"

BSIP SA/Alamy

In **directed masturbation training,** a woman is taught step by step how to masturbate effectively and eventually to reach orgasm during sexual interactions. The training includes the use of diagrams and reading material, private self-stimulation, erotic material and fantasies, "orgasm triggers" such as holding her breath or thrusting her pelvis, sensate focus with her partner, and sexual positioning that produces stimulation of the clitoris during intercourse. This training program appears to be highly effective: over 90 percent of female clients learn to have an orgasm during masturbation, about 80 percent during caressing by their partners, and about 30 percent during intercourse (Laan et al., 2013; Heiman, 2007).

As you read earlier, a lack of orgasm during intercourse is not necessarily a sexual dysfunction, provided the woman enjoys intercourse and can reach orgasm through caressing, either by her partner or by herself. For this reason some therapists believe that the wisest course is simply to educate women whose only concern is lack of orgasm during intercourse, informing them that they are quite normal.

Genito-Pelvic Pain/Penetration Disorder Specific treatment for involuntary contractions of the muscles around the vagina typically involves two approaches (Ter Kuile et al., 2015, 2013; Rosenbaum, 2011). First, a woman may practice tightening and relaxing her vaginal muscles until she gains more voluntary control over them. Second, she may receive gradual behavioral exposure treatment to help her overcome her fear of penetration, beginning, for example, by inserting increasingly large dilators in her vagina at home and at her own pace and eventually

▸ **directed masturbation training** A sex therapy approach that teaches women with female arousal or orgasmic problems how to masturbate effectively and eventually to reach orgasm during sexual interactions.

ending with the insertion of her partner's penis. Most clients treated with such procedures eventually have pain-free intercourse. Some medical interventions have also been used. For example, several clinical investigators have injected the problematic vaginal muscles with Botox to help reduce spasms in those muscles (Pacik, 2014; Fugl-Meyer et al., 2013). However, studies of this approach have been unsystematic.

Different approaches are used to treat the other form of genito-pelvic pain/penetration disorder—severe vaginal or pelvic pain during intercourse. As you saw earlier, the most common cause of this problem is physical, such as pain-causing scars, lesions, or infection aftereffects. When the cause is known, pain management procedures (see pages 273–275) and sex therapy techniques may be tried, including helping a couple to learn intercourse positions that avoid putting pressure on the injured area (Fugl-Meyer et al., 2013; Dewitte et al., 2011). Medical interventions—from topical creams to surgery—may also be tried, but typically they must be combined with other sex therapy techniques to overcome the years of sexual anxiety and lack of arousal (Archer et al., 2015; Goodman, 2013). Many experts believe that, in most cases, both forms of genito-pelvic pain/penetration disorder are best assessed and treated by a *team* of professionals, including a gynecologist, physical therapist, and sex therapist or other mental health professional (Berry & Berry, 2013; Rosenbaum, 2011, 2007).

What Are the Current Trends in Sex Therapy?

Sex therapists have now moved well beyond the approach first developed by Masters and Johnson. For example, today's sex therapists regularly treat partners who are living together but not married. They also treat sexual dysfunctions that arise from psychological disorders such as depression, mania, schizophrenia, and certain personality disorders (Leiblum, 2010, 2007). In addition, sex therapists no longer screen out clients with severe marital discord, the elderly, the medically ill, the physically handicapped, gay clients, or individuals who have no long-term sex partner (Rowen, 2013; Stevenson & Elliott, 2007). Sex therapists are also paying more attention to excessive sexuality, sometimes called *persistent sexuality disorder, hypersexuality,* or *sexual addiction* (Carvalho et al., 2013; Lee, 2011), although this condition is not listed as a disorder in DSM-5.

Many sex therapists have expressed concern about the sharp increase in the use of drugs and other medical interventions for sexual dysfunctions, particularly for the disorders characterized by low sexual desire and erectile disorder. Their concern is that therapists will increasingly choose the biological interventions rather than integrating biological, psychological, and sociocultural interventions. In fact, a narrow approach of any kind probably cannot fully address the complex factors that cause most sexual problems (Berry & Berry, 2013; Meana, 2012). It took sex therapists years to recognize the considerable advantages of an integrated approach to sexual dysfunctions. The development of new medical interventions should not lead to its abandonment.

➤ *Summing Up*

TREATMENTS FOR SEXUAL DYSFUNCTIONS In the 1970s, the work of William Masters and Virginia Johnson led to the development of sex therapy. Today sex therapy combines a variety of cognitive, behavioral, couple, and family systems therapies. It generally includes features such as careful assessment, education, acceptance of mutual responsibility, attitude changes, sensate-focus exercises, improvements in communication, and couple therapy. In addition, specific techniques have been developed for each of the sexual dysfunctions. The use of biological treatments for sexual dysfunctions is also increasing.

Paraphilic Disorders

Paraphilias are patterns in which people repeatedly have intense sexual urges or fantasies or display sexual behaviors that involve objects or situations outside the usual sexual norms. The sexual focus may, for example, involve nonhuman objects or the experience of suffering or humiliation. Many people with a paraphilia can become aroused only when a paraphilic stimulus is present, fantasized about, or acted out. Others need the stimulus only during times of stress or under other special circumstances. Some people with one kind of paraphilia have others as well (Seto, Kingston, & Bourget, 2014). The large consumer market in paraphilic pornography and growing trends such as sexting and cybersex lead clinicians to suspect that paraphilias are, in fact, quite common (Ahlers et al., 2011; Pipe, 2010) (see *MindTech* on the next page).

> **Is the availability of sex chat groups and other sexual material on the Internet psychologically healthy or damaging?**

According to DSM-5, a diagnosis of **paraphilic disorder** should be applied when paraphilias cause a person significant distress or impairment *or* when the satisfaction of the paraphilias places the person or other people at risk of harm—either currently or in the past (APA, 2013) (see Table 11-5 on page 369). People who initiate sexual contact with children, for example, warrant a diagnosis of *pedophilic disorder* regardless of how troubled the individuals may or may not be over their behavior. People whose paraphilic disorder involves children or nonconsenting adults often come to the attention of clinicians as a result of legal issues generated by their inappropriate actions.

Although theorists have proposed various explanations for paraphilic disorders, there is little formal evidence to support such explanations (Becker et al., 2012). Moreover, none of the many treatments applied to these disorders have received much research or proved clearly effective. Psychological and sociocultural treatments have been available the longest, but today's professionals are also using biological interventions.

Some practitioners administer drugs called *antiandrogens* that lower the production of testosterone, the male sex hormone, and reduce the sex drive (Assumpção et al., 2014). Although antiandrogens may indeed reduce paraphilic patterns, several of them disrupt normal sexual feelings and behavior as well. Thus the drugs tend to be used primarily when the paraphilic disorders are of particular danger either to the individuals themselves or to other people. Clinicians are also increasingly prescribing SSRIs, the serotonin-enhancing antidepressant medications, to treat people with paraphilic disorders, hoping that the SSRIs will reduce these compulsion-like sexual behaviors just as they help reduce other kinds of compulsions (Assumpção et al., 2014). In addition, of course, a common effect of the SSRIs is to lower sexual arousal.

A word of caution is in order before examining the various paraphilic disorders. The definitions of these disorders, like those of sexual dysfunctions, are strongly influenced by the norms of the particular society in which they occur (McManus et al., 2013). Some clinicians argue that except when other people are hurt by them, at least some paraphilic behaviors should not be considered disorders at all (De Block & Adriaens, 2013; Wright, 2010). Especially in light of the stigma associated with sexual disorders and the self-revulsion that many people feel when they believe they have such a disorder, we need to be very careful about applying these

▶ **paraphilias** Patterns in which a person has recurrent and intense sexual urges, fantasies, or behaviors involving nonhuman objects, children, nonconsenting adults, or experiences of suffering or humiliation.

▶ **paraphilic disorder** A disorder in which a person's paraphilia causes great distress, interferes with social or occupational activities, or places the person or others at risk of harm—either currently or in the past.

Playful context Dressing in clothes of the opposite sex does not necessarily convey a paraphilia. Here two members—both male—of Harvard University's Hasty Pudding Theatricals Club, known for staging musicals in which male undergraduates dress like women, plant a kiss on actress Anne Hathaway. Hathaway was receiving the club's 2010 Woman of the Year award.

AP Photo/Elise Amendola

MindTech

"Sexting": Healthy or Pathological?

"Sexting" is the sending of sexually explicit material—particularly, photos or text messages—between cell phones or other digital devices. The term "sexting" did not make its debut until 2005.

Surveys suggest that 20 percent of cell phone users have texted a sexually explicit photo of themselves and 40 percent have received a sexually explicit photo (McAfee, 2014; Strassberg et al., 2013). Half of all people save the sexual images and text messages they receive and more than 25 percent of recipients forward the sexual photos that they receive to others.

Naïve behavior? Not always. More than one-third of all sexters say they recognize that the act could lead to legal or personal problems. Young adults (18 to 24 years old) are the largest group of sexters. And males sext more often than females by a 3-to-2 margin.

Putting sexting on the map In 2011 New York congressman Anthony Weiner resigned his congressional seat and gave up his mayoral bid when his multiple episodes of sexting were revealed and widely reported in the media.

Richard Levine/Alamy

Is sexting a symptom of abnormal functioning? It depends. Certainly, some sexters fit the criteria for *exhibitionistic disorder*, the paraphilic pattern in which people act on urges to expose their genitals to others. Sixteen percent of sexters send sexual photos of themselves to complete strangers (McAfee, 2014). And like other forms of exhibitionism, sexting can cause psychological problems for nonconsenting recipients (Smith et al., 2014).

There are yet other ways in which sexting may reflect psychological or relationship problems. According to one study, people who sext to strangers or other nonconsenting recipients are more likely to have general problems with attachment or intimacy than other people (Drouin & Landgraff, 2012). In addition, research indicates that sexting (when done outside of one's marriage or monogamous relationship) is often a step toward infidelity. Some psychologists believe that sexting is itself a form of infidelity even though it does not involve physical contact. It has even been the grounds for divorce in some cases (Centeno, 2011; Cable, 2008).

On the other side of the coin, sexting can be a constructive activity, according to some psychologists. Many couples engage in it as an added dimension to their marriage or relationship. According to surveys, more than half of all couples have texted sexual photos or messages to their partners at least once, one-third more than once (Drouin & Landgraff, 2012). Research suggests that this often enhances the in-person romantic relationship, creates more bonding, and heightens sexual satisfaction in the relationship (Parker et al., 2012). 💬

labels to others or to ourselves. Keep in mind that for years clinicians considered homosexuality a paraphilic disorder, and their judgment was used to justify laws and even police actions against gay people (Drescher, 2015; Dickinson et al., 2012). Only when the gay rights movement helped change society's understanding of and attitudes toward homosexuality did clinicians officially stop considering it a disorder and remove it from the DSM—partly in 1973 and then fully in 1986. Even then, as you observed in Chapter 1, many clinicians continued for years to recommend *conversion,* or *reparative, therapy* to "fix" the sexual orientation of gay people. In the meantime, the clinical field had unintentionally contributed to the persecution, anxiety, and humiliation of millions of people because of personal sexual behavior that differed from the conventional norms.

Fetishistic Disorder

One relatively common paraphilic disorder is **fetishistic disorder.** Key features of this disorder are recurrent intense sexual urges, sexually arousing fantasies, or behaviors that involve the use of a nonliving object or nongenital body part, often to the exclusion of all other stimuli (APA, 2013). Usually the disorder, which is far more common in men than in women, begins in adolescence. Almost anything can be a fetish; women's underwear, shoes, and boots are particularly common. Some people with this disorder steal in order to collect as many of the desired objects as possible. The objects may be touched, smelled, worn, or used in some other way while the person masturbates, or the person may ask a partner to wear the object when they have sex (Marshall et al., 2008). Several of these features are seen in the following case:

A 32-year-old, single male . . . related that although he was somewhat sexually attracted by women, he was far more attracted by "their panties."

To the best of the patient's memory, sexual excitement began at about age 7, when he came upon a pornographic magazine and felt stimulated by pictures of partially nude women wearing "panties." His first ejaculation occurred at 13 via masturbation to fantasies of women wearing panties. He masturbated into his older sister's panties, which he had stolen without her knowledge. Subsequently he stole panties from her friends and from other women he met socially. He found pretexts to "wander" into the bedrooms of women during social occasions, and would quickly rummage through their possessions until he found a pair of panties to his satisfaction. He later used these to masturbate into, and then "saved them" in a "private cache." The pattern of masturbating into women's underwear had been his preferred method of achieving sexual excitement and orgasm from adolescence until the present consultation.

(Spitzer et al., 1994, p. 247)

Researchers have not been able to pinpoint the causes of fetishistic disorder. Behaviorists propose that fetishes are acquired through classical conditioning (Dozier, Iwata, & Worsdell, 2011; Roche & Quayle, 2007). In a pioneering behavioral study, male participants were shown a series of slides of nude women along with slides of boots (Rachman, 1966). After many trials, the participants became aroused by the boot photos alone. If early sexual experiences similarly occur in the presence of particular objects, perhaps the stage is set for the development of fetishes.

Behaviorists have sometimes treated fetishistic disorder with *aversion therapy* (Plaud, 2007; Krueger & Kaplan, 2002). In one study, an electric shock was administered to the arms or legs of participants with this disorder while they imagined their objects of desire (Marks & Gelder, 1967). After two weeks of therapy all men in the study showed at least some improvement. In another aversion technique, *covert sensitization,* people with fetishistic disorder are guided to *imagine* the pleasurable object and repeatedly to pair this image with an *imagined* aversive stimulus until the object of sexual pleasure is no longer desired.

Another behavioral treatment for fetishistic disorder is **masturbatory satiation** (Plaud, 2007). In this method, the client masturbates to orgasm while fantasizing

table: **11-5**

Dx Checklist

Paraphilic Disorder

1. For at least 6 months, individual experiences recurrent and intense sexually arousing fantasies, urges, or behaviors involving objects or situations outside the usual sexual norms (nonhuman objects; nongenital body parts; the suffering or humiliation of oneself or one's partner; or children or other nonconsenting persons).

2. Individual experiences significant distress or impairment over the fantasies, urges, or behaviors. (In some paraphilic disorders— pedophilic disorder, exhibitionistic disorder, voyeuristic disorder, frotteuristic disorder, and sexual sadism disorder—the performance of the paraphilic behaviors indicates a disorder, even in the absence of distress or impairment.)

(Information from: APA, 2013.)

▶**fetishistic disorder** A paraphilic disorder consisting of recurrent and intense sexual urges, fantasies, or behaviors that involve the use of a nonliving object or nongenital part, often to the exclusion of all other stimuli, accompanied by clinically significant distress or impairment.

▶**masturbatory satiation** A behavioral treatment in which a client masturbates for a long period of time while fantasizing in detail about a paraphilic object. The procedure is expected to produce a feeling of boredom that becomes linked to the object.

JOSEPH E. LEVINE PRESENTS A MIKE NICHOLS-LAWRENCE TURMAN PRODUCTION

This
is
Benjamin

He's
a little
worried
about
his
future

THE GRADUATE

STARRING

ANNE BANCROFT AND DUSTIN HOFFMAN · KATHARINE ROSS

SCREENPLAY BY
CALDER WILLINGHAM AND BUCK HENRY SONGS BY PAUL SIMON PERFORMED BY SIMON AND GARFUNKEL

PRODUCED BY
LAWRENCE TURMAN DIRECTED BY MIKE NICHOLS TECHNICOLOR® PANAVISION® United Artists

Embassy/The Kobal Collection

Mrs. Robinson's stockings The 1967 film *The Graduate* helped define a generation by focusing on the personal confusion, apathy, and sexual adventures of a young man in search of meaning. Marketers promoted this film by using a fetishistic-like photo of Mrs. Robinson putting on her stockings under Benjamin's watchful eye, a scene forever identified with the movie.

about a sexually appropriate object, then switches to fantasizing in detail about fetishistic objects while masturbating again and continues the fetishistic fantasy for an hour. The procedure is meant to produce a feeling of boredom, which in turn becomes linked to the fetishistic object.

Yet another behavioral approach to fetishistic disorder, also used for other paraphilias, is **orgasmic reorientation,** which teaches individuals to respond to more appropriate sources of sexual stimulation (Wright & Hatcher, 2006). People are shown conventional stimuli while they are responding to unconventional objects. A person with a shoe fetish, for example, may be instructed to obtain an erection from pictures of shoes and then to begin masturbating to a picture of a nude woman. If he starts to lose the erection, he must return to the pictures of shoes until he is masturbating effectively, then change back to the picture of the nude woman. When orgasm approaches, he must direct all attention to the conventional stimulus.

Transvestic Disorder

A person with **transvestic disorder,** also known as **transvestism** or **cross-dressing,** feels recurrent and intense sexual arousal from dressing in clothes of the opposite sex—arousal expressed through fantasies, urges, or behaviors (APA, 2013). In the following passage, a 42-year-old married father describes his pattern:

> I have been told that when I dress in drag, at times I look like Whistler's Mother [laughs], especially when I haven't shaved closely. I usually am good at detail, and I make sure when I dress as a woman that I have my nails done just so, and that my colors match. Honestly, it's hard to pin a date on when I began cross dressing. . . . If pressed, I would have to say it began when I was about 10 years of age, fooling around with and putting on my mom's clothes. . . . I was always careful to put everything back in its exact place, and in 18 years of doing this in her home, my mother never, I mean never, suspected, or questioned me about putting on her clothes. I belong to a transvestite support group . . . a group for men who cross dress. Some of the group are homosexuals, but most are not. A true transvestite—and I am one, so I know—is not homosexual. We don't discriminate against them in the group at all; hey,

we have enough trouble getting acceptance as normal people and not just a bunch of weirdos ourselves. They are a bunch of nice guys . . . really. Most of them are like me.

Most of [the men in the group] have told their families about their dressing inclinations, but those that are married are a mixed lot; some wives know and some don't, they just suspect. I believe in honesty, and told my wife about this before we were married. We're separated now, but I don't think it's because of my cross dressing. . . . Some of my friends, when I was growing up, suggested psychotherapy, but I don't regard this as a problem. If it bothers someone else, then they have the problem. . . . I function perfectly well sexually with my wife, though it took her some time to be comfortable with me wearing feminine underwear; yes, sometimes I wear it while making love, it just makes it more exciting.

(Janus & Janus, 1993, p. 121)

Like this man, the typical person with transvestic disorder, almost always a heterosexual male, begins cross-dressing in childhood or adolescence (Marshall et al., 2008; Långström & Zucker, 2005). He is the picture of characteristic masculinity in everyday life and is usually alone when he cross-dresses. A small percentage of such men cross-dress to visit bars or social clubs. Some wear a single item of women's clothing, such as underwear or hosiery, under their masculine clothes. Others wear makeup and dress fully as women. Some married men with transvestic disorder involve their wives in their cross-dressing. Transvestic disorder is often confused with *gender dysphoria,* but, as you will see, they are two separate patterns that overlap only in some individuals (Zucker et al., 2012).

The development of transvestic disorder sometimes seems to follow the behavioral principles of operant conditioning. In such cases, parents or other adults may openly encourage the child to cross-dress or even reward them for doing so. In one case, a woman was delighted to discover that her young nephew enjoyed dressing in girls' clothes. She had always wanted a niece, and she proceeded to buy him dresses and jewelry and sometimes dressed him as a girl and took him out shopping.

Exhibitionistic Disorder

A person with **exhibitionistic disorder** experiences recurrent and intense sexual arousal from exposing his genitals to an unsuspecting individual—arousal reflected by fantasies, urges, or behaviors (APA, 2013). Most often, the person wants to provoke shock or surprise rather than initiate sexual activity with the victim. Sometimes an exhibitionist will expose himself in a particular neighborhood at particular hours. In a survey of 2,800 men, 4.3 percent of them reported that they perform exhibitionistic behavior (Långström & Seto, 2006). Yet between one-third and half of all women report having seen or had direct contact with an exhibitionist, or so-called flasher (Marshall et al., 2008). The urge to exhibit typically becomes stronger when the person has free time or is under significant stress.

Generally, exhibitionistic disorder begins before age 18 and usually, but not always, is found among men (APA, 2013). Some studies suggest that those with the disorder are typically immature in their dealings with the opposite sex and have difficulty in interpersonal relationships (Marshall et al., 2008; Murphy & Page, 2006). Around 30 percent of them are married and another 30 percent divorced or separated; their sexual relations with their wives are not usually satisfactory (Doctor & Neff, 2001). Many have doubts or fears about their masculinity, and some seem to have a strong bond to a possessive mother. As with other paraphilic disorders, treatment generally includes aversion therapy and masturbatory satiation, possibly combined with orgasmic reorientation, social skills training, or cognitive-behavioral therapy (Assumpção et al., 2014; Federoff & Marshall, 2010).

▶ **orgasmic reorientation** A procedure for treating certain paraphilias by teaching clients to respond to new, more appropriate sources of sexual stimulation.

▶ **transvestic disorder** A paraphilic disorder consisting of repeated and intense sexual urges, fantasies, or behaviors that involve dressing in clothes of the opposite sex, accompanied by clinically significant distress or impairment. Also known as *transvestism* or *cross-dressing.*

▶ **exhibitionistic disorder** A paraphilic disorder in which persons have repeated sexually arousing urges or fantasies about exposing their genitals to others, and either act on these urges with nonconsenting individuals or experience clinically significant distress or impairment.

Lady Godiva and "Peeping Tom"
According to legend, Lady Godiva (shown in this 1890 illustration) rode naked through the streets of Coventry, England, in order to persuade her husband, the earl of Mercia, to stop taxing the city's poor. Although all townspeople were ordered to stay inside their homes with shutters drawn during her eleventh-century ride, a tailor named Tom "could not contain his sexual curiosity and drilled a hole in his shutter in order to watch Lady Godiva pass by" (Mann et al., 2008). Since then, the term "Peeping Tom" has been used to refer to people with voyeuristic disorder.

Voyeuristic Disorder

A person with **voyeuristic disorder** experiences recurrent and intense sexual arousal from observing an unsuspecting individual who is naked, disrobing, or engaging in sexual activity. As with other paraphilic disorders, this arousal takes the form of fantasies, urges, or behaviors (APA, 2013). The disorder usually begins before the age of 15 and tends to persist.

A person with voyeuristic disorder may masturbate during the act of observing or when thinking about it afterward but does not generally seek to have sex with the person being spied on. The vulnerability of the people being observed and the probability that they would feel humiliated if they knew they were under observation are often part of the enjoyment. In addition, the risk of being discovered adds to the excitement.

Voyeurism, like exhibitionism, is often a source of sexual excitement in fantasy; it can also play a role in normal sexual interactions, but in such cases it is engaged in with the partner's consent or understanding. The clinical disorder of voyeuristic disorder is marked by the repeated invasion of other people's privacy. Some people with the disorder are unable to have normal sexual relations; others have a normal sex life apart from their disorder.

Many psychodynamic clinicians propose that people with voyeuristic disorder are seeking by their actions to gain power over others, possibly because they feel inadequate or are sexually or socially shy (Metzl, 2004). Behaviorists explain the disorder as a learned behavior that can be traced to a chance and secret observation of a sexually arousing scene (Lavin, 2008). If the onlookers observe such scenes on several occasions while masturbating, they may develop a voyeuristic pattern.

Frotteuristic Disorder

A person with **frotteuristic disorder** experiences repeated and intense sexual arousal from touching or rubbing against a nonconsenting person. The arousal may, like with the other paraphilic disorders, take the form of fantasies, urges, or behaviors. Frottage (from French *frotter*, "to rub") is usually committed in a crowded place, such as a subway or a busy sidewalk (Guterman, Martin, & Rudes, 2010). The person, almost always a male, may rub his genitals against the victim's thighs or buttocks or fondle her genital area or breasts with his hands. Typically he fantasizes during the act that he is having a caring relationship with the victim. This paraphilia usually begins in the teenage years or earlier, often after the person observes others committing an act of frottage. After the age of about 25, people gradually decrease and often cease their acts of frottage (APA, 2000).

Pedophilic Disorder

A person with **pedophilic disorder** experiences equal or greater sexual arousal from children than from physically mature people. This arousal is expressed through fantasies, urges, or behaviors (APA, 2013). Those with the disorder may be attracted to prepubescent children (*classic* type), early pubescent children (*hebephilic* type), or both (*pedohebephilic* type). Some people with pedophilic disorder are satisfied by child pornography or seemingly innocent material such as children's underwear ads; others are driven to actually watch, touch, fondle, or engage in sexual intercourse with children (Babchishin, Hanson, & VanZuylen, 2014; Schmidt et al., 2014). Some people with the disorder are attracted only to children; others are attracted to adults as well. Both boys and girls can be pedophilic victims, but there is evidence suggesting that two-thirds are girls (Seto, 2008; Koss & Heslet, 1992).

People with pedophilic disorder usually develop their pattern of sexual need during adolescence (Farkas, 2013). Some were themselves sexually abused as children (Nunes et al., 2013), and many were neglected, excessively punished, or deprived of genuinely close relationships during their childhood. It is not unusual for them to be married and to have sexual difficulties or other frustrations in life that lead them to seek an area in which they can be masters. Often these individuals are immature: their social and sexual skills may be underdeveloped, and thoughts of normal sexual relationships fill them with anxiety (Marshall & Marshall, 2015; Seto, 2008).

Some people with pedophilic disorder also have distorted thinking, such as, "It's all right to have sex with children as long as they agree" (Roche & Quayle, 2007; Abel et al., 2001, 1984). It is not uncommon for pedophiles to blame the children for adult–child sexual contacts or to assert that the children benefited from the experience (Durkin & Hundersmarck, 2008; Lanning, 2001).

While many people with this disorder believe that their feelings are indeed wrong and abnormal, others consider adult sexual activity with children to be acceptable and normal. Some even have joined pedophile organizations that advocate abolishing the age-of-consent laws. The Internet has opened the channels of communication among such people, and there is now a wide range of Web sites, newsgroups, chat rooms, forums, and message boards centered on pedophilia and adult–child sex (Durkin & Hundersmarck, 2008).

Studies have found that most men with pedophilic disorder also display at least one additional psychological disorder (Farkas, 2013; McAnulty, 2006). Some theorists have proposed that pedophilic disorder may be related to biochemical or brain structure abnormalities, but such abnormalities have yet to receive consistent research support (Lucka & Dziemian, 2014; Wiebking & Northoff, 2013).

Most pedophilic offenders are imprisoned or forced into treatment if they are caught (Staller & Faller, 2010). After all, they are committing child sexual abuse when they take any steps toward sexual contact with a child (Farkas, 2013). There are now many residential registration and community notification laws across the United States that help law enforcement agencies and the public account for and control where convicted child sex offenders live and work (OJJDP, 2010).

▸ **voyeuristic disorder** A paraphilic disorder in which a person has repeated and intense sexual desires to observe unsuspecting people in secret as they undress or to spy on couples having intercourse, and either acts on these urges with nonconsenting people or experiences clinically significant distress or impairment.

▸ **frotteuristic disorder** A paraphilic disorder in which a person has repeated and intense sexual urges or fantasies that involve touching and rubbing against a nonconsenting person, and either acts on these urges with the nonconsenting person or experiences clinically significant distress or impairment.

▸ **pedophilic disorder** A paraphilic disorder in which a person has repeated and intense sexual urges or fantasies about watching, touching, or engaging in sexual acts with children, and either acts on these urges or experiences clinically significant distress or impairment.

Pedophilia, abuse, and justice People enter the courthouse in Angers, France, in 2005, to witness the largest child abuse trial ever held in France. The court found 65 defendants (39 men and 26 women) guilty of raping, molesting, and prostituting children. The victims ranged in age from 6 months to 14 years, and the defendants ranged from 27 to 73 years.

Treatments for pedophilic disorder include those already mentioned for other paraphilic disorders, such as aversion therapy, masturbatory satiation, orgasmic reorientation, cognitive-behavioral therapy, and antiandrogen drugs (Assumpção et al., 2014; Fromberger, Jordan, & Müller, 2013). One widely applied cognitive-behavioral treatment for this disorder, *relapse-prevention training,* is modeled after the relapse-prevention training programs used in the treatment of substance use disorders (see page 337). In this approach, clients identify the kinds of situations that typically trigger their pedophilic fantasies and actions (such as depressed mood or distorted thinking). They then learn strategies for avoiding those situations or coping with them more appropriately and effectively. Relapse-prevention training has sometimes, but not consistently, been of help in this and certain other paraphilic disorders (Marshall & Marshall, 2015; Federoff & Marshall, 2010).

Sexual Masochism Disorder

A person with **sexual masochism disorder** is repeatedly and intensely sexually aroused by the act of being humiliated, beaten, bound, or otherwise made to suffer (APA, 2013). Again, this arousal may take such forms as fantasies, urges, or behaviors. Many people have fantasies of being forced into sexual acts against their will, but only those who are very distressed or impaired by the fantasies receive this diagnosis. Some people with the disorder act on the masochistic urges by themselves, perhaps tying, sticking pins into, or even cutting themselves. Others have their sexual partners restrain, tie up, blindfold, spank, paddle, whip, beat, electrically shock, "pin and pierce," or humiliate them (APA, 2013).

An industry of products and services has arisen to meet the desires of people with the paraphilia or the paraphilic disorder of sexual masochism. Here a 34-year-old woman describes her work as the operator of a sadomasochism (S/M) facility:

© Brant Ward/San Francisco Chronicle/Corbis

A celebration of S/M Sexual sadism and sexual masochism have been viewed by the public with either bemusement or horror, depending on the circumstances and events that surround particular acts of these paraphilias. On the light side, the annual Folsom Street Fair in San Francisco is a very large event that celebrates S/M and invites people (like this participant) to go on stage, display their trademark outfits, and, in some cases, participate in whippings or spankings.

> I get people here who have been all over looking for the right kind of pain they feel they deserve. Don't ask me why they want pain, I'm not a psychologist; but when they have found us, they usually don't go elsewhere. It may take some of the other girls an hour or even two hours to make these guys feel like they've had their treatment—I can achieve that in about 20 minutes. . . .
>
> Among the things I do, that work really quickly and well, are: I put clothespins on their nipples, or pins in their [testicles]. Some of them need to see their own blood to be able to get off. . . .
>
> All the time that a torture scene is going on, there is constant dialogue. . . . I scream at the guy, and tell him what a no-good rotten bastard he is, how this is even too good for him, that he knows he deserves worse, and I begin to list his sins. It works every time. Hey, I'm not nuts, I know what I'm doing. I act very tough and hard, but I'm really a very sensitive woman. But you have to watch out for a guy's health . . . you must not kill him, or have him get a heart attack. . . . I know of other places that have had guys die there. I've never lost a customer to death, though they may have wished for it during my "treatment." Remember, these are repeat customers. I have a clientele and a reputation that I value.
>
> *(Janus & Janus, 1993, p. 115)*

In one form of sexual masochism disorder, *hypoxyphilia,* people strangle or smother themselves (or ask their partner to strangle them) in order to enhance their sexual pleasure. There have, in fact, been a disturbing number of clinical reports of *autoerotic asphyxia,* in which people, usually males and as young as 10 years old, may accidentally induce a fatal lack of oxygen by hanging, suffocating, or strangling themselves while masturbating (Sauvageau, 2014; Hucker, 2011, 2008). There is some debate as to whether the practice should be characterized as sexual masochism disorder, but it is at least sometimes accompanied by other acts of bondage.

Most masochistic sexual fantasies begin in childhood. However, the person does not act out the urges until later, usually by early adulthood. The pattern typically continues for many years. Some people practice more and more dangerous acts over time or during times of particular stress (Krueger, 2010).

In many cases, sexual masochism disorder seems to have developed through the behavioral process of classical conditioning (Stekel, 2010; Akins, 2004). A classic case study tells of a teenage boy with a broken arm who was caressed and held close by an attractive nurse as the physician set his fracture, a procedure done in the past without anesthesia (Gebhard, 1965). The powerful combination of pain and sexual arousal the boy felt then may have been the cause of his later masochistic urges and acts.

Sexual Sadism Disorder

A person with **sexual sadism disorder,** usually male, is repeatedly and intensely sexually aroused by the physical or psychological suffering of another individual (APA, 2013). This arousal may be expressed through fantasies, urges, or behaviors, including acts such as dominating, restraining, blindfolding, cutting, strangling, mutilating, or even killing the victim (Nitschke et al., 2013). The label is derived from the name of the famous Marquis de Sade (1740–1814), who tortured others in order to satisfy his sexual desires.

People who fantasize about sexual sadism typically imagine that they have total control over a sexual victim who is terrified by the sadistic act. Many carry out sadistic acts with a consenting partner, often a person with sexual masochism disorder. Some, however, act out their urges on nonconsenting victims (Mokros et al., 2014). A number of rapists and sexual murderers, for example, exhibit sexual sadism disorder (Knecht, 2014; Healey et al., 2013). In all cases, the real or fantasized victim's suffering is the key to arousal (Marshall & Marshall, 2015; Seto et al., 2012).

Fantasies of sexual sadism, like those of sexual masochism, may first appear in childhood or adolescence (Stone, 2010). People who engage in sadistic acts begin to do so by early adulthood (APA, 2013). The pattern is long-term. Some people with the disorder engage in the same level of cruelty in their sadistic acts over time, but often their sadism becomes more and more severe over the years (Robertson & Knight, 2014; Mokros et al., 2011). Obviously, people with severe forms of the disorder may be highly dangerous to others.

Some behaviorists believe that classical conditioning is at work in sexual sadism disorder (Akins, 2004). While inflicting pain, perhaps unintentionally, on an animal or person, a teenager may feel intense emotions and sexual arousal. The association between inflicting pain and being aroused sexually sets the stage for a pattern of sexual sadism. Behaviorists also propose that the disorder may result from modeling, when adolescents observe others achieving sexual satisfaction by inflicting pain. Many Internet sex sites and sexual videos, magazines, and books in our society make such models readily available (Brophy, 2010).

Both psychodynamic and cognitive theorists suggest that people with sexual sadism disorder inflict pain in order to achieve a sense of power or control, necessitated perhaps by underlying feelings of sexual inadequacy (Marshall & Marshall, 2015). The sense of power in turn increases their sexual arousal (Stekel, 2010; Rathbone, 2001). Alternatively, certain biological studies have found signs of possible brain and hormonal abnormalities in people with sexual sadism

▸ **sexual masochism disorder** A paraphilic disorder in which a person has repeated and intense sexual urges, fantasies, or behaviors that involve being humiliated, beaten, bound, or otherwise made to suffer, accompanied by clinically significant distress or impairment.

▸ **sexual sadism disorder** A paraphilic disorder in which a person has repeated and intense sexual urges or fantasies that involve inflicting suffering on others, and either acts on these urges with nonconsenting individuals or experiences clinically significant distress or impairment.

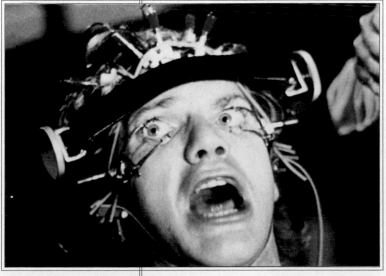

Cinematic introduction In one of filmdom's most famous scenes, Alex, the sexually sadistic character in *A Clockwork Orange*, is forced to observe violent images while he experiences painful stomach spasms.

The Everett Collection

BETWEEN THE LINES

Sex and the Law

In 1996 the California state legislature passed the first law in the United States allowing state judges to order *antiandrogen* drug treatments, often referred to as "chemical castration," for repeat sex crime offenders, such as men who repeatedly commit pedophilic acts or rape. Since then, at least seven other states also have passed laws permitting some form of coerced antiandrogen drug treatment.

(Harenski et al., 2012; Jacobs, 2011). None of these explanations, however, has been thoroughly investigated.

The disorder has been treated by aversion therapy. The public's view of and distaste for this procedure have been influenced by the novel and 1971 movie *A Clockwork Orange,* which depicts simultaneous presentations of violent images and drug-induced stomach spasms to a sadistic young man until he is conditioned to feel nausea at the sight of such images. It is not clear that aversion therapy is helpful in cases of sexual sadism disorder. However, relapse-prevention training, used in some criminal cases, may be of value (Federoff & Marshall, 2010; Bradford et al., 2008).

➤ *Summing Up*

PARAPHILIC DISORDERS Paraphilias are patterns characterized by recurrent and intense sexual urges, fantasies, or behaviors involving objects or situations outside the usual sexual norms—for example, nonhuman objects, children, nonconsenting adults, or experiences of suffering or humiliation. When an individual's paraphilia causes great distress, interferes with social or occupational functioning, or places the individual or others at risk of harm, a diagnosis of paraphilic disorder is applied. Paraphilic disorders are found primarily in men. The paraphilic disorders include fetishistic disorder, transvestic disorder, exhibitionistic disorder, voyeuristic disorder, frotteuristic disorder, pedophilic disorder, sexual masochism disorder, and sexual sadism disorder. Although various explanations have been proposed for these disorders, research has revealed little about their causes. A range of treatments have been tried, including aversion therapy, masturbatory satiation, orgasmic reorientation, and relapse-prevention training.

Gender Dysphoria

As children and adults, most people feel like and identify themselves as males or females—a feeling and identity that is consistent with their *assigned gender,* the gender to which they are born. But society has come to appreciate that many people do not experience such gender clarity. Instead, they have *transgender experiences*—a sense that their actual gender identity is different from their assigned gender or a sense that it lies outside the usual male versus female categories. It is estimated that 1.5 million people in the United States are transgender—0.5% of the population (Steinmetz, 2014). The prevalence in other countries is about the same (Kuyper & Wijsen, 2014). Many transgender people come to terms with their gender inconsistencies, but others experience extreme unhappiness with their assigned gender and may seek treatment for their problem. DSM-5 categorizes these people as having **gender dysphoria,** a disorder in which people persistently feel that a vast mistake has been made—they have been born to the wrong sex—and have clinically significant distress or impairment with this gender mismatch (see Table 11-6).

The DSM-5 categorization of gender dysphoria is controversial (Sennott, 2011). Many argue that since transgender experiences reflect alternative—not pathological—ways of experiencing one's gender identity, they should never be considered a psychological disorder, even when they bring significant unhappiness. At the other end of the spectrum, many argue that transgender experiences are in fact a medical problem that may produce personal unhappiness for some of the people with these experiences. According to this position, gender dysphoria should not be categorized as a psychological disorder, just as kidney disease and cancer,

▶ **gender dysphoria** A disorder in which a person persistently feels clinically significant distress or impairment due to his or her assigned gender and strongly wishes to be a member of another gender.

medical conditions that may also produce unhappiness, are not categorized as psychological disorders. Although one of these views may eventually prove to be an appropriate perspective, this chapter largely will follow DSM-5's position that (1) a transgender orientation is more than a variant lifestyle if it is accompanied by significant distress or impairment, and (2) a transgender orientation is far from a clearly defined medical problem. We will also examine what clinical theorists believe they know about gender dysphoria.

People with gender dysphoria typically would like to get rid of their primary and secondary sex characteristics—many of them find their own genitals repugnant—and acquire the characteristics of another sex (APA, 2013). Men with this disorder (i.e., "male-assigned people") outnumber women ("female-assigned people") by around 2 to 1. The individuals feel anxiety or depression and may have thoughts of suicide (Judge et al., 2014; Steinmetz, 2014). Such reactions may be related to the confusion and pain brought on by the disorder itself, or they may be tied to the prejudice typically faced by people who are transgender. According to an extensive survey across the United States, for example, 80 to 90 percent of transgender people have been harassed at school or work; 50 percent have been fired from a job, not hired, or not promoted; and 20 percent have been denied a place to live (Steinmetz, 2014). Studies also suggest that some people with gender dysphoria manifest a personality disorder (Singh et al., 2011). Today the term *gender dysphoria* has replaced the old term *transsexualism,* although the word "transsexual" is still sometimes used to describe those who desire and seek *full* gender change, often by surgery (APA, 2013).

Sometimes gender dysphoria emerges in children (Milrod, 2014; Nicholson & McGuinness, 2014). Like adults with this disorder, the children feel uncomfortable about their assigned gender and yearn to be members of another gender. This childhood pattern usually disappears by adolescence or adulthood, but in some cases it develops into adolescent and adult forms of gender dysphoria (Cohen-Kettenis, 2001). Thus adults with this disorder may have had a childhood form of gender dysphoria, but most children with the childhood form do not become adults with the disorder. Surveys of mothers indicate that about 1.5 percent of young boys wish to be a girl, and 3.5 percent of young girls wish to be a boy (Carroll, 2007; Zucker & Bradley, 1995), yet considerably less than 1 percent of adults manifest gender dysphoria (Zucker, 2010). This age shift in the prevalence of gender dysphoria is, in part, why leading experts on the disorder strongly recommend against any form of *irreversible*

A delicate matter A 5-year-old boy (left), who identifies and dresses as a girl and asks to be called "she," plays with a female friend. Sensitive to the gender identity rights movement and to the special needs of children with gender dysphoria, a growing number of parents, educators, and clinicians are now supportive of children like this boy.

table: **11-6**

Dx Checklist

Gender Dysphoria in Adolescents and Adults

1. For 6 months or more, individual's gender-related feelings and/or behaviors is at odds with those of his or her assigned gender, as indicated by two or more of the following symptoms: • Gender-related feelings and/or behaviors clearly contradict the individual's primary or secondary sex characteristics • Powerful wish to eliminate one's sex characteristics • Yearning for the sex characteristics of another gender • Powerful wish to be a member of another gender • Yearning to be treated as a member of another gender • Firm belief that one's feelings and reactions are those that characterize another gender.

2. Individual experiences significant distress or impairment.

(Information from: APA, 2013.)

physical treatment for this pattern until people reach adulthood, a recommendation upheld in the World Professional Association for Transgender Health Standards of Care (Milrod, 2014; HBIGDA, 2001). Nevertheless, some surgeons continue to perform such procedures for younger patients.

Explanations of Gender Dysphoria

Many clinicians suspect that biological factors—perhaps genetic or prenatal—play a key role in gender dysphoria (Rametti et al., 2011; Nawata et al., 2010). Consistent with a genetic explanation, the disorder does sometimes run in families. Research indicates, for example, that people whose siblings have gender dysphoria are more likely to have the same disorder than are people without such siblings (Gómez-Gil et al., 2010). Indeed, one study of 23 pairs of identical twins found that when one of the twins had gender dysphoria, the other twin had it as well in 9 of the pairs (Heylens et al., 2012).

Biological investigators have recently detected differences between the brains of control participants and participants with gender dysphoria. One study found, for example, that those with the disorder had heightened blood flow in the *insula* and reduced blood flow in the *anterior cingulate cortex* (Nawata et al., 2010). These brain areas are known to play roles in human sexuality and consciousness.

A biological study that was conducted around 20 years ago continues to receive considerable attention (Zhou et al., 1997, 1995). Dutch investigators autopsied the brains of six people who had changed their sex from male to female. They found that a cluster of cells in the hypothalamus called the *bed nucleus of stria terminalis* (*BST*) was only half as large in these people as it was in a control group of non-transgender men. Usually, a woman's BST is much smaller than a man's, so in effect the male-assigned people with gender dysphoria were found to have a female-sized BST. Scientists do not know for certain what the BST does in humans, but they know that it helps regulate sexual behavior in male rats. Thus it may be that male-assigned people who develop gender dysphoria have a key biological difference that leaves them very uncomfortable with their assigned sex characteristics.

Treatments for Gender Dysphoria

In order to more effectively assess and treat those with gender dysphoria, clinical theorists have tried to distinguish the most common patterns of the disorder encountered in clinical practice.

Client Patterns of Gender Dysphoria
Richard Carroll (2007), a leading theorist on gender dysphoria, has described the three patterns of gender dysphoria for which people most commonly seek treatment: (1) *female-to-male gender dysphoria,* (2) *male-to-female gender dysphoria: androphilic type,* and (3) *male-to-female gender dysphoria: autogynephilic type.*

FEMALE-TO-MALE GENDER DYSPHORIA People with a female-to-male gender dysphoria pattern are born female but appear or behave in a stereotypically masculine manner from early on—often as young as 3 years of age or younger. As children, they always play rough games or sports, prefer the company of boys, hate "girlish" clothes, and state their wish to be male. As adolescents, they become disgusted by the physical changes of puberty and are sexually attracted to females. However, lesbian relationships do not feel like a satisfactory solution to them because they want other women to be attracted to them as males, not as females.

MALE-TO-FEMALE GENDER DYSPHORIA: ANDROPHILIC TYPE People with an androphilic type of male-to-female gender dysphoria are born male but appear or behave in a stereotypically female manner from birth. As children, they are viewed as effeminate, pretty, and gentle; avoid rough games; and hate to dress in boys' clothing. As adolescents, they become sexually attracted to males, and they often come out as gay and develop gay relationships (the term "androphilic" means *attracted to males*). But by adulthood, it often becomes clear to them that such gay relationships do not truly address their gender dysphoric feelings because they want to be with heterosexual men who are attracted to them as women.

MALE-TO-FEMALE GENDER DYSPHORIA: AUTOGYNEPHILIC TYPE People with an autogynephilic type of male-to-female gender dysphoria are not sexually attracted to males; rather, they are attracted to the idea of themselves being female (the term "autogynephilic" means *attracted to oneself as a female*). Like males with the paraphilic disorder *transvestic disorder* (see pages 370–371), persons with this form of gender dysphoria behave in a stereotypically masculine manner as children, start to enjoy dressing in female clothing during childhood, and after puberty become sexually aroused when they cross-dress. Also, like males with transvestic disorder, they are attracted to females during and beyond adolescence. However, unlike people with transvestic disorder, these persons have desires of becoming female that become increasingly intense and overwhelming during adulthood.

In short, cross-dressing is characteristic of both men with transvestic disorder (the paraphilic disorder) and people with this type of male-to-female gender dysphoria (Zucker et al., 2012). But the former cross-dress strictly to become sexually aroused, whereas the latter develop much deeper reasons for cross-dressing, reasons of gender identity.

Types of Treatment for Gender Dysphoria

Many adults with gender dysphoria receive psychotherapy (Affatati et al., 2004), but a large number of them further seek to address their concerns through biological interventions (see *MediaSpeak* on the next page). For example, many transgender adults change their sexual characteristics by means of *hormone treatments* (Wierckx et al., 2014). Physicians prescribe the female sex hormone *estrogen* for male-assigned patients, causing breast development, loss of body and facial hair, and changes in body fat distribution. Some such patients also go to speech therapy, raising their tenor voice to alto

© Splash News/Corbis

Frazer Harrison/Getty Images

Hero to a new audience When he won the gold medal for the decathlon at the 1976 Olympics, Bruce Jenner became a national hero and was widely viewed as the personification of masculinity—the world's best male athlete—leading to lucrative contracts as the spokesperson for the popular cereal Wheaties (left), among other products. When in 2015 Jenner appeared in *Vanity Fair* magazine (right) as a transgender woman, Caitlyn, she became a hero to thousands of transgender persons who hoped that this high-profile revelation would reduce the public's misunderstanding of and prejudice against transgender individuals.

10:00 AM 75%

MediaSpeak
A Different Kind of Judgment

By Angela Woodall, *Oakland Tribune*

Few county judges command standing ovations before they say a word, nor do they compel hate mail from strangers halfway around the world.

Alameda County Superior Court Judge Victoria Kolakowski receives both. She is the first transgender person elected as a trial judge and one of the very few elected to any office. "No, I am not going to be able to get you out of things," she said jokingly to an audience of transgender advocates . . . two weeks after her upset victory. . . . "I had a chance to serve. If my being visible helps a community that is often ignored and looked down upon, then I am happy. If not me, then who?"

But it took years of rejection and perseverance to get from Michael Kolakowski to 49-year-old Judge Victoria Kolakowski, even though as a child she hoped and prayed to wake up in a female body. "I guess the prayer was answered," she said. "But not for a long time afterward." . . .

Kolakowski, a New York native, is a carefully groomed, mildly spoken brunette of average build who usually appears wearing glasses, modest makeup, dark pantsuits and pumps. In other words, she looks a lot like a conservatively dressed judge. . . .

[Back when she was a teenager], the Internet did not exist, and information about transsexuals was unavailable to minors, Kolakowski said. At Louisiana State University, she finally found some books in the college library about transsexuality and realized that she was not alone. But when she told her parents, they took her to the emergency room of the hospital. This started an on-again, off-again series of counseling and therapy that lasted for a decade.

Kolakowski eventually married, came out with her wife during law school and began her transition to becoming a woman on April 1, 1989. It was her last semester at LSU. She was 27. Three years later, she underwent surgery to complete her transition to a woman.

She was a 30-year-old lawyer with five degrees on her resume. So she had no problem attracting job offers—only to be rejected when she walked into the interview.

Rejection is one of the commonalities for transgender women and men, and the pain can run deep. Some

A new kind of role model Judge Victoria Kolakowski (left) waves during the 41st annual Gay Pride parade in San Francisco, June 26, 2011.

AP Photo/Jeff Chiu

of the transgender lawyers Kolakowski knew killed themselves.

Kolakowski attributes her resilience to her faith—she also holds a master's degree in divinity—and the support of "some very loving people." That includes her parents and her second wife. . . . They wed in 2006.

By then, Kolakowski had become an administrative law judge. . . . Her chance to run for the Superior Court bench came in 2008. . . . Kolakowski didn't win, but she tried again in 2010. "This time, things were different, and in June, I came in first," she said.

The spotlight turned in her direction because she became a symbol of success for the transgender community. But she also has become a target. The more successful you are, the more backlash you are likely to get, she said, "and that backlash can be violent.". . . [T]wo transgender women were killed in Houston last year, even though voters there elected a transgender municipal judge in November. . . . "We're dealing with people who don't know us and don't really understand who we are," she said.

Kolakowski is also mindful that she must be sensitive to the dignity of the office voters elected her to. Some people, she predicted, will accuse her of "acting inappropriately." But she said: "This is what it is. I was elected based on my qualifications. It just happens to be historic."

through training, and some have facial feminization surgery (Capitán et al., 2014; Steinmetz, 2014). In contrast, treatments with the male sex hormone *testosterone* are given to female-assigned patients with gender dysphoria, resulting in a deeper voice, increased muscle mass, and changes in facial and body hair.

These approaches enable many persons with the disorder to lead a fulfilling life in the gender that fits them. For others, however, this is not enough, and they seek out one of the most controversial practices in medicine: **sexual reassignment,** or **sex-change surgery** (Judge et al., 2014). This surgery, which is usually preceded by one to two years of hormone therapy, involves, for male-assigned persons, partial removal of the penis and restructuring of its remaining parts into a clitoris and vagina, a procedure called *vaginoplasty*. In addition, some individuals undergo face-changing plastic surgery. For female-assigned persons, surgery may include bilateral mastectomy and hysterectomy (Ott et al., 2010). The procedure for creating a functioning penis, called *phalloplasty*, is performed in some cases, but it is not perfected. Alternatively, doctors have developed a silicone prosthesis that can give patients the appearance of having male genitals. One review calculates that 1 of every 3,100 persons in the United States has had or will have sex-change surgery during their lifetime (Horton, 2008). For female-assigned persons, the incidence is 1 of every 4,200, and for male-assigned individuals, it is 1 of every 2,500. Many insurance companies refuse to cover these or even less invasive biological treatments for people with gender dysphoria, but a growing number of states now prohibit such insurance exclusions (Steinmetz, 2014).

Clinicians have debated heatedly whether sexual reassignment surgery is an appropriate treatment for gender dysphoria (Gozlan, 2011). Some consider it a humane solution, perhaps the most satisfying one to many people with the pattern. Others argue that sexual reassignment is a "drastic nonsolution" for a complex disorder. Either way, such surgery appears to be on the increase (Allison, 2010; Horton, 2008).

Research into the outcomes of sexual reassignment surgery has yielded mixed findings. On the one hand, in a number of studies, the majority of patients—both female-assigned and male-assigned—report satisfaction with the outcome of the surgery, improvements in self-satisfaction and interpersonal interactions, and improvements in sexual functioning (Judge et al., 2014; Johansson et al., 2010). On the other hand, several studies have yielded less favorable findings. A long-term follow-up study in Sweden, for example, found that although sexually reassigned participants did show a reduction in gender dysphoria, they also had a higher rate of psychological disorders and of suicide attempts than the general population (Dhejne et al., 2011). People with significant pretreatment psychological disturbances seem most likely to later regret the surgery (Carroll, 2007). All of this argues for careful screening prior to surgical interventions, continued research to better understand the impact of such procedures, and, more generally, better clinical care for transgender people.

Lea T. Transgender model Lea T. emerged in 2010 as the face of Givenchy, the famous French fashion brand. Born male, the Brazilian model has become a leading female figure in runway fashion shows and magazines, including *Vogue Paris, Cover* magazine, and *Love* magazine. In 2012 she underwent sexual reassignment surgery.

➤ *Summing Up*

GENDER DYSPHORIA People with gender dysphoria persistently feel that they have been born the wrong gender and, along with this, experience significant distress or impairment. The causes of this disorder are not well understood. Hormone treatments, facial surgery, speech therapy, and psychotherapy have been used to help some people adopt the gender role they believe to be right for them. Sex-change operations have also been performed, but the appropriateness of surgery as a form of treatment has been debated heatedly.

▶ **sex-change surgery** A surgical procedure that changes a person's sex organs, features, and, in turn, sexual identity. Also known as *sexual reassignment surgery*.

PUTTING IT...*together*

A Private Topic Draws Public Attention

For all the public interest in sexual and gender disorders, clinical theorists and practitioners have only recently begun to understand their nature and how to treat them. As a result of research done over the past few decades, people with sexual dysfunctions are no longer doomed to a lifetime of sexual frustration. At the same time, however, insights into the causes and treatment of paraphilic disorders and gender dysphoria remain limited.

Studies of sexual dysfunctions have pointed to many psychological, sociocultural, and biological causes. Often, as you have seen with so many disorders, the various causes may *interact* to produce a particular dysfunction, as in erectile disorder and female orgasmic disorder. For some dysfunctions, however, one cause alone is dominant, and integrated explanations may be inaccurate and unproductive. Some sexual pain dysfunctions, for example, have a physical cause exclusively.

Recent work has also yielded important progress in the treatment of sexual dysfunctions, and people with such problems are now often helped greatly by therapy. Sex therapy is usually a complex program tailored to the particular problems of an individual or couple. Techniques from the various models may be combined, although in some instances the particular problem calls primarily for one approach.

One of the most important insights to emerge from all of this work is that *education* about sexual dysfunctions can be as important as therapy. Sexual myths are still taken so seriously that they often lead to feelings of shame, self-hatred, isolation, and hopelessness—feelings that themselves contribute to sexual difficulty. Even a modest amount of education can help people who are in treatment.

In fact, most people can benefit from a more accurate understanding of sexual functioning. Public education about sexual functioning—through the Internet, books, television and radio, school programs, group presentations, and the like—has become a major clinical focus. It is important that these efforts continue and even increase in the coming years.

CLINICAL CHOICES

Now that you've read about disorders of sex and gender, try the interactive case study for this chapter. See if you are able to identify Charles's symptoms and suggest a diagnosis based on his symptoms. What kind of treatment would be most effective for Charles? Go to LaunchPad to access *Clinical Choices*.

KEY TERMS

sexual dysfunction, p. 348

desire phase, p. 348

male hypoactive sexual desire disorder, p. 349

female sexual interest/arousal disorder, p. 349

excitement phase, p. 351

erectile disorder, p. 352

nocturnal penile tumescence (NPT), p. 353

performance anxiety, p. 353

spectator role, p. 353

orgasm phase, p. 354

premature ejaculation, p. 355

delayed ejaculation, p. 355

female orgasmic disorder, p. 356

genito-pelvic pain/penetration disorder, p. 358

vaginismus, p. 358

dyspareunia, p. 358

sex therapy, p. 360

sensate focus, p. 361

flibanserin, p. 363

sildenafil (Viagra), p. 363

directed masturbation training, p. 365

paraphilia, p. 367

paraphilic disorder, p. 367

fetishistic disorder, p. 369

masturbatory satiation, p. 369

orgasmic reorientation, p. 370

transvestic disorder, p. 370

exhibitionistic disorder, p. 371

voyeuristic disorder, p. 372

frotteuristic disorder, p. 372

pedophilic disorder, p. 372

sexual masochism disorder, p. 374

sexual sadism disorder, p. 375

transgender experiences, p. 376

gender dysphoria, p. 376

hormone treatments, p. 379

sex-change surgery, p. 381

QuickQuiz

1. What sexual dysfunctions are associated with the desire phase of the sexual response cycle? How common are they, and what causes them? *pp. 348–351*

2. What are the symptoms and prevalence of erectile disorder? To which phase of the sexual response cycle is it related? *p. 352*

3. What are the possible causes of erectile disorder? *pp. 352–354*

4. Which sexual dysfunctions seem to involve performance anxiety and the spectator role? *pp. 353, 356*

5. What are the symptoms, rates, and leading causes of premature ejaculation, delayed ejaculation, and female orgasmic disorder? To which phase of the sexual response cycle are they related? *pp. 354–358*

6. Identify, describe, and explain disorders of sexual pain. *pp. 358–359*

7. What are the general features of modern sex therapy? What particular techniques are further used to treat specific sexual dysfunctions? *pp. 360–366*

8. List, describe, and explain the various paraphilic disorders. *pp. 367–375*

9. Describe the treatment techniques of aversion therapy, masturbatory satiation, orgasmic reorientation, and relapse-prevention training. Which paraphilic disorders have they been used to treat, and how successful are they? *pp. 369–376*

10. Distinguish transvestic disorder from gender dysphoria. What are the various types of gender dysphoria, and what are today's treatments for this disorder? *pp. 370–371, 376–381*

Visit *LaunchPad*

www.macmillanhighered.com/launchpad/comerfund8e

to access the e-book, new interactive case studies, videos, activities, and LearningCurve quizzes, as well as study aids including flashcards, FAQs, and research exercises.

Macmillan Education LaunchPad

Schizophrenia

Laura, 40 years old: *Laura's desire was to become independent and leave home . . . as soon as possible. . . . She became a professional dancer at the age of 20 . . . and was booked for . . . theaters in many European countries. . . .*

It was during one of her tours in Germany that Laura met her husband. . . . They were married and went to live in a small . . . town in France where the husband's business was. . . . She spent a year in that town and was very unhappy. . . . [Finally] Laura and her husband decided to emigrate to the United States. . . .

They had no children, and Laura . . . showed interest in pets. She had a dog to whom she was very devoted. The dog became sick and partially paralyzed, and veterinarians felt that there was no hope of recovery. . . . Finally [her husband] broached the problem to his wife, asking her "Should the dog be destroyed or not?" From that time on Laura became restless, agitated, and depressed. . . .

Later Laura started to complain about the neighbors. A woman who lived on the floor beneath them was knocking on the wall to irritate her. According to the husband, this woman had really knocked on the wall a few times; he had heard the noises. However, Laura became more and more concerned about it. She would wake up in the middle of the night under the impression that she was hearing noises from the apartment downstairs. She would become upset and angry at the neighbors. . . . Later she became more disturbed. She started to feel that the neighbors were now recording everything she said; maybe they had hidden wires in the apartment. She started to feel "funny" sensations. There were many strange things happening, which she did not know how to explain; people were looking at her in a funny way in the street. . . . She felt that people were planning to harm either her or her husband. . . . In the evening when she looked at television, it became obvious to her that the programs referred to her life. Often the people on the programs were just repeating what she had thought. They were stealing her ideas. She wanted to go to the police and report them.

(Arieti, 1974, pp. 165–168)

Richard, 23 years old: *In high school, Richard was an average student. After graduation from high school, he [entered] the army. . . . Richard remembered [the] period . . . after his discharge from the army . . . as one of the worst in his life. . . . Any, even remote, anticipation of disappointment was able to provoke attacks of anxiety in him. . . .*

Approximately two years after his return to civilian life, Richard left his job because he became overwhelmed by these feelings of lack of confidence in himself, and he refused to go look for another one. He stayed home most of the day. His mother would nag him that he was too lazy and unwilling to do anything. He became slower and slower in dressing and undressing and taking care of himself. When he went out of the house, he felt compelled "to give interpretations" to everything he looked at. He did not know what to do outside the house, where to go, where to turn. If he saw a red light at a crossing, he would interpret it as a message that he should not go in that direction. If he saw an arrow, he would follow the arrow interpreting it as a sign sent by God that he should go in that direction. Feeling lost and horrified, he would go home and stay there, afraid to go out because going out meant making decisions or choices that he felt unable to make. He reached the point where he stayed home most of the time. But even at home, he was tortured by his symptoms. He could not act; any motion that he felt like making seemed to him an insurmountable obstacle, because he did not know whether he should make it or not. He was increasingly afraid of doing the wrong thing. Such fears prevented him from dressing, undressing, eating, and so forth. He felt paralyzed and lay motionless in bed. He gradually became worse, was completely motionless, and had to be hospitalized. . . .

Being undecided, he felt blocked, and often would remain mute and motionless, like a statue, even for days.

(Arieti, 1974, pp. 153–155)

table: 12-1

Dx Checklist

Schizophrenia

1. For 1 month, individual displays two or more of the following symptoms much of the time:

   (a) Delusions
   (b) Hallucinations
   (c) Disorganized speech
   (d) Very abnormal motor activity, including catatonia
   (e) Negative symptoms

2. At least one of the individual's symptoms must be delusions, hallucinations, or disorganized speech.

3. Individual functions much more poorly in various life spheres than was the case prior to the symptoms.

4. Beyond this 1 month of intense symptomology, individual continues to display some degree of impaired functioning for at least 5 additional months.

(Information from: APA, 2013.)

Eventually, Laura and Richard each received a diagnosis of **schizophrenia** (APA, 2013). People with schizophrenia, though they previously functioned well or at least acceptably, deteriorate into an isolated wilderness of unusual perceptions, odd thoughts, disturbed emotions, and motor abnormalities. Like Laura and Richard, people with schizophrenia experience **psychosis,** a loss of contact with reality. Their ability to perceive and respond to the environment becomes so disturbed that they may not be able to function at home, with friends, in school, or at work (Harvey, 2014). They may have hallucinations (false sensory perceptions) or delusions (false beliefs), or they may withdraw into a private world. DSM-5 calls for a diagnosis of schizophrenia only after the symptoms of psychosis continue for six months or more (see Table 12-1).

As you saw in Chapter 10, taking LSD or abusing amphetamines or cocaine may produce psychosis. So may injuries or diseases of the brain. And so may other severe psychological disorders, such as major depressive disorder or bipolar disorder (Pearlson & Ford, 2014). Most commonly, however, psychosis appears in the form of schizophrenia.

Actually, there are a number of schizophrenia-like disorders listed in DSM-5, each distinguished by particular durations and sets of symptoms (see Table 12-2). Because these psychotic disorders all bear a similarity to schizophrenia, they—along with schizophrenia itself—are collectively called *schizophrenia spectrum disorders* (APA, 2013). Schizophrenia is the most prevalent of these disorders. Most of the explanations and treatments offered for schizophrenia are applicable to the other disorders as well (Potkin et al., 2014).

Approximately 1 of every 100 people in the world suffers from schizophrenia during his or her lifetime (Long et al., 2014). An estimated 26 million people worldwide are afflicted with it, including 3 million in the United States (MHF, 2015; NIMH, 2010). Its financial cost is enormous, and the emotional cost is even greater

table: 12-2

Schizophrenia Spectrum Disorders: An Array of Psychosis

Disorder	Key Features	Duration	Lifetime Prevalence
Schizophrenia	Various psychotic symptoms, such as delusions, hallucinations, disorganized speech, restricted or inappropriate affect, and catatonia	6 months or more	1.0%
Brief psychotic disorder	Various psychotic symptoms, such as delusions, hallucinations, disorganized speech, restricted or inappropriate affect, and catatonia	Less than 1 month	Unknown
Schizophreniform disorder	Various psychotic symptoms, such as delusions, hallucinations, disorganized speech, restricted or inappropriate affect, and catatonia	1 to 6 months	0.2%
Schizoaffective disorder	Marked symptoms of both schizophrenia and a major depressive episode or a manic episode	6 months or more	Unknown
Delusional disorder	Persistent delusions that are not bizarre and not due to schizophrenia; persecutory, jealous, grandiose, and somatic delusions are common	1 month or more	0.1%
Psychotic disorder due to another medical condition	Hallucinations, delusions, or disorganized speech caused by a medical illness or brain damage	No minimum length	Unknown
Substance/medication-induced psychotic disorder	Hallucinations, delusions, or disorganized speech caused directly by a substance, such as an abused drug	No minimum length	Unknown

(Information from: APA, 2013.)

(Kennedy et al., 2014). In addition, people with schizophrenia have an increased risk of suicide and of physical—often fatal—illness (Dickerson et al., 2014). On average, they live 20 fewer years than other people (Laursen et al., 2014).

Although schizophrenia appears in all socioeconomic groups, it is found more frequently at the lower economic levels (Burns, Tomita, & Kapadia, 2014; Sareen et al., 2011) (see Figure 12-1). This has led some theorists to believe that the stress of poverty is itself a cause of the disorder. However, it could be that schizophrenia causes its sufferers to fall from a higher to a lower socioeconomic level or to remain poor because they are unable to function effectively. This is sometimes called the *downward drift* theory.

Equal numbers of men and women are diagnosed with schizophrenia. The average age of onset for men is 23 years, compared with 28 years for women (Lindenmayer & Khan, 2012). Almost 3 percent of all those who are divorced or separated suffer from schizophrenia sometime during their lives, compared with 1 percent of married people and 2 percent of people who remain single. Again, however, it is not clear whether marital problems are a cause or a result (Solter et al., 2004).

People have long shown great interest in schizophrenia, flocking to plays and movies that explore or exploit our fascination with the disorder. Yet, as you will read, all too many people with schizophrenia are neglected in our country, their needs almost entirely ignored. Although effective interventions have been developed, those sufferers live without adequate treatment and may never fully fulfill their potential as human beings.

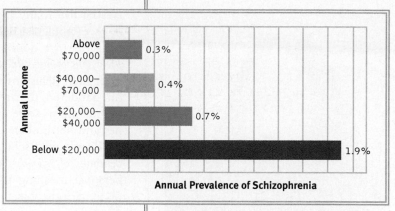

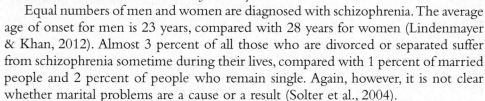

The Clinical Picture of Schizophrenia

The symptoms of schizophrenia vary greatly from sufferer to sufferer, and so do its triggers, course, and responsiveness to treatment (APA, 2013). In fact, a number of clinicians believe that schizophrenia is actually a group of distinct disorders that happen to have some features in common (Boutros et al., 2014). Regardless of whether schizophrenia is a single disorder or several disorders, the lives of people who struggle with its symptoms are filled with pain and turmoil.

What Are the Symptoms of Schizophrenia?

Think back to Laura and Richard, the two people described at the beginning of the chapter. Both of them deteriorated from a normal level of functioning to become ineffective in dealing with the world. Each had some of the symptoms found in schizophrenia. The symptoms can be grouped into three categories: *positive symptoms* (excesses of thought, emotion, and behavior), *negative symptoms* (deficits of thought, emotion, and behavior), and *psychomotor symptoms* (unusual movements or gestures). Some people with schizophrenia are more dominated by positive symptoms and others by negative symptoms, although most tend to have both kinds of symptoms to some degree. In addition, around half of those with schizophrenia have significant difficulties with memory and other kinds of cognitive functioning (Ragland et al., 2015; Eich et al., 2014).

Positive Symptoms **Positive symptoms** are "pathological excesses," or bizarre additions, to a person's behavior. *Delusions, disorganized thinking and speech, heightened perceptions and hallucinations,* and *inappropriate affect* are the ones most often found in schizophrenia.

figure 12-1
Socioeconomic class and schizophrenia
Poor people in the United States are more likely than wealthy people to experience schizophrenia. (Information from: Sareen et al., 2011.)

▸ **schizophrenia** A psychotic disorder in which personal, social, and occupational functioning deteriorate as a result of unusual perceptions, odd thoughts, disturbed emotions, and motor abnormalities.

▸ **psychosis** A state in which a person loses contact with reality in key ways.

▸ **positive symptoms** Symptoms of schizophrenia that seem to be excesses of or bizarre additions to normal thoughts, emotions, or behaviors.

Delusions of grandeur In 1892, an artist who was a patient at a mental hospital claimed credit for this painting, *Self-Portrait as Christ*. Although few people with schizophrenia have his artistic skill, a number have similar delusions of grandeur.

Famous, but rare, delusion In the MTV show *Teen Wolf*, a possessed man cries out in terror as his body changes into that of a wolf. *Lycanthropy*, the delusion of being an animal, is a rare psychological syndrome, but it has been the subject of many profitable books, movies, and TV shows over the years.

DELUSIONS Many people with schizophrenia develop **delusions,** ideas that they believe wholeheartedly but that have no basis in fact. Some people hold a single delusion that dominates their lives and behavior; others have many delusions. *Delusions of persecution* are the most common in schizophrenia (APA, 2013). People with such delusions believe they are being plotted or discriminated against, spied on, slandered, threatened, attacked, or deliberately victimized. Laura believed that her neighbors were trying to irritate her and that other people were trying to harm her and her husband.

People with schizophrenia may also have *delusions of reference:* they attach special and personal meaning to the actions of others or to various objects or events. Richard, for example, interpreted arrows on street signs as indicators of the direction he should take. People with *delusions of grandeur* believe themselves to be great inventors, religious saviors, or other specially empowered persons. And those with *delusions of control* believe their feelings, thoughts, and actions are being controlled by other people.

> Philosopher Friedrich Nietzsche said, "Insanity in individuals is something rare—but in groups, parties, nations and epochs, it is the rule." What did he mean?

DISORGANIZED THINKING AND SPEECH People with schizophrenia may not be able to think logically (Briki et al., 2014) and may speak in peculiar ways (Millier et al., 2014). These **formal thought disorders** can cause the sufferer great confusion and make communication extremely difficult. Often such thought disorders take the form of positive symptoms (pathological excesses), as in loose associations, neologisms, perseveration, and clang.

People who have *loose associations,* or *derailment,* the most common formal thought disorder, rapidly shift from one topic to another, believing that their incoherent statements make sense. A single, perhaps unimportant word in one sentence becomes the focus of the next. One man with schizophrenia, asked about his itchy arms, responded:

> *The problem is insects. My brother used to collect insects. He's now a man 5 foot 10 inches. You know, 10 is my favorite number. I also like to dance, draw, and watch television.*

Some people with schizophrenia use *neologisms,* made-up words that typically have meaning only to the person using them. One person said, for example, "I am here from a foreign university . . . and you have to have a *'plausity'* of all acts of amendment to go through for the children's code . . . it is an *'amorition'* law . . . the children have to have this *'accentuative'* law so they don't go into the *'mortite'* law of the church" (Vetter, 1969, p. 189). Others may have the formal thought disorder of *perseveration,* in which they repeat their words and statements again and again. Finally, some use *clang,* or rhyme, to think or express themselves. When asked how he was feeling, one man replied, "Well, hell, it's well to tell." Another described the weather as "So hot, you know it runs on a cot." Research suggests that some people may have disorganized speech or thinking long before their full pattern of schizophrenia unfolds (Remington et al., 2014; Covington et al., 2005).

HEIGHTENED PERCEPTIONS AND HALLUCINATIONS The perceptions and attention of some people with schizophrenia seem to intensify (Rossi-Arnaud et al., 2014). The persons may feel that their senses are being flooded by all the sights and sounds that surround them (Galderisi et al., 2014). This makes it almost impossible for them to attend to anything important. Such problems may develop years before the onset of

the actual disorder (Remington et al., 2014). It is possible that these problems further contribute to the memory impairments that are common to many people with schizophrenia (Ordemann et al., 2014).

Another kind of perceptual problem in schizophrenia consists of **hallucinations,** perceptions that a person has in the absence of external stimuli (see *InfoCentral* on the next page). People who have *auditory* hallucinations, by far the most common kind in schizophrenia, hear sounds and voices that seem to come from outside their heads. The voices may talk directly to the hallucinator, perhaps giving commands or warning of dangers, or they may be experienced as overheard.

Research suggests that people with auditory hallucinations actually produce the nerve signals of sound in their brains, "hear" them, and then believe that external sources are responsible (Chun et al., 2014; Sarin & Wallin, 2014). One study instructed six men with schizophrenia to press a button whenever they had an auditory hallucination (Silbersweig et al., 1995). PET scans revealed increased activity near the surfaces of their brains, in the tissues of the auditory cortex, the brain's hearing center, when they pressed the button.

Hallucinations can also involve any of the other senses. *Tactile* hallucinations may take the form of tingling, burning, or electric-shock sensations. *Somatic* hallucinations feel as if something is happening inside the body, such as a snake crawling inside one's stomach. *Visual* hallucinations may produce vague perceptions of colors or clouds or distinct visions of people or objects. People with *gustatory* hallucinations regularly find that their food or drink tastes strange, and people with *olfactory* hallucinations smell odors that no one else does, such as the smell of poison or smoke.

Hallucinations and delusional ideas often occur together (Cutting, 2015; Shiraishi et al., 2014). A woman who hears voices issuing commands, for example, may have the delusion that the commands are being placed in her head by someone else. Whatever the cause and whichever comes first, the hallucination and delusion eventually feed into each other.

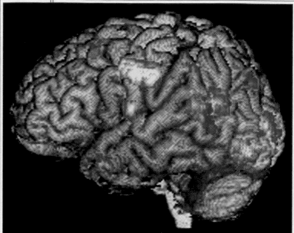

Reprinted by permission from Macmillan Publishers Ltd: Silbersweig, D.A., Stern, E., Frith, C. et al. A functional neuroanatomy of hallucinations in schizophrenia. Nature, Vol. 378, pp. 176–179 (1995). http://www.nature.com/index.html

The human brain during hallucinations This PET scan, taken at the moment a patient was having auditory hallucinations, shows heightened activity (yellow-orange) in Broca's area, a brain region that helps people produce speech, and in the auditory cortex, the brain area that helps people hear sounds (Silbersweig et al., 1995). Conversely, the front of the brain, which is responsible for determining the source of sounds, was quiet during the hallucinations. Thus people who are hallucinating seem to hear sounds produced by their own brains, but their brains cannot recognize that the sounds are actually coming from within (Juckel, 2014).

> *I thought the voices I heard were being transmitted through the walls of my apartment and through the washer and dryer and that these machines were talking and telling me things. I felt that the government agencies had planted transmitters and receivers in my apartment so that I could hear what they were saying and they could hear what I was saying.*
>
> *(Anonymous, 1996, p. 183)*

INAPPROPRIATE AFFECT Many people with schizophrenia display **inappropriate affect,** emotions that are unsuited to the situation (Taylor et al., 2014; Gard et al., 2011). They may smile when making a somber statement or upon being told terrible news, or they may become upset in situations that should make them happy. They may also undergo inappropriate shifts in mood. During a tender conversation with his wife, for example, a man with schizophrenia suddenly started yelling obscenities at her and complaining about her inadequacies.

In at least some cases, these emotions may be merely a response to other features of the disorder. Consider a woman with schizophrenia who smiles when told of her husband's serious illness. She may not actually be happy about the news; in fact, she may not be understanding or even hearing it. She could, for example, be responding instead to another of the many stimuli flooding her senses, perhaps a joke coming from an auditory hallucination.

▸ **delusion** A strange false belief firmly held despite evidence to the contrary.

▸ **formal thought disorder** A disturbance in the production and organization of thought.

▸ **hallucination** The experiencing of sights, sounds, or other perceptions in the absence of external stimuli.

▸ **inappropriate affect** Displays of emotions that are unsuited to the situation; a symptom of schizophrenia.

HALLUCINATIONS

Hallucinations are the experiencing of sights, sounds, smells, and other perceptions that occur in the absence of external stimuli.

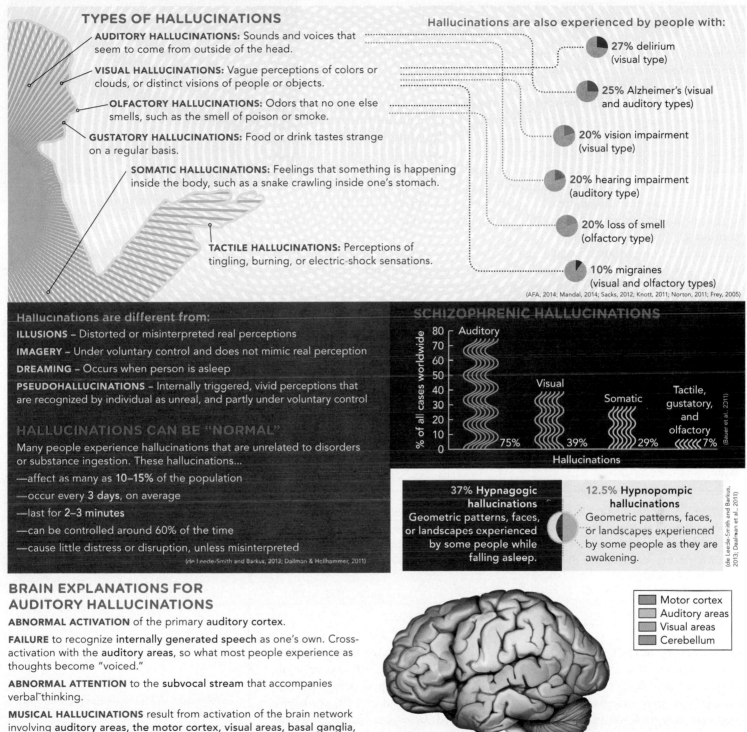

TYPES OF HALLUCINATIONS

AUDITORY HALLUCINATIONS: Sounds and voices that seem to come from outside of the head.

VISUAL HALLUCINATIONS: Vague perceptions of colors or clouds, or distinct visions of people or objects.

OLFACTORY HALLUCINATIONS: Odors that no one else smells, such as the smell of poison or smoke.

GUSTATORY HALLUCINATIONS: Food or drink tastes strange on a regular basis.

SOMATIC HALLUCINATIONS: Feelings that something is happening inside the body, such as a snake crawling inside one's stomach.

TACTILE HALLUCINATIONS: Perceptions of tingling, burning, or electric-shock sensations.

Hallucinations are also experienced by people with:

- **27%** delirium (visual type)
- **25%** Alzheimer's (visual and auditory types)
- **20%** vision impairment (visual type)
- **20%** hearing impairment (auditory type)
- **20%** loss of smell (olfactory type)
- **10%** migraines (visual and olfactory types)

(AFA, 2014; Mandal, 2014; Sacks, 2012; Knott, 2011; Norton, 2011; Frey, 2005)

Hallucinations are different from:

ILLUSIONS – Distorted or misinterpreted real perceptions

IMAGERY – Under voluntary control and does not mimic real perception

DREAMING – Occurs when person is asleep

PSEUDOHALLUCINATIONS – Internally triggered, vivid perceptions that are recognized by individual as unreal, and partly under voluntary control

HALLUCINATIONS CAN BE "NORMAL"

Many people experience hallucinations that are unrelated to disorders or substance ingestion. These hallucinations...

—affect as many as **10–15%** of the population

—occur every **3 days**, on average

—last for **2–3 minutes**

—can be controlled around **60%** of the time

—cause little distress or disruption, unless misinterpreted

(de Leede-Smith and Barkus, 2013; Dallman & Hollhommer, 2011)

SCHIZOPHRENIC HALLUCINATIONS

% of all cases worldwide

- Auditory — **75%**
- Visual — **39%**
- Somatic — **29%**
- Tactile, gustatory, and olfactory — **7%**

Hallucinations

(Bauer et al., 2011)

37% Hypnagogic hallucinations Geometric patterns, faces, or landscapes experienced by some people while falling asleep.

12.5% Hypnopompic hallucinations Geometric patterns, faces, or landscapes experienced by some people as they are awakening.

(de Leede-Smith and Barkus, 2013; Dallman et al., 2011)

BRAIN EXPLANATIONS FOR AUDITORY HALLUCINATIONS

ABNORMAL ACTIVATION of the primary **auditory cortex**.

FAILURE to recognize **internally generated speech** as one's own. Cross-activation with the **auditory areas**, so what most people experience as thoughts become "voiced."

ABNORMAL ATTENTION to the **subvocal stream** that accompanies verbal thinking.

MUSICAL HALLUCINATIONS result from activation of the brain network involving **auditory areas, the motor cortex, visual areas, basal ganglia, cerebellum, hippocampus,** and **amygdala.**

- Motor cortex
- Auditory areas
- Visual areas
- Cerebellum

HALLUCINATIONS OVER THE AGES

Ancient times: Attributed to gifts from the gods or the Muses.

Prior to 18th century: Caused by supernatural forces, such as gods or demons, angels or djinns.

Middle of 18th century: Caused by the overactivity of certain centers in the brain.

1990s: Resulting from a network of cortical and subcortical areas.

(Sachs, 2012; Shergill et al., 2000)

Negative Symptoms

Negative symptoms are those that seem to be "pathological deficits," characteristics that are lacking in a person. Poverty of speech, restricted affect, loss of volition, and social withdrawal are commonly found in schizophrenia (Azorin et al., 2014; Rocca et al., 2014). Such deficits greatly affect one's life and activities.

POVERTY OF SPEECH People with schizophrenia often have **alogia, or poverty of speech,** a reduction in speech or speech content. Some people with this negative kind of formal thought disorder think and say very little. Others say quite a bit but still manage to convey little meaning (Haas et al., 2014).

RESTRICTED AFFECT Many people with schizophrenia have a *blunted affect*—they show less anger, sadness, joy, and other feelings than most people (Rocca et al., 2014). And some show almost no emotions at all, a condition known as *flat affect*. Their faces are still, their eye contact is poor, and their voices are monotonous. In some cases, people with these problems may have *anhedonia,* a general lack of pleasure or enjoyment. In other cases, however, the restricted affect may reflect an inability to express emotions as others do. One study had participants view very emotional film clips. The participants with schizophrenia showed less facial expression than the others; however, they reported feeling just as much positive and negative emotion and in fact displayed more skin arousal (Kring & Neale, 1996).

LOSS OF VOLITION Many people with schizophrenia experience *avolition,* or apathy, feeling drained of energy and of interest in normal goals and unable to start or follow through on a course of action (Gard et al., 2014; Gold et al., 2014). This problem is particularly common in people who have had schizophrenia for many years, as if they have been worn down by it. Similarly, people with schizophrenia may feel *ambivalence,* or conflicting feelings, about most things. The avolition and ambivalence of Richard, the young man you read about earlier, made eating, dressing, and undressing impossible ordeals for him.

SOCIAL WITHDRAWAL People with schizophrenia may *withdraw from their social environment* and attend only to their own ideas and fantasies (Gard et al., 2014; Pinkham, 2014). Because their ideas are illogical and confused, the withdrawal has the effect of distancing them still further from reality. The social withdrawal seems also to lead to a breakdown of social skills, including the ability to recognize other people's needs and emotions accurately (Fogley et al., 2014; Lysaker et al., 2014).

Psychomotor Symptoms

People with schizophrenia sometimes experience *psychomotor symptoms,* for example, awkward movements or repeated grimaces and odd gestures that seem to have a private purpose—perhaps ritualistic or magical (Grover et al., 2015; Stegmayer et al., 2014). The psychomotor symptoms of schizophrenia may take certain extreme forms, collectively called **catatonia**.

People in a *catatonic stupor* stop responding to their environment, remaining motionless and silent for long stretches of time. Recall how Richard would lie motionless and mute in bed for days. People with *catatonic rigidity* maintain a rigid, upright posture for hours and resist efforts to be moved. Still others exhibit *catatonic posturing,* assuming awkward, bizarre positions for long periods of time. Finally, people with *catatonic excitement,* a different form of catatonia, move excitedly, sometimes wildly waving their arms and legs.

What Is the Course of Schizophrenia?

Schizophrenia usually first appears between the person's late teens and mid-thirties (Häfner, 2015; Lindenmayer & Khan, 2012). Although its course varies widely from case to case, many sufferers seem to go through three phases—prodromal, active, and residual (Fukumoto et al., 2014). During the *prodromal phase,* symptoms are

▸ **negative symptoms** Symptoms of schizophrenia that seem to be deficits in normal thought, emotions, or behaviors.

▸ **alogia** A decrease in speech or speech content; a symptom of schizophrenia. Also known as *poverty of speech*.

▸ **catatonia** A pattern of extreme psychomotor symptoms, found in some forms of schizophrenia, which may include catatonic stupor, rigidity, or posturing.

"Is there anybody out there?" Schizophrenia is often depicted in positive terms in the arts. Pink Floyd's hugely popular album and movie *The Wall,* for example, portrays the disorder as a social withdrawal and inward search undertaken by some people to cure themselves of confusion and unhappiness caused by society. Here former Pink Floyd band member Roger Waters tries to break down the societal wall during a recent concert.

© Robert Wagenhoffer/Corbis

The Oskar Diethelm Library, History of Psychiatry Section, Department of Psychiatry, Cornell University Medical College and the New York Hospital, New York

A catatonic pose These patients, photographed in the early 1900s, show features of catatonia, including catatonic posturing, in which they assume bizarre positions for long periods of time.

not yet obvious, but the person is beginning to deteriorate. He or she may withdraw socially, speak in vague or odd ways, develop strange ideas, or express little emotion. During the *active phase,* symptoms become apparent. Sometimes this phase is triggered by stress or trauma in the person's life. For Laura, the middle-aged woman described earlier, the immediate trigger was the loss of her cherished dog. Finally, many people with schizophrenia eventually enter a *residual phase* in which they return to a prodromal-like level of functioning. They may retain some negative symptoms, such as blunted emotion, but have a lessening of the striking symptoms of the active phase. Although 25 percent or more of patients recover completely from schizophrenia, the majority continue to have at least some residual problems for the rest of their lives (an der Heiden & Häfner, 2011).

A fuller recovery from schizophrenia is more likely in people who functioned quite well before the disorder; whose disorder is triggered by stress, comes on abruptly, or develops during middle age; and who receive early treatment (Remberk et al., 2015). Relapses are apparently more likely during times of life stress (Bebbington & Kuipers, 2011).

Many researchers believe that in order to help predict the course of schizophrenia, there should be a distinction between so-called Type I and Type II schizophrenia. People with *Type I schizophrenia* are thought to be dominated by positive symptoms, such as delusions, hallucinations, and certain formal thought disorders (Crow, 2008, 1995, 1985, 1980). Those with *Type II schizophrenia* have more negative symptoms, such as restricted affect, poverty of speech, and loss of volition. Type I patients generally seem to have been better adjusted prior to the disorder, to have later onset of symptoms, and to be more likely to show improvement, especially when treated with medications (Corves et al., 2014; Blanchard et al., 2011). In addition, as you will soon see, the positive symptoms of Type I schizophrenia may be linked more closely to *biochemical* abnormalities in the brain, while the negative symptoms of Type II schizophrenia may be tied largely to *structural* abnormalities in the brain.

➤ *Summing Up*

THE CLINICAL PICTURE OF SCHIZOPHRENIA Schizophrenia is a disorder in which functioning deteriorates as a result of disturbed thought processes, distorted perceptions, unusual emotions, and motor abnormalities. Approximately 1 percent of the world's population suffers from this disorder. The symptoms of schizophrenia fall into three groupings. Positive symptoms include delusions, certain formal thought disorders, hallucinations and other disturbances in perception and attention, and inappropriate affect. Negative symptoms include poverty of speech, restricted affect, loss of volition, and social withdrawal. Schizophrenia may also include psychomotor symptoms, collectively called catatonia in their extreme form. Schizophrenia usually emerges during late adolescence or early adulthood and tends to progress through three phases: prodromal, active, and residual.

////// BETWEEN THE LINES //////

In Their Words

"What's so great about reality?"

Person with schizophrenia, 1988

▌How Do Theorists Explain Schizophrenia?

As with many other kinds of disorders, biological, psychological, and sociocultural theorists have each proposed explanations for schizophrenia. So far, the biological explanations have received by far the most research support. This is not to say that psychological and sociocultural factors play no role in the disorder. Rather, a

diathesis-stress relationship may be at work: people with a biological predisposition will develop schizophrenia only if certain kinds of events or stressors are also present. Similarly, a diathesis-stress relationship often seems to be operating in the development of other kinds of psychotic disorders (see *PsychWatch* on the next page).

Biological Views

Perhaps the most enlightening research on schizophrenia during the past several decades has come from genetic and biological investigations. These studies have revealed the key roles of inheritance and brain activity in the development of schizophrenia and have opened the door to important treatment changes.

Genetic Factors Following the principles of the diathesis-stress perspective, genetic researchers believe that some people inherit a biological predisposition to schizophrenia and develop the disorder later when they face extreme stress, usually during late adolescence or early adulthood (Pocklington et al., 2014). The genetic view has been supported by studies of (1) relatives of people with schizophrenia, (2) twins with schizophrenia, (3) people with schizophrenia who are adopted, and (4) genetic linkage and molecular biology.

ARE RELATIVES VULNERABLE? Family pedigree studies have found repeatedly that schizophrenia and schizophrenia-like brain abnormalities are more common among relatives of people with the disorder (Scognamiglio et al., 2014). And the more closely related the relatives are to the person with schizophrenia, the more likely they are to develop the disorder (see Figure 12-2).

IS AN IDENTICAL TWIN MORE VULNERABLE THAN A FRATERNAL TWIN? Twins, who are among the closest of relatives, have in particular been studied by schizophrenia researchers. If both members of a pair of twins have a particular trait, they are said to be *concordant* for that trait. If genetic factors are at work in schizophrenia, identical twins (who share all their genes) should have a higher concordance rate for schizophrenia than fraternal twins (who share only some genes). This expectation has been supported consistently by research (Higgins & George, 2007; Gottesman, 1991). Studies have found that if one identical twin develops schizophrenia, there is a 48 percent chance that the other twin will do so as well. If the twins are fraternal, on the other hand, the second twin has approximately a 17 percent chance of developing the disorder.

> **What factors, besides genetic ones, might account for the elevated rate of schizophrenia among relatives of people with this disorder?**

ARE THE BIOLOGICAL RELATIVES OF AN ADOPTEE VULNERABLE? Adoption studies look at adults with schizophrenia who were adopted as infants and compare them with both their biological and their adoptive relatives. Because they were reared apart from their biological relatives, similar symptoms in those relatives would indicate genetic influences. Conversely, similarities to their adoptive relatives would suggest environmental influences. Researchers have repeatedly found that the biological relatives of adoptees with schizophrenia are more likely than their adoptive relatives to develop schizophrenia or another schizophrenia spectrum disorder (Andreasen & Black, 2006; Kety, 1988, 1968).

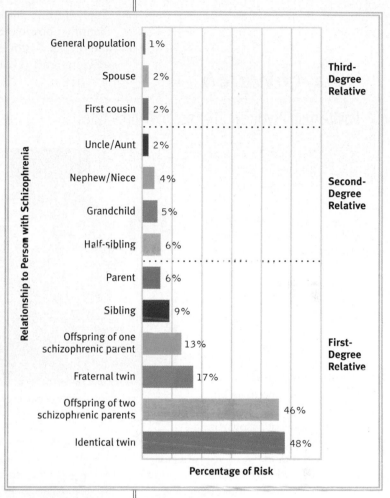

figure 12-2

Family links People who are biologically related to someone with schizophrenia have a heightened risk of developing the disorder during their lifetimes. The closer the biological relationship (that is, the more similar the genetic makeup), the greater the risk of developing the disorder. (Information from: Coon & Mitterer, 2007; Gottesman, 1991, p. 96.)

WHAT DO GENETIC LINKAGE AND MOLECULAR BIOLOGY STUDIES SUGGEST? As with bipolar disorders (see Chapter 6), researchers have run studies of *genetic linkage* and *molecular biology* to pinpoint the possible genetic factors in schizophrenia (Singh et al., 2014). In one approach, they select large families in which schizophrenia is very common, take blood and DNA samples from all members of the families, and then compare gene fragments from members with and without schizophrenia. Applying this procedure to families from around the world, various studies have identified possible gene defects on chromosomes 1, 2, 6, 8, 10, 13, 15, 18, 20, and 22 and on the X chromosome, each of which may help predispose a person to develop schizophrenia (Huang et al., 2014; Müller, 2014).

PsychWatch

Postpartum Psychosis: The Case of Andrea Yates

On the morning of June 20, 2001, the nation's television viewers watched in horror as officials escorted 36-year-old Andrea Yates to a police car. Just minutes before, she had called police and explained that she had drowned her five children in the bathtub because "they weren't developing correctly" and because she "realized [that she had not been] a good mother to them." Homicide sergeant Eric Mehl described how she looked him in the eye, nodded, answered with a polite "Yes, sir" to many of his questions, and twice recounted the order in which the children had died: first 3-year-old Paul, then 2-year-old Luke, followed by 5-year-old John and 6-month-old Mary. She then described how she had had to drag 7-year-old Noah to the bathroom and how he had come up twice as he fought for air. Later she told doctors she wanted her hair shaved so she could see the number 666—the mark of the Antichrist—on her scalp (Roche, 2002).

In Chapter 6 you read that as many as 80 percent of mothers experience "baby blues" soon after giving birth, while between 10 and 30 percent display the clinical syndrome of *postpartum depression*. Yet another postpartum disorder that has become all too familiar to the public in recent times, by way of cases such as that of Andrea Yates, is *postpartum psychosis* (Engqvist et al., 2014).

Postpartum psychosis affects about 1 to 2 of every 1,000 mothers who have

Family tragedy In this undated photograph, Andrea Yates poses with her husband and four of the five children she later drowned.

Photo courtesy of Yates family/Getty Images

recently given birth (Posmontier, 2010). The symptoms apparently are triggered by the enormous shift in hormone levels that takes place after delivery (Meinhard et al., 2014). Within days or at most a few months of childbirth, the woman develops signs of losing touch with reality, such as delusions (for example, she may become convinced that her baby is the devil); hallucinations (perhaps hearing voices); extreme anxiety, confusion, and disorientation; disturbed sleep; and illogical or chaotic thoughts (for example, thoughts about killing herself or her child).

Women with a history of bipolar disorder, schizophrenia, or depression are particularly vulnerable to the disorder (Di Florio et al., 2014). Women who have previously experienced postpartum depression or postpartum psychosis have an increased likelihood of developing postpartum psychosis after subsequent births (Bergink et al., 2012; Nonacs, 2007).

Andrea Yates had developed signs of postpartum depression (and perhaps postpartum psychosis) and had attempted suicide after the birth of her fourth child. At that time, however, she appeared to respond well to a combination of medications, including antipsychotic drugs, and so she and her husband later decided to conceive a fifth child. Although they were warned that she was at risk for serious postpartum symptoms once again, they believed that the same combination of medications would help if the symptoms were to recur (King, 2002).

After the birth of her fifth child, the symptoms did in fact recur, along with features of psychosis. Yates again attempted suicide. Although she was hospitalized twice and treated with various medications, her condition failed to improve. Six months after giving birth to Mary, her fifth child, she drowned all five of her children. Although only a fraction of women with postpartum psychosis actually harm their children (estimates run as high as 4 percent), the Yates case reminds us that such an outcome is possible (Posmontier, 2010) and that early detection and treatment are critical (O'Hara & Wisner, 2014).

On July 26, 2006, after an initial conviction for murder was overturned by an appeals court, Yates was found *not guilty by reason of insanity* and assigned to a state mental hospital, where she continues to receive treatment today.

These varied findings may indicate that some of the suspected gene sites are cases of mistaken identity and do not actually contribute to schizophrenia. Alternatively, it may be that different kinds of schizophrenia are linked to different genes. It is most likely, however, that schizophrenia, like a number of other disorders, is a *polygenic disorder,* caused by a combination of gene defects (Purcell et al., 2014).

How might genetic factors lead to the development of schizophrenia? Research has pointed to two kinds of biological abnormalities that could conceivably be inherited—*biochemical abnormalities* and *abnormal brain structure.*

Biochemical Abnormalities As you have read, the brain is made up of neurons whose electrical impulses (or "messages") are transmitted from one to another by neurotransmitters. After an impulse arrives at a receiving neuron, it travels down the axon of that neuron until it reaches the nerve ending. The nerve ending then releases neurotransmitters that travel across the synaptic space and bind to receptors on yet another neuron, thus relaying the message to the next "station." This neuron activity is known as "firing."

Over the past four decades, researchers have developed a **dopamine hypothesis** to explain their findings on schizophrenia: certain neurons that use the neurotransmitter dopamine fire too often and transmit too many messages, thus producing the symptoms of schizophrenia (Brisch et al., 2014; Düring et al., 2014). This hypothesis has undergone challenges and adjustments in recent years, but it is still the foundation for current biochemical explanations of schizophrenia (Rao & Remington, 2014). As you will see later in this chapter, the chain of events leading to this hypothesis began with the accidental discovery of **antipsychotic drugs,** medications that help remove the symptoms of schizophrenia. The first group of antipsychotic medications, the **phenothiazines,** was discovered in the 1950s by researchers who were looking for better *antihistamine* drugs to combat allergies. Although phenothiazines failed as antihistamines, it soon became obvious that they were effective in reducing schizophrenic symptoms, and clinicians began to prescribe them widely (Adams et al., 2014).

Researchers later learned that these early antipsychotic drugs often produce troublesome muscular tremors, symptoms that are identical to the central symptom of *Parkinson's disease,* a disabling neurological illness. This undesired reaction to antipsychotic drugs offered the first important clue to the biology of schizophrenia. Scientists already knew that people who suffer from Parkinson's disease have abnormally low levels of the neurotransmitter dopamine in some areas of the brain and that lack of dopamine is the reason for their uncontrollable shaking. If antipsychotic drugs produce Parkinsonian symptoms in people with schizophrenia while removing their psychotic symptoms, perhaps the drugs reduce dopamine activity. And, scientists reasoned further, if lowering dopamine activity helps remove the symptoms of schizophrenia, perhaps schizophrenia is related to excessive dopamine activity in the first place.

Since the 1960s, research has supported and helped clarify the dopamine hypothesis. It has been found, for example, that some people with Parkinson's disease develop schizophrenia-like symptoms if they take too much *L-dopa,* a medication that raises Parkinson's patients' dopamine levels (Brunelin et al., 2013). The L-dopa apparently raises the dopamine activity so much that it produces psychosis. Support has also come from research on *amphetamines,* drugs that, as you saw in Chapter 10, stimulate the central nervous system by increasing dopamine in the brain. Clinical investigators have observed that people who take high doses of amphetamines may develop *amphetamine psychosis*—a syndrome very similar to schizophrenia (Hawken & Beninger, 2014; Li et al., 2014).

Researchers have located areas of the brain that are rich in dopamine receptors and have found that phenothiazines and other antipsychotic drugs bind to many of these receptors (Yoshida et al., 2014). Apparently the drugs are dopamine *antagonists*—drugs

Whose Brain Has the Most Neurons?

Human	100,000,000,000 neurons
Octopus	300,000,000 neurons
Rat	21,000,000 neurons
Frog	16,000,000 neurons
Cockroach	1,000,000 neurons
Honey bee	850,000 neurons
Fruit fly	100,000 neurons
Ant	10,000 neurons

▶ **dopamine hypothesis** The theory that schizophrenia results from excessive activity of the neurotransmitter dopamine.

▶ **antipsychotic drugs** Drugs that help correct grossly confused or distorted thinking.

▶ **phenothiazines** A group of antihistamine drugs that became the first group of effective antipsychotic medications.

▸ **second-generation antipsychotic drugs** A relatively new group of antipsychotic drugs whose biological action is different from that of the traditional antipsychotic drugs. Also known as *atypical antipsychotic drugs*.

that bind to dopamine receptors, *prevent* dopamine from binding there, and so prevent the neurons from firing. Researchers have identified five kinds of dopamine receptors in the brain—called the D-1, D-2, D-3, D-4, and D-5 receptors—and have found that phenothiazines bind most strongly to the *D-2 receptors* (Chun et al., 2014).

These and related findings suggest that in schizophrenia, messages traveling from dopamine-sending neurons to dopamine receptors on other neurons, particularly to the D-2 receptors, may be transmitted too easily or too often. This theory is appealing because certain dopamine neurons are known to play a key role in guiding attention (Brisch et al., 2014). People whose attention is severely disturbed by excessive dopamine activity might well be expected to suffer from the problems of attention, perception, and thought found in schizophrenia (see *MindTech*).

MindTech

Can Computers Develop Schizophrenia?

One of the leading explanations for schizophrenia holds that people with this disorder are overwhelmed by the stimuli around them. According to this theory, excessive dopamine floods the brains of people with schizophrenia, leading them to process stimulus information at too high a rate. They are unable to disregard extraneous sensory information, which leads to a process dubbed

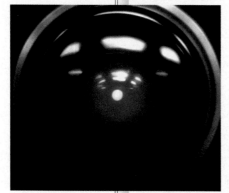

"Dave, my mind is going." These are the words spoken by the brilliant computer HAL (shown at right) to his colleague Dave Bowman, one of the astronauts aboard the Discovery One spacecraft in Stanley Kubrick's movie *2001: A Space Odyssey*.

MGM/Photofest

"hyperlearning." As a result of hyperlearning, people with schizophrenia cannot distinguish between reality and illusion or recognize the barriers between unrelated pieces of information or unrelated experiences (Boyle, 2011).

Researchers in the computer science department at the University of Texas at Austin created a study to test the hyperlearning theory (Hoffman et al., 2011). They built a computer neural network they called DISCERN and programmed it to store information in ways that parallel the ways the human brain organizes words, sentences, and other bits of information into knowledge and memories. The researchers then simulated the effects of a dopamine flood by programming the computer system to process information at a faster and faster rate, while at the same time programming it to ignore less and less data.

The researchers reported that after DISCERN had finished being reprogrammed, it began to display patterns of functioning that were similar to those found in people with schizophrenia. For example, while retelling stories that it had been programmed to recall, DISCERN began to place itself at the center of the retelling, often telling fantastical, delusional stories. In one instance, for example, the computer claimed that it had been responsible for a terrorist bombing. The researchers further found that the computer's delusional stories were similar to those produced by human participants with schizophrenia after they had been given similar pieces of information.

> Can you think of alternative—nonschizophrenic—explanations for the patterns of dysfunction displayed by the computer network DISCERN?

This study may bring to mind the famous film *2001: A Space Odyssey,* in which a computer named "HAL," with the capacity for artificial intelligence, develops a mental disorder when presented with orders that it could not logically reconcile. Of course, HAL's actions in that film still remain the stuff of science fiction, and the University of Texas study provides, at most, limited support for the hyperlearning model of schizophrenia. 💬

Though enlightening, the dopamine hypothesis has certain problems. The biggest challenge to it has come with the relatively recent discovery of a new group of antipsychotic drugs, initially referred to as **atypical antipsychotic drugs** and now called **second-generation antipsychotic drugs,** which are often more effective than the traditional ones. The new drugs bind not only to D-2 dopamine receptors, like the traditional antipsychotic drugs, but also to many D-1 and D-4 receptors and to receptors for other neurotransmitters such as *serotonin* (Waddington et al., 2011). Thus, it may be that schizophrenia is related to abnormal activity or interactions of both dopamine and other neurotransmitters, rather than to abnormal dopamine activity alone (Hashimoto, 2014; Juckel, 2014).

Abnormal Brain Structure During the past decade, researchers have also linked schizophrenia, particularly cases dominated by negative symptoms, to abnormalities in brain structure (Millan et al., 2014; Shinto et al., 2014). Using brain scans, they have found, for example, that many people with schizophrenia have *enlarged ventricles*—the brain cavities that contain cerebrospinal fluid (Hartberg et al., 2011).

It may be that enlarged ventricles are actually a sign that nearby parts of the brain have not developed properly or have been damaged, and perhaps these problems are the ones that help produce schizophrenia. In fact, studies suggest that some patients with schizophrenia also have smaller temporal and frontal lobes than other people, smaller amounts of cortical white and gray matter, and, perhaps most importantly, abnormal blood flow—either reduced or heightened—in certain areas of the brain (Lener et al., 2015; Kochunov & Hong, 2014). Still other studies have linked schizophrenia to abnormalities of the hippocampus, amygdala, and thalamus, among other brain structures (Arnold et al., 2014; Markota et al., 2014) (see Figure 12-3).

Viral Problems What might cause the biochemical and structural abnormalities found in many cases of schizophrenia? Various studies have pointed to genetic factors, poor nutrition, fetal development, birth complications, immune reactions, and toxins (Avramopoulos et al., 2015; Clarke et al., 2012). In addition, some investigators suggest that the brain abnormalities may result from exposure to *viruses* before birth. Perhaps the viruses enter the fetus' brain and interrupt proper brain development, or perhaps the viruses remain quiet until puberty or young adulthood, when, activated by changes in hormones or by another viral infection, they help to bring about schizophrenic symptoms (Brown, 2012; Fox, 2010; Torrey, 2001, 1991).

Some of the evidence for the viral theory comes from animal model investigations, and other evidence is circumstantial, such as the finding that an unusually large number of people with schizophrenia are born during the winter (Patterson, 2012). The winter birth rate among people with schizophrenia is 5 to 8 percent higher than among other people (Harper & Brown, 2012; Tamminga et al., 2008). This could be because of an increase in fetal or infant exposure to viruses at that time of year. More direct evidence comes from studies showing that mothers of people with schizophrenia were more likely to have been exposed to the influenza virus during pregnancy than were mothers of people without schizophrenia (Canetta et al., 2014). And, finally, studies have found antibodies to certain viruses in the blood of 40 percent of research participants with schizophrenia (Leweke et al., 2004; Torrey et al., 1994). The presence of such antibodies suggests that these people had at some time been exposed to those particular viruses.

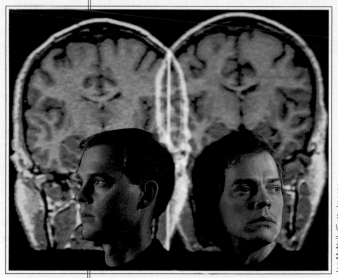

Joe McNally/Getty Images

Not-so-identical twins The man on the left does not have schizophrenia, while his identical twin, on the right, does. Magnetic resonance imaging (MRI), shown in the background, clarifies that the brain of the twin with schizophrenia is smaller overall than his brother's and has larger ventricles, indicated by the dark, butterfly-shaped spaces.

figure 12-3

Biology of schizophrenia Some studies show that people with schizophrenia have relatively small temporal and frontal lobes, as well as abnormalities in brain structures such as the hippocampus, amygdala, and thalamus.

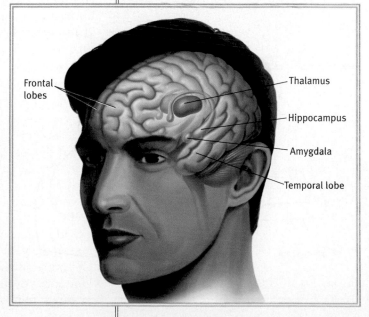

Frontal lobes

Thalamus

Hippocampus

Amygdala

Temporal lobe

Together, the biochemical, brain structure, and viral findings are shedding much light on the mysteries of schizophrenia. At the same time, it is important to recognize that many people who have these biological abnormalities never develop schizophrenia. Why not? Possibly, as you read earlier, because biological factors merely set the stage for schizophrenia, while key psychological and sociocultural factors must be present for the disorder to appear.

Psychological Views

When schizophrenia investigators began to identify genetic and biological factors during the 1950s and 1960s, many clinicians abandoned the psychological theories of the disorder. During recent decades, however, the tables have been turned and psychological factors are once again being considered as important pieces of the schizophrenia puzzle (Green et al., 2014). The most prominent psychological theories come from the psychodynamic and cognitive perspectives.

The Psychodynamic Explanation In the middle of the twentieth century, noted psychodynamic clinician Frieda Fromm-Reichmann (1948) elaborated on an earlier notion by Sigmund Freud (1924, 1915, 1914) that cold or unnurturing parents may set schizophrenia in motion. Fromm-Reichmann described the mothers of people who develop the disorder as cold, domineering, and uninterested in their children's needs. She claimed that these mothers may appear to be self-sacrificing but are actually using their children to meet their own needs. At once overprotective and rejecting, they confuse their children and set the stage for schizophrenic functioning. She called them **schizophrenogenic** (schizophrenia-causing) **mothers**. Fromm-Reichmann's theory has received little research support (Harrington, 2012; Willick, 2001). In fact, the majority of people with schizophrenia do not appear to have mothers who fit the schizophrenogenic description.

> Why have parents and family life so often been blamed for schizophrenia?

The Cognitive Explanation A leading cognitive explanation of schizophrenia is congruent with the biological view that during hallucinations and related perceptual difficulties, the brains of people with schizophrenia are actually producing strange and unreal sensations—sensations triggered by biological factors. According to the cognitive explanation, when people attempt to understand these unusual experiences, more features of their disorder emerge (Howes & Murray, 2014). When first confronted by voices or other troubling sensations, the individuals turn to friends and relatives. Naturally, the friends and relatives deny the reality of the sensations, and eventually the sufferers conclude that the others are trying to hide the truth. They begin to reject all feedback, and some develop beliefs (delusions) that they are being persecuted (Howes & Murray, 2014). In short, according to this theory, people with schizophrenia take a "rational path to madness" (Zimbardo, 1976). This process of drawing incorrect and bizarre conclusions (delusions) may be helped along by a cognitive bias that many people with schizophrenia have—a tendency to jump to conclusions (Sarin & Wallin, 2014).

Researchers have established that people with schizophrenia do indeed experience sensory and perceptual problems. As you saw earlier, many have hallucinations and most have trouble keeping their attention focused. But researchers have yet to provide clear, direct support for the cognitive notion that misinterpretations of such sensory problems actually produce a syndrome of schizophrenia.

"And only you can hear this whistle?"

Sociocultural Views

Sociocultural theorists, recognizing that people with mental disorders are subject to a wide range of social and cultural forces, believe that *multicultural factors, social labeling,* and *family dysfunctioning* all contribute to schizophrenia. Research has yet to clarify what the precise causal relationships might be.

Multicultural Factors Rates of schizophrenia appear to differ between racial and ethnic groups, particularly between African Americans and white Americans (Singh & Kunar, 2010). As many as 2.1 percent of African Americans receive a diagnosis of schizophrenia, compared with around 1.4 percent of white Americans (Lawson, 2008; Folsom et al., 2006). Similarly, studies suggest that African Americans with schizophrenia are overrepresented in state hospitals (Durbin et al., 2014; Barnes, 2004). For example, in Tennessee's state hospitals, 48 percent of those with a diagnosis of schizophrenia are African American, although only 16 percent of the state population is African American.

It is not clear why African Americans are more likely than white Americans to receive this diagnosis. One possibility is that African Americans are more prone to develop schizophrenia. Another is that clinicians from majority groups are unintentionally biased in their diagnoses of African Americans or misread cultural differences as symptoms of schizophrenia.

Yet another explanation for the difference between African Americans and white Americans may lie in the economic sphere. On average, African Americans are more likely than white Americans to be poor; when economic differences are controlled for, the prevalence rates of schizophrenia become closer for the two racial groups. Consistent with the economic explanation is the finding that Hispanic Americans, who also tend to be economically disadvantaged, appear to be much more likely to be diagnosed with schizophrenia than white Americans, although their diagnostic rate is not as high as that of African Americans (Blow et al., 2004).

> **How might bias by diagnosticians contribute to race-linked and culture-linked differences in the diagnosis of schizophrenia?**

It also appears that schizophrenia differs from country to country in key ways (Johnson et al., 2014; McLean et al., 2014). Although the overall prevalence of this disorder is stable—around 1 percent—in countries across the world, the *course* and *outcome* of the disorder may vary considerably. According to a 10-country study conducted by the World Health Organization (WHO), the 25 million schizophrenic patients who live in *developing* countries have better recovery rates than schizophrenic patients in Western and other *developed* countries (Vahia & Vahia, 2008; Jablensky, 2000). During the course of the two-year study, the schizophrenic patients from developing countries (Columbia, India, and Nigeria) were more likely than those in developed countries (the Czech Republic, Denmark, Ireland, Japan, Russia, the United Kingdom, and the United States) to recover from their disorder and less likely to have continuous symptoms, impaired social functioning, or require heavy antipsychotic drugs or hospitalization.

Some theorists believe that the psychosocial environments of developing countries tend to be more supportive and therapeutic than those of developed countries, leading to more favorable outcomes for people with schizophrenia (Vahia & Vahia, 2008; Jablensky, 2000). In developing countries, for example, there may be more

Silvia Izquierdo/AP Photo

Coming together Different countries and cultures each have their own way of viewing and interacting with schizophrenic people and those with other mental disturbances. Here patients and members of the community come together and dance during the annual Carnival parade in front of the Psychiatric Institute in Rio de Janeiro, Brazil.

▶ **schizophrenogenic mother** A type of mother—supposedly cold, domineering, and uninterested in the needs of her children—who was once thought to cause schizophrenia in her child.

What's in a name? The British band Madness entertains an audience in Italy in 2012, just as they have entertained millions of fans during their four decades of performing. Some social critics worry that band names like Madness, Bad Brains, the Insane Clown Posse, the Schizos, and Bark Psychosis serve to trivialize or romanticize the plight of people with schizophrenia and other psychotic disorders.

family and social support for people with schizophrenia; more relatives and friends available to help care for such people; and less judgmental, critical, and hostile attitudes toward people with schizophrenia. The Nigerian culture, for example, is generally more tolerant of the presence of voices than are Western cultures (Matsumoto & Juang, 2008).

Social Labeling Many sociocultural theorists believe that the features of schizophrenia are influenced by the diagnosis itself. In their opinion, society assigns the label "schizophrenic" to people who fail to conform to certain norms of behavior. Once the label is assigned, justified or not, it becomes a self-fulfilling prophecy that promotes the development of many schizophrenic symptoms (Omori, Mori, & White, 2014).

We have already seen the very real dangers of diagnostic labeling. In the famous Rosenhan (1973) study, discussed in Chapter 2, eight normal people presented themselves at various mental hospitals, complaining that they had been hearing voices utter the words "empty," "hollow," and "thud." They were quickly diagnosed as schizophrenic, and all eight were hospitalized. Although the pseudopatients then dropped all symptoms and behaved normally, they had great difficulty getting rid of the label and gaining release from the hospital.

The pseudopatients reported that staff members were authoritarian in their behaviors toward patients and also treated them as though they were invisible. "A nurse unbuttoned her uniform to adjust her brassiere in the presence

> **What kinds of ethical, legal, and therapeutic concerns does Rosenhan's study raise?**

of an entire ward of viewing men. One did not have the sense that she was being seductive. Rather, she didn't notice us." In addition, the pseudopatients described feeling powerless, bored, tired, and uninterested. The deceptive design and possible implications of this study have aroused the emotions of clinicians and researchers, pro and con. The investigation does demonstrate, however, that the label "schizophrenic" can itself have a negative effect not just on how people are viewed but also on how they themselves feel and behave.

Family Dysfunctioning Many studies suggest that schizophrenia, like a number of other mental disorders, is often linked to *family stress* (Cullen et al., 2014; Quah, 2014). Parents of people with schizophrenia often (1) display more conflict, (2) have more difficulty communicating with one another, and (3) are more critical of and overinvolved with their children than other parents.

Family theorists have long recognized that some families are high in **expressed emotion**—that is, members frequently express criticism, disapproval, and hostility toward each other and intrude on one another's privacy. People who are trying to recover from schizophrenia are almost four times more likely to relapse if they live with such a family than if they live with one low in expressed emotion (Koutra et al., 2015; Okpokoro et al., 2014). Do such findings mean that family dysfunctioning helps cause and maintain schizophrenia? Not necessarily. It is also the case that people with schizophrenia greatly disrupt family life (Friedrich et al., 2015). In so doing, they themselves may help produce the family problems that clinicians and researchers continue to observe (Hsiao et al., 2014).

"Bad news—we're all out of our minds. You're going to have to be the lone healthy person in this family."

Although the sociocultural causes of schizophrenia, like the psychological causes, have yet to be fully understood, many clinicians currently believe that such factors play an important role in the disorder. As you have seen, most hold a diathesis–stress view of schizophrenia, believing that biological factors set up a predisposition to the disorder, but that certain kinds of personal, family, or social stress are further needed for the syndrome to spring to life.

▸ **expressed emotion** The general level of criticism, disapproval, and hostility expressed in a family. People recovering from schizophrenia are considered more likely to relapse if their families rate high in expressed emotion.

➤ *Summing Up*

HOW DO THEORISTS EXPLAIN SCHIZOPHRENIA? The biological explanations of schizophrenia point to genetic, biochemical, structural, and viral causes. The genetic view is supported by studies of relatives, twins, adoptees, genetic linkage, and molecular biology. The leading biochemical explanation holds that the brains of people with schizophrenia experience excessive dopamine activity. Brain-imaging techniques have also detected abnormal brain structures in many people with schizophrenia. Finally, some researchers believe that schizophrenia is related to a virus that settles in the fetus.

The most prominent psychological explanations for schizophrenia come from the psychodynamic and cognitive models. In a once-influential psychodynamic explanation, Fromm-Reichmann proposed that schizophrenogenic mothers help produce schizophrenia. Cognitive theorists hold that when people with schizophrenia try to understand their strange biological sensations, they develop delusional thinking.

One sociocultural explanation holds that multicultural differences may influence the rate and character of schizophrenia, as well as recovery from this disorder, both within the United States and around the world. Another sociocultural explanation says that society expects people who are labeled as having schizophrenia to behave in certain ways and that these expectations actually lead to further symptoms. Still other sociocultural theorists point to family dysfunctioning as a cause of schizophrenia.

Most clinical theorists now agree that schizophrenia can be traced to a combination of biological, psychological, and sociocultural factors, operating in a diathesis-stress relationship.

How Are Schizophrenia and Other Severe Mental Disorders Treated?

Today's treatment picture for schizophrenia and other severe mental disorders is marked by miraculous triumphs for some, modest success for others, and heartbreaking failure for still others. It is typically characterized by medications, medication–linked health problems, compromised lifestyles, and a mixture of hope and frustration. Despite this, today's treatment outlook is vastly superior to that of past years. In fact, for much of human history, people with such disorders were considered beyond help. Few returned to any semblance of normal or functional living. Indeed, few returned home from the institutions to which they were sent.

Let us look at the case of Cathy, whose journey is typical of that of hundreds of thousands of people with schizophrenia and other severe mental disorders. To be sure, there are other patients whose efforts to overcome schizophrenia go more smoothly. And at the other end of the spectrum, there are many whose struggles against severe mental dysfunctioning never come close to Cathy's level of success. In between, there are the Cathys.

////// BETWEEN THE LINES //////

Treatment Delay

The average length of time between the first appearance of psychotic symptoms and the initiation of treatment is more than one year (Addington et al., 2015).

During [her] second year in college . . . her emotional troubles worsened. . . . and [Cathy was] put on Haldol and lithium.

For the next sixteen years, Cathy cycled in and out of hospitals. She "hated the meds"—Haldol stiffened her muscles and caused her to drool, while the lithium made her depressed—and often she would abruptly stop taking them. . . . The problem was that off the drugs, she would "start to decompensate and become disorganized."

In early 1994, she was hospitalized for the fifteenth time. She was seen as chronically mentally ill, occasionally heard voices now . . . and was on a cocktail of drugs: Haldol, Ativan, Tegretol, Halcion, and Cogentin, the last drug an antidote to Haldol's nasty side effects. But after she was released that spring, a psychiatrist told her to try Risperdal, a new antipsychotic that had just been approved by the FDA. "Three weeks later, my mind was much clearer," she says. "The voices were going away. I got off the other meds and took only this one drug. I got better. I could start to plan. I wasn't talking to the devil anymore. Jesus and God weren't battling it out in my head." Her father put it this way: "Cathy is back." . . .

She went back to school and earned a degree in radio, film, and television. . . . In 1998, she began dating the man she lives with today. . . . In 2005, she took a part-time job. . . . Still, she remains on SSDI (Social Security Disability Insurance)— "I am a kept woman," she jokes—and although there are many reasons for that, she believes that Risperdal, the very drug that has helped her so much, nevertheless has proven to be a barrier to full-time work. Although she is usually energetic by the early afternoon, Risperdal makes her so sleepy that she has trouble getting up in the morning. . . .

Risperdal has also taken a physical toll. . . . She has . . . developed some of the metabolic problems, such as high cholesterol, that the atypical antipsychotics regularly cause. "I can go toe-to-toe with an old lady with a recital of my physical problems," she says. "My feet, my bladder, my heart, my sinuses, the weight gain— I have it all." . . . But she can't do well without Risperdal. . . .

Such has been her life's course on medications. Sixteen terrible years, followed by fourteen pretty good years on Risperdal. She believes that this drug is essential to her mental health today, and indeed, she could be seen as a local poster child for promoting the wonders of that drug. Still, if you look at the long-term course of her illness . . . you have to ask: Is hers a story of a life made better by our drug-based . . . care for mental disorders, or a story of a life made worse? . . .

Cathy believes that this is a question that psychiatrists never contemplate.

"They don't have any sense about how these drugs affect you over the long term. They just try to stabilize you for the moment, and look to manage you from week to week, month to month. That's all they ever think about."

(Whitaker, 2010)

As Cathy's journey illustrates, schizophrenia is extremely difficult to treat, but clinicians are much more successful at doing so today than they were in the past. Much of the credit goes to *antipsychotic drugs*—imperfect, troubling, and even dangerous though they may be. These medications help many people with schizophrenia and other psychotic disorders to think clearly and to profit from psychotherapies that previously would have had little effect for them (Skelton et al., 2015; Miller et al., 2012).

To best convey the plight of people with schizophrenia, this chapter will depart from the usual format and discuss the treatments from a historical perspective. A look at how treatment has changed over the years will help us understand the nature, problems, and promise of today's approaches. As we consider past treatments for schizophrenia, it is important to keep in mind that throughout much of the twentieth century the label "schizophrenia" was assigned to most people with psychosis. Clinical theorists now realize that many people with psychotic symptoms are instead

▶ **state hospitals** Public mental hospitals in the United States, run by the individual states.

experiencing a severe form of bipolar disorder or major depressive disorder and that such people were in past times inaccurately diagnosed with schizophrenia (Tondo et al., 2015; Lake, 2012). Thus, our discussions of past treatments for schizophrenia, particularly the failures of institutional care, are as applicable to those other severe mental disorders as they are to schizophrenia. Similarly, our discussions about current approaches to schizophrenia, such as the community mental health movement, often apply to other severe mental disorders as well.

Institutional Care in the Past

For more than half of the twentieth century, most people diagnosed with schizophrenia were *institutionalized* in a public mental hospital. Because patients with schizophrenia did not respond to traditional therapies, the primary goals of these hospitals were to restrain them and give them food, shelter, and clothing. Patients rarely saw therapists and generally were neglected. Many were abused. Oddly enough, this state of affairs unfolded in an atmosphere of good intentions.

As you read in Chapter 1, the move toward institutionalization in hospitals began in 1793 when French physician Philippe Pinel "unchained the insane" at La Bicêtre asylum and began the practice of "moral treatment." For the first time in centuries, patients with severe disturbances were viewed as human beings who should be cared for with sympathy and kindness. As Pinel's ideas spread throughout Europe and the United States, they led to the creation of large mental hospitals rather than asylums to care for those with severe mental disorders (Goshen, 1967).

These new mental hospitals, typically located in isolated areas where land and labor were cheap, were meant to protect patients from the stresses of daily life and offer them a healthful psychological environment in which they could work closely with therapists (Grob, 1966). States throughout the United States were even required by law to establish public mental institutions, **state hospitals**, for patients who could not afford private ones.

Eventually, however, the state hospital system encountered serious problems. Between 1845 and 1955, nearly 300 state hospitals opened in the United States, and the number of hospitalized patients on any given day rose from 2,000 in 1845 to nearly 600,000 in 1955. During this expansion, wards became overcrowded, admissions kept rising, and state funding was unable to keep up.

Greg Wahl-Stephens/AP Photo

A graphic reminder During the 1800s and 1900s, tens of thousands of patients with severe mental disorders were abandoned by their families and spent the rest of their lives in the back wards of the public mental institutions. We are reminded of their tragic situation by the numerous brass urns filled with unclaimed ashes currently stored in a building at Oregon State Hospital.

© John Stanmeyer/VII/Corbis

Institutional life In a scene reminiscent of public mental hospitals in the United States during the first half of the twentieth century, these patients spend their days crowded together on a hospital ward in central Shanghai. Because of a shortage of therapists, only a small fraction of Chinese people with psychological disorders receive proper professional care today.

▶ **milieu therapy** A humanistic approach to institutional treatment based on the premise that institutions can help patients recover by creating a climate that promotes self-respect, responsible behavior, and meaningful activity.

▶ **token economy program** A behavioral program in which a person's desirable behaviors are reinforced systematically throughout the day by the awarding of tokens that can be exchanged for goods or privileges.

The priorities of the public mental hospitals, and the quality of care they provided, changed over those 110 years. In the face of overcrowding and understaffing, the emphasis shifted from giving humanitarian care to keeping order. In a throwback to the asylum period, difficult patients were restrained, isolated, and punished; individual attention disappeared. Patients were transferred to *back wards,* or chronic wards, if they failed to improve quickly (Bloom, 1984). Most of the patients on these wards suffered from schizophrenia (Häfner & an der Heiden, 1988). The back wards were human warehouses filled with hopelessness. Staff members relied on straitjackets and handcuffs to deal with difficult patients. More "advanced" forms of treatment included medical approaches such as *lobotomy* (see *PsychWatch* on the next page). Many patients not only failed to improve under these conditions but also developed additional symptoms, apparently as a result of institutionalization itself.

> **Why have people with schizophrenia so often been victims of horrific treatments such as overcrowded wards, lobotomy, and, later, deinstitutionalization?**

Institutional Care Takes a Turn for the Better

In the 1950s, clinicians developed two institutional approaches that finally brought some hope to patients who had lived in institutions for years: *milieu therapy,* based on humanistic principles, and the *token economy program,* based on behavioral principles. These approaches particularly helped improve the personal care and self-image of patients, problem areas that had been worsened by institutionalization. The approaches were soon adapted by many institutions and are now standard features of institutional care.

Milieu Therapy In 1953, Maxwell Jones, a London psychiatrist, converted a ward of patients with various psychological disorders into a therapeutic community—the first application of **milieu therapy** in a hospital setting. The premise of milieu therapy is that institutions can help patients by creating a social climate, or milieu, that promotes productive activity, self-respect, and individual responsibility. In such settings, patients are often given the right to run their own lives and make their own decisions. They may participate in community government, working with staff members to set up rules and decide penalties. Patients may also take on special projects, jobs, and recreational activities. In short, their daily schedule is designed to resemble life outside the hospital.

Since Jones' pioneering effort, milieu-style programs have since been set up in institutions throughout the Western world. The programs vary from setting to setting, but at a minimum, staff members try to encourage interactions (especially group interactions) between patients and staff, to keep patients active, and to raise their expectations about what they can accomplish.

Research over the years has shown that people with schizophrenia and other severe mental disorders in milieu hospital programs often improve and that they leave the hospital at higher rates than patients in programs offering primarily custodial care (Paul, 2000; Paul & Lentz, 1977). Many remain impaired, however, and must live in sheltered settings after their release. Despite its limitations, milieu therapy continues to be practiced in many institutions, often combined with other hospital approaches (Borge et al., 2013). Moreover, you will see later in this chapter that

Art that heals Art and other creative activities can be therapeutic for people with severe mental disorders. Here, artist William Scott paints a San Francisco cityscape at the Creative Growth Art Center in California. Scott, who has been diagnosed with schizophrenia and autism, sells paintings and sculptures around the world.

AP Photo/Paul Sakuma

PsychWatch

Lobotomy: How Could It Happen?

In 1935, a Portuguese neurologist named Egas Moniz performed a revolutionary new surgical procedure, which he called a *prefrontal leucotomy*, on a patient with severe mental dysfunctioning (Raz, 2013). The procedure, the first form of *lobotomy*, consisted of drilling two holes in either side of the skull and inserting an instrument resembling an ice-pick into the brain tissue to cut or destroy nerve fibers. Moniz believed that severe abnormal thinking—such as that on display in schizophrenia, depression, and obsessive-compulsive disorder—was the result of nerve pathways that carried such thoughts from one part of the brain to another. By cutting these pathways, Moniz believed, he could stop the abnormal thinking in its tracks and restore normal mental functioning.

After Moniz published a monograph describing 20 leucotomies that he had performed, an American neurologist, Walter Freeman, called the procedure to the attention of the medical community in the United States and performed it on many patients (Raz, 2013). In 1947 Freeman further developed a second kind of lobotomy called the *transorbital lobotomy*, in which the surgeon inserted a needle into the brain through the eye socket and rotated it in order to destroy the brain tissue.

From the early 1940s through the mid-1950s, the lobotomy was viewed as a miracle cure by most doctors and became a mainstream part of psychiatry (Levinson, 2011). An estimated 50,000 people in the United States alone eventually received lobotomies (Johnson, 2005).

We now know that the lobotomy was hardly a miracle treatment. Far from

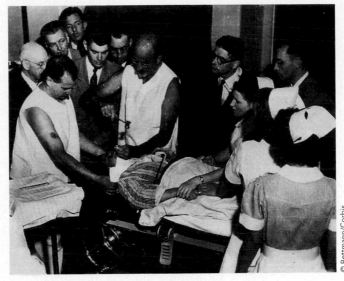

Lessons in psychosurgery Neuropsychiatrist Walter Freeman performs a lobotomy in 1949 before a group of interested onlookers by inserting a needle through a patient's eye socket into the brain.

"curing" people with mental disorders, the procedure left thousands upon thousands extremely withdrawn, subdued, and even stuporous. Why then was the procedure so enthusiastically accepted by the medical community in the 1940s and 1950s? Neuroscientist Elliot Valenstein (1986) points first to the extreme overcrowding in mental hospitals at the time. This crowding was making it difficult to maintain decent standards in the hospitals. Valenstein also points to the personalities of the inventors of the procedure as important factors. Although they were highly regarded, gifted, and dedicated physicians—in 1949 Moniz was awarded the Nobel Prize for his work—Valenstein believes that their professional ambitions led them to move too quickly in applying the procedure.

For years, physicians throughout the world were apparently misled by the seemingly positive findings of early studies of the lobotomy, which, as it turned out, were not based on sound methodology (Cooper, 2014). By the 1950s, however, better studies revealed that in addition to having a fatality rate of 1.5 to 6 percent, lobotomies could cause serious problems such as brain seizures, huge weight gain, loss of motor coordination, partial paralysis, incontinence, endocrine malfunctions, and very poor intellectual and emotional responsiveness (Lapidus et al., 2013). The discovery of effective antipsychotic drugs helped put an end to this inhumane treatment for mental disorders (Krack et al., 2010).

Today's psychosurgical procedures are greatly refined, used only as a last resort for various severe disorders, and hardly resemble the lobotomies of 60 years back (Nair et al., 2014; Lapidus et al., 2013). Even so, many professionals believe that any kind of surgery that destroys brain tissue is inappropriate and perhaps unethical and that it keeps alive one of the clinical field's most shameful and ill-advised efforts at cure.

---

many of today's halfway houses and other community programs for people with severe mental disorders apply the principles of milieu therapy.

The Token Economy In the 1950s, behaviorists discovered that the systematic use of *operant conditioning* techniques on hospital wards could help change the behaviors of patients (Ayllon, 1963; Ayllon & Michael, 1959). Programs that apply these techniques are called **token economy programs**.

In token economies, patients are rewarded when they behave acceptably and are not rewarded when they behave unacceptably. The immediate rewards for acceptable behavior are often tokens that can later be exchanged for food, cigarettes, hospital privileges, and other desirable items, all of which compose a "token economy." Acceptable behaviors likely to be included are caring for oneself and for one's possessions (making the bed, getting dressed), going to a work program, speaking normally, following ward rules, and showing self-control. Researchers have found that token economies do help reduce psychotic and related behaviors (Swartz et al., 2012; Dickerson et al., 2005).

Some clinicians have questioned the quality of the improvements made under token economy programs. Are behaviorists changing a patient's psychotic thoughts and perceptions or simply improving the patient's ability to *imitate* normal behavior? This issue is illustrated by the case of a middle-aged man named John, who had the delusion that he was the U.S. government. Whenever he spoke, he spoke as the government. "We are happy to see you. . . . We need people like you in our service. . . . We are carrying out our activities in John's body." When John's hospital ward converted to using a token economy, the staff members targeted his delusional statements and required him to identify himself properly to earn tokens. After a few months on the token economy program, John stopped referring to himself as the government. When asked his name, he would say, "John." Although staff members were understandably pleased with his improvement, John himself had a different view of the situation. In a private discussion he said:

> We're tired of it. Every damn time we want a cigarette, we have to go through their bullshit. "What's your name? Who wants the cigarette? Where is the government?" Today, we were desperate for a smoke and went to Simpson, the damn nurse, and she made us do her bidding. "Tell me your name if you want a cigarette. What's your name?" Of course, we said, "John." We needed the cigarettes. If we told her the truth, no cigarettes. But we don't have time for this nonsense. We've got business to do, international business, laws to change, people to recruit. And these people keep playing their games.
>
> *(Comer, 1973)*

Critics of the behavioral approach would argue that John was still delusional and therefore as psychotic as before. Behaviorists, however, would argue that at the very least, John's judgment about the consequences of his behavior had improved.

Token economy programs are no longer as popular as they once were, but they are still used in many mental hospitals, usually along with medication, and in many community residences as well (Kopelowicz et al., 2008). The approach has also been applied to other clinical problems, including intellectual disability, delinquency, and hyperactivity, as well as in other fields, such as education and business (Spiegler & Guevremont, 2015).

Antipsychotic Drugs

Milieu therapy and token economy programs helped improve the gloomy outlook for patients diagnosed with schizophrenia, but it was the discovery of *antipsychotic drugs* in the 1950s that truly revolutionized treatment for schizophrenia. These drugs eliminate many of its symptoms and today are almost always a part of treatment.

As you read earlier, the discovery of antipsychotic medications dates back to the 1940s, when researchers developed the first antihistamine drugs to combat allergies. The French surgeon Henri Laborit soon discovered that one group of antihistamines, *phenothiazines,* could also be used to help calm patients about to undergo surgery. Laborit suspected that the drugs might also have a calming effect on people with severe psychological disorders. One of the drugs, *chlorpromazine*, was eventually tested on six patients with psychotic symptoms and found to reduce their symptoms sharply. In 1954, chlorpromazine was approved for sale in the United States as an antipsychotic drug under the trade name Thorazine (Adams et al., 2014).

Since the discovery of the phenothiazines, other kinds of antipsychotic drugs have been developed. The ones developed throughout the 1960s, 1970s, and 1980s are now referred to as *"conventional" antipsychotic drugs* in order to distinguish them from the *"second-generation" antipsychotics* (also called *"atypical" antipsychotic drugs*) that have been developed in more recent decades. The conventional drugs are also known as **neuroleptic drugs** because they often produce undesired movement effects similar to the symptoms of neurological diseases. As you saw earlier, the conventional drugs reduce psychotic symptoms at least in part by blocking excessive activity of the neurotransmitter *dopamine,* particularly at the brain's dopamine D-2 receptors (Chun et al., 2014; Düring et al., 2014).

How Effective Are Antipsychotic Drugs?

Research has shown that antipsychotic drugs reduce symptoms in at least 65 percent of patients diagnosed with schizophrenia (Advokat et al., 2014; Geddes et al., 2011). Moreover, in direct comparisons the drugs appear to be a more effective treatment for schizophrenia than any of the other approaches used alone, such as psychotherapy, milieu therapy, or electroconvulsive therapy. In most cases, the drugs produce at least some improvement within weeks (Rabinowitz et al., 2014); however, symptoms may return if the patients stop taking the drugs too soon (Razali & Yusoff, 2014). The antipsychotic drugs, particularly the conventional ones, reduce the positive symptoms of schizophrenia (such as hallucinations and delusions) more completely, or at least more quickly, than the negative symptoms (such as restricted affect, poverty of speech, and loss of volition) (Millan et al., 2014; Stroup et al., 2012).

The Unwanted Effects of Conventional Antipsychotic Drugs

In addition to reducing psychotic symptoms, the conventional antipsychotic drugs sometimes produce disturbing movement problems (Kinon et al., 2014; Stroup et al., 2012). These effects are called **extrapyramidal effects** because they appear

▶ **neuroleptic drugs** Conventional antipsychotic drugs, so called because they often produce undesired effects similar to the symptoms of neurological disorders.

▶ **extrapyramidal effects** Unwanted movements, such as severe shaking, bizarre-looking grimaces, twisting of the body, and extreme restlessness, sometimes produced by conventional antipsychotic drugs.

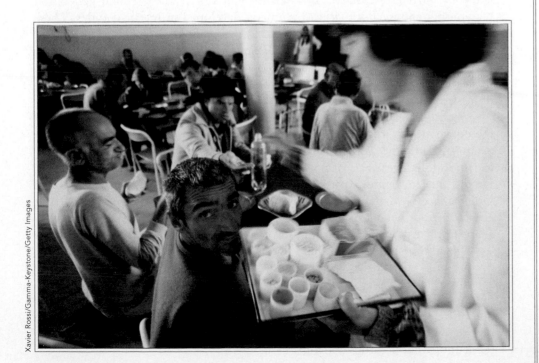

Xavier Rossi/Gamma-Keystone/Getty Images

The drug revolution Since the 1950s, medications have become a central part of treatment for patients with schizophrenia and other severe mental disorders. The medications have resulted in shorter hospitalizations that last weeks rather than years.

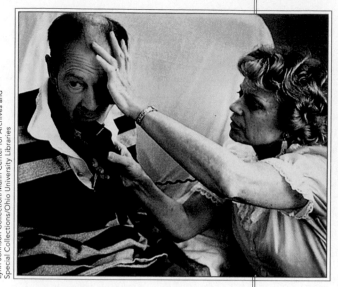

Unwanted effects This man has a severe case of Parkinson's disease, a disorder caused by low dopamine activity, and his muscle tremors prevent him from shaving himself. The conventional antipsychotic drugs often produce similar Parkinsonian symptoms.

table: **12-3**

Some Antipsychotic Drugs

Generic Name	Trade Name
Conventional antipsychotics	
Chlorpromazine	Thorazine
Trifluoperazine	Stelazine
Fluphenazine	Prolixin, Permitil
Perphenazine	Trilafon
Acetophenazine	Tindal
Chlorprothixene	Taractan
Thiothixene	Navane
Haloperidol	Haldol
Loxapine	Loxitane
Molindone hydrochloride	Moban, Lidone
Pimozide	Orap
Second-generation antipsychotics	
Risperidone	Risperdal
Clozapine	Clozaril
Olanzapine	Zyprexa
Quetiapine	Seroquel
Ziprasidone	Geodon
Aripiprazole	Abilify
Iloperidone	Fanapt
Lurasidone	Latuda
Paliperidone	Invega

to be caused by the drugs' impact on the extrapyramidal areas of the brain, areas that help control motor activity.

The most common extrapyramidal effects are *Parkinsonian symptoms,* reactions that closely resemble the features of the neurological disorder Parkinson's disease. At least half of patients on conventional antipsychotic drugs have muscle tremors and muscle rigidity at some point in their treatment; they may shake, move slowly, shuffle their feet, and show little facial expression (Geddes et al., 2011; Haddad & Mattay, 2011). Some also have related symptoms such as movements of the face, neck, tongue, and back; and a number experience significant restlessness and discomfort in their limbs.

Whereas most undesired drug effects appear within days or weeks, a reaction called **tardive dyskinesia** (meaning "late-appearing movement disorder") does not usually unfold until after a person has taken conventional antipsychotic drugs for more than a year (Tenback et al., 2015; Advokat et al., 2014). This reaction may include involuntary writhing or ticlike movements of the tongue, mouth, face, or whole body; involuntary chewing, sucking, and lip smacking; and jerky movements of the arms, legs, or entire body. It is believed that more than 10 percent of the people who take conventional antipsychotic drugs for an extended time develop tardive dyskinesia to some degree, and the longer the drugs are taken, the higher the risk becomes (Achalia, 2014). Patients over 50 years of age seem to be at greater risk. Tardive dyskinesia can be difficult, sometimes impossible, to eliminate (Combs et al., 2008).

Today clinicians are more knowledgeable and more cautious about prescribing conventional antipsychotic drugs than they were in the past (see Table 12–3). Previously, when patients did not improve with such a drug, their clinician would keep increasing the dose; today a clinician will typically add an additional drug to achieve a synergistic effect, stop the drug and try an alternative one, or stop all medications (Li et al., 2014; Roh et al., 2014). Today's clinicians also try to prescribe the lowest effective doses for each patient and to gradually reduce medications weeks or months after the patient begins functioning normally (Takeuchi et al., 2014).

Newer Antipsychotic Drugs As you read earlier, second-generation ("atypical") antipsychotic drugs have been developed in recent decades. These include *clozapine* (trade name Clozaril), *risperidone* (Risperdal), *olanzapine* (Zyprexa), *quetiapine* (Seroquel), *ziprasidone* (Geodon), and *aripiprazole* (Abilify). As noted earlier, these drugs are received at fewer dopamine D-2 receptors and more D-1, D-4, and serotonin receptors than the conventional antipsychotic drugs (Advokat et al., 2014; Nord & Farde, 2011).

Second-generation antipsychotic drugs appear to be more effective than the conventional drugs (Advokat et al., 2014; Bianchini et al., 2014). Recall, for example, Cathy, the woman whom we met earlier, and how well she responded to risperidone after years of doing poorly on conventional antipsychotic drugs. Unlike the conventional drugs, the new drugs reduce not only the positive symptoms of schizophrenia, but also the negative ones (Millan et al., 2014). Another major benefit of the second-generation antipsychotic drugs is that they cause fewer extrapyramidal symptoms and seem less likely to produce tardive dyskinesia, although some of them produce significant undesired effects of their own (Young et al., 2015; Waddington et al., 2011).

Given such advantages, more than half of all medicated patients with schizophrenia now take the second-generation drugs, which are considered the first line of treatment for the disorder (Barnes & Marder, 2011). Many patients with bipolar or other severe mental disorders also seem to be helped by several of these antipsychotic drugs (Advokat et al., 2014).

Psychotherapy

Before the discovery of antipsychotic drugs, psychotherapy was not really an option for people with schizophrenia. Most were too far removed from reality to profit from it. Today, however, psychotherapy is helpful to many such patients (Miller et al., 2012). By helping to relieve thought and perceptual disturbances, antipsychotic drugs allow many people with schizophrenia to learn about their disorder, participate actively in therapy (see *MindTech* on the next page), think more clearly, make changes in their behavior, and cope with stressors in their lives. The most helpful forms of psychotherapy include cognitive-behavioral therapy and two sociocultural interventions—family therapy and social therapy. Often the various approaches are combined.

Cognitive-Behavioral Therapy

As you read earlier, the cognitive explanation for schizophrenia starts with the premise that people with the disorder do indeed actually hear voices (or experience other kinds of hallucinations) as a result of biologically triggered sensations. According to this theory, the journey into schizophrenia takes shape when people try to make sense of these strange sensations and conclude incorrectly that the voices are coming from external sources, that they are being persecuted, or another such notion. These misinterpretations are essentially delusions.

With this explanation in mind, an increasing number of clinicians now employ a cognitive-behavioral treatment for schizophrenia that seeks to help change how people view and react to their hallucinations (Howes & Murray, 2014; Naeem et al., 2014). The therapists believe that if people can be guided to interpret such experiences in a more accurate way, they will not suffer the fear and confusion produced by their delusional misinterpretations. Thus, the therapists use a combination of behavioral and cognitive techniques:

1. They provide clients with education and evidence about the biological causes of hallucinations.

2. They help clients learn more about the "comings and goings" of their own hallucinations and delusions. The clients learn, for example, to identify which kinds of events and situations trigger the voices in their heads.

3. The therapists challenge their clients' inaccurate ideas about the power of their hallucinations, such as the idea that the voices are all-powerful and uncontrollable and must be obeyed. The therapists also have the clients conduct behavioral experiments to put such notions to the test. What happens, for example, if the clients occasionally resist following the orders from their hallucinatory voices?

4. The therapists teach clients to more accurately interpret their hallucinations. Clients may, for example, adopt alternative conclusions such as, "It's not a real voice, it's my illness."

5. The therapists teach clients techniques for coping with their unpleasant sensations (hallucinations). The clients may, for example, learn ways to reduce the physical arousal that accompanies hallucinations—using special breathing and relaxation techniques and the like. Similarly, they may learn to distract themselves whenever the hallucinations occur (Veiga-Martínez et al., 2008).

These behavioral and cognitive techniques often help schizophrenic people feel more control over their hallucinations and reduce their delusional ideas. Can anything be done further to lessen the hallucinations' unpleasant impact on the person? Yes, say *new-wave cognitive-behavioral therapists,* including practitioners of *acceptance and commitment therapy.*

▶ **tardive dyskinesia** Extrapyramidal effects involving involuntary movements that some patients have after they have taken conventional antipsychotic drugs for an extended time.

As you read in Chapters 2 and 4, new-wave cognitive-behavioral therapists believe that the most useful goal of treatment is often to help clients *accept* their streams of problematic thoughts rather than to judge them, act on them, or try fruitlessly to change them. The therapists, for example, help individuals with anxiety disorders to become *mindful* of the worries that engulf their thinking and to *accept* such negative thoughts as but harmless events of the mind (see pages 114–115). Similarly, in cases of schizophrenia, new-wave cognitive-behavioral therapists try to help clients become detached and comfortable observers of their hallucinations—merely mindful of the unusual sensations and accepting of them—while otherwise moving forward with the tasks and events of their lives (Bacon et al., 2015; Chien et al., 2014).

Studies indicate that the various cognitive-behavioral treatments are often very helpful to clients with schizophrenia (A-Tjak et al., 2015; Briki et al., 2014; Morrison et al., 2014). Many clients who receive such treatments report that they feel less distressed by their hallucinations and that they have fewer delusions. Indeed, they are often able to shed the diagnosis of schizophrenia. Rehospitalizations decrease by 50 percent among clients treated with cognitive-behavioral therapy.

MindTech

Putting a Face on Auditory Hallucinations

In Chapter 2, you read that a growing number of therapists are using *avatar therapy* to help clients overcome their psychological problems. In this form of cybertherapy, therapists have the clients interact with computer-generated on-screen virtual human figures. Perhaps the boldest application of avatar therapy is its use with schizophrenic patients. Clinical researcher Julian Leff and several colleagues have developed an approach that seems to offer particular promise for such people (Leff et al., 2014, 2013).

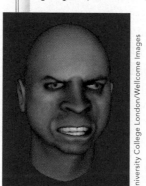

For a pilot study, the researchers selected 16 participants who were being tormented by imaginary voices (auditory hallucinations). In each case, the therapist presented the patient with a mean-sounding and mean-looking avatar. The avatar's voice pitch and appearance were designed based on the patient's description of what he was hearing and what he believed would be a corresponding face.

The patient was placed alone in a room with the computer simulation while the therapist generated the on-screen avatar from another room. Initially, the avatar spewed all sorts of frightening and upsetting statements at the patient. Then, the therapist encouraged the patient to fight back—to tell the avatar things such as, "I will not put up with this, what you are saying is nonsense, I don't believe these things, you must go away and leave me alone, and I do not need this kind of torment" (Leff et al., 2014, 2013; Kedmey, 2013).

After seven 30-minute sessions, most of the participants in the pilot study had less frequent and less intense auditory hallucinations and reported being less upset by the voices they did continue to hear. The participants also reported improvements in their feelings of depression and suicidal thinking. Three of the 16 actually reported a total cessation of their auditory hallucinations after the sessions. These promising results are now being followed up in a larger study with more participants. The results of that study should clarify whether confronting one's hallucinations in a virtual world can truly help people with schizophrenia. 💬

Voices spring to virtual life This is one of the sinister-looking avatars developed by clinical researcher Julian Leff and his colleagues in their new treatment for people with schizophrenia.

University College London/Wellcome Images

Family Therapy More than 50 percent of those who are recovering from schizophrenia and other severe mental disorders live with their families: parents, siblings, spouses, or children (Tsai et al., 2011; Barrowclough & Lobban, 2008). Generally speaking, people with schizophrenia who feel positive toward their relatives do better in treatment (Okpokoro et al., 2014). As you saw earlier, recovered patients living with relatives who display high levels of *expressed emotion*—that is, relatives who are very critical, emotionally overinvolved, and hostile—often have a much higher relapse rate than those living with more positive and supportive relatives. Moreover, for their part, family members may be very upset by the social withdrawal and unusual behaviors of a relative with schizophrenia (Friedrich et al., 2014; Quah, 2014).

To address such issues, clinicians now commonly include family therapy in their treatment of schizophrenia, providing family members with guidance, training, practical advice, psychoeducation about the disorder, and emotional support and empathy. In family therapy, relatives develop more realistic expectations and become more tolerant, less guilt-ridden, and more willing to try new patterns of communication. Family therapy also helps the person with schizophrenia cope with the pressures of family life, make better use of family members, and avoid troublesome interactions. Research has found that family therapy—particularly when it is combined with drug therapy—helps reduce tensions within the family and so helps relapse rates go down (Girón et al., 2015; Okpokoro et al., 2014).

The families of people with schizophrenia and other severe mental disorders may also turn to *family support groups* and *family psychoeducational programs* for encouragement and advice (Duckworth & Halpern, 2014). In such programs, family members meet with others in the same situation to share their thoughts and emotions, provide mutual support, and learn about schizophrenia.

Social Therapy Many clinicians believe that the treatment of people with schizophrenia should include techniques that address social and personal difficulties in the clients' lives. These clinicians offer practical advice; work with clients on problem solving, decision making, and social skills; make sure that the clients are taking their medications properly; and may even help them find work, financial assistance, appropriate health care, and proper housing (Granholm et al., 2014; Ordemann et al., 2014). Research finds that this practical, active, and broad approach, called *social therapy* or *personal therapy,* does indeed help keep people out of the hospital (Haddock & Spaulding, 2011; Hogarty, 2002).

The Community Approach

The broadest approach for the treatment of schizophrenia and other severe mental disorders is the *community approach*. In 1963, partly in response to the terrible conditions in public mental institutions and partly because of the emergence of antipsychotic drugs, the U.S. government ordered that patients be released and treated in the community. Congress passed the *Community Mental Health Act,* which provided that patients with psychological disorders were to receive a range of mental health services—outpatient therapy, inpatient treatment, emergency care, preventive care, and aftercare—in their communities rather than being transported to institutions far from home. The act was aimed at a variety of psychological disorders, but patients diagnosed with schizophrenia and other severe disorders, especially those who had been institutionalized for years, were affected most. Other countries around the world put similar sociocultural treatment programs into action shortly thereafter (Wiley-Exley, 2007).

Thus began several decades of **deinstitutionalization,** an exodus of hundreds of thousands of patients with schizophrenia and other long-term mental disorders

Spontaneous improvement? For reasons unknown, the symptoms of some people with schizophrenia lessen during old age, even without treatment. An example was the remarkable late-life improvement of John Nash, the subject of the book and movie *A Beautiful Mind*. Nash, seen here giving a presentation, received the 1994 Nobel Prize in Economic Science after struggling with schizophrenia for 35 years. He died in an automobile accident in 2015.

© João Relvas/epa/Corbis

▶ **deinstitutionalization** The discharge of large numbers of patients from long-term institutional care so that they might be treated in community programs.

Mental health on the streets In Indonesia, a police officer cuts the hair of a homeless person who he believes to have a severe mental disorder. The officer is a member of a special police unit that is trained to care for the homeless mentally ill and then take them to proper treatment facilities.

Healthy competition As part of the community mental health philosophy, people with schizophrenia and other severe mental disorders are also encouraged to participate in normal activities, athletic endeavors, and artistic undertakings. Here, for example, coached by former Napoli goalkeeper Enrico Zazzaro, patients from the Iflhan Rehabilitation Centre in Italy compete in a soccer league for people with psychological and intellectual disabilities.

from state institutions into the community. On a given day in 1955, close to 600,000 patients were living in state institutions; today fewer than 40,000 patients live in such facilities (Althouse, 2010). Clinicians have learned that patients recovering from schizophrenia and other severe disorders can profit greatly from community programs. As you will see, however, the actual quality of community care for these people has often been inadequate throughout the United States. The result is a "revolving door" pattern for many patients. They are released to the community, readmitted to an institution within months, released a second time, admitted yet again, and so on, over and over (Duhig et al., 2015; Burns & Drake, 2011).

> How might the "revolving door" pattern itself worsen the symptoms and outlook of people with schizophrenia?

What Are the Features of Effective Community Care? People recovering from schizophrenia and other severe disorders need medication, psychotherapy, help in handling daily pressures and responsibilities, guidance in making decisions, social skills training, residential supervision, and vocational counseling—a combination of services sometimes called *assertive community treatment* (Keller et al., 2014). Those whose communities help them meet these needs make more progress than those living in other communities (Malm, Ivarsson, & Allebeck, 2014; Swartz et al., 2012). Some of the key features of effective community care programs are (1) coordination of patient services, (2) short-term hospitalization, (3) partial hospitalization, (4) supervised residencies, and (5) occupational training.

COORDINATED SERVICES When the Community Mental Health Act was first passed, it was expected that community care would be provided by **community mental health centers**, treatment facilities that would supply medication, psychotherapy, and inpatient emergency care to people with severe disturbances, as well as coordinate the services offered by other community agencies. When community mental health centers are available and do provide these services, patients with schizophrenia and other severe disorders often make significant progress (Burns & Drake, 2011). Coordination of services is particularly important for so-called

mentally ill chemical abusers (*MICAs*), or *dual diagnosis* patients, individuals with psychotic disorders as well as substance use disorders (Drake et al., 2015; De Witte et al., 2014).

SHORT-TERM HOSPITALIZATION When people develop severe psychotic symptoms, today's clinicians first try to treat them on an outpatient basis, usually with a combination of anti-psychotic medication and psychotherapy. If this approach fails, they may try *short-term hospitalization*—in a mental hospital or a general hospital's psychiatric unit—that lasts a few weeks (rather than months or years) (Craig & Power, 2010). Soon after the patients improve, they are released for **aftercare**, a general term for follow-up care and treatment in the community.

PARTIAL HOSPITALIZATION People's needs may fall between full hospitalization and outpatient therapy, and so some communities offer **day centers**, or **day hospitals**, all-day programs in which patients return to their homes for the night. Such programs provide patients with daily supervised activities, therapy, and programs to improve social skills. People recovering from severe disorders in day centers often do better than those who spend extended periods in a hospital or in traditional outpatient therapy (Bales et al., 2014). Another kind of institution that has become popular is the *semihospital,* or *residential crisis center.* Semihospitals are houses or other structures in the community that provide 24-hour nursing care for people with severe mental disorders (Soliman et al., 2008).

SUPERVISED RESIDENCES Many people do not require hospitalization but are unable to live alone or with their families. **Halfway houses**, also known as *crisis houses* or *group homes,* often serve individuals well (Lindenmayer & Khan, 2012). Such residences may shelter between one and two dozen people. Live-in staff members usually are *paraprofessionals*—lay people who receive training and ongoing supervision from outside mental health professionals. The houses are usually run with a *milieu therapy* philosophy that emphasizes mutual support, resident responsibility, and self-government. Research indicates that halfway houses help many people recovering from schizophrenia and other severe disorders adjust to community life and avoid rehospitalization (Hansson et al., 2002; McGuire, 2000).

OCCUPATIONAL TRAINING AND SUPPORT Paid employment provides income, independence, self-respect, and the stimulation of working with others. It also brings companionship and order to one's daily life. For these reasons, occupational training and placement are important services for people with schizophrenia and other severe mental disorders (Johnsonn et al., 2014; Bell et al., 2011).

Many people recovering from such disorders receive occupational training in a **sheltered workshop**—a supervised workplace for employees who are not ready for competitive or complicated jobs. For some, the sheltered workshop becomes a permanent workplace. For others, it is an important step toward better-paying and more demanding employment or a return to a previous job. In the United States, however, occupational training is not consistently available to people with severe mental disorders.

An alternative work opportunity for people with severe psychological disorders is *supported employment,* in which vocational agencies and counselors help clients find competitive jobs in the community and provide psychological support while the clients are employed (Solar, 2014: Bell et al., 2011). Like sheltered workshops, supported employment opportunities are often in short supply.

Cause célèbre During the 1990s, Larry Hogue, nicknamed the "Wild Man of West 96th Street" by neighbors, roamed the streets of New York City's Upper West Side, screaming at, threatening, and frightening passers-by. Displaying the combined effects of schizophrenia and substance abuse, Hogue became the best known mentally ill chemical abuser (MICA) in the United States. His repeated cycles of imprisonment, hospitalization, and community placements exemplified the plight of thousands of people with severe mental disorders.

▶ **community mental health center** A treatment facility that provides medication, psychotherapy, and emergency care for psychological problems and coordinates treatment in the community.

▶ **aftercare** A program of posthospitalization care and treatment in the community.

▶ **day center** A program that offers hospital-like treatment during the day only. Also known as a *day hospital.*

▶ **halfway house** A residence for people with schizophrenia or other severe problems, often staffed by paraprofessionals. Also known as a *group home* or *crisis house.*

▶ **sheltered workshop** A supervised workplace for people who are not yet ready for competitive jobs.

▸ **case manager** A community therapist who offers a full range of services for people with schizophrenia or other severe disorders, including therapy, advice, medication, guidance, and protection of patients' rights.

How Has Community Treatment Failed? There is no doubt that effective community programs can help people with schizophrenia and other severe mental disorders recover. However, fewer than half of all the people who need them receive appropriate community mental health services (Addington et al., 2015; Burns & Drake, 2011). In fact, in any given year, 40 to 60 percent of all people with schizophrenia and other severe mental disorders receive no treatment at all (NIH, 2014; Torrey, 2001). Two factors are primarily responsible: *poor coordination* of services and a *shortage* of services.

POOR COORDINATION OF SERVICES The various mental health agencies in a community often fail to communicate with one another. There may be an opening at a nearby halfway house, for example, and the therapist at the community mental health center may not know about it. In addition, even within a community agency a patient may not have continuing contacts with the same staff members and may fail to receive consistent services. Still another problem is poor communication between state hospitals and community mental health centers, particularly at times of discharge (Torrey, 2001).

To help deal with such problems in communication and coordination, a growing number of community therapists have become **case managers** for people with schizophrenia and other severe mental disorders (Mas-Expósito et al., 2014; Burns, 2010). They try to coordinate available community services, guide clients through the community system, and help protect clients' legal rights. Like the social therapists described earlier, they also offer therapy and advice, teach problem-solving and social skills, ensure that clients are taking their medications properly, and keep an eye on possible health care needs. Many professionals now believe that effective case management is the key to success for a community program.

Changing the unacceptable A resident of a group home holds a sign during a rally in New York to protest the shortage of appropriate community residences for people with severe mental disorders. This shortage is one of the reasons that many such people have become homeless and/or imprisoned.

SHORTAGE OF SERVICES The number of community programs—community mental health centers, halfway houses, sheltered workshops—available to people with severe mental disorders falls woefully short (Zipursky, 2014; Burns & Drake, 2011). Moreover, the community mental health centers that do exist generally fail to provide adequate services for people with severe disorders. They tend to devote their efforts and money to people with less disabling problems, such as anxiety disorders or problems in social adjustment. Only a fraction of the patients treated by community mental health centers suffer from schizophrenia or other disorders marked by psychosis (Torrey, 2001).

There are various reasons for this shortage of services. The primary one is economic (Feldman et al., 2014; Covell et al., 2011). On the one hand, more public funds are available for people with psychological disorders now than in the past. In 1963 a total of $1 billion was spent in this area, whereas today approximately $171 billion in public funding is devoted each year to people with mental disorders (Rampell, 2013; Gill, 2010; Redick et al., 1992). This represents a significant increase even when inflation and so-called real dollars are factored in. On the other hand, rather little of the additional money is going to community treatment programs for people with severe disorders. Much of it goes instead to prescription drugs, monthly income payments such as social security disability income, services for people with mental disorders in nursing homes and general hospitals, and community services for people who are less disturbed. Today, the financial burden of providing community treatment for people with long-term severe disorders often falls on local governments and nonprofit organizations rather than the federal or state government, and local resources cannot always meet this challenge.

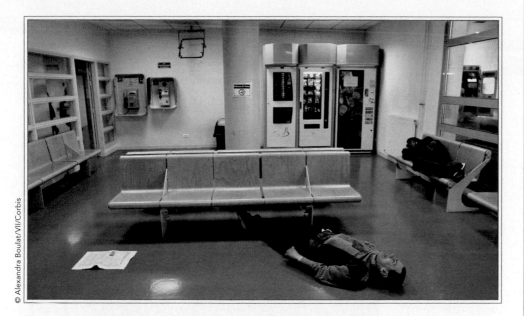

A long way to go A man with schizophrenia lies on the floor of the emergency room waiting area at Delafontaine Hospital near Paris, France. The plight of this patient is a reminder that, despite the development of various effective interventions, the overall treatment picture for many people with severe mental disorders leaves much to be desired.

What Are the Consequences of Inadequate Community Treatment?

What happens to people with schizophrenia and other severe disorders whose communities do not provide the services they need and whose families cannot afford private treatment (see Figure 12-4)? As you have read, a large number receive no treatment at all; many others spend a short time in a state hospital or semihospital and are then discharged prematurely, often without adequate follow-up treatment (Burns & Drake, 2011; Gill, 2010).

Many of the people with severe mental disorders return to their families and receive medication and perhaps emotional and financial support, but little else in the way of treatment (Barrowclough & Lobban, 2008). Around 8 percent enter an alternative institution such as a nursing home or rest home, where they receive only custodial care and medication (Torrey, 2001). As many as 18 percent are placed in privately run residences where supervision often is provided by untrained staff—foster homes (small or large), boardinghouses, care homes, and similar facilities (Lindenmayer & Khan, 2012). Another 34 percent of people with severe disorders live in totally unsupervised settings. Some are equal to the challenge of living alone, but many cannot really function independently and wind up in rundown single-room occupancy hotels (SROs) or rooming houses, often located in poor neighborhoods. They may live in conditions that are substandard and unsafe, which may exacerbate their disorder (Bowen et al., 2015; Bhavsar et al., 2014).

Finally, a great number of people with schizophrenia and other severe disorders have become homeless (Ogden, 2014; Kooyman & Walsh, 2011). There are between 400,000 and 800,000 homeless people in the United States, and approximately one-third have a severe mental disorder, commonly schizophrenia. Many have been released from hospitals; others are young adults who were never hospitalized in the first place. Another 135,000 or more people with severe mental disorders end up in prisons because their disorders have led them to break the law (Morrissey & Cuddeback, 2008; Peters et al., 2008) (see *MediaSpeak* on the next page). Certainly deinstitutionalization and the community mental health movement have failed these individuals, and many report actually feeling relieved if they are able to return to hospital life.

figure 12-4
Where do people with schizophrenia live? More than one-third live in unsupervised residences, 6 percent in jails, and 5 percent on the streets or in homeless shelters. (Information from Kooyman & Walsh, 2011; Torrey, 2001.)

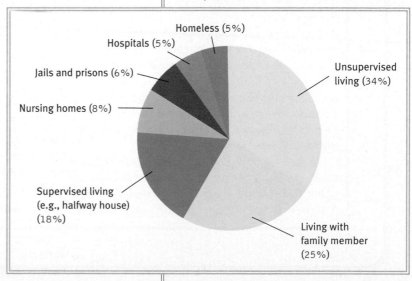

Homeless (5%)
Hospitals (5%)
Jails and prisons (6%)
Nursing homes (8%)
Supervised living (e.g., halfway house) (18%)
Unsupervised living (34%)
Living with family member (25%)

MediaSpeak

"Alternative" Mental Health Care

By Merrill Balassone, *Washington Post*, December 6, 2010

An 18-year-old schizophrenic pounds on the thick security glass of his single-man cell.

A woman lets out a long guttural scream to nobody in particular to turn off the lights.

A 24-year-old man drags his mattress under his bunk, fearful of the voices telling him to hurt himself.

This is not the inside of a psychiatric hospital. It's the B-Mental Health Unit [at a prison in California's] Stanislaus County. . . . Sheriff's deputy David Frost, who oversees the unit, says most of the inmates aren't difficult, just needy. "They do want help," Frost said.

Stanislaus County is not unique. Experts say U.S. prisons and jails have become the country's largest mental health institutions, its new asylums. Nearly four times more Californians with serious mental illnesses are housed in jails and prisons than in hospitals. . . . Nationally, 16 to 20 percent of prisoners are mentally ill, said Harry K. Wexler, a psychologist specializing in crime and substance abuse.

"I think it's a national tragedy," Wexler said. "Prisons are the institutions of last resort. The mentally ill are generally socially undesirable, less employable, more likely to be homeless and get on that slippery slope of repeated involvement in the criminal justice system."

Those who staff prisons and jails are understandably ill-equipped to be psychiatric caretakers. . . . Frost agrees. . . . "I'm not a mental health technician," he says, although he does hold a psychology degree. "I'm a sworn law enforcement officer." He walked the halls on a recent day, asking inmates if they were taking their medications and how they were feeling. . . .

Mentally ill offenders have higher recidivism rates than other inmates (they're called "frequent fliers" in the criminal justice world) because they receive little psychiatric care after their release. . . . Wexler said these inmates also are more likely to commit suicide. Because they're less capable of conforming to the rigid rules of a jailhouse, they can end up in isolation as punishment, Wexler said.

At 4:30 A.M. in the . . . jail—and again 12 hours later—it's "pill pass time," when the medical staff hands out about a dozen types of medications. . . . "You're making jailers our mental health treatment

Trying to help Sheriff's deputy David Frost talks with an inmate in the B-Mental Health Unit of the Public Safety Center, a prison in Stanislaus County, California.

personnel," said a forensic psychologist. "They're not trained to do that. . . . This population is not getting what they need." Because of the lack of hospital space, police are often forced to take the mentally ill who commit minor misdemeanors—from petty thefts to urinating in public—to jail instead. . . .

One nationally recognized solution is called a mental health treatment court, which gives offenders the choice between going to jail or following a treatment plan—including taking prescribed medications. [Such programs have had] success in decreasing the recidivism rate among mentally ill offenders and helping smooth their transition back into society. But at the same time, [the mental health treatment courts have been] forced to stop taking new offenders [because of budget cuts]. . . .

"We deal every day with this crisis of the mentally ill—in jail or out on the street," Frost said. "We do need the funding for these types of programs."

The Promise of Community Treatment Despite these very serious problems, proper community care has shown great potential for assisting people in recovering from schizophrenia and other severe disorders, and clinicians and many government officials continue to press to make it more available. In addition, a number of *national interest groups* have formed in countries around the world that push for better community treatment. In the United States, for example, the *National Alliance on Mental Illness* (*NAMI*) began in 1979 with 300 members and has expanded to 200,000 members in more than 1,000 chapters (NAMI, 2014). Made up largely of families and people affected by severe mental disorders, NAMI has become not only a source of information, support, and guidance for its members but also a powerful lobbying force in state and national legislatures, and it has pressured community mental health centers to treat more people with schizophrenia and other severe disorders.

Today, community care is a major feature of treatment for people recovering from severe mental disorders in countries around the world. Both in the United States and abroad, well-coordinated community treatment is seen as an important part of the solution to the problem of severe mental dysfunctioning (Wise, 2014; Burns & Drake, 2011).

A place to call home This man, recovering from schizophrenia and bipolar disorder, joyfully assumes a yoga pose in the living room of his new Chicago apartment. He found the residence with the help of a community program called Direct Connect.

➤ *Summing Up*

HOW ARE SCHIZOPHRENIA AND OTHER SEVERE MENTAL DISORDERS TREATED? For more than half of the twentieth century, the main treatment for schizophrenia and other severe mental disorders was institutionalization and custodial care. In the 1950s, two in-hospital approaches were developed, milieu therapy and token economy programs. They often brought improvement.

The discovery of antipsychotic drugs in the 1950s revolutionized the treatment of schizophrenia and other disorders marked by psychosis. Today they are almost always a part of treatment. Theorists believe that conventional antipsychotic drugs operate by reducing excessive dopamine activity in the brain. These drugs reduce the positive symptoms of schizophrenia more completely, or more quickly, than the negative symptoms.

The conventional antipsychotic drugs can also produce dramatic unwanted effects, particularly movement abnormalities. One such effect, tardive dyskinesia, apparently occurs in more than 10 percent of the people who take conventional antipsychotic drugs for an extended time and can be difficult or impossible to eliminate. In recent decades, atypical antipsychotic drugs have been developed; these seem to be more effective than the conventional drugs and to cause fewer or no extrapyramidal effects.

Today psychotherapy is often employed successfully in combination with antipsychotic drugs. Helpful forms include cognitive-behavioral therapy, family therapy, and social therapy.

A community approach to the treatment of schizophrenia and other severe mental disorders began in the 1960s, when a policy of deinstitutionalization in the United States brought about a mass exodus of hundreds of thousands of patients from state institutions into the community. Among the key elements of effective community care programs are coordination of patient services by a community mental health center, short-term hospitalization (followed by aftercare), day centers, halfway houses, occupational training and support, and case

(*continues on the next page*)

///// **BETWEEN THE LINES** /////

Schizophrenia and Jail

There are more people with schizophrenia and other severe mental disorders in jails and prisons than there are in all hospitals and other treatment facilities.

Chicago's Cook County Jail, where several thousand of the inmates require daily mental health services, is now in effect the largest mental institution in the United States.

(Pruchno, 2014; Balassone, 2011; Steadman et al., 2009; Morrissey & Cuddeback, 2008; Peters et al., 2008)

management. However, the quality and funding of community care for people with schizophrenia and other severe disorders have been inadequate throughout the United States, often resulting in a "revolving door" pattern. One result is that many people with such disorders are now homeless or in prison. Despite these problems, the potential of proper community care continues to capture the interest of clinicians and policy makers.

PUTTING IT...*together*

An Important Lesson

Schizophrenia—a bizarre and frightening disorder—was studied intensively throughout the twentieth century. Only since the discovery of antipsychotic drugs, however, have clinicians acquired any practical insight into its causes. As they do with most other psychological disorders, clinical theorists now believe that schizophrenia is probably caused by a combination of factors, though researchers have been far more successful in identifying the biological influences than the psychological and sociocultural ones. While biological investigations have closed in on specific genes, abnormalities in brain biochemistry and structure, and even viral infections, most of the psychological and sociocultural research has been able to cite only general factors, such as the roles of family conflict and diagnostic labeling. Clearly, researchers must identify psychological and sociocultural factors with greater precision if we are to gain a full understanding of schizophrenia.

The treatment picture for schizophrenia and other severe mental disorders has greatly improved in recent decades. After years of frustration and failure, clinicians now have an arsenal of weapons to use against these disorders—medication, institutional programs, psychotherapy, and community programs. It has become clear that antipsychotic medications open the door for recovery, but in most cases other kinds of treatment are also needed to help the recovery process along. The various approaches must be combined in a way that meets each individual's specific needs.

Working with schizophrenia and other severe disorders has taught therapists an important lesson: no matter how compelling the evidence for biological causation may be, a strictly biological approach to the treatment of psychological disorders is a mistake more often than not. Largely on the basis of pharmacological advances, hundreds of thousands of patients with schizophrenia and other severe mental disorders were released to their communities beginning in the 1960s. Little attention was paid to their psychological and sociocultural needs, and many have been trapped in their pathology ever since. Clinicians must remember this lesson, especially in today's climate, when managed care and government priorities often promote medication as the sole treatment for psychological problems.

When pioneering clinical researcher Emil Kraepelin described schizophrenia at the end of the nineteenth century, he estimated that only 13 percent of its victims ever improved. Today, even with shortages in community care, many more such people—at least three times as many—show improvement (Pinna et al., 2014). Certainly the clinical field has advanced considerably since Kraepelin's day, but it still has far to go. Studies suggest that the recovery rates—both partial and full—could be considerably higher (Zipursky, 2014). It is unacceptable that so many people with this and other severe mental disorders receive few or none of the effective community interventions that have been developed, worse still that tens of thousands have become homeless or prison inmates. It is now up to clinicians, along with public officials, to address the needs of all people with schizophrenia and other severe disorders.

CLINICAL CHOICES

Now that you've read about schizophrenia, try the interactive case study for this chapter. See if you are able to identify Randy's symptoms and suggest a diagnosis based on his symptoms. What kind of treatment would be most effective for Randy? Go to LaunchPad to access *Clinical Choices*.

KEY TERMS

schizophrenia, p. 386

psychosis, p. 386

schizophrenia spectrum disorders, p. 386

positive symptom, p. 387

delusion, p. 388

formal thought disorder, p. 388

loose associations, p. 388

hallucination, p. 389

inappropriate affect, p. 389

negative symptoms, p. 391

alogia, p. 391

restricted affect, p. 391

avolition, p. 391

catatonia, p. 391

dopamine hypothesis, p. 395

antipsychotic drug, p. 395

phenothiazines, p. 395

atypical antipsychotic drugs, p. 397

schizophrenogenic mother, p. 398

expressed emotion, p. 400

state hospital, p. 403

milieu therapy, p. 404

token economy program, p. 405

neuroleptic drugs, p. 407

extrapyramidal effects, p. 407

tardive dyskinesia, p. 408

social therapy, p. 409

deinstitutionalization, p. 410

assertive community treatment, p. 412

community mental health center, p. 412

mentally ill chemical abuser (MICA), p. 413

aftercare, p. 413

day center, p. 413

halfway house, p. 413

sheltered workshop, p. 413

case manager, p. 414

QuickQuiz

1. What is schizophrenia, and how prevalent is it? What is its relation to socioeconomic class and gender? *pp. 386–387*

2. What are the positive, negative, and psychomotor symptoms of schizophrenia? *pp. 387–391*

3. Describe the genetic, biochemical, brain structure, and viral explanations of schizophrenia, and discuss how they have been supported in research. *pp. 393–398*

4. What are the key features of the psychodynamic, cognitive, multicultural, social labeling, and family explanations of schizophrenia? *pp. 398–401*

5. Describe institutional care for people with schizophrenia and other severe mental disorders over the course of the twentieth century. How effective are the milieu and token economy treatment programs? *pp. 403–406*

6. How do antipsychotic drugs operate on the brain? How do conventional antipsychotic and atypical antipsychotic drugs differ? *pp. 406–408*

7. How effective are antipsychotic drugs in the treatment of schizophrenia? What are the unwanted effects of conventional antipsychotic drugs? *pp. 407–408*

8. What kinds of psychotherapy seem to help people with schizophrenia and other disorders marked by psychosis? *pp. 409–411*

9. What is deinstitutionalization? What features of community care seem critical for helping people with schizophrenia and other severe mental disorders? *pp. 411–414*

10. How and why has the community mental health approach been inadequate for many people with severe mental disorders? *pp. 414–416*

Visit *LaunchPad*

www.macmillanhighered.com/launchpad/comerfund8e
to access the e-book, new interactive case studies, videos, activities, and LearningCurve quizzes, as well as study aids including flashcards, FAQs, and research exercises.

Macmillan Education
LaunchPad

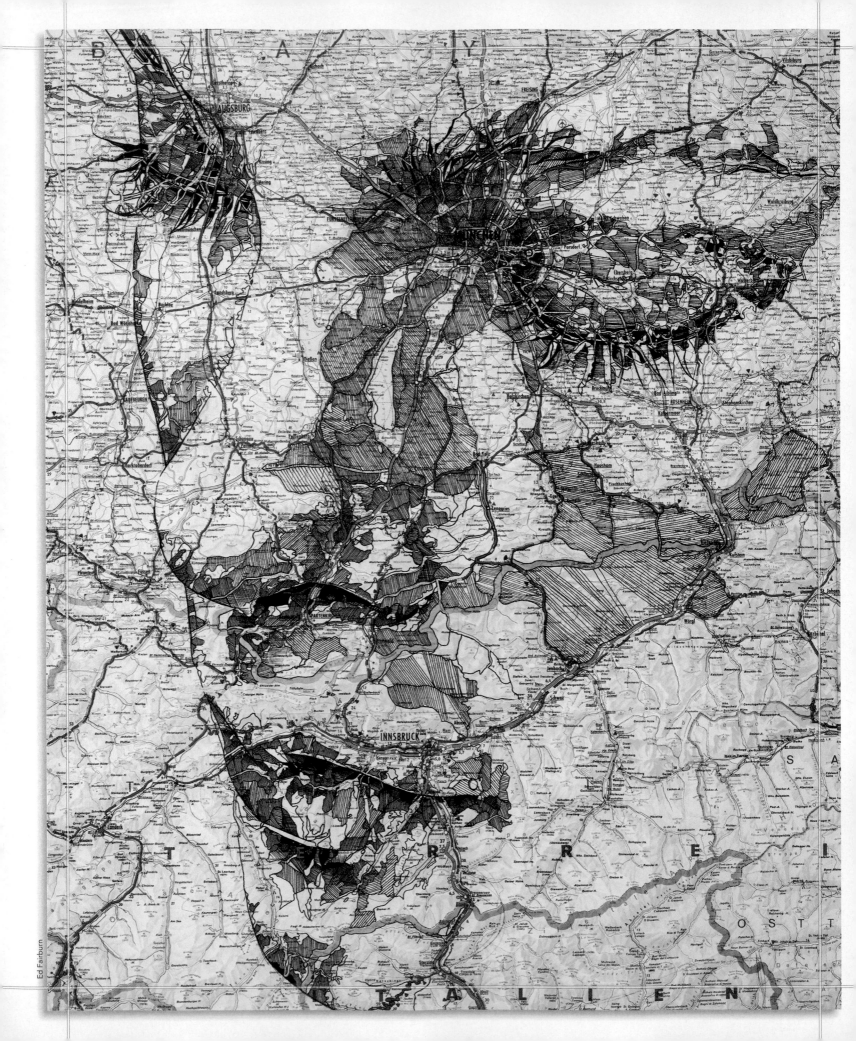

Ed Fairburn

Personality Disorders

*W*hile interviewing for the job of editor of a start-up news Web site, Frederick said, "This may sound self-serving, but I am extraordinarily gifted. I am certain that I will do great things in this position. I and the Osterman Post will soon set the standard for journalism and blogging in the country. Within a year, we'll be looking at the Huffington Post in the rearview mirror." The committee was impressed. Certainly, Frederick's credentials were strong, but even more important, his self-confidence and boldness had wowed them.

A year later, many of the same individuals were describing Frederick differently—arrogant, self-serving, cold, ego-maniacal, draining. He had performed well as editor (though not as spectacularly as he seemed to think), but that performance could not outweigh his impossible personality. Colleagues below and above him had grown weary of his manipulations, his emotional outbursts, his refusal ever to take the blame, his nonstop boasting, and his grandiose plans. Once again Frederick had outworn his welcome.

To be sure, Frederick had great charm, and he knew how to make others feel important, when it served his purpose. Thus he always had his share of friends and admirers. But in reality they were just passing through, until Frederick would tire of them or feel betrayed by their lack of enthusiasm for one of his self-serving interpretations or grand plans. Or until they simply could take Frederick no longer.

Bright and successful though he was, Frederick always felt entitled to more than he was receiving—to higher grades at school, greater compensation at work, more attention from girlfriends. If criticized even slightly, he reacted with fury and was certain that the critic was jealous of his superior intelligence, skill, or looks. At first glance, Frederick seemed to have a lot going for him socially. Typically, he could be found in the midst of a deep, meaningful romantic relationship—in which he might be tender, attentive, and seemingly devoted to his partner. But Frederick would always tire of his partner within a few weeks or months and would turn cold or even mean. Often he started affairs with other women while still involved with the current partner. The breakups—usually unpleasant and sometimes ugly—rarely brought sadness or remorse to him, and he would almost never think about his former partner again. He always had himself.

Each of us has a *personality*—a set of uniquely expressed characteristics that influence our behaviors, emotions, thoughts, and interactions. Our particular characteristics, often called *personality traits,* lead us to react in fairly predictable ways as we move through life. Yet our personalities are also flexible. We learn from experience. As we interact with our surroundings, we try out various responses to see which feel better and which are more effective. This is a flexibility that people who suffer from a personality disorder usually do not have.

People with a **personality disorder** display an enduring, rigid pattern of inner experience and outward behavior that impairs their sense of self, emotional experiences, goals, capacity for empathy, and/or capacity for intimacy (APA, 2013). Put another way, they have personality traits that are much more extreme and dysfunctional than those of most other people in their culture, leading to significant problems and psychological pain for themselves or others.

Frederick appears to display a personality disorder. For most of his life, his extreme narcissism, grandiosity, and insensitivity have led to poor functioning in both the personal and social realms. They have caused him to repeatedly feel angry and unappreciated, deprived him of close personal relationships,

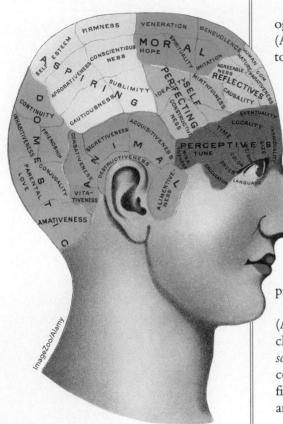

Early notions of personality In the popular nineteenth-century theory of phrenology, Franz Joseph Gall (1758–1828) suggested that the brain consists of distinct portions, each responsible for some aspect of personality. Phrenologists tried to assess personality by feeling bumps and indentations on a person's head.

and brought considerable pain to others. Witness the upset and turmoil felt by Frederick's coworkers and girlfriends.

The symptoms of personality disorders last for years and typically become recognizable in adolescence or early adulthood, although some start during childhood (APA, 2013). These disorders are among the most difficult psychological disorders to treat. Many people with the disorders are not even aware of their personality problems and fail to trace their difficulties to their maladaptive style of thinking and behaving. Surveys indicate that between 10 and 15 percent of all adults in the United States have a personality disorder (APA, 2013; Sansone & Sansone, 2011).

It is common for a person with a personality disorder to also suffer from another disorder, a relationship called *comorbidity*. As you will see later in this chapter, for example, many people with avoidant personality disorder, who fearfully shy away from all relationships, also display social anxiety disorder. Perhaps avoidant personality disorder predisposes people to develop social anxiety disorder. Or perhaps social anxiety disorder sets the stage for the personality disorder. Then again, some biological factor may create a predisposition to both the personality disorder and the anxiety disorder. Whatever the reason for the relationship, research indicates that the presence of a personality disorder complicates a person's chances for a successful recovery from other psychological problems (Fok et al., 2014).

DSM-5, like its predecessor, DSM-IV-TR, identifies 10 personality disorders (APA, 2013). Often these disorders are separated into three groups, or *clusters*. One cluster, marked by odd or eccentric behavior, consists of the *paranoid, schizoid,* and *schizotypal* personality disorders. A second cluster features dramatic behavior and consists of the *antisocial, borderline, histrionic,* and *narcissistic* personality disorders. The final cluster features a high degree of anxiety and includes the *avoidant, dependent,* and *obsessive-compulsive* personality disorders.

These 10 personality disorders are each characterized by a group of very problematic personality symptoms. For example, as you will soon see, *paranoid personality disorder* is diagnosed when a person has unjustified suspicions that others are harming him or her, has persistent unfounded doubts about the loyalty of friends, reads threatening meanings into benign events, persistently bears grudges, and has recurrent unjustified suspicions about the faithfulness of a life partner.

The DSM's listing of 10 distinct personality disorders is called a *categorical* approach. Like a light switch that is either on or off, this kind of approach assumes that (1) problematic personality traits are either present or absent in people, (2) a personality disorder is either displayed or not displayed by a person, and (3) a person who suffers from a personality disorder is not markedly troubled by personality traits outside of that disorder.

It turns out, however, that these assumptions are frequently contradicted in clinical practice. In fact, the symptoms of the personality disorders listed in DSM-5 overlap so much that clinicians often find it difficult to distinguish one disorder from another (see Figure 13-1), resulting in frequent disagreements about which diagnosis is correct for a person with a personality disorder. Diagnosticians sometimes even determine that particular people have more than one personality disorder (APA, 2013). This lack of agreement has raised serious questions about the *validity* (accuracy) and *reliability* (consistency) of the 10 DSM-5 personality disorder categories.

Given this state of affairs, many theorists have challenged the use of a categorical approach to personality disorders. They believe that personality disorders differ more in *degree* than in type of dysfunction and should instead be classified by the severity of personality traits rather than by the presence or absence of specific traits—a procedure called a *dimensional* approach (Morey, Skodol, & Oldham, 2014). In a dimensional approach, each trait is seen as varying along a continuum extending from nonproblematic to extremely problematic. People with a personality disorder

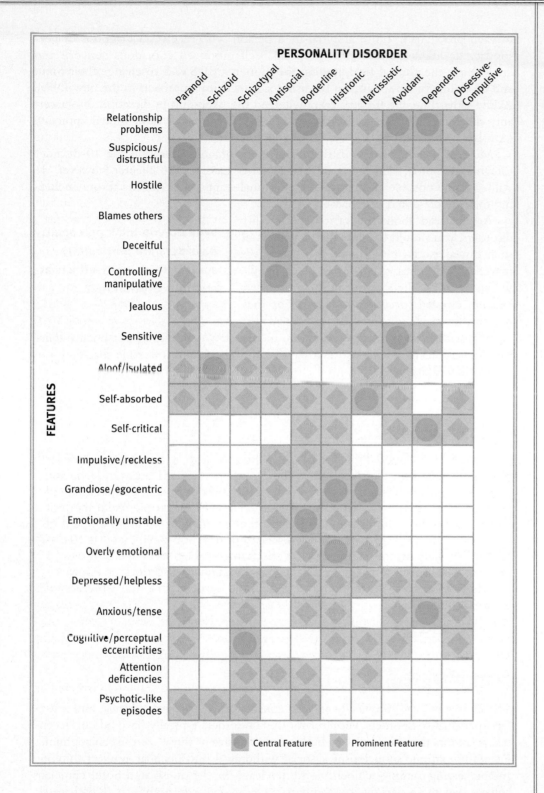

figure 13-1
Prominent and central features of the personality disorders in DSM-5 The symptoms of the various personality disorders often have significant overlap, leading to frequent misdiagnoses or to multiple diagnoses for a given client.

are those who display extreme degrees of problematic traits—degrees not commonly found in the general population (see Table 13-1 on the next page).

Given the inadequacies of a categorical approach and the growing enthusiasm for a dimensional one, the framers of DSM-5 initially proposed significant changes in how personality disorders should be classified. They proposed a largely dimensional system that would allow many additional kinds of personality problems to be classified as personality disorders and would require clinicians to assess the severity

▶ **personality disorder** An enduring, rigid pattern of inner experience and outward behavior that repeatedly impairs a person's sense of self, emotional experiences, goals, capacity for empathy, and/or capacity for intimacy.

table: **13-1**

Dx Checklist

Personality Disorder

1. Individual displays a long-term, rigid, and wide-ranging pattern of inner experience and behavior that leads to dysfunction in at least two of the following realms:
   • Cognition • Emotion • Social interactions • Impulsivity.

2. The individual's pattern is significantly different from ones usually found in his or her culture.

3. Individual experiences significant distress or impairment.

(Information from: APA, 2013)

of each problematic trait exhibited by a person who receives a diagnosis of personality disorder. However, this proposal itself produced enormous concern and criticism in the clinical field, leading the framers of DSM-5 to change their mind and to retain, for now, a classic 10-disorder categorical approach in the new DSM. At the same time, the framers acknowledged the likely future direction of personality disorder classifications by also describing an *alternative* dimensional approach (Anderson et al., 2014).

Most of the discussions in this chapter are organized around the 10-disorder categorical approach currently used in DSM-5. Later in the chapter, however, we will examine possible alternative—dimensional—approaches of the future, including the one presented in DSM-5.

As you read about the various personality disorders, you should be clear that diagnoses of such disorders can be assigned too often. We may catch glimpses of ourselves or of people we know in the descriptions of these disorders and be tempted to conclude that we or they have a personality disorder. In the vast majority of instances, such interpretations are incorrect. We all display personality traits. Only occasionally are they so maladaptive, distressful, and inflexible that they can be considered disorders.

> **Why do you think personality disorders are particularly subject to so many efforts at amateur psychology?**

➤ *Summing Up*

PERSONALITY DISORDERS AND DSM-5 People with a personality disorder display an enduring, rigid pattern of inner experience and outward behavior. Their personality traits are much more extreme and dysfunctional than those of most other people in their culture, resulting in significant problems for them or those around them. It has been estimated that as many as 10 to 15 percent of adults have such a disorder. DSM-5 uses a categorical approach that lists 10 distinct personality disorders. In addition, the framers of DSM-5 have proposed a dimensional approach to the classification of personality disorders, an approach that they assigned for further study and possible inclusion in a future revision of the DSM.

"Odd" Personality Disorders

The cluster of *"odd" personality disorders* consists of the *paranoid, schizoid,* and *schizotypal* personality disorders. People with these disorders typically have odd or eccentric behaviors that are similar to but not as extensive as those seen in schizophrenia, including extreme suspiciousness, social withdrawal, and peculiar ways of thinking and perceiving things. Such behaviors often leave the person isolated. Some clinicians believe that these personality disorders are related to schizophrenia (Rosell et al., 2014). In fact, schizotypal personality disorder is listed twice in DSM-5—as one of the schizophrenia spectrum disorders (see page 386) and as one of the personality disorders (APA, 2013). Directly related or not, people with an odd cluster personality disorder often qualify for an additional diagnosis of schizophrenia or have close relatives with schizophrenia (Chemerinski & Siever, 2011).

Clinicians have learned much about the symptoms of the odd cluster personality disorders but have not been so successful in determining their causes or how to treat them. In fact, as you'll soon see, people with these disorders rarely seek treatment.

Paranoid Personality Disorder

As you read earlier, people with **paranoid personality disorder** deeply distrust other people and are suspicious of their motives (APA, 2013). Because they believe that everyone intends them harm, they shun close relationships. Their trust in their own ideas and abilities can be excessive, though, as you can see in the case of Eduardo:

> *For Eduardo, a researcher at a genetic engineering company, this was the last straw. He had been severely chastised by his supervisor for deviating from the research procedure on a major study. He knew where this was coming from. He had been "ratted out" by his jealous, conniving lab colleagues. This time, Eduardo would not sit back quietly. He demanded a meeting with his supervisor and the three other researchers in the lab.*
>
> *At the outset of the meeting, Eduardo insisted that he would not leave the room until he was told the name of the person who had ratted him out. He acknowledged that he had, in fact, changed the study's design in key ways, maintaining that these changes would open the door to enormous medical gains. Eduardo quickly shifted the focus onto his lab colleagues. He stated that the other scientists were intimidated by his visionary ideas, and he accused them of trying to get him out of the way so they could continue to work in an unproductive, low-pressure atmosphere. He said that their desire to get rid of him was always apparent to him, revealed by their coldness toward him each and every day and their outright nastiness whenever he tried to correct them or offer constructive criticism. Nor did it escape his attention that they were always laughing at him, talking about him behind his back, and, on more than one occasion, trying to copy or destroy his notes.*
>
> *The other researchers were aghast as Eduardo laid out his suspicions. They pointed out that it was Eduardo, not they, who was always behaving in an unfriendly manner. He had stopped speaking to all of them two months ago and he regularly tried to antagonize them—giving them dirty looks and slamming doors.*
>
> *Next, Eduardo's supervisor, Lisa, spoke up. She said that in her objective opinion, none of Eduardo's accusations were true. First, none of his colleagues had informed on him. She herself had reviewed videos from the lab cameras as a matter of routine and had noticed him feeding rats that were supposed to be left hungry. Second, she said that it was his coworkers' account, not Eduardo's, that rang true. In fact, she had received many complaints from people outside the lab about Eduardo's cold and aloof manner.*
>
> *Later, in the privacy of her office, Lisa told Eduardo that she had no choice but to let him go. Eduardo was furious, but not completely surprised. His past two jobs had ended badly as well.*

Ever on guard and cautious and seeing threats everywhere, people like Eduardo continually expect to be the targets of some trickery (see Figure 13-2 on the next page). They find "hidden" meanings, which are usually belittling or threatening, in everything. In a study that required people to role-play, participants with paranoia were more likely than control participants to read hostile intentions into the actions of others (Turkat et al., 1990). In addition, they more often chose anger as the appropriate role-play response.

Quick to challenge the loyalty or trustworthiness of acquaintances, people with paranoid personality disorder remain cold and distant. A woman might avoid confiding in anyone, for example, for fear of being hurt, or a husband might, without any justification, persist in questioning his wife's faithfulness. Although inaccurate and inappropriate, their suspicions are not usually *delusional*; the ideas are not so bizarre or so firmly held as to clearly remove the individuals from reality (Millon, 2011).

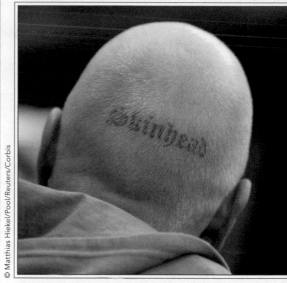

"Zero Degrees of Empathy" With the term "Skinhead" tattooed on the back of his head, this man awaits trial in Germany for committing neo-Nazi crimes against foreigners and liberals. Clinicians sometimes confront extreme racism and intolerance in their practices, particularly among clients with paranoid, antisocial and certain other personality disorders. Famous developmental psychologist Simon Baron-Cohen proposes in his book *Zero Degrees of Empathy* that the common element in all such behaviors is a total lack of empathy.

▶ **paranoid personality disorder** A personality disorder marked by a pattern of distrust and suspiciousness of others.

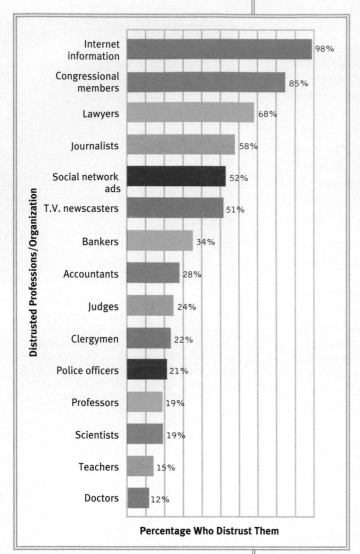

figure 13-2

Whom do you distrust? Although distrust and suspiciousness are the hallmarks of paranoid personality disorder, even people without this disorder are surprisingly untrusting. In various surveys, the majority of respondents said they distrust Internet information, members of Congress, lawyers, journalists, social network ads, and television newscasters. (Information from: YouGov, 2014; Harris Interactive, 2013, 2006; Press TV, 2013; Mancx, 2012).

People with this disorder are critical of weakness and fault in others, particularly at work (McGurk et al., 2013). They are unable to recognize their own mistakes, though, and are extremely sensitive to criticism. They often blame others for the things that go wrong in their lives, and they repeatedly bear grudges (Rotter, 2011). As many as 4.4 percent of adults in the United States experience this disorder, which is apparently more common in men than in women (APA, 2013; Sansone & Sansone, 2011).

How Do Theorists Explain Paranoid Personality Disorder? The theories that have been proposed to explain paranoid personality disorder, like those about most other personality disorders, have received little systematic research (Triebwasser et al., 2013). Psychodynamic theories, the oldest of these explanations, trace the pattern to early interactions with demanding parents, particularly distant, rigid fathers and overcontrolling, rejecting mothers (Caligor & Clarkin, 2010; Williams, 2010). (You will see that psychodynamic explanations for almost all the personality disorders begin the same way—with repeated mistreatment during childhood and lack of love.) According to one psychodynamic view, some people come to view their environment as hostile as a result of their parents' persistently unreasonable demands. They must always be on the alert because they cannot trust others, and they are likely to develop feelings of extreme anger. They also project these feelings onto others and, as a result, feel increasingly persecuted (Koenigsberg et al., 2001). Similarly, some cognitive theorists suggest that people with paranoid personality disorder generally hold broad maladaptive assumptions, such as "People are evil" and "People will attack you if given the chance" (Beck & Weishaar, 2014; Weishaar & Beck, 2006).

Biological theorists propose that paranoid personality disorder has genetic causes (APA, 2013; Bernstein & Useda, 2007). An early study that looked at self-reports of suspiciousness in 3,810 Australian twin pairs found that if one twin was excessively suspicious, the other had an increased likelihood of also being suspicious (Kendler et al., 1987). Once again, however, it is important to note that such similarities between twins might also be the result of common environmental experiences.

Treatments for Paranoid Personality Disorder People with paranoid personality disorder do not typically see themselves as needing help, and few come to treatment willingly (Millon, 2011). Furthermore, many who are in treatment view the role of patient as inferior and distrust and rebel against their therapists (Kellett & Hardy, 2014). Thus it is not surprising that therapy for this disorder, as for most other personality disorders, has limited effect and moves very slowly (Piper & Joyce, 2001).

Object relations therapists—the psychodynamic therapists who give center stage to relationships—try to see past the patient's anger and work on what they view as his or her deep wish for a satisfying relationship (Caligor & Clarkin, 2010). Cognitive and behavioral techniques have also been used to treat people with paranoid personality disorder and are often combined into an integrated cognitive-behavioral approach. On the behavioral side, therapists help clients to master anxiety-reduction techniques and to improve their skills at solving interpersonal problems. On the cognitive side, therapists guide the clients to develop more realistic interpretations of other people's words and actions and to become more aware of other people's points of view (Kellett & Hardy, 2014). Antipsychotic drug therapy seems to be of limited help (Birkeland, 2013).

Schizoid Personality Disorder

People with **schizoid personality disorder** persistently avoid and are removed from social relationships and demonstrate little in the way of emotion (APA, 2013). Like people with paranoid personality disorder, they do not have close ties with other people. The reason they avoid social contact, however, has nothing to do with paranoid feelings of distrust or suspicion; it is because they genuinely prefer to be alone. Take Eli:

> *Eli, a student at the local technical institute, had been engaged in several different Internet certificate programs over the past few years, and was about to engage in yet another, when his mother, confused as to why he would not apply for a traditional degree at a "real" college, insisted he seek therapy. A loner by nature, Eli preferred not to socialize in any traditional sense, having little to no desire to get to know much about the people in his immediate social context. The way Eli saw it, . . . "at least at my school you just go to class and go home."*
>
> *Routinely, he slept through much of his day and then spent his evenings, nights, and weekends at the school's computer lab, "chatting" with others over the Internet while not in class. Notably, people that he chatted with often sought to meet Eli, but he always declined these invitations, stating that he didn't really have any desire to learn more about them than what they shared over the computer In the chat rooms. He described a family life that was similar to that of his social surroundings; he was mostly oblivious of his younger brother and sister, two outgoing teens, despite the fact that they seemed to hold him in the highest regard, and he had recently alienated himself entirely from his father, who had left the family several years earlier. . . .*
>
> *A marked deficit in social interest was notable in Eli, as were frequent behavioral eccentricities. . . . At best, he had acquired a peripheral . . . role in social and family relationships. . . . Rather than venturing outward, he had increasingly removed himself from others and from sources of potential growth and gratification. Life was uneventful, with extended periods of solitude interspersed.*
>
> (Millon, 2011)

People like Eli, often described as "loners," make no effort to start or keep friendships, take little interest in having sexual relationships, and even seem indifferent to their families. They seek out jobs that require little or no contact with others. When necessary, they can form work relations to a degree, but they prefer to keep to themselves. Many live by themselves as well. Not surprisingly, their social skills tend to be weak. If they marry, their lack of interest in intimacy may create marital or family problems.

People with schizoid personality disorder focus mainly on themselves and are generally unaffected by praise or criticism. They rarely show any feelings, expressing neither joy nor anger. They seem to have no need for attention or acceptance; are typically viewed as cold, humorless, or dull; and generally succeed in being ignored. This disorder is present in 3.1 percent of the adult population (APA, 2013; Sansone & Sansone, 2011). Men are slightly more likely to experience it than are women, and men may also be more impaired by it.

How Do Theorists Explain Schizoid Personality Disorder?
Many psychodynamic theorists, particularly object relations theorists, propose that schizoid personality disorder has its roots in an unsatisfied need for human contact

► **schizoid personality disorder**
A personality disorder characterized by persistent avoidance of social relationships and little expression of emotion.

A darker knight In this scene from the popular 2008 movie *The Dark Knight*, Bruce Wayne confronts Batman, Wayne's alter ego and only real friend. True to the vision of comic book artist and writer Frank Miller, this film and its sequel, *The Dark Knight Rises*, present the crime-fighter as a singularly driven loner incapable of forming or sustaining relationships. Some clinical observers have argued that the current *Dark Knight* version of Batman often displays the features of schizoid personality disorder.

Warner Bros Pictures/Lengendary Pict./DC Comics/
Syncopy/Stephan Vaughn/Newscom

(Caligor & Clarkin, 2010). The parents of people with this disorder, like those of people with paranoid personality disorder, are believed to have been unaccepting or even abusive of their children. Whereas people with paranoid symptoms react to such parenting chiefly with distrust, those with schizoid personality disorder are left unable to give or receive love. They cope by avoiding all relationships.

Cognitive theorists propose, not surprisingly, that people with schizoid personality disorder suffer from deficiencies in their thinking. Their thoughts tend to be vague, empty, and without much meaning, and they have trouble scanning the environment to arrive at accurate perceptions (Kramer & Meystre, 2010). Unable to pick up emotional cues from others, they simply cannot respond to emotions. As this theory might predict, children with schizoid personality disorder develop language and motor skills very slowly, whatever their level of intelligence (APA, 2013; Wolff, 2000, 1991).

Treatments for Schizoid Personality Disorder Their social withdrawal prevents most people with schizoid personality disorder from entering therapy unless some other disorder, such as alcoholism, makes treatment necessary (Mittal et al., 2007). These clients are likely to remain emotionally distant from the therapist, seem not to care about their treatment, and make limited progress at best (Colli et al., 2014).

Cognitive-behavioral therapists have sometimes been able to help people with this disorder experience more positive emotions and more satisfying social interactions (Beck & Weishaar, 2011; Beck et al., 2004). On the cognitive end, their techniques include presenting clients with lists of emotions to think about or having them write down and remember pleasurable experiences. On the behavioral end, therapists have sometimes had success teaching social skills to such clients, using role-playing, exposure techniques, and homework assignments as tools. Group therapy is apparently useful when it offers a safe setting for social contact, although people with schizoid personality disorder may resist pressure to take part (Piper & Joyce, 2001). As with paranoid personality disorder, drug therapy seems to offer limited help (Silk & Jibson, 2010).

Schizotypal Personality Disorder

People with **schizotypal personality disorder** display a range of interpersonal problems marked by extreme discomfort in close relationships, very odd patterns of thinking and perceiving, and behavioral eccentricities (APA, 2013). Anxious around others, they seek isolation and have few close friends. Some feel intensely lonely. The disorder is more severe than the paranoid and schizoid personality disorders, as we see in the case of 41-year-old Kevin:

> Kevin was a night security guard at a warehouse, where he had worked since his high school graduation more than 20 years ago. His parents, both successful professionals, had been worried for many years, as Kevin seemed entirely disconnected from himself and his surroundings and had never taken initiative to make any changes, even toward a shift supervisory position. They therefore made the referral for therapy, and Kevin simply acquiesced. He explained that he liked his work, as it was a place where he could be by himself in a quiet atmosphere, away from anyone else. He described where he worked as "an empty warehouse; they don't use it no more but they don't want no one in there. It's nice; 'homey.'"
>
> Throughout the . . . interview, Kevin remained aloof, never once looking at the counselor, usually answering questions with either one-word responses or short phrases, and usually waiting to respond until a second question was asked or the

▶ **schizotypal personality disorder** A personality disorder characterized by extreme discomfort in close relationships, very odd patterns of thinking and perceiving, and behavioral eccentricities.

first question was repeated. He described, in . . . short, bizarre answers, a life devoid of almost any human interconnectedness, almost his only tangible contact being his brother, whom he saw only during major holidays. Living alone, he could only remember one significant relationship, and that was with a girl in high school. Very simply, he stated, "We graduated, and then I didn't see her anymore." He expressed no apparent loneliness, however, and appeared entirely emotionless regarding any aspect of his life. . . .

Kevin . . . often seemed to experience a separation between his mind and his physical body. There was a strange sense of nonbeing or nonexistence, as if his floating conscious awareness carried with it a depersonalized or identityless human form. Behaviorally, his tendency was to be drab, sluggish, and inexpressive. He . . . appeared bland, indifferent, unmotivated, and insensitive to the external world. . . . Most people considered him to be [a] strange person . . . who faded into the background, self-absorbed . . . and lost to the outside world. . . . Bizarre "telepathic" powers enabled him to communicate with mythical or distant others. . . . Kevin also occasionally decompensated when faced with too much, rather than too little, stimulation. . . . He would simply fade out, becoming blank, losing conscious awareness, and turning off the pressures of the outer world.

(Millon, 2011)

As with Kevin, the thoughts and behaviors of people with schizotypal personality disorder can be noticeably disturbed. These symptoms may include *ideas of reference*—beliefs that unrelated events pertain to them in some important way—and *bodily illusions,* such as sensing an external "force" or presence. A number of people with this disorder see themselves as having special extrasensory abilities, and some believe that they have magical control over others. Examples of schizotypal eccentricities include repeatedly arranging cans to align their labels, organizing closets extensively, or wearing an odd assortment of clothing. The emotions of these individuals may be inappropriate, flat, or humorless.

People with schizotypal personality disorder often have great difficulty keeping their attention focused. Correspondingly, their conversation is typically vague, even sprinkled with loose associations (Millon, 2011). Like Kevin, they tend to drift aimlessly and lead an idle, unproductive life (Hengartner et al., 2014). They are likely to choose undemanding jobs in which they can work below their capacity and are not required to interact with other people. Surveys suggest that 3.9 percent of adults—slightly more males than females—display schizotypal personality disorder (Rosell et al., 2014; Sansone & Sansone, 2011).

How Do Theorists Explain Schizotypal Personality Disorder?

Because the symptoms of schizotypal personality disorder so often resemble those of schizophrenia, researchers have hypothesized that similar factors may be at work in both disorders. A wide range of studies have supported such expectations (Hazlett et al., 2015; Rosell et al., 2015). Investigators have found that schizotypal symptoms, like schizophrenic patterns, are often linked to family conflicts and to psychological disorders in parents. They have also learned that defects in attention and short-term memory may contribute to schizotypal personality disorder, just as they apparently do to schizophrenia. For example, research participants with either disorder perform poorly on *backward masking,* a laboratory test of attention that requires a person to identify a visual stimulus immediately after a previous stimulus has flashed on and off the screen. People with these disorders have a hard time shutting out the first

Sipa Press

When personality disorders explode In this video, Seung-Hui Cho, a student at Virginia Tech, described the slights he experienced throughout his life. After mailing the video to NBC News, he proceeded, on April 16, 2007, to kill 32 people, including himself, and to wound 25 others in a massive campus shooting. Most clinical observers agree that he displayed a combination of features from the antisocial, borderline, paranoid, schizoid, schizotypal, and narcissistic personality disorders, including boundless fury and hatred, extreme social withdrawal, persistent distrust, strange thinking, intimidating behavior and arrogance, and disregard for others.

stimulus in order to focus on the second. Finally, researchers have linked schizotypal personality disorder to some of the same biological factors found in schizophrenia, such as high activity of the neurotransmitter dopamine, enlarged brain ventricles, smaller temporal lobes, and loss of gray matter (Lener et al., 2015; Ettinger et al., 2014). As you read in Chapter 12, there are indications that these biological factors may have a genetic base.

Although these findings do suggest a close relationship between schizotypal personality disorder and schizophrenia, the personality disorder also has been linked to disorders of mood (Lentz et al., 2010). More than half of people with schizotypal personality disorder also suffer from major depressive disorder at some point in their lives (APA, 2013). Moreover, relatives of people with depression have a higher than usual rate of schizotypal personality disorder, and vice versa. Thus, at the very least, this personality disorder is not tied exclusively to schizophrenia.

Treatments for Schizotypal Personality Disorder Therapy is as difficult in cases of schizotypal personality disorder as it is in cases of paranoid and schizoid personality disorders. Most therapists agree on the need to help these clients "reconnect" with the world and recognize the limits of their thinking and their powers. The therapists may thus try to set clear limits—for example, by requiring punctuality—and work on helping the clients recognize where their views end and those of the therapist begin. Other therapy goals are to increase positive social contacts, ease loneliness, reduce overstimulation, and help the individuals become more aware of their personal feelings (Colli et al., 2014; Sperry, 2003).

Cognitive-behavioral therapists further combine cognitive and behavioral techniques to help people with schizotypal personality disorder function more effectively. Using cognitive interventions, they try to teach clients to evaluate their unusual thoughts or perceptions objectively and to ignore the inappropriate ones (Beck & Weishaar, 2011; Weishaar & Beck, 2006). Therapists may keep track of clients' odd or magical predictions, for example, and later point out their inaccuracy. When clients are speaking and begin to digress, the therapists might ask them to sum up what they are trying to say. In addition, specific behavioral methods, such as speech lessons, social skills training, and tips on appropriate dress and manners, have sometimes helped clients learn to blend in better with and be more comfortable around others (Farmer & Nelson-Gray, 2005).

Antipsychotic drugs have been given to people with schizotypal personality disorder, again because of the disorder's similarity to schizophrenia. In low doses the drugs appear to have helped some people, usually by reducing certain of their thought problems (Rosenbluth & Sinyor, 2012).

➤ *Summing Up*

"ODD" PERSONALITY DISORDERS Three of the personality disorders in DSM-5 are marked by the kinds of odd or eccentric behaviors often seen in schizophrenia, although they are not as extensive as those found in schizophrenia. Some clinicians believe that these personality disorders are related to schizophrenia.

People with paranoid personality disorder display a broad pattern of distrust and suspiciousness. Those with schizoid personality disorder persistently avoid social relationships and show little emotional expression. People with schizotypal personality disorder display a range of interpersonal problems marked by extreme discomfort in close relationships, very odd forms of thinking and behavior, and various behavioral eccentricities. People with these three kinds of disorders usually are resistant to treatment, and treatment gains tend to be modest at best.

"Dramatic" Personality Disorders

The cluster of *"dramatic" personality disorders* includes the *antisocial, borderline, histrionic,* and *narcissistic* personality disorders. The behaviors of people with these problems are so dramatic, emotional, or erratic that it is almost impossible for them to have relationships that are truly giving and satisfying.

These personality disorders are more commonly diagnosed than the others. However, only the antisocial and borderline personality disorders have received much study, partly because they create so many problems for other people. The causes of the disorders, like those of the odd personality disorders, are not well understood. Treatments range from ineffective to moderately effective.

Antisocial Personality Disorder

Sometimes described as "psychopaths" or "sociopaths," people with **antisocial personality disorder** persistently disregard and violate others' rights (APA, 2013). Aside from substance use disorders, this is the disorder most closely linked to adult criminal behavior. DSM-5 stipulates that a person must be at least 18 years of age to receive this diagnosis; however, most people with antisocial personality disorder displayed some patterns of misbehavior before they were 15, including truancy, running away, cruelty to animals or people, and destroying property.

Robert Hare, a leading researcher of antisocial personality disorder, recalls an early professional encounter with a prison inmate named Ray:

In the early 1960s, I found myself employed as the sole psychologist at the British Columbia Penitentiary. . . . I wasn't in my office for more than an hour when my first "client" arrived. He was a tall, slim, dark-haired man in his thirties. The air around him seemed to buzz, and the eye contact he made with me was so direct and intense that I wondered if I had ever really looked anybody in the eye before. That stare was unrelenting—he didn't indulge in the brief glances away that most people use to soften the force of their gaze.

Without waiting for an introduction, the inmate—I'll call him Ray—opened the conversation: "Hey, Doc, how's it going? Look, I've got a problem. I need your help. I'd really like to talk to you about this."

Eager to begin work as a genuine psychotherapist, I asked him to tell me about it. In response, he pulled out a knife and waved it in front of my nose, all the while smiling and maintaining that intense eye contact.

Once he determined that I wasn't going to push the button, he explained that he intended to use the knife not on me but on another inmate who had been making overtures to his "protégé," a prison term for the more passive member of a homosexual pairing. Just why he was telling me this was not immediately clear, but I soon suspected that he was checking me out, trying to determine what sort of a prison employee I was. . . .

From that first meeting on, Ray managed to make my eight-month stint at the prison miserable. His constant demands on my time and his attempts to manipulate me into doing things for him were unending. On one occasion, he convinced me that he would make a good cook . . . and I supported his request for a transfer from the machine shop (where he had apparently made the knife). What I didn't consider was that the kitchen was a source of sugar, potatoes, fruit, and other ingredients that could be turned into alcohol. Several months after I had recommended the transfer, there was a mighty eruption below the floorboards directly under the warden's table. When the commotion died down, we found an elaborate system for distilling alcohol below the floor. Something had gone wrong and one of the pots had exploded. There was nothing unusual about the presence of a still in a

(continues on the next page)

Notorious disregard In 2009, financier Bernard Madoff was sentenced to 150 years in prison after defrauding thousands of investors, including many charities, of billions of dollars. Given his overwhelming disregard for others and other such qualities, some clinicians suggest that Madoff displays antisocial personality disorder.

Don Emmert/AFP/Getty Images

▸ **antisocial personality disorder** A personality disorder marked by a general pattern of disregard for and violation of other people's rights.

maximum-security prison, but the audacity of placing one under the warden's seat shook up a lot of people. When it was discovered that Ray was the brains behind the bootleg operation, he spent some time in solitary confinement.

Once out of "the hole," Ray appeared in my office as if nothing had happened and asked for a transfer from the kitchen to the auto shop—he really felt he had a knack, he saw the need to prepare himself for the outside world, if he only had the time to practice he could have his own body shop on the outside. . . . I was still feeling the sting of having arranged the first transfer, but eventually he wore me down.

Soon afterward I decided to leave the prison to pursue a Ph.D. in psychology, and about a month before I left Ray almost persuaded me to ask my father, a roofing contractor, to offer him a job as part of an application for parole.

Ray had an incredible ability to con not just me but everybody. He could talk, and lie, with a smoothness and a directness that sometimes momentarily disarmed even the most experienced and cynical of the prison staff. When I met him he had a long criminal record behind him (and, as it turned out, ahead of him); about half his adult life had been spent in prison, and many of his crimes had been violent. . . . He lied endlessly, lazily, about everything, and it disturbed him not a whit whenever I pointed out something in his file that contradicted one of his lies. He would simply change the subject and spin off in a different direction. Finally convinced that he might not make the perfect job candidate in my father's firm, I turned down Ray's request—and was shaken by his nastiness at my refusal.

Before I left the prison for the university, I took advantage of the prison policy of letting staff have their cars repaired in the institution's auto shop—where Ray still worked, thanks (he would have said no thanks) to me. The car received a beautiful paint job and the motor and drivetrain were reconditioned.

With all our possessions on top of the car and our baby in a plywood bed in the backseat, my wife and I headed for Ontario. The first problems appeared soon after we left Vancouver, when the motor seemed a bit rough. Later, when we encountered some moderate inclines, the radiator boiled over. A garage mechanic discovered ball bearings in the carburetor's float chamber; he also pointed out where one of the hoses to the radiator had clearly been tampered with. These problems were repaired easily enough, but the next one, which arose while we were going down a long hill, was more serious. The brake pedal became very spongy and then simply dropped to the floor—no brakes, and it was a long hill. Fortunately, we made it to a service station, where we found that the brake line had been cut so that a slow leak would occur. Perhaps it was a coincidence that Ray was working in the auto shop when the car was being tuned up, but I had no doubt that the prison "telegraph" had informed him of the owner of the car.

(Hare, 1993)

How do various institutions in our society—business, government, science, religion—view lying? How might such views affect lying by individuals?

Like Ray, people with antisocial personality disorder lie repeatedly (APA, 2013). Many cannot work consistently at a job; they are absent frequently and are likely to quit their jobs altogether (Hengartner et al., 2014). Usually they are also careless with money and frequently fail to pay their debts. They are often impulsive, taking action without thinking of the consequences (Lang et al., 2015). Correspondingly, they may be irritable, aggressive, and quick to start fights. Many travel from place to place.

Recklessness is another common trait: people with antisocial personality disorder have little regard for their own safety or for that of others, even their children. They are self-centered as well, and are likely to have trouble maintaining close relationships. Usually they develop a knack for gaining personal profit at the expense of other people. Because the pain or damage they cause seldom concerns them, clinicians commonly say that they lack a moral conscience. They think of their victims as weak and deserving of being conned, robbed, or even physically harmed (see *PsychWatch* on the next page).

Surveys indicate that 3.6 percent of adults in the United States meet the criteria for antisocial personality disorder (Sansone & Sansone, 2011). The disorder is as much as four times more common among men than women.

Because people with this disorder are often arrested, researchers frequently look for people with antisocial patterns in prison populations (Pondé et al., 2014). It is estimated that at least 40 percent of people in prison meet the diagnostic criteria for this disorder (Naidoo & Mkize, 2012). Among men in urban jails, the antisocial personality pattern has been linked strongly to past arrests for crimes of violence (De Matteo et al., 2005). The criminal behavior of many people with this disorder declines after the age of 40; some, however, continue their criminal activities throughout their lives (APA, 2013).

Studies and clinical observations also indicate that people with antisocial personality disorder have higher rates of alcoholism and other substance use disorders than do the rest of the population (Brook et al., 2014; Reese et al., 2010). Perhaps intoxication and substance misuse help trigger the development of antisocial personality disorder by loosening a person's inhibitions. Perhaps this personality disorder somehow makes a person more prone to abuse substances. Or perhaps antisocial personality disorder and substance use disorders both have the same cause, such as a deep-seated need to take risks. Interestingly, drug users with the personality disorder often cite the recreational aspects of drug use as their reason for starting and continuing it.

How Do Theorists Explain Antisocial Personality Disorder? Explanations of antisocial personality disorder come from the psychodynamic, behavioral, cognitive, and biological models. As with many other personality disorders, psychodynamic theorists propose that this one begins with an absence of parental love during infancy, leading to a lack of basic trust (Meloy & Yakeley, 2010; Sperry, 2003). In this view, some children—the ones who develop antisocial personality disorder—respond to the early inadequacies by becoming emotionally distant, and they bond with others through the use of power and destructiveness. In support of

Character Ingestion

As late as the Victorian era, many English parents believed babies absorbed personality and moral uprightness as they took in milk. Thus, if a mother could not nurse, it was important to find a wet nurse of good character.

(Asimov, 1997).

Popular sociopaths Television audiences seem to love characters with the symptoms of antisocial personality disorder. Legendary character Tony Soprano of *The Sopranos* (left) had hardly left our screens when he was replaced in the hearts of television viewers everywhere by the equally legendary Walter White of *Breaking Bad* (right).

Mary Evans/HBO/Soprano Productions/Ronald Grant/Everett Collection

Ursula Coyote/©AMC/Courtesy Everett Collection

PsychWatch

Mass Murders: Where Does Such Violence Come From?

In 2012, a young man entered the Sandy Hook Elementary School in Newtown, Connecticut, and killed 26 people—20 of them young children—in a shooting rampage. In the months prior to this massacre, gunmen killed 12 moviegoers at a *Batman* movie in Colorado and 6 churchgoers at a Sikh temple in Wisconsin. And in 2015 a young man shot and killed 9 people who were participating in a Bible study group at the Emanuel African Methodist Episcopal Church in Charleston, South Carolina. The clinical field has offered various theories about why individuals commit mass murders, but enlightening research and effective interventions have been elusive (Montaldo, 2014; Friedman, 2013).

What do we know about mass killings? We know they involve, by definition, the murder of four or more people in the same location and at around the same time. FBI records also indicate that, on average, mass killings occur in the United States every two weeks, 75 percent of them feature a lone killer, 67 percent involve the use of guns, and most are committed by males (Hoyer & Heath, 2012).

We also know that despite appearances, the number of mass killings is not on the rise *overall* (O'Neill, 2012). What is increasing, however, are certain settings for mass killings (e.g., schools) and certain patterns of mass murder. Although specific issues vary from mass murder to mass murder—racial or religious hatred, for example—two general patterns are on the rise. In one pattern, so-called pseudo-commando mass murders, the murderer "kills in public, often during the daytime, plans his offense well in advance, and comes prepared with a powerful arsenal of weapons. He has no escape planned and expects to be killed during the incident" (Knoll, 2010). In another pattern, "autogenetic" (self-generated) massacres, individuals kill people indiscriminately to fulfill a personal agenda (Bowers et al., 2010; Mullen, 2004).

Theorists have suggested a number of factors to help explain pseudocommando,

A nation grieves . . . again During a 2015 prayer vigil at a Washington, D. C. church, congregants hold up photographs of nine Bible study participants who had been shot and killed two days earlier at the Emanuel African Methodist Episcopal Church in Charleston, South Carolina.

Win McNamee/Getty Images

autogenetic, and other mass killings, including the availability of guns, bullying behavior, substance abuse, the proliferation of violent media and video games, dysfunctional homes, and contagion effects (Towers et al., 2015). Moreover, regardless of one's position on gun control, media violence, or the like, almost everyone, including most clinicians, believe that mass killers typically suffer from a mental disorder (Auxemery, 2015; Fox & Levin, 2014). Which mental disorder? On this, there is little agreement. Each of the following has been suggested:

➤ Antisocial, borderline, paranoid, or schizotypal personality disorder

➤ Schizophrenia or severe bipolar disorder

➤ Intermittent explosive disorder—an impulse-control disorder featuring repeated, unprovoked verbal and/or behavioral outbursts

➤ Severe depression, stress, or anxiety

Although these and yet other disorders have been proposed, none has received clear support in the limited research conducted on mass killings. On the other

hand, several psychological variables have emerged as a common denominator across the various studies: severe feelings of anger and resentment, feelings of being persecuted or grossly mistreated, and desires for revenge (Fox & Levin, 2014; Knoll, 2010). That is, regardless of which mental disorder a mass killer may display, he usually is driven by this set of feelings. For a growing number of clinical researchers, this repeated finding suggests that research should focus less on diagnosis and much more on identifying and understanding these particular feelings.

Clearly, clinical research must expand its focus on this area of enormous social concern. It is a difficult problem to investigate, partly because so few mass killers survive their crimes, but the clinical field has managed to gather useful insights about other elusive areas. And, indeed, in the aftermath of the horrific murders mentioned at the beginning of this box, a wave of heightened determination and commitment seems to have seized the clinical community.

the psychodynamic explanation, researchers have found that people with this disorder are more likely than others to have had significant stress in their childhoods, particularly in such forms as family poverty, family violence, child abuse, and parental conflict or divorce (Kumari et al., 2014; Martens, 2005).

Many behavioral theorists have suggested that antisocial symptoms may be learned through *modeling,* or imitation (Gaynor & Baird, 2007). As evidence, they point to the higher rate of antisocial personality disorder found among the parents of people with this disorder (APA, 2013). Other behaviorists have suggested that some parents unintentionally teach antisocial behavior by regularly rewarding a child's aggressive behavior (Kazdin, 2005). When the child misbehaves or becomes violent in reaction to the parents' requests or orders, for example, the parents may give in to restore peace. Without meaning to, they may be teaching the child to be stubborn and perhaps even violent.

The cognitive view says that people with antisocial personality disorder hold attitudes that trivialize the importance of other people's needs (Elwood et al., 2004). Such a philosophy of life, some theorists suggest, may be far more common in our society than people recognize (see Table 13-2). Cognitive theorists further propose that people with this disorder have genuine difficulty recognizing points of view or feelings other than their own (Herpertz & Bertsch, 2014).

Finally, studies suggest that biological factors may play an important role in antisocial personality disorder. Researchers have found that antisocial people, particularly those who are highly impulsive and aggressive, have lower serotonin activity than other people (Thompson et al., 2014). As you'll recall, both impulsivity and aggression also have been linked to low serotonin activity in other kinds of studies (see page 235), so the presence of this biological factor in people with antisocial personality disorder is not surprising.

Other studies indicate that individuals with this disorder display deficient functioning in their frontal lobes, particularly in the prefrontal cortex (Liu et al., 2014). Among other duties, this brain region helps people to plan and execute realistic strategies and to have personal characteristics such as sympathy, judgment, and empathy. These are, of course, all qualities found wanting in people with antisocial personality disorder.

In yet another line of research, investigators have found that people with antisocial personality disorder often feel less anxiety than other people, and so lack a key ingredient for learning (Blair et al., 2005). This would help explain why they have so much trouble learning from negative life experiences or tuning in to the emotional cues of others. Why should people with antisocial personality disorder experience less anxiety than other people? The answer may lie once again in the biological realm. Research participants with the disorder often respond to warnings or expectations of stress with low brain and bodily arousal (Thompson et al., 2014; Perdeci et al., 2010). Perhaps because of the low arousal, they easily tune out threatening or emotional situations, and so are unaffected by them.

It could also be argued that because of their physical underarousal, people with antisocial personality disorder would be more likely than other people to take risks and seek thrills. That is, they may be drawn to antisocial activity precisely because it meets an underlying biological need for more excitement and arousal. In support of this idea, as you read earlier, antisocial personality disorder often goes hand in hand with sensation-seeking behavior.

Treatments for Antisocial Personality Disorder Treatments for people with antisocial personality disorder are typically ineffective (Black, 2015). Major obstacles to treatment include the individuals' lack of conscience, desire to change, or respect for therapy (Colli et al., 2014; Kantor, 2006). Most of those in therapy have been forced to participate by an employer, their school, or the law,

> Can you point to attitudes and events in today's world that may trivialize people's needs?

table: **13-2**

Annual Hate Crimes in the United States

Group Attacked	Number of Reported Incidents
Racial/ethnic groups	4,119
LGBT* groups	1,318
Religious groups	1,166
Groups with disability	102

★Widely accepted acronym for Lesbian, Gay, Bisexual, and Transgender people

Information from: U.S. Department of Justice, Federal Bureau of Investigation, 2013, 2012

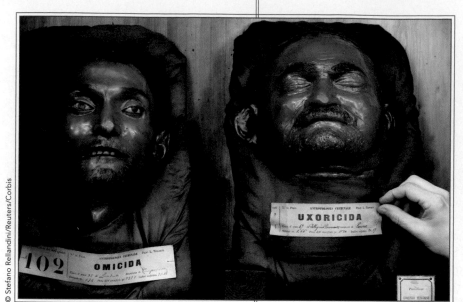

© Stefano Rellandini/Reuters/Corbis

Hardly a new disorder A worker attaches a tag that translates as "Killer of a Wife" to a wax-covered head at the Lombroso Museum in Turin, Italy. Hundreds of such heads, taken from prisons throughout Europe, line the museum's shelves, each with the tags like "Ladro" ("Thief") or "Omicida" ("Murderer"). The display comes from nineteenth-century psychiatrist Cesare Lombroso's crude but pioneering research into the nature of criminal and related antisocial behavior.

or they come to the attention of therapists when they also develop another psychological disorder (Agronin, 2006).

Some cognitive therapists try to guide clients with antisocial personality disorder to think about moral issues and about the needs of other people (Beck & Weishaar, 2011; Weishaar & Beck, 2006). In a similar vein, a number of hospitals and prisons have tried to create a therapeutic community for people with this disorder, a structured environment that teaches responsibility toward others (Harris & Rice, 2006). Some patients seem to profit from such approaches, but it appears that most do not. In recent years, clinicians have also used psychotropic medications, particularly atypical antipsychotic drugs, to treat people with antisocial personality disorder. Some report that these drugs help reduce certain features of the disorder, but systematic studies of this claim are still needed (Brown et al., 2014; Thompson et al., 2014).

Borderline Personality Disorder

People with **borderline personality disorder** display great instability, including major shifts in mood, an unstable self-image, and impulsivity (APA, 2013). These characteristics combine to make their relationships very unstable as well (Paris, 2010, 2005). Some of Ellen Farber's difficulties are typical:

> Ellen Farber, a 35-year-old, single insurance company executive, came to a psychiatric emergency room . . . with complaints of depression and the thought of driving her car off a cliff. An articulate, moderately overweight, sophisticated woman, Ms. Farber appeared to be in considerable distress. She reported a 6-month period of increasingly persistent dysphoria and lack of energy and pleasure. Feeling as if she were "made of lead," Ms. Farber had recently been spending 15–20 hours a day in her bed. She also reported daily episodes of binge eating, when she would consume "anything I can find.". . . She reported problems with intermittent binge eating since adolescence, but these had recently increased in frequency, resulting in a 20-pound weight gain. . . .
>
> She attributed her increasing symptoms to financial difficulties. Ms. Farber had been fired from her job two weeks before. . . . She claimed it was because she "owed a small amount of money." When asked to be more specific, she reported owing $150,000 to her former employers and another $100,000 to various local banks. . . . From age 30 to age 33, she had used her employer's credit cards to finance weekly "buying binges," accumulating the $150,000 debt. She . . . reported that spending money alleviated her chronic feelings of loneliness, isolation, and sadness. Experiencing only temporary relief, every few days she would impulsively buy expensive jewelry, watches, or multiple pairs of the same shoes. . . .
>
> In addition to lifelong feelings of emptiness, Ms. Farber described chronic uncertainty about what she wanted to do in life and with whom she wanted to be friends. She had many brief, intense relationships with both men and women, but her quick temper led to frequent arguments and even physical fights. Although she had always thought of her childhood as happy and carefree, when she became depressed, she began to recall [being abused verbally and physically by her mother].
>
> *(Spitzer et al., 1994, pp. 395–397)*

▶ **borderline personality disorder** A personality disorder characterized by repeated instability in interpersonal relationships, self-image, and mood and by impulsive behavior.

table: **13-3**

Comparison of Personality Disorders

	Cluster	Similar Disorders	Responsiveness to Treatment
Paranoid	Odd	Schizophrenia; delusional disorder	Modest
Schizoid	Odd	Schizophrenia; delusional disorder	Modest
Schizotypal	Odd	Schizophrenia; delusional disorder	Modest
Antisocial	Dramatic	Conduct disorder	Poor
Borderline	Dramatic	Depressive disorder; bipolar disorder	Moderate
Histrionic	Dramatic	Somatic symptom disorder; depressive disorder	Modest
Narcissistic	Dramatic	Cyclothymic disorder (mild bipolar disorder)	Poor
Avoidant	Anxious	Social anxiety disorder	Moderate
Dependent	Anxious	Separation anxiety disorder; depressive disorder	Moderate
Obsessive-compulsive	Anxious	Obsessive-compulsive disorder	Moderate

Like Ellen Farber, people with borderline personality disorder swing in and out of very depressive, anxious, and irritable states that last anywhere from a few hours to a few days or more (see Table 13-3). Their emotions seem to be always in conflict with the world around them. They are prone to bouts of anger, which sometimes result in physical aggression and violence (Martino et al., 2015; Scott et al., 2014). Just as often, however, they direct their impulsive anger inward and inflict bodily harm on themselves. Many seem troubled by deep feelings of emptiness.

Borderline personality disorder is a complex disorder, and it is fast becoming one of the more common conditions seen in clinical practice. Many of the patients who come to mental health emergency rooms are people with this disorder who have intentionally hurt themselves. Their impulsive, self-destructive activities may range from alcohol and substance abuse to delinquency, unsafe sex, and reckless driving (Kienast et al., 2014; Coffey et al., 2011). Many engage in self-injurious or self-mutilation behaviors, such as cutting or burning themselves or banging their heads (Turner et al., 2015). As you saw in Chapter 7, such behaviors typically cause immense physical suffering, but those with borderline personality disorder often feel as if the physical discomfort offers relief from their emotional suffering. It may serve as a distraction from their emotional or interpersonal upsets, "snapping" them out of an "emotional overload" (Sadeh et al., 2014). Many try to hurt themselves as a way of dealing with their chronic feelings of emptiness, boredom, and identity confusion. Scars and bruises also may provide them with a kind of concrete evidence of their emotional distress (Paris, 2010, 2005).

Suicidal threats and actions are also common (Amore et al., 2014; Zimmerman et al., 2014). Studies suggest that around 75 percent of people with borderline personality disorder attempt suicide at least once in their lives; as many as 10 percent actually commit suicide. It is common for people with this disorder to enter clinical treatment by way of the emergency room after a suicide attempt.

People with borderline personality disorder frequently form intense, conflict-ridden relationships in which their feelings are not necessarily shared by the other person. They may come to idealize another person's qualities and abilities after

BETWEEN THE LINES

Letting It Out

Expression of Anger Only 23 percent of adults report openly expressing their anger (Kanner, 2005, 1995). Around 39 percent say that they hide or contain their anger, and 23 percent walk away to try to collect themselves.

The Myth of Venting Contrary to the notion that "letting off steam" reduces anger, angry participants in one study acted much more aggressively after hitting a punching bag than did angry participants who first sat quietly for a while (Bushman et al., 1999).

just a brief first encounter. They also may violate the boundaries of relationships (Lazarus et al., 2014). They quickly feel rejected and may become furious when their expectations are not met, yet they remain very attached to the relationships (Berenson et al., 2011). In fact, they have recurrent fears of impending abandonment and frequently engage in frantic efforts to avoid real or imagined separations from important people in their lives (Gunderson, 2011). Sometimes they cut themselves or carry out other self-destructive acts to prevent partners from leaving.

People with borderline personality disorder typically have dramatic identity shifts. Because of this unstable sense of self, their goals, aspirations, friends, and even sexual orientation may shift rapidly (Westen et al., 2011; Skodol, 2005). They may at times have no sense of themselves at all, leading to the feelings of emptiness described earlier.

According to surveys, 5.9 percent of the adult population display borderline personality disorder (Zanarini et al., 2014; Sansone & Sansone, 2011). Close to 75 percent of the patients who receive the diagnosis are women (Gunderson, 2011). The course of the disorder varies from person to person. In the most common pattern, the person's instability and risk of suicide peak during young adulthood and then gradually wane with advancing age (APA, 2013). Given the chaotic and unstable relationships characteristic of borderline personality disorder, it is not surprising that the disorder tends to interfere with job performance even more than most other personality disorders do (Hengartner et al., 2014).

How Do Theorists Explain Borderline Personality Disorder?

Because a fear of abandonment tortures so many people with borderline personality disorder, psychodynamic theorists have looked once again to early parental relationships to explain the disorder (Gabbard, 2010). Object relations theorists, for example, propose that an early lack of acceptance by parents may lead to a loss of self-esteem, increased dependence, and an inability to cope with separation (Caligor & Clarkin, 2010).

Personality disorders—at the movies
In the 1999 film *Girl, Interrupted,* based on a best-selling memoir, Susanna Kaysen (left, played by actress Winona Ryder) is befriended by Lisa Rowe (played by Angelina Jolie) at a mental hospital. Kaysen received a diagnosis of borderline personality disorder at the hospital, while Rowe's diagnosis was antisocial personality disorder.

Suzanne Tenner/Columbia Tristar/The Kobal Collection

Research has found that this is consistent with the early childhoods of people with borderline personality disorder. In many cases, when they were children, their parents neglected or rejected them, verbally abused them, or otherwise behaved inappropriately (Martín-Blanco et al., 2014). Their childhoods were often marked by multiple parent substitutes, divorce, death, or traumas such as physical or sexual abuse (Newnham & Janca, 2014; Huang et al., 2010). At the same time, it is important to recognize that the vast majority of people with histories of physical, sexual, or psychological abuse do not go on to develop borderline personality disorder (Skodol, 2005).

Borderline personality disorder also has been linked to certain biological abnormalities, such as an overly reactive *amygdala,* the brain structure that is closely tied to fear and other negative emotions, and an underactive *prefrontal cortex,* the brain region linked to planning, self-control, and decision making (Mitchell et al., 2014; Stone, 2014). Moreover, people with borderline personality disorder who are particularly impulsive—those who attempt suicide or are very aggressive toward others—apparently have lower brain serotonin activity (Soloff et al., 2014). In accord with these various biological findings, close relatives of those with borderline personality disorder are five times more likely than the general population to have the same personality disorder (Amad et al., 2014; Torgersen, 2000, 1984).

A number of theorists currently use a *biosocial theory* to explain borderline personality disorder (Neacsiu & Linehan, 2014). According to this view, the disorder results from a combination of internal forces (for example, difficulty identifying and controlling one's emotions, social skill deficits, abnormal neurotransmitter reactions) and external forces (for example, an environment in which a child's emotions are punished, ignored, trivialized, or disregarded). Parents may, for instance, misinterpret their child's intense emotions as exaggerations or attempts at manipulation rather than as serious expressions of unsettled internal states. According to the biosocial theory, if children have intrinsic difficulty identifying and controlling their emotions and if their parents teach them to ignore their intense feelings, they may never learn how properly to recognize and control their emotional arousal or how to handle emotional distress (Herpertz & Bertsch, 2014; Lazarus et al., 2014). Such children will be at risk for the development of borderline personality disorder (Gill & Warburton, 2014).

Note that the biosocial theory is similar to one of the leading explanations for eating disorders. As you saw in Chapter 9, theorist Hilde Bruch proposed that children whose parents do not respond accurately to the children's internal cues may never learn to identify cues of hunger, thus increasing their risk of developing an eating disorder (see pages 289–290). Small wonder that a large number of people with borderline personality disorder also have an eating disorder (Gabriel & Waller, 2014). Recall, for example, Ellen Farber's dysfunctional eating pattern.

Finally, some sociocultural theorists suggest that cases of borderline personality disorder are particularly likely to emerge in cultures that change rapidly. As a culture loses its stability, they argue, it inevitably leaves many of its members with problems of identity, a sense of emptiness, high anxiety, and fears of abandonment. Family units may come apart, leaving people with little sense of belonging. Changes of this kind in society today may explain growing reports of the disorder (Millon, 2011).

Treatments for Borderline Personality Disorder

It appears that psychotherapy can eventually lead to some degree of improvement for people with borderline personality disorder (McMain, 2015; Neville, 2014). It is, however, extraordinarily difficult for a therapist to strike a balance between empathizing with the borderline client's dependency and anger and challenging his or her way of thinking (Goodman et al., 2014). The wildly fluctuating interpersonal attitudes of clients with the disorder can also make it difficult for therapists to establish collaborative working relationships with them. Moreover, clients with borderline personality disorder may violate the boundaries of the client–therapist relationship (for example, calling the therapist's emergency contact number to discuss matters of a less urgent nature) (Colli et al., 2014).

Over the past two decades, an integrative treatment for borderline personality disorder, called *dialectical behavior therapy* (*DBT*), has been receiving considerable research support and is now considered the treatment of choice in many clinical circles (Linehan et al., 2015, 2006, 2002, 2001). DBT, developed by psychologist Marsha Linehan, grows largely from the cognitive-behavioral treatment model (see *MediaSpeak* on the next page). It includes a number of the same cognitive and behavioral techniques that are applied to other disorders: homework assignments, psychoeducation, the teaching of social and other skills, modeling by the therapist, clear goal setting, reinforcements for appropriate behaviors, and collaborative examinations by the client and therapist of the client's ways of thinking.

DBT also borrows heavily from the humanistic and contemporary psychodynamic approaches, placing the client–therapist relationship itself at the center

© Reuters/Corbis

Troubled princess Admired by millions during her short life, particularly for her numerous charitable efforts and humane acts, Princess Diana also had a range of psychological problems that she herself disclosed in books and interviews. Diagnosing and explaining her problems has become a common practice—both inside and outside the clinical field—since her death in 1997. Her self-cutting, possible borderline personality functioning, and disordered eating behaviors have received the most attention.

////// BETWEEN THE LINES //////

Whither "Borderline"?

In 1938 the term "borderline" was introduced by psychoanalyst Adolph Stern. He used it to describe patients who were more disturbed than "neurotic" patients, yet not psychotic (Bateman, 2011; Stern, 1938). The term has since evolved to its present usage.

MediaSpeak
The Patient as Therapist

By Benedict Carey, *New York Times*, June 23, 2011

Marsha M. Linehan, 68 . . . told her story in public for the first time last week. . . .

Dr. Linehan . . . was driven by a mission to rescue people who are chronically suicidal, often as a result of borderline personality disorder, an enigmatic condition characterized in part by self-destructive urges. "I honestly didn't realize at the time that I was dealing with myself," she said. "But I suppose it's true that I developed a therapy that provides the things I needed for so many years and never got."

She learned the central tragedy of severe mental illness the hard way, banging her head against the wall of a locked room.

Marsha Linehan arrived at the Institute of Living on March 9, 1961, at age 17, and quickly became the sole occupant of the seclusion room on the unit known as Thompson Two, for the most severely ill patients. The staff saw no alternative: The girl attacked herself habitually, burning her wrists with cigarettes, slashing her arms, her legs, her midsection, using any sharp object she could get her hands on.

The seclusion room . . . had no such weapon. Yet her urge to die only deepened. . . .

"I was in hell," she said. "And I made a vow: when I get out, I'm going to come back and get others out of here.". . .

Radical Acceptance

. . . It was 1967, several years after she left the institute as a desperate 20-year-old whom doctors gave little chance of surviving outside the hospital. . . . "One night I was kneeling in [church], looking up at the cross, and the whole place became gold—and suddenly I felt something coming toward me," she said. "It was this shimmering experience, and I just ran back to my room and said, 'I love myself.' . . . I felt transformed.". . .

What had changed?

It took years of study in psychology—she earned a Ph.D. at Loyola in 1971—before she found an answer. On the surface, it seemed obvious: She had accepted herself as she was. . . . That basic idea—radical acceptance, she now calls it—became increasingly important as she began working with patients, first at a suicide clinic in Buffalo and later as a researcher. . . .

Psychologist Marsha Linehan

Damon Winter/The New York Times/Redux Pictures

No therapist could promise a quick transformation or even sudden "insight," much less a shimmering religious vision. But now Dr. Linehan was closing in on two seemingly opposed principles that could form the basis of a treatment: acceptance of life as it is, not as it is supposed to be; and the need to change, despite that reality and because of it. . . .

She chose to treat people with a diagnosis that she would have given her young self: borderline personality disorder. . . .

Yet even as she climbed the academic ladder, moving from the Catholic University of America to the University of Washington in 1977, she understood from her own experience that acceptance and change were hardly enough. . . . She relied on therapists herself, off and on over the years, for support and guidance. . . .

Dr. Linehan's own emerging approach to treatment—now called dialectical behavior therapy, or D.B.T.—would also have to include day-to-day skills. . . . She borrowed some of these from other behavioral therapies and added elements, like opposite action, in which patients act opposite to the way they feel when an emotion is inappropriate; and mindfulness meditation. . . .

In studies in the 1980s and '90s, researchers at the University of Washington and elsewhere tracked the progress of hundreds of borderline patients at high risk of suicide who attended weekly dialectical therapy sessions. Compared with similar patients who got other experts' treatments, those who learned Dr. Linehan's approach made far fewer suicide attempts, landed in the hospital less often and were much more likely to stay in treatment. D.B.T. is now widely used for a variety of clients, including juvenile offenders. . . .

Most remarkably, perhaps, Dr. Linehan has reached a place where she can stand up and tell her story, come what will. "I'm a very happy person now.". . . "I still have ups and downs, of course, but I think no more than anyone else."

of treatment interactions, making sure that appropriate treatment boundaries are adhered to and providing an environment of acceptance and validation of the client. Indeed, DBT therapists regularly empathize with their borderline clients and with the emotional turmoil they are experiencing, locate kernels of truth in the clients' complaints or demands, and examine alternative ways for them to address valid needs.

DBT is often supplemented by the clients' participation in social skill-building groups (Roney & Cannon, 2014). In these groups, clients practice new ways of relating to other people in a safe environment and receive validation and support from other group members.

DBT has received more research support than any other treatment for border-line personality disorder (Neacsiu & Linehan, 2014; Roepke et al., 2011). Many clients who receive DBT become more able to tolerate stress; develop new, more appropriate, social skills; respond more effectively to life situations; and develop a more stable identity. They also have significantly fewer suicidal behaviors and require fewer hospitalizations than those who receive other forms of treatment (Linehan et al., 2015). In addition, they are more likely to remain in treatment and to report less anger, more social gratification, improved work performance, and reductions in substance abuse (Rizvi et al., 2011).

Antidepressant, antibipolar, antianxiety, and antipsychotic drugs have helped calm the emotional and aggressive storms of some people with borderline personality disorder (Bridler et al., 2015; Knappich et al., 2014). However, given the numerous suicide attempts by people with this disorder, the use of drugs on an outpatient basis is controversial (Gunderson, 2011). Many professionals believe that psychotropic drug treatment for borderline personality disorder should be used largely as an adjunct to psychotherapy approaches, and indeed many clients seem to benefit from a combination of psychotherapy and drug therapy (Omar et al., 2014).

"You'll have to excuse me—I'm myself today."

Histrionic Personality Disorder

People with **histrionic personality disorder,** once called **hysterical personality disorder,** are extremely emotional—they are typically described as "emotionally charged"—and continually seek to be the center of attention (APA, 2013). Their exaggerated moods and neediness can complicate life considerably, as we see in the case of Lucinda:

> Unhappy over her impending divorce, Lucinda decided to seek counseling. She arrived at her first session wearing a very provocative outfit, including a revealing blouse and extremely short skirt. Her hair had been labored over, and she had on an excessive amount of makeup—very carefully applied.
>
> When asked to discuss her separation, Lucinda first insisted that the therapist call her Cindy, saying, "All my close friends call me that, and I like to think that you and I will become very good friends here." She said that her husband Morgan had suddenly abandoned her—"probably brainwashed by some young trollop." She proceeded to describe their break-up in a theatrical manner. Over a span of five minutes, her voice ranged from whispers to cries of agony and back again to whispers; she waved her arms dramatically while making some points and sat totally still while making others. She seemed to be on center stage.
>
> Lucinda said that when Morgan first told her that he wanted a divorce, she did not know whether she could go on. The pain was palpable. After all, they had been so "incredibly and irrevocably" close, and he had been so devoted to her. She said that initially she even had thoughts of doing away with herself. But, of course,

▶ **histrionic personality disorder** A personality disorder characterized by a pattern of excessive emotionality and attention seeking. Once called *hysterical personality disorder.*

(continues on the next page)

she knew that she had to pull herself together. So many people needed her to be strong. So many people relied on her, particularly her "dear friends" and her sister. She had deep and special relationships with them all.

She told the therapist that without Morgan she would now need a man to take care of her—emotionally and every other way. She asked the therapist if she looked like a 30-year-old woman. When he declined to answer, she said, "I know you're not supposed to say."

When the therapist attempted to steer the conversation back to Morgan, Lucinda asked, "Do we really need to talk about that abusive lout?" Pressed on the word "abusive," Lucinda replied that she was referring to "mental cruelty." Morgan had, after all, called her inadequate and worthless throughout their marriage and told her that everything good in her life had been due to him. When her therapist pointed out that this seemed to contradict the rosy picture she had just painted of Morgan and their married life, she quickly changed the subject.

As the session came to a close, Lucinda's therapist suggested that it might be useful for him to meet with Morgan. She loved the idea, saying, "Then he'll know the competition he has!"

When he met with Morgan a few days later, the therapist heard a very different story. Morgan said, "I really loved Cindy—still do—but she was always flying off the handle, telling me I'm no good or that I didn't care about her. She would often complain that I spent too much time at work—keep in mind that I never work more than 30 hours a week—and too little time attending to her needs. I just can't take life with her anymore. It's too draining."

Morgan also indicated that Lucinda had virtually no close friends. She and her sister might talk on the phone once a month and get together in person twice a year. He acknowledged that she drew a lot of attention from people. But, he noted "Look at how she dresses and her constant flirting. That'll get people's attention, keep them around for a while."

Transient hysterical symptoms These avid Harry Potter fans expressed themselves with exaggerated emotionality and lack of restraint at the midnight launch of one of the books in the series. Similar reactions, along with fainting, tremors, and even convulsions, have been common at concerts by musical idols dating back to the 1940s. Small wonder that expressive fans of this kind are regularly described as "hysterical" or "histrionic" by the press—the same labels applied to the personality disorder that is marked by such behaviors and symptoms.

© Jim Sugar/Corbis

People with histrionic personality disorder are always "on stage," using theatrical gestures and mannerisms and grandiose language to describe ordinary everyday events. Like chameleons, they keep changing themselves to attract and impress an audience, and in their pursuit they change not only their surface characteristics—according to the latest fads—but also their opinions and beliefs. In fact, their speech is actually scanty in detail and substance, and they seem to lack a sense of who they really are.

Approval and praise are their lifeblood; they must have others present to witness their exaggerated emotional states. Vain, self-centered, demanding, and unable to delay gratification for long, they overreact to any minor event that gets in the way of their quest for attention. Some make suicide attempts, often to manipulate others (APA, 2013).

People with histrionic personality disorder may draw attention to themselves by exaggerating their physical illnesses or fatigues. They may also behave very provocatively and try to achieve their goals through sexual seduction. Most obsess over how they look and how others will perceive them, often wearing bright, eye-catching clothes. They exaggerate the depth of their relationships, considering themselves to be the intimate friends of people who see them as no more than casual acquaintances. Often they become involved with romantic partners who may be exciting but who do not treat them well.

This disorder was once believed to be more common in women than in men, and clinicians long described the "hysterical wife" (Anderson et al., 2001). Research, however, has revealed gender bias in past diagnoses (APA, 2013). When evaluating case studies of people with a mixture of histrionic and antisocial traits, clinicians in several studies gave a diagnosis of histrionic personality disorder to women more than men. Surveys suggest that 1.8 percent of adults have this personality disorder, with males and females equally affected (APA, 2013; Sansone & Sansone, 2011).

How Do Theorists Explain Histrionic Personality Disorder?

The psychodynamic perspective was originally developed to help explain cases of hysteria (see Chapter 8), so it is no surprise that psychodynamic theorists continue to have a strong interest in histrionic personality disorder. Most psychodynamic theorists believe that as children, people with this disorder had cold and controlling parents who left them feeling unloved and afraid of abandonment (Horowitz & Lerner, 2010; Bender et al., 2001). To defend against deep-seated fears of loss, the children learned to behave dramatically, inventing crises that would require other people to act protectively.

Cognitive explanations look instead at the lack of substance and extreme suggestibility that people with histrionic personality disorder have. Cognitive theorists see these people as becoming less and less interested in knowing about the world at large because they are so self-focused and emotional. With no detailed memories of what they never learned, they must rely on hunches or on other people to provide them with direction in life (Blagov et al., 2007). Some cognitive theorists also believe that people with this disorder hold a general assumption that they are helpless to care for themselves, and so they constantly seek out others who will meet their needs (Weishaar & Beck, 2006; Beck et al., 2004).

Sociocultural, particularly multicultural, theorists believe that histrionic personality disorder is produced in part by cultural norms and expectations. Until recently, our society encouraged girls to hold on to childhood and dependency as they grew up. The vain, dramatic, and selfish behavior of the histrionic personality may actually be an exaggeration of femininity as our culture once defined it (Fowler et al., 2007). Similarly, some clinical observers claim that histrionic personality disorder is diagnosed less often in Asian and other cultures that discourage overt sexualization and more often in Hispanic American and Latin American cultures that are more tolerant of overt sexualization (Patrick, 2007; Trull & Widiger, 2003). Researchers have not, however, investigated this claim systematically.

Treatments for Histrionic Personality Disorder People with histrionic personality disorder are more likely than those with most other personality disorders to seek out treatment on their own (Tyrer et al., 2003). Working with them can be very difficult, however, because of the demands, tantrums, and seductiveness they are likely to deploy. Another problem is that these clients may pretend to have important insights or to change during treatment merely to please the therapist. To head off such problems, therapists must remain objective and maintain strict professional boundaries (Colli et al., 2014; Blagov et al., 2007).

Cognitive therapists have tried to help people with this disorder to change their belief that they are helpless and also to develop better, more deliberate ways of thinking and solving problems (Weishaar & Beck, 2006; Beck et al., 2004). Psychodynamic therapy and various group therapy formats have also been used (Horowitz & Lerner, 2010). In all these approaches, therapists ultimately aim to help the clients recognize their excessive dependency, find inner satisfaction, and become more self-reliant. Clinical case reports suggest that each of the approaches can be useful. Drug therapy appears less successful except as a means of relieving the depressive symptoms that some patients have (Bock et al., 2010; Grossman, 2004).

► **narcissistic personality disorder**
A personality disorder marked by a broad pattern of grandiosity, need for admiration, and lack of empathy.

Narcissistic Personality Disorder

People with **narcissistic personality disorder** are generally grandiose, need much admiration, and feel no empathy with others (APA, 2013). Convinced of their own great success, power, or beauty, they expect constant attention and admiration from those around them. Frederick, the man whom we met at the beginning of this chapter, was one such person. So is Steven, a 30-year-old artist, married, with one child:

Steven came to the attention of a therapist when his wife insisted that they seek marital counseling. According to her, Steve was "selfish, ungiving and preoccupied with his work." Everything at home had to "revolve about him, his comfort, moods and desires, no one else's." She claimed that he contributed nothing to the marriage, except a rather meager income. He shirked all "normal" responsibilities and kept "throwing chores in her lap," and she was "getting fed up with being the chief cook and bottlewasher, tired of being his mother and sleep-in maid."

On the positive side, Steven's wife felt that he was basically a "gentle and good-natured guy with talent and intelligence." But this wasn't enough. She wanted a husband, someone with whom she could share things. In contrast, he wanted, according to her, "a mother, not a wife"; he didn't want "to grow up, he didn't know how to give affection, only to take it when he felt like it, nothing more, nothing less."

Steve presented a picture of an affable, self-satisfied and somewhat disdainful young man. He was employed as a commercial artist, but looked forward to his evenings and weekends when he could turn his attention to serious painting. He claimed that he had to devote all of his spare time and energies to "fulfill himself," to achieve expression in his creative work. . . .

His relationships with his present co-workers and social acquaintances were pleasant and satisfying, but he did admit that most people viewed him as a "bit self-centered, cold and snobbish." He recognized that he did not know how to share his thoughts and feelings with others, that he was much more interested in himself than in them and that perhaps he always had "preferred the pleasure" of his own company to that of others.

(Millon, 1969, pp. 261–262)

People with narcissistic personality disorder have a grandiose sense of self-importance. They exaggerate their achievements and talents, expecting others to recognize them as superior, and often appear arrogant. They are very choosy about their friends and associates, believing that their problems are unique and can be appreciated only by other "special," high-status people. Because of their charm, they often make favorable first impressions, yet they can rarely maintain long-term relationships (Campbell & Miller, 2011).

Why do people often admire arrogant deceivers—art forgers, jewel thieves, or certain kinds of "con" artists, for example?

Like Steven, people with narcissistic personality disorder are seldom interested in the feelings of others. They may not even be able to empathize with such feelings (Marcoux et al., 2014; Roepke & Vater, 2014). Many take advantage of other people to achieve their own ends, perhaps partly out of envy; at the same time they believe others envy them. Though grandiose, some react to criticism or frustration with bouts of rage, humiliation, or embitterment (APA, 2013). Others may react with cold indifference. And still others become extremely pessimistic and filled with depression. They may have periods of zest that alternate with periods of disappointment (Ronningstam, 2011).

As many as 6.2 percent of adults display narcissistic personality disorder, up to 75 percent of them men (APA, 2013; Sansone & Sansone, 2011). Narcissistic-type behaviors and thoughts are common and normal among teenagers and do not usually lead to adult narcissism (see *MindTech* on page 446).

How Do Theorists Explain Narcissistic Personality Disorder? Psychodynamic theorists more than others have theorized about narcissistic personality disorder, and they again propose that the problem begins with cold, rejecting parents. They argue that some people with this background spend their lives defending against feeling unsatisfied, rejected, unworthy, ashamed, and wary of the world (Roepke & Vater, 2014; Bornstein, 2005). They do so by repeatedly telling themselves that they are actually perfect and desirable, and also by seeking admiration from others. Object relations theorists—the psychodynamic theorists who emphasize relationships—interpret the grandiose self-image as a way for these people to convince themselves that they are totally self-sufficient and without need of warm relationships with their parents or anyone else (Celani, 2014; Diamond & Meehan, 2013). In support of the psychodynamic theories, research has found that children who are abused or who lose parents through adoption, divorce, or death are at particular risk for the later development of narcissistic personality disorder (Kernberg, 2010, 1992, 1989). Studies also show that people with this disorder do indeed earn relatively high shame and rejection scores on various scales and believe that other people are basically unavailable to them (Ritter et al., 2014; Bender et al., 2001).

A number of cognitive-behavioral theorists propose that narcissistic personality disorder may develop when people are treated *too positively* rather than too negatively in early life. They hold that certain children acquire a superior and grandiose attitude when their "admiring or doting parents" teach them to "overvalue their self worth," repeatedly rewarding them for minor accomplishments or for no accomplishment at all (Millon, 2011; Sperry, 2003).

Many sociocultural theorists see a link between narcissistic personality disorder and "eras of narcissism" in society (Paris, 2014). They suggest that family values and social ideals in certain societies periodically break down, producing generations of young people who are self-centered and materialistic and have short attention spans. Western cultures in particular, which encourage self-expression, individualism, and competitiveness, are considered likely to produce such generations of narcissism. In fact, one worldwide study conducted on the Internet found that respondents from the United States had the highest narcissism scores, followed, in descending order, by those from Europe, Canada, Asia, and the Middle East (Foster et al., 2003).

> **What specific features of Western society may be contributing to today's apparent rise in narcissistic behavior?**

Treatments for Narcissistic Personality Disorder Narcissistic personality disorder is one of the most difficult personality patterns to treat because the clients are unable to acknowledge weaknesses, to appreciate the effect of their behavior on others, or to incorporate feedback from others (Campbell & Miller, 2011). The clients who consult therapists usually do so because of a related disorder such as depression (APA, 2013). Once in treatment, the clients may try to manipulate the therapist into supporting their sense of superiority. Some also seem to project their grandiose attitudes onto their therapists and develop a love-hate stance toward them (Colli et al., 2014; Shapiro, 2004).

Psychodynamic therapists seek to help people with this disorder recognize and work through their basic insecurities and defenses (Diamond & Meehan, 2013; Messer & Abbass, 2010). Cognitive therapists, focusing on the self-centered thinking of such individuals, try to redirect the clients' focus onto the opinions of others, teach them to interpret criticism more rationally, increase their ability to empathize, and change their all-or-nothing notions (Beck & Weishaar, 2014; Beck et al., 2004). None of the approaches have had clear success, however (Paris, 2014).

"I'm attracted to you, but then I'm attracted to me too."

Richard Cline/The New Yorker Collection/www.cartoonbank.com

Stolen Glances

22%   Percentage of people who regularly check their reflections in store windows and the like

69%   Those who steal glances at least occasionally

9%   Those who never look at themselves in public mirrors or windows

(Information from: Kanner, 2005, 1995)

MindTech

Selfies: Narcissistic or Not?

In the art world, people have been drawing self-portraits for centuries. In recent years, however, digital technology has ushered in the era of the *selfie,* a cousin to the self-portrait. Safe to say, just about every cell phone user has taken a selfie. In fact, more than 90 percent of all teens have now posted a photo of themselves online (Pew Research Foundation, 2014). These self-photos have created such a stir that the word "selfie" was elected "Word of the Year 2013" by the Oxford English Dictionary.

Peter Bernik/Shutterstock

As the selfie phenomenon has grown, opinions about selfies have intensified. It seems like people either love them or hate them. This is true in the field of psychology as well. Some psychologists view taking selfies as a form of narcissistic behavior, while others view them more positively.

First, the negative perspective. Many sociocultural theorists see a link between narcissistic personality disorder and "eras of narcissism" in society (Paris, 2014). They suggest that social values in society break down periodically, producing generations of self-centered, materialistic youth. Some of these theorists consider today's selfie generation a perfect example of a current era of narcissism. This theory has gained a large following, but it is not supported by research. One team of researchers, for example, found no relationship at all between how many selfies people post and how high they score on a narcissism personality scale (Alloway, 2014; Alloway et al., 2014).

This lack of support for the narcissism viewpoint does not mean that selfies, especially repeated selfie behaviors, are completely harmless. Sherry Turkle (2013), an influential technology psychologist, believes that the near-reflexive instinct to photograph oneself may limit deeper engagements with the environment or experiencing events to their fullest (Eisold, 2013). Turkle also suggests that people who post an endless stream of selfies are often seeking external validation of their self-worth, even if that pursuit may not rise to a level of clinical narcissism.

> **What other trends in behavior—digital or otherwise—might suggest that our society is currently in an era of narcissism?**

Psychologists also observe that posting too many "selfies" may alienate those who view the poster's social media profile (Miller, 2013). Studies have found, for example, that people often take a negative view of friends and family members who excessively post photos to their Facebook sites (Houghton, 2013).

On the positive side, a number of psychologists believe that the criticisms and concerns about the selfie movement have been overstated. Media psychologist Pamela Rutledge (2013) views selfies as an inevitable by-product of "technology-enabled self-expression." She believes that selfie behaviors are simply confusing to individuals of a predigital generation. Moreover, she concludes that the selfie trend, for digital natives, can enhance explorations of identity, help identify one's interests, develop artistic expression, help people craft a meaningful narrative of their life experiences, and even reflect more realistic body images (for example, posting "selfies" without makeup). In therapy, selfies can serve as a springboard to discuss issues that clients are reluctant to broach on their own (Sifferlin, 2013).

In short, like other technological trends you've read about, the selfie phenomenon has received mixed grades from psychology researchers and practitioners so far.

➤ *Summing Up*

"DRAMATIC" PERSONALITY DISORDERS Four of the personality disorders in DSM-5 are marked by highly dramatic, emotional, or erratic symptoms. People with antisocial personality disorder display a pattern of disregard for and violation of the rights of others. No known treatment is notably effective. People with borderline personality disorder display a pattern of instability in interpersonal relationships, self-image, and mood, along with extreme impulsivity. Treatment—particularly dialectical behavior therapy—apparently can be helpful and lead to some improvement. People with histrionic personality disorder display a pattern of extreme emotionality and attention seeking. Clinical case reports suggest that treatment is helpful on occasion. Finally, people with narcissistic personality disorder display a pattern of grandiosity, need for admiration, and lack of empathy. It is one of the most difficult disorders to treat.

"Anxious" Personality Disorders

The cluster of *"anxious" personality disorders* includes the *avoidant*, *dependent*, and *obsessive-compulsive personality disorders*. People with these patterns typically display anxious and fearful behavior. Although many of the symptoms of these personality disorders are similar to those of the anxiety and depressive disorders, researchers have not usually found direct links between this cluster and those disorders (O'Donohue et al., 2007). As with most of the other personality disorders, research support for the various explanations is very limited. At the same time, treatments for these disorders appear to be modestly to moderately helpful—considerably better than for other personality disorders.

Avoidant Personality Disorder

People with **avoidant personality disorder** are very uncomfortable and inhibited in social situations, overwhelmed by feelings of inadequacy, and extremely sensitive to negative evaluation (APA, 2013). They are so fearful of being rejected that they give no one an opportunity to reject them—or to accept them either:

> *Perhaps what made Malcolm pursue counseling was the painful awareness of his inability to socialize at a party hosted by a professor. A first-semester computer science graduate student, Malcolm watched other new students in his program fraternize at this gathering while he suffered in silence. He wanted desperately to join [in], but, as he described it, "I was totally at a loss as to how to go about talking to anyone." The best feeling in the world, he stated, was getting out of there. The following Monday, he came to the university counseling center, realizing he would have to be able to function in this group, but not before his first teaching experience that morning, which he described as "the most terrifying feeling I have ever encountered." As an undergrad, he spent most of his time alone in the computer lab working on new programs, which was what he most enjoyed as "no one was looking over my shoulder or judging me." In contrast to this, with his teaching assistantship duties . . . he felt he constantly ran the risk of being made to look like a fool in front of a large audience.*
>
> *When asked about personal relationships he had previously enjoyed, Malcolm admitted that any interaction was a source of frustration and worry. From the moment he left home for undergraduate school, he lived alone, attended functions alone, and*

▸ **avoidant personality disorder** A personality disorder characterized by consistent discomfort and restraint in social situations, overwhelming feelings of inadequacy, and extreme sensitivity to negative evaluation.

(continues on the next page)

found it nearly impossible to make conversation with anyone. . . . The expectancy that people would be rejecting . . . precipitated profound gloom. . . . Despite a longing to relate and be accepted, Malcolm . . . maintained a safe distance from all emotional involvement. [He] became remote from others and from needed sources of support. He . . . had learned to be watchful, on guard against ridicule, and ever alert . . . to the most minute traces of annoyance expressed by others.

(Millon, 2011)

Feelings of Shyness

Around 48 percent of people in the United States consider themselves to be shy to some degree.

(Carducci, 2000)

People like Malcolm actively avoid occasions for social contact. At the center of this withdrawal lies not so much poor social skills as a dread of criticism, disapproval, or rejection. They are timid and hesitant in social situations, afraid of saying something foolish or of embarrassing themselves by blushing or acting nervous. Even in intimate relationships they express themselves very carefully, afraid of being shamed or ridiculed.

People with this disorder believe themselves to be unappealing or inferior to others. They exaggerate the potential difficulties of new situations, so they seldom take risks or try out new activities. They usually have few or no close friends, though they actually yearn for intimate relationships, and frequently feel depressed and lonely. As a substitute, some develop an inner world of fantasy and imagination (Millon, 2011).

Avoidant personality disorder is similar to *social anxiety disorder* (see Chapter 4), and many people with one of these disorders also experience the other (Eikenaes et al., 2015, 2013). The similarities include a fear of humiliation and low confidence. Some theorists believe that there is a key difference between the two disorders—namely, that people with social anxiety disorder primarily fear social *circumstances,* while people with the personality disorder tend to fear close social *relationships* (Lampe & Sunderland, 2015; Kantor, 2010). Other theorists, however, believe that the two disorders reflect the same psychopathology and should be combined (Eikenaes et al., 2015, 2013).

Around 2.4 percent of adults have avoidant personality disorder, men as frequently as women (APA, 2013; Sansone & Sansone, 2011). Many children and

Just a stage This child sits alone on the steps of his school as other children pass by. That behavior could be a sign of being painfully shy, withdrawn, easily embarrassed, and uncomfortable with people. Early temperament is often linked to adult personality traits, but research has not yet clarified whether extreme shyness, a common and normal part of childhood, can in certain cases predict the development of avoidant or dependent personality disorder in adulthood.

© Michael Prince/Corbis

teenagers are also painfully shy and avoid other people, but this is usually just a normal part of their development.

How Do Theorists Explain Avoidant Personality Disorder?

Theorists often assume that avoidant personality disorder has the same causes as anxiety disorders—such as early traumas, conditioned fears, upsetting beliefs, or biochemical abnormalities. However, with the exception of social anxiety disorder, research has not yet tied the personality disorder directly to the anxiety disorders (Herbert, 2007). Psychodynamic, cognitive, and behavioral explanations of avoidant personality disorder are the most popular among clinicians.

Psychodynamic theorists focus mainly on the general sense of shame that people with avoidant personality disorder feel (Svartberg & McCullough, 2010). Some trace the shame to childhood experiences such as early bowel and bladder accidents. If parents repeatedly punish or ridicule a child for having such accidents, the child may develop a negative self-image. This may lead to the child's feeling unlovable throughout life and distrusting the love of others.

Similarly, cognitive theorists believe that harsh criticism and rejection in early childhood may lead certain people to assume that others in their environment will always judge them negatively. These people come to expect rejection, misinterpret the reactions of others to fit that expectation, discount positive feedback, and generally fear social involvements—setting the stage for avoidant personality disorder (Lampe, 2015; Weishaar & Beck, 2006). In several studies, participants with this disorder were asked to recall their childhood, and their descriptions supported both the psychodynamic and the cognitive theories (Carr & Francis, 2010; Herbert, 2007). They remembered, for example, feeling criticized, rejected, and isolated; receiving little encouragement from their parents; and experiencing few displays of parental love or pride.

Behavioral theorists suggest that people with avoidant personality disorder typically fail to develop normal social skills, a failure that helps maintain the disorder. In support of this position, several studies have found social skills deficits among people with avoidant personality disorder (Kantor, 2010; Herbert, 2007). Most behaviorists agree, however, that these deficits first develop as a result of the individuals avoiding so many social situations.

Treatments for Avoidant Personality Disorder

People with avoidant personality disorder come to therapy in the hope of finding acceptance and affection. Keeping them in treatment can be a challenge, however, for many of them soon begin to avoid the sessions. Often they distrust the therapist's sincerity and start to fear his or her rejection. Thus, as with several of the other personality disorders, a key task of the therapist is to gain the person's trust (Colli et al., 2014; Leichsenring & Salzer, 2014).

Beyond building trust, therapists tend to treat people with avoidant personality disorder much as they treat people with social anxiety disorder and other anxiety disorders. Such approaches have had at least modest success (Kantor, 2010; Porcerelli et al., 2007). Psychodynamic therapists try to help clients recognize and resolve the unconscious conflicts that may be operating (Leichsenring & Salzer, 2014). Cognitive therapists help them change their distressing beliefs and thoughts and improve their self-image (Rees & Pritchard, 2015, 2013; Weishaar & Beck, 2006). Behavioral therapists provide social skills training as well as exposure treatments that require people to gradually increase their social contacts (Herbert, 2007). Group therapy formats, especially groups that follow cognitive and behavioral principles, have the added advantage of providing clients with practice in social interactions (Herbert et al., 2005). Antianxiety and antidepressant drugs are sometimes useful in reducing the social anxiety of people with the disorder, although the symptoms may return when medication is stopped (Ripoll et al., 2011).

BETWEEN THE LINES

Shyness and the Arts

In recent years, the music industry has been strongly influenced by stars with extremely shy, reticent demeanors.

- The alternative rock band My Bloody Valentine often plays with their backs to the audience and spearheaded an influential pop movement called "shoegaze" based on their tendency to look away or at the floor during shows.

- In early shows, indie rock musician Sufjan Stevens would nervously applaud his audience when they clapped for him.

- For many of her initial concerts, folk singer Cat Power (Chan Marshall) would not look at the audience and would weep or run offstage during shows.

- Meg White, drummer for the two-piece rock band White Stripes, appeared uncomfortable and quiet both onstage and during rarely given interviews. The group disbanded after "acute anxiety" forced her to cancel a 2007 tour.

- Grammy-award winning singer Adele has revealed, "I'm scared of audiences. One show . . . I was so nervous, I escaped out the fire escape."

▶ **dependent personality disorder**
A personality disorder characterized by a pattern of clinging and obedience, fear of separation, and an ongoing need to be taken care of.

Dependent Personality Disorder

People with **dependent personality disorder** have a pervasive, excessive need to be taken care of (APA, 2013). As a result, they are clinging and obedient, fearing separation from their parent, spouse, or other person with whom they are in a close relationship. They rely on others so much that they cannot make the smallest decision for themselves. Matthew is a case in point.

> Matthew is a 34-year-old single man who lives with his mother and works as an accountant. He is . . . very unhappy after having just broken up with his girlfriend. His mother had disapproved of his marriage plans. . . . Matthew felt trapped and forced to choose between his mother and his girlfriend, and because "blood is thicker than water," he had decided not to go against his mother's wishes. . . . His mother . . . is a very domineering woman. . . . Matthew is afraid of disagreeing with [her] for fear that she will not be supportive of him and he will then have to fend for himself. He criticizes himself for being weak. . . . He alternates between resentment and a "Mother knows best" attitude. He feels that his own judgment is poor.
>
> Matthew works at a job several grades below what his education and talent would permit. On several occasions he has turned down promotions because he didn't want the responsibility of having to supervise other people or make independent decisions. He has worked for the same boss for 10 years . . . and is . . . highly regarded as a dependable and unobtrusive worker. He has two very close friends whom he has had since early childhood. He has lunch with one of them every single workday and feels lost if his friend is sick and misses a day.
>
> Matthew is the youngest of four children. . . . He had considerable separation anxiety as a child . . . difficulty falling asleep unless his mother stayed in the room . . . and unbearable homesickness when he occasionally tried "sleepovers." As a child he was teased by other boys because of his lack of assertiveness and was often called a baby. He has lived at home his whole life except for 1 year of college, from which he returned because of homesickness.
>
> *(Spitzer et al., 1994, pp. 179–180)*

////// **BETWEEN THE LINES** //////

In Their Words

"The deepest principle of human nature is the craving to be appreciated."

William James

It is normal and healthy to depend on others, but those with dependent personality disorder constantly need assistance with even the simplest matters and have extreme feelings of inadequacy and helplessness. Afraid that they cannot care for themselves, they cling desperately to friends or relatives.

As you just observed, people with avoidant personality disorder have difficulty *initiating* relationships. In contrast, people with dependent personality disorder have difficulty with *separation*. They feel completely helpless and devastated when a close relationship ends, and they quickly seek out another relationship to fill the void. Many cling persistently to relationships with partners who physically or psychologically abuse them (Loas et al., 2015, 2011).

Lacking confidence in their own ability and judgment, people with this disorder seldom disagree with others and allow even important decisions to be made for them (Millon, 2011). They may depend on a parent or spouse to decide where to live, what job to have, and which neighbors to befriend. Because they so fear rejection, they are overly sensitive to disapproval and keep trying to meet other people's wishes and expectations, even if it means volunteering for unpleasant or demeaning tasks.

Many people with dependent personality disorder feel distressed, lonely, and sad; often they dislike themselves. Thus they are at risk for depressive, anxiety, and eating disorders (Bornstein, 2012, 2007). Their fear of separation and their feelings of helplessness may leave them particularly prone to suicidal thoughts, especially when they believe that a current relationship is about to end (Bornstein, 2012; Kiev, 1989).

Surveys suggest that fewer than 1 percent of the population experience dependent personality disorder (APA, 2013; Sansone & Sansone, 2011). For years, clinicians have believed that more women than men display this pattern, but some research suggests that the disorder is just as common in men (APA, 2013).

How Do Theorists Explain Dependent Personality Disorder?

Psychodynamic explanations for dependent personality disorder are very similar to those for depression (Svartberg & McCullough, 2010). Freudian theorists argue, for example, that unresolved conflicts during the oral stage of development can give rise to a lifelong need for nurturance, thus heightening the likelihood of a dependent personality disorder (Bornstein, 2012, 2007, 2005). Similarly, object relations theorists say that early parental loss or rejection may prevent normal experiences of *attachment* and *separation,* leaving some children with fears of abandonment that persist throughout their lives (Caligor & Clarkin, 2010). Still other psychodynamic theorists suggest that, to the contrary, many parents of people with this disorder were overinvolved and overprotective, thus increasing their children's dependency, insecurity, and separation anxiety (Sperry, 2003).

Behaviorists propose that parents of people with dependent personality disorder unintentionally rewarded their children's clinging and "loyal" behavior, while at the same time punishing acts of independence, perhaps through the withdrawal of love. Alternatively, some parents' own dependent behaviors may have served as models for their children (Bornstein, 2012, 2007).

Cognitive theorists identify two maladaptive attitudes as helping to produce and maintain this disorder: (1) "I am inadequate and helpless to deal with the world," and (2) "I must find a person to provide protection so I can cope." Dichotomous (black-and-white) thinking may also play a key role: "If I am to be dependent, I must be completely helpless," or "If I am to be independent, I must be alone." Such thinking prevents sufferers from making efforts to be independent (Borge et al., 2010; Weishaar & Beck, 2006).

"My self-esteem was so low I just followed her around everywhere she would go."

Bruce Eric Kaplan/The New Yorker Collection/www.cartoonbank.com

Treatments for Dependent Personality Disorder In therapy, people with dependent personality disorder usually place all responsibility for their treatment and well-being on the clinician. Thus a key task of therapy is to help patients accept responsibility for themselves (Colli et al., 2014; Gutheil, 2005). Because the domineering behaviors of a spouse or parent may help foster a patient's symptoms, some clinicians suggest couple or family therapy as well, or even separate therapy for the partner or parent (Lebow & Uliaszek, 2010; Nichols, 2004).

Treatment for dependent personality disorder can be at least modestly helpful. Psychodynamic therapy for this pattern focuses on many of the same issues as therapy for depressed people, including the *transference* of dependency needs onto the therapist (Svartberg & McCullough, 2010). Cognitive-behavioral therapists combine behavioral and cognitive interventions to help the clients take control of their lives. On the behavioral end, the therapists often provide assertiveness training to help the individuals better express their own wishes in relationships (Farmer & Nelson-Gray, 2005). On the cognitive end, the therapists also try to help the clients challenge and change their assumptions of incompetence and helplessness (Borge et al., 2010; Beck et al., 2004). Antidepressant drug therapy has been helpful for people whose personality disorder is accompanied by depression (Fava et al., 2002).

As with avoidant personality disorder, a group therapy format can be helpful because it provides opportunities for the client to receive support from a number

▶ **obsessive-compulsive personality disorder** A personality disorder marked by such an intense focus on orderliness, perfectionism, and control that the person loses flexibility, openness, and efficiency.

of peers rather than from a single dominant person (Perry, 2005; Sperry, 2003). In addition, group members may serve as models for one another as they practice better ways to express feelings and solve problems.

Obsessive-Compulsive Personality Disorder

People with **obsessive-compulsive personality disorder** are so preoccupied with order, perfection, and control that they lose all flexibility, openness, and efficiency (APA, 2013). Their concern for doing everything "right" impairs their productivity, as in the case of Joseph:

> Joseph was advised to seek assistance from a therapist following several months of relatively sleepless nights and a growing immobility and indecisiveness at his job. When first seen, he reported feelings of extreme self-doubt and guilt and prolonged periods of tension and diffuse anxiety. It was established early in therapy that he always had experienced these symptoms; they were now merely more pronounced than before.
>
> The precipitant for this sudden increase in discomfort was a forthcoming change in his academic post. New administrative officers had assumed authority at the college, and he was asked to resign his deanship to return to regular departmental instruction. In the early sessions, Joseph spoke largely of his fear of facing classroom students again, wondered if he could organize his material well, and doubted that he could keep classes disciplined and interested in his lectures. It was his preoccupation with these matters that he believed was preventing him from concentrating and completing his present responsibilities.
>
> At no time did Joseph express anger toward the new college officials for the demotion he was asked to accept; he repeatedly voiced his "complete confidence" in the "rationality of their decision." Yet, when face-to-face with them, he observed that he stuttered and was extremely tremulous.
>
> Joseph was the second of two sons, younger than his brother by three years. His father was a successful engineer, and his mother a high school teacher. Both were "efficient, orderly, and strict" parents. Life at home was "extremely well planned," with "daily and weekly schedules of responsibility posted" and "vacations arranged a year or two in advance." Nothing apparently was left to chance. . . . Joseph adopted the "good boy" image. Unable to challenge his brother either physically, intellectually, or socially, he became a "paragon of virtue." By being punctilious, scrupulous, methodical, and orderly, he could avoid antagonizing his perfectionistic parents, and would, at times, obtain preferred treatment from them. He obeyed their advice, took their guidance as gospel, and hesitated making any decision before gaining their approval. Although he recalled "fighting" with his brother before he was 6 or 7, he "restrained my anger from that time on and never upset my parents again."
>
> *(Millon, 2011, 1969, pp. 278–279)*

In Joseph's concern with rules and order and doing things right, he has trouble seeing the larger picture. When faced with a task, he and others who have obsessive-compulsive personality disorder may become so focused on organization and details that they fail to grasp the point of the activity. As a result, their work is often behind schedule (some seem unable to finish any job), and they may neglect leisure activities and friendships.

People with this personality disorder set unreasonably high standards for themselves and others. Their behaviors extend well beyond the realm of conscientiousness. They can never be satisfied with their performance, but they typically refuse to seek help or to work with a team, convinced that others are too careless or incompetent to do the job right. Because they are so afraid of making mistakes, they may be reluctant to make decisions.

They also tend to be rigid and stubborn, particularly in their morals, ethics, and values. They live by a strict personal code and use it as a yardstick for measuring others. They may have trouble expressing much affection, and their relationships are sometimes stiff and superficial (Cain et al., 2015). In addition, they are often stingy with their time or money. Some cannot even throw away objects that are worn out or useless (APA, 2013).

According to surveys, as many as 7.9 percent of the adult population display obsessive-compulsive personality disorder, with white, educated, married, and employed people receiving the diagnosis most often (APA, 2013; Sansone & Sansone, 2011). Men are twice as likely as women to display the disorder.

Many clinicians believe that obsessive-compulsive personality disorder and *obsessive-compulsive disorder* are closely related. Certainly, the two disorders share a number of features, and many people who suffer from one of the disorders meet the diagnostic criteria for the other disorder (Pinto et al., 2014; Gordon et al., 2013). However, it is worth noting that people with the personality disorder are more likely to suffer from either major depressive disorder, generalized anxiety disorder, or a substance use disorder than from obsessive-compulsive disorder (APA, 2013; Peña-Garijo et al., 2013). In fact, researchers have not consistently found a specific link between obsessive-compulsive personality disorder and obsessive-compulsive disorder (Starcevic & Brakoulias, 2014; Gordon et al., 2013).

How Do Theorists Explain Obsessive-Compulsive Personality Disorder? Most explanations of obsessive-compulsive personality disorder borrow heavily from those of obsessive-compulsive disorder, despite the doubts concerning a link between the two disorders. As with so many of the personality disorders, psychodynamic explanations dominate and research evidence is limited.

Freudian theorists suggest that people with obsessive-compulsive personality disorder are *anal retentive.* That is, because of overly harsh toilet training during the anal stage, they become filled with anger, and they remain *fixated* at this stage. To keep their anger under control, they persistently resist both their anger and their instincts to have bowel movements. In turn, they become extremely orderly and restrained; many become passionate collectors. Other psychodynamic theorists suggest that any early struggles with parents over control and independence may ignite the aggressive impulses at the root of this personality disorder (Millon, 2011; Bartz et al., 2007).

Cognitive theorists have little to say about the origins of obsessive-compulsive personality disorder, but they do propose that illogical thinking processes help keep it going (Weishaar & Beck, 2006; Beck et al., 2004). They point, for example, to dichotomous—"all-or-nothing"—thinking, which may produce rigidity and perfectionism. Similarly, they note that people with this disorder tend to misread or exaggerate the potential outcomes of mistakes or errors.

Treatments for Obsessive-Compulsive Personality Disorder
People with obsessive-compulsive personality disorder do not usually believe there is anything wrong with them. They therefore are not likely to seek treatment unless they are also suffering from another disorder, most frequently an anxiety disorder or depression, or unless someone close to them insists that they get treatment (Bartz et al., 2007).

Toilet trouble According to Freud, toilet training often produces rage in a child. If parents are too harsh in their approach, the child may become fixated at the anal stage and prone to obsessive-compulsive functioning later in life.

Design Pics/Misty Bedwell/Getty Images

A Critical Difference

People with obsessive-compulsive disorder typically do not want or like their symptoms; those with obsessive-compulsive personality disorder often embrace their symptoms and rarely wish to resist them.

People with obsessive-compulsive personality disorder often respond well to psychodynamic or cognitive therapy (Messer & Abbass, 2010; Weishaar & Beck, 2006). Psychodynamic therapists typically try to help these clients recognize, experience, and accept their underlying feelings and insecurities and perhaps take risks and accept their personal limitations. Cognitive therapists focus on helping the clients to change their dichotomous thinking, perfectionism, indecisiveness, procrastination, and chronic worrying. A number of clinicians report that people with obsessive–compulsive personality disorder, like those with obsessive-compulsive disorder, respond well to serotonin-enhancing antidepressant drugs; however, researchers have yet to study this issue fully (Pinto et al., 2008).

➤ Summing Up

"ANXIOUS" PERSONALITY DISORDERS Three of the personality disorders in DSM-5 are marked by anxious and fearful behavior. People with avoidant personality disorder are consistently uncomfortable and restrained in social situations, overwhelmed by feelings of inadequacy, and extremely sensitive to negative evaluation. People with dependent personality disorder have a persistent need to be taken care of, are submissive and clinging, and fear separation. People with obsessive-compulsive personality disorder are so focused on order, perfection, and control that they lose their flexibility, openness, and efficiency. A variety of treatment strategies have been used for people with these disorders and apparently have been modestly to moderately helpful.

Multicultural Factors: Research Neglect

According to the current criteria of DSM-5, a pattern diagnosed as a personality disorder must "deviate markedly from the expectations of the individual's culture" (APA, 2013). Given the importance of culture in this diagnosis, it is striking how little multicultural research has been conducted on these problems. Clinical theorists have suspicions but little compelling evidence that there are cultural differences in this realm (Iacovino et al., 2014).

The lack of multicultural research is of special concern with regard to borderline personality disorder, the pattern characterized by extreme mood fluctuations, outbursts of intense anger, self-injurious behavior, feelings of emptiness, and problematic relationships because many theorists are convinced that gender and other cultural differences may be particularly important in both the development and diagnosis of this disorder.

Around 75 percent of all people who receive a diagnosis of borderline personality disorder are female. Although it may be that women are biologically more prone to the disorder or that diagnostic bias is at work, this gender difference may instead be a reflection of the extraordinary traumas to which many women are subjected as children (Daigre et al., 2015). Recall, for example, that the childhoods of people with borderline personality disorder tend to be filled with emotional trauma, victimization, violence, and abuse, at times sexual abuse. It may be, a number of theorists argue, that experiences of this kind are *prerequisites* to the development of borderline personality disorder, that women in our society are particularly subjected to such experiences, and that, in fact, the disorder should more properly be viewed and treated as a special form of posttraumatic stress disorder (Sherry & Whilde, 2008; Hodges, 2003). In the absence of systematic research, however, alternative explanations like this remain untested and corresponding treatments undeveloped.

Personality Disorder Demographics

19% Percentage of people with severe personality disorders who are racial or ethnic minority group members

59% People with severe personality disorders who are male

6% People with severe personality disorders who are unemployed

23% People with severe personality disorders who have never married

10% Impoverished people with borderline personality disorder

3% Wealthy people with borderline personality disorder

(Information from: Sareen et al., 2011; Cloninger & Svrakic, 2005)

In a related vein, some multicultural theorists believe that borderline personality disorder may be a reaction to persistent feelings of marginality, powerlessness, and social failure (Sherry & Whilde, 2008; Miller, 1999, 1994). That is, it may be attributable more to social inequalities (including sexism, racism, or homophobia) than to psychological factors.

Given such possibilities, it is most welcome that at least a few multicultural studies of borderline personality disorder have been conducted over the past decade (De Genna & Feske, 2013). In one, researchers assessed the rate of the personality disorder in racially diverse clinical populations from across the United States (Chavira et al., 2003). The study found that more Hispanic American clients qualified for a diagnosis of borderline personality disorder than did white or African American clients. Could it be that Hispanic Americans are more likely than other cultural groups to display this disorder, and—if so—why?

Finally, some multicultural theorists have argued that the features of borderline personality disorder may be perfectly acceptable traits and behaviors in certain cultures (APA, 2013). In Puerto Rican culture, for example, men are expected to display very strong emotions like anger, aggression, and sexual attraction (Sherry & Whilde, 2008; Casimir & Morrison, 1993). Could such culture-based characteristics help account for the higher rates of borderline personality disorder found among Hispanic American clients? And could these cultural-based characteristics also help explain the fact that Hispanic men and women demonstrate similar rates of this disorder, in contrast to the usual 3-to-1 female-to-male ratio found in other cultural groups (Chavira et al., 2003)?

Too little attention As illustrated by this diverse group of people, we live in a multicultural nation and world. The field of psychology has devoted considerable study to cultural and racial differences of various kinds. However, clinical researchers have given relatively little attention to multicultural differences in the development, features, and treatment of personality disorders.

Deborah Cheramie/Getty Images

➤ *Summing Up*

MULTICULTURAL FACTORS: RESEARCH NEGLECT Despite the field's growing focus on personality disorders, relatively little research has been done on gender and other multicultural influences. Nevertheless, many clinicians believe that multicultural factors may play key roles in the understanding, diagnosis and treatment of personality disorders, and researchers have recently begun to study this possibility.

Are There Better Ways to Classify Personality Disorders?

Most of today's clinicians believe that personality disorders represent important and troubling patterns. Yet, as you read at the beginning of this chapter, DSM-5's personality disorders are particularly hard to diagnose and easy to misdiagnose, difficulties that indicate serious problems with the validity and reliability of these categories. Consider, in particular, the following problems:

1. Some of the criteria used to diagnose the DSM-5 personality disorders cannot be observed directly. To separate paranoid from schizoid personality disorder, for example, clinicians must ask not only whether people avoid forming close relationships, but also *why*. In other words, the diagnoses often rely heavily on the impressions of the individual clinician.

2. Clinicians differ widely in their judgments about when a normal personality style crosses the line and deserves to be called a disorder. Some even believe that it is wrong ever to think of personality styles as mental disorders, however troublesome they may be.

3. The personality disorders often are very similar to one another. Thus it is common for people with personality problems to meet the diagnostic criteria for several DSM-5 personality disorders (Moore et al., 2012).

4. People with quite different personalities may qualify for the same DSM-5 personality disorder diagnosis.

In light of these problems, the leading criticism of DSM-5's approach to personality disorders is, as you read earlier, that the classification system defines such disorders by using *categories*—rather than *dimensions*—of personality. A growing number of theorists believe that personality disorders differ more in *degree* than in type of dysfunction. Therefore, they propose that the disorders should be classified by the severity of key personality traits (or dimensions) rather than by the presence or absence of specific traits (Morey et al., 2014). In such an approach, each key trait (for example, disagreeableness, dishonesty, or self-absorption) would be seen as varying along a continuum in which there is no clear boundary between normal and abnormal. People with a personality disorder would be those who display extreme degrees of several of these key traits—degrees not commonly found in the general population (see *InfoCentral* on the next page).

Which key personality dimensions should clinicians use to help identify people with personality problems? Some theorists believe that they should rely on the dimensions identified in the "Big Five" theory of personality, dimensions that have received enormous attention by personality psychologists over the years.

The "Big Five" Theory of Personality and Personality Disorders

A large body of research consistently suggests that the basic structure of personality may consist of five "supertraits," or factors—*neuroticism, extroversion, openness to experiences, agreeableness,* and *conscientiousness* (Curtis et al., 2014; Zuckerman, 2011). Each of these factors, which are frequently referred to as the "Big Five," consists of a number of subfactors. Anxiety and hostility, for example, are subfactors of the neuroticism factor, while optimism and friendliness are subfactors of the extroversion factor. Theoretically, everyone's personality can be summarized by a combination of these supertraits. One person may display high levels of neuroticism and agreeableness, medium extroversion, and low conscientiousness and openness to experiences. In contrast, another person may display high levels of agreeableness and conscientiousness, medium neuroticism and extroversion, and low openness to experiences. And so on.

Many proponents of the Big Five model have argued further that it would be best to describe all people with personality disorders as being high, low, or in between on the five supertraits and to drop the use of personality disorder categories altogether (Glover et al., 2012; Lawton et al., 2011). Thus a particular person who currently qualifies for a diagnosis of avoidant personality disorder might instead be described as displaying a high degree of neuroticism, medium degrees of agreeableness and conscientiousness, and very low degrees of extroversion and openness to new experiences. Similarly, a person currently diagnosed with narcissistic personality disorder might be described in the Big Five approach as displaying very high degrees of neuroticism and extroversion, medium degrees of conscientiousness and openness to new experiences, and a very low degree of agreeableness.

LYING

A **lie** is a false statement that a person makes in order to deliberately deceive another person. Everyone lies. But there is lying, and then there is "lying." Psychologists often distinguish several kinds of lying: **everyday lying**, **compulsive lying**, and **sociopathic lying**. Compulsive and sociopathic lying are often referred to, collectively, as **pathological lying**.

Everyday liars: Almost everyone lies on occasion

Compulsive liars: Some people consistently lie out of habit, even when nothing is gained by the lies.

Sociopathic liars: Some people lie incessantly, without any concern for others, in order to get their way.

EXCESSIVE LYING CAN DAMAGE RELATIONSHIPS

41% "I have lost several important relationships to the other person's lack of trust in me."

47% "I've been confronted by more than one person about my lying."

38% "I've had problems at work due to my lying."

(TAD, 2014)

PATHOLOGICAL LYING AND PERSONALITY DISORDERS

Pathological liars often ...

- Tell totally pointless lies
- Lie to seek attention
- Tell unbelievable stories
- Lie much or most of the time
- Seem unable to stay with the truth
- Lie to make themselves or situation look better
- Paint themselves as victims in their lies

Pathological lying is a common feature in

- Antisocial personality disorder
- Borderline personality disorder
- Histrionic personality disorder
- Narcissistic personality disorder

(Meyer, 2010)

EVERYDAY LYING

Everyone lies on occasion. The nature, motives for, and frequency of lying varies from person to person.

Motives for Everyday Lying

Offensive Motives
- Obtain a reward
- Gain advantage
- Win admiration
- Exercise control over others

Defensive Motives
- Avoid embarrassment or punishment
- Protect self or others from harm
- Escape awkward social situation
- Maintain privacy

Meyer, 2010; DePaulo et al., 2004; 1996; Feldman et al., 2002)

Which kinds of communication contain the most lies?

14%	21%	27%	37%
✉	🖱	👓	📱
e-mails	texts	face-to-face meetings	phone calls

(Meyer, 2010; Hancock et al., 2004)

THE BRAIN AND LYING

- The brain's prefrontal cortex becomes more active when people lie.
- Researchers have been able to detect when study participants are lying by observing prefrontal cortex activity on fMRIs.
- Beware: Just as polygraphs can be fooled, participants can lower the accuracy of fMRIs.

(Curley, 2013)

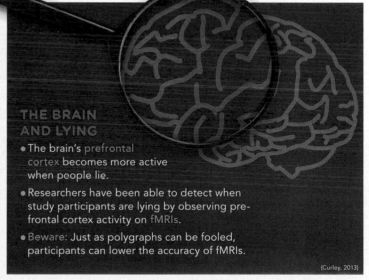

Who says ...

It is okay to lie to avoid hurting someone's feelings. 65%

They would lie in order to get a job. 85%

It is okay to lie to an insurance company. 25%

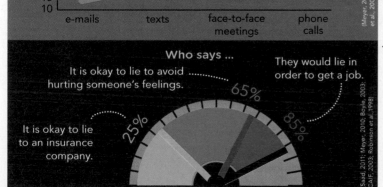

(Saad, 2011; Meyer, 2010; Boyle, 2003; CAIF, 2003; Robinson et al., 1998)

How many people lie to ...

parents	online dating site	friends	siblings	spouses	doctors	resumes
86%	81%	75%	73%	69%	45%	33-40%

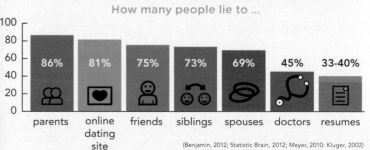

(Benjamin, 2012; Statistic Brain, 2012; Meyer, 2010: Kluger, 2002)

> **personality disorder—trait specified (PDTS)** A personality disorder currently undergoing study for possible inclusion in a future revision of DSM-5. People would receive this diagnosis if they had significant impairment in their functioning as a result of one or more very problematic traits.

"Personality Disorder—Trait Specified": Another Dimensional Approach

The "Big Five" approach to personality disorders is currently receiving study and may wind up being used in the next edition of the World Health Organization's International Classification of Diseases (ICD), the classification system for medical and psychiatric diagnoses used in many countries outside the United States (Aldhous, 2012). In the meantime, as you read earlier, the DSM-5 framers have designed their own *alternative* dimensional approach for possible use in a future revision of the DSM.

This approach begins with the notion that people whose traits significantly impair their functioning should receive a diagnosis called **personality disorder— trait specified (PDTS)** (APA, 2013). When assigning this diagnosis, clinicians would also identify and list the problematic traits and rate the severity of impairment caused by them. According to the proposal, five groups of problematic traits would be eligible for a diagnosis of PDTS: *negative affectivity, detachment, antagonism, disinhibition,* and *psychoticism.*

> **Negative Affectivity** People who display negative affectivity experience negative emotions frequently and intensely. In particular, they exhibit one or more of the following traits: *emotional lability* (unstable emotions), *anxiousness, separation insecurity, perseveration* (repetition of certain behaviors despite repeated failures), *submissiveness, hostility, depressivity, suspiciousness,* and *strong emotional reactions* (overreactions to emotionally arousing situations).

> **Detachment** People who manifest detachment tend to withdraw from other people and social interactions. They may exhibit any of the following traits: *restricted emotional reactivity* (little reaction to emotionally arousing situations), *depressivity, suspiciousness, withdrawal, anhedonia* (inability to feel pleasure or take interest in things), and *intimacy avoidance.* You'll note that two of the traits in this group—depressivity and suspiciousness—are also found in the negative affectivity group.

> **Antagonism** People who display antagonism behave in ways that put them at odds with other people. They may exhibit any of the following traits: *manipulativeness, deceitfulness, grandiosity, attention seeking, callousness,* and *hostility* (hostility is also found in the negative affectivity group).

> **Disinhibition** People who manifest disinhibition behave impulsively, without reflecting on potential future consequences. They may exhibit any of the following traits: *irresponsibility, impulsivity, distractibility, risk taking,* and *imperfection/ disorganization.*

> **Psychoticism** People who display psychoticism have unusual and bizarre experiences. They may exhibit any of the following traits: *unusual beliefs and experiences, eccentricity,* and *cognitive and perceptual dysregulation* (odd thought processes and sensory experiences).

If a person is impaired significantly by any of the five trait groups, or even by just 1 of the 25 traits that make up those groups, he or she would qualify for a diagnosis of *personality disorder—trait specified.* In such cases, the diagnostician would indicate which traits are impaired.

Consider, for example, Matthew, the unhappy 34-year-old accountant described on page 450. As you'll recall, Matthew meets the criteria for a diagnosis of dependent personality disorder under DSM-5's current categorical approach, based largely on his lifetime of extreme dependence on his mother, friends, and coworkers.

Using the alternative dimensional approach suggested in DSM-5, a diagnostician would instead observe that Matthew is significantly impaired by several of the traits that characterize the negative affectivity trait group. He is, for example, greatly impaired by "separation insecurity." This trait has prevented him from completing college, living on his own, marrying his girlfriend, ever disagreeing with his mother, advancing at work, and broadening his social life. In addition, Matthew seems to be impaired significantly by the traits of "anxiousness," "submissiveness," and "depressivity." Given this picture, his therapist might assign him a diagnosis of *personality disorder—trait specified, with problematic traits of separation insecurity, anxiousness, submissiveness, and depressivity.*

According to this dimensional approach, when clinicians assign a diagnosis of personality disorder—trait specified, they also must rate the degree of dysfunctioning caused by each of the person's traits, using a five-point scale ranging from "little or no impairment" (Rating = 0) to "extreme impairment" (Rating = 4).

Consider Matthew once again. He would probably warrant a rating of "0" on most of the 25 traits listed in the DSM-5 proposal, a rating of "3" on the trait of anxiousness and depressivity, and a rating of "4" on the traits of separation insecurity and submissiveness. Altogether, he would receive the following cumbersome, but informative, diagnosis:

Diagnosis: *Personality Disorder—Trait Specified*

Separation insecurity: Rating 4

Submissiveness: Rating 4

Anxiousness: Rating 3

Depressivity: Rating 3

Other traits: Rating 0

This dimensional approach to personality disorders may indeed prove superior to DSM-5's current categorical approach. Thus far, however, it has caused its own stir in the clinical community. Many clinicians believe that the proposed changes would give too much latitude to diagnosticians—allowing them to apply diagnoses of personality disorder to an enormous range of personality patterns. Still others worry that the requirements of the newly proposed system are too cumbersome or complicated. Only time and research will determine whether the alternative system is indeed a useful approach to the diagnosis of personality disorders.

© Joshua Sudock/ZUMA Press/Corbis

Photo courtesy of Everett Collection

Dysfunctional toons Today's animated film characters often display significant personality flaws or disorders. Some have a single dysfunctional trait, as is the case for Angry Birds, while others may have "clusters" of problematic traits, as shown by the *South Park* kids. Some critics suggest that the latter (especially Cartman, second from left) show enduring grumpiness, disrespect for authority, irreverence, self-absorption, disregard for the feelings of others, general lack of conscience, and a tendency to get into trouble.

➤ *Summing Up*

ARE THERE BETTER WAYS TO CLASSIFY PERSONALITY DISORDERS? The personality disorders listed in DSM-5 are commonly misdiagnosed, an indication of serious problems in the validity and reliability of the categories. Given the significant problems posed by the current categorical approach, a number of today's theorists believe that personality disorders should instead be described and classified by a dimensional approach. One such approach, the "Big Five" model, may be included in the next edition of the World Health Organization's International Classification of Diseases. Another dimensional approach, the "personality disorder—trait specified" model, is under study for possible inclusion in a future revision of DSM-5.

PUTTING IT...*together*

Disorders of Personality—Rediscovered and Reconsidered

During the first half of the twentieth century, clinicians believed deeply in the unique, enduring patterns we call personality, and they tried to define important personality traits. They then discovered how readily people can be shaped by the situations in which they find themselves, and a backlash developed. The concept of personality seemed to lose legitimacy, and for a while it became almost an obscene word in some circles. The clinical category of personality disorders went through a similar rejection. When psychodynamic and humanistic theorists dominated the clinical field, *neurotic character disorders*—a set of diagnoses similar to today's personality disorders—were considered useful clinical categories, but their popularity declined as other models grew in influence.

During the past 25 years, serious interest in personality and personality disorders has rebounded. In case after case, clinicians have concluded that rigid personality traits do seem to pose special problems, and they have developed new tests and interview guides to assess these disorders, setting in motion a wave of systematic research. So far, only the antisocial and borderline personality disorders have received much study. However, with DSM-5 now considering a new—dimensional—classification approach for possible use in the future, additional research is likely to follow. This may allow clinicians to better answer some pressing questions: How common are the various personality disorders? How useful are personality disorder categories? How effective is a dimensional approach to diagnosing these disorders? And which treatments are most effective?

One of the most important questions is, "Why do people develop troubled patterns of personality?" As you have read, psychological, as opposed to biological and sociocultural, theories have offered the most suggestions so far, but these explanations are not very precise and they do not have strong research support. Given the current enthusiasm for biological explanations, genetic and biological factors are beginning to receive considerable study, a shift in the waters that should soon enable researchers to determine possible interactions between biological and psychological causes. And one would hope that sociocultural factors will be studied as well. As you have seen, sociocultural theorists have only occasionally offered explanations for personality disorders, and multicultural factors have received little research. However, sociocultural factors may well play an important role in these disorders and certainly should be examined more carefully.

DSM-5's proposal of a dimensional classification approach eventually may lead to major changes in the field's understanding, diagnosis, and treatment of personality disorders. Now that clinicians have rediscovered personality disorders, they must determine the most appropriate ways to think about, explain, and treat them.

CLINICAL CHOICES

Now that you've read about personality disorders, try the interactive case study for this chapter. See if you are able to identify Alicia's symptoms and suggest a diagnosis based on her symptoms. What kind of treatment would be most effective for Alicia? Go to LaunchPad to access *Clinical Choices*.

KEY TERMS

QuickQuiz

1. What is a personality disorder? *pp. 421–424*

2. Describe the social relationship problems caused by each of the personality disorders. *pp. 421–454*

3. What are the three "odd" personality disorders, and what are the symptoms of each? *pp. 424–430*

4. What explanations and treatments have been applied to the paranoid, schizoid, and schizotypal personality disorders? *pp. 426–430*

5. What are the "dramatic" personality disorders, and what are the symptoms of each disorder? *pp. 431–445*

6. How have theorists explained antisocial personality disorder and borderline personality disorder? What are the leading treatments for these disorders, and how effective are they? *pp. 433–441*

7. What are the leading explanations and treatments for the histrionic and narcissistic personality disorders? How strongly does research support these explanations and treatments? *pp. 443–445*

8. What is the name of the cluster that includes the avoidant, dependent, and obsessive-compulsive personality disorders? What are the leading explanations and treatments for these

disorders, and to what extent are they supported by research? *pp. 447–454*

9. What kinds of problems have clinicians run into when using a categorical approach to the classification and diagnosis of personality disorders? *pp. 455–456*

10. Describe two dimensional approaches that have been proposed to identify and describe personality disorders. *pp. 456–459*

Visit *LaunchPad*
www.macmillanhighered.com/launchpad/comerfund8e
to access the e-book, new interactive case studies, videos, activities, and LearningCurve quizzes, as well as study aids including flashcards, FAQs, and research exercises.

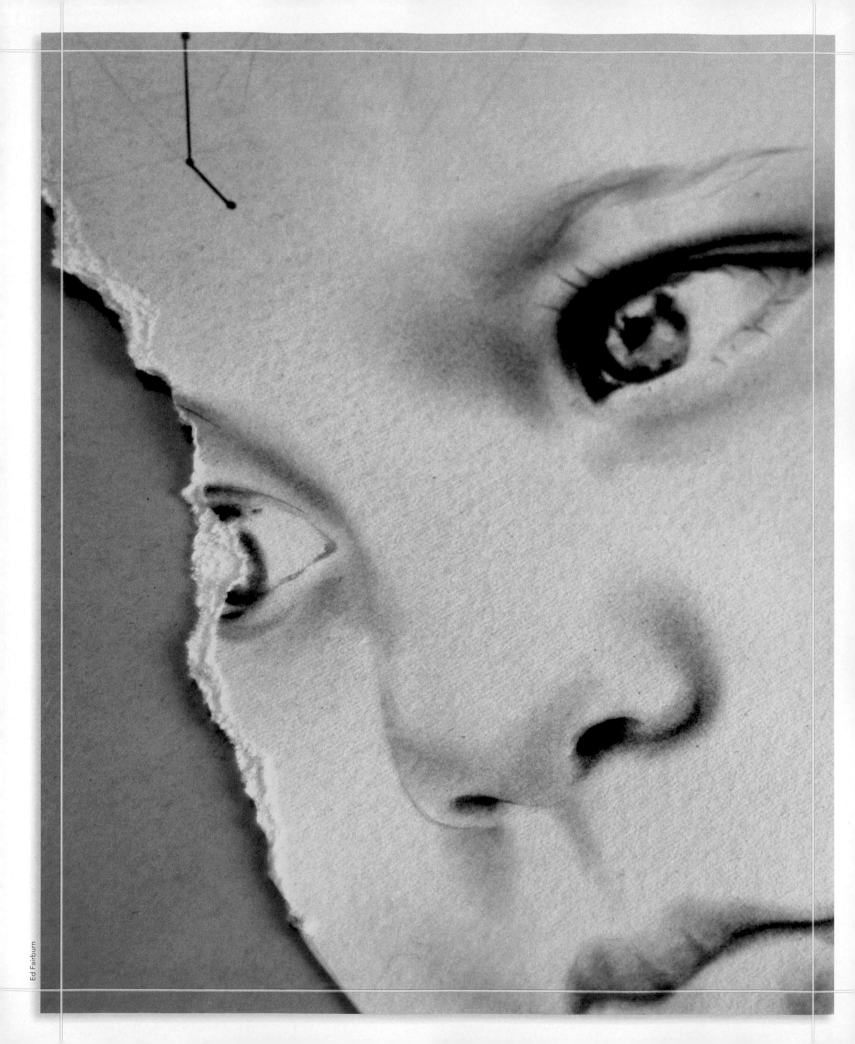

Ed Fairburn

Disorders Common Among Children and Adolescents

Billy, a 7-year-old . . . child, was brought to a mental health clinic by his mother because "he is unhappy and always complaining about feeling sick." . . . His mother describes Billy as a child who has never been very happy and never wanted to play with other children. From the time he started nursery school, he has complained about stomachaches, headaches, and various other physical problems. . . .

Billy did well in first grade, but in second grade he is now having difficulty completing his work. He takes a lot of time to do his assignments and frequently feels he has to do them over again so that they will be "perfect." Because of Billy's frequent somatic complaints, it is hard to get him off to school in the morning. If he is allowed to stay home, he worries that he is falling behind in his schoolwork. When he does go to school, he often is unable to do the work, which makes him feel hopeless about his situation. . . .

His worries have expanded beyond school, and frequently he is clinging and demanding of his parents. He is fearful that if his parents come home late or leave and go somewhere without him that something may happen to them. . . .

Although Billy's mother acknowledges that he has never been really happy, in the last 6 months, she feels, he has become much more depressed. He frequently lies around the house, saying that he is too tired to do anything. He has no interest or enjoyment in playing. His appetite has diminished. He has trouble falling asleep at night and often wakes up in the middle of the night or early in the morning. Three weeks ago, he talked, for the first time, about wanting to die. . . .

(Spitzer et al., 1994)

Ricky Smith was a 7-year-old. . . . During her initial call to the clinic, Mrs. Smith said her son was "out of control." She said Ricky "was all over the place" and "constantly getting into trouble." . . .

Ricky . . . said his teacher, Mrs. Candler, was always yelling at him and sending notes home to his mother. [He] initially said he did not know why the teacher yelled at him but then said it was mostly about not paying attention or following class rules. . . .

Ricky . . . said he had a few friends but often had to keep to himself. This was because Mrs. Candler made him spend much of the school day in a corner of the classroom to complete his work. Unfortunately, little of the work was successfully finished. Ricky said he felt bored, sad, tired, and angry in the classroom. . . .

Ricky said his mother yelled at him a lot. . . . He said he felt happiest when riding his bike because nobody yelled at him and he could "go wherever I want." . . .

Mrs. Smith said Ricky was almost intolerable in the classroom, . . . crying when asked to do something, stomping his feet, and being disrespectful to the teacher. . . . [She also] said her son was generally "out of control" at home. He would not listen to her commands and often ran around the house until he got what he wanted. She and her son often argued about his homework, chores, [and] misbehavior. . . . [In addition,] Ricky often fidgeted and lost many of his school materials. He was disorganized and paid little attention to long-term consequences. The child was also difficult to control in public places, such as a supermarket or church. . . .

Ricky's teacher . . . added that [his] attention was sporadic and insufficient. . . . Ricky was getting out of his seat more and more, requiring a constant response. . . .

(Kearney, 2013, pp. 62–64)

Billy and Ricky are both displaying psychological disorders. Their disorders are disrupting the boys' family ties, school performances, and social relationships, but each disorder does so in a particular way and for particular reasons. Billy, who may qualify for a diagnosis of *major depressive disorder*, struggles constantly with sadness, worry, and perfectionism, along with stomachaches and other physical ailments. Ricky's main problems, on the other hand, are that he cannot concentrate and is overly active and impulsive—difficulties that characterize *attention-deficit/hyperactivity disorder (ADHD)*.

Abnormal functioning can occur at any time in life. Some patterns of abnormality, however, are more likely to emerge during particular periods—during childhood, for example, or, at the other end of the spectrum, during old age. In this chapter you will read about disorders that commonly have their onset during childhood or early adolescence. In the next chapter you'll learn about problems that are more common among the elderly.

Childhood and Adolescence

People often think of childhood as a carefree and happy time—yet it can also be frightening and upsetting (see Figure 14-1). In fact, children of all cultures typically have at least some emotional and behavioral problems as they encounter new people and situations. Surveys reveal that *worry* is a common experience: close to half of all children in the United States have multiple fears, particularly concerning school, health, and personal safety (Jovanovic et al., 2014; Szabo & Lovibond, 2004). Bed-wetting, nightmares, temper tantrums, and restlessness are other problems that many

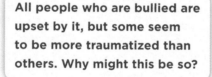

All people who are bullied are upset by it, but some seem to be more traumatized than others. Why might this be so?

children contend with. Adolescence can also be a difficult period. Physical and sexual changes, social and academic pressures, school violence, personal doubts, and temptations cause many teenagers to feel nervous, confused, and depressed.

A particular concern among children and adolescents is that of being bullied (see *InfoCentral* on page 466). Surveys throughout the world have revealed repeatedly that bullying ranks as a major problem in the minds of most young respondents, often a bigger problem than racism and peer pressure to try sex or alcohol (Hong et al., 2015; Isolan et al., 2013; Smith, 2011, 2010). More generally, over 25 percent of students report being bullied frequently, and more than 70 percent report having been bullied at least once.

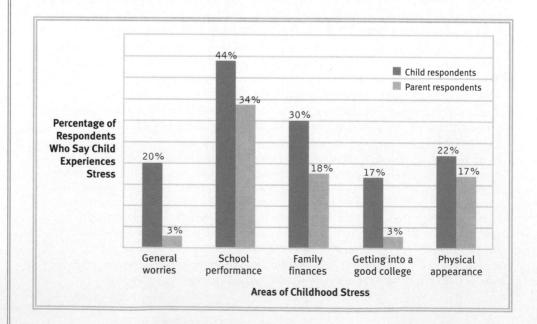

figure 14-1
Are parents aware of their children's stress? Not always, according to a large survey of parents and their children ages 8 to 17. For example, although 44 percent of the child respondents report that they worry about school, only 34 percent of the parent respondents believe that their children are worried about school. (Information from: Munsey, 2010.)

Typically, kids who have been bullied react with feelings of humiliation, anxiety, or dislike for school. Just as troubling, the technological advances of today's world have broadened the ways in which children and adolescents can be bullied, and *cyberbullying*—bullying and humiliating by e-mail, text messages, and Facebook—is now on the rise (Sampasa-Kanyinga et al., 2014).

Beyond these common concerns and psychological difficulties, at least one-fifth of all children and adolescents in North America also experience a diagnosable psychological disorder (NIMH, 2015; Winter & Bienvenu, 2011). Boys with disorders outnumber girls, even though most of the adult psychological disorders are more common among women.

Some disorders displayed by children—childhood anxiety disorders, childhood depression, and disruptive disorders—have adult counterparts, although they are also distinct in certain ways. Other childhood disorders—elimination disorders, for example—usually disappear or radically change form by adulthood. There are also disorders that begin at birth or in childhood and persist in stable forms into adult life. These include autism spectrum disorder and intellectual disability (previously called mental retardation), the former marked by a lack of responsiveness to the environment, the latter by an extensive disturbance in intellect.

Childhood Anxiety Disorders

Anxiety is, to a degree, a normal part of childhood. Since children have had fewer experiences than adults, their world is often new and scary. They may be frightened by common events, such as the beginning of school, or by special upsets, such as moving to a new house or becoming seriously ill. In addition, each generation of children is confronted by new sources of anxiety. Today's children, for example, are repeatedly warned, both at home and at school, about the dangers of Internet browsing and networking, child abduction, drugs, and terrorism.

Children may also be strongly affected by parental problems or inadequacies. If, for example, parents typically react to events with high levels of anxiety or if they overprotect their children, the children may be more likely to respond to the world

Targeted for Bullying

Surveys suggest that as many as 9 of 10 gay, lesbian, transgender, or bisexual middle and high school students are physically and/or verbally harassed each year (McKinley, 2010). The harassment ranges from taunts to beatings.

AP Photo/Charles Krupa

Multiple traumas A number of children in the Boston area developed posttraumatic stress disorder and/or other psychological disorders in the aftermath of the Boston Marathon bombing in 2013. It turns out that their disorders were triggered not only by witnessing (in person or on television) the devastation produced by the bombing, but also by the door-to-door searches for the suspects conducted by police in the days following the bombing (Comer, 2014). Here a woman carries her child from their home as a SWAT team enters to conduct one such search.

CHILD AND ADOLESCENT BULLYING

Bullying is the repeated infliction of force, threats, or coercion in order to intimidate, hurt, or dominate another—less powerful—person. It is particularly common among children and adolescents. Members of certain minority groups, such as LGBT individuals, are more likely to be bullied. Over the past decade, clinicians and educators have learned that bullying is much more common and more harmful than previously thought.

TYPES OF BULLYING

Physical — hitting, pushing, tripping

Verbal — name-calling, mean taunting, sexual comments, threatening

spreading rumors, posting embarrassing images, rejection from group

Relational/Social

BULLYING IS ON THE RISE...

39%	47%
Older than 50	Younger than 50

People bullied as teenagers

(Harris Interactive, 2014; Ratliffe, 2013; NFER, 2010)

BULLIES TEND TO:

Display antisocial behaviors
Perform poorly in school
Drop out of school
Bring weapons to school
Drink alcohol
Smoke cigarettes
Use drugs

(Hertz & Donato, 2013; CDC, 2011)

EFFECTS OF BULLYING:

Depression
Suicidal thinking and attempts
Anxiety
Low self-esteem
Sleep problems
Somatic symptoms
Substance use and abuse
School problems and/or phobias
Antisocial behavior

(CDC, 2013, 2011; Hertz & Donato, 2013)

SCHOOL BULLYING

Much bullying takes place at school. Around **2/3** of all school bullying occurs in hallways, schoolyards, bathrooms, cafeterias, or buses. A full **1/3** occurs in classrooms, while teachers are present (BSA, 2014). It is estimated that **40%** of school bullying goes unreported (BSA, 2014).

The Nature of School Bullying

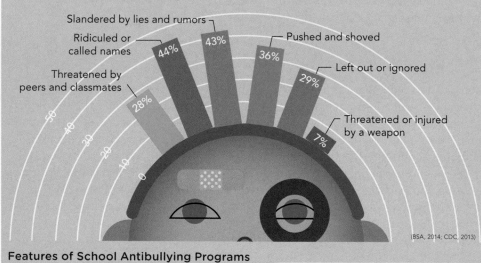

- Slandered by lies and rumors — 44%
- Ridiculed or called names — 43%
- Pushed and shoved — 36%
- Threatened by peers and classmates — 28%
- Left out or ignored — 29%
- Threatened or injured by a weapon — 7%

(BSA, 2014; CDC, 2013)

Features of School Antibullying Programs

- Increased supervision of students
- Delivery of consequences for bullying
- School-wide implementation of antibullying policies
- Cooperation among school staff, parents, and professionals across disciplines
- Identification of risk factors for bullying

Bullying prevention programs in schools reduce bullying up to **25%** (BSA, 2014).

(CDC, 2013; Hertz & Donato, 2013)

CYBERBULLYING

Cyberbullying takes place through email, text messaging, websites and apps, instant messaging, chat rooms or posted videos or photos (CDC, 2013). Around **40%** of all children and teens have been bullied online at least once. About **21%** are bullied online regularly. Girls are twice as likely as boys to be cyberbullied on a regular basis. (BSA, 2014; NSPCC, 2013; Sedghi, 2013; Hinduja & Patchin, 2010)

Like

Why do teens cyberbully?

Victim deserves it	58%
To get back at victim	58%
For entertainment	28%
To embarrass victim	21%
They want to be mean	14%
To show off for friends	11%

0 10 20 30 40 50 60 100 80 60 40 20 0

(BSA, 2014; Knowthenet, 2013)

Social Media and Cyberbullying

37%	Victims who report incidents to their social network
17%	Victims who initially tell a parent
1%	Victims who initially tell a teacher
95%	Users who witness cyberbullying on their social media site
35%	Witnesses who usually ignore cyberbullying on their social media site

(BSA, 2014; Knowthenet, 2013)

with anxiety (Platt, Williams, & Ginsburg, 2015). Similarly, if parents repeatedly reject, disappoint, or avoid their children, the world may seem an unpleasant and anxious place for them. And if parents are divorced, become seriously ill, or must be separated from their children for a long period, childhood anxiety may result. Beyond such environmental problems, there is genetic evidence that some children are prone to an anxious temperament (Rogers et al., 2013).

For some children, anxieties become long-lasting and overwhelming. These children may be suffering from an anxiety disorder. Surveys indicate that between 14 and 25 percent of all children and adolescents may experience an anxiety disorder (Mash & Wolfe, 2015; Mian, 2014). Some of the childhood anxiety disorders are similar to their adult counterparts. Childhood specific phobias, for example, usually look and operate just like the phobias of adulthood (Pilecki & McKay, 2011), and a number of untreated childhood phobias grow into adult ones.

More often, however, the anxiety disorders of childhood take on a somewhat different character from that of adult anxiety disorders. Typically they are dominated by behavioral and somatic symptoms rather than cognitive ones—symptoms such as clinging, sleep difficulties, and stomach pains (Morris & Ale, 2011; Schulte & Petermann, 2011). They tend to center on specific, sometimes imaginary, objects and events, such as monsters or thunderstorms, rather than broad concerns about the future or one's place in the world (APA, 2013; Davis & Ollendick, 2011). And they are more often than not triggered by current events and situations (Felix et al., 2011).

Separation Anxiety Disorder

Separation anxiety disorder, one of the most common anxiety disorders among children, follows this profile (APA, 2013). The disorder is common (but not unique) to childhood, begins as early as the preschool years, and at least 4 percent of all children experience it (Mash & Wolfe, 2015; APA, 2013). Sufferers feel extreme anxiety, often panic, whenever they are separated from home or a parent. Jonah's symptoms began when he was a preschooler and continued into kindergarten.

Oh, that first day! The first day of kindergarten is overwhelming for this child and perhaps also for his mother. Such anxiety reactions to the beginning of school and to being temporarily separated from one's parents are common among young children.

Steve Stoner/Fort Morgan Times/AP Photo

Jonah, age 4, began crying as soon as his parents tried to place him in the car for the 30-minute trip to his grandparents' house. This was going to be his first overnight weekend there. He had always been difficult on Tuesday afternoons when his grandmother came to his house to care for him—and, for that matter, whenever Mia, his mother, tried to take him to a play date—but this was an entirely new level of upset.

Jonah screamed that he would not get in the car. "I only want to be here with you! If you make me go, I'll never see you again! What if you like it better without me? What if Granny decides to keep me? What if you die?" Exasperated, Brandon, Jonah's father, picked up his son and carried him to the car. Jonah cried all the way to his grandparents' house. At their door, Jonah hugged his mother as though he would never let go.

Jonah finally went inside his grandparents' house. Eventually, Mia and Brandon left. Two hours later, they received a phone call from Mia's mother. An inconsolable Jonah had been crying nonstop since his parents had left. Reluctantly, Mia agreed to pick Jonah up, cancelling her and Brandon's weekend getaway.

That night, Jonah refused to sleep in his own room, insisting on sleeping between his parents. This was something they had tolerated occasionally in the past, but, beginning that night, it became a regular sleeping arrangement. During the

▶ **separation anxiety disorder** A disorder marked by excessive anxiety, even panic, whenever the person is separated from home, a parent, or another attachment figure.

(continues on the next page)

table: 14-1

Dx Checklist

Separation Anxiety Disorder

1. Individual displays fear or anxiety concerning separation from attachment figures, anxiety that is unreasonable or excessive for his or her age group.

2. Individual's excessive anxiety features three or more of the following symptoms:
   • Repeated separation-related upset • Repeated loss-related concern • Repeated fear of experiencing separation-caused events • Repeated resistance to leaving home • Repeated resistance to being alone • Repeated resistance to sleep-aways • Repeated separation-focused nightmares • Repeated separation-triggered physical symptoms.

3. Individual's symptoms last 4 or more weeks for children and at least 6 months for adults.

4. Significant distress or impairment.

(Information from: APA, 2013)

---

next several months, Jonah became hysterical every time Mia or Brandon tried to get him to leave the house for a play date or journey elsewhere.

Five months later, Jonah began kindergarten. That first day lasted all of two hours. The principal called, asking Mia to come get Jonah. Mia was hardly surprised. Her son had cried, screamed, and even kicked the whole ride to school, and his distress only escalated as she drove off. Though sympathetic, the principal explained that Jonah's nonstop crying was affecting all the other children. "Perhaps tomorrow Jonah will have a better day," he said. But the next day, Jonah's reaction was the same. And the next day. And the next day.

Children like Jonah have great trouble traveling away from their family, and they often refuse to visit friends' houses, go on errands, or attend camp or school (see Table 14–1). Many cannot even stay alone in a room and cling to their parent around the house. Some also have temper tantrums, cry, or plead to keep their parents from leaving them. The children may fear that they will get lost when separated from their parents or that the parents will meet with an accident or illness. As long as the children are near their parents and not threatened by separation, they may function quite normally. At the first hint of separation, however, the dramatic pattern of symptoms may be set in motion.

Separation anxiety disorder may further take the form of a *school phobia,* or *school refusal,* a common problem in which children fear going to school and often stay home for a long period (APA, 2013). Many cases of school phobia, however, have causes other than separation fears, such as social or academic fears, depression, and fears of specific objects or persons at school.

Treatments for Childhood Anxiety Disorders

Despite the high prevalence of childhood and adolescent anxiety disorders, around two-thirds of anxious children go untreated (Winter & Bienvenu, 2011). Among the children who do receive treatment, psychodynamic, cognitive-behavioral, family, and group therapies, separately or in combination, have been used most often. Each approach has had some degree of success; however, cognitive-behavioral therapy has fared the best across a number of studies (James et al., 2015; Mohatt et al., 2014). Such treatments parallel the adult anxiety approaches that you read about in Chapter 4, but they are tailored to the child's cognitive abilities, unique life situation, and limited control over his or her life. In addition, clinicians may offer psychoeducation, provide parent training, and arrange school interventions to treat anxious children (Lewin, 2011).

Clinicians have also used drug therapy in a number of cases of childhood anxiety disorders, often in combination with psychotherapy (Mohatt et al., 2014). Drug therapy often appears to be helpful, but it has begun only recently to receive much research attention (Comer et al., 2011, 2010).

Because children typically have difficulty recognizing and understanding their feelings and motives, many therapists, particularly psychodynamic therapists, use **play therapy** as part of treatment (Landreth, 2012). In this approach, the children play with toys, draw, and make up stories; in doing so they reveal the conflicts in their lives and their related feelings. The therapists then introduce more play and fantasy to help the children work through their conflicts and change their emotions and behavior. In addition, because children are often excellent hypnotic subjects, some therapists use *hypnotherapy* to help them overcome intense fears.

"This weekend I'm going to finally go through that closet and get rid of all those monsters."

➤ *Summing Up*

CHILDHOOD ANXIETY DISORDERS Emotional and behavioral problems are common in childhood and adolescence. A particular concern among children is that of being bullied. In addition, at least 20 percent of all children and adolescents in the United States have a diagnosable psychological disorder.

Anxiety disorders are particularly common among children and adolescents. This group of problems includes separation anxiety disorder, which is characterized by excessive anxiety, often panic, whenever a child is separated from a parent. Various treatments have been used for children with anxiety disorders, including play therapy.

▶ **play therapy** A treatment approach that helps children express their conflicts and feelings indirectly by drawing, playing with toys, and making up stories.

Childhood Depressive and Bipolar Disorders

Like Billy, the boy you read about at the beginning of this chapter, around 2 percent of children and 8 percent of adolescents currently experience a major depressive disorder (Mash & Wolfe, 2015). As many as 20 percent of adolescents experience at least one depressive episode during their teen years. In addition, many clinicians believe that children may experience bipolar disorder.

Major Depressive Disorder

Very young children lack some of the cognitive skills—a genuine sense of the future, for example—that help produce clinical depression (Hankin et al., 2008). Nevertheless, if life situations or biological predispositions are significant enough, even very young children sometimes have severe downward turns of mood (Tang et al., 2014). Depression in the young may be triggered by negative life events (particularly losses), major changes, rejection, or ongoing abuse. Childhood depression commonly features such symptoms as headaches, stomach pain, irritability, and a disinterest in toys and games (AACAP, 2013).

Clinical depression is much more common among teenagers than among young children. Adolescence is, under the best of circumstances, a difficult and confusing time, marked by angst, hormonal and bodily changes, mood changes, complex relationships, and new explorations (see *MindTech* on the next page). For some teens, these "normal" upsets of adolescence cross the line into clinical depression. As you read in Chapter 7, suicidal thoughts and attempts are particularly common among adolescents—one in eight teens persistently thinks about suicide each year—and depression is the leading cause of such thoughts and attempts (Nock et al., 2013; Spirito & Esposito-Smythers, 2008).

Interestingly, while there is no difference between the rates of depression in boys and girls before the age of 13, girls are twice as likely as boys to be depressed by the age of 16 (Frost et al., 2015; Merikangas et al., 2010). Why this gender shift? Several factors have been suggested, including hormonal changes and the fact that females increasingly experience more stressors than males. One explanation also focuses on teenage girls' growing dissatisfaction with their bodies. Whereas boys tend to like the increase in muscle mass and other body changes that accompany puberty, girls often detest the increases in body fat and weight gain that they experience during puberty and beyond. Raised in a society that values extreme thinness as the aesthetic female ideal, many adolescent girls feel imprisoned by their own bodies, have low self-esteem, and become depressed (Stice et al., 2000). Many also develop eating disorders, as you saw in Chapter 9.

Grief camp A number of "grief camps" have been developed around the country for children and teenagers who have lost a loved one. At one such program, this young girl, whose uncle was killed while fighting in Iraq, puts a clipping representing what she feels about his death into a bag.

AP Photo/Al Grillo

For years, it was generally believed that childhood and teenage depression would respond well to the same treatments that have been of help to depressed adults—cognitive-behavioral therapy and antidepressant drugs—and, in fact, many studies have indicated the effectiveness of such approaches (Straub et al., 2014; Vela et al., 2011). Some recent developments, however, have raised questions about these approaches for teenagers.

MindTech

Parent Worries on the Rise

Parents have always worried about their children—about their health, their safety, their grades, and their future. But in today's digital world, parent anxiety is rising to new heights as these traditional concerns are being joined by a major new focus—worry about their children's online experiences and behaviors (Fondas, 2014).

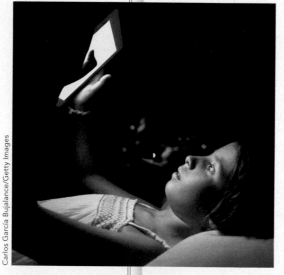

Carlos Garcia Bujalance/Getty Images

What exactly do parents worry about when their children go online, and who is worrying the most? Researchers Danah Boyd and Eszter Hargittai (2013) surveyed more than 1,000 parents across the United States and found that safety is at the heart of parents' anxiety. Almost two-thirds of the surveyed parents, whose children ranged in age from 10 to 14 years, were "extremely concerned" about their children being hurt by a stranger whom they might meet online. Additionally, many parents reported having extreme concern about their children being exposed to online pornography (57 percent of parents), being exposed to online violence (35 percent), and being the victim or perpetrator of online bullying (32 percent and 17 percent, respectively). Almost all of the surveyed parents expressed at least some degree of concern about each of these areas.

These areas of anxiety were not distributed evenly among parents. African American, Hispanic American, and Asian American parents were much more likely than white American parents to have these concerns. Urban parents were more fearful than suburban and rural parents. Lower-income parents had more anxiety about online bullying than did wealthier parents.

Mothers expressed more fear than fathers about their children being bullied online. Parents of daughters were more concerned than parents of sons about their children meeting harmful strangers and being exposed to violence online. And politically conservative and moderate parents expressed significantly more anxiety than liberal parents about their children viewing pornography or meeting strangers online.

In the early days of the Internet, parents would address concerns of this kind by supervising and restricting their children's online time and access. But those "good old days" are now gone, given the increasing number of U.S. teens who own a smartphone (almost half of them) and the easy access teens have to computers and tablets in so many locations outside the home (Fondas, 2014). In turn, parental anxiety continues to rise.

What can today's parents do to address their concerns about their children's online experiences and behaviors?

In one development, the National Institute of Mental Health recently sponsored a massive six-year study called the *Treatments for Adolescents with Depression Study* (*TADS*), which compared the effectiveness of cognitive-behavioral therapy alone, antidepressant therapy alone, cognitive-behavioral and antidepressant therapy combined, and placebo therapy for teenage depression (TADS, 2010, 2007, 2004). Three major surprises emerged from this highly regarded study. First, neither antidepressants alone nor cognitive-behavioral therapy alone was as effective for teenage depression as was a combination of antidepressants and cognitive-behavioral therapy. Second, antidepressants alone tended to be more helpful to depressed teens than cognitive-behavioral therapy alone. And third, cognitive-behavioral therapy alone was barely more helpful than placebo therapy. Many researchers believe that certain peculiarities in the participant population of the TADS study may have been responsible for the poor showing of cognitive-behavioral therapy. However, other clinical theorists believe that the TADS study is a definitive research undertaking and that many depressed teens may in fact respond less favorably to cognitive-behavioral therapy than adults do.

A second development has been the discovery that antidepressant drugs may be very dangerous for some depressed children and teenagers. As you read in Chapter 7, the U.S. Food and Drug Administration (FDA) concluded in 2004, based on a number of clinical reports, that the drugs may produce an increased risk of suicidal behavior for certain children and adolescents, especially during the first few months of treatment. Thus, the FDA ordered that all antidepressant containers carry "black box" warnings stating that the drugs "increase the risk of suicidal thinking and behavior in children."

Arguments about the wisdom of this FDA order have since followed. Although most clinicians agree that the drugs may indeed increase the risk of suicidal thoughts and attempts in as many as 2 to 4 percent of young patients, some have noted that the overall risk of suicide may actually be reduced for the vast majority of children who take the drugs (Isacsson & Rich, 2014; Vela et al., 2011). They point out, for example, that suicides among children and teenagers decreased by 30 percent in the decade leading up to 2004, as the number of antidepressant prescriptions provided to children and teenagers were soaring.

While the findings of the TADS study and questions about antidepressant drug safety continue to be sorted out, these two developments serve to highlight once again the importance of research, particularly in the treatment realm. We are reminded that treatments that work for individuals of a certain age, gender, race, or ethnic background may be ineffective or even dangerous for other groups of people.

Bipolar Disorder and Disruptive Mood Dysregulation Disorder

For decades, bipolar disorder was thought to be exclusively an *adult* disorder, and it was believed that its earliest age of onset is the late teens (APA, 2013). However, since the mid-1990s, clinical theorists have done an about-face, and many of them now believe that many children display bipolar disorder. A review of national diagnostic trends found that the number of children—often very young children—and adolescents diagnosed and treated for bipolar disorder in United States increased 40-fold from 1994 to 2003 (Moreno et al., 2007). For example, the number of private office visits for children with bipolar disorders increased from 20,000 in 1994 to 800,000 in 2003. And this rise has continued since 2003 (Mash & Wolfe, 2015).

Most theorists believe that these numbers reflect not an increase in the prevalence of bipolar disorders among children but rather a new diagnostic trend. The

Separation and depression This 3-year-old boy hugs his father as the soldier departs for deployment to Iraq. Given research evidence that extended family separations often produce depression in children, clinical theorists have been particularly worried about the thousands of children from military families who were left behind during the wars in Afghanistan and Iraq.

AP Photo/The Free Lance-Star, Mike Morones

Are children being medicated properly? A group of children in London protests against the common practice of prescribing adult medications and high dosages of medications for children with psychological disorders. Around half of all children treated for childhood bipolar disorder receive antipsychotic drugs.

© See Li/Demotix/Corbis

question is whether this trend is accurate. Many clinical theorists believe that the diagnosis of bipolar disorder is currently being overapplied to children and adolescents (Mash & Wolfe, 2015; Paris, 2014). They suggest that the label has become a clinical catchall that is being applied to almost every explosive, aggressive child. In fact, symptoms of rage and aggression, along with depression, dominate the clinical picture of most children who receive a bipolar diagnosis (Roy et al., 2013). The children may not even manifest the symptoms of mania or the mood swings that characterize adult bipolar disorder.

The DSM-5 task force agreed that the childhood bipolar label has in fact been overapplied over the past two decades. To help rectify this, DSM-5 now includes a new category, **disruptive mood dysregulation disorder,** which is used to describe children with patterns of severe rage (see Table 14-2). It is expected that more such children will receive this diagnosis in the coming years and that the number of childhood bipolar disorder diagnoses will decrease correspondingly.

This issue is particularly important because the rise in diagnoses of bipolar disorder has been accompanied by an increase in the number of children who are prescribed adult medications (Toteja et al., 2014; Chang et al., 2010; Grier et al., 2010). Around one-half of children in treatment for bipolar disorder receive an antipsychotic drug; one-third receive an antibipolar, or mood stabilizing, drug; and many others receive antidepressant or stimulant drugs. Yet relatively few of these drugs have been tested on and approved specifically for use with children.

table: 14-2

Dx Checklist

Disruptive Mood Dysregulation Disorder

1. For at least a year, individual repeatedly displays severe outbursts of temper that are extremely out of proportion to triggering situations and different from ones displayed by most other people of his or her age.

2. The outbursts occur at least three times per week and are present in at least two settings (home, school, with peers).

3. Individual repeatedly displays irritable or angry mood between the outbursts.

4. Individual receives initial diagnosis between 6 and 18 years of age.

(Information from: APA, 2013)

➤ Summing Up

CHILDHOOD DEPRESSIVE AND BIPOLAR DISORDERS Two percent of children and 8 percent of adolescents experience depression. In recent years, the TADS study and the FDA "black box" ruling have raised questions about the most appropriate treatments for teens with depression. In addition, the past two decades have witnessed an enormous increase in the number of children and adolescents who receive diagnoses of bipolar disorder. Such diagnoses are expected to decrease now that DSM-5 has added a new childhood category, disruptive mood dysregulation disorder.

Oppositional Defiant Disorder and Conduct Disorder

Most children break rules or misbehave on occasion. If they consistently display extreme hostility and defiance, however, they may qualify for a diagnosis of oppositional defiant disorder or conduct disorder. Those with **oppositional defiant disorder** are persistently argumentative or defiant, angry or irritable, and, in some cases, vindictive (APA, 2013). They may argue repeatedly with adults, ignore adult rules and requests, deliberately annoy other people, and feel much anger and resentment. As many as 10 percent of children qualify for a diagnosis of oppositional defiant disorder (Mash & Wolfe, 2015; Wilkes & Nixon, 2015). The disorder is more common in boys than in girls before puberty but equal in both sexes after puberty.

Children with **conduct disorder,** a more severe problem, repeatedly violate the basic rights of others (APA, 2013). They are often aggressive and may be physically cruel to people or animals, deliberately destroy other people's property, skip school, steal, or run away from home (see Table 14-3). Many threaten or harm their victims, committing such crimes as firesetting, shoplifting, forgery, breaking into buildings or cars, mugging, and armed robbery. As they get older, their acts of physical violence may include rape or, in rare cases, homicide. The symptoms of conduct disorder are apparent in this summary of a clinical interview with a 15-year-old boy named Derek:

> *Questioning revealed that Derek was getting into . . . serious trouble of late, having been arrested for shoplifting 4 weeks before. Derek was caught with one other youth when he and a dozen friends swarmed a convenience store and took everything they could before leaving in cars. This event followed similar others at [an electronics] store and a . . . clothing store. Derek blamed his friends for his arrest because they apparently left him behind as he straggled out of the store. He was charged only with shoplifting, however, after police found him holding just three candy bars and a bag of potato chips. Derek expressed no remorse for the theft or any care for the store clerk who was injured when one of the teens pushed her into a glass case. When informed of the clerk's injury, for example, Derek replied, "I didn't do it, so what do I care?"*
>
> *The psychologist questioned Derek further about other legal violations and discovered a rather extended history of trouble. Derek was arrested for vandalism 10 months earlier for breaking windows and damaging cars on school property. He received probation for 6 months because this was his first offense. Derek also boasted of other exploits for which he was not caught, including several shoplifting episodes, . . . joyriding, and missing school. Derek missed 23 days (50 percent) of school since the beginning of the academic year. In addition, he described break-in attempts of his neighbors' apartments. . . . Only rarely during the interview did Derek stray from his bravado.*
>
> *(Kearney, 2013, pp. 87–88)*

Conduct disorder usually begins between 7 and 15 years of age (APA, 2013). As many as 10 percent of children, three-quarters of them boys, qualify for this diagnosis (Mash & Wolfe, 2015; Nock et al., 2006). Children with a relatively mild conduct disorder often improve over time, but a severe case may continue into adulthood and develop into antisocial personality disorder or other psychological problems. Usually, the earlier the onset of the conduct disorder, the poorer the eventual outcome. Research indicates that more than 80 percent of those who develop conduct disorder first display a pattern of oppositional defiant disorder (APA, 2013; Lahey, 2008). More than one-third of children with conduct disorder also display

▶ **disruptive mood dysregulation disorder** A childhood disorder marked by severe recurrent temper outbursts and a persistent irritable or angry mood.

▶ **oppositional defiant disorder** A disorder in which children are persistently argumentative, defiant, angry, irritable, and perhaps vindictive.

▶ **conduct disorder** A disorder in which a child repeatedly violates the basic rights of others and displays significant aggression.

table: **14-3**

Dx Checklist

Conduct Disorder

1. Individual repeatedly behaves in ways that violate the rights of other people or ignores the norms or rules of society, beyond the violations displayed by most other people of his or her age.

2. At least three of the following features are present over the past year (and at least one in the past 6 months): • Frequent bullying or threatening of others • Frequent provoking of physical fights • Using dangerous weapons • Physical cruelty to people • Physical cruelty to animals • Stealing during confrontations with a victim • Forcing someone into sexual activity • Fire-setting • Deliberately destroying others' property • Breaking into a house, building, or car • Frequent lying • Stealing items of value under nonconfrontational circumstances • Frequent staying out beyond curfews, starting before the age of 13 • Running away from home overnight at least twice • Frequent truancy from school, starting before the age of 13.

3. Significant impairment.

(Information from: APA, 2013)

"Is this the story you want to tell on your college application?"

Lee Lorenz/The New Yorker Collection/www.cartoonbank.com

attention-deficit/hyperactivity disorder (ADHD), a disorder that you will read about shortly (Jiron, 2010).

Some clinical theorists believe that there are actually several kinds of conduct disorder, including (1) the *overt-destructive* pattern, in which individuals display openly aggressive and confrontational behaviors; (2) the *overt-nondestructive* pattern, dominated by openly offensive but nonconfrontational behaviors such as lying; (3) the *covert-destructive* pattern, characterized by secretive destructive behaviors such as violating other people's property, breaking and entering, and setting fires; and (4) the *covert-nondestructive* pattern, in which individuals secretly commit nonaggressive behaviors, such as being truant from school (McMahon et al., 2010; McMahon & Frick, 2007, 2005).

Other researchers distinguish yet another pattern of aggression found in certain cases of conduct disorder, *relational aggression,* in which the individual is socially isolated and primarily engages in social misdeeds such as slandering others, spreading rumors, and manipulating friendships (Ostrov et al., 2014). Relational aggression is more common among girls than boys.

Many children with conduct disorder are suspended from school, placed in foster homes, or incarcerated (Weyandt et al., 2011). When children between the ages of 8 and 18 break the law, the legal system often labels them *juvenile delinquents* (Wiklund et al., 2014; Jiron, 2010). Boys are much more involved in juvenile crime than girls, although the gap between them is narrowing. After steadily rising during the 1990s, the number of arrests of teenagers for serious crimes has fallen by one-third during the past decade (U.S. Department of Justice, 2014, 2010).

What Are the Causes of Conduct Disorder?

Many cases of conduct disorder, particularly those marked by destructive behaviors, have been linked to genetic and biological factors (Kerekes et al., 2014; Wallace et al., 2014). In addition, a number of cases have been tied to drug abuse, poverty, traumatic events, and exposure to violent peers or community violence (Wymbs et al., 2014; Weyandt et al., 2011). Most often, conduct disorder has been tied to troubled parent–child relationships, inadequate parenting, family conflict, marital conflict, and family hostility (Mash & Wolfe, 2015; Henggeler & Sheidow, 2012). Children whose parents reject, leave, coerce, or abuse them or fail to provide appropriate and consistent supervision are apparently more likely to develop conduct problems. Children also seem more prone to this disorder when their parents themselves are antisocial, display excessive anger, or have substance use, mood, or schizophrenic disorders (Advokat et al., 2014).

How Do Clinicians Treat Conduct Disorder?

Because aggressive behaviors become more locked in with age, treatments for conduct disorder are generally most effective with children younger than 13 (APA, 2013). A number of interventions, from sociocultural to child-focused, have been developed in recent years to treat children with the disorder. As you will see, several of these have had modest (and at times moderate) success, but clearly no one of them alone is the answer for this difficult problem. Today's clinicians are increasingly combining several approaches into a wide-ranging treatment program.

Sociocultural Treatments Given the importance of family factors in conduct disorder, therapists often use family interventions. One such approach, used with preschoolers, is called *parent–child interaction therapy* (Hembree-Kigin & McNeil,

2013; Zisser & Eyberg, 2010). Here therapists teach parents to work with their child positively, to set appropriate limits, to act consistently, to be fair in their discipline decisions, and to establish more appropriate expectations regarding the child. The therapists also try to teach the child better social skills. A related family intervention for very young children, *video modeling,* works toward the same goals with the help of video tools (Webster-Stratton & Reid, 2010).

When children reach school age, therapists often use a family intervention called *parent management training.* In this approach, (1) parents are again taught more effective ways to deal with their children, and (2) parents and children meet together in behavior-oriented family therapy (Kazdin, 2012, 2010, 2002; Forgatch & Patterson, 2010). Typically, the family and therapist target particular behaviors for change, then the parents are taught how to better identify problem behaviors, stop rewarding unwanted behaviors, and reward proper behaviors in a consistent manner. Like the family interventions for preschool-age children, parent management training has often achieved a measure of success.

Other sociocultural approaches, such as residential treatment in the community and programs at school, have also helped some children improve. In one such approach, *treatment foster care,* delinquent boys and girls with conduct disorder are assigned to a foster home in the community by the juvenile justice system (Henggeler & Sheidow, 2012). While there, the children, foster parents, and birth parents all receive training and treatment, followed by more treatment and support for the children and their biological parents after the children leave foster care.

> **How might juvenile training centers themselves contribute to the high recidivism rate among teenage criminal offenders?**

In contrast to these sociocultural interventions, institutionalization in so-called *juvenile training centers* has not met with much success (Stahlberg et al., 2010; Heilbrun et al., 2005). In fact, such institutions frequently serve to strengthen delinquent behavior rather than resocialize young offenders.

Child-Focused Treatments Treatments that focus primarily on the child with conduct disorder, particularly cognitive-behavioral interventions, have had some success in recent years (Kazdin, 2015, 2012, 2010, 2007). In an approach called *problem-solving skills training,* therapists combine modeling, practice, role-playing, and systematic rewards to help teach children constructive thinking and positive social behaviors. During therapy sessions, the therapists may play games and solve tasks with the children and later help the children apply the lessons and skills derived from the games and tasks to real-life situations.

In another child-focused approach, the *Coping Power Program,* children with conduct problems participate in group sessions that teach them to manage their anger more effectively, view situations in perspective, solve problems, become aware of their emotions, build social skills, set goals, and handle peer pressure.

Studies indicate that child-focused approaches such as these do indeed help reduce aggressive behaviors and prevent substance use in adolescence (Lochman et al., 2012, 2011, 2010). Recently, psychotropic medications have also been used for children with conduct disorder. Studies suggest, for example, that *stimulant drugs* may be helpful in reducing their aggressive behaviors at home and at school (Gorman et al., 2015).

Prevention It may be that the best hope for dealing with the problem of conduct disorder lies in *prevention* programs that begin in the earliest stages of childhood (Hektner et al., 2014).

Prevention: Scared straight Rather than waiting for children or adolescents to develop antisocial patterns, many clinicians call for better *prevention* programs. In one such program, "at risk" children visit nearby prisons where inmates describe how drugs, gang life, and other antisocial behaviors led to their imprisonment.

Craig Schreiner/Wisconsin State Journal/AP Photo

These programs try to change unfavorable social conditions before a conduct disorder is able to develop. The programs may offer training opportunities for young people, recreational facilities, and health care and may try to ease the stresses of poverty and improve parents' child-rearing skills. All such approaches work best when they educate and involve the family.

Elimination Disorders

Children with elimination disorders repeatedly urinate or pass feces in their clothes, in bed, or on the floor. They already have reached an age at which they are expected to control these bodily functions, and their symptoms are not caused by physical illness.

Enuresis

Enuresis is repeated involuntary (or in some cases intentional) bed-wetting or wetting of one's clothes. It typically occurs at night during sleep but may also occur during the day. Children must be at least 5 years of age to receive this diagnosis (APA, 2013). The problem may be triggered by stressful events, such as a hospitalization, entrance into school, or family problems. In some cases it is the result of physical or psychological abuse (see *PsychWatch* on page 478).

The prevalence of enuresis decreases with age. As many as 33 percent of 5-year-old children have some bed-wetting and as many as 10 percent meet the criteria for enuresis; in contrast, 3 to 5 percent of 10-year-olds and 1 percent of 15-year-olds have enuresis (Mash & Wolfe, 2015; APA, 2013). Those with enuresis typically have a close relative (parent, sibling) who has had or will have the same disorder.

Research has not favored one explanation for enuresis over the others (Kim et al., 2014; Friman, 2008). Psychodynamic theorists explain it as a symptom of broader anxiety and underlying conflicts. Family theorists point to disturbed family interactions. Behaviorists view the problem as the result of improper, unrealistic, or coercive toilet training. And biological theorists suspect that children with this disorder often have a small bladder capacity or weak bladder muscles.

Most cases of enuresis correct themselves even without treatment. However, therapy, particularly behavioral therapy, can speed up the process (Axelrod et al., 2014; Christophersen & Friman, 2010). In a widely used classical conditioning approach, the *bell-and-battery technique,* a bell and a battery are wired to a pad consisting of two metallic foil sheets, and the entire apparatus is placed under the child at bedtime (Mowrer & Mowrer, 1938). A single drop of urine sets off the bell, awakening the child as soon as he or she starts to wet. Thus the bell (unconditioned stimulus) paired with the sensation of a full bladder (conditioned stimulus) produces the response of waking. Eventually, a full bladder alone awakens the child.

Another effective behavioral treatment method is *dry-bed training,* in which children receive training in cleanliness and retention control, are awakened periodically during the night, practice going to the bathroom, and are appropriately rewarded. Like the bell-and-battery technique, this behavioral approach is often effective.

Encopresis

Encopresis, repeatedly defecating into one's clothing, is less common than enuresis, and it is also less well researched (Mash & Wolfe, 2015; APA, 2013). This problem seldom occurs at night during sleep. It is usually involuntary, starts at the age of 4 or older, and affects about 1.5 to 3 percent of all children (see Table 14-4). The disorder is much more common in boys than in girls.

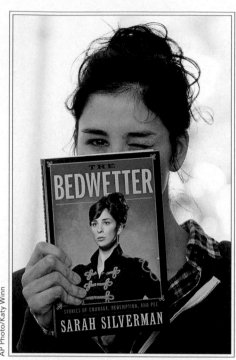

The Bedwetter Outrageous comedian Sarah Silverman holds up a copy of her best-selling 2010 book *The Bedwetter.* In this memoir, she writes extensively about her childhood experiences with enuresis and other emotional difficulties—always with a blend of self-revelation, pain, and humor.

AP Photo/Katy Winn

▶ **enuresis** A childhood disorder marked by repeated bed-wetting or wetting of one's clothes.

▶ **encopresis** A childhood disorder characterized by repeated defecating in inappropriate places, such as one's clothing.

table: **14-4**

Comparison of Childhood Disorders

Disorder	Usual Age of Identification	Prevalence Among All Children	Gender with Greater Prevalence	Elevated Family History	Recovery by Adulthood
Separation anxiety disorder	Before 12 years	4%–10%	Females	Yes	Usually
Conduct disorder	7–15 years	1%–10%	Males	Yes	Often
ADHD	Before 12 years	5%	Males	Yes	Often
Enuresis	5–8 years	5%	Males	Yes	Usually
Encopresis	After 4 years	1.5%–3%	Males	Unclear	Usually
Specific learning disorders	6–9 years	5%	Males	Yes	Often
Autism spectrum disorder	0–3 years	1.6%	Males	Yes	Sometimes
Intellectual disability	Before 10 years	1%–3%	Males	Unclear	Sometimes

Encopresis causes intense social problems, shame, and embarrassment (NLM, 2015; Mosca & Schatz, 2013). Children who suffer from it usually try to hide their condition and to avoid situations, such as camp or school, in which they might embarrass themselves. It may stem from stress, biological factors such as constipation, improper toilet training, or a combination of these factors. Because physical problems are so often linked to this disorder, a medical examination is typically conducted first.

The most common and successful treatments for encopresis are behavioral and medical approaches or a combination of the two (NLM, 2015; Collins et al., 2012; Christophersen & Friman, 2010). Treatment may include biofeedback training (see pages 118–119) to help the children better detect when their bowels are full; trying to eliminate the children's constipation; and stimulating regular bowel functioning with high-fiber diets, mineral oil, laxatives, and lubricants. Family therapy has also proved helpful.

"I wish I'd started therapy at your age."

PsychWatch

Child Abuse

A problem that affects all too many children and has an enormous impact on their psychological development is *child abuse*, the nonaccidental use of excessive physical or psychological force by an adult on a child, often with the intention of hurting or destroying the child. At least 5 percent of children in the United States are physically abused each year (Mash & Wolfe, 2015). Surveys suggest that 1 of every 10 children is the victim of severe violence, such as being kicked, bitten, hit, beaten, or threatened with a knife or a gun. In fact, some researchers believe that physical abuse and neglect are the leading causes of death among young children.

Overall, girls and boys are physically abused at approximately the same rate. Although such abuse occurs in all socio-economic groups, it is apparently more common among the poor (Romero-Martínez et al., 2014; Fowler et al., 2013).

Abusers are usually the child's parents (Ben-Natan et al., 2014). Clinical investigators have learned that abusive parents often have poor impulse control, low self-esteem, higher levels of depression, and weak parenting skills (Easterbrooks et al., 2013; Tolan et al., 2006). Many were abused themselves as children and have had poor role models (Romero-Martínez et al., 2014; McCaghy et al., 2006). In some cases, they are dealing with stressors such as marital discord or unemployment (Bor et al., 2013).

Studies suggest that the victims of child abuse may suffer immediate psychological effects such as anxiety, depression, bed-wetting, and performance and behavior problems in school (Keeshin et al., 2014; Buckingham & Daniolos, 2013). They may also experience long-term negative effects, including lack of social acceptance, more arrests during adolescence and adulthood, a higher number of medical and psychological disorders in their adult years, more abuse of alcohol and other substances, more impulsive and risk-taking behaviors, a heightened risk of becoming criminally violent, a higher unemployment rate, and a higher suicide rate (Afifi et al., 2014; Sujan et al., 2014; Faust et al., 2008). Moreover, as many as one-third of those who are abused grow up to be abusive, neglectful, or inadequate parents themselves (Romero-Martínez et al., 2014; Yaghoubi-Doust, 2013).

Two forms of child abuse have received special attention: psychological and sexual abuse. *Psychological abuse* may include severe rejection, excessive discipline, scapegoating and ridicule, isolation, and refusal to provide help for a child with psychological problems. It probably accompanies all forms of physical abuse and neglect and often occurs by itself. *Child sexual abuse*, the use of a child for gratification of adult sexual desires, may occur outside or within the home (Murray, Nguyen, & Cohen, 2014; Faust et al., 2008). Surveys suggest that at least 13 percent of women and 4 percent of men are forced into sexual contact with an adult during childhood, many of them with a parent or step-parent (Mash & Wolfe, 2015). Child sexual abuse appears to be equally common across all socioeconomic classes, races, and ethnic groups (Murray et al., 2014).

A variety of therapies have been used in cases of child abuse, including groups sponsored by *Parents Anonymous,* which help parents to develop insight into their behavior, provide training on alternatives to abuse, and teach coping and parenting skills (PA, 2014; Miller et al., 2007; Tolan et al., 2006). In addition, prevention programs, often in the form of home visitations and parent training, have proved promising (Beasley et al., 2014; Rubin et al., 2014).

Research suggests that the psychological needs of children who have been abused should be addressed as early as possible (Murray et al., 2014; Roesler & McKenzie, 1994). Clinicians and educators have launched valuable *early detection programs* that (1) educate all children about child abuse, (2) teach them skills for avoiding or escaping from abusive situations, (3) encourage children to tell another adult if they are abused, and (4) assure them that abuse is never their own fault (Miller et al., 2007; Finkelhor et al., 1995).

AP Photo/Chris Pizzello

"Memories so strong that I can smell and taste them now" That is how actor and filmmaker Tyler Perry (left) describes his recollections of the physical and sexual abuse he suffered as a child. Similarly, mega-celebrity and producer Oprah Winfrey (right) has publicly discussed her childhood experiences of sexual abuse. The two have collaborated to bring attention to child abuse.

➤ *Summing Up*

CONDUCT DISORDER AND ELIMINATION DISORDERS Children with oppositional defiant disorder and conduct disorder exceed the normal breaking of rules and act very aggressively. Those with oppositional defiant disorder argue repeatedly with adults, ignore adult rules and requests, and feel intense anger and resentment. Those with conduct disorder, a more severe pattern, repeatedly violate the basic rights of others. Children with this disorder often are violent and cruel and may deliberately destroy property, steal, and run away. Clinicians have treated children with conduct disorders by using approaches such as parent–child interaction therapy, parent management training, treatment foster care, problem-solving skills training, and the Coping Power Program. A number of prevention programs have been developed.

Children with an elimination disorder—enuresis or encopresis—repeatedly urinate or pass feces in inappropriate places. Behavioral approaches, such as the bell-and-battery technique, are effective treatments for enuresis.

Neurodevelopmental Disorders

Neurodevelopmental disorders are a group of disabilities in the functioning of the brain that emerge at birth or during very early childhood and affect the individual's behavior, memory, concentration, and/or ability to learn. As you read at the beginning of this chapter, many of the disorders first displayed during childhood subside as the person ages. However, the neurodevelopmental disorders often have a significant impact throughout the person's life. For example, at least half of those with *attention-deficit/hyperactivity disorder,* one of the neurodevelopmental disorders, carry some version of their disorder with them into adulthood. Moreover, the vast majority of those with *autism spectrum disorder* and *intellectual disability,* two other neurodevelopmental disorders, continue to display the symptoms of their disorders in largely unchanged form throughout adulthood.

Researchers have investigated each of these disorders extensively. In addition, although this was not always so, clinicians now have a range of treatment approaches that can make a major difference in the lives of people with these problems.

Attention-Deficit/Hyperactivity Disorder

Children with **attention-deficit/hyperactivity disorder (ADHD)** have great difficulty attending to tasks, or behave overactively and impulsively, or both (APA, 2013) (see Table 14-5 on the next page). ADHD often appears before the child starts school, as with Ricky, one of the boys we met at the beginning of this chapter. Steven is another child whose symptoms began very early in life:

> *Steven's mother cannot remember a time when her son was not into something or in trouble. As a baby he was incredibly active, so active in fact that he nearly rocked his crib apart. All the bolts and screws became loose and had to be tightened periodically. Steven was also always into forbidden places, going through the medicine cabinet or under the kitchen sink. He once swallowed some washing detergent and had to be taken to the emergency room. As a matter of fact, Steven had many more accidents and was more clumsy than his older brother and younger sister. . . . He always seemed to be moving fast. His mother recalls that Steven progressed from the crawling stage to a running stage with very little walking in between.*

▸ **neurodevelopmental disorders** A group of disabilities in the functioning of the brain that emerge at birth or during very early childhood and affect a person's behavior, memory, concentration, and/or ability to learn.

▸ **attention-deficit/hyperactivity disorder (ADHD)** A disorder marked by the inability to focus attention, or overactive and impulsive behavior, or both.

(continues on the next page)

Trouble really started to develop for Steven when he entered kindergarten. Since his entry into school, his life has been miserable and so has the teacher's. Steven does not seem capable of attending to assigned tasks and following instructions. He would rather be talking to a neighbor or wandering around the room without the teacher's permission. When he is seated and the teacher is keeping an eye on him to make sure that he works, Steven's body still seems to be in motion. He is either tapping his pencil, fidgeting, or staring out the window and daydreaming. Steven hates kindergarten and has few long-term friends; indeed, school rules and demands appear to be impossible challenges for him. The effects of this mismatch are now showing in Steven's schoolwork and attitude. He has fallen behind academically and has real difficulty mastering new concepts; he no longer follows directions from the teacher and has started to talk back.

(Gelfand, Jenson, & Drew, 1982, p. 256)

The symptoms of ADHD often feed into one another. Children who have trouble focusing attention may keep turning from task to task until they end up trying to run in several directions at once. Similarly, children who move constantly may find it hard to attend to tasks or show good judgment. In many cases, one of these symptoms stands out much more than the other. About half of the children with ADHD also have learning or communication problems; many perform poorly in school; a number have difficulty interacting with other children; and about 80 percent misbehave, often quite seriously (Mash & Wolfe, 2015; Goldstein, 2011). It is also common for these children to have anxiety or mood problems (Humphreys et al., 2015; Tsang et al., 2015).

Around 5 percent of all children display ADHD at any given time, as many as 70 percent of them boys (APA, 2013; Merikangas et al., 2011). The disorder usually

table: 14-5

Dx Checklist

Attention-Deficit/Hyperactivity Disorder

1. Individual presents one or both of the following patterns:
   (a) For 6 months or more, individual frequently displays at least six of the following symptoms of inattention, to a degree that is maladaptive and beyond that shown by most similarly aged persons: • Unable to properly attend to details, or frequently makes careless errors • Finds it hard to maintain attention • Fails to listen when spoken to by others • Fails to carry out instructions and finish work • Disorganized • Dislikes or avoids mentally effortful work • Loses items that are needed for successful work • Easily distracted by irrelevant stimuli • Forgets to do many everyday activities.
   (b) For 6 months or more, individual frequently displays at least six of the following symptoms of hyperactivity and impulsivity, to a degree that is maladaptive and beyond that shown by most similarly aged persons: • Fidgets, taps hands or feet, or squirms • Inappropriately wanders from seat • Inappropriately runs or climbs • Unable to play quietly • In constant motion • Talks excessively • Interrupts questioners during discussions • Unable to wait for turn • Barges in on others' activities or conversations.

2. Individual displayed some of the symptoms before 12 years of age.

3. Individual shows symptoms in more than one setting.

4. Individual experiences impaired functioning.

(Information from: APA, 2013)

persists throughout childhood. Many children show a marked lessening of symptoms as they move into mid-adolescence, but as many as 60 percent of affected children continue to have ADHD as adults (Weyandt et al., 2014). The symptoms of restlessness and overactivity are not usually as pronounced in adult cases.

ADHD is a difficult disorder to assess properly (Batstra et al., 2014). Ideally, the child's behavior should be observed in several environments (school, home, with friends) because the symptoms of hyperactivity and inattentiveness must be present across multiple settings in order for ADHD to be diagnosed (Burns et al., 2014; APA, 2013). Because children with ADHD often give poor descriptions of their symptoms, it is important to obtain reports of the child's symptoms from his or her parents and teachers. And, finally, although diagnostic interviews, ratings scales, and psychological tests can be helpful in the assessment of ADHD, studies suggest that many children receive their diagnosis from pediatricians or family physicians rather than mental health professionals and that at most one-third of such diagnoses are based on psychological or educational testing (Millichap, 2010).

What Are the Causes of ADHD?
Today's clinicians generally consider ADHD to have several interacting causes. Biological factors have been identified in many cases, particularly abnormal activity of the neurotransmitter *dopamine* and abnormalities in the *striatal* region of the brain (Advokat et al., 2014; Hale et al., 2010). The disorder has also been linked to high levels of stress and to family dysfunctioning (Montejo et al., 2015; Rapport et al., 2008). In addition, sociocultural theorists have noted that ADHD symptoms and a diagnosis of ADHD may themselves create social problems and produce additional symptoms in the child. That is, children who are hyperactive tend to be viewed negatively by their peers and by their parents, and they often view themselves negatively as well (Martin, 2014; Chandler, 2010).

How Is ADHD Treated?
Almost 80 percent of all children and adolescents with ADHD receive treatment (Winter & Bienvenu, 2011). There is, however, disagreement in the field about which kind of treatment is most effective. The most commonly used approaches are drug therapy, behavioral therapy, or a combination of the two (Sibley et al., 2014).

Millions of children and adults with ADHD are currently treated with **methylphenidate,** a stimulant drug that has been available for decades, or with certain other stimulants. Although a variety of manufacturers now produce methylphenidate, the drug continues to be known to the public by its most famous trade name, **Ritalin.** As researchers have confirmed Ritalin's quieting effect on children with ADHD and its ability to help them focus, solve complex tasks, perform better at school, and control aggression, use of the drug has increased enormously—according to some estimates, at least a threefold increase since 1990 alone (Mash & Wolfe, 2015; Sibley et al., 2014). Today, an estimated 2.2 million children in the United States, 3 percent of all schoolchildren, regularly take Ritalin or other stimulant drugs for ADHD. Collectively, the drugs are the most common treatment for the disorder.

> **Why has there been a sizable increase in the diagnosis and treatment of ADHD over the past few decades?**

Although widely used, Ritalin and other stimulant drugs have raised certain concerns. First, many clinicians worry about the possible long-term effects of the drugs (Berg et al., 2014; Waugh, 2013), and others question whether the favorable findings of the drug studies (most of which have been done on white American children) are applicable to children from minority

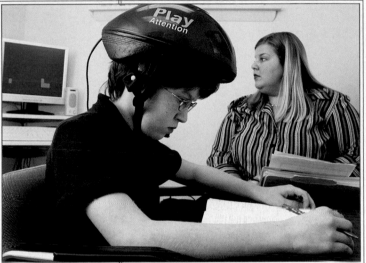

"Playing" attention A range of techniques have been used to help understand and treat children with ADHD, including a computer program called *Play Attention*. Here, under the watchful eye of a behavior specialist, a child wears a bike helmet that measures brain waves while she performs tasks that require attention.

▶ **methylphenidate** A stimulant drug, known better by the trade name *Ritalin*, commonly used to treat ADHD.

Jose Azel/Aurora

Behavioral intervention Educational programs use behavioral principles that clearly spell out targeted behaviors and program rewards and systematically reinforce appropriate behaviors. Such programs can be particularly helpful for children with ADHD.

groups. Second, investigations indicate that ADHD is overdiagnosed in the United States, so many children who are receiving the stimulants may, in fact, not really be in need of them (Batstra et al., 2014; Rapport et al., 2008).

Behavioral therapy has been used to help treat many people with ADHD. Parents and teachers learn how to reward children for their attentiveness or self-control, often by using a token economy program (Coates et al., 2015; DuPaul et al., 2011). Such operant conditioning treatments have been helpful for a number of children, especially when combined with stimulant drug therapy (Sibley et al., 2014; Dendy, 2011). Combining behavioral and drug therapies is also desirable because, according to research, children who receive both treatments require lower levels of medication, meaning, of course, that they are less subject to the medication's possible side effects (Hoza et al., 2008).

Multicultural Factors and ADHD Throughout this book, you have seen that race often affects how people are diagnosed and treated for various psychological disorders. Thus, you should not be totally surprised that race also seems to come into play with regard to ADHD.

A number of studies indicate that African American and Hispanic American children with significant attention and activity problems are less likely than white American children with similar symptoms to be assessed for ADHD, receive a diagnosis of ADHD, or undergo treatment for it (Morgan et al., 2014; Bussing et al., 2005, 2003, 1998). Moreover, among those who do receive such a diagnosis and treatment, children from racial minorities are less likely than white American children to be treated with stimulant drugs or a combination of stimulants and behavioral therapy—the interventions that seem to be of most help to those with ADHD (Pham et al., 2010). Finally, among those children who do receive stimulant drug treatment for ADHD, children from racial minorities are less likely than white American children to receive the promising (but more expensive) *long-acting* stimulant drugs that have been developed in recent years (Sugrue et al., 2014; Cooper, 2004).

In part, these racial differences are tied to economic factors. Studies consistently show that poorer children are less likely than wealthier ones to be identified as having ADHD and are less likely to receive effective treatment, and racial minority families have, on average, lower incomes and weaker insurance coverage than white American families. Some clinical theorists further believe that social bias and stereotyping may contribute to the racial differences in diagnosis and treatment. They argue that our society often views the symptoms of ADHD as medical problems when exhibited by white American children but as indicators of poor parenting, lower IQ, substance use, or violence when displayed by African American and Hispanic American children (Duval-Harvey & Rogers, 2010; Kendall & Hatton, 2002). This notion has been supported by the research finding that, all symptoms being equal, teachers and parents are more likely to conclude that overactive white American children have ADHD but that overactive African American or Hispanic American children have other kinds of difficulties (Hillemeier et al., 2007; Raymond, 1997; Samuel et al., 1997).

Whatever the reason—economic disadvantage, social bias, racial stereotyping, or other factors—it appears that children from racial minority groups are less likely to receive a proper ADHD diagnosis and treatment. While many of today's theorists correctly raise the possibility that ADHD may be generally overdiagnosed, it is important to recognize that children from certain segments of society may, in fact, be underdiagnosed and undertreated.

Autism Spectrum Disorder

Autism spectrum disorder, a pattern first identified by psychiatrist Leo Kanner in 1943, is marked by extreme unresponsiveness to other people, severe communication deficits, and highly rigid and repetitive behaviors, interests, and activities (APA, 2013) (see Table 14-6). These symptoms appear early in life, typically before 3 years of age. Just a few decades ago, the disorder seemed to affect around 1 out of every 2,000 children. However, in recent years there has been a steady increase in the number of children diagnosed with autism spectrum disorder, and it now appears that as many as 1 in 68 children display this pattern (CDC, 2015, 2014). Jennie is one such child:

> *[At school] Jennie was often nonresponsive to others, especially her classmates, and rarely made eye contact with anyone. When left alone, Jennie would usually stand, put her hands over her throat, stick out her tongue, and make strange but soft noises. This would last for hours if she were left alone. When seated, Jennie rocked back and forth in her chair but never fell. Her motor skills seemed excellent and she could use crayons and manipulate paper when asked to do so. Her dexterity was also evident in her aggression, however. Jennie often grabbed people's jewelry and eyeglasses and flung them across the room. She moved quickly enough to accomplish this in less than two seconds. . . . Jennie was most aggressive when introduced to something or someone new. . . .*
>
> *. . . Jennie did not speak and vocalized only when making her soft sounds. The volume of her sounds rarely changed. . . . [She] made no effort to communicate with others and was often oblivious to others. . . . Despite her lack of expressiveness, Jennie did understand and adhere to simple requests from others. She complied readily when told to get her lunch, use the bathroom, or retrieve an item in the classroom. . . .*
>
> *Jennie had a "picture book" with photographs of items she might want or need. . . . When shown the book and asked to point, Jennie either pushed the book onto the desk if she did not want anything or pointed to one of five photographs (i.e., a lunch box, cookie, glass of water, favorite toy, or toilet) if she did want something. . . .*
>
> *[Her parents] said Jennie "had always been like this." . . . Both said Jennie was "different" as a baby when she resisted being held and when she failed to talk by age 3 years. . . .*
>
> *(Kearney, 2013, pp. 125–126)*

Around 80 percent of all cases of autism spectrum disorder occur in boys. As many as 90 percent of children with the disorder remain significantly disabled into adulthood. They have great difficulty maintaining employment, performing household tasks, and leading independent lives (Sicile-Kira, 2014). Even the highest-functioning adults with autism typically have problems with closeness and empathy and have restricted interests and activities.

The individual's *lack of responsiveness and social reciprocity*—extreme aloofness, lack of interest in other people, low empathy, and inability to share attention with others—has long been considered a central feature of autism. Like Jennie, children with autism typically do not reach for their parents during infancy. Instead they may arch their backs when they are held and appear not to recognize or care about those around them. In a similar vein, unlike other children of the same age, autistic children typically do not include others in their play and do not represent social experiences when they are playing; they often fail to see themselves as others see them and have no desire to imitate or be like others (Bodison, 2015; Boyd et al., 2011).

Communication problems take various forms in autism spectrum disorder. Many autistic people have great difficulty understanding speech or using language for

table: 14-6

Dx Checklist

Autism Spectrum Disorder

1. Individual displays continual deficiencies in various areas of communication and social interaction, including the following:
   • Social-emotional reciprocity
   • Nonverbal communication
   • Development and maintenance of relationships.

2. Individual displays significant restriction and repetition in behaviors, interests, or activities, including two or more of the following: • Exaggerated and repeated speech patterns, movements, or object use • Inflexible demand for same routines, statements, and behaviors • Highly restricted, fixated, and overly intense interests • Over- or under-reactions to sensory input from the environment.

3. Individual develops symptoms by early childhood.

4. Individual experiences significant impairment.

(Information from: APA, 2013)

▶ **autism spectrum disorder** A developmental disorder marked by extreme unresponsiveness to others, severe communication deficits, and highly repetitive and rigid behaviors, interests, and activities.

Blocking out the world An 8-year-old child with autism spectrum disorder peers vacantly through a hole in the netting of a baseball batting cage, seemingly unaware of other children and activities at the playground.

conversational purposes. In fact, like Jennie, half fail to speak or develop effective language skills (Paul & Gilbert, 2011). Those who do talk may have rigid and repetitious speech patterns. One of the most common speech peculiarities is *echolalia,* the exact echoing of phrases spoken by others. The individuals repeat the words, but with no sign of understanding or intent of communicating. Another speech oddity is *pronominal reversal,* or confusion of pronouns—for example, the use of "you" instead of "I." When hungry, a child with autism spectrum disorder might say, "Do you want dinner?"

The nonverbal behaviors of these individuals are often at odds with their efforts at verbal communication. They may not, for example, use a proper tone when talking. It is also common for autistic persons to show few or no facial expressions or body gestures. In addition, a number are unable to maintain proper eye contact during interactions. Recall, for example, that Jennie "rarely made eye contact with anyone."

Autistic people also display a wide range of *highly rigid and repetitive behaviors, interests, and activities* that extend beyond speech patterns. Typically they become very upset at minor changes in objects, persons, or routines and resist any efforts to change their own repetitive behaviors. Recall that Jennie was most aggressive when introduced to something or someone new.

Similarly, some children with the disorder react with tantrums if a parent wears an unfamiliar pair of glasses, a chair is moved to a different part of the room, or a word in a song is changed. Kanner (1943) labeled such reactions a *perseveration of sameness.* Many also become strongly attached to particular objects—plastic lids, rubber bands, buttons, water. They may collect these objects, carry them, or play with them constantly. Some are fascinated by movement and may watch spinning objects, such as fans, for hours.

People with autism may display *motor movements* that are unusual, rigid, and repetitive. They may jump, flap their arms, twist their hands and fingers, rock, walk on their toes, spin, and make faces. These acts are called *self-stimulatory behaviors.* Some autistic individuals also perform *self-injurious behaviors,* such as repeatedly lunging into or banging their head against a wall, pulling their hair, or biting themselves (Aman & Farmer, 2011).

The symptoms of autism spectrum disorder suggest a very disturbed and contradictory pattern of reactions to stimuli (see *PsychWatch* on the next page). Sometimes the individuals seem overstimulated by sights and sounds and appear to be trying to block them out (called *hyperreactivity*), while at other times they seem understimulated and appear to be performing self-stimulatory actions (called *hyporeactivity*). They may, for example, fail to react to loud noises yet turn around when they hear soda being poured.

What Are the Causes of Autism Spectrum Disorder?

A variety of explanations have been offered for autism spectrum disorder. This is one disorder for which sociocultural explanations have probably been overemphasized. In fact, such explanations initially led investigators in the wrong direction. More recent work in the psychological and biological spheres has persuaded clinical theorists that cognitive limitations and brain abnormalities are the primary causes of this disorder.

SOCIOCULTURAL CAUSES At first, theorists thought that family dysfunction and social stress were the primary causes of autism spectrum disorder. When he first identified this disorder, for example, Kanner argued that particular personality characteristics of the parents created an unfavorable climate for development and contributed to the disorder (Kanner, 1954, 1943). He saw these parents as very intelligent yet

BETWEEN THE LINES

On the Rise: Estimates of Autism Prevalence

1985	1 per 2000 children
2000	1 per 150 children
2006	1 per 110 children
2012	1 per 88 children
2014	1 per 68 children

(CDC, 2015; Falco, 2014; Park, 2014; Rice et al., 2012)

cold—"refrigerator parents." These claims had enormous influence on the public and on the self-image of the parents themselves, but research has totally failed to support a picture of rigid, cold, rejecting, or disturbed parents (Sicile-Kira, 2014; Vierck & Silverman, 2011).

Similarly, some clinical theorists have proposed that a high degree of social and environmental stress is a factor in the disorder. Once again, however, research has not supported this notion. Investigators who have compared autistic children with nonautistic children have found no differences in the rate of parental death, divorce, separation, financial problems, or environmental stimulation (Landrigan, 2011).

PSYCHOLOGICAL CAUSES According to certain theorists, people with autism spectrum disorder have a central perceptual or cognitive disturbance that makes normal communication and interactions impossible. One influential explanation holds that those with the disorder fail to develop a **theory of mind**—an awareness that other people base their behaviors on their own beliefs, intentions, and other mental states, not on information that they have no way of knowing (Begeer et al., 2015; Kimhi et al., 2014).

By 3 to 5 years of age, most normal children can take the perspective of another person into account and use it to anticipate what the person will do. In a way, they learn to read others' minds. Let us say, for example, that we watch Jessica place a marble in a container and then we observe Frank move the marble to a nearby room while Jessica is taking a nap. We know that later Jessica will search first in the

▶ **theory of mind** An awareness that other people base their behaviors on their own beliefs, intentions, and other mental states, not on information that they have no way of knowing.

PsychWatch

A Special Kind of Talent

Most people are familiar with the savant syndrome, thanks to Dustin Hoffman's portrayal of a man with autism in the movie *Rain Man*. The savant skills that Hoffman portrayed—counting 246 toothpicks in the instant after they fall to the floor, memorizing the phone book through the Gs, and doing numerical calculations at lightning speed—were based on the astounding talents of certain real-life people who are otherwise limited by autism spectrum disorder or intellectual disability.

A *savant* (French for "learned" or "clever") is a person with a major mental disorder or intellectual handicap who has some spectacular ability. Often these abilities are remarkable only in light of the handicap, but sometimes they are remarkable by any standard (Treffert, 2014; Yewchuk, 1999). A common savant skill is calendar calculating, the ability to calculate what day of the week a date will fall on, such as New Year's Day in 2050. A common musical skill such people may possess is the ability to play a piece of classical music flawlessly from memory after hearing it only once. Other individuals can paint exact replicas of scenes they saw years ago.

Some theorists believe that savant skills do indeed represent special forms of cognitive functioning; others propose that the skills are merely a positive side to certain cognitive deficits (Treffert, 2014; Howlin, 2012; Scheuffgen et al., 2000). Special memorization skills, for example, may be facilitated by the very narrow and intense focus that people with autism often have.

Imke Lass/Redux Pictures

Special insights One of the highest-achieving autistic people in the world is Dr. Temple Grandin, a professor at Colorado State University. Applying her personal perspective and unique visualization skills, she has developed insight into the minds and sensitivities of cattle and has designed more humane animal-handling equipment and facilities. She argues that autistic savants and animals share cognitive similarities.

DSM-5 Controversy: Loss of Services?

Past editions of the DSM included a disorder called *Asperger's disorder,* a diagnosis given to individuals who displayed the severe social deficits and unusual behaviors found in autism but otherwise had normal language, adaptive, and cognitive skills. However, DSM-5 has eliminated Asperger's disorder as a distinct disorder. Individuals with that pattern now receive a diagnosis of either autism spectrum disorder or *social communication disorder*—a less severe disorder characterized by persistent problems in communication and social relationships. Many parents worry that children who receive this latter diagnosis will no longer qualify for the special educational services previously made available for children with Asperger's disorder.

container for the marble because she is not aware that Frank moved it. We know that because we take Jessica's perspective into account. A normal child would also anticipate Jessica's search correctly. An autistic child would not. He or she would expect Jessica to look in the nearby room because that is where the marble actually is. Jessica's own mental processes would be unimportant to the person.

Studies show that people with autism spectrum disorder do indeed have this kind of "mind-blindness," although they are not the only kinds of individuals with this limitation (Loukusa et al., 2014). They thus have great difficulty taking part in make-believe play, using language in ways that include the perspectives of others, developing relationships, or participating in human interactions. Why do autistic people have this and other cognitive limitations? Some theorists believe that they suffered early biological problems that prevented proper cognitive development.

BIOLOGICAL CAUSES For years researchers have tried to determine what biological abnormalities might cause theory-of-mind deficits and the other features of autism spectrum disorder. They have not yet developed a complete biological explanation, but they have uncovered some promising leads. First, examinations of the relatives of autistic people keep suggesting a *genetic factor* in this disorder (Egawa et al., 2015). The prevalence of autism among their siblings, for example, is as high as 1 per 10, a rate much higher than the general population's (Risch et al., 2014). Moreover, the prevalence of autism among the identical twins of autistic people is 60 percent.

Some studies have also linked autism spectrum disorder to *prenatal difficulties* or *birth complications* (Reichenberg et al., 2011). For example, the chances of developing the disorder are higher when the mother had rubella (German measles) during pregnancy, was exposed to toxic chemicals before or during pregnancy, or had complications during labor or delivery.

Finally, researchers have identified specific *biological abnormalities* that may contribute to autism spectrum disorder. One line of research has pointed to the **cerebellum** (Mosconi et al., 2015; Pierce & Courchesne, 2002, 2001). Brain scans and autopsies show abnormal development in this brain area occurring early in the life of autistic people. Scientists have long known that the cerebellum coordinates movement in the body, but they now suspect that it also helps control a person's ability to shift attention rapidly. It may be that people whose cerebellum develops abnormally will have great difficulty adjusting their level of attention, following verbal and facial cues, and making sense of social information—all key features of autism.

In a similar vein, neuroimaging studies indicate that many autistic children have increased brain volume and white matter and structural abnormalities in the brain's limbic system, brain stem nuclei, and amygdala (Travers et al., 2015; Bauman, 2011). Many people with autism spectrum disorder also have reduced activity in the brain's temporal and frontal lobes when they perform language and motor tasks (Taylor et al., 2014).

Given such findings, many researchers believe that this disorder may in fact have multiple biological causes (NINDS, 2015). Perhaps each of the relevant biological factors (genetic, prenatal, birth, and postnatal) can eventually lead to a common problem in the brain—a "final common pathway," such as neurotransmitter abnormalities, that produces the cognitive problems and other features of the disorder.

Finally, because it has received so much attention over the past 20 years, it is worth mentioning a biological explanation for autism spectrum disorder that has *not* been borne out—the *MMR vaccine* theory. In 1998 a team of investigators published a study suggesting that a *postnatal event*—the vaccine for measles, mumps, and rubella (*MMR vaccine*)—might produce autistic symptoms in some children (Wakefield et al., 1998). The researchers suggested that for certain children, this vaccine, which is usually given to children between the ages of 12 and 15 months, produces an increase in the measles virus throughout the body which in turn causes the onset of a powerful stomach disease and, ultimately, autism spectrum disorder.

▶ **cerebellum** An area of the brain that coordinates movement in the body and perhaps helps control a person's ability to shift attention rapidly.

However, virtually all research conducted since 1998 has argued against this theory (Taylor et al., 2014; Ahearn, 2010). First, epidemiological studies repeatedly have found that children throughout the world who receive the MMR vaccine have the same prevalence of autism as those who do not receive the vaccine. Second, according to research, children with autism do not have more measles viruses in their bodies than children without autism. Third, autistic children do not have the special stomach disease proposed by this theory. Finally, careful reexaminations of the original study have indicated that it was methodologically flawed and perhaps manipulated and that it actually failed to demonstrate any relationship between the MMR vaccine and the development of autism spectrum disorder (*Lancet,* 2010). Unfortunately, despite this clear refutation, many concerned parents now choose to withhold the MMR vaccine from their young children, leaving them highly vulnerable to diseases that can be extremely dangerous.

> **Why do many people still believe that the MMR vaccine causes autism spectrum disorder, despite so much evidence to the contrary?**

How Do Clinicians and Educators Treat Autism Spectrum Disorder?

Treatment can help people with autism spectrum disorder adapt better to their environment, although no treatment yet known totally reverses the autistic pattern. Treatments of particular help are *cognitive-behavioral therapy, communication training, parent training,* and *community integration.* In addition, psychotropic drugs and certain vitamins have sometimes helped when combined with other approaches (Sicile-Kira, 2014; Ristow et al., 2011).

COGNITIVE-BEHAVIORAL THERAPY Behavioral approaches have been used in cases of autism for more than 35 years to teach new, appropriate behaviors, including speech, social skills, classroom skills, and self-help skills, while reducing negative, dysfunctional ones. Most often, the therapists use modeling and operant conditioning. In modeling, they demonstrate a desired behavior and guide autistic individuals to imitate it. In operant conditioning, they reinforce desired behaviors, first by shaping them—breaking them down so they can be learned step by step—and then rewarding each step clearly and consistently. With careful planning and execution, these procedures often produce new, more functional behaviors.

A pioneering, long-term study compared the progress of two groups of children with autism spectrum disorder (Lovaas, 2003, 1987; McEachin et al., 1993). Nineteen received intensive behavioral treatments, and 19 served as a control group. The treatment began when the children were 3 years old and continued until they were 7. By the age of 7, the behavioral group was doing better in school and scoring higher on intelligence tests than the control group. Many were able to go to school in regular classrooms. The gains continued into the research participants' teenage years. Given the favorable findings of this and similar studies, many clinicians now consider early behavioral programs to be the preferred treatment for autism spectrum disorder (Boyd et al., 2014).

Therapies for people with autism spectrum disorder, particularly behavioral therapies, tend to provide the most benefit when they are started early in the children's lives (Estes et al., 2015). Very young autistic children often begin with services at home, but ideally, by the age of 3 they attend special programs outside the home. A federal law lists autism spectrum disorder as 1 of 10 disorders for which school districts must provide a free education from birth to age 22, in the least restrictive or most appropriate setting possible. Typically, services are provided by education,

Learning to communicate Behaviorists have had success teaching many children with autism spectrum disorder to communicate. Here a speech language specialist combines behavioral techniques with the use of a communication board to teach a 3-year-old child how to express herself better and understand others.

AP Photo/Albuquerque Journal, Pat Vasquez-Cunningham

health, or social service agencies until the children reach 3 years of age; then the department of education for each state determines which services will be offered.

Given the recent increases in the prevalence of autism spectrum disorder, many school districts are now trying to provide education and training for autistic children in special classes that operate at the district's own facilities (Iadarola et al., 2015). However, most school districts remain ill-equipped to meet the profound needs of students with autism. The most fortunate autistic students are sent by their school districts to attend special schools, where education and therapy are combined. At such schools, specially trained teachers help the children improve their skills, behaviors, and interactions with the world. Higher-functioning autistic students may eventually spend at least part of their school day returning to standard classrooms in their own school district (Hartford & Marcus, 2011).

COMMUNICATION TRAINING As you read earlier, even when given intensive behavioral treatment, half of the people with autism spectrum disorder remain speechless. To help address this, they are often taught other forms of communication, including *sign language* and *simultaneous communication,* a method combining sign language and speech. They may also learn to use **augmentative communication systems,** such as "communication boards" or computers that use pictures, symbols, or written words to represent objects or needs (Lerna et al., 2014; Prelock et al., 2011). A child may point to a picture of a fork to give the message "I am hungry," for instance, or point to a radio for "I want music." Recall, for example, the use of a "picture book" by Jennie, the child whose case introduced this section.

PARENT TRAINING Today's treatment programs for autism spectrum disorder involve parents in a variety of ways. Behavioral programs, for example, often train parents so that they can use behavioral techniques at home (Bearss et al., 2015; Sicile-Kira, 2014). Instruction manuals for parents and home visits by teachers and other professionals are typically included in such programs. Research consistently has demonstrated that the behavioral gains produced by trained parents are often equal to or greater than those generated by teachers.

In addition to parent-training programs, individual therapy and support groups are becoming more available to help the parents of autistic children deal with their own emotions and needs (Clifford & Minnes, 2013; Hastings, 2008). A number of parent associations and lobbies also offer emotional support and practical help.

COMMUNITY INTEGRATION Many of today's school-based and home-based programs for autism spectrum disorder teach self-help, self-management, and living, social, and work skills as early as possible to help the individuals function better in their communities. In addition, greater numbers of carefully run *group homes* and *sheltered workshops* are now available for teenagers and young adults with autism. These and related programs help those with autism become a part of their community; they also reduce the concerns of aging parents whose children will always need supervision.

AP Photo/Daily Herald, Bev Horne

The iPad breakthrough A child works on an iPad as his teacher looks on. A major new trend in the training and treatment of autism spectrum disorder is the use of electronic tablets. They are effective augmentative communication systems, and they also seem to provide enormous cognitive stimulation and pleasure for people with autism.

Intellectual Disability

Ed Murphy, aged 26, can tell us what it's like to be considered "mentally retarded":

What is retardation? It's hard to say. I guess it's having problems thinking. Some people think that you can tell if a person is retarded by looking at them. If you think that way you don't give people the benefit of the doubt. You judge a person by how they look or how they talk or what the tests show, but you can never really tell what is inside the person.

(Bogdan & Taylor, 1976, p. 51)

For much of his life Ed was labeled mentally retarded and was educated and cared for in special institutions. During his adult years, clinicians discovered that Ed's intellectual ability was in fact higher than had been assumed. In the meantime, however, he had lived the childhood and adolescence of a person labeled mentally retarded, and his statement reveals the kinds of difficulties often faced by people with this disorder.

In DSM-5, the term "mental retardation" has been replaced by *intellectual disability.* This term is applied to a varied population, including children in institutional wards who rock back and forth, young people who work in special job programs, and men and women who raise and support their families by working at undemanding jobs. As many as 3 of every 100 people meet the criteria for this diagnosis (NLM, 2015; APA, 2013). Around three-fifths of them are male, and the vast majority display a *mild* level of the disorder.

People receive a diagnosis of **intellectual disability (ID)** when they display general *intellectual functioning* that is well below average, in combination with poor *adaptive behavior* (APA, 2013). That is, in addition to having a low IQ (a score of 70 or below), a person with ID has great difficulty in areas such as communication, home living, self-direction, work, or safety. The symptoms also must appear before the age of 18 (see Table 14-7).

Assessing Intelligence Educators and clinicians administer intelligence tests to measure intellectual functioning (see Chapter 3). These tests consist of a variety of questions and tasks that rely on different aspects of intelligence, such as knowledge, reasoning, and judgment. Having difficulty in just one or two of these subtests or areas of functioning does not necessarily reflect low intelligence (see *PsychWatch* on page 491). It is an individual's overall test score, or **intelligence quotient (IQ),** that is thought to indicate general intellectual ability.

Many theorists have questioned whether IQ tests are indeed valid. Do they actually measure what they are supposed to measure? The correlation between IQ and school performance is rather high—around .50—indicating that many children with lower IQs do, as one might expect, perform poorly in school, while many of those with higher IQs perform better (Sternberg et al., 2001). At the same time, the correlation also suggests that the relationship is far from perfect. That is, a particular child's school performance is often higher or lower than his or her IQ might predict. Moreover, the accuracy of IQ tests at measuring extremely low intelligence has not been evaluated adequately, so it is difficult to properly assess people with severe intellectual disability (AAIDD, 2013, 2010).

Intelligence tests also appear to be socioculturally biased, as you read in Chapter 3. Children reared in households at the middle and upper socioeconomic levels tend to have an advantage on the tests because they are regularly exposed to the kinds of language and thinking that the tests evaluate. The tests rarely measure the "street sense" needed

Are there other kinds of intelligence that IQ tests might fail to assess?

▸ **augmentative communication system** A method for enhancing the communication skills of people with autism spectrum disorder, intellectual disability, or cerebral palsy by teaching them to point to pictures, symbols, letters, or words on a communication board or computer.

▸ **intellectual disability (ID)** A disorder marked by intellectual functioning and adaptive behavior that are well below average. Previously called *mental retardation.*

▸ **intelligence quotient (IQ)** A score derived from intelligence tests that theoretically represents a person's overall intellectual capacity.

table: **14-7**

Dx Checklist

Intellectual Disability

1. Individual displays deficient intellectual functioning in areas such as reasoning, problem-solving, planning, abstract thinking, judgment, academic learning, and learning from experience. The deficits are reflected by clinical assessment and intelligence tests.

2. Individual displays deficient adaptive functioning in at least one area of daily life, such as communication, social involvement, or personal independence, across home, school, work, or community settings. The limitations extend beyond those displayed by most other persons of his or her age and necessitate ongoing support at school, work, or independent living.

3. The deficits begin during the developmental period (before the age of 18).

(Information from: APA, 2013)

Getting a head start Studies suggest that IQ scores and school performances of children from poor neighborhoods can be improved by enriching their daily environments at a young age. The teachers in this classroom try to stimulate and enrich the lives of preschool children in a Head Start program in Oregon.

for survival by people who live in poor, crime-ridden areas—a kind of know-how that certainly requires intellectual skills. Members of cultural minorities and people for whom English is a second language also often appear to be at a disadvantage in taking these tests.

If IQ tests do not always measure intelligence accurately and objectively, then the diagnosis of intellectual disability also may be biased. That is, some people may receive the diagnosis partly because of test inadequacies, cultural differences, discomfort with the testing situation, or the bias of a tester.

Assessing Adaptive Functioning Diagnosticians cannot rely solely on a cutoff IQ score of 70 to determine whether a person suffers from intellectual disability. Some people with a low IQ are quite capable of managing their lives and functioning independently, while others are not. The cases of Brian and Jeffrey show the range of adaptive abilities.

> *Brian comes from a lower-income family. He always has functioned adequately at home and in his community. He dresses and feeds himself and even takes care of himself each day until his mother returns home from work. He also plays well with his friends. At school, however, Brian refuses to participate or do his homework. He seems ineffective, at times lost, in the classroom. Referred to a school psychologist by his teacher, he received an IQ score of 60.*

> *Jeffrey comes from an upper-middle-class home. He was always slow to develop and sat up, stood, and talked late. During his infancy and toddler years, he was put in a special stimulation program and given special help and attention at home. Still, Jeffrey has trouble dressing himself today and cannot be left alone in the backyard lest he hurt himself or wander off into the street. Schoolwork is very difficult for him. The teacher must work slowly and provide individual instruction for him. Tested at age 6, Jeffrey received an IQ score of 60.*

Brian seems well adapted to his environment outside school. However, Jeffrey's limitations are pervasive. In addition to his low IQ score, Jeffrey has difficulty meeting challenges at home and elsewhere. Thus a diagnosis of intellectual disability may be more appropriate for Jeffrey than for Brian.

Several scales have been developed to assess adaptive behavior. Here again, however, some people function better in their lives than the scales predict, while others fall short. Thus to properly diagnose intellectual disability, clinicians should probably observe the adaptive functioning of each individual in his or her everyday environment, taking both the person's background and the community's standards into account. Even then, such judgments may be subjective, as clinicians may not be familiar with the standards of a particular culture or community.

What Are the Features of Intellectual Disability? The most consistent feature of intellectual disability is that the person learns very slowly (Sturmey & Didden, 2014; AAIDD, 2013, 2010). Other areas of difficulty are attention, short-term memory, planning, and language. Those who are institutionalized with this disorder are particularly likely to have these limitations. It may be that the

▶ **mild ID** A level of intellectual disability (IQ between 50 and 70) at which people can benefit from education and can support themselves as adults.

PsychWatch

Reading and 'Riting and 'Rithmetic

Between 15 and 20 percent of children, boys more often than girls, develop slowly and function poorly compared with their peers in a single area such as learning, communication, or motor coordination (APA, 2013; Goldstein et al., 2011). The children do not suffer from intellectual disability, and in fact they are often very bright, yet their problems may interfere with school performance, daily living, and in some cases social interactions. Similar difficulties may be seen in the children's close biological relatives (APA, 2013; Watson et al., 2008). According to DSM-5, many of these children are suffering from a specific learning disorder, communication disorder, or developmental coordination disorder—each a kind of neurodevelopmental disorder (APA, 2013).

Children with a *specific learning disorder* have significant difficulties in acquiring reading, writing, arithmetic, or mathematical reasoning skills. Across the United States, children with such problems comprise the largest subgroup of those placed in special education classes (Watson et al., 2008). Some of these children read slowly or inaccurately or have difficulty understanding the meaning of what they are reading, difficulties also known as *dyslexia* (Boets, 2014). Others spell or write very poorly. And still others have great trouble remembering number facts, performing calculations, or reasoning mathematically.

The *communication disorders* include language disorder, speech sound disor-

A special pair of glasses One of several explanations for dyslexia is that some people with this disorder have a significant visual processing problem. Thus various kinds of special 3D glasses, modeled here by this child, have been developed to help diagnose and treat the disorder.

Sojka Libor/CTK via AP Images

der, and childhood-onset fluency disorder (stuttering) (APA, 2013). Children with *language disorder* have persistent difficulties acquiring, using, or comprehending spoken or written language. They may, for example, have trouble using language to express themselves, struggle at learning new words, confine their speech to short simple sentences, or show a general lag in language development. Children with *speech sound disorder* have persistent difficulties in speech production. Some, for example, cannot make correct speech sounds at an appropriate age, resulting in

speech that sounds like baby talk. People who display *stuttering* have a disturbance in the fluency and timing of their speech, characterized by repeating, prolonging, or interjecting sounds, pausing before finishing a word, or having excessive tension in the muscles they use for speech.

Finally, children with *developmental coordination disorder* perform coordinated motor activities at a level well below that of others their age (APA, 2013). Younger children with this disorder are very clumsy and slow to master skills such as tying shoelaces, buttoning shirts, and zipping pants. Older children with the disorder may have great difficulty assembling puzzles, building models, playing ball, and printing or writing.

Studies have linked these various disorders to genetic defects, brain abnormalities, birth injuries, lead poisoning, inappropriate diet, sensory or perceptual dysfunction, and poor teaching (Richlan, 2014; APA, 2013; Yeates et al., 2010; Golden, 2008). Research has been limited, however, and the precise causes of the disorders remain unclear.

Some of the disorders respond to special treatment approaches (McArthur et al., 2013; Feifer, 2010; Miller, 2010). Reading therapy, for example, is very helpful in mild cases of dyslexia, and speech therapy brings about complete recovery in many cases of speech sound disorder. Furthermore, the various disorders often disappear before adulthood, even without any treatment.

---

unstimulating environment and minimal interactions with staff in many institutions contribute to such difficulties. Traditionally, four levels of intellectual disability have been distinguished: *mild* (IQ 50–70), *moderate* (IQ 35–49), *severe* (IQ 20–34), and *profound* (IQ below 20).

MILD ID Some 80 to 85 percent of all people with intellectual disability fall into the category of **mild ID** (IQ 50–70). This is sometimes called the "educable" level because the individuals can benefit from schooling and can support themselves as adults. Mild ID is not usually recognized until children enter school and are assessed there. They demonstrate rather typical language, social, and play skills, but they need

AP Photo/Javier Galeano

Animal connection At the National Aquarium in Havana, Cuba, therapists host regular sessions of stroking and touching dolphins, sea tortoises, and sea lions for children. These sessions have helped many children with autism spectrum disorder and others with intellectual disability to become more spontaneous, independent, and sociable.

▶ **moderate ID** A level of intellectual disability (IQ between 35 and 49) at which people can learn to care for themselves and can benefit from vocational training.

▶ **severe ID** A level of intellectual disability (IQ between 20 and 34) at which people require careful supervision and can learn to perform basic work in structured and sheltered settings.

▶ **profound ID** A level of intellectual disability (IQ below 20) at which people need a very structured environment with close supervision.

▶ **Down syndrome** A form of intellectual disability caused by an abnormality in the 21st chromosome.

assistance when under stress—a limitation that becomes increasingly apparent as academic and social demands increase. Interestingly, the intellectual performance of individuals with mild ID often seems to improve with age; some even seem to leave the label behind when they leave school, and they go on to function well in the community (Sturmey & Didden, 2014; Sturmey, 2008). Their jobs tend to be unskilled or semiskilled.

Research has linked mild ID mainly to sociocultural and psychological causes, particularly poor and unstimulating environments during a child's early years, inadequate parent–child interactions, and insufficient learning experiences (Sturmey & Didden, 2014; Sturmey, 2008). These relationships have been observed in studies comparing deprived and enriched environments. In fact, some community programs have sent workers into the homes of young children with low IQ scores to help enrich the environment there, and their interventions have often improved the children's functioning. When continued, programs of this kind also help improve the person's later performance in school and adulthood (Ramey et al., 2012; Ramey & Ramey, 2007, 2004, 1992).

Although sociocultural and psychological factors seem to be the leading causes of mild ID, at least some biological factors also may be operating. Studies suggest, for example, that a mother's moderate drinking, drug use, or malnutrition during pregnancy may lower her child's intellectual potential (Hart & Ksir, 2014). Malnourishment during a child's early years also may hurt his or her intellectual development, although this effect can usually be reversed at least partly if a child's diet is improved before too much time goes by.

MODERATE, SEVERE, AND PROFOUND ID Approximately 10 percent of those with intellectual disability function at a level of **moderate ID** (IQ 35–49). They typically receive their diagnosis earlier in life than do individuals with mild ID, as they demonstrate clear deficits in language development and play during their preschool years. By middle school they further show significant delays in their acquisition of reading and number skills and adaptive skills. By adulthood, however, many individuals with moderate ID manage to develop a fair degree of communication skill, learn to care for themselves, benefit from vocational training, and can work in unskilled or semiskilled jobs, usually under supervision. Most also function well in the community if they have supervision (AAIDD, 2013, 2010).

Approximately 3 to 4 percent of people with intellectual disability display **severe ID** (IQ 20–34). They typically demonstrate basic motor and communication deficits during infancy. Many also show signs of neurological dysfunction and have an increased risk for brain seizure disorder. In school, they may be able to string together only two or three words when speaking. They usually require careful supervision, profit somewhat from vocational training, and can perform only basic work tasks in structured and sheltered settings. Their understanding of communication is usually better than their speech. Most are able to function well in the community if they live in group homes, in community nursing homes, or with their families (AAIDD, 2013, 2010).

Around 1 to 2 percent of all people with intellectual disability function at a level of **profound ID** (IQ below 20). This level is very noticeable at birth or early infancy. With training, people with profound ID may learn or improve basic skills such as walking, some talking, and feeding themselves. They need a very structured environment, with close supervision and considerable help, including a one-to-one relationship with a caregiver, in order to develop to the fullest (AAIDD, 2013, 2010).

Severe and profound levels of intellectual disability often appear as part of larger syndromes that include severe physical handicaps. The physical problems are often even more limiting than the individual's low intellectual functioning and in some cases can be fatal.

What Are the Biological Causes of Intellectual Disability?

As you read earlier, the primary causes of mild ID are environmental, although biological factors may also be operating in many cases. In contrast, the main causes of moderate, severe, and profound ID are biological, although people who function at these levels also are strongly affected by their family and social environment (Sturmey & Didden, 2014; Fletcher, 2011). The leading biological causes of intellectual disability are chromosomal abnormalities, metabolic disorders, prenatal problems, birth complications, and childhood diseases and injuries.

CHROMOSOMAL CAUSES The most common of the chromosomal disorders that lead to intellectual disability is **Down syndrome,** named after Langdon Down, the British physician who first identified it. Down syndrome occurs in around 1 of every 1,000 live births, but the rate increases significantly when the mother's age is

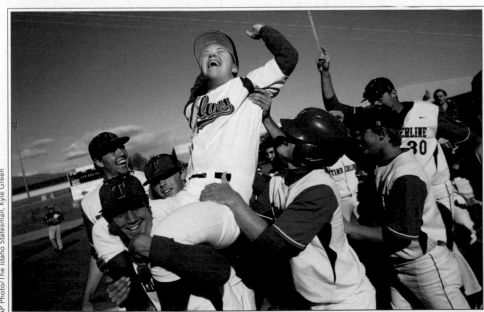

Reaching higher Today people with Down syndrome are viewed as individuals who can learn and accomplish many things in their lives. Eddie Gordon, a teenager with Down syndrome, is lifted into the air in celebration by his Timberline High School baseball teammates. He has just rounded the bases during his turn as an honorary lead-off batter.

over 35. Many older expectant mothers are now encouraged to undergo prenatal testing during the early months of pregnancy to identify Down syndrome and other chromosomal abnormalities.

People with Down syndrome may have a small head, flat face, slanted eyes, high cheekbones, and, in some cases, protruding tongue. The latter may affect their ability to pronounce words clearly. They are often very affectionate with family members but in general display the same range of personality characteristics as people in the general population.

Several types of chromosomal abnormalities may cause Down syndrome (NICHD, 2015). The most common type (94 percent of cases) is *trisomy 21,* in which the person has three free-floating 21st chromosomes instead of two. Most people with Down syndrome range in IQ from 35 to 55. The individuals appear to age early, and many even show signs of neurocognitive decline as they approach 40 (Powell et al., 2014; Lawlor et al., 2001). It may be that Down syndrome and early neurocognitive decline often occur together because the genes that produce them are located close to each other on chromosome 21 (Rohn et al., 2014; Lamar et al., 2011).

Fragile X syndrome is the second most common chromosomal cause of intellectual disability. Children born with a fragile X chromosome (that is, an X chromosome with a genetic abnormality that leaves it prone to breakage and loss) generally display mild to moderate degrees of intellectual dysfunctioning, language impairments, and, in some cases, behavioral problems (Hahn et al., 2015; Hagerman, 2011). Typically, they are shy and anxious.

METABOLIC CAUSES In metabolic disorders, the body's breakdown or production of chemicals is disturbed. The metabolic disorders that affect intelligence and development are typically caused by the pairing of two defective *recessive genes,* one from each parent. Although one such gene would have no influence if it were paired with a normal gene, its pairing with another defective gene leads to major problems for the child.

The most common metabolic disorder to cause intellectual disability is *phenylketonuria (PKU),* which strikes 1 of every 14,000 children. Babies with PKU appear normal at birth but cannot break down the amino acid *phenylalanine.* The chemical builds up and is converted into substances that poison the system, causing severe intellectual dysfunction and several other symptoms (NICHD, 2015; Waisbren, 2011). Today infants can be screened for PKU, and if started on a special diet before 3 months of age, they may develop normal intelligence.

Children with *Tay-Sachs disease,* another metabolic disorder resulting from a pairing of recessive genes, progressively lose their mental functioning, vision, and motor ability over the course of two to four years, and eventually die. One of every 30 persons of Eastern European Jewish ancestry carries the recessive gene responsible for this disorder, so that 1 of every 900 Jewish couples is at risk for having a child with Tay-Sachs disease.

PRENATAL AND BIRTH-RELATED CAUSES As a fetus develops, major physical problems in the pregnant mother can threaten the child's prospects for a normal life (AAIDD, 2013, 2010; Bebko & Weiss, 2006). When a pregnant woman has too little iodine in her diet, for example, her child may be born with *cretinism,* also called *severe congenital hypothyroidism,* marked by an abnormal thyroid gland, slow development, intellectual disability, and a dwarflike appearance. This condition is rare today because the salt in most diets now contains extra iodine. Also, any infant born with this problem may quickly be given thyroid extract to bring about normal development.

Other prenatal problems may also cause intellectual disability. As you saw in Chapter 10, children whose mothers drink too much alcohol during pregnancy may be born with **fetal alcohol syndrome,** a group of very serious problems that includes mild to severe ID (Bakoyiannis et al., 2014; Hart & Ksir, 2014). In fact, a generally safe level of alcohol consumption during pregnancy has not been established by research. In addition, certain maternal infections during pregnancy—*rubella* (German measles) and *syphilis,* for example—may cause childhood problems that include intellectual disability.

Birth complications also can lead to problems in intellectual functioning. A prolonged period without oxygen (*anoxia*) during or after delivery can cause brain damage and intellectual disability in a baby. In addition, although premature birth does not necessarily lead to long-term problems for children, researchers have found that some babies with a premature birth weight of less than 3.5 pounds display low intelligence (AAIDD, 2013, 2010; Taylor, 2010).

CHILDHOOD PROBLEMS After birth, particularly up to age 6, certain injuries and accidents can affect intellectual functioning and in some cases lead to intellectual disability. Poisonings, serious head injuries caused by accident or abuse, excessive exposure to X rays, and excessive use of certain drugs pose special dangers (AAIDD, 2013, 2010; Evans, 2006). For example, a serious case of *lead poisoning* from eating lead-based paints or inhaling high levels of automobile fumes can cause ID in children. Mercury, radiation, nitrite, and pesticide poisoning may do the same. In addition, certain infections, such as *meningitis* and *encephalitis,* can lead to intellectual disability if they are not diagnosed and treated in time (AAIDD, 2013, 2010; Durkin et al., 2000).

Interventions for People with Intellectual Disability
The quality of life attained by people with intellectual disability depends largely on sociocultural factors: where they live and with whom, how they are educated, and the growth opportunities available at home and in the community. Thus intervention programs for these individuals try to provide comfortable and stimulating residences, a proper education, and social and economic opportunities. At the same time, the programs seek to improve the self-image and self-esteem of those with intellectual disability. Once these needs are met, formal psychological or biological treatments are also of help in some cases.

WHAT IS THE PROPER RESIDENCE? Until recent decades, parents of children with intellectual disability would send them to live in public institutions—**state schools**—as early as possible (Harris, 2010). These overcrowded institutions provided basic care, but residents were neglected, often abused, and isolated from society.

During the 1960s and 1970s, the public became more aware of these sorry conditions and, as part of the broader *deinstitutionalization* movement (see Chapter 12), demanded that many people with intellectual disability be released from the state schools (Harris, 2010). In many cases, the releases were done without adequate preparation or supervision. Like people with schizophrenia who were suddenly deinstitutionalized, those with intellectual disability were virtually dumped into the community. Often they failed to adjust and had to be institutionalized once again.

Since that time, reforms have led to the creation of *small institutions* and other *community residences* (group homes, halfway houses, local branches of larger institutions, and independent residences) that teach self-sufficiency, devote more staff time to patient care, and offer educational and medical services. Many of these settings follow the principles of **normalization** first started in Denmark and Sweden—they attempt to provide living conditions similar

▶ **fetal alcohol syndrome** A group of problems in a child, including lower intellectual functioning, low birth weight, and irregularities in the hands and face, that result from excessive alcohol intake by the mother during pregnancy.

▶ **state school** A state-supported institution for people with intellectual disability.

▶ **normalization** The principle that institutions and community residences should provide people with intellectual disability types of living conditions and opportunities that are similar to those enjoyed by the rest of society.

Life lessons The normalization movement calls for people with intellectual disability to be taught whatever skills are needed for normal and independent living. Here a psychologist (left) gives cooking lessons to young adults with ID as part of a national program called You and I. The program also provides lessons in dating, self-esteem, social skills, and sex education.

AP Photo/Shiho Fukada

▸ **special education** An approach to educating children with intellectual disability in which they are grouped together and given a separate, specially designed education.

▸ **mainstreaming** The placement of children with intellectual disability in regular school classes. Also known as *inclusion*.

▸ **sheltered workshop** A protected and supervised workplace that offers job opportunities and training at a pace and level tailored to people with various psychological disabilities.

to those enjoyed by the rest of society; flexible routines; and normal developmental experiences, including opportunities for self-determination, sexual fulfillment, and economic freedom (Merrick et al., 2014; Hemmings, 2010).

Today the vast majority of children with intellectual disability live at home rather than in an institution. During adulthood and as their parents age, however, some people with intellectual disability require levels of assistance and opportunities that their families are unable to provide. A community residence becomes an appropriate alternative for them. Most people with intellectual disability, including almost all with mild ID, now spend their adult lives either in the family home or in a community residence (Sturmey & Didden, 2014; Sturmey, 2008).

WHICH EDUCATIONAL PROGRAMS WORK BEST? Because early intervention seems to offer such great promise, educational programs for people with intellectual disability may begin during the earliest years. The appropriate education depends on the person's level of functioning. Educators hotly debate whether special classes or mainstreaming is most effective once the children enter school (McKenzie et al., 2013; Hardman et al., 2002). In **special education,** children with intellectual disability are grouped together in a separate, specially designed educational program. In contrast, in **mainstreaming,** or **inclusion,** they are placed in regular classes with students from the general school population. Neither approach seems consistently superior. It may well be that mainstreaming is better for some areas of learning and for some children and that special classes are better for others.

> **What might be the benefits of mainstreaming compared with special education classes, and vice versa?**

Teacher preparedness is another factor that may play into decisions about mainstreaming and special education classes. Many teachers report feeling inadequately prepared to provide training and support for children with intellectual disability, especially children who have additional problems. Brief training courses for teachers appear to address such concerns (Hallahan et al., 2014; Campbell et al., 2003).

Teachers who work with students with intellectual disability often use operant conditioning principles to improve their students' self-help, communication, social, and academic skills (Sturmey & Didden, 2014; Sturmey, 2008; Ardoin et al., 2004). They break learning tasks down into small steps, giving positive reinforcement for each increment of progress. Additionally, many institutions, schools, and private homes have set up *token economy programs*—the operant conditioning programs that have also been used to treat institutionalized patients who have schizophrenia.

Working for money, independence, and self-respect This 28-year-old waiter serves beverages in a café in Slovakia. He is one of five waiters with intellectual disability who work at the café.

WHEN IS THERAPY NEEDED? Like anyone else, people with intellectual disability sometimes have emotional and behavioral problems. Around 30 percent or more have a psychological disorder other than intellectual disability (Sturmey & Didden, 2014; Bouras & Holt, 2010). Furthermore, some suffer from low self-esteem, interpersonal problems, and difficulties adjusting to community life. These problems are helped to some degree by either individual or group therapy. Large numbers of people with intellectual disability also take psychotropic medications (Sturmey & Didden, 2014). Many clinicians argue, however, that too often the medications are used simply for the purpose of making the individuals easier to manage.

HOW CAN OPPORTUNITIES FOR PERSONAL, SOCIAL, AND OCCUPATIONAL GROWTH BE INCREASED? People need to feel effective and competent in order to move forward in life. Those with intellectual disability are most likely to feel effective and competent if their communities allow them to grow and to make many of their own choices. Denmark and Sweden, where the normalization movement began, have again been leaders in this area, developing youth clubs that encourage those with intellectual disability to take risks and function independently. The Special Olympics program has also encouraged those with intellectual disability to be active in setting goals, to participate in their environment, and to interact socially with others (Crawford et al., 2015; Marks et al., 2010).

Socializing, sex, and marriage are difficult issues for people with intellectual disability and their families, but with proper training and practice, they usually can learn to use contraceptives and carry out responsible family planning. National advocacy organizations and a number of clinicians currently offer guidance in these matters, and some have developed *dating skills programs* (AAIDD, 2013, 2010, 2008; Segal, 2008).

Some states restrict marriage for people with intellectual disability. These laws are rarely enforced, though, and in fact many people with mild ID marry. Contrary to popular myths, the marriages can be very successful. And although some may be incapable of raising children, many are quite able to do so, either on their own or with special help and community services (Sturmey & Didden, 2014; AAIDD, 2013, 2010; Sturmey, 2008).

Finally, adults with intellectual disability—whatever the severity—need the personal and financial rewards that come with holding a job (AAIDD, 2013, 2010; Kiernan, 2000). Many work in **sheltered workshops,** protected and supervised workplaces that train them at a pace and level tailored to their abilities. After training in the workshops, many with mild or moderate ID move on to hold regular jobs.

Although training programs for people with intellectual disability have improved greatly in quality over the past 35 years, there are too few of them. Consequently, most participants do not receive a complete range of educational and occupational training services. Additional programs are required so that more people with intellectual disability may achieve their full potential, as workers and as human beings.

Normal needs People with intellectual disability have normal interpersonal and sexual needs, and many, such as this engaged couple, demonstrate considerable ability to express intimacy.

➤ *Summing Up*

NEURODEVELOPMENTAL DISORDERS Neurodevelopmental disorders are a group of disabilities in the functioning of the brain that emerge at birth or during very early childhood and affect the person's behavior, memory, concentration, and/or ability to learn.

Children with attention-deficit/hyperactivity disorder (ADHD) attend poorly to tasks, behave overactively and impulsively, or both. Ritalin and other stimulant drugs and behavioral programs are often effective treatments. The disorder extends into adulthood for many individuals.

People with autism spectrum disorder are extremely unresponsive to others, have severe communication deficits, and display very rigid and repetitive behaviors, interests, and activities. The leading explanations of this disorder point to cognitive deficits such as failure to develop a theory of mind and biological abnormalities such as abnormal development of the cerebellum. Although no treatment totally reverses the autistic pattern, significant help is available in the form of cognitive-behavioral treatments, communication training, training and treatment for parents, and community integration.

People with intellectual disability are significantly below average in intelligence and adaptive ability. Mild ID, by far the most common level of intellectual disability, has been linked primarily to environmental factors such as

(continues on the next page)

BETWEEN THE LINES

In Their Words

"The boy will come to nothing."

Jakob Freud, 1864 (referring to his 8-year-old son Sigmund, after he had urinated in his parents' bedroom)

unstimulating environments during a child's early years, inadequate parent–child interactions, and insufficient learning experiences. Moderate, severe, and profound ID are caused primarily by biological factors, although people who function at these levels also are affected enormously by their family and social environment. The leading biological causes of intellectual disability are chromosomal abnormalities, metabolic disorders, prenatal problems, birth complications, and childhood diseases and injuries.

Today intervention programs for people with intellectual disability emphasize the importance of a comfortable and stimulating residence, either the family home or a small institution or group home that follows the principles of normalization. Other important interventions include proper education, therapy for psychological problems, and programs offering training in socializing, sex, marriage, parenting, and occupational skills.

PUTTING IT...*together*

Clinicians Discover Childhood and Adolescence

Early in the twentieth century, mental health professionals virtually ignored children. At best, they viewed them as small adults and treated their psychological disorders as they would adult problems (Peterson & Roberts, 1991). Today the problems and needs of young people have caught the attention of researchers and clinicians. Although all of the leading models have been used to help explain and treat these problems, the sociocultural perspective—especially the family perspective—is considered to play a special role.

Because children and adolescents have limited control over their lives, they are particularly affected by the attitudes and reactions of family members. Clinicians must therefore deal with those attitudes and reactions as they try to address the problems of the young. Treatments for conduct disorder, ADHD, intellectual disability, and other problems common among children and adolescents typically fall short unless clinicians educate and work with the family as well.

At the same time, clinicians who work with children and adolescents have learned that a narrow focus on any one model can lead to problems. For years, autism spectrum disorder was explained exclusively by family factors, misleading theorists and therapists alike and adding to the pain of parents already devastated by their child's disorder. In addition, in the past, the sociocultural model often led professionals wrongly to accept anxiety among young children and depression among teenagers as inevitable, given the many new experiences confronted by the former and the latter group's preoccupation with peer approval.

The increased clinical focus on the young has also been accompanied by more attention to young people's human and legal rights. Clinicians and educators have called on government agencies to protect the rights and safety of this often powerless group. In doing so, they hope to fuel the fights for better educational resources and against child abuse and neglect, sexual abuse, malnourishment, and fetal alcohol syndrome.

As the problems and, at times, mistreatment of young people receive more attention, the special needs of these individuals are becoming more visible. Thus the study and treatment of psychological disorders common among children and adolescents are likely to continue at a rapid pace. Now that clinicians and public officials have "discovered" this population, they are not likely to underestimate their needs and importance again.

CLINICAL CHOICES

Now that you've read about disorders common among children and adolescents, try the interactive case study for this chapter. See if you are able to identify Gabriel's symptoms and suggest a diagnosis based on his symptoms. What kind of treatment would be most effective for Gabriel? Go to **LaunchPad** to access *Clinical Choices*.

KEY TERMS

separation anxiety disorder, p. 467

play therapy, p. 468

disruptive mood dysregulation disorder, p. 472

oppositional defiant disorder, p. 473

conduct disorder, p. 473

enuresis, p. 476

encopresis, p. 476

neurodevelopmental disorders, p. 479

attention-deficit/hyperactivity disorder (ADHD), p. 479

methylphenidate (Ritalin), p. 481

autism spectrum disorder, p. 483

echolalia, p. 484

theory of mind, p. 485

cerebellum, p. 486

augmentative communication system, p. 488

intellectual disability (ID), p. 489

intelligence quotient (IQ), p. 489

mild ID, p. 491

moderate ID, p. 492

severe ID, p. 493

profound ID, p. 493

Down syndrome, p. 493

fragile X syndrome, p. 494

recessive genes, p. 494

phenylketonuria (PKU), p. 494

fetal alcohol syndrome, p. 494

rubella, p. 495

syphilis, p. 495

state school, p. 495

normalization, p. 495

special education, p. 496

mainstreaming, p. 496

sheltered workshop, p. 497

QuickQuiz

1. What are the prevalence rates and gender ratios for the various disorders common among children and adolescents? *pp. 464–495*

2. What are the different kinds of childhood anxiety and mood-related disorders? What are today's leading explanations and treatments for these disorders? *pp. 465–472*

3. What is disruptive mood dysregulation disorder, and why might DSM-5's addition of this new category affect future diagnoses of childhood bipolar disorder? *p. 472*

4. Describe oppositional defiant disorder and conduct disorder. What factors help cause conduct disorder, and how is this disorder treated? *pp. 473–476*

5. What are enuresis and encopresis? How are these disorders treated? *pp. 476–477*

6. What are the symptoms of attention-deficit/hyperactivity disorder? What are today's leading explanations for it? What are the current treatments for ADHD, and how effective are they? *pp. 479–482*

7. What is autism spectrum disorder, and what are its possible causes? What are the overall goals of treatment for this disorder, and which interventions have been most helpful? *pp. 483–488*

8. Describe the different levels of intellectual disability. *pp. 490–493*

9. What are the leading environmental and biological causes of intellectual disability? *pp. 491–495*

10. What kinds of residences, educational programs, treatments, and community programs are helpful to persons with intellectual disability? *pp. 495–497*

Visit *LaunchPad*

www.macmillanhighered.com/launchpad/comerfund8e

to access the e-book, new interactive case studies, videos, activities, and LearningCurve quizzes, as well as study aids including flashcards, FAQs, and research exercises.

Macmillan Education LaunchPad

Disorders of Aging and Cognition

Harry appeared to be in perfect health at age 58. . . . He worked in the municipal water treatment plant of a small city, and it was at work that the first overt signs of Harry's mental illness appeared. While responding to a minor emergency, he became confused about the correct order in which to pull the levers that controlled the flow of fluids. As a result, several thousand gallons of raw sewage were discharged into a river. Harry had been an efficient and diligent worker, so after puzzled questioning, his error was attributed to the flu and overlooked.

Several weeks later, Harry came home with a baking dish his wife had asked him to buy, having forgotten that he had brought home the identical dish two nights before. Later that week, on two successive nights, he went to pick up his daughter at her job in a restaurant, apparently forgetting that she had changed shifts and was now working days. A month after that, he quite uncharacteristically argued with . . . the phone company; he was trying to pay a bill that he had already paid three days before. . . .

Months passed and Harry's wife was beside herself. She could see that his problem was worsening. Not only had she been unable to get effective help, but Harry himself was becoming resentful and sometimes suspicious of her attempts. He now insisted there was nothing wrong with him, and she would catch him narrowly watching her every movement. . . . Sometimes he became angry—sudden little storms without apparent cause. . . . More difficult for his wife was Harry's repetitiveness in conversation: He often repeated stories from the past and sometimes repeated isolated phrases and sentences from more recent exchanges. There was no context and little continuity to his choice of subjects. . . .

Two years after Harry had first allowed the sewage to escape, he was clearly a changed man. Most of the time he seemed preoccupied; he usually had a vacant smile on his face, and what little he said was so vague that it lacked meaning. . . . Gradually his wife took over getting him up, toileted, and dressed each morning. . . .

Harry's condition continued to worsen slowly. When his wife's school was in session, his daughter would stay with him some days, and neighbors were able to offer some help. But occasionally he would still manage to wander away. On those occasions he greeted everyone he met—old friends and strangers alike—with "Hi, it's so nice." That was the extent of his conversation, although he might repeat "nice, nice, nice" over and over again. . . . When Harry left a coffee pot on a unit of the electric stove until it melted, his wife, desperate for help, took him to see another doctor. Again Harry was found to be in good health. [However] the doctor ordered a [brain scan and eventually concluded] that Harry had "Pick-Alzheimer disease." . . . Because Harry was a veteran . . . [he qualified for] hospitalization in a . . . veterans' hospital about 400 miles away from his home. . . .

At the hospital the nursing staff sat Harry up in a chair each day and, aided by volunteers, made sure he ate enough. Still, he lost weight and became weaker. He would weep when his wife came to see him, but he did not talk, and he gave no other sign that he recognized her. After a year, even the weeping stopped. Harry's wife could no longer bear to visit. Harry lived on until just after his sixty-fifth birthday, when he choked on a piece of bread, developed pneumonia as a consequence, and soon died.

(Heston, 1992, pp. 87–90)

Harry suffered from a form of *Alzheimer's disease*. This term is familiar to almost everyone in our society. It seems as if each decade is marked by a disease that everyone dreads—a diagnosis no one wants to hear because it feels like a death sentence. Cancer used to be such a diagnosis, then AIDS. But medical

▶ geropsychology The field of psychology concerned with the mental health of elderly people.

science has made remarkable strides with those diseases, and patients who now develop them have reason for great hope. Alzheimer's disease, on the other hand, remains incurable and almost untreatable, although, as you will see later, researchers are currently making enormous progress toward understanding it and reversing, or at least slowing, its march.

What makes Alzheimer's disease particularly frightening is that it means not only eventual physical death but also, as in Harry's case, a slow psychological death—a progressive deterioration of one's memory and related cognitive faculties. Significant cognitive deterioration, previously called *dementia,* is now categorized as *neurocognitive disorder.* There are many types of neurocognitive disorders listed in DSM-5 (APA, 2013). Alzheimer's disease is the most common one.

Although neurocognitive disorders are currently the most publicized and feared psychological problems among the elderly, they are hardly the only ones. A variety of psychological disorders are tied closely to later life. As with childhood disorders, some of the disorders of old age are caused primarily by pressures that are particularly likely to appear at that time of life, others by unique traumatic experiences, and still others—like neurocognitive disorders—by biological abnormalities.

Old Age and Stress

Old age is usually defined in our society as the years past age 65. By this account, around 43 million people in the United States are "old," representing 13.6 percent of the total population; this is a 14-fold increase since 1900 (CDC, 2014; NCHS, 2014) (see Figure 15-1). It has also been estimated that there will be 70 million elderly people in the United States by the year 2030—more than 20 percent of the population. Not only is the overall population of the elderly on the rise, but also the number of people over 85 will double in the next 10 years. Indeed, people over 85 represent the fastest-growing segment of the population in the United States and in most countries around the world. Older women outnumber older men by almost 3 to 2 (NCHS, 2014).

Like childhood, old age brings special pressures, unique upsets, and major biological changes (Gerst-Emerson et al., 2014). People become more prone to illness and injury as they age (Nunes et al., 2014). About half of adults over 65 have two or three chronic illnesses, and 15 percent have four or more (NCHS, 2014). In addition, elderly people are likely to be contending with the stress of loss—the loss of spouses, friends, and adult children; of former activities and roles; of hearing and vision (Heine & Browning, 2014). Many lose their sense of purpose after they retire (Murayama et al., 2014). Some also have to adjust to the loss of favored pets and possessions.

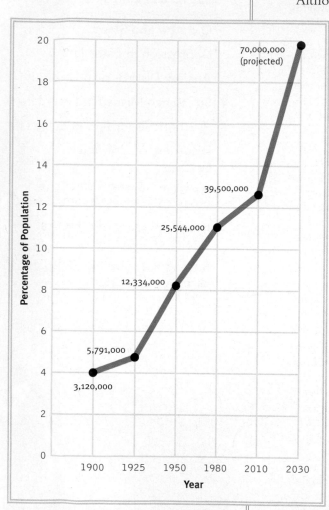

figure 15-1

On the rise The population of people age 65 and older in the United States has increased 14-fold since the beginning of the twentieth century. The percentage of elderly people in the population increased from 4 percent in 1900 to 13 percent in 2010. It is currently 13.6 percent and is expected to be more than 20 percent in 2030. (Information from: CDC, 2014; NCHS, 2014; U.S. Census Bureau, 2012; Cummings & Coffey, 2011; Edelstein et al., 2008.)

The stresses of aging need not necessarily cause psychological problems (see *PsychWatch* on the next page). In fact, some older people, particularly those who seek social contacts and those who maintain a sense of control over their lives, use the changes that come with aging as opportunities for learning and growth (Murayama et al., 2014). For example, the number of elderly—often physically limited—people who use the Internet to connect with people of similar ages and interests doubled between 2000 and 2004, doubled again between 2004 and 2007, and doubled yet again by 2010 (Oinas-Kukkonen & Mantila, 2010). For other elderly people, however, the stresses of old age do lead to psychological difficulties. Studies indicate that more than 20 percent of elderly people meet the criteria for a mental disorder and as many as half of all elderly people would benefit from some degree of mental health services, yet fewer than 20 percent actually receive them (APA, 2014). **Geropsychology,** the field of psychology dedicated to the mental health of elderly people, has developed almost entirely within the last four decades, and at present only 4 percent of clinicians work primarily with elderly persons (APA, 2014; Fiske et al., 2011).

The psychological problems of elderly people may be divided into two groups. One group consists of disorders that may be common among people in all age groups but are often connected to the process of aging when they occur in an elderly person. These include *depressive, anxiety,* and *substance use disorders.* The other group consists of disorders of cognition, such as *delirium, mild neurocognitive disorders,* and *major neurocognitive disorders* that result from brain abnormalities. As in Harry's case, these brain abnormalities are most often tied to aging, but they also can sometimes occur when people are younger. Elderly people with one of these psychological problems often display other such problems. For example, many who suffer from neurocognitive disorders also deal with depression and anxiety (Lebedeva et al., 2014).

> **What kinds of attitudes and activities might help people enter old age with peace of mind and positive anticipation?**

Depression in Later Life

Depression is one of the most common mental health problems of older adults. The features of depression are the same for elderly people as for younger people, including feelings of profound sadness and emptiness; low self-esteem, guilt, and pessimism; and loss of appetite and sleep disturbances. Depression is particularly common

PsychWatch

The Oldest Old

Clinicians suggest that aging need not inevitably lead to psychological problems. Nor apparently does it always lead to physical problems.

There are currently 65,000 *centenarians* in the United States—people who are 100 years old or older. When researchers have studied these people—often called the "oldest old"—they have been surprised to learn that centenarians are on average more healthy, positive, clear-headed, and agile than those in their 80s and early 90s (da Rosa et al., 2014; Zhou et al., 2011). Although some certainly experience cognitive decline, more than half remain perfectly alert. Many of the oldest old are, in fact, still employed, sexually active, and able to enjoy the outdoors and the arts. What is their greatest fear? The fear of significant cognitive decline. According to one study, many people in their 90s and older fear the prospect of mental deterioration more than they fear death (Boeve et al., 2003).

Some scientists believe that people who live this long carry "longevity" genes that make them resistant to disabling or

Welcome to the club A 100-year-old woman and a 99-year-old man chat during a party for centenarians in Woodbridge, Connecticut.

Peter Casolino/Alamy

terminal infections (Garatachea et al., 2014; He et al., 2014). Indeed, centenarians are 20 times more likely than other elderly people to have had a relative who also lived to a very old age (D.I., 2014). Other researchers point to engaged lifestyles and "robust" personalities that help the oldest old meet life's challenges with optimism and a sense of challenge (da Rosa et al., 2014; Martin et al., 2010,

2009). The centenarians themselves often credit a good frame of mind or regular behaviors that they have maintained for many years—for example, eating healthful food, getting regular exercise, and not smoking (D.I., 2014). Said one 96-year-old retired math and science teacher, "You can't sit. . . . You have to keep moving" (Duenwald, 2003).

Bereavement and Gender

11.4 million Number of widows in the
United States

2.8 million Number of widowers

(U.S. Census Bureau, 2010, 2005;
Etaugh, 2008)

among those who have recently undergone a trauma, such as the loss of a spouse or close friend or the development of a serious physical illness (Draper, 2014).

> *[Oscar] was an 83-year-old married man with an episode of major depressive disorder. . . . He said that about one and one-half years prior to beginning treatment, his brother had died. In the following months, two friends whom he had known since childhood died. Following these losses, he became increasingly anxious [and] grew more and more pessimistic. Reluctantly, he acknowledged, "I even thought about ending my life.". . .*
>
> *During . . . treatment, [Oscar] discussed his relationship with his brother. He discussed how distraught he was to watch his brother's physical deterioration from an extended illness. He described the scene at his brother's deathbed and the moment "when he took his final breath." He experienced guilt over the failure to carry out his brother's funeral services in a manner he felt his brother would have wanted. While initially characterizing his relationship with his brother as loving and amiable, he later acknowledged that he disapproved of many ways in which his brother acted. Later in therapy, he also reviewed different facets of his past relationships with his two deceased friends. He expressed sadness that the long years had ended. . . . [Oscar's] life had been organized around visits to his brother's home and outings with his friends. . . . [While] his wife had encouraged him to visit with other friends and family, it became harder and harder to do so as he became more depressed.*
>
> *(Hinrichsen, 1999, p. 433)*

Overall, as many as 20 percent of people become depressed at some point during old age (APA, 2014; Mathys & Belgeri, 2010). The rate is highest in older women. This rate among the elderly is about the same as that among younger adults—even lower, according to some studies (Dubovsky & Dubovsky, 2011). However, it climbs much higher (as high as 32 percent) among aged people who live in nursing homes, as opposed to those in the community (CDC, 2014; Mathys & Belgeri, 2010).

Several studies suggest that depression raises an elderly person's chances of developing significant medical problems (Taylor, 2014; Coffey & Coffey, 2011).

Making a difference To help prevent feelings of unimportance and low self-esteem, some older people now offer their expertise to young people who are trying to master new skills, undertake business projects, and the like (Murayama et al., 2014). This elderly man, who volunteers regularly at an elementary school, is teaching math to a first-grader.

© Owen Franken/Corbis

For example, older depressed people with high blood pressure are almost three times as likely to suffer a stroke as older nondepressed people with the same condition. Similarly, elderly people who are depressed recover more slowly and less completely from heart attacks, hip fractures, pneumonia, and other infections and illnesses. Small wonder that among the elderly, increases in clinical depression are tied to increases in the death rate (Aziz & Steffens, 2013).

> **Is it more likely that positive thinking leads to good health or that good health produces positive thinking?**

As you read in Chapter 7, elderly people are also more likely to commit suicide than young people, and often their suicides are related to depression (Draper, 2014). The overall rate of suicide in the United States is 12.1 per 100,000 people; among the elderly it is more than 16 per 100,000.

Like younger adults, older people who are depressed may be helped by cognitive-behavioral therapy, interpersonal therapy, antidepressant medications, or a combination of these approaches (Cleare et al., 2015; Dines et al., 2014). Both individual and group therapy formats have been used. More than half of elderly patients with depression improve with these various treatments. It is, however, sometimes difficult for older people to use antidepressant drugs effectively and safely because the body breaks the drugs down differently in later life (Dubovsky & Dubovsky, 2011). Moreover, among elderly people, antidepressant drugs have a higher risk of causing some cognitive impairment. Electroconvulsive therapy, applied with certain modifications, has been used for elderly people who are severely depressed and unhelped by other approaches (Coffey & Kellner, 2011).

The power of music The look on the face of this nursing home resident as she listens to music on her iPod underscores the repeated research finding that music helps improve the physical and emotional functioning of many elderly people.

Dan Reiland/The Eau Claire Leader-Telegram/AP Photo

Anxiety Disorders in Later Life

Anxiety is also common among elderly people (APA, 2014). At any given time, as many as 11 percent of elderly individuals in the United States experience at least one of the anxiety disorders. Surveys indicate that generalized anxiety disorder is particularly common, affecting up to 7 percent of all elderly people (ADAA, 2014). The rate of anxiety also increases throughout old age. For example, people over 85 years of age report higher rates of anxiety than those between 65 and 84 years. In fact, all of these numbers may be low, as anxiety in the elderly often goes unrecognized by healthcare professionals (APA, 2014; Jeste et al., 2005).

There are many things about aging that may heighten the anxiety levels of certain people (Bower et al., 2015; Lenze et al., 2011). Declining health, for example, has often been pointed to, and in fact, older persons who have significant medical illnesses or injuries report more anxiety than those who are healthy or injury-free. Researchers have not, however, been able to determine why some people who face such problems in old age become anxious while others in similar circumstances remain relatively calm (see *InfoCentral* on the next page).

Older adults with anxiety disorders have been treated with psychotherapy of various kinds, particularly cognitive-behavioral therapy (Bower et al., 2015; McKenzie & Teri, 2011). Many also receive antianxiety medications or certain antidepressant drugs, just as younger sufferers do. Again, however, all such drugs must be used cautiously with older people (Dubovsky & Dubovsky, 2011).

Substance Misuse in Later Life

Although alcohol use disorder and other substance use disorders are significant problems for many older persons, the prevalence of such patterns actually appears to decline after age 65, perhaps because of declining health or reduced income

THE AGING POPULATION

The number and proportion of elderly people in the United States and around the world are ever-growing. This acceleration has important consequences, requiring each society to pay particular attention to aging-related issues in healthcare, housing, the economy, and other such realms. In particular, as the number and proportion of elderly people increase, so too do the number and proportion of the population who experience aging-related psychological difficulties.

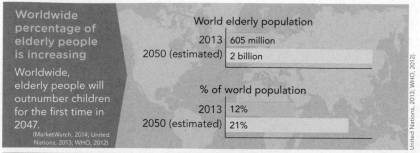

Worldwide percentage of elderly people is increasing

Worldwide, elderly people will outnumber children for the first time in 2047.
(MarketWatch, 2014; United Nations, 2013; WHO, 2012)

World elderly population

2013	605 million
2050 (estimated)	2 billion

% of world population

2013	12%
2050 (estimated)	21%

(United Nations, 2013; WHO, 2012)

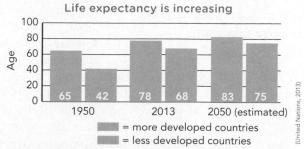

Life expectancy is increasing

	1950	2013	2050 (estimated)
more developed countries	65	78	83
less developed countries	42	68	75

= more developed countries
= less developed countries

(United Nations, 2013)

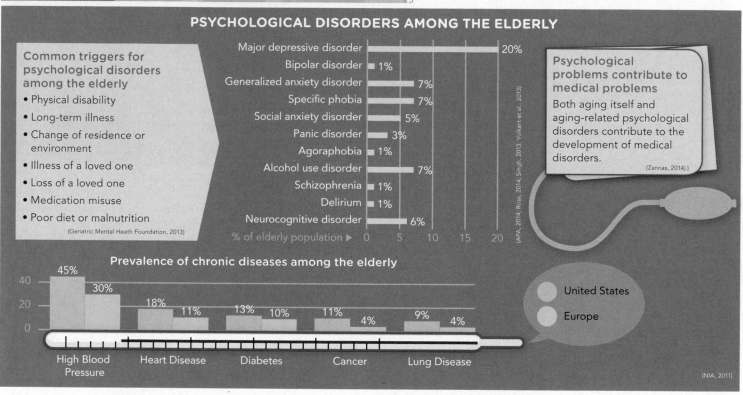

PSYCHOLOGICAL DISORDERS AMONG THE ELDERLY

Common triggers for psychological disorders among the elderly

- Physical disability
- Long-term illness
- Change of residence or environment
- Illness of a loved one
- Loss of a loved one
- Medication misuse
- Poor diet or malnutrition

(Geriatric Mental Heath Foundation, 2013)

% of elderly population ▶

Major depressive disorder	20%
Bipolar disorder	1%
Generalized anxiety disorder	7%
Specific phobia	7%
Social anxiety disorder	5%
Panic disorder	3%
Agoraphobia	1%
Alcohol use disorder	7%
Schizophrenia	1%
Delirium	1%
Neurocognitive disorder	6%

(APA, 2014; Ross, 2014; Singh, 2013; Volkert et al. 2013)

Psychological problems contribute to medical problems

Both aging itself and aging-related psychological disorders contribute to the development of medical disorders.

(Zannas, 2014].]

Prevalence of chronic diseases among the elderly

	United States	Europe
High Blood Pressure	45%	30%
Heart Disease	18%	11%
Diabetes	13%	10%
Cancer	11%	4%
Lung Disease	9%	4%

○ United States
○ Europe

(NIA, 2011)

THE ELDERLY POPULATION IS ITSELF AGING

80 years old and above

2013	14% of elderly people
2050 (estimated)	19% of elderly people

(MarketWatch, 2014; United Nations, 2013; WHO, 2012)

If you make it to age 80, you can expect to live an additional 8 years on average.
(MarketWatch, 2014; United Nations, 2013; WHO, 2012)

Aging and Gender
The world elderly population is predominantly female.

(NAELA, 2014; United Nations, 2013)

100:85 — 60+ years
100:62 — 80+ years

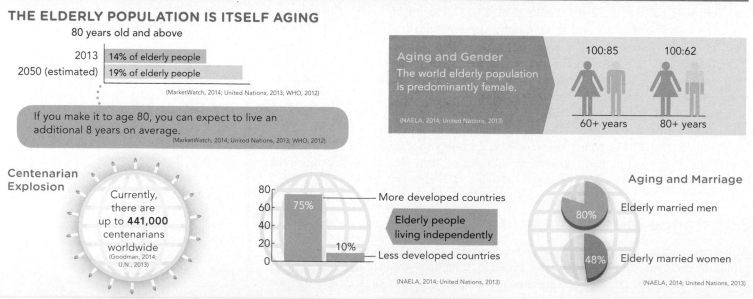

Centenarian Explosion

Currently, there are up to **441,000** centenarians worldwide
(Goodman, 2014; U.N., 2013)

Elderly people living independently

More developed countries — 75%
Less developed countries — 10%

(NAELA, 2014; United Nations, 2013)

Aging and Marriage

Elderly married men — 80%
Elderly married women — 48%

(NAELA, 2014; United Nations, 2013)

Racing to mental health Gerontologists propose that elderly people need to pursue pleasurable and personally meaningful activities. The elderly women on the left compete in a race at the 2013 National Senior Games in Ohio. In contrast, the elderly gentleman on the right, also interested in racing, watches a competition at the Saratoga Springs horse racing track with the daily racing form on his head. Which of these two activities might be more likely to contribute to successful psychological functioning during old age?

(Thompson, 2015). The majority of older adults do not misuse alcohol or other substances, despite the fact that aging can sometimes be a time of considerable stress and in our society people often turn to alcohol and drugs during times of stress. Accurate data about the rate of substance abuse among older adults are difficult to gather because many elderly people do not suspect or admit that they have such a problem.

Surveys find that 3 to 7 percent of older people, particularly men, have alcohol use disorder in a given year (Trevisan, 2014). Men under 30 are four times as likely as men over 60 to display a behavioral problem associated with excessive alcohol use, such as repeated falling, spells of dizziness or blacking out, secretive drinking, or social withdrawal. Older patients who are institutionalized, however, do display high rates of problem drinking. For example, alcohol problems among older people admitted to general and mental hospitals range from 15 percent to 49 percent, and estimates of alcohol-related problems among patients in nursing homes range from 10 percent to 20 percent (McConnaughey, 2014; Klein & Jess, 2002).

Researchers often distinguish between older problem drinkers who have had alcohol use disorder for many years, perhaps since their 20s, and those who do not start abusing alcohol until their 50s or 60s (in what is sometimes called "late-onset alcoholism") (Thompson, 2015; Volfson & Oslin, 2011). The latter group typically begins abusive drinking as a reaction to the negative events and pressures of growing older, such as the death of a spouse, living alone, or unwanted retirement. Alcohol use disorder in elderly people is treated much as it is in younger adults (see Chapter 10): through such interventions as detoxification, Antabuse, Alcoholics Anonymous (AA), and cognitive-behavioral therapy (APA, 2014).

A leading substance problem in the elderly is the *misuse of prescription drugs* (NIH, 2014). Most often the misuse is unintentional. In the United States, people over the age of 50 buy 77 percent of all prescription drugs and 61 percent of all over-the-counter drugs (NCHS, 2014; Statistic Brain, 2014). Elderly people—those who are over 65 years of age—receive twice as many prescriptions as younger persons (Dubovsky & Dubovsky, 2011). Around half take at least five prescription drugs and two over-the-counter drugs (NCHS, 2014). Thus their risk of confusing medications or skipping doses is high. To help address this problem, physicians and pharmacists often try to simplify medications, educate older patients about their prescriptions, clarify directions, and teach them to watch for undesired effects. However, physicians themselves are sometimes to blame in cases of prescription drug misuse, perhaps overprescribing medications for elderly patients or unwisely mixing certain medicines (Metsälä & Vaherkoski, 2014).

> **What changes in medical practice, patient education, or family interactions might reduce prescription drug misuse by the elderly?**

Yet another drug-related problem, apparently on the increase, is the misuse of powerful medications at nursing homes. Research suggests that antipsychotic drugs are currently being given to almost 30 percent of the total nursing home population in the United States, despite the fact that many of the residents do not display psychotic functioning (Mort et al., 2014; Lagnado, 2007). Apparently, these powerful and (for some elderly patients) dangerous drugs are often given to sedate and manage the patients.

Psychotic Disorders in Later Life

Elderly people have a higher rate of psychotic symptoms than younger people (Colijn et al., 2015; Devanand, 2011). Among aged people, these symptoms are usually caused by underlying medical conditions such as neurocognitive disorders, the disorders of cognition that you will read about in the next section. Some elderly people, though, suffer from *schizophrenia* or *delusional disorder.*

Actually, schizophrenia is less common in older people than in younger ones. In fact, many people with schizophrenia find that their symptoms lessen in later life (Dickerson et al., 2014). Improvement can occur in people who have had schizophrenia for 30 or more years, particularly in such areas as social skills and work capacity, as we are reminded by the remarkable late-life improvement of the Nobel Prize recipient John Nash, the subject of the book and movie *A Beautiful Mind.* Among those whose schizophrenia does emerge for the first time during old age, women outnumber men by at least 2 to 1 (Ames et al., 2010).

Another kind of psychotic disorder found among the elderly is delusional disorder, in which people develop beliefs that are false but not bizarre (Colijn et al., 2015). This disorder is rare in most age groups—around 2 of every 1,000

"All of a sudden, everyone seems younger than I am."

persons—but its prevalence appears to increase in the elderly population (APA, 2013). Older people with a delusional disorder may develop deeply held suspicions of persecution; they believe that other people—often family members, doctors, or friends—are conspiring against, cheating, spying on, or maligning them. They may become irritable, angry, or depressed or pursue legal action because of such ideas. It is not clear why this disorder increases among elderly people, but some clinicians suggest that the rise is related to the deficiencies in hearing, social isolation, greater stress, or heightened poverty with which many elderly persons contend.

> ► **delirium** A rapidly developing, acute disturbance in attention and orientation that makes it very difficult to concentrate and think in a clear and organized manner.

➤ *Summing Up*

DISORDERS OF LATER LIFE The problems of elderly people are often linked to the losses and other stresses and changes that accompany advancing age. As many as 50 percent of the elderly would benefit from mental health services, yet fewer than 20 percent receive them. Depression is a common mental health problem among those in this age group. Older people may also suffer from anxiety disorders. Between 4 and 6 percent exhibit alcohol use disorder in any given year, and many others misuse prescription drugs. In addition, some elderly people display psychotic disorders such as schizophrenia or delusional disorder.

Disorders of Cognition

Most of us worry from time to time that we are losing our memory and other mental abilities (Glauberman, 2014). You rush out the door without your keys, you meet a familiar person and cannot remember her name, or you forget that you have seen a particular film. Actually such mishaps are a common and quite normal feature of stress or of aging. As people move through middle age, these memory difficulties and lapses of attention increase, and they may occur regularly by the age of 60 or 70 (see *MindTech* on the next page). Sometimes, however, people have memory and other cognitive changes that are far more extensive and problematic.

In Chapter 5 you saw that problems in memory and related cognitive processes can occur without biological causes, in the form of *dissociative disorders*. More often, though, significant cognitive problems do involve biological factors, particularly when they appear late in life. The leading such disorders among the elderly are *delirium, major neurocognitive disorder,* and *mild neurocognitive disorder.*

Delirium

Delirium is a major disturbance in attention and orientation to the environment (see Table 15-1). As the person's focus becomes less clear, he or she has great difficulty concentrating and thinking in an organized way, leading to misinterpretations, illusions, and, on occasion, hallucinations (Lin et al., 2015). Sufferers may believe that it is morning in the middle of the night or that they are home when actually they are in a hospital room.

This state of massive confusion typically develops over a short period of time, usually hours or days (APA, 2013). Delirium may occur in any age group, including children, but is most common in elderly people. Fewer than 0.5 percent of the nonelderly population experience delirium, compared with 1 percent of people over 55 years of age and 14 percent of those over 85 years of age (Tune & DeWitt, 2011). When elderly people enter a hospital to be treated for a general medical condition, 1 in 10 of them shows the symptoms of delirium. At least another 10 percent develop delirium during their stay in the hospital (Bagnall & Faiz, 2014;

table: **15-1**

Dx Checklist
Delirium
1. Over the course of hours or a few days, individual experiences fast-moving and fluctuating disturbances in attention and orientation to the environment.
2. Individual also displays a significant cognitive disturbance.
(Information from: APA, 2013)

Inouye, 2006; Inouye et al., 2003). Around 17 percent of patients admitted for surgery develop delirium (de Castro et al., 2014). Sixty percent of nursing home residents older than 75 years of age have some delirium, compared with 35 percent of similar people living independently with the assistance of home health services (Tune & DeWitt, 2011).

Fever, certain diseases and infections, poor nutrition, head injuries, strokes, and stress (including the trauma of surgery) may all cause delirium (Lawlor & Bush, 2014; Eeles & Bhat, 2010). So may intoxication by certain substances, such as prescription drugs. Partly because older people face so many of these problems, they are more likely than younger ones to experience delirium. If a clinician accurately

MindTech

Remember to Tweet; Tweet to Remember

Social media sites such as Facebook and Twitter, and the Internet in general, are often thought of as the province of the young. However, elderly people are going online and joining social networking sites at increasing rates (Pew Internet, 2014). Some 45 percent of all elderly people online now use Facebook; 9 percent use Pinterest; 5 percent tweet, and 1 percent use Instagram—all sizable increases from previous years.

© Michel Gaillard/REA/Redux

Social networking among the elderly is much more than just an interesting statistic; it may be downright therapeutic. Several studies have found that online activity actually helps elderly people maintain and possibly improve their cognitive skills, coping skills, social pleasures, and emotions (Piatt, 2013; Szalavitz, 2013). Clinical theorists have offered several possible explanations for this phenomenon. It may be, for example, that the cognitive stimulation derived from Internet activity activates memory and other cognitive faculties or that the engagement with the world and family provided by the Internet through social networking directly satisfies social and emotional needs. Whatever the reason, more and more studies indicate that elderly people who are wired often function and feel better than those who do not pursue online activities.

One study in Italy, for example, focused on residents from two elder-care homes in the towns of Cremona and Brescia (Manuel-Logan, 2011). Some of the elderly residents were provided with laptops, given online tutorials, and set up with accounts on Facebook, Twitter, and other social networking sites. It turned out that, compared with other elderly residents at the facilities, those who used social networking displayed better memory and attention span and were generally "sharper" and more alert.

In another study, researchers at the University of Arizona recruited 42 adults, ages 68 to 91, and trained 14 of them on Facebook (Piatt, 2013; Wohltmann, 2013). The study found a 25 percent improvement in the cognitive performances of the 14 participants, including improvements in their mental "updating" skills—the ability to quickly add or delete material from their working memory.

Many elderly people resist the Internet and social networking, saying things like "It's not for me" or "You can't teach an old dog new tricks." However, this growing body of research suggests that they may want to embrace social networking and the Internet for better functioning and for better mental health. 💬

identifies delirium, it can often be easy to correct—by treating the underlying infection, for example, or changing the patient's drug prescription. However, the syndrome typically fails to be recognized for what it is (Traynor et al., 2015). One pioneering study on a medical ward, for example, found that admission doctors detected only 1 of 15 consecutive cases of delirium (Cameron et al., 1987). Incorrect diagnoses of this kind may contribute to a high death rate for older people with delirium (Dasgupta & Brymer, 2014).

Alzheimer's Disease and Other Neurocognitive Disorders

People with a **neurocognitive disorder** experience a significant decline in at least one (often more than one) area of cognitive functioning, such as memory and learning, attention, visual perception, planning and decision making, language ability, or social awareness (APA, 2013). Those who have certain types of neurocognitive disorders may also undergo personality changes—they may behave inappropriately, for example—and their symptoms may worsen steadily.

If the person's cognitive decline is substantial and interferes significantly with his or her ability to be independent, a diagnosis of **major neurocognitive disorder** is in order. If the decline is modest and does not interfere with independent functioning, the appropriate diagnosis is **mild neurocognitive disorder** (see Table 15-2).

There are currently 44 million people with neurocognitive disorders around the world, with 4.6 million new cases emerging each year (Hollingworth et al., 2011). The number of cases is expected to reach 135 million by 2050 unless a cure is found (Sifferlin, 2013). The occurrence of neurocognitive disorders is closely related to age (see Figure 15-2 on the next page). Among people 65 years of age, the prevalence is around 1 to 2 percent, increasing to as much as 50 percent among those over the age of 85 (ASHA, 2015; Apostolova & Cummings, 2008).

As you read earlier, **Alzheimer's disease** is the most common type of neurocognitive disorder, accounting for around two-thirds of all cases (Burke, 2011). Alzheimer's disease sometimes appears in middle age (*early onset*), but in the vast majority of cases it occurs after the age of 65 (*late onset*), and its prevalence increases markedly among people in their late 70s and early 80s (Zhao et al., 2014). At least 17 percent of those with Alzheimer's also experience major depressive disorder (Chi et al., 2014).

table: 15-2

Dx Checklist

Major Neurocognitive Disorder

1. Individual displays substantial decline in at least one of the following areas of cognitive function: • Memory and learning • Attention • Perceptual-motor skills • Planning and decision-making • Language ability • Social awareness.

2. Cognitive deficits interfere with the individual's everyday independence.

Mild Neurocognitive Disorder

1. Individual displays modest decline in at least one of the following areas of cognitive function: • Memory and learning • Attention • Perceptual-motor skills • Planning and decision-making • Language ability • Social awareness.

2. Cognitive deficits do not interfere with the individual's everyday independence.

(Information from: APA, 2013)

▶ **neurocognitive disorder** A disorder marked by a significant decline in at least one area of cognitive functioning.

▶ **major neurocognitive disorder** A neurocognitive disorder in which the decline in cognitive functioning is substantial and interferes with a person's ability to be independent.

▶ **mild neurocognitive disorder** A neurocognitive disorder in which the decline in cognitive functioning is modest and does not interfere with a person's ability to be independent.

▶ **Alzheimer's disease** The most common type of neurocognitive disorder, marked most prominently by memory impairment.

////// BETWEEN THE LINES //////

Universal Concern

In a survey of more than 3,000 adults across the United States, 84 percent of the respondents expressed concern that they or a family member would be affected by Alzheimer's disease (Shriver, 2014, 2011).

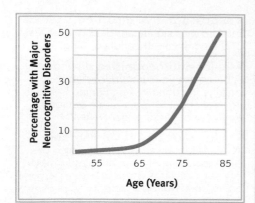

figure 15-2

Substantial cognitive decline and age
The occurrence of substantial cognitive decline is closely related to age. Fewer than 1 percent of all 60-year-olds have major neurocognitive disorders, compared with as many as 50 percent of those who are 85. (Information from: ASHA, 2015; Advokat et al., 2014; Ames et al., 2010; Nussbaum & Ellis, 2003.)

▸ **senile plaques** Sphere-shaped deposits of beta-amyloid protein that form in the spaces between certain brain cells and in certain blood vessels as people age. People with Alzheimer's disease have an excessive number of such plaques.

▸ **neurofibrillary tangles** Twisted protein fibers that form within certain brain cells as people age. People with Alzheimer's disease have an excessive number of such tangles.

Alzheimer's disease is a gradually progressive disease in which memory impairment is the most prominent cognitive dysfunction (APA, 2013). Technically, sufferers receive a DSM-5 diagnosis of *mild neurocognitive disorder due to Alzheimer's disease* during the early and mild stages of the syndrome and *major neurocognitive disorder due to Alzheimer's disease* during the later, more severe stages (see Table 15-3).

Alzheimer's disease is named after Alois Alzheimer, the German physician who formally identified it in 1907. Alzheimer first became aware of the syndrome in 1901 when a new patient, Auguste D., was placed under his care:

On November 25, 1901, a . . . woman with no personal or family history of mental illness was admitted to a psychiatric hospital in Frankfurt, Germany, by her husband, who could no longer ignore or hide quirks and lapses that had overtaken her in recent months. First, there were unexplainable bursts of anger, and then a strange series of memory problems. She became increasingly unable to locate things in her own home and began to make surprising mistakes in the kitchen. By the time she arrived at Städtische Irrenanstalt, the Frankfurt Hospital for the Mentally Ill and Epileptics, her condition was as severe as it was curious. The attending doctor, senior physician Alois Alzheimer, began the new file with these notes. . . .

She sits on the bed with a helpless expression.

"What is your name?"

Auguste.

"Last name?"

Auguste.

"What is your husband's name?"

Auguste, I think.

"How long have you been here?"

(She seems to be trying to remember.)

Three weeks.

It was her second day in the hospital. Dr. Alzheimer, a thirty-seven-year-old neuropathologist and clinician, . . . observed in his new patient a remarkable cluster of symptoms: severe disorientation, reduced comprehension, aphasia (language impairment), paranoia, hallucinations, and a short-term memory so incapacitated that when he spoke her full-name, Frau Auguste D____, and asked her to write it down, the patient got only as far as "Frau" before needing the doctor to repeat the rest.

He spoke her name again. She wrote "Augu" and again stopped.

When Alzheimer prompted her a third time, she was able to write her entire first name and the initial "D" before finally giving up, telling the doctor, "I have lost myself."

Her condition did not improve. It became apparent that there was nothing that anyone at this or any other hospital could do for Frau D. except to insure her safety and try to keep her as clean and comfortable as possible for the rest of her days. Over the next four and a half years, she became increasingly disoriented, delusional, and incoherent. She was often hostile.

"Her gestures showed a complete helplessness," Alzheimer later noted in a published report. "She was disoriented as to time and place. From time to time she would state that she did not understand anything, that she felt confused and totally lost. . . . Often she would scream for hours and hours in a horrible voice."

By November 1904, three and a half years into her illness, Auguste D. was bedridden, incontinent, and largely immobile. . . . Notes from October 1905 indicate that she had become permanently curled up in a fetal position with her knees drawn up to her chest, muttering but unable to speak, and requiring assistance to be fed.

(Shenk, 2001, pp. 12–14)

Although some people with Alzheimer's disease may survive for as many as 20 years, the time between onset and death is typically 8 to 10 years (Advokat et al., 2014; Soukup, 2006). It usually begins with mild memory problems, lapses of attention, and difficulties in language and communication. As symptoms worsen, the person has trouble completing complicated tasks or remembering important appointments. Eventually sufferers also have difficulty with simple tasks, forget distant memories, and have changes in personality that often become very noticeable. For example, a gentle man may become uncharacteristically aggressive.

People with Alzheimer's disease may at first deny that they have a problem, but they soon become anxious or depressed about their state of mind; many also become agitated. A woman from Virginia describes her memory loss as the disease progresses:

> *Very often I wander around looking for something which I know is very pertinent, but then after a while I forget about what it is I was looking for. . . . Once the idea is lost, everything is lost and I have nothing to do but wander around trying to figure out what it was that was so important earlier.*
>
> *(Shenk, 2001, p. 43)*

As the neurocognitive symptoms intensify, people with Alzheimer's disease show less and less awareness of their limitations. They may withdraw from others during the late stages of the disorder, become more confused about time and place, wander, and show very poor judgment. Eventually they become fully dependent on other people. They may lose almost all knowledge of the past and fail to recognize the faces of even close relatives. They also become increasingly uncomfortable at night and take frequent naps during the day (Ferman et al., 2015). During the late phases of the disorder, they require constant care.

People with Alzheimer's usually remain in fairly good health until the later stages of the disease. As their mental functioning declines, however, they become less active and spend much of their time just sitting or lying in bed. This makes them prone to develop illnesses such as pneumonia, which can result in death (Park et al., 2014). Alzheimer's disease is currently responsible for close to 84,000 deaths each year in the United States (NCHS, 2014), which makes it the sixth leading cause of death in the country, the third leading cause among the elderly (CDC, 2015).

In most cases, Alzheimer's disease can be diagnosed with certainty only after death, when structural changes in the person's brain, such as excessive *senile plaques and neurofibrillary tangles,* can be fully examined. **Senile plaques** are sphere-shaped deposits of a small molecule known as the *beta-amyloid protein* that form in the spaces *between* cells in the hippocampus, cerebral cortex, and certain other brain regions, as well as in some nearby blood vessels. The formation of plaques is a normal part of aging, but it is exceptionally high in people with Alzheimer's disease (Zhao et al., 2014; Selkoe, 2011, 2000, 1992). **Neurofibrillary tangles,** twisted protein fibers found *within* the cells of the hippocampus and certain other brain areas, also occur in all people as they age, but again people with Alzheimer's disease form an extraordinary number of them.

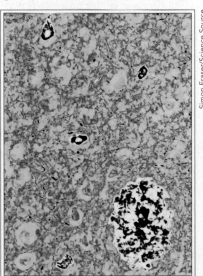

Simon Fraser/Science Source

Biological culprits Tissue from the brain of a person with Alzheimer's disease shows excessive amounts of plaque (large yellow-black sphere at lower right of photo) and neurofibrillary tangles (several smaller yellow blobs throughout photo).

table: 15-3

Dx Checklist

Neurocognitive Disorder Due to Alzheimer's Disease

1. Individual displays the features of major or mild neurocognitive disorder.

2. Memory impairment is a prominent feature.

3. Genetic indications or family history of Alzheimer's disease underscore diagnosis, but are not essential to diagnosis.

4. Symptoms are not due to other types of disorders or medical problems.

(Information from: APA, 2013)

Screening for Alzheimer's disease A neuropsychologist guides a patient through a psychomotor test—the gesture imitation test—to help screen for neurocognitive disorders such as Alzheimer's disease.

Scientists do not fully understand what role excessive numbers of plaques and tangles play in Alzheimer's disease, but they suspect they are very important. Today's leading explanations for this disease center on these plaques and tangles and on the various factors that may contribute to their formation.

What Are the Genetic Causes of Alzheimer's Disease?

To understand the genetic theories of Alzheimer's disease, we must first appreciate the nature and role of *proteins.* Proteins are fundamental components of all living cells, including, of course, brain cells. They are large molecules made up of chains of carbon, hydrogen, oxygen, nitrogen, and sulfur. There are many different kinds of proteins, each with a different function. Collectively, they are essential for the proper functioning of an organism.

The plaques and tangles that are so plentiful in the brains of Alzheimer's patients seem to occur when two important proteins start acting in a frenzied manner. Abnormal activity by the beta-amyloid protein is, as we noted above, key to the repeated formation of plaques. Abnormal activity by another protein, *tau,* is key to the excessive formation of tangles. One of the leading theories holds that the many plaques formed by beta-amyloid proteins cause tau proteins in the brain to start breaking down, resulting in tangles and the death of many neurons (Khan, 2015; Hughes, 2011).

What causes this chain of events? Genetic factors are a major culprit. However, the genetic factors that are responsible differ for the early-onset and late-onset types of Alzheimer's disease.

EARLY-ONSET ALZHEIMER'S DISEASE As we noted earlier, Alzheimer's disease occurs before the age of 65 in relatively few cases. Such cases typically run in families. Researchers have learned that this form of Alzheimer's disease can be caused by abnormalities in the genes responsible for the production of two proteins—the *beta-amyloid precursor protein* (*beta-APP*) and the *presenilin* protein. Apparently, some families transmit *mutations,* or abnormal forms, of one or both of these genes—mutations that lead ultimately to abnormal beta-amyloid protein buildups and, in turn, to plaque formations (Zhao et al., 2014).

LATE-ONSET ALZHEIMER'S DISEASE The vast majority of Alzheimer cases develop after the age of 65 and do not run in families. This late-onset form of the disease appears to result from a combination of genetic, environmental, and lifestyle factors. However, the genetic factor at play in late-onset Alzheimer's disease is different from those involved in early-onset Alzheimer's disease.

A gene called the *apolipoprotein E* (*ApoE*) *gene* is normally responsible for the production of a protein that helps carry various fats into the bloodstream. This gene comes in various forms. About 30 percent of the population inherit the form called *ApoE-4,* and those people may be particularly vulnerable to the development of Alzheimer's disease (Shu et al., 2014; Hollingworth et al., 2011). Apparently, the ApoE-4 gene form promotes the excessive formation of beta-amyloid proteins, helping to spur the formation of plaques and, in turn, the breakdown of the tau protein, the formation of numerous tangles, the death of many neurons, and, ultimately, the onset of Alzheimer's disease.

Although the ApoE-4 gene form appears to be a major contributor to the development of Alzheimer's disease, it is important to recognize that not everyone with this form of the gene develops the disease. Other factors—perhaps environmental, lifestyle, or stress-related—may also have a significant impact in the development of late-onset Alzheimer's disease (Chin-Chan et al., 2015; Nation et al., 2011).

BETWEEN THE LINES

Leading Causes of Death Among the Elderly

#1 Heart disease

#2 Cancer

#3 Chronic low respiratory disease

#4 Cerebrovascular disease

#5 Alzheimer's disease

(CDC, 2015)

AN ALTERNATIVE GENETIC THEORY OF ALZHEIMER'S DISEASE As you have just read, the leading genetic theories of Alzheimer's disease point to gene forms, such as ApoE-4, that produce abnormal beta-amyloid protein buildups and plaque formations, which, in turn, lead to abnormal activity of tau proteins and the formation of numerous tangles. In recent years, however, some researchers have come to believe that abnormal tau protein activity is not always the result of these abnormal beta-amyloid protein buildups (Peterson et al., 2014; Karch, Jeng, & Goate, 2013). These researchers have identified other gene forms in Alzheimer's patients that seem to be directly associated with tau protein abnormalities and tangle formations. Thus it may be that there are multiple genetic causes for the formation of numerous tangles and the onset of Alzheimer's disease: (1) gene forms that start the ball rolling by first promoting beta-amyloid protein formations and plaques and (2) gene forms that more directly promote tau protein abnormalities and tangle formations.

How Do Brain Structure and Biochemical Activity Relate to Alzheimer's Disease?
We know that genetic factors may predispose people to Alzheimer's disease, but we still need to know what abnormalities in brain structure and/or biochemical activity result from such factors and help promote Alzheimer's disease. Researchers have identified a number of possibilities.

Certain brain structures seem to be especially important in memory. Among the most important structures in short-term memory is the *prefrontal cortex,* located just behind the forehead; the *temporal lobes* (which include the *hippocampus* and *amygdala*); and the *diencephalon* (which includes the *mammillary bodies, thalamus,* and *hypothalamus*). Research indicates that Alzheimer's disease involves damage to or improper functioning of one or more of these brain structures (Hsu et al., 2015; Ishii & Iadecola, 2015) (see Figure 15-3).

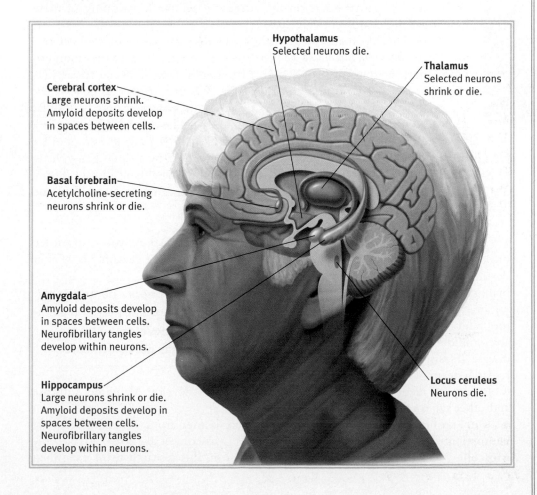

Hypothalamus
Selected neurons die.

Thalamus
Selected neurons shrink or die.

Cerebral cortex
Large neurons shrink. Amyloid deposits develop in spaces between cells.

Basal forebrain
Acetylcholine-secreting neurons shrink or die.

Amygdala
Amyloid deposits develop in spaces between cells. Neurofibrillary tangles develop within neurons.

Hippocampus
Large neurons shrink or die. Amyloid deposits develop in spaces between cells. Neurofibrillary tangles develop within neurons.

Locus ceruleus
Neurons die.

figure 15-3

The aging brain In old age, the brain undergoes changes that affect cognitive functions such as memory, learning, and reasoning to some degree. The same changes occur to an excessive degree in people with Alzheimer's disease. (Information from: Selkoe, 2011, 1992.)

Similarly, certain biochemical activities seem to be especially important in memory. In order for new information to be acquired and stored, certain proteins must be produced in key brain cells. Several chemicals—for example, *acetylcholine, glutamate, RNA (ribonucleic acid)*, and *calcium*—are responsible for the production of the memory-linked proteins. Researchers have found that if the activity of any of these chemicals is disturbed, the proper production of proteins may be prevented and the formation of memories interrupted (Canas et al., 2014; Berridge, 2011). Correspondingly, they have found that abnormal activity by these chemicals may contribute to the symptoms of Alzheimer's disease.

Other Explanations of Alzheimer's Disease Several lines of research suggest that certain substances found in nature may act as toxins, damage the brain, and contribute to the development of Alzheimer's disease. For example, researchers have detected high levels of *zinc* in the brains of some Alzheimer's patients (Xu et al., 2014; Schrag et al., 2011). This finding has gained particular attention because in some animal studies zinc has been observed to trigger a clumping of the beta-amyloid protein, similar to the plaques found in the brains of Alzheimer's patients.

Another line of research suggests that the environmental toxin *lead* may contribute to the development of Alzheimer's disease (Lee & Freeman, 2014; Ritter, 2008). Lead was phased out of gasoline products between 1976 and 1991, leading to an 80 percent drop of lead levels in people's blood. However, many of today's elderly were exposed to high levels of lead in the 1960s and 1970s, regularly inhaling air pollution from vehicle exhausts—an exposure that might have damaged or destroyed many of their neurons. Several studies suggest that this earlier absorption of lead and other pollutants may be having a negative effect on the current cognitive functioning of these individuals (Richardson et al., 2014).

Two other explanations for Alzheimer's disease have also been offered. One is the *autoimmune theory*. On the basis of certain irregularities found in the immune systems of people with Alzheimer's disease, several researchers have speculated that changes in aging brain cells may trigger an *autoimmune response* (that is, a mistaken attack by the immune system against itself) that helps lead to the disease (Marchese et al., 2014). The other explanation is a *viral theory*. Because Alzheimer's disease resembles *Creutzfeldt-Jakob disease*, another type of neurocognitive disorder that is known to be caused by a slow–acting virus, some researchers propose that a similar virus may cause Alzheimer's disease (Head, 2013; Prusiner, 1991). To date, however, no such virus has been detected in the brains of Alzheimer's victims.

Assessing and Predicting Alzheimer's Disease As you read earlier, most cases of Alzheimer's disease can be diagnosed with absolute certainty only after death, when an autopsy is performed. However, brain scans, which reveal abnormalities in the living brain, now are used commonly as assessment tools and often provide clinicians with considerable confidence in their diagnoses of Alzheimer's disease (Haris et al., 2015). In addition, several research teams currently are trying to develop tools that can identify those people who are likely to develop Alzheimer's disease and other types of neurocognitive disorders.

> **Would people be better off knowing that they will eventually develop a disease that has no known cure?**

One promising line of work, for example, comes from the laboratory of neuroscientist Lisa Mosconi and her colleagues (Mosconi et al., 2014, 2010, 2008; Mosconi, 2013). Using a special kind of PET scan, this research team examined

Slipping away Because of their short-term memory problems, people with advanced cases of Alzheimer's disease, one form of neurocognitive disorder, are often unable to draw or paint or do other simple tasks. In addition, their long-term memory deficits may prevent them from recognizing even close relatives or friends.

activity in certain parts of the *hippocampus* in dozens of elderly research participants and then conducted follow-up studies of them for up to 24 years. (Recall that the hippocampus plays a major role in memory.) Eventually, 43 percent of the study's participants developed either a mild or major neurocognitive disorder due to Alzheimer's disease. The researchers found that those who developed such cognitive impairments had displayed lower hippocampus activity on their initial PET scans than the participants who remained healthy. Overall, the PET scans, administered years before the onset of symptoms, predicted mild neurocognitive impairment with an accuracy rate of 71 percent and major neurocognitive impairment with an accuracy rate of 83 percent.

As you will see shortly, the most effective interventions for Alzheimer's disease and other types of neurocognitive disorders are those that help *prevent* these problems, or at least ones that are applied early. Clearly, then, it is essential to have tools that identify the disorders as early as possible, preferably years before the onset of symptoms (Rabin, 2013). That is what makes the research advances in assessment and diagnosis so exciting.

Other Types of Neurocognitive Disorders There are a number of neurocognitive disorders in addition to Alzheimer's disease (APA, 2013). *Vascular neurocognitive disorder*, for example, follows a cerebrovascular accident, or *stroke*, during which blood flow to specific areas of the brain was cut off, thus damaging the areas (Jia et al., 2014). In many cases, the patient may not even be aware of the stroke (Moorhouse & Rockwood, 2010). Like Alzheimer's disease, this disorder is progressive, but its symptoms begin suddenly rather than gradually. Moreover, the person's cognitive functioning may continue to be normal in areas of the brain that have not been affected by the stroke, in contrast to the broad cognitive deficiencies usually displayed by Alzheimer's patients. Some people have both Alzheimer's disease and vascular neurocognitive disorder.

Frontotemporal neurocognitive disorder, also known as *Pick's disease*, is a rare disorder that affects the frontal and temporal lobes. It has a clinical picture similar to Alzheimer's disease, but the two diseases can be distinguished at autopsy.

Neurocognitive disorder due to prion disease, also called *Creutzfeldt-Jakob disease*, has symptoms that include spasms of the body. As we observed earlier, this disorder is

AP Photo/Steve Ruark

Part of the game? National Football League great John Mackey shows off his Super Bowl V and Hall of Fame rings. Mackey died at age 69 in 2011 of frontotemporal neurocognitive disorder, a condition marked by extreme confusion and the need for full-time assistance. Many cases of neurocognitive disorder, like Mackey's, are apparently the result of repeated sports injuries to the head.

Victims of Parkinson's disease Two of today's most famous victims of Parkinson's disease, boxing legend Muhammad Ali (left) and actor Michael J. Fox (right), chat playfully prior to testifying before a Senate funding subcommittee about the devastating effects the disease has had on their lives and those of other people.

caused by a slow-acting virus that may live in the body for years before the disease develops. Once launched, however, the disease has a rapid course.

Neurocognitive disorder due to Huntington's disease is an inherited progressive disease in which memory problems, along with personality changes and mood difficulties, worsen over time. People with Huntington's have movement problems, too, such as severe twitching and spasms. Children of people with Huntington's disease have a 50 percent chance of developing it.

Parkinson's disease, the slowly progressive neurological disorder marked by tremors, rigidity, and unsteadiness, can result in *neurocognitive disorder due to Parkinson's disease,* particularly in older people or those whose cases are advanced.

Yet other neurocognitive disorders may be caused by *HIV infections, traumatic brain injury, substance abuse,* or various *medical conditions* such as meningitis or advanced syphilis.

What Treatments Are Currently Available for Alzheimer's Disease and Other Neurocognitive Disorders?

Treatments for the cognitive features of Alzheimer's disease and most other types of neurocognitive disorders have been at best modestly helpful. A number of approaches have been applied, including drug therapy, cognitive techniques, behavioral interventions, support for caregivers, and sociocultural approaches.

DRUG TREATMENT The drugs currently prescribed for Alzheimer's patients are designed to affect acetylcholine and glutamate, the neurotransmitters that play important roles in memory. Such drugs include *donepezil* (Aricept), *rivastigmine* (Exelon), *galantamine* (Razadyne), and *memantine* (Namenda). The short-term memory and reasoning ability of some Alzheimer's patients who take these drugs improve slightly, as do their use of language and their ability to cope under pressure (Jessen, 2014). Although the benefits of the drugs are limited and their side effects can be problematic, these drugs have been approved by the FDA. Clinicians believe that they may be of greatest use to people in the earlier, milder stages of Alzheimer's disease. Another approach, taking *vitamin E,* either alone or in combination with one of these drugs, also seems to help slow down cognitive decline among people in the milder stages of Alzheimer's disease (Dysken et al., 2014, 2009). Other possible drug treatments are being investigated currently (Medina & Avila, 2014).

The drugs just discussed are each prescribed *after* a person has developed Alzheimer's disease. In contrast, studies suggest that certain substances now available on the marketplace for other kinds of problems may help prevent or delay the onset of Alzheimer's disease. For example, some studies have found that women who took *estrogen,* the female sex hormone, for years after menopause cut their risk of developing Alzheimer's disease in half (Li et al., 2014; Kawas et al., 1997). Other studies have suggested that the long-term use of *nonsteroidal anti-inflammatory drugs* such as *ibuprofen* and *naprosyn* (drugs found in Advil, Motrin, Nuprin, and other pain relievers) may help reduce the risk of Alzheimer's disease, although recent findings on this possibility have been mixed (Advokat et al., 2014).

COGNITIVE TECHNIQUES Cognitive treatments have been used in cases of Alzheimer's disease, with some temporary success (Nelson & Tabet, 2015). In Japan, for example, a number of people with the disease meet regularly in classes, performing simple calculations and reading essays and novels aloud. Proponents of this approach claim that it serves as a mental exercise that helps rehabilitate those parts of the brain linked to memory, reasoning, and judgment. Similarly, some research suggests that cognitive activities, including computer-based cognitive stimulation programs, may help prevent or delay the onset of Alzheimer's disease (Szalavitz, 2013). One study of 700 people in their 80s found that those research participants who had pursued cognitive activities over a five-year period (for example, writing letters, following the news, reading books, or attending concerts or plays) were less likely to develop Alzheimer's disease than were mentally inactive participants (Wilson et al., 2012, 2007).

BEHAVIORAL INTERVENTIONS Behavioral interventions have also been somewhat successful in helping Alzheimer's patients. It has become increasingly clear across many studies that physical exercise helps improve cognitive functioning—for people of all ages and states of health. There is evidence that regular physical exercise may also help reduce the risk of developing Alzheimer's disease and other types of neurocognitive disorders (Paillard et al., 2015; Nation et al., 2011). Correspondingly, physical exercise is often a part of treatment programs for people with the disorders.

Behavioral interventions of a different kind have been used to help improve specific symptoms displayed by Alzheimer's patients. The approaches typically focus on changing everyday patient behaviors that are stressful for the family, such as wandering at night, loss of bladder control, demands for attention, and inadequate personal care (Lancioni et al., 2011; Lindsey, 2011). The behavioral therapists use a combination of role-playing exercises, modeling, and practice to teach family members how and when to use reinforcement in order to shape more positive behaviors.

SUPPORT FOR CAREGIVERS Caregiving can take a heavy toll on the close relatives of people with Alzheimer's disease and other types of neurocognitive disorders (Kang et al., 2014). Almost 90 percent of all people with Alzheimer's disease are cared for by their relatives (Alzheimer's Association, 2014, 2007). It is hard to take care of someone who is becoming increasingly lost, helpless, and medically ill. And it is very painful to witness mental and physical decline in someone you love.

© Christina Koci Hernandez/SFC/San Francisco Chronicle/Corbis

Cognitive fitness center A number of senior-living community programs now include cognitive fitness centers where elderly people sit at computers and work on memory and cognition software programs. Clinicians hope that "cognitive calisthenics" of this kind will help prevent or reverse certain symptoms of aging.

© Jodi Cobb/National Geographic Society/Corbis

Toll on caregivers A woman comforts her twin sister, who suffers from Alzheimer's disease. The psychological and physical burdens of caring for close relatives with neurocognitive disorders typically take a heavy toll on caregivers.

A therapeutic environment Some long-term care facilities have designed their buildings to address the cognitive and emotional needs of the elderly residents. In this facility, a woman with Alzheimer's disease is drawn to and touches some of her room's stimulating objects and is, at the same time, comforted by the room's soothing colors and decorations.

One of the most frequent reasons for the institutionalization of people with Alzheimer's disease is that overwhelmed caregivers can no longer cope with the difficulties of keeping them at home (Di Rosa et al., 2011; Apostolova & Cummings, 2008). Many caregivers experience anger and depression, and their own physical and mental health often declines (Kang et al., 2014). Clinicians now recognize that one of the most important aspects of treating Alzheimer's disease and other types of neurocognitive disorders is to focus on the emotional needs of the caregivers, including their needs for regular time out, education about the disease, and psychotherapy (Mittelman & Bartels, 2014). Some clinicians also provide caregiver support groups.

SOCIOCULTURAL APPROACHES Sociocultural approaches play an important role in treatment (Fouassier et al., 2015; Pongan et al., 2012) (see *MediaSpeak* on the next page). A number of *day-care facilities* for patients with neurocognitive disorders have been developed, providing treatment programs and activities for outpatients during the day and returning them to their homes and families at night. There are also many *assisted-living facilities* in which those suffering from neurocognitive impairment live in apartments tailored to their limitations, receive needed supervision, and take part in various activities that bring more joy and stimulation to their lives. Studies suggest that such facilities often help slow the cognitive decline of residents and enhance their enjoyment of life. In addition, a growing number of practical devices, such as tracking beacons worn on the wrists of Alzheimer's patients and shoes that contain a GPS tracker, have been developed to help locate patients who may wander off (Cavallo et al., 2015; Schiller, 2014).

Given the progress now unfolding in the understanding and treatment of Alzheimer's disease and other types of neurocognitive disorders, researchers are looking forward to important advances in the coming years. The brain changes responsible for these disorders are tremendously complex, but most investigators believe that exciting breakthroughs are just over the horizon.

Much more than a pet Bella, a smooth collie, is stroked by her owner, a man with Alzheimer's disease. Bella is one of many dogs trained to assist people with neurocognitive disorders in various tasks, including bringing them home if they get lost. The owner can command Bella to take him home, or his family can also summon the dog home with a special device.

10:00 AM   75%

MediaSpeak

Focusing on Emotions

By Pam Belluck, *New York Times*, January 1, 2011

Margaret Nance was, to put it mildly, a difficult case. Agitated, combative, often reluctant to eat, she would hit staff members and fellow residents at nursing homes, several of which kicked her out. But when Beatitudes nursing home agreed to an urgent plea to accept her, all that changed.

Disregarding typical nursing-home rules, Beatitudes allowed Ms. Nance, 96 and afflicted with Alzheimer's, to sleep, be bathed and dine whenever she wanted, even at 2 A.M. She could eat anything, too, no matter how unhealthy, including unlimited chocolate.

And she was given a baby doll, a move that seemed so jarring that a supervisor initially objected until she saw how calm Ms. Nance became when she rocked, caressed and fed her "baby," often agreeing to eat herself after the doll "ate" several spoonfuls.

Dementia patients at Beatitudes are allowed practically anything that brings comfort, even an alcoholic "nip at night," said Tena Alonzo, director of research. "Whatever your vice is, we're your folks," she said. . . .

It is an unusual posture for a nursing home, but Beatitudes is actually following some of the latest science. Research suggests that creating positive emotional experiences for Alzheimer's patients diminishes distress and behavior problems. . . . [Some studies also] recommend making cosmetic changes to rooms and buildings to affect behavior or mood. [One such study] found that brightening lights in dementia facilities decreased depression, cognitive deterioration and loss of functional abilities. . . .

One program for dementia patients cared for by relatives at home creates specific activities related to something they once enjoyed: arranging flowers, filling photo albums, snapping beans.

"A gentleman who loved fishing could still set up a tackle box, so we gave him a plastic tackle box" to set up every day, said the program's developer, Laura N. Gitlin, a sociologist . . . at Johns Hopkins University. . . .

Beatitudes, which takes about 30 moderate to severe dementia sufferers, introduced its program 12 years ago, focusing on individualized care. . . .

Finding the right activity This patient picks tomatoes from a garden at Résidence Les Aurélias, a residential treatment home for people with Alzheimer's disease in France. The staff recognized this patient's interest in horticulture and created a therapeutic garden where she could be active and find pleasure and satisfaction.

Stéphane Audras/REA/Redux Pictures

Beatitudes eliminated anything potentially considered restraining, from deep-seated wheelchairs that hinder standing up to bedrails (some beds are lowered and protected by mats). It drastically reduced antipsychotics and medications considered primarily for "staff convenience,". . . Ms. Alonzo said.

It encouraged keeping residents out of diapers if possible, taking them to the toilet to preserve feelings of independence . . . Beatitudes also changed activity programming, [instructing] staff members [to] conduct one-on-one activities: block-building, coloring, simply conversing. . . .

These days, hundreds of Arizona physicians, medical students, and staff members at other nursing homes have received Beatitudes' training, and several Illinois nursing homes are adopting it. . . .

> **If Alzheimer's disease is a biologically caused disorder, why would increasing patients' comfort levels make such a difference?**

➤ *Summing Up*

DISORDERS OF COGNITION Older people are more likely than people of other age groups to experience delirium, a fast-developing disturbance marked by great difficulty focusing attention, staying oriented, concentrating, and following an orderly sequence of thought.

Neurocognitive disorders, characterized by a significant decline in cognitive function, become increasingly common in older age groups. There are many types of neurocognitive disorders, the most common being Alzheimer's disease. Alzheimer's disease has been linked to an unusually high number of senile plaques and neurofibrillary tangles in the brain. According to a leading explanation of late-onset Alzheimer's disease—the most common kind of Alzheimer's disease—people who inherit ApoE-4, a particular form of the apolipoprotein E (ApoE) gene, are particularly vulnerable to the development of Alzheimer's disease.

A number of other causes have also been proposed for this disease, including high levels of zinc, lead, or other toxins; immune system problems; and a virus of some kind.

Researchers are making significant strides at better assessing Alzheimer's disease and other types of neurocognitive disorders and even at identifying those who will eventually develop these disorders. Drug, cognitive, and behavioral therapies have been used to treat Alzheimer's disease, with limited success. Addressing the needs of caregivers is now also recognized as a key part of treatment. In addition, sociocultural approaches such as day-care facilities are on the rise. Major treatment breakthroughs are expected in the coming years.

Issues Affecting the Mental Health of the Elderly

As the study and treatment of elderly people have progressed, three issues have raised concern among clinicians: the problems faced by elderly members of racial and ethnic minority groups, the inadequacies of long-term care, and the need for a health-maintenance approach to medical care in an aging world.

First, *discrimination based on race and ethnicity* has long been a problem in the United States (see Chapter 2), and many people suffer as a result, particularly those who are old. To be both old and a member of a minority group is considered a kind of "double jeopardy" by many observers. For older women in minority groups, the difficulties are sometimes termed "triple jeopardy," as many more older women than older men live alone, are widowed, and are poor. Clinicians must take into account their older patients' race, ethnicity, and gender as they try to diagnose and treat their mental health problems (Ng et al., 2014; Sirey et al., 2014) (see Figure 15-4).

Some elderly people in minority groups face language barriers that interfere with their medical and mental health care. Others may hold cultural beliefs that prevent them from seeking services. Additionally, many members of minority groups do not trust the majority establishment or do not know about medical and mental health services that are sensitive to their culture and their particular needs (Ayalon & Huyck, 2001). As a result, it is common for elderly members of racial and ethnic minority groups to rely largely on family members or friends for remedies and health care.

Today, 8 to 20 percent of elderly people live with their children or other relatives, usually because of increasing health problems (Keefer, 2015; Span, 2009). In the United States, this living arrangement is more common for elderly people from ethnic minority groups than for elderly white Americans. Elderly Asian Americans are most likely to live with their children, African Americans and Hispanic

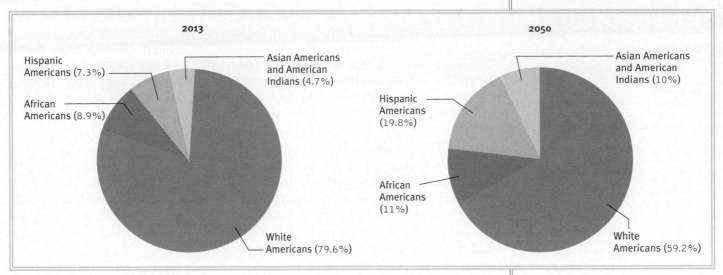

2013

Hispanic Americans (7.3%)

African Americans (8.9%)

Asian Americans and American Indians (4.7%)

White Americans (79.6%)

2050

Asian Americans and American Indians (10%)

Hispanic Americans (19.8%)

African Americans (11%)

White Americans (59.2%)

figure **15-4**

Ethnicity and old age The elderly population is becoming racially and ethnically more diverse. In the United States today, almost 80 percent of all people over the age of 65 are white Americans. By 2050, white Americans will comprise only 59 percent of the elderly. (Information from: NCHS, 2014; Pirkl, 2009; Hobbs, 1997.)

Americans are less likely to do so, and white Americans are least likely (Etaugh, 2008; Armstrong, 2001).

Second, many older people require *long-term care*, a general term that may refer variously to the services offered outside the family in a partially supervised apartment, a senior housing complex for mildly impaired elderly persons, or a nursing home where skilled medical and nursing care are available around the clock (Samos et al., 2010). The quality of care in such residences varies widely.

At any given time in the United States, only about 4 percent of the entire elderly population actually live in nursing homes (1.5 million people), but as many as 20 percent of people 85 years and older do eventually wind up being placed in such facilities (CDC, 2015). Thus many older adults live in fear of being "put away." They

Every little bit helps In line with research findings that all kinds of physical exercise help improve cognitive functioning, these elderly persons participate in an "arm chair" exercise program at the Dominica Association, a community center in Bradford, West Yorkshire, in the United Kingdom.

Paula Solloway/Alamy

fear having to move, losing independence, and living in a medical environment. Many also worry about the cost of long-term care facilities. Around-the-clock nursing care is expensive, and nursing home costs continue to rise. Most health insurance plans available today do not adequately cover the costs of long-term or permanent placement (Durso et al., 2010). Worry over these issues can greatly harm the mental health of older adults, perhaps leading to depression and anxiety as well as family conflict.

Finally, clinical scientists suggest that the current generation of young adults should take a *health-maintenance,* or *wellness promotion, approach* to their own aging process. In other words, they should do things that promote physical and mental health—avoid smoking, eat well-balanced and healthful meals, exercise regularly, engage in positive social relationships, and take advantage of psychoeducational, stress management, and other mental health programs (CDC, 2014). There is a growing belief that older adults will adapt more readily to changes and negative events if their physical and psychological health is good.

➤ *Summing Up*

ISSUES AFFECTING THE MENTAL HEALTH OF THE ELDERLY In studying and treating the problems of old age, clinicians have become concerned about three issues: the problems of elderly members of racial and ethnic minority groups, inadequacies of long-term care, and the need for health maintenance by young adults.

PUTTING IT...*together*

Clinicians Discover the Elderly

Early in the twentieth century, mental health professionals focused little on the elderly. But like the problems of children, those of aging people have now caught the attention of researchers and clinicians. Current work is changing how we understand and treat the psychological problems of the elderly. No longer do clinicians simply accept depression or anxiety in elderly people as inevitable. No longer do they overlook the dangers of prescription drug misuse by the elderly. And no longer do they underestimate the dangers of delirium or the prevalence of neurocognitive disorders. Similarly, geropsychologists have become more aware of the importance of addressing the health care and financial needs of the elderly as keys to their psychological well-being.

As the elderly population lives longer and grows ever larger, the needs of people in this age group are becoming more visible. Thus the study and treatment of their psychological problems will probably continue at a rapid pace. Clinicians and public officials are not likely to underestimate their needs and importance again.

Particularly urgent is neurocognitive impairment and its devastating impact on the elderly and their families. As you have read throughout the chapter, the complexity of the brain makes neurocognitive disorders difficult to understand, diagnose, and treat. However, researchers are now making important discoveries on a regular basis. To date, this research has largely focused on the biological aspects of these disorders, but the disorders have such a powerful impact on patients and their families that psychological and sociocultural investigations are also starting to grow by leaps and bounds.

CLINICAL CHOICES

Now that you've read about disorders of aging and cognition, try the interactive case study for this chapter. See if you are able to identify Fred's symptoms and suggest a diagnosis based on his symptoms. What kind of treatment would be most effective for Fred? Go to LaunchPad to access *Clinical Choices*.

KEY TERMS

geropsychology, p. 502
delirium, p. 509
neurocognitive disorder, p. 511
major neurocognitive disorder, p. 511
mild neurocognitive disorder, p. 511
Alzheimer's disease, p. 511
senile plaques, p. 513
beta-amyloid protein, p. 513
neurofibrillary tangles, p. 513
tau protein, p. 514
early-onset Alzheimer's disease, p. 514
beta-amyloid precursor protein, p. 514
presenilin, p. 514

late-onset Alzheimer's disease, p. 514
apolipoprotein E (ApoE) gene, p. 514
ApoE-4, p. 514
acetylcholine, p. 516
glutamate, p. 516
ribonucleic acid (RNA), p. 516
calcium, p. 516
zinc, p. 516
lead, p. 516
autoimmune theory, p. 516
viral theory, p. 516
vascular neurocognitive disorder, p. 517
Pick's disease, p. 517

Creutzfeld-Jakob disease, p. 517
Huntington's disease, p. 518
Parkinson's disease, p. 518
donepezil, p. 518
rivastigmine, p. 518
galantamine, p. 518
memantine, p. 518
vitamin E, p. 518
day-care facilities, p. 520
assisted-living facilities, p. 520
discrimination, p. 522
long-term care, p. 523
health-maintenance approach, p. 524

QuickQuiz

1. What is geropsychology? What kinds of special pressures and upsets are faced by elderly persons? *pp. 502–503*

2. How common is depression among the elderly? What are the possible causes of this disorder in aged persons, and how is it treated? *pp. 503–505*

3. How prevalent are anxiety disorders among the elderly? How do theorists explain the onset of these disorders in aged persons, and how do clinicians treat them? *p. 505*

4. Describe and explain the kinds of substance abuse patterns that sometimes emerge among the elderly. *pp. 505–508*

5. What kinds of psychotic disorders may be experienced by elderly persons? *pp. 508–509*

6. What is delirium? *pp. 509–511*

7. How common are neurocognitive disorders among the elderly? Describe the clinical features and course of Alzheimer's disease. *pp. 511–514*

8. What are the possible causes of Alzheimer's disease? *pp. 513–516*

9. Can Alzheimer's disease be predicted? What kinds of interventions are applied in cases of this and other neurocognitive disorders? *pp. 516–521*

10. What issues regarding aging have raised particular concern among clinicians? *pp. 522–524*

Visit *LaunchPad*
www.macmillanhighered.com/launchpad/comerfund8e
to access the e-book, new interactive case studies, videos, activities, and LearningCurve quizzes, as well as study aids including flashcards, FAQs, and research exercises.

 Macmillan Education LaunchPad

Ed Fairburn

Law, Society, and the Mental Health Profession

Dear Jodie:
There is a definite possibility that I will be killed in my attempt to get Reagan. It is for this very reason that I am writing you this letter now. As you well know by now, I love you very much. The past seven months I have left you dozens of poems, letters and messages in the faint hope you would develop an interest in me. . . . Jodie, I would abandon this idea of getting Reagan in a second if I could only win your heart and live out the rest of my life with you, whether it be in total obscurity or whatever. I will admit to you that the reason I'm going ahead with this attempt now is because I just cannot wait any longer to impress you. I've got to do something now to make you understand in no uncertain terms that I am doing all of this for your sake. By sacrificing my freedom and possibly my life I hope to change your mind about me. This letter is being written an hour before I leave for the Hilton Hotel. Jodie, I'm asking you please to look into your heart and at least give me the chance with this historical deed to gain your respect and love. I love you forever.

John Hinckley

John W. Hinckley Jr. wrote this letter to actress Jodie Foster in March 1981. Soon after writing it, he stood waiting, pistol ready, outside the Washington Hilton Hotel. Moments later, President Ronald Reagan came out of the hotel, and the popping of pistol fire was heard. As Secret Service agents pushed Reagan into the limousine, a police officer and the president's press secretary fell to the pavement. The president had been shot, and by nightfall most of America had seen the face and heard the name of the disturbed young man from Colorado.

As you have seen throughout this book, the psychological dysfunctioning of an individual does not occur in isolation. It is influenced—sometimes caused—by societal and social factors, and it affects the lives of relatives, friends, and acquaintances. The case of John Hinckley demonstrates in powerful terms that individual dysfunction may, in some cases, also affect the well-being and rights of people the person does not know.

By the same token, clinical scientists and practitioners do not conduct their work in isolation. As they study and treat people with psychological problems, they affect and are affected by other institutions of society. We have seen, for example, how the government regulates the use of psychotropic medications, how clinicians helped carry out the government's policy of deinstitutionalization, and how clinicians have called the psychological ordeals of Vietnam, Iraq, and Afghanistan combat veterans to the attention of society.

In short, like their clients, clinical professionals operate within a complex social system. Just as we must understand the social context in which abnormal behavior occurs in order to understand the behavior, so must we understand the context in which this behavior is studied and treated. This chapter focuses on the relationship between the mental health field and three major forces in society—the *legislative/judicial system*, the *business/economic* arena, and the world of *technology*.

Law and Mental Health

Two social institutions have a particularly strong impact on the mental health profession: the legislative and judicial systems. These institutions—collectively, the *legal field*—have long been responsible for protecting both the public good and the rights of individuals. Sometimes the relationship between the legal field and the mental health field has been friendly, and those in the two fields have worked together to protect the rights and meet the needs of troubled people and of society at large. At other times they have clashed, and one field has imposed its will on the other.

This relationship has two distinct aspects. On the one hand, mental health professionals often play a role in the criminal justice system, as when they are called upon to help the courts assess the mental stability of people accused of crimes. They responded to this call in the Hinckley case, as you will see, and in thousands of other cases. This aspect of the relationship is sometimes termed *psychology in law;* that is, clinical practitioners and researchers operate within the legal system. On the other hand, there is another aspect to the relationship, called *law in psychology.* The legislative and judicial systems act upon the clinical field, regulating certain aspects of mental health care. The courts may, for example, force some people to enter treatment, even against their will. In addition, the law protects the rights of patients.

The intersections between the mental health field and the legal and judicial systems are collectively referred to as **forensic psychology** (APA, 2015). Forensic psychologists or psychiatrists (or related mental health professionals) may perform such varied activities as testifying in trials, researching the reliability of eyewitness testimony, or helping police profile the personality of a serial killer on the loose.

How Do Clinicians Influence the Criminal Justice System?

To arrive at just and appropriate punishments, the courts need to know whether defendants are *responsible* for the crimes they commit and *capable* of defending themselves in court. If not, it would be inappropriate to find defendants guilty or punish them in the usual manner. The courts have decided that in some instances people who suffer from severe *mental instability* may not be responsible for their actions or may not be able to defend themselves in court, and so should not be punished in the usual way. Although the courts make the final judgment as to mental instability, their decisions are guided to a large degree by the opinions of mental health professionals.

When people accused of crimes are judged to be mentally unstable, they are usually sent to a mental institution for treatment, a process called **criminal commitment.** Actually there are several forms of criminal commitment. In one, people are judged mentally unstable *at the time of their crimes* and so innocent of wrongdoing. They may plead **not guilty by reason of insanity (NGRI)** and bring mental health professionals into court to support their claim. When people are found not guilty on this basis, they are committed for treatment until they improve enough to be released.

In a second form of criminal commitment, people are judged mentally unstable *at the time of their trial* and so are considered unable to understand the trial procedures and defend themselves in court. They are committed for treatment until they are competent to stand trial. Once again, the testimony of mental health professionals helps determine the defendant's psychological functioning.

These judgments of mental instability have stirred many arguments. Some people consider the judgments to be loopholes in the legal system that allow criminals to escape proper punishment for wrongdoing. Others argue that a legal system simply cannot be just unless it allows

Would-be assassin Few courtroom decisions have spurred as much debate or legislative action as the jury's verdict that John Hinckley, having been captured in the act of shooting President Ronald Reagan, was not guilty by reason of insanity.

AP/Wide World Photos

for extenuating circumstances, such as mental instability. The practice of criminal commitment differs from country to country. In this chapter you will see primarily how it operates in the United States. Although the specific procedures of each country may differ, most countries grapple with the same issues and decisions that you will read about here.

Criminal Commitment and Insanity During Commission of a Crime

Consider once again the case of John Hinckley. Was he insane at the time he shot the president? If insane, should he be held responsible for his actions? On June 21, 1982, 15 months after he shot four men in the nation's capital, a jury pronounced Hinckley not guilty by reason of insanity. Hinckley thus joined Richard Lawrence, a house painter who shot at Andrew Jackson in 1835, and John Schrank, a saloonkeeper who shot former president Teddy Roosevelt in 1912, as a would-be assassin who was found not guilty by reason of insanity.

It is important to recognize that "insanity" is a *legal* term. That is, the definition of "insanity" used in criminal cases was written by legislators, not by clinicians. Defendants may have mental disorders but not necessarily qualify for a legal definition of insanity. Modern Western definitions of insanity can be traced to the murder case of Daniel M'Naghten in England in 1843. M'Naghten shot and killed Edward Drummond, the secretary to British prime minister Robert Peel, while trying to shoot Peel. Because of M'Naghten's apparent delusions of persecution, the jury found him to be not guilty by reason of insanity. The public was outraged by this decision, and their angry outcry forced the British law lords to define the insanity defense more clearly. This legal definition, known as the **M'Naghten test,** or **M'Naghten rule,** stated that having a mental disorder at the time of a crime does not by itself mean that the person was insane; the defendant also had to be *unable to know right from wrong.* The state and federal courts in the United States adopted this test as well.

In the late nineteenth century some state and federal courts in the United States, dissatisfied with the M'Naghten rule, adopted a different test—the **irresistible impulse test.** This test, which had first been used in Ohio in 1834, emphasized the inability to control one's actions. A person who committed a crime during an uncontrollable "fit of passion" was considered insane and not guilty under this test.

For years state and federal courts chose between the M'Naghten test and the irresistible impulse test to determine the sanity of criminal defendants. For a while a third test, called the **Durham test,** also became popular, but it was soon replaced in most courts. This test, based on a decision handed down by the Supreme Court in 1954 in the case of *Durham v. United States,* stated simply that people are not criminally responsible if their "unlawful act was the product of mental disease or mental defect." This test was meant to offer more flexibility in court decisions, but it proved too flexible. Insanity defenses could point to such problems as alcoholism or other forms of substance abuse and conceivably even headaches or ulcers, which were listed as psychophysiological disorders in DSM-I.

In 1955 the American Law Institute (ALI) developed a test that combined aspects of the M'Naghten, irresistible impulse, and Durham tests. The **American Law Institute test** held that people are not criminally responsible if at the time of a crime they had a mental disorder or defect that prevented them from knowing right from wrong *or* from being able to control themselves and follow the law. For a time the new test became the most widely accepted legal test of insanity. After the Hinckley verdict, however, there was a public uproar over the "liberal" ALI guidelines, and people called for tougher standards.

Partly in response to this uproar, the American Psychiatric Association recommended in 1983 that people should be found not guilty by reason of insanity *only* if they did not know right from wrong at the time of the crime; an inability to control themselves and to follow the law should no longer be sufficient grounds

▶ **forensic psychology** The branch of psychology concerned with intersections between psychological practice and research and the judicial system.

▶ **criminal commitment** A legal process by which people accused of a crime are judged mentally unstable and sent to a treatment facility.

▶ **not guilty by reason of insanity (NGRI)** A verdict stating that defendants are not guilty of a crime because they were insane at the time of the crime.

▶ **M'Naghten test** A legal standard that holds people to be insane at the time they committed a crime if, because of a mental disorder, they did not know the nature of the act or did not know right from wrong.

▶ **irresistible impulse test** A legal standard that holds people to be insane at the time they committed a crime if they were driven to do so by an uncontrollable "fit of passion."

▶ **Durham test** A legal standard that holds people to be insane at the time they committed a crime if their act was the result of a mental disorder or defect.

▶ **American Law Institute test** A legal standard that holds people to be insane at the time they committed a crime if, because of a mental disorder, they did not know right from wrong or could not resist an uncontrollable impulse to act.

BETWEEN THE LINES

In Their Words

"I think John Hinckley will be a threat the rest of his life. He is a time bomb."

U.S. Attorney, 1982

"Without doubt, [John Hinckley] is the least dangerous person on the planet."

Attorney for John Hinckley, applying for increased privileges for his client, 2003

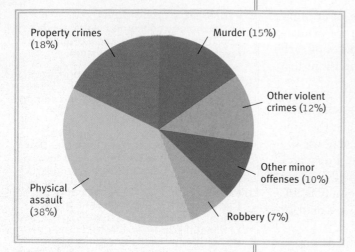

figure 16-1

Crimes for which people are found not guilty by reason of insanity (NGRI) Reviews of NGRI verdicts in a number of states show that most people who are acquitted on this basis had been charged with a violent crime. (Information from: Novak et al., 2007; APA, 2003; Steadman et al., 1993; Callahan et al., 1991.)

Pie chart labels: Property crimes (18%); Murder (15%); Other violent crimes (12%); Other minor offenses (10%); Robbery (7%); Physical assault (38%)

for a judgment of insanity. In short, the association was calling for a return to the M'Naghten test. This test now is used in all cases tried in federal courts and in about half of the state courts. The more liberal ALI standard is still used in the remaining state courts, except in Idaho, Kansas, Montana, and Utah, which have more or less done away with the insanity plea altogether.

People suffering from severe mental disorders in which confusion is a major feature may not be able to tell right from wrong or to control their behavior. It is therefore not surprising that around two-thirds of defendants who are acquitted of a crime by reason of insanity qualify for a diagnosis of schizophrenia (Almeida et al., 2010; Steadman et al., 1993). The vast majority of these acquitted defendants have a history of past hospitalization, arrest, or both. About half who successfully plead insanity are white, and 86 percent are male. Their mean age is 32 years. The crimes for which defendants are found not guilty by reason of insanity vary greatly, although approximately 65 percent are violent crimes of some sort. At least 15 percent of those acquitted are accused specifically of murder (see Figure 16-1).

WHAT CONCERNS ARE RAISED BY THE INSANITY DEFENSE? Despite the changes in the insanity tests, criticism of the insanity defense continues (MacKinnon & Fiala, 2015; Slovenko, 2011, 2004, 2002). One concern is the fundamental difference between the law and the science of human behavior. The law assumes that individuals have free will and are generally responsible for their actions. Several models of human behavior, in contrast, assume that physical or psychological forces act to determine the individual's behavior. Inevitably, then, legal definitions of insanity and responsibility will differ from those suggested by clinical research.

A second criticism points to the uncertainty of scientific knowledge about abnormal behavior. During a typical insanity defense trial, the testimony of defense clinicians conflicts with that of clinicians hired by the prosecution, and so the jury must weigh the claims of "experts" who disagree in their assessments. Some people see this lack of professional agreement as evidence that clinical knowledge in some areas may be too incomplete to be allowed to influence important legal decisions (Bartol & Bartol, 2015). Others counter that the field has made great strides—for example, developing several psychological scales to help clinicians discriminate more consistently between the sane and insane as defined by the M'Naghten standard (Pinals & Mossman, 2012; Rogers, 2008).

Even with helpful scales in hand, however, clinicians making judgments of legal insanity face a problem that is difficult to overcome: they must evaluate a defendant's state of mind during an event that took place weeks, months, or years earlier. Because mental states can and do change over time and across situations, clinicians can never be entirely certain that their assessments of mental instability at the time of the crime are accurate.

Perhaps the most common criticism of the insanity defense is that it allows dangerous criminals to escape punishment. Granted, some people who successfully plead insanity are released from treatment facilities just months after their acquittal. Yet the number of such cases is quite small (Asmar, 2014; Steadman et al., 1993; Callahan et al., 1991). According to surveys, the public dramatically overestimates the percentage of defendants who plead insanity, guessing it to be 30 to 40 percent, when in fact it is less than 1 percent. Moreover, only a minority of these defendants fake or exaggerate their psychological symptoms, and only 26 percent of those who plead insanity are actually found not guilty on this basis. In all, less than 1 of every 400 defendants in the United States is found not guilty by reason of insanity, and, in most such cases, the prosecution has agreed to the appropriateness of the plea (see *PsychWatch* on the next page).

PsychWatch

Famous Insanity Defense Cases

1977 In Michigan, Francine Hughes poured gasoline around the bed where her husband, Mickey, lay in a drunken stupor. Then she lit a match and set him on fire. At her trial she explained that he had beaten her repeatedly for 14 years and had threatened to kill her if she tried to leave him. The jury found her not guilty by reason of temporary insanity, making her into a symbol for many abused women across the nation.

1978 David "Son of Sam" Berkowitz, a serial killer in New York City, explained that a barking dog had sent him demonic messages to kill. Although two psychiatrists assessed him as psychotic, he was found guilty of his crimes. Long after his trial, he said that he had actually made up the delusions.

1979 Kenneth Bianchi, one of the pair known as the Hillside Strangler, entered a plea of not guilty by reason of insanity but was found guilty along with his cousin of sexually assaulting and murdering women in the Los Angeles area in late 1977 and early 1978. He claimed that he had multiple personalities.

1980 In December, Mark David Chapman murdered John Lennon. Chapman later explained that he had killed the rock music legend because he believed Lennon to be a "sell-out." Pleading not guilty by reason of insanity, he also described hearing the voice of God, considered himself his generation's "catcher in the rye" (from the J. D. Salinger novel), and compared himself with Moses. Chapman was convicted of murder.

1981 In an attempt to prove his love for actress Jodie Foster, John Hinckley Jr. tried to assassinate President Ronald Reagan. Hinckley was found not guilty by reason of insanity and was committed to St. Elizabeth's Hospital for the criminally insane in Washington, DC, where he remains today.

1992 Jeffrey Dahmer, a 31-year-old mass murderer in Milwaukee, was tried for

Rejecting the insanity plea James Holmes sits in a courtroom in Colorado in 2012, a few days after killing 12 moviegoers and injuring 70 others in the town of Aurora. In 2015, a jury rejected his plea of not guilty by reason of insanity, and, instead, found him guilty of murder and attempted murder.

AP Photo/Denver Post, RJ Sangosti

the killings of 15 young men. Dahmer apparently drugged some of his victims, performed crude lobotomies on them, and dismembered their bodies and stored their parts to be eaten. Despite a plea of not guilty by reason of insanity, the jury found him guilty as charged. He was beaten to death by another inmate in 1995.

1994 On June 23, 1993, 24-year-old Lorena Bobbitt cut off her husband's penis with a 12-inch kitchen knife while he slept. Her defense attorneys argued that after years of abuse by John Bobbitt, his wife suffered a brief psychotic episode and was seized by an "irresistible impulse" to cut off his penis after he came home drunk and raped her. In 1994, the jury found her not guilty by reason of temporary insanity. She was committed to a state mental hospital and released a few months later.

2003 For three weeks in October 2002, John Allen Muhammad and Lee Boyd Malvo went on a sniping spree in the

Washington, DC, area, shooting 10 people dead and wounding 3 others. Attorneys for Malvo, a teenager, argued that he had acted under the influence of the middle-aged Muhammad and that he should be found not guilty of the crimes by reason of insanity. The jury, though, found Malvo guilty of capital murder and sentenced him to life in prison.

2006 On June 20, 2001, Andrea Yates, a 36-year-old woman, drowned each of her five children in the bathtub. Yates had a history of *postpartum depression* and *postpartum psychosis:* she believed that she was the devil, that she had failed to be a good mother, and that her children were not developing correctly. She pleaded not guilty by reason of insanity. After an initial verdict of guilty was overturned, Yates was found not guilty by reason of insanity in 2006 and sent to a mental health facility for treatment.

2011 In 2002, Brian David Mitchell abducted a 14-year-old teenager named Elizabeth Smart from her home and held her until she was rescued nine months later. After years of trial delays, Mitchell was brought to trial for the crime of kidnapping. He pleaded not guilty by reason of insanity, saying that he was acting out delusions ("revelations from God") when he committed this crime. After deliberating for just five hours, the jury found him guilty of kidnapping. He was sentenced to life in prison without parole in 2011.

2012 On July 20, 2012, James Holmes, a 25-year-old neuroscience doctoral student, entered a cinema in Aurora, Colorado, and opened fire on the moviegoers, killing 12 and injuring 70. In the months after his arrest and incarceration, Holmes, who had no prior criminal record, tried to commit suicide three times. Although Holmes pleaded not guilty by reason of insanity, a jury found him guilty of multiple counts of murder and attempted murder in 2015. He was sentenced to life in prison without parole.

"Effectively misleading psychopath"
In 2002 Brian David Mitchell abducted a 14-year-old teenager named Elizabeth Smart at knifepoint from her home and held her until she was rescued nine months later. For seven years following his capture, Mitchell was declared incompetent to stand trial. Finally, in 2010, a federal court judge called him an "effectively misleading psychopath" and scheduled him for trial. Mitchell was found guilty of kidnapping and sentenced to life in prison, despite his not guilty by reason of insanity plea.

During most of U.S. history, a successful insanity plea amounted to the equivalent of a long-term prison sentence. In fact, treatment in a mental hospital often resulted in a longer period of confinement than a verdict of guilty would have brought (Bartol & Bartol, 2015). Because hospitalization resulted in little if any improvement, clinicians were reluctant to predict that the offenders would not repeat their crimes.

Today, however, offenders are being released from mental hospitals earlier and earlier. This trend is the result of the increasing effectiveness of drug therapy and other treatments in institutions, the growing reaction against extended institutionalization, and more emphasis on patients' rights (Slovenko, 2011, 2009, 2004). In 1992, in the case of *Foucha v. Louisiana*, the U.S. Supreme Court clarified that the *only* acceptable basis for determining the release of hospitalized offenders is whether or not they are still "insane"; they cannot be kept indefinitely in mental hospitals solely because they are dangerous. Some states are able to maintain control over offenders even after their release from hospitals. The states may insist on community treatment, monitor the patients closely, and rehospitalize them if necessary (Swanson & Swartz, 2014).

> After patients have been criminally committed to institutions, why might clinicians be hesitant to later declare them unlikely to commit the same crime again?

WHAT OTHER VERDICTS ARE AVAILABLE? Over the past four decades, at least 20 states have added another verdict option—**guilty but mentally ill.** Defendants who receive this verdict are found to have had a mental illness at the time of their crime, but the illness was not fully related to or responsible for the crime. The option of guilty but mentally ill enables jurors to convict a person they view as dangerous while also suggesting that the individual receive needed treatment. Defendants found to be guilty but mentally ill are given a prison term with the added recommendation that they also undergo treatment if necessary.

After initial enthusiasm for this verdict option, legal and clinical theorists have increasingly found it unsatisfactory. According to research, it has not reduced the number of not guilty by reason of insanity verdicts, and it often confuses jurors (Bartol & Bartol, 2015). In addition, as critics point out, appropriate mental health care is supposed to be available to all prisoners anyway, regardless of the verdict. That is, the verdict of guilty but mentally ill may differ from a guilty verdict in name only.

Some states allow still another kind of defense, *guilty with diminished capacity,* in which a defendant's mental dysfunctioning is viewed as an extenuating circumstance that the court should take into consideration in determining the precise crime of which he or she is guilty (Slovenko, 2011; Leong, 2000). The defense lawyer argues that because of mental dysfunctioning, the defendant could not have *intended* to commit a particular crime. The person can then be found guilty of a lesser crime—of manslaughter (unlawful killing without intent), say, instead of murder in the first degree (planned murder). The famous case of Dan White, who shot and killed Mayor George Moscone and City Supervisor Harvey Milk of San Francisco in 1978, illustrates the use of this verdict.

▶ **guilty but mentally ill** A verdict stating that defendants are guilty of committing a crime but are also suffering from a mental illness that should be treated during their imprisonment.

Defense attorney Douglas Schmidt argued that a patriotic, civic-minded man like Dan White—high school athlete, decorated war veteran, former fireman, policeman, and city supervisor—could not possibly have committed such an act unless something had snapped inside him. The brutal nature of the two final shots to each man's head only proved that White had lost his wits. White was not fully responsible for his actions because he suffered from "diminished capacity." Although White killed Mayor George Moscone and Supervisor Harvey Milk, he had not planned his

Bill Nation

actions. On the day of the shootings, White was mentally incapable of planning to kill, or even of wanting to do such a thing.

Well known in forensic psychiatry circles, Martin Blinder, professor of law and psychiatry at the University of California's Hastings Law School in San Francisco, brought a good measure of academic prestige to White's defense. White had been, Blinder explained to the jury, "gorging himself on junk food: Twinkies, Coca-Cola. . . . The more he consumed, the worse he'd feel and he'd respond to his ever-growing depression by consuming ever more junk food." Schmidt later asked Blinder if he could elaborate on this. "Perhaps if it were not for the ingestion of this junk food," Blinder responded, "I would suspect that these homicides would not have taken place." From that moment on, Blinder became known as the author of the Twinkie defense. . . .

Dan White was convicted only of voluntary manslaughter, and was sentenced to seven years, eight months. (He was released on parole January 6, 1984.) Psychiatric testimony convinced the jury that White did not wish to kill George Moscone or Harvey Milk.

The angry crowd that responded to the verdict by marching, shouting, trashing City Hall, and burning police cars was in good part homosexual. Gay supervisor Harvey Milk had worked well for their cause, and his loss was a serious setback for human rights in San Francisco. Yet it was not only members of the gay community who were appalled at the outcome. Most San Franciscans shared their feelings of outrage.

(Coleman, 1984, pp. 65–70)

Because of possible miscarriages of justice, many legal experts have argued against the "diminished capacity" defense. A number of states have even eliminated it, including California shortly after the Dan White verdict (Gado, 2008).

WHAT ARE SEX-OFFENDER STATUTES? Since 1937, when Michigan passed the first "sexual psychopath" law, a number of states have placed sex offenders in a special legal category (Perillo et al., 2014; Ewing, 2011). These states believe that some of those who are repeatedly found guilty of sex crimes have a mental disorder, so the states categorize them as *mentally disordered sex offenders*.

▶ **mental incompetence** A state of mental instability that leaves defendants unable to understand the legal charges and proceedings they are facing and unable to prepare an adequate defense with their attorney.

People classified in this way are convicted of a criminal offense and are thus judged to be responsible for their actions. Nevertheless, mentally disordered sex offenders are sent to a mental health facility instead of a prison. In part, such laws reflect a belief held by many legislators that such sex offenders are psychologically disturbed. On a practical level, the laws help protect sex offenders from the physical abuse that they often receive in prison society.

Over the past two decades, however, most states have been changing or abolishing their mentally disordered sex offender laws, and at this point only a handful still have them. There are several reasons for this trend. First, the state laws often require that in order to be classified as a mentally disordered sex offender, the person must be a good candidate for treatment, a judgment that is difficult for clinicians to make for this population (Marshall et al., 2011). Second, there is evidence that racial bias often affects the use of the mentally disordered sex offender classification. From a defendant's perspective, this classification is considered an attractive alternative to imprisonment—an alternative available to white Americans much more often than to members of racial minority groups. White Americans are twice as likely as African Americans or Hispanic Americans who have been convicted of similar crimes to be granted mentally disordered sex offender status.

But perhaps the primary reason that mentally disordered sex offender laws have lost favor is that state legislatures and courts are now less concerned than they used to be about the rights and needs of sex offenders, given the growing number of sex crimes taking place across the country (Laws & Ward, 2011), particularly ones in which children are victims. In fact, in response to public outrage over the high number of sex crimes, 21 states and the federal government have instead passed *sexually violent predator* laws (or *sexually dangerous persons* laws). These new laws call for certain sex offenders who have been convicted of sex crimes and have served their sentence in prison to be removed from prison before their release and committed involuntarily to a mental hospital for treatment if a court judges them likely to engage in further "predatory acts of sexual violence" as a result of "mental abnormality" or "personality disorder" (Perillo et al., 2014; Miller, 2010). That is, in contrast to the mentally disordered sex offender laws, which call for sex offenders to receive treatment *instead* of imprisonment, the sexually violent predator laws require certain sex offenders to receive imprisonment and then, *in addition,* be committed for a period of involuntary treatment. The constitutionality of the sexually violent predator laws was upheld by the Supreme Court in the 1997 case of *Kansas v. Hendricks* by a 5-to-4 margin.

Criminal Commitment and Incompetence to Stand Trial Regardless of their state of mind at the time of a crime, defendants may be judged to be **mentally incompetent** to stand trial. The competence requirement is meant to ensure that defendants understand the charges they are facing and can work with their lawyers to prepare and conduct an adequate defense (Ragatz et al., 2014; Reisner et al., 2013). This minimum standard of competence was specified by the Supreme Court in the case of *Dusky v. United States* (1960).

The issue of competence is most often raised by the defendant's attorney, although prosecutors, arresting police officers, and even the judge may raise it as well (Reisner et al., 2013). When the issue of competence is raised, the judge orders a psychological evaluation, usually on an inpatient basis (see Table 16-1). As many as 60,000 competency evaluations are conducted in the United States each year (Bartol & Bartol, 2015). Approximately 20 percent of defendants who receive such an evaluation are found to be incompetent to stand trial. If the court decides that the defendant is incompetent, he or she is typically assigned to a mental health facility until competent to stand trial.

A famous case of incompetence to stand trial is that of Jared Lee Loughner. On January 8, 2011, Loughner went to a political gathering at a shopping center

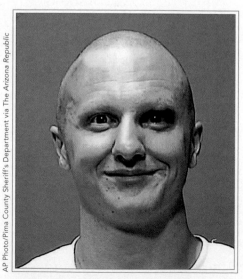

AP Photo/Pima County Sheriff's Department via The Arizona Republic

Incompetent to stand trial Jared Loughner, shown here in a police photo taken on the day of his shooting rampage in 2011 in Tucson, Arizona. For 18 months following his crime, Loughner was ruled incompetent to stand trial.

table: 16-1

Multicultural Issues: Race and Forensic Psychology

- Psychologically disturbed people from racial minority groups are more likely than disturbed white Americans to be sent to prison, as opposed to mental health facilities.

- Among defendants evaluated for competence to stand trial, those from racial minority groups are more likely than white American defendants to be referred for *inpatient* evaluations.

- When nonwhite and white defendants are evaluated for competence to stand trial, the defendants from racial minority groups are more likely to be found incompetent to stand trial.

- In New York State, 42 percent of all people ordered into *involuntary outpatient commitment* are African American, 34 percent are white American, and 21 percent are Hispanic American. In contrast, these three groups comprise, respectively, 17 percent, 61 percent, and 16 percent of New York's general population.

(Information from: Haroules, 2007; Pinals et al., 2004; Grekin et al., 1994; Arvanites, 1989)

in Tucson, Arizona, and opened fire on 20 people. Six were killed and 14 injured, including U.S. representative Gabrielle Giffords. Giffords, the apparent target of the attack, survived, although she was shot in the head. After Loughner underwent five weeks of psychiatric assessment, a judge ruled that he was incompetent to stand trial. It was not until 18 months later, after extended treatment with antipsychotic drugs, that Loughner was ruled competent to stand trial. In November 2012, he pleaded guilty to murder and was sentenced to life imprisonment.

Many more cases of criminal commitment result from decisions of mental incompetence than from verdicts of not guilty by reason of insanity (Roesch et al., 2010). However, the majority of criminals currently institutionalized for psychological treatment in the United States are not from either of these two groups. Rather, they are convicted inmates whose psychological problems have led prison officials to decide they need treatment, either in mental health units within the prison or in mental hospitals (Metzner & Dvoskin, 2010) (see Figure 16-2).

It is possible that an innocent defendant, ruled incompetent to stand trial, could spend years in a mental health facility with no opportunity to disprove the criminal accusations against him or her. Some defendants have, in fact, served longer "sentences" in mental health facilities awaiting a ruling of competence than they would have served in prison had they been convicted. Such a possibility was reduced when the Supreme Court ruled, in the case of *Jackson v. Indiana* (1972), that an incompetent defendant cannot be indefinitely committed. After a reasonable amount of time, he or she should either be found competent and tried, set free, or transferred to a mental health facility under *civil* commitment procedures.

Until the early 1970s, most states required that mentally incompetent defendants be committed to maximum security institutions for the "criminally insane." Under current law, however, the courts have more flexibility. In fact, when the charges are relatively minor, such defendants are often treated on an outpatient basis, an arrangement often called *jail diversion* because the disturbed person is "diverted" from jail to the community for mental health care (Hernandez, 2014).

figure 16-2

Prison and mental health According to studies conducted in several Western countries, psychological disorders are much more prevalent in prison populations than in the general population. For example, schizophrenia is four times more common and personality disorders (particularly antisocial personality disorder) are five times more common among prisoners than among nonprisoners. (Information from: Andreoli et al., 2014; Butler et al., 2006; Fazel & Danesh, 2002.)

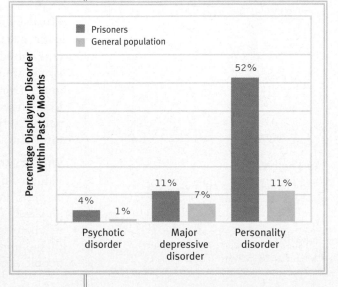

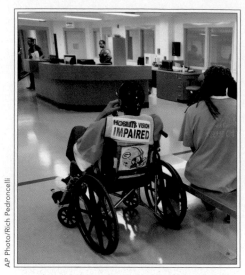

"Outpatient" care Prison inmates await treatment at a mental health treatment facility in California. The majority of those criminally committed for psychological treatment in the United States are prisoners who develop psychological disorders that have little or nothing to do with the crimes that led to their incarceration.

AP Photo/Rich Pedroncelli

➤ *Summing Up*

HOW DO CLINICIANS INFLUENCE THE CRIMINAL JUSTICE SYSTEM? One of the ways in which the mental health profession interacts with the legislative and judicial systems is that clinicians may help assess the mental stability of people accused of crimes. Evaluations by clinicians may help judges and juries decide whether defendants are responsible for crimes or capable of defending themselves in court.

If defendants are judged to have been mentally unstable at the time they committed a crime, they may be found not guilty by reason of insanity and placed in a treatment facility rather than a prison. In federal courts and about half the state courts, insanity is judged in accordance with the M'Naghten test. Other states use the broader American Law Institute test.

The insanity defense has been criticized on several grounds, and some states have added an additional option, guilty but mentally ill. Another verdict option is guilty with diminished capacity. A related category consists of convicted sex offenders, who are considered in some states to have a mental disorder and are therefore assigned to treatment in a mental health facility.

Regardless of their state of mind at the time of the crime, defendants may be found mentally incompetent to stand trial, that is, incapable of fully understanding the charges or legal proceedings that confront them. These defendants are typically sent to a mental hospital until they are competent to stand trial.

How Do the Legislative and Judicial Systems Influence Mental Health Care?

Just as clinical science and practice have influenced the legal system, so the legal system has had a major impact on clinical practice. First, courts and legislatures have developed the process of **civil commitment,** which allows certain people to be forced into mental health treatment. Although many people who show signs of mental disturbance seek treatment voluntarily, a large number are not aware of their problems or are simply not interested in undergoing therapy. For such people, civil commitment procedures may be put into action.

Second, the legal system, on behalf of the state, has taken on the responsibility of protecting patients' rights during treatment. This protection extends not only to patients who have been involuntarily committed but also to those who seek treatment voluntarily, even on an outpatient basis.

Civil Commitment Every year in the United States, large numbers of people with mental disorders are involuntarily committed to treatment. Typically they are committed to *mental institutions,* but 45 states also have some form of *outpatient* civil commitment laws that allow patients to be forced into community treatment programs (Morrissey et al., 2014; Swanson & Swartz, 2014). Civil commitments have long caused considerable debate. In some ways the law provides more protection for people suspected of being criminals than for people suspected of being psychotic (Strachan, 2008; Burton, 1990).

WHY COMMIT? Generally our legal system permits involuntary commitment of individuals when they are considered to be *in need of treatment* and *dangerous to themselves or others.* People may be dangerous to themselves if they are suicidal or if they act recklessly (for example, drinking a drain cleaner to prove that they are immune to its chemicals). They may be dangerous to others if they seek to harm them or if they unintentionally place others at risk. The state's authority to commit disturbed people rests on its duties to protect the interests of the individual and of society.

AFP/AFP/Getty Images

Dangerous to oneself The public often thinks that the term "dangerous to oneself" refers exclusively to those who are suicidal. There are, however, other ways that people may pose a danger to themselves, be in need of treatment, and be subject to civil commitment. This sequence of photos shows a man being attacked by a lion at the zoo after he crossed a barbed wire fence to "preach" to two of the animals.

WHAT ARE THE PROCEDURES FOR CIVIL COMMITMENT? Civil commitment laws vary from state to state. Some basic procedures, however, are common to most of these laws. Often family members begin commitment proceedings. In response to a son's psychotic behavior and repeated assaults on other people, for example, his parents may try to persuade him to seek admission to a mental institution. If the son refuses, the parents may go to court and seek an involuntary commitment order. If the son is a minor, the process is simple. The Supreme Court has ruled that a hearing is not necessary in such cases, as long as a qualified mental health professional considers commitment necessary. If the son is an adult, however, the process is more involved. The court usually will order a mental examination and allow the person to contest the commitment in court, often represented by a lawyer.

The Supreme Court has ruled that before an individual can be committed, there must be "clear and convincing" proof that he or she is mentally ill and has met the state's criteria for involuntary commitment. The ruling does not suggest what criteria should be used. That matter is still left to each state. But, whatever the state's criteria, clinicians must offer clear and convincing proof that the person meets those criteria. When is proof clear and convincing, according to the court? When it provides 75 percent certainty that the criteria of commitment have been met. This is far less than the near-total certainty ("beyond a reasonable doubt") required to convict people of committing a crime.

EMERGENCY COMMITMENT Many situations require immediate action; no one can wait for commitment proceedings when a life is at stake. Consider, for example, an emergency patient who is suicidal or hearing voices demanding hostile actions against others. He or she may need immediate treatment and round-the-clock supervision. If treatment could not be given in such situations without the patient's full consent, the consequences could be tragic.

Therefore, many states give clinicians the right to certify that certain patients need temporary commitment and medication. In past years, these states required certification by two *physicians* (not necessarily psychiatrists in some of the states). Today states may allow certification by other mental health professionals as well. The clinicians must declare that the state of mind of the patient makes them dangerous to themselves or others. By tradition, the certifications are often referred to

▶ **civil commitment** A legal process by which a person can be forced to undergo mental health treatment.

Failure to predict A school surveillance camera shows Dylan Klebold and Eric Harris in the midst of their killing rampage at Columbine High School in Littleton, Colorado, in 1999. Although the teenagers had built a violent Web site, threatened other students, had problems with the law, and, in the case of one of the boys, received treatment for psychological problems, professionals were not able to predict or prevent their violent behavior.

as *two-physician certificates,* or *2 PCs.* The length of such emergency commitments varies from state to state, but three days is often the limit. Should clinicians come to believe that a longer stay is necessary, formal commitment proceedings may be initiated during the period of emergency commitment.

WHO IS DANGEROUS? In the past, people with mental disorders were actually less likely than others to commit violent or dangerous acts. This low rate of violence was apparently related to the fact that so many such people lived in institutions. As a result of deinstitutionalization, however, hundreds of thousands of people with severe disturbances now live in the community, and many of them receive little, if any, treatment. Some are indeed dangerous to themselves or others.

Although approximately 90 percent of people with mental disorders are in no way violent or dangerous, studies now suggest at least a small relationship between severe mental disorders and violent behavior (Glied & Frank, 2014; Palijan et al., 2010). The disorders with the strongest relationships to violence are severe substance use disorder, impulse control disorder, antisocial personality disorder, and psychotic disorders (Ten Have et al., 2014; Volavka, 2013). Of these, substance use disorder appears to be the single most influential factor. For example, schizophrenia compounded by substance use disorder has a stronger relationship to violence than schizophrenia alone does.

A judgment of *dangerousness* is often required for involuntary civil commitment. But can mental health professionals accurately predict who will commit violent acts? Research suggests that psychiatrists and psychologists are wrong more often than right when they make *long-term* predictions of violence (Pistone, 2013; Mills et al., 2011; Palijan et al., 2010). Most often they overestimate the likelihood that a patient will eventually be violent. Their *short-term* predictions—that is, predictions of imminent violence—tend to be more accurate (Stanislaus, 2013; Otto & Douglas, 2010). Researchers are now working, with some success, to develop new assessment techniques that use statistical approaches and are more objective in their predictions of dangerousness than are the subjective judgments of clinicians (Pinals & Mossman, 2012).

WHAT ARE THE PROBLEMS WITH CIVIL COMMITMENT? Civil commitment has been criticized on several grounds (Evans & Salekin, 2014; Falzer, 2011; Winick, 2008). First is the difficulty of assessing a person's dangerousness. If judgments of dangerousness are often inaccurate, how can one justify using them to deprive people of liberty? Second, the legal definitions of "mental illness" and "dangerousness" are vague. The terms may be defined so broadly that they could be applied to almost anyone an evaluator views as undesirable. Indeed, many civil libertarians worry about involuntary commitment being used to control people, as was done in the former Soviet Union and now seems to be taking place in China, where mental hospitals house people with unpopular political views. A third problem is the sometimes questionable therapeutic value of civil commitment. Research suggests that many people committed involuntarily do not respond well to therapy.

TRENDS IN CIVIL COMMITMENT The flexibility of the involuntary commitment laws probably reached a peak in 1962. That year, in the case of *Robinson v. California,* the Supreme Court ruled that imprisoning people who suffered from drug addiction might violate the Constitution's ban on cruel and unusual punishment, and it recommended involuntary civil commitment to a mental hospital as a more reasonable action. This ruling encouraged the civil commitment of many kinds of "social deviants," and many such individuals found it difficult to obtain release from the hospitals to which they were committed.

> **How are people who have been institutionalized viewed and treated by other people in society today?**

During the late 1960s and early 1970s, reporters, novelists, civil libertarians, and others spoke out against the ease with which so many people were being unjustifiably committed to mental hospitals. As the public became more aware of these issues, state legislatures started to pass stricter standards about involuntary commitment (Pekkanen, 2007, 2002). Some states, for example, spelled out specific types of behavior that a person had to show before he or she could be determined to be dangerous. Rates of involuntary commitment then declined and release rates rose. Fewer people are institutionalized through civil commitment procedures today than in the past.

> ▶ **right to treatment** The legal right of patients, particularly those who are involuntarily committed, to receive adequate treatment.

Protecting Patients' Rights Over the past two decades, court decisions and state and federal laws have significantly expanded the rights of patients with mental disorders, in particular the *right to treatment* and the *right to refuse treatment* (Lepping & Raveesh, 2014).

HOW IS THE RIGHT TO TREATMENT PROTECTED? When people are committed to mental institutions and do not receive treatment, the institutions become, in effect, prisons for the unconvicted. To many patients in the late 1960s and the 1970s, large state mental institutions were just that, and some patients and their attorneys began to demand that the state honor their **right to treatment.** In the landmark case of *Wyatt v. Stickney,* a suit on behalf of institutionalized patients in Alabama in 1972, a federal court ruled that the state was constitutionally obligated to provide "adequate treatment" to all people who had been committed involuntarily. Because conditions in the state's hospitals were so terrible, the judge laid out goals that state officials had to meet, including more therapists, better living conditions, more privacy, more social interactions and physical exercise, and a more proper use of physical restraint and medication. Other states have since adopted many of these standards.

Another important decision was handed down in 1975 by the Supreme Court in the case of *O'Connor v. Donaldson.* After being held in a Florida mental institution for more than 14 years, Kenneth Donaldson sued for release. He argued that he and his fellow patients were receiving poor treatment, were being largely ignored by the staff, and were allowed little personal freedom. The Supreme Court ruled in his favor, fined the hospital's superintendent, and said that such institutions must review patients' cases periodically. The justices also ruled that the state cannot continue to institutionalize people against their will if they are not dangerous and are capable of surviving on their own or with the willing help of responsible family members or friends.

To help protect the rights of patients, Congress passed the Protection and Advocacy for Mentally Ill Individuals Act in 1986. This law set up *protection and advocacy systems* in all states and gave public advocates who worked for patients the power to investigate possible abuse and neglect and to correct those problems legally.

In recent years, public advocates have argued that the right to treatment also should be extended to the tens of thousands of people with severe mental disorders who are repeatedly released from hospitals into ill-equipped communities. Many such people have no place to go and are unable to care for themselves, often winding up homeless or in prisons (Ogden, 2014; Althouse, 2010). A number of advocates are now suing

Hospital neglect While some countries increasingly have attended to the rights of patients in recent decades, including their rights to treatment and to humane treatment conditions, other countries, especially poor ones, have lagged behind. This scene inside a government-run center for mental patients in Jakarta, Indonesia, underscores this point.

© John Stanmeyer/VII/Corbis

Neemah Aaron/AP Photo

Executing the mentally ill Charles Singleton, a man who killed a store clerk in Arkansas, was sentenced to death in 1979, and then developed schizophrenia at some point after the trial. Inasmuch as the United States does not allow executions if a person cannot understand why he or she is being executed, state officials wanted Singleton to take medications to clear up his psychosis. After years of legal appeals, the U.S. Supreme Court ruled in 2003 that Singleton was by then taking medications voluntarily, and he was executed by lethal injection in 2004.

▶**right to refuse treatment** The legal right of patients to refuse certain forms of treatment.

▶**malpractice suit** A lawsuit charging a therapist with improper conduct in the course of treatment.

federal and state agencies throughout the country, demanding that they fulfill the promises of the community mental health movement (see Chapter 12).

HOW IS THE RIGHT TO REFUSE TREATMENT PROTECTED? During the past two decades, the courts have also decided that patients, particularly those in institutions, have the **right to refuse treatment** (Ford & Rotter, 2014; Perlin, 2004, 2000). Most of the right-to-refuse-treatment rulings center on *biological treatments*. These treatments are easier to impose on patients without their cooperation than psychotherapy, and they often are more hazardous. For example, state rulings have consistently granted patients the right to refuse *psychosurgery*, the most irreversible form of physical treatment—and often the most dangerous.

Some states have also acknowledged a patient's right to refuse *electroconvulsive therapy (ECT)*, the treatment used in many cases of severe depression (see Chapter 6). However, the right-to-refuse issue is more complex with regard to ECT than to psychosurgery. ECT is very effective for many people with severe depression, yet it can cause great upset and can also be misused. Today many states grant patients— particularly voluntary patients—the right to refuse ECT. Usually a patient must be informed fully about the nature of the treatment and must give written consent to it. A number of states continue to permit ECT to be forced on committed patients, whereas others require the consent of a close relative or other third party in such cases.

In the past, patients did not have the right to refuse *psychotropic medications*. As you have read, however, many psychotropic drugs are very powerful, and some produce effects that are unwanted and dangerous. As these harmful effects have become more apparent, some states have granted patients the right to refuse medication. Typically, these states require physicians to explain the purpose of the medication to patients and obtain their written consent. If a patient's refusal is considered incompetent, dangerous, or irrational, the state may allow it to be overturned by an independent psychiatrist, medical committee, or local court. However, the refusing patient is supported in this process by a lawyer or other patient advocate.

WHAT OTHER RIGHTS DO PATIENTS HAVE? Court decisions have protected still other patient rights over the past several decades. Patients who perform work in mental institutions, particularly private institutions, are now guaranteed at least a *minimum wage*. In addition, according to a court decision, patients released from state mental hospitals have a right to *aftercare* and to an *appropriate community residence*, such as a group home. And more generally, people with psychological disorders should receive treatment in the *least restrictive facility* available. If an inpatient program at a community mental health center is available and appropriate, for example, then that is the facility to which they should be assigned, not a mental hospital.

THE "RIGHTS" DEBATE Certainly, people with psychological disorders have civil rights that must be protected at all times. However, many clinicians express concern that the patients' rights rulings and laws may unintentionally deprive these patients of opportunities for recovery. Consider the right to refuse medication. If medications can help a patient with a severe mental disorder to recover, doesn't the patient have the right to that recovery? If confusion causes the patient to refuse medication, can clinicians in good conscience delay medication while legal channels are cleared?

Despite such legitimate concerns, keep in mind that the clinical field has not always done an effective job of protecting patients' rights. Over the years, many patients have been overmedicated and received improper treatments. Furthermore, one must ask whether the field's present state of knowledge justifies clinicians' overriding of patients' rights. Can clinicians confidently say that a given treatment will help a patient? Can they predict when a treatment will have harmful effects? Since clinicians themselves often disagree, it seems appropriate for patients, their advocates, and outside evaluators to also play key roles in decision making.

➤ *Summing Up*

HOW DOES THE LEGAL SYSTEM INFLUENCE MENTAL HEALTH CARE? Courts may be called upon to commit noncriminals to mental hospitals for treatment, a process called civil commitment. Society allows such involuntary commitment for people considered to be in need of treatment and dangerous to themselves or others. Laws and criteria governing civil commitment procedures vary from state to state, but the Supreme Court has ruled that, whatever the state's criteria, clinicians must offer clear and convincing evidence that the individuals are mentally ill and meet the state's criteria for civil commitment.

The courts and legislatures also affect the mental health profession by specifying legal rights to which patients are entitled. The rights that have received the most attention are the right to treatment and the right to refuse treatment.

In What Other Ways Do the Clinical and Legal Fields Interact?

Mental health and legal professionals may influence each other's work in other ways as well. During the past 25 years, their paths have crossed in four key areas: *malpractice suits, professional boundaries, jury selection,* and *psychological research of legal topics.*

Malpractice Suits

The number of **malpractice suits** against therapists has risen sharply in recent years. Claims have been made against clinicians in response to a patient's attempted suicide, sexual activity with a patient, failure to obtain informed consent for a treatment, negligent drug therapy, omission of drug therapy that would speed improvement, improper termination of treatment, and wrongful commitment (Sher, 2015; Reich & Schatzberg, 2014). Studies suggest that malpractice suits, or the fear of them, can have significant effects on clinical decisions and practice, for better or for worse (Appelbaum, 2011; Feldman et al., 2005).

Professional Boundaries

Over the past two decades, the legislative and judicial systems have helped to change the *boundaries* that distinguish one clinical profession from another. In particular, they have given more authority to psychologists and blurred the lines that once separated psychiatry from psychology. A growing number of states, for example, are ruling that psychologists can admit patients to the state's hospitals, a power previously held only by psychiatrists.

> **Most psychiatrists oppose the idea of prescription rights for psychologists. Why do some psychologists also oppose this idea?**

In 1991, with the blessing of Congress, the Department of Defense (DOD) started to reconsider the biggest difference of all between the practices of psychiatrists and psychologists—the authority to prescribe drugs, a role previously denied to psychologists. The DOD set up a trial training program for Army psychologists. Given the apparent success of this trial program, the American Psychological Association later recommended that all psychologists be allowed to attend a special educational program in prescription services and receive certification to prescribe medications if they pass. New Mexico, Louisiana, Illinois, and the U.S. territory of Guam now do grant prescription privileges to psychologists who receive special pharmacology training (APA, 2014).

Jury Selection

During the past 30 years, more and more lawyers have turned to clinicians for psychological advice in conducting trials (Crouter, 2015; Hope, 2010). A new breed of clinical specialists, known as "jury specialists," has evolved. They advise lawyers about which potential jurors are likely to favor their side and which

Fear of litigation Psychologists are not the only ones who fear litigation for providing help to others. It is becoming a worldwide concern. A woman who fell off this escalator at a department store in Shanghai, China, was left unattended despite the presence of numerous onlookers. The reason? Fear of litigation. Incidents of good Samaritans becoming victims of litigation have become more frequent in China and other countries.

Zhou Junxiang/Imaginechina via AP Images

strategies are likely to win jurors' support during trials. The jury specialists make their suggestions on the basis of surveys, interviews, analyses of jurors' backgrounds and attitudes, and laboratory enactments of upcoming trials. However, it is not clear that a clinician's advice is more valid than a lawyer's instincts or that the judgments of either are particularly accurate.

Psychological Research of Legal Topics

Psychologists have sometimes conducted studies and developed expertise on topics of great importance to the criminal justice system. In turn, these studies influence how the system carries out its work. Psychological investigations of two topics, *eyewitness testimony* and *patterns of criminality,* have gained particular attention.

EYEWITNESS TESTIMONY In criminal cases, testimony by eyewitnesses is extremely influential. It often determines whether a defendant will be found guilty or not guilty. But how accurate is eyewitness testimony? This question has become urgent, as a troubling number of prisoners (many on death row) have had their convictions overturned after DNA evidence revealed that they could not have committed the crimes of which they had been convicted. It turns out that more than 75 percent of such wrongful convictions were based in large part on mistaken eyewitness testimony (Wise et al., 2014).

Most eyewitnesses undoubtedly try to tell the truth about what or who they saw. Yet research indicates that eyewitness testimony can be highly unreliable, partly because most crimes are unexpected and fleeting and therefore not the sort of events remembered well (Houston et al., 2013). During the crime, for example, lighting may be poor or other distractions may be present. Witnesses may have had other things on their minds, such as concern for their own safety or that of bystanders. Such concerns may greatly impair later memory.

In laboratory studies, researchers have found it easy to fool research participants who are trying to recall the details of an observed event simply by introducing misinformation (Morgan et al., 2013; Laney & Loftus, 2010). After a suggestive description by the researcher, stop signs can be transformed into yield signs, white cars into blue ones, and Mickey Mouse into Minnie Mouse (Pickel, 2004; Loftus, 2003). In addition, laboratory studies indicate that persons who are highly suggestible have the poorest recall of observed events (Liebman et al., 2002).

As for identifying actual perpetrators, research has found that accuracy is heavily influenced by the method used in identification (Bartol & Bartol, 2015; Garrett, 2011). The traditional police lineup, for example, is not always a highly reliable technique, and the errors that witnesses make when looking at lineups tend to stick (Wells et al., 2015, 2011; Wells, 2008). Researchers have also learned that witnesses' confidence is not necessarily related to accuracy (Wise et al., 2014; Ghetti et al., 2004). Witnesses who are "absolutely certain" may be no more correct in their recollections than those who are only "fairly sure." Yet the degree of a witness's confidence often influences whether jurors believe his or her testimony.

Psychological investigations into the memories of eyewitnesses have not yet undone the judicial system's reliance on or respect for those witnesses' testimony. Nor should it. The distance between laboratory studies and real-life events is often great, and the findings from such studies must be applied with care. Still, eyewitness research has begun to make an impact. Studies of hypnosis and of its ability to create false memories, for example, have led most states to prohibit eyewitnesses from testifying about events or details if their recall of the events was initially helped by hypnosis.

PATTERNS OF CRIMINALITY A growing number of television shows, movies, and books suggest that clinicians often play a major role in criminal investigations by providing police with *psychological profiles* of perpetrators—"He's probably white, in his 30s, has a history of animal torture, has few friends, and is subject to emotional outbursts." The study of criminal behavior patterns and of profiling has increased

Chuck Burton/AP Photo

Eyewitness error Psychological research indicates that eyewitness testimony is often invalid. Here a woman talks to the man whom she had identified as her rapist back in 1984. DNA testing eventually proved that a different person had raped her, and the incorrectly identified man was released — after having served 11 years of a life sentence in prison.

///// BETWEEN THE LINES /////

Popular TV Series Featuring Psychological Profilers

Criminal Minds

NCIS

The Mentalist

Law and Order: Special Victims Unit

Law and Order: Criminal Intent

in recent years; however, it is not nearly as revealing or influential as the media and the arts would have us believe (Kocsis & Palermo, 2013; Salfati, 2011).

On the positive side, researchers have gathered information about the psychological features of various criminals, and they have indeed found that perpetrators of particular kinds of crimes—serial murder or serial sexual assault, for example—frequently share a number of traits and background features (see *PsychWatch*). But while such traits are *often* present, they are not *always* present, and so applying profile information to a particular crime can be wrong and misleading (Hickey, 2015;

PsychWatch

Serial Murderers: Madness or Badness?

n late 2001, a number of anthrax-tainted letters were mailed to people throughout eastern parts of the United States, leading to five deaths and to severe illness in 13 other people. After years of work, in 2008 the FBI identified a biodefense researcher named Bruce Ivins as the killer. With a murder indictment imminent, Ivins committed suicide on July 29, 2008. It appeared that the FBI had finally found the perpetrator of these terrible deeds.

Although Ivins' suicide left behind unanswered questions, the FBI has concluded that this troubled man was indeed the anthrax killer. He appears to have been one of a growing list of serial killers who have fascinated and horrified Americans over the years: Theodore Kaczynski ("Unabomber"), Ted Bundy, David Berkowitz ("Son of Sam"), Albert DeSalvo, John Wayne Gacy, Jeffrey Dahmer, John Allen Muhammad, Lee Boyd Malvo, Dennis Rader ("BTK killer"), and more.

The FBI estimates that there are between 35 and 100 serial killers at large in the United States at any given time (FBI, 2014). Worldwide, 3,900 such killers have been identified since the year 1900 (Aamodt, 2014).

Each serial killer follows his or her own pattern, but many of them appear to have certain characteristics in common (Hickey, 2015; FBI, 2014; Fox & Levin, 2014). Most—but certainly not all—are white males between 25 and 34 years old, of average to high intelligence, generally clean-cut, smooth-talking, attractive, and skillful manipulators.

A number of serial killers seem to display severe personality disorders (Hickey,

Serial murder by mail In 2001, a hazardous-material worker sprays his colleagues as they depart the Senate Office Building after searching the building for traces of anthrax, an acute infectious disease caused by a spore-forming bacterium.

2015; Dogra et al., 2012; Waller, 2010). Lack of conscience and an utter disregard for people and the rules of society—key features of antisocial personality disorder—are typical. Narcissistic thinking is quite common as well. The feeling of being special may even give the killer an unrealistic belief that he will not get caught (Kocsis, 2008; Wright et al., 2006). Often it is this sense of invincibility that leads to his capture.

Sexual dysfunction and fantasy also seem to play a part (FBI, 2014; Arndt et al., 2004). Studies have found that vivid fantasies, often sexual and sadistic, may help drive the killer's behavior (Homant & Kennedy, 2006). Some clinicians also

believe that the killers may be trying to overcome general feelings of powerlessness by controlling, hurting, or eliminating those who are momentarily weaker (Fox & Levin, 2014). A number of the killers were abused as children—physically, sexually, and emotionally (Hickey, 2015; Wright et al., 2006).

Despite such profiles and suspicions, clinical theorists do not yet understand why serial killers behave as they do. But most agree with Park Dietz, a highly regarded forensic expert, when he asserts, "It's hard to imagine any circumstance under which they should be released to the public again" (Douglas, 1996, p. 349).

Misleading profile Police search for clues outside a Home Depot in Virginia in 2002, hoping to identify and capture the serial sniper who killed 10 people and terrorized residents throughout Washington, DC; Maryland; and Virginia. Psychological profiling in this case offered limited help and even misled the police in certain respects.

Aamodt, 2014). Increasingly, police are consulting psychological profilers, and this practice appears to be helpful as long as the limitations of profiling are recognized (Kocsis & Palermo, 2013).

A reminder of the limitations of profiling comes from the case of the snipers who terrorized the Washington, DC, area for three weeks in October 2002, shooting 10 people dead and seriously wounding 3 others. Most of the profiling done by FBI psychologists had suggested that the sniper was acting alone; it turned out that the attacks were conducted by a pair: a middle-aged man, John Allen Muhammad, and a teenage boy, Lee Boyd Malvo. Although profiles had suggested a young thrill-seeker, Muhammad was 41. Profilers had believed the attacker to be white, but neither Muhammad nor Malvo was white. The prediction of a *male* attacker was correct, but then again female serial killers are relatively rare.

> ➤ *Summing Up*

OTHER CLINICAL–LEGAL INTERACTIONS Mental health and legal professionals also cross paths in four other areas. First, malpractice suits against therapists have increased in recent years. Second, the legislative and judicial systems help define professional boundaries. Third, lawyers may solicit the advice of mental health professionals regarding the selection of jurors and case strategies. Fourth, psychologists may investigate legal phenomena such as eyewitness testimony and patterns of criminality.

What Ethical Principles Guide Mental Health Professionals?

Discussions of the legal and mental health systems may sometimes give the impression that clinicians as a group are uncaring and are considerate of patients' rights and needs only when they are forced to be. This, of course, is not true. Most clinicians care greatly about their clients and strive to help them while at the same time respecting their rights and dignity (Pope & Vasquez, 2016, 2011). In fact, clinicians do not rely exclusively on the legislative and court systems to ensure proper clinical practice. They also regulate themselves by continually developing and revising ethical guidelines for their work and behavior. Many legal decisions do nothing more than place the power of the law behind these already existing professional guidelines.

Each profession within the mental health field has its own **code of ethics.** The code of the American Psychological Association (2014, 2010, 2002) is typical. This code, highly respected by other mental health professionals and public officials, includes specific guidelines:

1. **Psychologists are permitted to offer advice** in self-help books, on DVDs, on television and radio programs, in newspaper and magazines, and in other places, provided they do so responsibly and professionally and base their advice on appropriate psychological literature and practices. Psychologists are bound by these same ethical requirements when they offer advice and ideas online, whether on individual Web pages, blogs, bulletin boards, or chat rooms. Internet-based professional advice has proved difficult to regulate, however,

➤ **code of ethics** A body of principles and rules for ethical behavior, designed to guide decisions and actions by members of a profession.

➤ **confidentiality** The principle that certain professionals will not divulge the information they obtain from a client.

because the number of such offerings keeps getting larger and larger and so many advice-givers do not appear to have any professional training or credentials.

2. **Psychologists may not conduct fraudulent research, plagiarize the work of others, or publish false data.** During the past 35 years cases of scientific fraud or misconduct have been discovered in all of the sciences, including psychology. These acts have led to misunderstandings of important issues, taken scientific research in the wrong direction, and damaged public trust. Unfortunately, the impressions created by false findings may continue to influence the thinking of both the public and other scientists for years.

3. **Psychologists must acknowledge their limitations** with regard to patients who are disabled or whose gender, ethnicity, language, socioeconomic status, or sexual orientation differs from that of the therapist. This guideline often requires psychotherapists to obtain additional training or supervision, consult with more knowledgeable colleagues, or refer clients to more appropriate professionals.

4. **Psychologists who make evaluations and testify in legal cases must base their assessments on sufficient information and substantiate their findings appropriately.** If an adequate examination of the individual in question is not possible, psychologists must make clear the limited nature of their testimony.

5. **Psychologists may not take advantage of clients and students, sexually or otherwise.** This guideline relates to the social problem of sexual harassment, as well as the problem of therapists who take sexual advantage of clients in therapy. The code specifically forbids a sexual relationship with a present or former therapy client for at least two years after the end of treatment—and even then such a relationship is permitted only in "the most unusual circumstances." Furthermore, psychologists may not accept as clients people with whom they have previously had a sexual relationship.

Research has clarified that clients may suffer great emotional damage from sexual involvement with their therapists (Pope & Vasquez, 2016, 2011; Pope & Wedding, 2014). How many therapists actually have a sexual relationship with a client? On the basis of various surveys, reviewers have estimated that 4 to 5 percent of today's therapists engage in some form of sexual misconduct with patients, down from 10 percent more than a decade ago.

Although the vast majority of therapists do not engage in sexual behavior of any kind with clients, their ability to control private feelings is apparently another matter. In surveys, more than 80 percent of therapists reported having been sexually attracted to a client, at least on occasion (Pope & Vasquez, 2016, 2011; Pope & Wedding, 2014). Although few of these therapists acted on their feelings, most of them felt guilty, anxious, or concerned about the attraction. Given such issues, it is not surprising that sexual ethics training is given high priority in many of today's clinical training programs.

6. **Psychologists must follow the principle of confidentiality.** All of the state and federal courts have upheld laws protecting therapist **confidentiality** (Fisher, 2013; Nagy, 2011). For peace of mind and to ensure effective therapy, clients must be able to trust that their private exchanges with a therapist will not be repeated to others. There are times, however, when the principle of confidentiality must be compromised (Pope & Vasquez, 2016, 2011). A therapist in training, for example, must discuss cases on a regular basis with a supervisor, and clients must be informed that such discussions are taking place.

Barry Brecheisen/WireImage/Getty Images

The ethics of giving professional advice Today's psychologists are bound by the field's ethics code to base their advice on psychological theories and findings. In 2006, the enormously popular Phil McGraw ("Dr. Phil") surrendered his Texas psychologist license so that he could be free to use his own best judgment when giving advice on television and in books.

Institutional ethics During the American Psychological Association Conference in 2007, these protesters rallied against participation by psychologists in "enhanced interrogations" (i.e., torture questioning) of suspected terrorists. Despite concerns of this kind, a 2015 report revealed that, over a period of several years, the APA did in fact aid the Department of Defense and the CIA in the development of such techniques, gave advice to interrogators, and adjusted professional guidelines to allow psychologist involvement in such interrogations. These revelations led to several changes in APA leadership and to an APA membership vote banning psychologists from direct and indirect involvement in all national security interrogations—both enhanced and noncoercive.

A second exception arises in cases of outpatients who are clearly dangerous. The 1976 case of *Tarasoff v. Regents of the University of California,* one of the most important cases to affect client–therapist relationships, concerned an outpatient at a University of California hospital. He had confided to his therapist that he wanted to harm his former girlfriend, Tanya Tarasoff. Several days after ending therapy, the former patient fulfilled his promise. He stabbed Tanya Tarasoff to death.

Should confidentiality have been broken in this case? The therapist, in fact, felt that it should. Campus police were notified, but the patient was released after some questioning. In their suit against the hospital and therapist, the victim's parents argued that the therapist should have also warned them and their daughter that the patient intended to harm Ms. Tarasoff. The California Supreme Court agreed: "The protective privilege ends where the public peril begins."

The current code of ethics for psychologists thus declares that therapists have a **duty to protect**—a responsibility to break confidentiality, even without the client's consent, when it is necessary "to protect the client or others from harm." Since the *Tarasoff* ruling, most states have passed "duty to protect" bills that clarify the rules of confidentiality for therapists and protect them from certain civil suits (Knoll, 2015).

Mental Health, Business, and Economics

The legislative and judicial systems are not the only social institutions with which mental health professionals interact. The *business* and *economic* fields are two other sectors that influence and are influenced by clinical practice and study.

Bringing Mental Health Services to the Workplace

Untreated psychological disorders are, collectively, among the 10 leading categories of work-related disorders and injuries (Negrini et al., 2014; Kemp, 1994). Almost one-third of all employees are estimated to experience psychological problems that are serious enough to affect their work (Larsen et al., 2010). Psychological problems contribute to 60 percent of all absenteeism from work, up to 90 percent of industrial accidents, and to 65 percent of work terminations. Alcohol abuse and other substance use disorders are particularly damaging. The business world has often turned to clinical professionals to help prevent and correct such problems.

Two common means of providing mental health care in the workplace are *employee assistance programs* and *stress-reduction seminars* (Sledge & Lazar, 2014; Merrick et al., 2011; Daw, 2001). **Employee assistance programs** are mental health services made available by a place of business. They are run either by mental health professionals who work directly for the company or by outside mental health agencies. **Stress-reduction,** or **problem-solving, seminars** are workshops or group sessions in which mental health professionals teach employees techniques for coping, solving problems, and handling and reducing stress. Businesses believe that employee assistance programs and stress-reduction seminars save them money in the long run by preventing psychological problems from interfering with work performance and by reducing employee insurance claims.

The Economics of Mental Health

You have already seen how economic decisions by the government may influence the clinical field's treatment of people with severe mental disorders. For example, the desire of the state and federal governments to reduce costs was an important consideration in the country's deinstitutionalization movement, which contributed to the premature release of hospital patients into the community. Economic decisions by government agencies may affect other kinds of clients and treatment programs as well.

As you read in Chapter 12, government funding for services to people with psychological disorders has risen sharply over the past five decades, from $1 billion in 1963 to around $171 billion today (Rampell, 2013; Gill, 2010). Around 30 percent of that money is spent on prescription drugs, but much of the rest is targeted for income support, housing subsidies, and other such expenses rather than direct mental health services (Feldman et al., 2014). The result is that government funding for mental health services is, in fact, insufficient. People with severe mental disorders are hit hardest by the funding shortage. The number of people on waiting lists for community-based services grew from 200,000 in 2002 to 393,000 in 2008 (Daly, 2010), and that number has continued to rise in recent years.

Government funding currently covers around two-thirds of all mental health services, leaving a mental health expense of tens of billions of dollars for individual patients and their private insurance companies (Rampell, 2013; Nordal, 2010; Mark et al., 2008, 2005). This large economic role of private insurance companies has had a significant effect on the way clinicians go about their work. As you'll remember from Chapter 1, to reduce their expenses, most of these companies have developed **managed care programs,** in which the insurance company decides which therapists clients may choose from, the cost of sessions, and the number of sessions for which a client may be reimbursed (Lustig et al., 2013; Turner, 2013). These and other insurance plans may also control expenses through the use of **peer review systems,** in which clinicians who work for the insurance company periodically review a client's treatment program and recommend that insurance benefits be either continued or stopped. Typically, insurers require reports or session notes from the therapist, often including intimate personal information about the patient.

> **What problems may result when insurance companies make decisions about the methods, frequency, and duration of treatment?**

As you also read in Chapter 1, many therapists and clients dislike managed care programs and peer reviews. They believe that the reports required of therapists breach confidentiality, even when efforts are made to protect anonymity, and that the importance of therapy in a given case is sometimes difficult to convey in a brief report. They also argue that the priorities of managed care programs inevitably shorten therapy, even if longer-term treatment would be advisable in particular cases. The priorities may also favor treatments that offer short-term results (for example, drug therapy) over more costly approaches that might yield more promising long-term improvement. As in the medical field, there are disturbing stories about patients who are prematurely cut off from mental health services by their managed care programs.

Yet another major problem with insurance coverage in the United States—both managed care and other insurance programs—is that reimbursements for mental disorders tend to be lower than those for medical disorders (Sipe et al., 2015). As you have read, the government has tried to address this problem in recent years by passing federal *parity* laws that direct insurance companies to provide equal coverage for mental and medical problems (see pages 17–18). The mental health provisions of the Affordable Care Act (ACA), commonly known as "Obamacare," designate mental health care as 1 of 10 types of "essential health benefits" that *must* be provided by all insurers (SAMHSA, 2014; Calmes & Pear,

▶ **duty to protect** The principle that therapists must break confidentiality in order to protect a person who may be the intended victim of a client.

▶ **employee assistance program** A mental health program offered by a business to its employees.

▶ **stress-reduction seminars** Workshops or group sessions offered by businesses, in which mental health professionals teach employees how to cope, solve problems, and/or reduce stress. Also known as *problem-solving seminars.*

▶ **managed care program** An insurance program in which the insurance company decides the cost, method, provider, and length of treatment.

▶ **peer review system** A system by which clinicians paid by an insurance company may periodically review a patient's progress and recommend the continuation or termination of insurance benefits.

Caught in an economic spiral Group home residents and mental health advocates rally at the legislative office building in Raleigh, North Carolina, to protest a Medicaid payment law change. This change could result in residents with severe mental disorders losing their group homes and having nowhere to live.

AP Photo/Gerry Broome

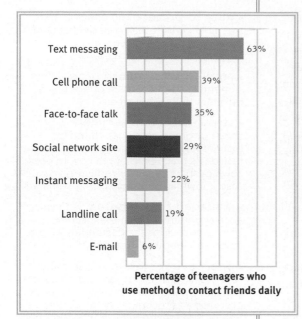

Percentage of teenagers who use method to contact friends daily

Text messaging	63%
Cell phone call	39%
Face-to-face talk	35%
Social network site	29%
Instant messaging	22%
Landline call	19%
E-mail	6%

figure 16-3

How do today's teenagers connect each day with their friends? A large survey of American teenagers reveals that 63 percent of teenagers use text messaging each day to connect with their friends, 35 percent talk face-to-face with them, and 6 percent e-mail them. (Information from: Pew Internet, 2013.)

Extending psychology's reach A child meets with a psychologist (left on screen) and physician (right) located several towns away. Long-distance therapy by Skype is an increasingly used form of cybertherapy.

2013). The act further requires mental health parity and demands that insurers allow new and continued membership to people with preexisting mental conditions. All of this is promising, but it is not yet clear that such provisions will, in fact, yield better treatment for people with psychological problems.

Technology and Mental Health

Technology is always changing and, like most other fields, the mental health field must work hard to keep pace with that change. This is not a new state of affairs. Technological change occurred 25, 50, 100 years ago and beyond. What is new, however, is the remarkable rate of technological change in the world today. As you have seen throughout this book, the digital and hyperconnected world in which we now live has had significant effects—both positive and negative—on the mental health field (see *MindTech* on the next page).

Consider for a moment the nature and breadth of technological change in today's world. Around 3.1 billion people across the world currently use the Internet—310 million in North America alone (IWS, 2015). It has become the primary medium through which people access all kinds of information. Closely aligned with the Internet, cell phone use has expanded. There are currently 6.8 billion cell phone owners worldwide—90 percent of the world population (Fernholz, 2014). Over 80 percent of all cell phone owners use them for texting, among other services—itself a relatively new form of technology (Duggan, 2013) (see Figure 16-3).

Video games have emerged as yet another force in our digital society. Sixty percent of Americans play such games on computers, cell phones, or consoles (ESA, 2015). Often gaming is a social experience: more than half of gamers play with other individuals in person, and some interact online with numerous other players in virtual game environments called MMOGs (Massively Multiplayer Online Games).

Finally, there is the spectacular growth of social networking among people of all ages. The number of social network users (on Facebook, Twitter, Pinterest, Tumblr, Instagram, and other such sites) is currently more than 2 billion worldwide and is continuing to rise (eBizMBA, 2015; Statista, 2015). Consider, for example, the remarkable growth of Twitter, the online social networking and micro-blogging service, launched less than a decade ago, that enables users to send and receive brief text-based messages to and from large numbers of friends, colleagues, and other

AP Photo/Nati Harnik

MindTech

New Ethics for a Digital Age

The American Psychological Association's code of ethics states that psychologists who operate on the Internet (offer cybertherapy, for example) are bound by the same ethical requirements as those who operate more conventionally. That seems reasonable enough, except for one thing: operating online opens up a world of brand-new ethical issues that the code of ethics does not even begin to cover.

Two leading clinical theorists, Kenneth Pope and Danny Wedding (2014), have spent the last decade compiling a list of ethical dilemmas and nightmares that can emerge as a by-product of therapists conducting therapy in the digital age. Let's say, for example, that a therapist in Boston and a client in Atlanta use Skype to conduct therapy sessions. Seems straightforward enough, but it turns out that this arrangement raises complex legal and ethical questions. Is the Massachusetts-based therapist actually practicing without a license in Georgia? Should the therapist follow Massachusetts' or Georgia's laws regarding confidentiality, duty to protect, and other therapist requirements? What happens if the laws in the therapist's state conflict with the laws in the client's state? Is long-distance online therapy covered by the therapist's malpractice insurance? And so on.

"Oops! I just deleted all your files. Can you repeat everything you've ever told me?"

Many therapists believe that because they do not conduct cybertherapy, they are untouched by digital concerns. Yet those same therapists likely use computers to keep notes of therapy sessions, maintain client billing information, score psychological tests, and the like. Thus, they might be alarmed to know that the following breaches of privacy have occurred more than a few times (Pope & Wedding, 2014):

➤ A laptop containing confidential patient information is hacked or is stolen from an office or car trunk.

➤ A virus, worm, or other kind of malware infects a therapist's computer and uploads confidential files to a Web site or to everyone listed in his or her address book.

➤ Someone reads a therapist's laptop monitor—and obtains confidential information—while sitting next to the therapist in an airport or on a flight.

➤ A therapist e-mails a message containing confidential client information to a colleague, but accidentally sends it to the wrong e-mail address.

➤ A therapist sells a computer, not realizing that confidential information is still recoverable because a truly thorough form of scrubbing was not used.

> **What other ethical problems might emerge as a result of the mental health field's increasing use of new technologies?**

The digital age in which therapists treat clients presents many new ethical concerns and potential problems. Certainly, the field's code of ethics must address these issues sooner rather than later. So too must each individual therapist. As Pope and Wedding (2014) point out, "When we use digital devices to handle the most sensitive and private information about our clients, we must remember to live up to an ancient precept: First, do no harm." 💬

"I can't wait to see what you're like online."

Paul Noth/The New Yorker Collection/www.cartoonbank.com

people. Currently, 500 million tweets (Twitter messages) are sent each day (DMR, 2015).

Given these changes and trends in technology, it is not surprising that the focus, tools, and research directions of the mental health field have themselves expanded over the past decade. As you have observed throughout this book, for example, our digital world provides new *triggers* for the expression of abnormal behavior: Internet gambling has intensified the problem of gambling disorder (see pages 342–343); the misuse of social networks and texting has fed problems such as bullying, sexual exhibitionism, and pedophilia (see pages 368, 465); violent video games may sometimes contribute to cases of antisocial behavior; and so on.

Similarly, our fast-moving digital world greatly affects clinical treatment. *Cybertherapy*—in such forms as long-distance therapy enabled by Skype (see page 57), virtual reality-enhanced treatments (see page 163), Internet-based support groups (see pages 57, 68), and countless mental health apps (see page 21)—has become a major force in mental health care. The options offered by cybertherapy have many virtues, but they have also produced serious problems such as poor quality control and the spread of psychological misinformation (see page 57).

Clearly, the growing impact of technological change on the mental health field presents significant challenges. Few of the technological applications discussed throughout this book are well understood, and few have been subjected to comprehensive research. Yet the relationship between technology and mental health is expected to expand still further in the coming years. It behooves everyone in the field to understand and be ready for this growth and its implications.

The Person Within the Profession

The actions of clinical researchers and practitioners not only influence and are influenced by other forces in society but also are closely tied to their personal needs and goals (see *InfoCentral* on the next page). You have seen that the human strengths, imperfections, wisdom, and clumsiness of clinical professionals may affect their theoretical orientations, their interactions with clients, and the kinds of clients with whom they choose to work. You have also seen how personal leanings may sometimes override professional standards and scruples and, in extreme cases, lead clinical scientists to commit research fraud and clinical practitioners to engage in sexual misconduct with clients.

Surveys of the mental health of therapists have found that as many as 84 percent report having been in therapy at least once (Pope & Wedding, 2014; Pope et al., 2006; Pope & Tabachnick, 1994). Their reasons are largely the same as those of other clients, with relationship problems, depression, and anxiety topping the list. It is not clear why so many therapists have psychological problems. Perhaps it is because their jobs are highly stressful; research suggests that therapists often experience some degree of job burnout (Clay, 2011; Rosenberg & Pace, 2006). Or perhaps therapists are simply more aware of their own negative feelings or are more likely to pursue treatment for their problems. Alternatively, people with personal concerns may be more inclined to choose clinical work as a profession. Whatever the reason, clinicians bring to their work a set of psychological issues that may, along with other important factors, affect how they listen and respond to clients.

The science and profession of abnormal psychology seek to understand, predict, and change abnormal functioning. But we must not lose sight of the fact that mental health researchers and clinicians are human beings, living within a society of human beings, working to serve human beings. The mixture of discovery, misdirection,

PERSONAL AND PROFESSIONAL ISSUES

Like everyone else, clinicians have personal needs, perspectives, goals, and problems, each of which may affect their work. Therapists typically try to minimize the impact of such variables on their interactions with clients—called **countertransference** by Freud. However, research suggests that, to at least some degree, personal therapist issues influence how clinicians deal with clients.

THE EARLY YEARS

Common events in the early lives of therapists

- Experiencing personal distress
- Witnessing the distress of others
- Observing the behaviors and emotions of others; becoming psychologically minded
- Reading
- Being in therapy
- Being a confidant to others
- Modeling the behavior of others
- Learning from a mentor

(Farber et al., 2005)

CLINICAL CAREERS

How satisfied are clinical psychologists with their careers?

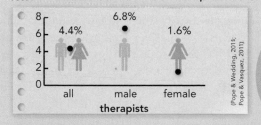

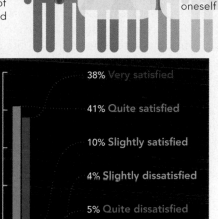

Top 5 reasons people become therapists

| help people | understand and help oneself | understand others | intellectual stimulation | professional autonomy |

(Farber et al., 2005; Norcross & Farber, 2005)

38%	Very satisfied
41%	Quite satisfied
10%	Slightly satisfied
4%	Slightly dissatisfied
5%	Quite dissatisfied
3%	Very dissatisfied

(Norcross et al., 2005)

How do clinical psychologists spend their professional time?

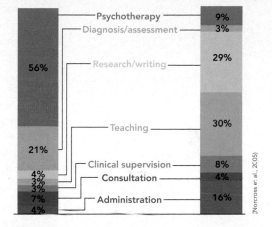

Private Practitioners / Academic Psychologists

	Private Practitioners	Academic Psychologists
Psychotherapy	56%	9%
Diagnosis/assessment		3%
Research/writing		29%
Teaching	21%	30%
Clinical supervision	4%	8%
Consultation	3%	4%
	3%	
Administration	7%	16%
	4%	

(Norcross et al., 2005)

ETHICS IN CLINICAL PRACTICE

Although the field's code of ethics explicitly forbids it, some therapists engage in sexual relationships with their clients. This is the profession's most egregious violation of trust and boundaries and typically causes significant psychological harm to clients.

Who has had a sexual relationship with a client?

	all	male	female
therapists	4.4%	6.8%	1.6%

(Pope & Wedding, 2014; Pope & Vasquez, 2011; Pope, 1994, 1988)

Effects on Clients

- Ambivalence
- Guilt
- Emptiness and isolation
- Sexual confusion
- Inability to trust
- Confusion of roles and boundaries
- Emotional damage
- Suppressed rage
- Heightened risk of suicide
- Cognitive dysfunction

CLINICIANS IN THERAPY

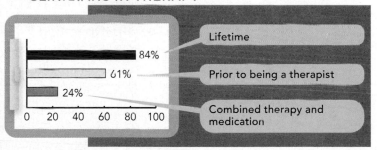

84%	Lifetime
61%	Prior to being a therapist
24%	Combined therapy and medication

? ? ?

Top qualities clinicians look for in choosing a therapist

- Competence
- Warmth and caring
- Clinical experience and professional reputation
- Openness
- Active therapeutic style
- Flexibility

(Norcross et al., 2009)

THE EMOTIONAL SIDE

Therapists' fears regarding clients

might commit suicide	condition might worsen	colleagues might criticize their work	malpractice complaint
97%	91%	88%	66%

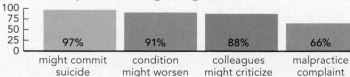

Therapists' anger toward clients

expressed anger toward a client	angry fantasies regarding a client	expressed disappointment toward a client
90%	63%	52%

(Pope & Vasquez, 2011; Pope & Tabachnick, 1993, Pope et al., 1987)

promise, and frustration that you have encountered throughout this book is thus to be expected. When you think about it, could the study and treatment of human behavior really proceed in any other way?

➤ *Summing Up*

ETHICAL, ECONOMIC, TECHNOLOGICAL, AND PERSONAL FACTORS Each clinical profession has a code of ethics. The psychologists' code includes prohibitions against engaging in fraudulent research and against taking advantage of clients and students, sexually or otherwise. It also establishes guidelines for respecting patient confidentiality. The case of *Tarasoff v. Regents of the University of California* helped to determine the circumstances in which therapists have a duty to protect clients or others from harm and must break confidentiality.

Clinical practice and study also intersect with the business and economic worlds. Clinicians often help address psychological problems in the workplace. In addition, private insurance companies often set up managed care programs whose procedures influence—sometimes adversely—the length, nature, and quality of therapy.

The remarkable technological advances of recent times have affected the mental health field, just as they have affected all other fields and professions. These advances have, for example, sometimes produced new triggers for psychopathology and have generated various kinds of cybertherapy.

Finally, mental health activities are affected by the personal needs, values, and goals of the human beings who provide the clinical services. These factors inevitably affect the choice, direction, and even quality of their work.

PUTTING IT...*together*

Operating Within a Larger System

At one time, clinical researchers and professionals conducted their work largely in isolation. Today their activities have numerous ties to the legislative, judicial, and economic systems and to technological forces as well. One reason for this growing interconnectedness is that the clinical field has reached a high level of respect and acceptance in our society. Clinicians now serve millions of people in many ways. They have much to say about almost every aspect of society, from education to ecology, and are widely looked to as sources of expertise. When a field becomes so prominent, it inevitably affects how other institutions are run. It also attracts public scrutiny, and various institutions begin to keep an eye on its activities.

When people with psychological problems seek help from a therapist, they are entering a complex system consisting of many interconnected parts. Just as their personal problems have grown within a social structure, so will their treatment be affected by the various parts of a larger system—the therapist's values and needs, legal and economic factors, societal attitudes, technological changes, and yet other forces. These many forces influence clinical research as well.

The effects of this larger system on an individual's psychological needs can be positive or negative, like a family's impact on each of its members. When the system protects a client's rights and confidentiality, for example, it is serving the client well. When economic, legal, or other societal forces limit treatment options, cut off treatment prematurely, or stigmatize a person, the system is adding to the person's problems.

Because of the enormous growth and impact of the mental health profession in our society, it is important that we understand the profession's strengths and weaknesses. As you have seen throughout this book, the field has gathered much knowledge, especially during the past several decades. What mental health professionals do not know and cannot do, however, still outweighs what they do know and can do. Everyone who turns to the clinical field—directly or indirectly—must recognize that it is young and imperfect. Society is vastly curious about behavior and often in need of information and help. What we as a society must remember, however, is that the field is still *putting it all together*.

KEY TERMS

forensic psychology, p. 528

criminal commitment, p. 528

not guilty by reason of insanity (NGRI), p. 528

M'Naghten test, p. 529

irresistible impulse test, p. 529

Durham test, p. 529

American Law Institute (ALI) test, p. 529

guilty but mentally ill, p. 532

guilty with diminished capacity, p. 532

mentally disordered sex offenders, p. 533

sexually violent predator laws, p. 534

mental incompetence, p. 535

civil commitment, p. 536

two-physician certificate (2 PC), p. 538

dangerousness, p. 538

right to treatment, p. 539

right to refuse treatment, p. 539

malpractice suit, p. 541

professional boundaries, p. 541

jury selection, p. 541

eyewitness testimony, p. 542

psychological profiles, p. 542

code of ethics, p. 544

confidentiality, p. 545

duty to protect, p. 546

employee assistance programs, p. 546

stress-reduction seminars, p. 546

managed care program, p. 547

peer review system, p. 547

cybertherapy, p. 549

QuickQuiz

1. Briefly explain the M'Naghten, irresistible impulse, Durham, and ALI tests of insanity. Which tests are used today to determine whether defendants are not guilty by reason of insanity? *pp. 529–530*

2. Explain the guilty but mentally ill, diminished capacity, mentally disordered sex offender, and sexually violent predator verdicts and laws. *pp. 532–534*

3. What are the reasons behind and the procedures for determining whether defendants are mentally incompetent to stand trial? *pp. 534–535*

4. What are the reasons for civil commitment, and how is it carried out? What criticisms have been made of civil commitment? *pp. 536–539*

5. What rights have court rulings and legislation guaranteed to patients with psychological disorders? *pp. 539–540*

6. How do the legislative and judicial systems affect the professional boundaries of clinical practice? *p. 541*

7. What have clinical researchers learned about eyewitness memories and about patterns of criminality? How accurate and influential is the practice of psychological profiling in criminal cases? *pp. 542–544*

8. What key issues are covered by the psychologist's code of ethics? Under what conditions must therapists break the principle of confidentiality? *pp. 544–546*

9. What kinds of programs for the prevention and treatment of psychological problems have been established in business settings? What trends have emerged in recent years in the funding and insurance of mental health care? *pp. 546–548*

10. Describe how the mental health field has been affected by and dealt with the technological advances of recent years. *pp. 548–550*

Visit *LaunchPad*

www.macmillanhighered.com/launchpad/comerfund8e
to access the e-book, new interactive case studies, videos, activities, and LearningCurve quizzes, as well as study aids including flashcards, FAQs, and research exercises.

GLOSSARY

ABAB design A single-subject experimental design in which behavior is measured during a baseline period, after a treatment has been applied, after baseline conditions have been reintroduced, and after the treatment has been reintroduced. Also called a *reversal design*.

Abnormal psychology The scientific study of abnormal behavior undertaken to describe, predict, explain, and change abnormal patterns of functioning.

Acceptance and commitment therapy A cognitive-behavioral therapy that teaches clients to accept and be mindful of (i.e., just notice) their dysfunctional thoughts or worries.

Acetylcholine A neurotransmitter that has been linked to depression and dementia.

Acute stress disorder A disorder in which fear and related symptoms are experienced soon after a traumatic event and last less than a month.

Addiction Persistent, compulsive dependence on a substance or behavior.

Adjustment disorders Disorders characterized by clinical symptoms such as depressed mood or anxiety in response to significant stressors.

Affect An experience of emotion or mood.

Aftercare A program of post-hospitalization care and treatment in the community.

Agoraphobia An anxiety disorder in which a person is afraid to be in public places or situations from which escape might be difficult (or embarrassing) or help unavailable if panic-like symptoms were to occur.

Agranulocytosis A life-threatening drop in white blood cells. This condition is sometimes produced by the atypical antipsychotic drug *clozapine*.

Alcohol Any beverage containing ethyl alcohol, including beer, wine, and liquor.

Alcohol dehydrogenase An enzyme that breaks down alcohol in the stomach before it enters the blood.

Alcohol use disorder A pattern of behavior in which a person repeatedly abuses or depends on alcohol. Also known as *alcoholism*.

Alcoholics Anonymous (AA) A self-help organization that provides support and guidance for people with alcoholism.

Alcoholism A pattern of behavior in which a person repeatedly abuses or depends on alcohol. Also known as *alcohol use disorder*.

Alogia A decrease in speech or speech content; a symptom of schizophrenia. Also known as *poverty of speech*.

Alprazolam A benzodiazepine drug shown to be effective in the treatment of anxiety disorders. Marketed as *Xanax*.

Altruistic suicide Suicide committed by people who intentionally sacrifice their lives for the well-being of society.

Alzheimer's disease The most common type of neurocognitive disorder, usually occurring after the age of 65, marked most prominently by memory impairment.

Amenorrhea The absence of menstrual cycles.

American Law Institute test A legal test for insanity that holds people to be insane at the time of committing a crime if, because of a mental disorder, they did not know right from wrong or could not resist an uncontrollable impulse to act.

Amnesia Loss of memory.

Amniocentesis A prenatal procedure used to test the amniotic fluid that surrounds the fetus for the possibility of birth defects.

Amphetamine psychosis A syndrome characterized by psychotic symptoms brought on by high doses of amphetamines. Similar to *cocaine psychosis*.

Amphetamines Stimulant drugs that are manufactured in the laboratory.

Amygdala A structure in the brain that plays a key role in emotion and memory.

Anal stage In psychoanalytic theory, the second 18 months of life, during which the child's focus of pleasure shifts to the anus.

Analog observation A method for observing behavior in which people are observed in artificial settings such as clinicians' offices or laboratories.

Analogue experiment A research method in which the experimenter produces abnormal-like behavior in laboratory participants and then conducts experiments on the participants.

Anesthesia A lessening or loss of sensation of touch or of pain.

Anomic suicide Suicide committed by individuals whose social environment fails to provide stability, thus leaving them without a sense of belonging.

Anorexia nervosa A disorder marked by the pursuit of extreme thinness and by an extreme loss of weight.

Anoxia A complication of birth in which the baby is deprived of oxygen.

Antabuse (disulfiram) A drug that causes intense nausea, vomiting, increased heart rate, and dizziness when taken with alcohol. It is often taken by people who are trying to refrain from drinking alcohol.

Antagonist drugs Drugs that block or change the effects of an addictive drug.

Antianxiety drugs Psychotropic drugs that help reduce tension and anxiety. Also called *minor tranquilizers* or *anxiolytics*.

Antibipolar drugs Psychotropic drugs that help stabilize the moods of people suffering from a bipolar disorder. Also known as *mood stabilizers*.

Antibodies Bodily chemicals that seek out and destroy foreign invaders such as bacteria or viruses.

Antidepressant drugs Psychotropic drugs that improve the mood of people with depression.

Antigen A foreign invader of the body, such as a bacterium or virus.

Antipsychotic drugs Drugs that help correct grossly confused or distorted thinking.

Antisocial personality disorder A personality disorder marked by a general pattern of disregard for and violation of other people's rights.

Anxiety The central nervous system's physiological and emotional response to a vague sense of threat or danger.

Anxiety disorder A disorder in which anxiety is a central symptom.

Anxiety sensitivity A tendency to focus on one's bodily sensations, assess them illogically, and interpret them as harmful.

Anxiolytics Drugs that reduce anxiety.

Arbitrary inference An error in logic in which a person draws negative conclusions on the basis of little or even contrary evidence.

Aripiprazole An atypical antipsychotic drug whose brand name is Abilify.

Asperger's disorder One of the patterns found in autism spectrum disorder, in which a person displays profound social impairment yet maintains a relatively high level of cognitive functioning and language skills.

Assertiveness training A cognitive-behavioral approach to increasing assertive behavior that is socially desirable.

Assessment The process of collecting and interpreting relevant information about a client or research participant.

Asthma A medical problem marked by narrowing of the trachea and bronchi, which results in shortness of breath, wheezing, coughing, and a choking sensation.

Asylum A type of institution that first became popular in the sixteenth century to provide care for persons with mental disorders. Most became virtual prisons.

Attention-deficit/hyperactivity disorder (ADHD) A disorder marked by the inability to focus attention, or overactive and impulsive behavior, or both.

Attribution An explanation of things we see going on around us that points to particular causes.

Atypical antipsychotic drugs A relatively new group of antipsychotic drugs whose biological action is different from that of the conventional antipsychotic drugs. Also known as *second-generation antipsychotic drugs*.

Auditory hallucination A hallucination in which a person hears sounds or voices that are not actually present.

Augmentative communication system A method for enhancing the communication skills of people with autism spectrum disorder, intellectual developmental disorder, or cerebral palsy by teaching them to point to pictures, symbols, letters, or words on a communication board or computer.

Aura A warning sensation that may precede a migraine headache.

Autism spectrum disorder A developmental disorder marked by extreme unresponsiveness to others, severe communication deficits, and highly repetitive and rigid behaviors, interests, and activities.

Autoerotic asphyxia A fatal lack of oxygen that people may unintentionally produce while hanging, suffocating, or strangling themselves during masturbation.

Automatic thoughts Numerous unpleasant thoughts that help to cause or maintain depression, anxiety, or other forms of psychological dysfunction.

Autonomic nervous system (ANS) The network of nerve fibers that connect the central nervous system to all the other organs of the body.

Aversion therapy A treatment in which clients are repeatedly presented with unpleasant stimuli while performing undesirable behaviors such as taking a drug.

Avoidant personality disorder A personality disorder characterized by consistent discomfort and restraint in social situations, overwhelming feelings of inadequacy, and extreme sensitivity to negative evaluation.

Avolition A symptom of schizophrenia marked by apathy and an inability to start or complete a course of action.

Axon A long fiber extending from the body of a neuron.

Barbiturates One group of sedative-hypnotic drugs that reduce anxiety and help produce sleep.

Baseline data A person's initial response level on a test or scale.

Basic irrational assumptions The inaccurate and inappropriate beliefs held by people with various psychological problems, according to Albert Ellis.

Battery A series of tests, each of which measures a specific skill area.

B-cell A lymphocyte that produces antibodies.

Behavioral medicine A field that combines psychological and physical interventions to treat or prevent medical problems.

Behavioral model A theoretical perspective that emphasizes behavior and the ways in which it is learned.

Behavioral therapy A therapeutic approach that seeks to identify problem-causing behaviors and change them. Also known as *behavior modification*.

Behaviors The responses an organism makes to its environment.

Bender Visual–Motor Gestalt Test A neuropsychological test in which a subject is asked to copy a set of nine simple designs and later reproduce the designs from memory.

Benzodiazepines The most common group of antianxiety drugs, which includes Valium and Xanax.

Bereavement The process of working through the grief that one feels when a loved one dies.

Beta-amyloid protein A small molecule that forms sphere-shaped deposits called senile plaques, linked to aging and to Alzheimer's disease.

"Big Five" theory of personality A leading theory that holds that personality can be effectively organized and described by five broad dimensions of personality—openness, conscientiousness, extraversion, agreeableness, and neuroticism.

Binge An episode of uncontrollable eating during which a person ingests a very large quantity of food.

Binge drinking A pattern of alcohol consumption in which a person consumes five or more drinks on a single occasion.

Binge-eating disorder A disorder marked by frequent binges but not extreme compensatory behaviors.

Binge-eating/purging-type anorexia nervosa A type of anorexia nervosa in which people have eating binges but still lose excessive weight by forcing themselves to vomit after meals or by abusing laxatives or diuretics.

Biofeedback A technique in which a client is given information about physiological reactions as they occur and learns to control the reactions voluntarily.

Biological challenge test A procedure used to produce panic in participants or clients by having them exercise vigorously or perform some other potentially panic-inducing task in the presence of a researcher or therapist.

Biological model The theoretical perspective that points to biological processes as the key to human behavior.

Biological therapy The use of physical and chemical procedures to help people overcome psychological problems.

Biopsychosocial theories Explanations that attribute the cause of abnormality to an interaction of genetic, biological, developmental, emotional, behavioral, cognitive, social, and societal influences.

Bipolar disorder A disorder marked by alternating or intermixed periods of mania and depression.

Bipolar I disorder A type of bipolar disorder marked by full manic and major depressive episodes.

Bipolar II disorder A type of bipolar disorder marked by mild manic (hypomanic) and major depressive episodes.

Birth complications Problematic biological conditions during birth that can affect the physical and psychological well-being of the child.

Blind design An experiment in which participants do not know whether they are in the experimental or the control condition.

Blunted affect A symptom of schizophrenia in which a person shows less emotion than most people.

Body dysmorphic disorder A disorder in which individuals become preoccupied with the belief that they have certain defects or flaws in their physical appearance. The perceived defects or flaws are imagined or greatly exaggerated.

Borderline personality disorder A personality disorder characterized by repeated instability in interpersonal relationships, self-image, and mood and by impulsive behavior.

Brain circuits Networks of brain structures that work together, triggering each other into action with the help of neurotransmitters.

Brain region A distinct area of the brain formed by a large group of neurons.

Brain wave The fluctuations of electrical potential that are produced by neurons in the brain.

Breathing-related sleep disorder A sleep disorder in which sleep is frequently disrupted by a breathing problem, causing excessive sleepiness or insomnia.

Brief psychotic disorder Psychotic symptoms that appear suddenly after a very stressful event or a period of emotional turmoil and last anywhere from a few hours to a month.

Brodmann Area 25 A brain structure whose abnormal activity has been linked to depression.

Bulimia nervosa A disorder marked by frequent eating binges that are followed by forced vomiting or other extreme compensatory behaviors to avoid gaining weight. Also known as *binge-purge syndrome*.

Caffeine The world's most widely used stimulant, most often consumed in coffee.

Cannabis Substance produced from the varieties of the hemp plant, *Cannabis sativa*. It causes a mixture of hallucinogenic, depressant, and stimulant effects.

Case manager A community therapist who offers a full range of services for people with schizophrenia or other severe disorders, including therapy, advice, medication, guidance, and protection of patients' rights.

Case study A detailed account of a person's life and psychological problems.

Catatonia A pattern of extreme psycho-motor symptoms, found in some forms of schizophrenia, which may include catatonic stupor, rigidity, or posturing.

Catatonic excitement A form of catatonia in which a person moves excitedly, sometimes with wild waving of the arms and legs.

Catatonic stupor A symptom associated with schizophrenia in which a person becomes almost totally unresponsive to the environment, remaining motionless and silent for long stretches of time.

Catharsis The reliving of past repressed feelings in order to settle internal conflicts and overcome problems.

Caudate nuclei Structures in the brain, within the region known as the basal ganglia, that help convert sensory information into thoughts and actions.

Central nervous system The brain and spinal cord.

Cerebellum An area of the brain that coordinates movement in the body and perhaps helps control a person's ability to shift attention rapidly.

Checking compulsion A compulsion in which people feel compelled to check the same things over and over.

Child abuse The nonaccidental use of excessive physical or psychological force by an adult on a child, often aimed at hurting or destroying the child.

Chlorpromazine A phenothiazine drug commonly used for treating schizophrenia. Marketed as *Thorazine*.

Chromosomes The structures, located within a cell, that contain genes.

Chronic headaches A medical problem marked by frequent intense aches in the head or neck that are not caused by another medical disorder.

Circadian rhythm disorder A sleep-wake disorder characterized by a mismatch between a person's sleep-wake pattern and the sleep-wake schedule of most other people.

Circadian rhythms Internal "clocks" consisting of repeated biological fluctuations.

Cirrhosis An irreversible condition, often caused by excessive drinking, in which the liver becomes scarred and begins to change in anatomy and functioning.

Civil commitment A legal process by which an individual can be forced to undergo mental health treatment.

Clang A rhyme used by some people with schizophrenia as a guide to forming thoughts and statements.

Classical conditioning A process of learning in which two events that repeatedly occur close together in time become tied together in a person's mind and so produce the same response.

Classification system A list of disorders, along with descriptions of symptoms and guidelines for making appropriate diagnoses.

Cleaning compulsion A common compulsion in which people feel compelled to keep cleaning themselves, their clothing, and their homes.

Client-centered therapy The humanistic therapy developed by Carl Rogers in which clinicians try to help clients by being accepting, empathizing accurately, and conveying genuineness.

Clinical interview A face-to-face encounter in which clinicians ask questions of clients, weigh their responses and reactions, and learn about them and their psychological problems.

Clinical psychologist A mental health professional who has earned a doctorate in clinical psychology.

Clinical psychology The study, assessment, treatment, and prevention of abnormal behavior.

Clitoris The female sex organ located in front of the urinary and vaginal openings. It becomes enlarged during sexual arousal.

Clozapine A commonly prescribed atypical antipsychotic drug.

Cocaine An addictive stimulant obtained from the coca plant. It is the most powerful natural stimulant known.

Code of ethics A body of principles and rules for ethical behavior, designed to guide decisions and actions by members of a profession.

Cognition The capacity to think, remember, and anticipate.

Cognitive behavior Thoughts and beliefs, many of which remain private.

Cognitive-behavioral therapies Therapy approaches that seek to help clients change both counterproductive behaviors and dysfunctional ways of thinking.

Cognitive model A theoretical perspective that emphasizes the process and content of thinking as causes of psychological problems.

Cognitive therapy A therapy developed by Aaron Beck that helps people identify and change the maladaptive assumptions and ways of thinking that help cause their psychological disorders.

Cognitive triad The three forms of negative thinking that theorist Aaron Beck theorizes lead people to feel depressed. The triad consists of a negative view of one's experiences, oneself, and the future.

Coitus Sexual intercourse.

Communication disorders Disorders characterized by marked impairment in language and/or speech.

Community mental health center A treatment facility that provides medication, psychotherapy, and emergency care to patients and coordinates treatment in the community.

Community mental health treatment A treatment approach that emphasizes community care.

Comorbidity The occurrence of two or more disorders in the same person.

Compulsion A repetitive and rigid behavior or mental act that persons feel driven to perform in order to prevent or reduce anxiety.

Compulsive ritual A detailed, often elaborate, set of actions that a person often feels compelled to perform, always in an identical manner.

Computerized axial tomography (CT scan) A composite image of the brain created by compiling X-ray images taken from many angles.

Concordance A statistical measure of the frequency with which family members (often both members of a pair of twins) have the same particular characteristic.

Concurrent validity The degree to which the measures gathered from one assessment tool agree with the measures gathered from other assessment techniques.

Conditioned response (CR) A response previously associated with an unconditioned stimulus that comes to be produced by a conditioned stimulus.

Conditioned stimulus (CS) A previously neutral stimulus that comes to be associated with a nonneutral stimulus and can then produce responses similar to those produced by the nonneutral stimulus.

Conditioning A simple form of learning.

Conditions of worth According to client-centered theorists, the internal standards by which a person judges his or her own lovability and acceptability, determined by the standards to which the person was held as a child.

Conduct disorder A disorder in which a child repeatedly violates the basic rights of others and displays aggression, characterized by symptoms such as physical cruelty to people or animals, the deliberate destruction of other people's property, and the commission of various crimes.

Confabulation A made-up description of one's experience to fill in a gap in one's memory.

Confederate An experimenter's accomplice, who helps create a particular impression in a study while pretending to be just another subject.

Confidentiality The principle that certain professionals will not divulge the information they obtain from a client.

Confound In an experiment, a variable other than the independent variable that is also acting on the dependent variable.

Continuous amnesia An inability to recall newly occurring events as well as certain past events.

Control group In an experiment, a group of participants who are not exposed to the independent variable.

Conversion disorder A disorder in which bodily symptoms affect voluntary motor and sensory functions, but the symptoms are inconsistent with known medical diseases.

Conversion therapy A treatment approach that attempts to change the sexual orientation of a person from homosexual or bisexual to heterosexual. Also called *reparative therapy*.

Convulsion A brain seizure.

Coronary arteries Blood vessels that surround the heart and are responsible for carrying oxygen to the heart muscle.

Coronary heart disease Illness of the heart caused by a blockage in the coronary arteries.

Correlation The degree to which events or characteristics vary along with each other.

Correlation coefficient (r) A statistical term that indicates the direction and the magnitude of a correlation, ranging from −1.00 to +1.00.

Correlational method A research procedure used to determine how much events or characteristics vary along with each other.

Corticosteroids A group of hormones, including cortisol, released by the adrenal glands at times of stress.

Cortisol A hormone released by the adrenal glands when a person is under stress.

Counseling psychology A mental health specialty similar to clinical psychology that offers its own graduate training program.

Countertransference A phenomenon of psychotherapy in which therapists' own feelings, history, and values subtly influence the way they interpret a patient's problems.

Couple therapy A therapy format in which the therapist works with two people who share a long-term relationship.

Covert desensitization Desensitization that focuses on imagining confrontations with the frightening objects or situations while in a state of relaxation.

Covert sensitization A behavioral treatment for eliminating unwanted behavior by pairing the behavior with unpleasant mental images.

Crack A powerful, ready-to-smoke freebase cocaine.

C-reactive protein (CRP) A protein that spreads throughout the body and causes inflammation and various illnesses and disorders.

Cretinism A disorder marked by intellectual deficiencies and physical abnormalities; caused by low levels of iodine in the mother's diet during pregnancy. Also known as *severe congenital hypothyroidism*.

Creutzfeldt-Jakob disease A form of neurocognitive disorder caused by a slow-acting virus that may live in the body for years before the disease unfolds.

Criminal commitment A legal process by which people accused of a crime are instead judged mentally unstable and sent to a mental health facility for treatment.

Crisis intervention A treatment approach that tries to help people in a psychological crisis view their situation more accurately, make better decisions, act more constructively, and overcome the crisis.

Critical incident stress debriefing Training in how to help victims of disasters or other horrifying events talk about their feelings and reactions to the traumatic incidents.

Cross-tolerance Tolerance that a person develops for a substance as a result of regularly using another substance similar to it.

Culture A people's common history, values, institutions, habits, skills, technology, and arts.

Culture-sensitive therapies Approaches that are designed to address the unique issues faced by members of minority groups.

Cyberbullying The use of e-mail, texting, chat rooms, cell phones, or other digital devices to harass, threaten, or intimidate people.

Cybertherapy The use of computer technology, such as Skype or avatars, to provide therapy.

Cyclothymic disorder A disorder marked by numerous periods of hypomanic symptoms and mild depressive symptoms.

Day center A program that offers hospital-like treatment during the day only. Also known as a *day hospital*.

Death darer A person who is ambivalent about the wish to die even as he or she attempts suicide.

Death ignorer A person who attempts suicide without recognizing the finality of death.

Death initiator A person who attempts suicide believing that the process of death is already under way and that he or she is simply quickening the process.

Death seeker A person who clearly intends to end his or her life at the time of a suicide attempt.

Deep brain stimulation (DBS) A treatment procedure for depression in which a pacemaker powers electrodes that have been implanted in Brodmann Area 25, thus stimulating that brain area.

Deinstitutionalization The discharge, begun during the 1960s, of large numbers of patients from long-term institutional care so that they might be treated in community programs.

Déjà vu The haunting sense of having previously seen or experienced a new scene or situation.

Delayed ejaculation A male dysfunction characterized by persistent inability to ejaculate or very delayed ejaculations during sexual activity with a partner.

Delirium A rapidly developing, acute disturbance in attention and orientation that makes it very difficult to concentrate and think in a clear and organized manner.

Delirium tremens (DTs) A dramatic withdrawal reaction experienced by some people with alcohol use disorder. It consists of confusion, clouded consciousness, and terrifying visual hallucinations.

Delusion A strange false belief firmly held despite evidence to the contrary.

Delusion of control The belief that one's impulses, feelings, thoughts, or actions are being controlled by other people.

Delusion of grandeur The belief that one is a great inventor, historical figure, or other specially empowered person.

Delusion of persecution The belief that one is being plotted or discriminated against, spied on, slandered, threatened, attacked, or deliberately victimized.

Delusion of reference A belief that attaches special and personal meaning to the actions of others or to various objects or events.

Delusional disorder A disorder consisting of persistent, nonbizarre delusions that are not part of a schizophrenic disorder.

Demonology The belief that abnormal behavior results from supernatural causes such as evil spirits.

Dendrite An extension located at one end of a neuron that receives impulses from other neurons.

Denial An ego defense mechanism in which a person fails to acknowledge unacceptable thoughts, feelings, or actions.

Dependent personality disorder A personality disorder characterized by a pattern of clinging and obedience, fear of separation, and an ongoing need to be taken care of.

Dependent variable The variable in an experiment that is expected to change as the independent variable is manipulated.

Depersonalization-derealization disorder A dissociative disorder marked by the presence of persistent and recurrent episodes of depersonalization, derealization, or both.

Depressant A substance that slows the activity of the central nervous system and in sufficient dosages causes a reduction of tension and inhibitions.

Depression A low, sad state marked by significant levels of sadness, lack of energy, low self-worth, guilt, or related symptoms.

Depressive disorders The group of disorders marked by unipolar depression.

Derailment A common thinking disturbance in schizophrenia, involving rapid shifts from one topic of conversation to another. Also called *loose associations*.

Desensitization See Systematic desensitization.

Desire phase The phase of the sexual response cycle consisting of an urge to have sex, sexual fantasies, and sexual attraction.

Detoxification Systematic and medically supervised withdrawal from a drug.

Developmental coordination disorder Disorder characterized by marked impairment in the development and performance of coordinated motor activities.

Deviance Variance from common patterns of behavior.

Diagnosis A determination that a person's problems reflect a particular disorder.

Diagnostic and Statistical Manual of Mental Disorders (DSM) The classification system for mental disorders developed by the American Psychiatric Association.

Dialectical behavior therapy A therapy approach developed by psychologist Marsha Linehan to treat people with borderline personality disorder and other psychological disorders, consisting of cognitive-behavioral techniques in combination with various emotion regulation, mindfulness, humanistic, and other techniques.

Diathesis-stress view The view that a person must first have a predisposition to a disorder and then be subjected to immediate psychosocial stress in order to develop the disorder.

Diazepam A benzodiazepine drug, marketed as *Valium*.

Dichotomous thinking Viewing problems and solutions in rigid "either/or" terms.

Diencephalon A brain area (consisting of the mammillary bodies, thalamus, and hypothalamus) that plays a key role in transforming short-term to long-term memory, among other functions.

Directed masturbation training A sex therapy approach that teaches women with female arousal or orgasmic disorders how to masturbate effectively and eventually reach orgasm during sexual interactions.

Disaster Response Network (DRN) A network of thousands of volunteer mental health professionals who mobilize to provide free emergency psychological services at disaster sites throughout North America.

Displacement An ego defense mechanism that channels unacceptable id impulses toward another, safer substitute.

Disruptive mood dysregulation disorder A childhood disorder marked by severe recurrent temper outbursts along with a persistent irritable or angry mood.

Dissociative amnesia A dissociative disorder marked by an inability to recall important personal events and information.

Dissociative disorders A group of disorders in which some parts of one's memory or identity seem to be dissociated, or separated, from other parts of one's memory or identity.

Dissociative fugue A form of dissociative amnesia in which a person travels to a new location and may assume a new identity, simultaneously forgetting his or her past.

Dissociative identity disorder A disorder in which a person develops two or more distinct personalities. Also known as *multiple personality disorder*.

Disulfiram (Antabuse) An antagonist drug used in treating alcohol abuse or dependence.

Dopamine The neurotransmitter whose high activity has been shown to be related to schizophrenia.

Dopamine hypothesis The theory that schizophrenia results from excessive activity of the neurotransmitter dopamine.

Double-bind hypothesis A theory that some parents repeatedly communicate pairs of messages that are mutually contradictory, helping to produce schizophrenia in their children.

Double-blind design Experimental procedure in which neither the participant nor the experimenter knows whether the participant has received the experimental treatment or a placebo.

Down syndrome A form of intellectual disability caused by an abnormality in the twenty-first chromosome.

Dream A series of ideas and images that form during sleep.

Drug Any substance other than food that affects the body or mind.

Drug maintenance therapy An approach to treating substance dependence in which clients are given legally and medically supervised doses of the drug on which they are dependent or a substitute drug.

Drug therapy The use of psychotropic drugs to reduce the symptoms of psychological disorders.

DSM-5 (Diagnostic and Statistical Manual of Mental Disorders, Fifth Edition) The newest edition of the DSM, published in 2013.

Durham test A legal test for insanity that holds people to be insane at the time they committed a crime if their act was the result of a mental disorder or defect.

Duty to protect The principle that therapists must break confidentiality in order to protect a person who may be the intended victim of a client.

Dyslexia A type of specific learning disorder in which people show a marked impairment in the ability to recognize words and to comprehend what they read.

Dyssomnias Sleep-wake disorders, such as insomnia disorder and hypersomnolence disorder, in which the amount, quality, or timing of sleep is disturbed.

Dysthymia A pattern of persistent depressive disorder that is chronic but less severe and less disabling than repeated episodes of major depression.

Eccentric A person who deviates from conventional norms in odd, irregular, or even bizarre ways, but is not displaying a psychological disorder.

Echolalia A symptom of autism or schizophrenia in which a person responds to statements by repeating the other person's words.

Ecstasy (MDMA) A drug chemically related to amphetamines and hallucinogens, used illicitly for its euphoric and hallucinogenic effects.

Ego According to Freud, the psychological force that employs reason and operates in accordance with the reality principle.

Ego defense mechanisms According to psychoanalytic theory, strategies developed by the ego to control unacceptable id impulses and to avoid or reduce the anxiety they arouse.

Ego theory The psychodynamic theory that emphasizes the ego and considers it an independent force.

Egoistic suicide Suicide committed by people over whom society has little or no control, people who are not concerned with the norms or rules of society.

Eidetic imagery A strong visual image of an object or scene that persists in some persons long after the object or scene is removed.

Ejaculation Contractions of the muscles at the base of the penis that cause sperm to be ejected.

Electra complex According to Freud, the pattern of desires all girls experience during the phallic stage, in which they develop a sexual attraction to their father.

Electroconvulsive therapy (ECT) A treatment for depression in which electrodes attached to a patient's head send an electrical current through the brain, causing a seizure.

Electroencephalograph (EEG) A device that records electrical impulses in the brain.

Electromyograph (EMG) A device that provides feedback about the level of muscular tension in the body.

Emergency commitment The temporary commitment to a mental hospital of a patient who is behaving in a bizarre or violent way.

Empirically supported treatment A movement in the clinical field that seeks to identify which therapies have received clear research support for each disorder, to develop corresponding treatment guidelines, and to spread such information to clinicians. Also known as *evidence-based treatment*.

Employee assistance program A mental health program offered by a business to its employees.

Encopresis A disorder characterized by repeated defecating in inappropriate places, such as one's clothing.

Endocrine system The system of glands located throughout the body that help control important activities such as growth and sexual activity.

Endogenous depression A depression that appears to develop without external reasons and is assumed to be caused by internal factors.

Endorphins Neurotransmitters that help relieve pain and reduce emotional tension. They are sometimes referred to as the body's own opioids.

Enmeshed family pattern A family system in which members are overinvolved with each other's affairs and overconcerned about each other's welfare.

Enuresis A disorder marked by repeated bed-wetting or wetting of one's clothes.

Epidemiological study A study that measures the incidence and prevalence of a disorder in a given population.

Erectile disorder A dysfunction in which a man persistently fails to attain or maintain an erection during sexual activity.

Ergot alkaloid A naturally occurring compound from which LSD is derived.

Essential hypertension High blood pressure caused by a combination of psychosocial and physiological factors.

Estrogen The primary female sex hormone.

Ethyl alcohol The chemical compound in all alcoholic beverages that is rapidly absorbed into the blood and immediately begins to affect the person's functioning.

Evoked potentials The brain response patterns recorded on an electroencephalograph while a person performs a task such as observing a flashing light.

Excitement phase The phase of the sexual response cycle marked by changes in the pelvic region, general physical arousal, and increases in heart rate, muscle tension, blood pressure, and rate of breathing.

Excoriation disorder A disorder in which persons repeatedly pick at their skin, resulting in significant sores or wounds. Also called *skin-picking disorder*.

Exhibitionistic disorder A paraphilic disorder in which persons have repeated sexually arousing urges or fantasies about exposing their genitals to others, and either act on these urges with nonconsenting individuals or experience clinically significant distress or impairment.

Existential anxiety According to existential theorists, a universal fear of the limits and responsibilities of one's existence.

Existential model The theoretical perspective that human beings are born with the total freedom either to face up to one's existence and give meaning to one's life or to shrink from that responsibility.

Existential therapy A therapy that encourages clients to accept responsibility for their lives and to live with greater meaning and value.

Exorcism The practice, common in early societies, of treating abnormality by coaxing evil spirits to leave the person's body.

Experiment A research procedure in which a variable is manipulated and the effect of the manipulation is observed.

Experimental group In an experiment, the participants who are exposed to the independent variable under investigation.

Exposure and response prevention A behavioral treatment for obsessive-compulsive disorder that exposes a client to anxiety-arousing thoughts or situations and then prevents the client from performing his or her compulsive acts. Also called *exposure and ritual prevention*.

Exposure treatments Behavioral treatments in which persons are exposed to the objects or situations they dread.

Expressed emotion The general level of criticism, disapproval, hostility, and intrusiveness expressed in a family. People recovering from schizophrenia are considered more likely to relapse if their families rate high in expressed emotion.

External validity The degree to which the results of a study may be generalized beyond that study.

Extrapyramidal effects Unwanted movements, such as severe shaking, bizarre-looking grimaces, twisting of the body, and extreme restlessness, sometimes produced by conventional antipsychotic drugs.

Eye movement desensitization and reprocessing (EMDR) An exposure treatment in which clients move their eyes in a rhythmic manner from side to side while flooding their minds with images of objects and situations they ordinarily avoid.

Factitious disorder A disorder in which a person feigns or induces symptoms, typically for the purpose of assuming the role of a sick person.

Family pedigree study A research design in which investigators determine how many and which relatives of a person with a disorder have the same disorder.

Family systems theory A theory that views the family as a system of interacting parts whose interactions exhibit consistent patterns and unstated rules.

Family therapy A therapy format in which the therapist meets with all members of a family and helps them to change in therapeutic ways.

Fantasy An ego defense mechanism in which a person uses imaginary events to satisfy unacceptable impulses.

Fear The central nervous system's physiological and emotional response to a serious threat to one's well-being.

Fear hierarchy A list of objects or situations that frighten a person, starting with those that are slightly feared and ending with those that are feared greatly; used in systematic desensitization.

Female orgasmic disorder A dysfunction in which a woman persistently fails to reach orgasm, has very low intensity orgasms, or has very delayed orgasms.

Female sexual interest/arousal disorder A female dysfunction marked by a persistent reduction or lack of interest in sex and low sexual activity, as well as, in some cases, limited excitement and few sexual sensations during sexual activity.

Fetal alcohol syndrome A cluster of problems in a child, including low birth weight, irregularities in the hands and face, and intellectual deficits, caused by excessive alcohol intake by the mother during pregnancy.

Fetishistic disorder A paraphilic disorder consisting of recurrent and intense sexual urges, fantasies, or behaviors that involve the use of a nonliving object or nongenital part, often to the exclusion of all other stimuli, accompanied by significant distress or impairment.

Fixation According to Freud, a condition in which the id, ego, and superego do not mature properly and are frozen at an early stage of development.

Flashback The recurrence of LSD-induced sensory and emotional changes long after the drug has left the body or, in posttraumatic stress disorder, the reexperiencing of past traumatic events.

Flat affect A symptom of schizophrenia in which the person shows almost no emotion at all.

Flibanserin A drug used to treat low sexual desire in women. Marketed as Addyi.

Flooding A treatment for phobias in which clients are exposed repeatedly and intensively to a feared object and made to see that it is actually harmless.

Forensic psychology The branch of psychology concerned with intersections between psychological practice and research and the judicial system. Also related to the field of *forensic psychiatry*.

Formal thought disorder A disturbance in the production and organization of thought.

Free association A psychodynamic technique in which the patient describes any thought, feeling, or image that comes to mind, even if it seems unimportant.

Freebase A technique for ingesting cocaine in which the pure cocaine basic alkaloid is chemically separated from processed cocaine, vaporized by heat from a flame, and inhaled through a pipe.

Free-floating anxiety Chronic and persistent feelings of anxiety that are not clearly attached to a specific, identifiable threat.

Frotteuristic disorder A paraphilic disorder in which a person has repeated and intense sexual urges or fantasies that involve touching and rubbing against a nonconsenting person and either acts on these urges with nonconsenting individuals or experiences clinically significant distress or impairment.

Functional magnetic resonance imaging (fMRI) A neuroimaging technique used to visualize internal functioning of the brain or body.

Fusion The final merging of two or more subpersonalities in multiple personality disorder.

GABA *See* Gamma-aminobutyric acid.

Gambling disorder A disorder marked by persistent and recurrent gambling behavior, leading to a range of life problems.

Gamma-aminobutyric acid (GABA) A neurotransmitter whose low activity has been linked to generalized anxiety disorder.

Gender dysphoria A disorder in which a person persistently feels clinically significant distress or impairment due to his or her assigned gender and strongly wishes to be a member of another gender.

Gender-sensitive therapies Approaches geared to the pressures of being a woman in Western society. Also called *feminist therapies*.

Gene Chromosome segments that control the characteristics and traits we inherit.

General paresis An irreversible medical disorder whose symptoms include psychological abnormalities, such as delusions of grandeur; caused by syphilis.

Generalized amnesia A loss of memory for events that occurred over a limited period of time as well as for certain events that occurred prior to that period.

Generalized anxiety disorder A disorder marked by persistent and excessive feelings of anxiety and worry about numerous events and activities.

Generic drug A marketed drug that is comparable to a trade-named drug in dosage form, strength, and performance.

Genetic linkage study A research approach in which extended families with high rates of a disorder over several generations are observed in order to determine whether the disorder closely follows the distribution pattern of other family traits.

Genital stage In Freud's theory, the stage beginning at approximately 12 years old, when the child begins to find sexual pleasure in heterosexual relationships.

Genito-pelvic pain/penetration disorder A sexual dysfunction characterized by significant physical discomfort during intercourse.

Geropsychology The field of psychology concerned with the mental health of elderly people.

Gestalt therapy The humanistic therapy developed by Fritz Perls in which clinicians actively move clients toward self-recognition and self-acceptance by using techniques such as role playing and self-discovery exercises.

Glia Brain cells that support the neurons.

Glutamate A common neurotransmitter that has been linked to memory and to dementia.

Grief The reaction a person experiences when a loved one is lost.

Group home A special home where people with disorders or disabilities live and are taught self-help, living, and working skills.

Group therapy A therapy format in which a group of people with similar problems meet together with a therapist to work on those problems.

Guided participation A modeling technique in which a client systematically observes and imitates the therapist while the therapist confronts feared items.

Guilty but mentally ill A verdict stating that defendants are guilty of committing a crime but are also suffering from a mental illness that should be treated during their imprisonment.

Guilty with diminished capacity A legal defense argument that states that because of limitations posed by mental dysfunctioning, a defendant could not have intended to commit a particular crime and thus should be convicted of a lesser crime.

Halfway house A residence for people with schizophrenia or other severe problems, often staffed by paraprofessionals. Also known as a *group home* or *crisis house*.

Hallucination The experiencing of imagined sights, sounds, or other perceptions in the absence of external stimuli.

Hallucinogen A substance that causes powerful changes primarily in sensory perception, including strengthening perceptions and producing illusions and hallucinations. Also called a *psychedelic drug*.

Hallucinosis A form of intoxication caused by hallucinogens, consisting of perceptual distortions and hallucinations.

Hardiness A set of positive attitudes and reactions in response to stress.

Health maintenance The principle that young adults should act to promote their physical and mental health to best prepare for the aging process. Also called *wellness*.

Helper T-cell A lymphocyte that identifies foreign invaders and then both multiplies and triggers the production of other kinds of immune cells.

Heroin One of the most addictive substances derived from opium.

High The pleasant feeling of relaxation and euphoria that follows the rush from certain recreational drugs.

Hippocampus A brain area located below the cerebral cortex that is involved in memory.

Histrionic personality disorder A personality disorder in which an individual displays a pattern of excessive emotionality and attention seeking. Once called *hysterical personality disorder*.

Hoarding disorder A disorder in which people feel compelled to save items and experience significant distress if they try to discard them, resulting in an excessive accumulation of items and possessions.

Hopelessness A pessimistic belief that one's present circumstances, problems, or mood will not change.

Hormones The chemicals released by endocrine glands into the bloodstream.

Humanistic model The theoretical perspective that human beings are born with a natural inclination to be friendly, cooperative, and constructive and are driven to self-actualize.

Humanistic therapy A system of therapy in which clinicians try to help clients look at themselves accurately and acceptingly so that they can fulfill their positive inborn potential.

Humors According to the Greeks and Romans, bodily chemicals that influence mental and physical functioning.

Huntington's disease An inherited disease, characterized by progressive problems in cognition, emotion, and movement, which results in neurocognitive disorder.

Hypersomnolence disorder A sleep-wake disorder characterized by an extreme need for extra sleep and feelings of excessive sleepiness.

Hypertension Chronic high blood pressure.

Hypnosis A sleeplike suggestible state during which a person can be directed to act in unusual ways, to experience unusual sensations, to remember seemingly forgotten events, or to forget remembered events.

Hypnotic amnesia Loss of memory produced by hypnotic suggestion.

Hypnotic therapy A treatment in which the patient undergoes hypnosis and is then guided to recall forgotten events or perform other therapeutic activities. Also known as *hypnotherapy*.

Hypnotism A procedure that places people in a trancelike mental state during which they become extremely suggestible.

Hypochondriasis A somatoform disorder in which people mistakenly fear that minor changes in their physical functioning indicate a serious disease. Now known as *illness anxiety disorder*.

Hypomanic episode An episode of mania in which the symptoms cause relatively little impairment.

Hypomanic pattern A pattern in which a person displays symptoms of mania, but the symptoms are less severe and cause less impairment than those of a manic episode.

Hypothalamic-pituitary-adrenal (HPA) pathway One route by which the brain and body produce arousal and fear.

Hypothalamus A part of the brain that helps maintain various bodily functions, including eating and hunger.

Hypothesis A hunch or prediction that certain variables are related in certain ways.

Hypoxyphilia A pattern in which people strangle or smother themselves, or ask their partners to strangle or smother them, to increase their sexual pleasure.

Hysteria A term once used to describe what are now known as conversion disorder, somatization disorder, and pain disorder associated with psychological factors.

Hysterical disorder A disorder in which physical functioning is changed or lost, without an apparent physical cause.

Iatrogenic Produced or caused inadvertently by a clinician.

Id According to Freud, the psychological force that produces instinctual needs, drives, and impulses.

Ideas of reference Beliefs that unrelated events pertain to oneself in some important way.

Identification Unconsciously incorporating the values and feelings of one's parents and fusing them with one's identity. Also, an ego defense mechanism in which a person takes on the values and feelings of a person who is causing them anxiety.

Idiographic understanding An understanding of the behavior of a particular individual.

Illness anxiety disorder A disorder in which people are chronically anxious about and preoccupied with the notion that they have or are developing a serious medical illness, despite the absence of somatic symptoms. Previously known as *hypochondriasis*.

Illogical thinking According to cognitive theories, illogical ways of thinking that may lead to self-defeating conclusions and psychological problems.

Immune system The body's network of activities and cells that identify and destroy antigens and cancer cells.

Inappropriate affect Display of emotions that are unsuited to the situation; a symptom of schizophrenia.

Incest Sexual relations between closely related individuals.

Incidence The number of new cases of a disorder occurring in a population over a specific period of time.

Independent variable The variable in an experiment that is manipulated to determine whether it has an effect on another variable.

Individual therapy A therapeutic approach in which a therapist sees a client alone for sessions that may last from 15 minutes to 2 hours.

Informed consent The requirement that researchers provide sufficient information to participants about the purpose, procedure, risks, and benefits of a study.

Insanity defense A legal defense in which a person charged with a criminal offense claims to be not guilty by reason of insanity at the time of the crime.

Insomnia Difficulty falling or staying asleep.

Insomnia disorder A sleep-wake disorder characterized by severe difficulty falling asleep or maintaining sleep at least three nights per week.

Institutional Review Board (IRB) An ethics committee formed in a research facility that is empowered to protect the rights and safety of human research participants. It reviews and may require changes in each proposed study at the facility before approving or disapproving the study.

Integrity test A test that is designed to measure whether the test taker is generally honest or dishonest.

Intellectual disability (ID) A disorder marked by intellectual functioning and adaptive behavior that are well below average. Previously called *mental retardation*.

Intelligence quotient (IQ) A score derived from intelligence tests that theoretically represents a person's overall intellectual capacity.

Intelligence test A test designed to measure a person's intellectual ability.

Intermittent explosive disorder An impulse-control disorder in which people periodically fail to resist aggressive impulses and commit serious assaults on others or destroy property.

Internal validity The accuracy with which a study can pinpoint one of various possible factors as the cause of a phenomenon.

International Classification of Diseases (ICD) The classification system for medical and mental disorders that is used by the World Health Organization.

Internet gaming disorder A disorder marked by persistent, recurrent, and excessive Internet gaming activity. Recommended for further study by the DSM study group.

Interpersonal psychotherapy (IPT) A treatment for unipolar depression that is based on the belief that clarifying and changing one's interpersonal problems will help lead to recovery.

Interrater reliability A measure of the reliability of a test or of research results in which the consistency of evaluations across different judges is assessed. Also called *interjudge reliability*.

Intoxication A cluster of undesirable behavioral or psychological changes, such as slurred speech or mood changes, that may develop during or shortly after the ingestion of a substance.

In vivo desensitization Desensitization that makes use of actual objects or situations, as opposed to imagined ones.

Ion An atom or group of atoms that has a positive or negative electrical charge.

Irresistible impulse test A legal test for insanity that holds people to be insane at the time they committed a crime if they were driven to do so by an uncontrollable "fit of passion."

Isolation An ego defense mechanism in which people unconsciously isolate and disown undesirable and unwanted thoughts, experiencing them as foreign intrusions.

Kleptomania An impulse-control disorder characterized by the recurrent failure to resist impulses to steal objects not needed for personal use or monetary value.

Korsakoff's syndrome An alcohol-related disorder marked by extreme confusion, memory impairment, and other neurological symptoms.

Latent content The symbolic meaning behind a dream's content.

Lateral hypothalamus (LH) A brain region that produces hunger when activated.

L-dopa A drug used in the treatment of Parkinson's disease, a disease in which dopamine is low.

Learned helplessness The perception, based on past experiences, that one has no control over one's reinforcements.

Libido The sexual energy that fuels the id.

Life change units (LCUs) A system for measuring the stress associated with various life events.

Light therapy A treatment for seasonal affective disorder in which patients are exposed to extra light for several hours. Also called *phototherapy*.

Lithium A metallic element that occurs in nature as a mineral salt and is an effective treatment for bipolar disorders.

Lobotomy Psychosurgery in which a surgeon cuts the connections between the brain's frontal lobes and the lower centers of the brain.

Localized amnesia An inability to recall any of the events that occurred over a limited period of time.

Locus ceruleus A small area of the brain that seems to be active in the regulation of emotions. Many of its neurons use norepinephrine.

Longitudinal study A study that observes the same participants on many occasions over a long period of time.

Long-term care Extended personal and medical support provided to elderly and other persons who may be impaired. It may range from partial support in a supervised apartment to intensive care at a nursing home.

Long-term memory The memory system that contains all the information that a person has stored over the years.

Loose associations A common thinking disturbance in schizophrenia, characterized by rapid shifts from one topic of conversation to another. Also known as *derailment*.

LSD (lysergic acid diethylamide) A hallucinogenic drug derived from ergot alkaloids.

Lycanthropy A condition in which persons believe themselves to be possessed by wolves or other animals.

Lymphocytes White blood cells that circulate through the lymph system and bloodstream, helping the body identify and destroy antigens and cancer cells.

Magnetic resonance imaging (MRI) A neuroimaging technique used to visualize internal structures of the brain or body.

Mainstreaming The placement of children with intellectual disability in regular school classes. Also known as *inclusion*.

Major depressive disorder A severe pattern of unipolar depression that is disabling and is not caused by such factors as drugs or a general medical condition.

Major neurocognitive disorder A neurocognitive disorder in which the decline in cognitive functioning is substantial and interferes with the ability to be independent.

Male hypoactive sexual desire disorder A male dysfunction marked by a persistent reduction or lack of interest in sex and hence a low level of sexual activity.

Malingering Intentionally faking illness to achieve some external gains, such as financial compensation or military deferment.

Malpractice suit A lawsuit charging a therapist with improper conduct or decision making in the course of treatment.

Managed care program A system of health care coverage in which the insurance company largely controls the nature, scope, and cost of medical or psychological services.

Mania A state or episode of euphoria or frenzied activity in which people may have an exaggerated belief that the world is theirs for the taking.

Manifest content The consciously remembered content of a dream.

Mantra A sound, uttered or thought, used to focus one's attention and to turn away from ordinary thoughts and concerns during meditation.

MAO inhibitor An antidepressant drug that prevents the action of the enzyme monoamine oxidase.

Marijuana One of the cannabis drugs, derived from the buds, leaves, and flowering tops of the hemp plant *Cannabis sativa*.

Marital therapy A therapy approach in which the therapist works with two people who share a long-term relationship. Also known as *couple therapy*.

Masturbation Self-stimulation of the genitals to achieve sexual arousal.

Masturbatory satiation A behavioral treatment in which a client masturbates for a very long period of time while fantasizing in detail about a paraphilic object. The procedure is expected to produce a feeling of boredom that becomes linked to the object.

Mean The average of a group of scores.

Meditation A technique of turning one's concentration inward and achieving a slightly changed state of consciousness.

Melancholia A condition described by early Greek and Roman philosophers and physicians as consisting of unshakable sadness. Today it is known as *depression*.

Melatonin A hormone released by the pineal gland when a person's surroundings are dark.

Memory The faculty for recalling past events and past learning.

Mental incompetence A state of mental instability that leaves defendants unable to understand the legal charges and proceedings they are facing and unable to prepare an adequate defense with their attorney.

Mental status exam A set of interview questions and observations designed to reveal the degree and nature of a client's psychological functioning.

Mentally disordered sex offender A legal category that some states apply to certain people who are repeatedly found guilty of sex crimes.

Mentally ill chemical abusers (MICAs) People suffering from both schizophrenia (or another severe psychological disorder) and a substance-related disorder. Also called *dual-diagnosis patients*.

Mesmerism The method employed by Austrian physician F. A. Mesmer to treat hysterical disorders; a precursor of *hypnotism*.

Meta-analysis A statistical method that combines results from multiple independent studies.

Metabolism An organism's chemical and physical breakdown of food and the process of converting it into energy. Also, an organism's biochemical transformation of various substances, as when the liver breaks down alcohol into acetylaldehyde.

Metaworry Worrying about the fact that one is worrying so much.

Methadone A laboratory-made opioid-like drug.

Methadone maintenance program An approach to treating heroin-centered substance use in which clients are given legally and medically supervised doses of a substitute drug, methadone.

Methamphetamine A powerful amphetamine drug that has experienced a surge in popularity in recent years, posing major health and law enforcement problems.

Methylphenidate A stimulant drug, known better by the trade name *Ritalin,* commonly used to treat ADHD.

Migraine headache A very severe headache that occurs on one side of the head, often preceded by a warning sensation and sometimes accompanied by dizziness, nausea, or vomiting.

Mild intellectual disability A level of intellectual disability (IQ between 50 and 70) at which people can benefit from education and can support themselves as adults.

Mild neurocognitive disorder Neurocognitive disorder in which the decline in cognitive functioning is modest and does not interfere with the ability to be independent.

Milieu therapy A humanistic approach to institutional treatment based on the premise that institutions can help patients recover by creating a climate that promotes self-respect, individual responsible behavior, and meaningful activity.

Mind-body dualism René Descartes's position that the mind is separate from the body.

Mindfulness-based cognitive therapy A type of therapy that teaches clients to be mindful of (just notice and accept) their dysfunctional thoughts or worries.

Mindfulness meditation A type of meditation in which people are mindful of (just notice) the various thoughts, emotions, sensations, and other private experiences that pass through their minds and bodies.

Minnesota Multiphasic Personality Inventory (MMPI) A widely used personality inventory consisting of a large number of statements that subjects mark as being true or false for them.

Mixed design A research design in which a correlational method is mixed with an experimental method. Also known as *quasi-experiment*.

M'Naghten test A widely used legal test for insanity that holds people to be insane at the time they committed a crime if, because of a mental disorder, they did not know the nature of the act or did not know right from wrong. Also known as the *M'Naghten rule*.

Model A set of assumptions and concepts that help scientists explain and interpret observations. Also called a *paradigm*.

Modeling A process of learning in which a person acquires responses by observing and imitating others. Also, a therapy approach based on the same principle.

Moderate intellectual disability A level of intellectual disability (IQ between 35 and 49) at which people can learn to care for themselves and can benefit from vocational training.

Monoamine oxidase (MAO) A body chemical that destroys the neurotransmitter norepinephrine.

Monoamine oxidase (MAO) inhibitors Antidepressant drugs that lower MAO activity and thus increase the level of norepinephrine activity in the brain.

Mood disorder A disorder affecting one's emotional state, including major depressive disorder and bipolar disorders.

Mood stabilizing drugs Psychotropic drugs that help stabilize the moods of people suffering from a bipolar mood disorder. Also known as *antibipolar drugs*.

Moral treatment A nineteenth-century approach to treating people with mental dysfunction that emphasized moral guidance and humane and respectful treatment.

Morphine A highly addictive substance derived from opium that is particularly effective in relieving pain.

Multicultural perspective The view that each culture within a larger society has a particular set of values and beliefs, as well as special external pressures, that help account for the behavior and functioning of its members. Also called *culturally diverse perspective*.

Multicultural psychology The field of psychology that examines the impact of culture, race, ethnicity, gender, and similar factors on our behaviors and thoughts and focuses on how such factors may influence the origin, nature, and treatment of abnormal behavior.

Multidimensional risk perspective A theory that identifies several kinds of risk factors that are thought to combine to help cause a disorder. The more factors present, the greater the risk of developing the disorder.

Munchausen syndrome An extreme and long-term form of factitious disorder in which a person produces symptoms, gains admission to a hospital, and receives treatment.

Munchausen syndrome by proxy A factitious disorder in which parents make up or produce physical illnesses in their children.

Muscle contraction headache A headache caused by the narrowing of muscles surrounding the skull. Also known as *tension headache*.

Muscle dysmorphobia Disorder in which people become obsessed with the incorrect belief that they are not muscular enough.

Narcissistic personality disorder A personality disorder marked by a broad pattern of grandiosity, need for admiration, and lack of empathy.

Narcolepsy A sleep-wake disorder characterized by a repeated sudden and irrepressible need to sleep during waking hours.

Narcotic Any natural or synthetic opioid-like drug.

Narcotic antagonist A substance that attaches to opioid receptors in the brain and, in turn, blocks the effects of opioids.

National Alliance on Mental Illness (NAMI) A nationwide grassroots organization that provides support, education, advocacy, and research for people with severe mental disorders and their families.

Natural experiment An experiment in which nature, rather than an experimenter, manipulates an independent variable.

Naturalistic observation A method of observing behavior in which clinicians or researchers observe people in their everyday environments.

Negative correlation A statistical relationship in which the value of one variable increases while the other variable decreases.

Negative symptoms Symptoms of schizophrenia that seem to be deficits in normal thought, emotions, or behaviors.

Neologism A made-up word that has meaning only to the person using it.

Nerve ending The region at the end of a neuron from which an impulse is sent to a neighboring neuron.

Neurocognitive disorder A disorder marked by a significant decline in at least one area of cognitive functioning.

Neurodevelopmental disorders A group of disabilities—including ADHD, autism spectrum disorder, and intellectual disability—in the functioning of the brain that emerge at birth or during very early childhood and affect an individual's behavior, memory, concentration, and/or ability to learn.

Neurofibrillary tangles Twisted protein fibers that form within certain brain cells as people age. People with Alzheimer's disease have an excessive number of such tangles.

Neuroimaging techniques Neurological tests that provide images of brain structure or activity, such as CT scans, PET scans, and MRIs. Also called *brain scans*.

Neuroleptic drugs An alternative term for conventional antipsychotic drugs, so called because they often produce undesired effects similar to the symptoms of neurological disorders.

Neuroleptic malignant syndrome A severe, potentially fatal reaction to antipsychotic drugs, marked by muscle rigidity, fever, altered consciousness, and autonomic dysfunction.

Neurological Relating to the structure or activity of the brain.

Neurological test A test that directly measures brain structure or activity.

Neuromodulator A neurotransmitter that helps modify or regulate the effect of other neurotransmitters.

Neuron A nerve cell.

Neuropsychological test A test that detects brain impairment by measuring a person's cognitive, perceptual, and motor performances.

Neurosis Freud's term for disorders characterized by intense anxiety, attributed to failure of a person's ego defense mechanisms to cope with unconscious conflicts.

Neurotransmitter A chemical that, released by one neuron, crosses the synaptic space to be received at receptors on the dendrites of neighboring neurons.

Neutralizing Attempting to eliminate thoughts that one finds unacceptable by thinking or behaving in ways that make up for those thoughts and so put matters right internally.

Nicotine An alkaloid (nitrogen-containing chemical) derived from tobacco or produced in the laboratory.

Nicotine patch A patch attached to the skin like a Band-Aid, with nicotine content that is absorbed through the skin, that supposedly eases the withdrawal reaction brought on by quitting cigarette smoking.

Nightmare disorder A parasomnia characterized by chronic distressful, frightening dreams.

Nocturnal penile tumescence (NPT) Erection during sleep.

Nomothetic understanding A general understanding of the nature, causes, and treatments of abnormal psychological functioning, in the form of laws or principles.

Nonsuicidal self-injury (NSSI) A disorder that is being studied for possible inclusion in a future edition of DSM-5, characterized by persons intentionally injuring themselves on five or more occasions over a one-year period, without the conscious intent of killing themselves.

Norepinephrine A neurotransmitter whose abnormal activity is linked to panic disorder and depression.

Normalization The principle that institutions and community residences should provide people with intellectual disability types of living conditions and opportunities that are similar to those enjoyed by the rest of society.

Norms A society's stated and unstated rules for proper conduct.

Not guilty by reason of insanity (NGRI) A verdict stating that defendants are not guilty of committing a crime because they were insane at the time of the crime.

Object relations theory The psychodynamic theory that views the desire for relationships as the key motivating force in human behavior.

Observer drift The tendency of an observer who is rating subjects in an experiment to change criteria gradually and involuntarily, thus making the data unreliable.

Obsession A persistent thought, idea, impulse, or image that is experienced repeatedly, feels intrusive, and causes anxiety.

Obsessive-compulsive disorder A disorder in which a person has recurrent and unwanted thoughts and/or a need to perform repetitive and rigid actions.

Obsessive-compulsive personality disorder A personality disorder marked by such an intense focus on orderliness, perfectionism, and control that the person loses flexibility, openness, and efficiency.

Obsessive-compulsive-related disorders A group of disorders in which obsessive-like concerns drive people to repeatedly and excessively perform specific patterns of behavior that greatly disrupt their lives.

Oedipus complex In Freudian theory, the pattern of desires emerging during the phallic stage in which boys become attracted to their mother as a sexual object and see their father as a rival they would like to push aside.

Olanzapine An atypical antipsychotic drug whose brand name is Zyprexa.

Operant conditioning A process of learning in which behavior that leads to satisfying consequences is likely to be repeated.

Opioid Opium or any of the drugs derived from opium, including morphine, heroin, and codeine.

Opium A highly addictive substance made from the sap of the opium poppy seed.

Oppositional defiant disorder A disorder in which children are repeatedly argumentative and defiant, angry and irritable, and, in some cases, vindictive.

Oral stage The earliest developmental stage in Freud's conceptualization of psychosexual development, during which the infant's main gratification comes from feeding and from the body parts involved in feeding.

Orbitofrontal cortex A region of the brain in which impulses involving excretion, sexuality, violence, and other primitive activities normally arise.

Orgasm A peaking of sexual pleasure, consisting of rhythmic muscular contractions in the pelvic region, during which a man's semen is ejaculated and the outer third of a woman's vaginal wall contracts.

Orgasm phase The phase of the sexual response cycle during which a person's sexual pleasure peaks and sexual tension is released as muscles in the pelvic region contract rhythmically.

Orgasmic reorientation A procedure for treating certain paraphilias by teaching clients to respond to new, more appropriate sources of sexual stimulation.

Outpatient A person who receives a diagnosis or treatment in a clinic, hospital, or therapist's office but is not hospitalized overnight.

Panic attacks Periodic, short bouts of panic that occur suddenly, reach a peak within minutes, and gradually pass.

Panic disorder An anxiety disorder marked by recurrent and unpredictable panic attacks.

Paranoid personality disorder A personality disorder marked by a pattern of extreme distrust and suspiciousness of others.

Paraphilias Patterns in which a person has recurrent and intense sexual urges, fantasies, or behaviors involving nonhuman objects, children, nonconsenting adults, or experiences of suffering or humiliation.

Paraphilic disorder A disorder in which a person's paraphilia causes great distress, interferes with social or occupational activities, or places the person or others at risk of harm—either currently or in the past.

Paraprofessional A person without previous professional training who provides services under the supervision of a mental health professional.

Parasomnias Sleep-wake disorders, such as sleepwalking, sleep terrors, and nightmare disorder, characterized by the occurrence of abnormal events during sleep.

Parasuicide A suicide attempt that does not result in death.

Parasympathetic nervous system The nerve fibers of the autonomic nervous system that help return bodily processes to normal.

Parkinsonian symptoms Symptoms similar to those found in Parkinson's disease. Patients with schizophrenia who take conventional antipsychotic medications may display one or more of these symptoms.

Parkinson's disease A slowly progressive neurological disease, marked by tremors and rigidity, that may also cause dementia.

Participant modeling A behavioral treatment in which people with fears observe a therapist (model) interacting with a feared object and then interact with the object themselves.

Pedophilic disorder A paraphilic disorder in which a person has repeated and intense sexual urges or fantasies about watching, touching, or engaging in sexual acts with children and either acts on these urges or experiences clinically significant distress or impairment.

Peer review system A system by which clinicians paid by an insurance company may periodically review a patient's progress and recommend the continuation or termination of insurance benefits.

Penile prosthesis A surgical implant consisting of a semi-rigid rod that produces an artificial erection.

Performance anxiety The fear of performing inadequately and a related tension experienced during sex.

Perseveration The persistent repetition of words and statements.

Persistent depressive disorder A chronic form of unipolar depression marked by ongoing and repeated symptoms of either major or mild depression.

Personality A unique and long-term pattern of inner experience and outward behavior that leads to consistent reactions across various situations.

Personality disorder An enduring, rigid pattern of inner experience and outward behavior that repeatedly impairs a person's sense of self, emotional experiences, goals, capacity for empathy, and/or capacity for intimacy.

Personality disorder—trait specified (PDTS) A personality disorder currently undergoing study for possible inclusion in a future revision of DSM-5. Individuals would receive this diagnosis if they display significant impairment in functioning as a result of one or more very problematic traits.

Personality inventory A test designed to measure broad personality characteristics, consisting of statements about behaviors, beliefs, and feelings that people evaluate as either characteristic or uncharacteristic of them.

Phallic stage In psychoanalytic theory, the period between the third and fourth years when the focus of sexual pleasure shifts to the genitals.

Phalloplasty A surgical procedure designed to create a functional penis.

Phenothiazines A group of antihistamine drugs that became the first group of effective antipsychotic medications.

Phenylketonuria (PKU) A metabolic disorder caused by the body's inability to break down the amino acid phenylalanine, resulting in intellectual disability and other symptoms.

Phobia A persistent and unreasonable fear of a particular object, activity, or situation.

Pick's disease A neurological disease that affects the frontal and temporal lobes, causing a neurocognitive disorder.

Placebo therapy A simulated treatment that the participant in an experiment believes to be genuine.

Play therapy An approach to treating childhood disorders that helps children express their conflicts and feelings indirectly by drawing, playing with toys, and making up stories.

Pleasure principle The pursuit of gratification that characterizes id functioning.

Plethysmograph A device used to measure sexual arousal.

Polygraph test A test that seeks to determine whether the test taker is telling the truth by measuring physiological responses such as respiration level, perspiration level, and heart rate. Also known as a *lie detector test*.

Polysubstance use The use of two or more substances at the same time.

Positive correlation A statistical relationship in which the values of two variables increase together or decrease together.

Positive psychology The study and enhancement of positive feelings, traits, and abilities.

Positive symptoms Symptoms of schizophrenia that seem to be excesses of or bizarre additions to normal thoughts, emotions, or behaviors.

Positron emission tomography (PET scan) A computer-produced motion picture showing rates of metabolism throughout the brain.

Postpartum depression An episode of depression experienced by some new mothers that begins within four weeks after giving birth.

Postpartum psychosis An episode of psychosis experienced by a small percentage of new mothers that begins within days or weeks after giving birth.

Posttraumatic stress disorder (PTSD) A disorder in which fear and related symptoms continue to be experienced long after a traumatic event.

Poverty of speech A decrease in speech or speech content found in some people with schizophrenia. Also known as *alogia*.

Predictive validity The ability of a test or other assessment tool to predict future characteristics or behaviors.

Predisposition An inborn or acquired vulnerability for developing certain symptoms or disorders.

Prefrontal lobes Regions of the brain that play a key role in short-term memory, among other functions.

Premature ejaculation A dysfunction in which a man persistently reaches orgasm and ejaculates within one minute of beginning sexual activity with a partner and before he wishes to. Also called *early* or *rapid ejaculation*.

Premenstrual dysphoric disorder A disorder marked by repeated experiences of significant depression and related symptoms during the week before menstruation.

Premenstrual syndrome (PMS) A common and normal cluster of psychological and physical discomforts that precede menses.

Premorbid The period prior to the onset of a disorder.

Preparedness A predisposition to develop certain fears.

Prevalence The total number of cases of a disorder occurring in a population over a specific period of time.

Prevention A key feature of community mental health programs that seek to prevent or minimize psychological disorders.

Primary gain In psychodynamic theory, the gain people achieve when their somatic symptoms keep their internal conflicts out of awareness.

Primary personality The subpersonality that appears more often than the others in individuals with dissociative identity disorder.

Primary prevention Prevention interventions that are designed to prevent disorders altogether.

Private psychotherapy An arrangement in which a person directly pays a therapist for counseling services.

Proband The person who is the focus of a genetic study.

Procedural memory Memory of learned skills that a person performs without needing to think about them.

Prodromal phase The period during which the symptoms of schizophrenia are not yet prominent, but the person has begun to deteriorate from previous levels of functioning.

Profound intellectual disability A level of intellectual disability (IQ below 20) at which people need a very structured environment with close supervision.

Projection An ego defense mechanism whereby individuals attribute to other people characteristics or impulses they do not wish to acknowledge in themselves.

Projective test A test consisting of ambiguous material that people interpret or respond to.

Protection and advocacy system The system by which lawyers and advocates who work for patients may investigate the patients' treatment and protect their rights.

Prozac The trade name for fluoxetine, a second-generation antidepressant.

Psychedelic drugs Substances such as LSD that cause profound perceptual changes. Also called *hallucinogenic drugs*.

Psychiatric social worker A mental health specialist who is qualified to conduct psychotherapy upon earning a master's degree or doctorate in social work.

Psychiatrist A physician who in addition to medical school has completed three to four years of residency training in the treatment of abnormal mental functioning.

Psychoanalysis Either the theory or the treatment of abnormal mental functioning that emphasizes unconscious psychological forces as the cause of psychopathology.

Psychodynamic model The theoretical perspective that sees all human functioning as being shaped by dynamic (interacting) psychological forces and explains people's behavior by reference to unconscious internal conflicts.

Psychodynamic therapy A system of therapy whose goals are to help clients uncover past traumatic events and the inner conflicts that have resulted from them, settle those conflicts, and resume personal development.

Psychogenic perspective The view that the chief causes of abnormal functioning are psychological.

Psychological autopsy A procedure used to analyze information about a deceased person, for example, in order to determine whether the person's death was a suicide.

Psychological debriefing A form of crisis intervention in which victims are helped to talk about their feelings and reactions to traumatic incidents. Also called *critical incident stress debriefing*.

Psychological profile A method of suspect identification that seeks to predict an unknown criminal's psychological, emotional, and personality characteristics based on the individual's pattern of criminal behavior and on research into the psychological characteristics of people who have committed similar crimes.

Psychology The study of mental processes and behaviors.

Psychomotor symptoms Disturbances in movement sometimes found in certain disorders such as schizophrenia.

Psychoneuroimmunology The study of the connections among stress, the body's immune system, and illness.

Psychopathology An abnormal pattern of functioning that may be described as deviant, distressful, dysfunctional, and/or dangerous.

Psychopathy *See* antisocial personality disorder.

Psychopharmacologist A psychiatrist who primarily prescribes medications. Also called *pharmacotherapist*.

Psychophysiological disorders Disorders in which biological, psychological, and sociocultural factors interact to cause or worsen a physical illness. Also known as *psychological factors affecting other medical conditions*.

Psychophysiological test A test that measures physical responses (such as heart rate and muscle tension) as possible indicators of psychological problems.

Psychosexual stages The developmental stages defined by Freud in which the id, ego, and superego interact.

Psychosis A state in which a person loses contact with reality in key ways.

Psychosurgery Brain surgery for mental disorders.

Psychotherapy A treatment system in which words and acts are used by a client (patient) and therapist in order to help the client overcome psychological difficulties.

Psychotropic medications Drugs that mainly affect the brain and reduce many symptoms of mental dysfunctioning.

Quasi-experiment An experiment in which investigators make use of control and experimental groups that already exist in the world at large. Also called a *mixed design*.

Random assignment A selection procedure that ensures that participants are randomly placed either in the control group or in the experimental group.

Rap group The initial term for group therapy sessions among veterans in which members meet to talk about and explore problems in an atmosphere of mutual support.

Rape Forced sexual intercourse or another sexual act committed against a nonconsenting person or intercourse with an underage person.

Rapid eye movement (REM) sleep The period of the sleep cycle during which the eyes move quickly back and forth, indicating that the person is dreaming.

Rapprochement movement An effort to identify a set of common strategies that run through the work of all effective therapists.

Rational-emotive therapy A cognitive therapy developed by Albert Ellis that helps clients identify and change the irrational assumptions and thinking that help cause their psychological disorder.

Rationalization An ego defense mechanism in which one creates acceptable reasons for unwanted or undesirable behavior.

Reaction formation An ego defense mechanism whereby a person counters an unacceptable desire by taking on a lifestyle that directly opposes the unwanted impulse.

Reactive depression A depression that appears to be triggered by clear events. Also known as *exogenous depression*.

Reactivity The extent to which the very presence of an observer affects a person's behavior.

Reality principle The recognition, characterizing ego functioning, that we cannot always express or satisfy our id impulses.

Receptor A site on a neuron that receives a neurotransmitter.

Regression An ego defense mechanism in which a person returns to a more primitive mode of interacting with the world.

Reinforcement The desirable or undesirable stimuli that result from an organism's behavior.

Relapse-prevention training A cognitive-behavioral approach to treating alcohol use disorder (and applied to certain other disorders) in which clients are taught to keep track of their drinking behavior, apply coping strategies in situations that typically trigger excessive drinking, and plan ahead for risky situations and reactions.

Relational psychoanalytic therapy A form of psychodynamic therapy that considers therapists to be active participants in the formation of patients' feelings and reactions and therefore calls for therapists to disclose their own experiences and feelings in discussions with patients.

Relaxation training A treatment procedure that teaches clients to relax at will so they can calm themselves in stressful situations.

Reliability A measure of the consistency of test or research results.

Repression A defense mechanism whereby the ego prevents unacceptable impulses from reaching consciousness.

Residential treatment center A place where people formerly addicted to drugs live, work, and socialize in a drug-free environment. Also called a *therapeutic community*.

Resiliency The ability to avoid or recover from the effects of negative circumstances.

Resistance An unconscious refusal to participate fully in therapy.

Resolution phase The fourth phase in the sexual response cycle, characterized by relaxation and a decline in arousal following orgasm.

Response inventories Tests designed to measure a person's responses in one specific area of functioning, such as affect, social skills, or cognitive processes.

Response prevention *See* Exposure and response prevention.

Response set A particular way of responding to questions or statements on a test, such as always selecting "true," regardless of the actual questions.

Restricting-type anorexia nervosa A type of anorexia nervosa in which people reduce their weight by severely restricting their food intake.

Reticular formation The brain's arousal center, which helps people to be awake, alert, and attentive.

Retrograde amnesia A lack of memory about events that occurred before the event that triggered amnesia.

Retrospective analysis A psychological autopsy in which clinicians and researchers piece together information about a person's suicide from the person's past.

Reversal design A single-subject experimental design in which behavior is measured to provide a baseline (A), then again after the treatment has been applied (B), then again after the conditions during baseline have been reintroduced (A), and then once again after the treatment is reintroduced (B). Also known as *ABAB design*.

Reward A pleasurable stimulus given to an organism that encourages a specific behavior.

Reward center A dopamine-rich pathway in the brain that produces feelings of pleasure when activated.

Reward-deficiency syndrome A condition, suspected to be present in some people, in which the brain's reward center is not readily activated by the usual events in their lives.

Right to refuse treatment The legal right of patients to refuse certain forms of treatment.

Right to treatment The legal right of patients, particularly those who are involuntarily committed, to receive adequate treatment.

Risperidone A commonly prescribed atypical antipsychotic drug.

Ritalin Trade name of methylphenidate, a stimulant drug that is helpful in many cases of attention-deficit/hyperactivity disorder (ADHD).

Role play A therapy technique in which clients are instructed to act out roles assigned to them by the therapist.

Rorschach test A projective test, in which a person reacts to inkblots designed to help reveal psychological features of the person.

Rosenthal effect The general finding that the results of any experiment often conform to the expectations of the experimenter.

Rush A spasm of warmth and ecstasy that occurs when certain drugs, such as heroin, are ingested.

Savant A person with a mental disorder or significant intellectual deficits who has some extraordinary ability despite the disorder or deficits.

Schizoaffective disorder A disorder in which symptoms of both schizophrenia and a mood disorder are prominent.

Schizoid personality disorder A personality disorder in which a person persistently avoids social relationships and shows little emotional expression.

Schizophrenia A psychotic disorder in which personal, social, and occupational functioning deteriorate as a result of strange perceptions, disturbed thought processes, unusual emotions, and motor abnormalities.

Schizophreniform disorder A disorder in which all of the key features of schizophrenia are present but last only between one and six months.

Schizophrenogenic mother A type of mother—supposedly cold, domineering, and uninterested in the needs of her children—who was once thought to cause schizophrenia in her child.

Schizotypal personality disorder A personality disorder characterized by extreme discomfort in close relationships, odd forms of thinking and perceiving, and behavioral eccentricities.

School phobia A pattern in which children fear going to school and often stay home for a long period of time. Also called *school refusal*.

Scientific method The process of systematically gathering and evaluating information through careful observations to gain an understanding of a phenomenon.

Seasonal affective disorder (SAD) A mood disorder in which mood episodes are related to changes in season.

Second-generation antidepressants A relatively new group of antidepressant drugs that differ structurally from tricyclics and MAO inhibitors.

Second-generation antipsychotic drugs A relatively new group of antipsychotic drugs whose biological action is different from that of the conventional antipsychotic drugs. Also known as *atypical antipsychotic drugs*.

Second messengers Chemical changes within a neuron just after the neuron receives a neurotransmitter message and just before it responds.

Secondary gain In psychodynamic theory, the gain people achieve when their somatic symptoms elicit kindness from others or provide an excuse for avoiding unpleasant activities.

Secondary prevention Prevention interventions that are designed to address disorders quickly, before they become more serious problems.

Sedative-hypnotic drug A drug used in low doses to calm people and in higher doses to help people sleep. Also called an *anxiolytic drug*.

Selective amnesia An inability to recall some of the events that occurred over a limited period of time.

Selective serotonin reuptake inhibitors (SSRIs) A group of second-generation antidepressant drugs that increase serotonin activity specifically, without affecting other neurotransmitters.

Self-actualization The humanistic process by which people fulfill their potential for goodness and growth.

Self-efficacy The belief that one can master and perform needed behaviors whenever necessary.

Self-help group A group made up of people with similar problems who help and support one another without the direct leadership of a clinician. Also called a *mutual help group*.

Self-hypnosis The process of hypnotizing oneself, sometimes for the purpose of forgetting unpleasant events.

Self-instruction training A cognitive treatment developed by Donald Meichenbaum that teaches people to use coping self-statements at times of stress, discomfort, or significant pain. Also called *stress inoculation training*.

Self-monitoring Clients' observation of their own behavior.

Self-statements According to some cognitive theorists, statements about oneself, sometimes counterproductive, that come to mind during stressful situations.

Self theory The psychodynamic theory that emphasizes the role of the self—a person's unified personality.

Senile plaques Sphere-shaped deposits of beta-amyloid protein that form in the spaces between certain brain cells and in certain blood vessels as people age. People with Alzheimer's disease have an excessive number of such plaques.

Sensate focus A treatment for sexual disorders that instructs couples to take the focus away from orgasm or intercourse and instead spend time concentrating on the pleasure achieved by such acts as kissing, hugging, and mutual massage. Also known as *nondemand pleasuring*.

Separation anxiety disorder A disorder marked by excessive anxiety, even panic, whenever the individual is separated from home, a parent, or another attachment figure.

Serial murders A series of two or more killings carried out separately by the same individual(s) over a period of time—usually a month or more.

Serotonin A neurotransmitter whose abnormal activity is linked to depression, obsessive-compulsive disorder, and eating disorders.

Severe intellectual disability A level of intellectual disability (IQ between 20 and 34) at which individuals require careful supervision and can learn to perform basic work in structured and sheltered settings.

Sex-change surgery A surgical procedure that changes a person's sex organs, features, and, in turn, sexual identity. Also known as *sexual reassignment surgery*.

Sex offender statute The presumption by some state legislatures that people who are repeatedly found guilty of certain sex crimes have a mental disorder and should be categorized as "mentally disordered sex offenders." Such laws have been changed or abolished by many states over the past two decades.

Sexual dysfunction A disorder marked by a persistent inability to function normally in some area of the human sexual response cycle.

Sexual masochism disorder A paraphilic disorder in which a person has repeated and intense sexual urges, fantasies, or behaviors that involve being humiliated, beaten, bound, or otherwise made to suffer, accompanied by clinically significant distress or impairment.

Sexual response cycle The general sequence of behavior and feelings that occurs during sexual activity, consisting of desire, excitement, orgasm, and resolution.

Sexual sadism disorder A paraphilic disorder in which a person has repeated and intense sexual urges or fantasies that involve inflicting suffering on others and either acts on these urges with nonconsenting individuals or experiences clinically significant distress or impairment.

Sexually violent predator laws Laws passed by the federal government and many states that call for certain sex offenders who have been convicted of sex crimes and have served their sentence in prison to be removed from prison before their release and committed involuntarily to a mental hospital for treatment if a court judges them likely to engage in further acts of sexual violence due to a mental or personality abnormality. Also called *sexually dangerous persons laws*.

Shaping A learning procedure in which successive approximations of the desired behavior are rewarded until finally the exact and complete behavior is learned.

Sheltered workshop A supervised workplace for people who are not yet ready for competitive jobs.

Short-term memory The memory system that collects new information. Also known as *working memory*.

Shuttle box A box separated in the middle by a barrier that an animal can jump over in order to escape or avoid shock.

Sildenafil A drug used to treat erectile disorder that helps increase blood flow to the penis during sexual activity. Marketed as Viagra.

Single-subject experimental design A research method in which a single participant is observed and measured both before and after the manipulation of an independent variable.

Situation anxiety The various levels of anxiety produced in a person by different situations. Also called *state anxiety*.

Sleep apnea disorder A sleep-wake disorder characterized by frequent awakenings each night due to periodic deprivation of oxygen to the brain during sleep.

Sleep terror disorder A parasomnia in which a person awakens suddenly during the first third of sleep, screaming out in extreme fear and agitation.

Sleepwalking disorder A parasomnia in which people repeatedly leave their beds and walk around without being conscious of the episode or remembering it later.

Social anxiety disorder A severe and persistent fear of social or performance situations in which embarrassment may occur.

Social communication disorder A disorder marked by persistent problems in communication and social relationships, but without significant language difficulties or cognitive impairment. The communication and social problems are different in nature and less severe than those in autism spectrum disorder.

Social skills training A therapy approach that helps people learn or improve social skills and assertiveness through role playing and rehearsing of desirable behaviors.

Social therapy An approach to therapy in which the therapist makes practical advice and life adjustment a central focus of treatment for schizophrenia. Therapy also focuses on problem solving, decision making, development of social skills, and management of medications. Also known as *personal therapy*.

Sociocultural model The theoretical perspective that emphasizes the effects of society, culture, and social and family groups on individual behavior.

Sociopathy *See* Antisocial personality disorder.

Sodium amobarbital (Amytal) A drug used to put people into a near-sleep state during which some can better recall forgotten events.

Sodium pentobarbital (Pentothal) *See* Sodium amobarbital.

Somatic symptom disorder A disorder in which people become excessively distressed, concerned, and anxious about bodily symptoms that they are experiencing, and their lives are greatly and disproportionately disrupted by the symptoms.

Somatogenic perspective The view that abnormal psychological functioning has physical causes.

Special education An approach to educating children with intellectual disability in which they are grouped together and given a separate, specially designed education.

Specific learning disorder A developmental disorder marked by impairments in cognitive skills such as reading, writing, arithmetic, or mathematical skills.

Specific phobia A severe and persistent fear of a specific object or situation (does not include agoraphobia and social anxiety disorder).

Spectator role A state of mind that some people experience during sex, focusing on their sexual performance to such an extent that their performance and their enjoyment are reduced.

Standardization The process in which a test is administered to a large group of people whose performance then serves as a standard or norm against which any individual's score can be measured.

State-dependent learning Learning that becomes associated with the conditions under which it occurred, so that it is best remembered under the same conditions.

State hospitals Public mental institutions in the United States, run by the individual states.

State school A state-supported institution for people with intellectual disability.

Statistical analysis The application of principles of probability to the findings of a study in order to learn how likely it is that the findings have occurred by chance.

Statistical significance A measure of the probability that a study's findings occurred by chance rather than because of the experimental manipulation.

Stimulant drug A substance that increases the activity of the central nervous system.

Stimulus generalization A phenomenon in which responses to one stimulus are also produced by similar stimuli.

Stress-management program An approach to treating generalized and other anxiety disorders that teaches clients techniques for reducing and controlling stress.

Stressor An event that creates a sense of threat by confronting a person with a demand or opportunity for change of some kind.

Stress-reduction and problem-solving seminar A workshop or series of group sessions offered by a business in which mental health professionals teach employees how to cope with and solve problems and reduce stress.

Stress response A person's particular reactions to stress.

Structured interview An interview format in which the clinician asks prepared questions.

Subintentional death A death in which the victim plays an indirect, hidden, partial, or unconscious role.

Subject An individual chosen to participate in a study. Also called a *participant*.

Sublimation In psychoanalytic theory, the rechanneling of id impulses into endeavors that are both socially acceptable and personally gratifying. Sublimation can also be used as an ego defense mechanism.

Subpersonalities The two or more distinct personalities found in individuals suffering with dissociative identity disorder. Also known as *alternate personalities*.

Substance use disorder A pattern of maladaptive behaviors and reactions brought about by repeated use of a substance, sometimes also including tolerance for the substance and withdrawal reactions.

Suicidal behavior disorder A classification being studied for possible inclusion in a future revision of DSM-5, in which individuals have tried to commit suicide within the last two years.

Suicide A self-inflicted death in which the person acts intentionally, directly, and consciously.

Suicide prevention program A program that tries to identify people who are at risk of killing themselves and to offer them crisis intervention.

Superego According to Freud, the psychological force that represents a person's values and ideals.

Supportive nursing care A treatment, used to help those with anorexia nervosa in particular, in which trained nurses conduct a day-to-day hospital program of increased caloric intake, nutrition education, support, and, in some programs, motivational interviewing.

Symbolic loss According to Freudian theory, the loss of a valued object (for example, a loss of employment) that is unconsciously interpreted as the loss of a loved one. Also called *imagined loss*.

Sympathetic nervous system The nerve fibers of the autonomic nervous system that quicken the heartbeat and produce other changes experienced as arousal and fear.

Symptom A physical or psychological sign of a disorder.

Synapse The tiny space between the nerve ending of one neuron and the dendrite of another.

Syndrome A cluster of symptoms that usually occur together.

Synergistic effect In pharmacology, an increase of effects that occurs when more than one substance is acting on the body at the same time.

Synesthesia A crossing over of sensory perceptions caused by LSD and other hallucinogenic drugs. For example, a loud sound may be seen or a color may be felt.

Systematic desensitization A behavioral treatment that uses relaxation training and a fear hierarchy to help clients with phobias react calmly to the objects or situations they dread.

Tarantism A disorder occurring throughout Europe between 900 and 1800 A.D. in which people would suddenly start to jump around, dance, and go into convulsions. Also known as *St. Vitus's dance*.

Tardive dyskinesia Extrapyramidal effects that appear in some patients after they have taken conventional antipsychotic drugs for an extended time.

Tay-Sachs disease A metabolic disorder that causes progressive loss of intellectual functioning, vision, and motor functioning, resulting in death.

Temporal lobes Regions of the brain that play a key role in transforming short-term memory to long-term memory, among other functions.

Tension headache *See* Muscle contraction headache.

Tertiary prevention Prevention interventions that are designed to provide effective treatment for moderate or severe disorders as soon as it is needed so that the disorders do not become long-term problems.

Test A device for gathering information about a few aspects of a person's psychological functioning from which broader information about the person can be inferred.

Testosterone The principal male sex hormone.

Tetrahydrocannabinol (THC) The main active ingredient of cannabis.

Thanatos According to the Freudian view, the basic death instinct that functions in opposition to the life instinct.

Thematic Apperception Test (TAT) A projective test consisting of pictures that show people in ambiguous situations that the client is asked to interpret.

Theory of mind One's awareness that other people base their behaviors on their own beliefs, intentions, and mental states, not on information they have no way of knowing.

Therapist A professional clinician who applies a system of therapy to help a person overcome psychological difficulties.

Therapy A systematic process for helping people overcome their psychological problems. Therapy consists of a patient, a trained therapist, and a series of contacts between them.

Token economy program A behavioral program in which a person's desirable behaviors are reinforced systematically throughout the day by the awarding of tokens that can be exchanged for goods or privileges.

Tolerance The adjustment that the brain and the body make to the regular use of certain drugs so that ever larger doses are needed to achieve the earlier effects.

Torture The use of brutal, degrading, and disorienting strategies to reduce victims to a state of utter helplessness.

Trait anxiety The general level of anxiety that a person brings to the various events in his or her life.

Tranquilizer A drug that reduces anxiety.

Transcranial magnetic stimulation (TMS) A treatment procedure for depression in which an electromagnetic coil, which is placed on or above a person's head, sends a current into the person's brain.

Transference According to psychodynamic theorists, the redirection toward the psychotherapist of feelings associated with important figures in a patient's life, now or in the past.

Transgender experience A sense that one's actual gender identity is different from one's assigned gender (i.e., the gender category to which one was born physically) or that it lies outside the usual male versus female categories.

Transvestic disorder A paraphilic disorder consisting of repeated and intense sexual urges, fantasies, or behaviors that involve dressing in clothes of the opposite sex, accompanied by clinically significant distress or impairment. Also known as *transvestism* or *cross-dressing*.

Treatment A systematic procedure designed to help change abnormal behavior into more normal behavior. Also called *therapy*.

Trephination An ancient operation in which a stone instrument was used to cut away a circular section of the skull, perhaps to treat abnormal behavior.

Trichotillomania A disorder in which people repeatedly pull out hair from their scalp, eyebrows, eyelashes, or other parts of their body. Also called *hair-pulling disorder*.

Tricyclic An antidepressant drug such as imipramine that has three rings in its molecular structure.

Trisomy A chromosomal abnormality in which a person has three chromosomes of one kind rather than the usual two.

Tube and intravenous feeding Forced nourishment sometimes provided to people with anorexia nervosa when their condition becomes life-threatening.

Type A personality style A personality pattern characterized by hostility, cynicism, drivenness, impatience, competitiveness, and ambition.

Type B personality style A personality pattern in which a person is more relaxed, less aggressive, and less concerned about time.

Type I schizophrenia According to some theorists, a type of schizophrenia dominated by positive symptoms, such as delusions, hallucinations, and certain formal thought disorders.

Type II schizophrenia According to some theorists, a type of schizophrenia dominated by negative symptoms, such as flat affect, poverty of speech, and loss of volition.

Tyramine A chemical that, if allowed to accumulate, can raise blood pressure dangerously. It is found in many common foods and is broken down by MAO.

Ulcer A lesion that forms in the wall of the stomach or of the duodenum.

Unconditional positive regard Full, warm acceptance of a person regardless of what he or she says, thinks, or feels; a critical component of client-centered therapy.

Unconditioned response (UCR) The natural, automatic response produced by an unconditioned stimulus.

Unconditioned stimulus (UCS) A stimulus that produces an automatic, natural response.

Unconscious The deeply hidden mass of memories, experiences, and impulses that is viewed in Freudian theory as the source of much behavior.

Undoing An ego defense mechanism in which a person unconsciously cancels out an unacceptable desire or act by performing another act.

Unilateral electroconvulsive therapy (ECT) A form of electroconvulsive therapy in which electrodes are attached to the head so that electrical current passes through only one side of the brain.

Unipolar depression Depression without a history of mania.

Unstructured interview An interview format in which the clinician asks spontaneous questions that are based on issues that arise during the interview.

Vagus nerve stimulation A treatment procedure for depression in which an implanted pulse generator sends regular electrical signals to a person's vagus nerve; the nerve, in turn, stimulates the brain.

Validity The accuracy of a test's or study's results; that is, the extent to which the test or study actually measures or shows what it claims.

Valium The trade name of diazepam, an anti-anxiety drug.

Variable Any characteristic or event that can vary across time, locations, or persons.

Ventromedial hypothalamus (VMH) A brain region that depresses hunger when activated.

Visual hallucinations Hallucinations in which a person may either experience vague visual perceptions, perhaps of colors or clouds, or have distinct visions of people, objects, or scenes that are not there.

Voyeuristic disorder A paraphilic disorder in which a person has repeated and intense sexual desires to observe unsuspecting people in secret as they undress or to spy on couples having intercourse and either acts on these urges with nonconsenting individuals or experiences clinically significant distress or impairment.

Weight set point The weight level that a person is predisposed to maintain, controlled in part by the hypothalamus.

Withdrawal Unpleasant, sometimes dangerous reactions that may occur when people who use a drug regularly stop taking or reduce their dosage of the drug.

Working through The psychoanalytic process of facing conflicts, reinterpreting feelings, and overcoming one's problems.

References

AA World Services. (2014). *2011 membership survey.* New York: Author.

AACAP (American Academy of Child & Adolescent Psychiatry). (2013). *Facts for families guide: The depressed child.* Washington, DC: AACAP.

AAIDD (American Association of Intellectual and Developmental Disabilities). (2008). *Sexuality.* Washington, DC: AAIDD.

AAIDD (American Association of Intellectual and Developmental Disabilities). (2010). *Intellectual disability: Definition, classification, and system of supports* (11th ed.). Washington, DC: AAIDD.

AAIDD (American Association of Intellectual and Developmental Disabilities). (2013). *Definition of intellectual disability.* Washington, DC: AAIDD.

Aamodt, M. G. (2014, September 6). *Serial killer statistics.* Retrieved from Aamodt website: http://maamodt.asp.radford.edu/serial_killer_information_center/project_description.htm.

Abbas, A. A., Kisely, S. R., Town, J. M., Leichsenring, F., Driessen, E., De Maat, S., . . . Crowe, E. (2014). Short-term psychodynamic psychotherapies for common mental disorders. *Cochrane Database of Systematic Reviews, 7,* CD004687.

Abbey, A. (2002). Alcohol-related sexual assault: A common problem among college students. *Journal of Studies on Alcohol, 14,* 118–128.

Abbey, A., Wegner, R., Woerner, J., Pegram, S. E., & Pierce, J. (2014). Review of survey and experimental research that examines the relationship between alcohol consumption and men's sexual aggression perpetration. *Trauma, Violence & Abuse, 15*(4), 265–282.

Abbey, S. E. (2005). Somatization and somatoform disorders. In J. L. Levenson (Ed.), *The American Psychiatric Publishing textbook of psychosomatic medicine* (pp. 271–296). Washington, DC: American Psychiatric Publishing.

Abel, G. G., Becker, J. V., & Cunningham-Rathner, J. (1984). Complications, consent, and cognitions in sex between children and adults. *International Journal of Law and Psychiatry, 7,* 89–103.

Abel, G. G., Jordan, A., Hand, C. G., Holland, L. A., & Phipps, A. (2001). Classification models of child molesters utilizing the Abel Assessment for child sexual abuse interest. *Child Abuse & Neglect, 25*(5), 703–718.

Aboujaoude, E., Savage, M. W., Starcevic, V., & Salame, W. O. (2015). Cyberbullying: Review of an old problem gone viral. *The Journal of Adolescent Health: Official Publication of the Society for Adolescent Medicine, 57*(1), 10–18.

Abraham, K. (1911). Notes on the psychoanalytic investigation and treatment of manic-depressive insanity and allied conditions. In *Selected papers on psychoanalysis* (pp. 137–156). New York: Basic Books. [Work republished 1960]

Abraham, K. (1916). The first pregenital stage of the libido. In *Selected papers on psychoanalysis* (pp. 248–279). New York: Basic Books. [Work republished 1960].

Abraham, S., & Llewellyn-Jones, D. (1984). *Eating disorders: The facts.* New York: Oxford University Press.

Abramowitz, J. S., & Braddock, A. E. (2011). *Hypochondriasis and health anxiety. Advances in psychotherapy—Evidence-based practice.* Cambridge, MA: Hogrefe Publishing.

Abramowitz, J. S., Deacon, B. J., & Whiteside, S. P. H. (2011). *Exposure therapy for anxiety: Principles and practice.* New York: Guilford Press.

Abramowitz, J. S., McKay, D., & Taylor, S. (Eds.) (2008). *Obsessive-compulsive disorder: Subtypes and spectrum conditions.* Oxford, England: Elsevier.

Abramson, L. Y., Alloy, L. B., Hankin, B. L., Haeffel, G. J., MacCoon, D. G., & Gibb, B. E. (2002). Cognitive vulnerability—Stress models of depression in a self-regulatory and psychobiological context. In I. H. Gotlib & C. L. Hammen (Eds.), *Handbook of depression* (pp. 268–294). New York: Guilford Press.

Abramson, L. Y., Metalsky, G. I., & Alloy, L. B. (1989). Hopelessness depression: A theory-based subtype of depression. *Psychological Review, 96*(2), 358–372.

Abramson, L. Y., Seligman, M. E., & Teasdale, J. D. (1978). Learned helplessness in humans: Critique and reformulation. *Journal of Abnormal Psychology, 87*(1), 49–74.

Achalia, R. M., Chaturvedi, S. K., Desai, G., Rao, G. N., & Prakash, O. (2014). Prevalence and risk factors associated with tardive dyskinesia among Indian patients with schizophrenia. *Asian Journal of Psychiatry, 9,* 31–35.

Acosta, M. C., Haller, D. L., & Schnoll, S. H. (2005). Cocaine and stimulants. In R. J. Frances, A. H. Mack, & S. I. Miller (Eds.), *Clinical textbook of addictive disorders* (3rd ed., pp. 184–218). New York: Guilford Press.

Acosta, M. C., Haller, D. L., & Schnoll, S. H. (2011). Cocaine and stimulants. In R. J. Frances, A. H. Mack, & S. I. Miller (Eds.), *Clinical textbook of addictive disorders* (3rd ed., pp. 184–218). New York: Guilford Press.

ADAA (Anxiety and Depression Association of America). (2014). *Facts and statistics.* Silver Spring, MD: ADAA.

Adam, K. S., Bouckoms, A., & Streiner, D. (1982). Parental loss and family stability in attempted suicide. *Archives of General Psychiatry, 39*(9), 1081–1085.

Adams, C. E., Awad, G. A., Rathbone, J., Thornley, B., & Soares-Weiser, K. (2014). Chlorpromazine versus placebo for schizophrenia. *Cochrane Database of Systematic Reviews, 1,* CD000284.

Adams, J. G. (2013). Sexual assault (Ch. 128). In J. G. Adams (Ed.), *Emergency medicine: Clinical essentials* (2nd ed.). Elsevier Health Services. [Kindle edition].

Adams, R. E., & Boscarino, J. A. (2005). Stress and well-being in the aftermath of the World Trade Center attack: The continuing effects of a communitywide disaster. *Journal of Community Psychology, 33*(2), 175–190.

Addington, J., Heinssen, R. K., Robinson, D. G., Schooler, N. R., Marcy, P., Brunette, M. F., . . . Kane, J. M. (2015). Duration of untreated psychosis in community treatment settings in the United States. *Psychiatric Services* (Washington, D.C.), *66*(7), 753–756.

Advokat, C. D., Comaty, J. E., & Julien, R. M. (2014). *Julien's primer of drug action.* New York: Worth Publishers.

AFA (Alzheimer's Foundation of America). (2014). *About dementia.* New York: AFA.

Affatati, V., Di Nicola, V., Santoro, M., Bellomo, A., Todarello, G., & Todarello, O. (2004). Psychotherapy of gender identity disorder: Problems and perspectives. *Medica Psicosomatica, 49*(1–2), 57–64.

Afifi, T. O., MacMillan, H. L., Boyle, M., Taillieu, T., Cheung, K., & Sareen, J. (2014). Child abuse and mental disorders in Canada. *Canadian Medical Association Journal, 186*(9), E324–E332.

AFSP (American Foundation for Suicide Prevention). (2014). Facts and figures for 2010: Suicide deaths. Retrieved from AFSP website: https://www.afsp.org/understanding-suicide/facts-and-figures.

AFSP (American Foundation for Suicide Prevention). (2014). Facts and figures for 2011: Suicide deaths. Retrieved from AFSP website: https://www.afsp.org/understanding-suicide/facts-and-figures.

Agras, S. (1985). *Panic: Facing fears, phobias, and anxiety.* New York: W. H. Freeman.

Agronin, M. E. (2006). Personality disorders. In D. V. Jeste & J. H. Friedman (Eds.), *Psychiatry for neurologists.* Totowa, NJ: Humana Press.

Aguilera, A., Garza, M. J., & Muñoz, R. F. (2010). Group cognitive-behavioral therapy for depression in Spanish: Culture-sensitive manualized treatment in practice. *Journal of Clinical Psychology, 66*(8), 857–867.

AHA (American Heart Association). (2011). Heart disease and stroke statistics—2010 update: A report from the American Heart Association. *Circulation, 121,* e-46–e-215.

Ahearn, W. H. (2010). What every behavior analyst should know about the "MMR uses autism" hypothesis. *Behavior Analysis in Practice, 3*(1), 46–50.

Ahern, G. L., Herring, A. M., Labiner, D. M., Weinand, M. E., & Hutzler, R. (2000). Affective self-report during the intracarotid sodium amobarbital test: Group differences. *Journal of the International Neuropsychological Society, 6*(6), 659–667.

Ahlers, C. J., Schaefer, G. A., Mundt, I. A., Roll, S., Englert, H., Willich, S. N., & Beier, K. M. (2011). How unusual are the contents of paraphilias? Paraphilia-associated sexual arousal patterns in a community-based sample of men. *Journal of Sexual Medicine, 8*(5), 1362–1370.

AI (Amnesty International). (2000). *Torture worldwide: An affront to human dignity.* New York: Amnesty International.

Aiken, C. B. (2010). Neuroprotection in bipolar depression. In M. C. Ritsner (Ed.), *Brain protection in schizophrenia, mood and cognitive disorders* (pp. 451–483). New York: Springer Science + Business Media.

Aiken, L. R. (1985). *Psychological testing and assessment* (5th ed.). Boston: Allyn & Bacon.

Ajdacic-Gross, V., Ring, M., Gadola, E., Lauber, C., Bopp, M., Gutzwiller, F., & Rössler, W. (2008). Suicide after bereavement: An overlooked problem. *Psychological Medicine, 38*(5), 673–676.

Akhtar, S., Wig, N. H., Verma, V. K., Pershod, D., & Verma, S. K. (1975). A phenomenological analysis of symptoms in obsessive-compulsive neuroses. *British Journal of Psychiatry, 127,* 342–348.

Akinbami, L. J., Moorman, J. E., & Liu, X. (2011, January 12). Asthma prevalence, health care use, and mortality: United States, 2005–2009. *National Health Statistics Report, 32,* 1–14.

Akins, C. K. (2004). The role of Pavlovian conditioning in sexual behavior: A comparative analysis of human and nonhuman animals. *International Journal of Comparative Psychology, 17*(2–3), 241–262.

Albala, I., Doyle, M., & Appelbaum, P. S. (2010). The evolution of consent forms for research: A quarter century of changes. *IRB: Ethics & Human Research, 32*(3), 7–11.

Alcalar, N., Ozkan, S., Kucucuk, S., Aslay, I., & Ozkan, M. (2012). Association of coping style, cognitive errors and cancer-related variables with depression in women treated for breast cancer. *Japanese Journal of Clinical Oncology, 42*(10), 940–947.

Alcántara, C., & Gone, J. P. (2008). Suicide in Native American communities: A transactional ecological formulation of the problem. In M. M. Leach & F. T. L. Leong (Eds.), *Suicide among racial and ethnic minority groups: Theory, research, and practice* (pp. 173–199). New York: Routledge/Taylor & Francis Group.

Aldhous, P. (2012, December 3). Personality disorder revamp ends in "horrible waste." *New Scientist.*

Alegría, M., Atkins, M., Farmer, E., Slaton, E., & Stelk, W. (2010). One size does not fit all: Taking diversity, culture and context seriously. *Administration and Policy in Mental Health and Mental Health Service Research, 37*(1-2), 48–60.

Alegría, M., Fortuna, L. R., Lin, J. Y., Norris, F. H., Gao, S., Takeuchi, D. T., . . . Valentine, A. (2013). Prevalence, risk, and correlates of posttraumatic stress disorder across ethnic and racial minority groups in the United States. *Medical Care, 51*(12), 1114–1123.

Alegría, M., Molina, K. M., & Chen, C. (2014). Neighborhood characteristics and differential risk for depressive and anxiety disorders across racial/ethnic groups in the United States. *Depression & Anxiety, 31*(1), 27–37.

Alegría, M., Mulvaney-Day, N., Torres, M., Polo, A., Cao, Z., & Canino, G. (2007). Prevalence of psychiatric disorders across Latino subgroups in the United States. *American Journal of Public Health, 97*(1), 68–75.

Alegría, M., Mulvaney-Day, N., Woo, M., & Miruell-Fuentes, E. A. (2012). Psychology of Latino adults: Challenges and an agenda for action. In E. C. Chang & C. A. Downey (Eds.). *Handbook of race and development in mental health* (pp. 279–306). New York: Springer Science & Business Media.

Alexander, J. F., Sexton, T. L., & Robbins, M. S. (2002). The developmental status of family therapy in family psychology intervention science. In H. A. Liddle, D. A. Santisteban, R. F. Levant, & J. H. Bray (Eds.), *Family psychology: Science-based interventions* (pp. 17–40) Washington, DC: American Psychological Association.

Alfano, C. A., & Beidel, D. C. (Eds.). (2011). *Social anxiety in adolescents and young adults: Translating developmental science into practice.* Washington, DC: American Psychological Association.

Algars, M., Santtila, P., Jern, P., Johansson, A., Westerlund, M., & Sandnabba, N. K. (2011). Sexual body image and its correlates: A population-based study of Finnish women and men. *International Journal of Sexual Health, 23*(1), 26–34.

Ali, M. M., Dwyer, D. S., & Rizzo, J. A. (2011). The social contagion effect of suicidal behavior in adolescents: Does it really exist? *Journal of Mental Health Policy and Economics, 14*(1), 3–12.

Ali, S., Jabeen, S., Pate, R. J., Shahid, M., Chinala, S., Nathani, M., & Shah, R. (2015). Conversion disorder—mind versus body: A review. *Innovations in Clinical Neuroscience, 12*(5-6), 27–33.

Alisic, E., Zalta, A. K., van Wesel, F., Larsen, S. E., Hafstad, G. S., Hassanpour, K., & Smid, G. E. (2014). Rates of post-traumatic stress disorder in trauma-exposed children and adolescents: Meta-analysis. *British Journal of Psychiatry, 204,* 335–340.

Allan, N. P., Capron, D. W., Raines, A. M., & Schmidt, N. B. (2014). Unique relations among anxiety sensitivity factors and anxiety, depression, and suicidal ideation. *Journal of Anxiety Disorders, 28*(2), 266–275.

Allan, R. (2014). John Hunter: Early association of Type A behavior with cardiac mortality. *The American Journal of Cardiology, 114*(1), 148–150.

Allderidge, P. (1979). Hospitals, madhouses and asylums: Cycles in the care of the insane. *British Journal of Psychiatry, 134,* 321–334.

Allen, D. F. (Ed.). (1985). *The cocaine crisis.* Plenum Press: New York.

Allison, R. (2010). Aligning bodies with minds: The case for medical and surgical treatment of gender dysphoria. *Journal of Gay & Lesbian Mental Health, 14*(2), 139–144.

Alloway, T. P. (2014, May 11). Selfies, Facebook, and narcissism: What's the link? *Psychology Today.*

Alloway, T. P., Runac, R., Qureshi, M., & Kemp, G. (2014). Is Facebook linked to selfishness?

Investigating the relationships among social media use, empathy, and narcissism. *Social Networking, 3*(3), 150–158.

Almeida, J., Graca, O., Vieira, F., Almeida, N., & Santos, J. C. (2010). Characteristics of offenders deemed not guilty by reason of insanity in Portugal. *Medicine, Science, and the Law, 50*(3), 136–139.

Alonzo, D., Thompson, R. G., Stohl, M., & Hasin, D. (2014). The influence of parental divorce and alcohol abuse on adult offspring risk of lifetime suicide attempt in the United States. *The American Journal of Orthopsychiatry, 84*(3), 316–320.

Alridge, J. (2012, May 17). How many people commit suicide due to depression. *Examiner.com.*

Alter, C. (2013, September 23). FDA to regulate health apps. *Time, Inc.*

Alter, C. (2014, March 10). Holder urges use of drug to combat heroin overdoses. *Time.*

Althof, S. E. (2007). Treatment of rapid ejaculation: Psychotherapy, pharmacotherapy, and combined therapy. In S. R. Leiblum, *Principles and practice of sex therapy* (4th ed., pp. 212–240). New York: Guilford Press.

Althof, S. E., Rosen, R. C., Perelman, M. A., & Rubio-Aurioles, E. (2013). Standard operating procedures for taking a sexual history. *Journal of Sexual Medicine, 10,* 26–35.

Althouse, R. (2010). Jails are nation's largest institutions for mentally ill. *National Psychologist, 19*(6), 1, 5.

Alvarenga, M. S., Koritar, P., Pisciolaro, F., Mancini, M., Cordás, T. A., & Scagliusi, F. B. (2014). Eating attitudes of anorexia nervosa, bulimia nervosa, binge eating disorder and obesity without eating disorder female patients: Differences and similarities. *Physiology & Behavior, 131,* 99–104.

Alzheimer's Association. (2007). Care in the U.S. Graph cited in *Newsweek, CXLIX*(25), 56.

Alzheimer's Association. (2014). *Alzheimer's disease.* New York: ALZ.org. Retrieved from Alzheimer's Assocation website: http://www.alz.org/alzheimers_disease_1973.asp.

AMA (American Medical Association). (2011). *Physician characteristics and distribution in the U.S.* Chicago, IL: AMA Press.

Amad, A., Ramoz, N., Thomas, P., Jardri, R., & Gorwood, P. (2014). Genetics of borderline personality disorder: Systematic review and proposal of an integrative model. *Neuroscience & Biobehavioral Reviews, 40,* 6–19.

Aman, M. G., & Farmer, C. A. (2011). Self-injury, aggression, and related problems. In E. Hollander, A. Kolevzon, & J. T. Coyle (Eds.), *Textbook of autism spectrum disorders.* (pp. 179–187). Arlington, VA: American Psychiatric Publishing, Inc.

Ambresin, A., Vust, S., Lier, F., & Michaud, P. (2014). Adolescents with an eating disorder: An evidence-based approach on the role of parents. *Revue Médicale Suisse, 10*(412-413), 66–68.

American Association of Fundraising Counsel. (2010). *Giving USA: 2009.* Chicago, IL: Author.

Ames, D., Chiu, E., Lindesay, J., & Shulman, K. I. (2010). *Guide to the psychiatry of old age.* New York: Cambridge University Press.

Amianto, F., Abbate-Doga, G., Morando, S., Sobrero, C., & Fassino, S. (2011). Personality traits that differentiate individuals with anorexia nervosa and their healthy siblings. *Clinician's Research Digest, 29*(3).

Amore, M., Innamorati, M., Vittorio, C. D., Weinberg, I., Turecki, G., Sher, L., . . . Pompili, M. (2014). Suicide attempts in major depressed patients with personality disorder. *Suicide & Life Threatening Behavior, 44*(2), 155–166.

ANAD (National Association of Anorexia Nervosa and Associated Disorders). (2014). *Binge eating disorder: The "new" eating disorder: Binge eating disorder (BED).* Retrieved from ANAD website: http://www.anad.org/get-information/get-informationbinge-eating.

ANAD (National Association of Anorexia Nervosa and Associated Disorders). (2015). *Eating disorders statistics.* Naperville, IL: ANAD.

an der Heiden, W., & Häfner, H. (2011). Course and outcomes. In D. R. Weinberg & P. Harrison (Eds.), *Schizophrenia* (pp. 104–141). Hoboken, NJ: Wiley-Blackwell.

Anders, S. L., Frazier, P. A., & Shallcross, S. L. (2012). Prevalence and effects of life event exposure among undergraduate and community college students. *Journal of Counseling Psychology, 59*(3), 449–457.

Anderson, G., Berk, M., Dean, O., Moylan, S., & Maes, M. (2014). Role of immune-inflammatory and oxidative and nitrosative stress pathways in the etiology of depression: Therapeutic implications. *CNS Drugs, 28*(1), 1–10.

Anderson, J., Snider, S., Sellbom, M., Krueger, R., & Hopwood, C. (2014). A comparison of the DSM-5 Section II and Section III personality disorder structures. *Psychiatry Research, 216*(3), 363–372.

Anderson, K. G., Sankis, L. M., & Widiger, S. A. (2001). Pathology versus statistical infrequency: Potential sources of gender bias in personality disorder criteria. *Journal of Nervous and Mental Disease, 189*(10), 661–668.

Anderson, N. (2014, July 1). Sex offense statistics show U.S. college reports are rising. *Washington Post.*

Anderson, P. L., Price, M., Edwards, S. M., Obasaju, M. A., Schmertz, S. K., Zimand, E., & Calamaras, M. R. (2013). Virtual reality exposure therapy for social anxiety disorder: A randomized controlled trial. *Journal of Consulting And Clinical Psychology, 81*(5), 751–760.

Andreasen, N. C., & Black, D. W. (2006). *Introductory textbook of psychiatry* (4th ed.). Washington, DC: American Psychiatric Publishing.

Andreoli, S. B., Dos Santos, M. M., Quintana, M. I., Ribeiro, W. S., Blay, S. L., Taborda, J. G., & de Jesus Mari, J. (2014). Prevalence of mental disorders among prisoners in the state of Sao Paulo, Brazil. *PLOS ONE, 9*(2), e88836.

Andresen, J. (2000). Meditation meets behavioral medicine: The story of experimental research on meditation. *Journal of Consciousness Studies, 7*(11–12), 17–73.

Andrews, J. A., & Hops, H. (2010). The influence of peers on substance use. In L. Scheier (Ed.), *Handbook of drug use etiology: Theory, methods, and empirical findings* (pp. 403–420). Washington, DC: American Psychological Association.

Andrews, V. (1998, December 14). Abducted by aliens? Or just a little schizoid? *HealthScout.*

Anestis, M. D., & Anestis J. C. (2015). Suicide rates and state laws regulating access and exposure to handguns. *American Journal of Public Health,* e1–e10. [Advance electronic publication.]

Annunziato, R. A., Lee, J. N., & Lowe, M. R. (2007). A comparison of weight-control behaviors in African American and Caucasian women. *Ethnicity & Disease, 17,* 262–267.

Anonymous. (1996). First person account: Social, economic, and medical effects of schizophrenia. *Schizophrenia Bulletin, 22*(1), 183.

Anonymous. (2006). On madness: A personal account of rapid cycling bipolar disorder. *British Journal of General Practice, 56*(530), 726–728.

Antal, H., Hossain, M. J., Hassink, S., Henry, S., Fuzzell, L., Taylor, A., & Wysocki, T. (2015). Audio-video recording of health care encounters for pediatric chronic conditions: Observational reactivity and its correlates. *Journal of Pediatric Psychology, 40*(1), 144–153.

Antony, M. M. (2014). Behavior therapy. In D. Wedding & R. J. Corsini (Eds.), *Current psychotherapies* (10th ed., pp. 193–230). Independence, KY: Cengage Publications.

Antony, M. M., & Barlow, D. H. (Eds.). (2004). *Handbook of assessment and treatment planning for psychological disorders*. New York: Guilford Press.

Antony, M. M., & Barlow, D. H. (Eds.). (2010). *Handbook of assessment and treatment planning for psychological disorders* (2nd ed.). New York: Guilford Press.

Antony, M. M., & Roemer, L. (2011). *Behavior therapy*. Washington, DC: American Psychological Association.

APA (American Psychiatric Association). (2000). *DSM-IV text revision*. Washington, DC: Author.

APA (American Psychiatric Association). (2003). Questions and answers on using "insanity" as a legal defense. *HealthyMinds.org*. Arlington, VA: American Psychiatric Association.

APA (American Psychiatric Association). (2013, May 13). *DSM-5 field trials*. Washington, DC: Author.

APA (American Psychiatric Association). (2013). *Diagnostic and statistical manual of mental disorders* (5th ed.). Washington, DC: Author.

APA (American Psychiatric Association). (2013). *The people behind DSM-5*. Washington, DC: Author.

APA (American Psychological Association). (1996). *Statement on the disclosure of test data*. Washington, DC: American Psychological Association.

APA (American Psychological Association). (2002). *Ethical principles of psychologists and code of conduct*. Washington, DC: Author.

APA (American Psychological Association). (2010). *Ethical principles of psychologists and code of conduct*. Washington, DC: Author.

APA (American Psychological Association). (2010). *Gender and stress: Stress on the rise for women*. Retrieved from APA website: http://www.apa.org.

APA (American Psychological Association). (2014). *APA applauds landmark Illinois law allowing psychologists to prescribe medications*. Washington, DC: Author.

APA (American Psychological Association). (2014). *Ethical principles of psychologists and code of conduct*. Washington, DC: Author.

APA (American Psychological Association). (2014). *Mental and behavioral health and older Americans*. Washington, DC: American Psychiatric Publishing, Inc. Retrieved from APA website: http://www.apa.org/about/gr/issues/aging/mental-health.aspx.

APA (American Psychological Association). (2015). *Eating disorders*. Washington, DC: APA.

APA (American Psychological Association). (2015). *Forensic psychology*. Washington, DC: Author.

Apfelbaum, B. (2000). Retarded ejaculation: A much misunderstood syndrome. In S. R. Leiblum & R. C. Rosen (Eds.), *Principles and practice of sex therapy* (3rd ed.). New York: Guilford Press.

Apostolova, L. G., & Cummings, J. L. (2008). Neuropsychiatric aspects of Alzheimer's disease and other dementing illnesses. In S. C. Yudofsky & R. E. Hales (Eds.), *The American psychiatric publishing textbook of neuropsychiatry and behavioral neurosciences* (5th ed.). Washington, DC: American Psychiatric Publishing.

Appelbaum, P. S. (2011). Law and psychiatry: Reforming malpractice: The prospects for change. *Psychiatric Services, 62*(1), 6–8.

Appelbaum, P. S. (2011). Law and psychiatry: SSRIs, suicide, and liability for failure to warn of medication risks. *Psychiatric Services, 62*(4), 347–349.

Apter, A., & Wasserman, D. (2007). Suicide in psychiatric disorders during adolescence. In R. Tatarelli, M. Pompili, & P. Girardi (Eds.), *Suicide in psychiatric disorders*. New York: Nova Science Publishers.

Arcelus, J., Witcomb, G. L., & Mitchell, A. (2014). Prevalence of eating disorders amongst dancers: A systemic review and meta-analysis. *European Eating Disorders Review, 22*(2), 92–101.

Archer, D. (2013). Reading between the (head)lines: Smartphone Addiction. *Psychology Today*. Retrieved from Psychology Today website: http://www.psychologytoday.com/blog/reading-between-the-headlines/2013077/smartphone-addiction.

Archer, D. F., Labrie, F., Bouchard, C., Portman, D. J., Koltun, W., Cusan, L., . . . Balser, J. (2015). Treatment of pain at sexual activity (dyspareunia) with intravaginal dehydroepiandrosterone (prasterone). *Menopause, 22*(9), 950–963.

Ardjmand, A., Rezayof, A., & Zarrindast, M-R. (2011). Involvement of central amygdala NMDA receptor mechanism in morphine state-dependent memory retrieval. *Neuroscience Research, 69*(1), 25–31.

Ardoin, S. P., Martens, B. K., Wolfe, L. A., Hilt, A. M., & Rosenthal, B. D. (2004). A method for conditioning reinforcer preferences in students with moderate mental retardation. *Journal of Developmental and Physical Disabilities, 16*(1), 33–51.

Arias, E., Anderson, R. N., Kung, H. C., Murphy, S. L., & Kochanek, K. D. (2003). Deaths: Final data for 2001. *National Vital Statistics Reports, 52*. Hyattsville, MD: National Center for Health Statistics.

Arias, I., Sorlozano, A., Villegas, E., de Dios Luna, J., McKenney, K., Cervilla, J., . . . Gutierrez, J. (2012). Infectious agents associated with schizophrenia: A meta-analysis. *Schizophrenia Research, 136* (1-3), 128–136.

Arieti, S. (1974). *Interpretation of schizophrenia*. New York: Basic Books.

Arieti, S., & Bemporad, J. (1978). *Severe and mild depression: The psychotherapeutic approach*. New York: Basic Books.

Aring, C. D. (1974). The Gheel experience: Eternal spirit of the chainless mind! *Journal of the American Medical Association, 230*(7), 998–1001.

Aring, C. D. (1975). Gheel: The town that cares. *Family Health, 7*(4), 54–55, 58, 60.

Armitage, R., & Arnedt, J. T. (2011). Sleep and circadian rhythms: An understudied area in treatment resistant depression. In J. F. Greden, M. B. Riba, & M. G. McInnis (Eds.), *Treatment resistant depression: A roadmap for effective care* (pp. 183–192). Arlington, VA: American Psychiatric Publishing.

Armour, C., Karstoft, K., & Richardson, J. D. (2014). The co-occurrence of PTSD and dissociation: Differentiating severe PTSD from dissociative-PTSD. *Social Psychiatry and Psychiatric Epidemiology, 49*(8), 1297–1306.

Armstrong, M. J. (2001). Ethnic minority women as they age. In J. D. Garner & S. O. Mercer (Eds.), *Women as they age* (2nd ed., pp. 97–114). New York: Haworth.

Arndt, W. B., Hietpas, T., & Kim, J. (2004). Critical characteristics of male serial murderers. *American Journal of Criminal Justice, 29*(1), 117–131.

Arnold, S. M., Ivleva, E. I., Gopal, T. A., Reddy, A. P., Jeon-Slaughter, H., Sacco, C. B., . . . Tamminga, C. A. (2014). Hippocampal volume is reduced in schizophrenia and schizoaffective disorder but not in psychotic bipolar I disorder demonstrated by both manual tracing and automated parcellation (FreeSurfer). *Schizophrenia Bulletin*. [Electronic publication.]

Aronow, E., Weiss, K. A., & Reznikoff, M. (2001). *A practical guide to the Thematic Apperception Test: The TAT in clinical practice*. New York: Routledge.

Arvanites, T. M. (1989). The differential impact of deinstitutionalization on white and nonwhite defendants found incompetent to stand trial. *Bulletin of the American Academy of Psychiatry Law, 17*, 311–320.

ASAPS (American Society for Aesthetic Plastic Surgery). (2015). Cosmetic surgery. *National Data Bank Statistics for 2014*.

Asberg, M., Traskman, L., & Thoren, P. (1976). 5 HIAA in the cerebrospinal fluid: A biochemical suicide predictor? *Archives of General Psychiatry, 33*(10), 1193–1197.

ASCA (American School Counselor Association). (2010). *Report on Counseling*. Alexandria, VA: Author.

Ash, R. (2001). *The top 10 of everything 2002* (American ed.). New York: DK Publishing.

ASHA (American Speech-Language-Hearing Association). (2015). *Dementia*. Rockville, MD: ASHA.

Ashraf, N., & Thevasagayam, M. S. (2014). Munchausen syndrome by proxy presenting as hearing loss, *Journal of Laryngology & Otology, 128*(6), 540–542.

Ashton, J. R., & Donnan, S. (1981). Suicide by burning as an epidemic phenomenon: An analysis of 82 deaths and inquests in England and Wales in 1978–9. *Psychological Medicine, 11*(4), 735–739.

Asimov, I. (1997). *Isaac Asimov's book of facts*. New York: Random House (Wings Books).

Asmar, M. (2014, February 6). What happens when accused killers plead insanity? *Denver Westword*.

Asnis, G. M., Kohn, S. R., Henderson, M., & Brown, N. L. (2004). SSRIs versus non-SSRIs in post-traumatic stress disorder: An update with recommendations. *Drugs, 64*(4), 383–404.

Assumpção, A. A., Garcia, F. D., Garcia, H. D., Bradford, J. W., & Thibaut, F. (2014). Pharmacologic treatment of paraphilias. *The Psychiatric Clinics of North America, 37*(2), 173–181.

Astbury, J. (2010). The social causes of women's depression: A question of rights violated? In D. C. Jack & A. Ali (Eds.), *Silencing the self across cultures: Depression and gender in the social world* (pp. 19–45). New York: Oxford University Press.

Atack, J. R. (2010). GABAA receptor α2/α3 subtype-selective modulators as potential nonsedating anxiolytics. In M. B. Stein & T. Steckler (Eds.), *Behavioral neurobiology of anxiety and its treatment*, (pp. 331–360). New York: Springer Science + Business Media.

A-Tjak, J. L., Davis, M. L., Morina, N., Powers, M. B., Smits, J. J., & Emmelkamp, P. G. (2015). A meta-analysis of the efficacy of acceptance and commitment therapy for clinically relevant mental and physical health problems. *Psychotherapy and Psychosomatics, 84*(1), 30–36.

Auxemery, Y. (2015). The mass murderer history: Modern classifications, sociodemographic and psychopathological characteristics, suicidal dimensions, and media contagion of mass murders. *Comprehensive Psychiatry, 56*, 149–154.

Avramopoulos, D., Pearce, B. D., McGrath, J., Wolyniec, P., Wang, R., Eckart, N., . . . Pulver, A. E. (2015). Infection and inflammation in schizophrenia and bipolar disorder: A genome wide study for interactions with genetic variation. *PLOS ONE, 10*(3), e0116696.

Axelrod, M. I., Tornehl, C., & Fontanini-Axelrod, A. (2014). Enhanced response using a multicomponent urine alarm treatment for nocturnal enuresis. *Journal for Specialists in Pediatric Nursing, 19*(2), 172–182.

Ayalon, L., & Huyck, M. H. (2001). Latino caregivers of relatives with Alzheimer's disease. *Clinical Gerontology, 24*(3–4), 93–106.

Ayd, F. J., Jr. (1956). A clinical evaluation of Frenquel. *Journal of Nervous and Mental Disease, 124*, 507–509.

Ayllon, T. (1963). Intensive treatment of psychotic behavior by stimulus satiation and food reinforcement. *Behavioral Research and Therapy, 1*, 53–62.

Ayllon, T., & Michael, J. (1959). The psychiatric nurse as a behavioural engineer. *Journal of Experimental Analytical Behavior, 2*, 323–334.

Ayoub, C. C. (2006). Munchausen by proxy. In T. G. Plante (Ed.), *Mental disorders of the new millenium: Biology and function* (Vol. 3, pp. 173–193). Westport, CT: Praeger Publishers/Greenwood Publishing.

Ayoub, C. C. (2010). Munchausen by proxy. In J. M. Brown & E. A. Campbell (Eds.), *The Cambridge handbook of forensic psychology* (pp. 690–699). New York: Cambridge University Press.

Ayoub, C. C. (2010). Munchausen by proxy. In R. J. Shaw & D. R. DeMaso (Eds.), *Textbook of pediatric psychosomatic medicine* (pp. 185–198). Arlington, VA: American Psychiatric Publishing.

Aziz, R., & Steffens, D. C. (2013). What are the causes of late-life depression? *Psychiatric Clinics of North America, 36*(4), 497–516.

Azorin, J., Belzeaux, R., & Adida, M. (2014). Negative symptoms in schizophrenia: Where we have been and where we are heading. *CNS Neuroscience & Therapeutics, 20*(9), 801–808.

Babchishin, K. M., Hanson, R. K., & Vanzuylen, H. (2014). Online child pornography offenders are different: A meta-analysis of the characteristics of online and offline sex offenders against children. *Archives of Sexual Behavior, 44*(1), 45–66.

Baca-Garcia, E., Perez-Rodriguez, M. M., Keyes, K. M., Oquendo, M. A., Hasin, D. S., Grant, B. F., & Blanco, C. (2011). Suicidal ideation and suicide attempts among Hispanic subgroups in the United States: 1991–1992 and 2001–2002. *Journal of Psychiatric Research, 45*(4), 512–518.

Bachelor, A. (1988). How clients perceive therapist empathy: A content analysis of "received" empathy. *Psychotherapy: Theory, Research, Practice, Training, 25*(2), 227–240.

Bacon, T., Farhall, J., & Fossey, E. (2014). The active therapeutic processes of acceptance and commitment therapy for persistent symptoms of psychosis: Clients' perspectives. *Behavioural and Cognitive Psychotherapy, 42*(4), 402–420.

Baer, L., & Blais, M. A. (Eds.). (2010). *Handbook of clinical rating scales and assessment in psychiatry and mental health.* Totowa, NJ: Humana Press.

Bagby, E. (1922). The etiology of phobias. *Journal of Abnormal Psychology, 17,* 16–18.

Bagnall, N., & Faiz, O. D. (2014). Delirium, frailty and IL-6 in the elderly surgical patient. *Langenbeck's Archives of Surgery/Deutsche Gesellschaft Für Chirurgie, 399*(6), 799–800.

Bai, Y., Chiou, W., Su, T., Li, C., & Chen, M. (2014). Pro-inflammatory cytokine associated with somatic and pain symptoms in depression. *Journal of Affective Disorders, 155,* 28–33.

Baig, M. R., Levin, T. T., Lichtenthal, W. G., Boland, P. J., & Breitbart, W. S. (2015). Factitious disorder (Munchausen's syndrome) in oncology: Case report and literature review. *Psycho-Oncology.* [Advance publication.]

Bailey, R. L., Gahche, J. J., Miller, P. E., Thomas, P. R., & Dwyer, J. T. (2013). Why U.S. adults use dietary supplements. *JAMA Internal Medicine, 173*(5), 355–361.

Bakalar, N. (2010) Happiness may come with age, study says. *New York Times, 159*(55, 058).

Bakalar, N. (2013, July 31). Moon phases tied to sleep cycles. *New York Times.*

Baker, K. (2010). From "it's not me" to "it was me, after all": A case presentation of a patient diagnosed with dissociative identity disorder. *Psychoanalytic Social Work, 17*(2), 79–98.

Baker, R. (1992). Psychosocial consequences for tortured refugees seeking asylum and refugee status in Europe. In M. Basoglu (Ed.), *Torture and its consequences: Current treatment approaches* (pp. 83–106). Cambridge, England: Cambridge University Press.

Baker, R. (2011). *Understanding panic attacks and overcoming fear* (3rd ed.). Oxford, UK: Lion Hudson.

Bakoyiannis, I., Gkioka, E., Pergialiotis, V., Mastroleon, I., Prodromidou, A., Vlachos, G. D., & Perrea, D. (2014). Fetal alcohol spectrum disorders and cognitive functions of young children. *Reviews in the Neurosciences, 25*(5), 631–639.

Balassone, M., (2011). Jails, prisons increasingly taking care of mentally ill. *Washington Post, 134*(49).

Baldessarini, R. J., & Tondo, L. (2007). Psychopharmacology for suicide prevention. In R. Tatarelli, M. Pompili, & P. Girardi (Eds.), *Suicide in psychiatric disorders.* New York: Nova Science Publishers.

Baldessarini, R. J., & Tondo, L. (2011). Psychopharmacology for suicide prevention. In M. Pompili & R. Tatarelli (Eds.), *Evidence-based practice in suicidology: A source book* (pp. 243–264). Cambridge MA: Hogrefe Publishing.

Baldinger, P., Lotan, A., Frey, R., Kasper, S., Lerer, B., & Lanzenberger, R. (2014). Neurotransmitters and electroconvulsive therapy. *The Journal of ECT, 30*(2), 116–121.

Baldwin, D. S., Ajel, K., Masdrakis, V. G., Nowak, M., & Rafiq, R. (2013). Pregabalin for the treatment of generalized anxiety disorder: An update. *Neuropsychiatric Disease and Treatment, 9,* 883–892.

Bales, D. L., Timman, R., Andrea, H., Busschbach, J. V., Verheul, R., & Kamphuis, J. H. (2014). Effectiveness of day hospital mentalization-based treatment for patients with severe borderline personality disorder: A matched control study. *Clinical Psychology & Psychotherapy.* [Advance online publication.]

Balhara, Y. S. (2014). A chart review based comparative study of retention rates for two dispensing regimens for buprenorphine for subjects with opioid dependence at a tertiary care substance use disorder treatment center. *Journal of Opioid Management, 10*(3), 200–206.

Bancroft, J., Loftus, J., & Long, J. S. (2003). Distress about sex: A national survey of women in heterosexual relationships. *Archives of Sexual Behavior, 32*(3), 193–208.

Bandelow, B., & Baldwin, D. S. (2010). Pharmacotherapy for panic disorder. In D. J. Stein, E. Hollander, & B. O. Rothbaum (Eds.), *Textbook of anxiety disorders* (2nd ed., pp. 399–416). Arlington, VA: American Psychiatric Publishing.

Bandelow, B., Reitt, M., Röver, C., Michaelis, S., Görlich, Y., & Wedekind, D. (2015). Efficacy of treatments for anxiety disorders: A meta-analysis. *International Clinical Psychopharmacology, 30*(4), 183–192.

Bandura, A. (1971). Psychotherapy based upon modeling principles. In A. E. Bergin & S. L. Garfield (Eds.), *Handbook of psychotherapy and behavior change.* New York: Wiley.

Bandura, A. (1977). Self-efficacy: Toward a unifying theory of behavioral change. *Psychological Review, 84*(2), 191–215.

Bandura, A. (2011). But what about that gigantic elephant in the room? In R. M. Arkin (Ed.), *Most underappreciated: 50 prominent social psychologists describe their most unloved work* (pp. 51–59). New York: Oxford University Press.

Bandura, A., & Rosenthal, T. (1966). Vicarious classical conditioning as a function of arousal level. *Journal of Personality and Social Psychology, 3,* 54–62.

Bandura, A., Adams, N. E., & Beyer, J. (1977). Cognitive processes mediating behavioral change. *Journal of Personality and Social Psychology, 35*(3), 125–139.

Bandura, A., Roth, D., & Ross, S. (1963). Imitation of film-mediated aggressive models. *Journal of Abnormal and Social Psychology, 66,* 3–11.

Barber, A. (1999, March). HerZines. Some yet-to-be exploited niches in the women's magazine market. *American Demographics.*

Barcott, B., & Scherer, M. (2015, May 25). The great pot experiment. *Time,* pp. 38–45.

Bareggi, S. R., Bianchi, L., Cavallaro, R., Gervasoni, M., Siliprandi, F., & Bellodi, L. (2004). Citalopram concentrations and response in obsessive-compulsive disorder: Preliminary results. *CNS Drugs, 18*(5), 329–335.

Barker, K. K. (2014). Mindfulness meditation: Do-it-yourself medicalization of every moment. *Social Science & Medicine (1982), 106,* 168–176.

Barlow, D. H. (2014). *Clinical handbook of psychological disorders: A step-by-step treatment manual* (5th ed.) New York: Guilford Press.

Barlow, M. R. (2011). Memory for complex emotional material in dissociative identity disorder. *Journal of Trauma & Dissociation, 12*(1), 53–66.

Barlow, M. R., & Chu, J. A. (2014). Measuring fragmentation in dissociative identity disorder: The integration measure and relationship to switching and time in therapy. *European Journal of Psychotraumatology, 5*(1). doi:10.3402/ejpt.v5.22250.

Barnes, A. (2004). Race, schizophrenia, and admission to state psychiatric hospitals. *Administration and Policy in Mental Health, 31*(3), 241–252.

Barnes, D. H. (2010). Suicide. In R. L. Hampton, T. P. Gullotta, & R. L. Crowel (Eds.), *Handbook of African American Health* (pp. 444–460). New York: Guilford Press.

Barnes, G. E., & Prosen, H. (1985). Parental death and depression. *Journal of Abnormal Psychology, 94*(1), 64–69.

Barnes, T. R. E., & Marder, S. R. (2011). Principles of pharmacological treatment in schizophrenia. In D. R. Weinberg & P. Harrison (Eds.), *Schizophrenia* (pp. 515–524). Hoboken, NJ: Wiley-Blackwell.

Barr, A. M., Boyda, H., & Procysbyn, R. C. (2011). Withdrawal. In M. C. Olmstead (Ed.), *Animal models of drug addiction. Springer protocols: Neuromethods* (pp. 431–459). Totowa, NJ: Humana Press.

Barrera, T. L., Wilson, K. P., & Norton, P. J. (2010). The experience of panic symptoms across racial groups in a student sample. *Journal of Anxiety Disorders, 24*(8), 873–878.

Barron, E., Sharma, A., Le Couteur, J., Rushton, S., Close, A., Kelly, T., . . . Le Couteur, A. (2014). Family environment of bipolar families: A UK study. *Journal of Affective Disorders, 152–154,* 522–525.

Barrowclough, C., & Lobban, F. (2008). Family intervention. In K. T. Mueser & D. V. Jeste (Eds.), *Clinical handbook of schizophrenia* (pp. 214–225). New York: Guilford Press.

Bartholomew, R. (2014). *Mass hysteria in schools: Worldwide since 1566.* Jefferson, NC: McFarland.

Bartol, C. R., & Bartol, A. M. (2015). *Psychology and Law: Research and Practice.* Los Angeles: Sage Publications.

Barton, A. (2004). Women and community punishment: The probation hostel as a semipenal institution for female offenders. *Howard J. Criminal Justice, 43*(2), 149–163.

Bartrop, R. W., Lockhurst, E., Lazarus, L., Kiloh, L. G., & Penny, R. (1977). Depressed lymphocyte function after bereavement. *Lancet, 1,* 834–836.

Bartz, J., Kaplan, A., & Hollander, E. (2007). Obsessive-compulsive personality disorder. In W. O'Donohue, K. A. Fowler, S. O. Lilienfeld (Eds.), *Personality disorders: Toward the DSM-V.* Los Angeles: Sage Publications.

Basaraba, S. (2014). How long can humans live? Maximum human lifespan: Actual vs. theoretical longevity. *About.com.* Retrieved from About.com website: http://www.about.com.

Basoglu, M., Jaranson, J. M., Mollica, R., & Kastrup, M. (2001). Torture and mental health: A research overview. In E. Gerrity, T. M. Keane, & F. Tuma (Eds.), *The mental health consequences of torture* (pp. 35–62). New York: Kluwer Academic/Plenum Publishers.

Bass, C., & Glaser, D. (2014). Early recognition and management of fabricated or induced illness in children. *Lancet, 383*(9926), 1412–1421.

Basson, R. (2007). Sexual desire/arousal disorders in women. In S. R. Leiblum (Ed.), *Principles and practice of sex therapy* (4th ed., pp. 25–53). New York: Guilford Press.

Bateman, A. W. (2011). Borderline personality disorder. In J. C. Norcross, G. R. VandenBos, & D. K. Freedheim (Eds.), History of psychotherapy: Continuity and change (2nd ed., pp. 588–600). Washington, DC: American Psychological Association.

Bates, G. W., Thompson, J. C., & Flanagan, C. (1999). The effectiveness of individual versus group induction of depressed mood. Journal of Psychology, 133(3), 245–252.

Batstra, L., Nieweg, E. H., Pij, S., Van Tol, C. G., & Haddeis-Algra, M. (2014). Childhood ADHD: A stepped diagnosis approach. Journal of Psychiatric Practice, 20(3),169–177.

Baucom, B. R., Atkins, D. C., Rowe, L. S., Doss, B. D., & Christensen, A. (2015). Prediction of treatment response at 5-year follow-up in a randomized clinical trial of behaviorally based couple therapies. Journal of Consulting and Clinical Psychology, 83(1), 103–114.

Baucom, B. R., Atkins, D. C., Simpson, L. E., & Christensen, A. (2009). Prediction of response to treatment in a randomized clinical trial of couple therapy: A 2-year follow-up. Journal of Consulting and Clinical Psychology, 77(1), 160–173.

Baucom, D. H., & Boeding, S. (2013). The role of theory and research in the practice of cognitive-behavioral couple therapy: If you build it, they will come. Behavior Therapy, 44(4), 592–602.

Baucom, D. H., Epstein, N. B., Kirby, J. S., & LaTaillade, J. J. (2010). Cognitive-behavioral couple therapy. In K. S. Dobson (Ed.), Handbook of cognitive-behavioral therapies (3rd ed., pp. 411–444). New York: Guilford Press.

Bauer, S., Percevic, R., Okon, E., Meermann, R., & Kordy, H. (2003). Use of text messaging in the aftercare of patients with bulimia nervosa. European Eating Disorders Review, 11(3), 279–290.

Baum, A., Trevino, L. A., & Dougall, A. L. (2011). Stress and the cancers. In R. J. Contrada & A. Baum (Eds.), The handbook of stress science: Biology, psychology, and health (pp. 411–423). New York: Springer Publishing.

Baum, A., Wallander, J. L., Boll, T. J., & Frank, R. G. (Eds.). (2004). Handbook of clinical health psychology, Vol. 3: Models and perspectives in health psychology. Washington, DC: American Psychological Association.

Bauman, M. L. (2011). Neuroanatomy of the brain in autism spectrum disorders. In E. Hollander, A. Kolevzon, & J. T. Coyle (Eds.), Textbook of autism spectrum disorders. (pp. 355–361). Arlington, VA: American Psychiatric Publishing, Inc.

Baxter, L. R., Jr., Ackermann, R. F., Swerdlow, N. R., Brody, A., Saxena, S., Schwartz, J. M., . . . Phelps, M. E. (2000). Specific brain system mediation of obsessive-compulsive disorder responsive to either medication or behavior therapy. In W. K. Goodman, M. V. Rudorfer, & J. D. Maser (Eds.), Obsessive-compulsive disorder: Contemporary issues in treatment (pp. 573–609). Mahwah, NJ: Lawrence Erlbaum.

Baxter, L. R., Jr., Clark, E. C., Iqbal, M., & Ackermann, R. F. (2001). Cortical-subcortical systems in the mediation of obsessive-compulsive disorder: Modeling the brain's mediation of a classic "neurosis." In D. G. Lichter & J. L. Cummings (Eds.), Frontal-subcortical circuits in psychiatric and neurological disorders (pp. 207–230). New York: Guilford Press.

Baxter, L. R., Jr., Schwartz, J. M., Bergman, K. S., Szuba, M. P., Guze, B. H., Mazziotta, J. C., . . . Phelps, M. E. (1992). Caudate glucose metabolic rate changes with both drug and behavior therapy for obsessive-compulsive disorder. Archives of General Psychiatry, 49, 681–689.

Baxter, L. R., Jr., Schwartz, J. M., Guze, B. H., Bergman, K., & Szuba, M. P. (1990). PET imaging in obsessive compulsive disorder with and without depression. Symposium: Serotonin and its effects on human behavior (1989, Atlanta, GA). Journal of Clinical Psychiatry, 51(Suppl.), 61–69.

Beardslee, W. R., Brent, D. A., Weersing, V. R., Clarke, G. N., Porta, G., Hollon, S. D., . . . Garber, J. (2013). Prevention of depression in at-risk adolescents: Longer-term effects. JAMA Psychiatry, 70(11), 1161–1170.

Bearss, K., Burrell, T. L., Stewart, L., & Scahill, L. (2015). Parent training in autism spectrum disorder: What's in a name? Clinical Child and Family Psychology Review, 18(2), 170–182.

Beasley, L. O., Silovsky, J. F., Owora, A., Burris, L., Hecht, D., DeMoraes-Huffine, P., . . . Tolma, E. (2014). Mixed-methods feasibility study on the cultural adaptation of a child abuse prevention model. Child Abuse & Neglect, 38(9), 1496–1507.

Bebbington, P. E., & Kuipers, E. (2011). Schizophrenia and psychosocial stresses. In D. R. Weinberg & P. Harrison (Eds.), Schizophrenia (pp. 599–624). Hoboken, NJ: Wiley-Blackwell.

Bebko, J. M., & Weiss, J. A. (2006). Mental retardation. In M. Hersen & J. C. Thomas (Series Eds.) & R. T. Ammerman (Vol. Ed.), Comprehensive handbook of personality and psychopathology, Vol. 3: Child psychopathology (pp. 233– 253). Hoboken, NJ: Wiley.

Beck, A. T. (1967). Depression: Clinical, experimental and theoretical aspects. New York: Harper & Row.

Beck, A. T. (1991). Cognitive therapy: A 30-year retrospective. American Psychologist, 46(4), 368–375.

Beck, A. T. (2002). Cognitive models of depression. In R. L. Leahy & E. T. Dowd (Eds.), Clinical advances in cognitive psychotherapy: Theory and application (pp. 29–61). New York: Springer.

Beck, A. T. (2004). Cognitive therapy, behavior therapy, psychoanalysis, and pharmacotherapy: A cognitive continuum. In M. J. Mahoney, P. DeVito, D. Martin, & A. Freeman (Eds.), Cognition and psychotherapy (2nd ed., pp. 197– 220). New York: Springer Publishing.

Beck, A. T., & Emery, G., with Greenberg, R. L. (1985). Differentiating anxiety and depression: A test of the cognitive content-specificity hypothesis. Journal of Abnormal Psychology, 96, 179–183.

Beck, A. T., & Weishaar, M. E. (2011). Cognitive Therapy. In R. J. Corsini & D. Wedding (Eds.), Current psychotherapies (9th ed.). Belmont, CA: Brooks/Cole.

Beck, A. T., & Weishaar, M. E. (2014). Cognitive therapy. In D. Wedding & R. J. Corsini (Eds.), Current psychotherapies (10th ed., pp. 231–264). Independence, KY: Cengage Publications.

Beck, A. T., Rush, A. J., Shaw, B. F., & Emery, G. (1979). Cognitive therapy of depression. New York: Guilford Press.

Beck, A. T., Ward, C. H., Mendelson, M., Mock, J. E., & Erbaugh, J. (1962). Reliability of psychiatric diagnosis: 2. A study of consistency of clinical judgments and ratings. American Journal of Psychiatry, 119, 351–357.

Becker, A. E., Burwell, R. A., Gilman, R. E., Herzog, D. B., & Hamburg, P. (2002). Eating behaviors and attitudes following prolonged exposure to television among ethnic Fijian adolescent girls. British Journal of Psychiatry, 180, 509–514.

Becker, A. E., Burwell, R. A., Navara, K., & Gilman, S. E. (2003). Binge eating and binge eating disorder in a small scale indigenous society: The view from Fiji. International Journal of Eating Disorders, 34, 423–431.

Becker, A. E., Fay, K. E., Agnew-Blais, J., Khan, A. N., Striegel-Moore, R. H., & Gilman, S. E. (2011). Social network media exposure and adolescent eating pathology in Fiji. British Journal of Psychiatry, 198(1), 43–50.

Becker, A. E., Fay, K. E., Gilman, S. E., & Stiegel-Moore, R. (2007). Facets of acculturation and their diverse relations to body shape concerns in Fiji. International Journal of Eating Disorders, 40(1), 42–50.

Becker, A. E., Grinspoon, S. K., Klibanski, A., & Herzog, D. B. (1999). Eating disorders. New England Journal of Medicine, 340, 1092–1098.

Becker, A. E., Roberts, A. L., Perloe, A., Bainivualiku, A., Richards, L. K., Gilman, S. E., & Striegel-Moore, R. H. (2010). Youth health-risk behavior assessment in Fiji: The reality of global school-based student health survey content adapted for ethnic Fijian girls. Ethnicity & Health, 15(2), 181–197.

Becker, J. V., Johnson, B. R., Parthasarathi, U., & Hategan, A. (2012). Gender identity disorders and paraphilias. In J. A. Bourgeois, U. Parthasarathi, & A. Hategan (Eds.), Psychiatry review and Canadian certification exam preparation guide (pp. 305–315). Arlington, VA: American Psychiatric Publishing.

Becker, P. M. (2015). Hypnosis in the management of sleep disorders. Sleep Medicine Clinics, 10(1), 85–92.

Becvar, D. S., & Becvar, R. J. (2012). Family therapy: A systemic integration (8th ed.). Boston: Pearson.

Begeer, S., Howlin, P., Hoddenbach, E., Clauser, C., Lindauer, R., Clifford, P., . . . Koot, H. M. (2015). Effects and moderators of a short theory of mind intervention for children with autism spectrum disorder: A randomized controlled trial. Autism Research. [Electronic publication.]

Behrman, A. (2014). Types of depression. About.com. Retrieved from About.com website: http://depression.about.com/od/mooddisordertypes/p/depression

Beier, E. G., & Young, D. M. (1984). The silent language of psychotherapy: Social reinforcement of the unconscious processes (2nd ed.). Hawthorne, New York: Aldine.

Bekkouche, N. S., Holmes, S., Whittaker, K. S., & Krantz, D. S. (2011). Stress and the heart: Psychosocial stress and coronary heart disease. In R. J. Contrada & A. Baum (Eds.), The handbook of stress science: Biology, psychology, and health (pp. 385–398). New York: Springer Publishing.

Belendiuk, K. A., & Riggs, P. (2014). Treatment of adolescent substance use disorders. Current Treatment Options in Psychiatry, 1(2), 175–188.

Bell, K., Lee, J., Foran, S., Kwong, S., & Christopherson, J. (2010). Is there an "ideal cancer" support group? Key findings from a qualitative study of three groups. Journal of Psychosocial Oncology, 28(4), 432–449.

Bell, M. D., Choi, J., & Lysaker, P. (2011). Psychological interventions to improve work outcomes for people with psychiatric disabilities. In R. Hagen, D. Turkington, T. Berge, & R. W. Grawe (Eds.), BT for psychosis: A symptom-based approach, International Society for the Psychological Treatments of the Schizophrenias and Other Psychoses (pp. 210–230). New York: Routledge/Taylor & Francis Group.

Belleville, G., Cousineau, H., Levrier, K., & St-Pierre-Delorme, M-E. (2011). Meta-analytic review of the impact of cognitive-behavior therapy for insomnia on concomitant anxiety. Clinical Psychology Review, 31(4), 638–652.

Bender, D. S., Farber, B. A., & Geller, J. D. (2001). Cluster B personality traits and attachment. Journal of the American Academy of Psychoanalysis, 29(4), 551–563.

Bender, E. (2006, June 16). APA, AACAP suggest ways to reduce high suicide rates in Native Americans. Psychiatric News, 41(12), 6.

Benjamin, K. (2012, May 7). 60% of people can't go 10 minutes without lying. Mental Floss.com. Retrieved from Mental Floss.com website: http://mentalfloss.com/article/30609/60.

Ben-Natan, M., Sharon, I., Barbashov, P., Minasyan, Y., Hanukayev, I., Kajdan, D., & Klein-Kremer, A. (2014). Risk factors for child abuse: Quantitative correlational design. Journal of Pediatric Nursing, 29(3), 220–227.

Bennett, M. D., & Olugbala, F. K. (2010). Don't bother me, I can't cope: Stress, coping, and problem behaviors among young African American males. In W. E. Johnson, Jr. (Ed.), *Social work with African American males: Health, mental health, and social policy* (pp. 179–194). New York: Oxford University Press.

Bennett, M. P. (1998). The effect of mirthful laughter on stress and natural killer cell cytotoxicity. *Dissertation Abstracts International: Section B: The Sciences and Engineering, 58*(7–B), 3553.

Berenson, K. R., Downey, G., Rafaeli, E., Coifman, K. G., & Leventhal Paquin, N. (2011). The rejection-rage contingency in borderline personality disorder. *Journal of Abnormal Psychology, 120*(3), 681–690.

Berg, A., Brätane, E., Odland, H. H., Brudvik, C., Rosland, B., & Hirth, A. (2014). Cardio-vascular risk assessment for the use of ADHD drugs in children. *Tidsskrift for den Norske Laegeforening, 134*(7), 710–714.

Bergado-Acosta, J. R., Müller, I., Richter-Levin, G., & Stork, O. (2014). The GABA-synthetic enzyme GAD65 controls circadian activation of conditioned fear pathways. *Behavioural Brain Research, 260*, 92–100.

Bergink, V., Bouvy, P. F., Vervoort, J. P., Koorengevel, K. M., Steegers, E. P., & Kushner, S. A. (2012). Prevention of postpartum psychosis and mania in women at high risk. *American Journal of Psychiatry, 169*(6), 609–615.

Bergler, E. (1951). *Neurotic counterfeit sex.* New York: Grune & Stratton.

Bergner, R. M., & Bunford, N. (2014). *Mental disorder is a disability concept, not a behavioral one: An empirical investigation.* Athens, OH: Ohio University.

Berk, S. N., & Efran, J. S. (1983). Some recent developments in the treatment of neurosis. In C. E. Walker (Ed.), *The handbook of clinical psychology: Theory, research, and practice* (Vol. 2). Homewood, IL: Dow Jones-Irwin.

Berlim, M. T., McGirr, A., Van den Eynde, F., Fleck, M. P., & Giacobbe, P. (2014). Effective-ness and acceptability of deep brain stimulation (DBS) of the subgenual cingulate cortex for treatment-resistant depression: A systematic review and exploratory meta-analysis. *Journal of Affective Disorders, 159*, 31–38.

Berman, A. L. (1986). Helping suicidal adolescents: Needs and responses. In C. A. Corr & J. N. McNeil (Eds.), *Adolescence and death.* New York: Springer.

Bernstein, D. P., & Useda, J. D (2007). Paranoid personality disorder. In W. O'Donohue, K. A. Fowler, & S. O. Lilienfeld (Eds.). *Personality disorders: Toward the DSM-V.* Los Angeles: Sage Publications.

Berrettini, W. (2006). Genetics of bipolar and unipolar disorders. In D. J. Stein, D. J. Kupfer, & A. F. Schatzberg (Eds.), *The American Psychiatric Publishing textbook of mood disorders.* Washington, DC: American Psychiatric Publishing.

Berridge, M. J. (2011). Calcium signaling and Alzheimer's disease. *Neurochemical Research, 36*(7), 1149–1156.

Berry, M. D., & Berry, P. D. (2013). Contemporary treatment of sexual dysfunction: Reexamining the biopsychosocial model. *Journal of Sexual Medicine, 10*, 2627–2643.

Berry, S. M., Broglio, K., Bunker, M., Jayewardene, A., Olin, B., & Rush, A. J. (2013). A patient-level meta-analysis of studies evalu-ating vagus nerve stimulation therapy for treatment-resistant depression. *Medical Devices: Evidence and Research*, 617–635.

Berthoud, H. (2012). The neurobiology of food intake in an obesogenic environment. *Proceedings of the Nutri-tion Society, 71*(4), 478–487.

Bertozzi, S., Londero, A. P., Fruscalzo, A., Driul, L., & Marchesoni, D. (2010). Preva-lence and risk factors for dyspareunia and unsatisfying sexual relationships in a cohort of primiparous and secondiparous women after 12 months postpartum. *International Journal of Sexual Health, 22*(1), 47–53.

Berzofsky, M., Krebs, C., Langton, L., Planty, M., & Smiley-McDonald, H. (2013). *Female victims of sexual violence, 1994–2010.* Washington, DC: Bureau of Justice Statistics.

Beutler, L. E. (2000). David and Goliath: When empirical and clinical standards of practice meet. *American Psychologist, 55*(9), 997–1007.

Beutler, L. E. (2002). The dodo bird is extinct. *Clinical Psychology: Science and Practice, 9*(1), 30–34.

Beutler, L. E. (2011). Prescriptive matching and systematic treatment selection. In J. C. Norcross, G. R. VandenBos, & D. K. Freedheim (Eds.), *History of psy-chotherapy: Continuity and change* (2nd ed., pp. 402–407). Washington, DC: American Psychological Association.

Beutler, L. E., Clarkin, J. F., & Bongar, B. (2000). *Guidelines for the systematic treatment of the depressed patient.* New York: Oxford University Press.

Beutler, L. E., Williams, R. E., Wakefield, P. J., & Entwistle, S. R. (1995). Bridging scientist and practitioner perspectives in clinical psychology. *American Psychologist, 50*(12), 984–994.

Bharani, N., & Lantz, M. S. (2008). New-onset agoraphobia in late life. *Clinical Geriatrics,* 1/17/08, 17–20.

Bhattacharya, R., Cross, S., & Bhugra, D. (Eds). (2010). *Clinical topics in cultural psychiatry.* London: Royal College of Psychiatrists.

Bhavsar, V., Boydell, J., Murray, R., & Power, P. (2014). Identifying aspects of neighbourhood deprivation associated with increased incidence of schizophrenia. *Schizophrenia Research, 156*(1), 115–121.

Bhutta, M. R., Hong, M. J., Kim, Y., & Hong, K. (2015). Single-trial lie detection using a combined fNIRS-polygraph system. *Frontiers in Psychology, 6*, 709.

Bianchini, O., Porcelli, S., Nespeca, C., Cannavò, D., Trappoli, A., Aguglia, E., . . . Serretti, A. (2014). Effects of antipsychotic drugs on insight in schizophrenia. *Psychiatry Research, 218* (1-2), 20–24.

Bigdeli, T. B., Maher, B. S., Zhao, Z., Sun, J., Medeiros, H., Akula, N., . . . Fanous, A. H. (2013). Association study of 83 candidate genes for bipolar disorder in chromosome 6q selected using an evidence-based prioritization algorithm. *American Journal of Medical Genetics. Part B, Neuropsychiatric Genetics, 162B*(8), 898–906.

Bills, C. B., & Li, G. (2005). Correlating homicide and suicide. *International Journal of Epidemiology, 34*(4), 837–845.

Bina, R. (2014). Seeking help for postpartum depres-sion in the Israeli Jewish orthodox community: Fac-tors associated with use of professional and informal help. *Women & Health, 54*(5), 455–473.

Binet, A., & Simon, T. (1916). *The development of intelligence in children (The Binet-Simon Scale).* Baltimore: Williams & Wilkins.

Biran, J., Tahor, M., Wircer, E., & Levkowitz, G. (2015). Role of developmental factors in hypothalamic function. *Frontiers in Neuroanatomy, 9*, 47.

Birkeland, S. F. (2013). Psychopharmacological treat-ment and course in paranoid personality disorder: A case series. *International Clinical Psychopharmacology, 28*(5), 283–285.

Biron, M., & Link, S. (2014). Stress, appraisal and work routine in wartime: Do men and women differ? *Anxiety, Stress, and Coping, 27*(2), 229–240.

Birrell, P. (2011). Review of memory matters: Contexts for understanding sexual abuse recollections. *Journal of Trauma & Dissociation, 12*(1), 107–109.

Bisaga, A., Sullivan, M. A., Glass, A., Mishlen, K., Pavlicova, M., Haney, M., . . . Nunes, E. V. (2015). The effects of dronabinol during detoxifi-cation and the initiation of treatment with extended re-lease naltrexone. *Drug and Alcohol Dependence, 154*, 38–45.

Bisson, J. I., & Deahl, M. P. (1994). Psychological debriefing and prevention of post-traumatic stress: More research is needed. *British Journal of Psychiatry, 165*(6), 717–720.

Bisson, J. I., Jenkins, P. L., Alexander, J., & Bannister, C. (1997). Randomised controlled trial of psychological debriefing for victims of acute burn trauma. *British Journal of Psychiatry, 171*, 78–81.

Bitter, J. R. (2013). *Theory and practice of family therapy and counseling.* Independence, KY: Cengage Learning.

Björgvinsson, T., & Hart, J. (2008). Obsessive-compulsive disorder. In M. Hersen & J. Rosqvist (Eds.), *Handbook of psychological assessment, case concep-tualization, and treatment, Vol. 1: Adults* (pp. 237–262). Hoboken, NJ: John Wiley & Sons.

Björkenstam, C., Johansson, L., Nordström, P., Thiblin, I., Fugelstad, A., Hallqvist, J., & Ljung, R. (2014). Suicide or undetermined intent? A register-based study of signs of misclassifica-tion. *Population Health Metrics, 12*, 11.

BJS (Bureau of Justice Statistics). (2013, March 7). *Female victims of sexual violence, 1994–2010* (NCJ 240655). Retrieved from http://www.bjs.gov/index.cfm?tv=pbdetail&iid=4594.

Black Youth Project. (2011). *The attitudes and behavior of young Black Americans: Research summary.* Retrieved from Black Youth Project website: www.blackyouthproject.com/survey findings.

Black, D. W. (2015). The natural history of antisocial personality disorder. *Canadian Journal of Psychiatry, 60*(7), 309–314.

Black, D. W., McCormick, B., Losch, M. E., Shaw, M., Lutz, G., & Allen, J. (2012). Prevalence of problem gambling in Iowa: Revisiting Shaffer's adaptation hypothesis. *Annals of Clinical Psy-chiatry, 24*(4), 279–284.

Black, M. C., Basile, K. C., Breiding, M. J., Smith, S. G., Walters, M. L., Merrick, M. T., . . . Stevens, M. R. (2011) *The National Intimate Partner and Sexual Violence Survey (NISVS): 2010 summary report.* Atlanta, GA: National Center for Injury Prevention and Control, CDC.

Blackmore, D. E., Hart, S. L., Albiani, J. J., & Mohr, D. C. (2011). Improvements in partner support predict sexual satisfaction among individuals with multiple sclerosis. *Rehabilitation Psychology, 56*(2), 117–122.

Blagov, P. S., Fowler K. A., & Lilienfeld, S. O. (2007). Histrionic personality disorder. In W. O'Donohue, K. A. Fowler, & S. O. Lilienfeld (Eds.). *Personality disorders: Toward the DSM-V.* Los Angeles: Sage Publications.

Blair, J., Mitchell, D., & Blair, K. (2005). *The psy-chopath: Emotion and the brain.* Malden, MA: Blackwell Publishing.

Blais, M. A., & Baer, L. (2010). Understanding rating scales and assessment instruments. In L. Baer & M. A. Blais (Eds.), *Handbook of clinical rating scales and assessment in psychiatry and mental health* (pp. 1–6). Totowa, NJ: Humana Press.

Blanchard, J. J., Kring, A. M., Horan, W. P., & Gur, R. (2011). Toward the next generation of negative symptom assessments: The collabora-tion to advance negative symptom assessment in schizophrenia. *Schizophrenia Bulletin, 37*(2), 291–299.

Blanken, I., Leusink, P., van Diest, S., Gijs, L., & van Lankveld, J. M. (2015). Outcome predic-tors of internet-based brief sex therapy for sexual dysfunctions in heterosexual men. *Journal of Sex & Marital Therapy, 45*(5), 531–543.

Blashfield, R. K., Keele, J. W., Flanagan, E. H., & Miles, S. R. (2014). The cycle, of classification: DSM-I through DSM-5. *Annual Review of Clinical Psychology, 10*, 25–51.

Blass, R. B. (2014). On the "fear of death" as the pri-mary anxiety: How and why Klein differs from Freud. *International Journal of Psycho-Analysis, 95*(4), 613–627.

Blatt, S. J. (2004). Developmental origins (distal antecedents). In S. J Blatt, *Experiences of depression: Theoretical, clinical, and research perspectives* (pp. 187–229). Washington, DC: American Psychological Association.

Bleiberg, K. L., & Markowitz, J. C. (2014). Interpersonal psychotherapy for depression. In D. H. Barlow (Ed.), (2014). *Clinical handbook of psychological disorders: A step-by-step treatment manual* (5th ed., Ch. 8). New York: Guilford Press.

Bliss, E. L. (1980). Multiple personalities: A report of 14 cases with implications for schizophrenia and hysteria. *Archives of General Psychiatry, 37*(12), 1388–1397.

Bliss, E. L. (1980). *Multiple personality, allied disorders and hypnosis.* New York: Oxford University Press.

Blodgett, J. C., Maisel, N. C., Fuh, I. L., Wilbourne, P. L., & Finney, J. W. (2014). How effective is continuing care for substance use disorders? A meta-analytic review. *Journal of Substance Abuse Treatment, 46*(2), 87–97.

Bloom, B. L. (1984). *Community mental health: A general introduction* (2nd ed.). Monterey, CA: Brooks/Cole.

Blow, F. C., Zeber, J. E., McCarthy, J. F., Valenstein, M., Gillon, L., & Bingham, C. R. (2004). Ethnicity and diagnostic patterns in veterans with psychoses. *Social Psychiatry and Psychiatric Epidemiology, 39*(10), 841–851.

Blow, J., & Cooper, T. V. (2014). Predictors of body dissatisfaction in a Hispanic college student sample. *Eating Behaviors, 15*(1), 1–4.

BLS (Bureau of Labor Statistics). (2015). *Economic News Release. Table A-3. Employment status of the Hispanic or Latino population by sex and age.* Retrieved from http://www.bls.gov/news.release.empsit.t03.htm.

Bluglass, K. (2001). Treatment of perpetrators. In G. Adshead & D. Brooke (Eds.), *Munchausen's syndrome by proxy: Current issues in assessment, treatment and research* (pp. 175–184). London: Imperial College Press.

Blum, K., Braverman, E. R., Holder, J. M., Lubar, J. F., Monastra, V. J., Miller, D., & Comings, D. E. (2000). Reward deficiency syndrome: A biogenetic model for the diagnosis and treatment of impulsive, addictive, and compulsive behaviors. *Journal of Psychoactive Drugs, 32*(Suppl.), 1–68.

Blum, K., Cull, J. G., Braverman, E. R., & Comings, D. E. (1996). Reward deficiency syndrome. *American Scientist, 84*(2), 132–144.

Blum, K., Noble, E. P., Sheridan, P. J., Montgomery, A., Ritchie, T., Jagadeeswaran, P., . . . Cohn, J. B. (1990). Allelic association of human dopamine D2 receptor gene in alcoholism. *Journal of the American Medical Association, 263*(15), 2055–2060.

Bock, C., Bukh, J. D., Vinberg, M., Gether, U., & Kessing, L. V. (2010). The influence of comorbid personality disorder and neuroticism on treatment outcome in first episode depression. *Psychopathology, 43*(3), 197–204.

Bodell, L. P., & Mayer, L. E. S. (2011). Percent body fat is a risk factor for relapse in anorexia nervosa: A replication study. *International Journal of Eating Disorders, 44*(2), 118–123.

Bodison, S. C. (2015). Developmental dyspraxia and the play skills of children with autism. *The American Journal of Occupational Therapy, 69*(5), 6905185060p1-6.

Boets, B. (2014, July 14). Dyslexia: Reconciling controversies within an integrative developmental perspective. *Trends in Cognitive Sciences, 18*(10), 501–503.

Boeve, B., McCormick, J., Smith, G., Ferman, T., Rummans, T., Carpenter, T., . . . Petersen, R. (2003). Mild cognitive impairment in the oldest old. *Neurology, 60*(3), 477–480.

Bogdan, R., & Taylor, S. (1976, January). The judged, not the judges: An insider's view of mental retardation. *American Psychologist, 31*(1), 47–52.

Bokor, G., & Anderson, P. D. (2014). Obsessive-compulsive disorder. *Journal of Pharmacy Practice, 27*(2), 116–130.

Bolgar, H. (1965). The case study method. In B. B. Wolman (Ed.), *Handbook of clinical psychology.* New York: McGraw-Hill

Bonanno, G. A. (2004). Loss, trauma, and human resilience. *American Psychologist, 59*(1), 20–28.

Bonanno, G. A., & Mancini, A. D. (2012). Beyond resilience and PTSD: Mapping the heterogeneity of responses to potential trauma. *Psychological Trauma: Theory, Research, Practice, and Policy, 4*(1), 74–83.

Bonelli, R. M., & Koenig, H. G. (2013). Mental disorders, religion and spirituality 1990 to 2010: A systematic evidence-based review. *Journal of Religion & Health, 52*(2), 657–673.

Bonetta, L. (2010). Study supports methadone maintenance in therapeutic communities. *NIDA Notes, 23*(3).

Boone, K. (2011). Somatoform disorders, factitious disorder, and malingering. In M. R. Schoenberg & J. G. Scott (Eds.), *The little black book of neuropsychology: Syndrome-based approach* (pp. 551–565). New York: Springer Science + Business Media.

Boone, L., Claes, L., & Luyten, P. (2014). Too strict or too loose? Perfectionism and impulsivity: The relation with eating disorder symptoms using a person-centered approach. *Eating Behaviors, 15*(1), 17–23.

Boone, L., Soenens, B., & Luyten, P. (2014). When or why does perfectionism translate into eating disorder pathology? A longitudinal examination of the moderating and mediating role of body dissatisfaction. *Journal of Abnormal Psychology, 123*(2), 412–418.

Bor, W., Stallman, H., Collerson, E., Boyle, C., Swenson, C. C., McDermott, B., & Lee, E. (2013). Therapy implications of child abuse in multi-risk families. *Australasian Psychiatry, 21*(4), 389–392.

Borden, L. A., Martens, M. P., McBride, M. A., Sheline, K. T., Bloch, K. K., & Dude, K. (2011). The role of college students' use of protective behavioral strategies in the relation between binge drinking and alcohol-related problems. *Psychology of Addictive Behaviors, 25*(2), 346–351.

Borge, F., Hoffart, A., Sexton, H., Martinsen, E., Gude, T., Hedley, L. M., & Abrahamsen, G. (2010). Pre-treatment predictors and in-treatment factors associated with change in avoidant and dependent personality disorder traits among patients with social phobia. *Clinical Psychology & Psychotherapy, 17*(2), 87–99.

Borge, L., Røssberg, J. I., & Sverdrup, S. (2013). Cognitive milieu therapy and physical activity: Experiences of mastery and learning among patients with dual diagnosis. *Journal of Psychiatric and Mental Health Nursing, 20*(10), 932–942.

Borges, S., Chen., Y., Laughren, T. P., Temple, R., Patel, H. D., David, P. A., . . . Khin, N. A. (2014). Review of maintenance trials for major depressive disorder: A 25-year perspective from the US Food and Drug Administration. *The Journal of Clinical Psychiatry, 75*(3), 205–214.

Borkovec, T. D., Alcaine, O. M., & Behar, E. (2004). Avoidance theory of worry and generalized anxiety disorder. In R. G. Heimberg, C. L. Turk, & D. S. Mennin (Eds.), *Generalized anxiety disorder: Advances in research and practice* (pp. 77–108). New York: Guilford Press.

Bornstein, R. F. (2005). Psychodynamic theory and personality disorders. In S. Strack (Ed.), *Handbook of personality and psychopathology* (pp. 164–180). Hoboken, NJ: Wiley.

Bornstein, R. F. (2007). Dependent personality disorder. In W. O'Donohue, K. A. Fowler, S. O. Lilienfeld (Eds.). *Personality disorders: Toward the DSM-V.* Los Angeles: Sage Publications.

Bornstein, R. F. (2007). Might the Rorschach be a projective test after all: Social projection of an undesired trait alters Rorschach oral dependency scores. *Journal of Personality Assessment, 88*(3), 354–367.

Bornstein, R. F. (2012). Illuminating a neglected clinical issue: Societal costs of interpersonal dependency and dependent personality disorder. *Journal of Clinical Psychology, 68*(7), 766–781

Borzekowski, D. L. G., Schenk, S., Wilson, J. L., & Peebles, R. (2010). e-Ana and e-Mia: A content analysis of pro-eating disorder web sites. *American Journal of Public Health, 100*(8), 1526–1534.

Bosco, D., Plastino, M., Colica, C., Bosco, F., Arianna, S., Vecchio, A., . . . Consoli, D. (2012). Opioid antagonist natrexone for the treatment of pathological gambling in Parkinson disease. *Clinical Neuropharmacology, 35*(3), 118–120.

Bott, E. (1928). Teaching of psychology in the medical course. *Bulletin of the Association of American Medical Colleges, 3,* 289–304.

Bouman, T. K. (2008). Hypochondriasis. In J. S. Abramowitz, D. McKay, & S. Taylor (Eds.), *Obsessive-compulsive disorder: Subtypes and spectrum conditions.* Oxford, England: Elsevier.

Bouras, N., & Holt, G. (Eds.). (2010). *Mental health services for adults with intellectual disability: Strategies and solutions. The Maudsley Series.* New York, Psychology Press.

Bourin, M., Malinge, M., & Guitton, B. (1995). Provocative agents in panic disorder. *Therapie 50*(4), 301–306. [French].

Bourne, E. J., Brownstein, A., & Garano, L. (2004). *Natural relief for anxiety: Complementary strategies for easing fear, panic and worry.* Oakland, CA: New Harbinger Publications.

Boutros, N. N., Mucci, A., Diwadkar, V., & Tandon, R. (2014). Negative symptoms in schizophrenia. *Clinical Schizophrenia & Related Psychoses, 8*(1), 28–35B.

Bowden, S. C., Saklofske, D. H., & Weiss, L. G. (2011). Invariance of the measurement model underlying the Wechsler Adult Intelligence Scale-IV in the United States and Canada. *Educational and Psychological Measurement, 71*(1), 186–199.

Bowen, E. A., Bowen, S. K., & Barman-Adhikari, A. (2015). Prevalence and covariates of food insecurity among residents of single room occupancy housing in Chicago, IL, USA. *Public Health Nutrition, 1–9.* [Electronic publication.]

Bowen, S., Witkiewitz, K., Clifasefi, S. L., Grow, J., Chawla, N., Hsu, S. H., . . . Larimer, M. E. (2014). Relative efficacy of mindfulness-based relapse prevention, standard relapse prevention, and treatment as usual for substance use disorders: A randomized clinical trial. *JAMA Psychiatry, 71*(5), 547–556.

Bower, B. (2013, November 2). The bright side, of sadness. *Science News.*

Bower, E. S., Wetherell, J. L., Mon, T., & Lenze, E. J. (2015). Treating anxiety disorders in older adults: Current treatments and future directions. *Harvard Review of Psychiatry, 23*(5), 329–342.

Bower, G. H. (1981). Mood and memory. *American Psychologist, 36*(2), 129–148.

Bowers, T. G., Holmes, E. S., & Rhom, A. (2010). The nature of mass murder and autogenic massacre. *Journal of Police and Criminal Psychology, 25,* pp. 59–66.

Boyd, B. A., Conroy, M. A., Asmus, J., McKenney, E. (2011). Direct observation of peer-related social interaction: Outcomes for young children with autism spectrum disorders. *Exceptionality, 19*(2), 94–108.

Boyd, B. A., Hume, K., McBee, M. T., Alessandri, M., Gutierrez, A., Johnson, L., . . . Odom, S. L. (2014). Comparative efficacy of LEAP, TEACCH, and non-model-specific special education programs for preschoolers with autism spectrum disorders. *Journal of Autism and Developmental Disorders, 44*(2), 366–380.

Boyd, D., & Hargittai, E. (2013). Connected and concerned: Variation in parents' online safety concerns. *Policy & Internet, 5*(3), 245–269.

Boyle, M. (2003, May 26). Liar! Liar! *Fortune.*

Boyle, R. (2011, May 6). Computer scientists induce schizophrenia in a neural network, causing it to make ridiculous claims. *Popular Science.*

Boysen, G. A., & VanBergen, A. (2013). A review of published research on adult dissociative identity disorder: 2000–2010. *The Journal of Nervous and Mental Disease, 201*(1), 5–11.

Boysen, G. A., & VanBergen, A. (2014). Simulation of multiple personalities: A review of research comparing diagnosed and simulated dissociative identity disorder. *Clinical Psychology Review, 34*(1), 14–28.

BPS (British Psychological Society). (2007). *Statement on the conduct of psychologists providing expert psychometric evidence to courts and lawyers.* Leicester, UK: British Psychological Society.

Bradford, J. M. W., Fedoroff, P., & Firestone, P. (2008). Sexual violence and the clinician. In R. I. Simon & K. Tardiff (Eds.), *Textbook of violence assessment and management* (pp. 441–460). Arlington, VA: American Psychiatric Publishing.

Brady, J. E., & Li, G. (2014). Trends in alcohol and other drugs detected in fatally injured drivers in the United States, 1999–2010. *American Journal of Epidemiology, 179*(6), 1093.

Brainerd, C. J., Reyna, V. F., & Ceci, S. J. (2008). Developmental reversals in false memory: A review of data and theory. *Psychological Bulletin, 134*(3), 343–382.

Brambrink, D. K. (2004). A comparative study for the treatment of anxiety in women using electromyographic biofeedback and progressive relaxation and coping with stress: A manual for women. *Dissertation Abstracts International: Section B: The Sciences and Engineering, 65*(6-B), 3146.

Brand, B. L., Loewenstein, R. J., & Spiegel, D. (2014). Dispelling myths about dissociative identity disorder treatment: An empirically based approach. *Psychiatry, 77*(2), 169–189.

Bratskeir, K. (2013, September 16). The habits of supremely happy people. *Huffington Post.*

Brauhardt, A., Rudolph, A., & Hilbert, A. (2014). Implicit cognitive processes in binge-eating disorder and obesity. *Journal of Behavior Therapy and Experimental Psychiatry, 45*(2), 285–290.

Braun, D. L. (1996, July 28). Interview. In S. Gilbert, More men may seek eating-disorder help. *New York Times.*

Braxton, L. E., Calhoun, P. S., Williams, J. E., & Boggs, C. D. (2007). Validity rates of the Personality Assessment Inventory and the Minnesota Multiphasic Personality Inventory-2 in a VA medical center setting. *Journal of Personality Assessment, 88*(1), 5–15.

Breitbart, W., Pessin, H., & Kolva, E. (2011). Suicide and desire for hastened death in people with cancer. In D. W. Kossane, M. Maj, & N. Sartorius (Eds.), *Depression and cancer, World Psychiatric Association titles on depression* (pp. 125–150). Hoboken, NJ: Wiley-Blackwell.

Bremner, J. D. (2002). *Does stress damage the brain? Understanding trauma-related disorders from a mind-body perspective.* New York: Norton.

Bremner, J. D., & Charney, D. S. (2010). Neural circuits in fear and anxiety. In D. J. Stein, E. Hollander & B. O. Rothbaum (Eds.), *Textbook of anxiety disorders* (2nd ed., pp. 55–71). Arlington, VA: American Psychiatric Publishing.

Bremner, J. D., Vythilingam, M., Vermetten, E., Vaccarino, V., & Charney, D. S. (2004). Deficits in hippocampal and anterior cingulate functioning during verbal declarative memory encoding in midlife major depression. *American Journal of Psychiatry, 161*(4), 637–645.

Brenot, P. (2011). Can a sexual symptom be fixed without taking account of the couple? *Sexologies: European Journal of Sexology and Sexual Health, 20*(1), 20–22.

Brent, D. A. (2001). Assessment and treatment of the youthful suicidal patient. In H. Hendin & J. J. Mann (Eds.), *The clinical science of suicide prevention* (Vol. 932, pp. 106–131). New York: Annals of the New York Academy of Sciences.

Breslau, J., Aguilar-Gaxiola, S., Kendler, K. S., Su, M., Williams, D., & Kessler, R. C. (2006). Specifying race-ethnic differences in risk for psychiatric disorder in a USA national sample. *Psychological Medicine, 36,* 57–68.

Bressi, C., Nocito, E. P., Milanese, E. A., Fronza, S., Della Valentina, P., Castagna, L., . . . Capra, G. A. (2014). Efficacy of short-term psychodynamic psychotherapy vs treatment as usual in a sample of patients with anxiety and depressive disorders. *Rivista Di Psichiatria, 49*(1), 28–33.

Brewer, J. (2014). Mindfulness in the military. *American Journal of Psychiatry, 171,* 803–806.

Brewerton, T. D., & Costin, C. (2011). Long-term outcome of residential treatment for anorexia nervosa and bulimia nervosa. *Eating Disorders: The Journal of Treatment & Prevention, 19*(2), 132–144.

Bridler, R., Häberle, A., Müller, S. T., Cattapan, K., Grohmann, R., Toto, S., . . . Greil, W. (2015). Psychopharmacological treatment of 2195 in-patients with borderline personality disorder: A comparison with other psychiatric disorders. *European Neuropsychopharmacology, 25*(6), 763–772.

Briki, M., Monnin, J., Haffen, E., Sechter, D., Favrod, J., Netillard, C., . . . Vandel, P. (2014). Metacognitive training for schizophrenia: A multicentre randomised controlled trial. *Schizophrenia Research, 157*(1-3), 99–106.

Brisch, R., Saniotis, A., Wolf, R., Bielau, H., Bernstein, H., Steiner, J., . . . Gos, T. (2014). The role of dopamine in schizophrenia from a neurobiological and evolutionary perspective: Old fashioned, but still in vogue. *Frontiers In Psychiatry, 5,* 47.

Britt, R. R. (2005, January 6). The odds of dying. *LiveScience.com.*

Brockmann, H., Zobel, A., Schuhmacher, A., Daamen, M., Joe, A., Biermann, K., . . . Boecker, H. (2011). Influence of 5-HTTLPR polymorphism on resting state perfusion in patients with major depression. *Journal of Psychiatric Research, 45*(4), 442–451.

Brook, J. S., Lee, J. Y., Rubenstone, E., Brook, D. W., & Finch, S. J. (2014). Triple comorbid trajectories of tobacco, alcohol, and marijuana use as predictors of antisocial personality disorder and generalized anxiety disorder among urban adults. *American Journal of Public Health, 104*(8), 1413–1420.

Brooks, A. C. (2013, December 14). A formula for happiness. *New York Times.*

Brooks, G. R., & Richardson, F. C. (1980). Emotional skills training: A treatment program for duodenal ulcer. *Behavior Therapist, 11*(2), 198–207.

Brooks, L., McCabe, P., & Schneiderman, N. (2011). Stress and cardiometabolic syndrome. In R. J. Contrada & A. Baum (Eds.), *The handbook of stress science: Biology, psychology, and health* (pp. 399–409). New York: Springer Publishing.

Brophy, M. (2010). Sex, lies, and virtual reality. In D. Monroe (Ed.), *Porn: How to think with kink, Philosophy for everyone* (pp. 204–218). Hoboken, NJ: Wiley-Blackwell.

Brown, A. (2012, April 27). *Chronic pain rates shoot up until Americans reach late 50s: Low-income and obese Americans more likely to have chronic pain.* Retrieved from Gallup website: http://www.gallup.com/poll/154169.

Brown, A. S. (2012). Maternal infection and schizophrenia. In A. S. Brown & P. H. Patterson (Eds.), *The origins of schizophrenia* (pp. 25–57). New York: Columbia University Press.

Brown, D., Larkin, F., Sengupta, S., Romero-Ureclay, J. L., Ross, C. C., Gupta, N., . . . Das, M. (2014). Clozapine: An effective treatment for seriously violent and psychopathic men with antisocial personality disorder in a UK high-security hospital. *CNS Spectrums, 19*(5), 391–402.

Brown, G. K., Stirman, S. W., & Spokas, M. (2010). Relapse prevention of suicide attempts: Application of cognitive therapy. In S. Richards & M. G. Perri (Eds.), *Relapse prevention for depression* (pp. 177–198). Washington, DC: American Psychological Association.

Brown, G. K., Wenzel, A., & Rudd, M. D. (2011). Cognitive therapy for suicidal patients. In K. Michel & D. A. Jobes (Eds.), *Building a therapeutic alliance with the suicidal patient* (pp. 273–291). Washington, DC: American Psychological Association.

Brown, G. W. (2002). Social roles, context and evolution in the origins of depression. *Journal of Health and Social Behavior, 43*(3), 255–276.

Brown, G. W., & Harris, T. O. (1978). *Social origins of depression: A study of psychiatric disorder in women.* London: Tavistock.

Brown, J. H., Henteleff, P., Barakat, S., & Rowe, C. J. (1986). Is it normal for terminally ill patients to desire death? *American Journal of Psychiatry, 143*(2), 208–211.

Brown, R. J., Schrag, A., & Trimble, M. R. (2005). Dissociation, childhood interpersonal trauma, and family functioning in patients with somatization disorder. *American Journal of Psychiatry, 162*(5), 899–905.

Brown, T. A., Holland, L. A., & Keel, P. K. (2014). Comparing operational definitions of DSM-5 anorexia nervosa for research contexts. *The International Journal of Eating Disorders, 47*(1), 76–84.

Brownley, K. A., Peat, C. M., La Via, M., & Bulik, C. M. (2015). Pharmacological approaches to the management of binge eating disorder. *Drugs, 75*(1), 9–32.

Bruch, H. (1962). Perceptual and conceptual disturbances in anorexia nervosa. *Psychosomatic Medicine, 24,* 187–194.

Bruch, H. (1973). *Eating disorders: Obesity, anorexia nervosa and the person within.* New York: Basic Books.

Bruch, H. (1978). *The golden cage: The enigma of anorexia nervosa.* Cambridge, MA: Harvard University Press.

Bruch, H. (1991). The sleeping beauty: Escape from change. In S. I. Greenspan & G. H. Pollock (Eds.), *The course of life, Vol. 4: Adolescence.* Madison, CT: International Universities Press.

Bruch, H. (2001). *The golden cage: The enigma of anorexia nervosa.* Cambridge, MA: Harvard University Press.

Bruffaerts, R., Demyttenaere, K., Kessler, R. C., Tachimori, H., Bunting, B., Hu, C., . . . Scott, K. M. (2015). The associations between preexisting mental disorders and subsequent onset of chronic headaches: A worldwide epidemiologic perspective. *The Journal of Pain, 16*(1), 42–52.

Brumberg, J. J. (1988). *Fasting girls: The history of anorexia nervosa.* New York: Penguin Books.

Brunelin, J., Fecteau, S., & Suaud-Chagny, M-F. (2013). Abnormal striatal dopamine transmission in schizophrenia. *Current Medicinal Chemistry, 20*(3), 397–404.

Bryant, R. A., Creamer, M., O'Donnell, M., Silove, D., McFarlane, A. C., & Forbes, D. (2015). A comparison of the capacity of DSM-IV and DSM-5 acute stress disorder definitions to predict posttraumatic stress disorder and related disorders. *The Journal of Clinical Psychiatry, 76*(4), 391–397.

Bryant, R. A., Moulds, M. L., Guthrie, R. M., & Nixon, R. D. V. (2005). The additive benefit of hypnosis and cognitive-behavioral therapy in treating acute stress disorder. *Journal of Consulting and Clinical Psychology, 73*(2), 334–340.

Bryner, J. (2011). Close friends less common today, study finds. *Live Science.* Retrieved from Live Science website: http://www.livescience.com/16879.

BSA (Boy Scouts of America). (2014). *Bullying statistics in America.* Retrieved from BSA website: http://nobullying.com/bullying-statistics/.

Buckingham, E. T., & Daniolos, P. (2013). Longitudinal outcomes for victims of child abuse. *Current Psychiatry Reports, 15*(2), 342.

Budney, A. J., Vandrey, R. L., & Fearer, S. (2011). Cannabis. In J. H. Lowinson & P. Ruiz (Eds.), *Substance abuse: A comprehensive textbook* (5th ed.). Philadelphia, PA: Lippincott, Williams, & Wilkins.

Buhlmann, U., Glaesmer, H., Mewes, R., Fama, J. M., Wilhelm, S., Brähler, E., & Rief, W. (2010). Updates on the prevalence of body dysmorphic disorder: A population-based survey. *Psychiatry Research, 178*(1), 171–175.

Bullen, C., Howe, C., Laugesen, M., McRobbie, H., Parag, V., Williman, J., & Walker, N. (2013). Electronic cigarettes for smoking cessation: A randomised controlled trial. *The Lancet, 382,* 1629–1637.

Bunaciu, L., Feldner, M. T., Babson, K. A., Zvolensky, M. J., & Eifert, G. H. (2012). Biological sex and panic-relevant anxious reactivity to abrupt increases in bodily arousal as a function of biological challenge intensity. *Journal of Behavior Therapy and Experimental Psychiatry, 43*(1), 526–531.

Bureau of Labor Statistics (BLS). (2011). *Occupational Outlook Handbook, 2010–11 Edition, Counselors.* Retrieved from http://www.bls.gov/oco/ocos067.htm.

Bureau of Labor Statistics (BLS). (2011). *Occupational Outlook Handbook, 2010–11 Edition, Psychologists.* Retrieved from http://www.bls.gov/oco/ocos056.htm.

Bureau of Labor Statistics (BLS). (2011). *Occupational Outlook Handbook, 2010–11 Edition, Social Workers.* Retrieved from http://www.bls.gov/oco/ocos060.htm.

Burgess, J. L. (2001). Phosphine exposure from a methamphetamine laboratory investigation. *Journal of Toxicology & Clinical Toxicology, 39,* 165.

Burijon, B. N. (2007). *Biological bases of clinical anxiety.* New York: W. W. Norton & Company.

Burke, A. (2011). Pathophysiology of behavioral and psychological disturbances in dementia. In P. McNamara (Ed.), *Dementia, Vols. 1–3; History and incidence. Science and biology, treatments and developments* (pp. 135–158). Santa Barbara, CA: Praeger/ABC-CLIO.

Burns, G. L., Servera, M., Bernad, M. M., Carrillo, J. M., & Geiser, C. (2014). Ratings of ADHD symptoms and academic impairment by mothers, fathers, teachers, and aides: Construct validity within and across settings as well as occasions. *Psychological Assessment, 26*(4), 1247–1258.

Burns, J. K., Tomita, A., & Kapadia, A. S. (2014). Income inequality and schizophrenia: Increased schizophrenia incidence in countries with high levels of income inequality. *International Journal of Social Psychiatry, 60*(2), 185–196.

Burns, T. (2010). Modern community care strategies for schizophrenia care: Impacts on outcome. In W. F. Gattaz & G. Busatto (Eds.), *Advances in schizophrenia research 2009* (pp. 417–427). New York: Springer Science + Business Media.

Burns, T., & Drake, B. (2011). Mental health services and patients with schizophrenia. In D. R. Weinberg & P. Harrison (Eds.), *Schizophrenia* (pp. 625–643). Hoboken, NJ: Wiley-Blackwell.

Burton, V. S. (1990). The consequences of official labels: A research note on rights lost by the mentally ill, mentally incompetent, and convicted felons. *Community Mental Health Journal, 26*(3), 267–276.

Busch, F. N., Milrod, B. L., & Shear, K. (2010). Psychodynamic concepts of anxiety. In J. Stein, E. Hollander, & B. O. Rothbaum (Eds.), *Textbook of anxiety disorders* (2nd ed., pp. 117–128). Arlington, VA: American Psychiatric Publishing.

Busch, F. N., Rudden, M. G., & Shapiro, T. (2004). *Psychodynamic treatment of depression.* Washington, DC: American Psychiatric Publishing.

Bushman, B. J., Baumeister, R. F., & Stack, A. D. (1999). Catharsis, aggression, and persuasive influence: Self-fulfilling or self-defeating prophecies? *Journal of Personality and Social Psychology, 76*(3), 367–376.

Bussing, R., Koro-Ljungberg, M. E., Gary, F., Mason, D. M., & Garvan, C. W. (2005). Exploring help-seeking for ADHD symptoms: A mixed-methods approach. *Harvard Review of Psychiatry, 13*(2), 85–101.

Bussing, R., Zima, B. T., & Belin, T. R. (1998). Differential access to care for children with ADHD in special education programs. *Psychiatric Services, 49*(9), 1226–1229.

Bussing, R., Zima, B. T., Gary, F. A., & Garvan, C. W. (2003). Barriers to detection, help-seeking, and service use for children with ADHD symptoms. *Journal of Behavioral Health Services & Research, 30*(2), 176–189.

Butcher, J. N. (2010). Personality assessment from the nineteenth to the early twenty-first century: Past achievements and contemporary challenges. *Annual Review of Clinical Psychology, 6,* 1–20.

Butcher, J. N. (2011). *A beginner's guide to the MMPI-2* (3rd ed.) Washington, DC: American Psychological Association.

Butler, T., Andrews, G., Allnutt, S., Sakashita, C., Smith, N. E., & Basson, J. (2006). "Mental disorders in Australian prisoners: A comparison with a community sample": Corrigendum. *Australian and New Zealand Journal of Psychiatry, 40*(8).

Byers, A. L., Covinsky, K. E., Neylan, T. C., & Yaffe, K. (2014). Chronicity of posttraumatic stress disorder and risk of disability in older persons. *JAMA Psychiatry, 71*(5), 540–546.

Bylsma, L. M., Taylor-Clift, A., & Rottenberg, J. (2011). Emotional reactivity to daily events in major and minor depression. *Journal of Abnormal Psychology, 120*(1), 155–167.

Cable, A. (2008, November 14). Divorced from reality: All three accounts of the Second Life love triangle that saw a woman separate from her husband for having a cyber affair. *Daily Mail, UK.*

Cachelin, F. M., Phinney, J. S., Schug, R. A., & Striegel-Moore, R. M. (2006). Acculturation and eating disorders in a Mexican American community sample. *Psychological Women Quarterly, 30*(4), 340–347.

Cadet, J. L., Bisagno, V., & Milroy, C. M. (2014). Neuropathology of substance use disorders. *Acta Neuropathologica, 127*(1), 91–107.

Cadge, W., & Fair, B. (2010). Religion, spirituality, health, and medicine: Sociological intersections. In C. E. Bird, P. Conrad, A. M. Fremont, & S. Timmermans (Eds.), *Handbook of medical sociology* (6th ed., pp. 341–362). Nashville, TN: Vanderbilt University Press.

CAIF (Coalition Against Insurance Fraud). (2003). Cited in *Accenture.* Retrieved from Accenture website: http://newsroom.accenture.com/article_display.cfm?article_id=3970.

Cain, N. M., Ansell, E. B., Simpson, H. B., & Pinto, A. (2015). Interpersonal functioning in obsessive-compulsive personality disorder. *Journal of Personality Assessment, 97*(1), 90–99.

Caligor, E., & Clarkin, J. F. (2010). An object relations model of personality and personality pathology. In J. F. Clarkin, P. Fonagy, & G. O. Gabbard (Eds.), *Psychodynamic psychotherapy for personality disorders: A clinical handbook* (pp. 3–36). Arlington, VA: American Psychiatric Publishing.

Calkins, S. D., & Dollar, J. M. (2014). Emotion: Commentary. A biopsychosocial perspective on maternal psychopathology and the development of child emotion regulation. *Journal of Personality Disorders, 28*(1), 70–77.

Callahan, L. A., Steadman, H. J., McGreevy, M. A., & Robbins, P. C. (1991). The volume and characteristics of insanity defense pleas: An eight-state study. *Bulletin of the American Academy of Psychiatry Law, 19*(4), 331–338.

Calmes, J., & Pear, R. (2013, November 8). Rules to require equal coverage for mental ills. *New York Times.*

Calugi, S., El Ghoch, M., Conti, M., & Dalle Grave, R. (2014). Depression and treatment outcome in anorexia nervosa. *Psychiatry Research, 218* (1-2), 195–200.

Cameron, D. J., Thomas, R. I., Mulvihill, M., & Bronheim, H. (1987). Delirium: A test of the Diagnostic and Statistical Manual III criteria on medical inpatients. *Journal of the American Geriatrics Society, 35,* 1007–1010.

Campbell, D. (2010). Pre-suicide states of mind. In P. Williams (Ed.), *The psychoanalytic therapy of severe disturbance, Psychoanalytic ideas* (pp. 171– 183). London: Karnac Books.

Campbell, J., Gilmore, L., & Cuskelly, M. (2003). Changing student teachers' attitudes towards disability and inclusion. *Journal of Intellectual & Developmental Disability, 28,* 369–379.

Campbell, S., Marriott, M., Nahmias, C., & MacQueen, G. M. (2004). Lower hippocampal volume in patients suffering from depression: A meta-analysis. *American Journal of Psychiatry, 161*(4), 598–607.

Campbell, W. K., & Miller, J. D. (Eds.). (2011). *The handbook of narcissism and narcissistic personality disorder: Theoretical approaches, empirical findings, and treatments.* Hoboken, NJ: John Wiley & Sons.

Canas, P. M., Simões, A. P., Rodrigues, R. J., & Cunha, R. A. (2014). Predominant loss of glutamatergic terminal markers in a b-amyloid peptide model of Alzheimer's disease. *Neuropharmacology, 76 Pt A,* 51–56.

Canetta, S., Sourander, A., Surcel, H., Hinkka-Yli-Salomäki, S., Leiviskä, J., Kellendonk, C., . . . Brown, A. S. (2014). Elevated maternal C-reactive protein and increased risk of schizophrenia in a national birth cohort. *American Journal of Psychiatry, 171*(9), 960–968.

Canetto, S. S. (2003). Older adulthood. In L. Slater, J. H. Daniel, & A. Banks (Eds.) *The complete guide to women and mental health* (pp. 56–64). Boston: Beacon Press.

Capitán, L., Simon, D., Kaye, K., & Tenorio, T. (2014). Facial feminization surgery: The forehead. Surgical techniques and analysis of results. *Plastic and Reconstructive Surgery, 134*(4), 609–619.

Capuzzi, D., & Gross, D. R. (Eds.). (2008). *Youth at risk: A prevention resource for counselors, teachers, and parents.* Alexandria, VA: American Counseling Association.

Carducci, B. (2000). Shyness: The new solution. *Psychology Today, 33*(1), 38–45.

CareerBuilder. (2012, April 18). 37% of companies use social networks to research potential job candidates. *CareerBuilder.* Retrieved from CareerBuilder website: http://www.careerbuilder.com/share/aboutus/pressreleasesdetail.

Carey, B. (2008, February 10). Making sense of the great suicide debate. *New York Times.* New York Times website: www.nytimes.com.

Carey, B. (2010, November 22). In cybertherapy, avatars assist with healing. *New York Times.*

Carey, B. (2011). Need therapy? A good man is hard to find. *The New York Times,* May 22. 160(55, 413).

Carlson, L. (2012). Mindfulness-based interventions for physical conditions: A narrative review evaluating levels of evidence. *ISRN Psychiatry,* 651583.

Caron, J., Julien, M., & Huang, J. H. (2008). Changes in suicide methods in Quebec between 1987 and 2000: The possible impact of Bill C-17 requiring safe storage of firearms. *Suicide & Life-Threatening Behavior, 38*(2), 195–208.

Carr, S. N., & Francis, A. J. P. (2010). Do early maladaptive schemas mediate the relationship between childhood experiences and avoidant personality disorder features? A preliminary investigation in a non-clinical sample. *Cognitive Therapy and Research, 34*(4), 343–358.

Carrobles, J. A., Gámez-Guadix, M., & Almendros, C. (2011). Sexual functioning, sexual satisfaction, and subjective and psychological well-being in Spanish women. *Anals de Psicologia, 27*(1), 27–33.

Carroll, K. M. (2008). Cognitive-behavioral therapies. In H. D. Kleber & M. Galanter (Eds.), *The American Psychiatric Publishing textbook of substance abuse treatment* (4th ed., pp. 349–360). Arlington, VA: American Psychiatric Publishing.

Carroll, K. M., & Kiluk, B. D. (2012). Integrating psychotherapy and pharmacotherapy in substance abuse treatment. In F. Rotgers, J. Morgenstern, & S. T. Walters (Eds.), *Treating substance abuse: Theory and technique* (3rd ed., pp. 319–354). Guilford Press: New York.

Carroll, M. E., & Meisch, R. A. (2011). Acquisition of drug self-administration. In M. C. Olmstead (Ed.), *Animal models of drug addiction. Springer protocols: Neuromethods* (pp. 237–265). Totowa, NJ: Humana Press.

Carroll, R. A. (2007). Gender dysphoria and transgender experiences. In S. R. Leiblum (Ed.), *Principles and practice of sex therapy* (4th ed., pp. 477–508). New York: Guilford Press.

Carroll, R. A. (2011). Psychological aspects of erectile dysfunction. In K. T. McVary (Ed.), *Contemporary treatment of erectile dysfunction: A clinical guide*. New York: Springer.

Carruthers, H. R., Morris, J., Tarrier, N., & Whorwell, P. J. (2010). The Manchester Color Wheel: Development of a novel way of identifying color choice and its validation in healthy, anxious and depressed individuals. *BMC Medical Research Methodology, 10*, 12.

Carvalho, J. P., & Hopko, D. R. (2011). Behavioral theory of depression: Reinforcement as a mediating variable between avoidance and depression. *Journal of Behavior Therapy and Experimental Psychiatry, 42*(2), 154–162.

Carvalho, J. P., Verissimo, A., & Nobre, P. J. (2013). Cognitive and emotional determinants characterizing women with persistent genital arousal disorder. *Journal of Sexual Medicine, 10*, 1549–1558.

Casey, P. (2001). Multiple personality disorder. *Primary Care Psychiatry, 7*(1), 7–11.

Cash, T. F., & Henry, P. E. (1995). Women's body images: The results of a national survey in the U. S. A. *Sex Roles, 33*(1/2), 19–28.

Casimir, G. J., & Morrison, B. J. (1993). Rethinking work with "multicultural populations." *Community Mental Health Journal, 29*, 547–559.

Catanesi, R., Martino, V., Candelli, C., Troccoli, G., Grattagliano, I., Di Vella, G., & Carabellese, F. (2013). Posttraumatic stress disorder: Protective and risk factors in 18 survivors of a plane crash. *Journal of Forensic Sciences, 58*(5), 1388–1392.

Cauwels, J. M. (1983). *Bulimia: The binge-purge compulsion*. New York: Doubleday.

Cavallo, F., Aquilano, M., & Arvati, M. (2015). An ambient assisted living approach in designing domiciliary services combined with innovative technologies for patients with Alzheimer's disease: A case study. *American Journal of Alzheimer's Disease and Other Dementias, 30*(1), 69–77.

Cayman, S. (2014). *Sex facts: 369 facts to blow you away*. Chichester, UK: Summersdale.

CBC. (2008, May 13). The world's worst natural disasters: Calamities of the 20th and 21st centuries. *CBC News.*

CDC (Centers for Disease Control and Prevention). (2010, December 3). QuickStats: Percentage of adults who had migraines or severe headaches, pain in the neck, lower back, or face/jaw, by sex. National Health Interview Survey, 2009. *Morbidity and Mortality Weekly Report, 59*(47), 1557.

CDC (Centers for Disease Control and Prevention). (2010). *Alzheimer's disease*. Atlanta, GA: CDC.

CDC (Centers for Disease Control and Prevention). (2010). *Chronic liver disease or cirrhosis*. Hyattsville, MD: NCHS.

CDC (Centers for Disease Control and Prevention). (2010). *Heart disease facts*. Retrieved from www.cdc.gov/heartdisease/facts.htm.

CDC (Centers for Disease Control and Prevention). (2010). *Suicide rates among persons ages 10 years and older, by race/ethnicity and sex, United States, 2002–2006. National Suicide Statistics at a Glance*. Atlanta, GA: CDC.

CDC (Centers for Disease Control and Prevention). (2011). Cited in NVSS, Deaths: Final Data for 2007. *National Vital Statistics Reports, 58*(19). Hyattsville, MD: National Center for Health Statistics.

CDC (Centers for Disease Control and Prevention). (2011). *Death rates from suicide by selected characteristics: 1990 to 2007*. Suitland, MD: US Department of Commerce, Bureau of the Census.

CDC (Centers for Disease Control and Prevention). (2011). *Health disparities and inequalities report—United States, 2011*. Atlanta, GA: Author.

CDC (Centers for Disease Control and Prevention). (2011). *High blood pressure facts*. Retrieved from http://www.cdc.gov/bloodpressure/facts.htm.

CDC (Centers for Disease Control and Prevention). (2011). *Key sleep disorders*. Retrieved from www.cdc.gov/sleep/about_sleep/key_disorders.htm.

CDC (Centers for Disease Control and Prevention). (2011). *Measuring bullying victimization, perpetration, and bystander experiences: A compendium of assessment tools*. Atlanta, GA: CDC, Division of Violence Prevention.

CDC (Centers for Disease Control and Prevention). (2011). *United States Life Tables*. Atlanta, GA: National Center for Health Statistics.

CDC (Centers for Disease Control and Prevention). (2012). *An estimated 1 in 10 U.S. adults report depression*. Washington, DC: Author.

CDC (Centers for Disease Control and Prevention). (2012). *Sexual violence: Facts at a Glance*. Atlanta, GA: CDC.

CDC (Centers for Disease Control and Prevention). (2013, May 2). Morbidity and Mortality Weekly Report, April 26. Cited in T. Parker-Pope, Suicide rates rise sharply in U.S. *The New York Times.*

CDC (Centers for Disease Control and Prevention). (2013). *Alcohol-related disease impact (ARDI)*. Atlanta, GA: CDC.

CDC (Centers for Disease Control and Prevention). (2013). *Asthma: Basic information*. Retrieved from http://www.cdc.gov/asthma/faqs.html.

CDC (Centers for Disease Control and Prevention). (2013). *Chronic liver disease and cirrhosis*. Retrieved from CDC website: http://www.cdc.gov/fastats/liver-disease.htm.

CDC (Centers for Disease Control and Prevention). (2013). *Leading causes of death*. Atlanta, GA: CDC.

CDC (Centers for Disease Control and Prevention). (2013). *Prescription sleep aid use among adults: United States, 2005–2010* (Number 127). Retrieved from http://www.cdc.gov/nchs/data/databriefs/db127.htm.

CDC (Centers for Disease Control and Prevention). (2013). *Statistics overview: HIS Surveillance Report: Diagnoses of HIV infection and AIDS in the United States and dependent areas, 2011, Vol. 23*. Atlanta, GA: CDC.

CDC (Centers for Disease Control and Prevention). (2013). *Suicide and self-inflicted injury*. Atlanta, GA: CDC.

CDC (Centers for Disease Control and Prevention). (2013). *Understanding bullying: Fact sheet*. Retrieved from http://www.cdc.gov/violenceprevention.

CDC (Centers for Disease Control and Prevention). (2014). *CDC and Million Hearts recognize 2013 hypertension control champions*. Retrieved from http://www.cdc.gov/media/releases/2014/p0205-million-hearts.html.

CDC (Centers for Disease Control and Prevention). (2014). *Data and statistics*. Washington, DC: CDC.

CDC (Centers for Disease Control and Prevention). (2014). *Heart disease facts*. Retrieved from http://www.cdc.gov/heartdisease/facts.html.

CDC (Centers for Disease Control and Prevention). (2014). *Morbidity and Mortality Weekly Report (MMWR). QuickStats: Percentage of users of long-term care services with a diagnosis of depression, by provider type—National study of long-term care providers, United States, 2011 and 2012*. Retrieved from http://www.cdc.gov/mmwr/preview/mmwrhtml/mm6304a7.htm.

CDC (Centers for Disease Control and Prevention). (2014). *National prevention strategy: America's plan for better health and wellness*. Retrieved from http://www.cdc.gov/features/preventionstrategy.

CDC (Centers for Disease Control and Prevention). (2014). *National suicide statistics at a glance*. Atlanta, GA: CDC.

CDC (Centers for Disease Control and Prevention). (2014). *New CDC study finds dramatic increase in e-cigarette-related calls to poison centers*. Retrieved from http://www.cdc.gov/media/releases/2014/p0403.

CDC (Centers for Disease Control and Prevention). (2014). *Older persons' health*. Washington, DC: CDC.

CDC (Centers for Disease Control and Prevention). (2014). *Traumatic brain injury in the United States: Fact Sheet*. Atlanta, GA: CDC.

CDC (Centers for Disease Control and Prevention). (2014, March 27). *CDC estimates 1 in 68 children has been identified with autism spectrum disorder*. CDC Newsroom, CDC Media Relations.

CDC (Centers for Disease Control and Prevention). (2015). *Autism and developmental disabilities monitoring (ADDM) network*. Retrieved from http://www.cdc.gov/ncbddd/autism/addm.html.

CDC (Centers for Disease Control and Prevention). (2015). *Chronic liver disease and cirrhosis*. Atlanta, GA: CDC. Retrieved from http://www.cdc.gov/nchs/fastats/liver-disease.htm.

CDC (Centers for Disease Control and Prevention). (2015). *FastStats: Adolescent Health*. Retrieved from http://www.cdc.gov//nchs/fastats/adolescent-health.htm.

CDC (Centers for Disease Control and Prevention). (2015). *Leading causes of death*. Retrieved from http://www.cdc.gov/nchs/fastats/leading-causes-of-death.htm.

CDC (Centers for Disease Control and Prevention). (2015). *Nursing home care*. Retrieved from http://www.cdc.gov/nchs/fastats/nursing-home-care.htm.

CDC (Centers for Disease Control and Prevention). (2015). *Vital signs: Leading causes of death, prevalence of diseases and risk factors, and use of health services among Hispanics in the United States—2009–2013*. Retrieved from http://www.cdc.gov/mmwr/preview/mmwrhtml/mm6417a5.htm.

Celani, D. P. (2014). A Fairbairnian structural analysis of the narcissistic personality disorder. *Psychoanalytic Review, 101*(3), 385–409.

Cénat, J. M., & Derivois, D. (2015). Long-term outcomes among child and adolescent survivors of the 2010 Haitian earthquake. *Depression & Anxiety, 32*(1), 57–63.

Centeno, D. (2011, June 13). Is Weiner's sexting scandal a valid ground for divorce? *New York Divorce News.*

Cerel, J., Moore, M., Brown, M. M., van de Venne, J., & Brown, S. L. (2015). Who leaves suicide notes? A six-year population-based study. *Suicide & Life-Threatening Behavior, 45*(3), 326–334.

CFJ (Center for Family Justice). (2012). *Sexual violence facts.* Bridgeport, CT: CFJ.

Chacón, F., & Vecina, M. L. (2007). The 2004 Madrid terrorist attack: Organizing a large-scale psychological response. In E. K. Carll (Ed.), *Trauma psychology: Issues in violence, disaster, health, and illness* (Vol. 1). Westport, CT: Praeger Publishers.

Chan, A. L. (2013, April 8). Mindfulness meditation benefits: 20 reasons why it's good for your mental and physical health. *Huffington Post.*

Chandler, C. (2010). *The science of ADHD: A guide for parents and professionals.* Hoboken, NJ: Wiley-Blackwell.

Chandola, T., & Marmot, M. G. (2011). Socioeconomic status and stress. In R. J. Contrada & A. Baum (Eds.), *The handbook of stress science: Biology, psychology, and health* (pp. 185–193). New York: Springer Publishing.

Chandra, A., Mosher, W. D., & Copen, C. (2011). Sexual behavior, sexual attraction, and sexual identity in the United States: Data from the 2006–2008 national survey of family growth. *National Health Statistics Reports, Report 36.*

Chang, K. D., Singh, M. K., Wang, P. W., & Howe, M. (2010). Management of bipolar disorders in children and adolescents. In T. A. Ketter (Ed.), *Handbook of diagnosis and treatment of bipolar disorders* (pp. 389–424). Arlington, VA: American Psychiatric Publishing.

Charney, D. S., Woods, S. W., Goodman, W. K., & Heninger, G. R. (1987). Neurobiological mechanisms of panic anxiety: Biochemical and behavioral correlates of yohimbine-induced anxiety. *American Journal of Psychiatry, 144*(8), 1030–1036.

Charney, D. S., Woods, S. W., Price, L. H., Goodman, W. K., Glazer, W. M., & Heninger, G. R. (1990). Noradrenergic dysregulation in panic disorder. In J. C. Ballenger (Ed.), *Neurobiology of panic disorder.* New York: Wiley-Liss.

Chase, M. (1993, May 28). Psychiatrists declare severe PMS a depressive disorder. *Wall Street Journal,* pp. B1, B6.

Chassin, L., Collins, R. L., Ritter, J., & Shirley, M. C. (2001). Vulnerability to substance use disorders across the life span. In R. E. Ingram & J. M. Price (Eds.), *Vulnerability to psychopathology: Risk across the lifespan* (pp. 165–172). New York: Guilford Press.

Chaudhry, M., & Ready, R. (2012). Differential effects of test anxiety and stress on the WAIS-IV. *Journal of Young Investigators, 24*(5), 60–66.

Chavira, D. A., Grilo, C. M., Shea, M. T., Yen, S., Gunderson, J. G., Morey, L. C., . . . McGlashan, T. H. (2003). Ethnicity and four personality disorders. *Comprehensive Psychiatry, 44*(6), 483–491.

Chekki, C. (2004, November 10). Treaty 3 cries for help. *The Chronicle Journal* (Thunder Bay, Ontario, Canada), p. A3.

Chemerinski, E., & Siever, L. J. (2011). The schizophrenia spectrum personality disorders. In D.R. Weinberger & P. Harrison (Eds.). *Schizophrenia.* Hoboken, NJ: Wiley-Blackwell.

Chen, C-H., Suckling, J., Lennox, B. R., Ooi, C., & Bullmore, E. T. (2011). A quantitative meta-analysis of fMRI studies in bipolar disorder. *Bipolar Disorders, 13*(1), 1–15.

Chen, C., O'Brien, M. S., & Anthony, J. C. (2005). Who becomes cannabis dependent soon after onset of use? Epidemiological evidence from the United States: 2000–2001. *Drug and Alcohol Dependence, 79*(1), 11–22.

Chen, L., Zhang, G., Hu, M., & Liang, X. (2015). Eye movement desensitization and reprocessing versus cognitive-behavioral therapy for adult posttraumatic stress disorder: Systematic review and metaanalysis. *The Journal of Nervous and Mental Disease, 203*(6), 443–451.

Chen, S., Zhou, R., Cui, H., & Chen, X. (2013). Deficits in cue detection underlie event-based prospective memory impairment in major depression: An eye tracking study. *Psychiatry Research, 209*(3), 453–458.

Cheng, A. T. A., Hawton, K., Lee, C. T. C., & Chen, T. H. H. (2007). The influence of media reporting of the suicide of a celebrity on suicide rates: A population-based study. *International Journal of Epidemiology, 36*(6), 1229–1234.

Cherner, R. A., & Reissing, E. D. (2013). A psychophysiological investigation of sexual arousal in women with lifelong vaginismus. *Journal of Sexual Medicine, 10,* 1291–1303.

Cherry, K. (2010). 10 facts about Sigmund Freud. *About.com.* Retrieved from About.com website: http://www.psychology.about.com/od/sigmundfreud/tp/facts-about-freud.htm.

Cherry, K. (2014). Employment of psychologists. *About.com.*

Cherry, K. (2014). How to become a counselor. *About.com.*

Cherry, K. (2014). Introduction to classical conditioning: *About.com.* Retrieved from About.com website: http://psychology.about.com/od/behavioralpsychology/a/classconditioning.

Cherry, K. (2014). Psychology employment trends. *About.com.*

Cherry, K. (2014). What is biological preparedness? *About.com.* Retrieved from About.com website: http://psychology.about.com/od/bindex/g/biological-preparedness.

Cherry, K. (2015). What is a projective test? *About Education.* Retrieved from About.com website: http://psychology.about.com/od/psychologicaltesting.

Cherry, K. (2015). What is personality testing? *About Education.* Retrieved from About.com website: http://psychology.about.com/od/personality-testing.

Cherry, K. E., Sampson, L., Nezat, P. F., Cacamo, A., Marks, L. D., & Galea, S. (2015). Long-term psychological outcomes in older adults after disaster: Relationships to religiosity and social support. *Aging & Mental Health, 19*(5), 430–443.

Chi, S., Yu, J., Tan, M., & Tan, L. (2014). Depression in Alzheimer's disease: Epidemiology, mechanisms, and management. *Journal of Alzheimer's Disease, 42*(3), 739–755.

Chien, W. T., & Thompson, D. R. (2014). Effects of a mindfulness-based psychoeducation programme for Chinese patients with schizophrenia: 2-year follow-up. *British Journal of Psychiatry, 205*(1), 52–59.

Chiesa, A., & Serretti, A. (2014). Are mindfulness-based interventions effective for substance use disorders? A systematic review of the evidence. *Substance Use & Misuse, 49*(5), 492–512.

Chin-Chan, M., Navarro-Yepes, J., & Quintanilla-Vega, B. (2015). Environmental pollutants as risk factors for neurodegenerative disorders: Alzheimer and Parkinson diseases. *Frontiers in Cellular Neuroscience, 9,* 124.

Chiu, L. H. (1971). Manifested anxiety in Chinese and American children. *Journal of Psychology, 79,* 273–284.

Chollet, J., Saragoussi, D., Clay, E., & François, C. (2013). A clinical research practice datalink analysis of antidepressant treatment patterns and health care costs in generalized anxiety disorder. *Value in Health, 16*(8), 1133–1139.

Christensen, A., Atkins, D. C., Baucom, B., & Yi, J. (2010). Marital status and satisfaction five years following a randomized clinical trial comparing traditional versus integrative behavioral couple therapy. *Journal of Consulting and Clinical Psychology, 78*(2), 225–235.

Christensen, A., Doss, B. D., & Jacobson, N. S. (2014). *Reconcilable differences: Rebuild your relationship by rediscovering the partner you love—without losing yourself* (2nd ed.). New York: Guilford Publications.

Christensen, B. S., Gronbaek, M., Osler, M., Pedersen, B. V., Graugaard, C., & Frisch, M. (2011). Sexual dysfunctions and difficulties in Denmark: Prevalence and associated sociodemographic factors. *Archives of Sexual Behavior, 40*(1), 121–132.

Christensen, J. (2014, February 4). How heroin kills you. *CNN.*

Christiansen, E., Agerbo, E., Bilenberg, N., & Stenager, E. (2015). SSRIs and risk of suicide attempts in young people: A Danish observational register-based historical cohort study, using propensity score. *Nordic Journal of Psychiatry, 1–9.* [Advance electronic publication.]

Christodoulou, M. (2012). Pro-anorexia websites pose public health challenge. *The Lancet, 379,* 110.

Christophersen, E. R., & Friman, P. C. (2010). *Elimination disorders in children and adolescents.* Cambridge, MA: Hogrefe Publishing.

Chun, S., Westmoreland, J. J., Bayazitov, I. T., Eddins, D., Pani, A. K., Smeyne, R. J., . . . Zakharenko, S. S. (2014). Specific disruption of thalamic inputs to the auditory cortex in schizophrenia models. *Science* (New York, N.Y.), *344*(6188), 1178–1182.

Chung, P. H., Ross, J. D., Wakhlu, S., & Adinoff, B. (2012). Neurobiological bases of addiction treatment. In S. T. Walters & F. Rotgers (Eds.), *Treating substance abuse: Theory and technique* (3rd Ed., pp. 281–318). New York: Guilford Press.

Chung, T., Sealy, L., Abraham, M., Ruglovsky, C., Schall, J., & Maisto, S. A. (2014). Personal network characteristics of youth in substance use treatment: Motivation for and perceived difficulty of positive network change. *Substance Abuse, 36*(3), 380–388.

Church, D. (2014). Reductions in pain, depression, and anxiety symptoms after PTSD remediation in veterans. *Explore, 10*(3), 162–169.

Ciraulo, D. A., Evans, J. A., Qiu, W. Q., Shader, R. I., & Salzman, C. (2011). Antidepressant treatment of geriatric depression. In D. A. Ciraulo & R. I. Shader, *Pharmacotherapy for depression* (2nd ed., pp 125–183). New York: Springer Science + Business Media.

Ciraulo, D. A., Shader, R. I., & Greenblatt, D. J. (2011). Clinical pharmacology and therapeutics of antidepressants. In D. A. Ciraulo & R. I. Shader (Eds.), *Pharmacotherapy of depression* (2nd ed., pp. 33–124). New York: Springer Science + Business Media.

CISCRP (Center for Information and Study on Clinical Research Participation). (2013). *Clinical trial facts and figures for health professionals.* Boston, MA: CISCRP.

Clark, D. A., & Beck, A. T. (2010). *Cognitive therapy of anxiety disorders: Science and practice.* New York: Guilford Press.

Clark, D. A., & Beck, A. T. (2012). *The anxiety and worry workbook: The cognitive behavioral solution.* New York: Guilford Press.

Clark, R., DeYoung, C. G., Sponheim, S. R., Bender, T. L., Polusny, M. A., Erbes, C. R., & Arbisi, P. A. (2013). Predicting post-traumatic stress disorder in veterans: Interaction of traumatic load with COMT gene variation. *Journal of Psychiatric Research, 47*(12), 1849–1856.

Clark, T. T. (2014). Perceived discrimination, depressive symptoms, and substance use in young adulthood. *Addictive Behaviors, 39*(6), 1021–1025.

Clarke, D. E., Narrow, W. E., Regier, D. A., Kuramoto, S. J., Kupfer, D. J., Kuhl, E. A., . . . Kraemer, H.C. (2013). DSM-5 field trials in the United States and Canada, Part I: Study design, sampling strategy, implementation, and analytic approaches. *American Journal of Psychiatry, 170,* 43–58.

Clarke, J. C., & Saunders, J. B. (1988). *Alcoholism and problem drinking: Theories and treatment.* Sydney: Pergamon Press.

Clarke, M., Roddy, S., & Cannon, M. (2012). Obstetric complications and schizophrenia: Historical overview and new directions. In A. S. Brown & P. H. Patterson (Eds.), *The origins of schizophrenia* (pp. 96–119). New York: Columbia University Press.

Claudino, A. M., & Morgan, C. M. (2012). Unravelling binge eating disorder. In J. Alexander and J. Treasure (Eds.), *A collaborative approach to eating disorders* (pp. 236–248). New York: Routledge/Taylor & Francis Group.

Clausen, L., Rosenvinge, J. H., Friborg, O., & Rokkedal, K. (2011). Validating the Eating Disorder Inventory-3 (EDI-3): A comparison between 561 female eating disorders patients and 878 females from the general population. *Journal of Psychopathology and Behavioral Assessment, 33*(1), 101–110.

Clay, R. A. (2011). A new day for parity. *Monitor on Psychology, 42*(1), 18–19.

Clay, R. A. (2011). Is stress getting to you? *Monitor on Psychology, 42*(1), 58–63.

Cleare, A., Pariante, C. M., Young, A. H., Anderson, I. M., Christmas, D., Cowen, P. J., . . . Uher, R. (2015). Evidence-based guidelines for treating depressive disorders with antidepressants: A revision of the 2008 British Association for Psychopharmacology guidelines. *Journal of Psychopharmacology, 29*(5), 459–525.

Clifford, T., & Minnes, P. (2013). Who participates in support groups for parents of children with autism spectrum disorders? The role of beliefs and coping style. *Journal of Autism and Developmental Disorders, 43*(1), 179–187.

Clinton, A. B., Fernandez, L., & Alicea, G. (2010). Interviewing, bias, and cultural considerations in Prevention Program Evaluation. Paper presented at APA 118th Annual Convention, San Diego, California, August 12–15.

Cloninger, C. F., & Svrakic, D. M. (2005). Personality disorders. In E. H. Rubin & C. F. Zorumski (Eds.), *Adult psychiatry* (2nd ed., pp. 290–306). Oxford, England: Blackwell Publishing.

CNCS (Corporation for National & Community Service). (2013). *New federal report finds 1 in 4 Americans volunteer.* Washington, DC: CNCS.

Coates, J., Taylor, J. A., & Sayal, K. (2015). Parenting interventions for ADHD: A systematic literature review and meta-analysis. *Journal of Attention Disorders, 19*(10), 831–843.

Cocotas, A. (2013, March 22). Chart of the day: Kids send a mind boggling number of texts every month. *Business Insider.*

Coffey, C. E., & Kellner, C. H. (2011). Electroconvulsive therapy. In C. E. Coffey, J. L. Cummings, M. S. George, & D. Weintraub (Eds.), *The American Psychiatric Publishing textbook of geriatric neuropsychiatry.* Arlington, VA: American Psychiatric Publishing, Inc.

Coffey, M. J., & Coffey, C. E. (2011). Mood disorders. In C. E. Coffey, J. L. Cummings, M. S. George, & D. Weintraub (Eds.), *The American Psychiatric Publishing textbook of geriatric neuropsychiatry.* Arlington, VA: American Psychiatric Publishing, Inc.

Coffey, S. F., Schumacher, J. A., Baschnagel, J. S., Hawk, L. W., & Holloman, G. (2011). Impulsivity and risk-taking in borderline personality disorder with and without substance use disorders. *Personality Disorders: Theory, Research, and Treatment, 2*(2), 128–141.

Cohen-Kettenis, P. T. (2001). Gender identity disorder in DSM? *Journal of the American Academy of Child & Adolescent Psychiatry, 40*(4), 391.

Cohen, N. (2009, July 28). "A Rorschach cheat sheet on Wikipedia?" *New York Times,* p. A1.

Cohen, S. (2002). Psychosocial stress, social networks, and susceptibility to infection. In H. G. Koenig & H. J. Cohen (Eds.), *The link between religion and health: Psychoneuroimmunology and the faith factor* (pp. 101–123). New York: Oxford University Press.

Cohen, S., Daniel O'Leary, K., Foran, H. M., & Kliem, S. (2014). Mechanisms of change in brief couple therapy for depression. *Behavior Therapy, 45*(3), 402–417.

Colburn, D. (1996, November 19). Singer's suicide doesn't lead to "copycat" deaths. *Washington Post Health,* p. 5.

Coleman, L. (1984). *The reign of error: Psychiatry, authority, and law.* Boston: Beacon.

Coleman, M. (2014, March 1). Philip Seymour Hoffman autopsy reveals actor died of toxic drug mix. *Rolling Stone.*

Colijn, M. A., Nitta, B. H., & Grossberg, G. T. (2015). Psychosis in later life: A review and update. *Harvard Review of Psychiatry, 23*(5), 354–367.

Colletti, G., Lynn, S. J., & Laurence, J.-R. (2010). Hypnosis and the treatment of dissociative identity disorder. In S. J. Lynn, J. W. Rhue, & I. Kirsch (Eds.), *Handbook of clinical hypnosis* (2nd ed., pp. 433–451). Washington, DC: American Psychological Association.

Colli, A., Tanzilli, A., Dimaggio, G., & Lingiardi, V. (2014). Patient personality and therapist response: An empirical investigation. *American Journal of Psychiatry, 171*(1), 102–108.

Collins, R. W., Levitt, M. A., Birnbaum, A. H., & Wruck, M. (2012). Encopresis: A medical and family approach. *Pediatric Nursing, 38*(4), 236–237.

Comas-Díaz, L. (2011). Multicultural approaches to psychotherapy. In J. C. Norcross, G. R. VandenBos, & D. K. Freedheim (Eds.), *History of psychotherapy: Continuity and change* (2nd ed., pp. 243–267). Washington, DC: American Psychological Association.

Comas-Díaz, L. (2011). Multicultural psychotherapies. In R. J. Corsini & D. Wedding (Eds.), *Current psychotherapies* (9th ed.). Belmont, CA: Brooks/Cole.

Comas-Díaz, L. (2012). *Multicultural care: A clinician's guide to cultural competence. Psychologists in independent practice* (Div. 42). Washington, DC: American Psychological Association.

Comas-Díaz, L. (2014). Multicultural psychotherapy. In F. T. L. Leong (Ed.), *APA handbook of multicultural psychology* (Ch. 25). Washington, DC: American Psychological Association.

Comas-Díaz, L. (2014). Multicultural theories of psychotherapy. In D. Wedding & R. J. Corsini (Eds.), *Current psychotherapies* (10th ed., pp. 533–568). Independence, KY: Cengage Publications.

Combs, D. R., Basso, M. R., Wanner, J. L., & Ledet, S. N. (2008). Schizophrenia. In M. Hersen & J. Rosqvist (Eds.), *Handbook of psychological assessment, case conceptualization and treatment, Vol. 1: Adults* (pp. 352–402). Hoboken, NJ: John Wiley & Sons.

Comer, J. S., Dantowitz, A., Chou, T., Edison, A. L., Elkins, R. M., Kerns, C., . . . Green, J. G. (2014). Adjustment among area youth after the Boston Marathon bombing and subsequent manhunt, *Pediatrics, 134*(1), 7–14.

Comer, J. S., Mojtabai, R., & Olfson, M. (2011). National trends in the antipsychotic treatment of psychiatric outpatients with anxiety disorders. *American Journal of Psychiatry, 168*(10), 1057–1065.

Comer, J. S., Olfson, M., & Mojtabai, R. (2010). National trends in child and adolescent psychotropic polypharmacy in office-based practice, 1996–2007. *Journal of the American Academy of Child & Adolescent Psychiatry, 49*(10), 1001–1010.

Comer, R. (1973). *Therapy interviews with a schizophrenic patient.* Unpublished manuscript.

Cone, J. E., Li, J., Kornblith, E., Gocheva, V., Stellman, S. D., Shaikh, A., . . . Bowler, R. M. (2015). Chronic probable PTSD in police responders in the World Trade Center health registry ten to eleven years after 9/11. *American Journal of Industrial Medicine, 58*(5), 483–493.

Conner, K. R., & Weisman, R. L. (2011). Embitterment in suicide and homicide-suicide. In M. Linden & A. Maercker (Eds.), *Embitterment: Societal, psychological, and clinical perspectives* (pp. 240–247). New York: Springer-Verlag Publishing.

Conrad, N. (1992). Stress and knowledge of suicidal others as factors in suicidal behavior of high school adolescents. *Issues in Mental Health Nursing, 13*(2), 95–104.

Constantino, J. N. (2011). Social impairment. In E. Hollander, A. Kolevzon & J. T. Coyle (Eds.), *Textbook of autism spectrum disorders* (pp. 139–145) Arlington, VA: American Psychiatric Publishing, Inc.

Conti, A. A. (2014). Western medical rehabilitation through time: A historical and epistemological review. *The Scientific World Journal, 2014,* 432506.

Conwell, Y., Caine, E. D., & Olsen, K. (1990). Suicide and cancer in late life. *Hospital Community Psychiatry, 43,* 1334–1338.

Cook, B. L., Zuvekas, S. H., Carson, N., Wayne, G. F., Vesper, A., & McGuire, T. G. (2014). Assessing racial/ethnic disparities in treatment across episodes of mental health care. *Health Services Research, 49*(1), 206–229.

Cook, C. H. (2014). Suicide and religion. *The British Journal of Psychiatry, 204,* 254–255.

Cool Infographics. (2013). Social network overload. Retrieved from Cool Infographics website: http://www.coolinfographics.com/blog/2013/4/2/social-network-overload.

Coon, D., & Mitterer, J. O. (2007). *Introduction to psychology: Gateways to mind and behavior* (11th ed.). Belmont, CA: Wadsworth.

Coons, P. M., & Bowman, E. S. (2001). Ten-year follow-up study of patients with dissociative identity disorder. *Journal of Trauma & Dissociation, 2*(1), 73–89.

Cooper, J. L. (2004). Treatment for children with attention-deficit/hyperactivity disorder. *Dissertation Abstracts International: Section B: The Sciences and Engineering, 65*(5-B), 2338.

Cooper, M. (2008). *Essential research findings in counselling and psychotherapy: The facts are friendly.* Los Angeles, CA: Sage Publications.

Cooper, R. (2014). On deciding to have a lobotomy: Either lobotomies were justified or decisions under risk should not always seek to maximize expected utility. *Medicine, Health Care, and Philosophy, 17*(1), 143–154.

Cooper, R., Hildebrandt, S., & Gerlach, A. L. (2014). Drinking motives in alcohol use disorder patients with and without social anxiety disorder. *Anxiety, Stress and Coping, 27*(1), 113–122.

Cooper, W. O., Callahan, S. T., Shintani, A., Fuchs, D. C., Shelton, R. C., Dudley, J. A., . . . Ray, W. A. (2014). Antidepressants and suicide attempts in children. *Pediatrics, 133*(2), 204–210.

Copley, J. (2008, May 8). Psychology of heavy metal music. *Suite101.com.* Retrieved from Suite101.com website: www.suite101.com.

Cordeau, D., & Courtois, F. (2014). Sexual disorders in women with MS: Assessment and management. *Annals of Physical and Rehabilitation Medicine, 57*(5), 337–347.

Corega, C., Vaida, L., Festila, D. G., Rigoni, G., Albanese, M., D'Agostino, A., . . . Bertossi, D. (2014). Dental white spots associated with bulimia nervosa in orthodontic patients. *Minerva Stomatologica.* [Electronic publication.]

Corey, G. (2004). *Theory and practice of counseling and psychotherapy (with web site, chapter quiz booklet, and InfoTrac.* Stanford, CT: Wadsworth Publishing.

Corey, G. (2012). *Theory and practice of counseling and psychotherapy.* Belmont, CA: Brooks Cole.

Corey, G. (2016). *Theory and practice of group counseling* (9th ed.). Independence, KY: Cengage Publications.

Corrie, S., & Callanan, M. M. (2001). Therapists' beliefs about research and the scientist-practitioner model in an evidence-based health care climate? A qualitative study. *British Journal of Medical Psychology, 74*(2), 135–149.

Corter, A., & Petrie, K. J. (2011). Expressive writing in patients diagnosed with cancer. In I. Nyklicek, A. Vingerhoets, & M. Zeelenberg (Eds.), *Emotion regulation and well-being* (pp. 297–306). New York: Springer Science + Business Media.

Corves, C., Engel, R. R., Davis, J., & Leucht, S. (2014). Do patients with paranoid and disorganized schizophrenia respond differently to antipsychotic drugs? *Acta Psychiatrica Scandinavica, 130*(1), 40–45.

Cosgrove, K. P. (2010). Imaging receptor changes in human drug abusers. In D. W. Self & J. K. Staley (Eds.), *Behavioral neuroscience of drug addiction* (pp. 199–217). New York: Springer Publishing.

Costa, E. (1983). Are benzodiazepine recognition sites functional entities for the action of endogenous effectors or merely drug receptors? *Advances in Biochemistry & Psychopharmacology, 38,* 249–259.

Costa, E. (1985). Benzodiazepine-GABA interactions: A model to investigate the neurobiology of anxiety. In A. H. Tuma & J. Maser (Eds.), *Anxiety and the anxiety disorders.* Hillsdale, NJ: Lawrence Erlbaum.

Costa, R., Carvalho, M., Cantini, J., Freire, R., & Nardi, A. (2014). Demographics, clinical characteristics and quality of life of Brazilian women with driving phobia. *Comprehensive Psychiatry, 55*(2), 374–379.

Costantino, G., Dana, R. H., & Malgady, R. G. (2007). *TEMAS (Tell-Me-A-Story) assessment in multicultural societies.* Mahwah, NJ: Lawrence Erlbaum.

Costantino, G., Malgady, R. G., Colon-Malgady, G., & Bailey, J. (1992). Clinical utility of the TEMAS with nonminority children. *Journal of Personality Assessment, 59*(3), 433–438.

Courtet, P., Samalin, L., & Olié, E. (2011). Antidepressants in bipolar disorder. *L'encéphale, 37 Suppl 3,* S196–S202.

Couturier, J., & Lock, J. (2006). Eating disorders: Anorexia nervosa, bulimia nervosa, and binge eating disorder. In T. G. Plante (Ed.), *Mental disorders of the new millennium, Vol. 3: Biology and function.* Westport, CT: Praeger Publishers.

Covell, N. H., Essock, S. M., & Frisman, L. K. (2011). Economics of the treatment of schizophrenia. In D. R. Weinberg & P. Harrison (Eds.), *Schizophrenia* (pp. 687–699). Hoboken, NJ: Wiley-Blackwell.

Covington, M. A., He, C., Brown, C., Naci, L., McClain, J. T., Fjordbak, B. S., . . . Brown, J. (2005). Schizophrenia and the structure of language: The linguist's view. *Schizophrenia Research, 77*(1), 85–98.

Coyne, J. C. (2001). Depression and the response of others. In W. G. Parrott (Ed.), *Emotions in social psychology: Essential readings* (pp. 231–238). Philadelphia: Psychology Press/Taylor & Francis.

CPA (Canadian Psychological Association). (2009). *Canadian Psychological Association position on publication and dissemination of psychological tests.* Ontario, Canada: Canadian Psychological Association.

Crabtree, S. (2011). *U.S. seniors maintain happiness highs with less social time* (Gallup poll 151457). *Gallup.* Retrieved from Gallup website: http://www.gallup.com/poll/151457.

Craig, K. J., & Chamberlain, S. R. (2010). The neuropsychology of anxiety disorders. In D. J. Stein, E. Hollander, & B. O. Rothbaum (Eds.), *Textbook of anxiety disorders* (2nd ed., pp. 87–102). Arlington, VA: American Psychiatric Publishing.

Craig, T., & Power, P. (2010). Inpatient provision in early psychosis. In P. French, J. Smith, D. Shiers, M. Reed, & M. Rayne (Eds.), *Promoting recovery in early psychosis: A practice manual* (pp. 17–26). Hoboken, NJ: Wiley-Blackwell.

Crandall, C. S., Preisler, J. J., & Aussprung, J. (1992). Measuring life event stress in the lives of college students: The Undergraduate Stress Questionnaire (USQ). *Journal of Behavioral Medicine, 15*(6), 627–662.

Craske, C. M., & Barlow, D. H. (2014). Panic disorder and agoraphobia. In D. H. Barlow, *Clinical handbook of psychological disorders* (5th ed.), (pp. 1–61). New York: Guilford Press.

Craske, M. G. (2010). *Cognitive–behavioral therapy.* Washington, DC: American Psychological Association.

Crawford, C., Burns, J., & Fernie, B. A. (2015). Psychosocial impact of involvement in the Special Olympics. *Research in Developmental Disabilities, 45-46,* 93–102.

CRCC (Cleveland Rape Crisis Center). (2014). *Sexual violence on college campuses.* Retrieved from CRCC website: http://www.clevelandrapecrisis.org/resources/statistics/sexual-violence-on-college-campuses.

Crighton, A. H., Wygant, D. B., Applegate, J. C., Umlauf, R. L., & Granacher, R. P. (2014). Can brief measures effectively screen for pain and somatic malingering? Examination of the Modified Somatic Perception Questionnaire and Pain Disability Index. *Spine Journal, 14*(9), 2042–2050.

Crits-Christoph, P., Lundy, C., Stringer, M., Gallop, R., & Gastfriend, D. R. (2015). Extended-release naltrexone for alcohol and opioid problems in Missouri parolees and probationers. *Journal of Substance Abuse Treatment, 56,* 54–60.

Cronin, E., Brand, B. L., & Mattanah, J. F. (2014). The impact of the therapeutic alliance on treatment outcome in patients with dissociative disorders. *European Journal of Psychotraumatology, 5d,* 226/6.

Crosby, A. E., Espitia-Hardeman, V., Hill, H. A., Ortega, L., & Clavel-Arcas, C. (2009). Alcohol and suicide among racial/ethnic populations—17 states, 2005–2006. *Journal of the American Medical Association, 302*(7), 733–734.

Crouter, F. (2015). *The psychology of jury selection.* Koko Books. [Electronic publication.]

Crow, T. J. (1980). Positive and negative schizophrenic symptoms and the role of dopamine: II. *British Journal of Psychiatry, 137,* 383–386.

Crow, T. J. (1985). The two-syndrome concept: Origins and current status. *Schizophrenia Bulletin, 11*(3), 471–486.

Crow, T. J. (1995). Brain changes and negative symptoms in schizophrenia. *Psychopathology, 28*(1), 18–21.

Crow, T. J. (2008). The "big bang" theory of the origin of psychosis and the faculty of language. *Schizophrenia Research, 102*(1–3), 31–52.

Crystal, S., Kleinhaus, K., Perrin, M., & Malaspina, D. (2012). Advancing paternal age and the risk of schizophrenia. In A. S. Brown & P. H. Patterson (Eds.), *The origins of schizophrenia* (pp. 140–155). New York: Columbia University Press.

Cuddeback, G. S., Shattell, M. M., Bartlett, R., Yoselle, J., & Brown, D. (2013). Consumers' perceptions of transitions from assertive community treatment to less intensive services. *Journal of Psychosocial Nursing and Mental Health Services, 51*(8), 39–45.

Cuijpers, P., Karyotaki, E., Weitz, E., Andersson, G., Hollon, S. D., & van Straten, A. (2014). The effects of psychotherapies for major depression in adults on remission, recovery and improvement: A meta-analysis. *Journal of Affective Disorders, 159,* 118–126.

Cuijpers, P., Sijbrandij, M., Koole, S. L., Andersson, G., Beekman, A. T., & Reynolds, C. (2014). Adding psychotherapy to antidepressant medication in depression and anxiety disorders: A meta-analysis. *World Psychiatry: Official Journal of the World Psychiatric Association (WPA), 13*(1), 56–67.

Cukrowicz, K. C., Cheavens, J. S., Van Orden, K. A., Ragain, R. M., & Cook, R. L. (2011). Perceived burdensomeness and suicide ideation in older adults. *Psychology and Aging, 26*(2), 331–338.

Cullen, A. E., Fisher, H. L., Roberts, R. E., Pariante, C. M., & Laurens, K. R. (2014). Daily stressors and negative life events in children at elevated risk of developing schizophrenia. *British Journal of Psychiatry, 204,* 354–360.

Culp, A. M., Clyman, M. M., & Culp, R. E. (1995). Adolescent depressed mood, reports of suicide attempts, and asking for help. *Adolescence, 30*(120), 827–837.

Culver, J. L., & Pratchett, L. C. (2010). Adjunctive psychosocial interventions in the management of bipolar disorders. In T. A. Ketter (Ed.), *Handbook of diagnosis and treatment of bipolar disorders* (pp. 661–676). Arlington, VA: American Psychiatric Publishing.

Cummings, J. L., & Coffey, C. E. (2011). Geriatric neuropsychiatry. In C. E. Coffey, J. L. Cummings, M. S. George, & D. Weintraub (Eds.), *The American Psychiatric Publishing textbook of geriatric neuropsychiatry.* Arlington, VA: American Psychiatric Publishing, Inc.

Cunha, M., & Paiva, M. J. (2012). Text anxiety in adolescents: The role of self-criticism and acceptance and mindfulness skills. *The Spanish Journal of Psychology, 15*(2), 533–543.

Cunningham, C. L., Groblewski, P. A., & Voorhees, C. M. (2011). Place conditioning. In M. C. Olmstead (Ed.), *Animal models of drug addiction. Springer protocols: Neuromethods* (pp. 167–189). Totowa, NJ: Humana Press.

Curley, A. (2013). The truth about lies: The science of deception. *BrainFacts.org.*

Curtis, R. G., Windsor, T. D., & Soubelet, A. (2014). The relationship between Big-5 personality traits and cognitive ability in older adults: A review. *Neuropsychology, Development, and Cognition. Section B, Aging, Neuropsychology and Cognition, 22*(1), 42–71.

Cutler, D. M., Glaeser, E. L., & Norberg, K. E. (2001). Explaining the rise in youth suicide. In J. Gruber (Ed.), *Risky behavior among youths: An economic analysis* (pp. 219–269). Chicago: University of Chicago Press.

Cutright, P., & Fernquist, R. M. (2001). The relative gender gap in suicide: Societal integration, the culture of suicide and period effects in 20 developed countries, 1955–1994. *Social Science Research, 30*(1), 76–99.

Cutting, J. (2015). First rank symptoms of schizophrenia: Their nature and origin. *History of Psychiatry, 26*(2), 131–146.

Cynkar, A. (2007). The changing gender composition of psychology. *The Monitor, 38*(6), 46.

Dagan, M., Sanderman, R., Schokker, M. C., Wiggers, T., Baas, P. C., van Haastert, M., & Hagedoorn, M. (2011). Spousal support and changes in distress over time in couples coping with cancer: The role of personal control. *Journal of Family Psychology, 25*(2), 310–318.

D'Agata, F., Caroppo, P., Amianto, F., Spalatro, A., Caglio, M. M., Bergui, M., . . . Fassino, S. (2015). Brain correlates of alexithymia in eating disorders: A voxel-based morphometry study. *Psychiatry and Clinical Neurosciences.* [Advance publication.]

Daigre, C., Rodríguez-Cintas, L., Tarifa, N., Rodríguez-Martos, L., Grau-López, L.,

Berenguer, M., . . . Roncero, C. (2015). History of sexual, emotional or physical abuse and psychiatric comorbidity in substance-dependent patients. *Psychiatry Research, 229*(3), 743–749.

Daine, K., Hawton, K., Singaravelu, V., Stewart, A., Simkin, S., & Montgomery, P. (2013). The power of the web: A systematic review of studies of the influence of the internet on self-harm and suicide in young people. *PLOS ONE, 8*(10), e77555.

Daitch, C. (2011). *Anxiety disorders: The go-to guide for clients and therapists.* New York: W. W. Norton & Co.

Daley, D. C., Marlatt, G. A., & Douaihy, A. (2011). Relapse prevention. In J. H. Lowinson & P. Ruiz (Eds.), *Substance abuse: A comprehensive textbook* (5th ed.). Philadelphia, PA: Lippincott, Williams, & Wilkins.

Dallman, M. F., & Hellhammer, D. (2011). Regulation of the hypothalamo-pituitary-adrenal axis, chronic stress, and energy: The role of brain networks. In R. J. Contrada & A. Baum (Eds.), *The handbook of stress science: Biology, psychology, and health* (pp. 11–36). New York: Springer Publishing.

Daly, M., Baumeister, R. F., Delaney, L., & MacLachlan, M. (2014). Self-control and its relation to emotions and psychobiology: Evidence from a Day Reconstruction Method study. *Journal of Behavioral Medicine, 37*(1), 81–93.

Daly, R. (2010). Shift to community care slowing in many states. *Psychiatric News, 45*(15), 8.

Dana, R. H. (2000). Culture and methodology in personality assessment. In I. Cuellar & F. A. Paniagua (Eds.), *Handbook of multicultural mental health* (pp. 97–120). San Diego, CA: Academic.

Dana, R. H. (2005). *Multicultural assessment: Principles, applications, and examples.* Mahwah, NJ: Lawrence Erlbaum.

Daniels, C. W. (2002). Legal aspects of polygraph admissibility in the United States. In M. Klener (Ed.), *The handbook of polygraph testing.* San Diego, CA: Academic.

Danquah, M. N-A. (1998). *Willow weep for me: A black woman's journey through depression.* New York: W. W. Norton.

Darke, S., Williamson, A., Ross, J., & Teesson, M. (2005). Attempted suicide among heroin users: 12-month outcomes from the Australian Treatment Outcome Study (ATOS). *Drug and Alcohol Dependence, 78*(2), 177–186.

D'Arienzo, J. A. (2010). Inoculation training for trauma and stress-related disorders. In S. S. Fehr (Ed.), *101 interventions in group therapy* (rev. ed., pp. 431–435). New York: Routledge/Taylor & Francis Group.

da Rosa, G., Martin, P., Gondo, Y., Hirose, N., Ishioka, Y., & Poon, L. (2014). Examination of important life experiences of the oldest-old: Cross-cultural comparisons of U.S. and Japanese centenarians. *Journal of Cross-Cultural Gerontology, 29*(2), 109–130.

Dasgupta, M., & Brymer, C. (2014). Prognosis of delirium in hospitalized elderly: Worse than we thought. *International Journal of Geriatric Psychiatry, 29*(5), 497–505.

da Silva, R. P., do Olival, G. S., Stievano, L. P., Toller, V. B., Jordy, S. S., Eloi, M., & Tilbery, C. P. (2015). Validation and cross-cultural adaptation of sexual dysfunction modified scale in multiple sclerosis for Brazilian population. *Arquivos De Neuro-Psiquiatria, 73*(8), 681–687.

Davey, M. (2010, May 13). Online talk, suicides and a thorny court case. *New York Times.*

Davey, M. (2010, May 14). Did he encourage suicide online? Retrieved from NDTV website: www.ndtv.com.

Davidson, L., & Chan, K. K. S. (2014). Common factors: Evidence-based practice and recovery. *Psychiatric Services, 65*(5), 675–677.

Davidson, L., Rakfeldt, J., & Strauss, J. (2010). *The roots of the recovery movement in psychiatry: Lessons learned.* Hoboken, NJ: John Wiley & Sons.

Davis, C. (2015). The epidemiology and genetics of binge eating disorder (BED). *CNS Spectrums,* 1–8.

Davis, M. (1992). Analysis of aversive memories using the fear potentiated startle paradigm. In M. Butters & L. R. Squire (Eds.), *The neuropsychology of memory* (2nd ed.). New York: Guilford Press.

Davis, R. E., Couper, M. P., Janz, N. K., Caldwell, C. H., & Resnicow, K. (2010). Interviewer effects in public health surveys. *Health Education Research, 25*(1), 14–26.

Davis, T. E., III, & Ollendick, T. H. (2011). Specific phobias. In D. McKay & E. A. Storch (Eds.), *Handbook of child and adolescent anxiety disorders* (pp. 231–244). New York: Springer Science & Business Media.

Daw, J. (2001). APA's disaster response network: Help on the scene. *Monitor on Psychology, 32*(10), 14–15.

Day, E., & Strang, J. (2011). Outpatient versus inpatient opioid detoxification: A randomized controlled trial. *Journal of Substance Abuse Treatment, 40*(1), 56–66.

Day, J. M. (2010). Religion, spirituality, and positive psychology in adulthood: A developmental view. *Journal of Adult Development, 17*(4), 215–229.

DeAngelis, T. (1993, September). Controversial diagnosis is voted into latest DSM. *APA Monitor, 24*(9), 32–33.

Deas, D., Gray, K., & Upadhyaya, H. (2008). Evidence-based treatments for adolescent substance use disorders. In R. G. Steele, T. D. Elkin, M. C. Roberts (Eds.), *Handbook of evidence-based therapies for children and adolescents,* (pp. 429–444). New York: Springer.

Deb, P., Li, C., Trivedi, P. K., & Zimmer, D. M. (2006). The effect of managed care on use of health care services: Results from two contemporaneous household surveys. *Health Economics, 15*(7), 743–760.

de Beurs, D. P., Bosmans, J. E., de Groot, M. H., de Keijser, J., van Duijn, E., de Winter, R. P., & Kerkhof, A. M. (2015). Training mental health professionals in suicide practice guideline adherence: Cost-effectiveness analysis alongside a randomized controlled trial. *Journal of Affective Disorders, 186,* 203–210.

De Block, A., & Adriaens, P. R. (2013). Pathologizing sexual deviance: A history. *Journal of Sex Research, 50*(3/4), 276–298.

de Castro, S. M., Ünlü, Ç., Tuynman, J. B., Honig, A., van Wagensveld, B. A., Steller, E. P., & Vrouenraets, B. C. (2014). Incidence and risk factors of delirium in the elderly general surgical patient. *American Journal of Surgery, 208*(1), 26–32.

De Genna, N. M., & Feske, U. (2013). Phenomenology of borderline personality disorder: The role of race and socioeconomic status. *The Journal of Nervous and Mental Disease, 201*(12), 1027–1034.

Degortes, D., Zanetti, T., Tenconi, E., Santonastaso, P., & Favaro, A. (2014). Childhood obsessive-compulsive traits in anorexia nervosa patients, their unaffected sisters and healthy controls: A retrospective study. *European Eating Disorders Review, 22*(4), 237–242.

Dehn, M. J. (2013) *Essentials of processing assessment.* Hoboken, NJ: Wiley.

Deitz, S. M. (1977). An analysis of programming DRL schedules in educational settings. *Behavioral Research and Therapy, 15*(1), 103–111.

De La Garza, R., II, & Kalechstein, A. D. (2012). Polydrug abuse. In T. R. Kosten, T. F. Newton, De La Garza, R. II, & Haile, C. N. (Eds.), *Cocaine and methamphetamine dependence: Advances in treatment* (pp. 155–173). Arlington, VA: American Psychiatric Publishing.

Delahanty, D. L. (2011). Toward the predeployment detection of risk for PTSD. *American Journal of Psychiatry, 168*(1), 9–11.

de Leede-Smith, S., & Barkus, E. (2013). A comprehensive review of auditory verbal hallucinations: Lifetime prevalence, correlates, and mechanisms in healthy and clinical individuals. *Frontiers in Human Neurosciences, 7,* 367.

De Leo, D., & Evans, R. (2004). *International suicide rates and prevention strategies.* Cambridge, MA: Hogrefe & Huber.

de l'Etoile, S. K. (2002). The effect of musical mood induction procedure on mood state-dependent word retrieval. *Journal of Music Therapy, 39*(2), 145–160.

Delforterie, M. J., Larsen, J. K., Bardone-Cone, A. M., & Scholte, R. J. (2014). Effects of viewing a pro-Ana website: An experimental study on body satisfaction, affect, and appearance self-efficacy. *Eating Disorders, 22*(4), 321–336.

Delinsky, S. S. (2011). Body image and anorexia nervosa. In T. F. Cash & L. Smolak, *Body image: A handbook of science, practice, and prevention* (Chap. 32). New York: Guilford Press.

Dell, P. F. (2010). Involuntariness in hypnotic responding and dissociative symptoms. *Journal of Trauma & Dissociation, 11*(1), 1–18.

De Matteo, D., Heilbrun, K., & Marczyk, G. (2005). Psychopathy, risk of violence, and protective factors in a noninstitutionalized and noncriminal sample. *International Journal of Forensic Mental Health, 4*(2), 147–157.

Dendy, C. A. Z. (2011). *Teaching teens with ADD, ADHD & executive function deficits: A quick reference guide for teachers and parents* (2nd ed.). Bethesda, MD: Woodbine House.

Dennis, C. (2014). The process of developing and implementing a telephone-based peer support program for postpartum depression: Evidence from two randomized controlled trials. *Trials, 15,* 131.

Dennis, J. P., & Brown, G. K. (2011). Suicidal older adults: Suicide risk assessments, safety planning, and cognitive behavioral therapy. In K. H. Sorocco & S. Lauderdale (Eds.), *Cognitive behavior therapy with older adults: Innovations across care settings* (pp. 95–123). New York: Springer Publishing.

DePaulo, B. (2013, April 5). *On getting married and (not) getting happier: What we know.* DePaulo website: http://belladepaulo.com/2013/04/05/on-getting-married-and-not-getting-happpier.

DePaulo, B. (2013, March 15). Marriage and happiness: 18 long-term studies. *Psychology Today.*

DePaulo, B. M., Ansfield, M, E., Kirkendol, S. E., & Boden, J. M. (2004). Serious lies. *Basic and Applied Social Psychology, 26*(2–3), 147–167.

DePaulo, B. M., Kashy, D. A., Kirkendol, S. E., Wyer, M. M., & Epstein, J. A. (1996). Lying in everyday life. *Journal of Personality and Social Psychology, 70*(5), 979–995.

Derenne, J. L., & Beresin, E. V. (2006). Body image, media, and eating disorders. *Academic Psychiatry, 30*(3), 257–261.

Dervic, K., Brent, D. A., & Oquendo, M. A. (2008). Completed suicide in childhood. *Psychiatric Clinics of North America, 31*(2), 271–291.

de Schipper, L. J., Vermeulen, M., Eeckhout, A. M., & Foncke, E. J. (2014). Diagnosis and management of functional neurological symptoms: The Dutch experience. *Clinical Neurology and Neurosurgery, 122,* 106–112.

Desmet, M. (2013). Some preliminary notes on an empirical test of Freud's theory on depression. *Frontiers in Psychology, 4,* 158.

de Sutter, P., Day, J., & Adam, F. (2014). Who are the orgasmic women? Exploratory study among a community sample of French-speaking women. *Sexologies, 23*(3), E51–e57. [Electronic publication.]

Devanand, D. P. (2011). Psychosis. In C. E. Coffey, J. L. Cummings, M. S. George, & D. Weintraub (Eds.), *The American Psychiatric Publishing textbook of geriatric neuropsychiatry.* Arlington, VA: American Psychiatric Publishing, Inc.

DeVeaugh-Geiss, J., Moroz, G., Biederman, J., Cantwell, D. P., Fontaine, R., Greist, J. H., . . . Landau, P. (1992). Clomipramine hydrochloride in childhood and adolescent obsessive compulsive disorder. A multicenter trial. *Journal of the American Academy of Child & Adolescent Psychiatry, 31*(1), 45–49.

Devineni, T., & Blanchard, E. B. (2005). A randomized controlled trial of an internet-based treatment for chronic headache. *Behavioral Research and Therapy, 43,* 277–292.

Dewitte, M., Van Lankveld, J., & Crombez, G. (2011). Understanding sexual pain: A cognitive-motivational account. *Pain, 152*(2), 251–253.

De Witte, N. A., Crunelle, C. L., Sabbe, B., Moggi, F., & Dom, G. (2014). Treatment for outpatients with comorbid schizophrenia and substance use disorders: A review. *European Addiction Research, 20*(3), 105–114.

Dey, J. K., Ishii, M., Phillis, M., Byrne, P. J., Boahene, K. O., & Ishii, L. E. (2015). Body dysmorphic disorder in a facial plastic and reconstructive surgery clinic: Measuring prevalence, assessing comorbidities, and validating a feasible screening instrument. *JAMA Facial Plastic Surgery, 17*(2), 137–143.

Dhabhar, F. S. (2011). Effects of stress on immune function: Implications for immunoprotection and immunopathology. In R. J. Contrada & A. Baum (Eds.), *The handbook of stress science: Biology, psychology, and health* (pp. 47–63). New York: Springer Publishing.

Dhabhar, F. S. (2014). Effects of stress on immune function: The good, the bad, and the beautiful. *Immunologic Research, 58*(2-3), 193–210.

Dhejne, C., Lichtenstein, P., Boman, M., Johansson, A. L. V., Langström, N., & Landén, M. (2011). Long-term follow-up of transsexual persons undergoing sex reassignment surgery: Cohort study in Sweden. *PLOS ONE, 6*(2), e16885.

D.I. (Daily Infographic). (2014). *Secrets of the world's oldest people.* Retrieved from D.I. website: http://www.dailyinfographic.com.

Diamond, D., & Meehan, K. B. (2013). Attachment and object relations in patients with narcissistic personality disorder: Implications for therapeutic process and outcome. *Journal of Clinical Psychology, 69*(11), 1148–1159.

Dickens, B. M., Boyle, J. M., Jr., & Ganzini, L. (2008). Euthanasia and assisted suicide. In A. M. Viens & P. A. Singer (Eds.), *The Cambridge textbook of bioethics* (pp. 72–77). New York: Cambridge University Press.

Dickerson, F. B., Schroeder, J., Stallings, C., Origoni, A., Katsafanas, E., Schwienfurth, L. A., . . . Yolken, R. (2014). A longitudinal study of cognitive functioning in schizophrenia: Clinical and biological predictors. *Schizophrenia Research, 156*(2/3), 248–253.

Dickerson, F. B., Stallings, C., Origoni, A., Schroeder, J., Khushalani, S., & Yolken, R. (2014). Mortality in schizophrenia: Clinical and serological predictors. *Schizophrenia Bulletin, 40*(4), 796–803.

Dickerson, F. B., Tenhula, W. N., & Green-Paden, L. D. (2005). The token economy for schizophrenia: Review of the literature and recommendations for future research. *Schizophrenia Research, 75*(2–3), 405–416.

Dickinson, T., Cook, M., Playle, J., & Hallett, C. (2012). "Queer" treatments: Giving a voice to former patients who received treatments for their "sexual deviations." *Journal of Clinical Nursing, 21*(9-10), 1345–1354.

DiClemente, C. C., Garay, M., & Gemmell, L. (2008). Motivational enhancement. In H. D.

Kleber & M. Galanter (Eds.), *The American Psychiatric Publishing textbook of substance abuse treatment* (4th ed., pp. 361–371). Arlington, VA: American Psychiatric Publishing.

Di Florio, A., Jones, L., Forty, L., Gordon-Smith, K., Blackmore, E. R., Heron, J., . . . Jones, I. (2014). Mood disorders and parity: A clue to the aetiology of the postpartum trigger. *Journal of Affective Disorders, 152-154,* 334–339.

DiGangi, J. A., Gomez, D., Mendoza, L., Jason, L. A., Keys, C. B., & Koenen, K. C. (2013). Pretrauma risk factors for posttraumatic stress disorder: A systematic review of the literature. *Clinical Psychology Review, 33*(6), 728–744.

Dilts, S. L., Jr., & Dilts, S. L. (2005). Opioids. In R. J. Frances, S. I. Miller, & A. H. Mack (Eds.), *Clinical textbook of addictive disorders* (3rd ed., pp. 138–156). New York: Guilford Publications.

Dilts, S. L., Jr., & Dilts, S. L. (2011) Opioids. In R. J. Frances, S. I. Miller, & A. H. Mack (Eds.), *Clinical textbook of addictive disorders* (3rd ed., Chap. 7). New York: Guilford Press.

Dimidjian, S., Martell, C. R., Herman-Dunn, R., & Hubley, S. (2014). Behavioral activation for depression. In D. H. Barlow, *Clinical handbook of psychological disorders* (5th ed., Ch. 9). New York: Guilford Press.

Dimsdale, J. E., & Creed, F. H. (2010). The proposed diagnosis of somatic symptom disorders in DSM-V to replace somatoform disorders in DSM-IV—A preliminary report. *Journal of Psychosomatic Research, 68*(1), 99–100.

Dimsdale, J. E., Sharma, N., & Sharpe, M. (2011). What do physicians think of somatoform disorders? *Psychosomatics: Journal of Consultation Liaison Psychiatry, 52*(2), 154–159.

Di Narzo, A. F., Kozlenkov, A., Roussos, P., Hao, K., Hurd, Y., Lewis, D. A., . . . Dracheva, S. (2014). A unique gene expression signature associated with serotonin 2C receptor RNA editing in the prefrontal cortex and altered in suicide. *Human Molecular Genetics, 23*(18), 4801–4813.

Dines, P., Hu, W., & Sajatovic, M. (2014). Depression in later-life: An overview of assessment and management. *Psychiatria Danubina, 26*(Suppl. 1), 78–84.

Ding, Y., Naganawa, M., Gallezot, J., Nabulsi, N., Lin, S., Ropchan, J., . . . Laruelle, M. (2014). Clinical doses of atomoxetine significantly occupy both norepinephrine and serotonin transports. Implications on treatment of depression and ADHD. *Neuroimage, 86,* 164–171.

Dingfelder, S. F. (2010). Time capsule: The first modern psychology study. *Monitor on Psychology, 41*(7).

Di Rosa, M., Kofahl, C., McKee, K., Bien, B., Lamura, G., Prouskas, C., Döhner, H., & Mnich, E. (2011). A typology of caregiving situations and service use in family careers of older people in six European countries: The EUROFAMCARE study. *GeroPsych: The Journal of Gerontopsychology and Geriatric Psychiatry, 24*(1), 5–18.

Dixon, L. B., & Schwarz, E. C. (2014). Fifty years of progress in community mental health in U.S.: The growth of evidence-based practices. *Epidemiology and Psychiatric Sciences, 23*(1), 5–9.

DMR. (2015, May). *By the numbers: 150+ amazing Twitter statistics.* Retrieved from Expanded Ramblings website: http://expandedramblings.com/index.php.

Doctor, R. M., & Neff, B. (2001). Sexual disorders. In H. S. Friedman (Ed.), *Specialty articles from the encyclopedia of mental health.* San Diego: Academic Press.

Dodes, L. M., & Khantzian, E. J. (2005). Individual psychodynamic psychotherapy. In R. J. Frances, A. H. Mack, & S. I. Miller (Eds.), *Clinical textbook of addictive disorders* (3rd ed., pp. 457–473). New York: Guilford Press.

Dodes, L. M., & Khantzian, E. J. (2011). Individual psychodynamic psychotherapy. In R. J. Frances, S. I. Miller, & A. H. Mack (Eds.), *Clinical textbook of addictive disorders* (3rd ed., Chap. 21). New York: Guilford Press.

Dogra, T. D., Leenaars, A. A., Chadha, R. K., Manju, M., Lalwani, S., Sood, M., . . . Behera, C. (2012). A psychological profile of a serial killer: A case report. *Omega, 65*(4), 299–316.

Dohrmann, R. J., & Laskin, D. M. (1978). An evaluation of electromyographic feedback in the treatment of myofascial pain-dysfunction syndrome. *Journal of the American Medical Association, 96,* 656–666.

Dolak, K., & Murphy, E. (2012, March 23). Whitney Houston cause of death: How cocaine contributes to heart disease. *ABC News.*

Dolan, E. (2011). *Facebook use and social anxiety: Are social behaviors different online and offline?* Retrieved from Associated Content website: www.associatedcontent.com.

Dole, V. P., & Nyswander, M. (1965). A medical treatment for heroin addiction. *Journal of the American Medical Association, 193,* 646–650.

Dole, V. P., & Nyswander, M. (1967). Heroin addiction, a metabolic disease. *Archives of Internal Medicine, 120,* 19–24.

Dolezsar, C. M., McGrath, J. J., Herzig, A. M., & Miller, S. B. (2014). Perceived racial discrimination and hypertension: A comprehensive systematic review. *Health Psychology, 33*(1), 20–34.

Domino, M. E. (2012). Does managed care affect the diffusion of psychotropic medications? *Health Economics, 21*(4), 428–443.

Dominus, S. (2012, March 7). What happened to the girls in Le Roy? *New York Times.*

Dorahy, M. J., Brand, B. L., Sar, V., Krüger, C., Stavropoulos, P., Martínez-Taboas, A., . . . Middleton, W. (2014). Dissociative identity disorder: An empirical overview. *The Australian and New Zealand Journal of Psychiatry, 48*(5), 402–417.

Dorahy, M. J., & Huntjens, R. J. C. (2007). Memory and attentional processes in dissociative identity disorder: A review of the empirical literature. In D. Spiegel, E. Vermetten, & M. Dorahy (Eds.), *Traumatic dissociation: Neurobiology and treatment* (pp. 55–75). Washington, DC: American Psychiatric Publishing.

Dossat, A. M., Bodell, L. P., Williams, D. L., Eckel, L. A., & Keel, P. K. (2015). Preliminary examination of glucagon-like peptide-1 levels in women with purging disorder and bulimia nervosa. *International Journal of Eating Disorders, 48*(2), 199–205.

Douglas, J. (1996). *Mind hunter: Inside the FBI's elite serial crime unit.* New York: Pocket Star.

Downey, L. A., Sands, H., Jones, L., Clow, A., Evans, P., Stalder, T., & Parrott, A. C. (2015). Reduced memory skills and increased hair cortisol levels in recent Ecstasy/MDMA users: Significant but independent neurocognitive and neurohormonal deficits. *Human Psychopharmacology, 30*(3), 199–207.

Dozier, C. L., Iwata, B. A., & Worsdell, A. S. (2011). Assessment and treatment of foot-shoe fetish displayed by a man with autism. *Journal of Applied Behavior Analysis, 44*(1), 133–137.

Draguns, J. G. (2006). Culture in psychopathology—psychopathology in culture: Taking a new look at an old problem. In T. G. Plante (Ed.), *Mental disorders of the new millennium, Vol. 2: Public and social problems.* Westport, CT: Praeger Publishers.

Drake, R. E., Luciano, A. E., Mueser, K. T., Covell, N. H., Essock, S. M., Xie, H., & McHugo, G. J. (2015). Longitudinal course of clients with co-occurring schizophrenia-spectrum and substance use disorders in urban mental health centers: A 7-year prospective study. *Schizophrenia Bulletin.* [Electronic publication.]

Draper, B. M. (2014). Suicidal behaviour and suicide prevention in later life. *Maturitas, 79*(2), 179–183.

Dray, J., Gilchrist, P., Singh, D., Cheesman, G., & Wade, T. D. (2014). Training mental health nurses to provide motivational interviewing on an inpatient eating disorder unit. *Journal of Psychiatric and Mental Health Nursing, 21*(7), 652–657.

Dreisbach, S. (2011). Shocking body-image news: 97% of women will be cruel to their bodies today. *Glamour.* Retrieved from Glamour website: http://www.glamour.com/health-fitness/2011/02.

Drescher, J. (2015). Queer diagnoses revisited: The past and future of homosexuality and gender diagnoses in DSM and ICD. *International Review of Psychiatry* (Abingdon, England), 1–10. [Electronic publication.]

Drouin, M., & Landgraff, C. (2012). Texting, sexting, attachment, and intimacy in college students' romantic relationships. *Computers in Human Behavior, 28,* 444–449.

Druss, B. G., & Bornemann, T. H. (2010). Improving health and health care for persons with serious mental illness: The window for US Federal policy change. *Journal of the American Medical Association, 303*(19), 1972–1973.

Dubovsky, S., & Dubovsky, A. (2011). Geriatric neuropsychopharmacology: Why does age matter? In C. E. Coffey, J. L. Cummings, M. S. George, & D. Weintraub (Eds.), *The American Psychiatric Publishing textbook of geriatric neuropsychiatry.* Arlington, VA: American Psychiatric Publishing, Inc.

Dubowitz, T., Bates, L. M., & Acevedo-Garcia, D. (2010). The Latino health paradox: Looking at the intersection of sociology and health. In C. E. Bird, P. Conrad, A. M. Fremont, & S. Timmermans (Eds.), *Handbook of medical sociology* (6th ed., pp. 106–123). Nashville, TN: Vanderbilt University Press.

Duckworth, K., & Halpern, L. (2014). Peer support and peer-led family support for persons living with schizophrenia. *Current Opinion in Psychiatry, 27*(3), 216–221.

Duenwald, M. (2003, March 18). "Oldest old" still show alertness. *New York Times.*

Dugas, M. J., Brillon, P., Savard, P., Turcotte, J., Gaudet, A., Ladouceur, R., Leblanc, R., & Gervais, N. J. (2010). A randomized clinical trial of cognitive-behavioral therapy and applied relaxation for adults with generalized anxiety disorder. *Behavior Therapy, 41*(1), 46–58.

Dugas, M. J., Buhr, K., & Ladouceur, R. (2004). The role of intolerance of uncertainty in etiology and maintenance. In R. G. Heimberg, C. L. Turk, & D. S. Mennin (Eds.), *Generalized anxiety disorder: Advances in research and practice* (pp. 143–163). New York: Guilford Press.

Dugas, M. J., Laugesen, N., & Bukowski, W. M. (2012). Intolerance of uncertainty, fear of anxiety, and adolescent worry. *Journal of Abnormal Child Psychology, 40*(6), 863–870.

Duggan, M. (2013). *Cell phone activities 2013.* Washington, DC: Pew Research Center.

Duhig, M., Gunasekara, I., & Patterson, S. (2015). Understanding readmission to psychiatric hospital in Australia from the service user's perspective: A qualitative study. *Health & Social Care in the Community.* [Electronic publication.]

Dukart, J., Regen, F., Kherif, F., Colla, M., Bajbouj, M., Heuser, I., . . . & Draganski, B. (2014). Electroconvulsive therapy-induced brain plasticity determines therapeutic outcome in mood disorders. *Proceedings of the National Academy of Sciences of the United States of America, 111*(3), 1156–1161.

Duman, R. S. (2014). Pathophysiology of depression and innovative treatments: Remodeling glutamatergic synaptic connections. *Dialogues in Clinical Neuroscience, 16*(1), 11–27.

Dunbar, F. (1948). *Synopsis of psychosomatic diagnosis and treatment.* St. Louis: Mosby.

Duncan, B. L., Miller, S. D., Wampold, B. E., & Hubble, M. A. (Eds.). (2010). *The heart and soul of change: Delivering what works in therapy* (2nd ed.). Washington, DC: American Psychological Association.

Dunn, J. (2013). Mysticism, motherhood, and pathological narcissism? A Kohutian analysis of Marie de l'Incarnation. *Journal of Religion and Health, 52*(2), 642–665.

Dunner, D. L., Aaronson, S. T., Sackeim, H. A., Janicak, P. G., Carpenter, L. L., Boyadjis, T., . . . Demitrack, M. A. (2014). A multisite, naturalistic, observational study of transcranial magnetic stimulation for patients with pharmacoresistant major depressive disorder: Durability of benefit over a 1-year follow-up period. *The Journal of Clinical Psychiatry, 75*(12), 1394–1401.

Dunsmoor, J. E., Ahs, F., Zielinski, D. J., & LaBar, K. S. (2014). Extinction in multiple virtual reality contexts diminishes fear reinstatement in humans. *Neurobiology of Learning and Memory, 113,* 157–164.

DuPaul, G. J., & Kern, L. (2011). Assessment and identification of attention-deficit/hyperactivity disorder. In G. J. DuPaul & K. Lee (2011). *Young children with ADHD: Early identification and intervention* (2nd ed., pp. 23–46). Washington, DC: American Psychological Association.

DuPaul, G. J., & Kern, L. (2011). Preschool-based behavioral intervention strategies. In G. J. DuPaul & K. Lee. (2011). *Young children with ADHD: Early identification and intervention* (2nd ed., pp. 87–106). Washington, DC: American Psychological Association.

DuPaul, G. J., & Kern, L. (2011). Support for families. In G. J. DuPaul & K. Lee (2011). *Young children with ADHD: Early identification and intervention* (2nd ed., pp. 167–183). Washington, DC: American Psychological Association.

Durbin, A., Rudoler, D., Durbin, J., Laporte, A., & Callaghan, R. C. (2014). Examining patient race and area predictors of inpatient admission for schizophrenia among hospital users in California. *Journal of Immigrant and Minority Health, 16*(6), 1025–1034.

Düring, S., Glenthøj, B. Y., Andersen, G. S., & Oranje, B. (2014). Effects of dopamine d2/d3 blockade on human sensory and sensorimotor gating in initially antipsychotic-naive, first-episode schizophrenia patients. *Neuropsychopharmacology, 39*(13), 3000–3008.

Durkheim, E. (1897). *Suicide.* New York: Free Press. [Work republished 1951.]

Durkin, K. F., & Hundersmarck, S. (2008). Pedophiles and child molesters. In E. Goode & D. A. Vail (Eds.), *Extreme deviance.* Los Angeles: Pine Forge Press.

Durkin, M. S., Khan, N. Z., Davidson, L. L., Huq, S., Munir, S., Rasul, I., & Zaman, S. S. (2000). Prenatal and postnatal risk factors for mental retardation among children in Bangladesh. *American Journal of Epidemiology, 152,* 1024–1032.

Durso, S., Bowker, L., Price, J., & Smith. S. (2010). *Oxford American handbook of geriatric medicine.* New York: Oxford University Press.

Duval-Harvey, J., & Rogers, K. M. (2010). Attention-deficit/hyperactivity disorder. In R. L. Hampton, T. P. Gullotta, & R. L. Crowel (Eds.), *Handbook of African American health* (pp. 375–418). New York: Guilford Press.

Dygdon, J. A., & Dienes, K. A. (2013). Behavioral excesses in depression: A learning theory hypothesis. *Depression & Anxiety, 30*(6), 598–605.

Dyl, J., Kittler, J., Phillips, K. A., & Hunt, J. I. (2006). Body dysmorphic disorder and other clinically significant body image concerns in adolescent psychiatric inpatients: Prevalence and clinical characteristics. *Child Psychiatry and Human Development, 36*(4), 369–382.

Dysken, M. W., Guarino, P. D., Vertrees, J. E., Asthana, S., Sano, M., Llorente, M., . . . Vatassery, G. (2014). Vitamin E and memantine in Alzheimer's disease: Clinical trial methods and baseline data. *Alzheimer's & Dementia, 10*(1), 36–44.

Dysken, M. W., Kirk, L. N., & Kuskowski, M. (2009). Changes in vitamin E prescribing for Alzheimer patients. *American Journal of Geriatric Psychiatry, 17*(7), 621–624.

Easterbrooks, M. A., Bartlett, J. D., Raskin, M., Goldberg, J., Contreras, M. M., Kotake, C., . . . Jacobs, F. H. (2013). Limiting home visiting effects: Maternal depression as a moderator of child maltreatment. *Pediatrics, 132*(2), 126–133.

eBizMBA. (2015, July). *Top 15 most popular social networking sites.* Retrieved from eBizMBA website: http://www.ebizmba.com.

Edelstein, B. A., Stoner, S. A., & Woodhead, E. (2008). Older adults. In M. Hersen & J. Rosqvist (Eds.), *Handbook of psychological assessment, case conceptualization and treatment, Vol. 1: Adults.* Hoboken, NJ: Wiley.

Edoka, I. P., Petrou, S., & Ramchandani, P. G. (2011). Healthcare costs of paternal depression in the postnatal period. *Journal of Affective Disorders, 133*(1–2), 356–360.

Eeles, E., & Bhat, R. S. (2010). Delirium. In H. M. Fillit, K. Rockwood, & K. Woodhouse (Eds.), *Brocklehurst's textbook of geriatric medicine and gerontology* (7th ed.). Philadelphia, PA: Saunders Publishers.

Egawa, J., Watanabe, Y., Sugimoto, A., Nunokawa, A., Shibuya, M., Igeta, H., . . . Someya, T. (2015). Whole-exome sequencing in a family with a monozygotic twin pair concordant for autism spectrum disorder and a follow-up study. *Psychiatry Research, 229*(1–2), 599–601.

Eggers, A. E. (2014). Treatment of depression with deep brain stimulation works by altering in specific ways the conscious perception of the core symptoms of sadness or anhedonia, not by modulating network circuitry. *Medical Hypotheses, 83*(1), 62–64.

Ehnvall, A., Parker, G., Hadzi, P. D., & Malhi, G. (2008). Perception of rejecting and neglectful parenting in childhood relates to lifetime suicide attempts for females—but not for males. *Acta Psychiatrica Scandinavica, 117*(1), 50–56.

Eich, T. S., Nee, D. E., Insel, C., Malapani, C., & Smith, E. E. (2014). Neural correlates of impaired cognitive control over working memory in schizophrenia. *Biological Psychiatry, 76*(2), 146–153.

Eifert, G. H., Greco, L. A., Heffner, M., & Louis, A. (2007). Eating disorders: A new behavioral perspective and acceptance-based treatment approach. In D. W. Woods & J. W. Kanter (Eds.), *Understanding behavior disorders: A contemporary behavioral perspective.* Reno, NV: Context Press.

Eikenaes, I., Hummelen, B., Abrahamsen, G., Andrea, H., & Wilberg, T. (2013). Personality functioning in patients with avoidant personality disorder and social phobia. *Journal of Personality Disorders, 27*(6), 746–763.

Eikenaes, I., Pedersen, G., & Wilberg, T. (2015). Attachment styles in patients with avoidant personality disorder compared with social phobia. *Psychology and Psychotherapy.* [Electronic publication.]

Eisold, K. (2013, December 21). Hidden motives: A look at the hidden factors that really drive our social interactions. *Psychology Today.*

Eker, C., Simsek, F., Yilmazer, E. E., Kitis, O., Cinar, C., Eker, O. D., . . . Gonul, A. S. (2014). Brain regions associated with risk and resistance for bipolar I disorder: A voxel-based MRI study of patients with bipolar disorder and their healthy siblings. *Bipolar Disorders, 16*(3), 249–261.

Ekern, J. (2014, April 28). *Eating disorder statistics and research.* Retrieved from Eating Disorder Hope website: http:www.eatingdisorderhope.com.

Ekman, P. (1971). Universals and cultural differences in facial expressions of emotion. In J. Cole (Ed.), *Nebraska Symposium on Motivation* (vol. 1, pp. 207–282). Lincoln, NE: University of Nebraska Press.

Ellenberger, H. F. (1970). *The discovery of the unconscious.* New York: Basic Books.

Ellenberger, H. F. (1972). The story of "Anna O.": A critical review with new data. *Journal of the History of the Behavioral Sciences, 8,* 267–279.

Ellis, A. (1962). *Reason and emotion in psychotherapy.* Secaucus, NJ: Lyle Stuart.

Ellis, A. (2002). The role of irrational beliefs in perfectionism. In G. L. Flett & P. L. Hewitt (Eds.) *Perfectionism: Theory, research, and treatment* (pp. 217–229). Washington, DC: American Psychological Association.

Ellis, A. (2005). Rational-emotive therapy. In R. Corsini & D. Wedding (Eds.), *Current psychotherapies* (7th ed., pp. 166–201). Boston: Thomson/Brooks-Cole.

Ellis, A. (2008). Rational emotive behavior therapy. In R. J. Corsini & D. Wedding (Eds.), *Current psychotherapies* (8th ed.). Belmont, CA: Thomson Brooks/Cole.

Ellis, A. (2014). Rational emotive behavior. In D. Wedding & R. J. Corsini (Eds.), *Current psychotherapies* (10th ed., pp. 151–192). Independence, KY: Cengage Publications.

Ellis, C. C., Peterson, M., Bufford, R., & Benson, J. (2014). The importance of group cohesion in inpatient treatment of combat-related PTSD. *International Journal of Group Psychotherapy, 64*(2), 208–226.

Elwood, C. E., Poythress, N. G., & Douglas, K. S. (2004). Evaluation of the Hare P-SCAN in a non-clinical population. *Personality and Individual Differences, 36*(4), 833–843.

Emig, D., Ivliev, A., Pustovalova, O., Lancashire, L., Bureeva, S., Nikolsky, Y., . . . Bessarabova, M. (2013). Drug target prediction and repositioning using an integrated network-based approach. *PLOS ONE, 8*(4), e60618.

Emmelkamp, P. G. (2011). Effectiveness of cybertherapy in mental health: A critical appraisal. *Studies in Health Technology and Informatics, 16,* 73–78.

Emmelkamp, P. M. (1982). Exposure in vivo treatments. In A. Goldstein & D. Chambless (Eds.), *Agoraphobia: Multiple perspectives on theory and treatment.* New York: Wiley.

Emmons, K. K. (2010). *Black dogs and blue words: Depression and gender in the age of self-care.* Piscataway, NJ: Rutgers University Press.

Enatescu, V., Enatescu, I., Craina, M., Gluhovschi, A., Papava, I., Romosan, R., . . . Bernad, E. (2014). State and trait anxiety as a psychopathological phenomenon correlated with postpartum depression in a Romanian sample: A pilot study. *Journal of Psychosomatic Obstetrics & Gynaecology, 35*(2), 55–61.

Endrass, T., Kloft, L., Kaufmann, C., & Kaufmann, N. (2011). Approach and avoidance learning in obsessive-compulsive disorder. *Depression & Anxiety, 28*(2), 166–172.

Engel, J. (2009). Migraines/chronic headaches. In W. T. O'Donohue & L. W. Tolle (Eds.), *Behavioral approaches to chronic disease in adolescence: A guide to integrative care* (pp. 155–161). New York: Springer Science + Business Media.

Engqvist, I., & Nilsson, K. (2014). The recovery process of postpartum psychosis from both the woman's and next of kin's perspective: An interview study in Sweden. *Open Nursing Journal, 8,* 8–16.

Epstein, R. (2001). In her own words. *Psychology Today, 34*(6), 36–37, 87.

Erikson, E. (1963). *Childhood and society.* New York: Norton.

Erlangsen, A., Vach, W., & Jeune, B. (2005). The effect of hospitalization with medical illnesses on the suicide risk in the oldest old: A population-based register study. *Journal of the American Geriatrics Society, 53*(5), 771–776.

Ernsberger, P. (2009). Does social class explain the connection between weight and health? In E. Rothblum & S. Solovay (Eds.), *The fat studies reader* (pp. 25–36). New York: University Press.

ESA (Entertainment Software Association). (2015). *2014 sales, demographic, and usage data: Essential facts about the computer and video game industry.* Washington, DC: ESA.

Escobar, J. I. (1995). Transcultural aspects of dissociative and somatoform disorders. *Psychiatric Clinics of North America, 18*(3), 555–569.

Escobar, J. I. (2004, April 15). Transcultural aspects of dissociative and somatoform disorders. *Psychiatric Times, XXI*(5), p. 10.

Escobar, J. I., Canino, G., Rubio-Stipec, M., & Bravo, M. (1992). Somatic symptoms after a natural disaster: A prospective study. *American Journal of Psychiatry, 149*(7), 965–967.

Escobar, J. I., Gara, M., Silver, R. C., Waitzkin, H., Holman, A., & Compton, W. (1998). Somatisation disorder in primary care. *British Journal of Psychiatry, 173,* 262–266.

Escobar, J. I., Randolph, E. T., Puente, G., Spiwak, F., Asamen, J. K., Hill, M., & Hough, R. L. (1983). Post-traumatic stress disorder in Hispanic Vietnam veterans: Clinical phenomenology and sociocultural characteristics. *Journal of Nervous and Mental Disease, 171,* 585–596.

Espada, J. P., Gonzálvez, M. T., Orgilés, M., Lloret, D., & Guillén-Riquelme, A. (2015). Meta-analysis of the effectiveness of school substance abuse prevention programs in Spain. *Psicothema, 27*(1), 5–12.

Estes, A., Munson, J., Rogers, S. J., Greenson, J., Winter, J., & Dawson, G. (2015). Long-term outcomes of early intervention in 6-year-old children with autism spectrum disorder. *Journal of the American Academy of Child and Adolescent Psychiatry, 54*(7), 580–587.

Etaugh, C. (2008). Women in the middle and later years. In F. L. Denmark & M. A. Paludi (Eds.), *Psychology of women: A handbook of issues and theories* (2nd ed.). Westport, CT: Praeger Publishers.

Etkin, A. (2010). Functional neuroanatomy of anxiety: A neural circuit perspective. In M. B. Stein & T. Steckler (Eds.), *Behavioral neurobiology of anxiety and its treatment. Current topics in behavioral neurosciences* (pp. 251–277). New York: Springer Science + Business Media.

Ettinger, U., Meyhöfer, I., Steffens, M., Wagner, M., & Koutsouleris, N. (2014). Genetics, cognition, and neurobiology of schizotypal personality: A review of the overlap with schizophrenia. *Frontiers in Psychiatry, 5,* 18.

Evans, G. W. (2006). Child development and the physical environment. *Annual Review of Psychology, 57,* 423–451.

Evans, J., & Waller, G. (2011). The therapeutic alliance in cognitive behavioural therapy for adults with eating disorders. In J. Alexander & J. Treasure (Eds.), *A collaborative approach to eating disorders* (pp. 163–176). New York: Taylor & Francis.

Evans, M., Donelle, L., & Hume-Loveland, L. (2012). Social support and online postpartum depression discussion groups: A content analysis. *Patient Education and Counseling, 87*(3), 405–410.

Evans, S. A., & Salekin, K. L. (2014). Involuntary civil commitment: Communicating with the court regarding "danger to other". *Law and Human Behavior, 38*(4), 325–336.

Everson, S. A., Goldberg, D. E., Kaplan, G. A., Cohen, R. D., Pukkata, E., Tuomilehto, J., & Salonen, J. T. (1996). Hopelessness and risk of mortality and incidence of myocardial infarction and cancer. *Psychosomatic Medicine, 58,* 113–121.

Ewing, C. P. (2011). *Justice perverted: Sex offense law, psychology, and public policy.* New York: Oxford University Press.

Fábrega, H., Jr. (1990). The concept of somatization as a cultural and historical product of Western medicine. *Psychosomatic Medicine, 52*(6), 653–672.

Fábrega, H., Jr. (2010). Understanding the evolution of medical traditions: Brain/behavior influences, enculturation, and the study of sickness and healing. *Neuropsychoanalysis, 12*(1), 21–27.

Fairbank, J. A., & Keane, T. M. (1982). Flooding for combat-related stress disorders: Assessment of anxiety reduction across traumatic memories. *Behavior Therapist, 13,* 499–510.

Fairburn, C. G. (1985). Cognitive-behavioural treatment for bulimia. In D. M. Garner & P. E. Garfinkel (Eds.), *Handbook of psychotherapy for anorexia nervosa and bulimia.* New York: Guilford Press.

Fairburn, C. G. (2013). *Overcoming binge eating: The proven program to learn why you binge and how you can stop* (2nd ed.). New York: Guilford Press.

Fairburn, C. G., Agras, W. S., Walsh, B. T., Wilson, G. T., & Stice, E. (2004). Prediction of outcome in bulimia nervosa by early change in treatment. *American Journal of Psychiatry, 161*(12), 2322–2324.

Fairburn, C. G., Bailey-Straebler, S., Basden, S., Doll, H. A., Jones, R., Murphy, R., . . . Cooper, Z. (2015). A transdiagnostic comparison of enhanced cognitive behavior therapy (CBT-E) and interpersonal psychotherapy in the treatment of eating disorders. *Behavior Research and Therapy, 70,* 64–71.

Fairburn, C. G., & Cooper, Z. (2014). Eating disorders: A transdiagnostic protocol. In D. H. Barlow, *Clinical handbook of psychological disorders* (5th ed., Ch. 17). New York: Guilford Press.

Fairburn, C. G., Cooper, Z., Shafran, R., & Wilson, G. T. (2008). Eating disorders: A transdiagnostic protocol. In D. H. Barlow (Ed.), *Clinical handbook of psychological disorders: A step-by-step treatment manual* (4th ed.). New York: Guilford Press.

Faje, A. T., Fazeli, P. K., Miller, K. K., Katzman, D. K., Ebrahimi, S., Lee, H., . . . Klibanski, A. (2014). Fracture risk and areal bone mineral density in adolescent females with anorexia nervosa. *International Journal of Eating Disorders, 47*(5), 458–466.

Falco, M. (2014). Autism rates now 1 in 68 U.S. children: CDC. *CNN.com.* Retrieved from CNN website: http://www.cnn.com/2014/03/27/health/cdc-autism.

Falzer, P. R. (2011). Expertise in assessing and managing risk of violence. The contribution of naturalistic decision making. In K. L. Mosier & U. M. Fischer (Eds.), *Informed by knowledge: Expert performance in complex situations. Expertise: Research and applications* (pp. 313–328). New York: Psychology Press.

Fang, A., & Wilhelm, S. (2015). Clinical features, cognitive biases, and treatment of body dysmorphic disorder. *Annual Review of Clinical Psychology, 11,* 187–212.

faqs.org. (2014). *Asylums.* Retrieved from FAQS website: http://www.faqs.org/health/topics/99/asylums.html.

Farber, B. A., Manevich, I., Metzger, J., & Saypol, E. (2005). Choosing psychotherapy as a career: Why did we cross that road? *Journal of Clinical Psychology, 61*(8), 1009–1031.

Farberow, N. L., & Litman, R. E. (1970). *A comprehensive suicide prevention program.* Unpublished final report, Suicide Prevention Center of Los Angeles, Los Angeles.

Fareed, A., Vayalapalli, S., Stout, S., Casarella, J., Drexler, K., & Bailey, S. P. (2011). Effect of methadone maintenance treatment on heroin craving, a literature review. *Journal of Addictive Diseases, 30*(1), 27–38.

Farkas, M. (2013). Pedophilia. *Psychiatria Hungarica: A Magyar Pszichiátriai Társaság Tudományos Folyóirata, 28*(2), 180–188.

Farmer, R. F., & Nelson-Gray, R. O. (2005). Behavioral treatment of personality disorders. In R. F. Farmer & R. O. Nelson-Gray (Eds.), *Personality-guided behavior therapy* (pp. 203–243). Washington, DC: American Psychological Association.

Faubion, S. S., & Rulo, J. E. (2015). Sexual dysfunction in women: A practical approach. *American Family Physician, 92*(4), 281–288.

Faust, D., & Ahern, D. C. (2012). Clinical judgment and prediction. In D. Faust (Ed.), *Coping with psychiatric and psychological testimony: Based on the original work by Jay Ziskin* (6th ed.) (pp. 147–208). New York: Oxford University Press.

Faust, J., Chapman, S., & Stewart, L. M. (2008). Neglected, physically abused, and sexually abused children. In D. Reitman (Ed.), *Handbook of psychological assessment, case conceptualization, and treatment, Vol. 2: Children and adolescents.* Hoboken, NJ: John Wiley & Sons.

Fava, M., Farabaugh, A. H., Sickinger, A. H., Wright, E., Alpert, J. E., Sonawalla, S., . . . Worthington, J. J., III. (2002). Personality disorders and depression. *Psychological Medicine, 32*(6), 1049–1057.

Fawcett, J. (2007). What has the "black box" done to reduce suicide? *Psychiatric Annals, 37*(10), 657, 662.

Fay, B. P. (1995). The individual versus society: The cultural dynamics of criminalizing suicide. *Hastings International and Comparative Law Review, 18,* 591–615.

Fazel, S., & Danesh, J. (2002). Serious mental disorder in 23,000 prisoners: A systematic review of 62 surveys. *Lancet, 359*(9306), 545–550.

Fazel, S., Grann, M., Kling, B., & Hawton, K. (2011). Prison suicide in 12 countries: An ecological study of 861 suicides during 2003–2007. *Social Psychiatry and Psychiatric Epidemiology, 46*(3), 191–195.

FBI (Federal Bureau of Investigation). (2010). About hate crime statistics, 2010. *Uniform crime reports.* http://www.fbi.gov/about-us/cjis/ucr/hate-crime/2010/index.

FBI (Federal Bureau of Investigation). (2010). Cyber investigations. Retrieved from http://www.fbi.gov/cyberinvest/cyberhome.

FBI (Federal Bureau of Investigation). (2012). *2012 hate crime statistics: Incidents and offenses.* Washington, DC: FBI.

FBI (Federal Bureau of Investigation). (2012). *Uniform crime reports: Crime in the United States.* Retrieved from http://www.fbi.gov/about-us/cjis/ucr.

FBI (Federal Bureau of Investigation). (2013, November 25). *Latest hate crime statistics: Annual report shows slight decrease.* Washington, DC: FBI.

FBI (Federal Bureau of Investigation). (2014) *Ten-year arrest trends. Totals, 2003–2012.* Washington, DC: Department of Justice, Criminal Justice Information Services.

FDA (Federal Drug Administration). (2014). *Consumer update: Understanding antidepressant medications.* Retrieved from http://www.fda.gov/forconsumers/consumerupdates/ucm095980.html.

FDA (Federal Drug Administration). (2014). *Development and approval process (drugs).* Retrieved from http://www.fda.gov/drugs/developmentapprovalprocess.

Federoff, J. P., & Marshall, W. L. (2010). Paraphilias. In D. McKay, J. S. Abramowitz, & S. Taylor (Eds.), *Cognitive-behavioral therapy for refractory cases: Turning failure into success* (pp. 369–384). Washington, DC: American Psychological Association.

Feifer, S. G. (2010). Assessing and intervening with children with reading disorders. In D. C. Miller (Ed.), *Best practices in school neuropsychology: Guidelines for effective practice, assessment, and evidence-based intervention* (pp. 483–505). Hoboken, NJ: John Wiley & Sons.

Feldman, M. D. (2004). *Playing sick? Untangling the web of Munchausen syndrome, Munchausen by proxy, malingering and factitious disorder.* New York: Routledge.

Feldman, M. D., & Feldman, J. M. (1995). Tangled in the web: Countertransference in the therapy of factitious disorders. *International Journal of Psychiatry in Medicine, 25,* 389.

Feldman, M. D., Ford, C. V., & Reinhold, T. (1994). *Patient or pretender: Inside the strange world of factitious disorders.* New York: Wiley.

Feldman, R. A., Bailey, R. A., Muller, J., Le, J., & Dirani, R. (2014). Cost of schizophrenia in the medicare program. *Population Health Management, 17*(3), 190–196.

Feldman, R. S., Forrest, J. A., & Happ, B. R. (2002). Self-presentation and verbal deception: Do self-presenters lie more? *Basic and Applied Social Psychology, 24*(2), 163–170.

Feldman, S. R., Moritz, S. H., & Benjamin, G. A. H. (2005). Suicide and the law: A practical overview for mental health professionals. *Women & Therapy, 28*(1), 95–103.

Felix, E., Hernández, L. A., Bravo, M., Ramirez, R., Cabiya, J., & Canino, G. (2011). Natural disaster and risk of psychiatric disorders in Puerto Rican children. *Journal of Abnormal Child Psychology, 39*(4), 589–600.

Fenichel, M. (2011). *Online psychotherapy: Technical difficulties, formulations and processes.* Retrieved from Fenichel website: http://www.fenichel.com/technical.shtml.

Fennig, S., Fennig, S., & Roe, D. (2002). Cognitive-behavioral therapy for bulimia nervosa: Time course and mechanisms of change. *General Hospital Psychiatry, 24*(2), 87–92.

Ferman, T. J., Smith, G. E., Dickson, D. W., Graff-Radford, N. R., Lin, S., Wszolek, Z., . . . Boeve, B. F. (2014). Abnormal daytime sleepiness in dementia with Lewy bodies compared to Alzheimer's disease using the Multiple Sleep Latency Test. *Alzheimer's Research & Therapy, 6*(9), 76.

Fernholz, T. (2014, February 25). *More people around the world have cell phones than ever had land-lines.* Quartz.com. Retrieved from Quartz website: http://qz.com/179897.

Fernquist, R. M. (2007). How do Durkheimian variables impact variation in national suicide rates when proxies for depression and alcoholism are controlled? *Archives of Suicide Research, 11*(4), 361–374.

Ferrari, R. (2006). *The whiplash encyclopedia: The facts and myths of whiplash.* Boston: Jones and Bartlett.

Fichter, M. M., Quadflieg, N., & Hedlund, S. (2008). Long-term course of binge eating disorder and bulimia nervosa: Relevance for nosology and diagnostic criteria. *International Journal of Eating Disorders, 41,* 577–586.

Field, A. P., & Purkis, H. M. (2012). Associative learning and phobias. In M. Haselgrove (Ed.), *Clinical applications of learning theory* (pp. 49–73). New York: Psychology Press.

Fields, J. (2004). *America's families and living arrangements, 2003.* Current Population Reports, P20-553. Washington, DC: U.S. Census Bureau.

Fieve, R. R. (1975). *Moodswing.* New York: Morrow.

Figley, C. R. (1978). Symptoms of delayed combat stress among a college sample of Vietnam veterans. *Military Medicine, 143*(2), 107–110.

Filip, M., Frankowska, M., Sadakierska-Chudy, A., Suder, A., Szumiec, Ł., Mierzejewski, P., . . . Cryan, J. F. (2015). GABAB receptors as a therapeutic strategy in substance use disorders: Focus on positive allosteric modulators. *Neuropharmacology, 88,* 36–47.

Fine, C. G., & Madden, N. E. (2000). Group psychotherapy in the treatment of dissociative identity disorder and allied dissociative disorders. In R. H. Klein & V. L. Schermer (Eds.), *Group psychotherapy for psychological trauma* (pp. 298–325). New York: Guilford Press.

Fink, D. S., Hu, R., Cerdá, M., Keyes, K. M., Marshall, B. L., Galea, S., & Martins, S. S. (2015). Patterns of major depression and nonmedical use of prescription opioids in the United States. *Drug and Alcohol Dependence, 153,* 258–264.

Fink, G. (2011). Stress controversies: Posttraumatic stress disorder, hippocampal volume, gastroduodenal ulceration. *Journal of Neuroendocrinology, 23*(2), 107–117.

Fink, M. (2007). What we learn about continuation treatments from the collaborative electroconvulsive therapy studies. *Journal of ECT, 23*(4), 215–218.

Fink, M. (2014). What was learned: Studies by the consortium for research in ECT (CORE) 1997–2011. *Acta Psychiatrica Scandinavica, 129*(6), 417–426.

Fink, M., Kellner, C. H., & McCall, W. V. (2014). The role of ECT in suicide prevention. *The Journal of ECT, 30*(1), 5–9.

Finkelhor, D., Asdigian, N., & Dziuba-Leatherman, J. (1995). Victimization prevention programs for children: A follow-up. *American Journal of Public Health, 85*(12), 1684–1689.

Finnegan, L. P., & Kandall, S. R. (2008). Perinatal substance abuse. In H. D. Kleber & M. Galanter (Eds.), *The American Psychiatric Publishing textbook of substance abuse treatment* (4th ed., pp. 565–580). Arlington, VA: American Psychiatric Publishing.

Fischer, B. A. (2012). Maltreatment of people with serious mental illness in the early 20th century: A focus on Nazi Germany and eugenics in America. *The Journal of Nervous and Mental Disease, 200*(12), 1096–1100.

Fischer, S., Meyer, A. H., Dremmel, D., Schlup, B., & Munsch, S. (2014). Short-term cognitive-behavioral therapy for binge eating disorder: Long-term efficacy and predictors of long-term treatment success. *Behaviour Research and Therapy, 58,* 36–42.

Fisher, M. A. (2013). *The ethics of conditional confidentiality: A practical model for mental health professionals.* New York: Oxford University Press.

Fisher, P. L., & Wells, A. (2011). Conceptual models of generalized anxiety disorder. *Psychiatric Annals, 41*(2), 127–132.

Fiske, A., Zimmerman, J. A., & Scogin, F. (2011). Geropsychology mentoring: A survey of current practices and perceived needs. *Educational Gerontology, 37*(5), 370–377.

Fitz, A. (1990). Religious and familial factors in the etiology of obsessive-compulsive disorder: A review. *Journal of Psychological Theology, 18*(2), 141–147.

Flaherty, E. G., & Macmillan, H. L. (2013). Caregiver-fabricated illness in a child: A manifestation of child maltreatment. *Pediatrics, 132*(3), 590–597.

Flanagan, D. P., Ortiz, S. O., & Alfonso, V. C. (2013). *Essentials of cross-battery assessment.* Hoboken, NJ: Wiley.

Flavin, D. K., Franklin, J. E., & Frances, R. J. (1990). Substance abuse and suicidal behavior. In S. J. Blumenthal & D. J. Kupfer (Eds.), *Suicide over the life cycle: Risk factors, assessment, and treatment of suicidal patients.* Washington, DC: American Psychiatry Press.

Fletcher, R. J. (Ed.). (2011). *Psychotherapy for individuals with intellectual disability.* Kingston, NY: NADD Press.

Flor, H. (2014). Psychological pain interventions and neurophysiology: Implications for a mechanism-based approach. *American Psychologist, 69*(2), 188–196.

Floyd, A., Dedert, E., Ghate, S., Salmon, P., Weissbecker, I., Studts, J. L., . . . Sephton, S. E. (2011). Depression may mediate the relationship between sense of coherence and quality of life in lung cancer patients. *Journal of Health Psychology, 16*(2), 249–257.

Fogley, R., Warman, D., & Lysaker, P. H. (2014). Alexithymia in schizophrenia: Associations with neurocognition and emotional distress. *Psychiatry Research, 218*(1-2), 1–6.

Fok, M. L., Stewart, R., Hayes, R. D., & Moran, P. (2014). The impact of co-morbid personality disorder on use of psychiatric services and involuntary hospitalization in people with severe mental illness. *Social Psychiatry and Psychiatric Epidemiology, 49*(10), 1631–1640.

Folsom, D. P., Fleisher, A. S., & Depp, C. A. (2006). Schizophrenia. In D.V. Jeste & J. H. Friedman (Eds.), *Psychiatry for neurologists* (pp. 59–66). Totowa, NJ: Humana Press.

Fonareva, I., & Oken, B. S. (2014). Physiological and functional consequences of caregiving for relatives with dementia. *International Psychogeriatrics, 26*(5), 725–747.

Fondas, N. (2014, January 10). The custom-fit workplace: Choose when, where, and how to work. *Psychology Today.* Retrieved from Psychologty Today website: http://www.psychologytoday.co /blog.

Foo, X. Y., Alwi, M. M., Ismail, S. F., Ibrahim, N., & Osman, Z. J. (2014). Religious commitment, attitudes toward suicide, and suicidal behaviors among college students of different ethnic and religious groups in Malaysia. *Journal of Religion & Health, 53*(3), 731–746.

Forcano, L., Alvarez, E., Santamaría, J. J., Jimenez-Murcia, S., Granero, R., Penelo, E., . . . Fernández-Aranda, F. (2010). Suicide attempts in anorexia nervosa subtypes. *Comprehensive Psychiatry, 52*(4), 352–358.

Ford, E., & Rotter, M. (2014). *Landmark cases in forensic psychiatry.* New York: Oxford University Press.

Ford, T. (2000). The influence of womanist identity on the development of eating disorders and depression in African American female college students. *Dissertation Abstracts International: Section A: Humanities and Social Sciences, 61,* 2194.

Foreyt, J. P., Poston, W. S. C., & Goodrick, G. K. (1996). Future directions in obesity and eating disorders. *Addictive Behavior, 21*(6), 767–778.

Forgas, J. F. (2013). Don't worry, be sad! On the cognitive, motivational, and interpersonal benefits of negative mood. *Current Directions in Psychological Science, 22*(3), 225–232.

Forgas, J. F. (2014, June 4). Four ways sadness may be good for you. *Greater Good.*

Forgatch, M. S., & Patterson, G. R. (2010). Parent management training—Oregon model: An intervention for antisocial behavior in children and adolescents. In J. R. Weisz & A. E. Kazdin (Eds.), *Evidence-based psychotherapies for children and adolescents* (2nd ed., pp. 159–177). New York: Guilford Press.

Forsén Mantilla, E., Bergsten, K., & Birgegård, A. (2014). Self-image and eating disorder symptoms in normal and clinical adolescents. *Eating Behaviors, 15*(1), 125–131.

Fortune, S. A., & Hawton, K. (2007). Suicide and deliberate self-harm in children and adolescents. *Paediatrics & Child Health, 17*(11), 443–447.

Foster, J. D., Campbell, W. K., & Twenge, J. M. (2003). Individual differences in narcissism: Inflated self-views across the lifespan and around the world. *Journal of Research in Personality, 37,* 469–486.

Fouassier, D., Suarez, F. G., Hamon, C., & Decoene, H. (2014). [A support group for Alzheimer's patients in a day care center]. *Soins Gérontologie* (106), 18–22.

Fowler, K. A., O'Donohue, W., Lilienfeld, S. O. (2007). Introduction: Personality disorders in perspective. In W. O'Donohue, K. A. Fowler, S. O. Lilienfeld (Eds.). *Personality disorders: Toward the DSM-V.* Los Angeles: Sage Publications.

Fowler, P. J., Henry, D. B., Schoeny, M., Landsverk, J., Chavira, D., & Taylor, J. J. (2013). Inadequate housing among families under investigation for child abuse and neglect: Prevalence from a national probability sample. *American Journal of Community Psychology, 52*(1-2), 106–114.

Fox, D. (2010, June 10). The insanity virus. *Discover, 31*(5).

Fox, J. A., & Levin, J. (2014). *Extreme killing: Understanding serial and mass murder* (3rd ed.). Los Angeles: Sage Publications.

Fox, M. D., Buckner, R. L., White, M. P., Greicius, M. D., & Pascual-Leone, A. (2012). Efficacy of transcranial magnetic stimulation targets for depression is related to intrinsic functional connectivity with the subgenual cingulate. *Biological Psychiatry, 72*(7), 595–603.

Frances, A. J. (2013). Frances's letter to editor. *New York Times.*

Frances, A. J. (2013, January 16). Bad news: DSM5 refuses to correct somatic symptom disorder. *Psychology Today* Blogs: DSM5 in distress.

Frances, A. J. (2013, July 3). Back to normal. *Psychology Today* Blogs: DSM5 in distress. Retrieved from Psychology Today website: http://www.psychologytoday.com/blog/dsm5-in-distress/201307/back-normal.

Frank, J. D. (1973). *Persuasion and healing* (Rev. ed.). Baltimore: Johns Hopkins University Press.

Franklin, M. E., & Foa, E. B. (2014). Obsessive compulsive disorder. In D. H. Barlow (Ed.), (2014). *Clinical handbook of psychological disorders: A step-by-step treatment manual* (5th ed., pp. 155–205). New York: Guilford Press.

Frazier, A. D., & Cross, T. L. (2011). Debunking the myths of suicide in gifted children. In J. L. Jolly, D. J. Treffinger, T. F. Inman, & J. F. Smutny (Eds.), *Parenting gifted children: The authoritative guide from the National Association for Gifted Children* (pp. 517–524). Waco, TX: Prufrock Press.

Frederickson, J. (2013). *Co-creating change: Effective dynamic therapy techniques.* Kansas City, MO: Seven Leaves Press.

Freitag, F. (2013). Managing and treating tension-type headache. *Medical Clinics of North America, 97*(2), 281–292.

Freud, S. (1894). The neuropsychoses of defense. In J. Strachey (Ed.), *The standard edition of the complete psychological works of Sigmund Freud* (Vol. 3). London: Hogarth Press. (Work republished 1962).

Freud, S. (1914). On narcissism. In *Complete psychological works* (Vol. 14). London: Hogarth Press. [Work republished 1957.]

Freud, S. (1915). A case of paranoia counter to psychoanalytic theory. In *Complete psychological works* (Vol. 14). London: Hogarth Press. [Work republished 1957.]

Freud, S. (1917). *A general introduction to psychoanalysis* (J. Riviere, Trans.). New York: Liveright. (Work republished 1963).

Freud, S. (1917). Mourning and melancholia. In *Collected papers* (Vol. 4, pp. 152–172). London: Hogarth Press and the Institute of Psychoanalysis. [Work republished 1950.]

Freud, S. (1924). The loss of reality in neurosis and psychosis. In *Sigmund Freud's collected papers* (Vol. 2, pp. 272–282). London: Hogarth Press.

Freud, S. (1933). *New introductory lectures on psychoanalysis.* New York: Norton.

Freud, S. (1961). *The future of an illusion.* New York: W. W. Norton.

Frey, R. (2005). Hallucination. In S. L. Chamberlin & B. Narins (Eds.), *Gale encyclopedia of neurological disorders.* Farmington Hills, MI: Thomson Gale.

Fried, E. I., Nesse, R. M., Guille, C., & Sen, S. (2015). The differential influence of life stress on individual symptoms of depression. *Acta Psychiatrica Scandinavica, 131*(6), 465–471.

Friedman, M. (2013). Mass murder: Is there a mental health issue? *Huffington Post.* Retrieved from Huffington Post website: http://www.huffingtonpost.com/michael-friedman-lmsw/mental.

Friedman, M., & Rosenman, R. (1959). Association of specific overt behavior pattern with blood and cardiovascular findings. *Journal of the American Medical Association, 169,* 1286.

Friedman, M., & Rosenman, R. (1974). *Type A behavior and your heart.* New York: Knopf.

Friedrich, F., Gross, R., Wrobel, M., Klug, G., Unger, A., Fellinger, M., . . . Wancata, J. (2014). Burden of mothers and fathers of persons with schizophrenia. *Psychiatrische Praxis, 42*(04), 208–215.

Friman, P. C. (2008). Evidence-based therapies for enuresis and encopresis. In R. G. Steele, T. D. Elkin, & M. C. Roberts (Eds.), *Handbook of evidence-based therapies for children and adolescents: Bridging science and practice.* New York: Springer.

Fromberger, P., Jordan, K., & Müller, J. L. (2013). Pedophilia: Etiology, diagnostics and therapy. *Der Nervenarzt, 84*(9), 1123–1135.

Fromm-Reichmann, F. (1948). Notes on the development of treatment of schizophrenia by psychoanalytic psychotherapy. *Psychiatry, 11,* 263–273.

Frosch, W. A., Robbins, E. S., & Stern, M. (1965). Untoward reactions to lysergic acid diethylamide (LSD) resulting in hospitalization. *New England Journal of Medicine, 273,* 1235–1239.

Frost, A., Hoyt, L. T., Chung, A. L., & Adam, E. K. (2015). Daily life with depressive symptoms: Gender differences in adolescents' everyday emotional experiences. *Journal of Adolescence, 43,* 132–141.

Frost, R. O., & Stekctee, G. (2001). Obsessive-compulsive disorder. In H. S. Friedman (Ed.), *Specialty articles from the encyclopedia of mental health.* San Diego: Academic Press.

Frost, R. O., Steketee, G., & Tolin, D. F. (2012). Diagnosis and assessment of hoarding disorder. *Annual Review of Clinical Psychology, 8,* 219–242.

Fugl-Meyer, K. S., Bohm-Starke, N., Petersen, C. D., Fugl-Meyer, A., Parish, S., & Giraldi, A. (2013). Standard operating procedures for female genital sexual pain. *Journal of Sexual Medicine, 10,* 83–93.

Fukumoto, M., Hashimoto, R., Ohi, K., Yasuda, Y., Yamamori, H., Umeda-Yano, S., . . . Takeda, M. (2014). Relation between remission status and attention in patients with schizophrenia. *Psychiatry and Clinical Neurosciences, 68*(3), 234–241.

Gabbard, G. O. (2010). Therapeutic action in the psychoanalytic psychotherapy of borderline personality disorder. In J. F. Clarkin, P. Fonagy, G. O. Gabbard (Eds.), *Psychodynamic psychotherapy for personality disorders: A clinical handbook.* Arlington, VA: American Psychiatric Publishing, Inc.

Gabriel, C., & Waller, G. (2014). Personality disorder cognitions in the eating disorders. *Journal of Nervous and Mental Disease, 202*(2), 172–176.

Gadalla, T. M. (2009). Eating disorders in men: A community-based study. *International Journal of Men's Health, 8*(1), 72–81.

Gado, M. (2008). The insanity defense: Twinkies as a defense. *trutv.com.* Retrieved from Tru TV website: http://www.trutv.com/library/crime/criminal_mind/psychology/insanity.

Galanter, M. (2014). Alcoholics Anonymous and twelve-step recovery: A model based on social and cognitive neuroscience. *American Journal on Addictions, 23*(3), 300–307.

Galanter, M., & Kleber, H. D. (Eds.). (2008). *The American Psychiatric Publishing textbook of substance abuse treatment* (4th ed.). Arlington, VA: American Psychiatric Publishing.

Galderisi, S., Vignapiano, A., Mucci, A., & Boutros, N. N. (2014). Physiological correlates of positive symptoms in schizophrenia. *Current Topics in Behavioral Neurosciences, 21,* 103–128.

Galea, S., Ahern, J., Resnick, H., Kilpatrick, D., Bucuvalas, M., Gold, J., & Vlahov, D. (2002). Psychological sequelae of the September 11 terrorist attacks in New York City. *New England Journal of Medicine, 13,* 982–987.

Galea, S., Ahern, J., Resnick, H., Kilpatrick, D., Bucuvalas, M., Gold, J., & Vlahov, D. (2007). Psychological sequelae of the September 11 terrorist attacks in New York City. In B. Trappler (Ed.), *Modern terrorism and psychological trauma* (pp. 14–24). New York: Gordian Knot Books/Richard Altschulerr & Associates.

Galling, B., Garvia, M. A., Osuchukwu, U., Hagi, K., & Correll, C. U. (2015). Safety and tolerability of antipsychotic-mood stabilizer co-treatment in the management of acute bipolar disorder: Results from a systematic review and exploratory meta-analysis. *Expert Opinion on Drug Safety, 14*(8), 1181–1199.

Gallo, L. C., Penedo, F. J., de los Monteros, K. E., & Arguelles, W. (2009). Resiliency in the face of disadvantage: Do Hispanic cultural characteristics protect health outcomes? *Journal of Personality, 77*(6), 1707–1746.

Gallup Poll. (2005). Three in four Americans believe in paranormal. *Gallup News Service.* http://www.gallup.com/poll/16915/three-four-americans-believe-paranormal.aspx.

Gallup Poll. (2013). *Most Americans practice charitable giving, volunteerism.* Retrieved from Gallup website: http://www.gallup.com/poll/166250.

Gallup Poll. (2013, May 29). *U.S. support for euthanasia hinges on how it's described.* (Poll 162815). Retrieved from Gallup website: http://www.gallup.com/poll/162815.

Gallup Poll. (2013, December 19). *In U.S., 40% get less than recommended amount of sleep.* (Poll 166553). Retrieved from Gallup website: http://www.gallup.com/poll/166553.

Galvez, J. F., Thommi, S., & Ghaemi, S. N. (2011). Positive aspects of mental illness: A review in bipolar disorder. *Journal of Affective Disorders, 28*(3), 185–190.

Gamble, A. L., Harvey, A. G., & Rapee, R. M. (2010). Specific phobia. In D. J. Stein, E. Hollander, & B. O. Rothbaum (Eds.), *Textbook of anxiety disorders* (2nd ed., pp. 525–541). Arlington, VA: American Psychiatric Publishing.

Gamwell, L., & Tomes, N. (1995). *Madness in America: Cultural and medical perceptions of mental illness before 1914.* Ithaca, NY: Cornell University Press.

Gao, K., Kemp, D. E., Wang, Z., Ganocy, S. J., Conroy, C., Serrano, M. B., . . . Calabrese, J. R. (2010). Predictors of nonstabilization during the combination therapy of lithium and divalproex in rapid cycling bipolar disorder: A post-hoc analysis of two studies. *Psychopharmacology Bulletin, 43*(1), 23–38.

Garatachea, N., Rodríguez, G., Pareja-Galeano, H., Sanchis-Gomar, F., Lucia, A., Santos-Lozano, A., . . . Emanuele, E. (2014). PTK2 rs7460 and rs7843014 polymorphisms and exceptional longevity: A functional replication study. *Rejuvenation Research, 17*(5), 430–438.

Garb, H. N. (2006). The conjunction effect and clinical judgment. *Journal of Social and Clinical Psychology, 25*(9), 1048–1056.

Garb, H. N. (2010). Clinical judgment and the influence of screening on decision making. In A. J. Mitchell & J. C. Coyne (Eds.), *Screening for depression in clinical practice: An evidence-based guide* (pp. 113–121). New York: Oxford University Press.

Gard, D. E., Cooper, S., Fisher, M., Genevsky, A., Mikels, J. A., & Vinogradov, S. (2011). Evidence for an emotion maintenance deficit in schizophrenia. *Psychiatry Research, 187*(1-2), 24–29.

Gard, D. E., Sanchez, A. H., Starr, J., Cooper, S., Fisher, M., Rowlands, A., & Vinogradov, S. (2014). Using self-determination theory to understand motivation deficits in schizophrenia: The 'why' of motivated behavior. *Schizophrenia Research, 156*(2-3), 217–222.

Garfield, J. B., Lubman, D. I., & Yücel, M. (2014). Anhedonia in substance use disorders: A systematic review of its nature, course and clinical correlates. *Australian and New Zealand Journal of Psychiatry, 48*(1), 36–51.

Garner, D. M. (1991). *Eating disorder inventory-2.* Odessa, FL: Psychological Assessment Resources.

Garner, D. M. (1997). The 1997 body image survey results. *Psychology Today, 30*(1), 30–44.

Garner, D. M. (2005). *Eating Disorder Inventory TM-3 (EDI TM-3).* Lutz, Florida: Psychological Assessment Resources, Inc. (PAR).

Garner, D. M., Garfinkel, P. E., Schwartz, D., & Thompson, M. (1980). Cultural expectations of thinness in women. *Psychological Reports, 47,* 483–491.

Garner, D. M., Olmsted, M. P., & Polivy, J. (1984). *The EDI.* Odessa, FL: Psychological Assessment Resources.

Garrett, B. L. (2011). *Convicting the innocent: Where criminal prosecutions go wrong.* Cambridge, MA: Harvard University Press.

Gaudiano, B. A. (2013, September 29). Psychotherapy's image problem. *New York Times.*

Gay, P. (1999, March 29). Psychoanalyst Sigmund Freud. *Time,* pp. 66–69.

Gay, P. (2006). *Freud: A life for our time.* New York: W. W. Norton & Co.

Gaynor, S. T., & Baird, S. C. (2007). Personality disorders. In D. W. Woods & J. W. Kanter (Eds.), *Understanding behavior disorders: A contemporary behavioral perspective.* Reno, NV: Context Press.

Gebhard, P. H. (1965). Situational factors affecting human sexual behavior. In F. Beach (Ed.), *Sex and behavior.* New York: Wiley.

Geddes, J. R., & Miklowitz, D. J. (2013). Treatment of bipolar disorder. *Lancet, 381*(9878), 1672–1682.

Geddes, J. R., Stroup, S., & Lieberman, J. A. (2011). Comparative efficacy and effectiveness in the drug treatment of schizophrenia. In D. R. Weinberg & P. Harrison (Eds.), *Schizophrenia* (pp. 525–539). Hoboken, NJ: Wiley-Blackwell.

Gelernter, J., & Kranzler, H. R. (2008). Genetics of addiction. In H. D. Kleber & M. Galanter (Eds.), *The American Psychiatric Publishing textbook of substance abuse treatment* (4th ed., pp. 17–27). Arlington, VA: American Psychiatric Publishing.

Gelfand, D. M., Jenson, W. R., & Drew, C. J. (1982). *Understanding child behavior disorders.* New York: Holt, Rinehart & Winston.

Gelfand, L., & Radomsky, A. (2013). Beliefs about control and the persistence of cleaning behaviour: An experimental analysis. *Journal of Behavior Therapy and Experimental Psychiatry, 44*(2), 172–178.

Gelkopf, M., Solomon, Z., & Bleich, A. (2013). A longitudinal study of changes in psychological responses to continuous terrorism. *The Israel Journal of Psychiatry and Related Sciences, 50*(2), 100–109.

Gentile, J. P., Dillon, K. S., & Gillig, P. M. (2013). Psychotherapy and pharmacotherapy for patients with dissociative identity disorder. *Innovations in Clinical Neuroscience, 10*(2), 22–29.

Gentile, J. P., Snyder, M., & Marie Gillig, P. (2014). Stress and trauma: Psychotherapy and pharmacotherapy for depersonalization/derealization disorder. *Innovations in Clinical Neuroscience, 11*(7-8), 37–41.

George, W. H., Davis, K. C., Heiman, J. R., Norris, J., Stoner, S. A., Schacht, R. L., . . . Kajumulo, K. F. (2011). Women's sexual arousal: Effects of high alcohol dosages and self-control instructions. *Hormones and Behavior, 59*(5), 730–738.

Gerard, N., Delvenne, V., & Nicolis, H. (2012). [The contagion of adolescent suicide: Culture, ethical and psychosocial aspects.] *Revue Médicale de Bruxelles, 33*(3), 164–170.

Geriatric Mental Health Foundation. (2013, October 7). *Causes and risk factors for senior mental illness.* Retrieved from A Place for Mom website: http://www.aplaceformom.com/blog.

Gerrity, E., Keane, T. M., & Tuma, F. (2001). Introduction. In E. Gerrity, T. M. Keane, & F. Tuma (Eds.), *The mental health consequences of torture* (pp. 3–12). New York: Kluwer Academic/Plenum Publishers.

Gershon, E. S., & Nurnberger, J. I. (1995). Bipolar illness. In J. M. Oldham & M. B. Riba (Eds.), *American Psychiatric Press review of psychiatry* (Vol. 14). Washington, DC: American Psychiatric Press.

Gerst-Emerson, K., Shovali, T. E., & Markides, K. S. (2014). Loneliness among very old Mexican Americans: Findings from the Hispanic established populations epidemiologic studies of the elderly. *Archives of Gerontology and Geriatrics, 59*(1), 145–149.

Gheorghiu, V. A., & Orleanu, P. (1982). Dental implant under hypnosis. *American Journal of Clinical Hypnosis, 25*(1), 68–70.

Ghetti, S., Schaaf, J. M., Qin, J., & Goodman, G. S. (2004). Issues in eyewitness testimony. In W. T. O'Donohue & E. R. Levensky (Eds.), *Handbook of forensic psychology: Resource for mental health and legal professionals* (pp. 513–554). New York: Elsevier Science.

Giesbrecht, T., & Merckelbach, H. (2009). Betrayal trauma theory of dissociative experiences: Stroop and directed forgetting findings. *American Journal of Psychology, 122*(3), 337–348.

Gifford, M., Friedman, S., & Majerus, R. (2010). *Alcoholism.* Santa Barbara, CA: Greenwood Press/ABC-CLIO.

Gilbert, K. L., Quinn, S. C., Ford, A. F., & Thomas, S. B. (2011). The urban context: A place to eliminate health disparities and build organizational capacity. *Journal of Prevention & Intervention in the Community, 39*(1), 77–92.

Gilbert, S. (2011). Eating disorders in women of African descent. In J. Alexander & J. Treasure (Eds.), *A collaborative approach to eating disorders* (pp. 249–261). New York: Taylor & Francis.

Gilbert, S. C., Keery, H., & Thompson, J. K. (2005). The media's role in body image and eating disorders. In J. H. Daniel & E. Cole (Eds.), *Featuring females: Feminist analyses of media* (pp. 41–56). Washington, DC: American Psychological Association.

Gill, A. D. (1982). Vulnerability to suicide. In E. L. Bassuk, S. C. Schoonover, & A. D. Gill (Eds.), *Lifelines: Clinical perspectives on suicide.* New York: Plenum Press.

Gill, D., & Warburton, W. (2014). An investigation of the biosocial model of borderline personality disorder. *Journal of Clinical Psychology, 70*(9), 866–873.

Gill, R. E. (2010, January/February). Practice opportunities available despite shrinking mental health dollars. *The National Psychologist, 1,* 3.

Gilman, S. E. (2013). Commentary: The causal and nosological status of loss in major depression. *Epidemiology, 24*(4), 616–618.

Giraldi, A., Rellini, A. H., Pfaus, J., & Laan, E. (2013). Female sexual arousal disorders. *Journal of Sexual Medicine, 10,* 58–73.

Girden, E. R., & Kabacoff, R. I. (2011). *Evaluating research articles: From start to finish* (3rd ed.). Thousand Oaks, CA: Sage Publications.

Girón, M., Nova-Fernández, F., Mañá-Alvarenga, S., Nolasco, A., Molina-Habas, A., Fernández-Yañez, A., . . . Gómez-Beneyto, M. (2015). How does family intervention improve the outcome of people with schizophrenia?

Social Psychiatry and Psychiatric Epidemiology, 50(3), 379–387.

Gist, R., & Devilly, G. J. (2010). Early intervention in the aftermath of trauma. In G. M. Rosen & B. C. Frueh (Eds.), *Clinician's guide to posttraumatic stress disorder* (pp. 153–175). Hoboken, NJ: John Wiley & Sons.

Gjini, K., Boutros, N. N., Haddad, L., Aikins, D., Javanbakht, A., Amirsadri, A., & Tancer, M. E. (2013). Evoked potential correlates of post-traumatic stress disorder in refugees with history of exposure to torture. *Journal of Psychiatric Research, 47*(10), 1492–1498.

Glasser, M. (2010). The history of managed care and the role of the child and adolescent psychiatrist. *Child and Adolescent Psychiatric Clinics of North America, 19*(1), 63–74.

Glauberman, N. (2014, January 29). On losing it (or not). *New York Times.*

Glied, S., & Frank, R. G. (2014). Mental illness and violence: Lessons from the evidence. *American Journal of Public Health, 104*(2), e5–e6.

Glina, S., Sharlip, I. D., & Hellstrom, W. J. G. (2013). Modifying risk factors to prevent and treat erectile dysfunction. *Journal of Sexual Medicine, 10,* 115–119.

Gloster, A. T., Gerlach, A. L., Hamm, A., Höfler, M., Alpers, G. W., Kircher, T., . . . Reif, A. (2015). 5HTT is associated with the phenotype psychological flexibility: Results from a randomized clinical trial. *European Archives of Psychiatry and Clinical Neuroscience, 265*(5), 399–406.

Gloster, A. T., Klotsche, J., Gerlach, A. L., Hamm, A., Ströhle, A., Gauggel, S., . . . Wittchen, H. (2014). Timing matters: change depends on the stage of treatment in cognitive behavioral therapy for panic disorder with agoraphobia. *Journal of Consulting and Clinical Psychology, 82*(1), 141–153.

Gloster, A. T., Wittchen, H-U., Einsle, F., Lang, T., Helbig-Lang, S., Fydrich, T., . . . Arolt, V. (2011). Psychological treatment for panic disorder with agoraphobia, A randomized controlled trial to examine the role of therapist-guided exposure in situ in CBT. *Journal of Consulting and Clinical Psychology, 79*(3), 406–420.

Glover, N. G., Crego, C., & Widiger, T. A. (2011). The clinical utility of the Five Factor Model of personality disorder. *Personality Disorders, 3*(2), 176–184.

Glovin, D. (2014, September 9). Baseball caught looking as fouls injure 17,500 fans a year. *Bloomberg.*

Godley, M. D., Godley, S. H., Dennis, M. L., Funk, R. R., Passetti, L. L., & Petry, N. M. (2014). A randomized trial of assertive continuing care and contingency management for adolescents with substance use disorders. *Journal of Consulting and Clinical Psychology, 82*(1), 40–51.

Gola, H., Engler, H., Schauer, M., Adenauer, H., Riether, C., Kolassa, S., . . . Kolassa, I. (2012). Victims of rape show increased cortisol responses to trauma reminders: A study in individuals with war- and torture-related PTSD. *Psychoneuroendocrinology, 37*(2), 213–220.

Gold, J. M., Kool, W., Botvinick, M. M., Hubzin, L., August, S., & Waltz, J. A. (2014). Cognitive effort avoidance and detection in people with schizophrenia. *Cognitive, Affective & Behavioral Neuroscience, 15*(1), 145–154.

Gold, S. N., & Castillo, Y. (2010). Dealing with defenses and defensiveness in interviews. In D. L. Segal & M. Hersen (Eds.), *Diagnostic interviewing* (pp. 89–102). New York: Springer Publishing.

Golden, C. J. (2008). Neurologically impaired children. In D. Reitman (Ed.), *Handbook of psychological assessment, case conceptualization, and treatment, Vol. 2: Children and adolescents.* Hoboken, NJ: John Wiley & Sons.

Goldenberg, I., Goldenberg, H., & Goldenberg Pelavin, E. (2014). Family therapy. In D.

Wedding & R. J. Corsini (Eds.), *Current psychotherapies* (10th ed., pp. 373–410). Independence, KY: Cengage Publications.

Goldfinger, K., & Pomerantz, A. M. (2014). *Psychological assessment and report writing* (2nd ed.). Los Angeles, CA: Sage Publications.

Goldiamond, I. (1965). Self-control procedures in personal behavior problems. *Psychological Reports, 17,* 851–868.

Goldin, P. R., Ziv, M., Jazaieri, H., Hahn, K., Heimberg, R., & Gross, J. J. (2013). Impact of cognitive behavioral therapy for social anxiety disorder on the neural dynamics of cognitive reappraisal of negative self-beliefs: randomized clinical trial. *JAMA Psychiatry, 70*(10), 1048–1056.

Goldin, P. R., Ziv, M., Jazaieri, H., Werner, K., Kraemer, H., Heimberg, R. G., & Gross, J. J. (2012, May 14). Cognitive reappraisal self-efficacy mediates the effects of individual cognitive-behavioral therapy for social anxiety disorder. *Journal of Consulting and Clinical Psychology, 80*(6),1034–1040.

Goldstein, D. J., Potter, W. Z., Ciraulo, D. A., & Shader, R. I. (2011). Biological theories of depression and implications for current and new treatments. In D. A. Ciraulo & R. I. Shader (Eds.), *Pharmacotherapy of depression* (2nd ed., pp. 1–32). New York: Springer Science + Business Media.

Goldstein, I. (2014). Unfair: Government-approved sexual medicine treatments only available for men. *Journal of Sexual Medicine, 11,* 317–320.

Goldstein, S. (2011). Attention-deficit/hyperactivity disorder. In S. Goldstein, & C. R. Reynolds (Eds.), *Handbook of neurodevelopmental and genetic disorders in children* (2nd ed., pp. 131–150). New York: Guilford Press.

Goldston, D. B., Molock, S. D., Whitbeck, B., Murakami, J. L., Zayas, L. H., & Hall, G. C. N. (2008). Cultural considerations in adolescent suicide prevention and psychosocial treatment. *American Psychologist, 63*(1), 14–31.

Gómez-Gil, E., Esteva, I., Almaraz, M. C., Pasaro, E., Segovia, S., & Guillamon, A. (2010). Familiarity of gender identity disorder in non-twin siblings. *Archives of Sexual Behavior, 39*(2), 546–552.

Gonçalves, J. B., Lucchetti, G., Menezes, P. R., & Vallada, H. (2015). Religious and spiritual interventions in mental health care: A systematic review and meta-analysis of randomized controlled clinical trials. *Psychological Medicine.* [Advance online publication.]

Gonidakis, F., Kravvariti, V., & Varsou, E. (2014). Sexual function of women suffering from anorexia nervosa and bulimia nervosa. *Journal of Sex & Marital Therapy, 41*(4), 368–378.

González, H. M., Tarraf, W., Whitfield, K. E., & Vega, W. A. (2010). The epidemiology of major depression and ethnicity in the United States. *Journal of Psychiatric Research, 44,* 1043–1051.

Good, G. E., & Brooks, G. R. (Eds.). (2005). *The new handbook of psychotherapy and counseling with men: A comprehensive guide to settings, problems, and treatment approaches* (Rev. & abridged ed.). San Francisco, CA: Jossey-Bass.

Goodman, G., Edwards, K., & Chung, H. (2014). Interaction structures formed in the psychodynamic therapy of five patients with borderline personality disorder in crisis. *Psychology & Psychotherapy, 87*(1), 15–31.

Goodman, M. (2013). Patient highlights: Female genital plastic/cosmetic surgery. *Journal of Sexual Medicine, 10*(8), 2125–2126.

Goodman, S. (2014). How many people live to 100 across the globe? *The Centenarian.* Retrieved from Centenarian website: http://www.thecentenarian.co.uk.

Goodwin, C. J., & Goodwin, K. A. (2012). *Research in psychology: Methods and design.* Hoboken, NJ: Wiley.

Gordon, D., Heimberg, R., Tellez, M., & Ismail, A. (2013). A critical review of approaches to the treatment of dental anxiety in adults. *Journal of Anxiety Disorders, 27*(4), 365–378.

Gordon, O. M., Salkovskis, P. M., Oldfield, V. B., & Carter, N. (2013). The association between obsessive compulsive disorder and obsessive compulsive personality disorder: Prevalence and clinical presentation. *British Journal of Clinical Psychology, 52*(3), 300–315.

Gorenstein, D. (2013, May 17). How much is the DSM-5 worth? Marketplace.org.

Gorman, D. A., Gardner, D. M., Murphy, A. L., Feldman, M., Bélanger, S. A., Steele, M. M., . . . Pringsheim, T. (2015). Canadian guidelines on pharmacotherapy for disruptive and aggressive behaviour in children and adolescents with attention-deficit hyperactivity disorder, oppositional defiant disorder, or conduct disorder. *Canadian Journal of Psychiatry, 60*(2), 72–76.

Goshen, C. E. (1967). *Documentary history of psychiatry: A source book on historical principles.* New York: Philosophy Library.

Gosling, S. (2011). Cited in M. L. Phillips, *Using social media in your research.* Washington, DC: American Psychological Association.

Goss, K., & Allan, S. (2009). Shame, pride and eating disorders. *Clinical Psychology & Psychotherapy, 16*(4), 303–316.

Goto, S., Terao, T., Hoaki, N., & Wang, Y. (2011). Cyclothymic and hyperthymic temperaments may predict bipolarity in major depressive disorder: A supportive evidence for bipolar II1/2 and IV. *Journal of Affective Disorders, 129*(1-3), 34–38.

Gottesman, I. I. (1991). *Schizophrenia genesis.* New York: Freeman.

Gouin, J-P, Glaser, R., Loving, T. J., Malarkey, W. B., Stowell, J., Houts, C., & Kiecolt-Glaser, J. K. (2009). Attachment avoidance predicts inflammatory responses to marital conflict. *Brain, Behavior, and Immunity, 23*(7), 898–904.

Gozlan, O. (2011). Transsexual surgery: A novel reminder and a navel remainder. *International Forum of Psychoanalysis, 20*(1), 45–52.

Graham, J. R. (2006). *MMPI-2: Assessing personality and psychopathology* (4th ed.). New York: Oxford University Press.

Graham, J. R. (2014). *MMPI-2: Assessing personality and psychopathology* (5th ed.). New York: Oxford University Press.

Granholm, E., Holden, J., Link, P. C., & McQuaid, J. R. (2014). Randomized clinical trial of cognitive behavioral social skills training for schizophrenia: Improvement in functioning and experiential negative symptoms. *Journal of Consulting and Clinical Psychology, 82*(6), 1173–1185.

Granitz, P. (2014, January 12). Four years after earthquake, many in Haiti remain displaced. *NPR.*

Granot, M., Zisman-Ilani, Y., Ram, E., Goldstick, O., & Yovell, Y. (2011). Characteristics of attachment style in women with dyspareunia. *Journal of Sex & Marital Therapy, 37*(1), 1–16.

Grant, J. E., Odlaug, B. L., Chamberlain, S. R., Keuthen, N. J., Lochner, C., & Stein, D. (2012). Skin picking disorder. *The American Journal of Psychiatry, 169*(11), 1143–1149.

Grant, J. E., Redden, S. A., Leppink, E. W., & Odlaug, B. L. (2015). Skin picking disorder with co-occurring body dysmorphic disorder. *Body Image, 15,* 44–48.

Gray, E. (2014, February 4). Heroin gains popularity as cheap doses flood the U.S. *Time.com.*

Gray, H. (1959). *Anatomy of the human body* (27th ed.). Philadelphia: Lea & Febiger.

Gray, J. A., & McNaughton, N. (1996). The neuropsychology of anxiety: Reprise. In D. A. Hope (Ed.),

The Nebraska symposium on motivation (Vol. 43). Lincoln: University of Nebraska Press.

Gray, N. A., Zhou, R., Du, J., Moore, G. J., & Manji, H. K. (2003). The use of mood stabilizers as plasticity enhancers in the treatment of neuropsychiatric disorders. *Journal of Clinical Psychiatry, 64*(Suppl. 5), 3–17.

Grayson, J. (2014). *Freedom from obsessive-compulsive disorder.* (Updated ed.). Berkley, MI: Berkley Trade.

Green, E. K., Hamshere, M., Forty, L., Gordon-Smith, K., Fraser, C., Russell, E., . . . Craddock, N. (2013). Replication of bipolar disorder susceptibility alleles and identification of two novel genome-wide significant associations in a new bipolar disorder case-control sample. *Molecular Psychiatry, 18*(12), 1302–1307.

Green, M. J., Girshkin, L., Teroganova, N., & Quidé, Y. (2014). Stress, schizophrenia and bipolar disorder. *Current Topics in Behavioral Neurosciences, 18,* 217–235.

Green, S. A. (1985). *Mind and body: The psychology of physical illness.* Washington, DC: American Psychiatric Press.

Green, S. M., Haber, E., Frey, B. N., & McCabe, R. E. (2015). Cognitive-behavioral group treatment for perinatal anxiety: A pilot study. *Archives of Women's Mental Health, 18*(4), 631–638.

Greenberg, G. (2011, December 27). Inside the battle to define mental illness. *Wired Magazine.*

Greenfield, S. F., Back, S. E., Lawson, K., & Brady, K. T. (2011). Women and addiction. In J. H. Lowinson & P. Ruiz (Eds.), *Substance abuse: A comprehensive textbook* (5th ed.). Philadelphia, PA: Lippincott, Williams, & Wilkins.

Greening, L., Stoppelbein, L., Fite, P., Dhossche, D., Erath, S., Brown, J., Cramer, R., & Young, L. (2008). Pathways to suicidal behaviors in childhood. *Suicide & Life-Threatening Behavior, 38*(1), 35–45.

Greer, S., Kramer, M. R., Cook-Smith, J. N., & Casper, M. L. (2014). Metropolitan racial residential segregation and cardiovascular mortality: Exploring pathways. *Journal of Urban Health, 91*(3), 499–509.

Gregg, L., Haddock, G., Emsley, R., & Barrowclough, C. (2014). Reasons for substance use and their relationship to subclinical psychotic and affective symptoms, coping, and substance use in a nonclinical sample. *Psychology of Addictive Behaviors, 28*(1), 247–256.

Grekin, P. M., Jemelka, R., & Trupin, E. W. (1994). Racial differences in the criminalization of the mentally ill. *Bulletin of the American Academy of Psychiatry Law, 22,* 411–420.

Griebel, G., & Holmes, A. (2013). 50 years of hurdles and hope in anxiolytic drug discovery. *Nature Reviews. Drug Discovery, 12*(9), 667–687.

Grier, B. C., Wilkins, M. L., & Jeffords, E. H. (2010). Diagnosis and treatment of pediatric bipolar disorder. In P. C. McCabe & S. R. Shaw (Eds.), *Psychiatric disorders: Current topics and interventions for educators* (pp. 17–27). Thousand Oaks, CA: Corwin Press.

Griffin, R. M. (2014). E-cigarettes 101. *WebMD.* Retrieved from WebMD website: http://www/webmd/com/smoking-cessation.

Grigg, J. R. (1988). Imitative suicides in an active duty military population. *Military Medicine, 153*(2), 79–81.

Grill, J. D., & Monsell, S. E. (2014). Choosing Alzheimer's disease prevention clinical trial populations. *Neurobiology of Aging, 35*(3), 466–471.

Grilo, C. M., Masheb, R. M., Brody, M., Toth, C., Burke-Martindale, C. H., & Rothschild, B. S. (2005). Childhood maltreatment in extremely obese male and female bariatric surgery candidates. *Obesity Research, 13,* 123–130.

Grilo, C. M., Masheb, R. M., White, M. A., Gueorguieva, R., Barnes, R. D., Walsh, B. T., . . . Garcia, R. (2014). Treatment of binge eating disorder in racially and ethnically diverse obese patients in primary care: Randomized placebo-controlled clinical trial of self-help and medication. *Behaviour Research and Therapy, 58,* 1–9.

Grimm, J. W. (2011). Craving. In M. C. Olmstead (Ed.), *Animal models of drug addiction. Springer protocols: Neuromethods* (pp. 311–336). Totowa, NJ: Humana Press.

Grob, G. N. (1966). *State and the mentally ill: A history of Worcester State Hospital in Massachusetts, 1830–1920.* Chapel Hill: University of North Carolina Press.

Groër, M. W., Kane, B., Williams, S. N., & Duffy, A. (2015). Relationship of PTSD symptoms with combat exposure, stress, and inflammation in American soldiers. *Biological Research for Nursing, 17*(3), 303–310.

Groër, M. W., Meagher, M. W., & Kendall-Tackett, K. (2010). An overview of stress and immunity. In K. Kendall-Tackett (Ed.), *The psychoneuroimmunology of chronic disease: Exploring the links between inflammation, stress, and illness* (pp. 9–22). Washington, DC: American Psychological Association.

Grohol, J. (2012). Top 25 psychiatric medication prescriptions for 2011. *Psych Central.* Retrieved from Psych Central website: http://psychcentral.com/lib/top-25-psychiatric-medication-prescriptions-for-2011/00012586.

Grossman, L. A. (2013). The origins of American health libertarianism. *Yale Journal of Health Policy, Law, and Ethics, 13*(1), 76–134.

Grossman, R. (2004). Pharmacotherapy of personality disorders. In J. J. Magnavita (Ed.), *Handbook of personality disorders: Theory and practice.* Hoboken, NJ: Wiley.

Grover, S., Chakrabarti, S., Ghormode, D., Agarwal, M., Sharma, A., & Avasthi, A. (2015). Catatonia in inpatients with psychiatric disorders: A comparison of schizophrenia and mood disorders. *Psychiatry Research, 229*(3), 919–925.

Grubin, D. (2010). Polygraphy. In J. M. Brown & E. A. Campbell (Eds.), *The Cambridge handbook of forensic psychology* (pp. 276–282). New York: Cambridge University Press.

Grucza, R. A., Przybeck, T. R., & Cloninger, C. R. (2007). Prevalence and correlates of binge eating disorder in a community sample. *Comprehensive Psychiatry, 48,* pp. 124–131.

Gruttadaro, D. (2005). Federal leaders call on schools to help. *NAMI Advocate, 3*(1), 7.

Guarnieri, P. (2009). Towards a history of the family care of psychiatric patients. *Epidemiologia e Psichiatria Sociale, 18*(1), 34–39.

Guimón, J. (2010). Prejudice and realities in stigma. *International Journal of Mental Health, 39*(3), 20–43.

Guintivano, J., Arad, M., Gould, T. D., Payne, J. L., & Kaminsky, Z. A. (2014). Antenatal prediction of postpartum depression with blood DNA methylation biomarkers. *Molecular Psychiatry, 19*(5), 560–567.

Gunderson, J. G. (2011). Borderline personality disorder. *New England Journal of Medicine, 364*(21), 2037–2042.

Güngörmüs, Z., Tanriverdi, D., & Gündoğan, T. (2014, May). The effect of religious belief on the mental health status and suicide probability of women exposed to violence. *Journal of Religion & Health, 54,* 1573–1583.

Guterman, J. T., Martin, C. V., & Rudes, J. (2011). A solution-focused approach to frotteurism. *Journal of Systemic Therapies, 30*(1), 59–72.

Gutheil, T. G. (2005). Boundary issues and personality disorders. *Journal of Psychiatric Practice, 11*(2), 88–96.

Gutman, D. A., & Nemeroff, C. B. (2011). Stress and depression. In R. J. Contrada & A. Baum (Eds.),

The handbook of stress science: Biology, psychology, and health (pp. 345–357). New York: Springer Publishing.

Guttmacher Institute. (2011). *Insurance coverage of contraceptives.* New York: Guttmacher Institute.

Haagen, J. G., Smid, G. E., Knipscheer, J. W., & Kleber, R. J. (2015). The efficacy of recommended treatments for veterans with PTSD: A metaregression analysis. *Clinical Psychology Review, 40,* 184–194.

Haaken, J., & Reavey, P. (Eds.). (2010). *Memory matters: Contexts for understanding sexual abuse recollections.* New York: Routledge/Taylor & Francis Group.

Haas, M. H., Chance, S. A., Cram, D. F., Crow, T. J., Luc, A., & Hage, S. (2014). Evidence of pragmatic impairments in speech and proverb interpretation in schizophrenia. *Journal of Psycholinguistic Research.* [Electronic publication.]

Haberman, C. (2007). It's not the stress, it's how you deal with it. *New York Times, 156*(54), 109.

Haddad, P. M., & Mattay, V. S. (2011). Neurological complications of antipsychotic drugs. In D. R. Weinberg & P. Harrison (Eds.), *Schizophrenia* (pp. 561–576). Hoboken, NJ: Wiley-Blackwell.

Haddock, G., & Spaulding, W. (2011). Psychological treatment of psychosis. In D. R. Weinberg & P. Harrison (Eds.), *Schizophrenia* (pp. 666–686). Hoboken, NJ: Wiley-Blackwell.

Hadland, S. E., & Baer, T. E. (2014). The racial and ethnic gap in substance use treatment: Implications for U.S. healthcare reform. *Journal of Adolescent Health, 54*(6), 627–628.

Häfner, H. (2015). What is schizophrenia? 25 years of research into schizophrenia—the Age Beginning Course Study. *World Journal of Psychiatry, 5*(2), 167–169.

Häfner, H., & an der Heiden, W. (1988). The mental health care system in transition: A study in organization, effectiveness, and costs of complementary care for schizophrenic patients. In C. N. Stefanis & A. D. Rabavilis (Eds.), *Schizophrenia: Recent biosocial developments.* New York: Human Sciences Press.

Hagerman, R. J. (2011). Fragile X syndrome and fragile X-associated disorders. In S. Goldstein & C. R. Reynolds (Eds.), *Handbook of neurodevelopmental and genetic disorders in children* (2nd ed., pp. 276–292). New York: Guilford Press.

Hagihara, A., Abe, T., Omagari, M., Motoi, M., & Nabeshima, Y. (2014). The impact of newspaper reporting of hydrogen sulfide suicide on imitative suicide attempts in Japan. *Social Psychiatry and Psychiatric Epidemiology, 49*(2), 221–229.

Hahn, L. J., Brady, N. C., Warren, S. F., & Fleming, K. K. (2015). Do children with fragile X syndrome show declines or plateaus in adaptive behavior? *American Journal on Intellectual and Developmental Disabilities, 120*(5), 412–432.

Haile, C. N. (2012). History, use, and basic pharmacology of stimulants. In T. R. Kosten, T. F. Newton, De La Garza, R. II, & Haile, C. N. (Eds.), *Cocaine and methamphetamine dependence: Advances in treatment* (pp. 13–84). Arlington, VA: American Psychiatric Publishing.

Hale, J. B., Reddy, L. A., Wilcox, G., McLaughlin, A., Hain, L., Stern, A., Henzel, J., & Eusebo, E. (2010). In D. C. Miller (Ed.), *Best practices in school neuropsychology: Guidelines for effective practice, assessment, and evidence-based intervention* (pp. 225–279). Hoboken, NJ: John Wiley & Sons.

Haliburn, J. (2005). Australian and New Zealand clinical practice guidelines for the treatment of anorexia nervosa. *Australian and New Zealand Journal of Psychiatry, 39*(7), 639–640.

Haliburn, J. (2010). Adolescent suicide and SSRI anti-depressants. *Australasian Psychiatry, 18*(6), 587.

Hall, K. (2007). Sexual dysfunction and childhood sexual abuse: Gender differences and treatment implications. In S. R. Leiblum (Ed.), *Principles and practice of sex therapy* (4th ed., pp. 350–370). New York: Guilford Press.

Hall, K. (2010). The canary in the coal mine: Reviving sexual desire in long-term relationships. In S. R. Leiblum (Ed.), *Treating sexual desire disorders: A clinical casebook* (pp. 61–74). New York: Guilford Press.

Hall, L., with Cohn, L. (1980). *Eat without fear.* Santa Barbara, CA: Gurze.

Hall, L., & Cohn, L. (2010). *Bulimia: A guide to recovery.* Carlsbad, CA: Gurze Books.

Hall-Flavin, D. K. (2011). *Nervous breakdown: What does it mean?* Rochester, MN: Mayo Foundation for Medical Education and Research.

Hallquist, M. N., Deming, A., Matthews, A., & Chaves, J. F. (2010). Hypnosis for medically unexplained symptoms and somatoform disorders. In S. J. Lynn, J. W. Rhue, & I. Kirsch (Eds.), *Handbook of clinical hypnosis* (2nd ed., pp. 615–639). Washington, DC: American Psychological Association.

Halverson, J. L., Bhalla, R. V., Andrew, L. B., Moraille-Bhalla, P., Leonard, R. C., Bi-enenfeld, D., . . . Walaszek, A. (2015). Depression: Practice essentials, background, pathophysiology, etiology, epidemiology, prognosis, patient education. *Medscape.* Retrieved from Medscape website: http://emedicine.medscape.com/article/286759-overview.

Hamilton, L. D., & Meston, C. M. (2013). Chronic stress and sexual function in women. *Journal of Sexual Medicine, 10,* 2443–2454.

Hammen, C. L., & Krantz, S. (1976). Effect of success and failure on depressive cognitions. *Journal of Abnormal Psychology, 85*(8), 577–588.

Hampel, P., Gemp, S., Mohr, B., Schulze, J., & Tlach, L. (2014). Long-term effects of a cognitive-behavioral intervention on pain coping among inpatient orthopedic rehabilitation of chronic low back pain and depressive symptoms. *Psychotherapie, Psychosomatik, Medizinische Psychologie, 64*(11), 439–447.

Hancock, J., Thom-Santelli, J., & Ritchie, T. (2004). *Deception and design: The impact of communication technology on lying behavior.* Paper presented at Computer-Human Interaction Conference in Vienna, Austria, April 2004.

Hankin, B. L., Grant, K. E., Cheeley, C., Wetter, E., Farahmand, F. K., & Wester-holm, R. I. (2008). Depressive disorders. In D. Reitman (Ed.), *Handbook of psychological assessment, case conceptualization, and treatment, Vol. 2: Children and adolescents.* Hoboken, NJ: John Wiley & Sons.

Hanna, D., Kershaw, K., & Chaplin, R. (2009). How specialist ECT consultants inform patients about memory loss. *Psychiatric Bulletin, 33*(11), 412–415.

Hansson, L., Middelboe, T., Sorgaard, K. W., Bengtsson, T. A., Bjarnason, O., Merinder, L., . . . Vinding, H. R. (2002). Living situation, subjective quality of life and social network among individuals with schizophrenia living in community settings. *Acta Psychiatrica Scandinavica, 106*(5), 343–350.

Hansson, L., Stjernswärd, S., & Svensson, B. (2014). Perceived and anticipated discrimination in people with mental illness—an interview study. *Nordic Journal of Psychiatry, 68*(2), 100–106.

Hanstede, M., Gidron, Y., & Nyklíček, I. (2008). The effects of a mindfulness intervention on obsessive-compulsive symptoms in a non-clinical student population. *The Journal of Nervous and Mental Disease, 196*(10), 776–779.

Hardin, S. B., Weinrich, S., Weinrich, M., Garrison, C., Addy, C., & Hardin, T. L. (2002). Effects of a long-term psychosocial nursing intervention on adolescents exposed to catastrophic stress. *Issues in Mental Health Nursing, 23*(6), 537–551.

Hardman, M. L., Drew, C. J., & Egan, M. W. (2002). *Human exceptionality: Society, school and family.* Boston: Allyn & Bacon.

Hare, R. D. (1993). *Without conscience: The disturbing world of the psychopaths among us.* New York: Pocket Books.

Harenski, C. L., Thornton, D. M., Harenski, K. A., Decety, J., & Kiehl, K. A. (2012). Increased frontotemporal activation during pain observation in sexual sadism: Preliminary findings. *Archives of General Psychiatry, 69*(3), 283–292.

Haris, M., Yadav, S. K., Rizwan, A., Singh, A., Cai, K., Kaura, D., . . . Borthakur, A. (2015). T1rho MRI and CSF biomarkers in diagnosis of Alzheimer's disease. *NeuroImage: Clinical, 7,* 598–604.

Harklute, A. (2010, July 26). Computer uses in clinical psychology. *eHOW.* Retrieved from eHOW website: www.ehow.com/print/list_6775537_computer-uses-clinical-psychology.html.

Harlapur, M., Abraham, D., & Shimbo, D. (2010). Cardiology. In J. M. Suls, K. W. Davidson, & R. M. Kaplan, (Eds.), *Handbook of health psychology and behavioral medicine* (pp. 411–425). New York: Guilford Press.

Haroules, B. (2007). Involuntary commitment is unconstitutional. In A. Quigley (Ed.), *Current controversies: Mental health.* Detroit: Greenhaven Press/Thomson Gale.

Harper, K. N., & Brown, A. S. (2012). Prenatal nutrition and the etiology of schizophrenia. In A. S. Brown & P. H. Patterson (Eds.), *The origins of schizophrenia* (pp. 58–95). New York: Columbia University Press.

Harrington, A. (2012). The fall of the schizophrenogenic mother. *The Lancet, 379*(9823), 1292–1293.

Harrington, B. C., Jimerson, M., Haxton, C., & Jimerson, D. C. (2015). Initial evaluation, diagnosis, and treatment of anorexia nervosa and bulimia nervosa. *American Family Physician, 91*(1), 46–52.

Harris Interactive. (2013). *Are Americans still serving up family dinners?* (Harris Poll #82). New York: Harris Interactive.

Harris International. (2011). *Large majorities support doctor assisted suicide for terminally ill patients in great pain.* (Poll No. 9, January 25, 2011). New York: Harris Interactive.

Harris International. (2013, July 16). *Less than half of Americans trust federal government with personal info.* (Poll No. 45). New York: Harris Interactive.

Harris International. (2014, February 19). *6 in 10 Americans say they or someone they know have been bullied.* (Harris Poll, No. 17)., New York: Harris Interactive.

Harris Poll. (2006, August 8). *Doctors and teachers most trusted among 22 occupations and professions: Fewer adults trust the president to tell the truth* (Harris Poll, No. 61). Retrieved from Harris Interactive website: http://www.harrisinteractive.com/harris_poll.

Harris Poll. (2008, February 8). *Three in ten Americans with a tattoo say having one makes them feel sexier* (Harris Poll, No. 15). New York: Harris Interactive.

Harris, G. (2008, January 24). F.D.A. requiring suicide studies in drug trials. *New York Times.* Retrieved from New York Times website: http://www.nytimes.com.

Harris, G. T., & Rice, M. E. (2006). Treatment of psychopathy: A review of empirical findings. In C. J. Patrick (Ed.), *Handbook of psychopathy.* New York: Guilford Press.

Harris, J. C. (2010). *Intellectual disability: A guide for families and professionals.* New York: Oxford University Press.

Harrison, E., & Petrakis, I. (2011). Naltrexone pharmacotherapy. In J. H. Lowinson & P. Ruiz (Eds.), *Substance abuse: A comprehensive textbook* (5th ed.). Philadelphia, PA: Lippincott, Williams, & Wilkins.

Hart, C., & Ksir, C. (2014). *Drugs, society, and human behavior* (15th ed.). East Windsor, NJ: McGraw-Hill Higher Education.

Hart, C., Ksir, C., & Ray, O. (2010). *Drugs, society, and human behavior.* New York: McGraw-Hill Humanities.

Hartberg, C. B., Sundet, K., Rimol, L. M., Haukvik, U. K., Lange, E. H., Nesvag, R., . . . Agartz, I. (2011). Subcortical brain volumes relate to neurocognition in schizophrenia and bipolar disorder and healthy controls. *Progress in Neuro-Psychopharmacology & Biological Psychiatry, 35*(4), 1122–1130.

Hartford, D., & Marcus, L. M. (2011). Educational approaches. In E. Hollander, A. Kolevzon & J. T. Coyle (Eds.), *Textbook of autism spectrum disorders.* (pp. 537–553). Arlington, VA: American Psychiatric Publishing, Inc.

Hartmann, A. S., Thomas, J. J., Greenberg, J. L., Matheny, N. L., & Wilhelm, S. (2014). A comparison of self-esteem and perfectionism in anorexia nervosa and body dysmorphic disorder. *The Journal of Nervous and Mental Disease, 202*(12), 883–888.

Hartmann, U., & Waldinger, M. D. (2007). Treatment of delayed ejaculation. In S. R. Leiblum (Ed.), *Principles and practice of sex therapy* (4th ed., pp. 241–276). New York: Guilford Press.

Hartney, E. (2014). *Addictions: Can marijuana cause infertility?* Retrieved from About.com website: http://addictions.about.com/od/legalissues/f/Can-Marijuana-Cause-Infertility.htm.

Harvey, P. D. (2014). Disability in schizophrenia: Contributing factors and validated assessments. *Journal of Clinical Psychiatry, 75*(Suppl. 1), 15–20.

Hashimoto, K. (2014). Targeting of NMDA receptors in new treatments for schizophrenia. *Expert Opinion on Therapeutic Targets, 18*(9), 1049–1063.

Hastings, R. P. (2008). Stress in parents of children with autism. In E. McGregor, M. Núñez, K. Cebula, & J. C. Gómez (Eds.), *Autism: An integrated view from neurocognitive, clinical, and intervention research.* Malden, MA: Blackwell Publishing.

Hawken, E. R., & Beninger, R. J. (2014). The amphetamine sensitization model of schizophrenia symptoms and its effect on schedule-induced polydipsia in the rat. *Psychopharmacology, 231*(9), 2001–2008.

Hawkins, J. R. (2004). The role of emotional repression in chronic back pain: A study of chronic back pain patients undergoing psychodynamically oriented group psychotherapy as treatment for their pain. *Dissertation Abstracts International: Section B: The Sciences and Engineering, 64*(8-B), 4038.

Hawks, E., Blumenthal, H., Feldner, M. T., Leen-Feldner, E. W., & Jones, R. (2011). An examination of the relation between traumatic event exposure and panic-relevant biological challenge responding among adolescents. *Behavior Therapy, 42*(3), 427–438.

Hayaki, J., Friedman, M. A., & Brownell, K. D. (2002). Shame and severity of bulimic symptoms. *Eating Behaviors, 3*(1), 73–83.

Hayden, L. A. (1998). Gender discrimination within the reproductive health care system: Viagra v. birth control. *Journal of Law and Health, 13,* 171–198.

Hayes, S. C., & Lillis, J. (2012). *Acceptance and commitment therapy: Theories of psychotherapy series.* Washington, DC: American Psychological Association.

Hayes, S. C., Levin, M. E., Plumb-Vilardaga, J., Villatte, J. L., & Pistorello, J. (2013). Acceptance and commitment therapy and contextual behavioral science: Examining the progress of a distinctive model of behavioral and cognitive therapy. *Behavior Therapy, 44*(2), 180–198.

Hayes, S. C., Luoma, J. B., Bond, F. W., Masuda, A., & Lillis, J. (2006). Acceptance and commitment therapy: Model, processes and outcomes. *Behavioral Research and Therapy, 44*, 1–25.

Hayes-Skelton, S. A., Roemer, L., Orsillo, S. M., & Borkovec, T. D. (2013). A contemporary view of applied relaxation for generalized anxiety disorder. *Cognitive Behaviour Therapy, 42*(4), 292–302.

Haynes, S. G., Feinleib, M., & Kannel, W. B. (1980). The relationship of psychosocial factors to coronary heart disease in the Framingham study: III. Eight-year incidence of coronary heart disease. *American Journal of Epidemiology, 111*, 37–58.

Hazlett, E. A., Rothstein, E. G., Ferreira, R., Silverman, J. M., Siever, L. J., & Olincy, A. (2015). Sensory gating disturbances in the spectrum: Similarities and differences in schizotypal personality disorder and schizophrenia. *Schizophrenia Research, 161*(2-3), 283–290.

HBIGDA (Harry Benjamin International Gender Dysphoria Association). (2001). The standards of care for gender identity disorders (6th version). *International Journal of Transgenderism, 5*(1).

He, Y., Lu, X., Wu, H., Cai, W., Yang, L., Xu, L., . . . Kong, Q. (2014). Mitochondrial DNA content contributes to healthy aging in Chinese: A study from nonagenarians and centenarians. *Neurobiology of Aging, 35*(7), 1779.e1–4.

Head, M. W. (2013). Human prion diseases: Molecular, cellular and population biology. *Neuropathology, 33*(3), 221–236.

Healey, J., Lussier, P., & Beauregard, E. (2013). Sexual sadism in the context of rape and sexual homicide: An examination of crime scene indicators. *International Journal of Offender Therapy and Comparative Criminology, 57*(4), 402–424.

Hedaya, R. J. (2011). Health matters: Connecting you to the sources of health. Panic disorders: Part 2. *Psychology Today*. Retrieved from Psychology Today website: http://www.psychologytoday.com/blog/health-matters/201102.

Heeramun-Aubeeluck, A., & Lu, Z. (2013). Neurosurgery for mental disorders: A review. *African Journal of Psychiatry, 16*(3), 177–181.

Heffron, T. M. (2014). *Insomnia Awareness Day facts and stats.* Retrieved from Sleep Education website: http://www.sleepeducation.com/news/2014/03/10/insomnia-awareness-day.

Hegerl, U., Schönknecht, P., & Mergl, R. (2012). "Are antidepressants useful in the treatment of minor depression: A critical update of the current literature": Erratum. *Current Opinion in Psychiatry, 25*(2), 163.

Heilbrun, K., Goldstein, N. E. S., & Redding, R. E. (Eds.). (2005). *Juvenile delinquency: Prevention, assessment, and intervention* (pp. 85–110). New York: Oxford University Press.

Heiman, J. R. (2002). Sexual dysfunction: Overview of prevalence, etiological factors, and treatments. *Journal of Sex Research, 39*(1), 73–78.

Heiman, J. R. (2007). Orgasmic disorders in women. In S. R. Leiblum (Ed.), *Principles and practice of sex therapy* (4th ed., pp. 84–123). New York: Guilford Press.

Heiman, J. R., Gladue, B. A., Roberts, C. W., & LoPiccolo, J. (1986). Historical and current factors discriminating sexually functional from sexually dysfunctional married couples. *Journal of Marital & Family Therapy, 12*(2), 163–174.

Heimberg, R. G., Brozovich, F. A., & Rapee, R. M. (2010). A cognitive-behavioral model of social anxiety disorder: Update and extension. In S. G. Hofmann & P. M. DiBartolo (Eds.), *Social anxiety: Clinical, developmental, and social perspectives.* New York: Academic Press.

Heimberg, R. G., Hofmann, S. G., Liebowitz, M. R., Schneier, F. R., Smits, J. J., Stein, M. B., . . . Craske, M. G. (2014). Social anxiety disorder in DSM-5. *Depression & Anxiety, 31*(6), 472–479.

Heimberg, R. G., & Magee, L. (2014). Social anxiety disorder. In D. H. Barlow (Ed.), *Clinical handbook of psychological disorders: A step-by-step treatment manual* (5th ed., pp. 114–154). New York: Guilford Press.

Heine, C., & Browning, C. J. (2014). Mental health and dual sensory loss in older adults: A systematic review. *Frontiers in Aging Neuroscience, 6*, 83.

Heir, T., Piatigorsky, A., & Weisaeth, L. (2010). Posttraumatic stress symptom clusters associations with psychopathology and functional impairment. *Journal of Anxiety Disorders, 24*(8), 936–940.

Hektner, J. M., August, G. J., Bloomquist, M. L., Lee, S., & Klimes-Dougan, B. (2014). A 10-year randomized controlled trial of the Early Risers conduct problems preventive intervention: Effects on externalizing and internalizing in late high school. *Journal of Consulting and Clinical Psychology, 82*(2), 355–360.

Hembree, E. A., & Foa, E. B. (2010). Cognitive behavioral treatments for PTSD. In G. M. Rosen & B. C. Frueh (Eds.), *Clinician's guide to posttraumatic stress disorder* (pp. 177–203). Hoboken, NJ: John Wiley & Sons.

Hembree-Kigin, T. L., & McNeil, C. B. (2013). *Parent-Child interaction therapy (Clinical Child Psychology Library).* New York: Springer Science + Business Media.

Hemmings, C. (2010). Service use and outcomes. In N. Bouras (Ed.), *Mental health services for adults with intellectual disability: Strategies and solutions. The Maudsley Series* (pp. 75–88). New York: Psychology Press.

Henderson, K., Buchholz, A., Obeid, N., Mossiere, A., Maras, D., Norris, M., . . . Spettigue, W. (2014). A family-based eating disorder day treatment program for youth: Examining the clinical and statistical significance of short-term treatment outcomes. *Eating Disorders, 22*(1), 1–18.

Henderson, V. (2010). Diminishing dissociative experiences for war veterans in group therapy. In S. S. Fehr (Ed.), *101 interventions in group therapy* (rev. ed., pp. 217–220). New York: Routledge/Taylor & Francis Group.

Hengartner, M., Müller, M., Rodgers, S., Rössler, W., & Ajdacic-Gross, V. (2014). Occupational functioning and work impairment in association with personality disorder trait-scores. *Social Psychiatry and Psychiatric Epidemiology, 49*(2), 327–335.

Henggeler, S. W., & Sheidow, A. J. (2012). Empirically supported family-based treatments for conduct disorder and delinquency in adolescents. *Journal of Marital & Family Therapy, 38*(1), 30–58.

Henn, F. (2013). Using brain imaging to understand the response to cognitive therapy in panic disorder. *American Journal of Psychiatry, 170*, 1235–1236.

Herbenick, D., Reece, M., Schick, V., Sanders, S. A., Dodge, B., & Fortenberry, J. D. (2010). Sexual behavior in the United States: Results from a national probability sample of men and women ages 14–94. *Journal of Sexual Medicine, 7*(5), 255–265.

Herbenick, D., Schick, V., Reece, M., Sanders, S. A., Smith, N., Dodge, B., & Fortenberry, J. D. (2013). Characteristics of condom and lubricant use among a nationally representative probability sample of adults ages 18–59 in the United States. *Journal of Sexual Medicine, 10*, 474–483.

Herbert, J. D. (2007). Avoidant personality disorder. In W. O'Donohue, K. A. Fowler, & S. O. Lilienfeld (Eds.), *Personality disorders: Toward the DSM-V.* Los Angeles: Sage Publications.

Herbert, J. D., Gaudiano, B. A., Rheingold, A., Harwell, V., Dalrymple, K., & Nolan, E. M. (2005). Social skills training augments the effectiveness of cognitive behavior group therapy for social anxiety disorder. *Behavior Therapy, 36*, 125–138.

Herman, N. J. (1999). Road rage: An exploratory analysis. *Michigan Sociological Review, 13*, 65–79.

Hermes, E. A., Hoff, R., & Rosenheck, R. A. (2014). Sources of the increasing number of Vietnam era veterans with a diagnosis of PTSD using VHA services. *Psychiatric Services, 65*(6), 830–832.

Hernandez, P. (2014, June 24). Jail diversion for mental health inmates. *Houston Public Media,* Houston, TX. Retrieved from Houston Public Media website: http://www.houstonpublicmedia.org/news.

Herne, M. A., Bartholomew, M. L., & Weahkee, R. L. (2014). Suicide mortality among American Indians and Alaska natives, 1999–2009. *American Journal of Public Health, (S3)*, S336–S342.

Herning, R. I., Better, W. E., Tate, K., & Cadet, J. L. (2005). Cerebrovascular perfusion in marijuana users during a month of monitored abstinence. *Neurology, 64*, 488–493.

Herpertz, S. C., & Bertsch, K. (2014). The social-cognitive basis of personality disorders. *Current Opinion in Psychiatry, 27*(1), 73–77.

Herrick, A. L., Marshal, M. P., Smith, H. A., Sucato, G., & Stall, R. D. (2011). Sex while intoxicated: A meta-analysis comparing heterosexual and sexual minority youth. *Journal of Adolescent Health, 48*(4), 306–309.

Hertz, M. F., & Donato, I. (2013). Bullying and suicide: A public health approach. *Journal of Adolescent Health, 53*, S1-S3.

Herzig, H. (2004). *Medical information.* Somerset, England: Somerset and Wessex Eating Disorders Association.

Herzog, T., Zeeck, A., Hartmann, A., & Nickel, T. (2004). Lower targets for weekly weight gain lead to better results in inpatient treatment of anorexia nervosa: A pilot study. *European Eating Disorders Review, 12*(3), 164–168.

Hess, A. (2009 June 16). *Huffington Post:* Sometimes a cigar is just a nipple is just sexist. *Washington City Paper.*

Heston, L. L. (1992). *Mending minds: A guide to the new psychiatry of depression, anxiety, and other serious mental disorders.* New York: W. H. Freeman.

Heylens, G., De Cuyper, G., Zucker, J. J., Schelfaut, C., Elaut, E., Vanden Bossche, H., . . . T'Sjoen, G. (2012). Gender identity disorder in twins: A review of the case report literature. *Journal of Sexual Medicine, 9*(3), 751–757.

Hickey, E. W. (2015). *Serial murderers and their victims* (7th ed.). Belmont, CA: Wadsworth.

Hickling, E. J., & Blanchard, E. B. (2007). Motor vehicle accidents and psychological trauma. In E. K. Carll (Ed.), *Trauma psychology: Issues in violence, disaster, health, and illness* (Vol. 2). Westport, CT: Praeger Publishers.

Hicks, B. M., Iacono, W. G., & McGue, M. (2014). Identifying childhood characteristics that underlie premorbid risk for substance use disorders: Socialization and boldness. *Development and Psychopathology, 26*(1), 141–157.

Hicks, K. (2014). A biocultural perspective on fictive kinship in the Andes: Social support and women's immune function in El Alto, Bolivia. *Medical Anthropology Quarterly, 28*(3), 440–445.

Higgins, E. S., & George, M. S. (2007). *The neuroscience of clinical psychiatry: The pathophysiology of behavior and mental illness.* Philadelphia: Wolters Kluwer/Lippincott Williams & Wilkins.

Higgins, S. T., Budney, A. J., Bickel, W. K., Hughes, J., Foerg, F., & Badger, G. (1993). Achieving cocaine abstinence with a behavioral approach. *American Journal of Psychiatry, 150*(5), 763–769.

Higgins, S. T., Sigmon, S. C., & Hiel, S. H. (2014). Drug use disorders. In D. H. Barlow, *Clinical handbook of psychological disorders* (5th ed., Ch. 14). New York: Guilford Press.

Higgins, S. T., Silverman, K., & Washio, Y. (2011). Contingency management. In M. Galanter & H. D. Kleber (Eds.), *Psychotherapy for the treatment of substance abuse* (pp. 192–218). Arlington, VA: American Psychiatric Publishing.

Hilbert, A., Hartmann, A. S., Czaja, J., & Schoebi, D. (2013). Natural course of preadolescent loss of control eating. *Journal of Abnormal Psychology, 122*(3), 684–693.

Hildebrandt, T., & Alfano, L. (2009). A review of eating disorders in males: Working towards an improved diagnostic system. *International Journal of Child and Adolescent Health, 2*(2), 185–196.

Hillemeier, M. M., Foster, E. M., Heinrichs, B., & Heier, B. (2007). Racial differences in parental reports of attention-deficit/hyperactivity disorder behaviors. *Journal of Developmental & Behavioral Pediatrics, 28*(5), 353–361.

Hinduja, S., & Patchin, J. W. (2010). Bullying, cyberbullying, and suicide. *Archives of Suicide Research, 14*(3), 206–221.

Hinrichsen, G. A. (1999). Interpersonal psychotherapy for late-life depression. In M. Duffy (Ed.), *Handbook of counseling and psychotherapy with older adults.* New York: Wiley.

Hinton, D. E., & Lewis-Fernández, R. (2011). The cross-cultural validity of posttraumatic stress disorder: Implications for DSM-5. *Depression & Anxiety, 28*(9), 783–801.

Hirsch, C. R., Hayes, S., Mathews, A., Perman, G., & Borkovec, T. (2012). The extent and nature of imagery during worry and positive thinking in generalized anxiety disorder. *Journal of Abnormal Psychology, 121*(1), 238–243.

Hobbs, F. B. (1997). *The elderly population. U.S. Census Bureau: The official statistics.* Washington, DC: U.S. Census Bureau.

Hodges, S. (2003). Borderline personality disorder and posttraumatic stress disorder: Time for integration? *Journal of Counseling & Development, 81*(4), 409–417.

Hodgson, R. J., & Rachman, S. (1972). The effects of contamination and washing in obsessional patients. *Behavioral Research and Therapy, 10*, 111–117.

Hofer, H., Frigerio, S., Frischknecht, E., Gassmann, D., Gutbrod, K., & Müri, R. M. (2013). Diagnosis and treatment of an obsessive-compulsive disorder following traumatic brain injury: A single case and review of the literature. *Neurocase, 19*(4), 390–400.

Hoff, P. (2015). The Kraepelinian tradition. *Dialogues in Clinical Neuroscience, 17*(1), 31–41.

Hoffman, J. (2011, Sept. 25). When your therapist is only a click away. *New York Times,* 160.

Hoffman, R. E., Grasemann, U., Gueorguieva, R., Quinlan, D., Lane, D., & Miikkulainen, R. (2011). Using computational patients to evaluate illness mechanisms in schizophrenia. *Biological Psychiatry, 69*(10), 997–1005.

Hofmann, S. G., & Barlow, D. H. (2014). Evidence-based psychological interventions and the common factors approach: The beginnings of a rapprochement? *Psychotherapy* (Chicago), *51*(4), 510–513.

Hogan, R. A. (1968). The implosive technique. *Behavioral Research and Therapy, 6*, 423–431.

Hogan, T. P. (2014). *Psychological testing: A practical introduction* (3rd ed.). Hoboken, NJ: Wiley.

Hogarty, G. E. (2002). *Personal therapy for schizophrenia and related disorders: A guide to individualized treatment.* New York: Guilford Press.

Hoge, C. W., Grossman, S. H., Auchterlonie, J. L., Riviere, L. A., Milliken, C. S., & Wilk, J. E. (2014). PTSD treatment for soldiers after combat deployment: Low utilization of mental health care and reasons for dropout. *Psychiatric Services, 65*(8), 997–1004.

Hoge, E. A., Bui, E., Marques, L., Metcalf, C. A., Morris, L. K., Robinaugh, D. J., . . . Simon, N. M. (2013). Randomized controlled trial of mindfulness meditation for generalized anxiety disorder: Effects on anxiety and stress reactivity. *The Journal of Clinical Psychiatry, 74*(8), 786–792.

Hogebrug, J., Koopmans, P. P., van Oostrom, I., & Schellekens, A. (2013). [Neurosyphilis, the great imitator: A diagnostic challenge]. *Nederlands Tijdschrift Voor Geneeskunde, 157*(30), A6033.

Holden, R. R., & Bernstein, I. H. (2013). Internal consistency: Reports of its death are premature. *Behavior Research Methods, 45*(4), 946–949.

Holinger, P. C., & Offer, D. (1982). Prediction of adolescent suicide: A population model. *American Journal of Psychiatry, 139,* 302–307.

Holinger, P. C., & Offer, D. (1991). Sociodemographic, epidemiologic, and individual attributes. In L. Davidson & M. Linnoila (Eds.), *Risk factors for youth suicide.* New York: Hemisphere.

Holinger, P. C., & Offer, D. (1993). *Adolescent suicide.* New York: Guilford Press.

Hollingworth, P., Harold, D., Jones, L., Owen, M. J., & Williams, J. (2011). Alzheimer's disease genetics: Current knowledge and future challenges. *International Journal of Geriatric Psychiatry, 26*(8), 793–802.

Hollon, S. D., & Cuijpers, P. (2013). Reviewing psychological treatments for adult depression. *Canadian Journal of Psychiatry, 58*(7), 373–375.

Hollon, S. D., & Ponniah, K. (2010). A review of empirically supported psychological therapies for mood disorders in adults. *Depression & Anxiety, 27*(10), 891–932.

Holm-Denoma, J. M., Hankin, B. L., & Young, J. F. (2014). Developmental trends of eating disorder symptoms and comorbid internalizing symptoms in children and adolescents. *Eating Behaviors, 15*(2), 275–279.

Holmes, L. (2014, July 14). Sadness is not depression. *About.com.*

Holmes, T. H., & Rahe, R. H. (1967). The Social Readjustment Rating Scale. *Journal of Psychosomatic Research, 11,* 213–218.

Holmes, T. H., & Rahe, R. H. (1989). The Social Readjustment Rating Scale. In T. H. Holmes & E. M. David (Eds.), *Life change, life events, and illness: Selected papers.* New York: Praeger.

Holowka, D. W., Marx, B. P., Gates, M. A., Litman, H. J., Ranganathan, G., Rosen, R. C., & Keane, T. M. (2014). PTSD diagnostic validity in Veterans Affairs electronic records of Iraq and Afghanistan veterans. *Journal of Consulting and Clinical Psychology, 82*(4), 569–579.

Holt, R., Beutler, L. E., Kimpara, S., Macias, S., Haug, N. A., Shiloff, N., . . . Stein, M. (2015). Evidence-based supervision: Tracking outcome and teaching principles of change in clinical supervision to bring science to integrative practice. *Psychotherapy* (Chicago, Ill.), *52*(2), 185–189.

Holtom-Viesel, A., & Allan, S. (2014). A systematic review of the literature on family functioning across all eating disorder diagnoses in comparison to control families. *Clinical Psychology Review, 34*(1), 29–43.

Hölzel, L., Härter, M., Reese, C., & Kriston, L. (2011). Risk factors for chronic depression—A systematic review. *Journal of Affective Disorders, 129*(1-3), 1–13.

Homant, R. J., & Kennedy, D. B. (2006). Serial murder: A biopsychosocial approach. In W. Petherick (Ed.), *Serial crime: Theoretical and practical issues in behavioral profiling* (pp. 189–228). San Diego, CA: Elsevier.

Hong, J. S., Kral, M. J., & Sterzing, P. R. (2015). Pathways from bullying perpetration, victimization, and bully victimization to suicidality among school-aged youth: A review of the potential mediators and a call for further investigation. *Trauma, Violence & Abuse, 16*(4), 379–390.

Hope, L. (2010). Eyewitness testimony. In G. J. Towl & D. A. Crighton (Eds.), *Forensic psychology* (pp. 160–177). Hoboken, NJ: Wiley-Blackwell.

Hopfer, C. (2011). Club drug, prescription drug, and over-the-counter medication abuse: Description, diagnosis, and intervention. In Y. Kaminer & K. C. Winters (Eds), *Clinical manual of adolescent substance abuse treatment* (pp. 187–212). Arlington, VA: American Psychiatric Publishing.

Hopko, D. R., Robertson, S. M. C., Widman, L., & Lejuez, C. W. (2008). Specific phobias. In M. Hersen & J. Rosqvist (Eds.), *Handbook of psychological assessment, case conceptualization, and treatment, Vol. 1: Adults* (pp. 139–170). Hoboken, NJ: John Wiley & Sons.

Horney, K. (1937). *The neurotic personality of our time.* New York: Norton.

Horowitz, J. A., Damato, E. G., Duffy, M. E., & Solon, L. (2005). The relationship of maternal attributes, resources, and perceptions of postpartum experiences to depression. *Research in Nursing & Health, 28*(2), 159–171.

Horowitz, J. A., Damato, E., Solon, L., Metzsch, G., & Gill, V. (1995). Postpartum depression: Issues in clinical assessment. *Journal of Perinatal Medicine, 15*(4), 268–278.

Horowitz, M. J., & Lerner, U. (2010). Treatment of histrionic personality disorder. In J. F. Clarkin, P. Fonagy, & G. O. Gabbard (Eds.), *Psychodynamic psychotherapy for personality disorders: A clinical handbook* (pp. 289–310). Arlington, VA: American Psychiatric Publishing.

Horton, M. A. (2008). *The incidence and prevalence of SRS among US residents.* Out & Equal Workplace Summit, San Francisco, CA September 2008. Retrieved from http://www.gender.net/taw/thbcost.html:prevalence.

Horwitz, A. G., Czyz, E. K., & King, C. A. (2014). Predicting future suicide attempts among adolescent and emerging adult psychiatric emergency patients. *Journal of Clinical Child & Adolescent Psychology, 53,* 1–11.

Horwitz, A. V., & Wakefield, J. C. (2007, December 9). Sadness is not a disorder. *The Philadelphia Inquirer,* pp. C1, C5.

Horwitz, A. V., & Wakefield, J. C. (2012). *The loss of sadness: How psychiatry transforms normal sorrow into depressive disorder.* New York: Oxford University Press.

Horwitz, S. (2014, March 9). The hard lives—and high suicide rate—of Native American children on reservations. *The Washington Post.*

Hoste, R. R., Lebow, J., & Le Grange, D. (2014). A bidirectional examination of expressed emotion among families of adolescents with bulimia nervosa. *International Journal of Eating Disorders.* [Electronic publication.]

Hou, Y., Hu, P., Zhang, Y., Lu, Q., Wang, D., Yin, L., . . . Zou, X. (2014). Cognitive behavioral therapy in combination with systemic family therapy improves mild to moderate postpartum depression. *Revista Brasileira De Psiquiatria* (São Paulo, Brazil: 1999), *36*(1), 47–52.

Houghton, D. (2013, August 12). Cited in T. Miller, Too many selfies on Facebook can damage relationships: Study. *New York Daily News.*

Houle, J. N., & Light, M. T. (2014). The home foreclosure crisis and rising suicide rates, 2005 to 2010. *American Journal of Public Health, 104*(6), 1073–1079.

Houston, K. A., Clifford, B. R., Phillips, L. H., & Memon, A. (2013). The emotional eyewitness: The effects of emotion on specific aspects of eyewitness recall and recognition performance. *Emotion, 13*(1), 118–128.

Howell, E. F. (2011). *Understanding and treating dissociative identity disorder: A rational approach.* New York: Routledge/Taylor & Francis Group.

Howes, O. D., & Murray, R. M. (2014). Schizophrenia: An integrated sociodevelopmental-cognitive model. *Lancet, 383*(9929), 1677–1687.

Howland, J., Rohsenow, D. J., Greece, J. A., Littlefield, C. A., Almeida, A., Heeren, T., . . . Hermos, J. (2010). The effects of binge drinking on college students' next-day academic test-taking performance and mood state. *Addiction, 105*(4), 655–665.

Howland, R. H. (2012). Dietary supplement drug therapies for depression. *Journal of Psychosocial Nursing and Mental Health Services, 50*(6), 13–16.

Howland, R. H. (2014). Vagus nerve stimulation. *Current Behavioral Neuroscience Reports, 1*(2), 64–73.

Howlin, P. (2012). Understanding savant skills in autism. *Developmental Medicine & Child Neurology, 54*(6), 484.

Hoyer, M., & Heath, B. (2012, December 19). A mass killing in U.S. occurs every 2 weeks. *USA Today.*

Hoza, B., Kaiser, N., & Hurt, E. (2008). Evidence-based treatments for attention-deficit/hyperactivity disorder (ADHD). In R. G. Steele, T. D. Elkin, & M. C. Roberts (Eds.), *Handbook of evidence-based therapies for children and adolescents: Bridging science and practice.* New York: Springer.

Hróbjartsson, A., Thomsen, A. S., Emanuelsson, F., Tendal, B., Rasmussen, J. V., Hilden, J., . . . Brorson, S. (2014). Observer bias in randomized clinical trials with time-to-event outcomes: Systematic review of trials with both blinded and non-blinded outcome assessors. *International Journal of Epidemiology, 43*(3), 937–948.

Hsiao, C., & Tsai, Y. (2014). Caregiver burden and satisfaction in families of individuals with schizophrenia. *Nursing Research, 63*(4), 260–269.

Hsu, J., Lee, W., Liao, Y., Lirng, J., Wang, S., & Fuh, J. (2015). Posterior atrophy and medial temporal atrophy scores are associated with different symptoms in patients with Alzheimer's disease and mild cognitive impairment. *PLOS ONE, 10*(9), e0137121.

Hsu, J., Lirng, J., Wang, S., Lin, C., Yang, K., Liao, M., & Chou, Y. (2014). Association of thalamic serotonin transporter and interleukin-10 in bipolar I disorder: A SPECT study. *Bipolar Disorders, 16*(3), 241–248.

Hsu, M. C., Schubiner, H., Lumley, M. A., Stracks, J. S., Clauw, D. J., & Williams, D. A. (2010). Sustained pain reduction through affective self-awareness in fibromyalgia: A randomized controlled trial. *Journal of General Internal Medicine, 25*(10), 1064–1070.

Hsu, W., Lin, S. J., Chang, S., Tseng, Y., & Chiu, N. (2014). Examining the diagnostic criteria for Internet addiction: Expert validation. *Journal of the Formosan Medical Association, Taiwan Yi Zhi.*

Hu, W., Zhou, P., Zhang, X., Xu, C., & Wang, W. (2015). Plasma concentrations of adrenomedullin and natriuretic peptides in patients with essential hypertension. *Experimental and Therapeutic Medicine, 9*(5), 1901–1908.

Huang, C., Cheng, M., Tsai, H., Lai, C., & Chen, C. (2014). Genetic analysis of GABRB3 at 15q12 as a candidate gene of schizophrenia. *Psychiatric Genetics, 24*(4), 151–157.

Huang, J-J., Yang, Y-P., & Wu, J. (2010). Relationships of borderline personality disorder and childhood trauma. *Chinese Journal of Clinical Psychology, 18*(6), 769–771.

Hucker, A., & McCabe, M. P. (2014). A qualitative evaluation of online chat groups for women completing a psychological intervention for female sexual dysfunction. *Journal of Sex & Marital Therapy, 40*(1), 58-68.

Hucker, A., & McCabe, M. P. (2015). Incorporating mindfulness and chat groups into an online cognitive behavioral therapy for mixed female sexual problems. *Journal of Sex Research, 52*(6), 627–639.

Hucker, S. J. (2008). Sexual masochism: Psychopathology and theory. In D. R. Laws & W. T. O'Donohue (Eds.), *Sexual deviance: Theory, assessment, and treatment* (2nd ed., pp. 250–263). New York: Guilford Press.

Hucker, S. J. (2011). Hypoxyphilia. *Archives of Sexual Behavior, 40*(6), 1323–1326.

Hudd, S., Dumlao, J., Erdmann-Sager, D., Murray, D., Phan, E., Soukas, N., & Yokozuka, N. (2000). Stress at college: Effects on health habits, health status and self-esteem. *College Student Journal, 34*(2), 217–227.

Hudson, J. L., & Rapee, R. M. (2004). From anxious temperament to disorder: An etiological model of generalized anxiety disorder. In R. G. Heimberg, C. L. Turk, & D. S. Mennin (Eds.), *Generalized anxiety disorder: Advances in research and practice* (pp. 51–74). New York: Guilford Press.

Hugdahl, K. (1995). *Psychophysiology: The mind-body perspective.* Cambridge, MA: Harvard University Press.

Hughes, K., Bullock, A., & Coplan, R. J. (2014). A person-centred analysis of teacher-child relationships in early childhood. *British Journal of Educational Psychology, 84*(Pt 2), 253–267.

Hughes, S. (2011). Untangling Alzheimer's. *The Pennsylvania Gazette, 109*(4), 30–41.

Huh, J., Le, T., Reeder, B., Thompson, H. J., & Demiris, G. (2013). Perspectives on wellness self-monitoring tools for older adults. *International Journal of Medical Informatics, 82*(11), 1092–1103.

Huijding, J., Borg, C., Weijmar-Schultz, W., & de Jong, P. J. (2011). Automatic affective appraisal of sexual penetration stimuli in women with vaginismus or dyspareunia. *Journal of Sexual Medicine, 8*(3), 806–813.

Humphrey, J. A. (2006). *Deviant behavior.* Upper Saddle River, NJ: Pearson/Prentice Hall.

Humphreys, K. L., Gleason, M. M., Drury, S. S., Miron, D., Nelson, C. E., Fox, N. A., & Zeanah, C. H. (2015). Effects of institutional rearing and foster care on psychopathology at age 12 years in Romania: Follow-up of an open, randomised controlled trial. *The Lancet Psychiatry, 2*(7), 625–634.

Humphry, D., & Wickett, A. (1986). *The right to die: Understanding euthanasia.* New York: Harper & Row.

Hunsley, J., & Lee, C. M. (2014). *Introduction to clinical psychology: An evidence-based approach* (2nd ed.). Hoboken, NJ: Wiley-Blackwell.

Hunt, C., & Andrews, G. (1995). Comorbidity in the anxiety disorders: The use of a life-chart approach. *Journal of Psychiatric Research, 29*(6), 467–480.

Hurd, N. M., Varner, F. A., Caldwell, C. H., & Zimmerman, M. A. (2014). Does perceived racial discrimination predict changes in psychological distress and substance use over time? An examination among Black emerging adults. *Developmental Psychology, 50*(7), 1910–1918.

Hurlbert, D. F. (1991). The role of assertiveness in female sexuality: A comparative study between sexually assertive and sexually nonassertive women. *Journal of Sex & Marital Therapy, 17*(3), 183–190.

Hurlbert, D. F. (1993). A comparative study using orgasm consistency training in the treatment of women reporting hypoactive sexual desire. *Journal of Sex & Marital Therapy, 19,* 41–55.

Hurst, C. S., Baranik, L. E., & Daniel, F. (2012). College student stressors: A review of the qualitative research. *Stress and Heart, 29,* 275–285.

Hyde, J. S. (1990). *Understanding human sexuality* (4th ed.). New York: McGraw-Hill.

Hyde, J. S. (2005). The genetics of sexual orientation. In J. S. Hyde (Ed.), *Biological substrates of human sexuality.* Washington, DC: American Psychological Association.

Iacovino, J. M., Jackson, J. J., & Oltmanns, T. F. (2014). The relative impact of socioeconomic status and childhood trauma on Black-White differences in paranoid personality disorder symptoms. *Journal of Abnormal Psychology, 123*(1), 225–230.

Iadarola, S., Hetherington, S., Clinton, C., Dean, M., Reisinger, E., Huynh, L., & Kasari, C. (2015). Services for children with autism spectrum disorder in three, large urban school districts: Perspectives of parents and educators. *Autism; The International Journal of Research and Practice, 19*(6), 694–703.

Iglesias, E. B., Fernández del Río, E., Calafat, A., & Fernández-Hermida, J. R. (2014). Attachment and substance use in adolescence: A review of conceptual and methodological aspects. *Adicciones, 26*(1), 77–86.

Igwe, M. N. (2013). Dissociative fugue symptoms in a 28-year-old male Nigerian medical student: A case report. *Journal of Medical Case Reports, 7,* 143.

Ihle, W., Jahnke, D., Heerwagen, A., & Neuperdt, C. (2005). Depression, anxiety, and eating disorders and recalled parental rearing behavior. *Kindheit Entwicklung, 14*(1), 30–38.

Ilahan, D. P., Kauffman, J. M., & Pullen, P. C. (2014). *Exceptional learners: An introduction to Special Education Access Card Package 13th.* New York: Pearson Education.

Ingram, R. E., Nelson, T., Steidtmann, D. K., & Bistricky, S. L. (2007). Comparative data on child and adolescent cognitive measures associated with depression. *Journal of Consulting and Clinical Psychology, 75*(3), 390–403.

Inman, A. G., & DeBoer Kreider, E. (2013). Multicultural competence: Psychotherapy practice and supervision. *Psychotherapy, 50*(3), 346–350.

Inouye, S. K. (2006). Delirium in older persons. *New England Journal of Medicine, 354*(11), 1157–1165.

Inouye, S. K., Bogardus, S. T., Jr., Williams, C. S., Leo-Summers, L., & Agostini, J. V. (2003). The role of adherence on the effectiveness of nonpharmacologic interventions: Evidence from the delirium prevention trial. *Archives of Internal Medicine, 163,* 958–964.

Insel, T. R., & Lieberman, J. A. (2013). *DSM-5 and RDoC: Shared interests.* Retrieved from http://www.nimh.nih.gov/news/science-news/2013.

Isacsson, G., & Adler, M. (2012). Randomized clinical trials underestimate the efficacy of antidepressants in less severe depression. *Acta Psychiatrica Scandinavica, 125*(6), 453–459.

Isacsson, G., Reutfors, J., Papadopoulos, F. C., Ösby, U., & Ahlner, J. (2010). Antidepressant medication prevents suicide in depression. *Acta Psychiatrica Scandinavica, 122*(6), 454–460.

Isacsson, G., & Rich, C. L. (2014). Antidepressant drugs and the risk of suicide in children and adolescents. *Pediatric Drugs, 16*(2), 115–122.

Isasi, C. R., Ostrovsky, N. W., & Wills, T. A. (2013). The association of emotion regulation with lifestyle behaviors in inner-city adolescents. *Eating Behaviors, 14*(4), 518–521.

Ishii, M., & Iadecola, C. (2015). Metabolic and non-cognitive manifestations of Alzheimer's disease: The hypothalamus as both culprit and target of pathology. *Cell Metabolism.* [Electronic publication.]

Islam, M. M., Conigrave, K. M., Day, C. A., Nguyen, Y., & Haber, P. S. (2014). Twenty-year trends in benzodiazepine dispensing in the Australian population. *Internal Medicine Journal, 44*(1), 57–64.

Isolan, L., Salum, G. A., Osowski, A. T, Zottis, G. H., & Manfro, G. G. (2013). Victims and bully-victims but not bullies are groups associated with anxiety symptomatology among Brazilian children and adolescents. *European Child & Adolescent Psychiatry, 22*(10), 641–648.

Isomaa, R., and Isomaa, A.-L. (2014). And then what happened? A 5-year follow-up of eating disorder patients. *Nordic Journal of Psychiatry, 68*(8), 567–572.

Ito, Y., & Sagara, J. (2014). Gender differences in measures of mental health associated with a marital relationship. *Shinrigaku Kenkyu: The Japanese Journal of Psychology, 84*(6), 612–617.

Iwadare, Y., Usami, M., Suzuki, Y., Ushijima, H., Tanaka, T., Watanabe, K., . . . Saito, K. (2014). Posttraumatic symptoms in elementary and junior high school children after the 2011 Japan earthquake and tsunami: Symptom severity and recovery vary by age and sex. *The Journal of Pediatrics, 164*(4), 917–921.e1.

IWS (Internet World Stats). (2011). *Top 20 countries with the highest number of internet users.* Retrieved from Internet World Stats website: http://www.internetworldstats.com/top20.htm.

IWS (Internet World Stats). (2015). *Internet users in the world: Distribution by world regions, 2014 Q4.* Retrieved from Internet World Stats website: http://www.internetworldstats.com/stats.htm.

Iza, M., Wall, M. M., Heimberg, R. G., Rodebaugh, T. L., Schneier, F. R., Liu, S., & Blanco, C. (2014). Latent structure of social fears and social anxiety disorders. *Psychological Medicine, 44*(2), 361–370.

Jablensky, A. (2000). Epidemiology of schizophrenia: The global burden of disease and disability. *European Archives of Psychiatry and Clinical Neuroscience, 250,* 274–285.

Jabr, F. (2013, October 15). How the brain gets addicted to gambling. *Scientific American.*

Jackson, B. R., & Bergeman, C. S. (2011). How does religiosity enhance well being? The role of perceived control. *Psychology of Religion and Spirituality, 3*(2), 149–161.

Jackson, M. L., Sztendur, E. M., Diamond, N. T., Byles, J. E., & Bruck, D. (2014). Sleep difficulties and the development of depression and anxiety: A longitudinal study of young Australian women. *Archives of Women's Mental Health, 17*(3), 189–198.

Jackson, S. L. (2012). *Research methods and statistics: A critical thinking approach.* (4th ed.). Independence, KY: Cengage Learning.

Jacob, M., Larson, M., & Storch, E. (2014). Insight in adults with obsessive-compulsive disorder. *Comprehensive Psychiatry, 55*(4), 896–903.

Jacobi, C., & Fittig, E. (2010). In W. S. Agras (Ed.), *The Oxford handbook of eating disorders. Oxford library of psychology* (pp. 123–136). New York: Oxford University Press.

Jacobs, D. (2011). *Analyzing criminal minds: Forensic investigative science for the 21st century. Brain, behavior, and evolution.* Santa Barbara, CA: Praeger/ABC-CLIO.

Jacobs, M. (2003). *Sigmund Freud.* London: Sage.

Jacobson, G. (1999). The inpatient management of suicidality. In D. G. Jacobs (Ed.), *The Harvard Medical School guide to suicide assessment and intervention.* San Francisco: Jossey-Bass.

Jaffe, S. L., & Klein, M. (2010). Medical marijuana and adolescent treatment. *American Journal on Addictions, 19*(5), 460–461.

Jager, L. R., & Leek, J. T. (2013). Empirical estimates suggest most published medical research is true. Ithaca, NY: Cornell University Library.

Jäger, M., Frasch, K., & Becker, T. (2013). [Syndromal versus nosological diagnosis]. *Der Nervenarzt, 84*(9), 1081.

James, A. C., James, G., Cowdrey, F. A., Soler, A., & Choke, A. (2015). Cognitive behavioural therapy for anxiety disorders in children and adolescents. *The Cochrane Database of Systematic Reviews, 2,* CD004690.

James, S. D. (2014, February 12). Neknomination deadly drinking game takes off on Internet. *ABC News online.*

James, W. (1890). *Principles of psychology* (Vol. 1). New York: Holt, Rinehart & Winston.

Jamison, K. R. (1995, February). Manic-depressive illness and creativity. *Scientific American,* pp. 63–67.

Jamison, K. R. (1995). *An unquiet mind.* New York: Vintage Books.

Janis, R. A. (2015). Collaborating with Alexander Scriabine and the Miles Institute for Preclinical Pharmacology. *Biochemical Pharmacology.* [Electronic publication.]

Jansen, R., Penninx, B. H., Madar, V., Xia, K., Milaneschi, Y., Hottenga, J. J., . . . Sullivan, P. F. (2015). Gene expression in major depressive disorder. *Molecular Psychiatry.* [Electronic publication.]

Janssen, S. J., Hearne, T. L., & Takarangi, M. T. (2015). The relation between self-reported PTSD and depression symptoms and the psychological distance of positive and negative events. *Journal of Behavior Therapy and Experimental Psychiatry, 48,* 177–184.

Janus, S. S., & Janus, C. L. (1993). *The Janus report on sexual behavior.* New York: Wiley.

Jefferson, D. J. (2005, August 8). America's most dangerous drug. *Newsweek, 146*(6), 40–48.

Jenike, M. A. (1992). New developments in treatment of obsessive-compulsive disorder. In A. Tasman & M. B. Riba (Eds.), *Review of psychiatry* (Vol. 11). Washington, DC: American Psychiatric Press.

Jensen, M. P., Day, M. A., & Miró, J. (2014). Neuromodulatory treatments for chronic pain: Efficacy and mechanisms. *Nature Reviews Neurology, 10*(3), 167–178.

Jensen, M. P., Ehde, D. M.,. Gertz, K. J., Stoelb, B. L., Dillworth, T. M., Hirsh, A. T., . . . Kraft, G. H. (2011). Effects of self-hypnosis training and cognitive restructuring on daily pain intensity and catastrophizing in individuals with multiple sclerosis and chronic pain. *International Journal of Clinical and Experimental Hypnosis, 59*(1), 45–63.

Jessen, F. (2014). Therapy for patients with dementia: Treatment strategies in the elderly. *Der Internist, 55*(7), 769–774.

Jeste, D. V., Blazer, D. G., & First, M. (2005). Aging-related diagnostic variations: Need for diagnostic criteria appropriate for elderly psychiatric patients. *Biological Psychiatry, 58*(4), 265–271.

Jhanjee, S. (2014). Evidence based psychosocial interventions in substance use. *Indian Journal of Psychological Medicine, 36*(2), 112–118.

Jia, J., Zhou, A., Wei, C., Jia, X., Wang, F., Li, F., . . . Dong, X. (2014). The prevalence of mild cognitive impairment and its etiological subtypes in elderly Chinese. *Alzheimer's & Dementia, 10*(4), 439–447.

Jiang, W., Krishnan, R., Kuchibhatla, M., Cuffe, M. S., Martsberger, C., Arias, R. M., & O'Connor, C. M. (2011). Characteristics of depression remission and its relation with cardiovascular outcome among patients with chronic heart failure (from the SAD-HART-CHF Study). *American Journal of Cardiology, 107*(4), 545–551.

Jiann, B.-P., Su, C.-C., & Tsai, J.-Y. (2013). Is female sexual function related to the male partners' erectile function? *Journal of Sexual Medicine, 10,* 420–429.

Jimenez, D. E., Alegria, M., Chen, C.-N., Chan, D., & Laderman, M. (2010). Prevalence of psychiatric illnesses in older ethnic minority adults. *Journal of the American Geriatrics Society, 38*(2), 256–264.

Jiron, C. (2010). Assessing and intervening with children with externalizing disorders. In D. C. Miller (Ed.), *Best practices in school neuropsychology: Guidelines for effective practice, assessment, and evidence-based intervention* (pp. 359–386). Hoboken, NJ: John Wiley & Sons.

Joe, S., Ford, B. C., Taylor, R. J., & Chatters, L. M. (2014). Prevalence of suicide ideation and attempts among Black Americans in later life. *Transcultural Psychiatry, 51*(2), 190–208.

Johansson, A., Sundborn, E., Höjerback, T., & Bodlund, O. (2010). A five-year follow-up study of Swedish adults with gender identity disorder. *Archives of Sexual Behavior, 39*(6), 1429–1437.

Johnson, D. P., & Whisman, M. A. (2013). Gender differences in rumination: A meta-analysis. *Personality and Individual Differences, 55*(4), 367–374.

Johnson, D. P., Whisman, M. A., Corley, R. P., Hewitt, J. K., & Friedman, N. P. (2014). Genetic and environmental influences on rumination and its covariation with depression. *Cognition & Emotion, 28*(7), 1270–1286.

Johnson, L. A. (2005, July 21). Lobotomy back in spotlight after 30 years. *Netscape News.*

Johnson, S., Sathyaseelan, M., Charles, H., & Jacob, K. S. (2014). Predictors of disability: A 5-year cohort study of first-episode schizophrenia. *Asian Journal of Psychiatry, 9,* 45–50.

Johnson, W. E., Jr. (Ed.). (2010). *Social work with African American males: Health, mental health, and social policy.* New York: Oxford University Press.

Johnston, L. D., O'Malley, P. M., Miech, R. A., Bachman, J. G., & Schulenberg, J. E. (2014). *Monitoring the future national results on drug use, 1975–2013: Overview, key findings on adolescent drug use.* Ann Arbor, MI: Institute for Social Research, University of Michigan.

Jones, M. C. (1968). Personality correlates and antecedents of drinking patterns in males. *Journal of Consulting and Clinical Psychology, 32,* 2–12.

Jones, M. C. (1971). Personality antecedents and correlates of drinking patterns in women. *Journal of Consulting and Clinical Psychology, 36,* 61–69.

Joshi, S. V., Hartley, S. N., Kessler, M., & Barstead, M. (2015). School-based suicide prevention: Content, process, and the role of trusted adults and peers. *Child and Adolescent Psychiatric Clinics of North America, 24*(2), 353–370.

Jovanovic, T., Nylocks, K. M., Gamwell, J. L., Smith, A., Davis, T. A., Norrholm, S. D., & Bradley, B. (2014). Development of fear acquisition and extinction in children: Effects of age and anxiety. *Neurobiology of Learning and Memory, 113,* 135–142.

Juan, W., Ziao-Juan, D., Jia-Ji, W., Xin-Wang, W., & Liang, X. (2011). How do risk-taking behaviors relate to suicide ideation and attempts in adolescents? *Clinician's Research Digest, 29*(1)

Juckel, G. (2014). Serotonin: From sensory processing to schizophrenia using an electrophysiological method. *Behavioural Brain Research, 277,* 121–124.

Judge, C., O'Donovan, C., Callaghan, G., Gaoatswe, G., & O'Shea, D. (2014). Gender dysphoria: Prevalence and co-morbidities in an Irish adult population. *Frontiers in Endocrinology, 5,* 87.

Kabat-Zinn, J. (2005). *Wherever you go, there you are: Mindfulness meditation in everyday life.* New York: Hyperion.

Kagan, J. (2003). Biology, context and developmental inquiry. *Annual Review of Psychology, 54,* 1–23.

Kagan, J. (2007). The limitations of concepts in developmental psychology. In G. W. Ladd (Ed.), *Appraising the human developmental sciences: Essays in honor of Merrill-Palmer Quarterly* (pp. 30–37). Detroit, MI: Wayne State University Press.

Kahn, A. P., & Fawcett, J. (1993). *The encyclopedia of mental health.* New York: Facts on File.

Kaij, L. (1960). Alcoholism in twins: Studies on the etiology and sequels of abuse of alcohol. Stockholm: Almquist & Wiksell.

Kaiser Family Foundation. (2010). *Distribution of U.S. population by race/ethnicity, 2010 and 2050.* Menlo Park, CA: Author.

Kalin, N. H. (1993, May). The neurobiology of fear. *Scientific American,* pp. 94–101.

Kalmbach, D. A., Kigsberg, S. A., & Ciesla, J. A. (2014). How changes in depression and anxiety symptoms correspond to variations in female sexual response in a nonclinical sample of young women: A daily diary study. *Journal of Sexual Medicine, 11*(12), 2915–2927.

Kambam, P., & Benedek, E. P. (2010). Testifying: The expert witness in court. In E. P. Benedek, P. Ash, & C. L. Scott (Eds.), *Principles and practice of child and adolescent forensic mental health* (pp. 41–51). Arlington, VA: American Psychiatric Publishing.

Kang, H. S., Myung, W., Na, D. L., Kim, S. Y., Lee, J., Han, S., . . . Kim, D. K. (2014). Factors associated with caregiver burden in patients with Alzheimer's disease. *Psychiatry Investigation, 11*(2), 152–159.

Kangelaris, K. N., Vittinghoff, E., Otte, C., Na, B., Auerbach, A. D., & Whooley, M. A. (2010). Association between a serotonin transporter gene variant and hopelessness among men in the Heart and Soul Study. *Journal of General Internal Medicine, 25*(10), 1030–1037.

Kanner, B. (1995). *Are you normal? Do you behave like everyone else?* New York: St. Martin's Press.

Kanner, B. (1998, February). Are you normal? Turning the other cheek. *American Demographics.*

Kanner, B. (2005). *Are you normal about sex, love, and relationships?* New York: St. Martin's Press.

Kanner, L. (1943). Autistic disturbances of affective contact. *Nervous Child, 2,* 217.

Kanner, L. (1954). To what extent is early infantile autism determined by constitutional inadequacies? In *Genetics and the Inheritance of Integrated Neurological and Psychiatric Patterns.* Baltimore: Williams and Wilkins.

Kantor, M. (2006). The psychopathy of everyday life. In T. G. Plante (Ed.), *Mental disorders of the new millennium, Vol. 1: Behavioral issues.* Westport, CT: Praeger Publishers.

Kantor, M. (2010). *The essential guide to overcoming avoidant personality disorder.* Santa Barbara, CA: Praeger/ABC-CLIO.

Kantrowitz, B., & Springen, K. (2004, August 9). What dreams are made of. *Newsweek, 144*(6), 40–47.

Kaplan, H. S. (1974). *The new sex therapy: Active treatment of sexual dysfunction.* New York: Brunner/Mazel.

Karch, C. M., Jeng, A. T., & Goate, A. M. (2013). Calcium phosphatase calcineurin influences tau metabolism. *Neurobiology of Aging, 34*(2), 374–386.

Kashdan, T. B., Adams, L., Savostyanova, A., Ferssizidis, P., McKnight, P. E., & Nezlek, J. B. (2011). Effects of social anxiety and depressive symptoms on the frequency and quality of sexual activity: A daily process approach. *Behaviour Research and Therapy, 49*(5), 352–360.

Kass, A. E., Kolko, R. P., & Wilfley, D. E. (2013). Psychological treatments for eating disorders. *Current Opinion in Psychiatry, 26*(6), 549–555.

Kassel, J. D., Wardle, M. C., Heinz, A. J., & Greenstein, J. E. (2010). Cognitive theories of drug effects on emotion. In J. D. Kassel (Ed.), *Substance abuse and emotion* (pp. 61–82). Washington, DC: American Psychological Association.

Kaufman, L. (2014, February 4). In texting era, crisis hotlines put help at youths' fingertips. *New York Times.*

Kaufman, S. B. (2013, October 3). The real link between creativity and mental illness. *Scientific American.*

Kawas, C., Resnick, S., Morrison, A., Brookmeyer, R., Corrada, M., Zonderman, A., . . . Metter, E. (1997). A prospective study of estrogen replacement therapy and the risk of developing Alzheimer's disease: The Baltimore Longtitudinal Study of Aging. *Neurology, 48*(6), 1517–1521.

Kaye, W. H. (2011). Neurobiology of anorexia nervosa. In D. Le Grange & J. Lock (Eds.), *Eating disorders in children and adolescents: A clinical handbook.* New York: Guilford Publications.

Kaye, W. H., Frank, G. K., Bailer, U. F., Henry, S. E., Meltzer, C. C., Price, J. C., . . . Wagner, A. (2005). Serotonin alterations in anorexia and bulimia nervosa: New insights from imaging studies. *Physiological Behavior, 85*(1), 73–81.

Kaye, W. H., Wierenga, C. E., Bailer, U. F., Simmons, A. N., & Bischoff-Grethe, A. (2013). Nothing tastes as good as skinny feels: The neurobiology of anorexia nervosa. *Trends in Neurosciences, 36*(2), 110–120.

Kazano, H. (2012). Asylum: The huge psychiatric hospital in the 19th century U.S. *Seishin Shinkeigaku Zasshi = Psychiatria Et Neurologia Japonica, 114*(10), 1194–1200.

Kazdin, A. E. (2002). Psychosocial treatments for conduct disorder in children and adolescents. In P. E. Nathan & J. M. Gorman (Eds.), *A guide to treatments that work* (2nd ed., pp. 57–85). London: Oxford University Press.

Kazdin, A. E. (2005). *Parent management training: Treatment for oppositional, aggressive, and antisocial behavior in children and adolescents.* New York: Oxford University Press.

Kazdin, A. E. (2006). Assessment and evaluation in clinical practice. In R. J. Sternberg, C. D. Goodheart, & A. E. Kazdin (Eds.), *Evidence-based psychotherapy: Where practice and research meet* (pp. 153–177). Washington, DC: American Psychological Association.

Kazdin, A. E. (2007). Psychosocial treatments for conduct disorder in children and adolescents. In P. E. Nathan & J. M. Gorman (Eds.), *A guide to treatments that work* (3rd ed., pp. 71–104). New York: Oxford University Press.

Kazdin, A. E. (2010). Problem-solving skills training and parent management training for oppositional defiant disorder and conduct disorder. In J. R. Weisz, & A. E. Kazdin (Eds.), *Evidence-based psychotherapies for children and adolescents* (2nd ed., pp. 211–226). New York: Guilford Press.

Kazdin, A. E. (2012). *Behavior modification in applied settings* (7th ed.). Long Grove, IL: Waveland Press.

Kazdin, A. E. (2013). Evidence-based treatment and usual care: Cautions and qualifications. *JAMA Psychiatry, 70*(7), 666–667.

Kazdin, A. E. (2015). Clinical dysfunction and psychosocial interventions: The interplay of research, methods, and conceptualization of challenges. *Annual Review of Clinical Psychology, 11,* 25–52.

Kearney, C. A. (2013). *Casebook in child behavior disorders* (5th ed.). Independence, KY: Cengage Publications.

Kedmey, D. (2013, June 5). Avatar therapy may silence schizophrenia sufferers' demons. *Time.*

Keefer, A. (2015, January 28). Elderly living with family. *Livestrong.com.* Retrieved from Live Strong website: http://www.livestrong.com/article/95828.

Keel, P. K., & McCormick, L. (2010). Diagnosis, assessment, and treatment planning for anorexia nervosa. In C. M. Grilo & J. E. Mitchell (Eds.), *The treatment of eating disorders: A clinical handbook* (pp. 3–27). New York: Guilford Press.

Keen, E. (1970). *Three faces of being: Toward an existential clinical psychology.* By the Meredith Corp. Reprinted by permission of Irvington Publishers.

Keeshin, B. R., Strawn, J. R., Luebbe, A. M., Saddana, S. N., Wehry, A. M., DelBello, M. P., & Putnam, F. W. (2014). Hospitalized youth and child abuse: A systematic examination of psychiatric morbidity and clinical severity. *Child Abuse & Neglect, 38*(1), 76–83.

Kelleher, E., & Campbell, A. (2011). A study of consultant psychiatrists' response to patients' suicide. *Irish Journal of Psychological Medicine, 28*(1), 35–37.

Keller, W. R., Fischer, B. A., McMahon, R., Meyer, W., Blake, M., & Buchanan, R. W. (2014). Community adherence to schizophrenia treatment and safety monitoring guidelines. *Journal of Nervous and Mental Disease, 202*(1), 6–12.

Kellett, S., & Hardy, G. (2014). Treatment of paranoid personality disorder with cognitive analytic therapy: A mixed methods single case experimental design. *Clinical Psychology & Psychotherapy, 21*(5), 452–464.

Kelley, M. L., Linden, A. N., Milletich, R. J., Lau-Barraco, C., Kurtz, E. D., D'Lima, G. M., . . . Sheehan, B. E. (2014). Self and partner alcohol-related problems among ACOAs and non-ACOAs: Associations with depressive symptoms and motivations for alcohol use. *Addictive Behaviors, 39*(1), 211–218.

Kelly, M. A., & Barry, L. M. (2010). Identifying and alleviating the stresses of college students through journal writing. In K. M. T. Collins, A. J. Onwuegbuzie, & Q. G. Jiao (Eds.), *Toward a broader understanding of stress and coping: Mixed methods approaches. Research on stress and coping in education* (pp. 343–370). Greenwich, VT: IAP Information Age Publishing.

Kemp, C. G., & Collings, S. C. (2011). Hyperlinked suicide: Assessing the prominence and accessibility of suicide websites. *Crisis: Journal of Crisis Intervention and Suicide Prevention, 32*(3), 143–151.

Kemp, D. R. (1994). *Mental health in the workplace: An employer's and manager's guide.* Westport, CT: Quorum Books.

Kendall-Tackett, K. A. (2010). *Depression in new mothers: Causes, consequences, and treatment alternatives* (2nd ed.). New York: Routledge/Taylor & Francis Group.

Kendall, J., & Hatton, D. (2002). Racism as a source of health disparity in families with children with attention deficit hyperactivity disorder. *Advances in Nursing Science, 25*(2), 22–39.

Kendler, K. S., Heath, A., & Martin, N. G. (1987). A genetic epidemiologic study of self-report suspiciousness. *Comprehensive Psychiatry, 28*(3), 187–196.

Kendler, K. S., Neale, M. C., Kessler, R. C., Heath, A. C., & Eaves, L. J. (1993). Panic disorder in women: A population-based twin study. *Psychological Medicine, 23,* 397–406.

Kendler, K. S., Ochs, A. L., Gorman, A. M., Hewitt, J. K., Ross, D. E., & Mirsky, A. F. (1991). The structure of schizotypy: A pilot multitrait twin study. *Psychiatry Research, 36*(1), 19–36.

Kendler, K. S., Walters, E. E., Neale, M. C., Kessler, R. C., Heath, A. C., & Eaves, L. J. (1995). The structure of the genetic and environmental risk factors for six major psychiatric disorders in women: Phobia, generalized anxiety disorder, panic disorder, bulimia, major depression, and alcoholism. *Archives of General Psychiatry, 52*(5), 374–383.

Kenedi, C., Sames, C., & Paice, R. (2013). A systematic review of factitious decompression sickness. *Undersea Hyperbaric Medicine, 40*(3), 267–274.

Kennedy, J. L., Altar, C. A., Taylor, D. L., Degtiar, I., & Hornberger, J. C. (2014). The social and economic burden of treatment-resistant schizophrenia: A systematic literature review. *International Clinical Psychopharmacology, 29*(2), 63–76.

Kerber, K., Taylor, K., & Riba, M. B. (2011). Treatment resistant depression and comorbid medical problems: Cardiovascular disease and cancer. In J. F. Greden, M. B. Riba, & M. G. McInnis (Eds.), *Treatment resistant depression: A roadmap for effective care* (pp. 137–156). Arlington, VA: American Psychiatric Publishing.

Kerekes, N., Lundström, S., Chang, Z., Tajnia, A., Jern, P., Lichtenstein, P., . . . Anckarsäter, H. (2014). Oppositional defiant- and conduct disorder-like problems: Neurodevelopmental predictors and genetic background in boys and girls, in a nationwide twin study. *Peer Journal, 22*(2), e359.

Kern, M. L., & Friedman, H. S. (2011). Personality and pathways of influence on physical health. *Social and Personality Psychology Compass, 5*(1), 76–87.

Kernberg, O. F. (1989). Narcissistic personality disorder in childhood. *Psychiatric Clinics of North America, 12*(3), 671–694.

Kernberg, O. F. (1992). *Aggression in personality disorders and its perversions.* New Haven, CT: Yale University Press.

Kernberg, O. F. (1997). Convergences and divergences in contemporary psychoanalytic technique and psychoanalytic psychotherapy. In E. S. Zeig (Ed.), *The evolution of psychotherapy: The third conference.* New York: Brunner/Mazel.

Kernberg, O. F. (2005). Object relations theories and technique. In E. S. Person, A. M. Cooper, & G. O. Gabbard (Eds.), *The American Psychiatric Publishing textbook of psychoanalysis* (pp. 57–75). Washington, DC: American Psychiatric Publishing.

Kernberg, O. F. (2010). Narcissistic personality disorder. In J. F. Clarkin, P. Fonagy, & G. O. Gabbard (Eds.), *Psychodynamic psychotherapy for personality disorders: A clinical handbook* (pp. 257–287). Arlington, VA: American Psychiatric Publishing.

Kerr, C. E., Sacchet, M. D., Lazar, S. W., Moore, C. I., & Jones, S. R. (2013). Mindfulness starts with the body: Somatosensory attention and top-down modulation of cortical alpha rhythms in mindfulness meditation. *Frontiers in Human Neuroscience, 7*(12), 1–15.

Kerr, J. H., Lindner, K. J., & Blaydon, M. (2007). *Exercise dependence.* London: Routledge.

Kessler, R. C. (2002). Epidemiology of depression. In I. H. Gotlib & C. L. Hammen (Eds.), *Handbook of depression* (pp. 23–42). New York: Guilford Press.

Kessler, R. C., Adler, L. A., Barkley, R., Biederman, J., Conners, C. K., Faraone, S. V., . . . Zaslavsky, A. M. (2005). Patterns and predictors of attention-deficit/hyperactivity disorder persistence into adulthood: Results from the National Comorbidity Survey Replication. *Biological Psychiatry, 57*(11), 1442–1451.

Kessler, R. C., Avenevoli, S., Green, J., Gruber, M. J., Guyer, M., He, Y., . . . Merikangas, K. R. (2009). National comorbidity survey replication adolescent supplement (NCS-A): III. concordance of DSM-IV/CIDI diagnoses with clinical reassessments. *Journal of the American Academy of Child & Adolescent Psychiatry, 48*(4), 386–399.

Kessler, R. C., Chiu, W. T., Jin, R., Ruscio, A. M., Shear, K., & Walters, E. E. (2006). The epidemiology of panic attacks, panic disorder, and agoraphobia in the National Comorbidity Survey Replication. *Archives of General Psychiatry, 63,* 415–424.

Kessler, R. C., Demier, O., Frank, R. G., Olfson, M., Pincus, H. A., Walters, E. E., . . . Zaslavsky, A. M. (2005). Prevalence and treatment of mental disorders, 1990 to 2003. *New England Journal of Medicine, 352*(24), 2515–2523.

Kessler, R. C., DuPont, R. L., Berglund, P., & Wittchen, H. U. (1999). Impairment in pure and comorbid generalized anxiety disorder and major depression at 12 months in two national surveys. *American Journal of Psychiatry, 156*(12), 1915–1923.

Kessler, R. C., Gruber, M., Hettema, J. M., Hwang, I., Sampson, N., & Yonkers, K. A. (2010). Major depression and generalized anxiety disorder in the National Comorbidity Survey follow-up survey. In D. Goldberg, K. S. Kendler, P. J. Sirovatka, & D. A. Regier (Eds.), *Diagnostic issues in depression and generalized anxiety disorder: Refining the research agenda for DSM-V* (pp. 139–170). Washington, DC: American Psychiatric Association.

Kessler, R. C., McGonagle, K. A., Zhao, S., Nelson, C. B., Hughes, M., Eshleman, S., . . . Kendler, K. S. (1994). Lifetime and 12-month prevalence of DSM-III-R psychiatric disorders among persons aged 15–54 in the United States: Results from the National Comorbidity Survey. *Archives of General Psychiatry, 51*(1), 8–19.

Kessler, R. C., Petukhova, M., Sampson, N. A., Zaslavsky, A. M., & Wittchen, H. (2012). Twelve-month and lifetime prevalence and lifetime morbid risk of anxiety and mood disorders in the United States. *International Journal of Methods in Psychiatric Research, 21*(3), 169–184.

Kessler, R. C., Ruscio, A. M., Shear, K., & Wittchen, H-U. (2010). Epidemiology of anxiety disorders. In M. B. Stein & T. Steckler (Eds.), *Behavioral neurobiology of anxiety and its treatment. Current topics in behavioral neurosciences* (pp. 21–35). New York: Springer Science + Business Media.

Kety, S. S. (1988). Schizophrenic illness in the families of schizophrenic adoptees: Findings from the Danish national sample. *Schizophrenia Bulletin, 14*(2), 217–222.

Kety, S. S., Rosenthal, D., Wender, P. H., & Schulsinger, F. (1968). The types and prevalence of mental illness in the biological and adoptive families of schizophrenics. *Journal of Psychiatric Research, 6,* 345–362.

Keuthen, N. J., Koran, L. M., Aboujaoude, E., Large, M. D., Serpe, R. T. (2010). The prevalence of pathologic skin picking in US adults. *Comprehensive Psychiatry, 51*(2), 183–186.

Keuthen, N. J., Rothbaum, B. O., Welch, S. S., Taylor, C., Falkenstein, M., Heekin, M., . . . Jernike, M. A. (2010). Pilot trial of dialectical behavior therapy-enhanced habit reversal for trichotillomania. *Depression & Anxiety, 27*(10), 953–959.

Keuthen, N. J., Siev, J., & Reese, H. (2012). Assessment of trichotillomania, pathological skin picking, and stereotypic movement disorder. In J. E. Grant, D. J. Stein, D. W. Woods, & N. J. Keuthen (Eds.), *Trichotillomania, skin picking, and other body-focused repetitive behaviors* (pp. 129–150). Arlington, VA: American Psychiatric Publishing.

Keys, A., Brozek, J., Henschel, A., Mickelson, O., & Taylor, H. L. (1950). *The biology of human starvation.* Minneapolis: University of Minnesota Press.

Keyser-Marcus, L., Alvanzo, A., Rieckmann, T., Thacker, L., Sepulveda, A., Forcehimes, A., . . . Svikis, D. S. (2015). Trauma, gender, and mental health symptoms in individuals with substance use disorders. *Journal of Interpersonal Violence, 30*(1), 3–24.

Khan, A. (2015). The amyloid hypothesis and potential treatments for Alzheimer's disease. *Journal of Quality Research in Dementia, 4.* Retrieved from Alzheimers website: http://www.alzheimers.org.uk.

Khatri, N., Marziali, E., Techernokov, I., & Shepherd, N. (2014). Comparing telehealth-based and clinic-based group cognitive behavioral therapy for adults with depression and anxiety: A pilot study. *Clinical Interventions in Aging, 9,* 765–770.

Khoury, B., Lecomte, T., Fortin, G., Masse, M., Therien, P., Bouchard, V., . . . Hofmann, S. G. (2013) Mindfulness-based therapy: A comprehensive meta-analysis. *Clinical Psychology Review, 33*(6), 763–771.

Kibler, J. L., Joshi, K., & Hughes, E. E. (2010). Cognitive and behavioral reactions to stress among adults with PTSD: Implications for immunity and health. In K. Kendall-Tackett (Ed.), *The psychoneuroimmunology of chronic disease: Exploring the links between inflammation, stress, and illness* (pp. 133–158). Washington, DC: American Psychological Association.

Kibria, A. A., & Metcalfe, N. H. (2014). A biography of William Tuke (1732–1822): Founder of the modern mental asylum. *Journal of Medical Biography.* [Electronic publication.]

Kiecolt-Glaser, J. K., Garner, W., Speicher, C., Penn, G. M., Holliday, J., & Glaser, R. (1984). Psychosocial modifiers of immunocompetence in medical students. *Psychosomatic Medicine, 46,* 7–14.

Kiecolt-Glaser, J. K., Glaser, R., Gravenstein, S., Malarkey, W. B., & Sheridan, J. (1996). Chronic stress alters the immune response to influenza virus vaccine in older adults. *Proceedings of the National Academy of Science, 93,* 3043–3047.

Kiecolt-Glaser, J. K., McGuire, L., Robles, S. F., & Glaser, R. (2002). Psychoneuroimmunology: Psychological influences on immune function and health. *Journal of Consulting and Clinical Psychology, 70*(3), 537–547.

Kienast, T., Stoffers, J., Bermpohl, F., & Lieb, K. (2014). Borderline personality disorder and comorbid addiction: Epidemiology and treatment. *Deutsches Ärzteblatt International, 111*(16), 280–286.

Kiernan, W. (2000). Where we are now: Perspectives on employment of persons with mental retardation. *Focus on Autism and Other Developmental Disabilities, 15*(2), 90–96.

Kiesler, D. J. (1966). Some myths of psychotherapy research and the search for a paradigm. *Psychological Bulletin, 65,* 110–136.

Kiesler, D. J. (1995). Research classic: Some myths of psychotherapy research and the search for a paradigm: Revisited. *Psychotherapy Research, 5*(2), 91–101.

Kiev, A. (1989). Suicide in adults. In J. G. Howells (Ed.), *Modern perspectives in the psychiatry of the affective disorders.* New York: Brunner/Mazel.

Kikuchi, H., Fujii, T., Abe, N., Suzuki, M., Takagi, M., Mugikura, S., . . . Mori, E. (2010). Memory repression: Brain mechanisms underlying dissociative amnesia. *Journal of Cognitive Neuroscience, 22*(3), 602–613.

Kim, D. R., Epperson, C. N., Weiss, A. R., & Wisner, K. L. (2014). Pharmacotherapy of postpartum depression: An update. *Expert Opinion on Pharmacotherapy, 15*(9), 1223–1234.

Kim, E. S., Chopik, W. J., & Smith, J. (2014). Are people healthier if their partners are more optimistic? The dyadic effect of optimism on health among older adults. *Journal of Psychosomatic Research, 76*(6), 447–453.

Kim, J., Han, J. Y., Shaw, B., McTavish, F., & Gustafson, D. (2010). The roles of social support and coping strategies in predicting breast cancer patients' emotional well-being: Testing mediation and moderation models. *Journal of Health Psychology, 15*(4), 543–552.

Kim, J. M., Park, J. W., & Lee, C. S. (2014). Evaluation of nocturnal bladder capacity and nocturnal urine volume in nocturnal enuresis. *Journal of Pediatric Urology, 10*(3), 559–563.

Kim, S., Ha, J. H., Yu, J., Park, D., & Ryu, S. (2014). Path analysis of suicide ideation in older people. *International Psychogeriatrics/IPA, 26*(3), 509–515.

Kim, S. M., Baek, J. H., Han, D. H., Lee, Y. S., & Yurgelun-Todd, D. A. (2015). Psychosocial-environmental risk factors for suicide attempts in adolescents with suicide ideation: Findings from a sample of 73,238 adolescents. *Suicide & Life-Threatening Behavior, 45*(4), 477–487.

Kimball, A. (1993). Nipping and tucking. In Skin deep: Our national obsession with looks. *Psychology Today, 26*(3), 96.

Kimhi, Y., Agam Bem-Artzi, G., Ben-Moshe, I., & Bauminger-Zviely, N. (2014). Theory of mind and executive function in preschoolers with typical development versus intellectually able preschoolers with autism spectrum disorder. *Journal of Autism and Developmental Disorders, 44*(9), 2341–2354.

King, A. P., Erickson, T. M., Giardino, N. D., Favorite, T., Rauch, S. A., Robinson, E., . . . Liberzon, I. (2013). A pilot study of group mindfulness-based cognitive therapy (MBCT) for combat veterans with posttraumatic stress disorder (PTSD). *Depression & Anxiety, 30*(7), 638–645.

King, L. (2002, March 19). Interview with Russell Yates. *Larry King Live, CNN.*

King, R. A. (2003). Psychodynamic approaches to youth suicide. In R. A. King & A. Apter (Eds.), *Suicide in children and adolescents* (pp. 150–169). New York: Cambridge University Press.

Kingsberg, S. A., Tkachenko, N., Lucas, J., Burbrink, A., Kreppner, W., & Dickstein, I. B. (2013). Characterization of orgasmic difficulties by women: Focus group evaluation. *Journal of Sexual Medicine, 10,* 2242–2250.

Kinon, B. J., Kollack-Walker, S., Jeste, D., Gupta, S., Chen, L., Case, M., . . . Stauffer, V. (2015). Incidence of tardive dyskinesia in older adult patients treated with olanzapine or conventional antipsychotics. *Journal of Geriatric Psychiatry and Neurology, 28*(1), 67–79.

Kirkcaldy, B. D., Richardson, R., & Merrick, J. (2010). Suicide risk. In J. M. Brown & E. A. Campbell (Eds.), *Cambridge Handbook of Forensic Psychology.* Cambridge: Cambridge University Press.

Kirmayer, L. J. (2001). Cultural variations in the clinical presentation of depression and anxiety: Implications for diagnosis and treatment. *Journal of Clinical Psychiatry, 62*(Suppl. 13), 22–28.

Kirmayer, L. J. (2002). The refugee's predicament. *Evolution Psychiatrique, 67*(4), 724–774.

Kirmayer, L. J. (2003). Failures of imagination: The refugee's narrative in psychiatry. *Anthropology and Medicine, 10*(2), 167–185.

Kiume, S. (2013). *Top 10 mental health apps: World of Psychology.* Retrieved from Wordpress website: http://mobilesocialwork.wordpress.com.

Kleespies, P. M., Van Orden, K. A., Bongar, B., Bridgeman, D., Bufka, L. F., Galper, D. I., Hillbrand, M., & Yufit, R. I. (2011). Psychologist suicide: Incidence, impact, and suggestions for prevention, intervention, and postvention. *Professional Psychology: Research and Practice, 42*(3), 244–251.

Klein, D. F. (1964). Delineation of two drug-responsive anxiety syndromes. *Psychopharmacologia, 5,* 397–408.

Klein, D. F., & Fink, M. (1962). Psychiatric reaction patterns to imipramine. *American Journal of Psychiatry, 119,* 432–438.

Klein, W. C., & Jess, C. (2002). One last pleasure? Alcohol use among elderly people in nursing homes. *Health & Social Work, 27*(3), 193–203.

Kleinman, A. (1987). Anthropology and psychiatry: The role of culture in cross-cultural research on illness. *British Journal of Psychiatry, 151,* 447–454.

Kleinman, A. (2004). Culture and depression. *New England Journal of Medicine, 351*(10), 951–953.

Kleinplatz, P. J. (2010). "Desire disorders" or opportunities for optimal erotic intimacy? In S. R. Leiblum (Ed.), *Treating sexual desire disorders: A clinical casebook* (pp. 92–113). New York: Guilford Press.

Kline, N. S. (1958). Clinical experience with iproniazid (Marsilid). *Journal of Clinical and Experimental Psychopathology, 19*(1, Suppl.), 72–78.

Kluft, R. P. (1987). The simulation and dissimulation of multiple personality disorder. *American Journal of Clinical Hypnosis, 30*(2), 104–118.

Kluft, R. P. (1988). The dissociative disorders. In J. Talbott, R. Hales, & S. Yudofsky (Eds.), *Textbook of psychiatry.* Washington, DC: American Psychiatric Press.

Kluft, R. P. (1991). Multiple personality disorder. In A. Tasman & S. M. Goldfinger (Eds.), *American Psychiatric Press review of psychiatry* (Vol. 10). Washington, DC: American Psychiatric Press.

Kluft, R. P. (1999). An overview of the psychotherapy of dissociative identity disorder. *American Journal of Psychotherapy, 53*(3), 289–319.

Kluft, R. P. (2000). The psychoanalytic psychotherapy of dissociative identity disorder in the context of trauma therapy. *Psychoanalytical Inquiry, 20*(2), 259–286.

Kluft, R. P. (2001). Dissociative disorders. In H. S. Friedman (Ed.), *Specialty articles from the encyclopedia of mental health.* San Diego: Academic Press.

Kluger, J. (2002, June 2). Pumping up your past. *Time.*

Knappich, M., Hörz-Sagstetter, S., Schwerthöffer, D., Leucht, S., & Rentrop, M. (2014). Pharmacotherapy in the treatment of patients with borderline personality disorder: Results of a survey among psychiatrists in private practices. *International Clinical Psychopharmacology, 29*(4), 224–228.

Knatz, S., Murray, S. B., Matheson, B., Boutelle, K. N., Rockwell, R., Eisler, I., & Kaye, W. H. (2015) A brief, intensive application of multi-family-based treatment for eating disorders. *Eating Disorders, 23*(4), 315–324.

Knecht, T. (2014). "Biastophilia"—rape as a form of paraphilia? *Archiv für Kriminologie, 233*(3-4), 130–135.

Knekt, P., Heinonen, E., Härkäpää, K., Järvikoski, A., Virtala, E., Rissanen, J., . . . The Helsinki Psychotherapy Study Group. (2015). Randomized trial on the effectiveness of long- and short-term psychotherapy on psychosocial functioning and quality of life during a 5-year-follow-up. *Psychiatry Research, 229*(1-2), 381–388.

Knoll, J. L. (2010). The "pseudocommando" mass murderer: Part I, the psychology of revenge and obliteration. *Journal of the American Academy of Psychiatry and the Law, 38,* 87–94.

Knoll, J. L. (2015). The psychiatrist's duty to protect. *CNS Spectrums, 20*(3), 215–222.

Knott, L. (2011). Delusions and hallucinations. *Patient.co.uk.* Retrieved from Patient website: http://www.patient.co.uk/print/1715.

Knott, L. (2011). Hypnagogic hallucinations. *Patient.co.uk.* Retrieved from Patient website: http://www.patient.co.uk/print/2297.

Knowthenet. (2013). Nineteen year old males revealed as top trolling target. *Knowthenet.org,* Retrieved from Know the Net website: http://www.knowthenet.org.uk/articles/nineteen-year-old-males-.

Knudson, R. M. (2006). Anorexia dreaming: A case study. *Dreaming, 16*(1), 43–52.

Koch, W. J., & Haring, M. (2008). Posttraumatic stress disorder. In M. Hersen & J. Rosqvist (Eds.), *Handbook of psychological assessment, case conceptualization, and treatment, Vol. 1: Adults* (pp. 263–290). Hoboken, NJ: John Wiley & Sons.

Kochunov, P., & Hong, L. E. (2014). Neurodevelopmental and neurodegenerative models of schizophrenia: White matter at the center stage. *Schizophrenia Bulletin, 40*(4), 721–728.

Kocsis, R. N. (2008). *Serial murder and the psychology of violent crimes.* Totowa, NJ: Humana Press.

Kocsis, R. N., & Palermo, G. B. (2013). Disentangling criminal profiling: Accuracy, homology, and the myth of trait-based profiling. *International Journal of Offender Therapy and Comparative Criminology,* December 12, 2013.

Koczor, C. A., Ludlow, I., Hight, R., Jiao, Z., Fields, E., Ludaway, T., . . . Lewis, W. (2015). Ecstasy (MDMA) alters cardiac gene expression and DNA methylation: Implications for circadian rhythm dysfunction in the heart. *Toxicological Sciences.* [Advance publication.]

Koenen, K. C., Lyons, M. J., Goldberg, J., Simpson, J., Williams, W. M., Toomey, R., . . . Tsuang, M. T. (2003). Co-twin control study of relationships among combat exposure, combat-related PTSD, and other mental disorders. *Journal of Traumatic Stress, 16*(5), 433–438.

Koenig, H. G. (2015). Religion, spirituality, and health: A review and update. *Advances in Mind-Body Medicine, 29*(3), 19–26.

Koenigsberg, H. W., Harvey, P., Mitropoulou, V., New, A. Goodman, M., Silverman, J., . . . Siever, L. J. (2001). Are the interpersonal and identity disturbances in the borderline personality disorder criteria linked to the traits of affectivity and impulsivity? *Journal of Personality Disorders, 15,* 358–370.

Koetting, C. (2015). Caregiver-fabricated illness in a child. *Journal of Forensic Nursing, 11*(2), 114–117.

Koetzle, D. (2014). Substance use and crime: Identifying and treating those in need. *International Journal of Offender Therapy and Comparative Criminology, 58*(6), 635–637.

Koh, M., Nishimatsu, Y., & Endo, S. (2000). Dissociative disorder. *Journal of International Society of Life Information Science, 18*(2), 495–498.

Koh, Y. W., Chui, C. Y., Tang, C. K., & Lee, A. M. (2014). The prevalence and risk factors of paternal depression from the antenatal to the postpartum period and the relationships between antenatal and postpartum depression among fathers in Hong Kong. *Depression Research and Treatment, 2014,* 127632.

Kohen, D. P., & Olness, K. (2011). *Hypnosis and hypnotherapy with children* (4th ed.). New York: Routledge/Taylor & Francis Group.

Kohut, H. (1977). *The restoration of the self.* New York: International Universities Press.

Kohut, H. (2001). On empathy. *European Journal for Psychoanalytic Therapy and Research, 2*(2), 139–146.

Kok, R., Avendano, M., Bago d'Uva, T., & Mackenbach, J. (2012). Can reporting heterogeneity explain differences in depressive symptoms across Europe? *Social Indicators Research, 105*(2), 191–210.

Kokish, R., Levenson, J. S., & Blasingame, G. D. (2005). Post-conviction sex offender polygraph examination: Client-reported perceptions of utility and accuracy. *Sexual Abuse: A Journal of Research and Treatment, 17*(2), 211–221.

Komaroff, A. L., Masuda, M., & Holmes, T. H. (1986). The Social Readjustment Rating Scale: A comparative study of Negro, white, and Mexican Americans. *Journal of Psychosomatic Research, 12,* 121–128.

Komaroff, A. L., Masuda, M., & Holmes, T. H. (1989). The Social Readjustment Rating Scale: A comparative study of Black, white, and Mexican Americans. In T. H. Holmes and E. M. David (Eds.), *Life change, life events, and illness.* New York: Praeger.

Konrath, S. (2013, December 18). Harnessing mobile media for good. *Psychology Today.*

Koo, K. H., Nguyen, H. V., Gilmore, A. K., Blayney, J. A., & Kaysen, D. L. (2014). Posttraumatic cognitions, somatization, and PTSD severity among Asian American and white college women in sexual trauma histories. *Psychological Trauma: Theory, Research, Practice and Policy, 6*(4), 337–344.

Kooyman, I., & Walsh, E. (2011). Societal outcomes in schizophrenia. In D. R. Weinberg & P. Harrison (Eds.), *Schizophrenia* (pp. 644–665). Hoboken, NJ: Wiley-Blackwell.

Kopelowicz, A., Liberman, R. P., & Zarate, R. (2008). Psychosocial treatments for schizophrenia. In K. T. Mueser & D. V. Jeste (Eds.), *Clinical handbook of schizophrenia* (pp. 243–269). New York: Guilford Press.

Korda, J. B., Goldstein, S. W., & Goldstein, I. (2010). The role of androgens in the treatment of hypoactive sexual desire disorder in women. In S. R. Leiblum (Ed.), *Treating sexual desire disorders: A clinical casebook* (pp. 201–218). New York: Guilford Press.

Kosinski, M., Stillwell, D., & Graepel, T. (2013). Private traits and attributes are predictable from digital records of human behavior. *Proceedings of the National Academy of Sciences of the United States of America, 110*(15), 5802–5805.

Koskinen, S. M., Ahveninen, J., Kujala, T., Kaprio, J., O'Donnell, B. F., Osipova, D., . . . Rose, R. J. (2011). A longitudinal twin study of effects of adolescent alcohol abuse on the neurophysiology of attention and orienting. *Alcoholism, Clinical and Experimental Research, 35*(7), 1339–1350.

Koss, M. P. (1993). Rape: Scope, impact, interventions, and public policy responses. *American Psychologist, 48*(10), 1062–1069.

Koss, M. P. (2005). Empirically enhanced reflections on 20 years of rape research. *Journal of Interpersonal Violence, 20*(1), 100–107.

Koss, M. P., Abbey, A., Campbell, R., Cook, S., Norris, J., Testa, M., . . . White, J. (2008). Revising the SES: A collaborative process to improve assessment of sexual aggression and victimization: Erratum. *Psychology of Women Quarterly, 32*(4), 493.

Koss, M. P., & Heslet, L. (1992). Somatic consequences of violence against women. *Archives of Family Medicine, 1*(1), 53–59.

Koss, M. P., White, J. W., & Kazdin, A. E. (2011). Violence against women and children: Perspectives and next steps. In M. P. Koss, J. W. White, & A. E. Kazdin (Eds.), *Violence against women and children, Vol. 2: Navigating solutions* (pp. 261–305). Washington, DC: American Psychological Association.

Kosten, T. R., George, T. P., & Kleber, H. D. (2005). The neurobiology of substance dependence: Implications for treatment. In R. J. Frances, A. H. Mack, & S. I. Miller (Eds.), *Clinical textbook of addictive disorders* (3rd ed., pp. 3–15). New York: Guilford Press.

Kosten, T. R., George, T. P., & Kleber, H. D. (2011). The neurobiology of substance dependence: Implications for treatment. In R. J. Frances, S. I. Miller, & A. H. Mack (Eds.), *Clinical textbook of addictive disorders* (3rd ed., Chap. 1). New York: Guilford Press.

Kosten, T. R., Sofuoglu, M., & Gardner, T. J. (2008). Clinical management: Cocaine. In H. D. Kleber & M. Galanter (Eds.), *The American Psychiatric Publishing textbook of substance abuse treatment* (4th ed., pp. 157–168). Arlington, VA: American Psychiatric Publishing.

Koukopoulos, A., & Sani, G. (2014). DSM-5 criteria for depression with mixed features: A farewell to mixed depression. *Acta Psychiatrica Scandinavica, 129*(1), 4–16.

Koutra, K., Triliva, S., Roumeliotaki, T., Basta, M., Simos, P., Lionis, C., & Vgontzas, A. N. (2015). Impaired family functioning in psychosis and its relevance to relapse: A two-year follow-up study. *Comprehensive Psychiatry, 62*, 1–12.

Kposowa, A. J., McElvain, J. P., & Breault, K. D. (2008). Immigration and suicide: The role of marital status, duration of residence, and social integration. *Archives of Suicide Research, 12*(1), 82–92.

Krack, P., Hariz, M. I., Baunez, C., Guridi, J., & Obeso, J. A. (2010). Deep brain stimulation: From neurology to psychiatry? *Trends in Neurosciences, 33*(10), 474–484.

Kraemer, K. M., McLeish, A. C., & Johnson, A. L. (2014). Associations between mindfulness and panic symptoms among young adults with asthma. *Psychology, Health & Medicine*, 1–10.

Kraines, S. H., & Thetford, E. S. (1972). *Help for the depressed*. Springfield, IL: Thomas.

Kramer, J., Boon, B., Schotanus-Dijkstra, M., van Ballegooijen, W., Kerkhof, A., & van der Poel, A. (2015). The mental health of visitors of web-based support forums for bereaved by suicide. *Crisis, 36*(1), 38–45.

Kramer, U., & Meystre, C. (2010). Assimilation process in a psychotherapy with a client presenting schizoid personality disorder. *Schweizer Archiv für Neurologie und Psychiatrie, 161*(4), 128–134.

Krapohl, D. J. (2002). The polygraph in personnel screening. In M. Kleiner (Ed.), *The handbook of polygraph testing*. San Diego, CA: Academic.

Krasnova, H., Wenninger, H., Widjaja, T., & Buxmann, P. (2013). Envy on Facebook: A hidden threat to users' life satisfaction? *Internationale Tagung Wirtschaftsinformatik, 27.02*. Retrieved from http://www.aisel.sidnrt.org/wi2013.

Krebs, G., Turner, C., Heyman, I., & Mataix-Cols, D. (2012). Cognitive behavior therapy for adolescents with body dysmorphic disorder: A case series. *Behavioural and Cognitive Psychotherapy, 40*(4), 452–461.

Kring, A. M., & Neale, J. M. (1996). Do schizophrenic patients show a disjunctive relationship among expressive, experiential, and psychophysiological components of emotion? *Journal of Abnormal Psychology, 105*(2), 249–257.

Krippner, S., & Paulson, C. M. (2006). Post-traumatic stress disorder among U.S. combat veterans. In T. G. Plante (Ed.), *Mental disorders of the new millennium: Vol. 2. Public and social problems*. Westport, CT: Praeger Publishers.

Kroemer, N. B., Guevara, A., Vollstädt-Klein, S., & Smolka, M. N. (2013). Nicotine alters food-cue reactivity via networks extending from the hypothalamus. *Neuropsychopharmacology, 38*(11), 2307–2314.

Kroon Van Diest, A. M., Tartakovsky, M., Stachon, C., Pettit, J. W., & Perez, M. (2014). The relationship between acculturative stress and eating disorder symptoms: Is it unique from general life stress? *Journal of Behavioral Medicine, 37*(3), 445–457.

Krueger, R. B. (2010). The DSM diagnostic criteria for sexual masochism. *Archives of Sexual Behavior, 39*(2), 346–356.

Krueger, R. G., & Kaplan, M. S. (2002). Behavioral and psychopharmacological treatment of the paraphilic and hypersexual disorders. *Journal of Psychiatric Practice, 8*(1), 21–32.

Kubera, M., Obuchowicz, E., Goehler, L., Brzeszcz, J., & Maes, M. (2011). In animal models, psychosocial stress-induced (neuro) inflammation, apoptosis and reduced neurogenesis are associated with the onset of depression. *Progress in Neuro-Psychopharmacology & Biological Psychiatry, 35*(3), 744–759.

Kuhn, R. (1958). The treatment of depressive states with G-22355 (imipramine hydrochloride). *American Journal of Psychiatry, 115*, 459–464.

Kuhn, T. S. (1962). *The structure of scientific revolutions.* Chicago: University of Chicago Press.

Kukla, L., Selesova, P., Okrajek, P., & Tulak, J. (2010). Somatoform dissociation and symptoms of traumatic stress in adolescents. *Activitas Nervosa Superior, 52*(1), 29–31.

Kulka, R. A., Schlesenger, W. E., Fairbank, J. A., Hough. R. L., Jordan, B. K., Marmar, C. R., & Weiss, D. S. (1990). *Trauma and the Vietnam War generation: Report of findings from the National Vietnam Veterans Readjustment Study.* New York: Brunner/Mazel.

Kumari, V., Uddin, S., Premkumar, P., Young, S., Gudjonsson, G. H., Raghuvanshi, S., . . . Das, M. (2014). Lower anterior cingulate volume in seriously violent men with antisocial personality disorder or schizophrenia and a history of childhood abuse. *Australian and New Zealand Journal of Psychiatry, 48*(2), 153–161.

Kunst, J. (2014, February 7). A headshrinker's guide to the galaxy: Psychoanalysis wisdom for everyday life. *Psychology Today.*

Kunst, M. J. J. (2011). Affective personality type, post-traumatic stress disorder symptom severity and post-traumatic growth in victims of violence. *Stress & Health: Journal of the International Society for the Investigation of Stress, 27*(1), 42–51.

Kurita, H., Maeshima, H., Kida, S., Matsuzaka, H., Shimano, T., Nakano, Y., . . . Arai, H. (2013). Serum dehydroepiandrosterone (DHEA) and DHEA-sulfate (S) levels in medicated patients with major depressive disorder compared with controls. *Journal of Affective Disorders, 146*(2), 205–212.

Kuyper, L., & Wijsen, C. (2014). Gender identities and gender dysphoria in the Netherlands. *Archives of Sexual Behavior, 43*(2), 377–385.

Kyaga, S., Landén, M., Boman, M., Hultman, C. M., Långström, N., & Lichtenstein, P. (2013). Mental illness, suicide and creativity: 40-year prospective total population study. *Journal of Psychiatric Research, 47*(1), 83–90.

Kyaga, S., Lichtenstein, P., Boman, M., Hultman, C., Långström, N., & Landén, M. (2011). Creativity and mental disorder: Family study of 300,000 people with severe mental disorder. *British Journal of Psychiatry, 199*(5), 373–379.

Laan, E., Rellini, A. H., & Barnes, T. (2013). Standard operating procedures for female orgasmic disorder: Consensus of the International Society for Sexual Medicine. *Journal of Sexual Medicine, 10*, 74–82.

Ladwig, K., Lederbogen, F., Albus, C., Angermann, C., Borggrefe, M., Fischer, D., & Herrmann-Lingen, C. (2014). Position paper on the importance of psychosocial factors in cardiology: Update 2013. *German Medical Science, 12*, Doc. 9.

Lagnado, L. (2007, December 4). Prescription abuse seen in U.S. nursing homes. *Wall Street Journal Online.* Retrieved from Wall Street Journal website: http://online.wsj.com/article/SB119672919018312521.html.

Lahey, B. B. (2008). Oppositional defiant disorder, conduct disorder, and juvenile delinquency. In S. P. Hinshaw & T. P. Beauchaine (Eds.), *Child and adolescent psychopathology* (pp. 335– 369). Hoboken, NJ: Wiley.

Lahmann, C., Henningsen, P., & Noll-Hussong, M. (2010). Somatoform pain disorder—Overview. *Psychiatria Danubina, 22*(3), 453–458.

Lai, C. Y., Zauszniewski, J. A., Tang, T., Hou, S. Y., Su, S. F., & Lai, P. Y. (2014). Personal beliefs, learned resourcefulness, and adaptive functioning in depressed adults. *Journal of Psychiatric and Mental Health Nursing, 21*(3), 280–287.

Lai, M. H., Maniam, T., Chan, L. F., & Ravindran, A. V. (2014). Caught in the web: A review of web-based suicide prevention. *Journal of Medical Internet Research, 16*(1), e30.

Lake, C. R. (2012). *Schizophrenia is a misdiagnosis: Implications for the DSM-5 and ICD11.* New York: Springer Science & Business Media.

Lake, N. (2014). *The caregivers: A support group's stories of slow loss, courage, and love.* New York: Scribner.

Lakhan, S. E., & Vieira, K. F. (2008). Nutritional therapies for mental disorders. *Nutrition Journal, 7*, 2.

Lamar, M., Foy, C. M. L., Beacher, F., Daly, E., Poppe, M., Archer, N., . . . Murphy, D. G. M. (2011). Down syndrome with and without dementia: An in vivo proton Magnetic Resonance Spectroscope study with implications for Alzheimer's disease. *NeuroImage, 57*(1), 63–68.

Lambdin, B. H., Masao, F., Chang, O., Kaduri, P., Mbwambo, J., Magimba, A., . . . Bruce, R. D. (2014). Methadone treatment for HIV prevention-feasibility, retention, and predictors of attrition in Dar es Salaam, Tanzania: A retrospective cohort study. *Clinical Infectious Diseases, 59*(5), 735–74.

Lambert, M. J. (2010). Using outcome data to improve the effects of psychotherapy: Some illustrations. In M. J. Lambert, *Prevention of treatment failure, The use of measuring, monitoring, and feedback in clinical practice* (pp. 203–242). Washington, DC: American Psychological Association.

Lambert, M. J., Shapiro, D. A., & Bergin, A. E. (1986). The effectiveness of psychotherapy. In S. L. Garfield & A. E. Bergin (Eds.), *Handbook of psychotherapy and behavioral change* (3rd ed.). New York: Wiley.

Lambert, M. J., Weber, F. D., & Sykes, J. D. (1993, April). Psychotherapy versus placebo. Poster presented at the annual meeting of the Western Psychological Association, Phoenix, AZ.

Lampe, L. (2015). Social anxiety disorders in clinical practice: Differentiating social phobia from avoidant personality disorder. *Australasian Psychiatry, 23*(4), 343–346.

Lampe, L., & Sunderland, M. (2015). Social phobia and avoidant personality disorder: Similar but different? *Journal of Personality Disorders, 29*(1), 115–130.

Lamprecht, F., Kohnke, C., Lempa, W., Sack, M., Matzke, M., & Munte, T. F. (2004). Event-related potentials and EMDR treatment of posttraumatic stress disorder. *Neuroscience Research, 49*(2), 267–272.

Lancet. (2010, February 2). Retraction—Ileal-lymphoid-nodular hyperplasia, non-specific colitis, and pervasive developmental disorder in children. *The Lancet.*

Lancioni, G. E., Singh, N. N., O'Reilly, M. F., Sigafoos, J., Bosco, A., Zonno, N., & Badagliacca, F. (2011). Persons with mild or moderate Alzheimer's disease learn to use urine alarms and prompts to avoid large urinary accidents. *Research in Developmental Disabilities, 32*(5), 1998–2004.

Landau, E. (2012, September 27). Smartphone apps become "surrogate therapists." *CNN.com.*

Landreth, G. L. (2012). *Play therapy: The art of relationship* (3rd ed.). New York: Routledge/Taylor & Francis Group.

Landrigan, P. J. (2011). Environment and autism. In E. Hollander, A. Kolevzon, & J. T. Coyle (Eds.), *Textbook of autism spectrum disorders* (pp. 247–264). Arlington, VA: American Psychiatric Publishing, Inc.

Lane, C. (2013, May 4). The NIMH withdraws support for DSM-5. *Psychology Today.*

Lane, K. L., Menzies, H. M., Bruhn, A. L., & Crnobori, M. (2011). Managing challenging behaviors in school: Research-based strategies that work. What works for specialneeds learners. New York: Guilford Press.

Laney, C., & Loftus, E. F. (2010). False memory. In J. M. Brown & E. A. Campbell (Eds.), *The Cambridge handbook of forensic psychology* (pp. 187–194). New York: Cambridge University Press.

Lang, E. V. (2010). Procedural hypnosis. In A. F. Barabasz, K. Olness, R. Boland, & S. Kahn (Eds.), *Medical hypnosis primer: Clinical and research evidence* (pp. 87–90). New York: Routledge/Taylor & Francis Group.

Lang, F. U., Otte, S., Vasic, N., Jäger, M., & Dudeck, M. (2015). [Impulsiveness among short-term prisoners with antisocial personality disorder.] *Psychiatrische Praxis, 42*(5), 274–277.

Lang, J. (1999, April 16). Local jails dumping grounds for mentally ill. *Detroit News.*

Lang, P. J., McTeague, L. M., & Bradley, M. M. (2014). Pathological anxiety and function/dysfunction in the brain's fear/defense circuitry. *Restorative Neurology and Neuroscience, 32*(1), 63–77.

Långström, N., & Seto, M. C. (2006). Exhibitionist and voyeuristic behavior in a Swedish national population survey. *Archives of Sexual Behavior, 35,* 427–435.

Långström, N., & Zucker, K. J. (2005). Transvestic fetishism in the general population: Prevalence and correlates. *Journal of Sex & Marital Therapy, 31*(2), 87–95.

Lanier, C. (2010). Structure, culture, and lethality: An integrated model approach to American Indian suicide and homicide. *Homicide Studies: An Interdisciplinary & International Journal, 14*(1), 72–78.

Lanning, K. V. (2001). *Child molesters: A behavioral analysis* (4th ed.). Washington, DC: National Center for Missing and Exploited Children.

Lapidus, K. B., Kopell, B. H., Ben-Haim, S., Rezai, A. R., & Goodman, W. K. (2013). History of psychosurgery: A psychiatrist's perspective. *World Neurosurgery, 80*(3-4), S27.e1-16.

Larsen, A., Boggild, H., Mortensen, J. T., Foldager, L., Hansen, J., Christensen, A., Arendt, M., & Munk-Jorgensen, P. (2010). Mental health in the workforce: An occupational psychiatric study. *International Journal of Social Psychiatry, 56*(6), 578–592.

Laska, K. M., Gurman, A. S., & Wampold, B. E. (2013). Expanding the lens of evidence-based practice in psychotherapy: A common factors perspective. *Psychotherapy* (Chicago), *51*(4), 467–481.

Latzer, Y., Katz, R., & Spivak, Z. (2011). *Facebook users more prone to eating disorders.* Retrieved from New Media website: http://newmedia-eng.haifa.ac.il/.

Laumann, E. O., Gagnon, J. H., Michael, R. T., & Michaels, S. (1994). *The social organization of sexuality.* Chicago: University of Chicago Press.

Laumann, E. O., Nicolosi, A., Glasser, D. B., Paik, A., Gingell, C., Moreira, E., & Wang, T. (2005). Sexual problems among women and men aged 40–80 years: Prevalence and correlates identified in the Global Study of Sexual Attitudes and Behaviors. *International Journal of Impotence Research, 17,* 39–57.

Laumann, E. O., Paik, A., & Rosen, R. C. (1999). Sexual dysfunction in the United States: Prevalence and predictors. *Journal of the American Medical Association, 281*(13), 1174.

Laursen, T. M., Nordentoft, M., & Mortensen, P. B. (2014). Excess early mortality in schizophrenia. *Annual Review of Clinical Psychology, 10,* 425–448.

Lavender, J. M., Wonderlich, S. A., Peterson, C. B., Crosby, R. D., Engel, S. G., Mitchell, J. E., . . . Berg, K. C. (2014). Dimensions of emotion dysregulation in bulimia nervosa. *European Eating Disorders Review, 22*(3), 212–216.

Lavin, M. (2008). Voyeurism: Psychopathology and theory. In D. R. Laws & W. T. O'Donohue (Eds.), *Sexual deviance: Theory, assessment, and treatment* (2nd ed., pp. 305–319). New York: Guilford Press.

Lawlor, A., & Kirakowski, J. (2014). When the lie is the truth: Grounded theory analysis of an online support group for factitious disorder. *Psychiatry Research, 218*(1-2), 209–218.

Lawlor, B. A., McCarron, M., Wilson, G., & McLoughlin, M. (2001). Temporal lobe-oriented CT scanning and dementia in Down's syndrome. *International Journal of Geriatric Psychiatry, 16*(4), 427–429.

Lawlor, P. G., & Bush, S. H. (2014). Delirium diagnosis, screening and management. *Current Opinion in Supportive and Palliative Care, 8*(3), 286–295.

Lawrence, P. J., & Williams, T. I. (2011). Pathways to inflated responsibility beliefs in adolescent obsessive-compulsive disorder: A preliminary investigation. *Behavioral and Cognitive Psychotherapy, 39*(2), 229–234.

Laws, D. R., & Ward, T. (2011). *Desistance from sex offending: Alternatives to throwing away the keys.* New York: Guilford Press.

Lawson, W. B. (2008). Schizophrenia in African Americans. In K. T. Mueser & D. V. Jeste (Eds.), *Clinical handbook of schizophrenia* (pp. 616–623). New York: Guilford Press.

Lawton, E. M., Shields, A. J., & Oltmanns, T. F. (2011). Five-factor model personality disorder prototypes in a community sample: Self- and informant-reports predicting interview-based DSM diagnoses. *Personality Disorders, 2*(4), 279–292.

Lazarov, O., Robinson, J., Tang, Y. P., Hairston, I. S., Korade-Mirnics, Z., Lee, V. M., . . . Sisodia, S. S. (2005). Environmental enrichment reduces A-beta levels and amyloid deposition in transgenic mice. *Cell, 120*(5), 572–574.

Lazarus, A. A. (1965). The treatment of a sexually inadequate man. In L. P. Ullman & L. Krasner (Eds.), *Case studies in behavior modification.* New York: Holt, Rinehart & Winston.

Lazarus, R. S., & Folkman, S. (1984). *Stress, appraisal, and coping.* New York: Springer Publishing.

Lazarus, S. A., Cheavens, J. S., Festa, F., & Zachary Rosenthal, M. (2014). Interpersonal functioning in borderline personality disorder: A systematic review of behavioral and laboratory-based assessments. *Clinical Psychology Review, 34*(3), 193–205.

Le, Q. A., Doctor, J. N., Zoellner, L. A., & Feeny, N. C. (2014). Cost-effectiveness of prolonged exposure therapy versus pharmacotherapy and treatment choice in posttraumatic stress disorder (the Optimizing PTSD Treatment Trial): A doubly randomized preference trial. *Journal of Clinical Psychiatry, 75*(3), 222–230.

Leahy, R. L. (2004). Cognitive-behavioral therapy. In R. G. Heimberg, C. J. Turk, & D. S. Mennin (Eds.), *Generalized anxiety disorder: Advances in research and practice.* New York: Guilford Press.

Lebedeva, A., Westman, E., Lebedev, A. V., Li, X., Winblad, B., Simmons, A., . . . Aarsland, D. (2014). Structural brain changes associated with depressive symptoms in the elderly with Alzheimer's disease. *Journal of Neurology, Neurosurgery, & Psychiatry, 85*(8), 930–935.

Lebow, J. L., Chambers, A. L., Christensen, A., & Johnson, S. M. (2012). Research on the treatment of couple distress. *Journal of Marital & Family Therapy, 38*(1), 145–168.

Lebow, J. L., & Uliaszek, A. A. (2010). Couples and family therapy for personality disorders. In J. J. Magnavita (Ed.), *Evidence-based treatment of personality dysfunction: Principles, methods, and processes* (pp. 193–221) Washington, DC: American Psychological Association.

Leclerc, A., Turrini, T., Sherwood, K., & Katzman, D. K. (2013). Evaluation of a nutrition rehabilitation protocol in hospitalized adolescents with restrictive eating disorders. *Journal of Adolescent Health, 53*(5), 585–589.

LeCroy, C. W., & Holschuh, J. (2012). *First person accounts of mental illness and recovery.* Hoboken, NJ: Wiley.

Ledoux, S., Miller, P., Choquet, M., & Plant, M. (2002). Family structure, parent-child relationships, and alcohol and other drug use among teenagers in France and the United Kingdom. *Alcohol Alcoholism, 37*(1), 52–60.

Lee, D. E. (1985). Alternative self-destruction. *Perceptual and Motor Skills, 61*(3, Part 2), 1065–1066.

Lee, E. B., An, W., Levin, M. E., & Twohig, M. P. (2015). An initial meta-analysis of acceptance and commitment therapy for treating substance use disorders. *Drug and Alcohol Dependence, 155,* 1–7.

Lee, J., & Freeman, J. L. (2014). Zebrafish as a model for investigating developmental lead (Pb) neurotoxicity as a risk factor in adult neurodegenerative disease: A mini-review. *Neurotoxicology, 43,* 57–64.

Lee, S., Yoon, S., Kim, J., Jin, S., & Chung, C. K. (2014). Functional connectivity of resting state EEG and symptom severity in patients with post-traumatic stress disorder. *Progress in Neuro-Psychopharmacology & Biological Psychiatry, 51,* 51–57.

Lee, T. (2011). A review on thirty days to hope & freedom from sexual addiction: The essential guide to beginning recovery and relapse prevention. *Sexual Addiction & Compulsivity, 18*(1), 52–55.

Leeman, R. F., Hoff, R. A., Krishnan-Sarin, S., Patock-Peckham, J. A., & Potenza, M. N. (2014). Impulsivity, sensation-seeking, and part-time job status in relation to substance use and gambling in adolescents. *Journal of Adolescent Health, 54*(4), 460–466.

Leenaars, A. A. (2004). Altruistic suicide: A few reflections. *Archives of Suicide Research, 8*(1), 1–7.

Leenaars, A. A. (2007). Gun-control legislation and the impact of suicide. *Crisis, 28*(Suppl. 1), 50–57.

Leenaars, A. A., & Lester, D. (2004). The impact of suicide prevention centers on the suicide rate in the Canadian provinces. *Crisis, 25*(2), 65–68.

Leff, J., Williams, G., Huckvale, M., Arbuthnot, M., & Leff, A. (2013). Computer-assisted therapy for medication-resistant auditory hallucinations: Proof-of-concept study. *British Journal of Psychiatry: The Journal of Mental Science, 202,* 428–433.

Leff, J., Williams, G., Huckvale, M., Arbuthnot, M., & Leff, A. P. (2014). Avatar therapy for persecutory auditory hallucinations: What is it and how does it work? *Psychosis, 6*(2), 166–176.

Leiblum, S. R. (2007). Sex therapy today: Current issues and future perspectives. In S. R. Leiblum (Ed.), *Principles and practice of sex therapy* (4th ed., pp. 3–22). New York: Guilford Press.

Leiblum, S. R. (2010). Introduction and overview: Clinical perspectives on and treatment for sexual desire disorders. In S. R. Leiblum (Ed.), *Treating sexual desire disorders: A clinical casebook* (pp. 1–22). New York: Guilford Press.

Leichsenring, F., & Salzer, S. (2014). A unified protocol for the transdiagnostic psychodynamic treatment of anxiety disorders: An evidence-based approach. *Psychotherapy, 51*(2), 224–245.

Lekander, M. (2002). Ecological immunology: The role of the immune system in psychology and neuroscience. *European Psychiatry, 7*(2), 98–115.

Lemma, A., Target, M., & Fonagy, P. (2011). The development of a brief psychodynamic intervention (dynamic interpersonal therapy) and its application to depression: A pilot study. *Psychiatry: Interpersonal and Biological Processes, 74*(1), 41–48.

Lemogne, C., Mayberg, H., Bergouignan, L., Volle, E., Delaveau, P., Lehéricy, S., Allilaire, J-F., & Fossati, P. (2010). Self-referential processing and the prefrontal cortex over the course of depression: A pilot study. *Journal of Affective Disorders, 124*(1-2), 196–201.

Lener, M. S., Wong, E., Tang, C. Y., Byne, W., Goldstein, K. E., Blair, N. J., . . . Hazlett, E. A. (2015). White matter abnormalities in schizophrenia and schizotypal personality disorder. *Schizophrenia Bulletin, 41*(1), 300–310.

Lentz, V., Robinson, J., & Bolton, J. M. (2010). Childhood adversity, mental disorder comorbidity, and suicidal behavior in schizotypal personality disorder. *Journal of Nervous and Mental Disease, 198*(11), 795–801.

Lenze, E. J., Wetherell, J. L., & Andreescu, C. (2011). Anxiety disorders. In C. E. Coffey, J. L. Cummings, M. S. George, & D. Weintraub (Eds.), *The American Psychiatric Publishing textbook of geriatric neuropsychiatry*. Arlington, VA: American Psychiatric Publishing, Inc.

Leong, F. T. L. (2013). *APA handbook of multicultural psychology: APA handbooks in psychology*. Washington, DC: American Psychological Association.

Leong, F. T. L. (2014). *APA handbook of multicultural psychology, Vol. 2: Applications and training*. Washington, DC: American Psychological Association.

Leong, G. B. (2000). Diminished capacity and insanity in Washington State: The battle shifts to admissibility. *Journal of the American Academy of Psychiatry and the Law, 28*(1), 77–81.

Lepp, A., Barkley, J. E., & Karpinski, A. C. (2014). The relationship between cell phone use, academic performance, anxiety, and satisfaction with life in college students. *Computers in Human Behavior, 31,* 343–350.

Lepping, P., & Raveesh, B. N. (2014). Overvaluing autonomous decision-making. *British Journal of Psychiatry, 204*(1), 1–2.

Lerna, A., Esposito, D., Conson, M., & Massagli, A. (2014). Long-term effects of PECS on social-communicative skills of children with autism spectrum disorders: A follow-up study. *International Journal of Language & Communication Disorders, 49*(4), 478–485.

Lerner, A. G., Rudinski, D., Bor, O., & Goodman, C. (2014) Flashbacks and HPPD: A clinical-oriented concise review. *The Israel Journal of Psychiatry and Related Sciences, 51*(4), 296–301.

Lerner, J. S., Li, Y., & Weber, E. U. (2013). The financial costs of sadness. *Psychological Sciences, 24*(1), 72–79.

Lester, D. (1985). The quality of life in modern America and suicide and homicide rates. *Journal of Social Psychology, 125*(6), 779–780.

Lester, D. (2000). *Why people kill themselves: A 2000 summary of research on suicide*. Springfield, IL: Charles C. Thomas.

Lester, D. (2011). Evidence-based suicide prevention by helplines: A meta-analysis. In M. Pompili & R. Tatarelli (Eds.), *Evidence-based practice in suicidology: A source book* (pp. 139–151). Cambridge MA: Hogrefe Publishing.

Lester, D. (2011). Evidence-based suicide prevention by lethal methods restriction. In M. Pompili & R. Tatarelli (Eds.), *Evidence-based practice in suicidology: A source book* (pp. 233–241). Cambridge MA: Hogrefe Publishing.

Lester, D., Innamorati, M., & Pompili, M. (2007). Psychotherapy for preventing suicide. In R. Tatarelli, M. Pompili, & P. Girardi (Eds.), *Suicide in psychiatric disorders*. New York: Nova Science Publishers.

Leung, G. M., Leung, T. K., & Ng, M. T. (2013). An outcome study of gestalt-oriented growth workshops. *International Journal of Group Psychotherapy, 63*(1), 117–125.

Levi, F., La Vecchia, C., Lucchini, F., Negri, E., Saxena, S., Maulik, P. K., & Saraceno, B. (2003). Trends in mortality from suicide, 1965–99. *Acta Psychiatrica Scandinavica, 108*(5), 341–349.

Levin, M. E., Pistorello, J., Hayes, S. C., Seeley, J. R., & Levin, C. (2015). Feasibility of an acceptance and commitment therapy adjunctive web-based program for counseling centers. *Journal of Counseling Psychology, 62*(3), 529–536.

Levin, M. E., Pistorello, J., Seeley, J. R., & Hayes, S. C. (2014). Feasibility of a prototype web-based acceptance and commitment therapy prevention program for college students. *Journal of American College Health, 62*(1), 20–30.

Levine, D. S., Himle, J. A., Taylor, R. J., Abelson, J. M., Matusko, N., Muroff, J., & Jackson, J. (2013). Panic disorder among African Americans, Caribbean blacks and non-Hispanic whites. *Social Psychiatry and Psychiatric Epidemiology, 48*(5), 711–723.

Levine, M. P., & Smolak, L. (2010) Cultural influences on body image and the eating disorders. In W. S. Agras (Ed.), *The Oxford handbook of eating disorders. Oxford library of psychology* (pp. 223–246). New York: Oxford University Press.

Levinson, D. F., & Nichols, W. E. (2014). *Major depression and genetics*. Stanford, CA: Stanford, School of Medicine.

Levinson, H. (2011, November 8). The strange and curious history of lobotomy. *BBC News Magazine*.

Levy, R. A., Ablon, J. S., & Kächele, H. (2011). *Psychodynamic psychotherapy research: Evidence-based practice and practice-based evidence (Current Clinical Psychiatry)*. Totowa, NJ: Humana Press.

Levy, T. B., Barak, Y., Sigler, M., & Aizenberg, D. (2011). Suicide attempts and burden of physical illness among depressed elderly inpatients. *Archives of Gerontology and Geriatrics, 52*(1), 115–117.

Leweke, F. M., Gerth, C. W., Koethe, D., Klosterkotter, J., Ruslanova, I., Krivogorsky, B., . . . Yolken, R. H. (2004). Antibodies to infectious agents in individuals with recent onset schizophrenia. *European Archives of Psychiatry and Clinical Neuroscience, 254*(1), 4–8.

Lewin, A. B. (2011). Parent training for childhood anxiety. In D. McKay & E. A. Storch (Eds.), *Handbook of child and adolescent anxiety disorders* (pp. 405–417). New York: Springer Science & Business Media.

Lewinsohn, P. M., Antonuccio, D. O., Steinmetz, J. L., & Teri, L. (1984). *The coping with depression course*. Eugene, OR: Castalia.

Lewinsohn, P. M., Clarke, G. N., Hops, H., & Andrews, J. (1990). Cognitive-behavioral treatment for depressed adolescents. *Behavior Therapist, 21,* 385–401.

Lewinsohn, P. M., Youngren, M. A., & Grosscup, S. J. (1979). Reinforcement and depression. In R. A. Depue (Ed.), *The psychobiology of the depressive disorders*. New York: Academic Press.

Lewis, R. W., Fugl-Meyer, K. S., Corona, G., Hayes, R. D., Laumann, E. O., Moreira, E. D., Jr., . . . Segraves, T. (2010). Definitions/epidemiology/risk factors for sexual dysfunction. *Journal of Sexual Medicine, 7,* 1598–1607.

Leyfer, O., Gallo, K. P., Cooper-Vince, C., & Pincus, D. B. (2013). Patterns and predictors of comorbidity of DSM-IV anxiety disorders in a clinical sample of children and adolescents. *Journal of Anxiety Disorders, 27*(3), 306–311.

Li, H., Lu, Q., Xiao, E., Li, Q., He, Z., & Mei, X. (2014). Methamphetamine enhances the development of schizophrenia in first-degree relatives of patients with schizophrenia. *Canadian Journal of Psychiatry, 59*(2), 107–113.

Li, L., Wu, M., Liao, Y., Ouyang, L., Du, M., Lei, D., . . . Gong, Q. (2014). Grey matter reduction associated with posttraumatic stress disorder and traumatic stress. *Neuroscience & Biobehavioral Reviews, 43,* 163–172.

Li, Q., Xiang, Y., Su, Y., Shu, L., Yu, X., Chiu, H. F., . . . Si, T. (2014). Antipsychotic polypharmacy in schizophrenia patients in China and its association with treatment satisfaction and quality of life: Findings of the third national survey on use of psychotropic medications in China. *Australian and New Zealand Journal of Psychiatry, 49*(2), 129–136.

Li, R., Cui, J., & Shen, Y. (2014). Brain sex matters: Estrogen in cognition and Alzheimer's disease. *Molecular and Cellular Endocrinology, 389*(1-2), 13–21.

Li, R., & El-Mallakh, R. S. (2004). Differential response of bipolar and normal control lymphoblastoid cell sodium pump to ethacrynic acid. *Journal of Affective Disorders, 80*(1), 1–17.

Liebman, J. I., McKinley-Pace, M. J., Leonard, A. M., Sheesley, L. A., Gallant, C. L., Renkey, M. E., & Lehman, E. B. (2002). Cognitive and psychosocial correlates of adults' eyewitness accuracy and suggestibility. *Personality and Individual Differences, 33*(1), 49–66.

Liera, S. J., & Newman, M. G. (2014). Rethinking the role of worry in generalized anxiety disorder: Evidence supporting a model of emotional contrast avoidance. *Behavior Therapy, 15*(3), 283–299.

Lightdale, H. A., Mack, A. H., & Frances, R. J. (2008). Psychodynamics. In H. D. Kleber & M. Galanter (Eds.), *The American Psychiatric Publishing textbook of substance abuse treatment* (4th ed., pp. 333–347). Arlington, VA: American Psychiatric Publishing.

Lightdale, H. A., Mack, A. H., & Frances, R. J. (2011). Psychodynamic psychotherapy. In M. Galanter & H. D. Kleber (Eds.), *Psychotherapy for the treatment of substance abuse* (pp. 219–247). Arlington, VA: American Psychiatric Publishing.

Lilenfeld, L. R. R. (2011). Personality and temperament. In R. A. H. Adan & W. H. Kaye (Eds.), *Behavioral neurobiology of eating disorders. Current topics in behavioral neurosciences* (pp. 3–16). New York: Springer-Verlag Publishing.

Lin, H., Eeles, E., Pandy, S., Pinsker, D., Brasch, C., & Yerkovich, S. (2015). Screening in delirium: A pilot study of two screening tools, the Simple Query for Easy Evaluation of Consciousness and Simple Question in Delirium. *Australasian Journal on Ageing*. [Electronic publication.]

Lin, L., & DeCusati, F. (2015). Muscle dysmorphia and the perception of men's peer muscularity preferences. *American Journal of Men's Health*. [Electronic publication.]

Lindau, S. T., Schumm, L. P., Laumann, E. O., Levinson, W., O'Muircheartaigh, C. A., & Waite, L. J. (2007). A study of sexuality and health among older adults in the United States. *New England Journal of Medicine, 357,* 762–774.

Lindenmayer, J. P., & Khan, A. (2012). Psychopathology. In J. A. Lieberman, T. S. Stroup, & D. O Perkins (Eds.), *Essentials of schizophrenia* (pp. 11–54). Arlington, VA: American Psychiatric Publishing.

Lindert, J., von Ehrenstein, O. S., Grashow, R., Gal, G., Braehler, E., & Weisskopf, M. G. (2014). Sexual and physical abuse in childhood is associated with depression and anxiety over the life course:

Systematic review and meta–analysis. *International Journal of Public Health, 59*(2), 359–372.

Lindhiem, O., Bernard, K., & Dozier, M. (2011). Maternal sensitivity: Within-person variability and the utility of multiple assessments. *Child Maltreatment, 16*(1), 41–50.

Lindner, M. (1968). *Hereditary and environmental influences upon resistance to stress.* Unpublished doctoral dissertation, University of Pennsylvania, Philadelphia.

Lindsay, J., Sykes, E., McDowell, I., Verreault, R., & Laurin, D. (2004). More than the epidemiology of Alzheimer's disease: Contributions of the Canadian Study of Health and Aging. *Canadian Journal of Psychiatry, 49*(2), 83–91.

Lindsey, P. (2011). Managing behavioral and psychological symptoms of dementia. In P. McNamara (Ed.), *Dementia, Vols. 1–3: History and incidence. Science and biology, treatments and developments* (pp. 73–91). Santa Barbara, CA: Praeger/ABC-CLIO.

Linehan, M. M., Cochran, B. N., & Kehrer, C. A. (2001). Dialectical behavior therapy for borderline personality disorder. In D. H. Barlow (Ed.), *Clinical handbook of psychological disorders* (3rd ed., pp. 470–522). New York: Guilford Press.

Linehan, M. M., Comtois, K. A., Murray, A., Brown, M. Z., Gallop, R. J., Heard, H. L., . . . Lindenboim, M. S. (2006). Two-year randomized trial + follow-up of dialectical behavior therapy vs. therapy by experts for suicidal behaviors and borderline personality disorder. *Archives of General Psychiatry, 63,* 757–766.

Linehan, M. M., Dimeff, L. A., Reynolds, S. K., Comtois, K. A., Welch, S. S., Heagerty, P., & Kivlahan, D. R. (2002). Dialectical behavior therapy versus comprehensive validation therapy plus 12-step for the treatment of opioid dependent women meeting criteria for borderline personality disorder. *Drug and Alcohol Dependence, 67*(1), 13–26.

Linehan, M. M., Korslund, K. E., Harned, M. S., Gallop, R. J., Lungu, A., Neacsiu, A. D., . . . Murray-Gregory, A. M. (2015). Dialectical behavior therapy for high suicide risk in individuals with borderline personality disorder: A randomized clinical trial and component analysis. *JAMA Psychiatry, 72*(5), 475–482.

Litjens, R. W., Brunt, T. M., Alderliefste, G., & Westerink, R. S. (2014). Hallucinogen persisting perception disorder and the serotonergic system: A comprehensive review including new MDMA-related clinical cases. *European Neuropsychopharmacology, 24*(8), 1309–1323.

Liu, A. (2007). *Gaining: The truth about life after eating disorders.* New York: Warner Books.

Liu, H., Liao, J., Jiang, W., & Wang, W. (2014). Changes in low-frequency fluctuations in patients with antisocial personality disorder revealed by resting-state functional MRI. *PLOS ONE, 9*(3), e89790.

Liu, X. V., Holtze, M., Powell, S. B., Terrando, N., Larsson, M. K., Persson, A., . . . & Erhardt, S. (2014). Behavioral disturbances in adult mice following neonatal virus infection or kynurenine treatment: Role of brain kynurenic acid. *Brain, Behavior, and Immunity, 36,* 80–89.

Lizarraga, L. E., Phan, A. V., Cholanians, A. B., Herndon, J. M., Lau, S. S., & Monks, T. J. (2014). Serotonin reuptake transporter deficiency modulates the acute thermoregulatory and locomotor activity response to 3,4-(6)-methylene-dioxymethamphetamine, and attenuates depletions in serotonin levels in SERT-KO rats. *Toxicological Sciences, 139*(2), 421–431.

Loas, G., Baelde, O., & Verrier, A. (2015). Relationship between alexithymia and dependent personality disorder: A dimensional analysis. *Psychiatry Research, 225*(3), 484–488.

Loas, G., Cormier, J., & Perez-Dias, F. (2011). Dependent personality disorder and physical abuse. *Psychiatry Research, 185*(1–2), 167–170.

Lochman, J. E., Barry, T., Powell, N., & Young, L. (2010). Anger and aggression. In D. W. Nangle, D. J. Hansen, C. A. Erdley & P. J. Norton (Eds.), *Practitioner's guide to empirically based measures of social skills* (pp. 155–166). New York: Springer Publishing Co.

Lochman, J. E., Boxmeyer, C. L., Powell, N. P., Barry, T. D., & Pardini, D. A. (2010). Anger control training for aggressive youths. In J. R. Weisz, & A. E. Kazdin (Eds.), *Evidence-based psychotherapies for children and adolescents* (2nd ed., pp. 227–242). New York: Guilford Press.

Lochman, J. E., Powell, N., Boxmeyer, C., Andrade, B., Stromeyer, S. L., & Jimenez-Camargo, L. A. (2012). Adaptations to the coping power program's structure, delivery settings, and clinician training. *Psychotherapy, 49*(2), 135–142.

Loewenthal, K. (2007). *Religion, culture and mental health.* New York: Cambridge University Press.

Loftus, E. F. (1993). The reality of repressed memories. *American Psychologist, 48,* 518–537.

Loftus, E. F. (2001). Imagining the past. *Psychologist, 14*(11), 584–587.

Loftus, E. F. (2003). Make-believe memories. *American Psychologist, 58*(11), 867–873.

Loftus, E. F. (2003). Our changeable memories: Legal and practical implications. *Nature Reviews Neuroscience, 4,* 231–234.

Loftus, E. F., & Cahill, L. (2007). Memory distortion: From misinformation to rich false memory. In J. S. Nairne (Ed.), *The foundations of remembering: Essays in honor of Henry L. Roediger, III.* New York: Psychology Press.

Lombardi, G., Celso, M., Bartelli, M., Cilotti, A., & Del Popolo, G. (2011). Female sexual dysfunction and hormonal status in multiple sclerosis patients. *Journal of Sexual Medicine, 8*(4), 1138–1146.

Long, J., Huang, G., Liang, W., Liang, B., Chen, Q., Xie, J., . . . Su, L. (2014). The prevalence of schizophrenia in mainland China: Evidence from epidemiological surveys. *Acta Psychiatrica Scandinavica, 130*(4), 244–256.

Loomer, H. P., Saunders, J. C., & Kline, N. S. (1957). A clinical and pharmacodynamic evaluation of iproniazid as a psychic energizer. *America Psychiatric Association Research Report, 8,* 129.

López, S. R., & Guarnaccia, P. J. (2000). Cultural psychopathology: Uncovering the social world of mental illness. *Annual Review of Psychology, 51,* 571–598.

López, S. R., & Guarnaccia, P. J. (2005). Cultural dimensions of psychopathology: The social world's impact on mental illness. In B. A. Winstead & J. E. Maddux, *Psychopathology: Foundations for a contemporary understanding* (pp. 19–37). Mahwah, NJ: Lawrence Erlbaum.

Lopez Molina, M. A., Jansen, K., Drews, C., Pinheiro, R., Silva, R., & Souza, L. (2014). Major depressive disorder symptoms in male and female young adults. *Psychology, Health & Medicine, 19*(2), 136–145.

LoPiccolo, J. (1991). Post-modern sex therapy for erectile failure. In R. C. Rosen & S. R. Leiblum (Eds.), *Erectile failure: Diagnosis and treatment.* New York: Guilford Press.

LoPiccolo, J. (1995). Sexual disorders and gender identity disorders. In R. J. Comer, *Abnormal psychology* (2nd ed.). New York: W. H. Freeman.

LoPiccolo, J. (1997). Sex therapy: A post-modern model. In S. J. Lynn & J. P. Garske (Eds.), *Contemporary psychotherapies: Models and methods* (2nd ed.). Columbus, OH: Merrill.

LoPiccolo, J. (2002). Postmodern sex therapy. In F. W. Kaslow (Ed.), *Comprehensive handbook of psychotherapy: Integrative/eclectic* (Vol. 4, pp. 411–435). New York: Wiley.

LoPiccolo, J. (2004). Sexual disorders affecting men. In L. J. Haas (Ed.), *Handbook of primary care psychology* (pp. 485–494). New York: Oxford University Press.

LoPiccolo, J., & Van Male, L. M. (2000). Sexual dysfunction. In A. E. Kazdin (Ed.), *Encyclopedia of psychology* (Vol. 7, pp. 246–251). Washington, DC: Oxford University Press/American Psychological Association.

Lorand, S. (1968). Dynamics and therapy of depressive states. In W. Gaylin (Ed.), *The meaning of despair.* New York: Jason Aronson.

Lorentzen, S., Fjeldstad, A., Ruud, T., Marble, A., Klungsøyr., O., Ulberg, R., & Høglend, P. A. (2015). The effectiveness of short- and long-term psychodynamic group psychotherapy on self-concept: Three years follow-up of a randomized clinical trial. *International Journal of Group Psychotherapy, 65*(3), 362–385.

Loukusa, S., Mäkinen, L., Kuusikko-Gauffin, S., Ebeling, H., & Moilanen, I. (2014). Theory of mind and emotion recognition skills in children with specific language impairment, autism spectrum disorder and typical development: Group differences and connection to knowledge of grammatical morphology, word-finding abilities and verbal working memory. *International Journal of Language & Communication Disorders, 49*(4), 498–507.

Lovaas, O. I. (1987). Behavioral treatment and normal educational/intellectual functioning in young autistic children. *Journal of Consulting and Clinical Psychology, 55,* 3–9.

Lovaas, O. I. (2003). *Teaching individuals with developmental delays: Basic intervention techniques.* Austin, TX: Pro-Ed.

Lovejoy, M. (2001). Disturbances in the social body: Differences in body image and eating problems among African-American and white women. *Gender & Society, 15*(2), 239–261.

Lublin, N. (2014, February 4). Cited in L. Kaufman, In texting era, crisis hotlines put help at youths' fingertips. *New York Times.*

Luborsky, E. B., O'Reilly-Landry, M., & Arlow, J. A. (2011). Psychoanalysis. In R. J. Corsini & D. Wedding (Eds.), *Current psychotherapies* (9th ed.). Belmont, CA: Brooks/Cole.

Luborsky, L. B. (1973). Forgetting and remembering (momentary forgetting) during psychotherapy. In M. Mayman (Ed.), *Psychoanalytic research and psychological issues* (Monograph 30). New York: International Universities Press.

Luborsky, L. B., Barrett, M. S., Antonuccio, D. O., Shoenberger, D., & Stricker, G. (2006). What else materially influences what is represented and published as evidence? In J. C. Norcross, L. E. Beutler, & R. F. Levant (Eds.), *Evidence-based practices in mental health: Debate and dialogue on the fundamental questions* (pp. 257–298). Washington, DC: American Psychological Association.

Luborsky, L. B., Rosenthal, R., Diguer, L., Andrusyna, T. P., Berman, J. S., Levitt, J. T., . . . Krause, E. D. (2002). The dodo bird verdict is alive and well—mostly. *Clinical Psychology: Science and Practice, 9*(1), 2–12.

Luborsky, L. B., Singer, B., & Luborsky, L. (1975). Comparative studies of psychotherapies. *Biological Psychiatry, 32,* 995–1008.

Lucas, G. (2006). Object relations and child psychoanalysis. [French]. *Revue Française de Psychanalyse, 70*(5), 1435–1473.

Lucka, I., & Dziemian, A. (2014). Pedophilia—a review of literature, casuistics, doubts. *Psychiatria Polska, 48*(1), 121–134.

Ludwig, A. M. (1995). *The price of greatness: Resolving the creativity and madness controversy.* New York: Guilford Press.

Lund, I. O., Brendryen, H., & Ravndal, E. (2014). A longitudinal study on substance use and related problems in women in opioid maintenance treatment from pregnancy to four years after giving birth. *Substance Abuse: Research and Treatment, 8,* 35–40.

Lundberg, U. (2011). Neuroendocrine measures. In R. J. Contrada & A. Baum (Eds.), *The handbook of* stress science: Biology, psychology, and health (pp. 531–542). New York: Springer Publishing.

Lundqvist, D., & Ohman, A. (2005). Emotion regulates attention: The relation between facial configurations, facial emotion, and visual attention. *Visual Cognition, 12*(1), 51–84.

Lundqvist, T. (2010). Imaging cognitive deficits in drug abuse. In D. W. Self & J. K. Staley (Eds.), *Behavioral neuroscience of drug addiction* (pp. 247–275). New York: Springer Publishing.

Lustig, S. L., Blank, A. R., Cirelli, R. J., Friedman, S. R., Green, F. C., Lopez, W. M., . . . Shampaine, V. C. (2013). Optimizing managed care peer reviews: Turning a "Doc to Doc" talk into better advocacy for psychiatric inpatients. *Psychiatric Services* (Washington, D.C.), *64*(8), 800–803.

Lyman, B. (1982). The nutritional values and food group characteristics of foods preferred during various emotions. *Journal of Psychology, 112,* 121–127.

Lynn, S. J., & Deming, A. (2010). The "Sybil tapes": Exposing the myth of dissociative identity disorder. *Theory & Psychology, 20*(2), 289–291.

Lysaker, P. H., Leonhardt, B. L., Brüne, M., Buck, K. D., James, A., Vohs, J., . . . Dimaggio, G. (2014). Capacities for theory of mind, metacognition, and neurocognitive function are independently related to emotional recognition in schizophrenia. *Psychiatry Research, 219*(1), 79–85.

Lysaker, P. H., Vohs, J., Hamm, J. A., Kukla, M., Minor, K. S., de Jong, S., . . . Dimaggio, G. (2014). Deficits in metacognitive capacity distinguish patients with schizophrenia from those with prolonged medical adversity. *Journal of Psychiatric Research, 55,* 126–132.

Macauley, A. (2010, December 3). Judging the bodies in ballet. *New York Times.*

MacDonald, W. L. (1998). The difference between blacks' and whites' attitudes toward voluntary euthanasia. *Journal for the Scientific Study of Religion, 37*(3), 411–426.

Mack, A., & Joy, J. (2001). *Marijuana as medicine? The science beyond the controversy.* Washington, DC: National Academy Press.

MacKinnon, B., & Fiala, A. (2016). *Ethics: Theory and contemporary issues, concise edition* (8th ed.) Independence, KY: Cengage Learning.

MacLaren, V. V. (2001). A qualitative review of the Guilty Knowledge Test. *Journal of Applied Psychology, 86*(4), 674–683.

MacLean, J., Kinley, D. J., Jacobi, F., Bolton, J. M., & Sareen, J. (2011). The relationship between physical conditions and suicidal behavior among those with mood disorders. *Journal of Affective Disorders, 130*(1-2), 245–250.

MacNeill, L. P., & Best, L. A. (2015). Perceived current and ideal body size in female undergraduates. *Eating Behaviors, 18,* 71–75.

Magee, C. L. (2007). The use of herbal and other dietary supplements and the potential for drug interactions in palliative care. *Palliative Medicine, 21*(6), 547–548.

Mäkinen, M., Puukko-Viertomies, L-R., Lindberg, N., Siirnes, M. A., & Aalberg, V. (2012). Body dissatisfaction and body mass in girls and boys transitioning from early to mid-adolescence: Additional role of self-esteem and eating habits. *BMC Psychiatry, 12,* 35.

Malhi, G. S., Tanious, M., Das, P., Coulston, C. M., & Berk, M. (2013). Potential mechanisms of action of lithium in bipolar disorder. *Current understanding. CNS Drugs, 27*(2), 135–153.

Maller, R. G., & Reiss, S. (1992). Anxiety sensitivity in 1984 and panic attacks in 1987. *Journal of Anxiety Disorders, 6*(3), 241–247.

Malm, U. I., Ivarsson, B. R., & Allebeck, P. (2014). Durability of the efficacy of integrated care in schizophrenia: A five-year randomized controlled study. *Psychiatric Services* (Washington, D.C.), *65*(8), 1054–1057.

Mamarde, A., Navkhare, P., Singam, A., & Kanoje, A. (2013). Recurrent dissociative fugue. *Indian Journal of Psychological Medicine, 35*(4), 400–401.

Manchanda, S. C., & Madan, K. (2014). Yoga and meditation in cardiovascular disease. *Clinical Research in Cardiology, 103*(9), 675–680.

Mancx. (2012, July 17). *Mancx survey: 98% of Americans distrust information on the internet.* San Francisco, CA: Mancx.

Mandal, A. (2014). Hallucination types. *NewsMedical.* Retrieved from News-Medical website: http://www.news-medical.net/health/hallucination-types.aspx.

Mandrioli, R., & Mercolini, L. (2015). Discontinued anxiolytic drugs (2009–214). *Expert Opinion on Investigational Drug, 24*(4), 557–573.

Manfredi, C., Caselli, G., Rovetto, F., Rebecchi, D., Ruggiero, G. M., Sassaroli, S., & Spada, M. M. (2011). Temperament and parental styles as predictors of ruminative brooding and worry. *Personality and Individual Differences, 50*(2), 186–191.

Manji, H. K., & Zarate, C. A., Jr. (Eds). (2011). *Behavioral neurobiology of bipolar disorder and its treatment.* Current topics in behavioral neurosciences. New York: Springer Science + Business Media.

Mann, A. P., Accurso, E. C., Stiles-Shields, C., Capra, L., Labuschagne, Z., Karnik, N. S., & Le Grange, D. (2014). Factors associated with substance use in adolescents with eating disorders. *Journal of Adolescent Health, 55*(2), 182–187.

Mann, J. J., & Currier, D. (2007). Neurobiology of suicidal behavior. In R. Tatarelli, M. Pompili, & P. Girardi (Eds.), *Suicide in psychiatric disorders.* New York: Nova Science Publishers.

Mann, M. (2009). The secrets behind the ten happiest jobs. *Excelle.* Retrieved from Excelle website: http://www.excelle.monster.com/benefits/articles/4033

Mann, R. E., Ainsworth, F., Al-Attar, Z., & Davies, M. (2008). Voyeurism: Assessment and treatment. In D. R. Laws & W. T. O'Donohue (Eds.), *Sexual deviance: Theory, assessment, and treatment* (2nd ed., pp. 320–335). New York: Guilford Press.

Manton, A., Wolf, L. A., Baker, K. M., Carman, M. J., Clark, P. R., Henderson, D., & Zavotsky, K. E. (2014). Ethical considerations in human subjects research. *Journal of Emergency Nursing, 40*(1), 92–94.

Manuel-Logan, R. (2011). Facebook helps stave off memory loss in elderly. *allfacebook.com.* Retrieved from Allfacebook website: http://allfacebook.com/facebook-helps-stave-off-memory-loss-in-elderly_b39329.

Marceaux, J. C., & Melville, C. L. (2011). Twelve-step facilitated versus mapping-enhanced cognitive-behavioral therapy for pathological gambling: A controlled study. *Journal of Gambling Studies, 27*(1), 171–190.

Marchand, W. R. (2014). Neural mechanisms of mindfulness and meditation: Evidence from neuroimaging studies. *World Journal of Radiology, 6*(7), 471–479.

Marchese, M., Cowan, D., Head, E., Ma, D., Karimi, K., Ashthorpe, V., . . . Sakic, B. (2014). Autoimmune manifestations in the 3xTg-AD model of Alzheimer's disease. *Journal of Alzheimer's Disease, 39*(1), 191–210.

Marcoux, L., Michon, P., Lemelin, S., Voisin, J. A., Vachon-Presseau, E., & Jackson, P. L. (2014). Feeling but not caring: Empathic alteration in narcissistic men with high psychopathic traits. *Psychiatry Research, 224*(3), 341–348.

Margo, J. L. (1985). Anorexia nervosa in adolescents. *British Journal of Medical Psychology, 58*(2), 193–195.

Maris, R. W. (2001). Suicide. In H. S. Friedman (Ed.), *Specialty articles from the encyclopedia of mental health.* San Diego: Academic Press.

Mark, T. L., Coffey, R. M., Vandivort-Warren, R., Harwood, H. J., & King, E. C. (2005, March 29). U.S. spending for mental health and substance treatment, 1991–2001. *Health Affairs, 24,* 133.

Mark, T. L., Harwood, H. J., McKusick, D. C., King, E. D., Vandivort-Warren, R., & Buck, J. A. (2008). Mental health and substance abuse spending by age, 2003. *Journal of Behavioral Health Services & Research, 35*(3), 279–289.

MarketWatch. (2014). Packaging for an aging population. *MarketWatch* press release, July 10, 2014.

Markota, M., Sin, J., Pantazopoulos, H., Jonilionis, R., & Berretta, S. (2014). Reduced dopamine transporter expression in the amygdala of subjects diagnosed with schizophrenia. *Schizophrenia Bulletin, 40*(5), 984–991.

Marks, B., Sisirak, J., Heller, T., & Wagner, M. (2010). Evaluation of community-based health promotion programs for Special Olympics athletes. *Journal of Policy and Practice in Intellectual Disabilities, 7*(2), 119–129.

Marks, I. M. (1977). Phobias and obsessions: Clinical phenomena in search of a laboratory model. In J. Maser and M. Seligman (Eds.), *Psychopathology: Experimental models.* San Francisco: Freeman.

Marks, I. M. (1987). *Fears, phobias and rituals: Panic, anxiety and their disorders.* New York: Oxford University Press.

Marks, I. M., & Gelder, M. G. (1967). Transvestism and fetishism: Clinical and psychological changes during faradic aversion. *British Journal of Psychiatry, 113,* 711–730.

Marks, J. W. (2014). *Peptic ulcer disease.* Retrieved from MedicineNet website: http://www.medicinenet.com/peptic_ulcer/article.

Marlatt, G. A., Kosturn, C. F., & Lang, A. R. (1975). Provocation to anger and opportunity for retaliation as determinants of alcohol consumption in social drinkers. *Journal of Abnormal Psychology, 84*(6), 652–659.

Marques, F. de A., Legal, E.-J., & Hofelmann, D. A. (2012). Body dissatisfaction and common mental disorders in adolescents. *Revista Paulista de Pediatria, 30*(4), 553–561.

Marsh, R., Horga, G., Parashar, N., Wang, Z., Peterson, B., & Simpson, H. (2014). Altered activation in fronto-striatal circuits during sequential processing of conflict in unmedicated adults with obsessive-compulsive disorder. *Biological Psychiatry, 75*(8), 615–622.

Marshall, J. J. (1997). Personal communication.

Marshall, T., Jones, D. P. H., Ramchandani, P. G., Stein, A., & Bass, C. (2007). Intergenerational transmission of health beliefs in somatoform disorders. *British Journal of Psychiatry, 191*(4), 449–450.

Marshall, W. L., & Marshall, L. E. (2015). Psychological treatment of the paraphilias: A review and an appraisal of effectiveness. *Current Psychiatry Reports, 17*(6). 47.

Marshall, W. L., Marshall, L. E., Serran, G. A., & O'Brien, M. D. (2011). *Rehabilitating sexual offenders: A strength-based approach.* Washington, DC: American Psychological Association.

Marshall, W. L., Serran, G. A., Marshall, L. E., & O'Brien, M. D. (2008). Sexual deviation. In M. Hersen & J. Rosqvist (Eds.), *Handbook of psychological assessment, case conceptualization and treatment, Vol. 1: Adults.* Hoboken, NJ: John Wiley & Sons.

Marsiglia, F. F., & Smith, S. J. (2010). An exploration of ethnicity and race in the etiology of substance use: A health disparities approach. In L. Scheier (Ed.), *Handbook of drug use etiology: Theory, methods, and empirical findings* (pp. 289–304). Washington, DC: American Psychological Association.

Marston, W. M. (1917). Systolic blood pressure changes in deception. *Journal of Experimental Psychology, 2,* 117–163.

Martell, C. R., Dimidjian, S., & Herman-Dunn, R. (2010). *Behavioral activation for depression: A clinician's guide.* New York: Guilford Press.

Martens, W. H. J. (2005). Multidimensional model of trauma and correlated antisocial personality disorder. *Journal of Loss and Trauma, 10*(2), 115–129.

Martin, A. J. (2014, May 12). The role of ADHD in academic adversity: Disentangling ADHD effects from other personal and contextual factors. *School Psychology Quarterly.*

Martin, A. L., Huelin, R., Wilson, D., Foster, T. S., & Mould, F. J. (2013). A systematic review assessing the economic impact of sildenafil citrate (Viagra) in the treatment of erectile dysfunction. *Journal of Sexual Medicine, 10,*1389–1400.

Martin, D. M., Gálvez, V., & Loo, C. K. (2015). Predicting retrograde autobiographical memory changes following electroconvulsive therapy: Relationships between individual, treatment, and early clinical factors. *The International Journal of Neuropsychopharmacology* 1–8. [Advance publication]

Martin, L. A., Neighbors, H. W., & Griffith, D. M. (2013). The experience of symptoms of depression in men vs. women: Analysis of the National Comorbidity Survey Replication. *JAMA Psychiatry, 70*(10), 1100–1106.

Martin, P., Baenziger, J., MacDonald, M., Siegler, I. C., & Poon, L. W. (2009). Engaged lifestyle, personality, and mental status among centenarians. *Journal of Adult Development, 16*(4), 199–208.

Martin, P., MacDonald, M., Margrett, J., & Poon, L. W. (2010). Resilience and longevity: Expert survivorship of centenarians. In P. S. Fry & L. M. Corey (Eds.), *New frontiers in resilient aging: Life-strengths and well-being in late life* (pp. 213–238). New York: Cambridge University Press.

Martin, P. L. (2000). Potency and pregnancy in Japan: Did Viagra push the pill? *Tulsa Lawyers Journal, 35,* 651–677.

Martin, S. A., Atlantis, E., Lange, K., Taylor, A. W., O'Loughlin, P., Wittert, G. A., and members of the Florey Adelaide Male Ageing Study (FAMAS). (2014). Predictors of sexual dysfunction incidence and remission in men. *Journal of Sexual Medicine, 11,* 1136–1147.

Martín-Blanco, A., Soler, J., Villalta, L., Feliu-Soler, A., Elices, M., Pérez, V., . . . Pascual, J. C. (2014). Exploring the interaction between childhood maltreatment and temperamental traits on the severity of borderline personality disorder. *Comprehensive Psychiatry, 55*(2), 311–318.

Martino, F., Caselli, G., Berardi, D., Fiore, F., Marino, E., Menchetti, M., . . . Sassaroli, S. (2015). Anger rumination and aggressive behaviour in borderline personality disorder. *Personality and Mental Health.* [Electronic publication.]

Martins, M. V., Peterson, B. D., Almeida, V., Mesquita-Guimarães, J., & Costa, M. E. (2014). Dyadic dynamics of perceived social support in couples facing infertility. *Human Reproduction* (Oxford, England), *29*(1), 83–89.

Martinsen, M., & Sundgot-Borgen, J. (2013). Higher prevalence of eating disorders among adolescent elite athletes than controls. *Medicine & Science in Sports and Exercise, 45*(6), 1188–1197.

Martlew, J., Pulman, J., & Marson, A. G. (2014). Psychological and behavioural treatments for adults with non-epileptic attack disorder. *Cochrane Database of Systematic Reviews, 2,* CD006370.

Mas-Expósito, L., Amador-Campos, J. A., Gómez-Benito, J., Mauri-Mas, L., & Lalucat-Jo, L. (2015). Clinical case management for patients with schizophrenia with high care needs. *Community Mental Health Journal, 51*(2), 165–170.

Mash, E. J., & Wolfe, D. A. (2015). *Abnormal child psychology* (6th ed.). Independence, KY: Cengage Publications.

Maslow, A. H. (1970). *Motivation and personality* (2nd ed.). New York: Harper & Row.

Masters, W. H., & Johnson, V. E. (1966). *Human sexual response.* Boston: Little, Brown.

Masters, W. H., & Johnson, V. E. (1970). *Human sexual inadequacy.* Boston: Little, Brown.

Mathew, J., & McGrath, J. (2002). Readability of consent forms in schizophrenia research. *Australian and New Zealand Journal of Psychiatry, 36*(4), 564–565.

Mathis, C. E. G. (2014). Anorexia Nervosa Health Center pro-anorexia web sites: The thin web line. *WebMD.* Retrieved from WebMD website: http://www.webmd.com/mental-health/eating-disorders/anorexia.

Mathys, M., & Belgeri, M. T. (2010). Psychiatric disorders. In L. C. Hutchison & R. B. Sleeper (Eds.), *Fundamentals of geriatric pharmacotherapy: An evidence-based approach.* Bethesda, MD: American Society of Health-Systems Pharmacists.

Matsumoto, D. (Ed.). (2001). *The handbook of culture and psychology.* New York: Oxford University Press.

Matsumoto, D. (2007). Culture, context, and behavior. *Journal of Personality, 75*(6), 1285–1320.

Matsumoto, D., & Hwang, H. S. (2011). Culture, emotion, and expression. In M. J. Gelfand, C-Y Chiu, & Y-Y. Hong (Eds.), *Advances in culture and psychology (Vol. 1), Advances in culture and psychology* (pp. 53–98). New York: Oxford University Press.

Matsumoto, D., & Hwang, H. S. (2012). Culture and emotion: The integration of biological and cultural contributions. *Journal of Cross-Cultural Psychology, 43*(1), 91–118.

Matsumoto, D., & Juang, L. (2008). *Culture and psychology* (4th ed.). Australia: Thomson Wadsworth.

Matsunaga, H., & Seedat, S. (2011). Obsessive-compulsive spectrum disorders: Crossnational and ethnic issues. In E. Hollander, J. Zohar, P. J. Sirovatka, & D. A. Regier (Eds.), *Obsessive-compulsive spectrum disorders: Refining the research agenda for DSM-V* (pp. 205–221). Washington, DC: American Psychiatric Publishing.

Maurice, W. L. (2007). Sexual desire disorders in men. In S. R. Leiblum (Ed.), *Principles and practice of sex therapy* (4th ed., pp. 181–210). New York: Guilford Press.

Mauthner, N. S. (2010). "I wasn't being true to myself ": Women's narratives of postpartum depression. In D. C. Jack & A. Ali (Eds.), *Silencing the self across cultures: Depression and gender in the social world* (pp. 459–484). New York: Oxford University Press.

Mayberg, H. S., Lozano, A. M., Voon, V., McNeely, H. E., Seminowicz, D., Hamani, C., . . . Kennedy, S. H. (2005). Deep brain stimulation for treatment-resistant depression. *Neuron, 45,* 651–660.

Mayo, C., & George, V. (2014). Eating disorder risk and body dissatisfaction based on muscularity and body fat in male university students. *Journal of American College Health, 62*(6), 407–415.

Maza, C. (2015, April 13). Tribes battle high teen suicide rates on native American reservations. *CSMonitor.* Retrieved from CS Monitor website: http://www.csmonitor.com/USA/USA-update/2015/0413.

McAfee. (2014). *Study reveals majority of adults share intimate details via unsecured digital devices.* Santa Clara, CA: Author.

McAnulty, R. D. (2006). Pedophilia. In R. D. McAnulty & M. M. Burnette (Eds.), *Sex and sexuality, Vol. 3: Sexual deviation and sexual offenses.* Westport, CT: Praeger Publishers.

McArthur, G., Castles, A., Kohnen, S., Larsen, L., Jones, K., Anandakumar, T., & Banales, E. (2013, October 13). Sight word and phonics training in children with dyslexia. *Journal of Learning Disabilities, 48*(4), 391–407.

McBride, J. J., Vlieger, A. M., & Anbar, R. D. (2014). Hypnosis in paediatric respiratory medicine. *Paediatric Respiratory Reviews, 15*(1), 82–85.

McCabe, C., & Mishor, Z. (2011). Antidepressant medications reduce subcortical-cortical resting-state functional connectivity in healthy volunteers. *Neuroimage, 57*(4), 1317–1323.

McCaghy, C. H., Capron, T. A., Jamieson, J. D., & Carey, S. H. (2006). *Deviant behavior: Crime, conflict, and interest groups* (7th ed.). New York: Pearson/Allyn & Bacon.

McCance-Katz, E. F. (2010). Drug interactions in the pharmacological treatment of substance use disorders. In E. V. Nunes, J. Selzer, P. Levounis, & C. A. Davies (Eds.), *Substance dependence and co-occurring psychiatric disorders: Best practices for diagnosis and treatment* (pp. 18-1– 18-36). Kingston, NJ: Civic Research Institute.

McCarthy, B., & McCarthy, E. (2012). *Sexual awareness: Your guide to healthy couple sexuality* (5th ed.). New York: Routledge/Taylor & Francis Group.

McCarthy, D. E., Curtin, J. J., Piper, M. E., & Baker, T. B. (2010). Negative reinforcement: Possible clinical implications of an integrative model. In J. D. Kassel (Ed.), *Substance abuse and emotion* (pp. 15–42). Washington, DC: American Psychological Association.

McClelland, S. (1998, September 21). Grief crisis counsellors under fire: Trauma teams were quick to descend on Peggy's Cove. Susan McClelland asks whether they do more harm than good. *Ottawa Citizen,* p. A4.

McCloud, A., Barnaby, B., Omu, N., Drummond, C., & Aboud, A. (2004). Relationship between alcohol use disorders and suicidality in a psychiatric population: In-patient prevalence study. *British Journal of Psychiatry, 184*(5), 439–445.

McClure, E. A., Gipson, C. D., Malcolm, R. J., Kalivas, P. W., & Gray, K. M. (2014). Potential role of N-acetylcysteine in the management of substance use disorders. *CNS Drugs, 28*(2), 95–106.

McConnaughey, J. (2014, May 17). Alcohol use may worsen in nursing homes. *ABC News.* Retrieved from ABC News website: http://abcnews.go.com/health.

McCrady, B. S. (2014). Alcohol use disorders. In D. H. Barlow, *Clinical handbook of psychological disorders* (5th ed., Ch. 13). New York: Guilford Press.

McDermott, B. E., Leamon, M. H., Feldman, M. D., & Scott, C. L. (2012). Factitious disorder and malingering. In J. A. Bourgeois, U. Parthasarathi, & A. Hategan (Eds.), *Psychiatry review and Canadian certification exam preparation guide* (pp. 267–276). Arlington, VA: American Psychiatric Publishing.

McDermott, B. M., & Jaffa, T. (2005). Eating disorders in children and adolescents: An update. *Current Opinions in Psychiatry, 18*(4), 407–410.

McDonald, J. A., Terry, M. B., & Tehranifar, P. (2014). Racial and gender discrimination, early life factors, and chronic physical health conditions in midlife. *Women's Health Issues: Official Publication of the Jacobs Institute of Women's Health, 24*(1), e5–e59.

McDowell, D. (2005). Marijuana, hallucinogens, and club drugs. In R. J. Frances, A. H. Mack, & S. I. Miller (Eds.), *Clinical textbook of addictive disorders* (3rd ed., pp. 157–183). New York: Guilford Press.

McDowell, D. (2011). Marijuana, hallucinogens, and club drugs. In R. J. Frances, S. I. Miller, & A. H. Mack (Eds.), *Clinical textbook of addictive disorders* (3rd ed., paperback, Ch. 8). New York: Guilford Press.

McEachin, J. J., Smith, T., & Lovaas, O. I. (1993). Long-term outcome for children with autism who received early intensive behavioral treatment. *American Journal of Mental Retardation, 97*(4), 359–372.

McEvoy, P. M. (2007). Effectiveness of cognitive behavioural group therapy for social phobia in a community clinic: A benchmarking study. *Behavioral Research and Therapy, 45*(12), 3030–3040.

McFeeters, D., Boyda, D., & O'Neill, S. (2015). Patterns of stressful life events: Distinguishing suicide ideators from suicide attempters. *Journal of Affective Disorders, 175,* 192–198.

McGlothlin, J. M. (2008). *Developing clinical skills in suicide assessment, prevention, and treatment.* Alexandria, VA: American Counseling Association.

McGoldrick, M., Loonan, R., & Wohlsifer, D. (2007). Sexuality and culture. In S. R. Leiblum (Ed.), *Principles and practice of sex therapy* (4th ed., pp. 416–441). New York: Guilford Press.

McGrath, R. E., & Carroll, E. J. (2012). The current status of "projective" "tests". In H. Cooper, P. M. Camic, D. L. Long, A. T. Panter, D. Rindskopf, & K. J. Sher (Eds.), *APA handbook of research methods in psychology. Vol. 1: Foundations, planning, measures, and psychometrics* (pp. 329–348). Washington, DC: American Psychological Association.

McGuffin, P. (2014). Different genetic factors influence specific symptom dimensions of DSM-IV major depression. *Evidence-Based Mental Health, 17*(1), 18.

McGuffin, P., Katz, R., Watkins, S., & Rutherford, J. (1996). A hospital-based twin register of the heritability of DSM-IV unipolar depression. *Archives of General Psychiatry, 53,* 129–136.

McGuire, P. A. (2000, February). New hope for people with schizophrenia. *Monitor on Psychology, 31*(2), 24–28.

McGurk, S. R., Mueser, K. T., Mischel, R., Adams, R., Harvey, P. D., McClure, M. M., . . . Siever, L. J. (2013). Vocational functioning in schizotypal and paranoid personality disorders. *Psychiatry Research, 210*(2), 498–504.

McIlvaine, R. (2011, January 25). 3-D software becoming safeware to returning soldiers with PTSD. *Army News Service.*

McKay, D., Gosselin, J. T., & Gupta, S. (2008). Body dysmorphic disorder. In J. S. Abramowitz, D. McKay, & S. Taylor (Eds.), *Obsessive-compulsive disorder: Subtypes and spectrum conditions.* Oxford, England: Elsevier.

McKay, D., Taylor, S., & Abramowitz, J. S. (2010). Cognitive-behavioral therapy and refractory cases: What factors lead to limited treatment response? In D. McKay, J. S. Abramowitz & S. Taylor (Eds.), *Cognitive-behavioral therapy for refractory cases: Turning failure into success* (pp. 3–10). Washington, DC: American Psychological Association.

McKenna, K., Gallagher, K. S., Forbes, P. W., & Ibezlako, P. (2015). Ready, set, relax: Biofeedback-assisted relaxation training (BART) in a pediatric psychiatry consultation service. *Psychosomatics, 56*(4), 381–389.

McKenzie, G., & Teri, L. (2011). Psychosocial therapies. In C. E. Coffey, J. L. Cummings, M. S. George, & D. Weintraub (Eds.), *The American Psychiatric Publishing textbook of geriatric neuropsychiatry.* Arlington, VA: American Psychiatric Publishing, Inc.

McKenzie, J. A., McConkey, R., & Adnams, C. (2013). Intellectual disability in Africa: Implications for research and service development. *Disability and Rehabilitation, 35*(20), 1750–1755.

McKinley, J. (2010, October 4). Several recent suicides put light on pressures facing gay teenagers. *New York Times.*

McLaughlin, K. A., Nandi, A., Keyes, K. M., Uddin, M., Aiello, A. E., Galea, S., & Koenen, K. C. (2012). Home foreclosure and risk of psychiatric morbidity during the recent financial crisis. *Psychological Medicine, 42*(7), 1441–1448.

McLay, R. N. (2013). How does virtual-reality therapy for PTSD work? *Scientific American, 24*(5).

McLay, R. N., Daylo, A. A., & Hammer, P. S. (2006). No effect of lunar cycle on psychiatric admissions or emergency evaluations. *Military Medicine, 17*(12), 1239–1242.

McLean, D., Thara, R., John, S., Barrett, R., Loa, P., McGrath, J., & Mowry, B. (2014). DSM-IV 'Criterion A' schizophrenia symptoms across ethnically different populations: Evidence for differing psychotic symptom content or structural organization? *Culture, Medicine and Psychiatry, 38*(3), 408–426.

McMahon, C. G., Jannini, E., Waldinger, M., & Rowland, D. (2013). Standard operating procedures in the disorders of orgasm and ejaculation. *Journal of Sexual Medicine, 1,* 204–229.

McMahon, R. J., & Frick, P. J. (2005). Evidence-based assessment of conduct problems in children and adolescents. *Journal of Clinical Child & Adolescent Psychology, 34,* 477–505.

McMahon, R. J., & Frick, P. J. (2007). Conduct and oppositional disorders. In E. J. Mash & R. A. Barkley (Eds.), *Assessment of childhood disorders* (4th ed., pp. 132–183). New York: Guilford Press.

McMahon, R. J., Witkiewitz, K., & Kotler, J. S. (2010). Predictive validity of callous-unemotional traits measured in early adolescence with respect to multiple antisocial outcomes. *Journal of Abnormal Psychology, 119*(4), 752–763.

McMain, S. F. (2015). Advances in the treatment of borderline personality disorder: An introduction to the special issue. *Journal of Clinical Psychology, 71*(8), 741–746.

McManus, M. A., Hargreaves, P., Rainbow, L., & Alison, L. J. (2013). Paraphilias: Definition, diagnosis and treatment. *F1000prime Reports, 5,* 36.

McNally, R. J. (2004, April 1). Psychological debriefing does not prevent posttraumatic stress disorder. *Psychiatric Times,* p. 71.

McNally, R. J., Clancy, S. A., Barrett, H. M., & Parker, H. A. (2005). Reality monitoring in adults reporting repressed, recovered, or continuous memories of childhood sexual abuse. *Journal of Abnormal Psychology, 114*(1), 147–152.

McNally, R. J., & Geraerts, E. (2009). A new solution to the recovered memory debate. *Perspectives on Psychological Science, 4*(2), 126–134.

McNeil, E. B. (1967). *The quiet furies.* Englewood Cliffs, NJ: Prentice Hall.

McPherson, M., Smith-Lovin, L., & Brashears, M. (2006). Social isolation in America: Changes in core discussion networks over two decades. *American Sociological Review, 71,* 353–375.

McSweeney, S. (2004). Depression in women. In L. Cosgrove & P. J. Caplan (Eds.), *Bias in psychiatric diagnosis* (pp. 183–188). Northvale, NJ: Jason Aronson.

Meana, M. (2012). *Sexual dysfunction in women: Advances in psychotherapy—Evidence-based practice.* Cambridge, MA: Hogrefe Publishing.

Medina, M., & Avila, J. (2014). New perspectives on the role of tau in Alzheimer's disease: Implications for therapy. *Biochemical Pharmacology, 88*(4), 540–547.

Mednick, S. A. (1971). Birth defects and schizophrenia. *Psychology Today, 4,* 48–50.

Meersand, P. (2011). Psychological testing and the analytically trained child psychologist. *Psychoanalytic Psychology, 28*(1), 117–131.

Mehta, D., Newport, D. J., Frishman, G., Kraus, L., Rex-Haffner, M., Ritchie, J. C., . . . Binder, E. B. (2014). Early predictive biomarkers for postpartum depression point to a role for estrogen receptor signaling. *Psychological Medicine,* 1–14.

Meichenbaum, D. H. (1975). A self-instructional approach to stress management: A proposal for stress inoculation training. In I. Sarason & C. D. Spielberger (Eds.), *Stress and anxiety* (Vol. 2). New York: Wiley.

Meichenbaum, D. H. (1977). *Cognitive-behavior modification: An integrative approach.* New York: Plenum Press.

Meichenbaum, D. H. (1993). Stress inoculation training: A 20-year update. In P. M. Lehrer & R. L. Woolfolk (Eds.), *Principles and practice of stress management* (2nd ed.). New York: Guilford Press.

Meijer, E. H., & Verschuere, B. (2010). The polygraph and the detection of deception. *Journal of Forensic Psychology Practice, 10*(4), 325–338.

Meinhard, N., Kessing, L. V., & Vinberg, M. (2014). The role of estrogen in bipolar disorder, a review. *Nordic Journal of Psychiatry, 68*(2), 81–87.

Meloy, J. R., & Yakeley, J. (2010). Psychodynamic treatment of antisocial personality disorder: Psychodynamic psychotherapy for personality disorders: A clinical handbook. In J. F. Clarkin, P. Fonagy, & G. O. Gabbard (Eds.), *Psychodynamic psychotherapy for personality disorders: A clinical handbook* (pp. 311–336). Arlington, VA: American Psychiatric Publishing.

Meltzer, H. Y. (2011). Evidence-based treatment for reducing suicide risk in schizophrenia. In M. Pompili & R. Tatarelli (Eds.), *Evidence-based practice in suicidology: A source book* (pp. 317–328). Cambridge MA: Hogrefe Publishing.

Melville, J. (1978). *Phobias and obsessions.* New York: Penguin.

Mendes, E. (2010). Uptick in high cholesterol and high blood pressure in U.S. *Gallup.* Retrieved from Gallup website: http://www.gallup.com/poll/127055.

Merenda, R. R. (2008). The posttraumatic and sociocognitive etiologies of dissociative identity disorder: A survey of clinical psychologists. *Dissertation Abstracts International: Section B: The Sciences and Engineering, 68*(8-B), 55–84.

Merikangas, K. R., He, J-P., Brody, D., Fisher, P. W., Bourdon, K., & Koretz, D. (2010). Prevalence and treatment of mental disorders among US children in the 2001–2004 NHANES. *Pediatrics, 125*(1), 75–81.

Merikangas, K. R., He, J., Rapoport, J., Vitiello, B., & Olfson, M. (2013). Medication use in U.S. youth with mental disorders. *JAMA Pediatrics, 167*(2), 141–148.

Merikangas, K. R., Jin, R., He, J-P., Kessler, R. C., Lee, S., Sampson, N. A., . . . & Zarkov, Z. (2011). Prevalence and correlates of bipolar spectrum disorder in the World Mental Health Survey Initiative. *Archives of General Psychiatry, 68*(3), 241–251.

Merikangas, K. R., & Swanson, S. A. (2010). Comorbidity in anxiety disorders. In M. B. Stein & T. Steckler (Eds.), *Behavioral neurobiology of anxiety and its treatment: Current topics in behavioral neurosciences* (pp. 37–59). New York: Springer Science + Business Media.

Merkl, A., Schubert, F., Quante, A., Luborzewski, A., Brakemeier, E-L., Grimm, S., Heuser, I., & Baibouj, M. (2011). Abnormal cingulate and prefrontal cortical neurochemistry in major depression after electroconvulsive therapy. *Biological Psychiatry, 69*(8), 772–779.

Merrick, E. S., Hodgkin, D., Hiatt, D., Horgan, C. M., Greenfield, S. F., & McCann, B. (2011). Integrated employee assistance program: Managed behavioral health plan utilization by persons with substance use disorders. *Journal of Substance Abuse Treatment, 40*(3), 299–306.

Merrick, J., Uldall, P., & Volther, J. (2014). Intellectual and developmental disabilities: Denmark, normalization, and de-institutionalization. *Frontiers in Public Health, 2,* 161.

Merrill, J. E., Carey, K. B., Lust, S. A., Kalichman, S. C., & Carey, M. P. (2014). "Do students mandated to intervention for campus alcohol–related violations drink more than non–mandated students?" *Psychology of Addictive Behaviors, 28*(4), 1265–1270.

Messer, S. B., & Abbass, A. A. (2010). Evidence-based psychodynamic therapy with personality disorders. In J. J. Magnavita (Ed.), *Evidence-based treatment of personality dysfunction: Principles, methods, and processes* (pp. 79–111) Washington, DC: American Psychological Association.

Messias, E. (2014). Standing on the shoulders of Pinel, Freud, and Kraepelin: A historiometric inquiry into the histories of psychiatry. *Journal of Nervous and Mental Disease, 202*(11), 788–792.

Metsälä, E., & Vaherkoski, U. (2014). Medication errors in elderly acute care: A systematic review. *Scandinavian Journal of Caring Sciences, 28*(1), 12–28.

Metzl, J. M. (2004). Voyeur nation? Changing definitions of voyeurism, 1950–2004. *Harvard Review of Psychiatry, 12*(q), 127–131.

Metzner, J. L., & Dvoskin, J. A. (2010). Correctional psychiatry. In R. I. Simon & L. H. Gold (Eds.), *The American Psychiatric Publishing textbook of forensic psychiatry* (2nd ed., pp. 395– 411). Arlington, VA: American Psychiatric Publishing.

Meyer, P. (2010). *Liespotting: Proven techniques to detect deception.* New York: St. Martin's Griffin.

Meyer, V. (1966). Modification of expectations in cases with obsessional rituals. *Behavioral Research and Therapy, 4,* 273–280.

MHA (Mental Health America). (2008). *Americans reveal top stressors, how they cope.* Alexandria, VA: Author.

MHA (Mental Health America). (2010). *Americans reveal top stressors.* New Mexico Health Association.

MHF (Mental Health Foundation). (2015). *Schizophrenia.* England: MHF.

MHF (Mental Health of the Future). (2014). *Suicide statistics and facts.* Retrieved from GenPsych website: http://www.genpsych.com/suicide-statistics-and-facts.

MHFA (Mental Health Foundation of Australia). (2014). *Sadness and depression.* Richmond, Canada: MHFA.

Mian, N. D. (2014). Little children with big worries: Addressing the needs of young, anxious children and the problem of parent engagement. *Clinical Child and Family Psychology Review, 17*(1), 85–96.

Michal, M. (2011). Review of depersonalization: A new look at a neglected syndrome. *Journal of Psychosomatic Research, 70*(2), 199.

Midgley, N., Cregeen, S., Hughes, C., & Rustin, M. (2013). Psychodynamic psychotherapy as treatment for depression in adolescence. *Child and Adolescent Psychiatric Clinics of North America, 22*(1), 67–82.

Millan, M. J., Fone, K., Steckler, T., & Horan, W. P. (2014). Negative symptoms of schizophrenia: Clinical characteristics, pathophysiological substrates, experimental models and prospects for improved treatment. *European Neuropsychopharmacology, 24*(5), 645–692.

Miller, A. (2015). The purpose of a clinical interview in a psychological assessment. *Chron.com.* Retrieved from Chron.com website: http://work.chron.com/purpose-clinical-interview-psychological.

Miller, A. L., McEvoy, J. P., Jeste, D. V., & Marder, S. R. (2012). Treatment of chronic schizophrenia. In J. A. Lieberman, T. S. Stroup, & D. O Perkins (Eds.), *Essentials of schizophrenia* (pp. 225–243). Arlington, VA: American Psychiatric Publishing.

Miller, D. C. (Ed.). (2010). *Best practices in school neuropsychology: Guidelines for effective practice, assessment, and evidence-based intervention.* Hoboken, NJ: John Wiley & Sons.

Miller, D. N. (2011). *Child and adolescent suicidal behavior: School-based prevention, assessment, and intervention. The Guilford practical intervention in the schools series.* New York: Guilford Press.

Miller, J. A. (2010). Sex offender civil commitment: The treatment paradox. *California Law Review, 98,* 2093–2128.

Miller, K. L., Dove, M. K., & Miller, S. M. (2007). *A counselor's guide to child sexual abuse: Prevention, reporting and treatment strategies.* Paper based on a program presented at the Association for Counselor Education and Supervision Conference, Columbus, OH.

Miller, M., & Kantrowitz, B. (1999, January 25). Unmasking Sybil: A re-examination of the most famous psychiatric patient in history. *Newsweek,* pp. 66–68.

Miller, N. E. (1948). Studies of fear as an acquirable drive: I. Fear as motivation and fear-reduction as reinforcement in the learning of new responses. *Journal of Experimental Psychology, 38,* 89–101.

Miller, P. M., Ingham, J. G., & Davidson, S. (1976). Life events, symptoms, and social support. *Journal of Psychiatric Research, 20*(6), 514–522.

Miller, S. G. (1994). Borderline personality disorder from the patient's perspective. *Hospital Community Psychiatry, 45*(12), 1215–1219.

Miller, S. G. (1999). Borderline personality disorder in cultural context: Commentary on Paris. *Psychiatry, 59*(2), 193–195.

Miller, T. (2013, August 12). Too many selfies on Facebook can damage relationships: Study. *New York Daily News.*

Miller, W. D., Sadegh-Nobari, T., & Lillie-Blanton, M. (2011). Healthy starts for all: Policy prescriptions. *American Journal of Preventive Medicine, 40*(1, Suppl 1), S19–S37.

Miller, W. R., & Seligman, M. E. (1975). Depression and learned helplessness in man. *Journal of Abnormal Psychology, 84*(3), 228–238.

Millichap, J. G. (2010). *Attention deficit hyperactivity disorder handbook: A physician's guide to ADHD* (2nd ed.). New York: Springer Science + Business Media.

Millier, A., Schmidt, U., Angermeyer, M. C., Chauhan, D., Murthy, V., Toumi, M., & Cadi-Soussi, N. (2014). Humanistic burden in schizophrenia: A literature review. *Journal of Psychiatric Research, 54,* 85–93.

Millon, T. (1969). *Modern psychopathology: A biosocial approach to maladaptive learning and functioning.* Philadelphia: Saunders.

Millon, T. (2011). *Disorders of personality: Introducing a DSM/ICD spectrum from normal to abnormal* (3rd ed.). Hoboken, NJ: John Wiley Sons.

Mills, J. F., Kroner, D. F., & Morgan, R. D. (2011). *Clinician's guide to violence risk assessment.* New York: Guilford Press.

Milner, A., Page, A., Morrell, S., Hobbs, C., Carter, G., Dudley, M., . . . Taylor, R. (2014). The effects of involuntary job loss on suicide and suicide attempts among young adults: Evidence from a matched case-control study. *The Australian and New Zealand Journal of Psychiatry, 48*(4), 333–340.

Milner, A., Spittal, M. H., Pirkis, J., & LaMontagne, A. D. (2013). Suicide by occupation: Systematic review and meta-analysis. *British Journal of Psychiatry: The Journal of Mental Science, 203*(6), 409–416.

Milrod, C. (2014). How young is too young: Ethical concerns in genital surgery of the transgender MTF adolescent. *Journal of Sexual Medicine, 11,* 338–346.

Miner, I. D., & Feldman, M. D. (1998). Factitious deafblindness: An imperceptible variant of factitious disorder. *General Hospital Psychiatry, 20,* 48–51.

Minnes, S., Singer, L., Min, M. O., Wu, M., Lang, A., & Yoon, S. (2014). Effects of prenatal cocaine/polydrug exposure on substance use by age 15. *Drug and Alcohol Dependence, 134,* 201–210.

Mintem, G. C., Horta, B. L., Domingues, M. R., & Gigante, D. P. (2015). Body size dissatisfaction among young adults from the 1982 Pelotas birth cohort. *European Journal of Clinical Nutrition, 69*(1), 55–61.

Minuchin, S. (1974). *Families and family therapy.* Cambridge, MA: Harvard University Press.

Minuchin, S. (1987). My many voices. In J. K. Zeig (Ed.), *The evolution of psychotherapy.* New York: Brunner/Mazel.

Minuchin, S. (2007). Jay Haley: My teacher. *Family Process, 46*(3), 413–414.

Minuchin, S., Lee, W-Y., & Simon, G. M. (2006). *Mastering family therapy: Journeys of growth and transformation* (2nd ed.). Hoboken, NJ: John Wiley & Sons.

Minzenberg, M. J., Yoon, J. H., & Carter, C. S. (2011). Schizophrenia. In R. E. Hales, S. C. Yudofsky, & G. O. Gabbard (Eds.), *Essentials of psychiatry* (3rd ed., pp. 111–150). Arlington, VA: American Psychiatric Publishing.

Miranda, J., Siddique, J., Belin, T. R., & Kohn-Wood, L. P. (2005). Depression prevalence in disadvantaged young black women: African and Caribbean immigrants compared to US-born African Americans. *Social Psychiatry and Psychiatric Epidemiology 40*(4), 253–258.

Miret, M., Nuevo, R., Morant, C., Sainz-Cortón, E., Jiménez-Arriero, M. A., López-Ibor, J. J., et al. (2011). The role of suicide risk in the decision for psychiatric hospitalization after a suicide attempt. *Crisis: Journal of Crisis Intervention and Suicide Prevention, 32*(2), 65–73.

Mirone, V., Longo, N., Fusco, F., Mangiapia, F., Granata, A. M., & Perretti, A. (2001). Can the BC reflex evaluation be useful for the diagnosis of primary premature ejaculation? *International Journal of Impotence Research, 13,* S47.

Mishak, P. B. (2014). IQ test, cognitive abilities test, predictive index test, general mental ability test, general intelligence test, mental aptitude test: Your basic guide to acing any eligibility index test. Amazon Media, EU. [Kindle version].

Mitchell, A. E., Dickens, G. L., & Picchioni, M. M. (2014). Facial emotion processing in borderline personality disorder: A systematic review and meta-analysis. *Neuropsychology Review, 24*(2), 166–184.

Mitchell, A. J. (2010). Overview of depression scales and tools. In J. Mitchell & J. C. Coyne (Eds.), *Screening for depression in clinical practice: An evidence-based guide* (pp. 29–56). New York: Oxford University Press.

Mitchell, A. J. (2010). Why do clinicians have difficulty detecting depression? In A. J. Mitchell & J. C. Coyne (Eds.), *Screening for depression in clinical practice: An evidence-based guide* (pp. 57–82). New York: Oxford University Press.

Mitchell, J. E., & Crow, S. J. (2010). Medical comorbidities of eating disorders. In W. S. Agras (Ed.), *The Oxford handbook of eating disorders. Oxford library of psychology* (pp. 259–266). New York: Oxford University Press.

Mitchell, J. T. (1983). When disaster strikes . . . the critical incident stress debriefing process. *Journal of Emergency Medical Services, 8,* 36–39.

Mitchell, J. T. (2003). *Crisis intervention & CISM: A research summary.* Retrieved from ICISF website: http://www.icisf.org/articles/cism_research_ summary.pdf.

Mitka, M. (2011). Study looks at PTSD among workers in Twin Towers during 9/11 attack. *Journal of the American Medical Association, 305*(9), 874–875.

Mittal, V. A., Kalus, O., Bernstein, D. P., & Siever, L. J. (2007). Schizoid personality disorder. In W. O'Donohue, K. A. Fowler, & S. O. Lilienfeld (Eds.), *Personality disorders: Toward the DSM-V.* Los Angeles: Sage Publications.

Mittelman, M. S., & Bartels, S. J. (2014). Translating research into practice: Case study of a community-based dementia caregiver intervention. *Health Affairs (Project Hope), 33*(4), 587–595.

Moberg, T., Nordström, P., Forslund, K., Kristiansson, M., Asberg, M., & Jokinen, J. (2011). Csf 5-hiaa and exposure to and expression of interpersonal violence in suicide attempters. *Journal of Affective Disorders, 125*(1-3), 388–392.

Modlin, T. (2002). Sleep disorders and hypnosis: To cope or cure? *Sleep and Hypnosis, 4*(1), 39–46.

Moffatt, F. W., Hodnett, E., Esplen, M. J., & Watt-Watson, J. (2010). Effects of guided imagery on blood pressure in pregnant women with hypertension: A pilot randomized controlled trial. *Birth: Issues in Perinatal Care, 37*(4), 296–306.

Mohatt, J., Bennett, S. M., & Walkup, J. T. (2014). Treatment of separation, generalized, and social anxiety disorders in youths. *American Journal of Psychiatry, 171*(7), 741–748.

Mohler, H., & Okada, T. (1977). Benzodiazepine receptor: Demonstration in the central nervous system. *Science, 198*(4319), 849–851.

Mohler, H., Richards, J. G., & Wu, J.-Y. (1981). Autoradiographic localization of benzodiazepine receptors in immunocytochemically identified c-aminobutyric synapses. *Proceedings of the National Academy of Science, 78*, 1935–1938.

Mokros, A., Osterheider, M., Hucker, S. J., & Nitschke, J. (2011). Psychopathy and sexual sadism. *Law and Human Behavior, 35*(3), 188–199.

Mokros, A., Schilling, F., Weiss, K., Nitschke, J., & Eher, R. (2014). Sadism in sexual offenders: Evidence for dimensionality. *Psychological Assessment, 26*(1), 138–147.

Mola, J. R. (2015). Erectile dysfunction in the older adult male. *Urologic Nursing, 35*(2), 87–93.

Moldavsky, D. (2004, June 1). Transcultural psychiatry for clinical practice. *Psychiatric Times, XXI*(7), p. 36.

Möller, J., Björkenstam, E., Liung, R., & Yngwe, M. A. (2011). Widowhood and the risk of psychiatric care, psychotropic medication and all-cause mortality: A cohort study of 658,022 elderly people in Sweden. *Aging & Mental Health, 15*(2), 259–266.

Momtaz, B. (2014, February 4). Cited in L. Kaufman, In texting era, crisis hotlines put help at youths' fingertips. *New York Times.*

Mond, J., Hall, A., Bentley, C., Harrison, C., Gratwick-Sarll, K., & Lewis, V. (2014). Eating-disordered behavior in adolescent boys: Eating disorder examination questionnaire norms. *International Journal of Eating Disorders, 47*(4), 335–341.

Monroe, S. M. (2010). Recurrence in major depression: Assessing risk indicators in the context of risk estimates. In C. S. Richards & L. C. Perri (Eds.), *Relapse prevention for depression* (pp. 27–49). Washington, DC: American Psychological Association.

Monroe, S. M., Slavich, G. M., & Gotlib, I. H. (2014). Life stress and family history for depression: The moderating role of past depressive episodes. *Journal of Psychiatric Research, 49*, 90–95.

Monson, C. M., Fredman, S. J., & Taft, C. T. (2011). Couple and family issues and interventions for veterans of the Iraq and Afghanistan wars. In J. I. Ruzek, P. P. Schnurr, J. J. Vasterling, & M. J. Friedman (Eds.), *Caring for veterans with deployment-related stress disorders* (pp. 151–169). Washington, DC: American Psychological Association.

Montaldo, C. (2014). *Multiple murderers.* Retrieved from About.com website: http://crime.about.com/od/serial/a/killer_types.htm.

Montejo, A.-L., Perahia, D. G. S., Spann, M. E., Wang, F., Walker, D. J., Yang, C. R., & Detke, M. J. (2011). Sexual function during long-term duloxetine treatment in patients with recurrent major depressive disorder. *Journal of Sexual Medicine, 8*(3), 773–782.

Montejo, J. E., Durán, M., Del Mar Martínez, M., Hilari, A., Roncalli, N., Vilaregut, A., . . . Ramos-Quiroga, J. A. (2015). Family functioning and parental bonding during childhood in adults diagnosed with ADHD. *Journal of Attention Disorders.* [Electronic publication.]

Moon, J. R., Glymour, M. M., Vable, A. M., Liu, S. Y., & Subramanian, S. V. (2014). Short- and long-term associations between widowhood and mortality in the United States: Longitudinal analyses. *Journal of Public Health* (Oxford, England), *36*(3), 382–389.

Moore, C. E., Radcliffe, J. D., & Liu, Y. (2014). Vitamin D intakes of adults differ by income, gender and race/ethnicity in the U.S.A., 2007 to 2010. *Public Health Nutrition, 17*(4), 756–763.

Moore, C. E., Radcliffe, J. D., & Liu, Y. (2014). Vitamin D intakes of children differ by race/ethnicity, sex, age, and income in the United States, 2007 to 2010. *Nutrition Research, 34*(6), 499–506.

Moore, E. A., Green, M. J., & Carr, V. J. (2012). Comorbid personality traits in schizophrenia:

Prevalence and clinical characteristics. *Journal of Psychiatric Research, 46*(3), 353–359.

Moore, P. J., Chrabaszcz, J. S., Peterson, R. A., Rohrbeck, C. A., Roemer, E. C., & Mercurio, A. E. (2014). Psychological resilience: The impact of affectivity and coping on state anxiety and positive emotions during and after the Washington, DC sniper killings. *Anxiety, Stress, and Coping, 27*(2), 138–155.

Moorhouse, P. A., & Rockwood, K. (2010). Vascular cognitive impairment. In H. M. Fillit, K. Rockwood, & K. Woodhouse. (Eds.), *Brocklehurst's textbook of geriatric medicine and gerontology* (7th ed.). Philadelphia, PA: Saunders Publishers.

Moreno, C., Laje, G., Blanco, C., Jiang, H., Schmidt, A. B., & Olfson, M. (2007). National trends in the outpatient diagnosis and treatment of bipolar disorder in youth. *Archives of General Psychiatry, 64*(9), 1032–1039.

Morey, L. C., Skodol, A. E., & Oldham, J. M. (2014). Clinician judgments of clinical utility: A comparison of DSM-IV-TR personality disorders and the alternative model for DSM-5 personality disorders. *Journal of Abnormal Psychology, 123*(2), 398–405.

Morgan, C. A., Southwick, S., Steffian, G., Hazlett, G. A., & Loftus, E. F. (2013). Misinformation can influence memory for recently experienced, highly stressful events. *International Journal of Law and Psychiatry, 36*(1), 11–17.

Morgan, C. D., & Murray, H. A. (1935). A method of investigating fantasies: The Thematic Apperception Test. *Archives of Neurological Psychiatry, 34,* 289–306.

Morgan, J. F. (2012). Male eating disorders. In J. Alexander and J. Treasure (Eds.), *A collaborative approach to eating disorders* (pp. 272–278). New York: Routledge/Taylor & Francis Group.

Morgan, L., Brittain, B., & Welch, J. (2015). Medical care following multiple perpetrator sexual assault: A retrospective review. *International Journal of STD & AIDS, 26*(2), 86–92.

Morgan, M., Lockwood, A., Steinke, D., Schleenbaker, R., & Botts, S. (2012). Pharmacotherapy regimens among patients with posttraumatic stress disorder and mild traumatic brain injury. *Psychiatric Services, 63*(2), 182–185.

Morgan, P. L., Hillemeier, M. M., Farkas, G., & Maczuga, S. (2014). Racial/ethnic disparities in ADHD diagnosis by kindergarten entry. *Journal of Child Psychology and Psychiatry, and Allied Disciplines, 55*(8), 905–913.

Morris, T. L., & Ale, C. M. (2011). Social anxiety. In D. McKay & E. A. Storch (Eds.), *Handbook of child and adolescent anxiety disorders* (pp. 289–301). New York: Springer Science & Business Media.

Morrison, A. P., Pyle, M., Chapman, N., French, P., Parker, S. K., & Wells, A. (2014). Metacognitive therapy in people with a schizophrenia spectrum diagnosis and medication resistant symptoms: A feasibility study. *Journal of Behavior Therapy and Experimental Psychiatry, 45*(2), 280–284.

Morrison, A. P., Turkington, D., Pyle, M., Spencer, H., Brabban, A., Dunn, G., . . . Hutton, P. (2014). Cognitive therapy for people with schizophrenia spectrum disorders not taking antipsychotic drugs: A single-blind randomised controlled trial. *Lancet, 383*(9926), 1395–1403.

Morrissey, J. P., & Cuddeback, G. S. (2008). Jail diversion. In K. T. Mueser & D. V. Jeste (Eds.), *Clinical handbook of schizophrenia* (pp. 524–532). New York: Guilford Press.

Morrissey, J. P., Desmarais, S. L., & Domino, M. E. (2014). Outpatient commitment and its alternatives: Questions yet to be answered. *Psychiatric Services, 65*(6), 812–815.

Mort, J. R., Sailor, R., & Hintz, L. (2014). Partnership to decrease antipsychotic medication use in

nursing homes: Impact at the state level. *South Dakota Medicine, 67*(2), 67–69.

Mosca, N. W., & Schatz, M. L. (2013). Encopresis: Not just an accident. *NASN School Nurse, 28*(3), 218–221.

Mosconi, L. (2013). Glucose metabolism in normal aging and Alzheimer's disease: Methodological and physiological considerations for PET studies. *Clinical and Translational Imaging: Reviews in Nuclear Medicine and Molecular Imaging, 1*(4), 217–233.

Mosconi, L., Berti, V., Glodzik, L., Pupi, A., De Santi, S., & de Leon, M. J. (2010). Pre-clinical detection of Alzheimer's disease using FDG-PET, with or without amyloid imaging. *Journal of Alzheimer's Disease, 20*(3), 843–854.

Mosconi, L., De Santi, S., Li, J., Tsui, W. H., Li, Y., Boppana, M., . . . de Leon, M. J. (2008). Hippocampal hypometabolism predicts cognitive decline from normal aging. *Neurobiology of Aging, 29*(5), 676–692.

Mosconi, L., Murray, J., Davies, M., Williams, S., Pirraglia, E., Spector, N., . . . de Leon, M. J. (2014). Nutrient intake and brain biomarkers of Alzheimer's disease in at-risk cognitively normal individuals: A cross-sectional neuroimaging pilot study. *BMJ Open, 4*(6), E004850.

Mosconi, M. W., Wang, Z, Schmitt, L. M., Tsai, P., & Sweeney, J. A. (2015). The role of cerebellar circuitry alterations in the pathophysiology of autism spectrum disorders. *Frontiers in Neuroscience, 9*, 296.

Moscovitch, D. A., Rowa, K., Paulitzki, J. R., Ierullo, M. D., Chiang, B., Antony, M. M., & McCabe, R. E. (2013). Self-portrayal concerns and their relation to safety behaviors and negative affect in social anxiety disorder. *Behaviour Research and Therapy, 51*(8), 476–486.

Moskowitz, E. S. (2001). *In therapy we trust: America's obsession with self-fulfillment.* Baltimore: Johns Hopkins University Press

Moskowitz, E. S. (2008). *In therapy we trust: America's obsession with self-fulfillment.* Baltimore, MD: Johns Hopkins University Press.

Mott, J. M., Barrera, T. L., Hernandez, C., Graham, D. P., & Teng, E. J. (2014). Rates and predictors of referral for individual psychotherapy, group psychotherapy, and medications among Iraq and Afghanistan veterans with PTSD. *The Journal of Behavioral Health Services & Research, 41*(2), 99–109.

Mowrer, O. H. (1939). A stimulus-response analysis of anxiety and its role as a reinforcing agent. *Psychological Review, 46*, 553–566.

Mowrer, O. H. (1947). On the dual nature of learning: A reinterpretation of "conditioning" and "problem-solving." *Harvard Education Review, 17*, 102–148.

Mowrer, O. H., & Mowrer, W. M. (1938). Enuresis: A method for its study and treatment. *American Journal of Orthopsychiatry, 8*, 436–459.

Moyano, O. (2010). A case of depersonalization-derealization in adolescence: Clinical study of dissociative disorders. *Neuropsychiatrie de l'Enfance et de l'Adolescence, 58*(3), 126–131.

Mucha, S. M., Varghese, L. A., French, R. E., & Shade, D. A. (2014). Separating fact from factitious hemoptysis: A case report. *Critical Care Nurse, 34*(4), 36–42.

Mueller, S. E., Petitjean, S., Boening, J., & Wiesbeck, G. A. (2007). The impact of self-help group attendance on relapse rates after alcohol detoxification in a controlled study. *Alcohol Alcoholism, 42*(2), 108–112.

Mulder, R. T. (2010). Antidepressants and suicide: Population benefit vs. individual risk. *Acta Psychiatrica Scandinavica, 122*(6), 442–443.

Mulhauser, G. (2010). *Disadvantages of counselling or therapy by email.* Retrieved from http://counsellingresource.com/counselling-service/online-disadvantages.html.

Mullen, P. E. (2004). The autogenic (self-generated) massacre. *Behavioral Sciences & the Law, 22*(3), 311–323.

Müller, C. A., Schäfer, M., Schneider, S., Heimann, H. M., Hinzpeter, A., Volkmar, K., Förg, A., Heinz, A., & Hein, J. (2010). Efficacy and safety of levetiracetam for outpatient alcohol detoxification. *Pharmacopsychiatry, 43*(5), 184–189.

Müller, N. (2014). Immunology of schizophrenia. *Neuroimmunomodulation, 21*(2-3), 109–116.

Munsey, C. (2010). The kids aren't all right. *Monitor on psychology, 41*(1), 22–25.

Murayama, Y., Ohba, H., Yasunaga, M., Nonaka, K., Takeuchi, R., Nishi, M., . . . Fujiwara, Y. (2014). The effect of intergenerational programs on the mental health of elderly adults. *Aging & Mental Health,* 1–9.

Murdock, K. K. (2013). Texting while stressed: Implications for students' burnout, sleep, and well-being. *Psychology of Popular Media Culture, 2,* 207–221.

Murphy, L., Mitchell, D., & Hallett, R. (2011). A comparison of client characteristics in cyber and in-person counseling. *Studies in Health Technology and Informatics, 167,* 149–153.

Murphy, R., Straebler, S., Cooper, Z., & Fairburn, C. G. (2010). Cognitive behavioral therapy for eating disorders. *Psychiatric Clinics of North America, 33*(3), 611–627.

Murphy, W. D., & Page, I. J. (2006). Exhibitionism. In R. D. McAnulty & M. M. Burnette (Eds.), *Sex and sexuality, Vol. 3: Sexual deviation and sexual offenses.* Westport, CT: Praeger Publishers.

Murray, D. E., Durazzo, T. C., Mon, A., Schmidt, T. P., & Meyerhoff, D. J. (2015). Brain perfusion in polysubstance users: Relationship to substance and tobacco use, cognition, and self-regulation. *Drug and Alcohol Dependence, 150,* 120–128.

Murray, K. E., & Nyp, S. S. (2011). Postpartum depression. *Journal of Developmental & Behavioral Pediatrics, 32*(2), 175.

Murray, L. K., Nguyen, A., & Cohen, J. A. (2014). Child sexual abuse. *Child and Adolescent Psychiatric Clinics of North America, 23*(2), 321–337.

Musa, R., Draman, S., Jeffrey, S., Jeffrey, I., Abdullah, N., Halim, N. M., . . . Sidi, H. (2014). Post tsunami psychological impact among survivors in Aceh and West Sumatra, Indonesia. *Comprehensive Psychiatry, 55 Suppl 1,* S13–S16.

Musiat, P., & Schmidt, U. (2010). Self-help and stepped care in eating disorders. In W. S. Agras (Ed.), *The Oxford handbook of eating disorders.* (pp. 386–401) New York: Oxford University Press.

Musikantow, R. (2011). Thinking in circles: Power and responsibility in hypnosis. *American Journal of Clinical Hypnosis, 54*(2), 83–85.

Nace, E. P. (2005). Alcohol. In R. J. Frances, A. H. Mack, & S. I. Miller (Eds.), *Clinical textbook of addictive disorders* (3rd ed., pp. 75–104). New York: Guilford Press.

Nace, E. P. (2011). Alcohol. In R. J. Frances, S. I. Miller, & A. H. Mack (Eds.), *Clinical textbook of addictive disorders* (3rd ed., paperback). New York: Guilford Press.

Naeem, F., Farooq, S., & Kingdon, D. (2014). Cognitive behavioural therapy (brief versus standard duration) for schizophrenia. *Cochrane Database of Systematic Reviews, 4,* CD010646.

NAELA (National Academy of Elder Law Attorneys). (2014). *Aging and special needs statistics.* Retrieved from NAELA website: http://www.naela.org/public/about_NAELA/Media/.

Nagy, T. F. (2011) Avoiding harm and exploitation. In T. F. Nagy, *Essential ethics for psychologists: A primer for understanding and mastering core issues* (pp. 127–144). Washington, DC: American Psychological Association.

Nagy, T. F. (2011). *Essential ethics for psychologists: A primer for understanding and mastering core issues.* Washington, DC: American Psychological Association.

Nagy, T. F. (2011). Ethics in research and publication. In T. F. Nagy, *Essential ethics for psychologists: A primer for understanding and mastering core issues* (pp. 199–216). Washington, DC: American Psychological Association.

NAHIC (National Adolescent Health Information Center). (2006). *Fact sheet on suicide: Adolescents & young adults.* San Francisco, CA: University of California, San Francisco.

Naidoo, S., & Mkize, D. L. (2012). Prevalence of mental disorders in a prison population in Durban, South Africa. *African Journal of Psychiatry, 15*(1), 30–35.

Nair, G., Evans, A., Bear, R. E., Velakoulis, D., & Bittar, R. G. (2014). The anteromedial GPi as a new target for deep brain stimulation in obsessive compulsive disorder. *Journal of Clinical Neuroscience, 21*(5), 815–821.

Nairn, S. (2012). A critical realistic approach to knowledge: Implications for evidence-based practice in and beyond nursing. *Nursing Inquiry, 19*(1), 6–17.

Najman, J. M., Khatun, M., Mamun, A., Clavarino, A., Williams, G. M., Scott, J., . . . Alati, R. (2014). Does depression experienced by mothers leads to a decline in marital quality: A 21-year longitudinal study. *Social Psychiatry and Psychiatric Epidemiology, 49*(1), 121–132.

NAMI (National Alliance on Mental Illness). (2014). *Find your local NAMI.* Arlington, VA: NAMI.

NAMI (National Alliance on Mental Illness). (2014). *The impact and cost of mental illness: The case of depression.* Arlington, VA: NAMI.

NAMI (National Alliance on Mental Illness). (2014). *The PACT advocacy guide.* Arlington, VA: NAMI.

Naninck, E. F. G., Lucassen, P. J., & Bakker, J. (2011). Sex differences in adolescent depression: Do sex hormones determine vulnerability? *Journal of Neuroendocrinology, 23*(5), 383–392.

Nardi, A. E., Valenca, A. M., Nascimento, I., & Zin, W. A. (2001). Hyperventilation challenge test in panic disorder and depression with panic attacks. *Psychiatry Research, 105,* 57–65.

Nathan, D. (2010). *Sybil exposed: The extraordinary story behind the famous multiple personality case.* New York: Free Press.

Nation, D. A., Hong, S., Jak, A. J., Delano-Wood, L., Mills, P. J., Bondi, M. W., & Dimsdale, J. E. (2011). Stress, exercise, and Alzheimer's disease: A neurovascular pathway. *Medical Hypotheses, 76*(6), 847–854.

National Center for PTSD. (2008). Appendix A. Case examples from Operation Iraqi Freedom. *Iraq War Clinician Guide.* Washington, DC: Department of Veteran Affairs.

National Highway Traffic Safety Administration. (2010). Early estimate of motor vehicle traffic fatalities for the first half (January-June) of 2010. *Traffic Safety Facts.* Washington, DC: U.S. Department of Transportation.

National Highway Traffic Safety Administration. (2010). *Fatality analysis reporting system (FARS).* Retrieved from NHTSA website: http://www.nhtsa.gov/FARS.

Nauert, R. (2014. May 7). Virtual reality therapy may reduce PTSD symptoms. *Psych Central.*

Nawata, H., Ogomori, K., Tanaka, M., Nishimura, R., Urashima, H., Yano, R., . . . Kuwabara, Y. (2010). Regional cerebral blood flow changes in female to male gender identity disorder. *Psychiatry and Clinical Neurosciences, 64*(2), 157–161.

Nazarian, M., & Craske, M. G. (2008). Panic and agoraphobia. In M. Hersen & J. Rosqvist (Eds.), *Handbook of psychological assessment, case conceptualization, and treatment, Vol. 1: Adults* (pp. 171–203). Hoboken, NJ: John Wiley & Sons.

NBC (National Broadcasting Company). (2012, February 2). Mystery teen illness grows in upstate New York. *NBC Nightly News.*

NCASA (National Center on Addiction and Substance Abuse at Columbia University). (2007, March). *Wasting the best and the brightest: Substance abuse at America's colleges and universities.* Washington, DC: Author.

NCHS (National Center for Health Statistics). (2014). *Health, United States, 2013; with special feature on prescription drugs.* Hyattsville, MD: NCHS.

NCHS (National Center for Health Statistics). (2014). *Older persons' health.* Hyattsville, MD: NCHS.

NCVS (National Crime Victimization Survey). (2013). *Data collection: National Crime Victimization Survey.* Washington, DC: Bureau of Justice Statistics.

NCVS (National Crime Victimization Survey). (2014). *National Crime Victimization Survey, 2013.* Washington, DC: Bureau of Justice Statistics.

NCVS (National Crime Victimization Survey). (2014). *Rape trauma syndrome.* Washington, DC: Bureau of Justice Statistics.

Neacsiu, A. D., & Linehan, M. M. (2014). Dialectical behavior therapy for borderline personality disorder. In D. H. Barlow (Ed.), *Clinical handbook of psychological disorders* (5th ed., pp. 394–461). New York: Guilford Press.

Neeleman, J., Wessely, S., & Lewis, G. (1998). Suicide acceptability in African- and white Americans: The role of religion. *Journal of Nervous and Mental Disease, 186*(1), 12–16.

Negrini, A., Perron, J., & Corbière, M. (2014). The predictors of absenteeism due to psychological disability: A longitudinal study in the education sector. *Work, 48*(2), 175–184.

Nelson, L., & Tabet, N. (2015). Slowing the progression of Alzheimer's disease: What works? *Ageing Research Reviews, 23*(Pt B), 193–209.

Nemecek, S. (1996, September). Mysterious maladies. *Scientific American,* 24–26.

Nenadic-Šviglin, K., Nedic, G., Nikolac, M., Kozaric-Kovacic, D., Stipcevic, T., Seler, D. M., & Pivac, N. (2011). Suicide attempt, smoking, comorbid depression, and platelet serotonin in alcohol dependence. *Alcohol, 45*(3), 209–216.

Neumark-Sztainer, D. R., Wall, M. M., Haines, J. I., Story, M. T., Sherwood, N. E., & van den Berg, P. A. (2007). Shared risk and protective factors for overweight and disordered eating in adolescents. *American Journal of Preventative Medicine, 33*(5), 359–369.

Neville, C. (2014). Psychological therapies for borderline personality disorder. *Nursing Times, 110*(4), 25.

Newcomb, M. E., & Mustanski, B. (2014). Diaries for observation or intervention of health behaviors: Factors that predict reactivity in a sexual diary study of men who have sex with men. *Annals of Behavioral Medicine: A Publication of the Society of Behavioral Medicine, 47*(3), 325–334.

Newman, M. G., Castonguay, L. G., Borkovec, T. D., Fisher, A. J., Boswell, J. F., Szkodny, L. E., & Nordberg, S. S. (2011). A randomized controlled trial of cognitive-behavioral therapy for generalized anxiety disorder with integrated techniques from emotion-focused and interpersonal therapies. *Journal of Consulting and Clinical Psychology, 79*(2), 171–181.

Newnham, E. A., & Janca, A. (2014). Childhood adversity and borderline personality disorder: A focus on adolescence. *Current Opinion in Psychiatry, 27*(1), 68–72.

Neziroglu, F., McKay, D., Todaro, J., & Yaryura-Tobias, J. A. (1996). Effect of cognitive behavior therapy on persons with body dysmorphic disorder and comorbid Axis II diagnoses. *Behavior Therapist, 27,* 67–77.

Neziroglu, F., Roberts, M., & Yaryura-Tobias, J. A. (2004). A behavioral model for body dysmorphic disorder. *Psychiatric Annals, 34*(12), 915–920.

Nezlek, J. B., Hampton, C. P., & Shean, G. D. (2000). Clinical depression and day-to-day social interaction in a community sample. *Journal of Abnormal Psychology, 109*(1), 11–19.

Nezu, A. M., Nezu, C., M., & Xanthopoulos, M. S. (2011). Stress reduction in chronically ill patients. In R. J. Contrada & A. Baum (Eds.), *The handbook of stress science: Biology, psychology, and health* (pp. 475–485). New York: Springer Publishing.

NFER (National Foundation for Educational Research). (2010). *Tellus4 national report* (DCSF Research Report 218). Retrieved from NFER website: http://www.nfer.ac.uk/publications/TEL01/.

Ng, J. H., Bierman, A. C., Elliott, M. N., Wilson, R. L., Xia, C., & Scholle, S. H. (2014). Beyond black and white: Race/ethnicity and health status among older adults. *The American Journal of Managed Care, 20*(3), 239–248.

NIA (National Institute of Aging). (2011). *Global health and aging.* Bethesda, MD: Author.

NIAAA (National Institute on Alcohol Abuse and Alcoholism). (2015). *Alcohol facts and statistics.* Retrieved from NIAAA website: http://www.niaaa.nih.gov/alcohol-health/overview-alcohol-consumption/alcohol-facts-and-statistics.

NICHD (National Institute of Child Health and Human Development). (2015). *What causes Down syndrome?* Washington, DC: NICHD.

NICHD (National Institute of Child Health and Human Development). (2015). *What causes phenylketonuria (PKU)?* Washington, DC: NICHD.

Nichols, M. P. (2013). *The essentials of family therapy* (6th ed.). Boston: Pearson.

Nichols, W. C. (2004). Integrative marital and family treatment of dependent personality disorders. In M. M. MacFarlane (Ed.), *Family treatment of personality disorders: Advances in clinical practice* (pp. 173–204). Binghamton, NY: Haworth Clinical Practice Press.

Nicholson, C., & McGuinness, T. M. (2014). Gender dysphoria and children. *Journal of Psychosocial Nursing and Mental Health Services, 52*(8), 27–30.

Nickel, R., Ademmer, K., & Egle, U. T. (2010). Manualized psychodynamic-interactional group therapy for the treatment of somatoform pain disorders. *Bulletin of the Menninger Clinic, 74*(3), 219–237.

NIDA (National Institute of Drug Abuse). (2014). *Heroin: Why does heroin use create special risk for contracting HIV/AIDS and hepatitis B and C?* Retrieved from NISA website: http://www.drugabuse.gov/publications/research-reports/heroin.

NIDA (National Institute on Drug Abuse). (2015). *DrugFacts: Marijuana.* Retrieved from NSA website: http://www.drugabuse.gov/publications/drugfacts/marijuana.

NIH (National Institutes of Health). (2011). Herbal medicine. *MedlinePlus.* Retrieved from http://www.nlm.nih.gov/medlineplus.herbalmedicine.html.

NIH (National Institutes of Health). (2014, January 3). *Severe mental illness tied to higher rates of substance use.* Retrieved from http://www.nih.gov/news/health/jan2014/nida-03.htm.

NIH (National Institutes of Health). (2014, July). *Prescription and illicit drug abuse.* Retrieved from http://nihseniorhealth.gov/drugabuse/improperuse/01.html.

NIH (National Institutes of Health). (2015). Cells and DNA. *Genetics Home Reference.* Retrieved from http://ghr.nlm.nih.gov/handbook/basics.

NIH (National Institutes of Health). (2015). *Cocaine. Also called: Blow, C, Coca, Coke, Crack, Flake, Snow.* Retrieved from https://www.nlm.nih.gov/medlineplus/cocaine.html.

NIJ (National Institute of Justice). (2010). *Human subject and privacy protection.* Retrieved from http://www.nij.gov/funding/humansubjects.

Nillni, Y. I., Rohan, K. J., & Zvolensky, M. J. (2012). The role of menstrual cycle phase and anxiety sensitivity in catastrophic misinterpretation of physical symptoms during a CO2 challenge. *Archives of Women's Mental Health,* August 25, pp. 1–10.

NIMH (National Institute of Mental Health). (2004). *Depression and cancer.* Bethesda, MD: Author.

NIMH (National Institute of Mental Health). (2004). *Depression and heart disease.* Bethesda, MD: Author.

NIMH (National Institute of Mental Health). (2004). *Depression and stroke.* Bethesda, MD: Author.

NIMH (National Institute of Mental Health). (2010). *Questions and answers about the NIMH Treatment for Adolescents with Depression Study (TADS).* Retrieved from http://www.nimh.nih.gov/trials/practical/tads/questions-and-answers.shtml.

NIMH (National Institute of Mental Health). (2010). *Schizophrenia.* Retrieved from http://www.nimh/nih/gov/statistics/1SCHIZ.shtml.

NIMH (National Institute of Mental Health). (2010). *Use of mental health services and treatment among adults.* Retrieved from http://www.nimh.nih.gov/statistics/3USE_MT_ADULT.shtml.

NIMH (National Institute of Mental Health). (2011). *Agoraphobia among adults.* Bethesda, MD: Author.

NIMH (National Institute of Mental Health). (2011). *Army study to assess risk and resilience in service members: A partnership between NIMH and the U.S. Army.* Retrieved from http://www.nimh/nih/gov/index.shtml.

NIMH (National Institute of Mental Health). (2011). *Director's blog: Antidepressants: A complicated picture.* Retrieved from http://www.nimh.nih.gov/about/director/2011/antidepressants.

NIMH (National Institute of Mental Health). (2011). *Generalized anxiety disorder among adults.* Bethesda, MD: Author.

NIMH (National Institute of Mental Health). (2011). *Treatment for Adolescents with Depression Study (TADS).* Retrieved from http://www.nimh.nih.gov/trials/practical/tads.index.shtml.

NIMH (National Institute of Mental Health). (2012). *Percentage of Americans with phobias.* Bethesda: MD: NIMH.

NIMH (National Institute of Mental Health). (2013). *Panic disorder: When fear overwhelms.* Retrieved from http://www.nimh.nih.gov/health/publications.

NIMH (National Institute of Mental Health). (2014). *Bipolar disorder among adults.* Retrieved from http://www.nimh.nih.gov/statistics/1bipolar_adult.shtml.

NIMH (National Institute of Mental Health). (2014). *Panic disorder among adults.* Bethesda, MD: NIMH.

NIMH (National Institute of Mental Health). (2014). *Social phobia among adults.* Bethesda, MD: NIMH.

NIMH (National Institute of Mental Health). (2014). *Specific phobia among adults.* Bethesda, MD: NIMH.

NIMH (National Institute of Mental Health). (2015). *Any disorder among children.* Retrieved from http://www.nimh.nih.gov/health/statistics/prevalence/_148474.pdf.

NIMH (National Institute of Mental Health). (2015). *Women and depression.* Retrieved from http://psychcentral.com/lib/women-and-depression.

NINDS (National Institute of Neurological Disorders and Stroke). (2015). *NIINDS autism information page.* Bethesda, MD: NINDS.

NISVS (National Intimate Partner and Sexual Violence Survey). (2010). *NISVS summary report.* Atlanta, GA: CDC.

Nitschke, J., Mokros, A., Osterheider, M., & Marshall, W. L. (2013). Sexual sadism: Current diagnostic vagueness and the benefit of behavioral definitions. *International Journal of Offender Therapy and Comparative Criminology, 57*(12), 1441–1453.

Niv, N., Shatkin, J. P., Hamilton, A. B., Unützer, J., Klap, R., & Young, A. S. (2010). The use of herbal medications and dietary supplements by people with mental illness. *Community Mental Health Journal, 46*(6), 563–569.

Nivoli, A. M. A., Colom, F., Murru, A., Pacchiarotti, I., Castro-Loli, P., González-Pinto, A., . . . Vieta, E. (2011). New treatment guidelines for acute bipolar depression: A systematic review. *Journal of Affective Disorders, 129*(1-3), 14–26.

NLM (National Library of Medicine). (2015). *Encopresis.* Retrieved from MedlinePlus website: https://www.nlm.nih.gov/medlineplus/ency/article/001570.htm.

NLM (National Library of Medicine). (2015). *Intellectual disability.* Retrieved from MedlinePlus website: https://www.nlm.nih.gov/medlineplus/ency/article/001523.htm.

NMHA (National Mental Health Association). (1999, June 5). Poll. *U.S. Newswire.*

Nobel Media. (2014). *Facts on the Nobel Prize.* Nobelprize.org.

Nock, M. K., Green, J. G., Hwang, I., McLaughlin, K. A., Sampson, N. A., Zaslavsky, A. M., & Kessler, R. C. (2013). Prevalence, correlates, and treatment of lifetime suicidal behavior among adolescents: Results from the National Comorbidity Survey Replication Adolescent Supplement. *JAMA Psychiatry, 70*(3), 300–310.

Nock, M. K., Kazdin, A. E., Hiripi, E., & Kessler, R. C. (2006). Prevalence, subtypes, and correlates of DSM-IV conduct disorder in the National Comorbidity Survey Replication. *Psychological Medicine, 36*(5), 699–710.

Nock, M. K., Stein, M. B., Heeringa, S. G., Ursano, R. J., Colpe, L. J., Fullerton, C. S., . . . Kessler, R. C. (2014). Prevalence and correlates of suicidal behavior among soldiers: Results from the Army Study to Assess Risk and Resilience in Servicemembers (Army STARRS). *JAMA Psychiatry, 71*(5), 514–522.

Noeker, M. (2004). Factitious disorder and factitious disorder by proxy. *Praxis der Kinderpsychologie und Kinderpsychiatrie, 53*(7), 449–467.

Noh, Y. (2009). Does unemployment increase suicide rates? the OECD panel evidence. *Journal of Economic Psychology, 30*(4), 575–582.

Nolen-Hoeksema, S. (1990). *Sex differences in depression.* Stanford, CA: Stanford University Press.

Nolen-Hoeksema, S. (2000). The role of rumination in depressive disorders and mixed anxiety/depressive symptoms. *Journal of Abnormal Psychology, 109,* 504–511.

Nolen-Hoeksema, S. (2002). Gender differences in depression. In I. H. Gotlib & C. L. Hammen (Eds.), *Handbook of depression* (pp. 492–509). New York: Guilford Press.

Noll-Hussong, M., Herberger, S., Grauer, M., Otti, A., & Gündel, H. (2013). Aspects of post-traumatic stress disorder after a traffic accident. *Versicherungsmedizin/Herausgegeben Von Verband Der Lebensversicherung-Unternehmen, 65*(3), 132–135.

Nonacs, R. M. (2007). Postpartum depression. *eMedicine Clinical Reference.* Retrieved from Emedicine website: http://www.emedicine.com/med/topic 3408.htm.

Noonan, D. (2003, June 16). A healthy heart. *Newsweek, 141*(24), 48–52.

Noonan, S. (2014). Veterinary wellness: Mindfulness-based stress reduction. *Canadian Veterinary Journal, 55,* 134–135.

Norcross, J. C. (Ed.) (2011). *Psychotherapy relationships that work evidence-based responsiveness* (2nd ed.). New York: Oxford University Press.

Norcross, J. C., Bike, D. H., & Evans, K. L. (2009). The therapist's therapist: A replication and extension 20 years later. *Psychotherapy Theory, Research, Practice, Training, 46*(1), 32–41.

Norcross, J. C., & Beutler, L. E. (2014). Integrative psychotherapies. In D. Wedding & R. J. Corsini (Eds.), *Current psychotherapies* (10th ed., pp. 499–532). Independence, KY: Cengage Publications.

Norcross, J. C., & Farber, B. A. (2005). Choosing psychotherapy as a career: Beyond "I want to help people." *Journal of Clinical Psychology, 61*(8), 939–943.

Norcross, J. C., & Goldfried, M. R. (Eds.). (2005). *Handbook of psychotherapy integration* (2nd ed.). New York: Oxford University Press.

Norcross, J. C., Karpiak, C. P., & Santoro, S. O. (2005). Clinical psychologists across the years: The division of clinical psychology from 1960 to 2003. *Journal of Clinical Psychology, 61*(12), 1467–1483.

Norcross, J. C., & Lambert, M. J. (2011). Psychotherapy relationships that work II. *Psychotherapy, 48*(1), 4–8.

Nord, M., & Farde, L. (2011). Antipsychotic occupancy of dopamine receptors in schizophrenia. *CNS Neuroscience & Therapeutics, 17*(2), 97–103.

Nordal, K. (2010, January–February). Interview with R. Gill. Practice opportunities available despite shrinking dollars. *National Psychologist, 1*–3.

North, C. S. (2005). Somatoform disorders. In E. H. Rubin & C. F. Zorumski (Eds.), *Adult psychiatry* (2nd ed., pp. 261–274). Oxford, England: Blackwell Publishing.

North, C. S., & Pfefferbaum, B. (2013). Mental health response to community disasters: A systematic review. *JAMA, 310*(5), 507–518.

Norton, A. (2011). Imagined smells can precede migraines. *Reuters*. Retrieved from Reuters website: http://www.reuters.om/assets/print?aid=USTRE79D4L120111014.

Novak, B., McDermott, B. E., Scott, C. L., & Guillory, S. (2007). Sex offenders and insanity: An examination of 42 individuals found not guilty by reason of insanity. *Journal of the American Academy of Psychiatry and the Law, 35*(4), 444–450.

Nowak, D. E., & Aloe, A. M. (2014). The prevalence of pathological gambling among college students: A meta-analytic synthesis, 2005–2013. *Journal of Gambling Studies, 30*(4), 819–843.

NPD Group. (2008). Entertainment Trends Report. Cited by Mike Antonucci in *San Jose Mercury News*, April 3, 2008.

NRC (National Research Council). (2014). Cited in C. Kruttschnitt, W. D. Kalsbeek, & C. C. House (Eds.). *Estimating the incidence of rape and sexual assault*. Washington, DC: Committee on National Statistics, Division of Behavioral and Social Sciences and Education.

NREPP (National Registry of Evidence-based Programs and Practices). (2014). *SAMHSA's national registry of evidence-based programs and practices.* Retrieved from http://www.nrepp.samhsa.gov/.

NSDUH (National Survey on Drug Use and Health). (2010). *Results from the 2009 National Survey on Drug Use and Health: Volume 1. Summary of national findings.* (Office of Applied Studies, NSDUH Series H-38a.) Rockville, MD: Substance Abuse and Mental Health Services Administration.

NSDUH (National Survey on Drug Use and Health). (2013). *Results from the 2012 National Survey on Drug Use and Health: Mental health findings,* NSDUH Series H-47, HHS Publication No. (SMA) 13-4805. Rockville, MD: Substance Abuse and Mental Health Services Administration.

NSF (National Sleep Foundation). (2014). *How much sleep do we really need?* Arlington, VA: NSF.

NSF (National Sleep Foundation). (2014). *Information about children's sleep for parents and teachers.* Retrieved from NSF website: http://www.sleepforkids.org/hml/uskids.html.

NSPCC (National Society for the Prevention of Cruelty to Children). (2013, August 11). Reported in *BBC News,* One in five children bullied online, says NSPCC survey.

Nugent, A. C., Bain, E. E., Carlson, P. J., Neumeister, A., Bonne, O., Carson, R. E., . . . Drevets, W. C. (2013). Reduced post-synaptic serotonin type 1A receptor binding in bipolar depression. *European Neuropsychopharmacology, 23*(8), 822–829.

Nunes, B. P., de Oliveira Saes, M., Siqueira, F. V., Tomasi, E., Silva, S. M., da Silveira, D. S., . . . Thumé, E. (2014). Falls and self-assessment of eyesight among elderly people: A population-based study in a south Brazilian municipality. *Archives of Gerontology and Geriatrics, 59*(1), 131–135.

Nunes, K. L., Hermann, C. A., Renee Malcom, J., & Lavoie, K. (2013). Childhood sexual victimization, pedophilic interest, and sexual recidivism. *Child Abuse & Neglect, 37*(9), 703–711.

Nussbaum, R. L., & Ellis, C. E. (2003). Alzheimer's disease and Parkinson's disease. *New England Journal of Medicine, 348,* 1356–1364.

NVSR (National Vital Statistics Reports). (2010, August 9). *Births: Final data for 2007, 58*(24).

NVSR (National Vital Statistics Reports). (2010). *Deaths: Final Data for 2007. National vital statistics reports, 58*(19). Hyattsville, MD: National Center for Health Statistics.

NVSR (National Vital Statistics Reports). (2011). *Deaths: Preliminary data for 2009. National vital statistics reports, 59*(4). Hyattsville, MD: National Center for Health Statistics.

O'Brien, C. P. (2013). Cited in NPR Staff, With addiction, breaking a habit means resisting a reflex. *Weekend Edition Sunday.* Retrieved from NPR website: http://www.npr.org/2013/10/20/238297311/with-addiction-breaking.

O'Brien, C. P., O'Brien, T. J., Mintz, J., & Brady, J. P. (1975). Conditioning of narcotic abstinence symptoms in human subjects. *Drug and Alcohol Dependence, 1,* 115–123.

Odlaug, B. L., & Grant, J. E. (2012). Pathological skin picking. In J. E. Grant, D. J. Stein, D. W. Woods, & N. J. Keuthen (Eds.), *Trichotillomania, skin picking, and other body-focused repetitive behaviors* (pp. 21–41). Arlington, VA: American Psychiatric Publishing, Inc.

O'Donohue, W., Fowler, K. A., & Lilienfeld, S. O. (Eds.). (2007). *Personality disorders: Toward the DSM-V.* Los Angeles: Sage Publications.

Oelschlager, J. R. (2014). *Sleep and college life.* Melbourne, FL: Florida Institute of Technology.

OFWW (Obesity, Fitness & Wellness Week). (2004, December 25). Drivers admit to experiencing road rage. *Obesity, Fitness & Wellness Week, 1209.*

Ogden, L. P. (2014). "Waiting to go home": Narratives of homelessness, housing and home among older adults with schizophrenia. *Journal of Aging Studies, 29,* 53–65.

Ogle, C. M., Rubin, D. C., & Siegler, I. C. (2014). Cumulative exposure to traumatic events in older adults. *Aging & Mental Health, 18*(3), 316–325.

O'Hara, M. W., & Wisner, K. L. (2014). Perinatal mental illness: Definition, description and aetiology. *Best Practice & Research. Clinical Obstetrics & Gynaecology, 28*(1), 3–12.

Ohman, A., & Mineka, S. (2003). The malicious serpent: Snakes as a prototypical stimulus for an evolved module of fear. *Current Directions in Psychological Science, 12*(1), 5–9.

Ohring, R., Graber, J. A., & Brooks-Gunn, J. (2002). Girls' recurrent and concurrent body dissatisfaction: Correlates and consequences over 8 years. *International Journal of Eating Disorders, 31*(4), 404–415.

Oinas-Kukkonen, H., & Mantila, L. (2010). *Lisa, Lisa the machine says I have performed an illegal action. Should I tell the police? A survey and observations of inexperienced elderly internet users.* Paper submitted to Journal of the Southern Association for Information Systems.

OJJDP (Office of Juvenile Justice and Delinquency Prevention). (2010, February). *In Focus: Girls' delinquency.* NCJ228414. Washington, DC: OJJDP.

Okawa, J. B., & Hauss, R. B. (2007). The trauma of politically motivated torture. In E. K. Carll (Ed.), *Trauma psychology: Issues in violence, disaster, health, and illness* (Vol. 1). Westport, CT: Praeger Publishers.

Okpokoro, U., Adams, C. E., & Sampson, S. (2014). Family intervention (brief) for schizophrenia. *Cochrane Database of Systematic Reviews, 3,* CD009802.

Ollendick, T. H. (2014). Advances toward evidence-based practice: where to from here? *Behavior Therapy, 45*(1), 51–55.

Olmsted, M. P., Kaplan, A. S., & Rockert, W. (1994). Rate and prediction of relapse in bulimia nervosa. *American Journal of Psychiatry, 151*(5), 738–743.

Olmsted, M. P., Kaplan, A. S., & Rockert, W. (2005). Defining remission and relapse in bulimia nervosa. *International Journal of Eating Disorders, 38*(1), 1–6.

Olson, D. (2011). FACES IV and the Circumplex Model: Validation study. *Journal of Marital & Family Therapy, 37*(1), 64–80.

Omar, H., Tejerina-Arreal, M., & Crawford, M. J. (2014). Are recommendations for psychological treatment of borderline personality disorder in current U.K. guidelines justified? Systematic review and subgroup analysis. *Personality and Mental Health, 8*(3), 228–237.

Omori, Y., Mori, C., & White, A. H. (2014). Self-stigma in schizophrenia: A concept analysis. *Nursing Forum, 49*(4), 259–266.

O'Neill, H. (2012, December 15). No rise in mass killings, but their impact is huge. *Associated Press.*

Ong, C., Pang, S., Sagayadevan, V., Chong, S. A., & Subramaniam, M. (2015). Functioning and quality of life in hoarding: A systemic review. *Journal of Anxiety Disorders, 32,* 17–30.

Onwuteaka-Philipsen, B. D., Brinkman-Stoppelenburg, A., Penning, C., de Jong-Krul, G. J. F., van Delden, J. J. M., & van der Heide, A. (2012). Trends in end-of-life practices before and after the enactment of the euthanasia law in the Netherlands from 1990 to 2010: A repeated cross-sectional survey. *The Lancet, 380*(9845), 908–915.

Opinion Research Corporation. (2004). National Survey Press Release. May 17, 2004.

Opinion Research Corporation Poll/CNN. (2011, March 18-20). Disaster preparedness and relief. *PollingReport.com.*

Oquendo, M. A., Dragatsi, D., Harkavy-Friedman, J., Dervic, K., Currier, D., Burke, A. K., . . . Mann, J. J. (2005). Protective factors against suicidal behavior in Latinos. *Journal of Nervous and Mental Disease, 193*(7), 438–443.

Oquendo, M. A., Lizardi, D., Greenwald. S., Weissman, M. M., & Mann, J. J. (2004). Rates of lifetime suicide attempt and rates of lifetime major depression in different ethnic groups in the United States. *Acta Psychiatrica Scandinavica, 110*(6), 446–451.

Oquendo, M. A., Russo, S. A., Underwood, M. D., Kassir, S. A., Ellis, S. P., Mann, J. J., & Arango, V. (2006). Higher post mortem prefrontal 5-HT2A receptor binding correlates with lifetime aggression in suicide. *Biological Psychiatry, 59,* 235–243.

Orbach, I., & Iohan, M. (2007). Stress, distress, emotional regulation and suicide attempts in female adolescents. In R. Tatarelli, M. Pompili, & P. Girardi (Eds.), *Suicide in psychiatric disorders*. New York: Nova Science Publishers.

Ordemann, G. J., Opper, J., & Davalos, D. (2014). Prospective memory in schizophrenia: A review. *Schizophrenia Research, 155*(1-3), 77–89.

O'Riley, A. A., Van Orden, K. A., He, H., Richardson, T. M., Podgorski, C., & Conwell, Y. (2014). Suicide and death ideation in older adults obtaining aging services. *The American Journal of Geriatric Psychiatry, 22*(6), 614–622.

ORR (Office of Refugee Resettlement). (2006). *Office of Refugee Resettlement (ORR). Services for Survivors of Torture Program: Program description*. Retrieved from http://www.acf.hhs.gov/programs/orr/programs/services_survivors_ torture.htm.

ORR (Office of Refugee Resettlement). (2011). *Services for survivors of torture*. Retrieved from http://www.acf.hhs.gov/programs/orr/programs/services_survivors_torture. htm.

Orri, M., Paduanello, M., Lachal, J., Falissard, B., Sibeoni, J., & Revah-Levy, A. (2014). Qualitative approach to attempted suicide by adolescents and young adults: The (neglected) role of revenge. *PLOS ONE, 9*(5), e96716.

Ostrov, J. M., Kamper, K. E., Hart, E. J., Godleski, S. A., & Blakely-McClure, S. J. (2014). A gender-balanced approach to the study of peer victimization and aggression subtypes in early childhood. *Development and Psychopathology, 26*(3), 575–587.

O'Sullivan, L F., Brotto, L. A., Byers, S., Majerovich, J. A., & Wuest, J. A. (2014). Prevalence and characteristics of sexual functioning among sexually experienced middle to late adolescents. *Journal of Sexual Medicine, 11*, 630–641.

Ott, J., van Trotsenburg, M., Kaufmann, U., Schrögendorfer, K., Haslik, W., Huber, J. C., & Wenzl, R. (2010). Combined hysterectomy/salpingo-oophorectomy and mastectomy is a safe and valuable procedure for female-to-male transsexuals *Journal of Sexual Medicine, 7*(6), 2130–2138.

Otto, R. K., & Douglas, K. S. (Eds.). (2010). *Handbook of violence risk assessment*. New York: Routledge/Taylor & Francis Group.

Ouellette, S. C., & DiPlacido, J. (2001). Personality's role in the protection and enhancement of health: Where the research has been, where it is stuck, how it might move. In A. Baum, T. A. Revenson, & J. E. Singer (Eds.), *Handbook of health psychology*. Mahwah, NJ: Lawrence Erlbaum.

Overton, D. (1964). State-dependent or "dissociated" learning produced with pentobarbital. *Journal of Comparative Physiology and Psychology, 57*, 3–12.

Overton, D. (1966). State-dependent learning produced by depressant and atropine-like drugs. *Psychopharmacologia, 10*, 6–31.

Owens, G. P., Held, P., Blackburn, L., Auerbach, J. S., Clark, A. A., Herrera, C. J., . . . Stuart, G. L. (2014). Differences in relationship conflict, attachment, and depression in treatment-seeking veterans with hazardous substance use, PTSD, or PTSD and hazardous substance use. *Journal of Interpersonal Violence, 29*(7), 1318–1337.

Owens, M., Herbert, J., Jones, P. B., Sahakian, A. J., Wilkinson, P. O., Dunn, V. J., . . . Goodyer, I. M. (2014). Elevated morning cortisol is a stratified population-level biomarker for major depression in boys only with high depressive symptoms. *Proceedings of the National Academy of Sciences of the United States of America, 111*(9), 3638–3643.

Ozden, A., & Canat, S. (1999). Factitious hemoptysis. *Journal of American Child and Adolescent Psychiatry, 38*, 356–357.

PA (Parents Anonymous). (2014). *Asking for help is a sign of strength*. Retrieved from PA website: http://www.parentsanonymous.org.

Pace, T. W. W., & Heim, C. M. (2011). A short review on the psychoneuroimmunology of posttraumatic stress disorder: From risk factors to medical comorbidities. *Brain, Behavior, and Immunity, 25*(1), 6–13.

Pacik, P. T. (2014). Understanding and treating vaginismus: A multimodal approach. *International Urogynecology Journal, 25*(12), 1613–1620.

Paczynski, R. P., & Gold, M. S. (2011). Cocaine and crack. In J. H. Lowinson & P. Ruiz (Eds.), *Substance abuse: A comprehensive textbook* (5th ed.). Philadelphia, PA: Lippincott Williams & Wilkins.

Padwa, L. (1996). *Everything you pretend to know and are afraid someone will ask*. New York: Penguin.

Pagliari, C., Burton, C., McKinstry, B., Szentatotai, A., David, D., Serrano Blanco, A., . . . Wolters, M. (2012). Psychosocial implications of avatar use in supporting therapy for depression. *Studies in Health Technology and Informatics, 181*, 329–333.

Paillard, T., Rolland, Y., & de Souto Barreto, P. (2015). Protective effects of physical exercise in Alzheimer's disease and Parkinson's disease: A narrative review. *Journal of Clinical Neurology, 11*(3), 212–219.

Palamar, J. J., & Kamboukos, D. (2014). An examination of sociodemographic correlates of ecstasy use among high school seniors in the United States. *Substance Use & Misuse, 49*(13), 1774–1783.

Palijan, T. Z., Radeljak, S., Kovac, M., & Kovacevic, D. (2010). Relationship between comorbidity and violence risk assessment in forensic psychiatry— The implication of neuroimaging studies. *Psychiatria Danubina, 22*(2), 253–256.

Palley, W. (2014, February 7). Data point: Digital distractions help drive Millennials to mindfulness. *JWT Intelligence*.

Pankevich, D. E., Teegarden, S. L., Hedin, A. D., Jensen, C. L., & Bale, T. L. (2010). Caloric restriction experience reprograms stress and orexigenic pathways and promotes binge eating. *Journal of Neuroscience, 30*(18), 16399–16407.

Paris, J. (2005). Borderline personality disorder. *Canadian Medical Association Journal, 172*(12), 1579–1583.

Paris, J. (2010). Estimating the prevalence of personality disorders in the community. *Journal of Personality Disorders, 24*(4), 405–411.

Paris, J. (2012). The rise and fall of dissociative identity disorder. *Journal of Nervous and Mental Disease, 200*(12), 1076–1079.

Paris, J. (2014). Modernity and narcissistic personality disorder. *Personality Disorders, 5*(2), 220–226.

Parish, B. S., & Yutsy, S. H. (2011). Somatoform disorders. In R. E. Hales, S. C. Yudofsky, & G. O. Gabbard, *Essentials of psychiatry* (3rd ed., pp. 229–254). Arlington, VA: American Psychiatric Publishing.

Park, A. (2014, March 27). U.S. autism rates jump 30% from 2012. *Time.com*.

Park, J. E., Lee, J., Suh, G., Kim, B., & Cho, M. J. (2014). Mortality rates and predictors in community-dwelling elderly individuals with cognitive impairment: An eight-year follow-up after initial assessment. *International Psychogeriatrics, 26*(8), 1295–1304.

Park, M., & Unützer, J. (2014). Hundred forty eight more days with depression: The association between marital conflict and depression-free days. *International Journal of Geriatric Psychiatry, 29*(12), 1271–1277.

Parker, G., & Hyett, M. (2010). Screening for depression in medical settings: Are specific scales useful? In A. J. Mitchell & J. C. Coyne (Eds.), *Screening for depression in clinical practice: An evidence-based guide* (pp. 191–201). New York: Oxford University Press.

Parker, S., Nichter, M., Vuckovic, N., Sims, C., & Ritenbaugh, C. (1995). Body image and weight concerns among African American and white adolescent females: Differences that make a difference. *Human Organization, 54*(2), 103–114.

Parker, T. S., Blackburn, K. M., Perry, M. S., & Hawks, J. M. (2012). Sexting as an intervention: Relationship satisfaction and motivational considerations. *American Journal of Family Therapy, 41*(1), 1–12.

Parrott, A. C., Montgomery, C., Wetherell, M. A., Downey, L. A., Stough, C., & Scholey, A. B. (2014). MDMA, cortisol, and heightened stress in recreational ecstasy users. *Behavioural Pharmacology, 25*(5-6), 458–472.

Paslakis, G., Graap, H., & Erim, Y. (2015). Media exposure and posttraumatic stress disorder: Review and implications for psychotherapy. [German] *Psychotherapie, Psychosomatik, Medizinische Psychologie*. [Advance publication.]

Patel, S. R., Humensky, J. L., Olfson, M., Simpson, H. B., Myers, R., & Dixon, L. B. (2014). Treatment of obsessive-compulsive disorder in a nationwide survey of office-based physician practice. *Psychiatric Services* (Washington, D.C.), 65(5), 681–684.

Patrick, C. J. (2007). Antisocial personality disorder and psychopathy. In W. O'Donohue, K. A. Fowler, & S. O. Lilienfeld (Eds.). *Personality disorders: Toward the DSM-V*. Los Angeles: Sage Publications.

Patterson, D. (2011). The linkage between secondary victimization by law enforcement and rape case outcomes. *Journal of Interpersonal Violence, 26*(2), 328–347.

Patterson, P. H. (2012). Animal models of the maternal infection risk factor for schizophrenia. In A. S. Brown & P. H. Patterson (Eds.), *The origins of schizophrenia* (pp. 255–281). New York: Columbia University Press.

Paul, G. L. (1967). The strategy of outcome research in psychotherapy. *Journal of Counseling Psychology, 31*, 109–118.

Paul, G. L. (2000). Milieu therapy. In A. E. Kazdin (Ed.), *Encyclopedia of psychology* (Vol. 5, pp. 250–252). New York: Oxford University Press.

Paul, G. L., & Lentz, R. (1977). *Psychosocial treatment of the chronic mental patient*. Cambridge, MA: Harvard University Press.

Paul, R., & Gilbert, K. (2011). Development of language and communication. In E. Hollander, A. Kolevzon & J. T. Coyle (Eds.), *Textbook of autism spectrum disorders* (pp. 147–157). Arlington, VA: American Psychiatric Publishing, Inc.

Paykel, E. S. (2003). Life events and affective disorders. *Acta Psychiatrica Scandinavica, 108*(Suppl. 418), 61–66.

Paykel, E. S. (2003). Life events: Effects and genesis. *Psychological Medicine, 33*(7), 1145–1148.

Paykel, E. S. (2006). Editorials: Depression: Major problem for public health. *Epidemiologia e Psichiatria Sociale, 15*(1), 4–10.

Paykel, E. S. (2008). Basic concepts of depression. *Dialogues in Clinical Neuroscience, 10*(3), 279–289.

Paykel, E. S., & Cooper, Z. (1992). Life events and social stress. In E. S. Paykel (Ed.), *Handbook of affective disorders*. New York: Guilford Press.

Payne, A. F. (1928). *Sentence completion*. New York: New York Guidance Clinics.

Pear, R. (2013, December 11). Fewer psychiatrists seen taking health insurance. *New York Times*.

Pearl, R. L., White, M. A., & Grilo, C. M. (2014). Overvaluation of shape and weight as a mediator between self-esteem and weight bias internalization among patients with binge eating disorder. *Eating Behaviors, 15*(2), 259–261.

Pearlson, G. D., & Ford, J. M. (2014). Distinguishing between schizophrenia and other psychotic disorders. *Schizophrenia Bulletin, 40*(3), 501–503.

Pearson, C. (2013, May 21). Oklahoma tornado PTSD: How survivors are coping. *Huffington Post*.

Pekkanen, J. (2002, July 2). Dangerous minds. *Washingtonian*.

Pekkanen, J. (2007). Involuntary commitment is essential. In A. Quigley (Ed.), *Current controversies: Mental health*. Detroit: Greenhaven Press/Thomson Gale.

Pelissolo, A., & Moukheiber, A. (2013). Open-label treatment with escitalopram in patients with social anxiety disorder and fear of blushing. *Journal of Clinical Psychopharmacology, 33*(5), 695–698.

Pena-Garijo, J., Edo Villamón, S., Meliá de Alba, A., & Ruipérez, M. Á. (2013). Personality disorders in obsessive-compulsive disorder: A comparative study versus other anxiety disorders. *Thescientificworldjournal, 2013*, 856846.

Pendery, M. L., Maltzman, I. M., & West, L. J. (1982). Controlled drinking by alcoholics? New findings and a reevaluation of a major affirmative study. *Science, 217*(4555), 169–175.

Peng, T. (2008, November 22). Pro-anorexia groups spread to Facebook. *Newsweek*.

Perdeci, Z., Gulsun, M., Celik, C., Erdem, M., Ozdemir, B., Ozdag, F., & Kilic, S. (2010). Aggression and the event-related potentials in antisocial personality disorder. *Bulletin of Clinical Psychopharmacology, 20*(4), 300–306.

Perilla, J. L., Norris, F. H., & Lavizzo, E. A. (2002). Ethnicity, culture, and disaster response: Identifying and explaining ethnic differences in PTSD six months after Hurricane Andrew. *Journal of Social and Clinical Psychology, 21*, 20–45.

Perillo, A. D., Spada, A. H., Calkins, C., & Jeglic, E. L. (2014). Examining the scope of questionable diagnostic reliability in sexually violent predator (SVP) evaluations. *International Journal of Law and Psychiatry, 37*(2), 190–197.

Perlin, M. L. (2000). *The hidden prejudice: Mental disability on trial*. Washington, DC: American Psychological Association.

Perlin, M. L. (2004). "Salvation" or a "lethal dose"? Attitudes and advocacy in right to refuse treatment cases. *Journal of Forensic Psychology Practice, 4*(4), 51–69.

Perrin, M., Vandeleur, C. L., Castelao, E., Rothen, S., Glaus, J., Vollenweider, P., & Preisig, M. (2014). Determinants of the development of post-traumatic stress disorder, in the general population. *Social Psychiatry and Psychiatric Epidemiology, 49*(3), 447–457.

Perry, J. C. (2005). Dependent personality disorder. In G. O. Gabbard, J. S. Beck & J. Holmes (Eds.), *Oxford textbook of psychotherapy* (pp. 321–328). New York: Oxford University Press.

Pervanidou, P., & Chrousos, G. P. (2012). Posttraumatic stress disorder in children and adolescents: Neuroendocrine perspectives. *Science Signaling, 5*(245), pt6.

Peteet, J. R., Lu, F. G., & Narrow, W. E. (Eds.). (2011). *Religious and spiritual issues in psychiatric diagnosis: A research agenda for DSM-V*. Washington, DC: American Psychiatric Association.

Peterlin, B. L., Rosso, A. L., Sheftell, F. D., Libon, D. J., Mossey, J. M., & Merikangas, K. R. (2011). Post-traumatic stress disorder, drug abuse and migraine: New findings from the National Comorbidity Survey Replication (NCS-R). *Cephalalgia, 31*(2), 235–244.

Peters, R. H., Sherman, P. B., & Osher, F. C. (2008). Treatment in jails and prisons. In K. T. Mueser & D. V. Jeste (Eds.), *Clinical handbook of schizophrenia* (pp. 354–364). New York: Guilford Press.

Petersen, J. L., & Hyde, J. S. (2011). Gender differences in sexual attitudes and behaviors: A review of meta-analytic results and large datasets. *Journal of Sex Research, 48*(2-3), 149–165.

Petersen, L., Mortensen, P. B., & Pedersen, C. B. (2011). Paternal age at birth of first child and risk of schizophrenia. *American Journal of Psychiatry, 168*(1), 82–88.

Petersen, L., Sørensen, T. A., Kragh Andersen, P., Mortensen, P. B., & Hawton, K. (2014). Genetic and familial environmental effects on suicide attempts: A study of Danish adoptees and their biological and adoptive siblings. *Journal of Affective Disorders, 155*, 273–277.

Peterson, D., Munger, C., Crowley, J., Corcoran, C., Cruchaga, C., Goate, A. M., . . . Kauwe, J. K. (2014). Variants in PPP3R1 and MAPT are associated with more rapid functional decline in Alzheimer's disease: The Cache County Dementia Progression Study. *Alzheimer's & Dementia, 10*(3), 366–371.

Peterson, L., & Roberts, M. C. (1991). Treatment of children's problems. In C. E. Walker (Ed.), *Clinical psychology: Historical and research foundations*. New York: Plenum Press.

Petrie, K. J., Fontanilla, I., Thomas, M. G., Booth, R. J., & Pennebaker, J. W. (2004). Effect of written emotional expression on immune function in patients with human immunodeficiency virus infection: A randomized trial. *Psychosomatic Medicine, 66*(2), 272–275.

Petrovich, G. D. (2011). Learning and the motivation to eat: Forebrain circuitry. *Physiology & Behavior, 104*(4), 582–589.

Pew Internet. (2013). *Social networking fact sheet*. Washington, DC: Pew Internet & American Life Project.

Pew Research Center. (2010). *8% of online Americans use Twitter*. Washington, DC: Author.

Pew Research Center. (2010). *Mobile Access 2010*. Washington, DC: Author.

Pew Research Center. (2010). Women, men and the new economics of marriage. *Pew Social Trends*. Retrieved from Pew Social Trends website: http://www.pewsocialtrends.org/2010/01/19.

Pew Research Center. (2011). Twitter, launched five years ago, delivers 350 billion tweets a day. *Media Mentions*. Washington, DC: Pew Internet & American Life Project.

Pew Research Center. (2013). 10 findings about women in the workplace. *Pew Social Trends*. Retrieved from Pew Social Trends website: http://www.pewsocialtrends.org/2013/12/11.

Pew Research Center. (2013). 50 years after the march on Washington, many racial divides remain: Personal experiences with discrimination. *Pew Social Trends*. Retrieved from Pew Social Trends website: http://www.pewsocialtrends.org/2013/08/22.

Pew Research Center. (2013). *Majority now supports legalizing marijuana*. Washington, DC: Pew Research Center for the People & the Press.

Pew Research Center. (2013). Modern parenthood. *Pew Social Trends*. Retrieved from Pew Social Trends website: http://www.pewsocialtrends.org/2013/03/14.

Pew Research Center. (2015, August 4). *Texting is most common way teens get in touch with closest friend*. Retrieved from Pew Internet website: http://www.pewinternet.org.

Pew Research Internet Project. (2014). *Social media update 2013: Main findings*. Washington, DC: Pew. Retrieved from Pew Internet website: http://www.pewinternet.org/2013/12/30/social-media-update-2013.

Pfeffer, C. R. (2003). Assessing suicidal behavior in children and adolescents. In R. A. King & A. Apter (Eds.), *Suicide in children and adolescents* (pp. 211–226). Cambridge, England: Cambridge University Press.

Pfefferbaum, B., Newman, E., & Nelson, S. D. (2014). Mental health interventions for children exposed to disasters and terrorism. *Journal of Child and Adolescent Psychopharmacology, 24*(1), 24–31.

Pham, A. V., Carlson, J. S., & Koschiulek, J. F. (2010). Ethnic differences in parental beliefs of attention–deficit/hyperactivity disorder and treatment. *Journal of Attention Disorders, 13*(6), 584–591.

Phillips, D. P. (1974). The influence of suggestion on suicide: Substantive and theoretical implications of the Werther effect. *American Sociological Review, 39*, 340–354.

Phillips, D. P., & Ruth, T. E. (1993). Adequacy of official suicide statistics for scientific research and public policy. *Suicide & Life-Threatening Behavior, 23*(4), 307–319.

Phillips, K., Keane, K., & Wolfe, B. E. (2014). Peripheral brain derived neurotrophic factor (BDNF) in bulimia nervosa: A systematic review. *Archives of Psychiatric Nursing, 28*(2), 108–113.

Phillips, K. A., McElroy, S. L., Keck, P. E., Jr., Pope, H. G., Jr., & Hudson, J. I. (1993). Body dysmorphic disorder: 30 cases of imagined ugliness. *American Journal of Psychiatry, 150*(2), 302–308.

Phillips, M. L. (2011). Treating postpartum depression. *Monitor on Psychology, 42*(2).

Phillips, M. L. (2011). *Using social media in your research*. Washington, DC: American Psychological Association.

Piatt, A. (2013). Facebook may improve working memory, cognition in elderly. *Neuropsychology*. Retrieved from Neuropsychology website: http://www.neuropsychology.com/2013/03/03/working-memory-.

Pickel, K. L. (2004). When a lie becomes the truth: The effects of self-generated misinformation on eyewitness memory. *Memory, 12*(1), 14–26.

Pickert, K. (2014, February 3). The art of being mindful, *Time*.

Pickover, C. A. (1999). *Strange brains and genius: The secret lives of eccentric scientists and madmen*. New York: HarperCollins/Quill.

Pierce, K., & Courchesne, E. (2001). Evidence for a cerebellar role in reduced exploration and stereotyped behavior in autism. *Biological Psychiatry, 49*(8), 655–664.

Pierce, K., & Courchesne, E. (2002). "A further support to the hypothesis of a link between serotonin, autism and the cerebellum": Reply. *Biological Psychiatry, 52*(2), 143.

Pieters, S., Van Der Zwaluw, C. S., Van Der Vorst, H., Wiers, R. W., Smeets, H., Lambrichs, E., . . . Engels, R. E. (2012). The moderating effect of alcohol-specific parental rule-setting on the relation between the dopamine D2 receptor gene (DRD2), the l-opioid receptor gene (OPRM1) and alcohol use in young adolescents. *Alcohol and Alcoholism* (Oxford, Oxfordshire), *47*(6), 663–670.

Pietrzak, R. H., el-Gabalawy, R., Tsai, J., Sareen, J., Neumeister, A., & Southwick, S. M. (2014). Typologies of posttraumatic stress disorder in the U.S. adult population. *Journal of Affective Disorders, 162*, 102–106.

Pigott, H. E., Leventhal, A. M., Alter, G. S., & Boren, J. J. (2010). Efficacy and effectiveness of antidepressants: Current status of research. *Psychotherapy and Psychosomatics, 79*(5), 267–279.

Pike, K. M., Carter, J. C., & Olmsted, M. P. (2010). Cognitive-behavioral therapy for anorexia nervosa. In C. M. Grilo & J. E. Mitchell (Eds.), *The treatment of eating disorders: A clinical handbook* (pp. 83–107). New York: Guilford Press.

Pike, K. M., Dunne, P. E., & Addai, E. (2013). Expanding the boundaries: Reconfiguring the demographics of the "typical" eating disordered patient. *Current Psychiatry Reports, 15*(11), 411.

Pilecki, B., & McKay, D. (2011). Cognitive behavioral models of phobias and pervasive anxiety. In D. McKay & E. A. Storch (Eds.), *Handbook of child and adolescent anxiety disorders* (pp. 39–48). New York: Springer Science & Business Media.

Pillay, B., Lee, S. J., Katona, L., Burney, S., & Avery, S. (2014). Psychosocial factors predicting survival after allogeneic stem cell transplant. *Supportive Care in Cancer, 22*(9), 2547–2555.

Pinals, D. A., & Mossman, D. (2012). *Evaluation for civil commitment: Best practices in forensic mental health assessment*. New York: Oxford University Press.

Pinals, D. A., Packer, I., Fisher, B., & Roy, K. (2004). Relationship between race and ethnicity and forensic clinical triage dispositions. *Psychiatric Services 55*, 873–878.

Pinkham, A. E. (2014). Social cognition in schizophrenia. *Journal of Clinical Psychiatry, 75*(Suppl 2), 14–19.

Pinna, F., Sanna, L., Perra, V., Pisu Randaccio, R., Diana, E., & Carpiniello, B. (2014). Long-term outcome of schizoaffective disorder: Are there any differences with respect to schizophrenia? *Rivista Di Psichiatria, 49*(1), 41–49.

Pinto, A., Eisen, J. L., Mancebo, M. C., & Rasmussen, S. A. (2008). Obsessive-compulsive personality disorder. In J. S. Abramowitz, D. McKay, & S. Taylor (Eds.), *Obsessive-compulsive disorder: Subtypes and spectrum conditions.* Oxford, England: Elsevier.

Pinto, A., Steinglass, J. E., Greene, A. L., Weber, E. U., & Simpson, H. B. (2014). Capacity to delay reward differentiates obsessive-compulsive disorder and obsessive-compulsive personality disorder. *Biological Psychiatry, 75*(8), 653–659.

Pipe, R. T. (2010). Something for everyone: Busty Latin anal nurses in leather and glasses. In D. Monroe (Ed.), *Porn: How to think with kink. Philosophy for everyone* (pp. 193–203). Hoboken, NJ: Wiley-Blackwell.

Piper, A., & Merskey, H. (2004). The persistence of folly: A critical examination of dissociative identity disorder. Part I. The excesses of an improbable concept. *Canadian Journal of Psychiatry, 49*(9), 592–600.

Piper, A., & Merskey, H. (2004). The persistence of folly: Critical examination of dissociative identity disorder. Part II: The defence and decline of multiple personality or dissociative identity disorder. *Canadian Journal of Psychiatry, 49*(10), 678–683.

Piper, A., & Merskey, H. (2005). Reply: The persistence of folly: A critical examination of dissociative identity disorder. *Canadian Journal of Psychiatry, 50*(12), 814.

Piper, W. E., & Joyce, A. S. (2001). Psychosocial treatment outcome. In W. J. Livesley (Ed.), *Handbook of personality disorders: Theory, research, and treatment* (pp. 323–343). New York: Guilford Press.

Pirkl, J. J. (2009). The demographics of aging. *Transgenerational Design Matters.* Retrieved from Transgenerational Design Matters website: http://transgenerational.org/aging/demographics.htm.

Pistone, R. A. (2012). A critical review of research methods used in: "in use of risk assessment instruments to predict violence and antisocial behavior in 73 samples involving 24,827 people". *Global Journal of Health Science, 5*(1), 87–89.

Planty, M., Hussar, W., Snyder, T., Provasnik, S., Kena, G., Dinkes, R., . . . Kemp, J. (2008). *The condition of education 2008.* Washington, DC: National Center for Education Statistics.

Platt, R., Williams, S. R., & Ginsburg, G. S. (2015). Stressful life events and child anxiety: Examining parent and child mediators. *Child Psychiatry and Human Development.* [Electronic publication].

Plaud, J. J. (2007). Sexual disorders. In P. Sturmey (Ed.), *Functional analysis in clinical treatment. Practical resources for the mental health professional* (pp. 357–377). San Diego, CA: Elsevier Academic Press.

Plaza, I., Demarzo, M. M. P., Herrera-Mercadal, P., & Garcia-Campayo, J. (2013). Mindfulness-based mobile applications: Literature review and analysis of current features. *Journal of Medical Internet Research, 1*(2), e24.

Pletcher, M. J., Vittinghoff, E., Kalhan, R., Richman, J., Safford, M., Sidney, S., Lin, F., & Kertesz, S. (2012). Association between marijuana exposure and pulmonary function over 20 years. *Journal of the American Medical Association, 307*(2), 173–181.

Pocklington, A. J., O'Donovan, M., & Owen, M. J. (2014). The synapse in schizophrenia. *European Journal of Neuroscience, 39*(7), 1059–1067.

Pole, N., Best, S. R., Weiss, D. S., Metzler, T., Liberman, A. J., & Fagan, J. (2001). Effects of gender and ethnicity on duty-related posttraumatic stress symptoms among urban police officers. *Journal of Nervous and Mental Disease, 189*(7), 442–448.

Pollack, M. H. (2005). The pharmacotherapy of panic disorder. *Journal of Clinical Psychiatry, 66*(4), 23–27.

Polo, A. J., Alegria, M., Chen, C-N., & Blanco, C. (2011). The prevalence and comorbidity of social anxiety disorder among United States Latinos: A retrospective analysis of data from 2 national surveys. *Journal of Clinical Psychiatry, 72*(8), 1096–1105.

Pompili, M., Innamorati, M., Girardi, P., Tatarelli, R., & Lester, D. (2011). Evidence-based interventions for preventing suicide in youths. In M. Pompili & R. Tatarelli (Eds.), *Evidence-based practice in suicidology: A source book* (pp. 171–209). Cambridge MA: Hogrefe Publishing.

Pompili, M., Lester, D., Leenaars, A. A., Tatarelli, R., & Girardi, P. (2008). Psychache and suicide: A preliminary investigation. *Suicide & Life-Threatening Behavior, 38*(1), 116–121.

Pondé, M. P., Caron, J., Mendonça, M. S., Freire, A. C., & Moreau, N. (2014). The relationship between mental disorders and types of crime in inmates in a Brazilian prison. *Journal of Forensic Sciences, 59*(5), 1307–1314.

Pongan, É., Padovan, C., Coste, M., Krolak-Salmon, P., & Rouch, I. (2012). Caring for young patients with Alzheimer's disease or associated disorders in day care centers of the Rhône-Alpes region. *Gériatrie et Psychologie Neuropsychiatrie du Vieillissement, 10*(3), 343–348.

Ponniah, K., Magiati, I., & Hollon, S. D. (2013). An update on the efficacy of psychological therapies in the treatment of obsessive-compulsive disorder in adults. *Journal of Obsessive-Compulsive and Related Disorders, 2*(2), 207–218.

Pope, H. G., Jr., Poliakoff, M. B., Parker, M. P., Boynes, M., & Hudson, J. I. (2007). Is dissociative amnesia a culture-bound syndrome? Findings from a survey of historical literature: Reply. *Psychological Medicine, 37*(7), 1065–1067.

Pope, K. S. (1988). How clients are harmed by sexual contact with mental health professionals. *Journal of Counseling & Development, 67*, 222–226.

Pope, K. S. (1994). *Sexual involvement with therapists: Patient assessment, subsequent therapy, forensics.* Washington, DC: APA.

Pope, K. S., Keith-Spiegel, P., & Tabachnick, B. G. (2006). Sexual attraction to clients: The human therapist and the (sometimes) inhuman training system. *Training and Education in Professional Psychology, 5*(2), 96–111.

Pope, K. S., & Tabachnick, B. G. (1993). Therapists' anger, hate, fear and sexual feelings: National survey of therapists' responses, client characteristics, critical events, formal complaints and training. *Professional Psychology: Research and Practice, 24*, 142–152.

Pope, K. S., & Tabachnick, B. G. (1994). Therapists as patients: A national survey of psychologists' experience, problems, and beliefs. *Professional Psychology: Research and Practice, 25*, 247–258.

Pope, K. S., Tabachnick, B. G., & Keith-Spiegel, P. (1987). Ethics of practice: The beliefs and behaviors of psychologists as therapists. *American Psychologist, 42*, 993–1006.

Pope, K. S., & Vasquez, M. J. T. (2011). *Ethics in psychotherapy and counseling: A practical guide* (4th ed.). Hoboken, NJ: John Wiley & Sons.

Pope, K. S., & Vasquez, M. J. T. (2016). *Ethics in psychotherapy and counseling: A practical guide* (5th ed.). Hoboken, NJ: Wiley.

Pope, K. S., & Wedding, D. (2014). Contemporary challenges and controversies. In D. Wedding & R. J. Corsini (Eds.), *Current psychotherapies* (10th ed., pp. 569–604). Independence, KY: Cengage Publications.

Porcerelli, J., Dauphin, B., Ablon, J. S., Leitman, S., & Bambery, M. (2007). Psychoanalysis of avoidant personality disorder: A systematic case study. *Psychotherapy, 44*, 1–13.

Poretz, M., & Sinrod, B. (1991). *Do you do it with the lights on?* New York: Ballantine Books.

Posmontier, B. (2010). The role of midwives in facilitating recovery in postpartum psychosis. *Journal of Midwifery & Women's Health, 55*(5), 430–437.

Pössel, P., & Black, S. W. (2014). Testing three different sequential mediational interpretations of Beck's cognitive model of the development of depression. *Journal of Clinical Psychology, 70*(1), 72–94.

Post, R. M. (2005). The impact of bipolar depression. *Journal of Clinical Psychiatry, 66*(Suppl. 5), 5–10.

Post, R. M. (2011). Treatment of bipolar depression. In D. A. Ciraulo & R. I. Shader (Eds.), *Pharmacotherapy of depression* (2nd ed., pp. 197–237). New York: Springer Science + Business Media.

Post, R. M., Ballenger, J. C., & Goodwin, F. K. (1980). Cerebrospinal fluid studies of neurotransmitter function in manic and depressive illness. In J. H. Wood (Ed.), *The neurobiology of cerebrospinal fluid* (Vol. 1). New York: Plenum Press.

Post, R. M., Lake, C. R., Jimerson, D. C., Bunney, J. H., Ziegler, M. G., & Goodwin, F. K. (1978). Cerebrospinal fluid norepinephrine in affective illness. *American Journal of Psychiatry, 135*(8), 907–912.

Potkin, S. G., Keator, D. B., Kesler-West, M. L., Nguyen, D. D., van Erp, T. M., Mukherjee, J., . . . Preda, A. (2014). D2 receptor occupancy following lurasidone treatment in patients with schizophrenia or schizoaffective disorder. *CNS Spectrums, 19*(2), 176–181.

Poulin, M. J., Holman, E. A., & Buffone, A. (2012). The neurogenetics of nice: Receptor genes for oxytocin and vasopressin interact with threat to predict prosocial behavior. *Psychological Science, 23*(5), 446–452.

Poulos, C. X., Le, A. D., & Parker, J. L. (1995). Impulsivity predicts individual susceptibility to high levels of alcohol self-administration. *Behavioral Pharmacology, 6*(8), 810–814.

Poulsen, S., Lunn, S., Daniel, S. F., Folke, S., Mathiesen, B. B., Katznelson, H., & Fairburn, C. G. (2014). A randomized controlled trial of psychoanalytic psychotherapy or cognitive-behavioral therapy for bulimia nervosa. *American Journal of Psychiatry, 171*(1), 109–116.

Powell, D., Caban-Holt, A., Jicha, G., Robertson, W., Davis, R., Gold, B. T., . . . Head, E. (2014). Frontal white matter integrity in adults with Down syndrome with and without dementia. *Neurobiology of Aging, 35*(7), 1562–1569.

Pratley, R. E., Fleck, P., & Wilson, C. (2014). Efficacy and safety of initial combination therapy with alogliptin plus metformin versus either as monotherapy in drug-naïve patients with type 2 diabetes: A randomized, double-blind, 6-month study. *Diabetes, Obesity and Metabolism, 16*(7), 613–621.

Prelock, P. A., Paul, R., & Allen, E. M. (2011). Evidence-based treatments in communication for children with autism spectrum disorders. In B. Reichow, P. Doehring, D. V. Cicchetti, & F. R. Volkmar (Eds.), *Evidence-based practices and treatments for children with autism* (pp. 93–169). New York: Springer Science + Business Media.

PressTV. (2013, January 9). New U.S. poll reveals 85% of Americans distrust congressmen. *PressTV.* Retrieved from Press TV website: http://www.presstv.ir/detail/2013/01/09/282571.

Preti, A. (2011). Animal model and neurobiology of suicide. *Progress in Neuro-Psychopharmacology & Biological Psychiatry, 35*(4), 818–830.

Preti, A. (2011). Do animals commit suicide? Does it matter? *Crisis: Journal of Crisis Intervention and Suicide Prevention, 32*(1), 1–4.

Preuss, U. W., Wurst, F. M., Ridinger, M., Rujescu, D., Fehr, C., Koller, G., . . . Zill, P. (2013). Association of functional DBH genetic variants with alcohol dependence risk and related depression and suicide attempt phenotypes: Results from a large multicenter association study. *Drug and Alcohol Dependence, 133*(2), 459–467.

Price, M. (2011). Upfront: Marijuana addiction a growing risk as society grows more tolerant. *Monitor on Psychology, 42*(5), 13.

Princeton Survey Research Associates. (1996). *Healthy steps for young children: Survey of parents.* Princeton: Author.

Prochaska, J. O., & Norcross, J. C. (2003). *Systems of psychotherapy: A transtheoretical analysis* (5th ed.). Pacific Grove, CA: Brooks/Cole.

Prochaska, J. O., & Norcross, J. C. (2006). *Systems of psychotherapy: A transtheoretical analysis.* (6th ed.) Pacific Grove, CA: Brooks/Cole.

Prochaska, J. O., & Norcross, J. C. (2010). *Systems of psychotherapy: A transtheoretical analysis* (7th ed.). Pacific Grove, CA: Brooks/Cole.

Prochaska, J. O., & Norcross, J. C. (2013). *Systems of psychotherapy: Transtheoretical analysis* (8th ed.). Independence, KY: Cengage Learning.

Prochwicz, K., & Sobczyk, A. (2011). [Dancing manias. Between culture and medicine]. *Psychiatria Polska, 45*(2), 277–287.

Protopopescu, X., Pan, H., Tuesher, O., Cloitre, M., Goldstein, M., Engelien, W., . . . Stern, E. (2005). Differential time courses and specificity of amygdala activity in posttraumatic stress disorder subjects and normal control subjects. *Biological Psychiatry, 57*(5), 464–473.

PROUD2BME. (2012, March 26). *Overall, do social networking sites like Facebook and Twitter help or hurt your body confidence?* Retrieved from PROUD2BME website: http://proud2bme.org.

Pruchno, R. (2014). All in the family: Prison or treatment for people with mental illness? *Psychology Today.* Retrieved from *Psychology Today* website: http://www.psychologytoday.com/blog.

Prusiner, S. B. (1991). Molecular biology of prion diseases. *Science, 252*, 1515–1522.

PRWeb. (2013). *Weight loss market in U.S. up 1.7% to $61 billion.* Beltville, MD: PrWeb. Retrieved from PR Web website: http://www.prweb.com/releases/2013/4/prweb10629316.htm.

Puhl, R. M., Latner, J. D., O'Brien, K., Luedicke, J., Danielsdottir, S., & Forhan, M. (2015). A multinational examination of weight bias: Predictors of anti-fat attitudes across four countries. *International Journal of Obesity, 39*(7), 1166–1173.

Punamäki, R., Qouta, S. R., & El Sarraj, E. (2010). Nature of torture, PTSD, and somatic symptoms among political ex-prisoners. *Journal of Traumatic Stress, 23*(4), 532–536.

Purcell, S. M., Moran, J. L., Fromer, M., Ruderfer, D., Solovieff, N., Roussos, P., . . . Sklar, P. (2014). A polygenic burden of rare disruptive mutations in schizophrenia. *Nature, 506*(7487), 185–190.

Putnam, F. W. (1984). The psychophysiologic investigation of multiple personality disorder. *Psychiatric Clinics of North America, 7*, 31–40.

Putnam, F. W. (2000). Dissociative disorders. In A. J. Sameroff, M. Lewis, & S. M, Miller (Eds.), *Handbook of developmental psychopathology* (2nd ed., pp. 739–754). New York: Kluwer Academic/Plenum Press.

Putnam, F. W. (2006). Dissociative disorders. In D. Cicchetti & D. J. Cohen (Eds.), *Developmental psychopathology, Vol. 3: Risk, disorder, and adaptation* (2nd ed., pp. 657–695). Hoboken, NJ: John Wiley & Sons.

Putnam, F. W., Zahn, T. P., & Post, R. M. (1990). Differential autonomic nervous system activity in multiple personality disorder. *Journal of Psychiatric Research, 31*(3), 251–260.

Quah, S. (2014). Caring for persons with schizophrenia at home: Examining the link between family caregivers' role distress and quality of life. *Sociology of Health & Illness, 36*(4), 596–612.

Quas, J. A., Malloy, L. C., Melinder, A., Goodman, G. S., D'Mello, M., & Schaaf, J. (2007). Developmental differences in the effects of repeated interviews and interviewer bias on young children's event memory and false reports. *Developmental Psychology, 43*(4), 823–837.

Queinec, R., Beitz, C., Contrad, B., Jougla, E., Leffondré, K., Lagarde, E., & Encrenaz, G. (2011). Copycat effect after celebrity suicides: Results from the French national death register. *Psychological Medicine: Journal of Research in Psychiatry and the Allied Sciences, 41*(3), 668–671.

Quillian, L., & Pager, D. (2010). Estimating risk: Stereotype amplification and the perceived risk of criminal victimization. *Social Psychology Quarterly, 73*(1), 79–104.

Qureshi, N. A., & Al-Bedah, A. M. (2013). Mood disorders and complementary and alternative medicine: A literature review. *Neuropsychiatric Disease and Treatment, 9*, 639–658.

Rabin, R. C. (2013, July 29). Concerns about dementia screening. *New York Times,* D4.

Rabinowitz, J., Werbeloff, N., Caers, I., Mandel, F. S., Stauffer, V., Ménard, F., . . . Kapur, S. (2014). Determinants of antipsychotic response in schizophrenia: Implications for practice and future clinical trials. *Journal of Clinical Psychiatry, 75*(4), e308–e316.

Raboch, J., Jr., & Raboch, J. (1992). Infrequent orgasm in women. *Journal of Sex & Marital Therapy, 18*(2), 114–120.

Rachman, S. (1966). Sexual fetishism: An experimental analog. *Psychological Record, 18*, 25–27.

Rachman, S. (1993). Obsessions, responsibility and guilt. *Behavioral Research and Therapy, 31*(2), 149–154.

Radford, B. (2009). Rorschach test: Discredited but still controversial. *Live Science,* July 31, 2009.

Ragatz, L., Vitacco, M. J., & Tross, R. (2014). Competency to proceed to trial evaluations and rational understanding. *International Journal of Offender Therapy and Comparative Criminology.* [Electronic publication.]

Ragland, J. D., Ranganath, C., Harms, M. P., Barch, D. M., Gold, J. M., Layher, E., . . . Carter, C. S. (2015). Functional and neuroanatomic specificity of episodic memory dysfunction in schizophrenia: A functional magnetic resonance imaging study of the relational and item-specific encoding task. *JAMA Psychiatry, 72*(9), 909–916.

RAINN (Rape, Abuse & Incest National Network). (2009). *Campus safety.* Retrieved from RAINN website: https://www.rainn.org/public-policy/campus-safety.

Raj, V., Rowe, A. A., Fleisch, S. B., Paranjape, S. Y., Arain, A. M., & Nicolson, S. E. (2014). Psychogenic pseudosyncope: Diagnosis and management. *Autonomic Neuroscience: Basic and Clinical, 184*, 66–72.

Rajkumar, R. P., & Kumaran, A. K. (2015). Depression and anxiety in men with sexual dysfunction: A retrospective study. *Comprehensive Psychiatry, 60*, 114–118.

Rametti, G., Carrillo, B., Gómez-Gil, E., Jungue, C., Segovia, S., Gomez, A., & Guillamon, A. (2011). White matter microstructure in female to male transsexuals before cross-sex hormonal treatment. A diffusion tensor imaging study. *Journal of Psychiatric Research, 45*(2), 199–204.

Ramey, C. T., & Ramey, S. L. (1992). Effective early intervention. *Mental Retardation, 30*(6), 337–345.

Ramey, C. T., & Ramey, S. L. (2004). Early learning and school readiness: Can early intervention make a difference? *Merrill-Palmer Quarterly, 50*(4), 471–491.

Ramey, C. T., & Ramey, S. L. (2007). Early learning and school readiness: Can early intervention make a difference? In G. W. Ladd, (Ed.), *Appraising the human developmental sciences: Essays in honor of Merrill-Palmer Quarterly, Landscapes of childhood* (pp. 329–350). Detroit, MI: Wayne State University Press.

Ramey, C. T., Sparling, J., & Ramey, S. (2012). Abecedarian: The ideas, the approach, and the findings. *CreateSpace Independent Publishing Platform.*

Ramirez, E., Ortega, A. R., Chamorro, A., & Colmenero, J. M. (2014). A program of positive intervention in the elderly: Memories, gratitude and forgiveness. *Aging & Mental Health, 18*(4), 463–470.

Rampell, C. (2013, July 2). Most U.S. health spending is exploding—but not for mental health. *New York Times.*

Ramsey, C. M., Spira, A. P., Mojtabai, R., Eaton, W. W., Roth, K., & Lee, H. B. (2013). Lifetime manic spectrum episodes and all-cause mortality: 26-year follow-up of the NIMH Epidemiologic Catchment Area Study. *Journal of Affective Disorders, 151*(1), 337–342.

Ramsland, K. & Kuter, R. (2011). Eve and Sybil. *Multiple Personalities: Crime and Defense.* Crime Library on truTV.com. Retrieved from TruTV: http://www.trutv.com/library/crime/criminal_mind/psychology/multiples/3.html.

RAND Corporation. (2008, April 17). 1 in 5 Iraq, Afghanistan vets has PTSD, major depression. *Science Blog.* Retrieved from Science Blog website: http://www.scienceblog.com/cms/1-5-iraqafghanistan-vet-has-ptsd-major-depressionrand-15954.html.

RAND Corporation. (2010). Studies' estimate of PTSD prevalence rates for returning service members vary widely. Retrieved from RAND website: http://www.rand.org/pubs/research_briefs/RB9509.html.

Randolph, J. J., Zheng, H., Avis, N. E., Greendale, G. A., & Harlow, S. D. (2015). Masturbation frequency and sexual function domains are associated with serum reproductive hormone levels across the menopausal transition. *The Journal of Clinical Endocrinology and Metabolism, 100*(1), 258–266.

Rao, N. P., & Remington, G. (2014). Targeting the dopamine receptor in schizophrenia: Investigational drugs in Phase III trials. *Expert Opinion on Pharmacotherapy, 15*(3), 373–383.

Rapee, R. M. (2014). Preschool environment and temperament as predictors of social and nonsocial anxiety disorders in middle adolescence. *Journal of the American Academy of Child and Adolescent Psychiatry, 53*(3), 320–328.

Rapport, M. D., Kofler, M. J., Alderson, R. M., & Raiker, J. S. (2008). Attention-deficit/hyperactivity disorder. In D. Reitman (Ed.), *Handbook of psychological assessment, case conceptualization, and treatment, Vol. 2: Children and adolescents.* Hoboken, NJ: John Wiley & Sons.

Rashid, T., & Seigman, M. (2014). Positive psychotherapy. In D. Wedding & R. J. Corsini (Eds.), *Current psychotherapies* (10th ed., pp. 461–498). Independence, KY: Cengage Publications.

Rasic, D., Hajek, T., Alda, M., & Uher, R. (2014). Risk of mental illness in offspring of parents with schizophrenia, bipolar disorder, and major depressive disorder: A meta-analysis of family high-risk studies. *Schizophrenia Bulletin, 40*(1), 28–38.

Raskin, D. C., & Honts, C. R. (2002). The comparison question test. In M. Kleiner (Ed.), *The handbook of polygraph testing.* San Diego, CA: Academic.

Raskin, N. J, Rogers, C. R., & Witty, M. C. (2014). Client-centered therapy. In D. Wedding & R. J. Corsini (Eds.), *Current psychotherapies* (10th ed., pp. 95–150). Independence, KY: Cengage Publications.

Ratcliffe, R. (2014). How do other countries tackle bullying? *The Guardian.* Retrieved from The Guardian website: http://www.theguardian/teacher-network/teacher-blog/2013.

Rathbone, C. J., Ellis, J. A., Baker, I., & Butler, C. R. (2014). Self, memory, and imagining the future in a case of psychogenic amnesia. *Neurocase, 21*(6), 727–737.

Rathbone, J. (2001). *Anatomy of masochism.* New York: Kluwer Academic/Plenum.

Rauch, S. M., Eftekhari, A., & Ruzek, J. I. (2012). Review of exposure therapy: A gold standard for PTSD treatment. *Journal of Rehabilitation Research & Development, 49*(5), 679–687.

Raveneau, G., Feinstein, R., Rosen, L. M., & Fisher, M. (2014). Attitudes and knowledge levels of nurses and residents caring for adolescents with an eating disorder. *International Journal of Adolescent Medicine and Health, 26*(1), 131–136.

Ravitz, P., Watson, P., & Grigoriadis, S. (2013). *Psychotherapy essentials to-go: Interpersonal therapy for depression.* New York: W. W. Norton.

Raviv, S. (2010). *Being Ana.* Bloomington, IN: iUniverse.

Raymond, K. B. (1997). The effect of race and gender on the identification of children with attention deficit hyperactivity disorder. *Dissertation Abstracts International: Section A: Humanities and Social Sciences, 57*(12-A), 5052.

Raz, M. (2013). *The lobotomy letters: The making of American psychosurgery (Rochester Studies in medical history).* NY: University of Rochester Press.

Razali, S. M., & Yusoff, M. M. (2014). Medication adherence in schizophrenia: A comparison between outpatients and relapse cases. *East Asian Archives of Psychiatry, 24*(2), 68–74.

Reamer, F. G. (2013). Social work in a digital age: Ethical and risk management challenges. *Social Work, 58*(2), 163–172.

Reas, D. L., Rø, Ø., Karterud, S., Hummelen, B., & Pedersen, G. (2013). Eating disorders in a large clinical sample of men and women with personality disorders. *International Journal of Eating Disorders, 46*(8), 801–809.

Recordon, N., & Kohl, J. (2014). [Sex therapy for sexual dysfunctions.] *Revue Médicale Suisse, 10*(422), 651–653.

Redding, A. J. (2014). *Cognitive behavioral therapy: A guide and techniques to CBT.* Amazon Digital Services. [Kindle version].

Redick, R. W., Witkin, M. J., Atay, J. E., & Manderscheid, R. W. (1992). Specialty mental health system characteristics. In R. W. Manderscheid & M. A. Sonnenschein (Eds.), *Mental health, United States, 1992.* Washington, DC: U.S. Department of Health and Human Services.

Redmond, D. E. (1977). Alterations in the function of the nucleus locus coeruleus: A possible model for studies of anxiety. In I. Hanin & E. Usdin (Eds.), *Animal models in psychiatry and neurology.* New York: Pergamon Press.

Redmond, D. E. (1979). New and old evidence for the involvement of a brain norepinephrine system in anxiety. In W. E. Fann, I. Karacan, A. D. Pokorny, & R. L. Williams (Eds.), *Phemenology and treatment of anxiety.* New York: Spectrum.

Redmond, D. E. (1981). Clonidine and the primate locus coeruleus: Evidence suggesting anxiolytic and anti-withdrawal effects. In H. Lal & S. Fielding (Eds.), *Psychopharmacology of clonidine.* New York: Alan R. Liss.

Redmond, D. E. (1985). Neurochemical basis for anxiety and anxiety disorders: Evidence from drugs which decrease human fear or anxiety. In A. H. Tuma & J. Maser (Eds.), *Anxiety and the anxiety disorders.* Hillsdale, NJ: Lawrence Erlbaum.

Rees, C. S., & Pritchard, R. (2013). Brief cognitive therapy for avoidant personality disorder. *Psychotherapy.* [Advance online publication.]

Rees, C. S., & Pritchard, R. (2015). Brief cognitive therapy for avoidant personality disorder. *Psychotherapy, 52*(1), 45–55.

Reese, J., Kraschewski, A., Anghelescu, I., Winterer, G., Schmidt, L. G., Gallinat, J., . . . Wernicke, C. (2010). Haplotypes of dopamine and serotonin transporter genes are associated with antisocial personality disorder in alcoholics. *Psychiatric Genetics, 20*(4), 140–152.

Regal, C. (2015). Erectile dysfunction. *HealthCentral.* Retrieved from Health Central website: http://www. healthcentral.com/slideshows.

Regier, D. A., Narrow, W. E., Clarke, D. E., Kraemer, H. C., Kuramoto, S. J., Kuhl, E. A. & Kupfer, D. J. (2013). DSM-5 field trials in the United States and Canada, Part II: Test-retest reliability of selected categorical diagnoses. *American Journal of Psychiatry, 170,* 59–70.

Regier, D. A., Narrow, W. E., Kuhl, E. A., & Kupfer, D. J. (Eds.). (2011). *The conceptual evolution of DSM-5.* Arlington, VA: American Psychiatric Publishing.

Regier, D. A., Narrow, W. E., Rae, D. S., Manderscheid, R. W., Locke, B. Z., & Goodwin, F. K. (1993). The de facto U.S. Mental and Addictive Disorders Service System: Epidemiologic Catchment Area prospective 1-year prevalence rates of disorders in services. *Archives of General Psychiatry, 50,* 85–94.

Reich, J., & Schatzberg, A. (2014). An empirical data comparison of regulatory agency and malpractice legal problems for psychiatrists. *Annals of Clinical Psychiatry, 26*(2), 91–96.

Reichenberg, A., Gross, R., Kolevzon, A., & Susser, E. S. (2011). Parental and perinatal risk factors for autism. In E. Hollander, A. Kolevzon & J. T. Coyle (Eds.), *Textbook of autism spectrum disorders.* (pp. 239–246) Arlington, VA: American Psychiatric Publishing, Inc.

Reif, S., George, P., Braude, L., Dougherty, R. H., Daniels, A. S., Ghose, S. S., & Delphin-Rittmon, M. E. (2014). Residential treatment for individuals with substance use disorders: Assessing the evidence. *Psychiatric Services* (Washington, D.C.), *65*(3), 301–312.

Reinares, M., Sánchez-Moreno, J., & Fountoulakis, K. N. (2014). Psychosocial interventions in bipolar disorder: What, for whom, and when. *Journal of Affective Disorders, 156,* 46–55.

Reinecke, A., Cooper, M., Favaron, E., Massey-Case, R., & Harmer, C. (2011). Attentional bias in untreated panic disorder. *Psychiatry Research, 185*(3), 387–393.

Reisch, T., Seifritz, E., Esposito, F., Wiest, R., Valach, L., & Michel, K. (2010). An fMRI study on mental pain and suicidal behavior. *Journal of Affective Disorders, 126*(1-2), 321–325.

Reisner, A. D., Piel, J., & Makey, M., Jr. (2013). Competency to stand trial and defendants who lack insight into their mental illness. *Journal of the American Academy of Psychiatry and the Law, 41*(1), 85–91.

Reitan, R. M., & Wolfson, D. (1996). Theoretical, methodological, and validational bases of the Halstead-Reitan neuropsychological test battery. In I. Grant & K. M. Adams (Eds.), *Neuropsychological assessment of neuropsychiatric disorders* (2nd ed., pp. 3–42). New York: Oxford University Press.

Reitan, R. M., & Wolfson, D. (2005). The effect of age and education transformations on neuropsychological test scores of persons with diffuse or bilateral brain damage. *Applied Neuropsychology, 12*(4), 181–189.

Remberk, B., Bazyn'ska, A. K., Bronowska, Z., Potocki, P., Krempa-Kowalewska, A., Niwin'ski, P., & Rybakowski, F. (2015). Which aspects of long-term outcome are predicted by positive and negative symptoms in early-onset psychosis? An exploratory eight-year follow-up study. *Psychopathology, 48,* 47–55.

Remington, G., Foussias, G., Fervaha, G., & Agid, O. (2014). Schizophrenia, cognition, and psychosis. *JAMA Psychiatry, 71*(3), 336–337.

Renaud, J., Berlim, M. T., McGirr, A., Tousignant, M., & Turecki, G. (2008). Current psychiatric morbidity, aggression/impulsivity, and personality dimensions in child and adolescent suicide: A case-control study. *Journal of Affective Disorders, 105*(1–3), 221–228.

Reuters. (2010, April 8). *They walk among us: 1 in 5 believe in aliens?* Retrieved from Reuters website: http://www.reuters.com/assets/print?aid.

Rhéaume, C., Arsenault, B. J., Després, J., Faha, Boekholdt, S. M., Wareham, N. J., . . . Chir, M. (2014). Impact of abdominal obesity and systemic hypertension on risk of coronary heart disease in men and women: The EPIC-Norfolk Population Study. *Journal of Hypertension, 32*(11), 2224–2230.

Rhebergen, D., & Graham, R. (2014). The relabelling of dysthymic disorder to persistent depressive disorder in DSM-5: Old wine in new bottles? *Current Opinion in Psychiatry, 27*(1), 27–31.

Rice, C. E., Rosanoff, M., Dawson, G., Durkin, M. S., Croen, L. A., Singer, A., & Yeargin-Allsopp, M. (2012). Evaluating changes in the prevalence of the autism spectrum disorders (ASDs). *Public Health Reviews, 34*(2), 1–22. [Electronic publication.]

Richard, M. (2005). Effective treatment of eating disorders in Europe: Treatment outcome and its predictors. *European Eating Disorders Review, 13*(3), 169–179.

Richards, S. B., Taylor, R., & Ramasamy, R. (2014). *Single subject research: Applications in educational and clinical settings* (2nd ed.). Independence, KY: Cengage.

Richardson, J. R., Roy, A., Shalat, S. L., von Stein, R. T., Hossain, M. M., Buckley, B., . . . German, D. C. (2014). Elevated serum pesticide levels and risk for Alzheimer disease. *JAMA Neurology, 71*(3), 284–290.

Richlan, F. (2014). Functional neuroanatomy of developmental dyslexia: The role of orthographic depth. *Frontiers in Human Neuroscience, 8,* 347.

Richtel, M. (2010, November 21). Growing up digital, wired for distraction. *New York Times.*

Rieber, R. W. (1999, March). Hypnosis, false memory, and multiple personality: A trinity of affinity. *History of Psychiatry, 10*(37), 3–11.

Rieber, R. W. (2002). The duality of the brain and the multiplicity of minds: Can you have it both ways? *History of Psychiatry 13*(49, pt1), 3–18.

Rieber, R. W. (2006). *The bifurcation of the self: The history and theory of dissociation and its disorders.* New York: Springer Science + Business Media.

Ries, R. K. (2010). Suicide and substance abuse. In E.V. Nunes, J. Selzer, P. Levounis, & C. A. Davies (Eds.), *Substance dependence and co-occurring psychiatric disorders: Best practices for diagnosis and treatment* (pp. 1–14). Kingston, NJ: Civic Research Institute.

Riesch, S. K., Jacobson, G., Sawdey, L., Anderson, J., & Henriques, J. (2008). Suicide ideation among later elementary school-aged youth. *Journal of Psychiatric and Mental Health Nursing, 15*(4), 263–277.

Riina, E. M., & McHale, S. M. (2014). Bidirectional influences between dimensions of coparenting and adolescent adjustment. *Journal of Youth and Adolescence, 43*(2), 257–269.

Ringer, J. (2010). "I'm not fat," says ballerina faulted for too many sugerplums. *Today.com.*

Ringer, J. (2014). Cited in P. Catton, Book in hand, a ballerina takes her bow. *Wall Street Journal Online.* Retrieved from Wall Street Journal Online website: http://online.wsj.com/news/articles/SB1000142405270230418.

Ringer, J. (2014, February 28). Cited in R. Ritzel, Opinions—Dancing through it: My journey in the ballet by Jenifer Ringer. *The Washington Post.*

Ringer, J. (2014, January 30). Cited in G. Kourlas, Jenifer Ringer talks about leaving New York City Ballet. *TimeOut New York.*

Ringstrom, P. A. (2014*). A relational psychoanalytic approach to couples psychotherapy (Relational Perspectives book series). New York:* Routledge.

Ringwood, S. (2013). Cheap and cheerful--can cybertherapy be compassionate too? Commentary on Fairburn & Wilson and Bauer & Moessner. *The International Journal of Eating Disorders, 46*(5), 522–524.

Ripoll, L. H., Triebwasser, J., & Siever, L. J. (2011). Evidence-based pharmacotherapy for personality disorders. *International Journal of Neuropsychopharmacology, 14*(9), 1257–1288.

Risch, N., Hoffmann, T. J., Anderson, M., Croen, L. A., Grether, J. K., & Windham, G. C. (2014). Familial recurrence of autism spectrum disorder: Evaluating genetic and environmental contributions. *American Journal of Psychiatry, 171*(11), 1206–1213.

Ristow, A., Westphal, A., & Scahill, L. (2011). Treating hyperactivity in children with pervasive developmental disorders. In E. Hollander, A. Kolevzon, & J. T. Coyle (Eds.)., *Textbook of autism spectrum disorders* (pp. 479– 486). Arlington, VA: American Psychiatric Publishing.

Ritter, K., Vater, A., Rüsch, N., Schröder-Abé, M., Schütz, A., Fydrich, T., . . . Roepke, S. (2014). Shame in patients with narcissistic personality disorder. *Psychiatry Research, 215*(2), 429–437.

Ritter, M. (2008, January 27). Lead linked to aging in older brains. *YAHOO! News.*

Ritter, M. R., Blackmore, M. A., & Heimberg, R. G. (2010). Generalized anxiety disorder. In D. McKay, J. S. Abramowitz, & S. Taylor (Eds.), *Cognitive-behavioral therapy for refractory cases: Turning failure into success* (pp. 111–137). Washington, DC: American Psychological Association.

Rivett, M. (2011). Embracing change in clinical practice. *Journal of Family Therapy, 33*(1), 1–2.

Rizvi, S. L., Dimeff, L. A., Skutch, J., Carroll, D., & Linehan, M. M. (2011). A pilot study of the DBT coach: An interactive mobile phone application for individuals with borderline personality disorder and substance use disorder. *Behavior Therapy, 42,* 589–600.

Robert, G., & Zadra, A. (2014). Thematic and content analysis of idiopathic nightmares and bad dreams. *Sleep, 37*(2), 409–417.

Robertson, C. A., & Knight, R. A. (2014). Relating sexual sadism and psychopathy to one another, non-sexual violence, and sexual crime behaviors. *Aggressive Behavior, 40*(1), 12–23.

Robinson, W. P., Shepherd, A., & Heywood, J. (1998). Truth, equivocation, concealment, and lies in job applications and doctor-patient communication. *Journal of Language and Social Psychology, 17*(2), 149–164.

Rocca, P., Montemagni, C., Zappia, S., Pìterà, R., Sigaudo, M., & Bogetto, F. (2014). Negative symptoms and everyday functioning in schizophrenia: A cross-sectional study in a real world-setting. *Psychiatry Research, 218*(3), 284–289.

Roche, B., & Quayle, E. (2007). Sexual disorders. In D. W. Woods & J. W. Kanter (Eds.), *Understanding behavior disorders: A contemporary behavioral perspective.* Reno, NV: Context Press.

Roche, T. (2002, January 20). The Yates odyssey. *TIME. com: Nation.*

Rocks, T., Pelly, F., & Wilkinson, P. (2014). Nutrition therapy during initiation of refeeding in underweight children and adolescent inpatients with anorexia nervosa: A systematic review of the evidence. *Journal of the Academy of Nutrition and Dietetics, 114*(6), 897–907.

Rodav, O., Levy, S., & Hamdan, S. (2014). Clinical characteristics and functions of nonsuicide self-injury in youth. *European Psychiatry, 29*(8), 503–508.

Rodriguez, B. F., Weisberg, R. B., Pagano, M. E., Machan, J. T., Culpepper, L., & Keller, M. B. (2004). Frequency and patterns of psychiatric comorbidity in a sample of primary care patients with anxiety disorders. *Comprehensive Psychiatry, 45*(2), 129–137.

Roelofs, K., Hoogduin, K. A. L., Keijsers, G. P. J., Naering, G. W. B., Moene, F. C., & Sandijck, P. (2002). Hypnotic susceptibility in patients with conversion disorder. *Journal of Abnormal Psychology, 111*(2), 390–395.

Roemer, L., & Orsillo, S. M. (2014). An acceptance-based behavioral therapy for generalized anxiety disorder. In D. H. Barlow, *Clinical handbook of psychological disorders* (5th ed.), (pp. 206–231). New York: Guilford Press.

Roepke, S., Schröder-Abé, M., Schütz, A., Jacob, G., Dams, A., Vater, A., . . . Lammers, C-H. (2011). Dialectic behavioural therapy has an impact on self-concept clarity and facets of self-esteem in women with borderline personality disorder. *Clinical Psychology & Psychotherapy, 18*(2), 148–158.

Roepke, S., & Vater, A. (2014). Narcissistic personality disorder: An integrative review of recent empirical data and current definitions. *Current Psychiatry Reports, 16,* 445.

Roesch, R. (1991). *The encyclopedia of depression.* New York: Facts on File.

Roesch, R., Zapf, P. A., & Hart, S. D. (2010). *Forensic psychology and law.* Hoboken, NJ: John Wiley & Sons.

Roesler, T. A., & McKenzie, N. (1994). Effects of childhood trauma on psychological functioning of adults sexually abused as children. *Journal of Nervous and Mental Disease, 182*(3), 145–150.

Rogers, C. R. (1951). *Client-centered therapy.* Boston: Houghton Mifflin.

Rogers, C. R. (1954). The case of Mrs. Oak: A research analysis. In C. R. Rogers & R. F. Dymond (Eds.), *Psychotherapy and personality change* (pp. 259–269). Chicago: University of Chicago Press.

Rogers, C. R. (1987). Rogers, Kohut, and Erickson: A personal perspective on some similarities and differences. In J. K. Zeig (Ed.), *The evolution of psychotherapy.* New York: Brunner/Mazel.

Rogers, J., Raveendran, M., Fawcett, G. L., Fox, A. S., Shelton, S. E., Oler, J. A., . . . Kalin, N. H. (2013). CRHR1 genotypes, neural circuits and the diathesis for anxiety and depression. *Molecular Psychiatry, 18*(6), 700–707.

Rogers, R. (2008). Insanity evaluations. In R. Jackson (Ed.), *Learning forensic assessment* (pp. 109–128). New York: Routledge/Taylor & Francis Group.

Rogler, L. H., Malgady, R. G., & Rodriguez, O. (1989). *Hispanics and mental health: A framework for research.* Malabar, FL: Krieger Publishing.

Roh, D., Chang, J., Kim, C., Cho, H., An, S. K., & Jung, Y. (2014). Antipsychotic polypharmacy and high-dose prescription in schizophrenia: A 5-year comparison. *Australian and New Zealand Journal of Psychiatry, 48*(1), 52–60.

Rohn, T. T., McCarty, K. L., Love, J. E., & Head, E. (2014). Is apolipoprotein E4 an important risk factor for dementia in persons with Down Syndrome? *Journal of Parkinson's Disease and Alzheimer's Disease, 1*(1), 7.

Romanelli, R. J., Wu, F. M., Gamba, R., Mojtabai, R., & Segal, J. B. (2014). Behavioral therapy and serotonin reuptake inhibitor pharmacotherapy in the treatment of obsessive-compulsive disorder: A systematic review and meta-analysis of head-to-head randomized controlled trials. *Depression & Anxiety, 31*(8), 641–652.

Romero-Martinez, A., Figueiredo, B., & Moya-Albiol, L. (2014). Childhood history of abuse and child abuse potential: The role of parent's gender and timing of childhood abuse. *Child Abuse & Neglect, 38*(3), 510–516.

Roney, T., & Cannon, J. (2014). Dialectical behavior group therapy for borderline personality disorder. *International Journal of Group Psychotherapy, 64*(3), 400–408.

Ronningstam, E. (2011). Narcissistic personality disorder: A clinical perspective. *Journal of Psychiatric Practice, 17*(2), 89–99.

Rook, K. S., August, K. J., & Sorkin, D. H. (2011). Social network functions and health. In R. J. Contrada & A. Baum (Eds.), *The handbook of stress science: Biology, psychology, and health* (pp. 123–135). New York: Springer Publishing.

Rose, T., Joe, S., & Lindsey, M. (2011). Perceived stigma and depression among black adolescents in outpatient treatment. *Children and Youth Services Review, 33*(1), 161–166.

Rosell, D. R., Futterman, S. E., McMaster, A., & Siever, L. J. (2014). Schizotypal personality disorder: A current review. *Current Psychiatry Reports, 16,* 452.

Rosell, D. R., Zaluda, L. C., McClure, M. M., Perez-Rodriguez, M. M., Strike, K. S., Barch, D. M., . . . Siever, L. J. (2015). Effects of the D1 dopamine receptor agonist dihydrexidine (DAR-0100A) on working memory in schizotypal personality disorder. *Neuropsychopharmacology, 40*(2), 446–453.

Rosellini, A. J., & Bagge, C. L. (2014). Temperament, hopelessness, and attempted suicide: Direct and indirect effects. *Suicide & Life-Threatening Behavior, 44*(4), 353–361.

Rosen, E. F., Anthony, D. L., Booker, K. M., Brown, T. L., Christian, E., Crews, R. C., . . . Petty, L. C. (1991). A comparison of eating disorder scores among African American and white college females. *Bulletin of Psychosomatic Society, 29*(1), 65–66.

Rosen, R. C. (2007). Erectile dysfunction: Integration of medical and psychological approaches. In S. R. Leiblum (Ed.), *Principles and practice of sex therapy* (4th ed., pp. 277–310). New York: Guilford Press.

Rosen, R. C., & Rosen, L. R. (1981). *Human sexuality.* New York: Knopf.

Rosenbaum, T. Y. (2007). Physical therapy management and treatment of sexual pain disorders. In S. R. Leiblum (Ed.), *Principles and practice of sex therapy* (4th ed., pp. 157–177). New York: Guilford Press.

Rosenbaum, T. Y. (2011). Addressing anxiety in vivo in physiotherapy treatment of women with severe vaginismus: A clinical approach. *Journal of Sex & Marital Therapy, 37*(2), 89–93.

Rosenberg, A., Ledley, D. R., & Heimberg, R. G. (2010). Social anxiety disorder. In D. McKay, J. S. Abramowitz, & S. Taylor (Eds.), *Cognitive-behavioral therapy for refractory cases: Turning failure into success* (pp. 65–88). Washington, DC: American Psychological Association.

Rosenberg, T., & Pace, M. (2006). Burnout among mental health professionals: Special considerations for the marriage and family therapist. *Journal of Marital & Family Therapy, 32*(1), 87–99.

Rosenbloom, S. (2007, December 17). On Facebook, scholars link up with data. *New York Times.*

Rosenblum, G. D., & Lewis, M. (1999). The relations among body image, physical attractiveness, and body mass in adolescence. *Child Development, 70*(1), 50–64.

Rosenbluth, M., & Sinyor, M. (2012). Off-label use of atypical antipsychotics in personality disorders. *Expert Opinion on Pharmacotherapy, 13*(11), 1575–1585.

Rosenhan, D. L. (1973). On being sane in insane places. *Science, 179*(4070), 250–258.

Rosenthal, R. (1966). *Experimenter effects in behavioral research.* New York: Appleton-Century-Crofts.

Rosenthal, R. N. (2011). Alcohol abstinence management. In J. H. Lowinson & P. Ruiz (Eds.), *Substance abuse: A comprehensive textbook* (5th ed.). Philadelphia, PA: Lippincott Williams & Wilkins.

Rosenthal, R. N., & Levounis, P. (2005). Polysubstance use, abuse, and dependence. In R. J. Frances, A. H. Mack, & S. I. Miller (Eds.), *Clinical textbook of addictive disorders* (3rd ed., pp. 245–270). New York: Guilford Press.

Roskar, S., Podlesek, A., Kuzmanic, M., Demsar, L. O., Zaletel, M., & Marusic, A. (2011). Suicide risk and its relationship to change in marital status. *Crisis: Journal of Crisis Intervention and Suicide Prevention, 32*(1), 24–30.

Rosky, J. W. (2013). The (f)utility of post-conviction polygraph testing. *Sexual Abuse: A Journal of Research and Treatment, 25*(3), 259–281.

Rosky, J. W. (2015). More polygraph futility: A comment on Jensen, Shafer, Roby, and Roby (2015). *Journal of Interpersonal Violence.* [Advance publication.]

Ross, C. A., & Gahan, P. (1988). Techniques in the treatment of multiple personality disorder. *American Journal of Psychotherapy, 42*(1), 40–52.

Ross, C. A., & Ness, L. (2010). Symptom patterns in dissociative identity disorder patients and the general population. *Journal of Trauma & Dissociation, 11*(4), 458–468.

Ross, S. (2014 October 20). Alcohol use disorders in the elderly. *Psychiatry Weekly.*

Rossi-Arnaud, C., Spataro, P., Saraulli, D., Mulligan, N. W., Sciarretta, A., Marques, V. S., & Cestari, V. (2014). The attentional boost effect in schizophrenia. *Journal of Abnormal Psychology, 123*(3), 588–597.

Rotenberg, K. J., Costa, P., Trueman, M., & Lattimore, P. (2012). An interactional test of the reformulated helplessness theory of depression in women receiving clinical treatment for eating disorders. *Eating Behaviors, 13*(3), 264–266.

Rothbaum, B. O., Foa, E. B., Riggs, D. S., Murdock, T., & Walsh, W. (1992). A prospective examination of posttraumatic stress disorder in rape victims. *Journal of Traumatic Stress, 5*(3), 455–475.

Rothbaum, B. O., Gerardi, M., Bradley, B., & Friedman, M. J. (2011). Evidence-based treatments for posttraumatic stress disorder in Operation Enduring Freedom and Operation Iraqi Freedom military personnel. In J. I. Ruzek, P. P. Schnurr, J. J. Vasterling, & M. J. Friedman (Eds.), *Caring for veterans with deployment-related stress disorders* (pp. 215–239). Washington, DC: American Psychological Association.

Rothbaum, B. O., Price, M., Jovanovic, T., Norrholm, S. D., Gerardi, M., Dunlop, B., . . . Ressler, K. J. (2014). A randomized, double-blind evaluation of D-cycloserine or alprazolam combined with virtual reality exposure therapy for posttraumatic stress disorder in Iraq and Afghanistan War veterans. *American Journal of Psychiatry, 171*(6), 640–648.

Rothschild, A. J. (2010). Major depressive disorder, severe with psychotic features. In C. B. Taylor (Ed.), *How to practice evidence-based psychiatry: Basic principles and case studies.* (pp. 195–202). Arlington, VA: American Psychiatric Publishing.

Rotter, M. (2011). Embitterment and personality disorder. In M. Linden & A. Maercker (Eds.), *Embitterment: Societal, psychological, and clinical perspectives* (pp. 177–186). New York: Springer-Verlag Publishing.

Rowan, P. (2005, July 31). Cited in J. Thompson, "Hungry for love": Why 11 million of us have serious issues with food. *Independent on Sunday.*

Rowen, T. S. (2013). Sexual health for people with disabilities. *The Journal of Sexual Medicine, 10*(6), 1667–1668.

Rowland, D. L. (2012). *Sexual dysfunction in men. Advances in psychotherapy—Evidence-based practice.* Cambridge, MA: Hogrefe Publishing.

Roy, A. (1992). Genetics, biology, and suicide in the family. In R. W. Maris, A. L. Berman, J. T. Maltsberger, & R. I. Yufitet (Eds.), *Assessment and prediction of suicide* (pp. xxii, 697). New York: Guilford Press.

Roy, A. (2011). Combination of family history of suicidal behavior and childhood trauma may represent correlate of increased suicide risk. *Journal of Affective Disorders, 130*(1-2), 205–208.

Roy, A. K., Klein, R. G., Angelsante, A., Bar-Haim, Y., Hulvershorn, L., . . . Spindel, C. (2013). Clinical features of young children referred for impairing temper outbursts. *Journal of Child and Adolescent Psychopharmacology, 23*(9), 588–596.

Roy-Byrne, P. P., Arguelles, L., Vitek, M. E., Goldberg, J., Keane, T. M., True, W. R., & Pitman, R. K. (2004). Persistence and change of PTSD symptomatology: A longitudinal co-twin control analysis of the Vietnam Era Twin Registry. *Social Psychiatry and Psychiatric Epidemiology, 39*(9), 681–685.

Rubin, D. M., Curtis, M. L., & Matone, M. (2014). Child abuse prevention and child home visitation: Making sure we get it right. *JAMA Pediatrics, 168*(1), 5–6.

Rubinstein, S., & Caballero, B. (2000). Is Miss America an undernourished role model? *Journal of the American Medical Association, 283*(12), 1569.

Rubio-Aurioloes, E., & Bivalacqua, T. J. (2012). Standard operational procedures for low sexual desire in men. *Journal of Sexual Medicine, 10,* 94–107.

Rudd, M. D., Berman, L., Joiner, T. E., Nock, M., Mandrusiak, M., Van Orden, K., . . . Witte, T. (2006). Warning signs for suicide: Theory, research, and clinical application. *Suicide & Life-Threatening Behavior, 36,* 255–262.

Rudd, M. D., & Brown, G. K. (2011). A cognitive theory of suicide: Building hope in treatment and strengthening the therapeutic relationship. In K. Michel & D. A. Jobes (Eds.), *Building a therapeutic alliance with the suicidal patient* (pp. 169–181). Washington, DC: American Psychological Association.

Rudd, M. D., Bryan, C. J., Wertenberger, E. G., Peterson, A. L., Young-McCaughan, S., Mintz, J., . . . Bruce, T. O. (2015). Brief cognitive-behavioral therapy effects on post-treatment suicide attempts in a military sample: Results of a randomized clinical trial with 2 year follow-up. *The American Journal of Psychiatry, 172*(5), 441–449.

Ruggero, C. J., Kotov, R., Callahan, J. L., Kilmer, J. N., Luft, B. J., & Bromet, E. J. (2013). PTSD symptom dimensions and their relationship to functioning in World Trade Center responders. *Psychiatry Research, 210*(3), 1049–1055.

Rüsch, N., Corrigan, P. W., Heekeren, K., Theodoridou, A., Dvorsky, D., Metzler, S., . . . Rössler, W. (2014). Well-being among persons at risk of psychosis: The role of self-labeling, shame, and stigma stress. *Psychiatric Services, 65*(4), 483–489.

Ruscio, A. M., Chiu, W. T., Roy-Byrne, P., Stang, P. E., Stein, D. J., Wittchen, H. U., & Kessler, R. C. (2007). Broadening the definition of generalized anxiety disorder: Effects on prevalence and associations with other disorders in the National Comorbidity Survey Replication. *Journal of Anxiety Disorders, 21*(5), 662–676.

Rusconi, E., & Mitchener-Nissen, T. (2013). Prospects of functional magnetic resonance imaging as lie detector. *Frontiers in Human Neuroscience, 7594.*

Rush, B. (2010). Selected writings of Benjamin Rush. In A. J. Milson, C. H. Bohan, P. L. Glanzer, & J. W. Null (Eds.), *American educational thought: Essays from 1640–1940* (2nd ed.), Readings in educational thought (pp. 53–70). Charlotte, NC: Information Age.

Russell, J. E. A. (2014, July 10). Practice mindfulness for better, and quite possibly longer, life. *Tampa Bay Times.*

Russo, F. (2014, January 14). What dreams are made of: Understanding why we dream (about sex and other things). *Time.*

Russo, N. F., & Tartaro, J. (2008). Women and mental health. In F. L. Denmark & M. A. Paludi (Eds.), *Psychology of women: A handbook of issues and theories* (2nd ed., pp. 440–483). Westport, CT: Praeger Publishers.

Rutledge, P. (2013, October 20). Positively media: How we connect and thrive through emerging technologies. *Psychology Today.*

Ruzek, J. I., & Batten, S. V. (2011). Enhancing systems of care for posttraumatic stress disorder: From private practice to large health care systems. In J. I. Ruzek, P. P. Schnurr, J. J. Vasterling, & M. J. Friedman (Eds.), *Caring for veterans with deployment-related stress disorders* (pp. 261–282). Washington, DC: American Psychological Association.

Ruzek, J. I., Schnurr, P. P., Vasterling, J. J., & Friedman, J. (Eds.). (2011). *Caring for veterans with deployment-related stress disorders.* Washington, DC: American Psychological Association.

Saad, G. (2011, November 30). How often do people lie in their daily lives? *Psychology Today.*

Saba, L. M., Flink, S. C., Vanderlinden, L. A., Israel, Y., Tampier, L., Colombo, G., . . . Tabakoff, B. (2015). The sequenced rat brain transcriptome—its use in identifying networks predisposing alcohol consumption. *The FEBS Journal.* [Electronic publication.]

Sacks, O. (2012). *Hallucinations.* New York: Vintage Books.

Sacks, O. (2012, November 3). Seeing things? Hearing things? Many of us do. *New York Times.*

Sadeh, N., Londahl-Shaller, E. A., Piatigorsky, A., Fordwood, S., Stuart, B. K., McNiel, D. E., . . . Yaeger, A. M. (2014). Functions of non-suicidal self-injury in adolescents and young adults with borderline personality disorder symptoms. *Psychiatry Research, 216*(2), 217–222.

Saedi, G. A. (2012, April 29). Millennial media: The media saturated generation Y. *Psychology Today.*

Sakinofsky, I. (2011). Evidence-based approaches for reducing suicide risk in major affective disorders. In M. Pompili & R. Tatarelli (Eds.), *Evidence-based practice in suicidology: A source book* (pp. 275–315). Cambridge, MA: Hogrefe Publishing.

Salari, A., Bakhtiari, A., & Homberg, J. R. (2015). Activation of GABA-A receptors during postnatal brain development increases anxiety- and depression-related behaviors in a time- and dose-dependent manner in adult mice. *European Neuropsychopharmacy: The Journal of the European College of Neuropsychopharmacology, 25*(8), 1260–1274.

Salfati, C. G. (2011). Criminal profiling. In B. Rosenfeld & S. D. Penrod (Eds.), *Research methods in forensic psychology* (pp. 122–134). Hoboken, NJ: John Wiley & Sons.

Salkovskis, P. M. (1985). Obsessional-compulsive problems: A cognitive-behavioural analysis. *Behavioral Research and Therapy, 23,* 571–584.

Salkovskis, P. M. (1999). Understanding and treating obsessive-compulsive disorder. *Behavioral Research and Therapy, 37*(Suppl. 1), S29–S52.

Salkovskis, P. M., Thorpe, S. J., Wahl, K., Wroe, A. L., & Forrester, E. (2003). Neutralizing increases discomfort associated with obsessional thoughts: An experimental study with obsessional patients. *Journal of Abnormal Psychology, 112*(4), 709–715.

Salzer, S., Winkelbach, C., Leweke, F., Leibing, E., & Leichsenring, F. (2011). Long-term effects of short-term psychodynamic psychotherapy and cognitive-behavioral therapy in generalized anxiety disorder: 12-month follow-up. *Canadian Journal of Psychiatry, 56*(8), 503–508.

Samek, D. R., Keyes, M. A., Hicks, B. M., Bailey, J., McGue, M., & Iacono, W. G. (2014). General and specific predictors of nicotine and alcohol dependence in early adulthood: Genetic and environmental influences. *Journal of Studies on Alcohol and Drugs, 75*(4), 623–634.

SAMHSA (Substance Abuse and Mental Health Services Administration). (2013). *Drug Abuse Warning Network, 2011: National estimates of drug-related emergency department visits.* HHS Publication No. (SMA) 13-4760, DAWN Series D-39. Rockville, MD: Substance Abuse and Mental Health Services Administration.

SAMHSA (Substance Abuse and Mental Health Services Administration). (2013). *National survey on drug use and health, 2011 and 2012.* Washington, DC: Department of Health and Human Services.

SAMHSA (Substance Abuse and Mental Health Services Administration). (2014). *Mental health parity and addiction equity.* Washington, DC: Department of Health and Human Services.

SAMHSA (Substance Abuse and Mental Health Services Administration). (2014). *Results from the 2013 National Survey on Drug Use and Health: Summary of national findings,* NSDUH Series H-48, HSS Publication No. (SMA) 14-4863. Rockville, MD: SAMHSA.

Samorodnitzky-Naveh, G., Geiger, S. B., & Levin, L. (2007). Patients' satisfaction with dental esthetics. *Journal of the American Dental Association, 138*(6), 805–808.

Samos, L. F., Aguilar, E., & Ouslander, J. G. (2010). Institutional long-term care in the United States. In H. M. Fillit, K. Rockwood, & K. Woodhouse (Eds.), *Brocklehurst's textbook of geriatric medicine and gerontology* (7th ed.). Philadelphia, PA: Saunders Publishers.

Sampasa-Kanyinga, H., Roumeliotis, P., & Xu, H. (2014). Associations between cyberbullying and school bullying victimization and suicidal ideation, plans and attempts among Canadian schoolchildren. *PLOS ONE, 9*(7), e102145.

Sample, I. (2005, November 30). Mental illness link to art and sex. *The Guardian.* Retrieved from The Guardian website: http://www.guardian.co.uk.

Samuel, V. J., Curtis, S., Thornell, A., George, P., Taylor, A., Brome, D. R., . . . Faraone, S. V. (1997). The unexplored void of ADHD and African-American research: A review of the literature. *Journal of Attention Disorders, 1*(4), 197–207.

Sanburn, J. (2013, September 13). Inside the National Suicide Hotline: Preventing the next tragedy. *Time.com.*

Sandler, I., Wolchik, S. A., Cruden, G., Mahrer, N. E., Ahn, S., Brincks, A., & Brown, C. H. (2014). Overview of meta-analyses of the prevention of mental health, substance use, and conduct problems. *Annual Review of Clinical Psychology, 10,* 243–273.

Sandler, M. (1990). Monoamine oxidase inhibitors in depression: History and mythology. *Journal of Psychopharmacology, 4*(3), 136–139.

Sanftner, J. L., & Tantillo, M. (2011). Body image and eating disorders: A compelling source of shame for women. In R. L. Dearing & J. P. Tangney (Eds.), *Shame in the therapy hour* (pp. 277–303). Washington, DC: American Psychological Association.

San Nicolas, A. C., & Lemos, N. P. (2015). Toxicology findings in cases of hanging in the City and County of San Francisco over the 3-year period from 2011 to 2013. *Forensic Science International, 255,* 146–55.

Sansone, A., Romanelli, F., Jannini, E. A., & Lenzi, A. (2015). Hormonal correlations of premature ejaculation. *Endocrine, 49*(2), 333–338.

Sansone, R. A., & Sansone, L. A. (2011). Personality disorders: A nation-based perspective on prevalence. *Innovations in Clinical Neuroscience, 8*(4), 13–18.

Santa-Cruz, N. (2010, June 10). Minority population growing in the United States, census estimates show. *Los Angeles Times.*

Santiseban, D. A., Muir-Malcolm, J. A., Mitrani, V. B., & Szapocznik, J. (2001). Chapter 16: Integrating the study of ethnic culture and family psychology intervention science. In H. A. Liddle, D. A. Santiseban, R. F. Levant, & J. H. Bray (Eds.), *Family psychology: Science-based interventions* (pp. 331–352). Washington, DC: American Psychological Association.

Sar, V., Onder, C., Kilincaslan, A., Zoroglu, S. S., & Alyanak, B. (2014). Dissociative identity disorder among adolescents: Prevalence in a university psychiatric outpatient unit. *Journal of Trauma & Dissociation, 15*(4), 402–419.

Sareen, J., Afifi, T. O., McMillan, K. A., & Asmundson, G. J. G. (2011). Relationship between household income and mental disorders: Findings from a population-based longitudinal study. *Archives of General Psychiatry, 68*(4), 419–426.

Sarin, F., & Wallin, L. (2014). Cognitive model and cognitive behavior therapy for schizophrenia: An overview. *Nordic Journal of Psychiatry, 68*(3), 145–153.

Sarver, N. W., Beidel, D. C., & Spitalnick, J. S. (2014). The feasibility and acceptability of virtual environments in the treatment of childhood social anxiety disorder. *Journal of Clinical Child & Adolescent Psychology, 43*(1), 63–73.

Satir, V. (1964). *Conjoint family therapy: A guide to therapy and technique.* Palo Alto, CA: Science & Behavior Books.

Satir, V. (1967). *Conjoint family therapy* (Rev. ed.). Palo Alto, CA: Science & Behavior Books.

Satir, V. (1987). Going behind the obvious: The psychotherapeutic journey. In J. K. Zeig (Ed.), *The evolution of psychotherapy.* New York: Brunner/Mazel.

Sauvageau, A. (2014). Current reports on autoerotic deaths: Five persistent myths. *Current Psychiatry Reports, 16*(1), 430.

Savitz, J., & Drevets, W. C. (2011). Neuroimaging and neuropathological findings in bipolar disorder. In C. A. Zarate, Jr. & H. K. Manji (Eds.), *Bipolar depression: Molecular neurobiology, clinical diagnosis and pharmacotherapy. Milestones in drug therapy* (pp. 201–225). Cambridge, MA: Birkhäuser.

Scelfo, J. (2005, June 13). Bad girls go wild. *Newsweek,* 66–67.

Schadenberg, A. (2012, September 25). Euthanasia is out of control in the Netherlands: New Dutch statistics. *LifeSite.* Retrieved from LifeSite website: http://www.lifesitenews.com/blogs/.

Schafer, J. A., Varano, S. P., Jarvis, J. P., & Cancino, J. M. (2010, July-August). Bad moon on the rise? Lunar cycles and incidents of crime. *Journal of Criminal Justice, 38*(4), 359–367.

Schattner, E., & Shahar, G. (2011). Role of pain personification in pain-related depression: An object relations perspective. *Psychiatry, 74*(1), 14–20.

Scheidt, C. E., Baumann, K., Katzev, M., Reinhard, M., Rauer, S., Wirsching, M., & Joos, A. (2014). Differentiating cerebral ischemia from functional neurological symptom disorder: A psychosomatic perspective. *BMC Psychiatry, 14*(1), 383–393.

Scheuerman, O., Grinbaum, I., & Garty, B. Z. (2013). Münchausen syndrome by proxy. *Harefuah, 152*(11), 639.

Scheuffgen, K., Happe, F., Anderson, M., & Frith, U. (2000). High "intelligence," low "IQ"? Speed of processing and measured IQ in children with autism. *Development and Psychopathology, 12*(1), 83–90.

Schienle, A., Hettema, J. M., Cáceda, R., & Nemeroff, C. B. (2011). Neurobiology and genetics of generalized anxiety disorder. *Psychiatric Annals, 41*(2), 133–123.

Schildkraut, J. J. (1965). The catecholamine hypothesis of affective disorders: A review of supporting evidence. *American Journal of Psychiatry, 122*(5), 509–522.

Schiller, B. (2014). *Hiding GPS inside shoes to keep track of wandering Alzheimer's patients.* New York: Co.Exist. Retrieved from Co.Exist website: http://www.fastcoexist.com/30225268.

Schilling, E. A., Lawless, M., Buchanan, L., & Aseltine, R. J. (2014). "Signs of Suicide" shows promise as a middle school suicide prevention program. *Suicide & Life-Threatening Behavior,* May 2, 2014.

Schmidt, A. F., Gykiere, K., Vanhoeck, K., Mann, R. E., & Banse, R. (2014). Direct and indirect measures of sexual maturity preferences differentiate subtypes of child sexual abusers. *Sexual Abuse, 26*(2), 107–128.

Schmidt, H. M., Munder, T., Gerger, H., Frühauf, S., & Barth, J. (2014). Combination of psychological interventions and phosphodiesterase-5 inhibitors for erectile dysfunction: A narrative review and meta-analysis. *Journal of Sexual Medicine, 11,* 1376–1391.

Schneider, K. J., & Krug, O. T. (2010). *Existential–humanistic therapy. Theories of psychotherapy.* Washington, DC: American Psychological Association.

Schneider, K. L., & Shenassa, E. (2008). Correlates of suicide ideation in a population-based sample of cancer patients. *Journal of Psychosocial Oncology, 26*(2) 49–62.

Schrag, M., Mueller, C., Oyoyo, U., Smith, M. A., & Kirsch, W. M. (2011). Iron, zinc and copper in the Alzheimer's disease brain: A quantitative meta-analysis. Some insight on the influence of citation bias on scientific opinion. *Progress in Neurobiology, 94*(3), 296–306.

Schreiber, F. R. (1973). *Sybil.* Chicago: Regnery.

Schreier, H. A., Ayoub, C. C., & Bursch, B. (2010). Forensic issues in Munchausen by Proxy. In E. P. Benedek, P. Ash, & C. L. Scott (Eds.), *Principles and practice of child and adolescent forensic mental health* (pp. 241–252). Arlington, VA: American Psychiatric Publishing.

Schroeder, M. J., & Hoffman, A. C. (2014). *Tobacco control: Electronic cigarettes and nicotine clinical pharmacology.* Retrieved from http://tobaccocontrol.bmj.com/content/23/suppl_2/ii30.

Schuch, J. J., Roest, A. M., Nolen, W. A., Penninx, B. H., & de Jonge, P. (2014). Gender differences in major depressive disorder: Results from the Netherlands study of depression and anxiety. *Journal of Affective Disorders, 156,* 156–163.

Schuel, H., Burkman, L. J., Lippes, J., Crickard, K., Mahony, M. C., Guiffrida, A., . . . Makriyannis, A. (2002). Evidence that anandamide-signalling regulates human sperm functions required for fertilization. *Molecular Reproduction and Development, 63,* 376–387.

Schulte, I. E., & Petermann, F. (2011). Somatoform disorders: 30 years of debate about criteria! What about children and adolescents? *Journal of Psychosomatic Research, 70*(3), 218–228.

Schultz, D. S., & Brabender, V. M. (2012). More challenges since Wikipedia: The effects of exposure to internet information about the Rorschach on selected comprehensive system variables. *Journal of Personality Assessment, 95*(2), 149–158.

Schultz, D. S., & Loving, J. L. (2012). Challenges since Wikipedia: The availability of Rorschach information online and internet users' reactions to online media coverage of the Rorschach-Wikipedia debate. *Journal of Personality Assessment, 94*(1), 73–81.

Schultz, G. (2007, May 24). Marital breakdown and divorce increases rates of depression, Stat-Can study finds. *LifeSiteNews.com.*

Schultz, L. T., Heimberg, R. G., & Rodebaugh, T. L. (2008). Social anxiety disorder. In M. Hersen & J. Rosqvist (Eds.), *Handbook of psychological assessment, case conceptualization, and treatment, Vol. 1: Adults* (pp. 204–236). Hoboken, NJ: John Wiley & Sons.

Schulz, S., & Laessle, R. G. (2012). Stress-induced laboratory eating behavior in obese women with binge eating disorder. *Appetite, 58*(2), 457–461.

Schumm, J. A., Koucky, E. M., & Bartel, A. (2014). Associations between perceived social reactions to trauma-related experiences with PTSD and depression among veterans seeking PTSD treatment. *Journal of Traumatic Stress, 27*(1), 50–57.

Schumm, J. A., Walter, K. H., Bartone, A. S., & Chard, K. M. (2015). Veteran satisfaction and treatment preferences in response to a posttraumatic stress disorder specialty clinic orientation group. *Behaviour Research and Therapy, 69,* 75–82.

Schwartz, C. E., Kunwar, P. S., Hirshfeld-Becker, D. R., Henin, A., Vangel, M. G., Rauch, S. L. . . . Rosenbaum, J. F. (2015). Behavioral inhibition in childhood predicts smaller hippocampal volume in adolescent offspring of parents with panic disorder. *Translational Psychiatry, 5,* e605.

Schwartz, M. (2011). The retrospective profile and the facilitated family retreat. In J. R. Jordan & J. L. McIntosh (Eds.), *Grief after suicide: Understanding the consequences and caring for the survivors. Series in death, dying and bereavement* (pp. 371–379). New York: Routledge/Taylor & Francis Group.

Schwartz, M. W. (2014). *Novel anti-diabetic actions of hypothalamic FGF19-FGFR1 signaling.* Washington, DC: NIH. Retrieved from http://grantome.com/grant/NIH/R01-DK101997-01.

Schwartz, N. (2011). Feelings-as-information. In P. Van Lange, A. W. Kruglanski, & E. T. Higgins (Eds.), *Handbook of theories of social psychology: Vol. 1.* London, UK: Sage.

Schwartz, S. (1993). *Classic studies in abnormal psychology.* Mountain View, CA: Mayfield Publishing.

Schwarzbach, M., Luppa, M., Forstmeier, S., König, H., & Riedel-Heller, S. G. (2014). Social relations and depression in late life—a systematic review. *International Journal of Geriatric Psychiatry, 29*(1), 1–21.

Scognamiglio, C., & Houenou, J. (2014). A meta-analysis of fMRI studies in healthy relatives of patients with schizophrenia. *Australian and New Zealand Journal of Psychiatry, 48*(10), 907–916.

Scott, L. N., Stepp, S. D., & Pilkonis, P. A. (2014). Prospective associations between features of borderline personality disorder, emotion dysregulation, and aggression. *Personality Disorders, 5*(3), 278–288.

Seaward, B. L. (2013). *Essentials of managing stress.* (3rd ed.). Burlington, MA: Jones & Bartlett Learning.

Sebert, K. R. (2014 July 17). Kesha reborn. *Elle Magazine* (UK edition).

Sedghi, A. (2013). 10 years of bullying data: What does it tell us? *The Guardian.* Retrieved from http://www.theguardian.com/news/datablog/2013/may/23/.

Segal, D. L., & Hersen, M. (Eds.). (2010). *Diagnostic interviewing.* New York: Springer Publishing.

Segal, D. L., June, A., & Marty, M. A. (2010). Basic issues in interviewing and the interview process. In D. L. Segal & M. Hersen (Eds.), *Diagnostic interviewing* (pp. 1–21). New York: Springer Publishing.

Segal, R. (2008). *The national association for retarded citizens.* Silver Spring, MD: The Arc.

Seiden, R. H. (1981). Mellowing with age: Factors influencing the nonwhite suicide rate. *International Journal of Aging and Human Development, 13,* 265–284.

Seligman, M. E. P. (1975). *Helplessness.* San Francisco: Freeman.

Seligman, M. E. P. (2002). *Authentic happiness: Using the new positive psychology to realize your potential for lasting fulfillment.* New York: Free Press.

Seligman, M. E. P., & Fowler, R. D. (2011). Comprehensive soldier fitness and the future of psychology. *American Psychologist, 66*(1), 82–86.

Selkoe, D. J. (1992). Alzheimer's disease: New insights into an emerging epidemic. *Journal of Geriatric Psychiatry, 25*(2), 211–227.

Selkoe, D. J. (2000). The origins of Alzheimer's disease: A is for amyloid. *Journal of the American Medical Association, 283*(12), 1615–1617.

Selkoe, D. J. (2011). Alzheimer's disease. *Cold Spring Harbor Perspectives in Biology, 3*(7).

Selling, L. S. (1940). *Men against madness.* New York: Greenberg.

Sennott, S. L. (2011). Gender disorder as gender oppression: A transfeminist approach to rethinking the pathologization of gender non-conformity. *Women & Therapy, 34*(1–2), 93–113.

Sergeant, S., & Mongrain, M. (2014). An online optimism intervention reduces depression in pessimistic individuals. *Journal of Consulting and Clinical Psychology, 82*(2), 263–274.

Seto, M. C. (2008). *Pedophilia and sexual offending against children: Theory, assessment, and intervention.* Washington, DC: American Psychological Association.

Seto, M. C., Kingston, D. A., & Bourget, D. (2014). Assessment of the paraphilias. *Psychiatric Clinics of North America, 37*(2), 149–161.

Seto, M. C., Lalumiere, M. L., Harris, G. T., & Chivers, M. L. (2012). The sexual responses of sexual sadists. *Journal of Abnormal Psychology, 121*(3), 739–753.

Shapiro, E. R. (2004). Discussion of Ernst Prelinger's "Thoughts on hate and aggression." *Psychoanalytic Study of the Child, 39,* 44–51.

Shapiro, J. R., Bauer, S., Andrews, E., Pisetsky, E., Bulik-Sullivan, B., Hamer, R. M., & Bulik, C. M. (2010). Text messaging in the treatment of bulimia nervosa. *Clinician's Research Digest, 28*(12).

Sharf, R. S. (2015). *Theories of psychotherapy and counseling: Concepts and cases.* Belmont, CA: Brooks/Cole.

Shaw, K. (2004). *Oddballs and eccentrics.* Edison, NJ: Castle Books.

Shaw, R. J., Spratt, E. G., Bernard, R. S., & DeMaso, D. R. (2010). Somatoform disorders. In R. J. Shaw & D. R. DeMaso (Eds.), *Textbook of pediatric psychosomatic medicine* (pp. 121–139). Arlington, VA: American Psychiatric Publishing.

Sheldon, P. (2008). The relationship between unwillingness-to-communicate and student's facebook use. *Journal of Media Psychology, 20*(2), 67–75.

Shenk, D. (2001). *The forgetting: Alzheimer's: Portrait of an epidemic.* New York: Doubleday.

Sher, L. (2015). Suicide medical malpractice: An educational overview. *International Journal of Adolescent Medicine and Health, 27*(2), 203–206.

Sher, L., Oquendo, M. A., Falgalvy, H. C., Grunebaum, M. F., Burke, A. K., Zalsman, G., & Mann, J. J. (2005). The relationship of aggression to suicidal behavior in depressed patients with a history of alcoholism. *Addictive Behavior, 30*(6), 1144–1153.

Sheras, P., & Worchel, S. (1979). *Clinical psychology: A social psychological approach.* New York: Van Nostrand.

Shergill, S. S., Brammer, M. J., Williams, S. R., Murray, R. M., & McGuire, P. K. (2000). Mapping auditory hallucinations in schizophrenia using functional magnetic resonance imaging. *Archives of General Psychiatry, 57*(11), 1033–1038.

Sherry, A., & Whilde, M. R. (2008). Borderline personality disorder. In M. Hersen & J. Rosqvist (Eds.), *Handbook of psychological assessment, case conceptualization and treatment, Vol. 1: Adults* (pp. 403–437). Hoboken, NJ: John Wiley & Sons.

Shinto, A. S., Kamaleshwaran, K. K., Srinivasan, D., Paranthaman, S., Selvaraj, K., Pranesh, M. B., . . . Prakash, B. (2014). "Hyperfrontality" as seen on FDG PET in unmedicated schizophrenia patients with positive symptoms. *Clinical Nuclear Medicine, 39*(8), 694–697.

Shiraishi, N., Watanabe, N., Kinoshita, Y., Kaneko, A., Yoshida, S., Furukawa, T. A., & Akechi, T. (2014). Brief psychoeducation for schizophrenia primarily intended to change the cognition of auditory hallucinations: An exploratory study. *Journal of Nervous and Mental Disease, 202*(1), 35–39.

Shiratori, Y., Tachikawa, H., Nemoto, K., Endo, G., Aiba, M., Matsui, Y., & Asada, T. (2014). Network analysis for motives in suicide cases: A cross-sectional study. *Psychiatry and Clinical Neurosciences, 68*(4), 299–307.

Shnaider, P., Pukay-Martin, N. D., Fredman, S. J., Macdonald, A., & Monson, C. M. (2014). Effects of cognitive-behavioral conjoint therapy for PTSD on partners' psychological functioning. *Journal of Traumatic Stress, 27*(2), 129–136.

Shneidman, E. S. (1963). Orientations toward death: Subintentioned death and indirect suicide. In R. W. White (Ed.), *The study of lives.* New York: Atherton.

Shneidman, E. S. (1979). An overview: Personality, motivation, and behavior theories. In L. D. Hankoff & B. Einsidler (Eds.), *Suicide: Theory and clinical aspects.* Littleton, MA: PSG Publishing.

Shneidman, E. S. (1981). Suicide. *Suicide & Life-Threatening Behavior, 11*(4), 198–220.

Shneidman, E. S. (1985). *Definition of suicide.* New York: Wiley.

Shneidman, E. S. (1987, March). At the point of no return. *Psychology Today.*

Shneidman, E. S. (1993). *Suicide as psychache: A clinical approach to self-destructive behavior.* Northvale, NJ: Jason Aronson.

Shneidman, E. S. (2001). *Comprehending suicide: Landmarks in 20th-century suicidology.* Washington, DC: American Psychological Association.

Shneidman, E. S. (2005). Anodyne psychotherapy for suicide: A psychological view of suicide. *Clinical Neuropsychiatry, 2*(1), 7–12.

Shneidman, E. S., & Farberow, N. (1968). The Suicide Prevention Center of Los Angeles. In H. L. P. Resnick (Ed.), *Suicidal behaviors: Diagnosis and management.* Boston: Little, Brown.

Shriver, M. (2011). *Alzheimer's in America: The Shriver Report on women and Alzheimer's.* New York: Free Press.

Shriver, M. (2014). Maria Shriver reports on the latest Alzheimer's research, sparked by The Shriver Report. *The Shriver Report,* March 20, 2014.

Shu, H., Yuan, Y., Xie, C., Bai, F., You, J., Li, L., . . . Zhang, Z. (2014). Imbalanced hippocampal functional networks associated with remitted geriatric depression and apolipoprotein e4 allele in nondemented elderly: A preliminary study. *Journal of Affective Disorders, 164,* 5–13.

Shultz, J. M., Besser, A., Kelly, F., Allen, A., Schmitz, S., Hausmann, V., . . . Neria, Y. (2012). Psychological consequences of indirect exposure to disaster due to the Haiti earthquake. *Prehospital and Disaster Medicine, 27*(4), 359–368.

Sibley, M. H., Kuriyan, A. B., Evans, S. W., Waxmonsky, J. G., & Smith, B. H. (2014). Pharmacological and psychosocial treatments for adolescents with ADHD: An updated systematic review of the literature. *Clinical Psychology Review, 34*(3), 218–232.

Sibrava, N. J., Beard, C., Bjornsson, A. S., Moitra, E., Weisberg, R. B., & Keller, M. B. (2013). Two-year course of generalized anxiety disorder, social anxiety disorder, and panic disorder in a longitudinal sample of African American adults. *Journal of Consulting and Clinical Psychology, 81*(6), 1052–1062.

Sicile-Kira, C. (2014). *Autism spectrum disorder (revised): The complete guide to understanding autism.* New York: Perigee Trade.

Siemens Healthcare. (2013, May 6). *Survey: The value of knowing.* Press Release.

Siep, N., Jansen, A., Havermans, R., & Roefs, A. (2011). Cognitions and emotions in eating disorders. In R. A. H. Adan & W. H. Kaye (Eds.), *Behavioral neurobiology of eating disorders. Current topics in behavioral neurosciences* (pp. 17–33). New York: Springer-Verlag Publishing.

Sifferlin, A. (2013, May 15). Looking good on Facebook: Social media leads to spikes in plastic surgery requests. *Time.*

Sifferlin, A. (2013, September 6). Social media: Why selfies matter. *Time*.

Sifferlin, A. (2013, December 5). Dementia causes expected to triple in coming decades. *Time*.

Sifferlin, A. (2014, January 15). Mashed up memory: How alcohol speeds memory loss in men. *Time*.

Sigerist, H. E. (1943). *Civilization and disease*. Ithaca, NY: Cornell University Press.

Silbersweig, D. A., Stern, E., Frith, C., Cahill, C., Holmes, A., Grootoonk, S, . . . Frackowiak, R. S. J. (1995). A functional neuroanatomy of hallucinations in schizophrenia. *Nature, 378*, 176–179.

Silk, K. R., & Jibson, M. D. (2010). Personality disorders. In M. D. Rothschild & J. Anthony (Eds.), *The evidence-based guide to antipsychotic medications* (pp. 101–124). Arlington, VA: American Psychiatric Publishing.

Simard, V., Nielsen, T. A., Tremblay, R. E., Boivin, M., & Montplaisir, J. Y. (2008). Longitudinal study of bad dreams in preschool-aged children: Prevalence, demographic correlates, risk and protective factors. *Sleep, 31*(1), 62–70.

Simmon, J. (1990). Media and market study. In skin deep: Our national obsession with looks. *Psychology Today, 26*(3), 96.

Simon, R. (Ed.) (2011). *Psychotherapy Networker*. Retrieved from www.psychotherapynetworker.org.

Simonelli, C., Eleuteri, S., Petruccelli, F., & Rossi, R. (2014). Female sexual pain disorders: Dyspareunia and vaginismus. *Current Opinion in Psychiatry, 27*(6), 406–412.

Simonton, D. K. (2010). So you want to become a creative genius? You must be crazy! In D. H. Cropley, A. J. Cropley, J. C. Kaufman, & M. A. Runco (Eds.), *The dark side of creativity* (pp. 218–234). New York: Cambridge University Press.

Simple, I. (2009 July 29). Testing times for Wikipedia after doctor posts secrets of the Rorschach inkblots. *The Guardian*.

Simpson, H. B., Foa, E. B., Liebowitz, M. R., Huppert, J. D., Cahill, S., Maher, M. J., . . . Campeas, R. (2013). Cognitive-behavioral therapy vs risperidone for augmenting serotonin reuptake inhibitors in obsessive-compulsive disorder: A randomized clinical trial. *JAMA Psychiatry, 70*(11), 1190–1199.

Singh, A. (2013, July 16). Dementia rate in the elderly has dropped 24% in past 20 years: What this means for coming generations. *Medical Daily.com*.

Singh, D., McMain, S., & Zucker, K. J. (2011). Gender identity and sexual orientation in women with borderline personality disorder. *Journal of Sexual Medicine, 8*(2), 447–454.

Singh, G. K., & Siahpush, M. (2014). Widening rural–urban disparities in all-cause mortality and mortality from major causes of death in the USA, 1969–2009. *Journal of Urban Health, 91*(2), 272–292.

Singh, S. P., & Kunar, S. S. (2010). Cultural diversity in early psychosis. In P. French, J. Smith, D. Shiers, M. Reed, & M. Rayne (Eds.), *Promoting recovery in early psychosis: A practice manual* (pp. 66–72). Hoboken, NJ: Wiley-Blackwell.

Singh, S. P., Kumar, A., Agarwal, S., Phadke, S. R., & Jaiswal, Y. (2014). Genetic insight of schizophrenia: Past and future perspectives. *Gene, 535*(2), 97–100.

Singhal, A., Ross, J., Seminog, O., Hawton, K., & Goldacre, M. J. (2014). Risk of self-harm and suicide in people with specific psychiatric and physical disorders: Comparisons between disorders using English national record linkage. *Journal of the Royal Society of Medicine, 107*(5), 194–204.

Sinkus, M. L., Graw, S., Freedman, R., Ross, R. G., Lester, H. A., & Leonard, S. (2015). The human CHRNA7 and CHRFAM7A genes: A review of the genetics, regulation, and function. *Neuropharmacology, 96*(Pt B), 274–288.

Sinton, M. M., & Taylor, C. B. (2010). Prevention: Current status and underlying theory. In W. S. Agras (Ed.), *The Oxford handbook of eating disorders. Oxford library of psychology* (pp. 307–330). New York: Oxford University Press.

Sipahi, L., Uddin, M., Hou, Z., Aiello, A. E., Koenen, K. C., Galea, S., & Wildman, D. E. (2014). Ancient evolutionary origins of epigenetic regulation associated with posttraumatic stress disorder, *Frontiers in Human Neuroscience, 8*, 284.

Sipe, T. A., Finnie, R. C., Knopf, J. A., Qu, S., Reynolds, J. A., Thota, A. B., . . . Nease, D. J. (2015). Effects of mental health benefits legislation: A community guide systematic review. *American Journal of Preventive Medicine, 48*(6), 755–766.

Sirey, J. A., Franklin, A. J., McKenzie, S. E., Ghosh, S., & Raue, P. J. (2014). Race, stigma, and mental health referrals among clients of aging services who screened positive for depression. *Psychiatric Services, 65*(4), 537–540.

Sitt, D. (2013, June 18). Dear Technology . . . Signed Mindfully. *Psychology Today*.

Sizemore, C. C. (1991). *A mind of my own: The woman who was known as "Eve" tells the story of her triumph over multiple personality disorder*. New York: William Morrow.

Sizemore, C. C., & Pitillo, E. S. (1977). *I'm Eve*. Garden City, NY: Doubleday.

Sjolie, I. I. (2002). A logotherapist's view of somatization disorder and a protocol. *International Forum for Logotherapy, 25*(1), 24–29.

Skelton, M., Khokhar, W. A., & Thacker, S. P. (2015). Treatment for delusional disorder. *The Cochrane Database of Systematic Reviews, 5*, CD009785.

Skodol, A. E. (2005). The borderline diagnosis: Concepts, criteria, and controversies. In J. G. Gunderson & P. D. Hoffman (Eds.), *Understanding and treating borderline personality disorder* (pp. 3–19). Washington, DC: American Psychiatric Publishing.

Slater, M. D., Kelly, K. J., Lawrence, F. R., Stanley, L. R., & Comello, M. L. G. (2011). Assessing media campaigns linking marijuana non-use with autonomy and aspirations: "Be under your own influence" and ONDCP's "above the influence." *Prevention Science, 12*(1), 12–22.

Sledge, W. H., & Lazar, S. G. (2014). Workplace effectiveness and psychotherapy for mental, substance abuse, and subsyndromal conditions. *Psychodynamic Psychiatry, 42*(3), 497–556.

Sloan, D. M. (2002). Does warm weather climate affect eating disorder pathology? *International Journal of Eating Disorders, 32*, 240–244.

Slopen, N., Fitzmaurice, G. M., Williams, D. R., & Gilman, S. E. (2012). Common patterns of violence experiences and depression and anxiety among adolescents. *Social Psychiatry and Psychiatric Epidemiology, 47*(10), 1591–1605.

Slovenko, R. (2002). *Psychiatry in law/Law in psychiatry*. New York: Brunner-Routledge.

Slovenko, R. (2002). The role of psychiatric diagnosis in the law. *Journal of Psychiatry & Law, 30*(3), 421–444.

Slovenko, R. (2004). A history of the intermix of psychiatry and law. *Journal of Psychiatry & Law, 32*(4), 561–592.

Slovenko, R. (2009). *Psychiatry in law/Law in psychiatry* (2nd ed.). New York: Routledge/Taylor & Francis Group.

Slovenko, R. (2011). *Psychotherapy testimonial privilege in criminal cases*. Presentation at American College of Forensic Psychiatry conference, San Diego, CA. March 23, 2011.

Slovenko, R. (2011). The DSM in litigation and legislation. *Journal of the American Academy of Psychiatry and the Law, 39*(1).

Sluhovsky, M. (2007). *Believe not every spirit: Possession, mysticism, & discernment in early modern Catholicism*. Chicago: University of Chicago Press.

Sluhovsky, M. (2011). Spirit possession and other alterations of consciousness in the Christian Western tradition. In E. Cardeña & M. Winkelman (Eds.), *Altering consciousness: Multidisciplinary perspectives (Vols. 1 and 2): History, culture, and the humanities. Biological and Psychological perspectives* (pp. 73–88). Santa Barbara, CA: Praeger/ABC-CLIO.

Smart-Richman, L., Pek, J., Pascoe, E., & Bauer, D. J. (2010). Discrimination is bad for your health. *Clinician's Research Digest, 28*(11).

Smink, F. E., van Hoeken, D., & Hoek, H. W. (2013). Epidemiology, course, and outcome of eating disorders. *Current Opinion in Psychiatry, 26*(6), 543–548.

Smith, A. (2013, September 4). Suicides kill more inmates than homicide, overdoses, accidents combined. *NBC News*.

Smith, A. (2014). *6 new facts about Facebook*. Washington, DC: Pew Research Center.

Smith, M. L., & Glass, G. V. (1977). Meta-analysis of psychotherapy outcome studies. *American Psychologist, 32*(9), 752–760.

Smith, M. L., Glass, G. V., & Miller, T. I. (1980). *The benefits of psychotherapy*. Baltimore: Johns Hopkins University Press.

Smith, P. K. (2010). Bullying in primary and secondary schools: Psychological and organizational comparisons. In S. R. Jimerson, S. M. Swearer, & D. L. Espelage (Eds.), *Handbook of bullying in schools: An international perspective*. (pp. 137–150) New York: Routledge/Taylor & Francis Group.

Smith, P. K. (2011). Bullying in schools: Thirty years of research. In C. P. Monks, & I. Coyne (Eds.), *Bullying in different contexts* (pp. 36–60). New York: Cambridge University Press.

Smith, P. K., Thompson, F., & Davidson, J. (2014). Cyber safety for adolescent girls: Bullying, harassment, sexting, pornography, and solicitation. *Current Opinion in Obstetrics & Gynecology, 26*(5), 360–365.

Smith, T. (2008, January 29). Real-life fears faced in online world: Helping alter-egos in "second life" helps people cope. *CBS News*. Retrieved from CBS News website: http:www.cbsnews.com/video/watch/?id=3764862.

Smith, T. W. (2007). *Job satisfaction in the United States*. Chicago, IL: University of Chicago.

Smyth, J. M., & Pennebaker, J. W. (2001). What are the health effects of disclosure? In A. Baum, T. A. Revenson, & J. E. Singer (Eds.), *Handbook of health psychology* (pp. 339–348). Mahwah, NJ: Lawrence Erlbaum.

Snyder, W. V. (1947). *Casebook of non-directive counseling*. Boston: Houghton Mifflin.

So, J. K. (2008). Somatization as cultural idiom of distress: Rethinking mind and body in a multicultural society. *Counselling Psychology Quarterly, 21*(2), 167–174.

Sobell, M. B., & Sobell, L. C. (1973). Individualized behavior therapy for alcoholics. *Behavior Therapist, 4*(1), 49–72.

Sobell, M. B., & Sobell, L. C. (1984). The aftermath of heresy: A response to Pendery et al.'s (1982) critique of "Individualized Behavior Therapy for Alcoholics." *Behavioral Research and Therapy, 22*(4), 413–440.

SOGC (Society of Obstetricians and Gynaecologists). (2014). *Female orgasms: Myths and facts*. Ottawa, ON: SOGC. Retrieved from SOGC website: http://sogc.org/publications.

Solar, A. (2014). A supported employment linkage intervention for people with schizophrenia who want a chance to work. *Australasian Psychiatry, 22*(3), 245–247.

Soliman, M., Santos, A. M., & Lohr, J. B. (2008). Emergency, inpatient, and residential treatment. In K. T. Mueser & D. V. Jeste (Eds.), *Clinical handbook of schizophrenia* (pp. 339–353). New York: Guilford Press.

Soloff, P. H., Chiappetta, L., Mason, N. S., Becker, C., & Price, J. C. (2014). Effects of serotonin-2A receptor binding and gender on personality traits and suicidal behavior in borderline personality disorder. *Psychiatry Research, 222*(3), 140–148.

Solter, V., Thaller, V., Bagaric, A., Karlovic, D., Crnkovic, D., & Potkonjak, J. (2004). Study of schizophrenia comorbid with alcohol addiction. *European Journal of Psychiatry, 18*(1), 15–22.

Sommers-Flanagan, J., & Sommers-Flanagan, R. (2013). *Clinical interviewing* (5th ed.). Hoboken, NJ: Wiley.

Soole, R., Kölves, K., & De Leo, D. (2015). Suicide in children: A systematic review. *Archives of Suicide Research, 19*(3), 285–304.

Soto, J. A., Dawson-Andoh, N. A., & BeLue, R. (2011). The relationship between perceived discrimination and generalized anxiety disorder among African Americans, Afro Caribbeans, and non-Hispanic Whites. *Journal of Anxiety Disorders, 25*(2), 258–265.

Soukup, J. E. (2006). Alzheimer's disease: New concepts in diagnosis, treatment, and management. In T. G. Plante (Ed.), *Mental disorders of the new millennium, Vol. 3: Biology and function.* Westport, CT: Praeger Publishers.

Spada, M. M., Giustina, L., Rolandi, S., Fernie, B. A., & Caselli, G. (2015). Profiling metacognition in gambling disorder. *Behavioural and Cognitive Psychotherapy, 43*(5), 614–622.

Span, P. (2009, March 24). They don't want to live with you, either. *New York Times, The New Old Age Blog.*

Spanton, T. (2008, July 28). UFOs: We believe. *The Sun.* Retrieved from The Sun website: http://www.thesun.co.uk/sol/homepage/news/ufos/article1477122.ece.

Speaking of Research. (2011). *Facts.* Retrieved from Speaking of Research website: http://speakingofresearch.com/facts/.

Speaking of Research. (2011). *Statistics.* Retrieved from Speaking of Research website: http://speakingofresearch.com/facts/statistics/.

Spence, J., Titov, N., Johnston, L., Jones, M. P., Dear, B. F., & Solley, K. (2014). Internet-based trauma-focused cognitive behavioural therapy for PTSD with and without exposure components. A randomised controlled trial. *Journal of Affective Disorders, 162*, 73–80.

Sperry, L. (2003). *Handbook of diagnosis and treatment of DSM-IV-TR personality disorders* (2nd ed.). New York: Brunner-Routledge.

Spiegel, D. (2009). Coming apart: Trauma and the fragmentation of the self. In D. Gordon (Ed.), *Cerebrum 2009: Emerging ideas in brain science* (pp. 1–11). Washington, DC: Dana Press.

Spiegler, M. D., & Guevremont, D. C. (2003). *Contemporary behavior therapy.* Belmont, CA: Thomson/Wadsworth.

Spielberger, C. D. (1966). Theory and research on anxiety. In C. D. Spielberger (Ed.), *Anxiety and behavior.* New York: Academic Press.

Spielberger, C. D. (1972). Anxiety as an emotional state. In C. D. Spielberger (Ed.), *Anxiety: Current xtrends in theory and research* (Vol. 1). New York: Academic Press.

Spielberger, C. D. (1985). Anxiety, cognition, and affect: A state-trait perspective. In A. H. Tuma & J. Maser (Eds.), *Anxiety and the anxiety disorders.* Hillsdale, NJ: Lawrence Erlbaum.

Spirito, A., & Esposito-Smythers, C. (2008). Evidence-based therapies for adolescent suicidal behavior. In R. G. Steele, T. D. Elkin, & M. C. Roberts (Eds.), *Handbook of evidence-based therapies for children and adolescents: Bridging science and practice.* New York: Springer.

Spirito, A., Simon, V., Cancilliere, M. K., Stein, R., Norcott, C., Loranger, K., &

Prinstein, M. J. (2011). Outpatient psychotherapy practice with adolescents following psychiatric hospitalization for suicide ideation or a suicide attempt. *Clinical Child Psychology and Psychiatry, 16*(1), 53–64.

Spitzer, R. L., Gibbon, M., Skodol, A. E., Williams, J. B. W., & First, M. B. (Eds.). (1994). *DSM-IV casebook: A learning companion to the diagnostic and statistical manual of mental disorders* (4th ed.). Washington, DC: American Psychiatric Press.

Spitzer, R. L., Skodol, A., Gibbon, M., & Williams, J. B. W. (1981). *DSM-III case book* (1st ed.). Washington, DC: American Psychiatric Press.

Spitzer, R. L., Skodol, A., Gibbon, M., & Williams, J. B. W. (1983). *Psychopathology: A case book.* New York: McGraw-Hill.

SPRC (Suicide Prevention Resource Center). (2013). *Suicide among racial/ethnic populations in the U.S.: American Indians/Alaska Natives.* Waltham, MA: Education Development Center, Inc.

Springman, R. E., Wherry, J. N., & Notaro, P. C. (2006). The effects of interviewer race and child race on sexual abuse disclosures in forensic interviews. *Journal of Child Sexual Abuse, 15*(3), 99–116.

Stacciarini, J. M. R., O'Keeffe, M., & Mathews, M. (2007). Group therapy as treatment for depressed Latino women: A review of the literature. *Issues in Mental Health Nursing, 28*(5), 473–488.

Stack, S. (2004). Emile Durkheim and altruistic suicide. *Archives of Suicide Research, 8*(1), 9–22.

Stack, S., & Wasserman, I. (2009). Gender and suicide risk: The role of wound site. *Suicide & Life-Threatening Behavior, 39*(1), 13–20.

Stahl, S. M. (2014). *Prescriber's guide: Stahl's essential psychopharmacology.* New York: Cambridge University Press.

Stahlberg, O., Anckarsater, H., & Nilsson, T. (2010). Mental health problems in youths committed to juvenile institutions: Prevalences and treatment needs. *European Child & Adolescent Psychiatry, 19*(12), 893–903.

Staller, K. M., & Faller, K. C. (Eds.). (2010). *Seeking justice in child sexual abuse: Shifting burdens and sharing responsibilities.* New York: Columbia University Press.

Stanislaus, A. (2013). Assessment of dangerousness in clinical practice. *Missouri Medicine, 110*(1), 61–64.

Stanley, B., Molcho, A., Stanley, M., Winchel, R., Gameroff, M. J., Parsons, B., & Mann, J. J. (2000). Association of aggressive behavior with altered serotonergic function in patients who are not suicidal. *American Journal of Psychiatry, 157*(4), 609–614.

Stanley, I. H., Horn, M. A., & Joiner, T. E. (2015). Mental health service use among adults with suicide ideation, plans, or attempts: Results from a national survey. *Psychiatric Services* (Washington, D.C.), app.ips 201400593. [Electronic publication.]

Starcevic, V. (2015). Trichotillomania: Impulsive, compulsive or both? *Australian and New Zealand Journal of Psychiatry, 49*(7), 660–661.

Starcevic, V., & Brakoulias, V. (2014). New diagnostic perspectives on obsessive-compulsive personality disorder and its links with other conditions. *Current Opinion in Psychiatry, 27*(1), 62–67.

Stares, J. (2005, November). Einstein, eccentric genius, smoked butts picked up off street. *The Telegraph.*

Starr, L. R., Hammen, C., Connolly, N. P., & Brennan, P. A. (2014). Does relational dysfunction mediate the association between anxiety disorders and later depression? Testing an interpersonal model of comorbidity. *Depression & Anxiety, 31*(1), 77–86.

Starr, T. B., & Kreipe, R. E. (2014). Anorexia nervosa and bulimia nervosa: Brains, bones and breeding. *Current Psychiatry Reports, 16*(5), 441.

Statista. (2015). *Leading social networks worldwide as of March 2015.* Retrieved from The Statistics Portal website: http://www.statista.com/statistics/272014.

Statistic Brain. (2012). *Bipolar disorder statistics.* Retrieved from Statistic Brain website: http://www.statistic.brain.com.

Statistic Brain. (2012). *College student alcohol drinking statistics.* Retrieved from Statistic Brain website: http://www.statisticbrain.com/college-student-alcohol-drinking-statistics/.

Statistic Brain. (2012). *Lying statistics.* Retrieved from Statistic Brain website: http://www.statisticbrain.com.

Statistic Brain. (2013). *Sex offender statistics.* Retrieved from Statistic Brain website: http://www.statisticbrain.com/sex-offender-statistics.

Statistic Brain. (2014). *Retirement statistics.* Retrieved from Statistic Brain website: http://www.statisticbrain.com/retirement-statistics.

Steadman, H. J., Monahan, J., Robbins, P. C., Appelbaum, P., Grisso, T., Klassen, D., . . . Roth, L. (1993). From dangerousness to risk assessment: Implications for appropriate research strategies. In S. Hodgins (Ed.), *Mental disorder and crime.* New York: Sage.

Steadman, H. J., Osher, F. C., Robbins, C. P., Case, B., & Samuels, S. (2009). Prevalence of serious mental illness among jail inmates. *Psychiatric Services 60*, 761–765.

Steele, H. (2011). Multiplicity revealed in the Adult Attachment Interview: When integration and coherence means death. In V. Sinason (Ed.), *Attachment, trauma and multiplicity: Working with dissociative identity disorder* (2nd ed., pp. 37–46). New York: Routledge/Taylor & Francis Group.

Steenkamp, M. M., Litz, B. T., Hoge, C. W., & Marmar, C. R. (2015). Psychotherapy for military-related PTSD: A review of randomized clinical trials. *Journal of the American Medical Association, 314*(5), 489–500.

Stegmayer, K., Horn, H., Federspiel, A., Razavi, N., Bracht, T., Laimböck, K., . . . Walther, S. (2014). Supplementary motor area (SMA) volume is associated with psychotic aberrant motor behaviour of patients with schizophrenia. *Psychiatry Research, 223*(1), 49–51.

Stein, C. H., Leith, J. E., Osborn, L. A., Greenberg, S., Petrowski, C. E., Jesse, S, . . . May, M. C. (2015). Mental health system historians: Adults with schizophrenia describe changes in community mental health care over time. *The Psychiatric Quarterly, 86*(1), 33–48.

Stein, D. J., & Fineberg, N. A. (2007). *Obsessive-compulsive disorder.* Oxford, England: Oxford University Press.

Stein, D. J., Hollander, E., & Rothbaum, B. O. (2010). *Textbook of anxiety disorders* (2nd ed.). Arlington, VA: American Psychiatric Publishing.

Stein, D. J., & Williams, D. (2010). Cultural and social aspects of anxiety disorders. In D. J. Stein, E. Hollander & B. O. Rothbaum (Eds.), *Textbook of anxiety disorders* (2nd ed., pp. 717–729). Arlington, VA: American Psychiatric Publishing.

Stein, J. (2003, August 4). Just say Om. *Time, 162*(5), pp. 48–56.

Stein, J. S., Johnson, P. S., Renda, C. R., Smits, R. R., Liston, K. J., Shahan, T. A., & Madden, G. J., (2013). Early and prolonged exposure to reward delay: Effects in impulsive choice and alcohol self-administration in male rats. *Experimental and Clinical Psychopharmacology, 21*(2), 172–180.

Steiner, H., Smith, C., Rosenkranz, R. T., & Litt, I. (1991). The early care and feeding of anorexics. *Child Psychiatry & Human Development, 21*(3), 163–167.

Steinhausen, H. C. (2002). The outcome of anorexia nervosa in the 20th century. *American Journal of Psychiatry, 159*(8), 1284–1293.

Steinhausen, H. C. (2009). Outcome of eating disorders. *Child and Adolescent Psychiatric Clinics of North America, 18*(1), 225–242.

Steinmetz, K. (2014, June 9). America's transition. *Time Magazine.*

Stekel, W. (2010). *Sadism and masochism: The psychopathology of sexual cruelty.* Chicago, IL: Solar Books/Solar Asylum.

Stene, L. E., & Dyb, G. (2015). Health service utilization after terrorism: A longitudinal study of survivors of the 2011 Utøya attack in Norway. *BMC Health Services Research, 15,* 158.

Stephens, R., Atkins, J., & Kingston, A. (2009). Swearing as a response to pain. *Neuro-Report, 20*(12). 1056–1060.

Stern, A. (1938). Psychoanalytic investigation and therapy in the borderline group of neuroses. *Psychoanalytical Quarterly, 7,* 467–489.

Sternberg, R. J., Grigorenko, E. L., & Bundy, D. A. (2001). The predictive value of IQ. *Merrill-Palmer Quarterly, 47*(1), 1–41.

Stevens, L. M., Lynm, C., & Glass, R. M. (2002). Postpartum depression. *Journal of the American Medical Association, 287*(6), 802.

Stevenson, R. W. D., & Elliott, S. L. (2007). Sexuality and illness. In S. R. Leiblum (Ed.), *Principles and practice of sex therapy* (4th ed., pp. 313–349). New York: Guilford Press.

Stewart, R. E., & Chambless, D. L. (2007). Does psychotherapy research inform treatment decisions in private practice. *Journal of Clinical Psychology, 63*(3), 267–281.

Stewart, T. M., & Williamson, D. A. (2008). Bulimia nervosa. In M. Hersen & J. Rosqvist (Eds.), *Handbook of psychological assessment, case conceptualization and treatment, Vol. 1: Adults.* Hoboken, NJ: John Wiley & Sons.

Stice, E., Hayward, C., Cameron, R. P., Killen, J. D., & Taylor, C. B. (2000). Body-image and eating disturbances predict onset of depression among female adolescents: A longitudinal study. *Journal of Abnormal Psychology, 109*(3), 438–444.

Stice, E., Marti, C. N., & Rohde, P. (2013). Prevalence, incidence, impairment, and course of the proposed DSM-5 eating disorder diagnoses in an 8-year prospective community study of young women. *Journal of Abnormal Psychology, 122*(2), 445–457.

Stice, E., & Presnell, K. (2010). Dieting and the eating disorders. In W. S. Agras (Ed.), *The Oxford handbook of eating disorders* (pp. 148–179). New York: Oxford University Press.

Stolberg, R. A., Clark, D. C., & Bongar, B. (2002). Epidemiology, assessment, and management of suicide in depressed patients. In I. H. Gotlib & C. L. Hammen (Eds.), *Handbook of depression* (pp. 581–601). New York: Guilford Press.

Stone, M. H. (2010). Sexual sadism: A portrait of evil. *Journal of the American Academy of Psychoanalysis & Dynamic Psychiatry, 38*(1), 133–157.

Stone, M. H. (2014). The spectrum of borderline personality disorder: A neurophysiological view. *Current Topics in Behavioral Neurosciences, 21,* 23–46.

Stoppler, M. C. (2014). Holiday depression and stress. *MedicineNet.com.*

Strachan, E. (2008). Civil commitment evaluations. In R. Jackson (Ed.), *Learning forensic assessment* (pp. 509–535). New York: Routledge/Taylor & Francis Group.

Strassberg, D. S., McKinnon, R. K., Sustaíta, M. A., & Rullo, J. (2013). Sexting by high school students: An exploratory and descriptive study. *Archives of Sexual Behavior, 42*(1), 15–21.

Stratemeier, M. W., & Vignogna, L. (2014). Peptic ulcers. Retrieved from emedicinehealth website: http://www.emedicinehealth.com.

Straub, J., Sproeber, N., Plener, P. L., Fegert, J. M., Bonenberger, M., & Koelch, M. G. (2014). A brief cognitive-behavioural group therapy programme for the treatment of depression in adolescent outpatients: A pilot study. *Child and Adolescent Psychiatry and Mental Health, 8*(1), 9.

Street, A. E., Bell, M. E., & Ready, C. B. (2011). Sexual assault. In D. M. Benedek, & G. H. Wynn (Eds.), *Clinical manual for management of PTSD.* (pp. 325–348) Arlington, VA: American Psychiatric Publishing.

Strickland, B. R., Hale, W. D., & Anderson, L. K. (1975). Effect of induced mood states on activity and self-reported affect. *Journal of Consulting and Clinical Psychology, 43*(4), 587.

Strober, M., Freeman, R., Lampert, C., Diamond, J., & Kaye, W. (2000). Controlled family study of anorexia nervosa and bulimia nervosa: Evidence of shared liability and transmission of partial syndromes. *American Journal of Psychiatry, 157*(3), 393–401.

Strober, M., Freeman, R., Lampert, C., Diamond, J., & Kaye, W. (2001). Males with anorexia nervosa: A controlled study of eating disorders in first-degree relatives. *International Journal of Eating Disorders, 29*(3), 264–269.

Strober, M., & Yager, J. (1985). A developmental perspective on the treatment of anorexia nervosa in adolescents. In D. M. Garner & P. E. Garfinkel (Eds.), *Handbook of psychotherapy for anorexia nervosa and bulimia.* New York: Guilford Press.

Stroup, T. S., Marder, S. R., & Lieberman, J. A. (2012). Pharmacotherapies. In J. A. Lieberman, T. S. Stroup, & D. O Perkins (Eds.), *Essentials of schizophrenia* (pp. 173–206). Arlington, VA: American Psychiatric Publishing.

Strümpfel, U. (2006). *Therapie der gefühle: For-schungsbefunde zur gestalttherapie.* Cologne, Germany: Edition Huanistiche Psychologie.

Stuart, S., Noyes, R., Jr., Starcevic, V., & Barsky, A. (2008). An integrative approach to somatoform disorders combining interpersonal and cognitive-behavioral theory and techniques. *Journal of Contemporary Psychotherapy, 38*(1), 45–53.

Stuber, J. P., Rocha, A., Christian, A., & Link, B. G. (2014). Conceptions of mental illness: Attitudes of mental health professionals and the general public. *Psychiatric Services, 65*(4), 490–497.

Štulhofer, A., Træen, B., & Carvalheira, A. (2013). Job-related strain and sexual health difficulties among heterosexual men from three European countries: The role of culture and emotional support. *Journal of Sexual Medicine, 10,* 747–756.

Stunkard, A. J. (1959). Eating patterns and obesity. *Psychiatric Quarterly, 33,* 284–295.

Sturmey, P. (2008). Adults with intellectual disabilities. In M. Hersen & J. Rosqvist (Eds.), *Handbook of psychological assessment, case conceptualization, and treatment, Vol. 1: Adults.* Hoboken, NJ: Wiley.

Sturmey, P., & Didden, R. (2014). *Evidence-based practice and intellectual disabilities.* Hoboken, NJ: Wiley.

Su, S., Wang, X., Kapuku, G. K., Treiber, F. A., Pollock, D. M., Harshfield, G. A., . . . Pollock, J. S. (2014). Adverse childhood experiences are associated with detrimental hemodynamics and elevated circulating endothelin-1 in adolescents and young adults. *Hypertension, 64*(1), 201–207.

Sue, D. W., & Sue, D. (2003) *Counseling the culturally diverse: Theory and practice* (4th ed.). New York: Wiley.

Sugrue, D., Bogner, R., & Ehret, M. J. (2014). Methylphenidate and dexmethylphenidate formulations for children with attention-deficit/hyperactivity disorder. *American Journal of Health-System Pharmacy, 71*(14). 1163–1170.

Sujan, A. C., Humphreys, K. L., Ray, L. A., & Lee, S. S. (2014, July 16). Differential association of child abuse with self-reported versus laboratory-based impulsivity and risk-taking in young adulthood. *Child Maltreatment, 19*(3-4), 145–155.

Suler, J. (2004). The online disinhibition effect. *Cyber Psychology and Behavior, 7*(3), 321–326.

Sullivan, E. L., Smith, M. S., & Grove, K. L. (2011). Perinatal exposure to high-fat diet programs energy balance, metabolism and behavior in adulthood. *Neuroendocrinology, 93*(1), 1–8.

Sullivan, E. M., Annest, J. L., Simon, T. R., Luo, F., & Dahlberg, L. L. (2015). Suicide trends among persons aged 10–24 years—United States, 1994–2012. *Morbidity and Mortality Weekly Report, 64*(8), 201–205.

Sullivan, H. S. (1953). *The interpersonal theory of psychiatry.* New York: Norton.

Sungur, M. Z., & Gündüz, A. (2014). A comparison of DSM-IV-TR and DSM-5 definitions for sexual dysfunctions: Critiques and challenges. *Journal of Sexual Medicine, 11,* 364–373.

Suokas, J. T., Suvisaari, J. M., Gissler, M., Löfman, R., Linna, M. S., Raevuori, A., & Haukka, J. (2013). Mortality in eating disorders: A follow-up study of adult eating disorder patients treated in tertiary care, 1995–2010. *Psychiatry Research, 210*(3), 1101–1106.

Suokas, J. T., Suvisaari, J. M., Grainger, M., Raevuori, A., Gissler, M., & Haukka, J. (2014). Suicide attempts and mortality in eating disorders: A follow-up study of eating disorder patients. *General Hospital Psychiatry, 36*(3), 355–357.

Suppes, T., Baldessarini, R. J., Faedda, G. L., & Tohen, M. (1991). Risk of recurrence following discontinuation of lithium treatment in bipolar disorder. *Archives of General Psychiatry, 48*(12), 1082–1088.

Sussman, S. (2010). Cognitive misperceptions and drug misuse. In L. Scheier (Ed.), *Handbook of drug use etiology: Theory, methods, and empirical findings* (pp. 617–629). Washington, DC: American Psychological Association.

Svartberg, M., & McCullough, L. (2010). Cluster C personality disorders: Prevalence, phenomenology, treatment effects, and principles of treatment. In J. F. Clarkin, P. Fonagy, & G. O. Gabbard (Eds.), *Psychodynamic psychotherapy for personality disorders: A clinical handbook* (pp. 337–367). Arlington, VA: American Psychiatric Publishing.

Swain, J., Hancock, K., Hainsworth, C., & Bowman, J. (2013). Acceptance and commitment therapy in the treatment of anxiety: A systematic review. *Clinical Psychology Review, 33*(8), 965–978.

Swan, L. K., & Heesacker, M. (2013). Evidence of a pronounced preference for therapy guided by common factors. *Journal of Clinical Psychology, 69*(9), 869–879.

Swanson, J. W., & Swartz, M. S. (2014). Why the evidence for outpatient commitment is good enough. *Psychiatric Services, 65*(6), 808–811.

Swartz, M. S., Frohberg, N. R., Drake, R. E., & Lauriello, J. (2012). Psychosocial therapies. In J. A. Lieberman, T. S. Stroup, & D. O Perkins (Eds.), *Essentials of schizophrenia* (pp. 207–224). Arlington, VA: American Psychiatric Publishing.

Syed-Abdul, S., Fernandez-Luque, L., Jian, W., Li, Y., Crain, S., Hsu, M., . . . Liou, D. (2013). Misleading health-related information promoted through video-based social media: Anorexia on YouTube. *Journal of Medical Internet Research, 15*(2), e30.

Syrjala, K. L., Jensen, M. P., Mendoza, M. E., Yi, J. C., Fisher, H. M., & Keefe, F. J. (2014). Psychological and behavioral approaches to cancer pain management. *Journal of Clinical Oncology, 32*(16), 1703–1711.

Szabo, M., & Lovibond, P. F. (2004). The cognitive content of thought-listed worry episodes in clinic-referred anxious and nonreferred children. *Journal of Clinical Child and Adolescent Psychology, 33*(3), 613–622.

Szalavitz, M. (2013, July 18). Apps for mastering your mood. *Time.*

Szalavitz, M. (2013, March 1). How Facebook improves memory. *Time.* Retrieved from Time website: http://healthland.time.com/2013/03/01.

Szasz, T. S. (1960). The myth of mental illness. *American Psychologist, 15,* 113–118.

Szasz, T. S. (1963). *The manufacture of madness.* New York: Harper & Row.

Szumilas, M., Wei, Y., & Kutcher, S. (2010). Psychological debriefing in schools. *Canadian Medical Association Journal, 182*(9), 883–884.

Tacón, A., & Caldera, Y. (2001). Behavior modification. In R. McComb & J. Jacalyn (Eds.), *Eating disorders in women and children: Prevention, stress management, and treatment* (pp. 263–272). Boca Raton, FL: CRC Press.

TAD [Truth About Deception]. (2014). Compulsive lying: Results summary. *TAD.* Retrieved from RAD website: http://www.truthaboutdeception.com/surveys/2-compulsive-lying.

TADS (Treatment for Adolescents with Depression Study Team, U.S.). (2004). Fluoxetine, cognitive behavioral therapy, and their combination for adolescents with depression: Treatment for Adolescents with Depression Study (TADS) randomized controlled trial. *Journal of the American Medical Association, 292*(7), 807–820.

TADS (Treatment for Adolescents with Depression Study Team, U.S.). (2007). The Treatment for Adolescents with Depression Study (TADS): Long-term effectiveness and safety outcomes. *Archives of General Psychiatry, 64*(10), 1132–1144.

TADS (Treatment for Adolescents with Depression Study Team, U.S.). (2010). *Treatment for Adolescents with Depression Study.* Retrieved from http://www.nimh.nih.gov/trials/practical/tads/index.shtml.

Taghva, A. S., Malone, D. A., & Rezai, A. R. (2013). Deep brain stimulation for treatment-resistant depression. *World Neurosurgery, 80*(3-4), S27.e17–24.

Takeuchi, H., Suzuki, T., Remington, G., Watanabe, K., Mimura, M., & Uchida, H. (2014). Lack of effect of risperidone or olanzapine dose reduction on subjective experiences in stable patients with schizophrenia. *Psychiatry Research, 218*(1-2), 244–246.

Tallis, F., Davey, G., & Capuzzo, N. (1994). The phenomenology of non-pathological worry: A preliminary investigation. In G. Davey & F. Tallis (Eds.), *Worrying: Perspectives on theory, assessment and treatment* (pp. 61–89). Chichester, England: John Wiley.

Tamminga, C. A., Shad, M. U., & Ghose, S. (2008). Neuropsychiatric aspects of schizophrenia. In S. C. Yudofsky & R. E. Hales (Eds.), *The American Psychiatric Publishing textbook of neuropsychiatry and behavioral neurosciences* (5th ed.). Washington, DC: American Psychiatric Publishing.

Tang, B., Liu, X., Liu, Y., Xue, C., & Zhang, L. (2014). A meta-analysis of risk factors for depression in adults and children after natural disasters. *BMC Public Health, 19*(14), 623.

Tantam, D. (2006). The machine as psychotherapist: Impersonal communication with a machine. *Advances in Psychiatric Treatment, 12,* 416–426.

Tasca, G. A., Hilsenroth, M., & Thompson-Brenner, H. (2014). Psychoanalytic psychotherapy or cognitive-behavioral therapy for bulimia nervosa. *American Journal of Psychiatry, 171*(5), 583–584.

Tashakova, O. (2011, March 25). Am I too fat? *Khaleej Times.*

Tashkin, D. P. (2001). Airway effects of marijuana, cocaine, and other inhaled illicit agents. *Current Opinions in Pulmonary Medicine, 7*(2), 43–61.

Taube-Schiff, M., & Lau, M. A. (2008). Major depressive disorder. In M. Hersen & J. Rosqvist (Eds.), *Handbook of psychological assessment, case conceptualization, and treatment, Vol. 1: Adults* (pp. 319–351). Hoboken, NJ: John Wiley & Sons.

Taycan, O., Sar, V., Celik, C., & Erdogan-Taycan, S. (2014). Trauma-related psychiatric comorbidity of somatization disorder among women in eastern Turkey. *Comprehensive Psychiatry, 55*(8), 1837–1846.

Taylor, B., Carswell, K., & Williams, A. C. (2013). The interaction of persistent pain and post-traumatic re-experiencing: A qualitative study in torture survivors. *Journal of Pain and Symptom Management, 46*(4), 546–555.

Taylor, L. E., Swerdfeger, A. L., & Eslick, G. D. (2014). Vaccines are not associated with autism: An evidence-based meta-analysis of case-control and cohort studies. *Vaccine, 32*(29), 3623–3629.

Taylor, M. J., Doesburg, S. M., & Pang, E. W. (2014). Neuromagnetic vistas into typical and atypical development of frontal lobe functions. *Frontiers in Human Neuroscience, 18*(8), 453.

Taylor, S. E. (2010). Health psychology. In R. F. Baumeister & E. J. Finkel (Eds.), *Advanced social psychology: The state of the science* (pp. 697–731). New York: Oxford University Press.

Taylor, S. E. (2010). Health psychology. In R. F. Baumeister & E. J. Finkel (Eds.), *Advanced social psychology: The state of the science* (pp. 697–731). New York: Oxford University Press.

Taylor, S. E. (2010). Health. In S. T. Fiske, D. T. Gilbert, & G. Lindzey (Eds.), *Handbook of social psychology, Vol. 1* (5th ed., pp. 698–723). Hoboken, NJ: John Wiley & Sons.

Taylor, S. F., Demeter, E., Phan, K. L., Tso, I. F., & Welsh, R. C. (2014). Abnormal GABAergic function and negative affect in schizophrenia. *Neuropsychopharmacology, 39*(4), 1000–1008.

Taylor, W. D. (2014). Depression in the elderly. *New England Journal of Medicine, 371,* 1228–1236.

Tellez, M., Potter, C., Kinner, D. G., Jensen, D., Waldron, E., Heimberg, R. G., . . . Ismail, A. I. (2015). Computerized tool to manage dental anxiety: A randomized clinical trial. *Journal of Dental Research, 94*(9 Suppl), 174S–80S.

Tenback, D. E., Bakker, P. R., & van Harten, P. N. (2015). [Risk factors for tardive movement disorders in schizophrenia] *Tijdschrift Voor Psychiatrie, 57*(2), 120–124.

Ten Have, M., de Graaf, R., van Weeghel, J., & van Dorsselaer, S. (2014). The association between common mental disorders and violence: To what extent is it influenced by prior victimization, negative life events and low levels of social support? *Psychological Medicine, 44*(7), 1485–1498.

Ten Have, M., Nuyen, J., Beekman, A., & de Graaf, R. (2013). Common mental disorder severity and its association with treatment contact and treatment intensity for mental health problems. *Psychological Medicine, 43*(10), 2203–2213.

Ter Kuile, M. M., Bulté, I., Weijenborg, P. T. M., Beekman, A., Melles, R., & Onghena, P. (2009). Therapist-aided exposure for women with life-long vaginismus: A replicated single-case design. *Journal of Consulting and Clinical Psychology, 77*(1), 149–159.

Ter Kuile. M. M., Melles, R., deGroot, H. E., Tuijnman-Raasveld, C. C., & van Lankveld, J. M. (2013). Therapist-aided exposure for women with lifelong vaginismus: A randomized waiting-list control trial of efficacy. *Journal of Consulting and Clinical Psychology, 81*(6), 1127–1136.

Thakker, J., & Ward, T. (1998). Culture and classification: The cross-cultural application of the DSM-IV. *Clinical Psychology Review, 18,* 501–529.

Thase, M. E., Trivedi, M. H., & Rush, A. J. (1995). MAOIs in the contemporary treatment of depression. *Neuropsychopharmacology, 12*(3), 185–219.

The Economist. (2010, December 16). Age and happiness: The U-bend of life. *The Economist.* Retrieved from Economist website: http://www.economist.com/node/17722567.

Thigpen, C. H., & Cleckley, H. M. (1957). *The three faces of Eve.* New York: McGraw-Hill.

Thomas, J. (2014, January/February). Most psychologists misinformed on "duty to warn." *The National Psychologist,* pp. 3–4.

Thomas, J., & Altareb, B. (2012). Cognitive vulnerability to depression: An exploration of dysfunctional attitudes and ruminative response styles in the United Arab Emirates. *Psychology & Psychotherapy, 85*(1), 117–121.

Thomasson, E. (2012, June 12). Right-to-die movement sees gain as world ages. *Reuters.*

Thompson, D. F., Ramos, C. L., & Willett, J. K. (2014). Psychopathy: Clinical features, developmental basis and therapeutic challenges. *Journal of Clinical Pharmacy and Therapeutics, 39*(5), 485–495.

Thompson, R. A., & Sherman, R. T. (2010). *Eating disorders in sport.* New York: Routledge/Taylor & Francis Group.

Thompson, W. (2015). *Alcoholism: Practice essentials, background, pathophysiology.* Retrieved from Medscape website: http://emedicine.medscape.com/article/285913-overview.

Thornton, L. M., Mazzeo, S. E., & Bulik, C. M. (2011). The heritability of eating disorders: Methods and current findings. In R. A. H. Adan & W. H. Kaye (Eds.), *Behavioral neurobiology of eating disorders. Current topics in behavioral neurosciences* (pp. 141–156). New York: Springer-Verlag Publishing.

Tiggemann, M., & Slater, A. (2013, September 5). NetTweens: The Internet and body image concerns in preteenage girls. *Journal of Early Adolescence.* [Online publication.]

Tilak, J. (2014, June 13). Canada is primed to be a global example for medical marijuana. *Business Insider.*

Tolan, P., Gorman-Smith, D., & Henry, D. (2006). Family violence. *Annual Review of Psychology, 57,* 557–583.

Tolmunen, T., Lehto, S. M., Julkunen, J., Hintikka, J., & Kauhanen, J. (2014). Trait anxiety and somatic concerns associate with increased mortality risk: A 23-year follow-up in aging men. *Annals of Epidemiology, 24*(6), 463–468.

Tondo, L., Vázquez, G. H., Baethge, C., Baronessa, C., Bolzani, L., Koukopoulos, A., . . . Baldessarini R. J. (2015). Comparison of psychotic bipolar disorder, schizoaffective disorder, and schizophrenia: An international, multisite study. *Acta Psychiatrica Scandinavica.* [Electronic publication.]

Torgersen, S. (1983). Genetic factors in anxiety disorders. *Archives of General Psychiatry, 40,* 1085–1089.

Torgersen, S. (1984). Genetic and nosological aspects of schizotypal and borderline personality disorders: A twin study. *Archives of General Psychiatry, 41,* 546–554.

Torgersen, S. (1990). Comorbidity of major depression and anxiety disorders in twin pairs. *American Journal of Psychiatry, 147,* 1199–1202.

Torgersen, S. (2000). Genetics of patients with borderline personality disorder. *Psychiatric Clinics of North America, 23*(1), 1–9.

Toro, J., Gila, A., Castro, J., Pombo, C., & Guete, O. (2005). Body image, risk factors for eating disorders and sociocultural influences in Spanish adolescents. *Eating and Weight Disorders, 10*(2), 91–97.

Torres, A. R., Shavitt, R. G., Torresan, R. C., Ferrão, Y. A., Miguel, E. C., & Fontenelle, L. F. (2013). Clinical features of pure obsessive-compulsive disorder. *Comprehensive Psychiatry, 54*(7), 1042–1052.

Torrey, E. F. (1991). A viral-anatomical explanation of schizophrenia. *Schizophrenia Bulletin, 17*(1), 15–18.

Torrey, E. F. (2001). *Surviving schizophrenia: A manual for families, consumers, and providers* (4th ed.). New York: HarperCollins.

Torrey, E. F., Bowler, A. E., Taylor, E. H., & Gottesman, I. I. (1994). *Schizophrenia and manic-depressive disorder.* New York: Basic Books.

Toteja, N., Gallego, J. A., Saito, E., Gerhard, T., Winterstein, A., Olfson, M., & Correll, C. U. (2013). Prevalence and correlates of antipsychotic polypharmacy in children and adolescents receiving antipsychotic treatment. *International Journal of Neuropsychopharmacy, 17*(7), 1095–1105.

Toth, S. L., Rogosch, F. A., Oshri, A., Gravener–Davis, J., Sturm, R., & Morgan–López, A. A. (2013). The efficacy of interpersonal psychotherapy for depression among economically disadvantaged mothers. *Development and Psychopathology, 25*(4 Pt 1), 1065–1078.

Touchette, E., Henegar, A., Godart, N. T., Pryor, L., Falissard, B., Tremblay, R. E., & Côté, S. M. (2011). Subclinical eating disorders and their comorbidity with mood and anxiety disorders in adolescent girls. *Psychiatry Research, 185*(1-2), 185–192.

Touyz, S. W., & Carney, T. (2010). Compulsory (involuntary) treatment for anorexia nervosa. In C. M. Grilo & J. E. Mitchell (Eds.), *The treatment of eating disorders: A clinical handbook* (pp. 212–224). New York: Guilford Press.

Towers, S., Gomez-Lievano, A., Khan, M., Mubayi, A., & Castillo-Chavez, C. (2015). Contagion in mass killings and school shootings. *PLOS ONE, 10*(7), e0117259.

Trapp, M., Trapp, E., Egger, J. W., Domej, W., Schillaci, G., Avian, A., . . . Baulmann, J. (2014). Impact of mental and physical stress on blood pressure and pulse pressure under normobaric versus hypoxic conditions. *PLOS ONE, 9*(5), e89005.

Trauer, J. M., Qian, M. Y., Doyle, J. S., Rajaratnam, S. W., & Cunnington, D. (2015). Cognitive behavioral therapy for chronic insomnia: A systematic review and meta-analysis. *Annals of Internal Medicine, 163*(3), 191–204.

Travers, B. G., Bigler, E. D., Tromp, D. M., Adluru, N., Destiche, D., Samsin, D., . . . Lainhart, J. E. (2015). Brainstem white matter predicts individual differences in manual motor difficulties and symptom severity in autism. *Journal of Autism and Developmental Disorders, 45*(9), 3030–3040.

Travis, C. B., & Meltzer, A. L. (2008). Women's health: Biological and social systems. In F. L. Denmark & M. A. Paludi (Eds.), *Psychology of women: A handbook of issues and theories* (2nd ed., pp. 353–399). Westport, CT: Praeger Publishers.

Travis, C. B., & Meltzer, A. L. (2008). Women's health: Biological and social systems. In F. L. Denmark & M. A. Paludi (Eds.), *Psychology of women: A handbook of issues and theories* (2nd ed., pp. 353–399). Westport, CT: Praeger Publishers.

Traynor, V., Cordato, N., Burns, P., Xu, Y., Britten, N., Duncan, K., . . . McKinnon, C. (2015). Is delirium being detected in emergency? *Australasian Journal on Ageing*. [Electronic publication.]

Treadway, M. T., & Pizzagalli, D. A. (2014). Imaging the pathophysiology of major depressive disorder—from localist models to circuit-based analysis. *Biology of Mood & Anxiety Disorders, 4*(1), 5.

Treffert, D. A. (2014). Savant syndrome: Realities, myths and misconceptions. *Journal of Autism and Developmental Disorders, 44*(3), 564–571.

Trevisan, L. A. (2014, May 9). Elderly alcohol use disorders: Epidemiology, screening, and assessment issues. *Psychiatric Times.*

Triebwasser, J., Chemerinski, E., Roussos, P., & Siever, L. J. (2013). Paranoid personality disorder. *Journal of Personality Disorders, 27*(6), 795–805.

Trifilieff, P., & Martinez, D. (2014). Blunted dopamine release as a biomarker for vulnerability for substance use disorders. *Biological Psychiatry, 76*(1), 4–5.

Tripoli, T. M., Sato, H., Sartori, M. G., de Arauio, F. F., Girao, M. J. B. C., & Schor, E. (2011). Evaluation of quality of life and sexual satisfaction in women suffering from chronic pelvic pain with or without endometriosis. *Journal of Sexual Medicine, 8*(2), 497–503.

True, W. R., & Lyons, M. J. (1999). Genetic risk factors for PTSD: A twin study. In R. Yehuda (Ed.), *Risk factors for posttraumatic stress disorder.* Washington, DC: American Psychiatric Press.

Trull, T. J., & Prinstein, M. (2012). *Clinical psychology.* Independence, KY: Cengage Learning.

Trull, T. J., & Widiger, T. A. (2003). Personality disorders. In G. Stricker, T. A. Widiger, & I. B. Wiener (Eds.), *Handbook of psychology: Clinical psychology.* New York: Wiley.

Tsai, J., Stroup, T. S., & Rosenheck, R. A. (2011). Housing arrangements among a national sample of adults with chronic schizophrenia living in the United States: A descriptive study. *Journal of Community Psychology, 39*(1), 76–88.

Tsai, J. L., Ying, Y. W., & Lee, P. A. (2001). Cultural predictors of self-esteem: A study of Chinese American female and male young adults. *Cultural Diversity & Ethnic Minority Psychology, 7,* 284–297.

Tsang, T. W., Kohn, M. R., Efron, D., Clarke, S. D., Clark, C. R., Lamb, C., & Williams, L. M. (2015). Anxiety in young people with ADHD: Clinical and self-report outcomes. *Journal of Attention Disorders, 19*(1), 18–26.

Tsuang, M., Domschke, K., Jerskey, B. A., & Lyons, M. J. (2004). Agoraphobic behavior and panic attack: A study of male twins. *Journal of Anxiety Disorders, 18*(6), 799–807.

Tsuang, M. T., Bar, J. L., Harley, R. M., & Lyons, M. J. (2001). The Harvard twin study of substance abuse: What we have learned. *Harvard Review of Psychiatry, 9*(6), 267–279.

Tuckey, M. R., & Scott, J. E. (2014). Group critical incident stress debriefing with emergency services personnel: A randomized controlled trial. *Anxiety, Stress, and Coping, 27*(1), 38–54.

Tune, L. E., & DeWitt, M. A. (2011). Delirium. In E. Coffey, J. L. Cummings, M. S. George, & D. Weintraub (Eds.), *The American Psychiatric Publishing textbook of geriatric neuropsychiatry.* Arlington, VA: American Psychiatric Publishing, Inc.

Turchik, J. A., & Hassija, C. M. (2014). Female sexual victimization among college students: Assault severity, health risk behaviors, and sexual functioning. *Journal of Interpersonal Violence, 29*(13), 2439–2457.

Turkat, I. D., Keane, S. P., & Thompson-Pope, S. K. (1990). Social processing errors among paranoid personalities. *Journal of Psychopathology and Behavioral Assessment, 12*(3), 263–269.

Turkle, S. (2012). *Alone together: Why we expect more from technology and less from each other.* New York: Basic Books.

Turkle, S. (2013, December 21). Cited in K. Eisold, Hidden motives: A look at the hidden factors that really drive our social interactions. *Psychology Today.*

Turkle, S. (2013, October 10). "We need to talk": Missed connections with hyperconnectivity. Cited in *NPR.* Retrieved from http://www.npr.org/2013/02/10/171490660.

Turner, B. H., Dixon-Gordon, K. L., Austin, S. B., Rodriguez, M. A., Rosenthal, M. Z., & Chapman, A. L. (2015). Non-suicidal self-injury with and without borderline personality disorder: Differences in self-injury and diagnostic comorbidity. *Psychiatry Research 230*(1), 28–35.

Turner, E. H., Matthews, A. M., Linardatos, E., Tell, R. A., & Rosenthal, R. (2008). Selective publication of antidepressant trials and its influence on apparent efficacy. *New England Journal of Medicine, 358,* 252–260.

Turner, L. J. (2013, October 9). The effect of Medicaid policies on the diagnosis and treatment of children's mental health problems in primary care. *Health Economics.*

Turner, S. M., Beidel, D. C., & Frueh, B. C. (2005). Multicomponent behavioral treatment of chronic combat-related post-traumatic stress disorder: Trauma management therapy. *Behavior Modification, 29*(1), 39–69.

Turney, K. (2011). Chronic and proximate depression among mothers: Implications for child well-being. *Journal of Marriage and Family, 73*(1), 149–163.

Turton, M. D., O'Shea, D., Gunn, I., Beak, S. A., Meeran, E. K., Choi, S. J. . . . Bloom, S. R. (1996, January 4). A role for glucagon-like peptide-1 in the central regulation of feeding. *Nature, 379,* 69–72.

Tusa, A. L., & Burgholzer, J. A. (2013). Came to believe: Spirituality as a mechanism of change in Alcoholics Anonymous: A review of the literature from 1992 to 2012. *Journal of Addictions Nursing, 24*(4), 237–246.

Tyrer, P., Mitchard, S., Methuen, C., & Ranger, M. (2003). Treatment rejecting and treatment seeking personality disorders: Type R and type S. *Journal of Personality Disorders, 17*(3), 263–268.

Tyson, A. S. (2006, December 20). Repeat Iraq tours raise risk of PTSD, Army finds. *Washington Post.* Retrieved from Washington Post website: http://www.washingtonpost.com.

U.S. Bureau of Justice Statistics (BJS). (2011). *Victims.* Retrieved from http://bjs.ojp.usdoj.gov/index.

U.S. Bureau of Labor Statistics (BLS). (2002). Counselors. In *Bureau of Labor Statistics, Occupational outlook handbook* (2004–05 ed.). Washington, DC: Author.

U.S. Bureau of Labor Statistics (BLS). (2002). Social workers. In *Bureau of Labor Statistics, Occupational outlook handbook* (2004–05 ed.). Washington, DC: Author.

U.S. Bureau of Labor Statistics (BLS). (2011). *Occupational Outlook Handbook, 2010-11 Edition, Counselors.* Retrieved from http://www.bls.gov/oco/ocos067.htm.

U.S. Bureau of Labor Statistics (BLS). (2011). *Occupational Outlook Handbook, 2010-11 Edition, Social Workers.* Retrieved from http://www.bls.gov/oco/ocos060.htm.

U.S. Bureau of Labor Statistics (BLS). (2014). *Occupational Outlook Handbook: Mental health counselors and marriage and family therapists.* Retrieved from http://www.bls.gov/ooh/.

U.S. Bureau of Labor Statistics (BLS). (2014). *Occupational Outlook Handbook: Psychologists.* Retrieved from http://www.bls.gov/ooh/.

U.S. Bureau of Labor Statistics (BLS). (2014). *Occupational Outlook Handbook: School and career counselors.* Retrieved from http://www.bls.gov/ooh/.

U.S. Bureau of Labor Statistics (BLS). (2014). *Occupational Outlook Handbook: Social workers.* Retrieved from http://www.bls.gov/ooh/.

U.S. Census Bureau. (2005). *Statistical abstract of the United States, 2006* (125th ed.). Washington, DC: Government Printing Office.

U.S. Census Bureau. (2010). *2010 Census data: Redistricting data.* Retrieved from http://2010.census.gov/2010census/data.

U.S. Census Bureau. (2010). Race and ethnicity. *American FactFinder.* (http://factfinder.census.gov/serviet/ACSSAFFPeople?).

U. S. Census Bureau. (2012). *The 2012 statistical abstract: The National Data Book.* Washington, DC: Author. Retrieved from http://www.census.gov/compendia/statab/.

U.S. Census Bureau. (2014). *Population projections. National population projections.* Retrieved from https://www.census.gov/population/projections/data/national.

U.S. Census Bureau. (2014). *USA QuickFacts: State and County QuickFacts.* Retrieved from http://quickfacts.census.gov/qfd/states/00000.html.

U.S. Department of Agriculture. (2014). Statistics received under Animal Welfare Act. Reported in *Speaking of Research,* 2014: USDA Statistics for Animals Used in Research in 2012.

U.S. Department of Justice. (2008). *Report: Girls study group, 2008.* Washington, DC: Author.

U.S. Department of Justice. (2010). Arrests. *Crime in the United States 2009.* http://www.fbi.gov/ucr/cius2009/arrests/index.html.

U.S. Department of Justice. (2010). National study of jail suicide: 20 years later. Washington, DC: National Institute of Corrections.

U.S. Department of Justice. (2014). *Crime in the United States 2013.* Retrieved from http://www.fbi.gov/about-us/cjis/ucr/crme-in-the-u.s./2013.

Udesky, L. (2014). Stroke and depression. *Health-Day.* Retrieved from Health-Day website: http://consumer.health-day.com/encyclopedia.

Ulrich, R. S. (1984). View from a window may influence recovery from surgery. *Science, 224,* 420–421.

Ungar, W. J., Mirabelli, C., Cousins, M., & Boydell, K. M. (2006). A qualitative analysis of a dyad approach to health-related quality of life measurement in children with asthma. *Social Science & Medicine, 63*(9), 2354–2366.

Unger, J. B., Schwartz, S. J., Huh, J., Soto, D. W., & Baezconde-Garbanati, L. (2014). Acculturation and perceived discrimination: Predictors of substance use trajectories from adolescence to emerging adulthood among Hispanics. *Addictive Behaviors, 39*(9), 1293–1296.

United Nations. (2013). *World population ageing 2013.* Geneva: UN, Department of Economic and Social Affairs, Population Division.

Urben, S., Baier, V., Mantzouranis, G., Pigois, E., Graap, C., Dutot, F., . . . Holzer, L. (2015). Predictors and moderators of clinical outcomes in adolescents with severe mental disorders after an assertive community treatment. *Child Psychiatry & Human Development.* [Electronic publication.]

Urcuyo, K. R., Boyers, A. E., Carver, C. S., & Antoni, M. H. (2005). Finding benefit in breast cancer: Relations with personality, coping, and concurrent well-being. *Psychology and Health, 20*(2), 175–192.

Uroševic´, S., Collins, P., Muetzel, R., Schissel, A., Lim, K. O., & Luciana, M. (2015). Effects of reward sensitivity and regional brain volumes on substance use initiation in adolescence. *Social Cognitive and Affective Neuroscience, 10*(1), 106–113.

Ursano, R. J., Boydstun, J. A., & Wheatley, R. D. (1981). Psychiatric illness in U.S. Air Force Vietnam prisoners of war: A five-year follow-up. *American Journal of Psychiatry, 138*(3), 310–314.

Ursano, R. J., McCarroll, J. E., & Fullerton, C. S. (2003). Traumatic death in terrorism and disasters: The effects of posttraumatic stress and behavior. In R. J. Ursano, C. S. Fullerton, & A. E. Norwood (Eds.), *Terrorism and disaster: Individual and community mental health interventions* (pp. 308–332). New York: Cambridge University Press.

USGS (U.S. Geological Survey). (2011, April 14). *Earthquakes with 1000 or more deaths since 1900.* Retrieved from http://earthquake/usgs/gov/earthquakes/world/world_deaths.php.

Vahia, V. N., & Vahia, I. V. (2008). Schizophrenia in developing countries. In K. T. Mueser & D.V. Jeste (Eds.), *Clinical handbook of schizophrenia* (pp. 549–555). New York: Guilford Press.

Valbak, K. (2001). Good outcome for bulimic patients in long-term group analysis: A single-group study. *European Eating Disorders Review, 9*(1), 19–32.

Valencia, M., Fresan, A., Juárez, F., Escamilla, R., & Saracco, R. (2013). The beneficial effects of combining pharmacological and psychosocial treatment on remission and functional outcome in outpatients with schizophrenia. *Journal of Psychiatric Research, 47*(12), 1886–1892.

Valenstein, E. S. (1986). *Great and desperate cures.* New York: Basic Books.

Vall, E., & Wade, T. D. (2015). Predictors of treatment outcome in individuals with eating disorders: A systematic review and meta-analysis. *International Journal of Eating Disorders.* [Electronic publication.]

van der Kruijs, S. M., Bodde, N. G., Carrette, E., Lazeron, R. C., Vonck, K. J., Boon, P. M., . . . Aldenkamp, A. P. (2014). Neurophysiological correlates of dissociative symptoms. *Journal of Neurology, Neurosurgery, & Psychiatry, 85*(2), 174–179.

van Deurzen, E. (2012). *Existential counseling and psychotherapy in practice.* Los Angeles, CA: Sage Publications.

van Duijl, M., Nijenhuis, E., Komproe, I. H., Gernaat, H. B. P. E., & de Jong, I. T. (2010). Dissociative symptoms and reported trauma among patients with spirit possession and matched healthy controls in Uganda. *Culture, Medicine and Psychiatry, 34*(2), 380–400.

Van Durme, K., Goossens, L., & Braet, C. (2012). Adolescent aesthetic athletes: A group at risk for eating pathology? *Eating Behaviors, 13*(2), 119–122.

van Geel, M., Vedder, P., & Tanilon, J. (2014). Relationship between peer victimization, cyberbullying, and suicide in children and adolescents: A meta-analysis. *JAMA Pediatrics, 168*(5), 435–442.

Van Orden, K. A., Witte, T. K., Selby, E. A., Bender, T. W., & Joiner, T. E., Jr. (2008). Suicidal behavior in youth. In J. R. Z. Abela & B. L. Hankin (Eds.), *Handbook of depression in children and adolescents.* New York: Guilford Press.

Van Praag, H. M. (2011). Commentary 4A on "Religious and spiritual issues in anxiety and adjustment disorders": A new psychiatric frontier? In J. R. Peteet, F. G. Lu, & W. E. Narrow (Eds.), *Religious and spiritual issues in psychiatric diagnosis: A research agenda for DSM-V* (pp. 97–99). Washington, DC: American Psychiatric Association.

van Son, G. E., van Kocken, D., van Furth, E. F., Donker, G. A., & Hoek, H. W. (2010). Course and outcome of eating disorders in a primary care-based cohort. *International Journal of Eating Disorders, 43*(2), 130–138.

Van Vonderen, K. E., & Kinnally, W. (2012). Media effects on body image: Examining media exposure in the broader context of internal and other social factors. *American Communication Journal, 14*(2), 41–57.

Vaz, S., Parsons, R., Passmore, A. E., Andreou, P., & Falkmer, T. (2013). Internal consistency, test-retest reliability and measurement error of the self report version of the social skills rating system in a sample of Australian adolescents. *PLOS ONE, 8*(9), e73924.

Veale, D., & Bewley, A. (2015). Body Dysmorphic disorder. *BMJ (Clinical Research Ed.), 240,* h2278.

Veiga-Martínez, C., Perez-Alvarez, M., & Garcia-Montes, J. M. (2008). Acceptance and commitment therapy applied to treatment of auditory hallucinations. *Clinical Case Studies, 7,* 118–135.

Vela, R. M., Glod, C. A., Rivinus, T. M., & Johnson, R. (2011). Antidepressant treatment of pediatric depression. In D. A. Ciraulo & R. I. Shader, *Pharmacotherapy for depression* (2nd ed., pp. 355–374). New York: Springer Science + Business Media.

Verdeli, H. (2014). Interpersonal psychotherapy. In D. Wedding & R. J. Corsini (Eds.), *Current psychotherapies* (10th ed., pp. 339–372). Independence, KY: Cengage Publications.

Vetter, H. J. (1969). *Language behavior and psychopathology.* Chicago: Rand McNally.

Via, E., Cardoner, N., Pujol, J., Alonso, P., López-Sola, M., Real, E., . . . Harrison, B. (2014). Amygdala activation and symptom dimensions in obsessive-compulsive disorder. *British Journal of Psychiatry, 204*(1), 61–68.

Vialou, V., Bagot, R. C., Cahill, M. E., Ferguson, D., Robison, A. J., Dietz, D. M., . . . Nestler, E. J. (2014). Prefrontal cortical circuit for depression- and anxiety-related behaviors mediated by cholecystokinin: Role of DFosB. *The Journal of Neuroscience, 34*(11), 3878–3887.

Vickrey, B. G., Samuels, M. A., & Ropper, A. H. (2010). How neurologists think: A cognitive psychology perspective on missed diagnoses. *Annals of Neurology, 67*(4), 425–433.

Victor, S. E., & Klonsky, E. D. (2014). Correlates of suicide attempts among self-injurers: A meta-analysis. *Clinical Psychology Review, 34*(4), 282–297.

Vierck, E., & Silverman, J. M. (2011). Family studies of autism. In E. Hollander, A. Kolevzon, & J.T. Coyle (Eds.), *Textbook of autism spectrum disorders* (pp. 299–312). Arlington, VA: American Psychiatric Publishing, Inc.

Vitaro, F., Hartl, A. C., Brendgen, M., Laursen, B., Dionne, G., & Boivin, M. (2014). Genetic and environmental influences on gambling and substance use in early adolescence. *Behavior Genetics, 44*(4), 347–355.

Vitelli, R. (2013). Can social media spread epidemics? *Psychology Today.* Retrieved from Psychology Today website: http://www.psychologytoday.com/blog/media-spotlight/201309/cann-social-media-spread-epidemics.

Voelker, R. (2010). Memories of Katrina continue to hinder mental health recovery in New Orleans. *Journal of the American Medical Association, 304*(8), 841–843.

Vogt, D. S., Dutra, L., Reardon, A., Zisserson, R., & Miller, M. W. (2011). Assessment of trauma, posttraumatic stress disorder, and related mental health outcomes. In J. I. Ruzek, P. P. Schnurr, J. J. Vasterling, & M. J. Friedman (Eds.), *Caring for veterans with deployment-related stress disorders* (pp. 59–85). Washington, DC: American Psychological Association.

Volavka, J. (2013). Violence in schizophrenia and bipolar disorder. *Psychiatria Danubina, 25*(1), 24–33.

Volfson, E., & Oslin, D. (2011). Addiction. In C. E. Coffey, J. L. Cummings, M. S. George, & D. Weintraub (Eds.), *The American Psychiatric Publishing textbook of geriatric neuropsychiatry.* Arlington, VA: American Psychiatric Publishing, Inc.

Volkert, J., Schulz, H., Härter, M., Wlodarczyk, O., & Andreas, S. (2013). The prevalence of mental disorders in older people in Western countries: A meta-analysis. *Ageing Research Reviews, 12,* 339–353.

Volkow, N. D., Fowler, J. S., & Wang, G. J. (2002). Role of dopamine in drug reinforcement and addiction in humans: Results from imaging studies. *Behavioral Pharmacology, 13,* 355–366.

Volkow, N. D., Fowler, J. S., & Wang, G. J. (2004). The addicted human brain viewed in the light of imaging studies: Brain circuits and treatment strategies. *Neuropharmacology, 47*(Suppl. 1), 3–13.

Volkow, N. D., Fowler, J. S., Wang, G. J., & Swanson, J. M. (2004). Dopamine in drug abuse and addiction: Results from imaging studies and treatment implications. *Molecular Psychiatry, 9*(6), 557–569.

Vos, J., Craig, M., & Cooper, M. (2015). Existential therapies: A meta-analysis of their effects on psychological outcomes. *Journal of Consulting and Clinical Psychology, 83*(1), 115–128.

Waddington, J. L., O'Tuathaigh, C. M. P., & Remington, G. J. (2011). Pharmacology and neuroscience of antipsychotic drugs. In D. R. Weinberg & P. Harrison (Eds.), *Schizophrenia* (pp. 483–514). Hoboken, NJ: Wiley-Blackwell.

Wade, T. D., & Tiggemann, M. (2013). The role of perfectionism in body dissatisfaction. *Journal of Eating Disorders, 1,* 2.

Wade, T. D., & Watson, H. J. (2012). Psychotherapies in eating disorders. In J. Alexander & J. Treasure (Eds.), *A collaborative approach to eating disorders* (pp. 125–135). New York: Taylor & Francis.

Wain, H., Kneebone, I. I., & Cropley, M., (2011). Attributional intervention for depression in two people with multiple sclerosis (MS): Single case design. *Behavioural and Cognitive Psychotherapy, 39*(1), 115–121.

Waisbren, S. E. (2011). Phenylketonuria. In S. Goldstein, & C. R. Reynolds (Eds.), *Handbook of neurodevelopmental and genetic disorders in children* (2nd ed., pp. 398–424) New York: Guilford Press.

Wakefield, A. J., Murch, S. H., Anthony, A., Linnell, J., Casson, D. M., Malik, M., . . . Walker-Smith, J. A. (1998). Retracted: Ileal-lymphoid-nodular hyperplasia, non-specific colitis, and pervasive developmental disorder in children. *The Lancet, 351*(9103), 637–641.

Wakefield, J. C. (2015). DSM-5, psychiatric epidemiology and the false positives problem. *Epidemiology and Psychiatric Sciences, 24*(3), 188–196.

Wakefield, J. C., & Horwitz, A. V. (2010). Normal reactions to adversity or symptoms of disorder? In G. M. Rosen & B. C. Frueh (Eds.), *Clinician's guide to post-traumatic stress disorder* (pp. 33–49). Hoboken, NJ: John Wiley & Sons.

Wallace, G. L., White, S. F., Robustelli, B., Sinclair, S., Hwang, S., Martin, A., & Blair, R. J. (2014). Cortical and subcortical abnormalities in youths with conduct disorder and elevated callous-unemotional traits. *Journal of the American Academy of Child and Adolescent Psychiatry, 53*(4), 456–465.

Waller, G., Gray, E., Hinrichsen, H., Mountford, V., Lawson, R., & Patient, E. (2014). Cognitive-behavioral therapy for bulimia nervosa and atypical bulimic nervosa: Effectiveness in clinical settings. *International Journal of Eating Disorders, 47*(1), 13–17.

Waller, S. (Ed.). (2010). *Serial killers: Being and killing. Philosophy for everyone.* Hoboken, NJ: Wiley-Blackwell.

Walsh, K., Resnick, H. S., Danielson, C. K., McCauley, J. L., Saunders, B. E., & Kilpatrick, D. G. (2014). Patterns of drug and alcohol use associated with lifetime sexual revictimization and current posttraumatic stress disorder among three national samples of adolescent, college, and household-residing women. *Addictive Behaviors, 39*(3), 684–689.

Walters, G. D. (2002). The heritability of alcohol abuse and dependence: A meta-analysis of behavior genetic research. *American Journal of Drug and Alcohol Abuse, 28*(3), 557–584.

Wambeam, R. A., Canen, E. L., Linkenbach, J., & Otto, J. (2014). Youth misperceptions of peer substance use norms: A hidden risk factor in state and community prevention. *Prevention Science, 15*(1), 75–84.

Wang, J., Korczykowski, M., Rao, H., Fan, Y., Pluta, J., Gur, R. C., . . . Detre, J. A. (2007). Gender difference in neural response to psychological stress. *Social Cognitive and Affective Neuroscience, 2*(3), 227–239.

Wang, L., Liu, L., Shi, S., Gao, J., Liu, Y., Li, Y., . . . Kendler, K. S. (2013). Cognitive trio: Relationship with major depression and clinical predictors in Han Chinese women. *Psychological Medicine, 43*(11), 2265–2275.

Wang, M., & Jiang, G-R. (2007). Psychopathological mechanisms and clinical assessment of dissociative identity disorder. *Chinese Journal of Clinical Psychology, 15*(4), 426–429.

Wang, P. S., Berglund, P., Olfson, M., Pincus, A., Wells, K. B., & Kessler, R. C. (2005). Failure and delay in initial treatment contact after first onset of mental disorders in the National Comorbidity Survey Replication. *Archives of General Psychiatry, 62,* 603–613.

Wang, P. S., Lane, M., Olfson, M., Pincus, H. A., Wells, K. B., & Kessler, R. C. (2005). Twelve-month use of mental health services in the United States. *Archives of General Psychiatry, 62,* 629–640.

Wang, S. S. (2007, September 25). Depression care: The business case. *Wall Street Journal Online.* Retrieved from Wall Street Journal Online website: http://blogs.wsj.com/health.

Wang, S. S. (2007, December 4). The graying of shock therapy. *Wall Street Journal Online.* Retrieved from Wall Street Journal Online website: http://online.wsg.com/public/article_print/SB1196737374406312767.html.

Wang, Y., & Gorenstein, C. (2013). Psychometric properties of the Beck Depression Inventory-II: A comprehensive review. *Revista Brasileira De Psiquiatria, 35*(4), 416–431.

Wang, Y., Katzmarzyk, P. T., Horswell, R., Zhao, W., Li, W., Johnson, J., . . . Hu, G. (2014). Racial disparities in cardiovascular risk factor control in an underinsured population with Type 2 diabetes. *Diabetic Medicine, 31*(10), 1230–1236.

Washburn, I. J., Capaldi, D. M., Kim, H. K., & Feingold, A. (2014). Alcohol and marijuana use in early adulthood for at-risk men: Time-varying associations with peer and partner substance use. *Drug and Alcohol Dependence, 140,* 112–117.

Washton, A. M., & Zweben, J. (2008). Treating alcohol and drug problems in psychotherapy practice: Doing what works. New York: Guilford Press.

Watkins, E. R., & Nolen-Hoeksema, S. (2014). A habit-goal framework of depressive rumination. *Journal of Abnormal Psychology, 123*(1), 24–34.

Watson, D. (2012). Objective tests as instruments of psychological theory and research. In H. Cooper, P. M. Camic, D. L. Long, A. T. Panter, D. Rindskopf, & K. J. Sher (Eds.), *APA handbook of research methods in psychology. Vol. 1: Foundations, planning, measures, and psychometrics* (pp. 349–369). Washington, DC: American Psychological Association.

Watson, J. B., & Rayner, R. (1920). Conditioned emotional reaction. *Journal of Experimental Psychology, 3,* 1–14.

Watson, J. C., Goldman, R. N., & Greenberg, L. S. (2011). Humanistic and experiential theories of psychotherapy. In J. C. Norcross, G. R. VandenBos, & D. K. Freedheim (Eds.), *History of psychotherapy: Continuity and change* (2nd ed., pp. 141–172). Washington, DC: American Psychological Association.

Watson, P. J., & Shalev, A. Y. (2005). Assessment and treatment of adult acute responses to traumatic stress following mass traumatic events. *CNS Spectrums, 10*(2), 123–131.

Watson, T. S., Watson, T. S., & Ret, J. (2008). Learning, motor, and communication disorders. In D. Reitman (Ed.), *Handbook of psychological assessment, case conceptualization, and treatment, Vol. 2: Children and adolescents.* Hoboken, NJ: John Wiley & Sons.

Watt, T. T. (2002). Marital and cohabiting relationships of adult children of alcoholics: Evidence from the National Survey of Family and Households. *Journal of Family Issues, 23*(2), 246–265.

Waugh, J. L. (2013). Acute dyskinetic reaction in a healthy toddler following methylphenidate ingestion. *Pediatric Neurology, 49*(1), 58–60.

Weaver, M. F., & Schnoll, S. H. (2008). Hallucinogens and club drugs. In H. D. Kleber & M. Galanter (Eds.), *The American Psychiatric Publishing textbook of substance abuse treatment* (4th ed., pp. 191–200). Arlington, VA: American Psychiatric Publishing.

Weber, T., & Ornstein, C. (2013). Half of drug company payoffs go to one "specialty"—psychiatry. *ProPublica.* Retrieved from ProPublica website: http://www.psychsearch.net.

Webster-Stratton, C., & Reid, M. J. (2010). The Incredible Years parents, teachers, and children training series: A multifaceted treatment approach for young children with conduct disorders. In J. R. Weisz & A. E. Kazdin (Eds.), *Evidence-based psychotherapies for children and adolescents* (2nd ed., pp. 194–210). New York: Guilford Press.

Wechsler, H., Davenport, A., Dowdall, G., Moeykens, B., & Castillo, S. (1994). Health and behavioral consequences of binge drinking in college. *Journal of the American Medical Association, 272*(21), 1672–1677.

Wechsler, H., Lee, J. E., Kuo, M., Seibring, M., Nelson, T. F., & Lee, H. (2002). Trends in alcohol use, related problems and experience of prevention efforts among US college students 1993 to 2001: Results from the 2001 Harvard School of Public Health College Alcohol Study. *Journal of American College Health, 50,* 203–217.

Wechsler, H., & Nelson, T. F. (2008). What we have learned from the Harvard School of Public Health College Alcohol Study: Focusing attention on college student alcohol consumption and the environmental conditions that promote it. *Journal of Studies on Alcohol and Drugs, 69,* 481–490.

Wechsler, H., Seibring, M., Liu, I. C., & Ahl, M. (2004). Colleges respond to student binge drinking: Reducing student demand or limiting access. *Journal of American College Health, 52*(4), 159–168.

Weck, F., Neng, J. B., Richtberg, S., Jakob, M., & Stangier, U. (2015). Cognitive therapy versus exposure therapy for hypochondriasis (health anxiety): A randomized controlled trial. *Journal of Consulting and Clinical Psychology, 83*(4), 665–676.

Wedding, D., & Corsini, R. J. (2014). *Current psychotherapies* (10th ed.). Independence, KY: Cengage Publishing.

Weeks, D., & James, J. (1995). *Eccentrics: A study of sanity and strangeness.* New York: Villard.

Wei, Y., Szumilas, M., & Kutcheer, S. (2010). Effectiveness on mental health of psychological debriefing for crisis intervention in schools. *Educational Psychology Review, 22*(3), 339–347.

Weichman, J. (2014, February 4). Cited in L. Kaufman, In texting era, crisis hotlines put help at youths' fingertips. *New York Times.*

Weinberger, J. (2014, August 11). Common factors are not so common and specific factors are not so specified: Toward an inclusive integration of psychotherapy research. *Psychotherapy (Chicago), 51*(4), 514–518.

Weiner, R. (2014, September 13). Colleges ramp up efforts to prevent sex assaults. *USA Today.* Retrieved from USA Today website: http://www.usatoday.com/story/news/nation/2014/09/13/.

Weinshenker, N. (2014). *Teenagers and body image: What's typical and what's not?* New York: NYU Child Study Center. Retrieved from NYU website: http://www.education.com.

Weinstein, Y., & Shanks, D. R. (2010). Rapid induction of false memory for pictures. *Memory, 18*(5), 533–542.

Weishaar, M. E., & Beck, A. T. (2006). Cognitive theory of personality and personality disorders. In S. Strack (Ed.), *Differentiating normal and abnormal personality* (2nd ed., pp. 113–135). New York: Springer Publishing Co.

Weiss, D. E. (1991). *The great divide.* New York: Poseidon Press/Simon & Schuster.

Weiss, F. (2011). Alcohol self-administration. In M. C. Olmstead (Ed.), *Animal models of drug addiction. Springer protocols: Neuromethods* (pp. 133–165). Totowa, NJ: Humana Press.

Weissman, M. M., Livingston, B. M., Leaf, P. J., Florio, L. P., & Holzer, C., III. (1991). Affective disorders. In L. N. Robins & D. A. Regier (Eds.), *Psychiatric disorders in America: The Epidemiologic Catchment Area Study.* New York: Free Press.

Weissman, S. W. (2000). America's psychiatric work force. *Psychiatric Times, 17*(11).

Wells, A. (2005). The metacognitive model of GAD: Assessment of meta-worry and relationship with DSM-IV generalized anxiety disorder. *Cognitive Therapy and Research, 29*(1), 107–121.

Wells, A. (2010). Metacognitive therapy: Application to generalized anxiety disorder. In D. Sookman & R. L. Leahy (Eds.), *Treatment resistant anxiety disorders: Resolving impasses to symptom remission* (pp. 1–29). New York: Routledge/Taylor & Francis Group.

Wells, A. (2011). Metacognitive therapy. In J. D. Herbert & E. M. Forman (Eds.), *Acceptance and mindfulness in cognitive behavior therapy: Understanding and applying the new therapies* (pp. 83–108). Hoboken, NJ: John Wiley & Sons Inc.

Wells, A. (2014). *Cognitive therapy of anxiety disorders: A practical guide* (2nd ed.). Hoboken, NJ: Wiley-Blackwell.

Wells, G. L. (2008). Field experiments on eyewitness identification: Towards a better understanding of pitfalls and prospects. *Law and Human Behavior, 32*(1), 6–10.

Wells, G. L., Steblay, N. K., & Dysart, J. E. (2011). *A test of the simultaneous vs. sequential lineup methods: An initial report of the AJS National Eyewitness Identification Field Studies.* Des Moines, Iowa: American Judicature Society.

Wells, G. L., Steblay, N. K., & Dysart, J. E. (2015). Double-blind photo lineups using actual eyewitnesses: An experimental test of a sequential versus simultaneous lineup procedure. *Law and Human Behavior, 39*(1), 1–14.

Welsh, C. J., & Liberto, J. (2001). The use of medication for relapse prevention in substance dependence disorders. *Journal of Psychiatric Practice, 7*(1), 15–31.

Werth, J. L., Jr. (2001). Policy and psychosocial considerations associated with non-physician assisted suicide: A commentary on Ogden. *International Journal of Eating Disorders, 25*(5), 403–411.

Werth, J. L., Jr. (2004). The relationships among clinical depression, suicide, and other actions that may hasten death. *Behavioral Sciences & the Law, 22*(5), 627–649.

Wertheimer, A. (2001). *A special scar: The experiences of people bereaved by suicide* (2nd ed.). East Sussex, England: Brunner-Routledge.

Wesner, A. C., Gomes, J. B., Detzel, T., Guimarães, L. P., & Heidt, E. (2015) Booster sessions after cognitive-behavioural group therapy for panic disorder: Impact on resilience, coping, and quality of life. *Behavioural and Cognitive Psychotherapy, 43*(5), 513 525.

Westen, D., Betan, E., & Defife, J. A. (2011). Identity disturbance in adolescence: Associations with borderline personality disorder. *Development and Psychopathology, 23*(1), 305–313.

Westermeyer, J. (1993). Substance use disorders among young minority refugees: Common themes in a clinical sample. *NIDA Research Monograph 130,* 308–320.

Westermeyer, J. (2001). Alcoholism and comorbid psychiatric disorders among American Indians. *American Indian and Alaska Native Mental Health Research, 10,* 27–51.

Westermeyer, J. (2004). Acculturation: Advances in theory, measurement, and applied research. *Journal of Nervous and Mental Disease, 192*(5), 391–392.

Westheimer, R. K., & Lopater, S. (2005). *Human sexuality: A psychosocial perspective* (2nd ed.). Baltimore, MD: Lippincott Williams & Wilkins.

Weyandt, L. L., Oster, D. R., Marraccini, M. E, Gundmundsdottir, B. G., Munro, B. A., Zavras, B. M., & Kuhar, B. (2014). Pharmacological interventions for adolescents and adults with ADHD: Stimulant and nonstimulant medications and misuse of prescription stimulants. *Psychology Research and Behavior Management, 7,* 223–249.

Weyandt, L. L., Verdi, G., & Swentosky, A. (2011). Oppositional, conduct, and aggressive disorders. In S. Goldstein, & C. R. Reynolds (Eds.), *Handbook of neurodevelopmental and genetic disorders in children* (2nd ed., pp. 151–170) New York: Guilford Press.

Wheeler, B. W., Gunnell, D., Metcalfe, C., Stephens, P., & Martin, R. M. (2008). The population impact on incidence of suicide and non-fatal self harm of regulatory action against the use of selective serotonin reuptake inhibitors in under 18s in the United Kingdom: Ecological study. *British Medical Journal, 336*(7643), 542.

Whiffen, V. E., & Demidenko, N. (2006). Mood disturbance across the life span. In J. Worell & C. D. Goodheart (Eds.), *Handbook of girls' and women's psychological health* (pp. 51–59). New York: Oxford University Press.

Whitaker, R. (2002). *Mad in America: Bad science, bad medicine, and the enduring mistreatment of the mentally ill.* Cambridge, MA: Perseus.

Whitaker, R. (2010). *Anatomy of an epidemic: Magic bullets, psychiatric drugs, and the astonishing rise of mental illness in America.* Norwalk, CT: Crown House Publishing Limited.

White, M. P., Alcock, I., Wheeler, B. W., & Depledge, M. H. (2013). Would you be happier living in a greener urban area? A fixed-effects analysis of panel data. *Psychological Science, 24*(6), 920–928.

White, P. (2009, July 31). Rorschach and Wikipedia: The battle of the inkblots. *The Globe and Mail.*

White House Task Force. (2014 April). *Not alone: The first report of the White House Task Force to protect students from sexual assault.* Washington, DC: The White House.

Whitney, S. D., Renner, L. M., Pate, C. M., & Jacobs, K. A. (2011). Principals' perceptions of benefits and barriers to school-based suicide prevention programs. *Children and Youth Services Review, 33*(6), 869–877.

Whitten, L. (2010). Marijuana linked with testicular cancer. *NIDA Notes, 23*(3).

Whitton, A., Henry, J., & Grisham, J. (2014). Moral rigidity in obsessive compulsive disorder: Do abnormalities in inhibitory control, cognitive flexibility and disgust play a role? *Journal of Behavior Therapy and Experimental Psychiatry, 45*(1), 152–159.

WHO (World Health Organization). (2011). *Suicide rates per 100,000 by country, year and sex* (Table). Retrieved from http://www.who.int/mental_health/prevention/suicide_rates/en/.

WHO (World Health Organization). (2012). *10 facts on ageing and the life course.* Retrieved from http://www.who.int/features/factfiles/.

WHO (World Health Organization). (2012). *About ageing and life course.* Retrieved from http://www.who.int/ageing/about/ageing_life_course/en/.

WHO (World Health Organization). (2012). *Depression.* Fact Sheet no. 369. Retrieved from http://www.who.int/mediacentre/factsheets/fs369/en/.

WHO (World Health Organization). (2013). *Asthma.* Fact sheet 307. Retrieved from http://www.who.int/mediacentre/factsheets/fs307/en/.

WHO (World Health Organization). (2014). 7. *Addiction to nicotine.* Retrieved from http:www.who.int/tobacco/publications/gender/women_tob_epidemic/en/.

WHO (World Health Organization). (2014). *Gender and women's mental health.* Retrieved from http://www.who.int/mental–health/prevention/genderwomen/en/.

WHO (World Health Organization). (2014). *Tobacco.* (Fact Sheet 339). Retrieved from http:www.who.int/mediacentre/factsheets/fs339/en/.

Wiebking, C., & Northoff, G. (2013). Neuroimaging in pedophilia. *Current Psychiatry Reports, 15*(4), 351.

Wiederman, M. W. (2001). "Don't look now": The role of self-focus in sexual dysfunction. *Family Journal: Counseling and Therapy for Couples and Families, 9*(2), 210–214.

Wierckx, K., Van Caenegem, E., Schreiner, T., Haraldsen, I., Fisher, A., Toye, K., . . . T'Sjoen, G. (2014). Cross-sex hormone therapy in trans persons is safe and effective at short-time follow-up: Results from the European network for the investigation of gender incongruence. *Journal of Sexual Medicine, 11*(8), 1999–2011.

Wiklund, G., Ruchkin, V. V., Koposov, R. A., & Af Klinteberg, B. (2014). Pro-bullying attitudes among incarcerated juvenile delinquents: Antisocial behavior, psychopathic tendencies and violent crime. *International Journal of Law and Psychiatry, 37*(3), 281–288.

Wilens, T. E., Yule, A., Martelon, M., Zulauf, C., & Faraone, S. V. (2014). Parental history of substance use disorders (SUD) and SUD in offspring: A controlled family study of bipolar disorder. *American Journal on Addictions, 23*(5), 440–446.

Wiley-Exley, E. (2007). Evaluations of community mental health care in low- and middle-income countries: A 10-year review of the literature. *Social Science & Medicine, 64*(6), 1231–1241.

Wilkes, T. C. R., & Nixon, M. K. (2015). Pharmacological treatment of children and adolescent disruptive behaviour disorders: Between the Scylla and Charybdis, what do the data say? *Canadian Journal of Psychiatry, 60*(2), 39–41.

Wilkinson, P., & Goodyer, I. (2011). Nonsuicidal self-injury. *European Child & Adolescent Psychiatry, 20*(2), 103–108.

Wilkinson, P., & Soares, I. (2014, February 18). Neknominate: "Lethal" drinking game sweeps social media. *CNN online.*

Wilkinson, T. (2011, January 12). Haiti still mired in post-quake problems. *Los Angeles Times.*

Williams, A. D., Grisham, J. R., Erskine, A., & Cassedy, E. (2012). Deficits in emotion regulation associated with pathological gambling. *British Journal of Clinical Psychology, 51*(2), 223–238.

Williams, C. L., & Butcher, J. N. (2011). *A beginner's guide to the MMPI-A.* Washington, DC: American Psychological Association.

Williams, P. (2010). Psychotherapeutic treatment of Cluster A personality disorders. In J. F. Clarkin, P. Fonagy, & G. O. Gabbard (Eds.), *Psychodynamic psychotherapy for personality disorders: A clinical handbook.* Arlington, VA: American Psychiatric Publishing, Inc.

Williams, P. G., Smith, T. W., Gunn, H. E., & Uchino, B. N. (2011). Personality and stress: Individual differences in exposure, reactivity, recovery, and restoration. In R. J. Contrada & A. Baum (Eds.), *The handbook of stress science: Biology, psychology, and health* (pp. 231–245). New York: Springer Publishing.

Williams, S., & Reid, M. (2010). Understanding the experience of ambivalence in anorexia nervosa: The maintainer's perspective. *Psychology & Health, 25*(5), 551–567.

Williams, T. M. (2008). *Black pain: It just looks like we're not hurting.* New York: Scribner.

Williams, W., Kunik, M. E., Springer, J., & Graham, D. P. (2013). Can personality traits predict the future development of heart disease in hospitalized psychiatric veterans? *Journal of Psychiatric Practice, 19*(6), 477–489.

Willick, M. S. (2001). Psychoanalysis and schizophrenia: A cautionary tale. *Journal of the American Psychoanalytical Association, 49*(1), 27–56.

Wills, T. A., & Ainette, M. G. (2010). Temperament, self-control, and adolescent substance use: A two-factor model of etiological processes. In L. Scheier (Ed.), *Handbook of drug use etiology: Theory, methods, and empirical findings* (pp. 127–146). Washington, DC: American Psychological Association.

Wilson, G. T. (2005). Psychological treatment of eating disorders. *Annual Review of Clinical Psychology, 1*(1), 439–465.

Wilson, G. T. (2010). Cognitive behavioral therapy for eating disorders. In W. S. Agras (Ed.), *The Oxford handbook of eating disorders. Oxford library of psychology* (pp. 331–347). New York: Oxford University Press.

Wilson, G. T. (2010). What treatment research is needed for bulimia nervosa? In C. M. Grilo & J. E.

Mitchell (Eds.), *The treatment of eating disorders: A clinical handbook* (pp. 544–553). New York: Guilford Press.

Wilson, K. R., Jordan, J. A., Kras, A. M., Tavkar, P., Bruhn, S., Asawa, L. E., . . . Trask, E. (2010). Adolescent measures: practitioner's guide to empirically based measure of social skills. In D. W. Nangle, D. J. Hansen, C. A. Erdley, & P. J. Norton (Eds.), *Practitioner's guide to empirically based measures of social skills* (pp. 327–381). New York: Springer Publishing.

Wilson, R. S., Scherr, P. A., Schneider, J. A., Tang, Y., & Bennett, D. A. (2007). Relation of cognitive activity to risk of developing Alzheimer disease. *Neurology, 69*(20), 1911–1920.

Wilson, R. S., Segawa, E., Boyle, P. A., & Bennett, D. A. (2012). Influence of late-life cognitive activity on cognitive health. *Neurology, 78*(15), 1123–1129.

Wincze, J. P., Bach, A. K., & Barlow, D. H. (2008). Sexual dysfunction. In D. H. Barlow (Ed.), *Clinical handbook of psychological disorders: A step-by-step treatment manual* (4th ed.). New York: Guilford Press.

Winick, B. J. (2008). A therapeutic jurisprudence approach to dealing with coercion in the mental health system. *Psychiatric and Psychological Law, 15*(1), 25–39.

Winslade, W. J., & Ross, J. (1983). *The insanity plea.* New York: Scribner's.

Winstock, A. R., Lintzeris, N., & Lea, T. (2011). "Should I stay or should I go?" Coming off methadone and buprenorphine treatment. *International Journal of Drug Policy, 22*(1), 77–81.

Winter, E. C., & Bienvenu, O. J. (2011). Temperament and anxiety disorders. In D. McKay & E. A. Storch (Eds.), *Handbook of child and adolescent anxiety disorders* (pp. 203–212). New York: Springer Science & Business Media.

Wise, J. (2014). Community based treatment for schizophrenia is effective in low income countries. *British Medical Journal, 348,* g1984.

Wise, R. A., Sartori, G., Magnussen, S., & Safer, M. A. (2014). An examination of the causes and solutions to eyewitness error. *Frontiers in Psychiatry, 5,* 102.

Wiste, A., Robinson, E. B., Milaneschi, Y., Meier, S., Ripke, S., Clements, C. C., . . . Perlis, R. H. (2014). Bipolar polygenic loading and bipolar spectrum features in major depressive disorder. *Bipolar Disorders, 16*(6), 608–616.

Witherow, M. P., Chandraiah, S., Seals, S. R., & Bugan, A. (2015). Relational intimacy and sexual frequency: A correlation or a cause? A clinical study of heterosexual married women. *Journal of Sex & Marital Therapy, 1-10.* [Electronic publication.]

Witkiewitz, K. A., & Marlatt, G. A. (2004). Relapse prevention for alcohol and drug problems: That was zen, this is tao. *American Psychologist, 59*(4), 224–235.

Witkiewitz, K. A., & Marlatt, G. A. (Eds.). (2007). *Therapist's guide to evidence-based relapse prevention.* San Diego, CA: Elsevier.

Wittayanukorn, S., Qian, J., & Hansen, R. A. (2014). Prevalence of depressive symptoms and predictors of treatment among U.S. adults from 2005 to 2010. *General Hospital Psychiatry, 36*(3), 330–336.

Witthöft, M., & Hiller, W. (2010). Psychological approaches to origins and treatments of somatoform disorders. *Annual Review of Clinical Psychology, 6,* 257–283.

Wohltmann, J. (2013). *Should grandma join Facebook?* Presentation at International Neuropsychological Society Annual Meeting. Hawaii.

Wolberg, L. R. (1967). *The technique of psychotherapy.* New York: Grune & Stratton.

Wolberg, L. R. (2005). *The technique of psychotherapy.* Lanham, MD: Jason Aronson.

Wolf, M. R., & Nochajski, T. H. (2013). Child sexual abuse survivors with dissociative amnesia: What's the difference? *Journal of Child Sexual Abuse, 22*(4), 462–480.

Wolff, S. (1991). Schizoid personality in childhood and adult life I: The vagaries of diagnostic labeling. *British Journal of Psychiatry, 159,* 615–620.

Wolff, S. (2000). Schizoid personality in childhood and Asperger syndrome. In S. S. Sparrow, A. Klin, & F. R. Volkmar (Eds.), *Asperger syndrome* (pp. 278–305). New York: Guilford Press.

Wolitzky, D. L. (2011). Psychoanalytic theories of psychotherapy. In J. C. Norcross, G. R. VandenBos, & D. K. Freedheim (Eds.), *History of psychotherapy: Continuity and change* (2nd ed., pp. 65–100). Washington, DC: American Psychological Association.

Wolpe, J. (1958). *Psychotherapy by reciprocal inhibition.* Stanford, CA: Stanford University Press.

Wolpe, J. (1969). *The practice of behavior therapy.* Oxford, England: Pergamon Press.

Wolpe, J. (1987). The promotion of scientific psychotherapy: A long voyage. In J. K. Zeig (Ed.), *The evolution of psychotherapy.* New York: Brunner/Mazel.

Wolpe, J. (1990). *The practice of behavior therapy* (4th ed.). Elmsford, NY: Pergamon Press.

Wolpe, J. (1995). Reciprocal inhibition: Major agent of behavior change. In W. T. O'Donohue & L. Krasner (Eds.), *Theories of behavior therapy: Exploring behavior change.* Washington, DC: American Psychological Association.

Wolpe, J. (1997). From psychoanalytic to behavioral methods in anxiety disorders: A continuing evolution. In J. K. Zeig (Ed.), *The evolution of psychotherapy: The third conference.* New York: Brunner/Mazel.

Wolrich, M. K. (2011). Body dysmorphic disorder and its significance to social work. *Clinical Social Work Journal, 39*(1), 101–110.

Wolters, F. J. (2013). [Harvey and his theory of circulation]. *Nederlands Tijdschrift Voor Geneeskunde, 157*(48), A6715.

Wonderlich, S. A., Peterson, C. B., Crosby, R. D., Smith, T. L., Klein, M. H., Mitchell, J. E., & Crow, S. J. (2014). A randomized controlled comparison of integrative cognitive-affective therapy (ICAT) and enhanced cognitive-behavioral therapy (CBT-E) for bulimia nervosa. *Psychological Medicine, 44*(3), 543–553.

Wong, J. P. S., Stewart, S. M., Claassen, C., Lee, P. W. H., Rao, U., & Lam, T. H. (2008). Repeat suicide attempts in Hong Kong community adolescents. *Social Science & Medicine, 66*(2), 232–241.

Wong, M. M., Brower, K. J., & Zucker, R. A. (2011). Sleep problems, suicidal ideation, and self-harm behaviors in adolescence. *Journal of Psychiatric Research, 45*(4), 505–511.

Wong, Y., & Huang, Y. (2000). Obesity concerns, weight satisfaction and characteristics of female dieters: A study on female Taiwanese college students. *Journal of American College Nutrition, 18*(2), 194–199.

Woodside, D. B., Bulik, C. M., Halmi, K. A., Fichter, M. M., Kaplan, A., Berrettini, W. H., . . . Kaye, W. H. (2002). Personality, perfectionism, and attitudes towards eating in parents of individuals with eating disorders. *International Journal of Eating Disorders, 31*(3), 290–299.

Wooldridge, T., Mok, C., & Chiu, S. (2014). Content analysis of male participation in pro-eating disorder web sites. *Eating Disorders, 22*(2), 97–110.

Worthen, M., Rathod, S. D., Cohen, G., Sampson, L., Ursano, R., Gifford, R., . . . Ahern, J. (2014). Anger problems and post-traumatic stress disorder in male and female National Guard and Reserve Service members. *Journal of Psychiatric Research, 5552–5558.*

Wortman, C. M., Wolff, K., & Bonanno, G. A. (2004). Loss of an intimate partner through death. In D. J. Mashek & A. Aron (Eds.), *Handbook of closeness and intimacy* (pp. 305–320). Mahwah, NJ: Lawrence Erlbaum.

Wright, J. J., & O'Connor, K. M. (2015). Female sexual dysfunction. *The Medical Clinics of North America, 99*(3), 607–628.

Wright, L. W., Jr., & Hatcher, A. P. (2006). Treatment of sex offenders. In R. D. McAnulty & M. M. Burnette (Eds.), *Sex and sexuality, Vol. 3: Sexual deviation and sexual offenses.* Westport, CT: Praeger Publishers.

Wright, L. W., Jr., Hatcher, A. P., & Willerick, M. S. (2006). Violent sex crimes. In R. D. McAnulty & M. M. Burnette (Eds.), *Sex and sexuality, Vol. 3: Sexual deviation and sexual offenses.* Westport, CT: Praeger Publishers.

Wright, S. (2010). Depathologizing consensual sexual sadism, sexual masochism, transvestic fetishism, and fetishism. *Archives of Sexual Behavior, 39*(6), 1229–1230.

Writer, B. W., Meyer, E. G., & Schillerstrom, J. E. (2014). Prazosin for military combat-related PTSD nightmares: A critical review. *Journal of Neuropsychiatry and Clinical Neurosciences, 26*(1), 24–33.

Wroble, M. C., & Baum, A. (2002). Toxic waste spills and nuclear accidents. In A. M. La Greca, W. K. Silverman, E. M. Vernberg, & M. C. Roberts (Eds.), *Helping children cope with disasters and terrorism* (pp. 207–221). Washington, DC: American Psychological Association.

Wu, G., & Shi, J. (2005). The problem of AIM and countermeasure for improvement in interviews. *Psychological Science (China), 28*(4), 952–955.

Wurst, F. M., Kunz, I., Skipper, G., Wolfersdorf, M., Beine, K. H., & Thon, N. (2011). The therapist's reaction to a patient's suicide: Results of a survey and implications for health care professionals' well-being. *Crisis: Journal of Crisis Intervention and Suicide Prevention, 32*(2), 99–105.

Wyatt, G. W., & Parham, W. D. (2007). The inclusion of culturally sensitive course materials in graduate school and training programs. *Psychotherapy: Theory, Research, Practice, Training, 22*(2, Suppl.) Sum 1985, 461–468.

Wymbs, B. T., McCarthy, C. A., Mason, W. A., King, K. M., Baer, J. S., Vander Stoep, A., & McCauley, E. (2014). Early adolescent substance use as a risk factor for developing conduct disorder and depression symptoms. *Journal of Studies on Alcohol and Drugs, 75*(2), 279–289.

Xu, H., Finkelstein, D. I., & Adlard, P. A. (2014). Interactions of metals and Apolipoprotein E in Alzheimer's disease. *Frontiers in Aging Neuroscience, 6,* 121.

Yaghoubi-Doust, M. (2013). Reviewing the association between the history of parental substance abuse and the rate of child abuse. *Addiction & Health, 5*(3-4), 126–133.

Yakushev, I. B., & Sidorov, P. I. (2013). [Philippe Pinel and the psychiatry of late XVII—early XIX centuries]. *Probl Sotsialnoi Gig Zdravookhranenniiai Istor Med., (1),* 57–59.

Yalom, I. D. (2014). Existential psychotherapy. In D. Wedding & R. J. Corsini (Eds.), *Current psychotherapies* (10th ed., pp. 299–338). Independence, KY: Cengage Publications.

Yap, M. H., Reavley, N., Mackinnon, A. J., & Jorm, A. F. (2013). Psychiatric labels and other influences on young people's stigmatizing attitudes: Findings from an Australian national survey. *Journal of Affective Disorders, 148*(2-3), 299–309.

Yeates, K. O., Ris, M. D., Taylor, H. G., & Pennington, B. F. (Eds.). (2010). *Pediatric neuropsychology: Research, theory, and practice* (2nd ed.) New York: Guilford Press.

Yehuda, R., & Bierer, L. M. (2007). Transgenerational transmission of cortisol and PTSD risk. *Progress in Brain Research, 167*, 121–135.

Yehuda, R., Flory, J. D., Bierer, L. M., Henn-Haase, C., Lehrner, A., Desarnaud, F., . . . Meaney, M. J. (2015). Lower methylation of glucocorticoid receptor gene promoter 1F in peripheral blood of veterans with posttraumatic stress disorder. *Biological Psychiatry, 77*(4), 356–364.

Yehuda, R., Golier, J. A., Bierer, L. M., Mikhno, A., Pratchett, L. C., Burton, C. L., . . . Mann, J. J. (2010). Hydrocortisone responsiveness in Gulf War veterans with PTSD: Effects on ACTH, declarative memory hippocampal [18F] FDG uptake on PET. *Psychiatry Research: Neuroimaging, 184*(2), 117–127.

Yewchuk, C. (1999). Savant syndrome: Intuitive excellence amidst general deficit. *Developmental Disabilities Bulletin, 27*(1), 58–76.

Yin, R. K. (2013). *Case study research: Design and methods (Applied social research methods).* London: Sage.

Yin, S. (2002, May 1). Coming up short. *American Demographics.*

Yontef, G., & Jacobs, L. (2014). Gestalt therapy. In D. Wedding & R. J. Corsini (Eds.), *Current psychotherapies* (10th cd., pp. 299–338). Independence, KY: Cengage Publications.

Yoo, Y., Cho, O., & Cha, K. (2014). Associations between overuse of the internet and mental health in adolescents. *Nursing & Health Sciences, 16*(2), 193–200.

Yoon, H-K., Kim, Y-K., Lee, H-J., Kwon, D-Y. & Kim, L. (2012). Role of cytokines in atypical depression. *Nordic Journal of Psychiatry, 66*(3), 183–188.

Yoon, J. H., Fintzy, R., & Dodril, C. L. (2012). Behavioral interventions. In T. R. Kosten, T. F. Newton, R. De La Garza II, & C. N. Haile (Eds.), *Cocaine and methamphetamine dependence: Advances in treatment* (pp. 105–142). Arlington, VA: American Psychiatric Publishing.

Yoshida, K., Bies, R. R., Suzuki, T., Remington, G., Pollock, B. G., Mizuno, Y., . . . Uchida, H. (2014). Tardive dyskinesia in relation to estimated dopamine D2 receptor occupancy in patients with schizophrenia: Analysis of the CATIE data. *Schizophrenia Research, 153*(1-3), 184–188.

You, S., Van Orden, K. A., & Conner, J. R. (2011). Social connections and suicidal thoughts and behavior. *Psychology of Addictive Behaviors, 25*(1), 180–184.

YouGov. (2014). Truth in advertising: 50% don't trust what they see, read, and hear. *YouGov.* Retrieved from YouGov website: http://research.yougov.com/news/2014/04/08/truth-advertising-50-dont-trust-what-they-see-read.

Young, C., & Skorga, P. (2011). Aspirin with or without an anti-emetic for migraine headaches in adults. *International Journal of Evidence-Based Healthcare, 9*(1), 74–75.

Young, J. E., Rygh, J. L., Weinberger, A. D., & Beck, A. T. (2014). Cognitive therapy for depression. In D. H. Barlow, *Clinical handbook of psychological disorders* (5th ed., Ch. 7). New York: Guilford Press.

Young, K. S. (2011). CBT-IA: The first treatment model for internet addiction. *Journal of Cognitive Psychotherapy, 25*(4), 304–312.

Young, K. S., & de Abreu, C. N. (Eds.) (2011). *Internet addiction: A handbook and guide to evaluation and treatment.* Hoboken, NJ: John Wiley & Sons.

Young, L., & Kemper, K. J. (2013). Integrative care for pediatric patients with pain. *Journal of Alternative and Complementary Medicine, 19*(7), 627–632.

Young, S. L., Taylor, M., & Lawrie, S. M. (2015). "First do no harm." A systematic review of the prevalence and management of antipsychotic adverse effects. *Journal of Psychopharmacology* (Oxford, England), *29*(4), 353–362.

Ystrom, E., Reichborn-Kjennerud, T., Neale, M. C., & Kendler, K. S. (2014). Genetic and environmental risk factors for illicit substance use and use disorders: Joint analysis of self and co-twin ratings. *Behavior Genetics, 44*(1), 1–13.

Yu, S., Zhu, L., Shen, Q., Bai, X., & Di, X. (2015). Recent advances in methamphetamine neurotoxicity mechanisms and its molecular pathophysiology. *Behavioural Neurology, 2015*, 103969.

Yu, Y., Vasselli, J. R., Zhang, Y., Mechanick, J. I., Korner, J., & Peterli, R. (2015). Metabolic vs. hedonic obesity: A conceptual distinction and its clinical implications. *Obesity Reviews, 16*(3), 234–247.

Yun, R. J., Stern, B. L., Lenzenweger, M. F., & Tiersky, L. A. (2013). Refining personality disorder subtypes and classification using finite mixture modeling. *Personality Disorders, 4*(2), 121–128.

Yusko, D. (2008). At home, but locked in war. Retrieved from *Times-Union* (Albany) Online.

Zakzanis, K. K., Campbell, Z., & Jovanovski, D. (2007). The neuropsychology of ecstasy (MDMA) use: A quantitative review. *Human Psychopharmacology: Clinical and Experimental, 22*(7), 427–435.

Zanarini, M. C., Horwood, J., Wolke, D., Waylen, A., Fitzmaurice, G., & Grant, B. F. (2011). Prevalence of DSM-IV borderline personality disorder in two community samples: 6,330 English 11-year-olds and 34,653 American adults. *Journal of Personality Disorders, 25*(5), 607–619.

Zannas, A. (2014, October 18). Why depression and aging are linked to increased disease risk. *European College of Neuropsychopharmacology.*

Zerbe, K. J. (2008). *Integrated treatment of eating disorders beyond the body betrayed.* New York: W. W. Norton.

Zerbe, K. J. (2010). Psycodynamic therapy for eating disorders. In C. M. Grilo & J. E. Mitchell (Eds.), *The treatment of eating disorders: A clinical handbook* (pp. 339–358). New York: Guilford Press.

Zerwas, S., Lund, B C., Von Holle, A., Thornton, L. M., Berrettini, W. H., Brandt, H., . . . Bulik. C. M. (2013). Factors associated with recovery from anorexia nervosa. *Journal of Psychiatric Research, 47*(7), 972–979.

Zeschel, E., Bingmann, T., Bechdolf, A., Krüger-Oezguerdal, S., Correll, C. U., Leopold, K., . . . Juckel, G. (2015). Temperament and prodromal symptoms prior to first manic/hypomanic episodes: Results from a pilot study. *Journal of Affective Disorders, 173*, 339–344.

Zhao, L. N., Lu, L., Chew, L. Y., & Mu, Y. (2014). Alzheimer's disease: A panorama glimpse. *International Journal of Molecular Sciences, 15*, 12631–12650.

Zheng, Y., Cleveland, H. H., Molenaar, P. M., & Harris, K. S. (2015). An alternative framework to investigating and understanding intraindividual processes in substance abuse recovery: An idiographic approach and demonstration. *Evaluation Review, 39*(2), 229–254.

Zhou, J. N., Hofman, M. A., Gooren, J. J. G., & Swaab, D. F. (1995). A sex difference in the human brain and its relation to transsexuality. *Nature, 378*, 68–70.

Zhou, J. N., Hofman, M. A., Gooren, L. J. G., & Swaab, D. F. (1997). A sex difference in the human brain and its relation to transsexuality. *International Journal of Transgenderism, 1*(1). Retrieved from http://www.symposion.com/ijt/ijtc0106.htm.

Zhou, X., Min, S., Sun, J., Kim, S. J., Ahn, J., Peng, Y., . . . Ryder, A. G. (2015). Extending a structural model of somatization to South Koreans: Culture values, somatization tendency, and the presentation of depressive symptoms. *Journal of Affective Disorders, 176*, 151–154.

Zhou, X., Peng, Y., Zhu, X., Yao, S., Dere, J., Chentsova-Dutton, Y. E., & Ryder, A. G. (2015). From culture to symptom: Testing a structural model of "Chinese somatization". *Transcultural Psychiatry.* [Advance publication.]

Zhou, Y., Flaherty, J. H., Huang, C., Lu, Z., & Dong, B. (2011). Association between body mass index and cognitive function among Chinese nonagenarians/centenarians. *Dementia and Geriatric Cognitive Disorders, 30*(6), 517–524.

Zhuo, J. N. (2010, November 29). Where anonymity breeds contempt. *New York Times.*

Zilboorg, G., & Henry, G. W. (1941). *A history of medical psychology.* New York: Norton.

Zimbardo, P. (1976). *Rational paths to madness.* Presentation at Princeton University, Princeton, NJ.

Zimmerman, M., Martinez, J., Young, D., Chelminski, I., Morgan, T. A., & Dalrymple, K. (2014). Comorbid bipolar disorder and borderline personality disorder and history of suicide attempts. *Journal of Personality Disorders, 28*(3), 358–364.

Zipursky, R. B. (2014). Why are the outcomes in patients with schizophrenia so poor? *Journal of Clinical Psychiatry, 75*(Suppl 2), 20–24.

Zisser, A., & Eyberg, S. M. (2010). Parent-child interaction therapy and the treatment of disruptive behavior disorders. In J. R. Weisz & A. E. Kazdin (Eds.), *Evidence-based psychotherapies for children and adolescents* (2nd ed., pp. 179–193). New York: Guilford Press.

Zoellner, T. (2000, November). "Don't get even, get mad." *Men's Health, 15*(9), 56.

Zoroya, G. (2013, December 10). PTSD hits civilians serving on war fronts, study finds. *USA Today.*

Zu, S., Xiang, Y., Liu, J., Zhang, L., Wang, G., Ma, X., . . . Li, Z. (2014). A comparison of cognitive-behavioral therapy, antidepressants, their combination and standard treatment for Chinese patients with moderate-severe major depressive disorders. *Journal of Affective Disorders, 152-154*, 262–267.

Zucker, K. J. (2010). Gender identity and sexual orientation. In M. K. Dulcan (Ed.), *Dulcan's textbook of child and adolescent psychiatry* (pp. 543–552). Arlington, VA: American Psychiatric Publishing.

Zucker, K. J., & Bradley, S. J. (1995). *Gender identity disorder and psychosexual problems in children and adolescents.* New York: Guilford Press.

Zucker, K. J., Bradley, S. J., Owen-Anderson, A., Kibblewhite, S. J., Wood, H., Singh, D., & Choi, K. (2012). Demographics, behavior problems, and psychosexual characteristics of adolescents with gender identity disorder or transvestic fetishism. *Journal of Sex & Marital Therapy, 38*(2), 151–189.

Zuckerman, M. (2011). Psychodynamic approaches. In M. Zuckerman, *Personality science: Three approaches to the causes and treatment of depression* (pp. 11–45). Washington, DC: American Psychological Association.

Zuckerman, M. (2011). Trait and psychobiological approaches. In M. Zuckerman (Ed.), *Personality Science: Three approaches and their applications to the causes and treatment of depression* (pp. 47–77). Washington, DC: American Psychological Association.

Credits

Used by permission of Crown Books, an imprint of the Crown Publishing Group, a division of Random House LLC. All rights reserved.

Chapter 13

pages 427, 429, 448, 452: Millon, T. (2011). *Disorders of personality: Introducing a DSM/ICD spectrum from normal to abnormal,* 3rd ed. Hoboken, NJ: Wiley. Reproduced with permission of John Wiley & Sons Inc.; **page 432:** Hare, R. D. (1993). *Without conscience: The disturbing world of the psychopaths among us.* New York: Pocket Books. Copyright Guilford Press. Reprinted with permission of The Guilford Press; **page 444:** Republished with permission of South-Western College Publishing, a division of Cengage Learning, from *Modern psychopathology: A biosocial approach to maladaptive learning and functioning,* Millon, T., 1969; permission conveyed through Copyright Clearance Center, Inc.

Chapter 14

pages 464, 473, 483: Republished with permission of South-Western College Publishing, a division of Cengage Learning, from *Casebook in child behavior disorders,* Kearney, C. A., 5th ed. (2013); permission conveyed through Copyright Clearance Center, Inc.; **page 480:** Republished with permission of South-Western College Publishing, a division of Cengage Learning, from *Understanding child behavior disorders,* Gelfand, D. M., Jenson, W. R., & Drew, C. J., 1982; permission conveyed through Copyright Clearance Center, Inc.

Chapter 15

page 501: Heston, L. L. (1992). *Mending minds: A guide to the new psychiatry of depression, anxiety, and other serious mental disorders.* New York: Worth Publishers, pp. 87–90. Reprinted with permission; **page 504:** Hinrichsen, G. A. (1999). Interpersonal psychotherapy for late-life depression. In M. Duffy (Ed.), *Handbook of counseling and psychotherapy with older adults.* New York: Wiley; **pages 512–513:** Excerpt from *The forgetting: Alzheimer's: Portrait of an epidemic,* by David Shenk, copyright © 2001, 2002 by David Shenk. Used by permission of Doubleday, an imprint of the Knopf Doubleday Publishing Group, a division of Random House LLC. All rights reserved. Reproduced with permission of ICM Partners.

Chapter 16

pages 533: Copyright 1984, Lee Coleman. Used by permission.

Name Index

McManus, D., 130
McManus, M. A., 367
McNally, R. J., 165, 169
McNaughton, N., 134
McNeil, C. B., 474, 475
McNeil, E. B., 137
McPherson, M., 198
McSweeney, S., 208
McTeague, L. M., 117
Meana, M., 357, 358, 363, 366
Medina, M., 518
Mednick, S. A., 26
Meehan, K. B., 445
Meersand, P., 90
Mehl, E., 394
Mehta, D., 190
Meichenbaum, D. H., 54, 275
Meijer, E. H., 87
Meinhard, N., 394
Meisch, R. A., 332
Mcloy, J. R., 433
Meltzer, A. L., 267, 290
Meltzer, H. Y., 230
Melville, C. L., 343
Melville, J., 120
Mendes, E., 267
Menninger, K., 232
Merckelbach, H., 175
Mercolini, L., 116
Merenda, R. R., 172
Merikangas, K. R., 7, 106, 213, 469, 480
Merkl, A., 192
Merrick, E. S., 546
Merrick, J., 496
Merrill, J. E., 5
Merskey, H., 172
Mesmer, F. A., 12, 13
Messer, S. B., 445, 454
Messias, E., 14
Meston, C. M., 351
Metcalfe, N. H., 10
Metsälä, E., 508
Metzl, J. M., 372
Metzner, J. L., 535
Meycr, P., 457
Meyer, V., 139
Meystre, C., 428
Mian, N. D., 467
Michael, J., 405
Michal, M., 178, 179
Micheletta, J., 65
Midgley, N., 198
Miklowitz, D. J., 216, 217
Milk, H., 532, 533
Millan, M. J., 397, 407, 408
Miller, A. L., 402, 409
Miller, A., 79, 80
Miller, D. C., 491
Miller, D. N., 236, 237
Miller, F., 427
Miller, J. A., 534
Miller, J. B., 154
Miller, J. D., 444, 445
Miller, K. L., 478
Miller, M., 172
Miller, N. E., 123
Miller, P. M., 25

Miller, S. G., 455
Miller, T. I., 99
Miller, T., 446
Miller, W. D., 71
Miller, W. R., 201
Millichap, J. G., 481
Millier, A., 388
Millon, T., 425, 426, 427, 429, 439, 444, 445, 448, 450, 452, 453
Mills, J. F., 538
Milner, A., 228
Milrod, C., 377, 378
Mineka, S., 124
Miner, I. D., 251
Minnes, P., 488
Minnes, S., 322
Mintem, G. C., 287
Minuchin, S., 69, 293
Minzenberg, M. J., 100
Miranda, J., 210
Miret, M., 246
Mirone, V., 355
Mishak, P. B., 89
Mishor, Z., 142
Mitchell, A., 292
Mitchell, A. E., 438
Mitchell, A. J., 97
Mitchell, B. D., 531, 532
Mitchell, J. E., 286, 301
Mitchell, J. T., 164, 165
Mitchener-Nissen, T., 87
Mitka, M., 157
Mittal, V. A., 428
Mittelman, M. S., 520
Mitterer, J. O., 393
Mkize, D. L., 433
M'Naghten, D., 529
Moberg, T., 235
Modlin, T., 274
Moffatt, F. W., 273
Mohatt, J., 468
Mohler, H., 116
Mokros, A., 375
Mola, J. R., 363
Moldavsky, D., 260
Möller, J., 268
Momtaz, B., 243
Mond, J., 297
Mongrain, M., 17
Moniz, A. E., 44
Moniz, E., 405
Monroe, M., 222, 231
Monroe, S. M., 23, 184
Monsell, S. E., 16
Monson, C. M., 154, 164
Montaldo, C., 434
Monteith, C., 329, 331
Montejo, A-L., 353, 356
Montejo, J. E., 481
Moon, J. R., 268
Moore, C. E., 107
Moore, E. A., 456
Moore, P. J., 152
Moorhouse, P. A., 517
Moreno, C., 471
Morey, L. C., 422, 456
Morgan, C. A., 542

Morgan, C. D., 82
Morgan, C. M., 305
Morgan, J. F., 297
Morgan, L., 157
Morgan, M., 162
Morgan, P. L., 482
Mori, C., 400
Morissette, A., 302
Morris, T. L., 467
Morrison, A. P., 410
Morrison, B. J., 455
Morrison, J., 331
Morrissey, J. P., 415, 417, 536
Mort, J. R., 508
Mosca, N. W., 477
Moscone, G., 532, 533
Mosconi, L., 516
Mosconi, M. W., 486
Moscovitch, D. A., 129, 130
Moses, 184, 531
Moskowitz, E. S., 57
Moss, K., 289
Mossman, D., 530, 538
Mott, J. M., 162, 164
Moukheiber, A., 130
Mowrer, O. H., 123, 476
Mowrer, W. M., 476
Moyano, O., 179
Mozart, W. A., 175
Mucha, S. M., 250
Mueller, S. E., 68
Muhammad, J. A., 531, 543, 544
Mulder, R. T., 238
Mulhauser, G., 57
Mullen, P. E., 434
Müller, C. A., 338
Müller, J. L., 374
Müller, N., 394
Munsey, C., 464
Murayama, Y., 502, 504
Murdock, K. K., 207
Murphy, E., 323
Murphy, L., 57
Murphy, R., 290
Murphy, W. D., 371
Murray, D. E., 328
Murray, H. A., 82
Murray, K. E., 209
Murray, L. K., 478
Murray, R. M., 398, 409
Musa, R., 30
Musiat, P., 306
Musikantow, R., 13
Mustanski, B., 91

Nace, E. P., 311, 314
Naeem, F., 409
Nagy, T. F., 545
Naidoo, S., 433
Nair, G., 405
Nairn, S., 98
Najman, J. M., 205
Naninck, E. F. G., 208
Nardi, A. E., 135
Narrow, W. E., 61
Nash, J., 411, 508
Nathan, D., 172
Nation, D. A., 514, 519

Nauert, R., 163
Nawata, H., 378
Nazarian, M., 108
Neacsiu, A. D., 438, 441
Neale, J. M., 391
Nebuchadnezzar, 184
Neeleman, J., 241
Neff, B., 371
Negrini, A., 546
Neighbors, H. W., 26
Nelson, L., 518
Nelson, S. D., 164
Nelson, T. F., 313
Nelson-Gray, R. O., 430, 451
Nemecek, S., 260
Nemeroff, C. B., 26, 197
Nenadic´-Šviglin, K., 229
Ness, L., 171, 173
Neumark-Sztainer, D. R., 293
Neville, C., 439
Newcomb, M. E., 91
Newman, E., 164
Newman, M. G., 112, 114
Newnham, E. A., 438
Neziroglu, F., 145
Nezlek, J. B., 205
Nezu, A. M., 273
Ng, J. H., 522
Ng, M. T., 61
Nguyen, A., 478
Nichols, M. P., 69
Nichols, W. C., 451
Nichols, W. E., 189
Nicholson, C., 377
Nickel, R., 257, 258, 260
Nietzsche, F., 388
Nijinsky, V., 214
Nillni, Y. I., 135
Nitschke, J., 375
Niv, N., 43
Nivoli, A. M. A., 217
Nixon, M. K., 473
Nochajski, T. H., 168, 169
Nock, M. K., 229, 236, 245, 469, 473
Noeker, M., 252
Noh, Y., 233
Nolen-Hoeksema, S., 204, 208
Noll-Hussong, M., 155
Nonacs, R. M., 394
Noonan, D., 145
Noonan, S., 115
Norcross, J. C., 50, 53, 56, 60, 61, 63, 67, 69, 72, 74, 99, 100, 101, 110, 198, 210, 551
Nord, M., 408
Nordal, K., 475, 547
North, C. S., 165, 257, 261
Northoff, G., 373
Norton, A., 390
Notaro, P. C., 81
Notaro, T., 272
Novak, B., 530
Nowak, D. E., 342
Nugent, A. C., 215
Nunes, B. P., 502
Nunes, K. L., 373
Nurnberger, J. I., 215

Subject Index

Note: Page numbers followed by f, t, and b indicate figures, tables, and boxes, respectively.

Milestones in Abnormal Psychology

Stone Age	Mental disorders treated by trephination. p. 8
430–377 B.C.	Hippocrates cites brain as source of mental disorders. p. 8
500–1450	Middle Ages adopts demonological explanations and treatments. pp. 8–9
1547	Bethlehem Hospital in London converted into asylum. p. 10
1693	Witch-hunting trials peak in Salem, Massachusetts. p. 9
1773	First American hospital exclusively for mental patients opens in Williamsburg, Virginia. p. 10
1793	Phillipe Pinel frees asylum patients at LaBicêtre in Paris. p. 10
1812	Benjamin Rush writes first American textbook on psychiatry. p. 10
1842	Dorothea Dix begins campaign to reform mental hospitals in the United States. pp. 10–11
1865	Gregor Mendel publishes theories of genetics. p. 40
1879	German professor Wilhelm Wundt establishes first laboratory for experimental study of psychology. p. 22
1883	Emil Kraepelin publishes textbook on psychiatry, likening mental disorders to physical diseases. pp. 11, 93
1892	American Psychological Association founded. p. 18
1893	Sigmund Freud, with Josef Breuer, publishes first chapters of On the Psychical Mechanisms of Hysterical Phenomena, launching psychoanalysis. pp. 13, 258
1896	Lightner Witmer establishes first psychological clinic in the U.S. at University of Pennsylvania. p. 13
1897	General paresis linked to physical cause, syphilis. pp. 11–12
1900	Freud publishes The Interpretation of Dreams. p. 49
1900	Morton Prince uses hypnosis to treat multiple personality disorder. p. 177
1901	Ivan Pavlov demonstrates classical conditioning. p. 51
1905	First intelligence test published. p. 89
1907	Alzheimer's disease identified by Dr. Alois Alzheimer. p. 512
1908	Clifford Beers writes autobiography A Mind That Found Itself, launching Mental Hygiene Movement in the United States. p. 404
1909	Freud makes his only visit to America and lectures at Clark University. pp. 13–14, 44–45
1913	Behaviorist John Watson argues that psychology should abandon study of consciousness. pp. 51, 123
1917	The U.S. Congress declares all nonmedical opioids illegal. p. 317
1921	Rorschach Test published. p. 82
1923	Freud publishes The Ego and the Id. p. 45
1929	EEG developed. p. 88
1935	Alcoholics Anonymous founded. p. 339
1935	First use of lobotomy for mental disorders. p. 405
1937	Marijuana made illegal in the United States. p. 327
1938	Electroconvulsive therapy introduced in Rome. p. 192
1938	B. F. Skinner proposes operant conditioning. p. 51
1939	The Wechsler-Bellevue Intelligence Scale published. p. 89
1943	LSD's hallucinogenic effects discovered. pp. 323–324
1943	Minnesota Multiphasic Personality Test (MMPI) published. p. 84
1943	Jean-Paul Sartre's existential book Being and Nothingness published. p. 58
1949	Lithium salts first used for bipolar disorder. p. 215
1951	Chlorpromazine, first antipsychotic drug, tested. p. 407
1951	Carl Rogers publishes Client-Centered Therapy. p. 59
1952	First edition of DSM published by the American Psychiatric Association. p. 93

Science Source

Stephane Audras / REA / Redux Pictures

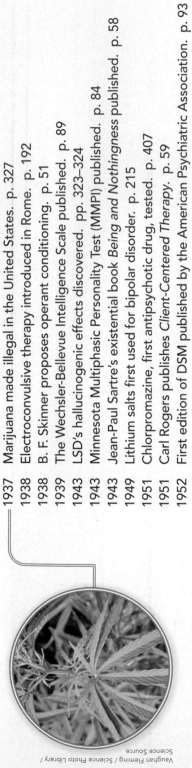

Vaughan Fleming / Science Photo Library / Science Source